W9-AQI-341

Index of American Periodical Verse: 1985

Rafael Catalá

and

James D. Anderson

assisted by

Sarah Park Anderson

and

Martha Park Sollberger

The Scarecrow Press, Inc.
Metuchen, N.J., & London
1987

Library of Congress Catalog Card No. 73-3060
ISBN 0-8108-2038-2
Copyright © 1987 by Rafael Catalá and James D. Anderson
Manufactured in the United States of America

CONTENTS

DEDICATION

To Rodrigo Molina
Professor Emeritus, New York University
His work has shaped the minds of
generations of students.

PREFACE

This, the fifteenth annual volume of the <u>Index</u> <u>of</u>
<u>American</u> <u>Periodical</u> <u>Verse</u>, was produced with the cooperation
of 224 participating English and Spanish language periodi-
cals from Canada, the United States, and Puerto Rico. More
than 5,000 entries for individual poets and translators,
15,000 entries for individual poems and 15,000 title entries
are included.

The importance of the <u>Index</u> grows as its necessity
becomes more apparent in circles of contemporary poetry
research. The increasing demand for inclusion corroborates
this fact. The <u>Index</u> constitutes an objective measure of
poetry in North America, recording not only the publication
of our own poets in Canada, the U.S. and Puerto Rico, but
also those from other lands and cultures and from other
times. Of course, the <u>Index</u>'s primary purpose is to show
what poems have been published by particular poets, what
poems have been translated by particular translators, and
who wrote poems with particular titles or first lines. But
taken together, the <u>Index</u> reveals trends and influences:
the ebb and flow of particular poets, as well as the influ-
ence of cultures of other lands and times as represented by
their poets published in North American journals.

James D. Anderson has made a major contribution to the
<u>Index</u> by designing and refining computer programs which have
greatly facilitated the indexing process, control of neces-
sary cross references, and page formatting. Also, I want to
express my sincere appreciation to Sarah Park Anderson and
Martha Park Sollberger for their valuable assistance.

Rafael Catalá
Co-Editor

v

INTRODUCTION

MICRO-COMPUTER COMPILATION

The 1985 Index was compiled using the Osborne 4 Vixen
micro-computer and the Wordstar word-processing program.
Once all indexing was complete, the entries were sorted and
formatted using a suite of programs written especially for
the Index in BASIC. The Osborne Vixen is data-compatible
with the IBM Personal Computer, so that after initial sort-
ing of entries on the Osborne, files could be moved to a
much larger IBM personal computer for final sorting. After
author and translator entries were sorted, entry numbers
were automatically generated and title entries were extract-
ed and sorted. Formatting programs created final entry
displays, inserted cross references, and formatted pages
with running heads. Finally, the Index was printed in
camera-ready form on a NEC Spinwriter printer.

The principal advantage in computer-based compilation
is eliminating the repetitive entry of the same data. With-
in a single issue of a journal, for example, the journal
citation will be the same for every poem, yet in the old
card-based method, the citation had to be rewritten on every
card. With the computer, it is simply copied, without re-
keying, to each entry. Similarly, translations no longer
call for a completely new entry for the translator. In-
stead, the original entry is simply modified, moving the
name of the translator to the lead position, and the author
to the note.

Persons interested in the precise details of compila-
tion, including the computer programs used, should write to
the editors at P.O. Box 38, New Brunswick, NJ 08903-0038.
The 1982, 1983, 1984 and 1985 Indexes are available from the
editors on 5-1/4" floppy disks.

NAMES AND CROSS REFERENCES

With the addition of many more poets with compound
surnames and surnames containing various prefixes, we have
recognized the need for systematic cross references from
alternative forms of surname to the form chosen for entry in
the Index. We have included these references whenever the
form used for entry did not fall under the last element. In
addition, many poets publish under different forms of the
same name, for example, with or without a middle initial.
Often these forms will file next to each other in the index.
In such cases, both forms are used, since it is often diffi-

cult, if not impossible, to determine with complete assurance whether it is the same poet or different poets with similar names. In such cases, "see also" cross references are used to remind users to check the variant forms of names which possibly refer to the same poet. When the poets are known to use different forms of the same name, alternative forms may be indicated by using the format authorized by the Anglo-American Cataloguing Rules, Second Edition. For example:

KNIGHT, Arthur W. (Arthur Winfield)

This heading indicates that this poet has poems published under two forms of name: Arthur W. Knight and Arthur Winfield Knight.

FORMAT AND ARRANGEMENT OF ENTRIES

The basic format and style of the Index remain unchanged. Poets are arranged alphabetically by surname and forenames. In creating this alphabetical sequence, we have adopted principles of the filing rules issued in 1980 by the American Library Association and the Library of Congress. Names are arranged on the basis of their spelling, rather than their pronunciation, so that, for example, names beginning with 'Mac' and 'Mc' are no longer interfiled. Similarly, the space consistently counts as a filing element, so that similar compound and prefixed surnames are often separated by some distance, as illustrated in the following examples. Note that "De BOLT" precedes "DeBEVOISE" by a considerable number of entries.

De ANGELIS	Van BRUNT
De BOLT	Van DUYN
De GRAVELLES	Van HALTEREN
De LOACH	Van TOORN
De PALCHI	Van TROYER
De RONSARD	Van WERT
De VAUL	Van WINCKEL
DEAL	VANCE
DeBEVOISE	Vander DOES
DeFOE	VANDERBEEK
DEGUY	VanDEVENTER
Del VECCHIO	
DeLISLE	
DeMOTT	
DENNISON	
Der HOVANESSIAN	
DESY	
DeYOUNG	

Abbreviations are also arranged on the basis of spelling, rather than pronunciation, so that "ST. JOHN" is not filed as "SAINT JOHN", but as "S+T+space+JOHN". Punctuation is not considered; a hyphen is filed as if it were a space and apostrophes and accents are ignored for purposes of filing. Finally, numerals are arranged in numerical order preceding alphabetical letters rather than as if they were spelled out.

Under each poet's name, poems are arranged alphabeti-
cally by title or, if there is no title, by first line.
Initial articles in the major languages are ignored in the
arrangement. Poem titles and first lines are placed within
quotation marks. All significant words of titles are capi-
talized, but in first lines, only the first word and proper
nouns are capitalized. Incomplete excerpts from larger
works are followed by the note "Excerpt" or, if they con-
sist of complete sections, by "Selection". The title, first
line or number of the excerpt follows if given in the
publication. For example:

WALCOTT, Derek
  "Midsummer" (Selections: XXXIV-XXXVI). <u>Agni</u> (18) 83, p. 5-
  7.

WEBB, Phyllis
  "The Vision Tree" (Selection: "I Daniel"). <u>PoetryCR</u> (5:2)
  Wint 83-84, p. 11.

WAINWRIGHT, Jeffrey
  "Heart's Desire" (Excerpt: "Some Propositions and Part of
  a Narrative"). <u>Agni</u> (18) 83, p. 37.

WATTEN, Barret
  "One Half" (Excerpts). <u>ParisR</u> (24:86) Wint 82, p. 112-113.

If an excerpt is a complete "sub-work", it receives an
independent entry, with reference to the larger work in a
note. For example:

ANDERSON, Jack
  "Magnets" (from The Clouds of That Country). <u>PoNow</u> (7:2,
  #38) 83, p. 23.

Notes about dedications, joint authors, translators,
and sources follow the title, enclosed in parentheses. A
poem with more than one author is entered under each author.
Likewise, a translated poem is entered under each transla-
tor, as well as its author(s). Each entry includes the
names of all authors and all translators. Multiple authors
or translators are indicated by the abbreviation "w.",
standing for "with". Translators are indicated by the ab-
breviation "tr. by", standing for "translated by", and ori-
ginal authors are indicated by the abbreviation "tr. of",
standing for "translation of". For example:

AGGESTAM, Rolf
  "Old Basho" (tr. by Erland Anderson and Lars Nordström).
  <u>NewRena</u> (16) Spr 83, p. 25.

ANDERSON, Erland
  "Old Basho" (tr. of Rolf Aggestam, w. Lars Nordström).
  <u>NewRena</u> (16) Spr 83, p. 25.

NORDSTROM, Lars
  "Old Basho" (tr. of Rolf Aggestam, w. Erland Anderson).
  <u>NewRena</u> (16) Spr 83, p. 25.

The journal citation includes an abbreviation standing for the journal title, followed by volume and issue numbers, date, and pages. The journal abbreviation is underlined. An alphabetical list of these journal abbreviations is included at the front of the volume, along with the full journal title, name of editor(s), address, the numbers of the issues indexed for this volume of the Index, and subscription information. A separate list of indexed periodicals is arranged by full journal title, with a reference to the abbreviated title. Volume and issue numbers are included within parentheses, e.g., (16:5) stands for volume 16, number 5; (21) refers to issue 21 for a journal which does not use volume numbers. Dates are given using abbreviations for months and seasons. Year of publication is indicated by the last two digits of the year, e.g. 85. Please see the separate list of abbreviations.

Compiling this year's Index has been an adventure into the wealth and variety of poetry published in U. S., Puerto Rican and Canadian periodicals as well as the intricacies of bringing this wealth together and organizing it into a consistent index. The world of poetry publication is a dynamic one, with new journals appearing, older journals declining, dying, reviving and thriving. This year saw the loss of eighteen journals and the addition of twenty-four new ones. These are listed at the front of the volume. Keeping up with these changes is a big order, and we solicit our reader's suggestions as to journals which should be included in future volumes of the Index, and also, journals which could be dropped. Editors who would like their journals considered for inclusion in future volumes should send sample issues to:

Rafael Català, Editor
Index of American Periodical Verse
P.O. Box 38
New Brunswick, NJ 08903-0038

Although indexing is indispensable for the organization of any literature so that particular works can be found when needed and scholarship and research facilitated, it is a tedious business. I know that we have made mistakes. We solicit your corrections and suggestions, which you may send to me at the above address.

James D. Anderson
Co-Editor

ABBREVIATIONS

dir., dirs.	director, directors
ed., eds.	editor, editors
(for.)	price for foreign countries
(ind.)	price for individuals
(inst.)	price for institutions
(lib.)	price for libraries
NS	new series
p.	page, pages
po. ed.	poetry editor
pub.	publisher
(stud.)	price for students
tr. by	translated by
tr. of	translation of
U.	University
w.	with

Months

Ja	January	Jl	July
F	February	Ag	August
Mr	March	S	September
Ap	April	O	October
My	May	N	November
Je	June	D	December

Seasons

Aut	Autumn	Spr	Spring
Wint	Winter	Sum	Summer

Years

83	1983	85	1985
84	1984	86	1986

PERIODICALS ADDED

Periodical acronyms are followed by the titles.

AmerV: THE AMERICAN VOICE
Conjunc: CONJUNCTIONS
ConnPR: THE CONNECTICUT POETRY REVIEW
Crazy: CRAZYHORSE
CrossCur: CROSSCURRENTS
CumbPR: CUMBERLAND POETRY REVIEW
GWR: THE G. W. REVIEW
HawaiiR: HAWAII REVIEW
Imagine: IMAGINE: International Chicano Poetry Journal
JamesWR: THE JAMES WHITE REVIEW
JlNJPo: THE JOURNAL OF NEW JERSEY POETS
Kaleid: KALEIDOSCOPE
LaurelR: LAUREL REVIEW
Oink: OINK!
PassN: PASSAGES NORTH
PoetryR: POETRY REVIEW
PortLES: THE PORTABLE LOWER EAST SIDE
Raccoon: RACCOON
Rampike: RAMPIKE
RiverS: RIVER STYX
SilverFR: SILVERFISH REVIEW
Temblor: TEMBLOR
Verse: VERSE
Zyzzyva: ZYZZYVA: The Last Word: West Coast Writers & Artists

PERIODICALS DELETED

The following periodicals have been deleted from the Index because (1) we have been notified that publication has ceased; (2) the periodical no longer publishes poetry; (3) no 1984 or 1985 issues have been received after repeated requests, or (4) it falls outside the scope of the Index.

Abatis: ABATIS -- No 1984 or 1985 issues.
Academe: ACADEME -- No longer publishes poetry.
Argo: ARGO -- Outside of scope.
BerksR: BERKSHIRE REVIEW -- No longer publishes poetry.
CEACritic: THE CEA CRITIC -- No longer publishes poetry.
Humanist: THE HUMANIST -- No longer publishes poetry.
Images: IMAGES -- No 1984 or 1985 issues.
Meadows: THE MEADOWS -- No 1984 or 1985 issues.
ModernPS: MODERN POETRY STUDIES -- Publication has ceased.
NewWR: NEW WORLD REVIEW -- Publication has ceased.
PoNow: POETRY NOW -- No 1984 or 1985 issues.
PortR: PORTLAND REVIEW -- Change in format.
Prismal: PRISMAL/CABRAL -- Publication has ceased.
Racata: JUNTE DEL TALLER RACATA -- Publication has ceased.
SunM: SUN & MOON -- No 1984 or 1985 issues.
Tele: TELEPHONE -- Publication has ceased.
Telescope: TELESCOPE -- Publication has ceased.
ThirdW: THE THIRD WIND -- Publication has ceased.

PERIODICALS INDEXED

Arranged by acronym, with names of editors, addresses, issues indexed, and subscription information. New titles added to the <u>Index</u> in 1985 are marked with an asterisk (*).

<u>13thM</u>: 13TH MOON, Marilyn Hacker, ed., P.O. Box 309, Cathedral Station, New York, NY 10025. Issues indexed: No 1985 issues received. Subscriptions: $19.50/3 volumes, $13.00/2 volumes; Single issues: $6.50.

<u>Abraxas</u>: ABRAXAS, Ingrid Swanberg, ed., 2518 Gregory St., Madison, WI 53711. Issues indexed: (33). Subscriptions: $12/4 issues.

<u>Agni</u>: THE AGNI REVIEW, Sharon Dunn, ed., P.O. Box 660, Amherst, MA 01004. Issues indexed: (22). Subscriptions: $21/3 yrs., $15/2 yrs., $8/yr., plus $1/yr. (for.); Single issues: $4.

<u>Amelia</u>: AMELIA, Frederick A. Raborg, Jr., ed., 329 "E" St., Bakersfield, CA 93304. Issues indexed: (2:1-2). Subscriptions: US, Canada, Mexico, $40/3 yrs., $28/2 yrs., $15/yr.; $75/3 yrs., $52/2 yrs., $27/yr. (for. air mail); Single issues: $4.75, $7 (for. air mail).

<u>AmerPoR</u>: THE AMERICAN POETRY REVIEW, David Bonanno, Stephen Berg, Arthur Vogelsang, eds., World Poetry, Inc., Temple U Center City, 1616 Walnut St., Room 405, Philadelphia, PA 19103. Issues indexed: (14:1-6). Subscriptions: $25/3 yrs., $30/3 yrs. (for.), $17/2 yrs., $21/2 yrs. (for.), $9.50/yr., $11.50/yr. (for.); classroom rate $6/yr. per student; Single issues: $1.95.

<u>AmerS</u>: THE AMERICAN SCHOLAR, Joseph Epstein, ed., United Chapters of Phi Beta Kappa, 1811 Q St. NW, Washington, DC 20009. Issues indexed: (54:1-4). Subscriptions: $39/3 yrs., $16/yr. plus $3/yr. (for.); Single issues: $4.75.

*<u>AmerV</u>: THE AMERICAN VOICE, Frederick Smock, ed., The Kentucky Foundation for Women, Inc., Heyburn Bldg., Suite 1215, Broadway at 4th Ave., Lousiville, KY 40202. Issues indexed: (1). Subscriptions: $12/yr. Single issues: $3.50.

<u>Annex</u>: ANNEX 21, Patrick Worth Gray, ed., UNO-Community Writer's Workshop, University of Nebraska at Omaha, Omaha, NE 68182. Issues indexed: No 1984 or 1985 issues received. "Temporarily discontinued"; Single issues: $4.95.

<u>Antaeus</u>: ANTAEUS, Daniel Halpern, ed., The Ecco Press, 18 W. 30th St., New York, NY 10001. Issues indexed: (54-55). Subscriptions: $20/4 issues, $37/8 issues, $53/12 issues; Single issues: $10.

<u>AntigR</u>: THE ANTIGONISH REVIEW, George Sanderson, ed., St. Francis Xavier U., Antigonish, Nova Scotia B2G 1C0 Canada. Issues indexed: (60-62/63). Subscriptions: $14/4 issues; Single issues: $4.

<u>AntR</u>: THE ANTIOCH REVIEW, Robert S. Fogarty, ed., David St. John, po. ed., P.O. Box 148, Yellow Springs, OH 45387. Issues indexed: (43:1-4). Subscriptions: $25/yr. (inst.), $18/yr. (ind.),

$30/yr. (for.); Single issues: $4.75; P.O. Box 1308-R, Ft. Lee, NJ 07024.

Areito: AREITO, Max Azicri, Emilio Bejel, et al., eds., GPO Box 2174, New York, NY 10116. Issues indexed: (9:36, 10:37-38). Subscriptions: $18/yr. (inst.), $12/yr. (ind)., $20/yr. (for.); Single issues: $3; Back issues: $3.50.

ArizQ: ARIZONA QUARTERLY, Albert Frank Gegenheimer, ed., U. of Arizona, Tucson, AZ 85721. Issues indexed: (41:1-4). Subscriptions: $10/3 yrs., $5/yr.; Single issues: $1.50.

Ascent: ASCENT, Daniel Curley, et al., eds., English Dept., U. of Illinois, 608 South Wright St., Urbana, IL 61801. Issues indexed: (10:2-3, 11:1). Subscriptions: $3/yr., $4.50/yr. (for.); Single issues: $1 (bookstore), $1.50 (mail).

Atlantic: THE ATLANTIC, William Whitworth, ed., Peter Davison, po. ed., 8 Arlington St., Boston, MA 02116. Issues indexed: (255:1-6, 256:1-6). Subscriptions: $29.95/3 yrs., $15.95/2 yrs., $9.95/yr., plus $3/yr. (Canada), $5/yr. (for.); Single issues: $2.

BallSUF: BALL STATE UNIVERSITY FORUM, Bruce W. Hozeski, Frances Mayhew Rippy, eds., Darlene Mathis-Eddy, po. ed., Ball State U., Muncie, IN 47306. Issues indexed: (24:4, 25:1-4, 26:2). Subscriptions: (vol. 25-26) $10/yr., Single issues: $3.; (vol. 27-) $15/yr., Single issues: $4.50.

BelPoJ: THE BELOIT POETRY JOURNAL, Marion K. Stocking, ed., RFD 2, Box 154, Ellsworth, ME 04605. Issues indexed: (35:3-4, 36:1-2). Subscriptions: $17/3 yrs., $6/yr.; Single issues: $1.50.

BilingR: THE BILINGUAL REVIEW/LA REVISTA BILINGUE, Gary D. Keller, ed., Box M, Campus Post Office, SUNY Binghampton, Binghampton, NY 13901. Issues indexed: (11:2-3). Subscriptions: $15/yr., $28/2 yrs., $39/3 yrs. (ind.); $20/yr. (inst., 1985), $24/yr. (inst., 1986).

BlackALF: BLACK AMERICAN LITERATURE FORUM, Joe Weixlmann, ed., Parsons Hall 237, Indiana State U., Terre Haute, IN 47809. Issues indexed: (19:1-4). Subscriptions: $12/yr. (ind.), $15/yr. (inst.), $15/yr. (for.), $18 (for. inst.). Single issues: $4.50.

BlackWR: BLACK WARRIOR REVIEW, Lynn Domina, ed., Janet McAdams, po. ed., U. of Alabama, P.O. Box 2936, University, AL 35486-2936. Issues indexed: (11:2, 12:1). Subscriptions: $6.50/yr. (ind.), $9/yr. (inst.); Single issues: $3.50 plus $.75 postage.

BlueBldgs: BLUE BUILDINGS: An International Magazine of Poetry and Translations, Tom Urban, Ruth Doty et al., eds., Dept. of English, Drake U., Des Moines, IA 50311. Issues indexed: (9). Subscriptions: $4/2 issues; Single issues: $2.

BlueBuf: BLUE BUFFALO, Roberts Hilles, David Maulsby, et al., eds., c/o Dandelion, 922 - 9 Avenue, S.E., Calgary, Alberta, Canada, T2G 0S4. Issues indexed: (2:2). Single issues: $1.

Blueline: BLUELINE, Alice Gilborn, ed. & publisher; Jane Z. Carroll & Gary McLouth, po. eds. Blue Mountain Lake, NY 12812. Issues indexed: (6:2, 7:1). Subscriptions: $5/yr. (U.S. & Canada), $6/yr. (for.); Back issues: $2.75.

<u>Bogg</u>: BOGG, John Elsberg, ed., 422 N. Cleveland St., Arlington, VA
   22201; George Cairncross, ed., 31 Belle Vue St., Filey, N. York-
   shire YO14 9HU, UK. Issues indexed: (53-54). Subscriptions:
   $8/3 issues; Single issues: $3.

<u>Bound</u>: BOUNDARY 2, William V. Spanos, ed., Dept. of English, State
   U. of New York, Binghamton, NY 13901. Issues indexed:
   (12:3/13:1, 13:2/3). Subscriptions: $25/yr. (inst.), $15/yr.
   (ind.), $13/yr (stud.), plus $2 (for.); Single issues: $8,
   Double issues: $10.

<u>Callaloo</u>: CALLALOO: A Tri-Annual Journal of Afro-American and Afri-
   can Arts and Letters, Charles H. Rowell, ed., Dept. of English,
   U. of Kentucky, Lexington, KY 40506-0027. Issues indexed: (8:1-
   2, issues 23-24). Subscriptions: $12/yr., $20/2 yrs, $30/3
   yrs., plus $12/yr. (for. bookrate), plus $21/yr. (for. airmail);
   Single issues: $7.

<u>CalQ</u>: CALIFORNIA QUARTERLY, Elliot L. Gilbert, ed., Mary L. Hower &
   Sarah-Hope Parmeter, po. eds., 100 Sproul Hall, U. of Californ-
   ia, Davis, CA 95616. Issues indexed: (26). Subscriptions:
   $10/yr.; Single issues: $2.

<u>Calyx</u>: CALYX: A Journal of Art and Literature by Women, Margarita
   Donnelly, Managing ed., P.O. Box B, Corvallis, OR 97339-0539.
   Issues indexed: (9:1). Subscriptions: $18/yr., $32/2 yrs., $42/3
   yrs., plus $4/yr. (for.), $9/yr. (for. airmail); $22.50/yr.
   (inst.); $15/yr. (low income individual); Single issue: $6.50-
   $12.

<u>CanLit</u>: CANADIAN LITERATURE, W. H. New, ed., U. of British Colum-
   bia, 2029 West Mall, Vancouver, B.C. V6T 1W5 Canada. Issues
   indexed: (104-107). Subscriptions: $20/yr. (ind.), $25/yr.
   (inst.) plus $5/yr. outside Canada; Single issues: $7.50.

<u>CapeR</u>: THE CAPE ROCK, Harvey Hecht, <u>et al.</u>, eds., Southeast Missou-
   ri State U., Cape Girardeau, MO 63701. Issues indexed: (20:1-
   2). Subscriptions: $3/yr.; Single issues: $2.

<u>CapilR</u>: THE CAPILANO REVIEW, Dorothy Jantzen, ed., Sharon Thesen,
   po. ed., Capilano College, 2055 Purcell Way, North Vancouver,
   B.C. V7J 3H5 Canada. Issues indexed: (34-37). Subscriptions:
   $17.50/8 issues (ind.), $9/4 issues (ind.), $10/4 issues (lib.),
   plus $1/4 issues (for.); Single issues: $3.

<u>CarolQ</u>: CAROLINA QUARTERLY, Stockard, Emily, ed., Margaret Bockting
   po. ed., Greenlaw Hall 066-A, U. of North Carolina, Chapel Hill,
   NC 27514. Issues indexed: (37:2-3, 38:1). Subscriptions:
   $12/yr. (inst.), $10/yr. (ind.), $11/yr. (for.); Single issues:
   $4, Back issues: $4, plus $1 postage.

<u>CentR</u>: THE CENTENNIAL REVIEW, Linda W. Wagner, ed., 110 Morrill
   Hall, Michigan State U., East Lansing, MI 48824-1036. Issues
   indexed: (29:2-4). Subscriptions: $8/2 yrs., $5/yr., plus $2/yr.
   (for.); Single issues: $1.50.

<u>CharR</u>: THE CHARITON REVIEW, Jim Barnes, ed., Division of Language
   and Literature, Northeast Missouri State U., Kirksville, MO
   63501. Issues indexed: (11:1-2). Subscriptions: $7/4 issues;
   Single issues: $2.

<u>Chelsea</u>: CHELSEA, Sonia Raiziss, ed., P.O. Box 5880, Grand Central
   Station, New York, NY 10163. Issues indexed: (44). Subscrip-
   tions: $9/2 issues or double issue, $10 (for.); Single issues:
   $5, $5.50 (for.).

ChiR: CHICAGO REVIEW, Robert Sitko, ed., Paul Baker & Michael
Donaghy, po. eds., U. of Chicago, Faculty Exchange, Box C,
Chicago, IL 60637. Issues indexed: (34:4, 35:1-2). Subscrip-
tions: $48/3 yrs., $32/2 yrs., $17/yr., $14/yr. (ind.), plus
$2/yr. (for.); Single issues: $4.50.

ChrC: THE CHRISTIAN CENTURY, James M. Wall, ed., 407 S. Dearborn
St., Chicago, IL 60605. Issues indexed: (102:1-40). Subscrip-
tions: $24/yr.; Single issues: $1.25.

CimR: CIMARRON REVIEW, Neil J. Hackett, ed., Michael J. Bugeja, po.
ed., 208 Life Sciences East, Oklahoma State U., Stillwater, OK
74078. Issues indexed: (70-73). Subscriptions: $10/yr.; Single
issues: $2.50.

ClockR: CLOCKWATCH REVIEW, James Plath, ed., 737 Penbrook Way,
Hartland, WI 53029. Issues indexed: (2:2). Subscriptions:
$6/yr.; Single issues: $3.

ColEng: COLLEGE ENGLISH, National Council of Teachers of English,
James C. Raymond, ed., James Tate, po. ed., P.O. Drawer AL, Uni-
versity, AL 35486. Issues indexed: (47:1-8). Subscriptions:
$35/yr. (inst.), $30/yr. (ind.), plus $4/yr. (for.); Single is-
sues: $4; NCTE, 1111 Kenyon Rd., Urbana, IL 61801.

Comm: COMMONWEAL, Peter Steinfels, ed., Rosemary Deen, po. ed., 232
Madison Ave., New York, NY 10016. Issues indexed: (112:1-22).
Subscriptions: $43/2 yrs., $47/2 yrs. (Canada), $53/2 yrs.
(for.), $24/yr., $26/yr. (Canada), $29/yr. (for.); Single is-
sues: $1.25.

ConcPo: CONCERNING POETRY, Ellwood Johnson, ed., Robert Huff, po.
ed., Dept. of English, Western Washington U., Bellingham, WA
98225. Issues indexed: (18:1/2). Subscriptions: $8/yr. (USA,
Canada), $10/yr. (for.); Single issues: $6.25.

Cond: CONDITIONS, Dorothy Allison, Cheryl Clarke, Nancy Clarke
Otter, Debbi Schaubman, eds., P.O. Box 56, Van Brunt Station,
Brooklyn, NY 11215. Issues indexed: (11/12). Subscriptions:
$25/3 issues (inst.), $15/3 issues (ind), $9/3 issues "hardship"
rate, plus $2 (for.); free to women in prisons and mental insti-
tutions; Single issues: $6 (ind.), $9 (inst.), plus $.50 (for.).

Confr: CONFRONTATION, Martin Tucker, ed., English Dept., C. W. Post
College, Long Island U., Greenvale, NY 11548. Issues indexed:
(29, 30/31). Subscriptions: $20/3 yrs., $15/2 yrs., $8/yr.;
Single issues: $5-6.

*Conjunc: CONJUNCTIONS, Bradford Morrow, ed., 33 West 9th St., New
York, NY 10011. Issues indexed: (7-8). Subscriptions: $16/yr.
(2 issues), $30/2 yrs.; $20/yr., $40/2 yrs. (inst.); $45/yr.,
$85/ 2 yrs. (cloth binding); plus $2.50/yr. (for.); Single
issues: $8.95.

*ConnPR: THE CONNECTICUT POETRY REVIEW, Christine Sennett, J. Clair
White, eds., P.O. Box 3783, Amity Station, New Haven, CT 06525.
Issues indexed: (3:1). Single issues: $2 (including postage).

CrabCR: CRAB CREEK REVIEW, Linda Clifton, ed., 806 N. 42nd, Seattle
WA 98103. Issues indexed: (2:2-3, 3:1). Subscriptions: $15/2
yrs., $8/yr.; Single issues: $3.

*Crazy: CRAZYHORSE, Russell Murphy, managing ed., Ralph Burns, po.
ed., Dept. of English, U. of Arkansas, Little Rock, AR 72204.

Issues indexed: (26-29). Subscriptions: $8/yr., $15/2 yrs., $22/3 yrs. Single issues: $4.

CreamCR: CREAM CITY REVIEW, Peter Hickey, ed., Marcia Hesselman, po. ed., English Dept., P.O. Box 413, U. of Wisconsin-Milwaukee, Milwaukee, WI 53201. Issues indexed: (10:1-2). Subscriptions: No information.

CropD: CROP DUST, Edward C. Lynskey ed., Route 5, Box 75, Warrenton, VA 22186. Issues indexed: No 1984 or 1985 issues published; next issue expected in 1986. Subscriptions: $5/2 issues (ind.), $8/2 issues (lib.); Single issues: $2.50.

CrossC: CROSS-CANADA WRITERS' QUARTERLY, Ted Plantos, ed., Box 277, Station F, Toronto, Ontario M4Y 2L7 Canada. Issues indexed: (7:1-3/4). Subscriptions: $14/yr. (ind.), $16/yr. (inst.), $18/yr (for.); Single issues: $3.95.

*CrossCur: CROSSCURRENTS, Linda Brown Michelson, ed., Elizabeth Bartlett, po. ed., 2200 Glastonbury Road, Westlake Village, CA 91361. Issues indexed: (4:1-3, 4:4/5:1, 5:2-3). Subscriptions: $15/yr., $22.50/2 yrs.; Single issues: $5.

*CumbPR: CUMBERLAND POETRY REVIEW, Bob Darrell, Sherry Darrell, Donald Davie, et al., eds., Poetics, Inc., P.O. Box 120128, Acklen Station, Nashville, TN 37212. Issues indexed: (5:1). Subscriptions: $9/yr, $18/2 yrs. (ind.); $12/yr., $24/2 yrs. (inst.); $18/yr., $36/2 yrs. (for.); Single issue: $5.

CutB: CUTBANK, Pamela Uschuk, eds., Dept. of English, U. of Montana, Missoula, MT 59812. Issues indexed: (23-24). Subscriptions: $12.50/2 yrs., $6.50/yr.; Single issues: $3.75.

Dandel: DANDELION, Robert Hilles & John McDermid, eds., John McDermid & Claire Harris, po. eds., Alexandra Centre, 922 - 9th Ave., S.E., Calgary, Alberta T2G 0S4 Canada. Issues indexed: (12:1-2). Subscriptions: $15/2 yrs., $8/yr., $12/yr. (inst.); Single issues: $4.

DekalbLAJ: THE DEKALB LITERARY ARTS JOURNAL, Frances S. Ellis, ed., DeKalb Community College, 555 N. Indian Creek Dr., Clarkston, GA 30021. Issues indexed: (18:1/2-3/4). Subscriptions: $10/volume, $12/volume (for.)

DenQ: DENVER QUARTERLY, David Milofsky, ed., U. of Denver, Denver, CO 80208. Issues indexed: (19:3-20:2). Subscriptions: $22/2 yrs., $12/yr., $14/yr. (inst.), plus $1/yr. (for.); Single issues: $4.

Descant: DESCANT, Karen Mulhallen, ed., P.O. Box 314, Station P, Toronto M5S 2S8, Ontario, Canada. Issues indexed: (16:1-16:4/17:1, issues 48-51). Subscriptions: $18/yr (ind.), $26/yr. (inst.); Single issues: $7.50-$12.

EngJ: ENGLISH JOURNAL, National Council of Teachers of English, Ken Donelson, Alleen Pace Nilsen, eds., College of Education, Arizona State U., Tempe, AZ 85287. Issues indexed: (74:1-8). Subscriptions: $35/yr. (inst.), $30/yr. (ind.), plus $4/yr. (for.); Single issues: $4; NCTE, 1111 Kenyon Rd., Urbana, IL 61801.

Epoch: EPOCH, C. S. Giscombe, ed., 251 Goldwin Smith Hall, Cornell U., Ithaca, NY 14853. Issues indexed: (34:2-3). Subscriptions: $8/yr., $10/yr. (for.); Single issues: $3.

EvergR: EVERGREEN REVIEW, Barney Rosset & Fred Jordan, eds., c/o Grove Press, 196 W. Houston St., New York, NY 10014; Issues indexed: "Suspended until 1987"; Single issues: $5.95.

Field: FIELD, Stuart Friebert, David Young, eds., Rice Hall, Oberlin College, Oberlin, OH 44074. Issues indexed: (32). Subscriptions: $12/2 yrs., $7/yr.; Single issues: $3.50; Back issues: $10.

FourQt: FOUR QUARTERS, John Christopher Kleis, ed., Richard Lautz, po. ed., La Salle U., 20th & Olney Aves., Philadelphia, PA 19141. Issues indexed: No 1985 issues received. Subscriptions: $13/2 yrs., $8/yr.; Single issues: $2.

Gargoyle: GARGOYLE MAGAZINE, Richard Peabody, Jr., ed./pub., Gretchen Johnsen, po. ed., Paycock Press, P.O. Box 3567, Washington, DC 20007. Issues indexed: (27). Subscriptions: $10/yr., 2 issues (ind.), $12/yr., 2 issues (inst.). Single issues: $5.95-7.95.

GeoR: GEORGIA REVIEW, Stanley W. Lindberg, ed., U. of Georgia, Athens, GA 30602. Issues indexed: (39:1-4). Subscriptions: $15/2 yrs., $9/yr., plus $3/yr. (for.); Single issues: $4.

Germ: GERMINATION, Allan Cooper, ed. & pub., Leigh Faulkner, Assoc. ed., 428 Yale Ave., Riverview, New Brunswick E1B 2B5, Canada. Issues indexed: (9:1-2) Subscriptions: $6/2 issues (ind.), $8/2 issues (inst.); Single issues: $3.50.

GrahamHR: GRAHAM HOUSE REVIEW, Peter Balakian & Bruce Smith, eds., Colgate U. Press, Box 5000, Colgate U., Hamilton, NY 13346; Issues indexed: (8-9); Subscriptions: $17/2 yrs; Single issues: $4.50.

Grain: GRAIN, Saskatchewan Writers Guild, Brenda Riches, ed., Garry Radison, po. ed., Box 1154, Regina, Saskatchewan S4P 3B4 Canada. Issues indexed: (13:1-4). Subscriptions: $15/2 yrs., $9/yr.; Single issues: $3.

GrandS: GRAND STREET, Ben Sonnenberg, ed., 50 Riverside Dr., New York, NY 10024. Issues indexed: (4:2-4, 5:1). Subscriptions: $20/yr. (ind.), $24/yr. (for.); $24/yr. (inst.), $28/yr. (for. inst.); Single issues: $5; Back issues, $6..

GreenfR: GREENFIELD REVIEW, Joseph Bruchac III, ed., R.D. 1, Box 80, Greenfield Center, NY 12833. Issues indexed: (12:3/4, 13:1/2). Subscriptions: $8/2 double issues; $10 (lib.); Single issues: $4.

*GWR: THE G. W. REVIEW, The Editor, Box 20, Marvin Center, The George Washington U., 800 21st St., N.W., Washington, DC 20052 (Editor changes annually). Issues indexed: (6:1). Subscriptions: $6/yr.; Single copies: $1.50.

HangL: HANGING LOOSE, Robert Hershon, et al., eds., 231 Wyckoff St., Brooklyn, NY 11217. Issues indexed: (47-46). Subscriptions: $18/9 issues, $12/6 issues, $6.50/3 issues; Single issues: $2.50.

Harp: HARPER'S MAGAZINE, Lewis H. Lapham, ed., Two Park Ave., New York, NY 10016. Issues indexed: (270:1616-1621, 271:1622-1627). Subscriptions: $18/yr., plus $2/yr. (USA possessions, Canada), plus $3/yr. (for.); Single issues: $2; P.O. Box 1937, Marion, OH 43305.

HarvardA: THE HARVARD ADVOCATE, Mark Csikszentmihalyi, Managing
ed., Eirc Selinger, po. ed., 21 South St., Cambridge, MA 02138.
Issues indexed: (118:3-119:2). Subscriptions: $10/yr. (ind.),
$12/yr. (inst.), $16/yr. (for.).

*HawaiiR: HAWAII REVIEW, Zdenek Kluzak, ed., Dean Honma, po. ed.,
U. of Hawaii at Manoa, Dept. of English, 1733 Donaghho Rd.,
Honolulu, HI 06822. Issues indexed: (17-18). Subscriptions:
$6/yr.; Single issue: $3.

HiramPoR: HIRAM POETRY REVIEW, English Dept., Hiram College, Hale
Chatfield & Carol Donley, eds., P.O. Box 162, Hiram, OH 44234.
Issues indexed: (38-39). Subscriptions: $4/yr.; Single issues:
$2.

HolCrit: THE HOLLINS CRITIC, John Rees Moore, ed., Hollins College,
VA 24020. Issues indexed: (22:1-5). Subscriptions: $5/yr., $9/2
yrs., $13/3 yrs.; $6.50/yr., $10.50/2 yrs., $14.50/3 yrs.
(for.).

Hudson: THE HUDSON REVIEW, Paula Deitz, Frederick Morgan, eds., 684
Park Ave., New York, NY 10021. Issues indexed: (38:1-3). Sub-
scriptions: $18/yr., $34/2 yrs., $50/3 yrs., plus $3/yr. (for.);
Single issues: $5.

*Imagine: IMAGINE: International Chicano Poetry Journal, Tino
Villanueva, ed., 89 Mass. Ave., Suite 270, Boston, MA 02115.
Issues indexed: (1:2, 2:1). Subscriptions: $8/yr., $14/2 yrs.
(ind.); $12/yr., $18/2 yrs. (inst.); plus $1/yr. (for.); Single
issues: $5.50-$8.

IndR: INDIANA REVIEW, Erin McGraw, ed., Christopher Cokinos,
Patrick Daily, Elizabeth Dodd, , po. eds., 316 N. Jordan Ave.,
Bloomington, IN 47405. Issues indexed: (8:1-3). Subscriptions:
$10/3 issues, $12/3 issues (inst.); $18/6 issues (ind.); $20/6
issues (inst.); Single issues: $4.

Inti: INTI, Revista de Literatura Hispanica, Roger B. Carmosino,
ed., Dept. of Modern Languages, Providence College, Providence,
RI 02918. Issues indexed: (16/17, 18/19, 20; Otoño 82-Oton~o
84). Subscriptions: $20/yr. (ind.), $25/yr. (for.); $25/yr.
(ind.), $30/yr. (for.); Single issues: $12 (ind.), $14 (for.),
$18 (special issues).

Iowa: IOWA REVIEW, David Hamilton, ed., 308 EPB, U. of Iowa, Iowa
City, IA 52242. Issues indexed: (15:1-3). Subscriptions:
$20/yr. (lib., inst.), $12/yr. (ind.), plus $3/yr. (for.); Sing-
le issues: $5.

*JamesWR: THE JAMES WHITE REVIEW, A Gay Men's Literary Quarterly,
Phil Willkie, David Lindahl, Greg Baysans, eds., P.O. Box 3356,
Traffic Station, Minneapolis, MN 55403. Issues indexed: (2:1-3,
3:1). Subscriptions: $8/yr., $14/2 yrs. (USA & Canada); $10/yr.
(inst.); $13/yr. (for.); Single issues: $2.

*JlNJPo: THE JOURNAL OF NEW JERSEY POETS, Marjorie Keyishian,
Managing ed., English Dept., Fairleigh Dickinson U., 285 Madison
Ave., Madison, NJ 07940. Issues indexed: (8:1). Subscriptions:
$3/2 issues. Single issues: $1.50.

*Kaleid: KALEIDOSCOPE, The International Literary & Fine Art Maga-
zine by Persons with Disabilities, Carson W. Heiner, Jr., Ed.,
United Cerebral Palsy and Services for the Handicapped, 326
Locust St., Akron, OH 44302. Issues indexed: (10-11). Subscrip-
tions: $8/yr. (2 issues); $9/yr. (for.). Single issues: $4; $5

(for.).

KanQ: KANSAS QUARTERLY, Harold Schneider, et al., eds., Dept. of
English, Denison Hall, Kansas State U., Manhattan, KS 66506.
Issues indexed: (17:1/2-4). Subscriptions: $27/2 yrs., $15/yr.
(USA, Canada, Latin America), $29/2 yrs., $16/yr. (other coun-
tries); Single issues: $4.

Kayak: KAYAK, George Hitchcock, Marjorie Simon, Gary Fisher, eds.,
325 Ocean View Ave., Santa Cruz, CA 95062. Issues indexed: (64)
"Final issue". Single issues: $2.

KenR: KENYON REVIEW, Philip D. Church, Galbraith M. Crump, eds.,
Kenyon College, Gambier, OH 43022. Issues indexed: No 1985
issues received. Subscriptions: Kenyon Review, P.O. Box 1308L,
Fort Lee, NJ 07024; $15/yr., $28/2 yrs., $39/3 yrs. (ind.);
$18/yr. (inst.); +$5 (for.); Single issues: $6.50; Back issues:
$3.

*LaurelR: LAUREL REVIEW, Mark DeFoe, ed., David McAleavey, et al.,
po. eds., Dept. of English, West Virginia Wesleyan College,
Buckhannon, WV 26201. Issues indexed: (19:1-2). Subscriptions:
$8/yr. (2 issues); Single issues: $4.

LetFem: LETRAS FEMENINAS, Asociacion de Literatura Femenina Hispan-
ica, Dr. Adelaida López de Martinez, Directora., Texas A & M U.,
Modern Languages Dept., College Station, TX 77843-4238. Issues
indexed: (11:1/2). Membership/Subscription: $20/yr.

LindLM: LINDEN LANE MAGAZINE, Belkis Cuza Male, ed., P.O. Box 2384,
Princeton, NJ 08540-0384. Issues indexed: (4:1-4). Subscrip-
tions: $10/yr. (ind.), $16/yr. (inst.), $20/yr. (for.); Single
issues: $2.

LitR: THE LITERARY REVIEW, Walter Cummins, ed., Fairleigh Dickinson
U., 285 Madison Ave., Madison, NJ 07940. Issues indexed: (28:2-
4, 29:1). Subscriptions: $12/yr., $15/yr. (for.), $22/2 yrs.
(ind.), $28/2 yrs. (for.); Single issues: $4.50, $5.50 (for.).

LittleBR: THE LITTLE BALKANS REVIEW, Gene DeGruson, po. ed., The
Little Balkans Press, Inc., 601 Grandview Heights Terr., Pitts-
burg, KS 66762. Issues indexed: (5:1). Subscriptions: $10/yr.;
Single issues: $3.50.

LittleM: THE LITTLE MAGAZINE, Kathryn Cramer, et al., eds, Dragon
Press, P.O. Box 78, Pleasantville, NY 10570. Issues Indexed:
(14:4-15:1). Subscriptions: $16/4 issues; Single issues: $4.50.

LittleR: THE LITTLE REVIEW, John McKernan, ed., Little Review
Press, Box 205, Marshall U., Huntington, WV 25701. Issues
indexed: No 1984 or 1985 issues received; next issue anticipated
in 1986. Subscriptions: $2.50/yr.; Single issues: $1.25.

Mairena: MAIRENA, Manuel de la Puebla, director, Himalaya 257,
Urbanizacín Monterrey, Río Piedras, PR 00926. Issues indexed:
(7:19). Subscriptions: $6/yr., $10/yr. (inst.), $10/yr. (for.),
$15/yr. (for. inst.).

MalR: THE MALAHAT REVIEW, Constance Rooke, ed., P.O. Box 1700,
Victoria, B. C., Canada V8W 2Y2. Issues indexed: (70-72).
Subscriptions: $40/3 yrs., $15/yr. (USA, Canada), $50/3 yrs.,
$20/yr. (other countries), $10/yr. (stud.); Single issues: $7
(USA, Canada), $8 (other countries).

ManhatR: THE MANHATTAN REVIEW, Philip Fried, ed., 304 Third Ave.,
Apt. 4A, New York, NY 10010. Issues indexed: No 1985 issues
published. Subscriptions: $8/2 issues (ind.), $12/2 issues
(inst.), plus $2.50/2 issues (outside USA & Canada); Back is-
sues: $4.

MassR: THE MASSACHUSETTS REVIEW, Mary Heath, John Hicks, Fred
Robinson, eds., Anne Halley, Paul Jenkins, po. eds., Memorial
Hall, U. of Massachusetts, Amherst, MA 01003. Issues indexed:
(26:1, 2/3, 4). Subscriptions: $12/yr., $14/yr. (for.); Single
issues: $4.

MemphisSR: MEMPHIS STATE REVIEW, William Page, ed., Dept. of Eng-
lish, Memphis State U., Memphis, TN 38152. Issues indexed:
(5:2, Spr 85). Subscriptions: $3/yr.; Single issues: $2.

Mester: MESTER, Kathleen Palatucci O'Donnell, directora, Dept. of
Spanish and Portuguese, U. of California, Los Angeles, CA 90024.
Issues indexed: (14:1). Subscriptions: $14/yr. (inst.), $8/yr.
(ind.), $5/yr. (stud.); Single issues: $7 (inst.), $4 (ind.)

Metam: METAMORFOSIS, Lauro Flores, Director, Centro de Estudios
Chicanos, GN-80, U. of Washington, Seattle, WA 98195. Issues
indexed: No 1985 issues received ("The journal is on hold").
Single issues: $5.

MichQR: MICHIGAN QUARTERLY REVIEW, Laurence Goldstein, ed., 3032
Rackham Bldg., U. of Michigan, Ann Arbor, MI 48109. Issues
indexed: (24:1-4). Subscriptions: $24/2 yr., $13/yr. (ind.),
$15/yr. (inst.); Single issues: $3.50; Back issues: $2.

MidAR: MID-AMERICAN REVIEW, Robert Early, ed., Ken Shedd, po. ed.,
106 Hanna Hall, Dept. of English, Bowling Green State U., Bowl-
ing Green, OH 43403. Issues indexed: (5:1-2). Subscriptions:
$6/yr. (2 issues), $10/2 yrs., $14/3 yrs.

MidwQ: THE MIDWEST QUARTERLY, James B. M. Schick, ed., Stephen E.
Meats, po. ed., Pittsburg State U., Pittsburg, KS 66762-5889.
Issues indexed: (26:2-4, 27:1). Subscriptions: $6/yr. plus $2
(for.); Single issues: $2.

MinnR: THE MINNESOTA REVIEW, Fred Pfeil, Michael Sprinker, eds,
Richard Daniels, Anne E. Krosby, po. eds., Dept. of English,
SUNY--Stony Brook, Stony Brook, NY 11794. Issues Indexed: (NS
24-25). Subscriptions: $20/2 yrs. (inst. & for.), $12/2 yrs.
(ind.), $12/yr. (inst. & for.), $7/yr. (ind.); Single issues:
$4.

MissouriR: THE MISSOURI REVIEW, Speer Morgan, ed., Sherod Santos &
Garrett Hongo, po. eds., Dept. of English, 231 Arts and Science,
U. of Missouri, Columbia, MO 65211. Issues indexed: (8:2-3).
Subscriptions: $18/2 yrs. (6 issues), $10/yr. (3 issues). Single
issues: $4.

MissR: MISSISSIPPI REVIEW, Frederick Barthelme, ed., The Center for
Writers, U. of Southern Mississippi, Southern Station, Box 5144,
Hattiesburg, MS 39406-5144. Issues indexed: (39-40/41). Sub-
scriptions: $26/3 yrs., $18/2 yrs., $10/yr., plus $2/yr. (for.);
Single issues: usually $5.

MoodySI: MOODY STREET IRREGULARS, Joy Walsh, ed., P.O. Box 157,
Clarence Center, NY 14032. Issues indexed: (15). Subscriptions:
$7/3 issues (ind.), $9/3 issues (lib.); Single issues: $3.

MSS: MSS, L. M. Rosenberg, Joanna Higgins, eds., State U. of NY at
   Binghamton, Binghamton, NY 13901. Issues indexed: (4:3). Sub-
   scriptions: $18/2 yrs. (ind.), $25/2 yrs. (lib.); $10/yr.
   (ind.), $15/yr. (lib.); Single issues: $4., Double issues: $6.

Mund: MUNDUS ARTIUM, Rainer Schulte, ed., U. of Texas at Dallas,
   Box 830688, MS J031, Richardson, TX 75080-0688. Issues indexed:
   (15:1/2, 16:1/2). Subscriptions: $10/2 issues (inst.), $8/2
   issues (ind.). Single issues: $4.50.

Nat: THE NATION, Victor Navasky, ed., Grace Schulman, po. ed., 72
   Fifth Ave., New York, NY 10011. Issues indexed: (240:1-25,
   241:1-22). Subscriptions: $81/2 yrs., $45/yr., plus $7/yr. (Mex-
   ico, Canada), plus $13/yr. (other for.); Single issues: $1.25;
   P.O. Box 1953, Marion, OH 43305.

NegC: NEGATIVE CAPABILITY, Sue Brannan Walker, ed., 6116 Timberly
   Road North, Mobile, AL 36609. Issues indexed: (5:1-4). Subscrip-
   tions: $12/yr. (ind.), $14/yr. (inst.), $14/yr. (for.); Single
   issues: $3.50.

NewEngR: NEW ENGLAND REVIEW AND BREAD LOAF QUARTERLY, Sydney Lea,
   Jim Schley, eds., Box 170, Hanover, NH 03755. Issues indexed:
   (7:3-4, 8:1-2). Subscriptions: $12/yr.; Single issues: $4; 13
   Dartmouth College Highway, Lyme, NH 03768..

NewL: NEW LETTERS, James McKinley, ed., U. of Missouri-Kansas City,
   5310 Harrison, Kansas City, MO 64110. Issues indexed: (51:3-4,
   52:1). Subscriptions: $50/5 yrs., $25/2 yrs., $15/yr. (ind.);
   $60/5 yrs., $30/2 yrs., $18/yr. (lib.); Single issues: $4.

NewOR: NEW ORLEANS REVIEW, John Mosier, et al., eds., Box 195,
   Loyola U., New Orleans, LA 70118. Issues indexed: (12:1-4).
   Subscriptions: $25/yr. (ind.), $30/yr. (inst.), $35/yr. (for.);
   Single issues: $7.

NewRena: THE NEW RENAISSANCE, Louise T. Reynolds, ed., Stanwood
   Bolton, po. ed., 9 Heath Road, Arlington, MA 02174. Issues
   indexed: (19). Subscriptions: $19/6 issues, $10/3 issues; $23/6
   issues, $12/3 issues (Canada, Mexico, Europe); $25/6 issues,
   $13/3 issues (elsewhere); Single issues: $5.75; $6 (Canada,
   Mexico & Europe); $6.20 (Elsewhere).

NewRep: THE NEW REPUBLIC. 1220 19th St. N.W., Washington, DC
   20036. Issues indexed: (192:1-25, 193:1-27). Subscriptions:
   $56/yr., $70 (Canada), $81 (elsewhere). Back issues: $2.50.
   Single issues: $1.95. Subscription Service Dept., The New
   Republic, P.O. Box 56515, Boulder, CO 80322.

NewYorker: THE NEW YORKER, 25 W. 43rd St., New York, NY 10036.
   Issues indexed: (60:47-53, 61:1-45). Subscriptions: $52/2 yrs.,
   $32/yr.; $44/yr. (Canada); $52/yr. (for.); Single issues: $1.50.

NewYRB: THE NEW YORK REVIEW OF BOOKS, Robert B. Silvers, Barbara
   Epstein, eds., 250 W. 57th St., New York, NY 10107. Issues
   indexed: (31:21/22, 32:1-20). Subscriptions: $30/yr.; Single
   issues: $2; Subscription Service Dept., P.O. Box 940, Farming-
   dale, NY 11737.

Nimrod: NIMROD, Francine Ringold, ed., Joan Flint, et al., po.
   eds., Arts and Humanities Council of Tulsa, 2210 S. Main St.,
   Tulsa, OK 74114. Issues indexed: (28:2, 29:1). Subscriptions:
   $10/yr., $13/yr. (for.); Single issues: $5.50, $7 (for.).

NoAmR: THE NORTH AMERICAN REVIEW, Robley Wilson, Jr., ed., Peter Cooley, po. ed., U. of Northern Iowa, Cedar Falls, IA 50614. Issues indexed: (270:1-4). Subscriptions: $11/yr., $12/yr. (Canada, Latin America), $14/yr. (elsewhere); Single issues: $3.

NoDaQ: NORTH DAKOTA QUARTERLY, Robert W. Lewis, ed., Don Eades, po. ed., Box 8237, U. of North Dakota, Grand Forks, ND 58202. Issues indexed: (53:1-4). Subscriptions: $10/yr.; Single issues: $4.

Northeast: NORTHEAST, John Judson, ed., Juniper Press, 1310 Shorewood Dr., La Crosse, WI 54601. Issues indexed: (Ser. 4: 1-2). Subscriptions: $25; Single issues: $3.

NowestR: NORTHWEST REVIEW, John Witte, ed., Maxine Scates, po. ed., 369 PLC, U. of Oregon, Eugene, OR 97403. Issues indexed: (23:1-3). Subscriptions: $30/3 yrs., $21/2 yrs., $11/yr.; $20/2 yrs., $10/yr. (stud.); plus $2/yr. (for.); Single issues: $4.

Obs: OBSIDIAN, Alvin Aubert, ed./pub., Wayne State U., Detroit, MI 48202. Issues indexed: No 1985 issues received. Subscriptions: $8.50/yr., $9.50/yr. (Canada), $11.50/yr. (for.); Single issues: $3; Double issues: $6.

OhioR: THE OHIO REIVEW, Wayne Dodd, ed., Ellis Hall, Ohio U., Athens, OH 45701-2979. Issues indexed: (34-35). Subscriptions: $30/3 yrs. (9 issues), $12/yr. (3 issues); Single issues: $4.25.

*Oink: OINK!, Maxine Chernoff and Paul Hoover, eds., 1446 Jarvis, Chicago, IL 60626. Issues indexed: (19). Subscriptions: $5/issue.

OntR: ONTARIO REVIEW, Raymond J. Smith, ed., 9 Honey Brook Dr., Princeton, NJ 08540. Issues indexed: (22-23). Subscriptions: $21/3 yrs., $15/2 yrs., $8/yr., plus $1/yr. (for.); Single issues: $3.95.

Open24: OPEN 24 HOURS, Kate Pipkin and Chris Toll, eds, 702 Homestead St., Baltimore, MD 21218. Issues indexed: (4) Subscriptions: $7/3 issues; Single issues: $3.

OP: OPEN PLACES, Eleanor M. Bender, ed., Box 2085, Stephens College, Columbia, MO 65215. Issues indexed: (38/39-40). Subscriptions: $15/2 yrs., $8/yr. (USA, Canada), plus $6/yr. (elsewhere); Single issue: $4-10.

Origin: ORIGIN. National Poetry Foundation. Cid Corman, ed., Michael Heller, USA ed., P.O. Box 981, Stuyvesant Sta., New York, NY 10009. Issues indexed: (Series 5:5). Subscriptions: $12/4 issues, $15/4 issues (Canadian currency), $21/4 issues (for.). Business Office: 305 Neville Hall, U. of Maine, Orono, ME 04469-0122.

OroM: ORO MADRE, Loss and Jan Glazier, eds., 4429 Gibraltar Dr., Fremont, CA 94536. Issues indexed: No 1985 issues received. Subscriptions: $12/4 issues; Single issues: $3.95.

Os: OSIRIS, Andrea Moorhead, ed., Box 297, Deerfield, MA 01342. Issues indexed: (20-21). Subscriptions: $6/2 issues (USA, Canada, Mexico), $7/2 issues (elsewhere, surface mail), $9/2 issues (elsewhere, airmail); Single issues: $3.

Outbr: OUTERBRIDGE, Charlotte Alexander, ed., English Dept. (A323), College of Staten Island, 715 Ocean Terrace, Staten Island, NY 10301. Issues indexed: (14/15). Sub-scriptions: $4/yr.; Single issues: $2.

Paint: PAINTBRUSH, Ben Bennani, ed., English & Foreign Languages,
   Georgia Southwestern College, Americus, GA 31709. Issues in-
   dexed: (11:21/12:24). Subscriptions: $20/3 yrs., $15/2 yrs.,
   $8/yr.; Single issues: $5; Back issues: $5.

PaintedB: PAINTED BRIDE QUARTERLY, Louis Camp, et al., eds., 230
   Vine St., Philadelphia, PA 19106. Issues indexed: (25-26/27).
   Subscriptions: $9/yr., $17/2 yrs., $15/yr. (lib, inst.); Single
   issues: $3.

ParisR: THE PARIS REVIEW, George A. Plimpton, et al., eds., Jona-
   than Galassi, po. ed., 541 East 72nd St., New York, NY 10021.
   Issues indexed: (27:95-98). Subscriptions: $1000/life, $48/12
   issues, $32/8 issues, $16/4 issues, plus $4/4 issues (for.);
   Single issues: $5; 45-39 171 Place, Flushing, NY 11358.

PartR: PARTISAN REVIEW, William Phillips, ed., Boston U., 141 Bay
   State Rd., Boston, MA 02215. Issues indexed: (52:2-4). Sub-
   scriptions: $39/3 yrs., $29/2 yrs., $16/yr.; $33/2 yrs., $18/yr.
   (for.); $22/yr. (inst.); Single issues: $4.50.

*PassN: PASSAGES NORTH, Elinor Benedict, ed., Bay Arts Writers'
   Guild of the William Bonifas Fine Arts Center, Inc., Escanaba,
   MI 49829. Issues indexed: (6:1-2). Subscriptions: $2/yr., $5/3
   yrs; Single issues: $1.50.

Paunch: PAUNCH, Arthur Efron, ed., Mili Clark, po. ed., 123 Wood-
   ward Ave., Buffalo, NY 14214. Issues indexed: No 1985 issues
   received. Subscriptions: $7 (ind.), $10 (lib.), $4 (stud.)

Peb: PEBBLE, Greg Kuzma, ed., The Best Cellar Press, Dept. of
   English, U. of Nebraska, Lincoln, NE 68588. Issues indexed: No
   1985 issues received. Subscriptions: $15/4 issues (lib.), $12/4
   issues (ind.); single issue: $4.

Pequod: PEQUOD, Mark Rudman, ed., Dept. of English, Room 200, New
   York U., 19 University Place, New York, NY 10003. Issues in-
   dexed: (18, 19/20/21). Subscriptions: $16/2 yrs. (4 issues),
   $9/yr. (2 issues) (ind.); $20/2 yrs., $10/yr. (lib).; plus
   $2/yr. (for.); Single issues: $8. The National Poetry Founda-
   tion, 305 Neville Hall, U. of Maine, Orono, ME 04469-0122.

Pig: PIG IRON, Rose Sayre & Jim Villani, eds., Pig Iron Press, P.O.
   Box 237, Youngstown, OH 44501. Issues indexed: (13). Single
   issues: $5.95.

PikeF: THE PIKESTAFF FORUM, James R. Scrimgeour, Robert D. Suther-
   land, eds./pubs., P.O. Box 127, Normal, IL 61761. Issues in-
   dexed: No 1985 issues published; next issue no. 7, 1986. Sub-
   scriptions: $10/6 issues; Single issues: $2; Back issues: $2.

Playb: PLAYBOY, Hugh M. Hefner, ed./pub., 919 N. Michigan Ave.,
   Chicago, IL 60611. Issues indexed: (32:1-12). Subscriptions:
   $22/yr., $36/2 yrs., $35 (for.); Single issues: varies.

Ploughs: PLOUGHSHARES, DeWitt Henry, Peter O'Malley, Directors,
   Div. of Creative Writing and Literature, Emerson College, 100
   Beacon St., Boston, MA 02116; 214A Waverly Ave., Watertown, MA
   02172. Issues indexed: (11:1, 2/3, 4). Subscriptions: $14/yr.,
   $16/yr. (for.); Single issues: $5.95.

Poem: POEM, Huntsville Literary Association, Robert L. Welker &
   Nancy F. Dillard, eds., P.O. Box 919,, Huntsville, AL 35804.
   Issues indexed: (53-54). Subscriptions: $7.50/yr., $10/yr.
   (for.); Back issues: $5.

PoetC: POET AND CRITIC, Michael Martone, ed., 203 Ross Hall, Iowa
State U., Ames, IA 50011. Issues indexed: (16:2-3, 17:1).
Subscriptions: 9/yr., plus $1/yr. (for.); Single issues: $3;
Iowa State U. Press, South State St., Ames, IA 50010.

PoeticJ: POETIC JUSTICE: Contemporary American Poetry, Alan Enge-
bretsen, ed., 8220 Rayford Dr., Los Angeles, CA 90045. Issues
indexed: (9-12). Subscriptions: $10/yr.; Single issues: $3.

PoetL: POET LORE, Philip K. Jason, Barbara Lefcowitz, Roland Flint,
Executive eds., Heldref Publications, 4000 Albemarle St., N.W.,
Washington, DC 20016. Issues indexed: (79:4, 80:1-3). Subscrip-
tions: $12/yr., $20/yr. (inst.), plus $5/yr. (for.); Single
issues: $4.50.

Poetry: POETRY, Joseph Parisi, ed., 601 S. Morgan St., P.O. Box
4348, Chicago, IL 60680. Issues indexed: (145:4-6, 146:1-6,
147:1-3). Subscriptions: $22/yr., $27/yr. (for.); Single issues:
$2.50 plus $.75 postage; Back issues: $3 plus $.75 postage.

PoetryCR: POETRY CANADA REVIEW, Robert Billings, ed., 307 Coxwell
Ave., Toronto, Ontario M4L 3B5 Canada. Issues indexed: (6:3-4,
7:1-2). Subscriptions: $14/yr., $26/2 yrs. (ind.); $30/yr. $56/2
yrs. (inst.); Single issues: $2.50.

PoetryE: POETRY EAST, Richard Jones, Kate Daniels, eds., Star Route
1, Box 50, Earlysville, VA 22936. Issues indexed: (16/17-18).
Subscriptions: $10/yr.; Single issues: $3.50-$6.

PoetryNW: POETRY NORTHWEST, David Wagoner, ed., U. of Washington,
4045 Brooklyn Ave., NE, Seattle, WA 98105. Issues indexed:
(26:1-4). Subscriptions: $8/yr., $9/yr. (for.); Single issues:
$2, $2.25 (for.).

*PoetryR: POETRY REVIEW, A magazine of poetry, translations of
poetry, and essays, Poetry Society of America, Jerome Mazzaro,
ed., 15 Gramercy Park, New York, NY 10003. Issues Indexed: (2:2
& Issue No. 5); publication ceased following No. 5.

*PortLES: THE PORTABLE LOWER EAST SIDE, Kurt Hollander, ed., 463
West St., #344, New York, NY 10014. Issues indexed: (2:1).
Subscriptions: $8/yr. (2 issues); Single issues: $4.

PottPort: THE POTTERSFIELD PORTFOLIO, Peggy Amirault, Barbara Cot-
trell, Robin Metcalfe, Donalee Moulton-Barrett, eds., Crazy
Quilt Press, c/o 19 Oakhill Drive, Halifax, Nova Scotia B3M 2V3
Canada. Issues indexed: (7). Subscriptions: $10/3 yrs.

PraF: PRAIRIE FIRE, Andris Taskans, managing ed., 374 Donald St.,
3rd Floor, Winnipeg, Manitoba R3B 2J2 Canada. Issues indexed:
(6:1-4). Subscriptions: $15/yr. (ind.), $20/yr. (inst.), plus
$4 (for.); Single issues: $4.95.

PraS: PRAIRIE SCHOONER, Hugh Luke, ed., Hilda Raz, po. ed., 201
Andrews Hall, U. of Nebraska, Lincoln, NE 68588. Issues in-
dexed: (59:1-4). Subscriptions: $29/3 yrs., $20/2 yrs., $11/yr.
(ind.); $15/yr. (lib.); Single issues: $3.25.

Prima: PRIMAVERA, Ann Grearen, Rebecca Hecht-Lewis, Jeanne Krinsley
et al., eds., 1212 East 59th, Chicago, IL 60637. Issues in-
dexed: (9). Single issues: $5.

Quarry: QUARRY, Bob Hilderley, ed., Box 1061, Kingston, Ontario K7L
4Y5 Canada. Issues indexed: (34:1-4). Subscriptions: $16/yr. (4
issues), $28/2 yrs. (8 issues); Single issues: $4.

QRL: QUARTERLY REVIEW OF LITERATURE, T. & R. Weiss, 26 Haslet Ave., Princeton, NJ 08540. Issues indexed: No 1985 issues published. Subscriptions: $15/2 volumes (paper), $20/volume (cloth, inst.); Single issues: $10 (paper).

QW: QUARTERLY WEST, Christopher Merrill, Ann Snodgrass, eds.; Scott, Cairns, Kevin Cantwell, po. eds. 317 Olpin Union, U. of Utah, Salt Lake City, UT 84112. Issues indexed: (20-21). Subscriptions: $12/2 yrs. 4 issues), $6.50/yr. (2 issues); Single issues: $3.50.

*Raccoon: RACCOON, David Spicer, ed., 323 Hodges Street, Memphis, TN 38111. Issues indexed: (17-18). Subscriptions: $10/yr.; Single issues: $5.00; St. Luke's Press, Suite 401, Mid-Memphis Tower, 1407 Union Avenue, Memphis, TN 38104.

RagMag: RAG MAG, Beverly Voldseth, ed., Box 12, Goodhue, MN 55027. Issues indexed: (4:1-2). Subscriptions: $5/yr.; Single issues: $3.

*Rampike: RAMPIKE, Karl Jirgens, David McFadden, Terrence McCubbin, eds., 95 Rivercrest Road, Toronto, Ontario M6S 4H7 Canada. Issues indexed: (4:2/3). Subscriptions: $14/3 issues; Single issues: $6.

Raritan: RARITAN, Richard Poirier, ed., Rutgers U., 165 College Ave., New Brunswick, NJ 08903. Issues indexed: (4:3-4, 5:1-2). Subscriptions: $12/yr., $21/2 yrs. (ind.); $16/yr., $26/2 yrs. (inst.); plus $4/yr (for.); Single issues: $4; Back issues: $5.

RevChic: REVISTA CHICANO-RIQUENA, Julián Olivares, ed., U. of Houston, University Park, Houston, TX 77004. With 14:1 (Spr 86) title changed to THE AMERICAS REVIEW: A Review of Hispanic Literature and Art of the USA. Issues indexed: (12:1-3/4, 13:1-3/4). Subscriptions: $15/yr., $20/yr. (inst.); Single issues: $5.

*RiverS: RIVER STYX, Jan Garden Castro, Quincy Troupe, eds., 7420 Cornell, St. Louis, MO 63130 (Castro); 1925 7th Ave., H4, 7L, New York, NY 10026 (Troupe). Issues indexed: (16-18). Subscriptions: $9/yr. (2 issues, ind.); $17/yr., $26/2 yrs. (inst.); Single issues: $5; Big River Association, 7420 Cornell, St. Louis, MO 63130.

Salm: SALMAGUNDI, Robert Boyers, ed., Peggy Boyers, Exec. ed., Skidmore College, Saratoga Springs, NY 12866. Issues indexed: (66, 67, 68/69). Subscriptions: $12/yr., $18/2 yrs.; Single issues: $5.

Sam: SAMISDAT, Merritt Clifton, Robin Michelle Clifton, eds., Box 129, Richford, VT 05476. Issues indexed: (41:3-43:3, releases 163-171). Subscriptions: $150/all future issues, $25/1000 pages, $15/500 pages; Single issues: varies.

SanFPJ: SAN FERNANDO POETRY JOURNAL, Richard Cloke, ed., 18301 Halsted St., Northridge, CA 91324. Issues indexed: (7:2-4). Subscriptions: $10/yr., $18/2 yrs., $25/3 yrs.; Single issues: $3.

SecC: SECOND COMING, A. D. Winans, ed./pub., Box 31249, San Francisco, CA 94131. Issues indexed: (12:1-2, 13:1-2). Subscriptions: $8.50/yr. (lib.), $6/yr. (ind.), $11 (for.).

SenR: SENECA REVIEW, Deborah Tall, ed., Hobart & William Smith Colleges, Geneva, NY 14456. Issues indexed: (15:1-2). Subscriptions: $6/yr.; Single issues: $3.50.

SewanR: THE SEWANEE REVIEW, George Core, ed., U. of the South, Sewanee, TN 37375. Issues indexed: (93:1-4). Subscriptions: $48/3 yrs., $33/2 yrs., $18/yr. (inst.); $28/3 yrs., $20/2 yrs., $12/yr. (ind.); plus $3/yr. (for.); Single issues: $4; Back issues: $5-10, plus $.75/copy postage & handling.

Shen: SHENANDOAH, James Boatwright, ed., Richard Howard, po. ed., Washington and Lee U., Box 722, Lexington, VA 24450. Issues indexed: (36:1). Subscriptions: $25/3 yrs., $18/2 yrs., $11/yr.; $33/3 yrs., $24/2 yrs., $14/yr. (for.); Single issues: $3.50; Back issues: $6.

*SilverFR: SILVERFISH REVIEW, Rodger Moody, ed., P.O. Box 3541, Eugene, OR 97403. Issues indexed: (10). Subscriptions: $9/3 issues, $15/6 issues, $25/lifetime; Single issues: $3.

SinN: SIN NOMBRE, Nilita Vientòs Gastòn, Dir., Box 4391, San Juan, PR 00905-4391. Issues indexed: (14:4). Subscriptions: $20/yr. (inst.), $15/yr. (ind.), $10/yr. (stud., Puerto Rico); Single issues: $4.25; Special issues: $6.

SmPd: THE SMALL POND MAGAZINE OF LITERATURE, Napoleon St. Cyr, ed./pub., P.O. Box 664, Stratford, CT 06497. Issues indexed: (22:1-3, issues 63-65). Subscriptions: $5.50/yr., $10.25/2 yrs., $15/3 yrs.; Single issues: $2.50.

SnapD: SNAPDRAGON, Gail Eckwright, Tina Foriyes, Margaret Snyder, Co-eds., Library-Humanities, U. of Idaho, Moscow, ID 83843. Issues indexed: (8:2, 9:1). Subscriptions: $3.50 (ind.), $4.50 (inst.).

SoCaR: SOUTH CAROLINA REVIEW, Richard J. Calhoun, ed., Dept. of English, Clemson U., Clemson, SC 29634-1503. Issues indexed: (17:2, 18:1). Subscriptions: $9/2 yrs., $5/yr. (USA, Canada, Mexico); $10/2 yrs., $5.50/yr. (elsewhere); Back issues: $5.

SoDakR: SOUTH DAKOTA REVIEW, John R. Milton, ed., Dept. of English, U. of South Dakota, Box 111, U. Exchange, Vermillion, SD 57069. Issues indexed: (23:1-4). Subscriptions: $17/2 yrs., $10/yr. (USA, Canada); $20/2 yrs., $12/yr. (elsewhere); Single issues: $3.

SouthernHR: SOUTHERN HUMANITIES REVIEW, Dan R. Latimer, Thomas L. Wright, eds., 9088 Haley Center, Auburn U., Auburn, AL 36849. Issues indexed: (19:1-4). Subscriptions: $9/yr.; Single issues: $3.

SouthernPR: SOUTHERN POETRY REVIEW, Robert Grey, ed., English Dept., U. of North Carolina, Charlotte, NC 28223. Issues indexed: (25:1-2; 25:2 (Fall 85) labeled 26:2 in error?). Subscriptions: $5/yr.; Single issues: $3.

SouthernR: SOUTHERN REVIEW, James Olney, Lewis P. Simpson, eds., Louisiana State U., 43 Allen Hall, Baton Rouge, LA 70893. Issues indexed: (21:1-4). Subscriptions: $21/3 yrs., $16/2 yrs., $9/yr.; Single issues: $2.50.

SouthwR: SOUTHWEST REVIEW, Willard Spiegelman, ed., Southern Metho-dist U., Box 4374, Dallas, TX 75275. Issues indexed: (70:1-4). Subscriptions: $25/3 yrs., $18/2 yrs., $10/yr. (ind.); Single issues: $3.

Sparrow: SPARROW PRESS POVERTY PAMPHLETS, Felix Stefanile, ed./Pub., Sparrow Press, 103 Waldron St., West Lafayette, IN 47906. Issues indexed: (48-49). Subscriptions: $7.50/3 issues; Single issues: $2.50.

Spirit: THE SPIRIT THAT MOVES US, Morty Sklar, ed., P.O. Box 1585, Iowa City, IA 52244. Issues indexed: No 1985 issues received; (8:2) due in March 1987. Single issues: $9.60-$13.60.

SpiritSH: SPIRIT, David Rogers, ed., Seton Hall U., South Orange, NJ 07079. Issues indexed: (51). Subscriptions: $4/yr.; Single issues: $2; Back issues: $3.

SpoonRQ: THE SPOON RIVER QUARTERLY, David R. Pichaske, ed., P.O. Box 1443, Peoria, IL 61655. Issues indexed: (10:2-4, 11:1). Subscriptions: $10/yr.; Single issues: $3.

Stand: STAND, Jon Silkin, et al., eds., 179 Wingrove Road, Newcastle upon Tyne NE4 9DA, England; Howard Fink, Canadian ed., 4054 Melrose Ave., Montreal, Quebec H4A 2S4 Canada; Lawrence Joseph, USA ed., Apt. 8, 275 Water St., New York, NY 10038. Issues indexed: (26:1-4). Subscriptions: $12/yr.; $10/yr. (students, unwaged); Single issues: $3; Stand Magazine USA, P.O. Box 648, Concord, MA 01742,

Stepp: STEPPINGSTONE, James B. Gwyne, ed., Box 1856, Harlem, NY 10027. Issues indexed: No 1985 issues received. Single issues: $5.

StoneC: STONE COUNTRY, Judith Neeld, ed., The Nathan Mayhew Seminars of Martha's Vineyard, P.O. Box 132, Menemsha, MA 02552. Issues indexed: (12:2/3, 13:1/2). Subscriptions: $15/4 issues, $8/2 issues; Single issues: $4.50; Back issues: $3.50.

Sulfur: SULFUR, Clayton Eshleman, ed., English Dept., Eastern Michigan U., Ypsilanti, MI 48197. Issues indexed: (4:2[i.e.3], 5:1-2, issues 12-14). Subscriptions: $22/yr. - 3 issues (inst.), $15/yr. - 3 issues (ind.), plus $3/yr. (for.); Single issues: $6.

Swallow: SWALLOW'S TALE, Joe Taylor, ed., P.O. Box 4328, Tallahassee, FL 32315-4328. Issues indexed: (4). Subscriptions: Final issue, No. 5, $5; Back issues: $4.

TarRP: TAR RIVER POETRY, Peter Makuck, ed., Dept. of English, Austin Bldg., East Carolina U., Greenville, NC 27834. Issues indexed: 24:2 & 25:1 (1985) received too late for indexing; will be included in 1986 volume. Subscriptions: $5/yr., $8/2 yrs.; Single issues: $2.50.

*Temblor: TEMBLOR, Contemporary Poets, Leland Hickman, ed., 4624 Cahuenga Blvd., #307, North Hollywood, CA 91602. Issues indexed: (1-2). Subscriptions: $16/2 issues, $30/4 issues (ind.); $20/2 issues, $40/4 issues (inst.); Single issues: $8.50.

Tendril: TENDRIL, George E. Murphy, Jr., managing ed., Box 512, Green Harbor, MA 02041. Issues indexed: (19/20). Subscriptions: $27/9 issues, $19/6 issues, $12/3 issues (ind.); $14/yr. (inst.); Single issues: $5.95-$10.95.

TexasR: TEXAS REVIEW, Paul Ruffin, ed., Division of English and Foreign Language, Sam Houston State U., Huntsville, TX 77341. Issues indexed: (6:1/2-3/4). Subscriptions: $4/yr., $4.25/yr. (Canada), $4.50/yr. (for.); Single issues: $2.

13thM: 13TH MOON. See entry at beginning of list, prior to the 'A' entries.

ThRiPo: THREE RIVERS POETRY JOURNAL, Gerald Costanzo, ed., Three Rivers Press, P.O. Box 21, Carnegie-Mellon U., Pittsburgh, PA 15213. Issues indexed: (25/26). Subscriptions: $10/4 issues; Single issues: $2.50; Double issues: $5.

Thrpny: THE THREEPENNY REVIEW, Wendy Lesser, ed./pub., P.O. Box 9131, Berkeley, CA 94709. Issues indexed: (20-23). Subscriptions: $13/2 yrs., $8/yr., $16/yr. (surface for.), $24/yr. (airmail for.); Single issues: $2.

TriQ: TRIQUARTERLY, Reginald Gibbons, ed., Northwestern U., 1735 Benson Ave., Evanston, IL 60201. Issues indexed: (62-64). Subscriptions: $100/life (ind.), $200/life (inst.), $28/2 yrs. (ind.), $40/2 yrs. (inst.), $16/yr. (ind.), $22/yr. (inst.), plus $4/yr. (for.); Single issues: usually $6.95; Sample copies: $3.

UnderRM: UNDERGROUND RAG MAG. See: RagMag: RAG MAG.

US1: US 1 WORKSHEETS, US 1 Poets Cooperative, 21 Lake Dr., Roosevelt, NJ 08555. Issues indexed: (18/19). Subscriptions: $5/4 issues; Single issues: $2.50; Back issues: Prices on request.

Veloc: VELOCITIES, Andrew Joron, ed., 1509 Le Roy Ave., Berkeley, CA 94708. Issues indexed: No 1985 issues received. Single issues: $3.50.

*Verse: VERSE, Henry Hart, U. S. ed., English Dept., College of William and Mary, Williamsburg, VA 23185. Issues indexed: (1-4). Subscriptions: $9/3 issues; Single issues: $3.

VirQR: THE VIRGINIA QUARTERLY REVIEW, Staige D. Blackford, ed., Gregory Orr, po. consultant., One West Range, Charlottesville, VA 22903. Issues indexed: (61:1-4). Subscriptions: $24/3 yrs., $18/2 yrs., $10/yr., plus $.50/yr. (Canada), $1/yr. (elsewhere); Single issues: $3.

Vis: VISIONS, Bradley R. Strahan, po. ed./pub., Black Buzzard Press, 4705 South 8th Rd., Arlington, VA 22204. Issues indexed: (17-19). Subscriptions: $8.50/yr., $16/2 yrs.; $25/3 yrs. (lib.); Single issues: $3.

Waves: WAVES, Bernice Lever, ed., Gay Allison, po. ed., 79 Denham Drive, Richmond Hill, Ontario L4C 6H9 Canada. Issues indexed: (13:2/3-4, 14:1/2). Subscriptions: $8/yr. (ind.), $12/yr. (lib.); Single issues: $3; Back issues: $2.

WebR: WEBSTER REVIEW, Nancy Schapiro, ed., Pamela White Hadas & Jerred Metz, po. eds., Webster U., 470 E. Lockwood, Webster Groves, MO 63119. Issues indexed: (10:1-2). Subscriptions: $5/yr.; Single issues: $2.50.

WestB: WEST BRANCH, Karl Patten & Robert Taylor, eds., Dept. of English, Bucknell U., Lewisburg, PA 17837. Issues indexed: (16-17). Subscriptions: $5/yr., 2 issues, $8/2 yrs.; Single issues: $3.

WestCR: WEST COAST REVIEW, Fred Candelaria, ed., English Dept., Simon Fraser U., Burnaby, B.C. V5A 1S6 Canada. Issues indexed: (19:3-4, 20:1-2). Subscriptions: $12/yr. (Canada), $15/yr. (USA, for.), $16/yr. (inst.); Single issues: $3.50 (Canada), $4 (USA, for.).

WestHR: WESTERN HUMANITIES REVIEW, Jack Garlington, ed., U. of Utah, Salt Lake City, UT 84112. Issues indexed: (39:1-4). Subscriptions: $20/yr. (inst.), $15/yr. (ind.); Single issues: $4.

Wind: WIND, Quentin R. Howard, ed., RFD Route 1, Box 809K, Pikeville, KY 41501. Issues indexed: (14:53-55). Subscriptions: $7/3 issues (inst.), $6/3 issues (ind.), $10.50/3 issues (for.); Single issues: $2; $3 (for.).

WindO: THE WINDLESS ORCHARD, Robert Novak, ed., English Dept., Indiana U.-Purdue U., Fort Wayne, IN 46805. Issues indexed: (45-46). Subscriptions: $7/yr. (4 issues), $20/3 yrs., $4/yr. (stud.); Single issues: $2.

WoosterR: WOOSTER REVIEW, Gordon Landefeld, Marjorie Saul, Warren Hedges (poetry), eds., The College of Wooster, Wooster, OH 44691. Issues indexed: (3-4). Subscriptions: $5/yr., $8/2 yrs.; Single issues: $2.50.

WorldO: WORLD ORDER, Firuz Kazemzadeh, Betty J. Fisher, Howard Garey, James D. Stokes, eds., National Spiritual Assembly of the Baha'is of the United States, 415 Linden Ave., Wilmette, IL 60091. Issues indexed: (19:1-2). Subscriptions: $18/2 yrs., $10/yr.; $34/2 yrs., $18/yr. (for.); Single issues: $3.

WormR: THE WORMWOOD REVIEW, Marvin Malone, ed., P.O. Box 8840, Stockton, CA 95208-0840. Issues indexed: (24:1-4, issues 97-100). Subscriptions: $20/4 issues (patrons), $7/4 issues (inst.), $6/4 issues (ind.); Back issues: $3; Single issues: $3..

Writ: WRIT, Roger Greenwald, ed., Innis College, U. of Toronto, 2 Sussex Ave., Toronto, Canada M5S 1JS. Issues indexed: No. 17 (1985, c1986) received too late for indexing; will be included in the 1986 volume. Subscriptions: $12/2 issues (US funds outside Canada); Back issues: $5-10.

WritersL: WRITER'S LIFELINE, Stephen Gill, ed., Box 1641, Cornwall, Ontario K6H 5V6 Canada. Issues indexed: No 1985 issues received. Subscriptions: $18/yr; Single issues: $2.

YaleR: THE YALE REVIEW, Kai Erikson, ed., J. D. McClatchy, po. ed., 1902 A Yale Station, New Haven, CT 06520. Issues indexed: (74:2-4, 75:1). Subscriptions: $22/yr. (inst.), $14/yr. (ind.), plus $3/yr. (for.); Single issues: $5; Back issues: Prices on request; Yale University Press, 92 A Yale Station, New Haven, CT 06520.

YellowS: YELLOW SILK: Journal of Erotic Arts, Lily Pond, ed., P.O. Box 6374, Albany, CA 94706. Issues indexed: (14-17). Subscriptions: $12-$40/yr. (ind., sliding scale), $15/yr. (lib., inst.), plus $5/yr. (for. surface), plus $10/yr. (for. air). Single issues: $3.50.

YetASM: YET ANOTHER SMALL MAGAZINE, Candace Catlin Hall, ed., Box 14353, Hartford, CT 06114. Issues indexed: Vol. 4 (1985) received too late for indexing; will be included in the 1986 volume. Single issues: $1.98.

*Zyzzyva: ZYZZYVA: The Last Word: West Coast Writers & Artists, Howard Junker, ed, 55 Sutter St., Suite 400, San Francisco, CA 94104. Issues indexed: (1:1-4). Subscriptions: $20/yr.; Single copies: $6 post paid.

ALPHABETICAL LIST OF JOURNALS INDEXED, WITH ACRONYMS

13TH MOON: 13thM

ABRAXAS: Abraxas
THE AGNI REVIEW: Agni
AMELIA: Amelia
THE AMERICAN POETRY REVIEW: AmerPoR
THE AMERICAN SCHOLAR: AmerS
THE AMERICAN VOICE: AmerV
ANNEX 21: Annex
ANTAEUS: Antaeus
THE ANTIGONISH REVIEW: AntigR
THE ANTIOCH REVIEW: AntR
AREITO: Areito
ARIZONA QUARTERLY: ArizQ
ASCENT: Ascent
THE ATLANTIC: Atlantic

BALL STATE UNIVERSITY FORUM: BallSUF
THE BELOIT POETRY JOURNAL: BelPoJ
THE BILINGUAL REVIEW/LA REVISTA BILINGUE: BilingR
BLACK AMERICAN LITERATURE FORUM: BlackALF
BLACK WARRIOR REVIEW: BlackWR
BLUE BUFFALO: BlueBuf
BLUE BUILDINGS: BlueBldgs
BLUELINE: Blueline
BOGG: Bogg
BOUNDARY 2: Bound

CALIFORNIA QUARTERLY: CalQ
CALLALOO: Callaloo
CALYX: Calyx
CANADIAN LITERATURE: CanLit
THE CAPE ROCK: CapeR
THE CAPILANO REVIEW: CapilR
CAROLINA QUARTERLY: CarolQ
THE CENTENNIAL REVIEW: CentR
THE CHARITON REVIEW: CharR
CHELSEA: Chelsea
CHICAGO REVIEW: ChiR
THE CHRISTIAN CENTURY: ChrC
CIMARRON REVIEW: CimR
CLOCKWATCH REVIEW: ClockR
COLLEGE ENGLISH: ColEng
COMMONWEAL: Comm
CONCERNING POETRY: ConcPo
CONDITIONS: Cond
CONFRONTATION: Confr
CONJUNCTIONS: Conjunc
THE CONNECTICUT POETRY REVIEW: ConnPR
CRAB CREEK REVIEW: CrabCR
CRAZYHORSE: Crazy
CREAM CITY REVIEW: CreamCR
CROP DUST: CropD
CROSS-CANADA WRITERS' QUARTERLY: CrossC
CROSSCURRENTS: CrossCur
CUMBERLAND POETRY REVIEW: CumbPR
CUTBANK: CutB

DANDELION: Dandel
THE DEKALB LITERARY ARTS JOURNAL: DekalbLAJ
DENVER QUARTERLY: DenQ
DESCANT: Descant

ENGLISH JOURNAL: EngJ
EPOCH: Epoch
EVERGREEN REVIEW: EvergR

FIELD: Field
FOUR QUARTERS: FourQt

THE G. W. REVIEW: GWR
GARGOYLE MAGAZINE: Gargoyle
GEORGIA REVIEW: GeoR
GERMINATION: Germ
GRAHAM HOUSE REVIEW: GrahamHR
GRAIN: Grain
GRAND STREET: GrandS
GREENFIELD REVIEW: GreenfR

HANGING LOOSE: HangL
HARPER'S MAGAZINE: Harp
THE HARVARD ADVOCATE: HarvardA
HAWAII REVIEW: HawaiiR
HIRAM POETRY REVIEW: HiramPoR
THE HOLLINS CRITIC: HolCrit
THE HUDSON REVIEW: Hudson

IMAGINE: Imagine
INDIANA REVIEW: IndR
INTI: Inti
IOWA REVIEW: Iowa

THE JAMES WHITE REVIEW: JamesWR
THE JOURNAL OF NEW JERSEY POETS: JlNJPo

KALEIDOSCOPE: Kaleid
KANSAS QUARTERLY: KanQ
KAYAK: Kayak
KENYON REVIEW: KenR

LAUREL REVIEW: LaurelR
LETRAS FEMENINAS: LetFem
LINDEN LANE MAGAZINE: LindLM
THE LITERARY REVIEW: LitR
THE LITTLE BALKANS REVIEW: LittleBR
THE LITTLE MAGAZINE: LittleM
THE LITTLE REVIEW: LittleR

MAIRENA: Mairena
THE MALAHAT REVIEW: MalR
THE MANHATTAN REVIEW: ManhatR
THE MASSACHUSETTS REVIEW: MassR
MEMPHIS STATE REVIEW: MemphisSR
MESTER: Mester
METAMORFOSIS: Metam
MICHIGAN QUARTERLY REVIEW: MichQR
MID-AMERICAN REVIEW: MidAR
THE MIDWEST QUARTERLY: MidwQ
THE MINNESOTA REVIEW: MinnR
MISSISSIPPI REVIEW: MissR
THE MISSOURI REVIEW: MissouriR
MOODY STREET IRREGULARS: MoodySI
MSS: MSS

MUNDUS ARTIUM: <u>Mund</u>

THE NATION: <u>Nat</u>
NEGATIVE CAPABILITY: <u>NegC</u>
NEW ENGLAND REVIEW AND BREAD LOAF QUARTERLY: <u>NewEngR</u>
NEW LETTERS: <u>NewL</u>
NEW ORLEANS REVIEW: <u>NewOR</u>
THE NEW RENAISSANCE: <u>NewRena</u>
THE NEW REPUBLIC: <u>NewRep</u>
THE NEW YORK REVIEW OF BOOKS: <u>NewYRB</u>
THE NEW YORKER: <u>NewYorker</u>
NIMROD: <u>Nimrod</u>
THE NORTH AMERICAN REVIEW: <u>NoAmR</u>
NORTH DAKOTA QUARTERLY: <u>NoDaQ</u>
NORTHEAST: <u>Northeast</u>
NORTHWEST REVIEW: <u>NowestR</u>

OBSIDIAN: <u>Obs</u>
THE OHIO REIVEW: <u>OhioR</u>
OINK!: <u>Oink</u>
ONTARIO REVIEW: <u>OntR</u>
OPEN 24 HOURS: <u>Open24</u>
OPEN PLACES: <u>OP</u>
ORIGIN: <u>Origin</u>
ORO MADRE: <u>OroM</u>
OSIRIS: <u>Os</u>
OUTERBRIDGE: <u>Outbr</u>

PAINTBRUSH: <u>Paint</u>
PAINTED BRIDE QUARTERLY: <u>PaintedB</u>
THE PARIS REVIEW: <u>ParisR</u>
PARTISAN REVIEW: <u>PartR</u>
PASSAGES NORTH: <u>PassN</u>
PAUNCH: <u>Paunch</u>
PEBBLE: <u>Peb</u>
PEQUOD: <u>Pequod</u>
PIG IRON: <u>Pig</u>
THE PIKESTAFF FORUM: <u>PikeF</u>
PLAYBOY: <u>Playb</u>
PLOUGHSHARES: <u>Ploughs</u>
POEM: <u>Poem</u>
POET AND CRITIC: <u>PoetC</u>
POET LORE: <u>PoetL</u>
POETIC JUSTICE: <u>PoeticJ</u>
POETRY: <u>Poetry</u>
POETRY CANADA REVIEW: <u>PoetryCR</u>
POETRY EAST: <u>PoetryE</u>
POETRY NORTHWEST: <u>PoetryNW</u>
POETRY REVIEW: <u>PoetryR</u>
THE PORTABLE LOWER EAST SIDE: <u>PortLES</u>
THE POTTERSFIELD PORTFOLIO: <u>PottPort</u>
PRAIRIE FIRE: <u>PraF</u>
PRAIRIE SCHOONER: <u>PraS</u>
PRIMAVERA: <u>Prima</u>

QUARRY: <u>Quarry</u>
QUARTERLY REVIEW OF LITERATURE: <u>QRL</u>
QUARTERLY WEST: <u>QW</u>

RACCOON: <u>Raccoon</u>
RAG MAG: <u>RagMag</u>
RAMPIKE: <u>Rampike</u>
RARITAN: <u>Raritan</u>
REVISTA CHICANO-RIQUENA: <u>RevChic</u>
RIVER STYX: <u>RiverS</u>

SALMAGUNDI: Salm
SAMISDAT: Sam
SAN FERNANDO POETRY JOURNAL: SanFPJ
SECOND COMING: SecC
SENECA REVIEW: SenR
THE SEWANEE REVIEW: SewanR
SHENANDOAH: Shen
SILVERFISH REVIEW: SilverFR
SIN NOMBRE: SinN
THE SMALL POND MAGAZINE OF LITERATURE: SmPd
SNAPDRAGON: SnapD
SOUTH CAROLINA REVIEW: SoCaR
SOUTH DAKOTA REVIEW: SoDakR
SOUTHERN HUMANITIES REVIEW: SouthernHR
SOUTHERN POETRY REVIEW: SouthernPR
SOUTHERN REVIEW: SouthernR
SOUTHWEST REVIEW: SouthwR
SPARROW PRESS POVERTY PAMPHLETS: Sparrow
SPIRIT: SpiritSH
THE SPIRIT THAT MOVES US: Spirit
THE SPOON RIVER QUARTERLY: SpoonRQ
STAND: Stand
STEPPINGSTONE: Stepp
STONE COUNTRY: StoneC
SULFUR: Sulfur
SWALLOW'S TALE: Swallow

TAR RIVER POETRY: TarRP
TEMBLOR: Temblor
TENDRIL: Tendril
TEXAS REVIEW: TexasR
13TH MOON. See entry at beginning of list
THREE RIVERS POETRY JOURNAL: ThRiPo
THE THREEPENNY REVIEW: Thrpny
TRIQUARTERLY: TriQ

UNDERGROUND RAG MAG. See: RAG MAG
US 1 WORKSHEETS: US1

VELOCITIES: Veloc
VERSE: Verse
THE VIRGINIA QUARTERLY REVIEW: VirQR
VISIONS: Vis

WAVES: Waves
WEBSTER REVIEW: WebR
WEST BRANCH: WestB
WEST COAST REVIEW: WestCR
WESTERN HUMANITIES REVIEW: WestHR
WIND: Wind
THE WINDLESS ORCHARD: WindO
WOOSTER REVIEW: WoosterR
WORLD ORDER: WorldO
THE WORMWOOD REVIEW: WormR
WRIT: Writ
WRITER'S LIFELINE: WritersL

THE YALE REVIEW: YaleR
YELLOW SILK: YellowS
YET ANOTHER SMALL MAGAZINE: YetASM

ZYZZYVA: Zyzzyva

THE AUTHOR INDEX

1. AAL, Katharyn Machan
    "Call." CreamCR (10:2) [85?], p. 45.
    "Jet." GreenfR (13:1/2) Fall-Wint 85, p. 60.
    "Little Elk Is Dead." NegC (5:4) Fall 85, p. 73.
    "Phantasia for J." CreamCR (10:1) 85, p. 32.
    "Supermarket." GreenfR (13:1/2) Fall-Wint 85, p. 61.
2. AARNES, William (See also AARNES, William A.)
    "Economy." Swallow (4) 85, p. 96.
    "Name These Things." CapeR (20:1) Spr 85, p. 19.
    "November." Swallow (4) 85, p. 97.
3. AARNES, William A. (See also AARNES, William)
    "Fluster." SoCaR (17:2) Spr 85, p. 35.
    "Rapt." SoCaR (17:2) Spr 85, p. 34.
4. ABBEY, Lloyd
    "Signs." CanLit (107) Wint 85, p. 69.
5. ABBOTT, Tony
    "Echoes of This Place." SouthernPR (26, i.e. 25:2) Fall 85,
       p. 16-18.
ABDUL MALIK de COTEAU, Delano
       See MALIK (DELANO ABDUL MALIK DE COTEAU)
6. ABERCOMBIE, V. T.
    "People, Love, Friendship, Functioning Things." Poem (53) Mr
       85, p. 39.
    "Second Hand Man." Poem (53) Mr 85, p. 40.
    "Vail." Poem (53) Mr 85, p. 41.
7. ABINADER, Elmaz
    "Arabic Music." Amelia (2:1) Ap 85, p. 67.
    "Pigeon Rock: Lebanon." Amelia (2:1) Ap 85, p. 67-68.
8. ABRAHAMSON, Dick
    "New England Boys Grow Up." EngJ (74:6) O 85, p. 36.
9. ABSE, Dannie
    "Bloody Horse." Poetry (146:4) Jl 85, p. 225-226.
    "In the Old-Age Home Where He Says He's Resting." GeoR
       (39:3) Fall 85, p. 526.
10. ACCROCCA, Elio Filippo
    "Delft" (tr. by Giuliano Dego and Margaret Straus). LitR
       (29:1) Fall 85, p. 91.
    "Faces by Rembrandt" (tr. by Giuliano Dego and Margaret
       Straus). LitR (29:1) Fall 85, p. 90.
    "Geometry Is in the Air" (tr. by P. F. Paolini). LitR
       (29:1) Fall 85, p. 92.
    "North Sea" (tr. by Giuliano Dego and Margaret Straus).
       LitR (29:1) Fall 85, p. 91.
    "Provos" (tr. by Giuliano Dego and Margaret Straus). LitR
       (29:1) Fall 85, p. 90.
11. ACHARYA, Pradip
    "In the Quiet of Blood" (tr. of Hiren Bhattacharjya). Verse
       (2) 85, p. 38.
    "Untranslatable" (tr. of Hiren Bhattacharjya). Verse (2)
       85, p. 38.
12. ACKER, Peter
    "A Bestiary of Poets" (Selections: "Seal," "Mink"). AntigR
       (62/63) Sum-Aut 85, p. 38-39.
13. ACKERMAN, Diane
    "For the Ride." PraS (59:1) Spr 85, p. 18.
    "Grand Canyon." MichQR (24:2) Spr 85, p. 289-291.
    "In the Green Purse of the Yard This Loose Red Change."

PraS (59:1) Spr 85, p. 17-18.
"Poem in Winter." PraS (59:1) Spr 85, p. 19-20.
"Pumping Iron." PraS (59:1) Spr 85, p. 21-22.
14. ADAM, Ian
"Canlit Conference." Quarry (34:4) Aut 85, p. 88-91.
"The Grandfathers -- a Poem for Voices." Dandel (12:1) 85,
p. 45-48.
15. ADAMCZYK, Terri
"Hieroglyphics." ColEng (47:5) S 85, p. 502-503.
16. ADAMS, B. B.
"The Promiscuous Tigress." NegC (5:2) Spr 85, p. 94-95.
"Restoration Project." WoosterR (3) Spr 85, p. 34.
17. ADAMS, Chelsea
"The Thin Outer Air." Wind (15:53) 85, p. 49.
18. ADAMS, Doreen
"Shadows." Quarry (34:3) Sum 85, p. 77-78.
19. ADAMSON, Jill
"Hunting in the Rain." CrossC (7:2) 85, p. 18.
20. ADCOCK, Betty
"Remembering Brushing My Grandmother's Hair." NegC (5:4)
Fall 85, p. 52-53.
21. ADDONIZIO, Kim
"After His Funeral." PoetL (80:3) Fall 85, p. 150.
22. ADILMAN, Mona Elaine
"Full-Time Employment." PoetryCR (7:2) Wint 85-86, p. 16.
23. ADISA, Opal Palmer
"She Travelin." NewEngR (7:4) Sum 85, p. 601.
ADORNO, Pedro López
See LOPEZ-ADORNO, Pedro
24. ADRES, Benjamin
"For Steph." LittleM (14:4) 85, p. 12.
25. AFIF, Fatimah
"Old Asia." AmerPoR (14:3) My-Je 85, p. 48.
26. AGARD, John
"English Girl Eats Her First Mango" (a kind of love poem).
NewEngR (7:4) Sum 85, p. 518-520.
27. AGGESTAM, Rolf
"Apples of Knowledge" (tr. by Erland Anderson and Lars
Nordström). GreenfR (12:3/4) Wint-Spr 85, p. 120.
"I took strands of hair from your heads" (tr. by Erland
Anderson and Lars Nordström). GreenfR (12:3/4) Wint-
Spr 85, p. 119.
"It Has Taken Me Many Years to Build This House" (tr. by
Erland Anderson and Lars Nordström). LitR (29:1) Fall
85, p. 26-27.
"Proof of God" (tr. by Erland Anderson and Lars Nordstrom).
NowestR (23:2) 85, p. 36.
"The recalcitrant" ("Untitled, tr. by Erland Anderson and
Lars Nordstrom). NowestR (23:2) 85, p. 36.
AGHA SHAHID ALI
See ALI, Agha Shahid
28. AGOOS, Julie
"An Early Translation." Crazy (28) Spr 85, p. 50-51.
"Preparing to Move." QW (21) Fall-Wint 85, p. 74-75.
29. AGOSIN, Marjorie
"Antonia's Questions" (tr. by Susan L. Taracido). NewL
(51:4) Sum 85, p. 111.
"Gina's Lover" (tr. by Susan L. Taracido). NewL (51:4) Sum
85, p. 113.
"Gracias, Querido Mío." BilingR (11:2) My-Ag 84 [c1986],
p. 75.
"León" (Para Leonidas). BilingR (11:2) My-Ag 84 [c1986],
p. 76.
"Letters" (tr. by Susan L. Taracido). NewL (51:4) Sum 85,
p. 111.
"Lo Que Somos." BilingR (11:2) My-Ag 84 [c1986], p. 51.

"The Married Woman" (tr. by Susan L. Taracido). NewL (51:4)
    Sum 85, p. 112.
"Medieval House" (tr. by Susan L. Taracido). NewL (51:4)
    Sum 85, p. 113-114.
"Memorial de las Locas en la Plaza de Mayo" (a la memoria de
    Marta Traba). Mund (15:1/2) 85, p. 62, 64.
"Mi Estómago." BilingR (11:2) My-Ag 84 [c1986], p. 10.
"Nueva Versión del Paraíso." BilingR (11:2) My-Ag 84
    [c1986], p. 51-53.
"Pene." BilingR (11:2) My-Ag 84 [c1986], p. 58.
"Penélope I." BilingR (11:2) My-Ag 84 [c1986], p. 59.
"Remembering the Madwomen of the Plaza de Mayo" (Written in
    memory of Marta Traba, died in the Avianca crash, Madrid,
    1983, tr. by Cola Franzen). Mund (15:1/2) 85, p. 63, 65.
"La Suicida." BilingR (11:2) My-Ag 84 [c1986], p. 41-42.
"Thresholds" (tr. by Cola Franzen). Mund (15:1/2) 85, p. 65.
"La Tortura" (Para Rosa Montero y para aquellos que le
    contaron sus historias). Mund (15:1/2) 85, p. 58, 60.
"Torture" (For Rosa Montero and all those who told her their
    stories, tr. by Cola Franzen). Mund (15:1/2) 85, p. 59,
    61.
"Umbrals." Mund (15:1/2) 85, p. 64.
"Virginia." Mund (15:1/2) 85, p. 58.
"Virginia" (tr. by Cola Franzen). Mund (15:1/2) 85, p. 59.
30. AGRELLA, Catherine Vance
    "Story River." LaurelR (19:1) Wint 85, p. 46.
31. AGTE, Bruce
    "Blue City." Raccoon (17) Mr 85, p. 19.
    "Horses." OhioR (34) 85, p. 42.
32. AGUERO, Kathleen
    "Beating Up Billy Murphy in Fifth Grade." WestB (17) 85, p.
    98.
    "Betrothal." HangL (47) Spr 85, p. 3.
    "Helping Grandma to Bed." HangL (47) Spr 85, p. 4.
33. AGUILA, Pancho
    "Death Wish." SecC (12:2) 84?, p. 1.
    "Halloween." AmerPoR (14:4) Jl-Ag 85, p. 29.
    "Shivo." SecC (12:2) 84?, p. 13.
    "Simple." AmerPoR (14:4) Jl-Ag 85, p. 29.
34. AGUILAR, Mila D.
    "Disillusionment." MinnR (N.S. 25) Fall 85, p. 65.
35. AGUIRRE, Francisca
    "Flamenco." Mund (15:1/2) 85, p. 162.
    "Flamenco" (tr. by Catherine Lawson). Mund (15:1/2) 85, p.
    163.
    "The Other Music" (tr. by Catherine Lawson). Mund (15:1/2)
    85, p. 165.
    "La Otra Música." Mund (15:1/2) 85, p. 164.
36. AGYEYA
    "The Dissenter" (tr. by the author). NewL (51:4) Sum 85, p.
    136.
    "Friendship" (tr. by the author). NewL (51:4) Sum 85, p.
    137.
    "Heroes" (tr. by the author). NewL (51:4) Sum 85, p. 136.
37. AHO, Margaret
    "On the Uses of Flour and Eggs." CutB (23) Fall-Wint 85, p.
    56.
38. AI
    "Elegy" (for John, 1946-1967). Crazy (26) Spr 84, p. 63-64.
    "The Man with the Saxophone." AmerV (1) 85, p. 66-67.
    "More" (For James Wright). Crazy (26) Spr 84, p. 65-66.
    "The Testimony of J. Robert Oppenheimer" (A Fiction).
    MichQR (24:2) Spr 85, p. 368--370.
39. AI, Qing
    "When Dawn Has Put Her White Cloak On" (7 poems in Chinese
    and English, tr. by Li Jia Hu, Ken Letko, and Michael Karl

(Ritchie)). <u>MidAR</u> (5:2) 85, p. 47-63.
40. AIELLO, Kate
   "Rosa (1961-1962)." <u>Bogg</u> (53) 85, p. 32.
   "Zealot." <u>Bogg</u> (53) 85, p. 14.
41. AISENBERG, Nadya
   "At Akumal." <u>Agni</u> (22) 85, p. 19-20.
   "Listening to Schubert." <u>Agni</u> (22) 85, p. 17-18.
42. AKHMATOVA, Anna
   "Alexander at Thebes" (Zh. 471, tr. by Judith Hemschemeyer).
      <u>NowestR</u> (23:3) 85, p. 67.
   "And all day, terrified by its own moans" (Zh. 234, tr. by
      Judith Hemschemeyer). <u>Ploughs</u> (11:4) 85, p. 178.
   "Apparition" (Zh. 290, tr. by Judith Hemschemeyer). <u>Ploughs</u>
      (11:4) 85, p. 180.
   "Around the neck is a string of find beads" (#232, in
      Russian). <u>NowestR</u> (23:3) 85, p. 54.
   "Around the neck is a string of find beads" (Zh. 232, tr. by
      Judith Hemschemeyer). <u>NowestR</u> (23:3) 85, p. 55.
   "Because sin is what I glorified" (Zh. 516, tr. by Judith
      Hemschemeyer). <u>NowestR</u> (23:3) 85, p. 57.
   "Cast-iron fence" (Zh. 278, tr. by Judith Hemschemeyer).
      <u>NowestR</u> (23:3) 85, p. 59.
   "Confusion" (tr. by Judith Hemschemeyer). <u>NewL</u> (51:4) Sum
      85, p. 47.
   "Creativity" (From Mysteries of Craft, tr. by Marianne
      Andrea). <u>Waves</u> (14:1/2) Fall 85, p. 71.
   "Don't torment your heart with the joys of earth" (Zh. 244,
      tr. by Judith Hemschemeyer). <u>Ploughs</u> (11:4) 85, p. 178.
   "Farewell Song" (Zh. 461, tr. by Judith Hemschemeyer).
      <u>NowestR</u> (23:3) 85, p. 65.
   "He whispers: I won't even apologize" (Zh. 255, tr. by Judith
      Hemschemeyer). <u>Ploughs</u> (11:4) 85, p. 179.
   "How terribly the body has changed" (tr. by Judith
      Hemschemeyer). <u>NewL</u> (51:4) Sum 85, p. 47.
   "I Asked a Nearby Cuckoo" (tr. by Neva Herrington and Gale
      Vathing). <u>NewL</u> (51:4) Sum 85, p. 49.
   "I Didn't Ask for the Praise" (tr. by Neva Herrington and
      Gale Vathing). <u>NewL</u> (51:4) Sum 85, p. 48.
   "I will leave your white house and peaceful garden" (Zh. 113,
      tr. by Judith Hemschemeyer). <u>Ploughs</u> (11:4) 85, p. 177.
   "Latest Return" (Zh. 408, tr. by Judith Hemschemeyer).
      <u>NowestR</u> (23:3) 85, p. 64.
   "The Leningrad Elegy" (tr. by Lenore Mayhew and William
      McNaughton). <u>DevQ</u> (19:3) Wint 85, p. 19-20.
   "Like the angel moving upon the water" (tr. by Judith
      Hemschemeyer). <u>NewL</u> (51:4) Sum 85, p. 47-48.
   "Listening to Singing" (Zh. 582, tr. by Judith Hemschemeyer).
      <u>NowestR</u> (23:3) 85, p. 68.
   "Mayakovsky in 1913" (Zh. 330, tr. by Judith Hemschemeyer).
      <u>NowestR</u> (23:3) 85, p. 63.
   "More about this Summer" (Excerpt, tr. by Marianne Andrea).
      <u>DevQ</u> (19:3) Wint 85, p. 27.
   "Native Land" (Zh. 478, tr. by Judith Hemschemeyer).
      <u>NowestR</u> (23:3) 85, p. 66.
   "Over the snowdrift's hard crust" (Tsarskoye Selo, tr. by J.
      Hemschemeyer). <u>Mund</u> (15:1/2) 85, p. 199.
   "Parting (2)" (Zh. 328, tr. by Judith Hemschemeyer).
      <u>NowestR</u> (23:3) 85, p. 61.
   "Parting (3)" (Zh. 329, tr. by Judith Hemschemeyer).
      <u>NowestR</u> (23:3) 85, p. 62.
   "Secrets of the Trade" (Excerpts, tr. by Lenore Mayhew).
      <u>DevQ</u> (19:3) Wint 85, p. 21-26.
   "Suddenly it's become still in the house" (tr. by Judith
      Hemschemeyer). <u>NewL</u> (51:4) Sum 85, p. 47.
   "Sweetbriar Blooms" (From "The Burnt Notebook", tr. by
      Marianne Andrea). <u>BlueBldgs</u> (9) [85?], p. 31.

"Three times it came to torment me" (Tsarskoye Selo, tr. by
    J. Hemschemeyer). Mund (15:1/2) 85, p. 199.
"The Voice of Another" (Tsarskoye Selo, tr. by J.
    Hemschemeyer). Mund (15:1/2) 85, p. 200.
"Voronezh" (To Osip Mandelstam, 1936, tr. by Marianne
    Andrea). DevQ (19:3) Wint 85, p. 28.
"We Don't Know How to Say Goodbye" (tr. by Joan Aleshire).
    NewL (51:4) Sum 85, p. 49.
"Why then did I used to" (Zh. 196, tr. by Judith
    Hemschemeyer). NowestR (23:3) 85, p. 58.
"Willow" (Zh. 322, tr. by Judith Hemschemeyer). NowestR
    (23:3) 85, p. 60.
"You know, I languish in captivity" (Zh. 83, tr. by Judith
    Hemschemeyer). NowestR (23:3) 85, p. 56.
43. ALABAU, Magaly
    "Aqui." LindLM (4:2) Ap-Je 85, p. 27.
44. ALARCON, Francisco X.
    "I Used to Be Much Much Darker." Zyzzyva (1:3) Fall 85, p.
    54-56.
45. ALARCON, Norma
    "Nine Lines: A Self-Portrait." Imagine (1:2) Wint 84, p.
    102.
    "Rosa's Window" (after Lorca). Imagine (1:2) Wint 84, p.
    100-101.
46. ALBERHASKY, Peggy Sue
    "Newly Arrived." SouthernPR (26, i.e. 25:2) Fall 85, p. 13.
47. ALBERT ROBATTO, Matilde
    "Convenimos en el desamor." Mairena (7:19) 85, p. 96.
48. ALBERTSON, Julie
    "The Two Girls" (tr. of Eugenio Florit). Vis (18) 85, p. 39.
49. ALBRECHT, Sheila
    "Moon Chant." Northeast (Series 4:1) Sum 85, p. 5.
50. ALCOSSER, Sandra
    "The Banker's House." WestHR (19:3) Aut 85, p. 226-227.
    "First Flowers." WestHR (19:3) Aut 85, p. 232-233.
    "The Sawyer's Wife." WestHR (19:3) Aut 85, p. 228-231.
51. ALDAN, Daisy
    "The Blond Nets." PoetryR (2:2) Ap 85, p. 80.
52. ALDRICH, Jonathan
    "Wade's Wait" (A narrative poem. Chapbook 18). BelPoJ
    (36:1) Fall 85, p. 1-71.
53. ALEIXANDRE, Vicente
    "Vida" (manuscript facsimile). Mairena (7:19) 85, p. 60.
54. ALESHIRE, Joan
    "Feeding the Birds." SenR (15:2) 85, p. 45.
    "Fine Line." Tendril (19/20) 85, p. 44.
    "I met the new year alone" (tr. of Marina Tsvetayeva). NewL
    (51:4) Sum 85, p. 42.
    "Images from the Floating World" (After a print by Haronobu).
    Poetry (147:3) D 85, p. 149.
    "Last Thing." SenR (15:2) 85, p. 44.
    "Nausikaa." Poetry (147:3) D 85, p. 147-148.
    "Orion." Poetry (147:3) D 85, p. 148.
    "We Don't Know How to Say Goodbye" (tr. of Anna Akhmatova).
    NewL (51:4) Sum 85, p. 49.
    "A White Horse, The New Moon." Tendril (19/20) 85, p. 43.
55. ALEXANDER, Donald
    "Downtown." AntigR (61) Spr 85, p. 112.
56. ALEXANDER, Francis W.
    "Infinity." BlackALF (19:3) Fall 85, p. 113.
    "Justice - The Rules of the Game." SanFPJ (7:2) 85, p. 48.
    "Justify the Cause" (A Certain Administration's Illogical
    Meanderings). SanFPJ (7:2) 85, p. 45.
    "Parallelism." SanFPJ (7:4) 85, p. 20.
    "Redundancies." SanFPJ (7:4) 85, p. 21.
    "Where's the (Bleeped) Empirical Experimental Findings?"

SanFPJ (7:2) 85, p. 46-47.
57. ALEXANDER, Meena
   "Theater" (for Svati Joshi). GreenfR (12:3/4) Wint-Spr 85,
      p. 19.
   "A Time of Difficulty" (for Svati Joshi). GreenfR (12:3/4)
      Wint-Spr 85, p. 20-21.
58. ALEXANDER, Pamela
   "City House Built As a Series of Additions." YaleR (74:4)
      Sum 85, p. 523-524.
59. ALEXANDROU, Aris
   "The First Anatomist" (tr. by Peter Mackridge). Verse (4)
      85, p. 45.
   "Make Sure" (tr. by Peter Mackridge). Verse (4) 85, p. 44.
   "Promotion" (tr. by Peter Mackridge). Verse (4) 85, p. 44.
60. ALEXIS, Austin
   "Calculations." JamesWR (2:1) Fall 84, p. 5.
   "Know." JamesWR (2:1) Fall 84, p. 5.
ALFONSO, Antonio d'
   See D'ALFONSO, Antonio
61. ALFRED, William
   "To Robert Fitzgerald" (on his birthday, 20 October 1984).
      HarvardA (119:1) N 85, p. 18.
62. ALI, Agha Shahid
   "A Call." CimR (70) Ja 85, p. 53.
   "The Dacca Gauzes." Crazy (27) Fall 84, p. 20-21.
   "A Lost Memory of Delhi." Crazy (27) Fall 84, p. 18-19.
   "Memoir." QW (21) Fall-Wint 85, p. 72-73.
63. ALLAN, Pat
   "Recurring Dream." Descant 49 (16:2) Sum 85, p. 23-25.
64. ALLAN-HARE, Jannis
   "Sea Side Strolling." Quarry (34:1) Wint 85, p. 27.
65. ALLBERY, Debra
   "Dream near Extinction." Iowa (15:3) Fall 85, p. 28-29.
   "Instinct." Iowa (15:3) Fall 85, p. 29-30.
   "Next-Door Neighbors." Iowa (15:3) Fall 85, p. 27-28.
   "Produce." Iowa (15:3) Fall 85, p. 26-27.
   "Protection." PoetryNW (26:4) Wint 85-86, p. 25.
   "Stone Soup." Iowa (15:3) Fall 85, p. 25-26.
66. ALLEN, Deborah
   "A Room in Winter." StoneC (12:2/3) Spr-Sum 85, p. 23.
67. ALLEN, Dick
   "The Physicist to His Lost Love." MichQR (24:2) Spr 85, p.
      273-274.
68. ALLEN, Elizabeth
   "Changing Place." CanLit (107) Wint 85, p. 59.
69. ALLEN, Gilbert
   "A Poem Is, After All, a Redneck Entering" (from the
      transcript of a taped interview). Swallow (4) 85, p. 1.
70. ALLEN, Henry
   "Idyll #6." Gargoyle (27) 85, p. 66.
   "Japanese Ambassador." PoetL (79:4) Wint 85, p. 201.
   "Nostalgia." PoetL (79:4) Wint 85, p. 202.
   "Poets and Their Phonographs." PoetL (79:4) Wint 85, p. 202.
71. ALLEN, James
   "Camping among Ferns." SouthernHR (19:1) Wint 85, p. 62.
72. ALLEN, Margaret Vanderharr
   "What They Seek." AmerPoR (14:3) My-Je 85, p. 46.
73. ALLEN, Paula Gunn
   "Taking a Visitor to See the Ruins" (for Joe Bruchac). OP
      (38/39) Spr 85, p. 201.
74. ALLEN, Samuel
   "About Poetry and South Africa." Imagine (1:2) Wint 84, p.
      87.
   "Conquistador." Imagine (1:2) Wint 84, p. 85-86.
   "Definitions." Imagine (1:2) Wint 84, p. 86-87.
   "The Lawyer." Imagine (1:2) Wint 84, p. 88.

75. ALLISON, Carrie
    "Soldier, 1978." WoosterR (4) Fall 85, p. 12.
    "Summers." WoosterR (4) Fall 85, p. 11.
76. ALLISON, Dorothy
    "Crossing the River." Cond (11/12) 85, p. 65.
    "Diminishing." Cond (11/12) 85, p. 64.
    "Etymology Is Not Destiny." Cond (11/12) 85, p. 62-63.
    "Whispers." Cond (11/12) 85, p. 66.
77. ALMANZA, Antonion
    "Azrael." Wind (15:54) 85, p. 47.
ALONSO, Emilio V. Lopez
    See LOPEZ-ALONSO, Emilio V.
78. ALONSO, Oscar
    "I Had Heard about You" (tr. by Kent Johnson). MinnR (N.S.
    25) Fall 85, p. 45.
79. ALSINA, Maria Elena
    "Junio 7." LetFem (11:1/2) Prim-Otoño 85, p. 101.
    "Paisaje en Honduras." LetFem (11:1/2) Prim-Otoño 85, p.
    103-104.
    "Poema de la Soledad." LetFem (11:1/2) Prim-Otoño 85, p.
    101-102.
    "Por un Final y un Comienzo." LetFem (11:1/2) Prim-Otoño
    85, p. 102-103.
80. ALTHAUS, Keith
    "The Ambulance." Tendril (19/20) 85, p. 45.
    "Listening to Music" (for Tomas Tranströmer). Crazy (27)
    Fall 84, p. 60-61.
81. ALTMAN, Julie
    "Colette." Imagine (2:1) Sum 85, p. 98.
    "Daddy." Imagine (2:1) Sum 85, p. 97-98.
82. ALURISTA
    "Ga Yo Ga." Imagine (1:2) Wint 84, p. 62.
    "There Will B No Bullfights This Fall." Imagine (1:2) Wint
    84, p. 63-66.
ALVARADO, Abbey Melec
    See MELEC ALVARADO, Abbey
83. ALVARADO DELGADO, Angel
    "La Unica Luz." Mairena (7:19) 85, p. 102.
84. ALVAREZ BRAVO, Armando
    "Casi un Sueño." LindLM (4:3) Jl-S 85, p. 6.
    "Mañana." LindLM (4:3) Jl-S 85, p. 6.
    "Marina." LindLM (4:3) Jl-S 85, p. 6.
    "Musica para Dos" (Selecciones del libro inédito, Memorias
    de un merodeador nocturno). LindLM (4:3) Jl-S 85, p. 6.
    "Noche en Fragmentos." LindLM (4:3) Jl-S 85, p. 6.
    "Texto en la Lluvia." LindLM (4:3) Jl-S 85, p. 6.
85. ALVAREZ LEZAMA, Manuel
    "The Creation." LindLM (4:1) Ja-Mr 85, p. 18.
    "The Word and the Hummingbird." LindLM (4:1) Ja-Mr 85, p.
    18.
86. AMABILE, George
    "Sleeping Beauty." Grain (13:1) F 85, p. 16-19.
    "Tao." Grain (13:1) F 85, p. 20.
87. AMAR, Mubarak Anwar
    "July in Lebanon, 1983." KanQ (17:4) Fall 85, p. 100-101.
88. AMATO, Joseph
    "Cathy." SpoonRQ (10:2) Spr 85, p. 56.
    "Soft Times." SpoonRQ (10:2) Spr 85, p. 56.
    "Spring at the Front." SpoonRQ (10:2) Spr 85, p. 56.
89. AMBRUSO, Diane
    "Daddy's Girl." NegC (5:3) Sum 85, p. 122.
90. AMEN, Grover
    "Hotel Paintings." GrandS (4:3) Spr 85, p. 190.
AMESTOY, Lida Aronne
    See ARONNE-AMESTOY, Lida

91. AMICHAI, Yehuda
    "And That Is Your Glory" (Phrase from the liturgy of the Days
       of Awe, tr. by Stephen Mitchell). ParisR (27:98) Wint
       85, p. 20.
    "The Art of Loving" (tr. by Chana Bloch). NewL (51:4) Sum
       85, p. 19.
    "The Bull Returns" (tr. by Stephen Mitchell). ParisR
       (27:98) Wint 85, p. 22.
    "Farewell" (tr. by Stephen Mitchell). ParisR (27:98) Wint
       85, p. 19.
    "My Mother Told Me Once" (tr. by Stephen Mitchell). MissR
       (40/41) Wint 85, p. 114.
    "National Thoughts" (tr. by Stephen Mitchell). ParisR
       (27:98) Wint 85, p. 23.
    "Now in the Storm" (tr. by Stephen Mitchell). MissR (40/41)
       Wint 85, p. 115.
    "A Pity. We Were Such a Good Invention" (tr. by Stephen
       Mitchell). MissR (40/41) Wint 85, p. 116.
    "Poem without an End" (tr. by Chana Bloch). NewL (51:4) Sum
       85, p. 18.
    "Poems for a Woman" (tr. by Stephen Mitchell). Zyzzyva
       (1:4) Wint 85, p. 74-77.
    "Reinforcements" (tr. by Chana Bloch). NewL (51:4) Sum 85,
       p. 18-19.
    "Resurrection" (tr. by Stephen Mitchell). ParisR (27:98)
       Wint 85, p. 21.
    "Six Poems for Tamar" (tr. by Stephen Mitchell). ParisR
       (27:98) Wint 85, p. 17-18.
    "Travels" (Excerpt, tr. by Ruth Nevo). Pequod (19/20/21)
       85, p. 19-24.
    "The U.N. Headquarters in the High Commissioner's House in
       Jerusalem" (tr. by Stephen Mitchell). Thrpny (6:3, issue
       23) Fall 85, p. 8.
92. AMIDON, Richard
    "A Consumer's Guide to Church Going." SmPd (22:3) Fall 85,
       p. 30-31.
    "Surviving Freshman Comp." EngJ (74:8) D 85, p. 69.
93. AMMONS, A. R.
    "Chiseled Clouds." Epoch (34:3) 84-85, p. 196.
    "Coming Round." CarolQ (37:3) Spr 85, p. 34.
    "Construing Deconstruction." Verse (4) 85, p. 8-9.
    "Day Ghosts." NewYorker (61:8) 15 Ap 85, p. 49.
    "Loft." Epoch (34:3) 84-85, p. 194.
    "Plain Divisions." Verse (3) 85, p. 3.
    "Possibility along a Line of Difference." TriQ (63) Spr-Sum
       85, p. 136-137.
    "Standing Light Up." Verse (3) 85, p. 3.
    "Taking Place." Verse (4) 85, p. 8.
    "Tracing Out." Epoch (34:3) 84-85, p. 193.
    "Whitelash of Air Rapids." Epoch (34:3) 84-85, p. 195.
94. AMPRIMOZ, Alexandre L.
    "All Soldiers Unknown." PoetryCR (6:4) Sum 85, p. 21.
    "The Generation Race." CanLit (106) Fall 85, p. 43.
    "He Must Exist a Little." CanLit (106) Fall 85, p. 43-44.
    "Les Invalides." Bogg (54) 85, p. 7.
    "Sad Wedding of Two Seasons." PoetryCR (6:4) Sum 85, p. 21.
95. ANANIA, Pablo
    "Del Orden en Que Suceden las Cosas." Inti (20) Otoño 84,
       p. 111-112.
    "Eliot." Inti (20) Otoño 84, p. 112-113.
    "Quevedo." Inti (20) Otoño 84, p. 111.
96. ANCEVSKI, Zoran
    "The Black Dream of the Elm" (tr. of Slavko Janevski, w.
       James McKinley). NewL (51:4) Sum 85, p. 23-24.
    "The Carvers" (tr. by the author and James McKinley). NewL
       (51:4) Sum 85, p. 32.

"A Child Talking in Its Sleep" (tr. of Vlada Urosevic, w.
    James McKinley). NewL (51:4) Sum 85, p. 25.
"The Desert Woman" (Excerpt from a sequence of poems, tr. of
    Bogomil Gjuzel, w. James McKinley). NewL (51:4) Sum 85,
    p. 27.
"Droughts" (tr. of Slavko Janevski, w. James McKinley).
    NewL (51:4) Sum 85, p. 23.
"For Aunt A.K." (tr. by the author and James McKinley).
    NewL (51:4) Sum 85, p. 30.
"Night Song" (tr. by the author and James McKinley). NewL
    (51:4) Sum 85, p. 31-32.
"Poem of the Inscriptions" (tr. of Vlada Urosevic, w. James
    McKinley). NewL (51:4) Sum 85, p. 25.
"Reader of Dreams" (tr. of Vlada Urosevic, w. James
    McKinley). NewL (51:4) Sum 85, p. 24.
"The Rebellion of the Seeds" (tr. of Radovan Pavlovski, w.
    James McKinley). NewL (51:4) Sum 85, p. 26.
"A Stranger at Home, at Home Elsewhere" (tr. of Bogomil
    Gjuzel, w. James McKinley). NewL (51:4) Sum 85, p. 28.
"Travelling to Ithaca" (tr. by the author and James
    McKinley). NewL (51:4) Sum 85, p. 29-30.
"The Turtle" (tr. of Radovan Pavlovski, w. James McKinley).
    NewL (51:4) Sum 85, p. 26-27.
ANCZEL, Paul
    See CELAN, Paul
97. ANDERMANN, Guri
    "Three A.M." PassN (6:1) Fall-Wint 85, p. 16.
98. ANDERS, Shirley B.
    "Jacob Come Lately." Wind (15:53) 85, p. 51.
    "Wifman." KanQ (17:4) Fall 85, p. 94-95.
99. ANDERSON, Barbara
    "Junk City." Crazy (29) Fall 85, p. 21-22.
    "The Subject of My Pain" (for my therapist). NoAmR (270:3)
        S 85, p. 16.
    "Weekday Matinees." Tendril (19/20) 85, p. 46-47.
100. ANDERSON, C. M.
    "Carvings." LittleBR (5:1) Fall-Wint 84-85, p. 20.
101. ANDERSON, Clifford
    "Now a Major Motion Picture." CarolQ (37:2) Wint 85, p. 49.
102. ANDERSON, Clifton
    "A Sunday in Early Summer." SnapD (9:1) Fall 85, p. 15.
103. ANDERSON, Erland
    "Apples of Knowledge" (tr. of Rolf Aggestam, w. Lars
        Nordström). GreenfR (12:3/4) Wint-Spr 85, p. 120.
    "I took strands of hair from your heads" (tr. of Rolf
        Aggestam, w. Lars Nordström). GreenfR (12:3/4) Wint-
        Spr 85, p. 119.
    "It Has Taken Me Many Years to Build This House" (tr. of
        Rolf Aggestam, w. Lars Nordström). LitR (29:1) Fall
        85, p. 26-27.
    "Proof of God" (tr. of Rolf Aggestam, w. Lars Nordstrom).
        NowestR (23:2) 85, p. 36.
    "The recalcitrant" ("Untitled, tr. of Rolf Aggestam, w.
        Lars Nordstrom). NowestR (23:2) 85, p. 36.
104. ANDERSON, Jack
    "The Condemned." Chelsea (44) 85, p. 70.
    "The Great Days of Ballooning." HangL (47) Spr 85, p. 7-8.
    "The Icebergs." Confr (30/31) N 85, p. 253.
    "Instructions for Visiting a Strange City." Chelsea (44)
        85, p. 70.
    "The Real World." HangL (47) Spr 85, p. 9-10.
    "Retirement." HangL (47) Spr 85, p. 5-6.
105. ANDERSON, Kath M.
    "About Talking." Geor (39:2) Sum 85, p. 327.
106. ANDERSON, Ken
    "Elizabeth and Henry." JamesWR (3:1) Fall 85, p. 14.

"The Mariners." <u>JamesWR</u> (2:2) Wint 85, p. 12.
107. ANDERSON, Maggie
    "Country Wisdoms." <u>PraS</u> (59:4) Wint 85, p. 94.
    "In Singing Weather." <u>NowestR</u> (23:2) 85, p. 40-46.
    "Walker Evans: Among Elms and Maples, Morgantown, West
        Virginia, August, 1935." <u>NowestR</u> (23:1) 85, p. 47.
    "Walker Evans: House and Graveyard, Rowlesburg, West
        Virginia, 1935." <u>NowestR</u> (23:1) 85, p. 48.
    "Walker Evans: Independence Day, Terra Alta, West Virginia,
        1935." <u>NowestR</u> (23:1) 85, p. 46.
    "Walker Evans: Mining Camp, Residents, West Virginia, July,
        1935." <u>NowestR</u> (23:1) 85, p. 45.
    "With Wine." <u>PraS</u> (59:4) Wint 85, p. 93.
108. ANDERSON, Mark
    "Night Flight" (tr. of Ingeborg Bachmann). <u>ParisR</u> (27:95)
        Spr 85, p. 133-134.
109. ANDERSON, Martin
    "Swamp Fever." <u>AntigR</u> (60) Wint 85, p. 73.
    "The Tree." <u>AntigR</u> (60) Wint 85, p. 74.
110. ANDERSON, Michael
    "Foreplay." <u>KanQ</u> (17:1/2) Wint-Spr 85, p. 262.
111. ANDERSON, Nathalie
    "Gazelles." <u>PraS</u> (59:4) Wint 85, p. 91-92.
    "Lost Sisters." <u>PraS</u> (59:4) Wint 85, p. 90.
    "Oralee Dantzler." <u>PraS</u> (59:4) Wint 85, p. 89.
112. ANDERSON, T. J., III
    "Inventory." <u>BlackALF</u> (19:3) Fall 85, p. 113-114.
113. ANDERSON, Tammy
    "Economics." <u>PoeticJ</u> (10) 85, p. 32.
    "January's Hades." <u>Sam</u> (42:4, 168th release) 85, p. 40-41.
    "Jimmy." <u>PoeticJ</u> (11) 85, p. 11.
    "That Afternoon." <u>PoeticJ</u> (9) 85, p. 5.
114. ANDRADE, Carlos Drummond de
    "Death of the Houses in Ouro Preto" (tr. by Thomas Colchie).
        <u>ParisR</u> (27:97) Fall 85, p. 26-28.
    "The Disappearance of Luisa Porto" (tr. by Thomas Colchie).
        <u>NewYRB</u> (32:19) 5 D 85, p. 25.
    "Indications" (tr. by Thomas Colchie). <u>NewYRB</u> (32:12) 18
        Jl 85, p. 30.
    "Morning Street" (tr. by Thomas Colchie). <u>ParisR</u> (27:97)
        Fall 85, p. 32-33.
    "The Package" (tr. by Thomas Colchie). <u>ParisR</u> (27:97) Fall
        85, p. 29-31.
115. ANDRADE, Eugenio de
    "Almost Mother-of-Pearl" (tr. by Alexis Levitin). <u>PoetryR</u>
        (2:2) Ap 85, p. 64.
    "Ao acordar já por aí andavam" (XI). <u>CumbPR</u> (5:1) Fall
        85, p. 56.
    "Children" (tr. by Alexis Levitin). <u>BlueBldgs</u> (9) [85?],
        p. 25.
    "História de Verão." <u>SouthernHR</u> (19:1) Wint 85, p. 39.
    "The House" (tr. by Alexis Levitin). <u>BlueBldgs</u> (9) [85?],
        p. 25.
    "I'm Satisfied" (tr. by Alexis Levitin). <u>NowestR</u> (23:1)
        85, p. 50.
    "Não há ninguém à entrada de novembro" (XLV).
        <u>CumbPR</u> (5:1) Fall 85, p. 58.
    "On Awakening" (tr. by Alexis Levitin). <u>CumbPR</u> (5:1) Fall
        85, p. 57.
    "On the Greenness of Clover" (tr. by Alexis Levitin). <u>SenR</u>
        (15:1) 85, p. 28.
    "Other Afternoons" (tr. by Alexis Levitin). <u>PoetryR</u> (2:2)
        Ap 85, p. 64.
    "Paestum, with New Moon" (tr. by Alexis Levitin). <u>NewL</u>
        (51:4) Sum 85, p. 87.
    "Rain" (tr. by Alexis Levitin). <u>SenR</u> (15:1) 85, p. 24.

"Sheltered from Harm" (tr. by Alexis Levitin). SenR (15:1)
    85, p. 27.
"Sometimes One Enters" (tr. by Alexis Levitin). NowestR
    (23:1) 85, p. 49.
"South" (tr. by Alexis Levitin). BlueBldgs (9) [85?], p.
    24.
"Still-Life with Fruit" (tr. by Alexis Levitin). NewL
    (51:4) Sum 85, p. 87.
"A Tale of Summer" (tr. by Alexis Levitin). SouthernHR
    (19:1) Wint 85, p. 39.
"There Is No One at the Entrance of November" (tr. by Alexis
    Levitin). CumbPR (5:1) Fall 85, p. 59.
"To the Memory of Ruy Belo" (tr. by Alexis Levitin). NewL
    (51:4) Sum 85, p. 88.
"Vast Fields" (tr. by Alexis Levitin). QW (20) Spr-Sum 85,
    p. 115.
"The Visit of the Prince" (tr. by Alexis Levitin). SenR
    (15:1) 85, p. 26.
"Voyage" (tr. by Alexis Levitin). SenR (15:1) 85, p. 25.
116. ANDREA, Marianne
"Auden Remembered." Wind (15:55) 85, p. 2.
"Creativity" (From Mysteries of Craft, tr. of Anna
    Akhmatova). Waves (14:1/2) Fall 85, p. 71.
"Flight I." Wind (15:55) 85, p. 2-3.
"Gathering of Poets." Wind (15:55) 85, p. 1.
"Lines for Late Evening." Waves (14:1/2) Fall 85, p. 70.
"More about this Summer" (Excerpt, tr. of Anna Akhmatova).
    DevQ (19:3) Wint 85, p. 27.
"Sweetbriar Blooms" (From "The Burnt Notebook", tr. of Anna
    Akhmatova). BlueBldgs (9) [85?], p. 31.
"Voronezh" (To Osip Mandelstam, 1936, tr. of Anna
    Akhmatova). DevQ (19:3) Wint 85, p. 28.
"With Friends in Moscow" (1936). BlueBldgs (9) [85?], p.
    32.
117. ANDRESEN, Sophia de Mello Breyner
"Christmas Letter to Murilo Mendes" (tr. by Alexis Levitin).
    SenR (15:1) 85, p. 29.
"I believe in the trees whose roots sink" (in Portuguese and
    English, tr. by Lisa Sapinkopf). StoneC (13:1/2) Fall-
    Wint 85-86, p. 50-51.
"Inert margins spread their arms" (in Portuguese and
    English, tr. by Lisa Sapinkopf). StoneC (13:1/2) Fall-
    Wint 85-86, p. 48-49.
"Nine Poems" (tr. by Lisa Sapinkopf). Ploughs (11:4) 85,
    p. 230-232.
"Our fingers opened closed hands" (in Portuguese and
    English, tr. by Lisa Sapinkopf). StoneC (13:1/2) Fall-
    Wint 85-86, p. 48-49.
"The pinetrees moan at the passing wind" (in Portuguese and
    English, tr. by Lisa Sapinkopf). StoneC (13:1/2) Fall-
    Wint 85-86, p. 50-51.
"Shake off the clouds that settle on your hair" (from
    Coral, tr. by Lisa Sapinkopf). Abraxas (33) 85, p. 27.
"Torso" (tr. by Alexis Levitin). SenR (15:1) 85, p. 30.
"Yes, To your rooms lined with moonlight" (from Coral, tr.
    by Lisa Sapinkopf). Abraxas (33) 85, p. 27.
118. ANDREWS, Linda
"Anna." SmPd (22:3) Fall 85, p. 32.
119. ANDREWS, Michael
"Lao Tzu Selling Water." SnapD (9:1) Fall 85, p. 14.
120. ANDROLA, Ron
"An Oracular Ode to Poetry." Bogg (53) 85, p. 41.
"Sound." Bogg (53) 85, p. 7.
"Steel." Bogg (54) 85, p. 45.
121. ANDRUS, David
"The Blind." Waves (13:4) Spr 85, p. 40.

"Mansong." AntigR (62/63) Sum-Aut 85, p. 44.
"Only White Silence." AntigR (62/63) Sum-Aut 85, p. 45.
122. ANDRUS, R. Blain
"The Signing." Amelia (2:2) O 85, p. 81-82.
123. ANDRYSSON, Susan
"The Condition of the Laughing Animal." Imagine (2:1) Sum
85, p. 88-89.
"Mother at 19, Unmarried." Imagine (2:1) Sum 85, p. 88.
124. ANGEL, Ralph
"Committing Sideways." Ploughs (11:1) 85, p. 33-34.
"Fragile Hardware." NewOR (12:1) Spr 85, p. 97.
"You Are the Place You Cannot Move." Ploughs (11:1) 85, p.
31-32.
ANGELIS, Milo de
See De ANGELIS, Milo
125. ANGELL, Roger
"Greetings, Friends!" NewYorker (61:44) 23 D 85, p. 31.
126. ANGLESEY, Zoe
"Companion" (1981, tr. of Julio Cortazar). RiverS (18) 85,
p. 106.
127. ANGST, Bim
"Driving Home at Night" (Honorable Mention, International
Poetry Contest). WestB (17) 85, p. 21.
128. ANONYMOUS
"Ahi Ali Baba" (Bektashi dervish origin, tr. by Joe Malone).
Paint (11:21/12:24) 84-85, p. 57.
"The Avenger's Wife" (tr. of the Old English poem called
"The Wife's Lament" by Marijane Osborn). LitR (28:4)
Sum 85, p. 586-587.
"Cock" (Korean Sijo Poem, tr. by Graeme Wilson). DenQ
(20:1) Sum 85, p. 16.
"Dawn" (Korean Sijo Poem, tr. by Graeme Wilson). DenQ
(20:1) Sum 85, p. 15.
"Jose Feeding Her Baby." Stand (26:1) Wint 84-85, p. 33.
"On the Tomb of the Cuckold Menoitios" (tr. by Elliot
Richman). WindO (46) Fall 85, p. 3.
"The Pigeons of Dubrovnik" (tr. out of the Serbo-Croatian by
William McLaughlin). KanQ (17:1/2) Wint-Spr 85, p. 147.
"Secret Service" (from the underground, tr. out of the Serbo-
Croatian by William McLaughlin). KanQ (17:1/2) Wint-Spr
85, p. 146.
"The Subject in a Virtuoso Dark" (from the Croato-Serbian by
William McLaughlin). WoosterR (3) Spr 85, p. 60-61.
"Virtue Rewarded" (Korean Sijo Poem, tr. by Graeme Wilson).
DenQ (20:1) Sum 85, p. 19.
"Wind chimes die." SecC (12:2) 84?, p. 2.
129. ANSON, John (See also ANSON, John S.)
"A Little World" (For my daughter). Thrpny (5:4, issue 20)
Wint 85, p. 26.
130. ANSON, John S. (See also ANSON, John)
"Edward Thomas." ArizQ (41:4) Wint 85, p. 337.
131. ANTHONY, George
"First Communion." OP (38/39) Spr 85, p. 10.
"Mon Frère Délicat." OP (38/39) Spr 85, p. 170.
"Poet." OP (38/39) Spr 85, p. 116.
132. ANTLER
"Catching the Sunrise." Abraxas (33) 85, p. 40.
"Enskyment." Blueline (7:1) Sum-Fall 85, p. 7.
133. ANTONIO, Norberto
"Daños Utiles." Mairena (7:19) 85, p. 49-50.
"Sudario." Mairena (7:19) 85, p. 47-48.
134. ANZALDUA, Gloria
"Tihuique (Now Let Us Go)." BilingR (11:2) My-Ag 84
[c1986], p. 54.
135. APONICK, Kathleen
"Ancestor." Os (21) 85, p. 5.

"Winter Fever Dying Out." <u>Os</u> (21) 85, p. 4.
136. APPEL, Cathy
     "Bedtime." <u>HangL</u> (47) Spr 85, p. 11.
     "Photographic Memory." <u>HangL</u> (47) Spr 85, p. 12.
137. APPLEMAN, Philip
     "Are You Saved?" <u>Poetry</u> (146:5) Ag 85, p. 288.
     "Euphorias." <u>Tendril</u> (19/20) 85, p. 48-51.
     "A Little Heart-to-Heart on Valentines's Day." <u>Poetry</u>
       (145:5) F 85, p. 270.
     "On the Seventh Day." <u>Confr</u> (30/31) N 85, p. 87-88.
     "Watching Her Sleep." <u>PartR</u> (52:4) 85, p. 431-432.
138. APPLEWHITE, James
     "A Change of Light." <u>CarolQ</u> (37:3) Spr 85, p. 79.
     "Collards." <u>VirQ</u> (61:3) Sum 85, p. 421-422.
     "The Emporium." <u>NoAmR</u> (270:4) D 85, p. 47.
     "Grading an Old Friend." <u>CrossCur</u> (5:3) 85, p. 127.
     "Tree of Babel." <u>SouthernPR</u> (26, i.e. 25:2) Fall 85, p. 59-
       60.
139. ARBONA DE MARTINEZ, Maria Isabel
     "Genesis." <u>Mairena</u> (7:19) 85, p. 94.
140. ARBOR, Ann
     "A Poem for Maria on the Death of Her Father." <u>CalQ</u> (26)
       Sum 85, p. 52.
141. ARCHER, Nuala
     "Between Swilly and Sewanee" (for Naomi). <u>CreamCR</u> (10:2)
       [85?], p. 51.
     "Here in Oklahoma." <u>Nimrod</u> (28:2) Spr-Sum 85, p. 70-71.
     "In Bright Gray and Lavender Fissures." <u>Nimrod</u> (28:2) Spr-
       Sum 85, p. 73-74.
     "The Lost Glove Is Happy." <u>Nimrod</u> (28:2) Spr-Sum 85, p. 71-
       72.
     "Uncounted Coming." <u>CreamCR</u> (10:2) [85?], p. 52-53.
142. ARENAS, A. T. (<u>See also</u> ARENAS, Andrea-Teresa)
     "A la Noche del Semilunio." <u>RevChic</u> (13:2) Sum 85, p. 36.
     "The Decade." <u>RevChic</u> (13:2) Sum 85, p. 35.
     "National Hype." <u>RevChic</u> (13:2) Sum 85, p. 34.
143. ARENAS, Andrea-Teresa (<u>See also</u> ARENAS, A. T.)
     "Curve Ball." <u>BilingR</u> (11:2) My-Ag 84 [c1986], p. 74.
     "House Calls on 15th Street." <u>BilingR</u> (11:2) My-Ag 84
       [c1986], p. 73.
144. ARENAS, Reinaldo
     "Aportes." <u>LindLM</u> (4:1) Ja-Mr 85, p. 19.
145. ARES, Mercedes
     "Mañana de Ciudad" (en Miami). <u>LindLM</u> (4:1) Ja-Mr 85, p.
       12.
     "Saludos a Don Vicente" (para Gisela). <u>LindLM</u> (4:1) Ja-Mr
       85, p. 12.
     "Voy a Combinar." <u>LindLM</u> (4:1) Ja-Mr 85, p. 12.
146. ARGUELLES, Ivan
     "The Drowning in March." <u>YellowS</u> (16) Aut 85, p. 38.
     "Eminent Domain." <u>YellowS</u> (16) Aut 85, p. 37.
     "Headache." <u>BlueBldgs</u> (9) [85?], p. 12.
     "Heat." <u>YellowS</u> (16) Aut 85, p. 40.
     "High School." <u>Abraxas</u> (33) 85, p. 16-17.
     "In the Mausoleum." <u>Pig</u> (13) 85, p. 59.
     "Jihad." <u>AmerPoR</u> (14:3) My-Je 85, p. 56.
     "Lethe." <u>Northeast</u> (Series 4:1) Sum 85, p. 48.
     "Lust for Life." <u>YellowS</u> (16) Aut 85, p. 42.
     "Muddy Waters" (Obit April 20 1983). <u>GreenfR</u> (13:1/2) Fall-
       Wint 85, p. 22.
     "The Poem Written for the Secret: On Her Cheeks a
       Constellation of Roses." <u>YellowS</u> (16) Aut 85, p. 41.
     "The Poetry Reading." <u>Abraxas</u> (33) 85, p. 17.
     "Remembering the Uncertainties." <u>Wind</u> (15:55) 85, p. 4-5.
     "This Year Will End Near Palo Alto." <u>AmerPoR</u> (14:3) My-Je
       85, p. 56.

"Vital Signs." <u>BlueBldgs</u> (9) [85?], p. 12.
"Which Shall I Choose?" <u>YellowS</u> (16) Aut 85, p. 39.
147. ARGYLE, Gisela
    "Fall" (tr. of Venceslav Sprager). <u>Waves</u> (14:1/2) Fall 85,
        p. 74.
    "Spring" (tr. of Venceslav Sprager). <u>Waves</u> (14:1/2) Fall
        85, p. 72.
    "Summer" (tr. of Venceslav Sprager). <u>Waves</u> (14:1/2) Fall
        85, p. 73.
    "Winter" (in German and English, tr. of Venceslav Sprager).
        <u>Waves</u> (14:1/2) Fall 85, p. 75.
148. ARIZA, René
    "AMEOP." <u>LindLM</u> (4:4) O-D 85, p. 25.
    "Primer Soneto a las Chinches." <u>LindLM</u> (4:4) O-D 85, p. 25.
149. ARMANTROUT, Rae
    "Context." <u>Temblor</u> (2) 85, p. 85.
    "Disown." <u>Temblor</u> (2) 85, p. 83-84.
    "Necromance." <u>Temblor</u> (2) 85, p. 85.
    "Range." <u>Temblor</u> (2) 85, p. 86.
150. ARMITAGE, Barri
    "The Bouquet." <u>Paint</u> (11:21/12:24) 84-85, p. 14.
151. ARMSTRONG, Bruce
    "Morning, Noon, and Night." <u>PottPort</u> (7) 85-86, p. 25.
152. ARMSTRONG, Tim
    "Poem." <u>Bogg</u> (54) 85, p. 16.
153. ARNAUT, Abdel Kader
    "Your Eyes Are Autumn Grey" (from <u>Ashes on a Cold Earth</u>,
        tr. by Mirene Ghossein). <u>NewRena</u> (19) Fall 85, p. 79.
    "Your Eyes Are Autumn Grey" (in Arabic). <u>NewRena</u> (19) Fall
        85, p. 78.
154. ARNETT, Gogisgi/Carroll
    "The Grant Boys." <u>NoDaQ</u> (53:2) Spr 85, p. 204-205.
    "Sweat." <u>NoDaQ</u> (53:2) Spr 85, p. 205.
155. ARNOLD, Les
    "The Blue Boat" (after Tu Fu). <u>Grain</u> (13:3) Ag 85, p. 19.
    "The Church at Polstead." <u>Grain</u> (13:2) My 85, p. 13-14.
    "Night Cairn." <u>Grain</u> (13:3) Ag 85, p. 14.
    "Skulls." <u>Grain</u> (13:3) Ag 85, p. 40.
    "The Tunnel." <u>Grain</u> (13:2) My 85, p. 12.
    "A Winter Dream" (after Rimbaud's 'Rêve pour l'hiver').
        <u>Grain</u> (13:3) Ag 85, p. 15.
156. ARONNE-AMESTOY, Lida
    "Destiempos." <u>Inti</u> (20) Otoño 84, p. 107-108.
    "Exilios." <u>Inti</u> (20) Otoño 84, p. 106-107.
157. ARROWSMITH, William
    "Boats on the Marne" (tr. of Eugenio Montale). <u>Pequod</u> (18)
        85, p. 131-132.
    "Correspondences" (tr. of Eugenio Montale). <u>SenR</u> (15:1)
        85, p. 89.
    "Eastbourne" (tr. of Eugenio Montale). <u>GrandS</u> (4:4) Sum
        85, p. 138-139.
    "Gerti's Carnival" (tr. of Eugenio Montale). <u>SenR</u> (15:1)
        85, p. 84-86.
    "In the Rain" (tr. of Eugenio Montale). <u>SenR</u> (15:1) 85, p.
        87.
    "New Stanzas" (tr. of Eugenio Montale). <u>Pequod</u> (18) 85, p.
        135-136.
    "News from Amiata" (tr. of Eugenio Montale). <u>PartR</u> (52:2)
        85, p. 60-62.
    "Old Verses" (tr. of Eugenio Montale). <u>SenR</u> (15:1) 85, p.
        82-83.
    "Stanzas" (tr. of Eugenio Montale). <u>Pequod</u> (18) 85, p. 133-
        134.
    "Summer" (tr. of Eugenio Montale). <u>SenR</u> (15:1) 85, p. 88.
158. ARROYO VICENTE, Arminda
    "El Alma en los Brazos." <u>Mairena</u> (7:19) 85, p. 22.

"Cuando Llegue la Hora." <u>Mairena</u> (7:19) 85, p. 20.
"El Eco de Tu Aliento." <u>Mairena</u> (7:19) 85, p. 19.
"No Creo Lo Que Soy." <u>Mairena</u> (7:19) 85, p. 19.
"No Hables, Voz." <u>Mairena</u> (7:19) 85, p. 21.
"La Noche." <u>Mairena</u> (7:19) 85, p. 21.
"Oscuras Amapolas." <u>Mairena</u> (7:19) 85, p. 20.
"Tus Palabras." <u>Mairena</u> (7:19) 85, p. 18.
"La Vida." <u>Mairena</u> (7:19) 85, p. 18.
159. ARTHUR, Elizabeth
"Filling Canvas." <u>Shen</u> (36:1) 85-86, p. 18.
160. ARVEY, Michael
"The Recommendation." <u>SouthernPR</u> (25:1) Spr 85, p. 47.
"Winter Bus-Stop." <u>SoDakR</u> (23:2) Sum 85, p. 75.
161. ARVILLA, Mark
"Unexpected Intimacy." <u>RagMag</u> (4:2) Fall 85, p. 21.
"The Woman." <u>RagMag</u> (4:2) Fall 85, p. 20.
162. ARVIO, Sarah
"Coral Washed Up at Golindano, Venezuela." <u>NewYorker</u>
    (61:40) 25 N 85, p. 48.
163. ASARNOW, Herman
"Why I Want to Play It with Feeling" (for my brother).
    <u>LaurelR</u> (19:1) Wint 85, p. 30-31.
164. ASCRIZZI, Lynn Ann
"Wasp." <u>WorldO</u> (19:1/2) Fall 85-Wint 84-85, p. 58.
165. ASCROFT, Steve
"Later." <u>AntigR</u> (62/63) Sum-Aut 85, p. 167.
"Upstairs." <u>AntigR</u> (62/63) Sum-Aut 85, p. 167.
166. ASEKOFF, L. S.
"Winter Geese." <u>NewYorker</u> (61:3) 11 Mr 85, p. 40.
167. ASH, John
"Landscape with Artists." <u>NewYorker</u> (61:33) 7 O 85, p. 44.
"The Other Great Composers." <u>NewYorker</u> (61:14) 27 My 85,
    p. 40.
168. ASH, Karin (<u>See also</u> ASH, Karin T.)
"On Getting Sick." <u>Pequod</u> (18) 85, p. 114.
"Ordinary Love." <u>Pequod</u> (18) 85, p. 112.
"A Portrait." <u>Pequod</u> (18) 85, p. 113.
"Your Wild Earth." <u>Pequod</u> (18) 85, p. 115-116.
169. ASH, Karin T. (<u>See also</u> ASH, Karin)
"Death of Your Baby." <u>SenR</u> (15:2) 85, p. 83-84.
"Diabetes." <u>SenR</u> (15:2) 85, p. 82.
"The Leper" (for Kandaki). <u>SenR</u> (15:2) 85, p. 81.
"Subway Beggar." <u>SenR</u> (15:2) 85, p. 80.
"Turbulence." <u>SenR</u> (15:2) 85, p. 78-79.
170. ASH, Maureen
"Signs" (after a death). <u>Prima</u> (9) 85, p. 12.
171. ASHANTI, Asa Paschal
"Dust to Dust." <u>BlackALF</u> (19:3) Fall 85, p. 102.
"Mere Anarchy." <u>BlackALF</u> (19:3) Fall 85, p. 101.
"Non-Grata." <u>BlackALF</u> (19:3) Fall 85, p. 102.
"Note from Haran" (for Jackie Gogan). <u>BlackALF</u> (19:3) Fall
    85, p. 102.
172. ASHBERY, John
"The Bushiness of Infinity." <u>YaleR</u> (74:4) Sum 85, p. 518-
    519.
"The Double Dream of Spring" (for Gerrit Henry). <u>TriQ</u> (63)
    Spr-Sum 85, p. 140.
"Down by the Station, Early in the Morning." <u>Nat</u> (241:12)
    19 O 85, p. 387.
"Dream Overture." <u>YaleR</u> (74:4) Sum 85, p. 518.
"Imperfect Sympathies." <u>MemphisSR</u> (5:2) Spr 85, p. 13-14.
"The Romantic Entanglement." <u>NewYorker</u> (61:39) 18 N 85, p.
    46.
"Trefoil." <u>Nat</u> (241:12) 19 O 85, p. 387.
"Vetiver." <u>NewYorker</u> (61:44) 23 D 85, p. 36.

173. ASHE, Lynne
     "Holi/day Sho(pping)." _Swallow_ (4) 85, p. 73.
     "When Time Shall Once Again Be the Answer." _Swallow_ (4)
        85, p. 74.
174. ASHTON, Charlie
     "At the Knacker's." _Stand_ (26:3) Sum 85, p. 60.
175. ASKINS, Justin
     "Clowns." _CapeR_ (20:1) Spr 85, p. 21.
     "Daemons" (For Gyorgyi). _CapeR_ (20:1) Spr 85, p. 20.
176. ASPENSTROM, Werner
     "The Mill" (tr. by Robin Fulton). _Verse_ (3) 85, p. 41.
177. ASPER, Douglas (_See_ also ASPER, Douglas M.)
     "The Final Word." _KanQ_ (17:4) Fall 85, p. 67.
     "Mission." _KanQ_ (17:4) Fall 85, p. 66-67.
     "Solitude." _DenQ_ (19:3) Wint 85, p. 46.
     "This Indeterminacy Bothers You." _DenQ_ (19:3) Wint 85, p.
        45.
178. ASPER, Douglas M. (_See_ also ASPER, Douglas)
     "Wristwatch." _KanQ_ (17:1/2) Wint-Spr 85, p. 242.
179. ASPINWALL, Dorothy
     "The Minuet" (tr. of Tristan Klingsor). _WebR_ (10:2) Fall
        85, p. 35.
     "Never Anyone But You" (tr. of Robert Desnos). _WebR_ (10:2)
        Fall 85, p. 33.
     "Under Cover of Night" (tr. of Robert Desnos). _WebR_ (10:2)
        Fall 85, p. 34.
     "The Voice of Robert Desnos" (tr. of Robert Desnos). _WebR_
        (10:2) Fall 85, p. 31-32.
180. ASTOR, Susan
     "Bathwater Baby." _Confr_ (30/31) N 85, p. 133.
     "Construction." _PoetL_ (79:4) Wint 85, p. 216-217.
     "Ode to Her Thumb." _Confr_ (30/31) N 85, p. 133.
181. ATKINS, Priscilla
     "Spumoni" (for Mary Bell Sard). _HawaiiR_ (18) Fall 85, p.
        60-61.
182. ATKINSON, Charles
     "After Slapping a Child at Bedtime." _SouthernR_ (21:1) Wint
        85, p. 111-112.
     "At the Park after Work, Listen." _SouthernR_ (21:1) Wint
        85, p. 113-114.
     "Drive by Instinct." _ColEng_ (47:7) N 85, p. 713.
     "A Mother Falls Asleep." _SouthernR_ (21:1) Wint 85, p. 112-
        113.
183. ATKINSON, Jennifer
     "Letter from Uji Village, 1011." _LitR_ (29:1) Fall 85, p.
        16.
     "Pattaconk Pond" (in memory of Martha Hale). _Tendril_
        (19/20) 85, p. 52.
     "Philosophy Class." _Poetry_ (147:3) D 85, p. 142-144.
     "Pig Alley." _Tendril_ (19/20) 85, p. 53.
184. ATMANAM
     "Reconsideration" (tr. by M. S. Ramaswami). _Stand_ (26:3)
        Sum 85, p. 6.
ATSUKO, Fujino
     See FUJINO, Atsuko
185. ATTANASIO, Rob (_See_ also ATTANASIO, Robert)
     "Barbell Remembered." _WindO_ (46) Fall 85, p. 32.
186. ATTANASIO, Robert (_See_ also ATTANASIO, Rob)
     "The Buddha." _LaurelR_ (19:2) Sum 85, p. 68.
187. ATWATER, Anne
     "Who then fashioned this." _Bogg_ (53) 85, p. 44.
188. ATWOOD, Margaret
     "Doorway." _Iowa_ (15:1) Wint 85, p. 45-46.
     "Galiano Coast: Four Entrances." _MemphisSR_ (5:2) Spr 85,
        p. 23-24.
     "The Saints." _Iowa_ (15:1) Wint 85, p. 44-45.

"Women's Novels" (for Lenore). <u>OP</u> (38/39) Spr 85, p. 95-96.
189. AUBERT, Jimmy
    "Alligator Gar" (Third Award Poem, 1984/1985). <u>KanQ</u>
        (17:1/2) Wint-Spr 85, p. 23.
    "From a Boat, Neosho River." <u>KanQ</u> (17:1/2) Wint-Spr 85, p.
        23.
    "Silo." <u>Wind</u> (15:55) 85, p. 6-7.
    "Something Grew." <u>Wind</u> (15:55) 85, p. 6.
190. AUBREY, Daniel
    "Joseph Leidy" (for my mother). <u>PoetL</u> (80:3) Fall 85, p.
        142-143.
191. AUBREY, Keith
    "Birds on a Pond at Dust, Turnbull Wildlife Refuge, May
        1984." <u>HolCrit</u> (22:3) Je 85, p. 18.
192. AUGUSTIN, Michael
    "Exaggerated Consequence" (tr. by Margitt Lebhert).
        <u>Ploughs</u> (11:1) 85, p. 36.
    "An Excellent Sentence" (tr. by Margitt Lebhert). <u>Ploughs</u>
        (11:1) 85, p. 38.
    "Immaculatus" (tr. by Margitt Lebhert). <u>Ploughs</u> (11:1) 85,
        p. 37.
    "Self-Portrait" (tr. by Margitt Lebhert). <u>Ploughs</u> (11:1)
        85, p. 37.
    "Sleepwalking" (tr. by Margitt Lebhert). <u>Ploughs</u> (11:1)
        85, p. 36.
    "A Terrible Disappointment" (tr. by Margitt Lebhert).
        <u>Ploughs</u> (11:1) 85, p. 35.
193. AUSTIN, Penelope
    "Demolition Derby." <u>QW</u> (20) Spr-Sum 85, p. 82-83.
    "Margaret Hammond" (December 8, 1916 - April 21, 1972).
        <u>AntR</u> (43:2) Spr 85, p. 194-197.
194. AVE JEANNE
    "The autumn wind." <u>NegC</u> (5:4) Fall 85, p. 107.
    "Canvas on Tuesday." <u>PoeticJ</u> (10) 85, p. 37.
    "Letter to the Editor #2." <u>SanFPJ</u> (7:3) 84 [i.e. 85], p. 9.
    "Measuring Up." <u>SanFPJ</u> (7:3) 84 [i.e. 85], p. 12.
    "One Moment Please." <u>SanFPJ</u> (7:3) 84 [i.e. 85], p. 20.
195. AVERETT, Joy
    "Amethyst August." <u>Waves</u> (14:1/2) Fall 85, p. 108.
196. AVERILL, Diane
    "Music Lover." <u>Calyx</u> (9:1) Spr-Sum 85, p. 46.
197. AVICOLLI, Tommi
    "For Charlie Howard" (a gay man killed by teenagers in
        Maine). <u>JamesWR</u> (2:1) Fall 84, p. 3.
198. AVILA, Kay
    "Climbing Party" (For G.P. & P.W.). <u>Amelia</u> (2:2) O 85, p.
        71.
199. AVISON, Margaret
    "Coming Back." <u>PoetryCR</u> (7:1) Aut 85, p. 9.
    "Known." <u>PoetryCR</u> (7:1) Aut 85, p. 9.
200. AWAD, Joseph
    "For Jude's Lebanon." <u>SmPd</u> (22:2) Spr 85, p. 33-34.
    "For My Irish Grandfather." <u>Poem</u> (53) Mr 85, p. 22-24.
    "I'm beginning a novena to St. Jude." <u>SmPd</u> (22:1) Wint 85,
        p. 10.
    "Story." <u>Wind</u> (15:55) 85, p. 22.
201. AXELROD, David
    "Abandoned Migrant Dorm." <u>CrabCR</u> (3:1) Fall-Wint 85, p. 12.
    "The Lives of Our Fathers." <u>CrabCR</u> (3:1) Fall-Wint 85, p.
        10.
    "One for My Father." <u>Confr</u> (30/31) N 85, p. 181.
    "Solstice, Upper Gold Creek Homestead." <u>LaurelR</u> (19:2) Sum
        85, p. 41.
202. AXINN, Donald Everett
    "Stalls." <u>Confr</u> (30/31) N 85, p. 138.

203. AYHAN, Ece
     "Orthodoxies I" (Excerpts, tr. by Murat Nemet-Nejat).
        Chelsea (44) 85, p. 148.
204. AYLSWORTH, Peggy
     "The Daily Visit." LaurelR (19:2) Sum 85, p. 17.
205. AYRES, Gail W.
     "For Maggie." NegC (5:1) Wint 85, p. 47-49.
206. BABAD, Katharine Heath
     "The Belle of Vines" (for Frances Mayes). CapeR (20:2)
        Fall 85, p. 41.
     "Drowning." CapeR (20:1) Spr 85, p. 32.
     "The Familiar Gecko." CapeR (20:1) Spr 85, p. 31.
     "Overturned." CapeR (20:2) Fall 85, p. 40.
     "Writing an Avalanche." CapeR (20:1) Spr 85, p. 30.
207. BACA, Jimmy-Santiago
     "Martin III." RevChic (13:1) Spr 85, p. 49-53.
208. BACH, Emmon
     "Five Sonnets." MassR (26:1) Spr 85, p. 58-60.
209. BACHAM, Paul
     "Until Now." SanFPJ (7:4) 85, p. 87.
210. BACHMANN, Ingeborg
     "Nachtflug." CumbPR (5:1) Fall 85, p. 30-31.
     "Night Flight" (tr. by Mark Anderson). ParisR (27:95) Spr
        85, p. 133-134.
     "Nightflight" (tr. by Siegfried Mandel). CumbPR (5:1) Fall
        85, p. 32-33.
     "Stars in March" (tr. by Siegfried Mandel). CumbPR (5:1)
        Fall 85, p. 29.
     "Sterne im März." CumbPR (5:1) Fall 85, p. 28.
211. BACKMAN, John L. D.
     "Like God with Adam, Your Image." CapeR (20:1) Spr 85, p.
        18.
     "Snow Calls Us to the Things of This World." Poem (54) N
        85, p. 50.
212. BADIKIAN, Beatriz
     "Elements for an Autobiographical Poem." Imagine (1:2)
        Wint 84, p. 122.
     "Paris, 24 de diciembre." Imagine (1:2) Wint 84, p. 120-
        121.
     "Rosas Marchitas." Imagine (2:1) Sum 85, p. 64.
     "Things to Do While Waiting for a Lover" (fill in the
        blanks, please). Imagine (2:1) Sum 85, p. 64.
     "Womanscapes." Imagine (1:2) Wint 84, p. 119-120.
213. BADOR, Bernard
     "Dialogues" (tr. of Michel Deguy). Temblor (2) 85, p. 68.
     "Pleasures of the Threshold" (tr. of Michel Deguy).
        Temblor (2) 85, p. 69.
     "Space" (tr. of Michel Deguy). Temblor (2) 85, p. 68-69.
214. BAECHTEL, Mark H.
     "For Weldon Kees." PoetL (80:3) Fall 85, p. 135.
     "Horus." PoetL (80:3) Fall 85, p. 136.
     "Staying." PoetL (80:3) Fall 85, p. 137.
215. BAEHR, Anne-Ruth Ediger
     "Carlisle School" (1890). PoetryR (5) S 85, p. 36-37.
     "I Am Dancing with My Mennonite Father" (The Mary Elinore
        Smith Poetry Prize). AmerS (54:3) Sum 85, p. 326-327.
     "Mother and Daughter." Confr (30/31) N 85, p. 163.
216. BAER, William
     "Nightcry." AntR (43:4) Fall 85, p. 464.
217. BAEZ, Luis A.
     "Epitafio 2." RevChic (13:2) Sum 85, p. 29-33.
218. BAHR, A. H.
     "Epitaph." Wind (15:53) 85, p. 42.
     "Rain." Wind (15:53) 85, p. 27.
219. BAIGENT, Beryl
     "The Lost Children of Abergan." PoetryCR (7:2) Wint 85-86,

p. 52.
220. BAILEY, Charles
    "Freighter." _Wind_ (15:54) 85, p. 32.
221. BAILEY, Don
    "Easter." _Germ_ (9:2) Fall-Wint 85, p. 27.
    "For Daile." _Germ_ (9:2) Fall-Wint 85, p. 26.
222. BAILEY, Thomas S.
    "Mary Appleberry." _Wind_ (15:55) 85, p. 8-9.
223. BAILLARGEON, Gary (_See also_ BAILLARGEON, Gerald)
    "Shortwave." _Germ_ (9:2) Fall-Wint 85, p. 23-24.
224. BAILLARGEON, Gerald (_See also_ BAILLARGEON, Gary)
    "Beulah." _AntigR_ (60) Wint 85, p. 30.
    "Seamstress." _AntigR_ (60) Wint 85, p. 30.
225. BAIRD, Bonnie
    "Impressions." _PottPort_ (7) 85-86, p. 19.
    "Son." _PottPort_ (7) 85-86, p. 51.
226. BAKER, David
    "Chimney." _CharR_ (11:1) Spr 85, p. 68-69.
    "Fireworks." _SewanR_ (93:4) Fall 85, p. 526-527.
    "Going on Instincts." _KanQ_ (17:1/2) Wint-Spr 85, p. 26.
    "Hunters: The Planting." _KanQ_ (17:1/2) Wint-Spr 85, p. 25-
       26.
    "New Campers at Dusk." _CharR_ (11:1) Spr 85, p. 69.
    "Rest Stop." _CimR_ (71) Ap 85, p. 45-51.
    "Waking after Snow." _WestHR_ (19:3) Aut 85, p. 266.
    "Web." _NoAmR_ (270:2) Je 85, p. 49.
227. BAKER, Houston A., Jr.
    "Carolina, Coltrane, and Love." _SouthernR_ (21:3) Sum 85,
       p. 855-856.
    "Double South Spring." _SouthernR_ (21:3) Sum 85, p. 857-858.
    "My Mother's Mother's House." _SouthernR_ (21:3) Sum 85, p.
       854.
    "Prodigal." _SouthernR_ (21:3) Sum 85, p. 858-859.
    "Socializing: Roots: Or When My Wife Surprised the Dinner
       Party with Talk of Her Youth." _SouthernR_ (21:3) Sum 85,
       p. 855.
    "Sr/Sd: for an African Chronicle." _SouthernR_ (21:3) Sum
       85, p. 857.
228. BAKER, June Frankland
    "Attending the Garage Sale" (after your death at 92). _CutB_
       (23) Fall-Wint 85, p. 35.
    "Poem, in Case I Am Ever Asked to Read at Graduation."
       KanQ (17:4) Fall 85, p. 109.
    "Poetry Reading, Fort Worden" (for William Stafford). _KanQ_
       (17:4) Fall 85, p. 109.
229. BAKKEN, Dick
    "House." _YellowS_ (15) Sum 85, p. 39.
    "Jalopy." _YellowS_ (15) Sum 85, p. 39.
    "Lagoon." _YellowS_ (15) Sum 85, p. 39.
    "Marge." _YellowS_ (15) Sum 85, p. 39.
    "Midnight." _YellowS_ (15) Sum 85, p. 39.
    "Poem for My Wife." _YellowS_ (15) Sum 85, p. 39.
    "Ripe Cherries." _YellowS_ (15) Sum 85, p. 39.
230. BALABAN, John
    "Dedication" (To Tamara, tr. of Luchesar Elenkov). _Mund_
       (15:1/2) 85, p. 142.
    "Song between the Sea and Sky" (tr. of Kolyo Sevov). _Mund_
       (15:1/2) 85, p. 143.
    "Toas Mountain." _PoetryR_ (2:2) Ap 85, p. 39.
    "A Woman Alone on the Road" (tr. of Blaga Dimitrova). _Mund_
       (15:1/2) 85, p. 144-145.
231. BALAKIAN, Peter
    "The Oriental Rug" (For my daughter, Sophia). _Poetry_
       (147:2) N 85, p. 78-84.
    "Visitation." _ThRiPo_ (25/26) 85, p. 18-19.

232. BALAZ, Joseph P.
   "On That Same Beach beneath a Full Moon." HawaiiR (17) Spr
      85, p. 74-75.
233. BALAZS, Mary
   "After Twenty-Two Years." Wind (15:54) 85, p. 1-2.
   "Diagnosis." CapeR (20:1) Spr 85, p. 11.
   "For My Son, Adolescent." Wind (15:54) 85, p. 2.
   "Grief, and Winter's Burdens." CapeR (20:2) Fall 85, p. 4.
234. BALBO, Ned Clark
   "Kristina, Listen." StoneC (12:2/3) Spr-Sum 85, p. 24.
   "Red Eft." SoCaR (18:1) Fall 85, p. 74-75.
   "The Third Rail." NegC (5:3) Sum 85, p. 146.
235. BALDWIN, Joseph
   "Sarabande." SouthwR (70:1) Wint 85, p. 113.
236. BALDWIN, Sy Margaret
   "Barbed Wire." Calyx (9:1) Spr-Sum 85, p. 32.
   "First Loves." Calyx (9:1) Spr-Sum 85, p. 29.
   "Shady Lakes." HangL (47) Spr 85, p. 13.
   "Trinity." Calyx (9:1) Spr-Sum 85, p. 28.
   "Yellow Tulips." Calyx (9:1) Spr-Sum 85, p. 30-31.
237. BALDWIN, Tama
   "I Went to Her House to Remember What Happened and Thus What
      Will." Raccoon (17) Mr 85, p. 22-23.
238. BALESTRIERI, Elizabeth
   "Red Tulips." CreamCR (10:1) 85, p. 48.
239. BALESTRINI, Nanni
   "Instinct of Self-preservation" (tr. by Annalisa Saccà).
      LitR (28:2) Wint 85, p. 207.
240. BALK, Christianne
   "Elegy." Pequod (19/20/21) 85, p. 68-69.
   "The Young Widow Studies the Sky." Pequod (19/20/21) 85,
      p. 66-67.
241. BALL, Angela
   "Filings." HawaiiR (18) Fall 85, p. 33-34.
   "One Sunday Afternoon." CrossCur (5:3) 85, p. 85-86.
   "Wife." IndR (8:1) Wint 85, p. 52-53.
242. BALL, Joseph B.
   "And This Is So." YellowS (16) Aut 85, p. 8.
   "A Little Like Love." HiramPoR (39) Fall-Wint 85, p. 7.
243. BALLINGER, Susan George
   "Genitals." Bogg (53) 85, p. 19.
244. BALTENSPERGER, Peter
   "Ghost Town Sequence." Germ (9:2) Fall-Wint 85, p. 33-35.
245. BANGERT, Sharon
   "Abstract #3." WestCR (20:2) O 85, p. 18.
   "Scavenging." WestCR (20:2) O 85, p. 17.
246. BANKER, Ashok K.
   "Between Nightmares." Mund (15:1/2) 85, p. 128-129.
247. BANKIER, Joanna
   "Black Postcards" (tr. of Tomas Transtromer). Thrpny (6:2,
      issue 22) Sum 85, p. 6.
248. BANKS, Kenneth
   "The Kneeling Brook." AntigR (62/63) Sum-Aut 85, p. 40.
249. BANKS, Leigh
   "You Mortals, Breathe Your Sighs No More" (tr. of Pierre
      Guedron, w. W. D. Snodgrass). NegC (5:1) Wint 85, p. 78.
250. BANKS, Loy
   "Attending Toas." SoDakR (23:1) Spr 85, p. 51.
   "Near the Convent." LittleBR (5:1) Fall-Wint 84-85, p. 45.
251. BANKS, M. Anne
   "Progressions: Aunt Lena." PottPort (7) 85-86, p. 39.
252. BANTING, Pamela
   "Pamela" (Selections). PraF (6:3) Sum 85, p. 40-45.
253. BARAKA, Amiri
   "Courageousness." SouthernR (21:3) Sum 85, p. 810.
   "I Investigate the Sun." SouthernR (21:3) Sum 85, p. 811.

"Why's / Wise" (Selections: "What about Literature? W-15,"
   "A Note to President Pasadoekeeoh! & His Wise Ass Reply W-
   16"). SouthernR (21:3) Sum 85, p. 801-809.
254. BARANCZAK, Stanislaw
   "Along with the Dust" (tr. by Reginald Gibbons and the
   author). TriQ (63) Spr-Sum 85, p. 566.
   "The Answer" (tr. of Ryszard Krynicki, w. Clare Cavanagh).
   Ploughs (11:4) 85, p. 134.
   "Atlantis" (tr. by Richard Lourie). Ploughs (11:4) 85, p.
   138.
   "By Saying" (tr. of Ryszard Krynicki, w. Clare Cavanagh).
   Ploughs (11:4) 85, p. 133.
   "The Heart" (tr. of Ryszard Krynicki, w. Clare Cavanagh).
   Ploughs (11:4) 85, p. 135.
   "History" (The first protest leaflet, June, 1956, tr. by
   Richard Lourie). Ploughs (11:4) 85, p. 139.
   "How Far" (tr. of Ryszard Krynicki, w. Clare Cavanagh).
   Ploughs (11:4) 85, p. 135.
   "If China" (tr. by Reginald Gibbons and the author). TriQ
   (63) Spr-Sum 85, p. 567.
   "If It Comes to Pass" (tr. of Ryszard Krynicki, w. Clare
   Cavanagh). Ploughs (11:4) 85, p. 136.
   "I'll Remember That" (tr. of Ryszard Krynicki, w. Clare
   Cavanagh). Ploughs (11:4) 85, p. 136.
   "Inscription on a China Dish" (tr. of Ryszard Krynicki, w.
   Clare Cavanagh). Ploughs (11:4) 85, p. 137.
   "N.N. Records Something on the Back of a Cigarette Pack" (In
   Polish and English, tr. by Leonard Kress). CrossCur
   (4:2) 84, p. 12-13.
   "Rumor Has It" (tr. of Ryszard Krynicki, w. Clare Cavanagh).
   Ploughs (11:4) 85, p. 133.
   "This Moment" (tr. of Ryszard Krynicki, w. Clare Cavanagh).
   Ploughs (11:4) 85, p. 137.
   "The Time of Trial" (tr. of Ryszard Krynicki, w. Clare
   Cavanagh). Ploughs (11:4) 85, p. 137.
255. BARANOW, Joan
   "American Childhood" (Excerpt). USl (18/19) Wint 85, p. 11.
   "On Your Mother's Death" (for Lex Allen). LittleM (14:4)
   85, p. 13.
   "Ophelia Speaks to the River." USl (18/19) Wint 85, p. 11.
256. BARBARESE, J. T.
   "Firewood Talk, 23 October 1983." CarolQ (38:1) Fall 85,
   p. 25-27.
   "Sunshine." DenQ (20:1) Sum 85, p. 67.
   "That Last Spring" (for M.J.). CarolQ (37:2) Wint 85, p.
   71.
   "Through the Sunshower off Stage Point." IndR (8:1) Wint
   85, p. 20-21.
257. BARBER, David
   "Small Hours." MissouriR (8:2) 85, p. 20.
   "Sudden Clarity at the Artichoke Stands." MissouriR (8:2)
   85, p. 18-19.
258. BARBER, Jennifer
   "The Letter." GeoR (39:4) Wint 85, p. 806.
   "Long Engagement" (from Chekhov's letters to Olga).
   PoetryR (2:2) Ap 85, p. 91.
259. BARD, Karen S.
   "The Small Actions of Household." SmPd (22:3) Fall 85, p.
   10.
260. BARENBLATT, Daniel
   "Twenty-third Street Station Two A.M." HarvardA (118:4) My
   85, p. 12.
261. BARGE, Shelly
   "Educator." EngJ (74:6) O 85, p. 76.
262. BARGEN, Walter
   "Eve's Rib." WebR (10:1) Spr 85, p. 62-63.

"New Franklin Tornado." <u>KanQ</u> (17:4) Fall 85, p. 103.
"Second Going." <u>CapeR</u> (20:2) Fall 85, p. 8.
263. BARI, Károly
    "By the Gypsies' Graves" (tr. by Laura Schiff). <u>Zyzzyva</u>
        (1:4) Wint 85, p. 79.
264. BARKER, David
    "Green Socks." <u>WormR</u> (25:1, issue 97) 85, p. 6-7.
    "Last Days in L.A." <u>WormR</u> (25:1, issue 97) 85, p. 5-6.
    "Mad April." <u>WormR</u> (25:1, issue 97) 85, p. 5.
    "Me and Howard Hughes." <u>WormR</u> (25:1, issue 97) 85, p. 8.
    "Over the Hills to Mexico." <u>WormR</u> (25:1, issue 97) 85, p.
        7-8.
    "Paper." <u>WormR</u> (25:3, issue 99) 85, p. 91-92.
265. BARKER, Wendy
    "Black Sheep, Red Stars." <u>Poetry</u> (146:1) Ap 85, p. 11-12.
    "Dancing Lessons." <u>Imagine</u> (2:1) Sum 85, p. 84.
    "I See You in That Light." <u>Imagine</u> (2:1) Sum 85, p. 85.
    "Night Song." <u>Poetry</u> (146:1) Ap 85, p. 13.
    "The Swallow Watcher" (for Larry and Elliot). <u>AmerS</u> (54:3)
        Sum 85, p. 344.
266. BARLOW, Stanley
    "Swimming Laps in August." <u>Outbr</u> (14/15) Fall 84-Spr 85,
        p. 46.
267. BARNES, Dick
    "Cuscuta Californica." <u>Zyzzyva</u> (1:4) Wint 85, p. 111.
268. BARNES, Jim
    "Decades." <u>NoDaQ</u> (53:2) Spr 85, p. 193.
    "Icons" (For Sam, briefly met). <u>NewL</u> (51:3) Spr 85, p. 51-
        53.
    "The Poor Fox." <u>NoDaQ</u> (53:2) Spr 85, p. 191.
    "Postcard to Terence Moser in Exile." <u>NoDaQ</u> (53:2) Spr 85,
        p. 191.
    "Surviving the Storm." <u>NoDaQ</u> (53:2) Spr 85, p. 192.
269. BARNES, Richard
    "The Assassin." <u>Poetry</u> (146:2) My 85, p. 84-85.
    "To a Child Who Cut His Finger for the First Time." <u>Poetry</u>
        (146:2) My 85, p. 82-83.
    "You." <u>Poetry</u> (146:2) My 85, p. 83-84.
270. BARNES, S. Brandi
    "Blackberries in the China Cabinet." <u>BlackALF</u> (19:3) Fall
        85, p. 103.
    "We Got Stuff" (for the sisterhood). <u>BlackALF</u> (19:3) Fall
        85, p. 103.
271. BARNES, W. J.
    "Angelico's Magi." <u>Quarry</u> (34:3) Sum 85, p. 73-75.
    "Budgie at the Bank." <u>Quarry</u> (34:3) Sum 85, p. 72-73.
272. BARNETT, Anthony
    "Seedport" (9 selections). <u>Temblor</u> (1) 85, p. 20-22.
273. BARNETT, Ruth Anderson
    "Aubade." <u>PoeticJ</u> (11) 85, p. 8.
    "Crow Mother Songs." <u>NegC</u> (5:2) Spr 85, p. 60-62.
    "Humidity." <u>PoeticJ</u> (11) 85, p. 36.
    "Into Winter" (For my grandfather). <u>PoeticJ</u> (12) 85, p. 30.
    "Oregon Fog on Highway Five." <u>PoeticJ</u> (9) 85, p. 2.
    "Waiting for Winter." <u>PoeticJ</u> (10) 85, p. 13.
    "Westering" (to Seamus Heaney). <u>PoeticJ</u> (10) 85, p. 14-15.
274. BARNIE, John
    "Cwm Bryn-Arw." <u>PoetryCR</u> (6:3) Spr 85, p. 33.
275. BARNSTONE, Aliki
    "Impossible Blue." <u>Raccoon</u> (17) Mr 85, p. 29-30.
276. BARNSTONE, Willis
    "Antonio Machado in Soria (Jotting in a Copybook)." <u>ChiR</u>
        (35:2) Wint 85, p. 32.
    "Winter Rain." <u>Raccoon</u> (17) Mr 85, back cover.
277. BARON, E.
    "Saturday Matinee, 1944." <u>CrossCur</u> (4:4/5:1) 85, p. 53.

278. BARON, Mary
     "Messmate." GreenfR (13:1/2) Fall-Wint 85, p. 39.
279. BARON, Todd
     "Go or Come Again." Temblor (1) 85, p. 118.
     "Location." Temblor (1) 85, p. 118.
     "A Wave in Which." Gargoyle (27) 85, p. 91.
280. BARQUET, Jesus J.
     "El Libro de las Estaciones." LindLM (4:2) Ap-Je 85, p. 21.
281. BARR, Allan
     "In the Playground by the School for the Deaf." Waves
     (13:2/3) Wint 85, p. 77.
282. BARR, Tina
     "The Crossing." AmerPoR (14:3) My-Je 85, p. 45.
     "North of Kennebunkport." Ploughs (11:1) 85, p. 39-40.
     "Public Garden above the Rhone." Ploughs (11:1) 85, p. 41-
     42.
283. BARRACK, Jack
     "Hollywood Extra." GrandS (4:2) Wint 85, p. 200.
     "Monster." GrandS (4:2) Wint 85, p. 202.
     "On One Who Never Learned to Read." GrandS (4:2) Wint 85,
     p. 201.
284. BARRESI, Dorothy
     "Thanksgiving." PoetryNW (26:4) Wint 85-86, p. 23.
     "Vacation, 1969." ColEng (47:6) O 85, p. 611.
285. BARRETT, Carol
     "A Family Affair." Cond (11/12) 85, p. 11-12.
     "Ghost Story." WoosterR (4) Fall 85, p. 72.
     "Milk" (for Alice Evans). PoetL (80:2) Sum 85, p. 97-98.
     "Overcoming the Ordinary" (w. Peggy Schrader). WoosterR
     (4) Fall 85, p. 73.
286. BARRETT, Joseph
     "Woman Playing a Juke Box." LaurelR (19:1) Wint 85, p. 61.
287. BARRETT, Linda
     "344" (tr. of Marina Tsvetaeva). GrahamHR (8) Wint 85, p.
     43-44.
288. BARRETT, Lou
     "Interrupted Night." PoeticJ (9) 85, p. 14.
289. BARRIE, Jill
     "Song of the Jilted Girl." ConnPR (3:1) 84, p. 28.
     "Walter's Insomnia." CrabCR (2:2) Wint 85, p. 16.
290. BARRIER, Don
     "Hands 1." Vis (19) 85, p. 18.
291. BARRIOS, Marilyn Horton
     "Blackberry Morning." Wind (15:55) 85, p. 10.
292. BARRY, Paul
     "Anatomical Illustration." Poetry (145:5) F 85, p. 271-272.
     "The Blind Girl Speaks of the Marvelous Things." Poetry
     (145:5) F 85, p. 272-273.
293. BARST, Fran
     "Desert." StoneC (13:1/2) Fall-Wint 85-86, p. 34-35.
     "The Hunter." Amelia (2:2) O 85, p. 78-79.
294. BARTKOWECH, R.
     "Series of Silence Holding." NoDaQ (53:1) Wint 85, p. 97-
     98.
     "A Silly Syndicate of Lies Comes Forth." NoDaQ (53:1) Wint
     85, p. 98-101.
BARTLETT, Catherine Vallejos
     See VALLEJOS BARTLETT, Catherine
295. BARTLETT, Elizabeth
     "1 x 1 x 1." Imagine (2:1) Sum 85, p. 82.
     "The All of One." CrossCur (4:4/5:1) 85, p. 94.
     "Fight of Flight." CumbPR (5:1) Fall 85, p. 25.
     "One and All" (In English and Japanese, tr. by Keiko Matsui
     Gibson). CrossCur (4:2) 84, p. 58-59.
     "A Penny's Worth." PoetL (80:1) Spr 85, p. 45-46.
     "Proclamation." StoneC (13:1/2) Fall-Wint 85-86, p. 18-19.

"Summer Is the Hardest Time." StoneC (13:1/2) Fall-Wint 85-
86, p. 19-20.
"The Sunday Paper." Wind (15:54) 85, p. 3.
296. BARTLETT, Martha-Elizabeth
"At the Nursing Home." Paint (11:21/12:24) 84-85, p. 25.
"Suicide's Daughter." Paint (11:21/12:24) 84-85, p. 24.
297. BARTON, David
"In This Climate." JamesWR (3:1) Fall 85, p. 15.
298. BARTOW, Stuart, Jr.
"The Ghost." Poem (53) Mr 85, p. 14.
"Glowworms." Poem (53) Mr 85, p. 15.
"The Vanished Ones." Poem (53) Mr 85, p. 13.
299. BASINSKI, Michael
"The Secret." YellowS (14) Spr 85, p. 9.
300. BASNEY, Lionel
"Fallward." CumbPR (5:1) Fall 85, p. 55.
BASORA, Neli Jo Carmona
See CARMONA BASORA, Neli Jo
301. BASS, Madeline Tiger
"Art History: A Hieroglyph." NegC (5:2) Spr 85, p. 31.
"Elegy." NegC (5:1) Wint 85, p. 113.
"La Grande Jatte" (for Elizabeth Herrera & Gemma Finn).
GreenfR (13:1/2) Fall-Wint 85, p. 58-59.
"The Word Process" (for Arthur Binder). GreenfR (13:1/2)
Fall-Wint 85, p. 57.
302. BASSHAM, Tod
"Walpurgisnacht." Nimrod (28:2) Spr-Sum 85, p. 141.
303. BASTIAN, Heiner
"Before Margins" (tr. by Rosemarie Waldrop). NewL (51:4)
Sum 85, p. 59.
"Observations in the Aerial Ocean" (tr. by Rosemarie
Waldrop). NewL (51:4) Sum 85, p. 60-61.
304. BASTIAN, Richard
"Sisyphus in Parsippany." PoetryR (2:2) Ap 85, p. 44.
305. BATAILLE, Gabriel
"Qui Veut Chasser une Migraine." NegC (5:1) Wint 85, p. 81.
"Who Wants to Cure a Migraine?" (tr. by W. D. Snodgrass).
NegC (5:1) Wint 85, p. 82.
306. BATEMAN, David
"There Once Was." Bogg (54) 85, p. 9.
307. BATEROWICZ, Marek
"Rescued Graines" (11 poems in Polish and English, tr. by
Victor Contoski, The Mid-American Review Translation
Chapbook Series, Number 3). MidAR (5:1) 85, p. 81-103.
308. BATHANTI, Joseph
"The Bull." HolCrit (22:1) F 85, p. 20.
"Moses at the Egyptian Restaurant." CarolQ (37:3) Spr 85,
p. 69.
"Raskolnikov." GreenfR (13:1/2) Fall-Wint 85, p. 18.
309. BATT, Tina
"Channel Childhood." BlueBldgs (9) [85?], p. 34.
310. BATTIN, Wendy
"In the Solar Wind." Tendril (19/20) 85, p. 54-59.
311. BATUR, Enis
"Lot's Woman" (tr. by Talat Sait Halman). GreenfR (13:1/2)
Fall-Wint 85, p. 84-85.
312. BAUER, Steven
"Heat Lightning." CharR (11:1) Spr 85, p. 88-89.
313. BAUGH, Edward
"Dusk Poem." GreenfR (12:3/4) Wint-Spr 85, p. 126.
"Nigger Sweat." GreenfR (12:3/4) Wint-Spr 85, p. 127-128.
"An Open Letter to Feelings of Insecurity." GreenfR
(12:3/4) Wint-Spr 85, p. 127.
314. BAUGH, Gabrielle
"My Room." AmerPoR (14:3) My-Je 85, p. 21.

315. BAUMGAERTNER, Jill P.
     "Upon Finding a Photo of My Second Grade Class." Vis (19)
        85, p. 5.
316. BAUTISTA, Jacquelin
     "Tales of Psychosurgery." Pig (13) 85, p. 34.
317. BAUTISTA PAIZ, Juan
     "Egrets" (tr. by Kent Johnson). MinnR (N.S. 25) Fall 85,
        p. 47.
318. BAVIS, Ed
     "The Holy Wire." Open24 (4) 85, p. 52-53.
319. BAWER, Bruce
     "The View from an Airplane at Night, over California."
        ArizQ (41:3) Aut 85, p. 196.
320. BAYEZ-SNYDER, E. Bernardine
     "Privation." SanFPJ (7:4) 85, p. 88.
321. BAYSA, Fred
     "Cane Fire." HawaiiR (18) Fall 85, p. 88-91.
322. BBB
     "The Early Farmhouse Summer." Wind (15:55) 85, p. 11-14.
323. BEACHLER, Lea
     "The Shadow." SouthernPR (26, i.e. 25:2) Fall 85, p. 19-20.
324. BEAKE, Fred
     "Tree with Old Woman." Stand (26:2) Spr 85, p. 63.
325. BEALL, Sandra
     "In Einstein's House, in the Closet." Sulfur (12) 85, p.
        102-103.
     "In Praise of Whatnot." Sulfur (12) 85, p. 105.
     "Mother Goose." Sulfur (12) 85, p. 103-104.
326. BEAM, Jeffery
     "Antinous in Egypt." CarolQ (37:3) Spr 85, p. 70-71.
     "The Monk." JamesWR (2:3) Spr-Sum 85, p. 10.
BEAR, Ray A. Young
     See YOUNG BEAR, Ray A.
327. BEARDSLEY, Doug
     "Baby Poem" (for Anna Maura). AntigR (62/63) Sum-Aut 85,
        p. 168.
     "The House beneath the Surface of Things." AntigR (62/63)
        Sum-Aut 85, p. 168.
     "An Image of Christ Ascending into the Heavens." Waves
        (14:1/2) Fall 85, p. 61.
     "Vivaldi's Four Sonnets." CanLit (107) Wint 85, p. 17-19.
328. BEASLEY, Bruce
     "Lazarus." StoneC (12:2/3) Spr-Sum 85, p. 9.
     "A Thing among Things." StoneC (12:2/3) Spr-Sum 85, p. 9.
329. BEASLEY, Conger, Jr.
     "A Story about Maurice Ravel." Oink (19) 85, p. 105.
330. BEAUCHAMP, Steve
     "In Evening." DeKalbLAJ (18:3/4) 85, p. 30.
331. BEAUDOIN, Kenneth Lawrence
     "Chorale in December" (tr. of Claude Vigée, w. J. R.
        LeMaster). Mund (15:1/2) 85, p. 179, 181.
     "Heart Lost in the World" (tr. of Claude Vigée, w. J. R.
        LeMaster). Mund (15:1/2) 85, p. 177, 179.
     "Living Tomb" (tr. of Claude Vigée, w. J. R. LeMaster).
        WebR (10:1) Spr 85, p. 31-32.
     "Patience" (tr. of Claude Vigée, w. J. R. LeMaster).
        Mund (15:1/2) 85, p. 183.
332. BEAUDOUIN, David
     "The Art of Narrative." Open24 (4) 85, p. 25.
     "For Basil Bunting." Open24 (4) 85, p. 56.
     "Rune." Open24 (4) 85, p. 39.
333. BEAUSOLEIL, Claude
     "Désinformer, le mot existe" (with Michael Delisle).
        Rampike (4:2/3) 85-86, p. 6.
334. BECK, John Peter
     "Get All Over You Like a Cheap Suit." PassN (6:2) Spr-Sum

85, p. 15.
335. BECKER, Carol
"Life along the Delaware and Raritan Canal." PoetryR (2:2)
Ap 85, p. 70.
336. BECKER, Marjorie
"Bones." CapeR (20:1) Spr 85, p. 41.
BEEK, Edith van
See Van BEEK, Edith
337. BEGIN, Tom
"Farm Mornings." PottPort (7) 85-86, p. 23.
"On the Shores of the Kennetcook" (In Memory of Alden
Nowlan). PottPort (7) 85-86, p. 19.
338. BEHAN, Marie
"Set." Confr (29) Wint 85, p. 137-138.
339. BEHM, Richard
"Conversations." SouthwR (70:4) Aut 85, p. 488.
"The Swimmer." KanQ (17:1/2) Wint-Spr 85, p. 81.
"Trying to Make Something of It." Wind (15:54) 85, p. 4-5.
"Woman Raking." Amelia (2:2) O 85, p. 45.
340. BEHN, Robin
"After Love." Crazy (26) Spr 84, p. 42-43.
"Four Years after Your Deliberate Drowning." Poetry
(145:6) Mr 85, p. 337.
"Last Page." Tendril (19/20) 85, p. 79.
341. BEHRENDT, Stephen C.
"Flying over Nebraska by Night." NoDaQ (53:4) Fall 85, p.
180.
"The Garden of Questionable Delights." PraS (59:2) Sum 85,
p. 55.
"Homage à Robbe-Grillet." PraS (59:2) Sum 85, p. 56.
"In Memory of My Grandfather." PraS (59:2) Sum 85, p. 52-
54.
"Life Sketch." PraS (59:2) Sum 85, p. 51-52.
"The Spirits." PraS (59:2) Sum 85, p. 54-55.
BEKY, Ivan Halasz de
See De BEKY, Ivan Halasz
342. BELANGER, Dann
"Jack Kerouac." MoodySI (15) Spr 85, p. 27.
343. BELCHER, Diane
"Come, Live with Her, and Be My Love." YellowS (16) Aut
85, p. 9.
344. BELFIELD, Judy
"Cyclist." Sam (42:3, 167th release) 85, back cover.
"Stream of Subconscious." LittleBR (5:1) Fall-Wint 84-85,
p. 30.
345. BELITT, Ben
"Crossing the Ice: Acapulco." PoetryR (5) S 85, p. 33.
"Esmiss Esmoor: Passage from India" (Homage to E.M.
Forster). Salm (68/69) Fall-Wint 85-86, p. 3-5.
"This Rock." PoetryR (5) S 85, p. 34.
346. BELL, Carolyn Light
"One of My Stories." KanQ (17:4) Fall 85, p. 128.
"We Go in Stages" (to Patti Steger, Arctic Explorer).
Prima (9) 85, p. 88.
347. BELL, Donald
"Imagine the Man." Ploughs (11:1) 85, p. 44.
"Introduction of Dolphins." Ploughs (11:1) 85, p. 43.
348. BELL, John
"Reagan's Reaganarok: A Video Game." PottPort (7) 85-86,
p. 50.
"West River Cemetery." PoetryCR (7:2) Wint 85-86, p. 10.
349. BELL, Marvin
"Don't Let It End Here." CrossCur (4:2) 84, p. 78.
"Half-Time Poems." OP (38/39) Spr 85, p. 198-199.
"Instructions to be Left Behind." TriQ (63) Spr-Sum 85, p.
545-546.

"Long Island." AmerPoR (14:1) Ja-F 85, p. 16.
"Quilt, Dutch China Plate." SouthwR (70:2) Spr 85, p. 215.
"Tideline." SouthwR (70:2) Spr 85, p. 214.
"The Tradition." OP (38/39) Spr 85, p. 109.
"What I Did in Paris in the Twenties." OP (38/39) Spr 85,
    p. 109.
350. BELLADONNA
    "Stacked Deck." YellowS (17) Wint 85, p. 37.
351. BELLAMY, Joe David
    "From the Biography of the Hummingbird." SouthernPR (25:1)
        Spr 85, p. 9.
352. BELLEZZA, Dario
    "A Private Story" (Excerpt, tr. by Giuliano Dego and
        Margaret Straus). LitR (29:1) Fall 85, p. 93-94.
353. BELLI, Carlos Germán
    "Algun Dia el Amor." Inti (18/19) Otoño 83-Prim. 84, p.
        136.
    "Amanuense." Inti (18/19) Otoño 83-Prim. 84, p. 139.
    "Asir la Forma Que Se Va." Inti (18/19) Otoño 83-Prim.
        84, p. 135.
    "El Atarantado." Inti (18/19) Otoño 83-Prim. 84, p. 141-
        142.
    "Boda de la Pluma y la Letra." Inti (18/19) Otoño 83-
        Prim. 84, p. 143-144.
    "La Cara de Mis Hijas." Inti (18/19) Otoño 83-Prim. 84,
        p. 143.
    "Cepo de Lima." Inti (18/19) Otoño 83-Prim. 84, p. 139-
        140.
    "Cuanta Existencia Menos!" Inti (18/19) Otoño 83-Prim.
        84, p. 138.
    "Fisco." Inti (18/19) Otoño 83-Prim. 84, p. 140.
    "Las Formulas Magicas." Inti (18/19) Otoño 83-Prim. 84,
        p. 136.
    "Ha Llegado el Domingo." Inti (18/19) Otoño 83-Prim. 84,
        p. 138.
    "Mis Ajos." Inti (18/19) Otoño 83-Prim. 84, p. 140-141.
    "Oh Alma Mia Empedrada!" Inti (18/19) Otoño 83-Prim. 84,
        p. 137.
    "Oh Hada Cibernetica!" Inti (18/19) Otoño 83-Prim. 84,
        p. 139.
    "Oh Padres, Sabedlo Bien!" Inti (18/19) Otoño 83-Prim.
        84, p. 137-138.
    "Papá, Mamá." Inti (18/19) Otoño 83-Prim. 84, p. 137.
    "Poema." Inti (18/19) Otoño 83-Prim. 84, p. 135.
    "Segragacion No. 1" (a modo de un pintor primitivo culto).
        Inti (18/19) Otoño 83-Prim. 84, p. 135-136.
    "Sextina de los Desiguales." Inti (18/19) Otoño 83-Prim.
        84, p. 142-143.
    "Villanela." Inti (18/19) Otoño 83-Prim. 84, p. 144-145.
354. BELLINI, Giorgio
    "I Cenno: Genova." Os (20) 85, p. 16.
    "II Cenno: Venezia." Os (20) 85, p. 16.
    "III Cenno: Milano." Os (20) 85, p. 17.
    "IV Cenno: Siena." Os (20) 85, p. 17.
355. BEN, Menahem
    "When Winter Comes" (tr. of David Jaffin, w. David Ben
        Gershon). CrossCur (4:2) 84, p. 35-36.
BEN GERSHON, David
    See GERSHON, David Ben
356. BENEDIKT, Michael
    "The Displaced Energy Blues." Agni (22) 85, p. 78-87.
    "Of the Gravity That Does Not Bring Us Down." Telescope
        (4:1) Wint 85, p. 9.
    "Ominous Omelettes." OP (38/39) Spr 85, p. 89.
    "Unisex?" (for L.B.Z./1984). Telescope (4:2) Spr 85, p. 59-
        60.

"The Wheel" (tr. of Aimé Césaire). <u>TriQ</u> (63) Spr-Sum
  85, p. 207.
"Xmas on Bay State Road, Boston, by B.U., 1978" (In fond
  Memory, Alice Hoop). <u>MassR</u> (26:2/3) Sum-Aut 85, p. 373-
  378.
357. BENEDIKTSSON, Tom
"Ishi's Song." <u>Paint</u> (11:21/12:24) 84-85, p. 27-28.
"Shepherd's Song." <u>Paint</u> (11:21/12:24) 84-85, p. 26.
358. BENERT, Annette Larson
"Desert." <u>Wind</u> (15:54) 85, p. 6.
"Life and Art." <u>Wind</u> (15:54) 85, p. 6.
359. BENN, Gottfried
"Full Circle" (tr. by Stuart Miller). <u>NewL</u> (51:4) Sum 85,
  p. 68.
"Pet Peeves" (tr. by Stuart Miller). <u>NewL</u> (51:4) Sum 85,
  p. 69.
360. BENNERS, Jane
"Child." <u>TexasR</u> (6:1/2) Spr-Sum 85, p. 121.
361. BENNETT, Bruce
"Advice." <u>NegC</u> (5:2) Spr 85, p. 42.
362. BENNETT, Debbie
"Magician Tricks." <u>WestCR</u> (20:2) O 85, p. 36.
"Woman behind Glass." <u>WestCR</u> (20:2) O 85, p. 37.
363. BENNETT, John M.
"Pencil." <u>SmPd</u> (22:2) Spr 85, p. 30.
"Shoe Boiling." <u>SmPd</u> (22:2) Spr 85, p. 31.
364. BENNETT, Maria
"Men in the City" (tr. of Julia de Burgos). <u>CrabCR</u> (2:2)
  Wint 85, p. 13.
"Saturday" (tr. of Alfonsina Storni). <u>CrabCR</u> (3:1) Fall-
  Wint 85, p. 7.
"Sweet Torture" (After a poem by Alfonsina Storni). <u>CrabCR</u>
  (3:1) Fall-Wint 85, p. 8.
"To Julia de Burgos" (tr. of Julia de Burgos). <u>CrabCR</u>
  (3:1) Fall-Wint 85, p. 6-7.
"To Julia de Burgos" (tr. of Julia de Burgos). <u>NewL</u> (51:4)
  Sum 85, p. 89-90.
"What Women Carry." <u>Amelia</u> (2:1) Ap 85, p. 25.
365. BENNICK, Tom
"Killdeer." <u>NegC</u> (5:2) Spr 85, p. 120.
366. BENOIT, Jacques
"Last Tour before Dawn." <u>PottPort</u> (7) 85-86, p. 18.
367. BENSEN, Robert
"An Ordinary Evening in Havana." <u>RiverS</u> (18) 85, p. 96.
368. BENSKO, John
"The Dancing Islands." <u>PoetryNW</u> (26:3) Aut 85, p. 14-15.
"The Elk Uncovers the Heavens." <u>QW</u> (20) Spr-Sum 85, p. 96.
"Our Friend, the Photographer of Our Wedding." <u>PoetryNW</u>
  (26:3) Aut 85, p. 13.
369. BENSKO, Rosemary
"Frances at Virginia Beach" (for the poet). <u>CarolQ</u> (37:2)
  Wint 85, p. 52.
"The Husband Comes Home from Work." <u>HawaiiR</u> (18) Fall 85,
  p. 32.
"Induction." <u>SouthernPR</u> (26, i.e. 25:2) Fall 85, p. 21-22.
370. BENSON, Peter
"Homage to Henry--2." <u>NoDaQ</u> (53:3) Sum 85, p. 66-67.
"Homage to Henry--9." <u>NoDaQ</u> (53:3) Sum 85, p. 66.
"Homage to Henry--18" (Henry's Burning Song of Love).
  <u>NoDaQ</u> (53:3) Sum 85, p. 67.
371. BENSON, Robert
"Hunting Wild and Tame." <u>SewanR</u> (93:4) Fall 85, p. 528.
372. BENTLEY, Beth
"Letters to Lost Children." <u>BlueBldgs</u> (9) [85?], p. 38-41.
"Our Parents." <u>PoetryNW</u> (26:4) Wint 85-86, p. 20-21.
"The Possibilities." <u>PoetryNW</u> (26:4) Wint 85-86, p. 19-20.

373. BENTLEY, Roy
     "Ralph Waldo Emerson Addresses the ICBM Silos at Minot,
        North Dakota." IndR (8:1) Wint 85, p. 79.
374. BENTTINEN, Ted
     "Above Punta Arenas" (for Chile, in memoriam). Tendril
        (19/20) 85, p. 80-81.
     "Snow." Confr (29) Wint 85, p. 60.
375. BERAY, Patrice
     "130-140." Rampike (4:2/3) 85-86, p. 13.
376. BERG, Charles Ramírez
     "The Pachuco Stroll: Sunset Heights -- April, 1959."
        RevChic (12:2) Sum 84, p. 28-29.
     "Rainstory." RevChic (12:2) Sum 84, p. 31.
     "Salsa Woman." RevChic (12:2) Sum 84, p. 30.
377. BERG, Lora
     "Passion Play." Vis (18) 85, p. 24-25.
378. BERG, Nancy
     "Requiem for California." CrossCur (4:4/5:1) 85, p. 97.
379. BERG, Sharon
     "Coming of Age" (for Pam and Sara). PoetryCR (7:2) Wint 85-
        86, p. 11.
380. BERG, Stephen
     "From the Bridge." Poetry (147:1) O 85, p. 4-5.
     "Last Elegy." Iowa (15:1) Wint 85, p. 86-87.
     "Nights after Reading." Poetry (147:1) O 85, p. 6.
381. BERGE, Carol
     "The Accident" (for Steve Dixon). Amelia (2:1) Ap 85, p.
        15.
     "Apotheosis." Abraxas (33) 85, p. 53.
     "The Doyennes." Abraxas (33) 85, p. 52-53.
     "Genetics & the Laws of Nature As Subject to Civilization."
        OP (38/39) Spr 85, p. 75.
382. BERGER, Bruce
     "Departure." PoetryNW (26:4) Wint 85-86, p. 14.
     "Revisited." PoetryNW (26:4) Wint 85-86, p. 12-13.
383. BERGER, Jim
     "For Weeks I Forestalled." PoetryR (5) S 85, p. 68.
     "Portrait of a Painter." PoetryR (5) S 85, p. 67.
384. BERGLAND, Martha
     "The Rabbit Killer" (First Prize, Poetry Award). Prima (9)
        85, p. 60-61.
385. BERGMAN, David
     "Fenway Court." MidAR (5:1) 85, p. 37-38.
     "The Great Transatlantic Hot-Air Balloon Race." MidAR
        (5:1) 85, p. 36.
     "The Hunger of Battersea Park." Raritan (4:4) Spr 85, p.
        92-93.
     "Ode on a Grecian Urning." MidAR (5:2) 85, p. 90-91.
     "Old Man Sitting in a Shopping Mall." AmerS (54:1) Wint 84-
        85, p. 97.
     "Primal Scene." Raritan (4:4) Spr 85, p. 91.
     "Seduction at Camden Passage." Raritan (4:4) Spr 85, p. 94-
        95.
     "Urban Renewal." Raritan (4:4) Spr 85, p. 96.
386. BERGMAN, Susan
     "According to These Maps." PoetC (17:1) Fall 85, p. 34-35.
     "Irreducibly." PoetryNW (26:3) Aut 85, p. 17-18.
     "Wanting, Sometimes, to Be Animal, Vegetable, Mineral."
        PoetryNW (26:3) Aut 85, p. 18-19.
387. BERGSTROM, Vera
     "Among the Layers of Evening." Bogg (53) 85, p. 56.
388. BERKE, Judith
     "The Child." CalQ (26) Sum 85, p. 53.
     "Eve." SouthwR (70:2) Spr 85, p. 245-246.
     "We Know Now." PartR (52:3) 85, p. 248-249.

389. BERLIND, Bruce
      "The Christmas of Long Walks" (tr. of Desző Tandori).
        Ploughs (11:4) 85, p. 216-217.
      "Clearance Sale" (tr. of Günther Grass). Ploughs (11:4)
        85, p. 140-141.
      "Grip" (tr. of Gyula Illyés). NewL (51:4) Sum 85, p. 38.
      "The Salvation of the Damned" (tr. of Gyula Illyés).
        NewL (51:4) Sum 85, p. 37.
      "World Collapse" (tr. of Gyula Illyés). NewL (51:4) Sum
        85, p. 38.
390. BERMAN, Ruth
      "Noah's Animals." SouthernHR (19:2) Spr 85, p. 170.
391. BERNARD, April
      "Against Biography." NewYRB (32:12) 18 Jl 85, p. 41.
392. BERNARD, Kenneth
      "Gypsy Trick." GrandS (4:4) Sum 85, p. 210.
393. BERNHARDT, Suzanne
      "Pearl Street." HangL (47) Spr 85, p. 14.
394. BERNIER, Jack
      "Barnacles Know They Know." SanFPJ (7:4) 85, p. 46.
      "The Prophecy of Muse Melpomene." SanFPJ (7:4) 85, p. 48.
      "Touching Can Start an Epidemic." SanFPJ (7:4) 85, p. 47.
395. BERNLEF, J.
      "Winter Roads" (Selections, tr. by Maria Jacobs: "Hotel
        Guest," "Before It Starts," "Winter Roads," "With and
        Without Snow"). PoetryCR (7:1) Aut 85, p. 50.
      "Winterwegen" (Selections: "Hotelgast," "Voor Het Begint,"
        "Winterwegen," "Met en Zonder Sneeuw"). PoetryCR (7:1)
        Aut 85, p. 50.
396. BERNSTEIN, Charles
      "Entitlement" (Cast: Liubov Popova, Jenny Lind, John
        Milton). Rampike (4:2/3) 85-86, p. 96-97.
      "Foam Post." Sulfur (13) 85, p. 118-119.
      "The Harbor of Illusion." Sulfur (13) 85, p. 117.
      "Safe Methods of Business." Sulfur (13) 85, p. 119-125.
      "Surface Reflectance." Temblor (2) 85, p. 74-82.
397. BERRY, D. C.
      "Alexander Pope." ChiR (35:1) Aut 85, p. 38.
      "Baby." Poetry (146:2) My 85, p. 81.
      "Blisters." TexasR (6:1/2) Spr-Sum 85, p. 21.
      "The Creek Book: A Week on the Chunky and Chickasawhay" (an
        excerpt from "Thursday"). TexasR (6:3/4) Fall-Wint 85,
        p. 36-42.
      "Daddy." Poetry (146:2) My 85, p. 79.
      "Dancer." Poetry (146:2) My 85, p. 80.
      "DC Berry, Sr." (5 May 1911-9 March 1984). SouthernPR
        (25:1) Spr 85, p. 12-18.
      "Sir Walter Ralegh and the Milkweed." Poetry (146:2) My
        85, p. 79-80.
398. BERRY, James
      "What Is No Good?" Poetry (146:4) Jl 85, p. 224.
399. BERRY, Paul
      "Corylus Avellana, Flower of." Bogg (54) 85, p. 25-26.
400. BERRY, Wendell
      "A Difference." Hudson (38:3) Aut 85, p. 446.
      "The Record." Hudson (38:3) Aut 85, p. 445-446.
401. BERSSENBRUGGE, Mei-mei
      "Emphathy." Conjunc (7) 85, p. 169-172.
402. BERTOLINO, James
      "Clam Bombs." KanQ (17:1/2) Wint-Spr 85, p. 44.
      "Five Views of the New History." Gargoyle (27) 85, p. 65.
      "Junior Gulls." KanQ (17:1/2) Wint-Spr 85, p. 44.
      "Letter from the Island" (for Melina Costello). NewL
        (52:1) Fall 85, p. 44.
403. BERTOLUCCI, Attilio
      "Portrait of a Sick Man" (tr. by Annalisa Saccà). LitR

(28:2) Wint 85, p. 208.
404. BERTRAND, Claudine
     "La Rue Réclame Sa Propagande." Rampike (4:2/3) 85-86,
        p. 64.
405. BERZINS, Rai
     "Chewing the Fuse." Quarry (34:3) Sum 85, p. 9.
     "A Mother's Love." WestCR (19:4) Ap 85, p. 33.
     "Postscript to a Miscarriage of Affections." WestCR (19:4)
        Ap 85, p. 33-34.
406. BESONEN, Julie
     "Face of amber belly of jade wife of bitterness" (tr. of
        Jacques Crickillon). Mund (15:1/2) 85, p. 137.
     "Kings and Castles" (tr. of Sylvain Garneau). Mund
        (15:1/2) 85, p. 139.
407. BESSERMAN, Ellen
     "A Wedding." PoeticJ (11) 85, p. 30.
408. BETHEL, Gar
     "After Work at the Processing Plant." PraS (59:4) Wint 85,
        p. 85.
     "I Take Up Living." PraS (59:4) Wint 85, p. 83-84.
     "Rain at the Fair." PraS (59:4) Wint 85, p. 86-88.
     "A Romantic in Maine." KanQ (17:1/2) Wint-Spr 85, p. 239.
     "When I Was a Framer." WebR (10:1) Spr 85, p. 69.
409. BETTARINI, Mariella
     "Psychograph" (tr. by Giuliano Dego and Margaret Straus).
        LitR (29:1) Fall 85, p. 94.
410. BEUCE, Evelyn
     "The Promised Land for Uncle Harold." ChrC (102:20) 5-12
        Je 85, p. 575.
411. BEUM, Robert
     "An Old Movie." SewanR (93:1) Wint 85, p. 56.
412. BEVAN, Patricia
     "Basking." Wind (15:55) 85, p. 15.
413. BEYER, William
     "The Meeting." CrossCur (4:1) 84, p. 89.
     "Wind and a Question." Wind (15:55) 85, p. 29.
414. BEYERS, Joanna
     "Concertos for Insomnia." Waves (14:1/2) Fall 85, p. 36.
415. BHAT, V. G.
     "The Image" (tr. by K. Raghavendra Rao). NewL (51:4) Sum
        85, p. 133.
416. BHATTACHARJYA, Hiren
     "In the Quiet of Blood" (tr. by Pradip Acharya). Verse (2)
        85, p. 38.
     "Untranslatable" (tr. by Pradip Acharya). Verse (2) 85, p.
        38.
417. BIALOSKY, Jill
     "Oh Giant Flowers." AntR (43:2) Spr 85, p. 205.
418. BIARUJIA, Javant
     "On Shealing Hill." JamesWR (3:1) Fall 85, p. 14.
419. BICKNELL, John
     "Half a Billion Children." SanFPJ (7:2) 85, p. 56.
     "We Listen No More for Beautiful Words." SanFPJ (7:2) 85,
        p. 53.
420. BIDART, Frank
     "Dark Night" (John of the Cross). Antaeus (55) Aut 85, p.
        85-86.
     "Guilty of Dust." Thrpny (6:2, issue 22) Sum 85, p. 7.
421. BIEN, Peter
     "The Fourth Dimension" (tr. of Stylianos Harkianakis).
        Verse (1) 84, p. 42.
     "Keep Left" (tr. of Stylianos Harkianakis). Verse (1) 84,
        p. 41.
422. BIERDS, Linda
     "Reviving the Geyser, Reykjavik, Iceland, 1935." NewYorker
        (61:15) 3 Je 85, p. 44.

"The Terms of Endurance." <u>CarolQ</u> (38:1) Fall 85, p. 7-8.
423. BIERMANN, Wolf
    "Everlasting Peace" (tr. by Maurice Taylor). <u>MalR</u> (71) Je
        85, p. 80.
424. BIGGER, Duff
    "The Galaxy." <u>NewL</u> (52:1) Fall 85, p. 122.
    "I Chose the Buddha over Christ." <u>NewL</u> (52:1) Fall 85, p.
        122.
    "I Know a Man." <u>NewL</u> (52:1) Fall 85, p. 122.
    "Mission Impossible Goes off the TV." <u>NewL</u> (52:1) Fall 85,
        p. 123.
    "The Sun Will Flame Out, Fail." <u>NewL</u> (52:1) Fall 85, p.
        123-124.
425. BILGERE, George
    "August." <u>SouthwR</u> (70:1) Wint 85, p. 111.
    "Before the Museum of Modern Art." <u>KanQ</u> (17:4) Fall 85, p.
        53.
    "Cross Country." <u>KanQ</u> (17:4) Fall 85, p. 54-55.
    "Emily." <u>KanQ</u> (17:4) Fall 85, p. 54.
    "Journal of the Country Wife." <u>WebR</u> (10:1) Spr 85, p. 57-
        59.
    "Nova." <u>PraS</u> (59:3) Fall 85, p. 65-66.
    "Potato Digging." <u>SouthwR</u> (70:1) Wint 85, p. 111-113.
    "Song for Morning." <u>QW</u> (20) Spr-Sum 85, p. 120.
426. BILICKE, Tom
    "Mystery Solved by Deft Duo." <u>Bogg</u> (53) 85, p. 32.
    "True Confessions." <u>Open24</u> (4) 85, p. 13.
427. BILLINGS, Philip
    "On a Bad Day." <u>StoneC</u> (12:2/3) Spr-Sum 85, p. 30-31.
428. BILLINGS, Robert
    "Black River." <u>Waves</u> (13:4) Spr 85, p. 86-87.
    "Open Winter." <u>Waves</u> (13:4) Spr 85, p. 86.
    "The songbirds' voices catch in the small bones of the ear."
        <u>Waves</u> (13:4) Spr 85, p. 87.
429. BINGHAM, Sallie
    "Toad." <u>Chelsea</u> (44) 85, p. 42.
430. BINGHAM, Tom
    "Doing Time." <u>Bogg</u> (54) 85, p. 13.
431. BIRCHARD, Guy
    "Cold Mine." <u>Grain</u> (13:1) F 85, p. 5-13.
    "Coup de Poing." <u>Quarry</u> (34:4) Aut 85, p. 84.
    "Coup de Poing." <u>Waves</u> (13:4) Spr 85, p. 75.
    "Coup de Stylo." <u>Quarry</u> (34:4) Aut 85, p. 85.
    "Coup de Stylo." <u>Waves</u> (13:4) Spr 85, p. 75.
    "Coup de Tête." <u>Quarry</u> (34:4) Aut 85, p. 84.
    "Coup de Tête." <u>Waves</u> (13:4) Spr 85, p. 75.
    "Coup de Torchon." <u>Quarry</u> (34:4) Aut 85, p. 85.
    "Coups de Brosse." <u>Quarry</u> (34:4) Aut 85, p. 84-85.
432. BIRDSALL, Jane
    "Experience." <u>Tendril</u> (19/20) 85, p. 82.
433. BIRNBAUM, Saul
    "The Gas Business." <u>SanFPJ</u> (7:2) 85, p. 68.
    "A Man Was Tossed." <u>SanFPJ</u> (7:2) 85, p. 67.
434. BIRNEY, Earle
    "Copernican Fix" (Selections: 6 poem). <u>PoetryCR</u> (7:2) Wint
        85-86, p. 27.
435. BIRO, Fred
    "Clay to Dust." <u>AntigR</u> (60) Wint 85, p. 32.
    "Halls of China." <u>AntigR</u> (60) Wint 85, p. 32.
436. BISENIEKS, Guntis
    "Ephemera." <u>Wind</u> (15:54) 85, p. 38.
437. BISHOP, W. (<u>See also</u> BISHOP, Wendy)
    "Cache Creek." <u>PraS</u> (59:2) Sum 85, p. 63.
    "The Ferryman." <u>ColEng</u> (47:5) S 85, p. 501.
    "For Months." <u>MissR</u> (13:3, issue 39) Spr 85, p. 70-71.
    "A Ghastly Record." <u>CapeR</u> (20:2) Fall 85, p. 44.

"If over Your Shoulder the Hangnail Moon." <u>PraS</u> (59:2) Sum 85, p. 62.
"Mountains by Moonrise." <u>MissR</u> (13:3, issue 39) Spr 85, p. 69.
438. BISHOP, Wendy (<u>See</u> <u>also</u> BISHOP, W.)
"Taking Photographs." <u>Tendril</u> (19/20) 85, p. 83-84.
439. BISSETT, Bill
"Canada Gees Mate for Life" (Selections: "Th nite th ammunishyun dump xplodid ...," "Halifax nova scotia," "It sz in th tondon free press ..."). <u>PoetryCR</u> (7:2) Wint 85-86, p. 24-25.
"Typewriter Pomes." <u>Rampike</u> (4:2/3) 85-86, p. 32-33.
440. BITNEY, Kate
"Sakharov Meets Nikola Tesla in a Dream." <u>PoetryCR</u> (6:4) Sum 85, p. 45.
441. BIXLER, Bernice
"The Army Has Cleared Out." <u>WoosterR</u> (3) Spr 85, p. 46.
442. BIZZARO, Patrick
"In the Niagara River." <u>Gargoyle</u> (27) 85, p. 66.
"Newer Bodies, Darker Dreams." <u>LaurelR</u> (19:1) Wint 85, p. 68.
443. BLACK, Candace
"Safe Passage." <u>CharR</u> (11:2) Fall 85, p. 105-106.
444. BLACK, J. David
"A Poem for Primitives." <u>PoetryCR</u> (7:2) Wint 85-86, p. 55.
445. BLACK, Leslie Schultz
"Gilbert's Hobby." <u>NegC</u> (5:3) Sum 85, p. 138-139.
"The Letter" (Mary Cassatt). <u>StoneC</u> (13:1/2) Fall-Wint 85-86, p. 30.
446. BLACK, Ralph
"Cairning." <u>StoneC</u> (13:1/2) Fall-Wint 85-86, p. 70-71.
447. BLACKBURN, Richard
"The Musician Plays for Richard." <u>PoetL</u> (80:2) Sum 85, p. 110-111.
448. BLACKSHEAR, Helen
"The Exiles." <u>NegC</u> (5:2) Spr 85, p. 65.
449. BLACKSHER, James
"May 29, 1984." <u>NegC</u> (5:3) Sum 85, p. 96.
450. BLACKWELL, Marian
"Husbandry." <u>SoCaR</u> (18:1) Fall 85, p. 40.
451. BLADES, Joe
"Venezia." <u>AntigR</u> (60) Wint 85, p. 75-76.
452. BLAIKIE, John
"Seven and Seventeen." <u>AntigR</u> (60) Wint 85, p. 52.
453. BLAIN, Derrel R.
"Echoes, Nothing Dissipates." <u>AntigR</u> (62/63) Sum-Aut 85, p. 14.
454. BLAIR, John
"After the Storm." <u>SouthernPR</u> (25:1) Spr 85, p. 57-58.
"Old Man, Walking." <u>GeoR</u> (39:3) Fall 85, p. 550.
"Pig Days." <u>BlackWR</u> (11:2) Spr 85, p. 66-67.
"Weathering." <u>TexasR</u> (6:1/2) Spr-Sum 85, p. 118-119.
455. BLAKER, Margaret C.
"Slow Down for Fast Copies." <u>PoeticJ</u> (12) 85, p. 35.
BLANC, Gérald Le
<u>See</u> LeBLANC, Gérald
456. BLANCHE, Ella
"Dissertation." <u>PoeticJ</u> (9) 85, p. 8.
"In the Fall." <u>PoeticJ</u> (9) 85, p. 9.
457. BLANKENBURG, Gary
"Mr. Electric." <u>Open24</u> (4) 85, p. 12.
458. BLASING, Randy
"Kingdom Come." <u>Poetry</u> (146:6) S 85, p. 333-334.
"North End." <u>Poetry</u> (145:4) Ja 85, p. 206-207.
"Pirated Version." <u>Poetry</u> (146:6) S 85, p. 332-333.

459. BLAUNER, Laurie
    "A Housewife's Old-Fashioned Fire." BlackWR (12:1) Fall
        85, p. 62.
460. BLAZEK, Douglas
    "Chloe's Bookstore" (for Philip and Gail). CrossCur (4:2)
        84, p. 107.
    "Edvard Munch." RiverS (17) 85, p. 23.
    "I Startle Myself Taking a Walk." RiverS (17) 85, p. 22.
    "Inner Marathons." OP (38/39) Spr 85, p. 196.
    "The Morning Atavism." RiverS (17) 85, p. 23.
    "Peach." Raccoon (17) Mr 85, inside front cover.
461. BLEHERT, Dean
    "Cloning." KanQ (17:4) Fall 85, p. 161.
462. BLESSING, Tom
    "Hiding." PoeticJ (10) 85, p. 33.
    "On Being a Father." Amelia (2:2) O 85, p. 50.
463. BLESSINGTON, Francis
    "The Abandoned Monastery on Skellig Michael" (off the Irish
        coast). CumbPR (5:1) Fall 85, p. 64.
    "Eye Shadow." CumbPR (5:1) Fall 85, p. 65.
    "Mowing Italy." StoneC (13:1/2) Fall-Wint 85-86, p. 23.
464. BLOCH, Chana
    "The Art of Loving" (tr. of Yehuda Amichai). NewL (51:4)
        Sum 85, p. 19.
    "The Ghost." Field (32) Spr 85, p. 34.
    "Hunger." Field (32) Spr 85, p. 33.
    "Poem without an End" (tr. of Yehuda Amichai). NewL (51:4)
        Sum 85, p. 18.
    "Reinforcements" (tr. of Yehuda Amichai). NewL (51:4) Sum
        85, p. 18-19.
465. BLODGETT, E. D.
    "Bestiare." CapilR (36) 85, p. 48-54.
    "Fugue of Che Guevara." Dandel (12:1) 85, p. 24-32.
    "Night Thoughts on Clausewitz' On War." Dandel (12:2)
        85, p. 50-53.
466. BLOMAIN, Karen
    "Summer House." PassN (6:2) Spr-Sum 85, p. 10.
467. BLOSSOM, Laurel
    "Company." Confr (30/31) N 85, p. 269.
    "How." Confr (30/31) N 85, p. 268.
468. BLUE, Jane
    "At Work." Tendril (19/20) 85, p. 85-86.
469. BLUE, Keith
    "Drunk at 3 A.M." (Obscene Acrostic, w. Delilah Shepherd).
        Open24 (4) 85, p. 44.
470. BLUGER, Marianne
    "By Bricks." PoetryCR (7:2) Wint 85-86, p. 12.
    "Canon Denton." PoetryCR (6:3) Spr 85, p. 12.
    "Kenneth Patchen." PoetryCR (7:2) Wint 85-86, p. 12.
    "Life and Literature." PoetryCR (6:3) Spr 85, p. 12.
    "The Poplars." PoetryCR (6:3) Spr 85, p. 12.
    "Portrait of Maji." PoetryCR (7:2) Wint 85-86, p. 12.
471. BLUMENTHAL, Michael
    "Advice to My Students: How to Write a Poem." Poetry
        (145:5) F 85, p. 274.
    "Halved." Nat (241:17) 23 N 85, p. 558.
    "Lucky." AmerS (54:3) Sum 85, p. 328.
    "A Man Grieves Always for the Ships He Has Missed." AmerV
        (1) 85, p. 76.
    "The Scullers." Nat (241:9) 28 S 85, p. 284.
472. BLY, Robert
    "The Cypress Root." NewL (51:3) Spr 85, p. 38.
    "A Dream about Sam." NewL (51:3) Spr 85, p. 28.
    "The Forgotten Commander" (tr. of Tomas Tranström̈er).
        Ploughs (11:4) 85, p. 240-241.
    "Letter to Miguel Otero Silva, in Caracas (1948)" (Tr. of

           Pablo Neruda, from Canto General, Section 12). NewL
           (51:4) Sum 85, p. 103-106.
473. BLY, Ruth Counsell
        "For Sam." NewL (51:3) Spr 85, p. 39.
BODET, Jaime Torres
        See TORRES BODET, Jaime
474. BOE, Deborah
        "Attack of the Polka-Dot Girls." HangL (48) Fall 85, p. 42-
           43.
        "Daughter." BlueBldgs (9) [85?], p. 26.
        "In Praise of Polka Dots." SmPd (22:1) Wint 85, p. 26.
        "Invisible Girl." Tendril (19/20) 85, p. 87.
        "Laughter." SmPd (22:1) Wint 85, p. 25.
        "The Living Sister." HangL (48) Fall 85, p. 41.
        "Magic Slate." PoetryNW (26:2) Sum 85, p. 7.
        "My Sister of the Horses." BlueBldgs (9) [85?], p. 28.
        "My Sister of the Horses." HangL (48) Fall 85, p. 39-40.
        "On My Birthday, Gifts from Two Grandmothers." SmPd (22:1)
           Wint 85, p. 24.
        "Paper Stars." PoetryNW (26:2) Sum 85, p. 8.
        "Remembering the Ukulele" (for my grandfather). PoetryNW
           (26:2) Sum 85, p. 7-8.
        "Sickness, or Quilt." PoetryNW (26:2) Sum 85, p. 6.
        "The Small Blessings among Us." HangL (48) Fall 85, p. 44.
        "Why I Haven't Been Writing" (for Liz, while house-sitting).
           USl (18/19) Wint 85, p. 2.
475. BOEBEL, Charles
        "Melville on Billy Budd." ArizQ (41:2) Sum 85, p. 100.
BOER, David C. den
        See DenBOER, David C.
476. BOERSMA, Ann
        "Sunland Center." PoeticJ (9) 85, p. 32-33.
477. BOES, Don
        "Thirst." PraS (59:4) Wint 85, p. 102.
        "The World Since Yesterday." LaurelR (19:1) Wint 85, p. 42.
478. BOGAN, James
        "Clara Franz." Vis (17) 85, p. 17-19.
479. BOGGIS, Jay
        "Aphorisms and Observations" (tr. of Friedrich Hebbel).
           Ploughs (11:4) 85, p. 148-150.
480. BOGIN, George
        "Cottontail." NewL (52:1) Fall 85, p. 69.
        "The Eisenhower Cubes." NewL (52:1) Fall 85, p. 70.
481. BOGIN, Nina
        "The Caught Fish Speaks." Stand (26:1) Wint 84-85, p. 6.
        "In the North." Stand (26:1) Wint 84-85, p. 7.
        "Under." Stand (26:1) Wint 84-85, p. 7.
482. BOISSEAU, Michelle
        "Arbor Day." Poetry (147:1) O 85, p. 32.
        "Counting." Poetry (147:1) O 85, p. 31.
        "The Gloss Avenue Ghost." NewEngR (8:1) Aut 85, p. 39-44.
        "Mental Hospital Graveyard." Poetry (145:6) Mr 85, p. 324-
           325.
        "The Night of the Breaking Glass." Crazy (29) Fall 85, p.
           16-17.
        "Sisters." Poetry (145:6) Mr 85, p. 326-327.
        "Snorkling" (for Jeff). Crazy (26) Spr 84, p. 44.
        "Votary." Poetry (145:6) Mr 85, p. 325-326.
483. BOLAND, Eavan
        "The Bottle Garden." Stand (26:2) Spr 85, p. 5.
        "Self-Portrait on a Summer Evening." OntR (22) Spr-Sum 85,
           p. 15-16.
484. BOLLS, Imogene L.
        "The House across the Street." KanQ (17:1/2) Wint-Spr 85,
           p. 67.

485. BOLSTRIDGE, Alice
     "Dinner Time." <u>CimR</u> (73) O 85, p. 46.
486. BOLT, Jeffrey
     "Just the Sound." <u>RagMag</u> (4:1) Spr 85, p. 39.
     "Setting a Canoe into the Kickapoo." <u>RagMag</u> (4:1) Spr 85,
          p. 36-37.
     "The Snow Is a White Poem, the Sky a Magic Blue." <u>RagMag</u>
          (4:1) Spr 85, p. 38.
     "Visiting New In-Laws in Illinois." <u>RagMag</u> (4:1) Spr 85,
          p. 37.
BOLT, William Walter de
     <u>See</u> de BOLT, William Walter
487. BOND, Adrienne
     "Early Warning." <u>SouthernR</u> (21:1) Wint 85, p. 131-132.
     "Metastasis." <u>SouthernR</u> (21:1) Wint 85, p. 130-131.
488. BOND, Anita (<u>See</u> <u>also</u> BOND, Anita Cortez)
     "Wading." <u>MidAR</u> (5:2) 85, p. 84.
     "Winter-kill." <u>MidAR</u> (5:2) 85, p. 85.
489. BOND, Anita Cortez (<u>See</u> <u>also</u> BOND, Anita)
     "Receiving Holy Communion." <u>MidAR</u> (5:1) 85, p. 60.
490. BOND, Joan
     "Tall structures of grey concrete." <u>Waves</u> (13:4) Spr 85,
          p. 21.
491. BONDS, Diane
     "Statuary." <u>SouthernHR</u> (19:1) Wint 85, p. 21.
492. BONHONA, Mark
     "When We Lived Together." <u>JamesWR</u> (3:1) Fall 85, p. 15.
493. BONNEFOY, Yves
     "The Almond Tree" (tr. by Richard Pevear). <u>NewYorker</u>
          (60:49) 21 Ja 85, p. 36.
     "The Beautiful Summer" (tr. by Lisa Sapinkopf). <u>Ploughs</u>
          (11:4) 85, p. 112.
     "Delphi the Second Day" (tr. by Lisa Sapinkopf). <u>Ploughs</u>
          (11:4) 85, p. 113.
     "Dialogue of Anguish and Desire" (Excerpts, from <u>Words</u> <u>in</u>
          <u>Stone</u>, tr. by Lisa Sapinkopf). <u>PartR</u> (52:3) 85, p. 241-
          242.
     "The Foliage Lit Up" (from <u>Yesterday's</u> <u>Barren</u> <u>Kingdom</u>, tr.
          by Lisa Sapinkopf). <u>Abraxas</u> (33) 85, p. 30-31.
     "Hier Règnant Désert" (tr. by Anthony Rudolf). <u>Stand</u>
          (26:3) Sum 85, p. 46.
     "The Iron Bridge" (tr. by Lisa Sapinkopf). <u>Ploughs</u> (11:4)
          85, p. 115.
     "The Lure of the Threshold" (tr. by Richard Pevear).
          <u>ParisR</u> (27:95) Spr 85, p. 117-126.
     "The Ravine" (tr. by Lisa Sapinkopf). <u>Ploughs</u> (11:4) 85,
          p. 114.
     "The River" (tr. by Richard Pevear). <u>Pequod</u> (18) 85, p. 26-
          28.
     "Threats of the Witness" (from <u>Yesterday's</u> <u>Barren</u> <u>Kingdom</u>,
          tr. by Lisa Sapinkopf). <u>Abraxas</u> (33) 85, p. 28-29.
     "Veneranda" (tr. by Lisa Sapinkopf). <u>Ploughs</u> (11:4) 85, p.
          113.
     "A Voice" (tr. by Lisa Sapinkopf). <u>Ploughs</u> (11:4) 85, p.
          115.
494. BONNELL, Paula
     "Eurydice" (1984 Narrative Poetry Prize: Honorable Mention).
          <u>PoetL</u> (80:1) Spr 85, p. 26-31.
495. BONOMO, Jacquelyn
     "The Cold, the Dark." <u>Chelsea</u> (44) 85, p. 147.
     "Hens." <u>Chelsea</u> (44) 85, p. 146.
496. BONSPIEL, Jean-Luc
     "Sans les Choses." <u>Rampike</u> (4:2/3) 85-86, p. 61.
497. BOOTH, Philip
     "Among Houses." <u>Tendril</u> (19/20) 85, p. 88.
     "Ganglia." <u>OntR</u> (22) Spr-Sum 85, p. 74.

"Over Antarctica." OntR (22) Spr-Sum 85, p. 74-75.
"Playing Around." OP (38/39) Spr 85, p. 202.
"Prime" (Correction: The final line in the 3rd stanza should
    read: "and to listen my share of third-coffee talk:" --
    (27) p. 5). Crazy (26) Spr 84, p. 26.
"Saying It." Poetry (147:1) O 85, p. 13-14.
"Species." OntR (22) Spr-Sum 85, p. 75-76.
"Where Tide." Geor (39:2) Sum 85, p. 350-351.
498. BORCHERDT, Ronald W.
    "Aslan." CrossCur (4:1) 84, p. 99.
499. BORCHERS, Elisabeth
    "The Song" (tr. by Anneliese Wagner). Paint (11:21/12:24)
        84-85, p. 58.
    "Summer Begins" (tr. by Anneliese Wagner). Paint
        (11:21/12:24) 84-85, p. 59.
500. BORCZON, Matthew
    "Joan of Arc's Last Stand." HangL (47) Spr 85, p. 54.
    "Summer Nights." HangL (47) Spr 85, p. 52.
    "We made love like a parade." HangL (47) Spr 85, p. 53.
501. BORDAO, Rafael
    "1." LindLM (4:2) Ap-Je 85, p. 30.
502. BORGES, Jorge Luis
    "The Labyrinth" (adapted by Kevin Orth). PoetryR (2:2) Ap
        85, p. 67.
    "The Sea" (tr. by John Updike). TriQ (63) Spr-Sum 85, p.
        111.
    "Sherlock Holmes" (tr. by Richard Outram). Descant 51
        (16:4/17:1) Wint 85-86, p. 10-11.
503. BORINSKY, Alicia
    "Strip-Tease." Imagine (2:1) Sum 85, p. 55.
504. BORNSTEIN, Miriam
    "Basurero Nacional." BilingR (11:2) My-Ag 84 [c1986], p.
        60.
    "El Lugar de la Mujer." BilingR (11:2) My-Ag 84 [c1986],
        p. 49.
505. BORSON, Roo
    "After Argument." PoetryCR (7:1) Aut 85, p. 27.
    "Intent, or the Weight of the World." PoetryCR (7:1) Aut
        85, p. 26.
    "Of the Conch, of the Snail." PoetryCR (7:1) Aut 85, p. 27.
    "Pine." PoetryCR (7:1) Aut 85, p. 27.
506. BORUCH, Marianne
    "After Supper in Madison, Wisconsin." Field (32) Spr 85,
        p. 43-44.
    "Bending Every Bush to Black." NowestR (23:2) 85, p. 38.
    "Blur in the Attic." ColEng (47:8) D 85, p. 826-827.
    "A Chair in Raw Hope." ColEng (47:8) D 85, p. 827.
    "The Fat One in Her Lifetime." ColEng (47:8) D 85, p. 825-
        826.
    "First Snow." Field (32) Spr 85, p. 41.
    "Letter." AmerPoR (14:1) Ja-F 85, p. 45.
    "The Monstrous House." ColEng (47:8) D 85, p. 824.
    "Noon" (after a painting by Doris Lee, 1935). NowestR
        (23:2) 85, p. 39.
    "Plain Overalls of Another Century." ColEng (47:8) D 85,
        p. 825.
    "Stranger in Your Room." Field (32) Spr 85, p. 42.
    "A Summer Shower" (after the painting by Edith Hallyer,
        1883). BelPoJ (36:2) Wint 85-86, p. 9.
    "This Moment of Raven." PraS (59:2) Sum 85, p. 58.
    "The Violinist Beginning to Fly" (after Chagall). AmerPoR
        (14:1) Ja-F 85, p. 45.
507. BOSNICK, David
    "Passover." MSS (4:3) Spr 85, p. 23.
    "Queen of the Hill." MSS (4:3) Spr 85, p. 22.
    "Second Wind at Lourdes." MSS (4:3) Spr 85, p. 24.

508. BOSS, Laura
      "At the Faculty Christmas Party." <u>Vis</u> (17) 85, p. 40.
509. BOTELHO, Eugene G. E.
      "Reflections in an Ancient Forest." <u>PoeticJ</u> (9) 85, p. 30.
510. BOTTOMS, David
      "Appearances." <u>Poetry</u> (146:2) My 85, p. 91.
      "A Dream of Grand Cayman." <u>ClockR</u> (2:2) 85, p. 25.
      "Homage to Lester Flatt." <u>Poetry</u> (146:2) My 85, p. 92.
      "The Hurdler." <u>ClockR</u> (2:2) 85, p. 26.
      "An Old Hymn for Ian Jenkins." <u>NoAmR</u> (270:4) D 85, p. 17.
      "A War, A Home Front." <u>ClockR</u> (2:2) 85, p. 24.
      "White Shrouds." <u>NewYorker</u> (61:41) 2 D 85, p. 113.
511. BOUCHER, Alan
      "A Habitat by the Sea" (Excerpt, tr. of Hannes Petursson).
        <u>Vis</u> (19) 85, p. 7.
      "Staves" (tr. of Snorri Hjartarson). <u>Vis</u> (18) 85, p. 20.
512. BOUCHERON, Robert
      "Aquashorts." <u>JamesWR</u> (2:1) Fall 84, p. 15.
513. BOULDREY, Brian D.
      "Invitation." <u>CrossCur</u> (4:1) 84, p. 104-106.
      "The Translators." <u>LittleM</u> (14:4) 85, p. 63.
514. BOURKE, Lawrence
      "April 25, 1985." <u>PoetryCR</u> (7:1) Aut 85, p. 30.
515. BOURNE, Daniel
      "City" (tr. of Tomasz Jastrum). <u>CharR</u> (11:2) Fall 85, p.
        107-108.
      "The Detention Camp" (a poem for a book published under
        censorship, tr. of Tomasz Jastrun). <u>CutB</u> (24) Spr-Sum
        85, p. 52.
      "Farewell to Business As Usual." <u>StoneC</u> (13:1/2) Fall-Wint
        85-86, p. 72.
      "Foraging." <u>SpoonRQ</u> (10:4) Fall 85, p. 2.
      "Freedom" (tr. of Tomasz Jastrum). <u>CharR</u> (11:2) Fall 85,
        p. 108.
      "From a Shipyard in a Bottle." <u>MinnR</u> (N.S. 25) Fall 85, p.
        85.
      "Goodby to the Poetry of James Wright Elegies." <u>PoetryNW</u>
        (26:3) Aut 85, p. 37.
      "The Household Gods." <u>SpoonRQ</u> (10:4) Fall 85, p. 1.
      "National Stew." <u>Paint</u> (11:21/12:24) 84-85, p. 9.
      "Poetry for Physicists." <u>PoetryNW</u> (26:3) Aut 85, p. 36-37.
516. BOUVARD, Marguerite
      "The Republic of Brittany." <u>WestB</u> (16) 85, p. 81-84.
517. BOWERING, George
      "Brown Cup, Dirty Glasses." <u>CanLit</u> (105) Sum 85, p. 68.
      "Delayed Mercy: Late Night Poems" (Sections IV & V). <u>Epoch</u>
        (34:3) 84-85, p. 165-178.
      "On the Radio" (From an upcoming book called <u>77 Poems for
        People</u>). <u>Rampike</u> (4:2/3) 85-86, p. 8.
518. BOWERING, Marilyn
      "Marilyn Monroe: Anyone Can See I Love You" (Selections: 19
        poems). <u>MalR</u> (71) Je 85, p. 99-125.
519. BOWERS, Neal
      "90." <u>SouthernPR</u> (25:1) Spr 85, p. 20.
      "Living the Parable." <u>Poetry</u> (147:2) N 85, p. 101.
      "Losses." <u>Poetry</u> (147:1) O 85, p. 7.
      "Museo del Oro, Bogotá." <u>BallSUF</u> (26:2) Spr 85, p. 60.
      "Notes from the Morticians' Convention." <u>SewanR</u> (93:1)
        Wint 85, p. 1-4.
      "The Rest." <u>SouthernPR</u> (26, i.e. 25:2) Fall 85, p. 28.
      "Terminal." <u>Poetry</u> (147:2) N 85, p. 100.
520. BOWIE, Robert
      "Antlers." <u>CalQ</u> (26) Sum 85, p. 43.
      "Arrowheads." <u>Amelia</u> (2:1) Ap 85, p. 72.
      "Black Roses." <u>Paint</u> (11:21/12:24) 84-85, p. 20-21.
      "The Music of Wolves." <u>PaintedB</u> (26/27) Sum-Fall 85, p. 41.

"Skins." <u>Amelia</u> (2:1) Ap 85, p. 72.
"Very." <u>PoetL</u> (80:3) Fall 85, p. 139-140.
521. BOWLER, C. A.
"The Lightning Show." <u>SanFPJ</u> (7:3) 84 [i.e. 85], p. 29.
"Right to Die Directive." <u>SanFPJ</u> (7:3) 84 [i.e. 85], p. 32.
522. BOX, Thad
"Poet's Release." <u>Bogg</u> (53) 85, p. 41.
"Saturday Morning." <u>Bogg</u> (53) 85, p. 29.
523. BOYCHUK, Bohdan
"Look into the Faces of Dead Poets" (tr. by David Ignatow
and the author). <u>GrandS</u> (4:3) Spr 85, p. 131.
524. BOYCHUK, Bohdan
"Graves" (tr. by David Ignatow and the author). <u>GrandS</u>
(4:3) Spr 85, p. 130.
"How life lulls us" (tr. of Boris Pasternak, w. Mark
Rudman). <u>Pequod</u> (19/20/21) 85, p. 260-263.
"Landscapes" (tr. by Mark Rudman and the author). <u>GrandS</u>
(4:3) Spr 85, p. 132.
"Stone Women" (tr. by David Ignatow and the author).
<u>GrandS</u> (4:3) Spr 85, p. 130.
525. BOYLAN, Matthew
"Cheap Seats." <u>WormR</u> (25:4, issue 100) 85, p. 132.
"Passing Grade." <u>WormR</u> (25:4, issue 100) 85, p. 132.
"Slow Poetry." <u>WormR</u> (25:4, issue 100) 85, p. 131.
526. BOZANIC, Nick
"At the Frederic Inn" (for Michael Delp). <u>HawaiiR</u> (17) Spr
85, p. 92-93.
"September." <u>PassN</u> (6:2) Spr-Sum 85, p. 20.
527. BRACKENBURY, Alison
"Hips." <u>Verse</u> (3) 85, p. 6.
"Peggy." <u>Verse</u> (3) 85, p. 5.
528. BRADBURY, Peter
"Night Train to Paris." <u>SewanR</u> (93:2) Spr 85, p. 185.
"Your Absence." <u>SewanR</u> (93:2) Spr 85, p. 186.
529. BRADBURY, Ray
"Manet/Renoir: Two Views." <u>OP</u> (38/39) Spr 85, p. 215.
530. BRADLEY, George
"E Pur Si Muove." <u>Antaeus</u> (55) Aut 85, p. 87.
"Its Bladderlike Sail." <u>GrandS</u> (4:4) Sum 85, p. 109-110.
"La Vie Bohèmienne." <u>Shen</u> (36:1) 85-86, p. 28-29.
531. BRAGA, Thomas J.
"Voy al Algua." <u>LindLM</u> (4:2) Ap-Je 85, p. 30.
532. BRAND, Alice G.
"Some Sundays." <u>LitR</u> (28:4) Sum 85, p. 579.
"The Twist of the Place." <u>LitR</u> (28:4) Sum 85, p. 578.
533. BRANDER, John M.
"The Pimp." <u>Amelia</u> (2:2) O 85, p. 50.
534. BRANDON, Leroy N., III
"Contradictions." <u>SanFPJ</u> (7:4) 85, p. 61.
"Dust to Dust." <u>SanFPJ</u> (7:3) 84 [i.e. 85], p. 62.
"What Will We Leave for Posterity?" <u>SanFPJ</u> (7:4) 85, p. 76.
"Why So Much Interest in Nicaragua?" <u>SanFPJ</u> (7:4) 85, p.
62.
535. BRANNEN, Jonathan
"Sharing." <u>BlueBldgs</u> (9) [85?], p. 61.
536. BRATHWAITE, Edward Kamau
"Jah Music." <u>GreenfR</u> (12:3/4) Wint-Spr 85, p. 130-136.
"Metaphors of Underdevelopment: A Proem for Hernan Cortez."
<u>NewEngR</u> (7:4) Sum 85, p. 453-476.
537. BRAULT, Jacques
"Within the Mystery" (Excerpt, tr. by Gertrude Sanderson).
<u>AntigR</u> (61) Spr 85, p. 92-95.
538. BRAVERMAN, Kate
"True Story." <u>Zyzzyva</u> (1:3) Fall 85, p. 137-138.
BRAVO, Armando Alvarez
<u>See</u> ALVAREZ BRAVO, Armando

539. BRAXTON, Charles R. (See also BRAXTON, Charlie & Charlie R.)
     "First World People Shall Inherit the Earth." SanFPJ (7:4)
     85, p. 30-32.
540. BRAXTON, Charlie (See also BRAXTON, Charles R. & Charlie R.)
     "Poem for Warrior Spirits." SanFPJ (7:3) 84 [i.e. 85], p.
     93.
541. BRAXTON, Charlie R. (See also BRAXTON, Charles R. & Charlie)
     "The Bird Cage Bunch" (For Those Who Don't Believe in the
     Freeze). BlackALF (19:3) Fall 85, p. 114.
     "W. W. II" (the prelude to holocaust). BlackALF (19:3)
     Fall 85, p. 114.
542. BREBNER, Diana
     "Always, in the Middle of Winter." Waves (14:1/2) Fall 85,
     p. 109.
     "The Artist, Surrounded by Children." Grain (13:3) Ag 85,
     p. 33.
     "Green Country." PoetryCR (6:3) Spr 85, p. 6.
     "Philosophical Argument." Grain (13:3) Ag 85, p. 32.
543. BRECCIA, Estela
     "Aunque lo lime al verbo." Inti (20) Otoño 84, p. 101.
     "Desnúdate." Inti (20) Otoño 84, p. 102.
     "Legado." Inti (20) Otoño 84, p. 101.
     "Palabra -- Lejos." Inti (20) Otoño 84, p. 100-101.
544. BRECHT, Bertolt
     "Anecdotes from Herr Keuner" (tr. by Bert Cardullo). WebR
     (10:1) Spr 85, p. 17.
     "Entirely Because of the Growing Confusion" (tr. by Ed
     Ochester). NewL (51:4) Sum 85, p. 62.
     "On Swimming in Lakes and Rivers" (tr. by Ed Ochester).
     CharR (11:2) Fall 85, p. 85-86.
     "On the Infanticide: Marie Farrar" (tr. by Ed Ochester).
     Telescope (4:2) Spr 85, p. 55-58.
     "On This Spot Old Walls Stood Fast" (tr. by Bert Cardullo).
     WebR (10:1) Spr 85, p. 17.
     "The Ship" (tr. by Ed Ochester). NewL (51:4) Sum 85, p. 63-
     64.
     "The Shopper" (tr. by Ed Ochester). NewL (51:4) Sum 85, p.
     62-63.
     "The Song of Flux" (tr. by Bert Cardullo). WebR (10:1) Spr
     85, p. 15-16.
     "Traveling in a Comfortable Car" (tr. by Ed Ochester).
     NewL (51:4) Sum 85, p. 61.
545. BREEDEN, David
     "Céline Blues" (for Ma Rainey). WormR (25:1, issue 97)
     85, p. 10-11.
     "Dinner." Outbr (14/15) Fall 84-Spr 85, p. 38.
     "First Morning." WormR (25:1, issue 97) 85, p. 11.
     "Foxhole." Outbr (14/15) Fall 84-Spr 85, p. 40.
     "Germany May 18, 1945." Outbr (14/15) Fall 84-Spr 85, p.
     37.
     "Personality Improvement." Outbr (14/15) Fall 84-Spr 85,
     p. 39.
     "Porch." DeKalbLAJ (18:1/2) 85, p. 66.
     "Prisoners." Outbr (14/15) Fall 84-Spr 85, p. 39.
546. BREEN, Nancy
     "Mammogram Vs. the Thing." Amelia (2:2) O 85, p. 36.
547. BREHM, John
     "In Her Darkness." NewEngR (8:2) Wint 85, p. 204.
     "My Grandmother a Few Moments before Learning of Her Son's
     Death." GrahamHR (8) Wint 85, p. 14.
548. BREMAULT, Gerard
     "In a Bus Shack on an Autumn Day." PraF (6:2) Spr 85, p.
     60.
     "Not Just Walking by the River." PraF (6:2) Spr 85, p. 60.
549. BREMNER, Lary
     "$ en Direct & Stars/Stripes Rien." Rampike (4:2/3) 85-86,

p. 69.
550. BRENNAN, Lucy
    "The Listeners." AntigR (62/63) Sum-Aut 85, p. 153.
    "My First Loons." PoetryCR (6:3) Spr 85, p. 34.
551. BRENNAN, Matthew
    "Jealousy." CapeR (20:2) Fall 85, p. 31.
    "Nights Our House Comes to Life." PassN (6:1) Fall-Wint
        85, p. 10.
    "Winter Scene, Past Midnight." CapeR (20:2) Fall 85, p. 30.
552. BRENNER, Summer
    "From Berkshire Elegy" (Selections: VI-XI). Zyzzyva (1:1)
        Spr 85, p. 50-52.
553. BRESLIN, Carol
    "Anniversary Waltz." EngJ (74:6) O 85, p. 55.
554. BRESLIN, Paul
    "Résumé." Poetry (146:5) Ag 85, p. 253-255.
555. BRETON, André
    "Earthlight" (Selections: 15 poems tr. by Bill Zavatsky and
        Zack Rogow). AmerPoR (14:1) Ja-F 85, p. 3-10.
    "Maps on the Dunes" (To Giuseppe Ungaretti, tr. by Bill
        Zavatsky and Zack Rogow). Antaeus (55) Aut 85, p. 90.
    "On the Road to San Romano" (tr. by Richard Tillinghast).
        Ploughs (11:4) 85, p. 123-124.
    "The Reptile Houseburglars" (To Janine, tr. by Bill Zavatsky
        and Zack Rogow). Antaeus (55) Aut 85, p. 88-89.
    "Shrivelled Love" (tr. by Bill Zavatsky and Zack Rogow).
        Antaeus (55) Aut 85, p. 90.
    "The Verb to Be" (tr. by Bill Zavatsky and Zack Rogow).
        ParisR (27:95) Spr 85, p. 131-132.
556. BRETT, Brian
    "Narcissus and the Downtown Traffic." Dandel (12:2) 85, p.
        27.
    "Raptor." Dandel (12:2) 85, p. 28.
557. BRETT, Peter
    "Chapultapec." HolCrit (22:2) Ap 85, p. 19.
    "Hundred Year Fences." Wind (15:53) 85, p. 1.
    "The Invitation of Time" (Dusk, Mojave). CrabCR (2:3) Sum
        85, p. 4.
    "Needles." Zyzzyva (1:1) Spr 85, p. 148.
    "Walking at Dawn" (Farmington, N. M.). SnapD (8:2) Spr 85,
        p. 38-39.
    "Walking at Dawn" (Farmington, N.M.). Wind (15:53) 85, p.
        2.
558. BREWER, Kenneth (See also BREWER, Kenneth W.)
    "To Know and Then to Die." RiverS (17) 85, p. 39.
559. BREWER, Kenneth W. (See also BREWER, Kenneth)
    "Walking Backwards." NegC (5:4) Fall 85, p. 113.
560. BREWTON, Catherine
    "My Father's Greenhouse." Confr (29) Wint 85, p. 60.
    "Stitching." NewRena (19) Fall 85, p. 82.
    "The Visitation." KanQ (17:4) Fall 85, p. 102.
BREYNER, Sophia de Mello
    See ANDRESEN, Sophia de Mello Breyner
BREYNER ANDRESEN, Sophia de Mello
    See ANDRESEN, Sophia de Mello Breyner
561. BRICUTH, John
    "Conflicting Descriptions." AntR (43:1) Wint 85, p. 69-72.
562. BRIDGFORD, Kim
    "A Brief Flowering." Paint (11:21/12:24) 84-85, p. 6-7.
    "Just One Part of the Road." TexasR (6:1/2) Spr-Sum 85, p.
        122.
    "No Solid Ground." NegC (5:3) Sum 85, p. 116-117.
    "The Other Side of Our Lives." Waves (14:1/2) Fall 85, p.
        99.
    "Out of the Dust." NewOR (12:1) Spr 85, p. 42-43.
    "Suicide." AntigR (61) Spr 85, p. 111.

"The Walls of Time." <u>Mund</u> (15:1/2) 85, p. 112-113.
"Weathering." <u>Ascent</u> (11:1) 85, p. 17.
563. BRIERY, Randy
"Waving Good-Bye." <u>NegC</u> (5:1) Wint 85, p. 26-28.
564. BRINGHURST, Robert
"Riddle." <u>CanLit</u> (105) Sum 85, p. 15.
565. BRINSON-PINEDA, Barbara
"Amoroso." <u>Imagine</u> (1:2) Wint 84, p. 134.
"Dustdevils." <u>Imagine</u> (1:2) Wint 84, p. 133.
"Speak to Me from Dreams." <u>Imagine</u> (1:2) Wint 84, p. 132.
566. BRISTOW, Christine
"Seasonal." <u>CutB</u> (24) Spr-Sum 85, p. 72-73.
567. BRISTOW, Margaret Smith
"A Poet Conducts a Workshop." <u>EngJ</u> (74:7) N 85, p. 45.
568. BRITO, S. J.
"Charm for an Eagle Medicine Man." <u>NoDaQ</u> (53:2) Spr 85, p. 67.
"Native American Trickster." <u>NoDaQ</u> (53:2) Spr 85, p. 66.
"Tranceformation." <u>NoDaQ</u> (53:2) Spr 85, p. 67.
569. BRITTON, Donald
"In the Empire of the Air." <u>ParisR</u> (27:97) Fall 85, p. 103-104.
"Virgule." <u>ParisR</u> (27:97) Fall 85, p. 105.
570. BRITTON, Mariah
"Reports." <u>PoetryR</u> (2:2) Ap 85, p. 19.
571. BRIZENDINE, Ellanor
"Rehearsals." <u>EngJ</u> (74:4) Ap 85, p. 28.
572. BROCK, James
"The Growth of Mathematics." <u>ColEng</u> (47:2) F 85, p. 140.
573. BROCK, Randall
"Cold Dark." <u>Open24</u> (4) 85, p. 49.
"Inside." <u>Open24</u> (4) 85, p. 49.
574. BROCK, Van K.
"The Hindenberg." <u>NewEngR</u> (8:2) Wint 85, p. 205.
575. BROCKLEBANK, Ian
"The Refugee." <u>Open24</u> (4) 85, p. 25.
576. BROCKMAN, Gary
"A Note to the Curious." <u>Amelia</u> (2:2) O 85, p. 33.
577. BRODSKY, Joseph
"Enigma for an Angel" (tr. by George L. Kline). <u>TriQ</u> (63) Spr-Sum 85, p. 172-174.
"Galatea Encore." <u>NewYorker</u> (61:33) 7 O 85, p. 38.
"To a Friend: In Memoriam" (tr. from the Russian by the author). <u>NewYorker</u> (61:11) 6 My 85, p. 44.
578. BRODSKY, Louis Daniel
"An Autumnal" (for Hayden Carruth). <u>KanQ</u> (17:1/2) Wint-Spr 85, p. 39.
"Parachutes." <u>KanQ</u> (17:1/2) Wint-Spr 85, p. 40.
579. BRODWICK, Malcolm S.
"Strictly Biological" (For Paul O'Lague and Sue Huttner). <u>ConcPo</u> (18:1/2) 85, p. 132-133.
580. BRODY, Harry
"Alternate Occasional: For Birth, for Death, for Hagen." <u>LaurelR</u> (19:2) Sum 85, p. 53.
"Over the Iowa River after a Hearty Supper with a Woman I Want to Know Better." <u>PaintedB</u> (26/27) Sum-Fall 85, p. 49.
581. BROMLEY, Anne (<u>See also</u> BROMLEY, Anne C.)
"Autumn Vigil: Flagstaff, AZ). <u>ThRiPo</u> (25/26) 85, p. 21.
"Woman Holding a Balance" (after Jan Vermeer). <u>ThRiPo</u> (25/26) 85, p. 20.
582. BROMLEY, Anne C. (<u>See also</u> BROMLEY, Anne)
"Messages." <u>PoetL</u> (80:3) Fall 85, p. 155-156.
583. BRONK, William
"Polar Projection." <u>Pequod</u> (19/20/21) 85, p. 98.
"Where We Are, Or Getting There Is Only Half the Fun."

Pequod (19/20/21) 85, p. 97.
584. BROOK, Donna
"Pink Diapers." Cond (11/12) 85, p. 105.
585. BROOKHOUSE, Christopher
"1945-   ." CarolQ (37:3) Spr 85, p. 39.
"Reply." CarolQ (37:3) Spr 85, p. 38.
586. BROOKS, Alan
"Indra's Net." BelPoJ (35:3) Spr 85, p. 3-4.
"Winter Rain." BelPoJ (35:3) Spr 85, p. 2.
587. BROOKS, Eunice
"Housework." CrossC (7:2) 85, p. 28.
588. BROSMAN, Catharine Savage
"Longboat Key." SouthwR (70:2) Spr 85, p. 246-248.
"Vézelay: The Abbey." SoDakR (23:2) Sum 85, p. 64-65.
"The Window." SoDakR (23:2) Sum 85, p. 63.
"Woman in Red: Vogue Cover, 1919." SouthernR (21:2) Spr
85, p. 439-440.
589. BROUGHTON, T. Alan
"Beyond Change." CharR (11:2) Fall 85, p. 96-98.
"Overture." BelPoJ (35:4) Sum 85, p. 14-16.
"Recreation Hour." Confr (30/31) N 85, p. 237.
"A Simple Death." CharR (11:2) Fall 85, p. 94-96.
590. BROUMAS, Olga
"Field Poetry." Calyx (9:1) Spr-Sum 85, p. 4--8.
"Pax San Tropezana" (tr. of Odysseas Elytis). Zyzzyva
(1:4) Wint 85, p. 87-88.
591. BROWN, Arthur
"A Trumpet in the Morning" (Special Issue). RiverS (16)
85, 60 p.
592. BROWN, Beulah
"Crossing Water." GreenfR (12:3/4) Wint-Spr 85, p. 138-139.
"For Steve Biko in Memoriam" (in response to Molefe Pheto's
"When they come"). GreenfR (12:3/4) Wint-Spr 85, p. 140.
593. BROWN, Bill
"Less Than an Apple" (for Clay). Vis (18) 85, p. 12-13.
594. BROWN, Clarence
"My age, my animal" (tr. of Osip Mandelstam). TriQ (63)
Spr-Sum 85, p. 175.
"Night outside. An uppercrust lie" (tr. of Osip Mandelstam).
TriQ (63) Spr-Sum 85, p. 175.
595. BROWN, Emerson
"The 1984 Landslide." SanFPJ (7:4) 85, p. 89.
"The Last Negro." SanFPJ (7:2) 85, p. 9.
"A Word with You, Mr. Mighty Man!" SanFPJ (7:3) 84 [i.e.
85], p. 96.
596. BROWN, George Mackay
"Cragsmen." PoetryCR (7:1) Aut 85, p. 19.
597. BROWN, Glen H.
"Moon Horror." WindO (45) Spr 85, p. 15.
"The Newspaper Man." WindO (45) Spr 85, p. 14.
598. BROWN, Harriet
"Rist Canyon" (Second Prize, International Poetry Contest).
WestB (17) 85, p. 13-14.
599. BROWN, Simon
"Rob's Place." Bogg (54) 85, p. 24.
600. BROWN, Spencer
"Letter to a Young Poet." SewanR (93:1) Wint 85, p. 138-
139.
601. BROWN, Victor H.
"Moth Dancing." PoetryCR (6:3) Spr 85, p. 33.
602. BROWN, W. S. (See also BROWN, Wesley)
"I Saw a Torn and Empty Envelope . . ." (Textual Image).
Rampike (4:2/3) 85-86, p. 72.
603. BROWN, Wesley (See also BROWN, W. S.)
"My Uuglee Ways." OP (38/39) Spr 85, p. 21.
"That Hussy Called Justice." OP (38/39) Spr 85, p. 71.

604. BROWNE, Barbara
      "Spiritual Jousting." _Imagine_ (2:1) Sum 85, p. 89.
BROWNE, Nicholas Mason
      See MASON-BROWNE, Nicholas
605. BROZIO, Gary
      "Santa Cruz, the Wharf." _MissouriR_ (8:3) 85, p. 38-39.
606. BRUCE, Debra
      "Aging Mother at the Health Club." _OP_ (40) Fall-Wint 85,
         p. 36-37.
      "Aunt Judith and Her Housemate, Ann." _OP_ (40) Fall-Wint
         85, p. 38.
      "The Centauress" (The Rodin Museum, Philadelphia). _AmerPoR_
         (14:4) Jl-Ag 85, p. 18.
      "Emergency Room 2 A.M." _MinnR_ (N.S. 24) Spr 85, p. 39.
      "Mid-life Crisis." _AmerPoR_ (14:4) Jl-Ag 85, p. 18.
      "Morning Swim." _OP_ (40) Fall-Wint 85, p. 33-35.
      "My Father's Visits." _PraS_ (59:4) Wint 85, p. 81.
      "The Restaurant Where We Lived." _PraS_ (59:4) Wint 85, p.
         82-83.
607. BRUCHAC, Joseph (_See_ _also_ BRUCHAC, Joseph, III)
      "Altamira." _CrossCur_ (4:3) 84, p. 44-45.
      "Captain Kidd's Treasure." _WestB_ (17) 85, p. 77.
      "Climbing." _CrossCur_ (4:3) 84, p. 43.
      "For Sam Ray." _NewL_ (51:3) Spr 85, p. 57.
      "Walking in November across the Stream to the Sweat Lodge"
         (In memory of Sam Ray). _NewL_ (51:3) Spr 85, p. 56-57.
      "Wild Hogs." _Raccoon_ (17) Mr 85, p. 43-44.
608. BRUCHAC, Joseph, III (_See_ _also_ BRUCHAC, Joseph)
      "The Broken Rainbow." _NoDaQ_ (53:2) Spr 85, p. 138-159.
609. BRUGALETTA, John J.
      "Grandfather's Voice: Sepia." _NegC_ (5:2) Spr 85, p. 71-72.
      "To My Pagan Ancestors." _NegC_ (5:2) Spr 85, p. 73-74.
610. BRUMMELS, J. V.
      "Bloodstorm." _CharR_ (11:2) Fall 85, p. 86-89.
      "Exile." _CharR_ (11:2) Fall 85, p. 89-90.
BRUNT, H. L. van
      See Van BRUNT, H. L.
BRUNT, Lloyd van
      See Van BRUNT, Lloyd
611. BRUSH, Thomas
      "In the Badlands." _PoetryNW_ (26:3) Aut 85, p. 45.
      "Last Summer." _Nimrod_ (29:1) Fall-Wint 85, p. 67.
      "Long Distance" (for Mike Bigley). _Nimrod_ (29:1) Fall-Wint
         85, p. 68.
612. BRUTEN, Avril
      "A Lesson." _Verse_ (2) 85, p. 20.
613. BRYAN, Jeanne
      "Ian Calls Out from a Nightmare." _Abraxas_ (33) 85, p. 12.
      "The Moment of Learning Demeter." _Abraxas_ (33) 85, p. 13.
614. BRYAN, Sharon
      "Breaking and Entering." _Nat_ (240:25) 29 Je 85, p. 808.
615. BUCHANAN, Carl
      "After Reading the Archeologist's Verse." _KanQ_ (17:1/2)
         Wint-Spr 85, p. 123.
      "Drunk Car." _KanQ_ (17:1/2) Wint-Spr 85, p. 122-123.
616. BUCK, Paul
      "Lust II" (Excerpt: "Lust / The Lost World"). _Temblor_ (1)
         85, p. 69-72.
      "The Translation Begins" (tr. of Jacqueline Risset).
         Temblor (1) 85, p. 124-129.
      "Vertical Letter" (tr. of Bernard Noel). _Temblor_ (1) 85,
         p. 130-132.
617. BUCKLAND, Karen
      "Off Duty." _Bogg_ (54) 85, p. 8.
618. BUCKLEY, Christopher
      "Leonardo's 'Genevra de' Benci'." _SewanR_ (93:4) Fall 85,

p. 529-530.
"Memory." <u>Crazy</u> (26) Spr 84, p. 14-15.
"Photographing Flower Fields outside Lompoc, California."
    <u>PoetryR</u> (2:2) Ap 85, p. 85-86.
"Picasso: Two Self-Portraits--1901, 1907." <u>SewanR</u> (93:4)
    Fall 85, p. 531-532.
"Rain." <u>PoetryR</u> (2:2) Ap 85, p. 87.
"To Begin Again" (for Katie in Santa Barbara). <u>SenR</u> (15:1)
    85, p. 8-10.
619. BUDENZ, Julia
    "Flora Baum, Mathematician." <u>SouthwR</u> (70:1) Wint 85, p.
        106-107.
620. BUGEJA, Michael (<u>See also</u> BUGEJA, Michael J.)
    "Autobiography." <u>PassN</u> (6:2) Spr-Sum 85, p. 8.
    "East, West" (for Lena). <u>PoetryE</u> (18) Fall 85, p. 41.
621. BUGEJA, Michael J. (<u>See also</u> BUGEJA, Michael)
    "Adoption & Fulfillment" (for Erin Marie, 1/6/83). <u>Amelia</u>
        (2:1) Ap 85, p. 26-27.
    "The Cheat." <u>GreenfR</u> (13:1/2) Fall-Wint 85, p. 182.
    "Eurasian." <u>Amelia</u> (2:2) O 85, p. 48-49.
    "Humor & Prophecy." <u>Amelia</u> (2:1) Ap 85, p. 43.
    "Language of the Guitar." <u>KanQ</u> (17:4) Fall 85, p. 22-23.
    "Lullaby, with Balloons." <u>LaurelR</u> (19:2) Sum 85, p. 80.
    "The Music Miser." <u>WestB</u> (16) 85, p. 85.
    "Musicians, Aware" (For L.S.). <u>Amelia</u> (2:2) O 85, p. 48.
    "On Your Imminent Graduation." <u>NegC</u> (5:4) Fall 85, p. 94-
        95.
    "Platonic Love." <u>WestB</u> (17) 85, p. 91.
    "The Watched Vial." <u>IndR</u> (8:3) Fall 85, p. 13.
622. BUKOWSKI, Charles
    "462-0614." <u>SecC</u> (12:2) 84?, p. 6.
    "Fun Times." <u>WormR</u> (25:3, issue 99) 85, p. 115-116.
    "Good Stuff" (Special Section). <u>WormR</u> (25:4, issue 100)
        85, p. 133-148.
    "The Ladies Who Rip Men Apart." <u>SecC</u> (12:2) 84?, p. 12.
    "The Man at the Piano." <u>WormR</u> (25:1, issue 97) 85, p. 34-
        35.
    "Message." <u>WormR</u> (25:1, issue 97) 85, p. 37.
    "The Miracle Man." <u>WormR</u> (25:1, issue 97) 85, p. 35.
    "My Big Fling." <u>WormR</u> (25:1, issue 97) 85, p. 33-34.
    "Purple." <u>WormR</u> (25:3, issue 99) 85, p. 114-115.
    "Puzzle?" <u>WormR</u> (25:3, issue 99) 85, p. 116-117.
    "The Sadness of the News." <u>WormR</u> (25:3, issue 99) 85, p.
        118.
    "Unloading the Goods." <u>WormR</u> (25:1, issue 97) 85, p. 36.
623. BULLA, Hans Georg
    "Childhood Image" (tr. by D. H. Wilson and the author).
        <u>Stand</u> (26:2) Spr 85, p. 22.
624. BUNDY, Elroy L.
    "Olympians 3" (For Theron of Akragas, winner in the chariot
        race, tr. of Pindar, edited and revised by Helen
        Pinkerton). <u>ChiR</u> (35:1) Aut 85, p. 88-90.
625. BUNNIMIT, Joan
    "Burnt Offerings." <u>SanFPJ</u> (7:3) 84 [i.e. 85], p. 35.
    "Death's Garden." <u>SanFPJ</u> (7:4) 85, p. 64.
    "Shroud." <u>SanFPJ</u> (7:4) 85, p. 64.
626. BUNTING, Basil
    "A Song for Rustam." <u>Sulfur</u> (14) 85, p. 7.
627. BURCH, Edward
    "Old Man Alone." <u>Wind</u> (15:53) 85, p. 3.
628. BURCHARD, Rachael C.
    "Angel Gatherer." <u>SpoonRQ</u> (10:2) Spr 85, p. 55.
629. BURCIAGA, José Antonio
    "El Juan Cuéllar de Sanjo" (5 febrero 1983). <u>Imagine</u>
        (1:2) Wint 84, p. 117-118.
    "El Retefeminismo" (8 febrero 1982). <u>Imagine</u> (1:2) Wint

                    84, p. 116.
630. BURD, Cindy
        "Blue Mystery." USl (18/19) Wint 85, p. 7.
BUREN, David van
        See Van BUREN, David
631. BURGAUD, Christian
        "Au Travers de L'Ecriture." Os (21) 85, p. 3.
632. BURGESS, Dean
        "Wisteria Seen through a Small Window." Wind (15:54) 85,
        p. 7.
633. BURGESS, Lynne Hume
        "Triptych." RagMag (4:2) Fall 85, p. 11.
634. BURGOS, Julia de
        "Men in the City" (tr. by Maria Bennett). CrabCR (2:2)
        Wint 85, p. 13.
        "To Julia de Burgos" (tr. by Maria Bennett). CrabCR (3:1)
        Fall-Wint 85, p. 6-7.
        "To Julia de Burgos" (tr. by Maria Bennett). NewL (51:4)
        Sum 85, p. 89-90.
635. BURK, Ronnie
        "Mictlán." RevChic (12:2) Sum 84, p. 36-38.
636. BURKARD, Michael
        "Absolute Love Affair." QW (21) Fall-Wint 85, p. 41.
        "Biography." Pequod (18) 85, p. 83.
        "Black Wing." Telescope (4:1) Wint 85, p. 4.
        "Enigma." Pequod (18) 85, p. 82.
        "The Family." Ploughs (11:1) 85, p. 48-49.
        "Horse Light." QW (21) Fall-Wint 85, p. 39-40.
        "I wanted to love those" ("Untitled"). Telescope (4:1)
        Wint 85, p. 1.
        "It is in the nature of the other I" ("Untitled").
        Telescope (4:1) Wint 85, p. 2.
        "The Man Alone." Telescope (4:1) Wint 85, p. 3.
        "Mornings Like a Vase." Ploughs (11:1) 85, p. 47.
        "My Sister's Room." Pequod (18) 85, p. 86.
        "Pentimento." Ploughs (11:1) 85, p. 50-51.
        "Sequence of the Horses." Pequod (18) 85, p. 84-85.
        "Side with Stars." Ploughs (11:1) 85, p. 46.
        "Star for a Glass." Ploughs (11:1) 85, p. 45.
        "Street to the North." QW (21) Fall-Wint 85, p. 28.
637. BURKE, Kate
        "The Bog" (for Leo Marx Leva, 1946-1984). PoetL (80:3)
        Fall 85, p. 165.
638. BURNESS, Don
        "The Tennis Players." Confr (29) Wint 85, p. 79.
639. BURNHAM, Deborah
        "Calling Them Back." CutB (23) Fall-Wint 85, p. 65.
640. BURNS, Gerald
        "A Book of Spells II." Temblor (1) 85, p. 33-48.
641. BURNS, Jim
        "After the Rain." HangL (48) Fall 85, p. 6.
        "Proletarian Nights" (Excerpt). HangL (48) Fall 85, p. 7.
        "Sardines." HangL (48) Fall 85, p. 4-5.
642. BURNS, Michael
        "A Finale of Seem" (on the fifth day of the search for David
        Tate, Neo-nazi and accused killer hiding in the Missouri
        Ozarks). CharR (11:2) Fall 85, p. 72.
        "Healing." NoDaQ (53:4) Fall 85, p. 182.
        "A Jimmie Rodgers Blue Yodel." NegC (5:2) Spr 85, p. 75.
        "Letter to Death." CharR (11:2) Fall 85, p. 72.
        "The Rice Farmer's Vacation." NoDaQ (53:4) Fall 85, p. 181-
        182.
        "The Way Where Light Dwells." MidwQ (26:4) Sum 85, p. 452-
        453.
643. BURR, Gray
        "French Impressionists" (Engagement calendar). PoetryR

(2:2) Ap 85, p. 73.
"Owl." PoetryR (2:2) Ap 85, p. 74.
644. BURRIS, Sidney
"Warehouse Thoughts." PraS (59:3) Fall 85, p. 104.
"The Widow." PraS (59:3) Fall 85, p. 105.
645. BURRITT, Jonathan
"North of the French River, Canada." Wind (15:55) 85, p.
16.
646. BURRITT, Mary
"Cythera, the Cedars." Raccoon (17) Mr 85, p. 15.
647. BURROUGHS, C.
"Persephone's Gown." PoetryR (2:2) Ap 85, p. 63.
648. BURROWS, E. G.
"Evening Grosbeaks One Afternoon of April." Ascent (11:1)
85, p. 47-48.
"Projections." PoetryNW (26:1) Spr 85, p. 38.
"Reading the Sea at Mukilteo." Ascent (11:1) 85, p. 44-47.
"Words for the Imperilled." CharR (11:1) Spr 85, p. 83.
649. BURSK, Christopher
"Signaling" (for my son). PaintedB (25) Spr 85, p. 11.
"Timothy." PaintedB (25) Spr 85, p. 12.
650. BURT, John
"Songs of Innocence" (Newport, 1886). CumbPR (5:1) Fall
85, p. 66.
"Trucks on Hill in Winter." CumbPR (5:1) Fall 85, p. 67.
651. BURT, Kathryn
"Earthworms." PoetryNW (26:1) Spr 85, p. 27.
652. BURTON, David
"Singing." CrossCur (4:1) 84, p. 103.
653. BUSAILAH, Reja-E
"At an Old Market" (Damascus, 1984). RagMag (4:2) Fall 85,
p. 41.
"Too Late." RagMag (4:2) Fall 85, p. 40.
654. BUSCH, Trent
"As Literature Comes of Age." Poetry (146:5) Ag 85, p. 271-
272.
"Country Wife." Paint (11:21/12:24) 84-85, p. 18.
"The Jilting of Mary Brown." Comm (112:13) 12 Jl 85, p.
399.
"Oak Ridge." Vis (19) 85, p. 30-31.
"Reunion." ChiR (35:2) Wint 85, p. 70-71.
655. BUSCHEK, John
"Cream o' Wheat." Poem (53) Mr 85, p. 20.
"Missing Persons." Poem (53) Mr 85, p. 19.
656. BUSHKOWSKY, Aaron
"To Walk on Water." PoetryCR (7:2) Wint 85-86, p. 17.
657. BUTKIE, Joseph D.
"At Bomosan Temple." Amelia (2:1) Ap 85, p. 64-65.
"Before Parting." JamesWR (2:1) Fall 84, p. 15.
"Before Parting." JamesWR (2:3) Spr-Sum 85, p. 19.
"From Scratch." EngJ (74:3) Mr 85, p. 73.
"In Bunraku." ColEng (47:3) Mr 85, p. 262-263.
"On a Bus Ride: Getting a Seat" (Two Haiku). Amelia (2:2)
O 85, p. 64.
658. BUTLER, Earl
"Demon Haze Demon Haze You Return Here Here." Pig (13) 85,
p. 88.
"Melting Fantasy." Pig (13) 85, p. 68.
"Vicarian Newspeak, OK? Yaknow, OK? Yaknow." Pig (13) 85,
p. 59.
659. BUTLER, Elvie L.
"The Old Hostess." AntigR (60) Wint 85, p. 122.
660. BUTLER, Paris K.
"Concerning Cerebral Trivialities." NoDaQ (53:2) Spr 85,
p. 208.

661. BUTSCHER, Edward
     "How the West Is Won." <u>Confr</u> (30/31) N 85, p. 178.
662. BUTTERBRODT, Larry E.
     "Let's Hope." <u>SanFPJ</u> (7:4) 85, p. 18-19.
     "Weagan's War." <u>SanFPJ</u> (7:4) 85, p. 17.
663. BUTTERICK, George
     "Repartee with the Mummy" (Excerpts). <u>Temblor</u> (2) 85, p.
     132.
664. BYER, Kathryn Stripling
     "Childbirth." <u>CarolQ</u> (37:3) Spr 85, p. 24.
665. BYLSMA, Jan
     "When You're Fifteen" (tr. by Rod Jellema). <u>PoetL</u> (79:4)
     Wint 85, p. 235.
666. BYLSMA, Meindert
     "Old Skipper" (tr. by Rod Jellema). <u>PoetL</u> (79:4) Wint 85,
     p. 234.
667. BYRNE, Edward
     "Winslow Homer: Prout's Neck, Maine." <u>AmerS</u> (54:2) Spr 85,
     p. 206.
668a. BYRNE, Elena Karina
     "The Collector Calls." <u>Ploughs</u> (11:1) 85, p. 52.
     "The Sound of Sheep before Shearing." <u>Ploughs</u> (11:1) 85,
     p. 53.
C., R.
     <u>See</u> R. C.
CABAN, David Cortés
     <u>See</u> CORTES CABAN, David
668b. CABEL, Jesus
     "Abre ese corazón." <u>Mairena</u> (7:19) 85, p. 56.
     "Amarte mi muchacha." <u>Mairena</u> (7:19) 85, p. 59.
     "Diferente tu sonrisa." <u>Mairena</u> (7:19) 85, p. 58.
     "Es tu voz aferrada." <u>Mairena</u> (7:19) 85, p. 57.
     "Galopo sobre los copos." <u>Mairena</u> (7:19) 85, p. 56-57.
     "No tener nombre propio." <u>Mairena</u> (7:19) 85, p. 58.
     "Oh tú la carne cintileante." <u>Mairena</u> (7:19) 85, p. 59.
     "Recuerdo tu voz ajada." <u>Mairena</u> (7:19) 85, p. 60.
669. CABRI, Louis
     "The Checker Meets Mr. Magic" (for P. McCormick my friend).
     <u>AntigR</u> (62/63) Sum-Aut 85, p. 258.
670. CACCIATORE, Edoardo
     "Excessus" (tr. by Annalisa Saccà). <u>LitR</u> (28:2) Wint 85,
     p. 214.
     "Nothingness, Part II" (tr. by Annalisa Saccà). <u>LitR</u>
     (28:2) Wint 85, p. 213.
671. CADDEL, Richard
     "From Wreay Churchyard." <u>Conjunc</u> (8) 85, p. 211.
672. CADER, Teresa
     "Gooseflesh." <u>Tendril</u> (19/20) 85, p. 100.
     "Insomnia." <u>Tendril</u> (19/20) 85, p. 97-98.
     "Zach's Cliffs, Gay Head." <u>Tendril</u> (19/20) 85, p. 99.
673. CADNUM, Michael
     "Afternoons That Go On Forever." <u>SoDakR</u> (23:2) Sum 85, p.
     66.
     "Farm." <u>Comm</u> (112:7) 5 Ap 85, p. 213.
     "Hot October." <u>SouthwR</u> (70:3) Sum 85, p. 395.
     "Midwinter." <u>GeoR</u> (39:4) Wint 85, p. 738.
     "Twilight." <u>Amelia</u> (2:1) Ap 85, p. 60.
674. CADSBY, Heather
     "As Real As Yesterday." <u>PoetryCR</u> (6:3) Spr 85, p. 17.
     "Crazy July." <u>Quarry</u> (34:3) Sum 85, p. 70.
     "Neighbourhood Party." <u>PoetryCR</u> (6:3) Spr 85, p. 17.
675. CAGE, John
     "Theme and Variations" (New York City, March 1984). <u>AntigR</u>
     (62/63) Sum-Aut 85, p. 126-132.
676. CAIN, Michael Scott
     "The Treasure of Sierra Madre." <u>Pig</u> (13) 85, p. 43.

677. CAIRNS, Scott
     "Approaching Judea." CarolQ (37:2) Wint 85, p. 27.
     "Homeland of the Foreign Tongue." Atlantic (256:2), Ag 85,
        p. 52.
678. CAKLAIS, Maris
     "Dolce Maria" (Excerpt, tr. by Inara Cedrins). ConnPR
        (3:1) 84, p. 26.
679. CALDERON, Teresa
     "De las Aves sin Nombre." Mund (15:1/2) 85, p. 204.
     "Of the Nameless Birds" (tr. by Steven White). Mund
        (15:1/2) 85, p. 205.
680. CALDERWOOD, James L.
     "Sea Watch." SouthwR (70:3) Sum 85, p. 334-335.
681. CALDWELL, S. F.
     "Oral Report." EngJ (74:1) Ja 85, p. 37.
     "Unruly Being: a Concept of Duty" (#4). SanFPJ (7:2) 85,
        p. 58.
     "V.i.c.t.o.r.y." SanFPJ (7:2) 85, p. 59.
682. CALHOUN, Archell
     "Fall." AmerPoR (14:3) My-Je 85, p. 21.
683. CALHOUN, Harry
     "Island." Bogg (53) 85, p. 46.
684. CALLAGHAN, Tom
     "Epitaph." Conjunc (8) 85, p. 218.
685. CALLEIRO, Mary
     "Orden Futurista." LindLM (4:2) Ap-Je 85, p. 26.
686. CALMAN, Nancy Harris
     "Orchids When the Moon." Gargoyle (27) 85, p. 33.
687. CALVERT, Laura
     "Poems on Andean Indian Themes" (I. "Serenade," II. "Song,"
        III. "Elegy of the Quechua Princes"). NoDaQ (53:2) Spr
        85, p. 82-83.
688. CAMERON, Juan
     "Beach" (tr. by Steven White). Mund (15:1/2) 85, p. 37.
     "Canto 7" (from Cámera Oscura). Mund (15:1/2) 85, p.
        40.
     "Canto 7" (from the long poem Cámera Oscura, tr. by
        Steven White). Mund (15:1/2) 85, p. 41.
     "Caso." Mund (15:1/2) 85, p. 38.
     "Cuando Se Acabe." Mund (15:1/2) 85, p. 34.
     "Duro Oficio." Mund (15:1/2) 85, p. 38.
     "Event" (tr. by Steven White). Mund (15:1/2) 85, p. 39.
     "Hard Work" (tr. by Steven White). Mund (15:1/2) 85, p. 39.
     "Heraclito." Mund (15:1/2) 85, p. 36.
     "Heraclitus" (tr. by Steven White). Mund (15:1/2) 85, p.
        37.
     "Mosquito" (tr. by Steven White). Mund (15:1/2) 85, p. 39.
     "Playa." Mund (15:1/2) 85, p. 36.
     "When It's Over" (tr. by Steven White). Mund (15:1/2) 85,
        p. 35.
     "Zancudo." Mund (15:1/2) 85, p. 38.
689. CAMP, James
     "An Academic Affair." OP (38/39) Spr 85, p. 52.
     "An Academic Divorce." OP (38/39) Spr 85, p. 52.
     "Marx in Algiers." MissouriR (8:3) 85, p. 60-61.
     "The Task." Chelsea (44) 85, p. 113-114.
     "The Trilobite in the Stylobate." OP (38/39) Spr 85, p.
        176-177.
690. CAMPBELL, Andrew
     "Paris Airport." AntigR (62/63) Sum-Aut 85, p. 248.
     "La Plage." AntigR (62/63) Sum-Aut 85, p. 249.
691. CAMPBELL, Anthony
     "Mad House" (I imagine New York, tr. by Kent Johnson).
        MinnR (N.S. 25) Fall 85, p. 46.
692. CAMPBELL, Mary Belle
     "Transformation." NegC (5:4) Fall 85, p. 58.

693. CAMPBELL, Rick
   "Footnotes." <u>Pig</u> (13) 85, p. 24.
   "For the Valley, Friends, and a Bar in Rochester,
      Pennsylvania." <u>Pig</u> (13) 85, p. 47.
   "Poem to the Waitress at the Coffee Shop." <u>Pig</u> (13) 85, p.
      28.
694. CAMPION, Dan
   "Handful of Stars." <u>NoDaQ</u> (53:1) Wint 85, p. 81.
   "Hastings, Nebraska, 1920." <u>PoetL</u> (80:2) Sum 85, p. 101-
      102.
   "Lapidary." <u>LaurelR</u> (19:1) Wint 85, p. 34.
   "Moonshine." <u>Vis</u> (17) 85, p. 42.
   "The Nightship." <u>NegC</u> (5:2) Spr 85, p. 89.
695. CAMPOS CARR, Irene
   "Mujer." <u>RevChic</u> (12:2) Sum 84, p. 26.
   "La Señorita." <u>RevChic</u> (12:2) Sum 84, p. 25.
696. CANDELARIA, Cordelia
   "Festival of the Winds." <u>Imagine</u> (1:2) Wint 84, p. 140.
   "Object." <u>Imagine</u> (2:1) Sum 85, p. 79.
   "A Prayer, A Dios." <u>Imagine</u> (1:2) Wint 84, p. 139.
697. CANDOW, James
   "Blood Test." <u>PottPort</u> (7) 85-86, p. 47.
698. CANNON, Melissa
   "Dry thunder." <u>Amelia</u> (2:1) Ap 85, p. 8.
699. CANTRELL, Charles
   "The Cold Depths." <u>SpoonRQ</u> (10:2) Spr 85, p. 51.
   "A Hell for Animals" (after James Dickey's "The Heaven of
      Animals"). <u>Nimrod</u> (29:1) Fall-Wint 85, p. 25-26.
   "Homage to the House." <u>PassN</u> (6:1) Fall-Wint 85, p. 11.
   "Underneath" (for L. G.). <u>SpoonRQ</u> (10:4) Fall 85, p. 44.
700. CAPPELLO, Mary
   "To Sharon." <u>AmerPoR</u> (14:3) My-Je 85, p. 44.
701. CAPRONI, Giorgio
   "Birthday" (tr. by Annalisa Saccà). <u>LitR</u> (28:2) Wint 85,
      p. 222.
   "Experience" (tr. by Annalisa Saccà). <u>LitR</u> (28:2) Wint
      85, p. 222.
   "Homecoming" (tr. by Annalisa Saccà). <u>LitR</u> (28:2) Wint
      85, p. 221.
   "The Last Hamlet" (tr. by Annalisa Saccà). <u>LitR</u> (28:2)
      Wint 85, p. 220-221.
   "Sure Direction" (To the foreigner who had asked for the
      hotel, tr. by Annalisa Saccà). <u>LitR</u> (28:2) Wint 85,
      p. 221.
CARBEAU, Mitchell les
   <u>See</u> LesCARBEAU, Mitchell
702. CARDARELLI, Joe
   "For the Song's Space." <u>Open24</u> (4) 85, p. 11.
   "Poem after Other Not Poems." <u>Open24</u> (4) 85, p. 20.
703. CARDENAL, Ernesto
   "2 AM." <u>Inti</u> (18/19) Otoño 83-Prim. 84, p. 118-119.
   "Apocalipsis." <u>Inti</u> (18/19) Otoño 83-Prim. 84, p. 123-
      127.
   "Las Ciudades Perdidas." <u>Inti</u> (18/19) Otoño 83-Prim. 84,
      p. 127-130.
   "Como Latas de Cerveza Vacias." <u>Inti</u> (18/19) Otoño 83-
      Prim. 84, p. 119.
   "Epigramas." <u>Inti</u> (18/19) Otoño 83-Prim. 84, p. 115-116.
   "Jose Dolores Estrada" (A todos los exilados
      nicaragüenses). <u>Inti</u> (18/19) Otoño 83-Prim. 84, p.
      127.
   "Oración por Marilyn Monroe." <u>Inti</u> (18/19) Otoño 83-
      Prim. 84, p. 121-122.
   "Salmo 1." <u>Inti</u> (18/19) Otoño 83-Prim. 84, p. 119.
   "Salmo 5." <u>Inti</u> (18/19) Otoño 83-Prim. 84, p. 119-120.
   "Somoza Desveliza la Estatua de Somoza en el Estadio

Somoza." <u>Inti</u> (18/19) Otoño 83-Prim. 84, p. 117-118.
"The U.S. Congress Approves Aid to the Contras" (tr. by
Stephen Kessler). <u>Zyzzyva</u> (1:4) Wint 85, p. 130-134.
704. CARDENAS, Esteban Luis
"Apuntes de una Carta." <u>LindLM</u> (4:4) O-D 85, p. 5.
705. CARDILLO, Joe
"All of the Days and Nights Ahead." <u>RagMag</u> (4:2) Fall 85,
p. 44.
"Athens." <u>CrabCR</u> (2:2) Wint 85, p. 27.
"Sometimes, Just at Dawn." <u>RagMag</u> (4:2) Fall 85, p. 45.
706. CARDULLO, Bert
"Anecdotes from Herr Keuner" (tr. of Bertolt Brecht). <u>WebR</u>
(10:1) Spr 85, p. 17.
"On This Spot Old Walls Stood Fast" (tr. of Bertolt Brecht).
<u>WebR</u> (10:1) Spr 85, p. 17.
"The Song of Flux" (tr. of Bertolt Brecht). <u>WebR</u> (10:1)
Spr 85, p. 15-16.
707. CAREY, Barbara
"Blood or Time." <u>PoetryCR</u> (7:2) Wint 85-86, p. 10.
"In the Latest Photo" (WQ Editors' First Prize Winner --
Poetry). <u>CrossC</u> (7:1) 85, p. 18.
"Prodigal Ways." <u>Quarry</u> (34:3) Sum 85, p. 44-46.
"Sorting." <u>PoetryCR</u> (6:3) Spr 85, p. 22.
"Undressing the Dark." <u>PoetryCR</u> (6:3) Spr 85, p. 22.
708. CAREY, Michael A.
"Last Chance." <u>PoetC</u> (17:1) Fall 85, p. 22-23.
"Last Rites." <u>PoetC</u> (17:1) Fall 85, p. 18-19.
"Separate Joy." <u>PoetC</u> (17:1) Fall 85, p. 20-21.
709. CARGAS, Harry James
"Retreat" (for Jim Schulte). <u>WebR</u> (10:1) Spr 85, p. 76.
710. CARIELLO, Matthew
"In October." <u>J1NJPo</u> (8:1) 85, p. 44.
"What Sal Did" (Selection: 18). <u>J1NJPo</u> (8:1) 85, p. 45.
711. CARIS, Jane Godard
"Portia and the Apricots" (for Portia Weiskel). <u>CarolQ</u>
(37:3) Spr 85, p. 23.
712. CARLETON, Bill
"A Sequence of Diverted Sonnets." <u>CarolQ</u> (37:3) Spr 85, p.
35-37.
713. CARLILE, Henry
"Merlin." <u>Iowa</u> (15:1) Wint 85, p. 98.
714. CARLISLE, Thomas John
"Just Like Joseph." <u>ChrC</u> (102:40) 18-25 D 85, p. 1166.
715. CARLSON, Martha
"The Silversmith." <u>CarolQ</u> (37:3) Spr 85, p. 28-29.
716. CARLSON, Ralph S.
"The Lover." <u>NegC</u> (5:1) Wint 85, p. 115-116.
717. CARLSON, Thomas C. (<u>See also</u> CARLSON, Tom)
"Burned Forest" (tr. of Nichita Stanescu, w. Vasile
Poenaru). <u>StoneC</u> (13:1/2) Fall-Wint 85-86, p. 46-47.
718. CARLSON, Tom (<u>See also</u> CARLSON, Thomas C.)
"Bas-Relief with Heroes" (tr. of Nichita Stanescu, w. Vasile
Poenaru). <u>Mund</u> (16:1/2) 85, p. 75.
"My Mother and Her Soldier" (tr. of Nichita Stanescu, w.
Vasile Poenaru). <u>Mund</u> (16:1/2) 85, p. 73.
"Of Course" (tr. of Nichita Stanescu, w. Vasile Poenaru).
<u>Mund</u> (16:1/2) 85, p. 77.
"Star Roar" (tr. of Petre Ghelmez, w. Vasile Poenaru).
<u>Mund</u> (16:1/2) 85, p. 59.
719. CARMELL, Pamela
"I Buy Old Furniture: Chairs, Beds, Bed Springs" (tr. of
Belkis Cuza Malé). <u>NewEngR</u> (7:4) Sum 85, p. 491.
"My Mother's Homeland" (tr. of Belkis Cuza Malé).
<u>NewEngR</u> (7:4) Sum 85, p. 492.
"Still Life" (tr. of Belkis Cuza Malé). <u>NewEngR</u> (7:4)
Sum 85, p. 493.

720. CARMODY-WYNNE, Diane
    "Banalities." <u>Imagine</u> (2:1) Sum 85, p. 86-87.
    "The Bracelet." <u>Imagine</u> (2:1) Sum 85, p. 87.
721. CARMONA BASORA, Neli Jo
    "Mujer sin Tiempo ni Edad" (A Susana Seidman). <u>Mairena</u>
        (7:19) 85, p. 97.
722. CARPATHIOS, Neil
    "Nightfall over Fields I Love." <u>Wind</u> (15:54) 85, p. 8.
    "Waiting in December." <u>CrabCR</u> (2:2) Wint 85, p. 12.
    "Wanderers." <u>CrabCR</u> (3:1) Fall-Wint 85, p. 23.
723. CARPELAN, Bo
    "The Dream" (tr. by Robin Fulton). <u>Verse</u> (3) 85, p. 38.
    "In That House" (tr. by Robin Fulton). <u>Verse</u> (3) 85, p. 39.
    "They Are Alive" (tr. by Robin Fulton). <u>Verse</u> (3) 85, p.
        39.
724. CARPENTER, Bogdana
    "Beethoven" (tr. of Zbigniew Herbert, w. John Carpenter).
        <u>Antaeus</u> (55) Aut 85, p. 115.
    "Mr. Cogito -- the Return" (tr. of Zbigniew Herbert, w. John
        Carpenter). <u>Antaeus</u> (55) Aut 85, p. 121-123.
    "Mr. Cogito's Soul" (tr. of Zbigniew Herbert, w. John
        Carpenter). <u>Antaeus</u> (55) Aut 85, p. 119-120.
    "The Murderers of Kings" (tr. of Zbigniew Herbert, w. John
        Carpenter). <u>Antaeus</u> (55) Aut 85, p. 118.
    "The Power of Taste" (For Professor Izydora Dambska, tr. of
        Zbigniew Herbert, w. John Carpenter). <u>Antaeus</u> (55) Aut
        85, p. 116-117.
    "Report from the Besieged City" (tr. of Zbigniew Herbert, w.
        John Carpenter). <u>Antaeus</u> (55) Aut 85, p. 110-112.
    "To Ryszard Krynicki -- a Letter" (tr. of Zbigniew Herbert,
        w. John Carpenter). <u>Antaeus</u> (55) Aut 85, p. 113-114.
725. CARPENTER, J. D. (<u>See also</u> CARPENTER, John)
    "Birdwatching." <u>Dandel</u> (12:2) 85, p. 44-45.
    "Eulogy for H. MacKay." <u>CanLit</u> (107) Wint 85, p. 45-47.
    "Pond below the Camp." <u>Dandel</u> (12:2) 85, p. 42-43.
726. CARPENTER, John (<u>See also</u> CARPENTER, J. D.)
    "Beethoven" (tr. of Zbigniew Herbert, w. Bogdana Carpenter).
        <u>Antaeus</u> (55) Aut 85, p. 115.
    "Mr. Cogito -- the Return" (tr. of Zbigniew Herbert, w.
        Bogdana Carpenter). <u>Antaeus</u> (55) Aut 85, p. 121-123.
    "Mr. Cogito's Soul" (tr. of Zbigniew Herbert, w. Bogdana
        Carpenter). <u>Antaeus</u> (55) Aut 85, p. 119-120.
    "The Murderers of Kings" (tr. of Zbigniew Herbert, w.
        Bogdana Carpenter). <u>Antaeus</u> (55) Aut 85, p. 118.
    "The Power of Taste" (For Professor Izydora Dambska, tr. of
        Zbigniew Herbert, w. Bogdana Carpenter). <u>Antaeus</u> (55)
        Aut 85, p. 116-117.
    "Report from the Besieged City" (tr. of Zbigniew Herbert, w.
        Bogdana Carpenter). <u>Antaeus</u> (55) Aut 85, p. 110-112.
    "To Ryszard Krynicki -- a Letter" (tr. of Zbigniew Herbert,
        w. Bogdana Carpenter). <u>Antaeus</u> (55) Aut 85, p. 113-114.
727. CARPENTER, Tom
    "The Swimming Lesson." <u>Quarry</u> (34:4) Aut 85, p. 54-55.
    "The Truth at Bacon Tank." <u>Quarry</u> (34:4) Aut 85, p. 54.
728. CARPER, Thomas
    "Catching Fireflies." <u>Poetry</u> (146:3) Je 85, p. 165.
    "Creation." <u>Poetry</u> (146:3) Je 85, p. 166.
    "Laundry at Night." <u>Poetry</u> (146:3) Je 85, p. 165.
729. CARR, Dana Elaine
    "Chimney Nests." <u>PoeticJ</u> (11) 85, p. 41.
CARR, Irene Campos
    <u>See</u> CAMPOS CARR, Irene
730. CARRADICE, Phil
    "Magic Maggie." <u>Bogg</u> (54) 85, p. 60.
    "Modern Nursery Rhyme." <u>Bogg</u> (54) 85, p. 12.

731. CARRANZA, Eduardo
       "Elegia Pura." Mairena (7:19) 85, p. 112.
       "Llano Llanero." Mairena (7:19) 85, p. 112-113.
       "El Olvidado." Mairena (7:19) 85, p. 114.
732. CARRIE, LeAnn Jackson
       "Women Snapping Beans." Prima (9) 85, p. 30-31.
733. CARROLL, Jim
       "NYC Variations" (Excerpts). ParisR (27:98) Wint 85, p.
       153-155.
734. CARROLLTON, Chris
       "Something Plowed Out and Planted In" (DeKalb County High
       Schools, Literary award winners: second place, poetry).
       DeKalbLAJ (18:3/4) 85, p. 46.
735. CARRUTH, Hayden
       "At the Back of the North Wind." Pequod (18) 85, p. 11-12.
       "The Avenue Lined with American Chestnut Trees Is More Than
       a Textbook." Sulfur (13) 85, p. 49.
       "Carnations for C." Pequod (18) 85, p. 7.
       "An Excursus of Reassurance in Begonia Time" (for C.).
       Pequod (18) 85, p. 8-10.
       "For Papa." Tendril (19/20) 85, p. 101.
       "How To." GreenfR (12:3/4) Wint-Spr 85, p. 17-18.
       "Meditation in the Presence of 'Ostrich Walk'." Sulfur
       (13) 85, p. 48.
       "Mother" (Margery Carruth, 1896-1981). SewanR (93:1) Wint
       85, p. 116-127.
       "Not by Any Means Have I Now for the First Time." Sulfur
       (13) 85, p. 50.
       "On the Truistical and Fashionable Eyes of Albert Camus."
       OhioR (34) 85, p. 59.
       "The Opposing Concepts of Spontaneity and Expediency in
       Improvisation." VirQ (61:2) Spr 85, p. 249-251.
       "Ovid, Old Buddy, I Would Discourse with You a While."
       VirQ (61:2) Spr 85, p. 251-252.
       "Plain Song." GreenfR (12:3/4) Wint-Spr 85, p. 14-16.
       "Prolegomenon to a Fantasized Propaedeutics for Kathleen
       Roberts." Sulfur (13) 85, p. 49-50.
       "Sonnet." OP (38/39) Spr 85, p. 205.
       "Une Présence Absolue." OhioR (34) 85, p. 58.
       "What She Said." Pequod (18) 85, p. 13.
736. CARSON, Anne
       "The Fall of Rome" (A Traveller's Guide: Excerpts). CanLit
       (106) Fall 85, p. 76-79.
737. CARTER, Ellin E.
       "Goddesses." NegC (5:2) Spr 85, p. 157.
       "Mind Power." NegC (5:4) Fall 85, p. 86-87.
738. CARTER, Jared
       "Love Song for Oscillating Universe." PaintedB (26/27) Sum-
       Fall 85, p. 14.
       "Preparations." LittleBR (5:1) Fall-Wint 84-85, p. 22-23.
       "Starlings." PaintedB (26/27) Sum-Fall 85, p. 15-16.
739. CARTER, Martin
       "Our Number." RiverS (18) 85, p. 99.
740. CARTER, Richard E.
       "The Last Fisherman." SpoonRQ (10:2) Spr 85, p. 46-47.
741. CARTER, Stephen
       "Syncretistic Poem." CarolQ (38:1) Fall 85, p. 47.
742. CARVER, Raymond
       "An Afternoon." Ploughs (11:4) 85, p. 79.
       "Anathema." Tendril (19/20) 85, p. 427.
       "Asia." Ploughs (11:4) 85, p. 78-79.
       "Ask Him." Tendril (19/20) 85, p. 407-408.
       "Away." OhioR (34) 85, p. 11.
       "Away." Tendril (19/20) 85, p. 406.
       "Balsa Wood." Poetry (146:6) S 85, p. 346.
       "Blood." GrandS (4:2) Wint 85, p. 89.

"Bonnard's Nudes." <u>Crazy</u> (27) Fall 84, p. 9.
"Cadillacs and Poetry." <u>Ploughs</u> (11:4) 85, p. 80.
"The Cranes." <u>NewL</u> (51:3) Spr 85, p. 63.
"Elk Camp." <u>Tendril</u> (19/20) 85, p. 423-424.
"Energy." <u>Crazy</u> (27) Fall 84, p. 10.
"Energy." <u>Tendril</u> (19/20) 85, p. 428.
"The Eve of Battle." <u>Tendril</u> (19/20) 85, p. 416.
"Extirpation." <u>Tendril</u> (19/20) 85, p. 417.
"The Fishing Pole of the Drowned Man." <u>Tendril</u> (19/20) 85,
     p. 429.
"For Tess." <u>Poetry</u> (145:5) F 85, p. 252.
"The Garden." <u>Tendril</u> (19/20) 85, p. 410-411.
"The Gift" (for Tess). <u>SenR</u> (15:2) 85, p. 50-51.
"Grief." <u>Poetry</u> (145:5) F 85, p. 254.
"Happiness." <u>Poetry</u> (145:5) F 85, p. 251.
"The Hat." <u>Tendril</u> (19/20) 85, p. 418-419.
"In Switzerland." <u>Tendril</u> (19/20) 85, p. 425-426.
"In the Lobby of the Hotel del Mayo." <u>Tendril</u> (19/20) 85,
     p. 420.
"Interview." <u>Tendril</u> (19/20) 85, p. 405.
"The Juggler" (Or, The Scene to Remember from <u>Heaven's</u>
     <u>Gate</u>, for Michael Cimino). <u>Tendril</u> (19/20) 85, p. 414.
"Kafka's Watch." <u>NewYorker</u> (61:35) 21 O 85, p. 117.
"Late Night with Fog and Horses." <u>OhioR</u> (34) 85, p. 6-7.
"Late Night with Fog and Horses." <u>Tendril</u> (19/20) 85, p.
     422.
"Locking Yourself Out, Then Trying to Get Back In." <u>Pequod</u>
     (18) 85, p. 48-49.
"Mesopotamia." <u>Poetry</u> (147:3) D 85, p. 128.
"Money." <u>Poetry</u> (145:5) F 85, p. 252-253.
"Mother." <u>Poetry</u> (147:3) D 85, p. 127.
"My Crow." <u>Poetry</u> (145:5) F 85, p. 253.
"My Death." <u>OhioR</u> (34) 85, p. 13.
"Next Door." <u>Tendril</u> (19/20) 85, p. 421.
"Next Year." <u>GrandS</u> (4:2) Wint 85, p. 88.
"The Old Days." <u>Pequod</u> (18) 85, p. 50-51.
"Our First House in Sacramento." <u>Pequod</u> (18) 85, p. 47.
"The Pen." <u>Zyzzyva</u> (1:3) Fall 85, p. 121-122.
"The Prize." <u>NowestR</u> (23:1) 85, p. 44.
"The Rest." <u>Poetry</u> (146:6) S 85, p. 347.
"The Sensitive Girl." <u>Poetry</u> (146:6) S 85, p. 344-436.
"Shiftless." <u>Poetry</u> (146:6) S 85, p. 344.
"Stupid." <u>Poetry</u> (147:3) D 85, p. 129.
"This Morning." <u>Ploughs</u> (11:4) 85, p. 81.
"To Begin With." <u>OhioR</u> (34) 85, p. 8-10.
"Tomorrow." <u>OhioR</u> (34) 85, p. 12.
"Union Street: San Francisco, Summer 1975." <u>Ploughs</u> (11:4)
     85, p. 82-83.
"Venice." <u>Tendril</u> (19/20) 85, p. 415.
"Vigil." <u>Ploughs</u> (11:4) 85, p. 84.
"Wenas Ridge." <u>Tendril</u> (19/20) 85, p. 412-413.
"Where the Groceries Went." <u>SenR</u> (15:2) 85, p. 46-47.
"Where Water Comes Together with Other Water." <u>Tendril</u>
     (19/20) 85, p. 403.
"The White Field." <u>SenR</u> (15:2) 85, p. 48-49.
"Yesterday, Snow." <u>GrandS</u> (4:2) Wint 85, p. 87.
"The Young Fire Eaters of Mexico City." <u>Crazy</u> (27) Fall
     84, p. 11.
"The Young Fire Eaters of Mexico City." <u>Tendril</u> (19/20)
     85, p. 404.
"The Young Girls." <u>Tendril</u> (19/20) 85, p. 409.
743. CASAS, Walter de las
"A Annie Reibel." <u>LindLM</u> (4:4) O-D 85, p. 3.
"Insomnio." <u>LindLM</u> (4:4) O-D 85, p. 3.
"Mi Vida" (A Michael Franks y Antonio Carlos Jobim).
     <u>LindLM</u> (4:4) O-D 85, p. 3.

"Otro Poema" (A José Olivio Jiménez). <u>LindLM</u> (4:4) O-D
    85, p. 3.
744. CASEY, Deb
    "12 October." <u>NoAmR</u> (270:4) D 85, p. 50.
    "Old Shoe." <u>GreenfR</u> (13:1/2) Fall-Wint 85, p. 56.
745. CASEY, Michael
    "Fragging." <u>ColEng</u> (47:7) N 85, p. 716.
    "Monkey House." <u>GrahamHR</u> (8) Wint 85, p. 29.
    "Sniperscope." <u>ColEng</u> (47:7) N 85, p. 715-716.
746. CASEY, Raymond O.
    "Weight Lifting Mike." <u>WindO</u> (46) Fall 85, p. 47-48.
747. CASSELLS, Cyrus
    "Atlantic Window" (for Stanley Kunitz). <u>SouthernR</u> (21:3)
        Sum 85, p. 819-820.
748. CASSELMAN, Barry
    "Alkaline Helicopters." <u>GreenfR</u> (13:1/2) Fall-Wint 85, p.
        20-21.
749. CASSITY, Turner
    "The Aswan Rowing Club." <u>Poetry</u> (146:3) Je 85, p. 162.
    "Imputations." <u>Poetry</u> (146:3) Je 85, p. 161-162.
    "Keepers." <u>ChiR</u> (35:1) Aut 85, p. 36-37.
    "Why Fortune Is the Empress of the World." <u>Poetry</u> (146:3)
        Je 85, p. 161.
750. CASTAÑO, Wilfredo
    "Jules, Two Years Old" (To my sons Jules and Gilbert).
        <u>AmerPoR</u> (14:4) Jl-Ag 85, p. 30.
    "To People Who Pick Food." <u>AmerPoR</u> (14:4) Jl-Ag 85, p. 30.
751. CASTEDO, Elena
    "Agonizó Franco?" <u>LindLM</u> (4:1) Ja-Mr 85, p. 27.
752. CASTELLANOS, Yolanda Gracia
    "Cuando la Luz Se Cuaja sobre la Geografia" (fragmento).
        <u>Mairena</u> (7:19) 85, p. 81.
    "Hoy-Quiero." <u>Mairena</u> (7:19) 85, p. 82.
    "Transformaciones." <u>Mairena</u> (7:19) 85, p. 81-82.
753. CASTILLO, Amelia del
    "Dime" (A mis hijos). <u>LindLM</u> (4:2) Ap-Je 85, p. 25.
754. CASTILLO, Ofelia
    "Los Amantes." <u>Mund</u> (15:1/2) 85, p. 22.
    "Del Poeta y Su Rio" (a Juan L. Ortiz). <u>Mund</u> (15:1/2) 85,
        p. 20, 22.
    "Fragmentos." <u>Mund</u> (15:1/2) 85, p. 16, 18.
    "Fragments" (tr. by H. E. Francis). <u>Mund</u> (15:1/2) 85, p.
        17, 19.
    "The Lovers" (tr. by H. E. Francis). <u>Mund</u> (15:1/2) 85, p.
        23.
    "Of the Poet and His River" (tr. by H. E. Francis). <u>Mund</u>
        (15:1/2) 85, p. 21, 23.
    "The Poem" (tr. by H. E. Francis). <u>Mund</u> (15:1/2) 85, p. 17.
    "El Poema." <u>Mund</u> (15:1/2) 85, p. 16.
755. CASTLE, Sandie
    "Apt. 3-G." <u>Open24</u> (4) 85, p. 43.
    "Roll Out the Barrel." <u>Open24</u> (4) 85, p. 42.
756. CASTNER, Lorale E.
    "It's Still the Same Old World." <u>SanFPJ</u> (7:4) 85, p. 39-40.
757. CATHERS, Ken
    "At the Duncan Turn-Off." <u>Waves</u> (13:4) Spr 85, p. 74.
    "Ida." <u>Quarry</u> (34:4) Aut 85, p. 9-10.
758. CATLIN, Alan
    "Betting Football with the Village Idiot." <u>WormR</u> (25:3,
        issue 99) 85, p. 88.
    "Bingo Players in the Rain." <u>WoosterR</u> (3) Spr 85, p. 41.
    "The Dresser." <u>WormR</u> (25:3, issue 99) 85, p. 87.
    "Extending Joe Dimaggio's Streak." <u>WormR</u> (25:3, issue 99)
        85, p. 90-91.
    "The Fan." <u>WormR</u> (25:3, issue 99) 85, p. 89.
    "Hot Stuff." <u>WormR</u> (25:3, issue 99) 85, p. 89.

"Long Island (N.Y.) Images." <u>Vis</u> (17) 85, p. 25.
"Shelley and the Romantics." <u>WormR</u> (25:3, issue 99) 85, p.
90.
"Shrine of the Blessed Virgin Mary Still Life, Montreal,
Canada 1963." <u>Open24</u> (4) 85, p. 56.
"Sojourner Truth in the Schenectady Public Library." <u>WormR</u>
(25:3, issue 99) 85, p. 89.
"Speed Demon." <u>WormR</u> (25:3, issue 99) 85, p. 91.
"Still Life with Handgrenade" (Utica, N.Y. 1970). <u>Vis</u> (19)
85, p. 31.
"The Village Idiot." <u>WormR</u> (25:3, issue 99) 85, p. 87-88.
"The Weaver." <u>Open24</u> (4) 85, p. 57.
759. CAVAFY, C. P.
"Ta'en" (March 1921, tr. by Stavros Deligiorgis). <u>Iowa</u>
(15:2) Spr-Sum 85, p. 83-84.
"The Town" (tr. by Stephen Spender and Nikos Stangos).
<u>TriQ</u> (63) Spr-Sum 85, p. 102.
760. CAVALIERI, Grace
"After Taking the Train to Martinsburg" (for Angel). <u>Vis</u>
(19) 85, p. 10.
"It's Like Putting Cologne on a Pig." <u>PoetL</u> (80:2) Sum 85,
p. 124-125.
761. CAVALIERO, Glen
"Good Angel." <u>LittleBR</u> (5:1) Fall-Wint 84-85, p. 34.
"On the Library Steps: Persephone." <u>LittleBR</u> (5:1) Fall-
Wint 84-85, p. 32.
"On the Piazza." <u>LittleBR</u> (5:1) Fall-Wint 84-85, p. 31.
"Solo." <u>LittleBR</u> (5:1) Fall-Wint 84-85, p. 32.
"Valse Bleu." <u>LittleBR</u> (5:1) Fall-Wint 84-85, p. 33.
762. CAVALLARO, Carol
"Dissolution by a Northern Ocean." <u>Nat</u> (241:2) 20-27 Jl
85, p. 58.
"Giotto's Maesta." <u>CutB</u> (23) Fall-Wint 85, p. 40-41.
"The Neighboring House." <u>Nimrod</u> (29:1) Fall-Wint 85, p. 69.
763. CAVANAGH, Clare
"The Answer" (tr. of Ryszard Krynicki, w. Stanislaw
Baranczak). <u>Ploughs</u> (11:4) 85, p. 134.
"By Saying" (tr. of Ryszard Krynicki, w. Stanislaw
Baranczak). <u>Ploughs</u> (11:4) 85, p. 133.
"The Heart" (tr. of Ryszard Krynicki, w. Stanislaw
Baranczak). <u>Ploughs</u> (11:4) 85, p. 135.
"How Far" (tr. of Ryszard Krynicki, w. Stanislaw Baranczak).
<u>Ploughs</u> (11:4) 85, p. 135.
"If It Comes to Pass" (tr. of Ryszard Krynicki, w. Stanislaw
Baranczak). <u>Ploughs</u> (11:4) 85, p. 136.
"I'll Remember That" (tr. of Ryszard Krynicki, w. Stanislaw
Baranczak). <u>Ploughs</u> (11:4) 85, p. 136.
"Inscription on a China Dish" (tr. of Ryszard Krynicki, w.
Stanislaw Baranczak). <u>Ploughs</u> (11:4) 85, p. 137.
"Rumor Has It" (tr. of Ryszard Krynicki, w. Stanislaw
Baranczak). <u>Ploughs</u> (11:4) 85, p. 133.
"This Moment" (tr. of Ryszard Krynicki, w. Stanislaw
Baranczak). <u>Ploughs</u> (11:4) 85, p. 134.
"The Time of Trial" (tr. of Ryszard Krynicki, w. Stanislaw
Baranczak). <u>Ploughs</u> (11:4) 85, p. 137.
764. CAWLEY, Kevin
"Distinguish." <u>Poem</u> (53) Mr 85, p. 46.
"Queen of Cats." <u>Poem</u> (53) Mr 85, p. 45.
765. CAYLE
"Whited Out." <u>CrossCur</u> (4:4/5:1) 85, p. 162.
766. CAYLE (JEFF LOO)
"Rejoice!" (for a poet-brother who's drying out). <u>AmerPoR</u>
(14:3) My-Je 85, p. 47.
767. CECIL, Edythe
"Fall at Bailey Pond." <u>Confr</u> (30/31) N 85, p. 22.

768. CECIL, Richard
     "Applications." <u>Ploughs</u> (11:1) 85, p. 57-58.
     "The Call." <u>Ploughs</u> (11:1) 85, p. 54-56.
     "Einstein's Brain." <u>AmerPoR</u> (14:3) My-Je 85, p. 18.
     "Railroad Death." <u>Telescope</u> (4:1) Wint 85, p. 18-19.
     "Widower." <u>AmerPoR</u> (14:3) My-Je 85, p. 19.
769. CECILIONE, Michael
     "A Dream by the Sea in Three Parts." <u>JlNJPo</u> (8:1) 85, p.
        42.
     "Driving through the Country at Twilight." <u>JlNJPo</u> (8:1)
        85, p. 43.
770. CEDERING, Siv
     "Aubade, Ending with an Imperfect Sestina, in Spring."
        <u>SouthernPR</u> (26, i.e. 25:2) Fall 85, p. 52-55.
     "Dead Wood." <u>Confr</u> (30/31) N 85, p. 122.
771. CEDRINS, Inara
     "Dolce Maria" (Excerpt, tr. of Maris Caklais). <u>ConnPR</u>
        (3:1) 84, p. 26.
772. CELAN, Paul
     "Everything's Different" (tr. by Michael Hamburger). <u>Stand</u>
        (26:3) Sum 85, p. 48.
     "Matière de Bretagne" (tr. by Michael Hamburger). <u>Verse</u>
        (2) 85, p. 40.
     "Sonnet IV" (in German and English, tr. by Tom Mandel).
        <u>Zyzzyva</u> (1:3) Fall 85, p. 128-130.
     "Uprising of Smoke Banners" (tr. by Michael Hamburger).
        <u>Stand</u> (26:3) Sum 85, p. 47.
     "Windmills" (tr. by Michael Hamburger). <u>Stand</u> (26:3) Sum
        85, p. 49.
773. CELLI, Roberto
     "The Cobra and the Mongoose." <u>NewL</u> (51:3) Spr 85, p. 89.
     "That Wall." <u>NewL</u> (51:3) Spr 85, p. 89.
774. CERMAC, Rick
     "Rictus." <u>AntigR</u> (62/63) Sum-Aut 85, p. 255.
     "So, So." <u>AntigR</u> (62/63) Sum-Aut 85, p. 256.
     "What Luck." <u>AntigR</u> (62/63) Sum-Aut 85, p. 257.
775. CESAIRE, Aimé
     "The Wheel" (tr. by Michael Benedikt). <u>TriQ</u> (63) Spr-Sum
        85, p. 207.
776. CESARANO, James
     "Revisiting Old Poetry." <u>NegC</u> (5:3) Sum 85, p. 142-143.
777. CHACE, Joel
     "Rain." <u>ConnPR</u> (3:1) 84, p. 44.
778. CHADWICK, Jerah
     "Absence Wild." <u>CrabCR</u> (3:1) Fall-Wint 85, p. 28.
     "The Life to Come." <u>JamesWR</u> (2:3) Spr-Sum 85, p. 8.
     "Stove." <u>PassN</u> (6:1) Fall-Wint 85, p. 11.
779. CHAMBERLAND, Paul
     "Future Exterminé." <u>Rampike</u> (4:2/3) 85-86, p. 12.
780. CHAMBERS, Douglas
     "A Haiku for Basil, Riving the Apples of Elysium." <u>Conjunc</u>
        (8) 85, p. 197.
781. CHAMBERS, Leland H.
     "Big John." <u>Imagine</u> (1:2) Wint 84, p. 127.
     "Toys." <u>Imagine</u> (1:2) Wint 84, p. 126.
782. CHANDLER, Jim
     "Aged Like Old Beef." <u>Open24</u> (4) 85, p. 10.
     "Slipping." <u>Open24</u> (4) 85, p. 6.
783. CHANDLER, Joyce A.
     "Empathy." <u>PoeticJ</u> (11) 85, p. 6.
     "Features." <u>BlueBldgs</u> (9) [85?], p. 56.
784. CHANDRA, G. S. Sharat
     "Ars Poetica." <u>NoAmR</u> (270:2) Je 85, p. 41.
     "An Indian Razor Advertisement." <u>NewL</u> (52:1) Fall 85, p.
        46.
     "Shiva Winding a Wreath of Victory Round a Devotee-King's

Head" (Stone carving in a temple in Tanjore, Madras).
NewL (52:1) Fall 85, p. 45.

785. CHANG, Diana
    "The Earth Turns a Thousand Miles an Hour." CrossCur (5:3)
        85, p. 12-13.

786. CHAPPEL, Allen H.
    "Everything Went Quite Well Again" (tr. of Gabriele
        Wohmann). NewOR (12:1) Spr 85, p. 90-91.

787. CHAPPELL, Fred
    "Aubade." DevQ (19:3) Wint 85, p. 5-7.
    "Score." DevQ (19:3) Wint 85, p. 8.
    "Teller." DevQ (19:3) Wint 85, p. 9-10.

788. CHAR, René
    "Course of Clay" (tr. by Charles Guenther). NewL (51:4)
        Sum 85, p. 149.
    "Cur Secessisti?" (tr. by Michael O'Brien). NewL (51:4)
        Sum 85, p. 150.
    "The Legitimate Order Is Sometimes Inhuman" (tr. by Michael
        O'Brien). NewL (51:4) Sum 85, p. 150.
    "Let's Dance at the Barronies" (tr. by Charles Guenther).
        NewL (51:4) Sum 85, p. 149.
    "Penumbra" (tr. by Michael O'Brien). NewL (51:4) Sum 85,
        p. 150.
    "Say" (tr. by Michael O'Brien). NewL (51:4) Sum 85, p. 151.
    "To Bloom in Winter" (From La Nuit Talismanique 1972, tr.
        by Charles Guenther). WebR (10:2) Fall 85, p. 39.

789. CHARACH, Ron
    "As Foreign Couples Rise." PraF (6:3) Sum 85, p. 52-53.
    "The Error." AntigR (62/63) Sum-Aut 85, p. 114-115.
    "A Heater from Space." AntigR (62/63) Sum-Aut 85, p. 118.
    "Herb Woodley Is Dead." Quarry (34:4) Aut 85, p. 57-59.
    "I Was Glad." AntigR (62/63) Sum-Aut 85, p. 117.
    "A Madison Avenue Emergency." AntigR (62/63) Sum-Aut 85,
        p. 116-117.
    "Why Not Stall?" AntigR (62/63) Sum-Aut 85, p. 115.

790. CHARD, John V.
    "Barnegat Decoys." JlNJPo (8:1) 85, p. 17.
    "Beach Rhythms." JlNJPo (8:1) 85, p. 16.
    "Sic Transit Gloria Mundi" (Thus the glory of this world
        passes away). JlNJPo (8:1) 85, p. 15.

791. CHARENTS, Eghishe
    "Dante-esque Legend" (Dedicated to Mihran Markarian, Stepan
        Ghazarian and Ashod Millionchian . . ., tr. by Diana Der
        Hovanessian). GrahamHR (8) Wint 85, p. 48-67.

792. CHARLTON, Lindsey
    "Barb Wire Roses." PoetryCR (6:4) Sum 85, p. 47.
    "The Quality of Light." PoetryCR (6:4) Sum 85, p. 47.

793. CHARTERS, Samuel
    "The Boat -- The Village" (tr. of Tomas Tranströmer).
        Antaeus (55) Aut 85, p. 172.
    "For Mats and Laila" (tr. of Tomas Tranströmer).
        Antaeus (55) Aut 85, p. 173.
    "The Gallery" (tr. of Tomas Tranströmer). Antaeus (55)
        Aut 85, p. 176-179.
    "Gogol" (tr. of Tomas Tranströmer). Antaeus (55) Aut
        85, p. 171.
    "Memory Sees Me" (tr. of Tomas Tranströmer). Antaeus
        (55) Aut 85, p. 174.
    "Molokai" (tr. of Tomas Tranströmer). Antaeus (55) Aut
        85, p. 175.
    "The Station" (tr. of Tomas Tranströmer). Antaeus (55)
        Aut 85, p. 174.
    "The Winter's Glance" (tr. of Tomas Tranströmer).
        Antaeus (55) Aut 85, p. 175.

794. CHASE, Kim
    "Stages." NegC (5:4) Fall 85, p. 93.

795. CHASE, Naomi Feigelson
       "How It Would Happen." <u>Prima</u> (9) 85, p. 75.
       "The Sound of My Voice." <u>Prima</u> (9) 85, p. 75.
796. CHE-LAN-VIEN
       "On the Way Home" (tr. by Mai-Lan and Robert Crawford).
          <u>Verse</u> (1) 84, p. 40.
797. CHEATHAM, Karyn
       "For the Mother on the Cover of the News Magazine with her
          Druze Son in Her Arms." <u>Wind</u> (15:54) 85, p. 9-10.
798. CHECUTI, V.
       "Poem: 120 degrees in the shade." <u>SanFPJ</u> (7:3) 84 [i.e.
          85], p. 36.
       "Poem: There's a video show on the radio." <u>SanFPJ</u> (7:3) 84
          [i.e. 85], p. 36.
       "Sounds of a Nuclear City." <u>SanFPJ</u> (7:3) 84 [i.e. 85], p.
          22-23.
799. CHEN, Jingrong
       "Coming Back from Bada Pass" (tr. by Chiu Yee Ming and
          Martha Kennedy). <u>DenQ</u> (19:3) Wint 85, p. 47-48.
       "Sowing" (tr. by Chiu Yee Ming and Martha Kennedy). <u>DenQ</u>
          (19:3) Wint 85, p. 47-48.
800. CHERNOFF, Maxine
       "Monday." <u>Epoch</u> (34:2) 84-85, p. 99.
       "Then B." <u>Epoch</u> (34:2) 84-85, p. 97-98.
801. CHERRY, Kelly
       "My House." <u>CrossCur</u> (4:2) 84, p. 161.
802. CHESS, Richard
       "After the Bar Mitzvah." <u>PaintedB</u> (26/27) Sum-Fall 85, p.
          53.
       "Introduction to the New Revised Prayer Book" (Excerpt).
          <u>Shen</u> (36:1) 85-86, p. 23.
803. CHETCUTI, Vince
       "Prop-A-Ganda." <u>Rampike</u> (4:2/3) 85-86, p. 99.
CH'I-CHI, Hsin
       <u>See</u> HSIN, Ch'i-chi
804. CHIA, Tao
       "After Rain, I Stay at a Pond-Pagoda of Liu, Minister of
          War" (tr. by Sam Suen). <u>NewL</u> (51:4) Sum 85, p. 144.
       "Lamenting the Monk, P'o-yen" (tr. by Sam Suen). <u>NewL</u>
          (51:4) Sum 85, p. 144.
       "Thoughts on Hearing the Cicada" (tr. by Sam Suen). <u>NewL</u>
          (51:4) Sum 85, p. 144.
805. CHIASSON, Hermenègilde
       "Boredom Cake" (tr. by Martine Jacquot). <u>Germ</u> (9:2) Fall-
          Wint 85, p. 13.
       "Inventory Number Two" (tr. by Martine Jacquot). <u>Germ</u>
          (9:2) Fall-Wint 85, p. 15.
       "Rimbaud from the Bottom of the Night" (tr. by Martine
          Jacquot). <u>Germ</u> (9:2) Fall-Wint 85, p. 14.
806. CHIESURA, Giorgio
       "The Chess Set" (tr. by Rina Ferrarelli). <u>Mund</u> (15:1/2)
          85, p. 169, 171, 173, 175.
       "Gli Scacchi." <u>Mund</u> (15:1/2) 85, p. 168, 170, 172, 174.
       "A Morning" (tr. by Rina Ferrarelli). <u>LitR</u> (29:1) Fall 85,
          p. 95.
       "Useless Things" (tr. by Rina Ferrarelli). <u>LitR</u> (29:1)
          Fall 85, p. 96.
807. CHILL, Maureen
       "Berthelot's River." <u>CanLit</u> (107) Wint 85, p. 101.
808. CHINELLY, Cynthia
       "You." <u>MidAR</u> (5:2) 85, p. 22.
809. CHING, Laureen
       "Fever" (for Mona). <u>HawaiiR</u> (17) Spr 85, p. 97.
810. CHINMOY, Sri
       "You Can Transform." <u>ArizQ</u> (41:4) Wint 85, p. 310.

811. CHIRIRNOS, Eduardo
     "The Last Crusader" (tr. by John Olver Simon). <u>Chelsea</u>
        (44) 85, p. 89.
812. CHIU, Yee Ming
     "Coming Back from Bada Pass" (tr. of Chen Jingrong, w.
        Martha Kennedy). <u>DenQ</u> (19:3) Wint 85, p. 47-48.
     "Sowing" (tr. of Chen Jingrong, w. Martha Kennedy). <u>DenQ</u>
        (19:3) Wint 85, p. 47-48.
813. CHOCK, Eric
     "Lily Pond." <u>HawaiiR</u> (18) Fall 85, p. 62-63.
     "The Meaning of Fishing." <u>HawaiiR</u> (18) Fall 85, p. 64.
814. CHOI, Christine
     "Torture and Culture." <u>SecC</u> (12:2) 84?, p. 14.
815. CHOINIERE, Camille M.
     "So sad, so sweet." <u>WindO</u> (45) Spr 85, p. 13.
CHOL, Chong
     See CHONG, Chol
816. CHONG, Chol
     "Chalice" (Korean Sijo Poem, tr. by Graeme Wilson). <u>DenQ</u>
        (20:1) Sum 85, p. 18.
CHONGJU, So
     See SO, Chongju
817. CHORLTON, David
     "Again I climb down into the crater of fear" (tr. of
        Christine Lavant). <u>NegC</u> (5:2) Spr 85, p. 144.
     "Buy us a grain of reality!" (tr. of Christine Lavant).
        <u>NegC</u> (5:2) Spr 85, p. 140.
     "Crown Prince Rudolph Stands over the Body of Mary Vetsera
        in the Hunting Lodge at Mayerling." <u>WebR</u> (10:2) Fall
        85, p. 47-48.
     "Heaven's Road" (A response to poems by Christine Lavant).
        <u>PoetL</u> (80:3) Fall 85, p. 178.
     "Das Ich Dem Mond Mein Gemüt Uberliess" ("Because I Leave
        My Spirit to the Moon," tr. of Christine Lavant). <u>PoetL</u>
        (80:3) Fall 85, p. 173.
     "Im Finsteren Hohlweg" ("Along the Dark Pass," tr. of
        Christine Lavant). <u>PoetL</u> (80:3) Fall 85, p. 177.
     "In Line." <u>PoeticJ</u> (11) 85, p. 27.
     "Kafka." <u>Abraxas</u> (33) 85, p. 15.
     "Listen closely at the place that remembers you" (tr. of
        Christine Lavant). <u>NegC</u> (5:2) Spr 85, p. 146.
     "Odessa." <u>WebR</u> (10:2) Fall 85, p. 49.
     "So Eine Kopflose Nacht!" ("What a Headless Night," tr. of
        Christine Lavant). <u>PoetL</u> (80:3) Fall 85, p. 172.
     "Strange blood in the heart of the night" (tr. of Christine
        Lavant). <u>NegC</u> (5:2) Spr 85, p. 138.
     "Strenge Nächtigung über dem Ort" ("A Harsh Night's Rest
        over the Village," tr. of Christine Lavant). <u>PoetL</u>
        (80:3) Fall 85, p. 175.
     "Through these glazed afternoons" (tr. of Christine Lavant).
        <u>NegC</u> (5:2) Spr 85, p. 142.
     "Trotzdem der Himmel ein Bleisarg Wird" ("Although Heaven
        Turns," tr. of Christine Lavant). <u>PoetL</u> (80:3) Fall 85,
        p. 174.
     "Weighing Souls." <u>Abraxas</u> (33) 85, p. 15.
     "Zerschlage die Glocke in Meinem Gehör" ("Shatter the Bell
        in My Ear," tr. of Christine Lavant). <u>PoetL</u> (80:3) Fall
        85, p. 176.
818. CHOYCE, Lesley
     "The Apple Tree." <u>PottPort</u> (7) 85-86, p. 52.
     "The Best Watermelon Since the First World War." <u>AntigR</u>
        (62/63) Sum-Aut 85, p. 263.
     "Guerilla Tactics." <u>PottPort</u> (7) 85-86, p. 16.
     "Interruptions from Kubla Khan." <u>CanLit</u> (104) Spr 85, p.
        34.
     "Local History." <u>Germ</u> (9:1) Spr-Sum 85, p. 23.

"Lost Creek." AntigR (62/63) Sum-Aut 85, p. 264.
"The Man Who Borrowed the Bay of Fundy." Germ (9:1) Spr-
    Sum 85, p. 24.
"Poetry Reading: Privateer's Wharf." AntigR (62/63) Sum-
    Aut 85, p. 262.
"The Uses of Emptiness." PottPort (7) 85-86, p. 9.
819. CHRISTENSEN, Erleen J.
    "Uncle Sven" (Honorable Mention Poem, 1984/1985). KanQ
        (17:1/2) Wint-Spr 85, p. 24.
820. CHRISTENSEN, Nadia
    "The Cry" (tr. of Stein Mehren). Ploughs (11:4) 85, p. 246.
    "Little Girls Riding Bikes on the Sidewalk" (tr. of Stein
        Mehren). Ploughs (11:4) 85, p. 247.
821. CHRISTENSEN, Owen
    "Patience" (for Sam). NewL (51:3) Spr 85, p. 40.
822. CHRISTENSEN, Paul
    "Break-Down." Sulfur (14) 85, p. 85-86.
    "Desire." Sulfur (14) 85, p. 87.
823. CHRISTIAN, Eddena
    "Oops!" PoeticJ (12) 85, p. 13.
824. CHRISTINA-MARIE
    "Making Magic." PoetryR (2:2) Ap 85, p. 92.
825. CHRISTOPHER, Nicholas
    "At the Station." Nat (240:23) 15 Je 85, p. 744.
    "Black and White." Nat (240:23) 15 Je 85, p. 744.
    "Icarus." Nat (240:11) 23 Mr 85, p. 341.
    "Leaving Town: A Short Story." NewYorker (61:10) 29 Ap 85,
        p. 116.
    "Lineage." GrandS (5:1) Aut 85, p. 104-105.
    "Losing Altitude." NewYorker (61:2) 4 Mr 85, p. 46.
    "The Public Gardens." NewYorker (61:19) 1 Jl 85, p. 28.
    "Watching the Cane-Cutters." Nat (240:7) 23 F 85, p. 218.
826. CHRISTOPHERSEN, Bill
    "Hardanger Nocturnes." ChiR (35:2) Wint 85, p. 67.
    "Letter from God to Wassily Kandinsky." KanQ (17:3) Sum
        85, p. 16.
CHUANG, Wei
    See WEI, Chuang
827. CHUBBS, Boyd
    "There Is Nothing Else, Here." PottPort (7) 85-86, p. 41.
828. CHUMLEY, Janis
    "Confessional" (After Akmatova). WestCR (19:4) Ap 85, p.
        14.
    "The Crossing." WestCR (19:4) Ap 85, p. 17.
    "End of Summer." WestCR (19:4) Ap 85, p. 15.
    "Everest" (Goddess of the Wind). WestCR (19:4) Ap 85, p.
        16.
    "Just before Rain." WestCR (19:4) Ap 85, p. 13.
829. CHUTE, Robert M.
    "The Convalescent." BelPoJ (36:2) Wint 85-86, p. 27.
    "Forced March to the Front: Poland, July 19, 1919" (A
        Photograph by André Kertèsz). BelPoJ (36:2) Wint 85-
        86, p. 27.
CICCO, Pier Giorgio di
    See Di CICCO, Pier Giorgio
830. CIFUENTES, Julia
    "Hoy Está el Mar Impreciso." LindLM (4:2) Ap-Je 85, p. 3.
831. CIOFFARI, Philip
    "Second Honeymoon." SouthernPR (26, i.e. 25:2) Fall 85, p.
        48.
832. CIORDIA, Javier
    "Elegia sin Nombre." Mairena (7:19) 85, p. 100.
833. CIRINO, Leonard
    "As graces go." Amelia (2:2) O 85, p. 72.
    "White Moon Beach." Amelia (2:1) Ap 85, p. 71.
    "Young man walking on." Amelia (2:1) Ap 85, p. 78.

834. CISNEROS, Antonio
"Apendice del Poema sobre Jonas y los Desalienados" (Para
Ricardo Luna). Inti (18/19) Otoño 83-Prim. 84, p. 277.
"La Araña Cuelga Demasiado Lejos de la Tierra." Inti
(18/19) Otoño 83-Prim. 84, p. 277-278.
"Canto Ceremonial contra un Oso Hormiguero" (Para Javier
Montori). Inti (18/19) Otoño 83-Prim. 84, p. 279-281.
"Consejo para un Viajero." Inti (18/19) Otoño 83-Prim.
84, p. 275-276.
"Cuando el Diablo Me Rondaba Anunciando Tus Rigores." Inti
(18/19) Otoño 83-Prim. 84, p. 276.
"Denuncia de los Elefantes (Demasiado Bien Considerados en
los Ultimos Tiempos)." Inti (18/19) Otoño 83-Prim.
84, p. 282-283.
"Domingo en Santa Cristina de Budapest y Frutería al
Lado." Inti (18/19) Otoño 83-Prim. 84, p. 285-286.
"Karl Marx Died 1883 Aged 65." Inti (18/19) Otoño 83-
Prim. 84, p. 278-279.
"Una Muerte del Niño Jesús" (Chilca 1950). Inti
(18/19) Otoño 83-Prim. 84, p. 284.
"Quo Vadis Cesar Vallejo." Inti (18/19) Otoño 83-Prim.
84, p. 284-285.
"Sol (Bornemouth)." Inti (18/19) Otoño 83-Prim. 84, p.
283-284.
"Tercer Movimiento (Affettuosso) contra la Flor de la
Canela." Inti (18/19) Otoño 83-Prim. 84, p. 281.
835. CISNEROS, Sandra
"Ass" (for David). Imagine (1:2) Wint 84, p. 75-76.
"One Last Poem for Richard." Imagine (1:2) Wint 84, p. 77-
78.
"Postcard to the Lace Man -- The Old Market, Antibes."
Imagine (1:2) Wint 84, p. 76.
"Rodrigo de Barro" (from The Rodrigo Poems). RevChic
(12:1) Spr 84, p. 31-32.
"Rodrigo in the Dark" (from The Rodrigo Poems). RevChic
(12:1) Spr 84, p. 33.
"To Cesare, Goodbye." Imagine (1:2) Wint 84, p. 79.
"Valparaiso" (from The Rodrigo Poems). RevChic (12:1) Spr
84, p. 34-35.
"A Woman Cutting Celery." RevChic (12:1) Spr 84, p. 36.
836. CITINO, David
"Basic Writing: Marion Correctional Institution." PoetryNW
(26:4) Wint 85-86, p. 37-38.
"The Beauticians Who Style the Hair of the Dead."
SouthernPR (25:1) Spr 85, p. 21.
"Believing There's No Cleveland." BelPoJ (35:3) Spr 85, p.
18.
"Flying into Billings to Read My Poetry." KanQ (17:1/2)
Wint-Spr 85, p. 55.
"Letter from the shaman: the Tribe with No Myth." LitR
(29:1) Fall 85, p. 40-41.
"My Father's Violin." WestB (17) 85, p. 70.
"Official Press Release from the Front." WestB (16) 85, p.
62.
"Poem to My Sons on the Feast of St. Simon of Crèpy."
Salm (68/69) Fall-Wint 85-86, p. 13.
"Prosopagnosia." SouthernHR (19:1) Wint 85, p. 22.
"Recluse." CharR (11:1) Spr 85, p. 78-79.
"Sister Mary Appassionata Addresses the Eighth Grade Boys
and Girls during a Field Trip to the Museums of Natural
History and Art." Wind (15:53) 85, p. 5.
"Sister Mary Appassionata Addresses the Psychic Research
Guild of Marion, Ohio." BelPoJ (35:3) Spr 85, p. 19-20.
"Sister Mary Appassionata Addresses the V. F. W." Wind
(15:53) 85, p. 4-5.
"Sister Mary Appassionata Lectures the Biology Class:

Natural Selection and the Evolution of Fear." <u>LitR</u>
(29:1) Fall 85, p. 39.
"Sister Mary Appassionata Lectures the Criminology Class:
Homage to the Coroner." <u>Wind</u> (15:53) 85, p. 4.
"Sister Mary Appassionata Lectures the Eighth Grade Girls:
Cooking with Sweet Basil." <u>NoDaQ</u> (53:3) Sum 85, p. 87.
"Sister Mary Appassionata Lectures the Eighth Grade Girls:
Furrow, Cave, Cowry, Home." <u>Tendril</u> (19/20) 85, p. 102.
"Sister Mary Appassionata Lectures the Ethics Class."
<u>SoDakR</u> (23:2) Sum 85, p. 53.
"Sister Mary Appassionata Lectures the History of Film
Class: Rebel without a Cause." <u>SoDakR</u> (23:2) Sum 85, p.
56.
"Sister Mary Appassionata Lectures the Meteorology Class."
<u>SoDakR</u> (23:2) Sum 85, p. 55.
"Sister Mary Appassionata Lectures the Mortuary Science
Class: Feeding the Dead." <u>MidAR</u> (5:2) 85, p. 26.
"Sister Mary Appassionata Lectures the Studio Art Class:
Doctrines of Nakedness." <u>Tendril</u> (19/20) 85, p. 104-105.
"Sister Mary Appassionata on the Nature of Sound."
<u>Telescope</u> (4:2) Spr 85, p. 49.
"Sister Mary Appassionata Responds to Questions from the
Floor." <u>NoDaQ</u> (53:3) Sum 85, p. 88.
"Sister Mary Appassionata Speaks During the Retreat of the
Eighth Grade Boys and Girls." <u>Tendril</u> (19/20) 85, p.
103.
"Sister Mary Appassionata to the Human Awareness Class: One
Fate Worse." <u>SoDakR</u> (23:2) Sum 85, p. 54.
"Sister Mary Appassionata to the Ornithology Class."
<u>Telescope</u> (4:2) Spr 85, p. 50.
"St. John the Dwarf." <u>KanQ</u> (17:1/2) Wint-Spr 85, p. 56.
"To Kenneth Arnold, Pilot, Who Reported the First Flying
Saucers, June 24, 1947." <u>SouthernHR</u> (19:4) Fall 85, p.
323.
"Watching the Nightly News with the Sound Turned Down."
<u>CentR</u> (29:2) Spr 85, p. 205-206.
837. CLAMPITT, Amy
"Athene." <u>Poetry</u> (145:6) Mr 85, p. 334.
"Babel Aboard the Hellas International Express." <u>GrandS</u>
(4:4) Sum 85, p. 17-20.
"Clotho." <u>RiverS</u> (17) 85, p. 29.
"Dallas - Fort Worth: Redbud and Mistletoe." <u>SouthwR</u>
(70:2) Spr 85, p. 242.
"A Hermit Thrush." <u>NewYorker</u> (61:18) 24 Je 85, p. 32.
"Hippocrene." <u>NewYorker</u> (60:51) 4 F 85, p. 44.
"Knickknack Time." <u>RiverS</u> (18) 85, p. 90.
"Lights in a Cold Season." <u>RiverS</u> (17) 85, p. 30.
"Medusa." <u>Poetry</u> (145:6) Mr 85, p. 331-332.
"On Finding an Abandoned Burial Ground." <u>RiverS</u> (17) 85,
p. 28.
"Perseus." <u>Poetry</u> (145:6) Mr 85, p. 332-334.
"Scrooge in a Manger." <u>OP</u> (38/39) Spr 85, p. 113.
838. CLARE, Josephine
"How shall we know it -- death?" ("Untitled," In Memory of
Sam Ray). <u>NewL</u> (51:3) Spr 85, p. 61.
839. CLARK, Arthur
"Origami." <u>Open24</u> (4) 85, p. 38.
840. CLARK, Brian C.
"Saving the World." <u>PoeticJ</u> (10) 85, p. 10-11.
841. CLARK, G. O.
"Earthbound." <u>WormR</u> (25:4, issue 100) 85, p. 131.
"Turning Eleven." <u>WormR</u> (25:4, issue 100) 85, p. 131.
842. CLARK, J. Wesley
"American Earth." <u>Bogg</u> (53) 85, p. 8.
"The Man Who Loved Rita Coolidge." <u>Bogg</u> (54) 85, p. 31.

843. CLARK, Joanne
   "This man has not spoken for fifteen years." Grain (13:2)
      My 85, p. 4.
844. CLARK, Patricia
   "Second Marriage." Crazy (27) Fall 84, p. 46.
   "Winter Landscape, Missoula." NoAmR (270:3) S 85, p. 57.
845. CLARK, Sheila Seiler (See also SEILER, Sheila)
   "Bits of Perfection." PoeticJ (12) 85, p. 32.
846. CLARK, Tom
   "Bed at Tor House." Zyzzyva (1:3) Fall 85, p. 59.
   "Interesting Losers" (for Bill Veeck). OP (38/39) Spr 85,
      p. 7-8.
   "Jazz for Jack." MoodySI (15) Spr 85, p. 22.
   "Thinking about Pound on Shattuck Avenue." Zyzzyva (1:1)
      Spr 85, p. 134-135.
847. CLARKE, Cheryl
   "IV." Cond (11/12) 85, p. 90.
   "Funeral Thoughts." HangL (47) Spr 85, p. 15-17.
   "Kittatinny." Cond (11/12) 85, p. 93.
   "Living As a Lesbian at 35." Cond (11/12) 85, p. 91-92.
   "Nothing." Cond (11/12) 85, p. 94.
848. CLARKE, Gerald
   "Sonoran Frost." NegC (5:4) Fall 85, p. 90.
849. CLARKE, John
   "Basking in the Beams of Light and Love." Temblor (1) 85,
      p. 15.
   "Beginning the Other Side." Temblor (1) 85, p. 16.
   "Completing the Circuit of Circe." Temblor (1) 85, p. 13.
   "The Furnace of Ophelia." Temblor (1) 85, p. 15.
   "If This Be Heat." Temblor (1) 85, p. 14.
   "The Kouretes Reach the Bed Chamber." Temblor (1) 85, p.
      16.
   "The Torn Leaf." Temblor (1) 85, p. 14.
850. CLARKE, Peter P.
   "Klondike in Winter." CapeR (20:1) Spr 85, p. 29.
851. CLARKE, Terence
   "Passage." MidAR (5:1) 85, p. 12.
852. CLARY, Killarney
   "Green beetles tick against the lighted windows." ParisR
      (27:98) Wint 85, p. 129.
   "He said, 'Remember what it is you are afraid of'." ParisR
      (27:98) Wint 85, p. 130.
853. CLEARY, Brendan
   "Life Chances." Stand (26:4) Aut 85, p. 20.
854. CLEARY, Michael
   "Plastic Flamingos." SouthernPR (26, i.e. 25:2) Fall 85,
      p. 47.
855. CLEARY, Suzanne
   "The Heart as Dog" (for Carita). Geor (39:2) Sum 85, p.
      270-271.
856. CLEMENT, Jennifer Sibley
   "For a Certified Public Accountant." LittleM (14:4) 85, p.
      14.
857. CLEMENTS, Arthur
   "Entering." Blueline (6:2) Wint-Spr 85, p. 39.
858. CLEWELL, David
   "New Year's Eve Letter to Friends." Poetry (145:4) Ja 85,
      p. 227-228.
   "Two Alley Songs for the Vegetable Man: St. Louis." Poetry
      (145:4) Ja 85, p. 224-226.
859. CLIFTON, Lucille
   "Miss Rosie." PoetryR (2:2) Ap 85, p. 20.
860. CLIFTON, Merritt
   "Handyman." Sam (41:4, 164th release) 85, p. 5-11.
861. CLINTON, Robert
   "Boy at Seven." PraS (59:3) Fall 85, p. 57.

"Gypsies." PraS (59:3) Fall 85, p. 56.
"In Church." SenR (15:1) 85, p. 37.
"The Men I Know." Tendril (19/20) 85, p. 106.
"North." PraS (59:3) Fall 85, p. 55.
862. CLOKE, Richard (See also R. C.)
    "Message" (Phase A134, A138). SanFPJ (7:3) 84 [i.e. 85],
        p. 60-61.
    "Message" (Phase A135). SanFPJ (7:4) 85, p. 28.
    "Message" (Phase A136-137). SanFPJ (7:2) 85, p. 62-63.
    "Message" (Phase A139-140). SanFPJ (7:4) 85, p. 93-95.
    "What to Do." SanFPJ (7:4) 85, p. 74-75.
863. COAKLEY, William Leo
    "Invasion of the Animals." OP (38/39) Spr 85, p. 195.
864. COALE, Howard S. L.
    "The Beginning." SenR (15:1) 85, p. 67.
    "Split-Level Tyrant." SenR (15:1) 85, p. 68.
865. COCCIMIGLIO, Vic
    "Another Man." BlueBldgs (9) [85?], p. 7.
    "The Child Who Carries Her Own Grave." BlueBldgs (9)
        [85?], p. 7.
866. COCHRANE, Guy R.
    "Freedom." WormR (25:3, issue 99) 85, p. 105.
    "Plastic Rap." WormR (25:3, issue 99) 85, p. 105.
    "Soap Fable." WormR (25:3, issue 99) 85, p. 105.
867. COCKELREAS, Charles E.
    "Flint and Stone." CutB (24) Spr-Sum 85, p. 42.
868. CODRESCU, Andrei
    "En Passant." Open24 (4) 85, p. 34.
    "Volcanic Dirge & Co." (for e.b.). Open24 (4) 85, p. 34.
869. COE, Dina
    "Anywhere, Now." USl (18/19) Wint 85, p. 4.
    "Burpee's Double and Single French." USl (18/19) Wint 85,
        p. 4.
    "Driving Home through Etra." USl (18/19) Wint 85, p. 4.
870. COFER, Judith Ortiz
    "Claims." PraS (59:1) Spr 85, p. 32.
    "La Fe." RevChic (12:2) Sum 84, p. 24.
    "Holly" (for Tanya at eleven). PassN (6:2) Spr-Sum 85, p.
        9.
    "Letter from a Caribbean Island." Tendril (19/20) 85, p.
        107.
    "Las Malas Lenguas." RevChic (12:2) Sum 84, p. 24.
    "La Maldad." RevChic (12:2) Sum 84, p. 23.
    "My Brother's Son" (for Alexander Miguel, born 10/18/84).
        SoCaR (17:2) Spr 85, p. 74.
    "Night Driving." SoCaR (17:2) Spr 85, p. 74-75.
    "The Other." BilingR (11:2) My-Ag 84 [c1986], p. 43.
    "They Say." BilingR (11:2) My-Ag 84 [c1986], p. 12-13.
    "To My Student." SoCaR (17:2) Spr 85, p. 75.
    "Why There Are No Unicorns." NegC (5:2) Spr 85, p. 122.
    "The Woman Who Was Left at the Altar." PraS (59:1) Spr 85,
        p. 33.
871. COFFEE REPOSA, Carol
    "Mother and Child: An Art Song." Imagine (2:1) Sum 85, p.
        58.
    "Women and Writing" (For Virginia Woolf). Imagine (2:1)
        Sum 85, p. 59.
872. COFFIN, Lyn
    "She Longs for Her White Lover." HolCrit (22:5) D 85, p.
        20.
873. COGGESHALL, Rosanne
    "'Motions of the Heart' --Pascal" (for AG). SouthernR
        (21:2) Spr 85, p. 437-438.
874. COGSWELL, Fred
    "Brave Heart." Stand (26:2) Spr 85, p. 65.
    "Edges." PoetryCR (6:4) Sum 85, p. 11.

"I Have Not Heard." Waves (14:1/2) Fall 85, p. 62.
"Kiltarlity." Quarry (34:4) Aut 85, p. 75-76.
"A Revelation." Descant 50 (16:3) Fall 85, p. 11-12.
"A Tribute." CanLit (105) Sum 85, p. 134-135.
"The Walk." Germ (9:1) Spr-Sum 85, p. 26.
"Wall." Descant 50 (16:3) Fall 85, p. 13-14.
"We Are Those." Waves (14:1/2) Fall 85, p. 62-63.
"Wordsworth Country." PoetryCR (6:4) Sum 85, p. 11.
875. COHEN, Bruce
"The Day Off." LaurelR (19:1) Wint 85, p. 64.
"Driving to Hartford." LaurelR (19:1) Wint 85, p. 63.
876. COHEN, Gerald
"Sonnet: For Teen-Age Dogs in Winter." Wind (15:53) 85, p.
41.
877. COHEN, Marion Deutsche
"Women Who Have Lost Babies." AmerPoR (14:3) My-Je 85, p.
45.
878. COHEN, Miriam A.
"Of Other Dreams" (A Human Potential Fantasy!). PoeticJ
(11) 85, p. 16.
"Rare." PoeticJ (10) 85, p. 25.
879. COLANDER, Valerie Nieman
"At the Union Picnic." LaurelR (19:1) Wint 85, p. 39.
"Baptismal." Wind (15:55) 85, p. 17-18.
880. COLBY, Joan
"Anniversary Song." Amelia (2:1) Ap 85, p. 62.
"The Apples of the Hesperides." HolCrit (22:2) Ap 85, p.
13-14.
"Blue Moon of Ixtab." Poetry (146:1) Ap 85, p. 33-34.
"The Disgrace." NewRena (19) Fall 85, p. 44-45.
"Geese." NewRena (19) Fall 85, p. 31.
"Geography." Poetry (146:1) Ap 85, p. 31.
"Kay" (1938-1982). Poetry (146:1) Ap 85, p. 32-33.
"Sinking in the Botannical Gardens." NewRena (19) Fall 85,
p. 43-44.
"Six White Birds" (Poetry Award). Prima (9) 85, p. 56.
"Symbiosis" (The Phillips Poetry Award, Fall/Winter
1984/85). StoneC (12:2/3) Spr-Sum 85, p. 73.
881. COLCHIE, Thomas
"Death of the Houses in Ouro Preto" (tr. of Carlos Drummond
de Andrade). ParisR (27:97) Fall 85, p. 26-28.
"The Disappearance of Luisa Porto" (tr. of Carlos Drummond
de Andrade). NewYRB (32:19) 5 D 85, p. 25.
"Indications" (tr. of Carlos Drummond de Andrade). NewYRB
(32:12) 18 Jl 85, p. 30.
"Morning Street" (tr. of Carlos Drummond de Andrade).
ParisR (27:97) Fall 85, p. 32-33.
"The Package" (tr. of Carlos Drummond de Andrade). ParisR
(27:97) Fall 85, p. 29-31.
882. COLE, Henri
"The Buoyant Ending." GrandS (5:1) Aut 85, p. 71-72.
"Diana and the Adder." GrandS (5:1) Aut 85, p. 70-71.
"Father's Jewelry Box." Poetry (146:6) S 85, p. 327-328.
"Of Island Animals." Nat (240:14) 13 Ap 85, p. 442.
883. COLE, Kevin
"Fire Heart." JamesWR (2:3) Spr-Sum 85, p. 14.
"Main View Bar." JamesWR (2:3) Spr-Sum 85, p. 14.
"Return." Poetry (146:1) Ap 85, p. 28.
884. COLE, Michael
"286" (tr. of Osip Mandelstam, w. Karen Kimball). MinnR
(N.S. 24) Spr 85, p. 102.
"341" (tr. of Osip Mandelstam, w. Karen Kimball). MinnR
(N.S. 24) Spr 85, p. 102.
"349" (tr. of Osip Mandelstam, w. Karen Kimball). MinnR
(N.S. 24) Spr 85, p. 103.
"For me, winter feels like a belated gift" (tr. of Osip

Mandelstam, w. Karen Kimball). NewL (51:4) Sum 85, p.
    42.
"I don't know when this song began" (131, of Osip
    Mandelstam, w. Karen Kimball). StoneC (12:2/3) Spr-Sum
    85, p. 14-15.
"Poem" (tr. of Osip Mandelstam, w. Karen Kimball). Stand
    (26:2) Spr 85, p. 41.
"Today is yellow-beaked, inexperienced" (329, of Osip
    Mandelstam, w. Karen Kimball). StoneC (12:2/3) Spr-Sum
    85, p. 12-13.
885. COLE, Richard
"In New York the Women Are Dreaming." Telescope (4:2) Spr
    85, p. 35-37.
886. COLE FALTO, Evelyn
"Textos Robados." Mairena (7:19) 85, p. 99.
887. COLEMAN, Andrew
"Alone with Gloucester." AntigR (62/63) Sum-Aut 85, p. 160.
888. COLEMAN, Jane
"Flowering Almond." WestB (16) 85, p. 86-87.
889. COLEMAN, Wanda
"Lady of the Cans." OP (38/39) Spr 85, p. 86.
"On That Stuff That Ain't Nevah Been Long Enuff for No Damn
    Body" (chain braids). BlackALF (19:3) Fall 85, p. 109.
"Refugee from Vacaville." Zyzzyva (1:2) Sum 85, p. 89--90.
890. COLES, Don
"Gone Out Is Part of Sanity." PoetryCR (7:2) Wint 85-86,
    p. 6.
"Small Mortalities." PoetryCR (6:4) Sum 85, p. 15.
"Walking in the Snowy Night." PoetryCR (6:4) Sum 85, p. 15.
891. COLES, Katharine
"At Klondike Bluffs, Utah" (for Kay). PoetryNW (26:1) Spr
    85, p. 23.
"Blessing." Vis (18) 85, p. 28.
"Declension." PoetryNW (26:1) Spr 85, p. 20-22.
"Domestic Comforts." Vis (19) 85, p. 22-23.
"The Gardens." Vis (19) 85, p. 20-21.
"Impulse Shopping." Vis (18) 85, p. 26-27.
"The Rapist's Wife." PoetryNW (26:1) Spr 85, p. 22.
"The Rapist's Wife." Vis (19) 85, p. 24.
892. COLLAZO, Hiram
"??" Mairena (7:19) 85, p. 79.
"Con el Ala Cargada." Mairena (7:19) 85, p. 80.
"Lugar Comun." Mairena (7:19) 85, p. 79.
893. COLLIER, Michael
"Aquarium." NewRep (192:16) 22 Ap 85, p. 41.
"Boats near Luxor." Poetry (146:5) Ag 85, p. 274.
"Tonight." Poetry (146:5) Ag 85, p. 273.
894. COLLIER, Phyllis K.
"The Tides That Pull Us." Nimrod (28:2) Spr-Sum 85, p. 15.
895. COLLINS, Billy
"Inferno." WormR (25:3, issue 99) 85, p. 78.
"Introduction to Poetry." CrossCur (5:3) 85, p. 11.
"The Rival Poet." WormR (25:3, issue 99) 85, p. 77.
"Schoolsville." WormR (25:3, issue 99) 85, p. 78-79.
896. COLLINS, Bridey
"St. Vincent's Home for Unwanted Children." SanFPJ (7:3)
    84 [i.e. 85], p. 17.
"Success." SanFPJ (7:3) 84 [i.e. 85], p. 16.
897. COLLINS, Chris
"Developed Negative." PoetryCR (7:2) Wint 85-86, p. 10.
898. COLLINS, Floyd
"Night Song." SouthernHR (19:1) Wint 85, p. 23.
899. COLLINS, Martha
"3 AM." StoneC (12:2/3) Spr-Sum 85, p. 26.
"Affliction." WestB (17) 85, p. 35.
"Alone, One Must Be Careful" (from A Catastrophe of

Rainbows). StoneC (12:2/3) Spr-Sum 85, p. 29.
"Christmas Visit." Crazy (29) Fall 85, p. 62.
"First Snow." WestB (17) 85, p. 34.
"Her Rage" (from A Catastrophe of Rainbows). StoneC
    (12:2/3) Spr-Sum 85, p. 28-29.
"Inquiry." StoneC (12:2/3) Spr-Sum 85, p. 25.
"May." SoCaR (18:1) Fall 85, p. 62.
"Mozart." QW (21) Fall-Wint 85, p. 78.
"Novel." OP (38/39) Spr 85, p. 98.
"Passage." Swallow (4) 85, p. 60.
"River." SenR (15:2) 85, p. 94-95.
"Summer Visit." Crazy (29) Fall 85, p. 63.
"The Trains Are Running, We Will Not Miss Them" (from A
    Catastrophe of Rainbows). StoneC (12:2/3) Spr-Sum 85,
    p. 27.
"Visitor." ConnPR (3:1) 84, p. 43.
"Waiting." Telescope (4:1) Wint 85, p. 10.
"Warmer." SoCaR (17:2) Spr 85, p. 109.
"Wind Chill." SenR (15:2) 85, p. 96-97.
900. COLLINS, Michael
    "The Cafeteria." MalR (72) S 85, p. 97-98.
    "The Lightning Rods." MalR (72) S 85, p. 94-96.
901. COLLINS, Robert
    "Invisible Runner." ColEng (47:3) Mr 85, p. 263-264.
    "The Jump Shot" (for Walt Meyer). ColEng (47:1) Ja 85, p.
        57.
902. COLOMBO, John Robert
    "Behaviourism" (tr. of George Faludy). PoetryCR (7:1) Aut
        85, p. 17.
903. COLON RUIZ, José O.
    "Canto." Mairena (7:19) 85, p. 96.
904. COLSON, Theodore
    "Two Wisdoms." PoetryCR (7:2) Wint 85-86, p. 25.
905. COLTER, Cyrus
    "Triste Past Tense." NewL (52:1) Fall 85, p. 41-42.
    "The War That Summer." NewL (52:1) Fall 85, p. 42-43.
906. COLVIN, Gerald
    "Japanese Gardens, Ft. Worth." KanQ (17:4) Fall 85, p. 159.
    "Prospography." KanQ (17:4) Fall 85, p. 160.
907. COMBELLICK, Henry
    "Serious Chili." SmPd (22:2) Spr 85, p. 6-7.
908. COMPAGNONE, Luigi
    "And listen: as soon as night turns deep in the sky" (tr. by
        Bruce Cutler). NewL (51:4) Sum 85, p. 168.
    "And look: that street shrine" (tr. by Bruce Cutler). NewL
        (51:4) Sum 85, p. 167.
    "At day's end, when the sun paints the familiar roundness of
        the barrels red" (tr. by Bruce Cutler). NewL (51:4) Sum
        85, p. 166.
    "At times a flight of doves arrives" (tr. by Bruce Cutler).
        NewL (51:4) Sum 85, p. 168.
    "Here in every house there are little family cemeteries"
        (tr. by Bruce Cutler). NewL (51:4) Sum 85, p. 166.
    "The mother keeps the plate of food in a drawer for her son"
        (tr. by Bruce Cutler). NewL (51:4) Sum 85, p. 169.
    "Then one day I meet my father in the street" (tr. by Bruce
        Cutler). NewL (51:4) Sum 85, p. 169.
    "There he is, my father, Oblomov" (tr. by Bruce Cutler).
        NewL (51:4) Sum 85, p. 167.
909. COMPTON, Gayle
    "Barbaric Yawp." Wind (15:53) 85, p. 6-7.
    "Leaving at Daybreak." Wind (15:53) 85, p. 7.
910. CONKLING, Helen
    "There Was an Angel." OhioR (34) 85, p. 43.
911. CONN, Jan
    "The Fabulous Disguise of Ourselves" (Selections: 6 poems).

PoetryCR (7:1) Aut 85, p. 43.
912. CONNELLAN, Leo
"The End of the World." GreenfR (12:3/4) Wint-Spr 85, p.
10.
"Garbage Truck." GreenfR (12:3/4) Wint-Spr 85, p. 11.
"Indians." GreenfR (12:3/4) Wint-Spr 85, p. 11.
"On the Eve of My Becoming a Father." GreenfR (12:3/4)
Wint-Spr 85, p. 10.
"Schwartz, in Three Worlds, Delmore, You Said 'Keep Your
Head'." GreenfR (12:3/4) Wint-Spr 85, p. 12.
"To War Dead." GreenfR (12:3/4) Wint-Spr 85, p. 8.
"What Can I Leave for You to Feel of Me." GreenfR (12:3/4)
Wint-Spr 85, p. 9.
913. CONNOLLY, Geraldine
"Climbing Up to the Attic" (for Lish Mahler). PoetL (80:1)
Spr 85, p. 44.
"The Hardware of the Brain." MichQR (24:2) Spr 85, p. 291-
292.
914. CONOLEY, Gillian
"Alias." Ploughs (11:1) 85, p. 60.
"The Cousin at the Funeral." Tendril (19/20) 85, p. 113.
"Insomnia." Tendril (19/20) 85, p. 112.
"New in Town." Tendril (19/20) 85, p. 108-109.
"Patsy Cline." Tendril (19/20) 85, p. 110.
"Some Gangster Pain." Ploughs (11:1) 85, p. 59.
"Woman Speaking inside Film Noir." Tendril (19/20) 85, p.
111.
915. CONOVER, Carl
"The Madagascar Dragon Plant." HolCrit (22:5) D 85, p. 19.
916. CONRAD, David
"The Visitor." AntigR (61) Spr 85, p. 104.
917. CONRAD, James
"Harvest." JamesWR (2:1) Fall 84, p. 7.
"May Day." JamesWR (2:1) Fall 84, p. 7.
"The Tattoo" (for Carol, who now claims to know better).
JamesWR (2:1) Fall 84, p. 7.
918. CONRAD, Nick
"The Cyanean Sea." LitR (28:4) Sum 85, p. 572.
"Now Seven Years Have Passed." LitR (28:4) Sum 85, p. 572.
919. CONSTANTINE, David
"At Dinas." PoetryCR (6:3) Spr 85, p. 33.
"Sunken Cities" (For Lynne Williamson). Poetry (146:4) Jl
85, p. 200.
"Wet lilac, drifts of hail." PoetryCR (6:4) Sum 85, p. 42.
920. CONTOSKI, Victor
"Rescued Graines" (11 poems, tr. of Marek Baterowicz, The
Mid-American Review Translation Chapbook Series, Number
3). MidAR (5:1) 85, p. 81-103.
921. CONTRERAS VEGA, Mario Enrique
"Escritos para el Futuro." Mairena (7:19) 85, p. 10.
"Esta Ciudad a La Que Amo." Mairena (7:19) 85, p. 11.
"Metamorfosis." Mairena (7:19) 85, p. 8-9.
"Sueño." Mairena (7:19) 85, p. 11.
"Tarea." Mairena (7:19) 85, p. 10.
"El Tiempo de las Malas Noticias." Mairena (7:19) 85, p. 7-
8.
"Los Tiempos Pasados." Mairena (7:19) 85, p. 9.
922. CONWAY, Jack
"Common Ground" (An Italian Sonnet). Amelia (2:1) Ap 85,
p. 78.
"Harvest." PoeticJ (10) 85, p. 17.
"Spring House, Block Island." Blueline (7:1) Sum-Fall 85,
p. 26-27.
923. COOK, Gregory
"Epilogue: Among the Living." PottPort (7) 85-86, p. 27.
"My Family" (After Seamus Heaney's Selected Poems).

PottPort (7) 85-86, p. 26.
"Stranger." PottPort (7) 85-86, p. 26-27.
924. COOK-LYNN, Elizabeth
"Ghazal #1." GreenfR (12:3/4) Wint-Spr 85, p. 89.
"Ghazal #2." GreenfR (12:3/4) Wint-Spr 85, p. 89.
"Ghazal #3." GreenfR (12:3/4) Wint-Spr 85, p. 90.
"Spider As She Used to Be" (and might someday be again).
GreenfR (12:3/4) Wint-Spr 85, p. 93-96.
"We Stood." GreenfR (12:3/4) Wint-Spr 85, p. 92.
"The World He Lived In." GreenfR (12:3/4) Wint-Spr 85, p.
91.
925. COOKE, Robert P.
"They Pass By in the Dark, Dry Air." SouthernPR (25:1) Spr
85, p. 45.
926. COOLEY, Dennis
"After the Dance." PoetryCR (7:2) Wint 85-86, p. 21.
"Behind the Door." Dandel (12:2) 85, p. 31-33.
"Burnt Out." PoetryCR (7:2) Wint 85-86, p. 21.
"Dear Valentine." PraF (6:1) Wint 85, p. 51.
"Driving into Blues." PoetryCR (7:2) Wint 85-86, p. 21.
"Feeding the Pigs." PoetryCR (7:2) Wint 85-86, p. 21.
"The Glass Bead Game I." Dandel (12:2) 85, p. 34-35.
"I Met a Poem." Quarry (34:4) Aut 85, p. 83.
"Love Potion No 9." PoetryCR (7:2) Wint 85-86, p. 21.
"Youre in My Dreams Nightly." PraF (6:1) Wint 85, p. 50.
927. COOLEY, Peter
"Fourteen Lines." BlackWR (12:1) Fall 85, p. 40.
"The Girl before the Mirror." SewanR (93:1) Wint 85, p. 57-
58.
"Old Couple." NewOR (12:1) Spr 85, p. 57.
"The Southern Demons." Shen (36:1) 85-86, p. 27.
"A Spring Poem." NewOR (12:1) Spr 85, p. 98.
"Tableau." PraS (59:2) Sum 85, p. 60.
"To a Daughter." CrossCur (4:3) 84, p. 85.
"Under Heaven." PraS (59:2) Sum 85, p. 59-60.
"Van Gogh, 'Orchard with Peach Blossom'." QW (20) Spr-Sum
85, p. 114.
"Van Gogh, 'Pieta'." ThRiPo (25/26) 85, p. 24.
"Van Gogh, 'Self-Portrait'." SouthernPR (26, i.e. 25:2)
Fall 85, p. 23.
"Van Gogh, 'Still Life with Open Bible'." ThRiPo (25/26)
85, p. 23.
"Van Gogh, 'The Loom'." ThRiPo (25/26) 85, p. 22.
"Van Gogh, 'The Potato Eaters'." GeoR (39:1) Spr 85, p. 89.
928. COOLIDGE, Clark
"Coasts." Temblor (1) 85, p. 54.
"Dimes Are Loose, and Other Sense." Temblor (1) 85, p. 50.
"Hommage à Ron Padgett." Temblor (1) 85, p. 51.
"A Residue." Temblor (1) 85, p. 53.
"Rugged Loaf off Coal" (after the Captain's Ice Cream for
Crow). Temblor (1) 85, p. 50.
"Strike of the Ability." Temblor (1) 85, p. 52.
929. COOLIDGE, Miles
"What." HarvardA (119:2) D 85, p. 37.
930. COONEY, Ellen
"Princess Mary Stuart of Orange Listens to Purcell's Funeral
Music for Her Niece Queen Mary II." PoetL (80:2) Sum
85, p. 82-83.
"Reagan's Twelve Days of Christmas." SecC (12:1) 84, p. 7.
"Witch at the Stake." PoetL (80:2) Sum 85, p. 84.
931. COOP, Mahlon
"Birdcall." KanQ (17:4) Fall 85, p. 70.
932. COOPER, Allan
"Remembering Issa's Poem about the Foal." AntigR (62/63)
Sum-Aut 85, p. 46.

933. COOPER, Daniel
     "Memorial Day." <u>PaintedB</u> (26/27) Sum-Fall 85, p. 51.
934. COOPER, Darius
     "Bread." <u>GreenfR</u> (13:1/2) Fall-Wint 85, p. 174-175.
     "Touch Wood." <u>GreenfR</u> (13:1/2) Fall-Wint 85, p. 173-174.
935. COOPER, Jane Todd
     "The Animated Woman in the Mirror." <u>PoetL</u> (80:2) Sum 85,
         p. 91-92.
936. COOPER, Wyn
     "Perdido." <u>WestHR</u> (39:4) Wint 85, p. 357-358.
937. COOPERMAN, Robert
     "The Camera's Eye." <u>CapeR</u> (20:1) Spr 85, p. 7.
     "Early Memory." <u>HolCrit</u> (22:5) D 85, p. 16.
     "Eating Habits." <u>GWR</u> (6:1) 85?, p. 20.
     "Eavesdropping." <u>CutB</u> (23) Fall-Wint 85, p. 60.
     "Father Kriek Sees Mary McCormick after Her Confession."
         <u>CumbPR</u> (5:1) Fall 85, p. 23.
     "Father Matthews Hears the Confession of Mary McCormick."
         <u>CumbPR</u> (5:1) Fall 85, p. 21-22.
     "The Geology Teacher." <u>WindO</u> (45) Spr 85, p. 21.
     "Heaven" (For Earle Wescott). <u>NegC</u> (5:3) Sum 85, p. 88-89.
     "Heredity." <u>GWR</u> (6:1) 85?, p. 22.
     "Lord Randal's Wife Tells Her Story." <u>HiramPoR</u> (39) Fall-
         Wint 85, p. 8-9.
     "A Mother's Love." <u>Wind</u> (15:54) 85, p. 11.
     "My Cousin's Heart Attack." <u>CumbPR</u> (5:1) Fall 85, p. 19-20.
     "My Only Meeting with Thomas Carlyle." <u>WindO</u> (45) Spr 85,
         p. 22.
     "Renoir's Women." <u>GWR</u> (6:1) 85?, p. 21.
     "Reprieve." <u>SouthernPR</u> (25:1) Spr 85, p. 19.
     "A Small Storm." <u>CumbPR</u> (5:1) Fall 85, p. 18.
     "Telling Life from Art." <u>CutB</u> (23) Fall-Wint 85, p. 58-59.
     "Visits of Obligation." <u>Confr</u> (29) Wint 85, p. 149.
     "Wordsworth's Cuckoo Clock." <u>ColEng</u> (47:6) O 85, p. 609-
         610.
938. COPELAND, R. F. (<u>See also</u> COPELAND, Robert)
     "Christmas." <u>JamesWR</u> (2:1) Fall 84, p. 3.
939. COPELAND, Robert (<u>See also</u> COPELAND, R. F.)
     "Around Art Students" (first place poetry entry in the
         Northstar competition). <u>JamesWR</u> (2:3) Spr-Sum 85, p. 4.
     "We Visited Dresden" (first place poetry entry in the
         Northstar competition). <u>JamesWR</u> (2:3) Spr-Sum 85, p. 4.
940. CORBETT, William
     "Biking: Fog." <u>Oink</u> (19) 85, p. 78.
     "Cross My Heart." <u>Imagine</u> (1:2) Wint 84, p. 103-104.
     "Reading." <u>Agni</u> (22) 85, p. 146-147.
     "The Shoe." <u>Imagine</u> (1:2) Wint 84, p. 105-107.
     "Smoke." <u>Oink</u> (19) 85, p. 79-80.
941. CORDERO, Ricardo
     "Me Esperaras." <u>Mairena</u> (7:19) 85, p. 77-78.
     "La Muerte de Ate." <u>Mairena</u> (7:19) 85, p. 78.
     "La Muerte de Piro." <u>Mairena</u> (7:19) 85, p. 77.
942. CORDING, Robert
     "Christmas, 1954." <u>QW</u> (21) Fall-Wint 85, p. 97.
     "Palm Gardens." <u>QW</u> (20) Spr-Sum 85, p. 116-117.
943. CORMAN, Cid
     "Bunting." <u>Conjunc</u> (8) 85, p. 195.
     "Three Things on the Commode" (tr. of Dominique Fourcade w.
         the author). <u>Origin</u> (Series 5:5) Spr 85, p. 74-76.
     "The Unangular Sky" (Selections: 38, 42, 45, tr. of
         Dominique Fourcade w. the author). <u>Origin</u> (Series 5:5)
         Spr 85, p. 67-74.
CORMIER-SHEKERJIAN, Regina de
     <u>See</u> DeCORMIER-SHEKERJIAN, Regina
944. CORN, Alfred
     "Before They Wake." <u>Nat</u> (240:11) 23 Mr 85, p. 340.

"From the United Provinces, 1632-1677." <u>Shen</u> (36:1) 85-86,
    p. 34.
945. CORNELL, Birdtee
    "When a Liar Cooked a Lie." <u>OP</u> (38/39) Spr 85, p. 200.
946. CORPI, Lucha
    "Ambito y Jornada." <u>Imagine</u> (1:2) Wint 84, p. 82-84.
    "Mariana." <u>Imagine</u> (1:2) Wint 84, p. 80-81.
    "Marina" (tr. by Catherine Rodriguez-Nieto). <u>AmerPoR</u>
        (14:4) Jl-Ag 85, p. 31.
    "The Protocol of Vegetables" (tr. by Catherine Rodriguez-
        Nieto). <u>AmerPoR</u> (14:4) Jl-Ag 85, p. 31.
    "Voces." <u>Imagine</u> (1:2) Wint 84, p. 80.
947. CORRIE, Dan
    "The Endless Insistence." <u>IndR</u> (8:3) Fall 85, p. 93-98.
    "The Sunbathers." <u>SoDakR</u> (23:2) Sum 85, p. 67.
    "A Wall of Bees." <u>CapeR</u> (20:2) Fall 85, p. 42.
948. CORRIGAN, Paul
    "Into the Woods." <u>Blueline</u> (7:1) Sum-Fall 85, p. 17.
949. CORT, John
    "In the Library: Studying for Generals" (after Rexroth).
        <u>Abraxas</u> (33) 85, p. 34.
950. CORTAZAR, Enrique
    "Agosto." <u>Imagine</u> (1:2) Wint 84, p. 123.
    "Park Street y la Tarde" (Boston, 1981). <u>Imagine</u> (1:2)
        Wint 84, p. 124.
    "Tarde en Cambridge con Michelle y la Noche." <u>Imagine</u>
        (1:2) Wint 84, p. 125.
951. CORTAZAR, Julio
    "Companion" (1981, tr. by Zoe Anglesey). <u>RiverS</u> (18) 85,
        p. 106.
952. CORTES CABAN, David
    "Cuando el Amor se Acaba." <u>Mairena</u> (7:19) 85, p. 72-73.
    "Diles Que Ya No Puedo Sujetarme a Tu Sombra." <u>Mairena</u>
        (7:19) 85, p. 73-74.
    "Es Inutil la Ira." <u>Mairena</u> (7:19) 85, p. 72.
    "Morir No Es Esta Oscura Fabula." <u>Mairena</u> (7:19) 85, p. 73.
    "Pero Este Es Mi Pueblo" (a Diana Ramírez de Arellano).
        <u>Mairena</u> (7:19) 85, p. 74.
953. CORVAIA, Vince
    "Calm at Harvest." <u>CimR</u> (72) Jl 85, p. 40.
    "Love Poem." <u>KanQ</u> (17:1/2) Wint-Spr 85, p. 91.
    "Renting a Bathtub." <u>KanQ</u> (17:1/2) Wint-Spr 85, p. 91-92.
    "Taking Liberties." <u>KanQ</u> (17:1/2) Wint-Spr 85, p. 90.
954. CORY, James
    "Abandoned Gun Emplacement, Cape May Point." <u>PaintedB</u> (25)
        Spr 85, p. 39.
    "Dakota." <u>PaintedB</u> (25) Spr 85, p. 44-45.
    "Driving through Central Pennsylvania: Suite." <u>PaintedB</u>
        (25) Spr 85, p. 29-30.
    "Drunk Dream." <u>PaintedB</u> (25) Spr 85, p. 38.
    "For Frank Robinson." <u>PaintedB</u> (25) Spr 85, p. 31-33.
    "Ginkgo." <u>PaintedB</u> (25) Spr 85, p. 47.
    "Homeless, 30th St. Station, Philadelphia." <u>PaintedB</u> (25)
        Spr 85, p. 46.
    "Die-Off at Higbee Beach." <u>PaintedB</u> (25) Spr 85, p. 40.
    "Postcard." <u>PaintedB</u> (25) Spr 85, p. 34.
    "Someone." <u>PaintedB</u> (25) Spr 85, p. 35.
    "Teeth." <u>PaintedB</u> (25) Spr 85, p. 42-43.
    "When I Saw You." <u>PaintedB</u> (25) Spr 85, p. 36.
    "Who Are They?" <u>PaintedB</u> (25) Spr 85, p. 41.
    "Who I'll Be." <u>PaintedB</u> (25) Spr 85, p. 37.
955. COSENS, Susan M.
    "Hilde's Birth, Pappy's Diary, March 4, 1914." <u>RagMag</u>
        (4:1) Spr 85, p. 10.
    "Making Pickles." <u>CapeR</u> (20:2) Fall 85, p. 3.
    "Woman's Slope" (Oberg Mountain Trail, Minnesota). <u>CapeR</u>

(20:2) Fall 85, p. 2.
956. COSIER, Tony
"The Morningstone." CapeR (20:2) Fall 85, p. 50.
"William Blackthorn Lived in a Leanto on a Hill." PoetryCR
(6:4) Sum 85, p. 44.
957. COSTA, Marithelma
"Bien Sabemos" (a Garnata quinientos años mas tarde).
LindLM (4:1) Ja-Mr 85, p. 25.
COTEAU, Delano Abdul Malik de
See MALIK (DELANO ABDUL MALIK DE COTEAU)
958. COTTAGE, Steve
"They'll Plant Tulips around the Smoke House." Vis (18)
85, p. 11.
959. COTTAM, Mary
"Only a Rose." Bogg (54) 85, p. 17-18.
960. COTTERILL, Sarah
"Among Other Places They Leave Their Bodies." AmerPoR
(14:1) Ja-F 85, p. 17.
"Susan at the State Hospital." KanQ (17:1/2) Wint-Spr 85,
p. 134-135.
961. COTTON, Rickey
"Somehow It's True" (To My Father). Wind (15:54) 85, p. 5.
962. COUCH, Larry
"Accident" (for David). Vis (17) 85, p. 35.
963. COULTER, Page
"Rain." PoetryR (2:2) Ap 85, p. 79.
964. COURT, Wesli
"Letter to a Hall-of-Famer" (First Award Poem, 1984/1985).
KanQ (17:1/2) Wint-Spr 85, p. 8-9.
965. COUZYN, Jeni
"A Death in Winter" (for Maureen). PoetryCR (6:3) Spr 85,
p. 28.
966. COWSER, Robert
"For the Joads and Their Descendants." EngJ (74:2) F 85,
p. 39.
967. COX, C. B. (See also COX, Carol)
"Foundlings." SewanR (93:2) Spr 85, p. 187-188.
"LSD." SewanR (93:2) Spr 85, p. 188.
"Threshing." SewanR (93:2) Spr 85, p. 189.
968. COX, Carol (See also COX, C. B.)
"Domesticity" (December 28). CimR (71) Ap 85, p. 52.
969. COX, Celeste O.
"King of the White Swan Hotel." PoeticJ (9) 85, p. 34.
970. COY, David
"A Farmer Remembers His Former Wife after Seeing Her Name in
the Phonebook." SpoonRQ (10:4) Fall 85, p. 50.
"Proposing a Toast." SpoonRQ (10:4) Fall 85, p. 43.
"The Witch of Middlefork." SpoonRQ (10:2) Spr 85, p. 52.
971. COZY, David
"Now." SanFPJ (7:3) 84 [i.e. 85], p. 24.
"Work." SanFPJ (7:4) 85, p. 49.
CRABBE, Chris Wallace
See WALLACE-CRABBE, Chris
972. CRAGO, William
"Memo to MacLeish" (Copy to Keats and Thomas). Wind
(15:53) 85, p. 3.
973. CRAIG, Christine
"Day of the Ibo." GreenfR (12:3/4) Wint-Spr 85, p. 143.
"A House with a Bridge." GreenfR (12:3/4) Wint-Spr 85, p.
142-143.
974. CRAIG, David
"For the Duration." NegC (5:1) Wint 85, p. 20.
975. CRAIG, Dennis
"By the Hudson, New York." GreenfR (12:3/4) Wint-Spr 85,
p. 145-146.
"Roots" (revisited from Jamaica, with apologies to Alex

Haley). <u>GreenfR</u> (12:3/4) Wint-Spr 85, p. 146-147.
976. CRAMER, Steven
"Ailanthus." <u>AntR</u> (43:4) Fall 85, p. 468.
"Garlic." <u>SenR</u> (15:1) 85, p. 71-72.
"To Francis Jammes." <u>AntR</u> (43:4) Fall 85, p. 469.
977. CRANE, Margaret
"After-Effects." <u>Stand</u> (26:2) Spr 85, p. 64.
978. CRANSTON, Philip
"The Sleeping Lake" (tr. of Jules Supervielle). <u>GrahamHR</u>
(9) Fall 85, p. 88.
"Sleepless" (tr. of Jules Supervielle). <u>GrahamHR</u> (9) Fall
85, p. 90-91.
"This Pure Child" (tr. of Jules Supervielle). <u>GrahamHR</u> (9)
Fall 85, p. 87.
"Whisper in Agony" (tr. of Jules Supervielle). <u>GrahamHR</u>
(9) Fall 85, p. 89.
979. CRAVEN, Rodney A.
"The Luminiferous Ether." <u>CarolQ</u> (37:3) Spr 85, p. 25.
980. CRAWFORD, John W.
"I Prefer Not To." <u>ArizQ</u> (41:2) Sum 85, p. 151.
981. CRAWFORD, Robert
"Christmas Night 1984." <u>NegC</u> (5:1) Wint 85, p. 46.
"Clearances." <u>Verse</u> (1) 84, p. 28.
"Dishes." <u>Verse</u> (4) 85, p. 42.
"On the Way Home" (tr. of Che-Lan-Vien, w. Mai-lan). <u>Verse</u>
(1) 84, p. 40.
"Passages." <u>Verse</u> (4) 85, p. 40-41.
982. CREELEY, Robert
"Life" (for Basil). <u>Conjunc</u> (8) 85, p. 198.
"Old." <u>Stand</u> (26:2) Spr 85, p. 4.
"Picture." <u>Stand</u> (26:2) Spr 85, p. 4.
983. CREESE, Richard
"Assent." <u>PraS</u> (59:4) Wint 85, p. 97.
"Bluebell Canyon." <u>PraS</u> (59:4) Wint 85, p. 100-101.
"Wild Goats." <u>PraS</u> (59:4) Wint 85, p. 98-99.
984. CREIGHTON, Jane
"The Bone Bank." <u>Waves</u> (14:1/2) Fall 85, p. 95.
985. CRESPO, José Antonio
"A Vicente Aleixandre" (In Memoriam). <u>Mairena</u> (7:19) 85,
p. 66.
986. CREW, Louie
"Auction." <u>PoetL</u> (80:2) Sum 85, p. 89-90.
"Surveillance 20 Years Ago." <u>Swallow</u> (4) 85, p. 72.
"This Boy." <u>JamesWR</u> (3:1) Fall 85, p. 15.
987. CREWS, Judson
"The Delays That Dimmed the Lights Out." <u>WormR</u> (25:3,
issue 99) 85, p. 107.
"I Once Did a Hilariously Funny." <u>WormR</u> (25:3, issue 99)
85, p. 107.
"It's a Kind of Plague That Diseases My Mind." <u>WormR</u>
(25:3, issue 99) 85, p. 106.
988. CRICKILLON, Jacques
"Face of amber belly of jade wife of bitterness" (tr. by
Julie Besonen). <u>Mund</u> (15:1/2) 85, p. 137.
"Visage d'ambre ventre de jade épouse d'amertume." <u>Mund</u>
(15:1/2) 85, p. 136.
989. CRINNIN, Gerry
"Animal, Cries of." <u>WestB</u> (16) 85, p. 45.
990. CRIST, Vonnie
"Trundle On." <u>Open24</u> (4) 85, p. 57.
991. CROFT, Patricia
"Tea Time." <u>Amelia</u> (2:1) Ap 85, p. 41.
992. CROGHAN, Melissa
"Communion." <u>MassR</u> (26:1) Spr 85, p. 10.
993. CRONIN, Orion
"Dead Elm." <u>Vis</u> (18) 85, p. 10.

994. CROOKER, Barbara
    "Skating after School." WestB (17) 85, p. 106-107.
    "Small Game Season." StoneC (13:1/2) Fall-Wint 85-86, p.
        62.
995. CROOKES, Joyce
    "Renewal." Sam (42:4, 168th release) 85, p. 46.
    "Teri." Sam (42:3, 167th release) 85, p. 38.
996. CROSBY, Philip D.
    "Spenard Lake." PoeticJ (12) 85, p. 22.
    "Two Sonnets to Stage Fright." Amelia (2:2) O 85, p. 83.
997. CROSS, Ronald Anthony
    "American Fairy Tales" (No. 1 The Poor Little Black Girl).
        Rampike (4:2/3) 85-86, p. 84.
998. CROW, Mary
    "Blue and White." WoosterR (3) Spr 85, p. 42.
    "Derivations of light" (tr. of Roberto Juarroz). Mund
        (15:1/2) 85, p. 187, 189.
    "End of the World" (tr. of Jorge Teillier). NewL (51:4)
        Sum 85, p. 108.
    "A fly walks head down on the roof" (To Paul Eluard, tr. of
        Roberto Juarroz). Mund (15:1/2) 85, p. 189, 191.
    "The Last Blackberry." PraS (59:3) Fall 85, p. 28.
    "Life sketches a tree" (tr. of Roberto Juarroz). Mund
        (15:1/2) 85, p. 185, 187.
    "More Remains Unspoken." PraS (59:3) Fall 85, p. 27.
    "Night Train." HawaiiR (18) Fall 85, p. 83-84.
    "Platforms" (tr. of Jorge Teillier). NewL (51:4) Sum 85,
        p. 107.
    "Rite" (tr. of Marco Martos). Mund (15:1/2) 85, p. 141.
999. CROWELL, Doug
    "My Mother's Eyes." LaurelR (19:1) Wint 85, p. 43.
1000. CROZIER, Lorna
    "After Watching the Late Night News." Waves (14:1/2) Fall
        85, p. 84.
    "Deer Mouse." PraF (6:3) Sum 85, p. 17.
    "Driving Home." PraF (6:3) Sum 85, p. 17.
    "Flight of Cranes." Waves (14:1/2) Fall 85, p. 85.
    "The Garden Going on Without Us" (Selections: 7 poems).
        PoetryCR (7:1) Aut 85, p. 5.
    "The Horizon Is a Line." Waves (14:1/2) Fall 85, p. 84.
    "In the Cypress Hills." Waves (14:1/2) Fall 85, p. 85.
    "Jameson's Irish Whiskey" (for Sean). Dandel (12:1) 85,
        p. 11.
    "Searching for the Poem." Waves (14:1/2) Fall 85, p. 82-
        83.
    "When the Sky Got Sick." PraF (6:3) Sum 85, p. 16.
1001. CRUMMETT, Vance
    "Improvisation." NewL (51:3) Spr 85, p. 118.
1002. CRUZ, Emilio
    "Night Store." RiverS (17) 85, p. 58.
1003. CRUZ, Grethel
    "Caferino the Peasant" (tr. by Kent Johnson). MinnR (N.S.
        25) Fall 85, p. 42-43.
1004. CRUZ, Juana Inés de la, Sor
    "Philosophical Satire" (tr. by Amanda Powell). Imagine
        (2:1) Sum 85, p. 95-96.
1005. CRUZ, Pete
    "Voodoo Doll." SnapD (8:2) Spr 85, p. 36-37.
1006. CRUZKATZ, Ida
    "The Hands." WindO (45) Spr 85, p. 18.
    "Questioning the Host." WindO (45) Spr 85, p. 19.
1007. CRYER, Jim
    "Painting Bamboo" (tr. of Hsü Wei). CarolQ (37:3) Spr
        85, p. 77.
    "Peach Leaf Ferry" (tr. of Hsü Wei). CarolQ (37:3) Spr
        85, p. 76.

CSAMER 98

1008. CSAMER, Mary Ellen
    "Neon/Off." PoetryCR (6:4) Sum 85, p. 47.
1009. CSOORI, Sándor
    "The First Moment of Resurrection" (tr. by Ivan Halasz de
        Beky). Rampike (4:2/3) 85-86, p. 16.
    "Fragment from the Seventies" (tr. by Ivan Halasz de Beky).
        Rampike (4:2/3) 85-86, p. 16.
    "In the Root Cellar" (tr. by Nicholas Kolumban). NewL
        (51:4) Sum 85, p. 36.
    "Message" (tr. by Ivan Halasz de Beky). Rampike (4:2/3)
        85-86, p. 16.
1010. CUADRA, Pablo Antonio
    "September: The Shark" (tr. by Steven White). NowestR
        (23:1) 85, p. 95-113.
    "Septiembre: El Tiburon." NowestR (23:1) 85, p. 94-112.
1011. CULLY, Barbara
    "Eve." AmerPoR (14:5) S-O 85, p. 30.
    "In This Way We" (for G. Threefoot). AmerPoR (14:5) S-O
        85, p. 30.
1012. CUMMING, Peter
    "Letter from Away." PottPort (7) 85-86, p. 39.
    "Song of Radiation." PottPort (7) 85-86, p. 42.
1013. CUMMINGS, Darcy
    "Meditations on Instructions for Surviving a Shark Attack"
        (Selections: 2-5). CarolQ (38:1) Fall 85, p. 14-16.
1014. CUMMINS, Richard
    "The Supplication." NoAmR (270:2) Je 85, p. 8.
CUMPIAN, Cynthia Gallaher
    See GALLAHER-CUMPIAN, Cynthia
1015. CUMPIANO, Ina
    "Chickens Stink." AntR (43:2) Spr 85, p. 206-207.
    "Getting the Boat Ready." BilingR (11:2) My-Ag 84
        [c1986], p. 17-18.
1016. CUNNINGHAM, J. V.
    "Refrain." OP (38/39) Spr 85, p. 186.
    "Trees." OP (38/39) Spr 85, p. 186.
1017. CUNNINGHAM, James W.
    "The Want to Write." EngJ (74:1) Ja 85, p. 84.
1018. CURRAN, Ann
    "Lace Curtain Dreams." ThRiPo (25/26) 85, p. 25-26.
1019. CURRIER, Douglas K.
    "Welcome." LaurelR (19:1) Wint 85, p. 40.
1020. CURTIS, Tony
    "Worm." Stand (26:4) Aut 85, p. 65.
1021. CUSHING, James
    "Blue Room." WindO (45) Spr 85, p. 39.
1022. CUTHBERT, Terry
    "Text 77." Bogg (54) 85, p. 17.
1023. CUTLER, Bruce
    "And listen: as soon as night turns deep in the sky" (tr.
        of Luigi Compagnone). NewL (51:4) Sum 85, p. 168.
    "And look: that street shrine" (tr. of Luigi Compagnone).
        NewL (51:4) Sum 85, p. 167.
    "At day's end, when the sun paints the familiar roundness
        of the barrels red" (tr. of Luigi Compagnone). NewL
        (51:4) Sum 85, p. 166.
    "At times a flight of doves arrives" (tr. of Luigi
        Compagnone). NewL (51:4) Sum 85, p. 168.
    "Black Market, 1944" (from The Book of Naples). BelPoJ
        (36:2) Wint 85-86, p. 12-15.
    "Here in every house there are little family cemeteries"
        (tr. of Luigi Compagnone). NewL (51:4) Sum 85, p. 166.
    "Landscape with Food, 1944" (from The Book of Naples).
        Northeast (Series 4:1) Sum 85, p. 12.
    "The mother keeps the plate of food in a drawer for her
        son" (tr. of Luigi Compagnone). NewL (51:4) Sum 85, p.

169.
"Nightingales" (from The Book of Naples). _Northeast_
    (Series 4:1) Sum 85, p. 11.
"The Stonk, 1943" (from The Book of Naples). _Northeast_
    (Series 4:1) Sum 85, p. 10.
"Then one day I meet my father in the street" (tr. of Luigi
    Compagnone). _NewL_ (51:4) Sum 85, p. 169.
"There he is, my father, Oblomov" (tr. of Luigi
    Compagnone). _NewL_ (51:4) Sum 85, p. 167.
1024. CUTTS, Simon
"Ode: Schubert Impromptu in F Minor." _Conjunc_ (8) 85, p.
    213.
1025. CUZA MALE, Belkis
"I Buy Old Furniture: Chairs, Beds, Bed Springs" (tr. by
    Pamela Carmell). _NewEngR_ (7:4) Sum 85, p. 491.
"My Mother's Homeland" (tr. by Pamela Carmell). _NewEngR_
    (7:4) Sum 85, p. 492.
"Still Life" (tr. by Pamela Carmell). _NewEngR_ (7:4) Sum
    85, p. 493.
1026. CYRUS, Della
"Gone." _Ploughs_ (11:1) 85, p. 62.
"Mirage." _Ploughs_ (11:1) 85, p. 61-62.
"River Trip." _Ploughs_ (11:1) 85, p. 63-64.
1027. CZAPLA, Cathy Young
"Envoy." _RagMag_ (4:2) Fall 85, p. 9.
"Odanak" (After the destruction of the Abenaqui village by
    Major Robert Rogers, October 4, 1757). _RagMag_ (4:2)
    Fall 85, p. 8.
"Orchard Hill." _NoDaQ_ (53:4) Fall 85, p. 183.
1028. CZUMA, Michael
"Father Praying." _MalR_ (71) Je 85, p. 73.
"Notes." _MalR_ (71) Je 85, p. 76-77.
"Painter." _MalR_ (71) Je 85, p. 74-75.
1029. CZURY, Craig
"Again" (for Watson-Costelloe). _Origin_ (Series 5:5) Spr
    85, p. 90.
"Bells Like Sad Angels" (for the pigeons). _Origin_ (Series
    5:5) Spr 85, p. 94.
"Cards, Kielbasy." _Origin_ (Series 5:5) Spr 85, p. 92.
"Coalscape" (for Barnes). _Origin_ (Series 5:5) Spr 85, p.
    91.
"Coalscape" (for Monk). _Origin_ (Series 5:5) Spr 85, p. 91.
"Zola in Shamokin." _Origin_ (Series 5:5) Spr 85, p. 93.
Da SILVA, Humberto
    See SILVA, Humberto da
1030. DABNEY, Stuart
"Groundwork." _OhioR_ (35) 85, p. 101.
"What the Humpbacked Man Carries in His Hump." _OhioR_ (35)
    85, p. 100.
1031. DABYDEEN, Cyril
"Algorithm." _AntigR_ (62/63) Sum-Aut 85, p. 103-104.
"The Calypsonian." _CanLit_ (104) Spr 85, p. 93-94.
1032. DACEY, Philip
"I-70, Missouri." _SpoonRQ_ (10:2) Spr 85, p. 18.
"I-90, Wisconsin." _SpoonRQ_ (10:2) Spr 85, p. 18.
"The Movie: A Book of Poems" (Selections: 1-5). _Chelsea_
    (44) 85, p. 106-108.
"The Poets at Yaddo" (with apologies to Gwendolyn Brooks).
    SpoonRQ (10:2) Spr 85, p. 17.
"Rental." _SpoonRQ_ (10:2) Spr 85, p. 20.
"Why I No Longer Teach Creative Writing." _SpoonRQ_ (10:2)
    Spr 85, p. 19.
1033. DAFIEWARE, Esiri
"Fable." _Rampike_ (4:2/3) 85-86, p. 69.
1034. DAHL, Chris
"The Great Blue Heron Once Again." _PoetryNW_ (26:4) Wint

85-86, p. 29-30.
"I'm Writing Another Impossible Love Poem." <u>PoetryNW</u>
    (26:4) Wint 85-86, p. 28.
"Washing Windows." <u>PoetryNW</u> (26:4) Wint 85-86, p. 29.
"When Grandmothers Die." <u>CrabCR</u> (2:2) Wint 85, p. 12.
1035. DAHLQUIST, Daniel
"The Golden Hour." <u>PraS</u> (59:4) Wint 85, p. 72-73.
"With the Road." <u>PraS</u> (59:4) Wint 85, p. 74-75.
1036. DAIGON, Ruth
"Anniversary." <u>GreenfR</u> (13:1/2) Fall-Wint 85, p. 55.
"Immigrant Days." <u>Vis</u> (17) 85, p. 12.
"Mathematics." <u>GreenfR</u> (13:1/2) Fall-Wint 85, p. 54.
"Names." <u>PoetL</u> (79:4) Wint 85, p. 214.
"Royalty." <u>GreenfR</u> (13:1/2) Fall-Wint 85, p. 53-54.
1037. DAILEY, Joel
"Lumber, Words, Time." <u>Confr</u> (29) Wint 85, p. 38.
1038. DALASHINSKY, Steve
"Bird in Paradise" (dedicated to: Jack Kerouac -- born
    3/12/ , Charlie Parker -- died 3/12). <u>MoodySI</u> (15)
    Spr 85, p. 19.
1039. DALE, David W.
"My Brothers." <u>CutB</u> (24) Spr-Sum 85, p. 71.
1040. DALES, Kim
"Before Battle." <u>PraF</u> (6:4) Aut-Wint 85, p. 27.
"Duck Lake Massacre." <u>PraF</u> (6:4) Aut-Wint 85, p. 30.
"Dumont Was a Great Shot." <u>PraF</u> (6:4) Aut-Wint 85, p. 26.
"Fort Garry Beverage Room, 1886." <u>PraF</u> (6:4) Aut-Wint 85,
    p. 28.
"Mister Dumas Says Riels Better Because." <u>PraF</u> (6:4) Aut-
    Wint 85, p. 29.
"When Dumont." <u>PraF</u> (6:4) Aut-Wint 85, p. 24.
"Why We Call It 'Batoche'." <u>PraF</u> (6:4) Aut-Wint 85, p. 29.
"The Wild West Show." <u>PraF</u> (6:4) Aut-Wint 85, p. 28.
"You have to be fast" ("Untitled"). <u>PraF</u> (6:4) Aut-Wint
    85, p. 27.
1041. D'ALFONSO, Antonio
"For Louis Dudek." <u>CanLit</u> (106) Fall 85, p. 42.
"The Machine." <u>CanLit</u> (106) Fall 85, p. 54.
"Per Pier Giorgio Di Cicco." <u>CanLit</u> (106) Fall 85, p. 41.
1042. DALIBARD, Jill
"Possessions" (for Naio and George). <u>AntigR</u> (62/63) Sum-
    Aut 85, p. 187-188.
1043. DALTON, Dorothy
"Encounter with Toad." <u>Abraxas</u> (33) 85, p. 54.
1044. DALVEN, Rae
"Platytera" (Byzantize Madonna, tr. of Alexandra
    Placotari). <u>Poetry</u> (145:6) Mr 85, p. 335.
1045. DAMACION, Kenneth Zamora (<u>See also</u> DAMACION, Kenny)
"In August." <u>WebR</u> (10:2) Fall 85, p. 81.
"Parable." <u>VirQ</u> (61:3) Sum 85, p. 426-427.
"Tadpole Fishing." <u>Tendril</u> (19/20) 85, p. 114.
1046. DAMACION, Kenny (<u>See also</u> DAMACION, Kenneth Zamora)
"Innocence." <u>SenR</u> (15:2) 85, p. 151-152.
"Migrant Labor." <u>SenR</u> (15:2) 85, p. 153-154.
1047. DAMAS, Léon
"Hiccups" (tr. by Beverly Mitchell). <u>NewEngR</u> (7:4) Sum
    85, p. 495-497.
1048. DAMON, Kris
"Nightmare." <u>NoDaQ</u> (53:2) Spr 85, p. 208.
1049. DAMON, S. Foster
"Thy Hand, Great Anarch." <u>MichQR</u> (24:2) Spr 85, p. 371.
1050. DANA, Robert
"At the Vietnam War Memorial." <u>Poetry</u> (146:5) Ag 85, p.
    285-287.
1051. DANAHY, Michael
"Fuse with it." <u>Swallow</u> (4) 85, p. 3.

1052. DANGEL, Leo
"Country Church First Communion." SpoonRQ (10:2) Spr 85,
p. 8.
"A Cowboy's Complaint." SpoonRQ (10:2) Spr 85, p. 7.
1053. DANIEL, Hal J., III
"Kitty Boy's New Girlfriend." JamesWR (3:1) Fall 85, p.
11.
"Mrs. Leach." RagMag (4:1) Spr 85, p. 8.
"My New Room in the Boring Old Fart Clubhouse." Open24
(4) 85, p. 58.
"Sloup." RagMag (4:1) Spr 85, p. 9.
1054. DANIEL, John
"Coyote Bloodsong." SoDakR (23:1) Spr 85, p. 53.
"Ourselves." SoDakR (23:1) Spr 85, p. 52.
1055. DANIELS, Jim
"Bar Time." KanQ (17:1/2) Wint-Spr 85, p. 113.
"First Job." ThRiPo (25/26) 85, p. 27.
"Flea Market." WestB (16) 85, p. 59.
"A Good Customer." Wind (15:54) 85, p. 12.
"My Grandfather's Tools." GreenfR (12:3/4) Wint-Spr 85,
p. 50-51.
"My Mother Walks." GreenfR (12:3/4) Wint-Spr 85, p. 49.
"Recycled Lunchbucket." PassN (6:1) Fall-Wint 85, p. 6.
"Riding Double Home from the Dairy." Agni (22) 85, p. 23-
24.
"Still Lives in Detroit, #5." CutB (23) Fall-Wint 85, p.
52.
"Taking the Bus to Veracruz." Agni (22) 85, p. 21-22.
"Two Visions of Love, or a Poem for Ike Snopes." NegC
(5:3) Sum 85, p. 115.
"Winter Poem 4." HiramPoR (38) Spr-Sum 85, p. 7.
"Winter Poem 5." HiramPoR (38) Spr-Sum 85, p. 8.
1056. DANIELS, Richard
"A Rosy Future." CutB (24) Spr-Sum 85, p. 51.
DAO, Jia
See JIA, Dao
1057. DAOUST, Jean-Paul
"Panneau-Réclame." Rampike (4:2/3) 85-86, p. 62.
1058. DARLING, Charles W.
"Tying Knots" (Stave Island, Summer, 1983). Tendril
(19/20) 85, p. 115-116.
1059. DARNELL, Cheryl Parsons
"Honeymoon." TexasR (6:1/2) Spr-Sum 85, p. 41.
1060. DARR, Ann
"What Do You Want from the Country?" PoetL (80:3) Fall
85, p. 151-154.
1061. DAS, Jagannath Prasad
"The Corpse" (tr. by Jayanta Mahapatra). NewL (51:4) Sum
85, p. 134.
1062. DASSANOWSKY-HARRIS, Robert von
"Modernes Kinderlied." Os (20) 85, p. 18.
"Zerbrochenes Glas." Os (20) 85, p. 19.
1063. DAUGHADAY, Charles H.
"Leafing through the Day." LaurelR (19:2) Sum 85, p. 33.
1064. DAUNT, Jon
"Alive in a Tropical Country." MissR (13:3, issue 39) Spr
85, p. 68.
"American Dreams." MissR (13:3, issue 39) Spr 85, p. 66-
67.
"The Cat's Revenge." CalQ (26) Sum 85, p. 48-49.
"The Dragon of an Arsonist's Thought." CapeR (20:2) Fall
85, p. 13.
"My Uncle's Voice." PraS (59:3) Fall 85, p. 29-30.
"Rebuilding Viet Nam." PraS (59:3) Fall 85, p. 31.
"With Cobra Speed." CapeR (20:2) Fall 85, p. 12.

1065. DAUZAT, Thomas
        "The Spangled Braces" (tr. of Jacques Reda). <u>Verse</u> (2)
            85, p. 28.
1066. DAVENPORT, Guy
        "We Often Think of Lenin at the Clothespin Factory."
            <u>Conjunc</u> (8) 85, p. 46-57.
1067. DAVENPORT, Richard
        "Diminution." <u>JlNJPo</u> (8:1) 85, p. 31.
1068. DAVENPORTE, Denise
        "Winter Poem." <u>NoDaQ</u> (53:2) Spr 85, p. 209.
1069. DAVID, Almitra
        "Six Post-scripts." <u>AmerPoR</u> (14:3) My-Je 85, p. 47.
1070. DAVID, Becky
        "January is." <u>LittleBR</u> (5:1) Fall-Wint 84-85, p. 4.
1071. DAVIDSON, Michael
        "The Endurance of Resolve." <u>Sulfur</u> (13) 85, p. 111-113.
        "The Fall (Tentative)." <u>Temblor</u> (2) 85, p. 100-102.
        "The Memo." <u>Temblor</u> (2) 85, p. 103.
        "Ready to Hand." <u>Zyzzyva</u> (1:3) Fall 85, p. 108-109.
        "Subject Matter." <u>Temblor</u> (2) 85, p. 102.
1072. DAVIDSON, Ronald
        "Testing, 1, 2, 3." <u>HangL</u> (47) Spr 85, p. 18.
1073. DAVIDSON-SHADDOX, Brenda
        "Coming of Age." <u>Imagine</u> (2:1) Sum 85, p. 99.
1074. DAVIE, Donald
        "For Bunting." <u>Conjunc</u> (8) 85, p. 153.
        "Helena Morley." <u>TriQ</u> (64) Fall 85, p. 49-50.
        "A Measured Tread" (for Kenneth Millar dead). <u>TriQ</u> (64)
            Fall 85, p. 51.
        "Reminded of Bougainville" (for Howard Erskine-Hill).
            <u>AmerS</u> (54:3) Sum 85, p. 360-362.
        "Wombwell on Strike." <u>TriQ</u> (64) Fall 85, p. 52-53.
1075. DAVIES, Mary
        "Looking at Schiller's Pen" (tr. of Günter Eich). <u>Field</u>
            (32) Spr 85, p. 35.
        "Yellow" (tr. of Günter Eich). <u>Field</u> (32) Spr 85, p. 36.
DAVILA, Marcos Reyes
        <u>See</u> REYES DAVILA, Marcos
1076. DAVILA LOPEZ, Antonio
        "IX." <u>Mairena</u> (7:19) 85, p. 75.
        "X." <u>Mairena</u> (7:19) 85, p. 75.
        "XI." <u>Mairena</u> (7:19) 85, p. 76.
        "XII." <u>Mairena</u> (7:19) 85, p. 76.
1077. DAVIS, Alan
        "Flood Drums." <u>SouthernPR</u> (26, i.e. 25:2) Fall 85, p. 39-
            40.
        "Hudson Street." <u>Vis</u> (18) 85, p. 30.
1078. DAVIS, Barbara Nector
        "In the Face of the Nuclear Build-Up." <u>SanFPJ</u> (7:2) 85,
            p. 36.
        "When They Say You Have to Be Stronger Than the Russians."
            <u>SanFPJ</u> (7:2) 85, p. 33-34.
1079. DAVIS, Christopher
        "The Murderer." <u>ChiR</u> (35:1) Aut 85, p. 72.
1080. DAVIS, Cynthia C.
        "Garden-child" (for W. R. D.). <u>IndR</u> (8:2) Spr 85, p. 102-
            103.
1081. DAVIS, David
        "My night is but a star's wink" ("Untitled"). <u>Amelia</u>
            (2:1) Ap 85, p. 55.
1082. DAVIS, Dick
        "Ibn Battuta." <u>ParisR</u> (27:98) Wint 85, p. 88.
1083. DAVIS, Ed
        "Appalachian Day." <u>Sam</u> (41:3, 163rd release) 85, 16 p.
1084. DAVIS, Frances
        "Edges." <u>Waves</u> (14:1/2) Fall 85, p. 103.

1085. DAVIS, John (<u>See</u> <u>also</u> DAVIS, Jon)
       "Campaign Speech." <u>CrabCR</u> (2:2) Wint 85, p. 27.
1086. DAVIS, Jon (<u>See</u> <u>also</u> DAVIS, John)
       "The Arena of Civilization" (after Mark Tobey). <u>OntR</u> (23)
          Fall-Wint 85-86, p. 39-41.
       "The Artist Reveals His Method and His Fear." <u>MidAR</u> (5:1)
          85, p. 28.
       "The Astronaut Remembers His First Space Walk" (after Dick
          Allen). <u>CrossCur</u> (4:3) 84, p. 97.
       "At Clem's Cabin." <u>LitR</u> (29:1) Fall 85, p. 15.
       "Cats." <u>MidAR</u> (5:1) 85, p. 27.
       "Driving Red Bush Lane." <u>Tendril</u> (19/20) 85, p. 117-120.
       "James Lee Howell, Trucker, Reconsiders His Profession."
          <u>MidAR</u> (5:2) 85, p. 86.
       "Picking Fieldstone" (for Joe). <u>TexasR</u> (6:1/2) Spr-Sum
          85, p. 120.
       "Picnic at the Farm." <u>PaintedB</u> (26/27) Sum-Fall 85, p. 42.
       "Proposition and Lament." <u>MinnR</u> (N.S. 24) Spr 85, p. 62.
       "The Return." <u>PaintedB</u> (26/27) Sum-Fall 85, p. 43-44.
       "The Unmetaphysical Esteves" (after Fernando Pessoa).
          <u>IndR</u> (8:1) Wint 85, p. 55.
       "White Body, Green Moss." <u>Poetry</u> (146:2) My 85, p. 88-90.
       "The World." <u>OntR</u> (23) Fall-Wint 85-86, p. 37-38.
1087. DAVIS, Lloyd
       "Bealington." <u>OhioR</u> (34) 85, p. 68.
       "A Vision of Loveliness." <u>OhioR</u> (34) 85, p. 69.
1088. DAVIS, Lydia
       "The Dog Man." <u>ParisR</u> (27:97) Fall 85, p. 107.
       "The Fish." <u>ParisR</u> (27:97) Fall 85, p. 108.
       "What She Knew." <u>ParisR</u> (27:97) Fall 85, p. 106.
1089. DAVIS, Melody
       "A Plague on My Typewriter" (which punches through the
          paper on every "o"). <u>MalR</u> (71) Je 85, p. 60-61.
       "Socrates' Wife's Revenge." <u>MalR</u> (71) Je 85, p. 62-63.
       "Through Lancaster." <u>GrahamHR</u> (9) Fall 85, p. 24.
1090. DAVIS, Nancy DePass
       "In Your Room." <u>SoCaR</u> (18:1) Fall 85, p. 80-82.
1091. DAVIS, William Virgil
       "The Caller." <u>Pig</u> (13) 85, p. 10.
       "The Lesson." <u>CentR</u> (29:4) Fall 85, p. 440-441.
       "Shark." <u>KanQ</u> (17:4) Fall 85, p. 240-241.
       "Testament." <u>SouthernPR</u> (25:1) Spr 85, p. 22.
       "Topiary." <u>SouthernPR</u> (25:1) Spr 85, p. 22.
       "Twilight." <u>SouthernHR</u> (19:2) Spr 85, p. 157.
1092. DAVISON, Peter
       "The Farm Animals' Desertion." <u>MassR</u> (26:2/3) Sum-Aut 85,
          p. 358.
       "Second Nesting" (for J. E. G.). <u>MassR</u> (26:2/3) Sum-Aut
          85, p. 357.
       "Taking Pleasure." <u>Atlantic</u> (256:4), O 85, p. 62.
1093. DAWSON, Fielding
       "Lost Horizon." <u>Open24</u> (4) 85, p. 33.
1094. DAY, Cynthia
       "Often a Particular Evening, a Particular Instant, Seems
          Like the Beginning of Autumn." <u>WestB</u> (16) 85, p. 44.
       "A Radical Activist in a Remote Part of Maine." <u>WestB</u>
          (16) 85, p. 42-43.
De . . . <u>See</u> <u>also</u> names beginning with "De" without the following
          space, filed below in their alphabetic positions,
          e.g., DeFOE.
De ANDRADE, Carlos Drummond
       <u>See</u> ANDRADE, Carlos Drummond de
De ANDRADE, Eugenio
       <u>See</u> ANDRADE, Eugenio de
1095. De ANGELIS, Milo
       "The Dream of the Dancing Cat" (tr. by Lawrence Venuti).

AmerPoR (14:1) Ja-F 85, p. 48.
"Foreweb" (tr. by Lawrence Venuti). AmerPoR (14:1) Ja-F
    85, p. 48.
"Neither Point nor Line" (tr. by Lawrence Venuti).
    AmerPoR (14:1) Ja-F 85, p. 48.
"The Train Corridor" (tr. by Lawrence Venuti). AmerPoR
    (14:1) Ja-F 85, p. 48.
1096. De BEKY, Ivan Halasz
"Adominition" (of János Pilinszky). Rampike (4:2/3) 85-
    86, p. 17.
"Come Back" (tr. of Mihály Ladány). Rampike (4:2/3)
    85-86, p. 14.
"The First Moment of Resurrection" (tr. of Sándor
    Csoóri). Rampike (4:2/3) 85-86, p. 16.
"Fragment from the Seventies" (tr. of Sándor Csoóri).
    Rampike (4:2/3) 85-86, p. 16.
"Inventory" (tr. of Mihály Ladány). Rampike (4:2/3)
    85-86, p. 14.
"Message" (tr. of Sándor Csoóri). Rampike (4:2/3) 85-
    86, p. 16.
"The Pack" (tr. of Mihály Ladány). Rampike (4:2/3) 85-
    86, p. 14.
"Roving on a Celestial Body" (tr. of László Kálnoky).
    Rampike (4:2/3) 85-86, p. 15.
"Scaffold in Winter" (of János Pilinszky). Rampike
    (4:2/3) 85-86, p. 17.
"Solitude" (tr. of László Kálnoky). Rampike (4:2/3)
    85-86, p. 15.
"Through a Whole Life" (of János Pilinszky). Rampike
    (4:2/3) 85-86, p. 17.
"What Man Could Do on Earth" (tr. of László Kálnoky).
    Rampike (4:2/3) 85-86, p. 15.
1097. De BOLT, William Walter
"Thesis." NegC (5:4) Fall 85, p. 74.
De BURGOS, Julia
    See BURGOS, Julia de
De COTEAU, Delano Abdul Malid
    See MALIK (DELANO ABDUL MALIK DE COTEAU)
De ESPINOZA, Juana Meléndez
    See MELENDEZ de ESPINOZA, Juana
De FRANCHY GAVIÑO, Carlos
    See GAVIÑO de FRANCHY, Carlos
De JESUS, Luis F.
    See JESUS, Luis F. de
De la CRUZ, Juana Inés, Sor
    See CRUZ, Juana Inés de la, Sor
De la PUEBLA, Manuel
    See PUEBLA, Manuel de la
De LACERDA, Alberto
    See LACERDA, Alberto de
De las CASAS, Walter
    See CASAS, Walter de las
De LEON, Grace
    See LEON, Grace de
1098. De LEON, Kathie
"A Room Is Waiting." Wind (15:54) 85, p. 13-14.
De LEON, Nephtalí
    See LEON, Nephtalí de
1099. De MARIS, Ron
"Something Domestic." NewOR (12:1) Spr 85, p. 53.
"Sudden Storm." PoetryNW (26:1) Spr 85, p. 36.
De MARTINEZ, María Isabel Arbona
    See ARBONA DE MARTINEZ, María Isabel
De MORAES, Vinicius
    See MORAES, Vinicius de

De OLIVEIRA, Celso
    See OLIVEIRA, Celso de
De ORY, Carlos Edmundo
    See ORY, Carlos Edmundo de
1100. De PALCHI, Alfredo
    "& as in the bible I betroth" (tr. by S. Raiziss). NewL
        (51:4) Sum 85, p. 162.
    "In the fluster of buds & birds" (tr. by S. Raiziss).
        NewL (51:4) Sum 85, p. 162.
    "Smokestacks fertilizer" (tr. by S. Raiziss). NewL (51:4)
        Sum 85, p. 162.
1101. De RACHEWILTZ, Mary
    "A Tessera for Basil Bunting's Library." Conjunc (8) 85,
        p. 193.
De RONSARD, Pierre
    See RONSARD, Pierre de
De SENA, Jorge
    See SENA, Jorge de
De URIARTE, Miriam
    See URIARTE, Miriam de
De VILLEGAS, Nestor Díaz
    See DIAZ de VILLEGAS, Nestor
1102. De VRIES, Carrow
    "Anti Running and Weight-Lifting Unless You Enjoy It."
        WindO (46) Fall 85, p. 36.
    "Epicurus Jogs in Oregon." WindO (46) Fall 85, p. 36.
1103. De VRIES, N.
    "Were it Spring again." Amelia (2:1) Ap 85, p. 51.
De VRIES, Theun
    See VRIES, Theun de
1104. De YAMPERT, Rick
    "On Walking through Bryce Cemetery." NegC (5:2) Spr 85,
        p. 70.
1105. DEAL, Susan Strayer
    "Edges." NowestR (23:1) 85, p. 13-14.
    "Everything Is a Thought." MidAR (5:1) 85, p. 117.
    "In Appeasement." CrossCur (4:4/5:1) 85, p. 32-33.
    "The Look of Things." MidAR (5:1) 85, p. 116.
1106. DEAN, Harry
    "Afternoon." CumbPR (5:1) Fall 85, p. 14.
1107. DEAN, Mick
    "An Aimless Seduction." JamesWR (2:1) Fall 84, p. 6.
    "Another Bar Closing Poem." JamesWR (2:1) Fall 84, p. 6.
    "No Reply." JamesWR (2:1) Fall 84, p. 6.
    "Placebo" (second place poetry entry in the Northstar
        competition). JamesWR (2:3) Spr-Sum 85, p. 4.
    "The View." JamesWR (2:2) Wint 85, p. 2-3.
1108. DEAN, Peter
    "Conversation." PoeticJ (10) 85, p. 22.
    "Dream." PoeticJ (10) 85, p. 18.
    "Stain." DeKalbLAJ (18:3/4) 85, p. 30.
1109. DEAN, Richard
    "Emily Dickinson Home Robbed of Clocks, Silver." PoetryNW
        (26:3) Aut 85, p. 38-39.
    "Users of the Curved Line." PoetryNW (26:3) Aut 85, p. 37-
        38.
1110. DEANS, G. N.
    "After Balthus." Bogg (54) 85, p. 10.
1111. DECAVALLES, Andonis
    "Crimes or Genesis II" (in Greek and English, tr. by Kimon
        Friar). LitR (28:4) Sum 85, p. 542-543.
    "The Fingers" (in Greek and English, tr. by Kimon Friar).
        LitR (28:4) Sum 85, p. 540-541.
    "Next Time" (1973). JlNJPo (8:1) 85, p. 10-11.
    "Oceanids" (1969). JlNJPo (8:1) 85, p. 9.
    "Resurrection of a Dean Man" (1948). JlNJPo (8:1) 85, p.

7-8.
"Waterdrops and Drummer" (in Greek and English, tr. by
    Kimon Friar). <u>LitR</u> (28:4) Sum 85, p. 538-539.
1112. DECEMBER, John
"Festival Queen." <u>WindO</u> (45) Spr 85, p. 43.
"Home, Evening." <u>WindO</u> (45) Spr 85, p. 43.
"Rituals of Earth." <u>WindO</u> (45) Spr 85, p. 44.
1113. DECKER, Samuel
"Nameless Poem." <u>KanQ</u> (17:4) Fall 85, p. 148.
"St. Joe." <u>KanQ</u> (17:4) Fall 85, p. 147.
1114. DeCORMIER-SHEKERJIAN, Regina
"From the Journal of an Unknown Lady-in-Waiting." <u>MassR</u>
    (26:1) Spr 85, p. 139-140.
"In the Round Clearing" (The poet is jester to the king).
    <u>NegC</u> (5:2) Spr 85, p. 18-19.
"Modi" (1984 Narrative Poetry Prize: Honorable Mention).
    <u>PoetL</u> (80:1) Spr 85, p. 32-38.
1115. DEDORA, Brian
"Discoloured: His Story." <u>Rampike</u> (4:2/3) 85-86, p. 82-83.
1116. DEE, Denise
"Sadness (Down the River of Dreams)" (Excerpt). <u>Zyzzyva</u>
    (1:3) Fall 85, p. 31-33.
1117. DeFOE, Mark
"At a Rest Stop in Iowa." <u>CrossCur</u> (4:4/5:1) 85, p. 12-14.
"Diving for the Cripples at the VFW Lake" (for J. D.
    Hansard). <u>NoDaQ</u> (53:4) Fall 85, p. 185-186.
"The Druggist Considers His Town." <u>MemphisSR</u> (5:2) Spr
    85, p. 40.
"In the Tourist Cave." <u>MidAR</u> (5:1) 85, p. 129-130.
"Photo: Women's Rifle Team, Cornell--1934." <u>MidAR</u> (5:1)
    85, p. 128.
"Piano Lesson." <u>ThRiPo</u> (25/26) 85, p. 28.
"Quaint and Rustic." <u>NoDaQ</u> (53:4) Fall 85, p. 184-185.
"The Sultan." <u>MidAR</u> (5:2) 85, p. 89.
"Through the Cemetery: Jogging Early." <u>MemphisSR</u> (5:2)
    Spr 85, p. 41-42.
"Two Old Coaches Hang-out at the Mall." <u>MidAR</u> (5:2) 85,
    p. 88.
1118. DeFREES, Madeline
"Beside Mill River." <u>CrossCur</u> (4:2) 84, p. 105.
"Dominance: A Museum Guide." <u>AmerPoR</u> (14:4) Jl-Ag 85, p.
    16.
"The Dream of Double Life." <u>IndR</u> (8:1) Wint 85, p. 16-17.
"In the Locker Room." <u>AmerPoR</u> (14:4) Jl-Ag 85, p. 16.
"Like the Astronomer's Tame Elk, It May Be the Only Thing
    Missing." <u>AmerPoR</u> (14:4) Jl-Ag 85, p. 17.
"Stirrups." <u>IndR</u> (8:1) Wint 85, p. 18-19.
"Whale Watch." <u>MassR</u> (26:2/3) Sum-Aut 85, p. 402-404.
"The Whaling Wife Awaits the Captain's Return Home."
    <u>MassR</u> (26:2/3) Sum-Aut 85, p. 401-402.
"Whaling Wives" (Selections: "Jenny Martinson, Whaling
    Captain's Widow . . .," "Whaling Wives: Submit
    Claiborne"). <u>Nimrod</u> (29:1) Fall-Wint 85, p. 22-24.
1119. DeGENNARO, Lorraine S.
"The Tattooed Lady." <u>PoeticJ</u> (11) 85, p. 4-5.
1120. DEGO, Giuliano
"And Then We Learn" (tr. of Alfredo Giuliani, w. Margaret
    Straus). <u>LitR</u> (28:2) Wint 85, p. 244.
"Camel" (tr. of Mario Lunetta, w. Margaret Straus). <u>LitR</u>
    (28:2) Wint 85, p. 249-250.
"Delft" (tr. of Elio Filippo Accrocca w. Margaret Straus).
    <u>LitR</u> (29:1) Fall 85, p. 91.
"Faces by Rembrandt" (tr. of Elio Filippo Accrocca, w.
    Margaret Straus). <u>LitR</u> (29:1) Fall 85, p. 90.
"North Sea" (tr. of Elio Filippo Accrocca w. Margaret
    Straus). <u>LitR</u> (29:1) Fall 85, p. 91.

"The (Portable) Rite of Sleep" (Selections: 1-4, 12, 17,
   tr. of Giuliano Gramigna, w. Margaret Straus). LitR
   (29:1) Fall 85, p. 101-103.
"A Private Story" (Excerpt, tr. of Dario Bellezza w.
   Margaret Straus). LitR (29:1) Fall 85, p. 93-94.
"Provos" (tr. of Elio Filippo Accrocca w. Margaret Straus).
   LitR (29:1) Fall 85, p. 90.
"Psychograph" (tr. of Mariella Bettarini, w. Margaret
   Straus). LitR (29:1) Fall 85, p. 94.
"La Storia in Rima" (an epic poem, in progress: Excerpt,
   tr. by the author and Margaret Straus). LitR (29:1)
   Fall 85, p. 97-100.
"When I Was Young" (tr. of Alfredo Giuliani, w. Margaret
   Straus). LitR (28:2) Wint 85, p. 243.
M. "Huddle with a Hyena" (tr. of Alberto M. Moriconi, w.
   Margaret Straus). LitR (29:1) Fall 85, p. 112.
1121. DeGRAVELLES, Charles
   "Little Clouds But Low." GreenfR (13:1/2) Fall-Wint 85,
      p. 19.
   "The Movement This Joy Makes." GeoR (39:4) Wint 85, p.
      836-837.
   "What Reduces, What Remains." SmPd (22:2) Spr 85, p. 28.
1122. DEGUY, Michel
   "Dialogues" (tr. by Bernard Bador). Temblor (2) 85, p. 68.
   "Passim" (tr. by Clayton Eshleman). Verse (2) 85, p. 26.
   "Pleasures of the Threshold" (tr. by Bernard Bador).
      Temblor (2) 85, p. 69.
   "Space" (tr. by Bernard Bador). Temblor (2) 85, p. 68-69.
   "When the World Confines" (to Breughel, tr. by Clayton
      Eshleman). Verse (2) 85, p. 25.
1123. DEKIN, Timothy
   "Elegy at Donner Hot Springs." SouthwR (70:3) Sum 85, p.
      381-383.
   "For a Friend, Randomly Murdered in L.A." ChiR (34:4) 85,
      p. 63.
   "Imagine." TriQ (64) Fall 85, p. 165.
   "The Meeting" (for Ken). TriQ (64) Fall 85, p. 166-167.
Del CASTILLO, Amelia
   See CASTILLO, Amelia del
Del PINO, Salvador Rodriguez
   See RODRIGUEZ DEL PINO, Salvador
DELGADO, Angel Alvarado
   See ALVARADO DELGADO, Angel
1124. DELIGIORGIS, Stavros
   "After Some Hits." Iowa (15:2) Spr-Sum 85, p. 81-82.
   "Ta'en" (March 1921, tr. of C. P. Cavafy). Iowa (15:2)
      Spr-Sum 85, p. 83-84.
1125. DELISLE, Michael
   "Désinformer, le mot existe" (with Claude Beausoleil).
      Rampike (4:2/3) 85-86, p. 6.
1126. DELORME, Alain-Gilles
   "Fragments." AntigR (60) Wint 85, p. 42-44.
1127. DELP, Michael
   "Killings." HawaiiR (18) Fall 85, p. 98.
   "The Language of Wind." PassN (6:1) Fall-Wint 85, p. 21.
1128. DeMARTINI, Brenda
   "A Domestic Crisis." OP (38/39) Spr 85, p. 57.
1129. DEMING, Alison
   "Fiber Optics and the Heart." MichQR (24:2) Spr 85, p.
      307.
1130. DEMIROVIC, Hamdija
   "Charge on Transience" (tr. by Robert Mezey and the
      author). AmerPoR (14:2) Mr-Ap 85, p. 21.
   "From the water, life" (tr. by Robert Mezey and the
      author). AmerPoR (14:2) Mr-Ap 85, p. 21.
   "Your nights are all too clear" (tr. by Robert Mezey and

the author). <u>AmerPoR</u> (14:2) Mr-Ap 85, p. 21.
1131. DEMPSEY, Ivy
"Fear of Heights." <u>Nimrod</u> (28:2) Spr-Sum 85, p. 130-131.
"Remembering Cesar Franck's Symphony in D Minor." <u>Nimrod</u>
(28:2) Spr-Sum 85, p. 129.
1132. DEMPSTER, Barry
"The Astronaut." <u>Quarry</u> (34:4) Aut 85, p. 73-74.
"Blue Collar." <u>CrossC</u> (7:2) 85, p. 10.
"The Fire Hydrant." <u>Quarry</u> (34:4) Aut 85, p. 72-73.
"The Lion's Dream." <u>Waves</u> (13:4) Spr 85, p. 82.
"Neighbourhoods." <u>CrossC</u> (7:2) 85, p. 10.
"The Waiting Room." <u>Waves</u> (13:4) Spr 85, p. 82-83.
1133. DENBERG, Ken
"Another Story." <u>SouthernPR</u> (25:1) Spr 85, p. 59-60.
1134. DenBOER, David C.
"Dawn." <u>MSS</u> (4:3) Spr 85, p. 119.
"October: Baseball Field Theory." <u>NegC</u> (5:1) Wint 85, p.
123-134.
1135. DENBY, Edwin
"Poem." <u>NewYRB</u> (32:14) 26 S 85, p. 31.
1136. DENDINGER, Lloyd
"Freud." <u>NegC</u> (5:3) Sum 85, p. 45.
1137. DeNIORD, Chard
"The Death of a Cow." <u>CutB</u> (23) Fall-Wint 85, p. 48-49.
"No Moon." <u>CutB</u> (24) Spr-Sum 85, p. 60-61.
1138. DENNIS, Carl
"Beauty Exposed." <u>Salm</u> (66) Wint-Spr 85, p. 147.
"Captain Cook." <u>Pequod</u> (19/20/21) 85, p. 122-123.
"The Dig." <u>NewRep</u> (192:20) 20 My 85, p. 32.
"The Greenhouse Effect." <u>Poetry</u> (146:5) Ag 85, p. 266.
"Heinrich Schliemann." <u>Poetry</u> (147:3) D 85, p. 146.
"Letchworth State Park." <u>Pequod</u> (19/20/21) 85, p. 124-125.
"Little League." <u>Poetry</u> (146:3) Je 85, p. 158.
"The Meek." <u>MichQR</u> (24:4) Fall 85, p. 622.
"Puritans" (for Robert Daly). <u>Salm</u> (66) Wint-Spr 85, p.
145-146.
"Winter Light." <u>Poetry</u> (147:3) D 85, p. 145.
1139. DENNIS, Michael
"In Laughter and Again in Fear." <u>Dandel</u> (12:1) 85, p. 44.
1140. DENNY, David
"Holden Caulfield at the Car Wash." <u>BelPoJ</u> (35:3) Spr 85,
p. 34-36.
DeNORD, Chard
<u>See</u> DeNIORD, Chard
1141. DENTINGER, Philip
"Black Widow." <u>Ascent</u> (11:1) 85, p. 60-61.
"Castaway." <u>Ascent</u> (11:1) 85, p. 61-62.
1142. DEPPE, Theodore
"Counting the Stations" (lines after the suicide of a
favorite teacher). <u>CumbPR</u> (5:1) Fall 85, p. 5-7.
"The Gatekeeper." <u>BelPoJ</u> (35:3) Spr 85, p. 4-5.
"Starry Night on the Rhone." <u>Comm</u> (112:6) 22 Mr 85, p.
186.
1143. DEPTA, Victor M.
"The Egotism of Death." <u>CharR</u> (11:1) Spr 85, p. 80-81.
"The Litigation." <u>CrossCur</u> (4:4/5:1) 85, p. 108.
1144. Der HOVANESSIAN, Diana
"The Bath" (tr. of Siamanto). <u>GrahamHR</u> (9) Fall 85, p. 77-
78.
"Dante-esque Legend" (Dedicated to Mihran Markarian, Stepan
Ghazarian and Ashod Millionchian . . ., tr. of Eghishe
Charents). <u>GrahamHR</u> (8) Wint 85, p. 48-67.
"A Handful of Ash" (To the Memory of Akn, tr. of Siamanto).
<u>GrahamHR</u> (9) Fall 85, p. 84-85.
"In a Landscape without Humans." <u>Agni</u> (22) 85, p. 35.
"The Mulberry Tree" (tr. of Siamanto). <u>GrahamHR</u> (9) Fall

85, p. 81-83.
"New York, London 1983." OP (38/39) Spr 85, p. 140.
"Orphan" (tr. of Hovhaness Shiraz). Mund (15:1/2) 85, p.
    70.
"Portrait" (tr. of Yrui Sahakian). GrahamHR (8) Wint 85,
    p. 45-46.
"Silence Is Golden" (tr. of Gevorg Emin). GrahamHR (8)
    Wint 85, p. 47.
"Songs of Bread." GrahamHR (9) Fall 85, p. 17.
"The Strangling" (tr. of Siamanto). GrahamHR (9) Fall 85,
    p. 79-80.
"Thirst" (tr. of Siamanto). GrahamHR (9) Fall 85, p. 76.
"Twenty Years after His Drowning." LitR (29:1) Fall 85,
    p. 41.
"Your Shadow Falls on My Life" (tr. of Yuri Sahakian).
    Mund (15:1/2) 85, p. 69.
1145. DERRICOTTE, Toi
"Allen Ginsberg." USl (18/19) Wint 85, p. 3.
"Constructing a Dream." RiverS (17) 85, p. 40-41.
"New Jersey Poet." USl (18/19) Wint 85, p. 3.
"The Promise." Pequod (18) 85, p. 106-107.
"Saturday Night." Pequod (18) 85, p. 108.
"Tiedown." BelPoJ (36:2) Wint 85-86, p. 31.
1146. DERSLEY, Keith
"Am I a Bob Hope figure in your life." HangL (48) Fall
    85, p. 9.
"His Alamo of Crocketts." HangL (48) Fall 85, p. 9.
"Though pessimistic about ever being able to change the
    world." HangL (48) Fall 85, p. 10.
1147. DeRUGERIS, C. K.
"Hot City Sunday." Bogg (53) 85, p. 21.
"Jesus." JamesWR (3:1) Fall 85, p. 10.
1148. DESCH, Robert
"Graven Image." ChrC (102:14) 24 Ap 85, p. 405.
1149. DESHLER, Timothy
"Seraphim Wounded." Amelia (2:2) O 85, p. 55.
1150. DESIDERI, Franco
"The Cock on the Barrel" (tr. by Annalisa Saccà). LitR
    (28:2) Wint 85, p. 232.
"I Have Nothing to Give You" (tr. by Annalisa Saccà).
    LitR (28:2) Wint 85, p. 231.
"In This Scent" (tr. by Annalisa Saccà). LitR (28:2)
    Wint 85, p. 231.
"Not Even the Greeting" (tr. by Annalisa Saccà). LitR
    (28:2) Wint 85, p. 231.
"The Squalor" (tr. by Annalisa Saccà). LitR (28:2) Wint
    85, p. 232.
1151. DESKINS, David
"4 A.M. and." Wind (15:55) 85, p. 19-20.
1152. DESNOS, Robert
"Never Anyone But You" (tr. by Dorothy Aspinwall). WebR
    (10:2) Fall 85, p. 33.
"Under Cover of Night" (tr. by Dorothy Aspinwall). WebR
    (10:2) Fall 85, p. 34.
"The Voice of Robert Desnos" (tr. by Dorothy Aspinwall).
    WebR (10:2) Fall 85, p. 31-32.
1153. DESY, Peter
"At Thoreau's Grave, 1974." SoCaR (18:1) Fall 85, p. 35.
"Autumn Burnings." SouthernHR (19:4) Fall 85, p. 322.
"Dog, This Dog." StoneC (12:2/3) Spr-Sum 85, p. 34.
"Explanation." EngJ (74:5) S 85, p. 74.
"The Voyeur." MemphisSR (5:2) Spr 85, p. 30.
"Your G Spot." SoCaR (18:1) Fall 85, p. 35.
1154. DEUMER, Joseph
"Sunday Morning." Tendril (19/20) 85, p. 121-122.

1155. DeVALL, Sally
      "Mothers." PoeticJ (12) 85, p. 3.
      "We Meet." PoeticJ (9) 85, p. 44.
1156. DEVET, Rebecca McClanahan
      "The Other Woman." PaintedB (26/27) Sum-Fall 85, p. 48.
1157. DEVET, Rebecca, McClanahan
      "When It Slips Away." CarolQ (37:3) Spr 85, p. 74-75.
1158. DeVIEW, Lucille S.
      "The Knowledge of Good and Evil." SanFPJ (7:3) 84 [i.e.
         85], p. 52.
      "Liberal Distance." SanFPJ (7:3) 84 [i.e. 85], p. 49.
1159. DEVOL, Jond
      "Inuit Woman." Tendril (19/20) 85, p. 124.
      "Inuits." Tendril (19/20) 85, p. 123.
1160. DHOMHNAILL, Nuala Ni
      "The Visitor" (tr. by Joe Malone). Paint (11:21/12:24) 84-
         85, p. 56.
Di . . . See also names beginning with "Di" without the following
         space, filed below in their alphabetic positions, e.g.,
         DiPALMA
1161. Di CICCO, Pier Giorgio
      "Going Back." CanLit (106) Fall 85, p. 75.
      "Mattina." CrossC (7:1) 85, p. 13.
      "Multicultural Blues" (for Alberto DiGiovanni). CanLit
         (106) Fall 85, p. 18.
      "Paesani." CanLit (106) Fall 85, p. 44.
1162. Di MICHELE, Mary
      "Beauty and Dread in 1959." MalR (72) S 85, p. 45-51.
      "Blue Brassieres." PoetryCR (6:4) Sum 85, p. 31.
      "Children of Unwanted Parents." MalR (72) S 85, p. 52.
      "Colour and a Man's Eyes." PoetryCR (6:4) Sum 85, p. 31.
      "Maps of All We Have Been." CrossC (7:3/4) 85, p. 53.
      "Nightingale Tongues." CrossC (7:3/4) 85, p. 52.
      "Sex and Death." MalR (72) S 85, p. 43-44.
      "Snapshot." CrossC (7:3/4) 85, p. 52.
      "Starlight Theatre" (for Susan Glickman). PoetryCR (6:4)
         Sum 85, p. 31.
      "Translated World." CanLit (106) Fall 85, p. 55-56.
      "X-Rated Romance." PoetryCR (6:3) Spr 85, p. 17.
1163. Di PIERO, W. S.
      "I-80." SouthernR (21:1) Wint 85, p. 140-142.
      "June Harvest." TriQ (63) Spr-Sum 85, p. 541-542.
      "The Keeper" (in memoriam: R. G. Vliet). SouthwR (70:4)
         Aut 85, p. 487.
      "The One-Year-Old Lemon Tree." AmerS (54:3) Sum 85, p.
         403.
      "The Pool at Eden Falls." SouthwR (70:4) Aut 85, p. 486.
      "Something Understood." SouthernR (21:1) Wint 85, p. 142-
         143.
      "Summer Returns." Agni (22) 85, p. 36-37.
1164. DIAMONDSTONE, Esther
      "Local Gods." AmerPoR (14:3) My-Je 85, p. 21.
1165. DIAZ, Rosemary
      "Amelia: Eyes in the Landscape." NoDaQ (53:2) Spr 85, p.
         211.
1166. DIAZ de VILLEGAS, Néstor
      "Bolero." LindLM (4:2) Ap-Je 85, p. 26.
1167. DIAZ MARQUEZ, Luis
      "Ayer -Hoy." Mairena (7:19) 85, p. 31-32.
      "Del Album Familiar" (a Edgardo Rodríguez Julía).
         Mairena (7:19) 85, p. 35.
      "Llegas Siempre." Mairena (7:19) 85, p. 31.
      "Quisiera, Luz." Mairena (7:19) 85, p. 32-33.
      "Soy Romero Incansable." Mairena (7:19) 85, p. 33.
      "Y Conocí a un Poeta." Mairena (7:19) 85, p. 34-35.

1168. DIAZ VILLAMIL, Maria de los A.
    "La Noche de Los Mil y Un Unicornios." LindLM (4:2) Ap-Je
    85, p. 29.
1169. DICKEMAN, Nancy
    "All Souls." PoetryNW (26:4) Wint 85-86, p. 42.
    "Confirmation." PoetryNW (26:4) Wint 85-86, p. 43-44.
1170. DICKEY, Bill A.
    "I need for me alone -- what?" LittleBR (5:1) Fall-Wint
    84-85, p. 53.
1171. DICKEY, James
    "Air." Verse (2) 85, p. 3.
    "Owned Eye." Raccoon (17) Mr 85, p. 39.
    "To Be Done in Winter by Those Surviving Truman Capote."
    ParisR (27:97) Fall 85, p. 190.
1172. DICKSON, John
    "The Aragon Ballroom." TriQ (63) Spr-Sum 85, p. 654-655.
    "The Burr Oak Tree." NegC (5:2) Spr 85, p. 68-69.
    "Fossil Fuel." Poetry (147:1) O 85, p. 8.
    "On Living Too Close to the Music School." SpoonRQ (10:2)
    Spr 85, p. 59.
    "Perfect Crimes." SpoonRQ (10:2) Spr 85, p. 58.
    "The Picture on the Stairs." PassN (6:2) Spr-Sum 85, p. 9.
    "Rites of Printemps." StoneC (13:1/2) Fall-Wint 85-86, p.
    21.
    "Subject Matter." SpoonRQ (10:4) Fall 85, p. 18-19.
    "They." SpoonRQ (10:4) Fall 85, p. 20.
    "The Victors." NegC (5:2) Spr 85, p. 66-67.
1173. DICKSON, Ray Clark
    "Coming In." BelPoJ (35:4) Sum 85, p. 9-10.
    "The Day They Shot Sakharov." BelPoJ (36:2) Wint 85-86,
    p. 6.
    "The Garimpeiro: A Translation." BelPoJ (35:4) Sum 85, p.
    10-11.
    "Uncle Voychek's Vodka" (to Marysia Maziarz). BelPoJ
    (36:2) Wint 85-86, p. 7-8.
1174. DIEGO, Eliseo
    "A Mis Calles de la Habana" (a Bella). Inti (18/19)
    Otoño 83-Prim. 84, p. 57.
    "El Agua." Inti (18/19) Otoño 83-Prim. 84, p. 53.
    "Asombro." Inti (18/19) Otoño 83-Prim. 84, p. 57-58.
    "El Cofrecillo Blanco." Inti (18/19) Otoño 83-Prim. 84,
    p. 56.
    "Como la Noche." Inti (18/19) Otoño 83-Prim. 84, p. 50-
    51.
    "La Dicha." Inti (18/19) Otoño 83-Prim. 84, p. 54.
    "La Estancia." Inti (18/19) Otoño 83-Prim. 84, p. 52.
    "Fragmento." Inti (18/19) Otoño 83-Prim. 84, p. 53.
    "Frente al Espejo." Inti (18/19) Otoño 83-Prim. 84, p.
    56.
    "Hacia la Constelación de Hércules." Inti (18/19)
    Otoño 83-Prim. 84, p. 55.
    "El Lunes." Inti (18/19) Otoño 83-Prim. 84, p. 50.
    "Nunca Le Ve la Cara." Inti (18/19) Otoño 83-Prim. 84,
    p. 53-54.
    "Pantomima." Inti (18/19) Otoño 83-Prim. 84, p. 51.
    "The Pauses" (tr. by Kent Johnson). BlueBldgs (9) [85?],
    p. 8.
    "El Pez." Inti (18/19) Otoño 83-Prim. 84, p. 52.
    "Queja." Inti (18/19) Otoño 83-Prim. 84, p. 51-52.
    "El Saco." Inti (18/19) Otoño 83-Prim. 84, p. 50.
    "The Vase" (tr. by Kent Johnson). BlueBldgs (9) [85?], p.
    8.
    "Versiones." Inti (18/19) Otoño 83-Prim. 84, p. 51.
    "Versions" (tr. by Kent Johnson). BlueBldgs (9) [85?], p.
    9.
    "Y Cuando, en Fin, Todo Está Dicho." Inti (18/19)

Otoño 83-Prim. 84, p. 54-55.
1175. DiFALCO, Salvatore
"Amenities." <u>PoetryCR</u> (7:2) Wint 85-86, p. 22.
"At My Desk / Fri. Night." <u>Pig</u> (13) 85, p. 1.
"Disclosures." <u>Pig</u> (13) 85, p. 45.
"Losing the Sea at Last." <u>PoetryCR</u> (7:2) Wint 85-86, p.
22.
"Mesteño." <u>Waves</u> (13:2/3) Wint 85, p. 66-68.
"Le Songe d'une Nuit D'êtê." <u>PoetryCR</u> (6:3) Spr 85,
p. 35.
1176. DIFALCO, Sam
"Lunch on the Green." <u>AntigR</u> (62/63) Sum-Aut 85, p. 247.
"Predomination at the Quarry." <u>AntigR</u> (62/63) Sum-Aut 85,
p. 246.
1177. DIGBY, John
"A Collage Poem for Doctor Edmond Halley's Comet." <u>Confr</u>
(30/31) N 85, p. 126.
1178. DIGGES, Deborah
"Ancestral Lights." <u>NewYorker</u> (61:43) 16 D 85, p. 44.
"Brides of Christ." <u>DenQ</u> (20:1) Sum 85, p. 47-48.
"Bums." <u>Tendril</u> (19/20) 85, p. 125.
"Crimes." <u>Crazy</u> (27) Fall 84, p. 49-50.
"I Begin to Believe We Are Born for Some Things." <u>Crazy</u>
(27) Fall 84, p. 47-48.
"The Leaves." <u>DenQ</u> (20:1) Sum 85, p. 44-46.
"The New World." <u>NewYorker</u> (61:30) 16 S 85, p. 44.
"Stealing Lilacs in the Cemetery" (for my son). <u>DenQ</u>
(20:1) Sum 85, p. 49.
1179. DILLARD, Annie
"Language for Everyone." <u>OP</u> (38/39) Spr 85, p. 118-121.
1180. DILLON, Andrew
"William Stafford." <u>NegC</u> (5:4) Fall 85, p. 57.
1181. DILLON, Norma
"An Archetypal Rape." <u>PraF</u> (6:3) Sum 85, p. 50.
"A Buoyant Menagerie." <u>PraF</u> (6:3) Sum 85, p. 47.
"Rose White and Snow Red." <u>PraF</u> (6:3) Sum 85, p. 51.
"Rosebud Was Here." <u>PraF</u> (6:3) Sum 85, p. 48.
"Sometimes, Love" ("Untitled"). <u>PraF</u> (6:3) Sum 85, p. 51.
"Wetscape." <u>PraF</u> (6:3) Sum 85, p. 49.
1182. DiMAGGIO, Jill
"Cookie's Eyes." <u>PoeticJ</u> (12) 85, p. 5.
"Juan." <u>PoeticJ</u> (12) 85, p. 4.
1183. DIMITROVA, Blaga
"Introduction to the Beyond" (tr. by Jascha Kessler and
Alexander Shurbanov). <u>Ploughs</u> (11:4) 85, p. 220.
"A Woman Alone on the Road" (tr. by John Balaban). <u>Mund</u>
(15:1/2) 85, p. 144-145.
1184. DINE, Carol
"Morning / Afternoon." <u>Tendril</u> (19/20) 85, p. 126.
1185. DINGS, Fred
"Blackbirds Flocked in Evergreens." <u>PoetryNW</u> (26:4) Wint
85-86, p. 8.
DiNIORD, Chard
See DeNIORD, Chard
1186. DINO
"Ave de Paso, Cañazo!" <u>RevChic</u> (13:2) Sum 85, p. 40-41.
"Et in Arcadia Ego." <u>RevChic</u> (13:2) Sum 85, p. 42.
"Sicut Minerva Strix." <u>RevChic</u> (13:2) Sum 85, p. 43.
1187. DION, Marc Munroe
"Mill Strike - 1909." <u>NewL</u> (52:1) Fall 85, p. 118.
1188. DIONNE, Craig
"Of Sonic Booms and Goose Eggs." <u>SnapD</u> (9:1) Fall 85, p.
10-11.
1189. DiPASQUALE, E.
"Ancestral Chimera." <u>Poem</u> (54) N 85, p. 29.
"The Dead Speak." <u>Poem</u> (54) N 85, p. 30.

"A Mother's Preparation for Her Dead Child." <u>Poem</u> (54) N
   85, p. 31.
1190. DiSANTO, Alex
   "Dictators." <u>Open24</u> (4) 85, p. 21-22.
1191. DISCH, Tom
   "Brief Lives." <u>ChiR</u> (34:4) 85, p. 67.
   "The Return to Nature." <u>Poetry</u> (146:3) Je 85, p. 125-132.
1192. DISCHELL, Stuart
   "At the Summit." <u>Ploughs</u> (11:1) 85, p. 67-68.
   "Auteuil." <u>AntR</u> (43:4) Fall 85, p. 456.
   "Elegy for L.S.M., 1909-1981." <u>Crazy</u> (27) Fall 84, p. 35.
   "Fish Pier." <u>Ploughs</u> (11:1) 85, p. 70.
   "History Lessons" (Henry Adams). <u>PartR</u> (52:3) 85, p. 244-
     246.
   "Interstates." <u>Ploughs</u> (11:1) 85, p. 69.
   "Land's End" (for Franz). <u>AntR</u> (43:4) Fall 85, p. 455.
   "Little Songs of the Hanged Man." <u>SenR</u> (15:2) 85, p. 149.
   "Mal de Tete." <u>SenR</u> (15:2) 85, p. 147.
   "Manifesto." <u>SenR</u> (15:2) 85, p. 150.
   "Penny Serenade." <u>Ploughs</u> (11:1) 85, p. 65-66.
   "Shrine." <u>SenR</u> (15:2) 85, p. 148.
1193. DISEND, David S.
   "English Teachers." <u>LittleM</u> (14:4) 85, p. 19.
   "Every Ten Years an Identity Crisis." <u>LittleM</u> (14:4) 85,
     p. 19.
1194. DISKIN, Lahna
   "Bird I Was." <u>GrahamHR</u> (9) Fall 85, p. 15-16.
1195. DISKO, Toni
   "Ancient Hidings." <u>LitR</u> (28:4) Sum 85, p. 574.
1196. DISTELHEIM, Rochelle
   "Taking a Daughter to Princeton." <u>Vis</u> (17) 85, p. 13.
1197. DITSKY, John
   "Aprillic." <u>Open24</u> (4) 85, p. 51.
   "Edging the Lawn." <u>AntigR</u> (62/63) Sum-Aut 85, p. 155.
   "Fathering." <u>CumbPR</u> (5:1) Fall 85, p. 10.
   "The Gap." <u>CrossCur</u> (4:3) 84, p. 93.
   "A Hail of Gunfire." <u>LaurelR</u> (19:1) Wint 85, p. 65.
   "Julie." <u>Open24</u> (4) 85, p. 51.
   "Learning the Graces." <u>Outbr</u> (14/15) Fall 84-Spr 85, p. 54.
   "MIA." <u>CumbPR</u> (5:1) Fall 85, p. 9.
   "The Other." <u>CanLit</u> (104) Spr 85, p. 84.
   "Smiles of a Summer Night." <u>AntigR</u> (62/63) Sum-Aut 85, p.
     154.
   "To the Revelers." <u>PoetryCR</u> (7:2) Wint 85-86, p. 54.
   "Tom, Doubting." <u>CumbPR</u> (5:1) Fall 85, p. 11.
   "Touch." <u>OntR</u> (23) Fall-Wint 85-86, p. 44.
   "The young girl dancing in the mirror" (16). <u>Paint</u>
     (11:21/12:24) 84-85, p. 15.
1198. DITTBERNER, Hugo
   "Der Längste Tag." <u>Mund</u> (15:1/2) 85, p. 158, 160.
   "The Longest Day" (tr. by Walter Kreeger). <u>Mund</u> (15:1/2)
     85, p. 159, 161.
   "On the Utility of Love" (tr. by Walter Kreeger). <u>Mund</u>
     (15:1/2) 85, p. 159.
   "Vom Nutzen der Liebe." <u>Mund</u> (15:1/2) 85, p. 158.
1199. DITZANI, Rami
   "Les Enfants du R. P. G." (Rocket-Propelled Grenade, tr. by
     Ruth Whitman). <u>Ploughs</u> (11:4) 85, p. 171-172.
   "From West Beirut" (September 1982, in connection with non-
     standard and negligent building in Lebanon, tr. by Ruth
     Whitman). <u>Ploughs</u> (11:4) 85, p. 172.
1200. DiVENTI, Tom
   "Sleep Is Fun Forever." <u>Open24</u> (4) 85, p. 15-16.
   "When I Wear My Dress." <u>Open24</u> (4) 85, p. 28.
1201. DIXON, Melvin
   "After Prayers at Twilight." <u>SouthernR</u> (21:3) Sum 85, p.

845.
"Altitudes" (for Richard: centripetal, earth signs).
    SouthernR (21:3) Sum 85, p. 847-848.
"Mother's Tour." SouthernR (21:3) Sum 85, p. 846.
"Winter Gardens." SouthernR (21:3) Sum 85, p. 845-846.
1202. DJANIKIAN, Gregory
"The Theft." Poetry (145:4) Ja 85, p. 216-217.
"These Are the Gifts" (For my daughter, 2-1/2). Poetry
    (145:4) Ja 85, p. 217-218.
1203. DOBBS, C. K.
"Nine Years Old near Hannibal on the Mississippi." CarolQ
    (37:2) Wint 85, p. 50-51.
1204. DOBLER, Patricia
"Book Circle." PraS (59:2) Sum 85, p. 105.
"The Ghost." PraS (59:2) Sum 85, p. 106.
"The Mill in Winter." BlackWR (12:1) Fall 85, p. 61.
"Two Photographs." PraS (59:2) Sum 85, p. 106-107.
"What Mother Wanted for Me." CrossCur (5:2) 85, p. 47.
"World without End" (1984 AWP Award-Winning Poem).
    Tendril (19/20) 85, p. 37.
1205. DOBRAN, Michael Evan
"Ambient 28." CreamCR (10:1) 85, p. 36-37.
1206. DOBYNS, Stephen
"Cemetery Nights III." SenR (15:1) 85, p. 21.
"Cemetery Nights IV." SenR (15:1) 85, p. 22-23.
"Creeping Intelligence." SenR (15:1) 85, p. 19-20.
"The Face in the Ceiling." Ploughs (11:1) 85, p. 71-72.
"Freak" (For Byron Burford). Ploughs (11:1) 85, p. 79-80.
"How to Like It." Ploughs (11:1) 85, p. 77-78.
"Pony Express." Ploughs (11:1) 85, p. 73-74.
"Spider Web." Ploughs (11:1) 85, p. 75-76.
"Spiritual Chickens." SenR (15:1) 85, p. 17-18.
1207. DOCHERTY, John
"John Torrington." TexasR (6:3/4) Fall-Wint 85, p. 93.
1208. DODD, Elizabeth
"Another Season." Tendril (19/20) 85, p. 127.
"As If an Arm Could Always Reach through Pain or Distance."
    WestB (17) 85, p. 93-94.
"As If Life Mirrored Art." WestB (17) 85, p. 92-93.
1209. DODD, Wayne
"Again." Iowa (15:1) Wint 85, p. 81-82.
"Winter Poems." Iowa (15:1) Wint 85, p. 80.
1210. DOELE, Sikke
"Dictators" (tr. by Rod Jellema). PoetL (79:4) Wint 85,
    p. 238.
1211. DOERING, Steven
"Flash of Confusion." Bogg (53) 85, p. 20.
"Middles." WormR (25:4, issue 100) 85, p. 154-155.
"Piece of Ass." WormR (25:4, issue 100) 85, p. 154.
"There Is Much of Me." RagMag (4:1) Spr 85, p. 5.
1212. DOLAN, John D.
"Capital Losses." JamesWR (2:3) Spr-Sum 85, p. 12.
1213. DOLAN, Karen Deirdre
"Resisting Rain" (for David). CrossCur (4:4/5:1) 85, p.
    109-110.
1214. DOLAN, Pam Stratton
"Elegy for Mother." EngJ (74:5) S 85, p. 92.
1215. DOMINA, Lynn
"Objects for Still Lives" (Selection: II. "The Pear: The
    Creation of Habit"). Nimrod (29:1) Fall-Wint 85, p. 96.
"The Offering." CimR (73) O 85, p. 45.
"The Wedding Feast." HawaiiR (18) Fall 85, p. 35-36.
1216. DONAGHY, Michael
"The Tuning." MissR (13:3, issue 39) Spr 85, p. 81-82.
1217. DONAHUE, Joseph
"Guest Plus Host Equals Ghost." Temblor (2) 85, p. 122.

"Lou Reed." <u>Temblor</u> (2) 85, p. 123.
1218. DONALDSON, Jeffery
        "Movements from an Unfinished Symphony." <u>GrandS</u> (4:4) Sum
        85, p. 61-72.
1219. DONALDSON, Stephen R.
        "Elegy." <u>WoosterR</u> (3) Spr 85, p. 74-75.
1220. DONNELLY, Susan
        "Field Guides to the Birds." <u>PraS</u> (59:4) Wint 85, p. 95.
        "Forced Forsythia." <u>PraS</u> (59:4) Wint 85, p. 95-96.
1221. DONOVAN, Deirdre
        "Mary Decker." <u>WindO</u> (46) Fall 85, p. 11.
1222. DONOVAN, Diane C.
        "Perpetual Motion." <u>Amelia</u> (2:2) O 85, p. 28.
1223. DONOVAN, Laurence
        "Donovan's Tarot." <u>SpiritSH</u> (51) 85, 45 p.
1224. DONOVAN, Loretta
        "Early Morning Roof Horizontals." <u>Vis</u> (18) 85, p. 34.
        "The Inevitable Background Information." <u>Vis</u> (18) 85, p.
        33-34.
1225. DONOVAN, Stewart
        "Dublin's McLuhan" (In Memoriam). <u>AntigR</u> (62/63) Sum-Aut
        85, p. 125.
        "Immigrants." <u>AntigR</u> (60) Wint 85, p. 110.
        "In Our Time Too." <u>AntigR</u> (60) Wint 85, p. 110.
1226. DORAN, Jim
        "Twilight Performance." <u>CutB</u> (24) Spr-Sum 85, p. 48-49.
1227. DORESKI, William
        "April First." <u>Outbr</u> (14/15) Fall 84-Spr 85, p. 55.
        "Black Ice." <u>MassR</u> (26:2/3) Sum-Aut 85, p. 475.
        "A Field of Sculpture." <u>LitR</u> (29:1) Fall 85, p. 14-15.
        "Sea-Lavender." <u>LitR</u> (29:1) Fall 85, p. 12.
        "A Sense of Your Body." <u>Outbr</u> (14/15) Fall 84-Spr 85, p.
        56.
        "Stonington Harbor." <u>MassR</u> (26:2/3) Sum-Aut 85, p. 476.
        "Turtle Eggs." <u>LitR</u> (29:1) Fall 85, p. 13.
1228. DORFMAN, Nina
        "Buttons" (1943). <u>HiramPoR</u> (38) Spr-Sum 85, p. 9.
        "New Widow." <u>HiramPoR</u> (38) Spr-Sum 85, p. 10.
1229. DORMAN, Sonya
        "The Old Country." <u>WestB</u> (16) 85, p. 40.
1230. DORNEY, Dennis M.
        "Flight from Churubusco." <u>Tendril</u> (19/20) 85, p. 135.
        "Sunday with the Game On." <u>Tendril</u> (19/20) 85, p. 136.
1231. DORRIS, Michael
        "Dangerous Waters" (For Henrietta). <u>NoDaQ</u> (53:2) Spr 85,
        p. 173.
1232. DORSET, Gerald
        "A Lover Running for Office." <u>Bogg</u> (53) 85, p. 36.
1233. DORSETT, Robert
        "Camper's Theorem" (found in <u>The Death of Adam</u>, by John
        C. Greene, Mentor 1959). <u>KanQ</u> (17:4) Fall 85, p. 93.
        "Confession" (tr. of Wen I-To). <u>LitR</u> (28:4) Sum 85, p. 589.
        "The Death of Orpheus." <u>SouthernHR</u> (19:3) Sum 85, p. 204.
1234. DORSETT, Thomas
        "The Answer." <u>SmPd</u> (22:2) Spr 85, p. 8.
        "The Difference between Dust and Snow." <u>WebR</u> (10:2) Fall
        85, p. 59.
        "Nobody's Haircut." <u>Amelia</u> (2:2) O 85, p. 75.
1235. DOTY, Mark
        "A Catalogue for Cooks." <u>Agni</u> (22) 85, p. 88-90.
        "Charlie Howard's Descent." <u>PoetryNW</u> (26:3) Aut 85, p. 46-
        47.
        "Shaker Orchard." <u>Poetry</u> (147:1) O 85, p. 33-34.
        "Turtle, Swan." <u>Crazy</u> (28) Spr 85, p. 64-66.
1236. DOUGHERTY, Fred
        "Ballad of the Vietnam Vet." <u>SanFPJ</u> (7:2) 85, p. 93.

1237. DOUGHERTY, Jay
        "Before and After the Blast." <u>PoetryE</u> (18) Fall 85, p. 85-
            86.
        "Conversation from Another Planet." <u>WormR</u> (25:4, issue
            100) 85, p. 128-129.
        "Coveringdeertrackswithwords." <u>WormR</u> (25:4, issue 100)
            85, p. 127.
        "Let Me Tell You How I Got Those." <u>Bogg</u> (53) 85, p. 40.
        "Road Not the Taken." <u>WormR</u> (25:4, issue 100) 85, p. 128.
        "The Teacher" (for Reed Whittemore). <u>Wind</u> (15:54) 85, p.
            56.
1238. DOVE, Rita
        "Aircraft." <u>CutB</u> (23) Fall-Wint 85, p. 29.
        "La Chapelle. 92nd Division. Ted." <u>SouthernR</u> (21:3) Sum
            85, p. 849-850.
        "Daystar." <u>Agni</u> (22) 85, p. 71.
        "Dog Days, Jerusalem." <u>SouthernR</u> (21:3) Sum 85, p. 853.
        "Falling Asleep with a Cold." <u>OP</u> (38/39) Spr 85, p. 25.
        "Fifth Grade Autobiography." <u>SouthernR</u> (21:3) Sum 85, p.
            852-853.
        "The Gorge." <u>SouthernR</u> (21:3) Sum 85, p. 850-852.
        "Lightnin' Blues." <u>ParisR</u> (27:96) Sum 85, p. 102.
        "Obedience." <u>CutB</u> (23) Fall-Wint 85, p. 28.
        "Old Folk's Home, Jerusalem" (For Harry Timar). <u>Poetry</u>
            (147:1) O 85, p. 12.
        "The Satisfaction Coal Company." <u>ParisR</u> (27:96) Sum 85,
            p. 103-104.
        "Turning Thirty, I Contemplate Students Bicycling Home."
            <u>Iowa</u> (15:1) Wint 85, p. 24.
        "Weathering Out." <u>Agni</u> (22) 85, p. 69-70.
        "Wingfoot Lake" (Independence Day, 1964). <u>ParisR</u> (27:96)
            Sum 85, p. 105-106.
1239. DOWKER, David Joseph
        "Doldrums." <u>PoetryCR</u> (6:4) Sum 85, p. 47.
1240. DOWNER, Ann Elizabeth
        "Practical Holiness." <u>Gargoyle</u> (27) 85, p. 91.
1241. DOWNIE, Glen
        "Evolution." <u>PraF</u> (6:2) Spr 85, p. 38.
        "Splitting." <u>PraF</u> (6:2) Spr 85, p. 39.
        "Spring Cleaning." <u>WestCR</u> (20:2) O 85, p. 38.
        "Stone Men." <u>PraF</u> (6:2) Spr 85, p. 40.
1242. DOXEY, W. S.
        "Being Here." <u>Mund</u> (15:1/2) 85, p. 68.
        "Edges." <u>Mund</u> (15:1/2) 85, p. 68.
1243. DOYLE, Donna
        "They're Talking Days Now." <u>AntigR</u> (62/63) Sum-Aut 85, p.
            37.
1244. DOYLE, James
        "The Beast." <u>BlueBldgs</u> (9) [85?], p. 33.
        "The Course." <u>BlueBldgs</u> (9) [85?], p. 33.
        "The Metaphors of the Dead." <u>StoneC</u> (12:2/3) Spr-Sum 85,
            p. 47.
        "Salomê." <u>CutB</u> (23) Fall-Wint 85, p. 64.
1245. DOYLE, P. J.
        "How to Train a Mistress." <u>RagMag</u> (4:1) Spr 85, p. 22-23.
1246. DOYLE, Suzanne J.
        "After Swan Lake, Act II at the San Francisco Ballet."
            <u>ChiR</u> (35:1) Aut 85, p. 58-59.
1247. DRAGOMOSHCHENKO, Arkadii
        "Accidia" (tr. by Lyn Hejinian and Michael Molnar).
            <u>Sulfur</u> (14) 85, p. 116-122.
        "I dread my dreams" (tr. by Lyn Hejinian and Michael
            Molnar). <u>Sulfur</u> (14) 85, p. 131.
        "Obscure Bases of Narration" (example readings, tr. by Lyn
            Hejinian and Michael Molnar). <u>Sulfur</u> (14) 85, p. 123-
            127.

"A Sentimental Elegy" (a gift for Anna, tr. by Lyn Hejinian
   and Michael Molnar). <u>Sulfur</u> (14) 85, p. 128-130.
"Study of Dimension" (tr. by Lyn Hejinian and Michael
   Molnar). <u>Sulfur</u> (14) 85, p. 131.
1248. DRAKE, Barbara
   "The Bed." <u>Sulfur</u> (13) 85, p. 126-128.
1249. DRAKE, Jack
   "A Brief Reactive Psychosis." <u>NegC</u> (5:4) Fall 85, p. 133-
      134.
   "Germans, Jews, John Cohen, and Me." <u>NegC</u> (5:4) Fall 85,
      p. 131-132.
   "An Old Man Talks at the Yellow Creek Boat Landing." <u>NegC</u>
      (5:4) Fall 85, p. 127-128.
   "The Viet Nam War 1984." <u>NegC</u> (5:4) Fall 85, p. 129-131.
1250. DRAPEAU, Francis Xavier
   "No Swimming." <u>ConnPR</u> (3:1) 84, p. 34-35.
1251. DRESCHER, Elizabeth
   "The Body As Concept." <u>Pig</u> (13) 85, p. 95.
   "A Rhetoric of Modern Art." <u>Pig</u> (13) 85, p. 76.
1252. DRESMAN, Paul
   "Willow Work." <u>SoDakR</u> (23:1) Spr 85, p. 50.
1253. DREW, Bettina
   "A Relief to be Back." <u>Wind</u> (15:54) 85, p. 15.
1254. DREW, George
   "103 Mountain Avenue." <u>Blueline</u> (7:1) Sum-Fall 85, p. 5.
   "Burning Trash." <u>Blueline</u> (7:1) Sum-Fall 85, p. 4.
   "The Knowledge of Bruised Fruit." <u>Blueline</u> (6:2) Wint-Spr
      85, p. 47.
1255. DREWRY, Elizabeth
   "For Dan." <u>Raccoon</u> (17) Mr 85, p. 12.
1256. DRISCOLL, Frances
   "If it rains, what will we do?" (tr. of Thérèse
      Plantier). <u>WebR</u> (10:1) Spr 85, p. 29.
   "The Night Dance." <u>HolCrit</u> (22:2) Ap 85, p. 14-15.
   "Night on earth and love" (tr. of Thérèse Plantier).
      <u>WebR</u> (10:1) Spr 85, p. 30.
   "There is no one season to sow the body" (tr. of
      Thérèse Plantier). <u>WebR</u> (10:1) Spr 85, p. 29.
1257. DRISCOLL, Jack
   "Driving towards Sleep." <u>HawaiiR</u> (18) Fall 85, p. 97.
   "The Electric Fence." <u>PoetryNW</u> (26:1) Spr 85, p. 34.
   "The Love and Fear of Fire." <u>PassN</u> (6:2) Spr-Sum 85, p. 3.
1258. DRISKELL, Leon
   "Like Maenads." <u>NegC</u> (5:1) Wint 85, p. 40-44.
1259. DROBNIES, Adrienne
   "Sabertooth." <u>Waves</u> (14:1/2) Fall 85, p. 26.
   "Two Views of Winter." <u>PoetryCR</u> (6:4) Sum 85, p. 45.
DRUMMOND de ANDRADE, Carlos
   <u>See</u> ANDRADE, Carlos Drummond de
1260. DRURY, John
   "The Biblical Garden." <u>MissouriR</u> (8:3) 85, p. 114-116.
   "Evensong." <u>QW</u> (20) Spr-Sum 85, p. 118.
1261. DU, Fu
   "Going to the Palace with a Friend at Dawn" (tr. by Sam
      Hamill). <u>PoetryE</u> (18) Fall 85, p. 68.
   "Looking at Mount T'ai" (tr. by Sam Hamill). <u>PoetryE</u> (18)
      Fall 85, p. 67.
   "Passing Mr. Sung's Old House" (tr. by Sam Hamill).
      <u>PoetryE</u> (18) Fall 85, p. 70.
   "Random Pleasures, III" (tr. by Sam Hamill). <u>PoetryE</u> (18)
      Fall 85, p. 66.
   "Random Pleasures, IV" (tr. by Sam Hamill). <u>PoetryE</u> (18)
      Fall 85, p. 69.
   "Visiting the Monastery at Lung-men" (tr. by Sam Hamill).
      <u>PoetryE</u> (18) Fall 85, p. 65.

1262. DUBIE, Norman
        "Currier & Ives." AntR (43:1) Wint 85, p. 78.
        "The Huts at Esquimaux." MissR (13:3, issue 39) Spr 85,
            p. 62-63.
        "Oration: Half Moon in Vermont." MissR (13:3, issue 39)
            Spr 85, p. 60-61.
        "The Trolley from Xochimilco." Crazy (28) Spr 85, p. 55-
            58.
1263. DUBNOV, Eugene
        "How the snow's dry prickles lash across" (For Carol
            Rumens). SouthwR (70:3) Sum 85, p. 359.
        "So to Speak" (tr. by Christopher Newman). Rampike
            (4:2/3) 85-86, p. 74.
1264. DUBRAVA, Patricia
        "Women's Work." GreenfR (13:1/2) Fall-Wint 85, p. 158.
1265. DUDDY, Patrick
        "Massacre at Martin's Hundred." Thrpny (5:4, issue 20)
            Wint 85, p. 21.
1266. DUDEK, Louis
        "Advertisement." Rampike (4:2/3) 85-86, p. 9.
        "The Future." Waves (13:4) Spr 85, p. 64.
        "Hilary Our Kitten." Waves (13:4) Spr 85, p. 64.
        "Regret, Regret." AntigR (61) Spr 85, p. 14.
        "To a Young Woman." AntigR (61) Spr 85, p. 13.
1267. DUDLEY, Deborah
        "Missing in the 20th Century." PoetryCR (7:1) Aut 85, p.
            15.
1268. DUEHR, Gary
        "Another Life." NegC (5:2) Spr 85, p. 86.
        "Cure." PraS (59:3) Fall 85, p. 32.
        "Modern Problems" (Excerpts). Telescope (4:1) Wint 85, p.
            11-13.
        "Still, I Look Around." PraS (59:3) Fall 85, p. 33.
        "To Teach." NewL (51:3) Spr 85, p. 120.
1269. DUFF, Marnie
        "Islands in Bed." AntigR (60) Wint 85, p. 55.
1270. DUFFIN, K. E.
        "Commute." Verse (3) 85, p. 18.
1271. DUGAN, Alan
        "Mock Translation from the Greek." Ploughs (11:4) 85, p.
            15.
        "On the Summer Goddess Who Should Be Nameless." Ploughs
            (11:4) 85, p. 256-257.
1272. DUKES, Norman
        "Delphi on a Winter Evening." Agni (22) 85, p. 49.
        "Marx's Tomb in Highgate Cemetery." Agni (22) 85, p. 44.
        "Moving Day." Agni (22) 85, p. 48.
        "Portrait of Father in a Dust Storm." Agni (22) 85, p. 46-
            47.
        "Science Center." Agni (22) 85, p. 50.
        "To the Reader, to the Writer." Agni (22) 85, p. 51.
        "Two Pictures of a Rose in the Dark." Agni (22) 85, p. 43.
        "Wedge." Agni (22) 85, p. 42.
        "The Year" (For my mother, 1908-1970). Agni (22) 85, p.
            45.
1273. DULIN, Jane L.
        "Telegrams and Anger." Open24 (4) 85, p. 47.
1274. DUMAINE, Christine
        "The Death of Rachel" (Poetry Award). Prima (9) 85, p. 24.
1275. DUMARAN, Adele
        "Dear Ginger." HawaiiR (17) Spr 85, p. 76-77.
        "Moorea" (for William Sawyer). HawaiiR (17) Spr 85, p. 78.
1276. DUNBAR, Jan
        "Big Moment." EngJ (74:1) Ja 85, p. 72.
1277. DUNCAN, Graham
        "Toad." Vis (18) 85, p. 15.

1278. DUNCAN, Robert
        "After a Long Illness." <u>SouthernR</u> (21:1) Wint 85, p. 49-
            51.
        "A Paris Visit: Poems" (Drawings and Afterword by R. B.
            Kitaj). <u>Conjunc</u> (8) 85, p. 8-21.
1279. DUNGEY, Christopher
        "Girls Running Cross-Country." <u>WindO</u> (46) Fall 85, p. 22.
        "His Sermon to the Graduates." <u>Wind</u> (15:54) 85, p. 16.
        "My Dentist, Running." <u>WindO</u> (46) Fall 85, p. 23.
1280. DUNMORE, Helen
        "In Deep Water." <u>Stand</u> (26:1) Wint 84-85, p. 56.
1281. DUNN, Douglas
        "Abernethy." <u>Verse</u> (4) 85, p. 3.
        "S. Frediano's." <u>NewYorker</u> (61:1) 25 F 85, p. 36.
1282. DUNN, Millard
        "At the Ninth Grade Prom." <u>SouthernPR</u> (26, i.e. 25:2)
            Fall 85, p. 6.
1283. DUNN, Sharon
        "Creation." <u>AmerPoR</u> (14:2) Mr-Ap 85, p. 13.
1284. DUNN, Stephen
        "Accident in the Snow on the Way to <u>Amadeus</u>." <u>QW</u> (20)
            Spr-Sum 85, p. 52-53.
        "After the Argument." <u>QW</u> (20) Spr-Sum 85, p. 50-51.
        "At the Smithville Methodist Church." <u>PoetryNW</u> (26:2) Sum
            85, p. 24-25.
        "He / She." <u>GeoR</u> (39:1) Spr 85, p. 167-168.
        "Ignorance." <u>Poetry</u> (146:5) Ag 85, p. 259.
        "Leaning toward Grandfather." <u>Raccoon</u> (17) Mr 85, p. 5-6.
        "Local Time." <u>Crazy</u> (28) Spr 85, p. 30-38.
        "Portrait." <u>Poetry</u> (146:5) Ag 85, p. 260-261.
        "Round Trip." <u>NewEngR</u> (7:3) Spr 85, p. 361-368.
        "Saints." <u>Poetry</u> (146:5) Ag 85, p. 260.
        "Toward the Verrazano." <u>Antaeus</u> (55) Aut 85, p. 91.
        "Tucson." <u>Crazy</u> (28) Spr 85, p. 29.
1285. DUNNE, Carol
        "All the Way to Ireland to Win One." <u>Wind</u> (15:54) 85, p.
            42.
        "Catalina." <u>WindO</u> (45) Spr 85, p. 11.
        "Child without the Warring Parts." <u>Outbr</u> (14/15) Fall 84-
            Spr 85, p. 48.
        "Coming Home to Damion." <u>WebR</u> (10:1) Spr 85, p. 52.
        "The Foxing of Black Priscilla." <u>CumbPR</u> (5:1) Fall 85, p.
            12.
        "Frances and Elizabeth." <u>WindO</u> (45) Spr 85, p. 12.
        "The Jilt." <u>CumbPR</u> (5:1) Fall 85, p. 13.
        "The Man Who Is Patient with Seascapes." <u>StoneC</u> (13:1/2)
            Fall-Wint 85-86, p. 9.
        "The Men of My Miles." <u>WebR</u> (10:1) Spr 85, p. 53.
        "Sessions." <u>Outbr</u> (14/15) Fall 84-Spr 85, p. 47.
1286. DUNNING, Stephen
        "At the Boulderado." <u>MichQR</u> (24:4) Fall 85, p. 620.
        "Hide and Seek." <u>BelPoJ</u> (35:4) Sum 85, p. 36.
        "Independence Day" (for Buffy). <u>BelPoJ</u> (35:4) Sum 85, p.
            37.
        "Moves." <u>LaurelR</u> (19:2) Sum 85, p. 32.
        "News." <u>NewL</u> (52:1) Fall 85, p. 39-40.
1287. DUNSMORE, Roger
        "Blood House" (from Nancy by Roger for Jack). <u>PraS</u> (59:4)
            Wint 85, p. 46-47.
        "For Nelly." <u>PraS</u> (59:4) Wint 85, p. 45-46.
        "Humus" (for Willie). <u>PraS</u> (59:4) Wint 85, p. 48-49.
        "The Junco" (a self-respect poem). <u>PraS</u> (59:4) Wint 85,
            p. 50.
1288. DUPREE, Edison
        "At Your Hanging." <u>Ploughs</u> (11:1) 85, p. 82.
        "The Donation." <u>Ploughs</u> (11:1) 85, p. 83.

"A Life of Crime" (for John Vargas). Ploughs (11:1) 85, p. 84.

"None Other" (Matthew 27.50,51). Ploughs (11:1) 85, p. 81.

"To the Glistening Center of a Period, on a Page of the Newspaper." Ploughs (11:1) 85, p. 85.

"Water Music." WestHR (19:2) Sum 85, p. 119.

1289. DURBIN, William
"Summer Carpenter." Confr (29) Wint 85, p. 100.

1290. DUREN, Brian
"Fadings." Rampike (4:2/3) 85-86, p. 100-103.

1291. DURHAM, Jimmie
"1886 / Haymarket / Prairie Grasses." MinnR (N.S. 25) Fall 85, p. 5-6.

1292. DURNO, Janet
"Ghost Shirt." Quarry (34:4) Aut 85, p. 15-17.

1293. DUTTON, Sandra
"The Festival of the Broken Body." Wind (15:53) 85, p. 8-9.

1294. DuVAL, John
"Ana Maria" (tr. of Nicolás Guillén, w. Gastón Fernández-Torriente). NewEngR (7:4) Sum 85, p. 541.

"Force of Habit" (tr. of Trilussa). Mund (15:1/2) 85, p. 153.

"The Grand Zoo" (Selections: "Winds," "The Great Bear," "Aconcagua," "KKK," "Rivers", tr. of Nicolás Guillén, w. Gastón Fernández-Torriente). NewEngR (7:4) Sum 85, p. 542-544.

"Happiness" (tr. of Trilussa). Mund (15:1/2) 85, p. 153.

"Sensemayah" (Snake-killing song, tr. of Nicolás Guillén, w. Gastón Fernández-Torriente). NewEngR (7:4) Sum 85, p. 540-541.

1295. DWORKIN, Martin S.
"Voice Over." LaurelR (19:1) Wint 85, p. 60.

1296. DWYER, Augusta
"When This War Should End" (tr. of Nain Nómez). Waves (13:2/3) Wint 85, p. 70, 72.

1297. DWYER, David
"To Kathleen, with a Rabbit." PraS (59:3) Fall 85, p. 75-77.

1298. DWYER, T. J.
"A Man & a Woman on a Beach." Wind (15:54) 85, p. 34.

1299. DYAK, Miriam
"China Sparklers" (for Ray). YellowS (14) Spr 85, p. 24.

1300. DYCK, E. F.
"My Dark Darling, My Dolphin" (after a line by Nana Issaia). Dandel (12:1) 85, p. 23.

"Yin-Yang Dolphin." Dandel (12:1) 85, p. 22.

1301. DYE, Bru
"Rimbaud's Motorcycle." JamesWR (3:1) Fall 85, p. 5.

1302. DYE, Vesna
"Coral Returned to the Sea" (tr. of Vesna Parun, w. Peter Kastmiler). WebR (10:2) Fall 85, p. 38.

1303. DYER, Linda
"Grandmother Rogers' Bed." Nimrod (29:1) Fall-Wint 85, p. 37.

1304. DYLAN, Bob
"I Believe in You." Kaleid (10) Spr 85, p. 44.

1305. DYMENT, Margaret
"There Is No West Coast." Quarry (34:3) Sum 85, p. 71.

1306. EADY, Robert
"Bluebeard's Theatre." PoetryCR (6:3) Spr 85, p. 9.

"Satan." PoetryCR (6:3) Spr 85, p. 9.

1307. EARLS, Terrence D.
"Epiphanies." EngJ (74:6) O 85, p. 84.

1308. EARLY, Gerald
"The Dreadful Bop of Flyers." NowestR (23:3) 85, p. 33-37.

1309. EATON, Charles Edward
    "The Axle." _Chelsea_ (44) 85, p. 115.
    "The Blowgun." _Tendril_ (19/20) 85, p. 137-138.
    "Discs." _Poem_ (53) Mr 85, p. 2.
    "Down by the Riverside." _WebR_ (10:1) Spr 85, p. 80-81.
    "Folk Song." _ConcPo_ (18:1/2) 85, p. 134.
    "Geisha." _CrossCur_ (5:2) 85, p. 91-92.
    "The Glioma." _ChiR_ (34:4) 85, p. 26-27.
    "Hacienda." _HawaiiR_ (18) Fall 85, p. 59.
    "Imago." _Poem_ (53) Mr 85, p. 1.
    "In Xanadu." _HiramPoR_ (38) Spr-Sum 85, p. 11.
    "The Luck of the Zeppelin." _Salm_ (68/69) Fall-Wint 85-86,
        p. 14-15.
    "The Odometer." _CharR_ (11:1) Spr 85, p. 66.
    "The Prompter." _Poem_ (53) Mr 85, p. 3.
    "The Soft Spot." _KanQ_ (17:1/2) Wint-Spr 85, p. 110.
    "Special Effects." _Salm_ (68/69) Fall-Wint 85-86, p. 16.
    "The Stretcher." _HolCrit_ (22:5) D 85, p. 17.
    "Sunflower Souvenir." _SouthwR_ (70:2) Spr 85, p. 243.
    "The Veil of Breath." _DeKalbLAJ_ (18:1/2) 85, p. 67-68.
    "Writing Letters on a Train." _CrossCur_ (4:2) 84, p. 75.
1310. EBERHART, Richard
    "21st Century Man." _NewEngR_ (7:3) Spr 85, p. 298.
    "The Angels." _NegC_ (5:4) Fall 85, p. 81-82.
    "Boat Race Speculation." _OP_ (38/39) Spr 85, p. 216.
    "The Hand" (for Helen Vendler). _MichQR_ (24:3) Sum 85, p.
        390.
    "To the Harps." _Verse_ (2) 85, p. 9.
    "White Pines, Felled 1984." _NegC_ (5:4) Fall 85, p. 83-84.
1311. EBERT, Gwen
    "Psalmist." _CreamCR_ (10:1) 85, p. 38.
1312. ECELBERGER, Dana
    "Between the Lines." _Confr_ (29) Wint 85, p. 135.
1313. ECKBLAD, Peter
    "The Poet's Pipe." _Wind_ (15:54) 85, p. 17.
EDDY, Darlene Mathis
    See MATHIS-EDDY, Darlene
1314. EDDY, Gary
    "Why the Shakers Didn't Write Poetry." _Geor_ (39:2) Sum
        85, p. 242.
1315. EDEL, Marjorie
    "Hulihee." _HawaiiR_ (17) Spr 85, p. 44.
1316. EDELMAN, Lee
    "Glacial Valley, Late July." _Nat_ (240:14) 13 Ap 85, p.
        440.
1317. EDGARLEECHIADES OF SPOONIA
    "On the Tomb of Gladiator Butchweldedes" (tr. by Elliot
        Richman). _WindO_ (46) Fall 85, p. 4.
1318. EDGERTON, Becky R.
    "Old Tricks." _IndR_ (8:1) Wint 85, p. 51.
1319. EDGU, Ferit
    "Classroom Notes" (Selections, tr. by Talat Sait Halman).
        GreenfR (13:1/2) Fall-Wint 85, p. 86-90.
1320. EDMO, Ed
    "Indian Mask." _GreenfR_ (12:3/4) Wint-Spr 85, p. 73.
1321. EDMONDS, Dale
    "Cedar Crest Lodge" (January, 1964). _NegC_ (5:4) Fall 85,
        p. 136-138.
    "To My Daughter" (or son, aged two months, who died on the
        higway between Indianapolis, Ind., and Columbus, O., on
        May 15, 1959). _NegC_ (5:4) Fall 85, p. 135.
1322. EDMONDSON, Gary
    "Holocene Memories." _WebR_ (10:2) Fall 85, p. 80.
1323. EDMUNDS, Martin
    "Fever." _Agni_ (22) 85, p. 99-100.

1324. EDSON, Russell
       "The Egg Layers." <u>MidAR</u> (5:2) 85, p. 87.
1325. EDWARDS, Frank John
       "Post-Traumatic Stress Syndrome Blues." <u>VirQ</u> (61:4) Aut
          85, p. 620-623.
       "The Sound of Branches Cut." <u>VirQ</u> (61:4) Aut 85, p. 623-
          624.
1326. EDWARDS, Joan
       "Coleus." <u>Wind</u> (15:53) 85, p. 16.
1327. EDWARDS, Mary Uzzell
       "The Hedge." <u>NegC</u> (5:3) Sum 85, p. 134-135.
1328. EDWARDS, Paul
       "The Artist at the Menai Straits" (for Irene). <u>HangL</u> (48)
          Fall 85, p. 14.
       "Holiday in Tokyo." <u>HangL</u> (48) Fall 85, p. 11-12.
       "West Coast Split-Up." <u>HangL</u> (48) Fall 85, p. 13.
1329. EEN, Andrea
       "Turned Around." <u>RagMag</u> (4:2) Fall 85, p. 34.
1330. EGGELING, J. L. S.
       "The Ganymede Equation." <u>JamesWR</u> (3:1) Fall 85, p. 14.
1331. EHRHART, W. D.
       "Awaiting the Harvest." <u>StoneC</u> (12:2/3) Spr-Sum 85, p. 23.
       "Flying to the Moon." <u>PaintedB</u> (25) Spr 85, p. 19.
       "Home Is the Hunter" (Longmont Municipal Airport, Colorado,
          December 1979). <u>ConnPR</u> (3:1) 84, p. 45.
       "On the Plain of Marathon" (Marine Corps Marathon,
          Washington, DC, 6 November 1983). <u>StoneC</u> (13:1/2) Fall-
          Wint 85-86, p. 29.
       "Responsibility." <u>Sam</u> (42:3, 167th release) 85, p. 20-21.
       "Winter Bells." <u>PaintedB</u> (26/27) Sum-Fall 85, p. 8.
1332. EHRLICH, Maurice
       "The Abandoned." <u>SanFPJ</u> (7:4) 85, p. 77.
       "To Whom It May Concern." <u>SanFPJ</u> (7:4) 85, p. 80.
1333. EHRLICH, Shelley
       "Goldfinch in April." <u>Northeast</u> (Series 4:1) Sum 85, p. 9.
       "Hummingbird." <u>Northeast</u> (Series 4:1) Sum 85, p. 8.
       "Naamah and the Ark" (Selections: "Dailiness in the Ark,"
          "The Notion," "From Naamah's Notebook"). <u>PraS</u> (59:4)
          Wint 85, p. 51-54.
1334. EHRMAN, S. (<u>See</u> also EHRMAN, Sally)
       "Berry Poem." <u>GreenfR</u> (13:1/2) Fall-Wint 85, p. 155.
1335. EHRMAN, Sally (<u>See</u> also EHRMAN, S.)
       "Local Farmer." <u>WindO</u> (45) Spr 85, p. 20.
1336. EICH, Günter
       "Looking at Schiller's Pen" (tr. by Mary Davies). <u>Field</u>
          (32) Spr 85, p. 35.
       "Pigeons" (In German and English, tr. by Teo Savory).
          <u>CrossCur</u> (4:4/5:1) 85, p. 100-101.
       "Yellow" (tr. by Mary Davies). <u>Field</u> (32) Spr 85, p. 36.
1337. EICHHORN, Doug
       "Ithaca, 1966." <u>NewL</u> (51:3) Spr 85, p. 47.
1338. EIGNER, Larry
       "Absence of the dead tree" (#1477). <u>Sulfur</u> (14) 85, p. 42.
       "Breathing invisible smoke" (#1403). <u>Sulfur</u> (14) 85, p.
          43.
       "Death this great impediment." <u>Kaleid</u> (11) Sum 85, p. 27.
       "Down the block" (#1496). <u>Sulfur</u> (14) 85, p. 43.
       "End History about like any other point" (#1506). <u>Sulfur</u>
          (14) 85, p. 42.
       "Forget days." <u>Kaleid</u> (11) Sum 85, p. 27.
       "The most productive agricultural county in the East"
          (#1460). <u>Sulfur</u> (14) 85, p. 44.
       "Sometimes it's surprising how I don't think of death."
          <u>Kaleid</u> (11) Sum 85, p. 27.
       "The woman's muscle inside him." <u>Kaleid</u> (11) Sum 85, p.
          27.

1339. EIMERS, Nancy
        "The First Photographer." _CutB_ (24) Spr-Sum 85, p. 36.
1340. EINZIG, Barbara
        "After Wim Wenders' _Die Angst Des Tormanns Beim Elfmeter_"
        ("The Fear of the Goalie before the Penalty"). _Conjunc_
        (8) 85, p. 22-23.
1341. EISENBERG, Ruth F.
        "Oppositions." _GreenfR_ (13:1/2) Fall-Wint 85, p. 55.
1342. EKLUND, Jane
        "Here and Here." _PoetC_ (16:3) Spr 85, p. 7-8.
        "In the Hospital Storeroom." _PoetC_ (16:3) Spr 85, p. 9.
        "Indiana Blues." _PoetC_ (16:3) Spr 85, p. 6.
        "The Metamorphosis." _Tendril_ (19/20) 85, p. 140.
        "The Mill Worker's Daughter, 1933." _Tendril_ (19/20) 85,
        p. 139.
1343. ELAGIN, Ivan
        "Birch Tree" (in Russian and English, tr. by Helen
        Matveyeff). _WoosterR_ (4) Fall 85, p. 32-33.
        "I Stand Here, Filled with Sawdust" (in Russian and
        English, tr. by Helen Matveyeff). _WoosterR_ (4) Fall
        85, p. 34-37.
1344. ELDRIDGE, Kevin Joe
        "Hay Making." _SouthernPR_ (26, i.e. 25:2) Fall 85, p. 10-
        11.
        "I Was a Teen-Aged Baptist." _SouthernPR_ (26, i.e. 25:2)
        Fall 85, p. 8-9.
1345. ELENBOGEN, Dina
        "Chilled Mulberries." _Prima_ (9) 85, p. 78.
1346. ELENKOV, Luchesar
        "Dedication" (To Tamara, tr. by John Balaban). _Mund_
        (15:1/2) 85, p. 142.
1347. ELIAS, Megan
        "Limpid." _HangL_ (47) Spr 85, p. 55.
1348. ELIAS, Vic
        "Something for Karson" (revised). _Quarry_ (34:3) Sum 85,
        p. 27-28.
1349. ELIOT, Eileen
        "Changes." _Vis_ (18) 85, p. 38.
1350. ELKIND, Sue Saniel
        "Changing Direction." _PoeticJ_ (12) 85, p. 40.
        "A Hard Wind." _Wind_ (15:55) 85, p. 21-22.
        "The Silence of the World." _Wind_ (15:55) 85, p. 21.
1351. ELLEDGE, Jim
        "Halloween Morning." _Poem_ (54) N 85, p. 58.
        "A Last Evening in London." _GrahamHR_ (9) Fall 85, p. 27.
        "Myths." _Poem_ (54) N 85, p. 57.
        "Rock & Roll Confidential" (for Susan Del Guidice).
        SpoonRQ (10:2) Spr 85, p. 45.
        "Souvenir." _GrahamHR_ (9) Fall 85, p. 28.
1352. ELLIOTT, Carmen
        "Child of Jairus." _CarolQ_ (37:3) Spr 85, p. 72-73.
1353. ELLIOTT, William D.
        "Crossing the Front Campus, October 21." _PraF_ (6:1) Wint
        85, p. 59.
        "Wednesday." _NewL_ (52:1) Fall 85, p. 61.
1354. ELLIOTT, William I.
        "Artichoke." _Amelia_ (2:1) Ap 85, p. 43.
1355. ELLIS, Melanie
        "Mutation." _NoDaQ_ (53:2) Spr 85, p. 210.
        "Night Sun." _NoDaQ_ (53:2) Spr 85, p. 211.
1356. ELLISON, Jessie T.
        "Clean Kid." _WindO_ (45) Spr 85, p. 17.
1357. ELMAN, Richard
        "Sonnet on Discourse." _Confr_ (30/31) N 85, p. 71.
1358. ELMSLIE, Kenward
        "Puce Parrot." _Oink_ (19) 85, p. 82-85.

1359. ELMUSA, Sharif S.
    "Rain." <u>GreenfR</u> (13:1/2) Fall-Wint 85, p. 177.
    "Shapshots." <u>GreenfR</u> (13:1/2) Fall-Wint 85, p. 178.
1360. ELON, Florence
    "Imprint." <u>Confr</u> (29) Wint 85, p. 33.
    "Looking Eastward." <u>Confr</u> (29) Wint 85, p. 32.
1361. ELOVIC, Barbara
    "3/4 Time." <u>Poetry</u> (146:6) S 85, p. 339.
    "Light Years." <u>Poetry</u> (146:6) S 85, p. 338.
    "Lights." <u>Amelia</u> (2:1) Ap 85, p. 74.
    "Sarah." <u>GreenfR</u> (12:3/4) Wint-Spr 85, p. 32.
    "Trying." <u>GreenfR</u> (12:3/4) Wint-Spr 85, p. 33.
1362. ELSBERG, John
    "Ode to Stephen Crane." <u>Amelia</u> (2:2) O 85, p. 6.
1363. ELYTIS, Odysseus
    "Deep Blue" (tr. by Martin McKinsey). <u>Ploughs</u> (11:4) 85,
        p. 16.
    "The Garden Was Entering the Sea" (tr. by Martin McKinsey).
        <u>Ploughs</u> (11:4) 85, p. 18-19.
    "The Monogram" (Selection: VII, tr. by Edward Morin and
        Lefteris Pavlides). <u>NewL</u> (51:4) Sum 85, p. 13.
    "Pax San Tropezana" (tr. by Olga Broumas). <u>Zyzzyva</u> (1:4)
        Wint 85, p. 87-88.
    "Violet" (tr. by Martin McKinsey). <u>Ploughs</u> (11:4) 85, p.
        17.
1364. EMANS, Elaine V.
    "I'll Tell You How Deep the Snow Is." <u>KanQ</u> (17:1/2) Wint-
        Spr 85, p. 218.
    "Oh, to Wear the Bones of a Bird Inside." <u>TexasR</u> (6:3/4)
        Fall-Wint 85, p. 104.
    "Rite for a Squirrel." <u>KanQ</u> (17:1/2) Wint-Spr 85, p. 218.
    "Snow-Cave." <u>CapeR</u> (20:1) Spr 85, p. 43.
    "Talking to Peonies." <u>CentR</u> (29:3) Sum 85, p. 325-326.
    "The Two-Crow Recital." <u>Wind</u> (15:53) 85, p. 24.
    "Wood Duck." <u>KanQ</u> (17:4) Fall 85, p. 108.
1365. EMANUEL, Lynn
    "Apology." <u>Iowa</u> (15:1) Wint 85, p. 35.
1366. EMERY, Lillie A.
    "An Assembly Line Star." <u>SanFPJ</u> (7:4) 85, p. 55-56.
1367. EMERY, Michael J.
    "On Lifting." <u>WindO</u> (46) Fall 85, p. 11.
1368. EMIN, Gevorg
    "Silence Is Golden" (tr. by Diana Der Hovanessian).
        <u>GrahamHR</u> (8) Wint 85, p. 47.
1369. EMMANUEL, Pierre
    "Chansons du Dé à Coudre" (Selections: "Autumn,"
        "Somewhere in the empty house," tr. by Brian Merrikin
        Hill). <u>Verse</u> (1) 84, p. 39.
    "Magdalen in the Garden" (tr. by Brian Merrikin Hill).
        <u>Verse</u> (1) 84, p. 38.
1370. ENDO, Russell
    "Susumu, My Name." <u>AmerPoR</u> (14:3) My-Je 85, p. 44.
1371. ENGEBRETSEN, Alan C.
    "Disbelief." <u>Amelia</u> (2:1) Ap 85, p. 84.
1372. ENGEL, Peter
    "Ein Nicht Geheurer Freitag." <u>Mund</u> (15:1/2) 85, p. 154.
    "Not Your Usual Friday" (tr. by Billie R. Engels). <u>Mund</u>
        (15:1/2) 85, p. 155.
1373. ENGELS, Billie R.
    "Not Your Usual Friday" (tr. of Peter Engel). <u>Mund</u>
        (15:1/2) 85, p. 155.
1374. ENGELS, John
    "The Ash Grove in October." <u>MassR</u> (26:2/3) Sum-Aut 85, p.
        263-264.
    "Dead Dog." <u>Antaeus</u> (55) Aut 85, p. 92-93.

1375. ENGLAND, Jayne
      "Loss of a Child" (for Terry). <u>LaurelR</u> (19:2) Sum 85, p.
      61.
1376. ENGLE, Bruce
      "Letter to My Brother" (for Dan). <u>PassN</u> (6:2) Spr-Sum 85,
      p. 11.
1377. ENGLER, Robert Klein
      "Zoo Poem." <u>LaurelR</u> (19:1) Wint 85, p. 66.
1378. ENGLISH, Maurice
      "Wading In." <u>CrossCur</u> (4:2) 84, p. 57.
1379. ENNIS, Lamar Wallace
      "Angry Blood." <u>DeKalbLAJ</u> (18:3/4) 85, p. 31.
1380. ENNS, Victor Jerrett
      "Correct in This Culture" (Selections: "The Boy Who Loved,
      Counting," "Dick & Jane Blues," "Where Smiles Go at
      Night"). <u>PraF</u> (6:3) Sum 85, p. 24-26.
1381. ENOS, Anya Dozier
      "Final Visits." <u>NoDaQ</u> (53:2) Spr 85, p. 212.
1382. ENRIQUEZ, Credo James
      "Pleasure." <u>Abraxas</u> (33) 85, p. 6.
      "Superman." <u>Abraxas</u> (33) 85, p. 7.
      "Tornado." <u>Abraxas</u> (33) 85, p. 5.
1383. ENSLIN, Theodore
      "Axes 82." <u>Conjunc</u> (7) 85, p. 87-91.
1384. ENTREKIN, Charles
      "Fort Mason Bar, Northern California." <u>USl</u> (18/19) Wint
      85, p. 14.
1385. ENZENSBERGER, Hans Magnus
      "Bathroom" (tr. by Felix Pollak and Reinhold Grimm). <u>NewL</u>
      (51:4) Sum 85, p. 67.
      "The Dark Room" (tr. by Felix Pollak and Reinhold Grimm).
      <u>NewL</u> (51:4) Sum 85, p. 65.
      "Dirge for the Apple" (tr. by Felix Pollak and Reinhold
      Grimm). <u>NewL</u> (51:4) Sum 85, p. 68.
      "The Divorce" (tr. by Felix Pollak and Reinhold Grimm).
      <u>NewL</u> (51:4) Sum 85, p. 66.
      "In Memory of William Carlos Williams" (tr. by Felix Pollak
      and Reinhold Grimm). <u>LitR</u> (28:4) Sum 85, p. 585.
      "Misogyny" (tr. by Felix Pollak and Reinhold Grimm). <u>LitR</u>
      (28:4) Sum 85, p. 584.
1386. EPLING, Kathy
      "Dark Side of the Moon." <u>CrossCur</u> (4:1) 84, p. 87.
      "Kindling." <u>KanQ</u> (17:1/2) Wint-Spr 85, p. 112.
      "Miscarriage." <u>KanQ</u> (17:1/2) Wint-Spr 85, p. 112-113.
      "Planting Vegetables." <u>PraS</u> (59:3) Fall 85, p. 34.
      "Singing You Simply." <u>CrossCur</u> (4:1) 84, p. 88.
      "Winter Child." <u>PraS</u> (59:3) Fall 85, p. 35.
1387. EPSTEIN, Daniel Mark
      "The American White Pelican." <u>MichQR</u> (24:4) Fall 85, p.
      570-571.
      "The Sorceress." <u>Confr</u> (30/31) N 85, p. 242.
1388. EPSTEIN, Elaine
      "Desire." <u>CutB</u> (24) Spr-Sum 85, p. 56.
1389. EQUI, Elaine
      "Crime and the Classics." <u>NoAmR</u> (270:2) Je 85, p. 57.
      "Puritans." <u>AmerV</u> (1) 85, p. 30-31.
1390. ESCOBAR GALINDO, David
      "Estampilla Postal." <u>Mund</u> (16:1/2) 85, p. 12.
      "Nocturnes of Trafalgar Place" (Selections: III, V, tr. by
      Elizabeth Gamble Miller). <u>Mund</u> (16:1/2) 85, p. 11, 13.
      "Nocturnos de Trafalgar Place" (Selecciones: III, V).
      <u>Mund</u> (16:1/2) 85, p. 10, 12.
      "Picture Postcard" (tr. by Elizabeth Gamble Miller). <u>Mund</u>
      (16:1/2) 85, p. 13.
1391. ESCUDERO, Bettina
      "You" (tr. of Juana Meléndez de Espinoza). <u>NewL</u> (51:4)

Sum 85, p. 114.
1392. ESENIN, Sergey
"Song about a Dog" (tr. by Robert L. Smith). BlueBldgs
(9) [85?], p. 24.
1393. ESHE, Aisha
"Child Abuse." Amelia (2:2) O 85, p. 72.
1394. ESHLEMAN, Clayton
"Ariadne's Reunion." Temblor (2) 85, p. 3-15.
"Auto------." Temblor (1) 85, p. 63-64.
"The Excavation of Artaud." Sulfur (14) 85, p. 105.
"I so much want no meaning as part of composition."
Temblor (1) 85, p. 62.
"A Night with Hamlet" (Excerpts, tr. of Vladimir Holan, w.
Frantisek Galan). Sulfur (12) 85, p. 4-11.
"A Night with Hamlet" (Excerpts, tr. of Vladimir Holan, w.
Frantisek Galan). Sulfur (13) 85, p. 129-134.
"A Night with Hamlet" (Excerpts, tr. of Vladimir Holan, w.
Frantisek Galan). Sulfur (14) 85, p. 74-80.
"O-shock of a fresh deadman discovering" (after Munch).
Conjunc (7) 85, p. 209.
"Passim" (tr. of Michel Deguy). Verse (2) 85, p. 26.
"Turned off" (after Bacon). Conjunc (7) 85, p. 209.
"Tuxedoed Groom on Canvas Bride." Sulfur (13) 85, p. 21-
27.
"When the World Confines" (to Breughel, tr. of Michel
Deguy). Verse (2) 85, p. 25.
1395. ESPADA, Martín
"Again the Mercenaries: Atlantic Coast of Nicaragua, 4th of
July 1982." RevChic (12:2) Sum 84, p. 34.
"David Leaves the Saints for Paterson." RevChic (12:2)
Sum 84, p. 35.
"The Jeep Driver" (for Fernando Reñazco, Nicaragua,
Summer 1982). RevChic (12:2) Sum 84, p. 32-33.
"The Spanish of Our Out-Loud Dreams" (A Nora Elena).
Imagine (1:2) Wint 84, p. 142-143.
"La Tormenta." Imagine (1:2) Wint 84, p. 141.
1396. ESPAILLAT, Rhina P.
"Intensive Care." PoetL (79:4) Wint 85, p. 211.
"So Many." PoetL (80:3) Fall 85, p. 166.
1397. ESPAILLAT, Rhina R.
"Biography" (A poem composed of five sedokas). Amelia
(2:2) O 85, p. 51.
ESPINOZA, Juana Meléndez de
See MELENDEZ de ESPINOZA, Juana
1398. ESPOSITO, María del Carmen
"Ausencia." Mairena (7:19) 85, p. 29.
"Conversando." Mairena (7:19) 85, p. 28-29.
"Derecho de Ampara." Mairena (7:19) 85, p. 28.
"Nos Despojaron." Mairena (7:19) 85, p. 30.
"Poder de Sintesis." Mairena (7:19) 85, p. 29.
"Por Si Vuelven." Mairena (7:19) 85, p. 27.
"Rebelion." Mairena (7:19) 85, p. 30.
1399. ESPOSITO, Nancy
"Cancún City." Imagine (2:1) Sum 85, p. 43.
"Jungle Taxi." Nat (240:11) 23 Mr 85, p. 341.
1400. ESTAVER, Paul
"Bestler Justifies His Position Description." StoneC
(13:1/2) Fall-Wint 85-86, p. 67.
"Hierarchy." StoneC (13:1/2) Fall-Wint 85-86, p. 66.
1401. ESTES, Carolyn
"Things to Do While Listening to Commencement Platitudes."
EngJ (74:4) Ap 85, p. 37.
1402. ETCHEVERRY, Jorge
"Fragment IX" (tr. by Christine Shantz). Waves (13:4) Spr
85, p. 102.
"Rue de Grand Pre" (tr. by Christine Shantz). Waves

           (13:4) Spr 85, p. 103.
1403. ETHRIDGE, Judy
        "He Searched the Matrix of His Brain." <u>Poem</u> (54) N 85, p.
           6.
        "She Stalks Her Ideal." <u>Poem</u> (54) N 85, p. 5.
1404. ETROG, Sorel
        "Propaganda" (Images from Etrog's film <u>Spiral</u> Broadcast
           on C.B.C. 1975). <u>Rampike</u> (4:2/3) 85-86, p. 115-118.
1405. ETTER, Carol A.
        "Being Found Out." <u>Open24</u> (4) 85, p. 14.
        "Her Mind Will Scare You." <u>Open24</u> (4) 85, p. 53.
1406. ETTER, Dave
        "AA." <u>SpoonRQ</u> (10:2) Spr 85, p. 5.
        "Apple Wine." <u>GreenfR</u> (13:1/2) Fall-Wint 85, p. 79.
        "Charlie Parker." <u>SpoonRQ</u> (10:4) Fall 85, p. 3.
        "Cherokee Street." <u>SpoonRQ</u> (10:2) Spr 85, p. 2.
        "Couple." <u>CharR</u> (11:1) Spr 85, p. 76.
        "Drawing of a Happy Face." <u>SpoonRQ</u> (10:4) Fall 85, p. 5.
        "Failing." <u>SpoonRQ</u> (10:2) Spr 85, p. 1.
        "Hannibal, Missouri: Summer 1846." <u>ClockR</u> (2:2) 85, p. 9.
        "House Party." <u>SpoonRQ</u> (10:4) Fall 85, p. 7.
        "Howling Walter." <u>CharR</u> (11:1) Spr 85, p. 77.
        "Loose." <u>CharR</u> (11:1) Spr 85, p. 77.
        "Picasso." <u>SpoonRQ</u> (10:4) Fall 85, p. 6.
        "Post Office." <u>SpoonRQ</u> (10:2) Spr 85, p. 3.
        "Real Farmers." <u>OP</u> (38/39) Spr 85, p. 197.
        "Suburban." <u>SpoonRQ</u> (10:2) Spr 85, p. 4.
        "Tallgrass Township." <u>KanQ</u> (17:4) Fall 85, p. 21.
        "Trombone." <u>CharR</u> (11:1) Spr 85, p. 78.
        "Witness." <u>SpoonRQ</u> (10:2) Spr 85, p. 6.
        "Young in Toledo." <u>SpoonRQ</u> (10:4) Fall 85, p. 4.
1407. EUDY, Julie
        "November Widow." <u>CarolQ</u> (37:3) Spr 85, p. 58.
1408. EULBERG, Mary Thomas, Sister
        "Haiku" (2 poems). <u>WindO</u> (46) Fall 85, p. 35.
1409. EVANS, Bill
        "From the Ancient Chinese." <u>AntR</u> (43:3) Sum 85, p. 338-
           339.
1410. EVANS, Bradford
        "Coming in Two Seconds." <u>LaurelR</u> (19:1) Wint 85, p. 41.
1411. EVANS, David
        "I Saw an Old Acquaintance." <u>EngJ</u> (74:4) Ap 85, p. 29.
1412. EVANS, George
        "Blues on Elegy." <u>Oink</u> (19) 85, p. 100-102.
        "In Asia." <u>Epoch</u> (34:3) 84-85, p. 197-198.
        "Uji." <u>Epoch</u> (34:3) 84-85, p. 199.
        "A View from Space." <u>Sulfur</u> (14) 85, p. 81-84.
        "Whalesong." <u>Stand</u> (26:3) Sum 85, p. 61.
        "Wrecking." <u>Stand</u> (26:3) Sum 85, p. 61.
        "Xenakis's Psappho" (a percussion). <u>Thrpny</u> (5:4, issue
           20) Wint 85, p. 16.
1413. EVANS, Kathy
        "At Alpha Beta." <u>Imagine</u> (2:1) Sum 85, p. 93.
1414. EVANS, Mari
        "Cellblock Blues." <u>PoetryR</u> (2:2) Ap 85, p. 12.
1415. EVANS, Sally
        "Raasay Wood" (English adaption of Sorley MacLean). <u>Verse</u>
           (3) 85, p. 44-49.
1416. EVASON, Greg
        "Paint." <u>PoetryCR</u> (7:2) Wint 85-86, p. 7.
        "Steps." <u>PoetryCR</u> (7:2) Wint 85-86, p. 7.
        "Storm." <u>PoetryCR</u> (7:2) Wint 85-86, p. 7.
1417. EVERETT, Graham
        "Changes at Baiting Hollow." <u>Confr</u> (30/31) N 85, p. 180.
1418. EVERETT, Joann Marie
        "The Color Red." <u>SanFPJ</u> (7:3) 84 [i.e. 85], p. 58.

"Doomed." <u>SanFPJ</u> (7:3) 84 [i.e. 85], p. 58.
"Edges and Angles." <u>PoeticJ</u> (9) 85, p. 38.
"November Mists." <u>PoeticJ</u> (9) 85, p. 38.
"A Thought on Civilization." <u>SanFPJ</u> (7:3) 84 [i.e. 85],
    p. 59.
1419. EWART, Gavin
"The Dugong" (Lewis Carroll watches television). <u>GrandS</u>
    (4:2) Wint 85, p. 67-68.
"Dying." <u>GrandS</u> (5:1) Aut 85, p. 243.
"High Potato Land." <u>GrandS</u> (4:3) Spr 85, p. 92.
"The Mating of Pseudoscorpions." <u>GrandS</u> (4:2) Wint 85, p.
    70.
"Sadomasochism" (A Black Ballad). <u>GrandS</u> (5:1) Aut 85, p.
    241-242.
"The Song Sung in the Wendy-House." <u>GrandS</u> (5:1) Aut 85,
    p. 239-240.
"Sonnet: Nice." <u>GrandS</u> (4:2) Wint 85, p. 69.
"What's in a Marriage?" <u>GrandS</u> (4:2) Wint 85, p. 66.
1420. EWING, Jim
"Ne'erday" (New Year's Day in Glasgow, Scotland). <u>TexasR</u>
    (6:3/4) Fall-Wint 85, p. 95.
1421. EWING, Sharon D.
"Classified" (for Helga). <u>StoneC</u> (12:2/3) Spr-Sum 85, p.
    16.
"Dakota Crossing." <u>SoDakR</u> (23:2) Sum 85, p. 72-73.
"Remington Journal" (From the Greenhouse). <u>SoDakR</u> (23:2)
    Sum 85, p. 74.
1422. FABIAN, R. Gerry
"Pagan Reactors." <u>SanFPJ</u> (7:3) 84 [i.e. 85], p. 41.
1423. FAGAN, Kathy
"Night Flowers." <u>Tendril</u> (19/20) 85, p. 141.
"The Sleep of the Apostles." <u>Tendril</u> (19/20) 85, p. 142.
1424. FAGLES, Robert
"Death" (after an Egyptian poem of the Twelfth Dynasty).
    <u>GrandS</u> (5:1) Aut 85, p. 53.
"Relativity" (C.D.F. 1897-1947). <u>SouthernR</u> (21:1) Wint
    85, p. 120-121.
1425. FAGNAN, Tracy Jon
"Trick." <u>CreamCR</u> (10:1) 85, p. 62.
"Trick." <u>JamesWR</u> (3:1) Fall 85, p. 15.
1426. FAHEY, W. A.
"Come In." <u>YellowS</u> (15) Sum 85, p. 25.
"Invention of a Color." <u>Confr</u> (30/31) N 85, p. 127.
"Invention of a Sound" (For Seth). <u>Confr</u> (30/31) N 85, p.
    127.
"Pinturas Negras." <u>YellowS</u> (17) Wint 85, p. 24.
"The Pleasures of Portals." <u>YellowS</u> (15) Sum 85, p. 24.
"Snow." <u>YellowS</u> (17) Wint 85, p. 24.
1427. FAHY, Christopher
"Thinking of Buying the Watchmaker's House." <u>CharR</u> (11:2)
    Fall 85, p. 79.
1428. FAINLIGHT, Ruth
"Flies." <u>Thrpny</u> (6:1, issue 21) Spr 85, p. 11.
"The Limitations of Tiredness." <u>CumbPR</u> (5:1) Fall 85, p.
    15.
"Ocean." <u>CumbPR</u> (5:1) Fall 85, p. 16-17.
1429. FAIRCHILD, B. H.
"Cars." <u>CalQ</u> (26) Sum 85, p. 40-41.
"Desire." <u>SouthernPR</u> (25:1) Spr 85, p. 62.
"Portrait of My Father As a Young Man" (after Rilke).
    <u>SouthernPR</u> (25:1) Spr 85, p. 63.
1430. FAIRCHOK, Sherry
"The Church Road Lilac Bush." <u>Blueline</u> (7:1) Sum-Fall 85,
    p. 23.
1431. FAIRLEY, Bruce F.
"The Cry." <u>Grain</u> (13:3) Ag 85, p. 48.

1432. FAIZ, Faiz Ahmed
       "The Day Death Comes" (tr. by the author and Naomi Lazard).
          NewL (51:4) Sum 85, p. 125.
       "Do What You Have To" (tr. by Daud Kamal). PoetryE (18)
          Fall 85, p. 63.
       "The Frozen Country" (tr. by Daud Kamal). PoetryE (18)
          Fall 85, p. 62.
       "If You Look at the City from Here" (tr. by Naomi Lazard
          and the author). GrandS (4:4) Sum 85, p. 51.
       "Once Again the Mind" (tr. by Naomi Lazard and the author).
          GrandS (4:4) Sum 85, p. 50.
       "Where Will You Go" (tr. by Daud Kamal). PoetryE (18)
          Fall 85, back cover.
       "Why Pray for Eternal Life?" (tr. by Daud Kamal). PoetryE
          (18) Fall 85, p. 61.
       "You Tell Us What to Do" (tr. by Naomi Lazard and the
          author). GrandS (4:4) Sum 85, p. 52.
1433. FALCO, Edward
       "Bodies." GreenfR (13:1/2) Fall-Wint 85, p. 150-151.
       "A Child before St. Jerome." MidAR (5:1) 85, p. 5.
       "Delivery." MidAR (5:1) 85, p. 4.
       "Harsh Thunder." Pequod (19/20/21) 85, p. 130.
FALCO, Salvatore di
       See DiFALCO, Salvatore
1434. FALCON, Juan Ramon
       "During Somocismo" (tr. by Kent Johnson). MinnR (N.S. 25)
          Fall 85, p. 40.
       "Lorena Faber (Known as 'Linda')" (tr. by Sesshu Foster).
          NewL (51:4) Sum 85, p. 95-96.
1435. FALCONE, James
       "The Fire This Time." PottPort (7) 85-86, p. 50.
       "Illusion." PottPort (7) 85-86, p. 19.
       "Liberty Avenue, Queens." PottPort (7) 85-86, p. 15.
1436. FALES, David
       "The Mall." Sam (42:3, 167th release) 85, p. 42.
1437. FALK, Marcia
       "For G. and A." OP (40) Fall-Wint 85, p. 48.
       "Green." OP (40) Fall-Wint 85, p. 46.
       "The Storm." OP (40) Fall-Wint 85, p. 47.
       "To M., a Postscript." OP (40) Fall-Wint 85, p. 45.
       "The Walls of My House." OP (40) Fall-Wint 85, p. 44.
FALTO, Evelyn Cole
       See COLE FALTO, Evelyn
1438. FALUDY, George
       "Behaviourism" (tr. by John Robert Colombo). PoetryCR
          (7:1) Aut 85, p. 17.
       "Birch Tree in Winter" (tr. by Robin Skelton). PoetryCR
          (7:1) Aut 85, p. 17.
       "Closed Freight Car" (tr. by Robin Skelton). PoetryCR
          (7:1) Aut 85, p. 17.
       "Reading Chinese Poems" (tr. by Robin Skelton). PoetryCR
          (7:1) Aut 85, p. 17.
       "Refugee in Morocco 1940" (tr. by Robin Skelton).
          PoetryCR (7:1) Aut 85, p. 17.
       "Sonnet Twenty Seven" (tr. by Robin Skelton). PoetryCR
          (7:1) Aut 85, p. 17.
1439. FANDEL, John
       "I Felt." Confr (29) Wint 85, p. 17.
FANG-HU, Sung
       See SUNG, Fang-Hu
1440. FANZONE, Joseph, Jr.
       "Warranties." Open24 (4) 85, p. 37.
1441. FAREWELL, Patricia
       "Running." WestB (16) 85, p. 22-23.
1442. FARGAS, Laura
       "The Protection of Dust." AmerS (54:4) Aut 85, p. 500.

1443. FARKAS, Endre
"After Seeing Breaker Morant" (for K.T.). PoetryCR
(6:3) Spr 85, p. 31.
"A First Tooth." PoetryCR (6:3) Spr 85, p. 31.
"For Katie: Some Notes on These Times." PoetryCR (7:2)
Wint 85-86, p. 16.
"Ultra Sound Poem." CrossC (7:2) 85, p. 18.
1444. FARLEY, Susan
"The House Alone under the Pecan Trees." HangL (48) Fall
85, p. 60.
1445. FARNSWORTH, Jane
"The Seasons." Quarry (34:4) Aut 85, p. 35-36.
1446. FARNSWORTH, Robert
"Against Snapshots." Crazy (27) Fall 84, p. 25.
1447. FARRAR, Winifred Hamrick
"To Lanier at Brunswick." NegC (5:3) Sum 85, p. 144.
1448. FARRELL, M. A.
"The Kittins." HawaiiR (18) Fall 85, p. 78-79.
"Kramskoy's Portrait of Shishkin." HawaiiR (18) Fall 85,
p. 82.
"Whitehawk's Masts at Twilight." HawaiiR (18) Fall 85, p.
80-81.
1449. FASULO, Anne
"After Christmas Is Over." CrabCR (3:1) Fall-Wint 85, p.
27.
1450. FAUCHER, Réal
"After the Introductions." Open24 (4) 85, p. 30.
"Working Man." NewL (51:3) Spr 85, p. 112-113.
1451. FAULKNER, Leigh
"Peace." PottPort (7) 85-86, p. 24.
"The Silence of Things in Their Place." PottPort (7) 85-
86, p. 9.
1452. FAUSEL, Raymond L.
"Anne's Poem." AntigR (61) Spr 85, p. 98.
"Weather or Not." AntigR (61) Spr 85, p. 97.
1453. FAY, Julie
"Oregon" (for Suzi Aufderheide - Poetry Award). Prima (9)
85, p. 21.
"Three Swimmers" (after Matisse's The Swimming Pool).
Prima (9) 85, p. 11.
1454. FECTEAUX, T. Joan
"Listen." SanFPJ (7:3) 84 [i.e. 85], p. 77-78.
"The Shadow." SanFPJ (7:4) 85, p. 52.
1455. FEDERHART, Doug
"Below Stairs" (to Tom, the first of them). JamesWR (2:2)
Wint 85, p. 6.
1456. FEDERMAN, Raymond
"Before That." CrossCur (5:2) 85, p. 48-49.
"Le Démon de Maxwell" (pour Michel Serres). Os (20) 85,
p. 27.
1457. FEENY, Thomas
"Lying in Wait." StoneC (12:2/3) Spr-Sum 85, p. 66-67.
"Night Run to Norfolk." MalR (71) Je 85, p. 81.
1458. FEHLER, Gene
"Play Rehearsal." Bogg (54) 85, p. 41.
1459. FEIN, Cheri
"Still in Love on My Birthday But Aging." LaurelR (19:2)
Sum 85, p. 60.
1460. FEINBERG, Chaim
"Roadside Sage." Vis (19) 85, p. 14.
1461. FEIRSTEIN, Frederick
"Renee's Husband." OntR (23) Fall-Wint 85-86, p. 30-32.
"The Shawl." OntR (23) Fall-Wint 85-86, p. 33-34.
1462. FELDMAN, Irving
"The Flight from the City." GrandS (4:2) Wint 85, p. 30-
43.

"Meeting Hall of the Sociedad Anarquista, 1952." TriQ
   (63) Spr-Sum 85, p. 100-101.
1463. FELDMAN, Ruth
   "Anniversary with Agaves" (tr. of Margherita Guidacci).
      Ploughs (11:4) 85, p. 55.
   "Appointment to Look at the Moon" (from Hymn to Joy 1983,
      tr. of Margherita Guidacci). WebR (10:1) Spr 85, p. 11.
   "The Catherine-Wheels" (tr. of Rocco Scotellaro, w. Brian
      Swann). Ploughs (11:4) 85, p. 58.
   "Chess I" (May 9, 1984, tr. of Primo Levi). Ploughs
      (11:4) 85, p. 50.
   "Chess II" (June 23, 1984, tr. of Primo Levi). Ploughs
      (11:4) 85, p. 51.
   "A Different Latitude" (from Hymn to Joy 1983, tr. of
      Margherita Guidacci). WebR (10:1) Spr 85, p. 10.
   "Fiction." StoneC (13:1/2) Fall-Wint 85-86, p. 10-11.
   "Flight" (tr. of Primo Levi). Stand (26:4) Aut 85, p. 7.
   "Greeting" (tr. of Rocco Scotellaro, w. Brian Swann).
      Ploughs (11:4) 85, p. 56-57.
   "Libyan Sibyl" (br. of Margherita Guidacci). Mund
      (15:1/2) 85, p. 167.
   "The Life That Has Made You" (from Contrappunto, tr. of
      Piera Simeoni). StoneC (12:2/3) Spr-Sum 85, p. 32-33.
   "Like the Migrant" (tr. of Andrea Genovese). CrossCur
      (4:2) 84, p. 55.
   "Partisan" (tr. of Primo Levi). Stand (26:4) Aut 85, p. 6.
   "Passover" (tr. of Primo Levi). Stand (26:4) Aut 85, p. 7.
   "Sunflower" (from Hymn to Joy 1983, tr. of Margherita
      Guidacci). WebR (10:1) Spr 85, p. 11.
   "To Don Quixote" (tr. of Piera Simeoni). CrossCur (4:2)
      84, p. 91.
   "Unfinished Business" (April 19, 1981, tr. of Primo Levi).
      Ploughs (11:4) 85, p. 48-49.
1464. FELLOWES, Peter
   "Fall Term." TriQ (64) Fall 85, p. 47-48.
1465. FENTON, James
   "The Ballad of the Imam and the Shah." Harp (271:1624) S
      85, p. 41.
1466. FEREBEE, Gideon, Jr.
   "Comsat Papers II." JamesWR (3:1) Fall 85, p. 11.
1467. FERENCZ, Amalia
   "The Great Hungarian Lowland." CrabCR (2:2) Wint 85, p.
      28.
1468. FERGUSON, Gordon
   "I'm Listening to the Slow Part of an Old Tape." CreamCR
      (10:1) 85, p. 25.
1469. FERICANO, Paul
   "Stoogism." SecC (12:2) 84?, p. 8.
   "The Woman Who Calls Me Crazy." SecC (12:2) 84?, p. 11.
1470. FERNANDEZ RETAMAR, Roberto
   "The Other" (tr. by Arnold Odio). NewEngR (7:4) Sum 85,
      p. 521.
1471. FERNANDEZ-TORRIENTE, Gastòn
   "Ana Maria" (tr. of Nicolàs Guillèn, w. John DuVal).
      NewEngR (7:4) Sum 85, p. 541.
   "The Grand Zoo" (Selections: "Winds," "The Great Bear,"
      "Aconcagua," "KKK," "Rivers", tr. of Nicolàs
      Guillèn, w. John DuVal). NewEngR (7:4) Sum 85, p.
      542-544.
   "Sensemayah" (Snake-killing song, tr. of Nicolàs
      Guillèn, w. John DuVal). NewEngR (7:4) Sum 85, p.
      540-541.
1472. FERRARA, Patricia
   "Fragile." DeKalbLAJ (18:1/2) 85, p. 68.
1473. FERRARELLI, Rina
   "The Chess Set" (tr. of Giorgio Chiesura). Mund (15:1/2)

85, p. 169, 171, 173, 175.
"Milan, August 1943" (tr. of Salvatore Quasimodo). NewL
    (51:4) Sum 85, p. 165.
"A Morning" (tr. of Giorgio Chiesura). LitR (29:1) Fall
    85, p. 95.
"San Babila" (tr. of Leonardo Sinisgalli). NewL (51:4)
    Sum 85, p. 172.
"September's New Moon" (tr. of Leonardo Sinisgalli). NewL
    (51:4) Sum 85, p. 172.
"The Sun Will Not Stop" (tr. of Leonardo Sinisgalli).
    NewL (51:4) Sum 85, p. 173.
"Useless Things" (tr. of Giorgio Chiesura). LitR (29:1)
    Fall 85, p. 96.
1474. FERREE, Joel
"Allowing Lesser Powers." ChrC (102:19) 29 My 85, p. 556.
"This Is That Day in August When." ChrC (102:25) 14-21 Ag
    85, p. 733.
1475. FERRY, David
"In Balance" (after Jorge Guillén). Imagine (1:2) Wint
    84, p. 224-225.
1476. FERRY, W. H.
"An Epitaph, Perhaps, for Beloved Baz." Conjunc (8) 85,
    p. 222.
1477. FESSENDEN, Anne
"4000 Year Old Skier." NewL (52:1) Fall 85, p. 101.
1478. FETHERLING, Doug
"Accumulated Wisdom." Germ (9:2) Fall-Wint 85, p. 36.
"Ancient Beliefs." Germ (9:2) Fall-Wint 85, p. 37.
"It seemed obvious." Germ (9:2) Fall-Wint 85, p. 38.
1479. FICKERT, Kurt J.
"A Modern Odyssey." Wind (15:54) 85, p. 18-19.
1480. FICOWSKI, Jerzy
"Blind Intimacy" (tr. by Andrew Gorski). Os (21) 85, p.
    13.
"Bliskość Niewidoma." Os (21) 85, p. 12.
"Grzech Unikniony." Os (21) 85, p. 14.
"A Sin Avoided" (tr. by Andrew Gorski). Os (21) 85, p. 15.
1481. FIECHTER, Stan Leon
"Disbelief." WindO (45) Spr 85, p. 28.
1482. FIELD, Edward
"Music Lessons." Nat (241:20) 14 D 85, p. 658.
1483. FIELDER, William
"At the Beach" (tr. of Kemal Ozer, w. O. Yalim and Dionis
    Riggs). NewL (51:4) Sum 85, p. 14.
"In Clouded Water" (tr. of Oktay Rifat, w. Ozcan Yalim and
    Dionis Coffin Riggs). StoneC (13:1/2) Fall-Wint 85-86,
    p. 44-45.
"Night and Night" (tr. of Ismail Uyaroglu, w. O. Yalim and
    Dionis Riggs). NewL (51:4) Sum 85, p. 14.
"To My Wife" (tr. of Ozcan Yalim, w. O. Yalim and Dionis
    Riggs). NewL (51:4) Sum 85, p. 15.
1484. FIELDS, Kenneth
"Arkansas Stone Medium." ChiR (35:1) Aut 85, p. 45.
"A Short History." ChiR (35:1) Aut 85, p. 46.
"Two from the Book of Odysseus." ChiR (35:1) Aut 85, p.
    47-48.
1485. FIGMAN, Elliot
"The Silence" (For William Figman, 1916-1980). Poetry
    (146:6) S 85, p. 326.
"This Life." PoetryR (2:2) Ap 85, p. 61.
"This Morning." Poetry (146:6) S 85, p. 324.
"The Tunnel." Poetry (146:6) S 85, p. 325.
"Your Own Good Leg." PoetryR (2:2) Ap 85, p. 62.
1486. FIGUEROA, John
"Goodbye, Despedida" (El niño come naranjas, Garcia
    Lorca). GreenfR (12:3/4) Wint-Spr 85, p. 149.

"Problems of a Writer Who Does Not Quite." GreenfR
    (12:3/4) Wint-Spr 85, p. 149-150.
1487. FIGURSKI, Jan
    "The Edge" (August). Waves (13:4) Spr 85, p. 97.
    "Shadow Song" (September). Waves (13:4) Spr 85, p. 96.
1488. FILIP, Raymond
    "Arm Swingers." PoetryCR (6:3) Spr 85, p. 5.
    "Brown Study in Autumn." PoetryCR (6:3) Spr 85, p. 5.
    "Mademoiselle among Immortelles." PoetryCR (6:3) Spr 85,
        p. 5.
    "MMMM, Maple Leaves" (For Claudine). PoetryCR (6:3) Spr
        85, p. 5.
    "Stepfather's Dance." PoetryCR (6:3) Spr 85, p. 5.
1489. FILKINS, Peter
    "The Puzzle" (for Leslie & Mimi). PoetryR (2:2) Ap 85, p.
        81-82.
1490. FILLINGHAM, George
    "Cleopatra, to Her Asp." NegC (5:2) Spr 85, p. 118.
1491. FILSON, B. K.
    "Angel Din." AntigR (60) Wint 85, p. 40.
    "The Day Is Done." AntigR (60) Wint 85, p. 41.
    "A Note." AntigR (60) Wint 85, p. 40-41.
1492. FINALE, Frank
    "Garage Organist." Vis (19) 85, p. 40.
1493. FINCH, Casey
    "Against Poetics." OhioR (35) 85, p. 76-77.
1494. FINCH, Roger
    "At Kasuga Shrine." LaurelR (19:2) Sum 85, p. 77.
    "Cormorant Fishing" (Ozu, August 1984). PoetL (80:1) Spr
        85, p. 39.
    "Eve" (Romanesque Art, Early 12th Century, Musée Rollin,
        Autun). BelPoJ (36:2) Wint 85-86, p. 2.
    "F Is for Fairy." KanQ (17:4) Fall 85, p. 83.
    "The Giant Panda." WindO (45) Spr 85, p. 3.
    "Hyacinth Room." KanQ (17:1/2) Wint-Spr 85, p. 150.
    "Incertezza del Poeta" (Giorgio de Chirico, 1888-1978).
        Gargoyle (27) 85, p. 98.
    "Katsurahama Beach." HiramPoR (39) Fall-Wint 85, p. 10.
    "Learning to Apply Gilt." CimR (70) Ja 85, p. 40.
    "Matsushima." PoetL (80:1) Spr 85, p. 40.
    "The Moon Moth." PoetryCR (7:1) Aut 85, p. 6.
    "Patterns in Sunlight" (at Grandmother's farmhouse, 6 mi.
        north of Butler, Pa.). KanQ (17:4) Fall 85, p. 81-83.
    "Please Touch This Poem." Bogg (54) 85, p. 37.
    "Poem Including a Poem Entitled 'This Candle' by Ngwe Ta
        Yi." HiramPoR (39) Fall-Wint 85, p. 11.
    "Sketch of an Angel." WindO (45) Spr 85, p. 25.
    "Studies on Arden's Tamil Grammar" ("Chapter IV:
        Conjunctions -- The Water Sports of Krishna"). BelPoJ
        (36:2) Wint 85-86, p. 3.
    "A Taste of Hebrew." CapeR (20:1) Spr 85, p. 22.
    "They Can Not Be Mended with Wax." PraS (59:4) Wint 85,
        p. 103.
    "Wanting Is a White Museum." YellowS (16) Aut 85, p. 30.
    "We Weavers." WebR (10:2) Fall 85, p. 54.
    "What Is Written in Glass." PraS (59:4) Wint 85, p. 104.
1495. FINCH, Steven
    "Theme and Variation." JamesWR (2:2) Wint 85, p. 7.
1496. FINCKE, Gary
    "Breaking Glass." PaintedB (25) Spr 85, p. 16-17.
    "The Brief Abduction." WestB (17) 85, p. 105.
    "The Bum's Lecture." Amelia (2:2) O 85, p. 59.
    "The Cold Shoes." WebR (10:1) Spr 85, p. 87.
    "Exit Interview." CapeR (20:1) Spr 85, p. 38.
    "The First Armed Robbery in Selinsgrove." MidAR (5:2) 85,
        p. 17.

"He Had Just Been Born." <u>Vis</u> (17) 85, p. 36.
"The Highway a Mile from Home." <u>PraS</u> (59:4) Wint 85, p. 77.
"How to Verify God." <u>CimR</u> (71) Ap 85, p. 37-38.
"The Local Cemetery." <u>Poetry</u> (146:2) My 85, p. 68-69.
"A Murder of Crows." <u>Poetry</u> (146:2) My 85, p. 69-70.
"My Mother Calls, Complains about Shingles." <u>LitR</u> (29:1) Fall 85, p. 24.
"My Name Where I Will Never Return." <u>CapeR</u> (20:1) Spr 85, p. 39.
"The One Minute Almanac." <u>BlueBldgs</u> (9) [85?], p. 43.
"One of Those Commencement Speeches." <u>WebR</u> (10:1) Spr 85, p. 85-86.
"The Phone Call." <u>PraS</u> (59:4) Wint 85, p. 76.
"The Previous Tenant." <u>WebR</u> (10:1) Spr 85, p. 86.
1497. FINK, Eloise Bradley
"Quote." <u>CreamCR</u> (10:1) 85, p. 10.
1498. FINKEL, Donald
"Election Day." <u>Tendril</u> (19/20) 85, p. 144.
"No News" (from <u>The Detachable Man</u>). <u>Tendril</u> (19/20) 85, p. 143.
1499. FINKELSTEIN, Caroline
"Blind-Spot." <u>Tendril</u> (19/20) 85, p. 145.
1500. FINLAYSON, D. (<u>See also</u> FINLAYSON, Douglas)
"Young Pup on the Wrong Road." <u>DeKalbLAJ</u> (18:3/4) 85, p. 32.
1501. FINLAYSON, Douglas (<u>See also</u> FINLAYSON, D.)
"The Siege of Atlanta." <u>Rampike</u> (4:2/3) 85-86, p. 80.
1502. FINLEY, C. Stephen
"Easter-Song." <u>SouthernPR</u> (26, i.e. 25:2) Fall 85, p. 57.
"The Ferry." <u>MissR</u> (13:3, issue 39) Spr 85, p. 73.
"Mens Angelica." <u>MissR</u> (13:3, issue 39) Spr 85, p. 72.
"Ruth-Song." <u>SouthernPR</u> (26, i.e. 25:2) Fall 85, p. 58.
"Sledding in the Dark." <u>MissR</u> (13:3, issue 39) Spr 85, p. 74.
1503. FINLEY, Michael
"The Bale-Door Ledge." <u>WoosterR</u> (4) Fall 85, p. 16-17.
"The Campaign." <u>PoetryR</u> (5) S 85, p. 77.
"Centipede on Chop Suey." <u>ConnPR</u> (3:1) 84, p. 19.
"Dance of the Dog." <u>KanQ</u> (17:4) Fall 85, p. 150.
"The Ghost." <u>PoetryR</u> (5) S 85, p. 78.
"The Heighth of the Drought." <u>NoDaQ</u> (53:4) Fall 85, p. 187.
"Homeopener." <u>HiramPoR</u> (38) Spr-Sum 85, p. 12.
"My Baby." <u>NegC</u> (5:4) Fall 85, p. 124.
"Old Stone Enters into Heaven" (The Master Calls Him to His Reward). <u>KanQ</u> (17:4) Fall 85, p. 151.
"One Week before High School Graduation, I Make a Visit to Marblehead Peninsula." <u>IndR</u> (8:1) Wint 85, p. 77.
"Steamboat's Ledge." <u>ConnPR</u> (3:1) 84, p. 18.
"The Two Thieves." <u>Poem</u> (53) Mr 85, p. 54.
1504. FINLEY, Robert
"Altovise / The Reunion." <u>Grain</u> (13:4) N 85, p. 14.
"Temerity." <u>Grain</u> (13:4) N 85, p. 13.
1505. FINNEGAN, James
"Twilights of This Third Planet." <u>StoneC</u> (13:1/2) Fall-Wint 85-86, p. 28.
1506. FINNELL, Dennis
"Altar Boys." <u>CharR</u> (11:2) Fall 85, p. 92-93.
"Near the Ruins of Dunstanburg Castle." <u>CharR</u> (11:2) Fall 85, p. 91.
1507. FINNEY, Bernard
"The Fading Blue of Summer." <u>NegC</u> (5:3) Sum 85, p. 22.
1508. FIRER, Susan
"The Pear Tree" (for Erin). <u>Abraxas</u> (33) 85, p. 32-33.

1509. FIRKE, Lisa
    "Re-Tinting the Daguerrotype" (for Margaret and Gertrude).
        PassN (6:2) Spr-Sum 85, p. 10.
FIRMAT, Gustavo Pérez
    See PEREZ FIRMAT, Gustavo
1510. FISCHER, Olga Howard
    "On Composing with My Computer." EngJ (74:7) N 85, p. 34.
1511. FISET, Joan
    "Eggshell Mosaic." NegC (5:3) Sum 85, p. 114.
1512. FISH, Karen
    "Signs of Life." Crazy (26) Spr 84, p. 22-23.
    "Sunday Morning." Crazy (26) Spr 84, p. 21.
1513. FISHER, Allen
    "Bel Air." Sulfur (12) 85, p. 50-57.
1514. FISHER, Lori
    "Along the Danube in Fog" (tr. of Reiner Kunze). NewL
        (51:4) Sum 85, p. 50.
    "Erasmus of Rotterdam" (tr. of Reiner Kunze). NewL (51:4)
        Sum 85, p. 50.
    "Love Poem after Takeoff, or In the Same Plane with You"
        (tr. of Reiner Kunze). NewL (51:4) Sum 85, p. 51.
    "A Small Account of Moravia" (for Jan Skacel, tr. of Reiner
        Kunze). Mund (16:1/2) 85, p. 15.
    "Solace at Ten Thousand Meters" (tr. of Reiner Kunze).
        NewL (51:4) Sum 85, p. 50.
1515. FISHER, Roy
    "A Furnace" (Excerpt). Stand (26:3) Sum 85, p. 4-5.
    "News for the Ear." Conjunc (8) 85, p. 164.
1516. FISHMAN, Charles
    "Blue Garden Ball" (tr. of Sarah Kirsch, w. Marina
        Roscher). NewL (51:4) Sum 85, p. 70-71.
    "Keys to the City." BlueBldgs (9) [85?], p. 16.
    "Mist." Confr (30/31) N 85, p. 146.
    "Motionless" (tr. of Sarah Kirsch, w. Marina Roscher).
        NewL (51:4) Sum 85, p. 72.
    "South of the Border" (El Salvador, 1982). NewL (52:1)
        Fall 85, p. 68.
    "Stoneheart" (tr. of Sarah Kirsch, w. Marina Roscher).
        NewL (51:4) Sum 85, p. 70.
    "Two Boys at the Seashore." Confr (30/31) N 85, p. 145.
    "The Vessel." BlueBldgs (9) [85?], p. 17.
    "Winter Promenade" (tr. of Sarah Kirsch, w. Marina
        Roscher). NewL (51:4) Sum 85, p. 71.
1517. FISKIN, Jeffrey
    "Burning Ship" (tr. of Jaroslav Seifert, w. Erik
        Vestville). Antaeus (55) Aut 85, p. 158.
    "Mortar Salvos" (tr. of Jaroslav Seifert, w. Erik
        Vestville). Antaeus (55) Aut 85, p. 159-160.
    "When the Ashes" (tr. of Jaroslav Seifert, w. Erik
        Vestville). Antaeus (55) Aut 85, p. 157.
1518. FISTER, Mary P.
    "Cumbrian Herd." Ploughs (11:1) 85, p. 86-87.
    "Sounding." Ploughs (11:1) 85, p. 88-90.
1519. Fitz GERALD, Gregory
    "For Moses, Who Must Have Learned It on the Mountain."
        Amelia (2:1) Ap 85, p. 14.
    "Lines Composed for a Lady Who Pushed the Poet into the
        Freezer Along with the Spumoni." Amelia (2:2) O 85, p.
        75.
1520. FITZGERALD, Frank S.
    "Have you ever been window shopping." YellowS (15) Sum
        85, p. 11.
1521. FitzPATRICK, Kevin
    "Favorite Recipe." Vis (18) 85, p. 18.
1522. FITZPATRICK, Mark
    "Quem Quaeritis." Poem (53) Mr 85, p. 66.

1523. FITZPATRICK, Vince
       "Harsh Climate." Open24 (4) 85, p. 39.
1524. FLACK, Brian L.
       "Icicles & Stalagmites." Quarry (34:3) Sum 85, p. 65-66.
       "Images on My Mind." Quarry (34:3) Sum 85, p. 66.
       "Talk." Quarry (34:3) Sum 85, p. 67.
1525. FLAGG, John S.
       "Elegy Written in a Swivel Chair." PoetryNW (26:3) Aut
       85, p. 10-12.
       "For Joy." PoetryNW (26:3) Aut 85, p. 8-10.
1526. FLANAGAN, Jim
       "I Am the Sentinel of Snow Beach." StoneC (13:1/2) Fall-
       Wint 85-86, p. 24-25.
1527. FLANAGAN, Katherine
       "Another Trick with Mirrors." Open24 (4) 85, p. 5.
       "Proceedings." PoeticJ (11) 85, p. 26.
       "Remembering." PoeticJ (11) 85, p. 29.
1528. FLANDERS, Jane
       "Anatomy Theater, 1945." Chelsea (44) 85, p. 58.
       "John Keats, Apothecary." PoetL (80:2) Sum 85, p. 72-73.
       "Milk Valley." Chelsea (44) 85, p. 57.
1529. FLANNER, Hildegarde
       "Concerto No. 2 in A Flat Major" (John Field, 1782 Ireland -
       - 1837 Moscow). ParisR (27:97) Fall 85, p. 174.
       "Image on a Curving Surface Seen in Evening Traffic."
       ParisR (27:97) Fall 85, p. 173.
       "A Kind of Getting Up." Salm (66) Wint-Spr 85, p. 135-136.
       "The Old Lady." Salm (66) Wint-Spr 85, p. 132-133.
       "On Board the Zephyr." Salm (66) Wint-Spr 85, p. 134.
       "Waiting for the Griddle to Smoke." Salm (66) Wint-Spr
       85, p. 133-134.
1530. FLECK, Polly
       "Coyote as a Shape-shifter." Dandel (12:1) 85, p. 35.
       "Coyote as Poet." Dandel (12:1) 85, p. 34.
       "Fuji-San." PoetryCR (6:4) Sum 85, p. 9.
       "Spider Moon." PoetryCR (6:4) Sum 85, p. 9.
1531. FLECK, Richard C., Jr.
       "The Black Nebula." GreenfR (13:1/2) Fall-Wint 85, p. 66-
       67.
1532. FLEMING, Gerald
       "The Beekeeper's Beard." WebR (10:1) Spr 85, p. 90.
       "Death of a White-Haired Friend." WebR (10:1) Spr 85, p.
       89.
       "Landscape after a Painting by Arthur Dove." WebR (10:1)
       Spr 85, p. 89.
1533. FLEMING, Jack
       "Are You There?" WebR (10:2) Fall 85, p. 58.
       "Spectral." WebR (10:2) Fall 85, p. 57.
1534. FLEMING, L. A.
       "Aquarius." CapeR (20:1) Spr 85, p. 46.
1535. FLETCHER, Ann
       "Brave." PraS (59:1) Spr 85, p. 35.
       "New World Pastorale." PraS (59:1) Spr 85, p. 36.
       "Persian New Year at the Waldorf." CimR (70) Ja 85, p. 17-
       18.
1536. FLETCHER, Lynne Yamaguchi
       "This Riven World." GreenfR (13:1/2) Fall-Wint 85, p. 37-
       38.
       "Yangshuo, July 7, 1983." GreenfR (13:1/2) Fall-Wint 85,
       p. 36-37.
1537. FLIEGER, Verlyn
       "North Face." PoetL (79:4) Wint 85, p. 207.
1538. FLINN, Eugene C.
       "O's." CapeR (20:1) Spr 85, p. 37.
1539. FLINT, Charles
       "Dreams." Nimrod (28:2) Spr-Sum 85, p. 54.

"The Furious and Sad Old Surrealist Master Disowning His
    Establishment Daughter." Nimrod (28:2) Spr-Sum 85, p.
    55.
1540. FLINT, Roland
    "Aubade." TriQ (63) Spr-Sum 85, p. 510.
    "Pigeon in the Night." NewL (51:3) Spr 85, p. 59.
    "A Poem Called George, Sometimes." NewL (51:3) Spr 85, p.
        58.
    "Under Pressure Pigeon Stops Fighting It." NewL (51:3)
        Spr 85, p. 59.
1541. FLOCK, Miriam
    "The Dark Lady" (Selections: V, VI). ChiR (35:2) Wint 85,
        p. 54.
1542. FLOOK, Maria
    "The Beautiful Illness." Ploughs (11:1) 85, p. 92-93.
    "The Improper Persons." Poetry (145:5) F 85, p. 259-260.
    "Memory." Ploughs (11:1) 85, p. 91.
    "The Past." Ploughs (11:1) 85, p. 94.
    "The Stone." Ploughs (11:1) 85, p. 95-96.
1543. FLORES PEREGRINO, José
    "Poet." Imagine (1:2) Wint 84, p. 59.
    "To a Crow" (a healing poem). Imagine (1:2) Wint 84, p.
        60-61.
1544. FLORIT, Eugenio
    "Con Marti." LindLM (4:2) Ap-Je 85, p. 5.
    "The Two Girls." Vis (18) 85, p. 39.
1545. FLOSDORF, Jim
    "Cement-Man." Blueline (6:2) Wint-Spr 85, p. 49.
    "City." Blueline (6:2) Wint-Spr 85, p. 49.
    "Osprey" (for Doris Allen). Blueline (7:1) Sum-Fall 85,
        p. 14.
1546. FLYNN, David
    "Double Distance." KanQ (17:1/2) Wint-Spr 85, p. 114.
    "The Ocean of the Rivers of Desire." KanQ (17:1/2) Wint-
        Spr 85, p. 114.
1547. FLYNN, Richard
    "Defining Gravity." Gargoyle (27) 85, p. 50.
FOE, Mark de
    See DeFOE, Mark
1548. FOERSTER, Richard
    "EEG." Poetry (146:3) Je 85, p. 163.
    "The Hohntor" (Bad Neustadt/Saale). PoetryR (5) S 85, p.
        46.
    "On Hearing a Phoebe's Call in Early March." SouthernHR
        (19:1) Wint 85, p. 64.
    "Riding the Changes." Nat (240:18) 11 My 85, p. 566.
    "Transfigured Nights." Poetry (146:3) Je 85, p. 164.
1549. FOIX, J. V.
    "Les Irreals Omegues" (Selection: XVI). AntigR (61) Spr
        85, p. 54.
    "Les Irreals Omegues" (Selection: XVI, English tr. by
        Shelley Quinn). AntigR (61) Spr 85, p. 55.
1550. FOLEY, Sylvia
    "To My Father." Cond (11/12) 85, p. 109.
1551. FOLKESTAD, Marilyn
    "Between Hoodoo and Silver Falls." CutB (23) Fall-Wint
        85, p. 63.
    "Collage." PoetryNW (26:1) Spr 85, p. 11-12.
    "The Lady Who Set My Son Down in Oil." PoetryNW (26:1)
        Spr 85, p. 13-15.
    "The Mad Women of the Plaza de Mayo." PoetryNW (26:1) Spr
        85, p. 16-17.
    "The Portrait." PoetryNW (26:1) Spr 85, p. 15-16.
1552. FOLKS, Jeffrey
    "Evidence." Wind (15:53) 85, p. 10.

1553. FOLLAIN, Jean
      "Life" (tr. by W. S. Merwin). TriQ (63) Spr-Sum 85, p.
      137.
1554. FONSECA, Aguinaldo
      "Drought" (tr. by Charles Philip Thomas). WebR (10:2)
      Fall 85, p. 36.
1555. FONT, María Cecilia
      "Arbol de la Vida." Mairena (7:19) 85, p. 46.
      "Ayer, la Patria." Mairena (7:19) 85, p. 42.
      "Forma del Aire." Mairena (7:19) 85, p. 43.
      "Homenaje a Jorge Guillen." Mairena (7:19) 85, p. 26.
      "El Mendigo." Mairena (7:19) 85, p. 43-44.
      "Profanacion de la Cripta." Mairena (7:19) 85, p. 45.
      "Señal sin Pulso." Mairena (7:19) 85, p. 44.
      "Vecinos a la Costa." Mairena (7:19) 85, p. 44-45.
1556. FORD, Adrian Robert
      "Three Lake Poems." JamesWR (2:2) Wint 85, p. 4.
1557. FORD, Terri L.
      "6/11/58." CapeR (20:2) Fall 85, p. 35.
      "Losing Her." CarolQ (37:2) Wint 85, p. 58.
1558. FORD, William
      "Adult Church Camp." WestB (16) 85, p. 67.
      "April Rain." BlueBldgs (9) [85?], p. 11.
      "Crossing Indian Land" (Fidalgo Island, Washington).
      Poetry (145:4) Ja 85, p. 209.
      "The Eskimo Ivory Exhibition." Poetry (145:4) Ja 85, p.
      208.
      "A Natural Childbirth." BlueBldgs (9) [85?], p. 11.
1559. FORDYCE, Richard
      "What I Did on Thursday, March 16th, 1956." OP (38/39)
      Spr 85, p. 9.
1560. FORNOFF, Frederick H.
      "Beside What Doesn't Die" (tr. of Antonio Hernández).
      NewOR (12:4) Wint 85, p. 44-46.
1561. FORST, Graham
      "Corporal Punishment" (from Margaret Lawrence, A Jest of
      God). WestCR (19:4) Ap 85, p. 31.
      "Moving Quiety, Cautiously toward a Drink." WestCR (19:4)
      Ap 85, p. 32.
      "Their Hands Touch, by Accident." WestCR (19:4) Ap 85, p.
      31.
1562. FORTH, Steven
      "Apple Requital." Waves (13:2/3) Wint 85, p. 82.
      "Give the People Back" (tr. Sankichi Toge). AmerPoR
      (14:4) Jl-Ag 85, p. 9.
      "Glass Country" (tr. of Tsuneko Yoshikawa). Waves
      (13:2/3) Wint 85, p. 84.
      "A Healing." Waves (13:2/3) Wint 85, p. 83.
      "If You" (tr. Tsuneko Yoshikawa). AmerPoR (14:4) Jl-Ag
      85, p. 10.
      "Long Summer" (tr. of Tsuneko Yoshikawa). Waves (13:2/3)
      Wint 85, p. 86.
      "Vow" (tr. of Atsuko Fujino). AmerPoR (14:4) Jl-Ag 85, p.
      9.
      "Water Please" (tr. of Tamiki Hara). AmerPoR (14:4) Jl-Ag
      85, p. 9.
FORTIN, Cher Holt
      See HOLT-FORTIN, Cher
1563. FORTUNATO, Peter
      "Adirondack Visit." Blueline (7:1) Sum-Fall 85, p. 24-25.
      "Some Words for Snow." CrossCur (5:2) 85, p. 141.
1564. FOSS, Phillip
      "The Condition of the Soil, the Digression of Mountains."
      BlueBldgs (9) [85?], p. 35.
      "Virga./Icy Gate" (6 selections). Temblor (2) 85, p. 110-
      112.

1565. FOSTER, Robert
      "Tanglewood" (Ivan Eyre, 1973, Winnipeg Art Gallery).
          PraF (6:1) Wint 85, p. 58-59.
      "What Love Teaches." PraF (6:1) Wint 85, p. 57.
1566. FOSTER, Sesshu
      "Commander Two" (tr. of Daisy Zamora). NewL (51:4) Sum
          85, p. 95.
      "Commander Two" (tr. of Daisy Zamora). Open24 (4) 85, p.
          31.
      "The Final Years of Lil Milagro Ramirez" (Selection: #6).
          SanFPJ (7:2) 85, p. 51.
      "Lines in Red and White Lights for L.A." (Selection: #12).
          SanFPJ (7:2) 85, p. 50.
      "Lorena Faber (Known as 'Linda')" (tr. of Juan Ramon
          Falcon). NewL (51:4) Sum 85, p. 95-96.
1567. FOUGERE, Norman
      "The Mind of Roses." PottPort (7) 85-86, p. 50.
1568. FOURCADE, Dominique
      "Three Things on the Commode" (tr. by Cid Corman and the
          author). Origin (Series 5:5) Spr 85, p. 74-76.
      "The Unangular Sky" (Selections: 38, 42, 45, tr. by Cid
          Corman and the author). Origin (Series 5:5) Spr 85, p.
          67-74.
1569. FOURNIER, Merci
      "Bone Structures There in the Sky." AntigR (61) Spr 85,
          p. 11.
      "Cosmos." AntigR (61) Spr 85, p. 11.
1570. FOWLER, Anne Carroll
      "Missing Person." LitR (28:4) Sum 85, p. 575.
      "On the Nova Scotia Coast." KanQ (17:4) Fall 85, p. 225.
      "Seduction Song / Vegetable Love." Wind (15:54) 85, p. 20.
1571. FOWLER, Gene
      "Truck Stop Dance" (Nov. 73-Feb. 74). SecC (12:2) 84?, p.
          7.
1572. FOWLER, Jay Bradford, Jr.
      "Dawn." AmerPoR (14:2) Mr-Ap 85, p. 30.
      "There Are No Bells in This House." PoetL (80:1) Spr 85,
          p. 43.
1573. FOWLER, Karen Joy
      "Rites of Intensification" (To My Daughter). CalQ (26)
          Sum 85, p. 34.
1574. FOWLER, Russell T.
      "Ars Moriendi." SouthernHR (19:3) Sum 85, p. 230.
      "Positions." SouthernHR (19:3) Sum 85, p. 236.
1575. FOWLIE, Wallace
      "The Inferno" (Selections: "The Jovial Friars" -- from
          canto 23, "Fortuna" -- from canto 7). SewanR (93:2)
          Spr 85, p. 183-184.
1576. FOX, Anne Valley
      "Snake." AmerV (1) 85, p. 86.
1577. FOX, Gail
      "17 Monarch Park Avenue." Waves (13:2/3) Wint 85, p. 97.
      "The Deepening of the Colours." Waves (13:2/3) Wint 85,
          p. 96.
      "The Deepening of the Colours" (Selections: 6 Poems).
          PoetryCR (6:4) Sum 85, p. 5.
      "Terror on Wednesday." PoetryCR (7:2) Wint 85-86, p. 17.
1578. FOX, Graham
      "Eden, Eden, Eden" (Excerpt, tr. of Pierre Guyotat).
          Temblor (1) 85, p. 122-123.
1579. FOX, Hugh
      "Humanpoems" (Selections: 26, 51). Open24 (4) 85, p. 60.
1580. FRALEY, Bernard
      "Barroom Stories." Wind (15:53) 85, p. 12.
1581. FRAME, Cynthia Solt
      "A Kodak Calamity." Bogg (54) 85, p. 45.

"Modern Lover." Bogg (53) 85, p. 6.
FRANCHY GAVIÑO, Carlos de
      See GAVIÑO de FRANCHY, Carlos
1582. FRANCIA, Héctor
      "Nuevamente la Alondra." Mairena (7:19) 85, p. 102.
1583. FRANCIS, H. E.
      "Fragments" (tr. of Ofelia Castillo). Mund (15:1/2) 85,
            p. 17, 19.
      "The Lovers" (tr. of Ofelia Castillo). Mund (15:1/2) 85,
            p. 23.
      "Of the Poet and His River" (tr. of Ofelia Castillo).
            Mund (15:1/2) 85, p. 21, 23.
      "The Poem" (tr. of Ofelia Castillo). Mund (15:1/2) 85, p.
            17.
1584. FRANCIS, Lee
      "Twentieth Century Buccaneer." Bogg (54) 85, p. 15.
      "Unfinished Poem." Bogg (54) 85, p. 25.
1585. FRANCISCO, Dorman E.
      "Mawdren Man" (fed accidentally into a word processor).
            DeKalbLAJ (18:3/4) 85, p. 33-34.
1586. FRANCOEUR, Lucien
      "The Future Is Now" (for Ken Norris and Endre Farkas).
            Rampike (4:2/3) 85-86, p. 60.
1587. FRANK, Edwin
      "Snake Train" (for Joseph Shea, after Velemir Khlebnikov).
            NewYRB (32:3) 28 F 85, p. 36.
1588. FRANZEN, Cola
      "Edifice Dedicated to Silence" (tr. of Saul Yurkievich).
            Sulfur (14) 85, p. 107-109.
      "I Myself" (tr. of Saul Yurkievich). Sulfur (14) 85, p.
            106.
      "Ratifies" (tr. of Saúl Yurkievich). Temblor (1) 85, p.
            115.
      "Remembering the Madwomen of the Plaza de Mayo" (Written in
            memory of Marta Traba, died in the Avianca crash,
            Madrid, 1983, tr. of Marjorie Agosin). Mund (15:1/2)
            85, p. 63, 65.
      "Reverieriver" (tr. of Saúl Yurkievich). Temblor (1)
            85, p. 115.
      "Rolling Stones" (tr. of Saúl Yurkievich). Temblor (1)
            85, p. 116.
      "Sentence" (tr. of Saul Yurkievich). Sulfur (14) 85, p.
            106-107.
      "Story" (tr. of Saúl Yurkievich). Temblor (1) 85, p.
            116.
      "They force me to play" (tr. of Saul Yurkievich). Sulfur
            (14) 85, p. 106.
      "Thresholds" (tr. of Marjorie Agosin). Mund (15:1/2) 85,
            p. 65.
      "Torture" (For Rosa Montero and all those who told her
            their stories, tr. of Marjorie Agosin). Mund (15:1/2)
            85, p. 59, 61.
      "Tumbles and Rumbles" (tr. of Saúl Yurkievich). Temblor
            (1) 85, p. 116.
      "Virginia" (tr. of Marjorie Agosin). Mund (15:1/2) 85, p.
            59.
1589. FRASER, Caroline
      "In the Night, What Things Move." AmerPoR (14:4) Jl-Ag
            85, p. 16.
      "On the Coast." AmerPoR (14:4) Jl-Ag 85, p. 15.
1590. FRATICELLI, Marco
      "Haiku: I wait in your bed." CrossC (7:1) 85, p. 28.
      "Two Haiku" (in computer program form: #3, #9). CanLit
            (106) Fall 85, p. 16-17.
      "The Wind Is My Canvas" (The Journal of Jesus Christ:
            Exceprts, 1-5). CanLit (106) Fall 85, p. 29-30.

1591. FRAZEE, James
   "The Bathrobe." NegC (5:1) Wint 85, p. 109-110.
   "Beyond Lorca." Iowa (15:3) Fall 85, p. 36-37.
   "Intimate Lighting." Iowa (15:3) Fall 85, p. 33-34.
   "The Laughing Boy." Iowa (15:3) Fall 85, p. 31-33.
   "The Laughter of Boys." Iowa (15:3) Fall 85, p. 37-38.
   "The Orange Grove" (for Barry Bell). SenR (15:2) 85, p.
      73.
   "The Privilege of Light." SenR (15:2) 85, p. 74.
   "Second Person." NegC (5:1) Wint 85, p. 111-112.
   "Stranded." PassN (6:1) Fall-Wint 85, p. 15.
   "Three Shots." SenR (15:2) 85, p. 75-77.
   "The Windmill." AmerPoR (14:2) Mr-Ap 85, p. 28.
   "Women in Black." Iowa (15:3) Fall 85, p. 34-36.
1592. FRAZIER, Beverly
   "Winter." LittleBR (5:1) Fall-Wint 84-85, p. 12.
1593. FRAZIER, Mark J.
   "Vacation Couple." Ascent (11:1) 85, p. 54-55.
1594. FRECHETTE, Jean-Marc
   "A Mère Meera." Os (20) 85, p. 20.
1595. FREEDMAN, William
   "The Greatest." AntR (43:4) Fall 85, p. 462-463.
   "Momentum." CumbPR (5:1) Fall 85, p. 36.
1596. FREEMAN, Sunil
   "Tabloid Nightmares" ("Romantic Misadventures with Prince
      Andy, Soft Porn Queen Tells All"). Bogg (53) 85, p. 9.
FREES, Madeline de
   See DeFREES, Madeline
1597. FRENCH, Larry
   "Cornfields." NewOR (12:4) Wint 85, p. 60.
1598. FREUND, Edith
   "The History of Electricity." Vis (17) 85, p. 6-8.
1599. FREW, Glenn
   "YREFFACCM EVETS OT." Rampike (4:2/3) 85-86, p. 50.
1600. FREY, Charles
   "Theory's a Trojan Horse" (Wittig). NegC (5:2) Spr 85, p.
      160-161.
1601. FRIAR, Kimon
   "Anti-Nebula" (tr. of Nikos Karoúzos). Mund (15:1/2)
      85, p. 133.
   "Behavior" (tr. of Nikos Karoúzos). Mund (15:1/2) 85,
      p. 131.
   "Crimes or Genesis II" (tr. of Andonis Decavalles). LitR
      (28:4) Sum 85, p. 543.
   "Daredevil Motorcycling" (tr. of Nikos Karoúzos).
      Mund (15:1/2) 85, p. 131-132.
   "Degrees of Sensation" (tr. of Yánnis Rítsos). Mund
      (15:1/2) 85, p. 52.
   "Endless Winter" (tr. of Nikos Karoúzos). Mund
      (15:1/2) 85, p. 132-133.
   "The Fingers" (tr. of Andonis Decavalles). LitR (28:4)
      Sum 85, p. 541.
   "The Idiot" (tr. of Yánnis Rítsos). Mund (15:1/2) 85,
      p. 51.
   "An Invalid's Day" (tr. of Yánnis Rítsos). Mund
      (15:1/2) 85, p. 52.
   "The Lesser Angel" (tr. of Nikos Karoúzos). Mund
      (15:1/2) 85, p. 130.
   "Need of Proof" (tr. of Yánnis Rítsos). Mund (15:1/2)
      85, p. 50.
   "Opposite the Rock" (tr. of Yannis Ritsos, w. Kostas
      Myrsiades). ArizQ (41:4) Wint 85, p. 318.
   "Process" (tr. of Yánnis Rítsos). Mund (15:1/2) 85,
      p. 50.
   "The Sum of Ambition" (tr. of Nikos Karoúzos). Mund
      (15:1/2) 85, p. 130-131.

FRIAR 142

"The Suspect" (tr. of Yánnis Rítsos). Mund (15:1/2)
    85, p. 51.
"Waterdrops and Drummer" (tr. of Andonis Decavalles).
    LitR (28:4) Sum 85, p. 539.
1602. FRICK, Thomas
"Grodek" (Trakl's last poem, tr. of Georg Trakl). Ploughs
    (11:4) 85, p. 143.
"Melancholia" (tr. of Georg Trakl). Ploughs (11:4) 85, p.
    142.
1603. FRIEBERT, Stuart
"Air" (tr. of Karl Krolow). Ploughs (11:4) 85, p. 144.
"Coney Island." Iowa (15:1) Wint 85, p. 50.
"Hard & Easy." PoetL (80:3) Fall 85, p. 133.
"Harvey Tells Us about Frohman the Butcher" (For & with
    HG). MidwQ (27:1) Aut 85, p. 74.
"Haven't You Noticed?" (tr. of Karl Krolow). Field (32)
    Spr 85, p. 38.
"Holding Hands at the Mall." NewL (52:1) Fall 85, p. 57.
"In Flight" (tr. of Karl Krolow). Ploughs (11:4) 85, p.
    147.
"It's Plain." PoetL (80:3) Fall 85, p. 133.
"Lines under Your Eyes, under My Mouth." MSS (4:3) Spr
    85, p. 118.
"My Brother's Keeper." MidwQ (27:1) Aut 85, p. 72-73.
"People on the Move" (tr. of Karl Krolow). Ploughs (11:4)
    85, p. 146.
"Psalmody." MidwQ (27:1) Aut 85, p. 75.
"Sir Thomas Tucker." ConnPR (3:1) 84, p. 36.
"Some Exceptions" (tr. of Karl Krolow). Field (32) Spr
    85, p. 39.
"Stranger's Hand in Your Pocket" (tr. of Karl Krolow).
    Ploughs (11:4) 85, p. 145.
"There. Not Here." NoAmR (270:1) Mr 85, p. 69.
"Think I Heard Something" (tr. of Karl Krolow). Field
    (32) Spr 85, p. 40.
"The Time We Thought We Could Steal." QW (21) Fall-Wint
    85, p. 47-48.
"The Will." QW (21) Fall-Wint 85, p. 49.
1604. FRIED, Philip
"Application & Resume." HolCrit (22:1) F 85, p. 16-17.
"Death of a Scientist, Birth of a Believer." ConnPR (3:1)
    84, p. 24-25.
"The Good Book." PoetL (80:2) Sum 85, p. 75.
"Patch-/Work." NegC (5:3) Sum 85, p. 95 NegC (5:3) Sum
    85, p. 95.
"Syndrome." PoetL (80:2) Sum 85, p. 74.
1605. FRIEDLAND, Linda
"For E.K." Dandel (12:1) 85, p. 37.
"Spider wheels." Dandel (12:1) 85, p. 36.
1606. FRIEDLANDER, Benjamin
"A Mechanism." Zyzzyva (1:2) Sum 85, p. 150-151.
1607. FRIEDMAN, Jeff
"Monologue on the 7 Train Moving East over Queens." AntR
    (43:2) Spr 85, p. 208.
1608. FRIEDMAN, Robert J.
"I'm a Degenerate for Your Love" (The Lost Puppy). Open24
    (4) 85, p. 58.
1609. FRIEDRICH, Paul
"Five Stages." Wind (15:53) 85, p. 11-12.
"Generation." KanQ (17:4) Fall 85, p. 69.
1610. FRIESEN, Jim
"Dark Mirror." WestCR (20:2) O 85, p. 21-22.
"The Moon Goes Down." WestCR (20:2) O 85, p. 22-23.
1611. FRIESEN, Patrick
"Fool's Week." CanLit (105) Sum 85, p. 43-45.

1612. FRIGGIERI, Joe
        "Departing." <u>Vis</u> (19) 85, p. 17.
1613. FRIMAN, Alice
        "Myself." <u>CreamCR</u> (10:2) [85?], p. 60.
        "Turning Fifty." <u>CreamCR</u> (10:2) [85?], p. 61-62.
1614. FRITCHIE, Barbara
        "Museum Piece." <u>SouthernPR</u> (25:1) Spr 85, p. 30.
1615. FROST, Carol
        "Bluejay." <u>ThRiPo</u> (25/26) 85, p. 30.
        "The Gardener Delivers a Fawn." <u>NowestR</u> (23:1) 85, p. 8.
        "The Gardener Must Mow near the Dead Rabbit." <u>NowestR</u>
          (23:1) 85, p. 7.
        "The Gardener Praises Rain." <u>NowestR</u> (23:1) 85, p. 6.
        "The Invention of Music." <u>ThRiPo</u> (25/26) 85, p. 29-30.
1616. FROST, Richard
        "Kisses." <u>Raccoon</u> (17) Mr 85, p. 25.
1617. FRUMKIN, Gene
        "The Age Now Ending." <u>Conjunc</u> (7) 85, p. 168.
        "Androgynous Mind." <u>HawaiiR</u> (17) Spr 85, p. 47.
        "Bowing to the Rigid Applause." <u>Conjunc</u> (7) 85, p. 166.
        "The Caterpillar." <u>Chelsea</u> (44) 85, p. 118.
        "Embrace in an Open Field." <u>Chelsea</u> (44) 85, p. 120.
        "Erotic Woman." <u>Chelsea</u> (44) 85, p. 117-118.
        "A Figure of Immutable Force." <u>Chelsea</u> (44) 85, p. 34.
        "The Hallway." <u>Conjunc</u> (7) 85, p. 167.
        "In the Desert Alone at Night." <u>Chelsea</u> (44) 85, p. 35.
        "The Islands." <u>HawaiiR</u> (17) Spr 85, p. 46.
        "Origins." <u>HawaiiR</u> (17) Spr 85, p. 50-51.
        "Revolution." <u>Chelsea</u> (44) 85, p. 36.
        "Saddened by the Death of Francois Truffaut." <u>HawaiiR</u>
          (17) Spr 85, p. 48-49.
        "Several Descriptions of Their Life Together." <u>Chelsea</u>
          (44) 85, p. 119.
        "Shaping." <u>CharR</u> (11:1) Spr 85, p. 65.
        "The Singer of Manoa Street." <u>CharR</u> (11:1) Spr 85, p. 64.
        "View of the Riders." <u>Chelsea</u> (44) 85, p. 37.
1618. FRUTKIN, Mark
        "A Cup of Chai." <u>Quarry</u> (34:3) Sum 85, p. 68.
        "Etymon." <u>Descant</u> 49 (16:2) Sum 85, p. 20.
        "Gilgamesh." <u>Descant</u> 49 (16:2) Sum 85, p. 18.
        "Phosphor Ghost." <u>Descant</u> 49 (16:2) Sum 85, p. 16.
        "Photography." <u>Descant</u> 49 (16:2) Sum 85, p. 17.
        "Red-Winged." <u>Descant</u> 49 (16:2) Sum 85, p. 22.
        "River of Dreams." <u>Quarry</u> (34:3) Sum 85, p. 68-69.
        "Skeleton Song." <u>Descant</u> 49 (16:2) Sum 85, p. 21.
        "A Sliver of Brightness." <u>Waves</u> (13:4) Spr 85, p. 89.
        "Sounds." <u>Descant</u> 49 (16:2) Sum 85, p. 15.
        "Spontaneous Combustion" (9 selected poems). <u>Descant</u> 49
          (16:2) Sum 85, p. 14-22.
        "Text." <u>Descant</u> 49 (16:2) Sum 85, p. 19.
        "Untouchable Heat." <u>Descant</u> 49 (16:2) Sum 85, p. 14.
        "What Appollinaire's Friends Said about Him." <u>Waves</u>
          (13:4) Spr 85, p. 88-89.
1619. FRY, L. R.
        "Hello." <u>AntigR</u> (61) Spr 85, p. 102.
        "Westbound." <u>AntigR</u> (61) Spr 85, p. 102.
1620. FRY, Nan
        "Riddle." <u>NegC</u> (5:2) Spr 85, p. 170.
1621. FRYKBERG, Susan
        "Roberta the Robot." <u>Rampike</u> (4:2/3) 85-86, p. 108.
1622. FRYM, Gloria
        "In the Museum." <u>Zyzzyva</u> (1:4) Wint 85, p. 62.
FU, Du
        <u>See</u> DU ,Fu
FU, Tu
        <u>See</u> DU ,Fu

1623. FUJINO, Atsuko
      "Vow" (tr. by Steven Forth). AmerPoR (14:4) Jl-Ag 85, p.
      9.
1624. FULKER, Tina
      "Saturday Night." Vis (18) 85, p. 32.
1625. FULLER, John
      "Aubade." Poetry (146:4) Jl 85, p. 191.
      "Bud." Poetry (146:4) Jl 85, p. 192.
      "The Curable Romantic." Poetry (146:4) Jl 85, p. 187-190.
1626. FULLER, William
      "Some White Ship." CumbPR (5:1) Fall 85, p. 47.
1627. FULTON, Alice
      "603 West Liberty St." YaleR (74:3) Spr 85, p. 450-451.
      "Fables from the Random" (To Hank). Ploughs (11:1) 85, p.
      99-100.
      "Fierce Girl Playing Hopscotch." Poetry (145:6) Mr 85, p.
      340.
      "For Phyllis, Whose Name Means 'Leafy'." SoCaR (18:1)
      Fall 85, p. 32-33.
      "The Ice Storm." NewYorker (60:47) 7 Ja 85, p. 32.
      "Mary Studies the Apple Tree" (Poetry Award). Prima (9)
      85, p. 62.
      "Never Leave Elation Unattended." SoCaR (18:1) Fall 85,
      p. 34.
      "Nugget and Dust." Poetry (145:6) Mr 85, p. 340-341.
      "On the Charms of Absentee Gardens." Ploughs (11:1) 85,
      p. 101-103.
      "Risk Management." MichQR (24:1) Wint 85, p. 91-92.
      "Semaphores and Hemispheres" (To Hank. Third Prize,
      International Poetry Contest). WestB (17) 85, p. 15-19.
      "Well, Pain's Wildwood Looks Refined." SoCaR (18:1) Fall
      85, p. 31.
      "Works on Paper." Ploughs (11:1) 85, p. 97-98.
1628. FULTON, La Vendee
      "Making Your Own." EngJ (74:7) N 85, p. 102.
1629. FULTON, Robin
      "The Aspen" (tr. of Olav Hauge). Verse (3) 85, p. 41.
      "The Barn" (tr. of Lennart Sjogren). Verse (3) 85, p. 42.
      "The Birch" (tr. of Olav Hauge). Verse (3) 85, p. 40.
      "The Dream" (tr. of Bo Carpelan). Verse (3) 85, p. 38.
      "The Forgotten Captain" (tr. of Tomas Transtromer). Verse
      (3) 85, p. 37.
      "A Grain" (tr. of Olav Hauge). Verse (3) 85, p. 40.
      "In That House" (tr. of Bo Carpelan). Verse (3) 85, p. 39.
      "Lasting." Verse (3) 85, p. 32.
      "The Mill" (tr. of Werner Aspenstrom). Verse (3) 85, p.
      41.
      "The Nightingale in Badelunda" (tr. of Tomas Transtromer).
      Verse (3) 85, p. 38.
      "Stare Miasto" (the old part of Warsaw, tr. of Olav Hauge).
      Verse (3) 85, p. 40.
      "They Are Alive" (tr. of Bo Carpelan). Verse (3) 85, p.
      39.
1630. FUNGE, Robert
      "Easter Sunday." Tendril (19/20) 85, p. 146.
      "For My Daughter's Birthday" (Feb. 6, 1985). SpoonRQ
      (10:4) Fall 85, p. 53.
      "Guilt & Love, Guilt & Love" (from John/Henry). StoneC
      (13:1/2) Fall-Wint 85-86, p. 26.
      "John / Henry" (4 poems: "The Ping-Pong Song," "The
      Floods," "A Sunday Song," "The Confrontation"). NewL
      (51:3) Spr 85, p. 96-98.
      "John / Henry" (Four poems). KanQ (17:4) Fall 85, p. 188-
      190.
      "John / Henry" (Selection: "5th of July, 1982"). GreenfR
      (13:1/2) Fall-Wint 85, p. 50.

"John Henry" (Excerpt). <u>Tendril</u> (19/20) 85, p. 147.
1631. FUNK, Allison
"The Marsh." <u>Antaeus</u> (55) Aut 85, p. 95.
"New England Walls." <u>Antaeus</u> (55) Aut 85, p. 94.
1632. FUNSTEN, Kenneth
"Daniel Boone." <u>Open24</u> (4) 85, p. 40.
"Industrial Accident." <u>WormR</u> (25:4, issue 100) 85, p. 149.
"She Wanted Me To." <u>WormR</u> (25:4, issue 100) 85, p. 149-
150.
"Sonnet Abortion." <u>Bogg</u> (53) 85, p. 35.
1633. FURNIVAL, John
"Basil Leaves." <u>Conjunc</u> (8) 85, p. 196.
1634. FURTNEY, Diane
"If Asked for a Definition of Poetry." <u>Wind</u> (15:55) 85,
p. 25.
1635. GABBARD, G. N.
"Tabella Defixa." <u>Bogg</u> (54) 85, p. 60.
1636. GACH, G. G.
"Lakeshore" (tr. of Ren Yu, w. C. H. Kwock). <u>Zyzzyva</u>
(1:1) Spr 85, p. 40.
"To the Tune of Half & Half" (tr. of Sung Fang-Hu, w. C. H.
Kwock). <u>Zyzzyva</u> (1:1) Spr 85, p. 41.
1637. GADOL, Peter
"The Dream of a New Language: Antique Lamps from the Rue
Jacob." <u>HarvardA</u> (119:1) N 85, p. 9.
1638. GADOUTSIS, Helen
"First Place." <u>Waves</u> (13:2/3) Wint 85, p. 69.
1639. GALAN, Frantisek
"A Night with Hamlet" (Excerpts, tr. of Vladimir Holan, w.
Clayton Eshleman). <u>Sulfur</u> (12) 85, p. 4-11.
"A Night with Hamlet" (Excerpts, tr. of Vladimir Holan, w.
Clayton Eshleman). <u>Sulfur</u> (13) 85, p. 129-134.
"A Night with Hamlet" (Excerpts, tr. of Vladimir Holan, w.
Clayton Eshleman). <u>Sulfur</u> (14) 85, p. 74-80.
1640. GALAND, René
"Ar Steredenn Du." <u>Imagine</u> (1:2) Wint 84, p. 130.
"Black Star" (tr. by the author). <u>Imagine</u> (1:2) Wint 84,
p. 131.
"Nightfall in the Desert" (tr. by the author). <u>Imagine</u>
(1:2) Wint 84, p. 129.
"Serr-noz er Gouelec'h." <u>Imagine</u> (1:2) Wint 84, p. 128.
1641. GALASSI, Jonathan
"Cuttlefish Bones" (tr. of Eugenio Montale). <u>Ploughs</u>
(11:4) 85, p. 43-47.
"The Look of Things" (for Katha Pollitt). <u>ParisR</u> (27:97)
Fall 85, p. 137-139.
"Morning Run" (Villa Doria Pamphili, Rome). <u>AntR</u> (43:1)
Wint 85, p. 66-68.
"A Paris Suite." <u>Pequod</u> (19/20/21) 85, p. 131-134.
"A Paris Suite" (Excerpt). <u>CrossCur</u> (4:3) 84, p. 15.
"A Poem" (tr. of Eugenio Montale). <u>NewYRB</u> (32:13) 15 Ag
85, p. 14.
1642. GALE, Joseph Michael
"Wooden Bridge." <u>PottPort</u> (7) 85-86, p. 25.
GALINDO, David Escobar
<u>See</u> ESCOBAR GALINDO, David
1643. GALIOTE, Salvatore
"Anarchic." <u>SanFPJ</u> (7:2) 85, p. 42.
"The good Old Days - Remember?" <u>SanFPJ</u> (7:2) 85, p. 41.
"I Scream in Silence." <u>SanFPJ</u> (7:2) 85, p. 43.
1644. GALIOTO, Salvatore
"Fascism in the Air." <u>SanFPJ</u> (7:4) 85, p. 73.
"I Have Run along the River." <u>SanFPJ</u> (7:4) 85, p. 81.
1645. GALLAGHER, Dan
"The Gentle Heart." <u>CreamCR</u> (10:2) [85?], p. 56.

1646. GALLAGHER, Tess
        "The Borrowed Ones." NewYorker (61:17) 17 Je 85, p. 46.
        "The Hat." Antaeus (55) Aut 85, p. 99.
        "His Shining Helmet, Its Horsehair Crest." Antaeus (55)
            Aut 85, p. 98.
        "Into the Known" (For Bill Knott). Antaeus (55) Aut 85,
            p. 96-97.
        "With Stars" (For M.K.). Antaeus (55) Aut 85, p. 100.
1647. GALLAHER-CUMPIAN, Cynthia
        "Portrait of a Woman." Imagine (2:1) Sum 85, p. 80.
1648. GALLEGO, Laura
        "A Juan Antonio Corretjer." Mairena (7:19) 85, p. 84.
1649. GALLER, David
        "Bristol." SouthwR (70:4) Aut 85, p. 498.
        "The Event." MidAR (5:1) 85, p. 126-127.
        "Keep Away!" HolCrit (22:4) O 85, p. 20.
1650. GALLIANO, Alina
        "A Tientas." LindLM (4:3) Jl-S 85, p. 23.
        "XXV." LindLM (4:3) Jl-S 85, p. 23.
1651. GALLOWAY, Priscilla
        "The Bicycle of My Mood." CrossC (7:1) 85, p. 31.
        "For all that time he asked her." Waves (14:1/2) Fall 85,
            p. 91.
1652. GALVIN, Brendan
        "The Apple Trees." GeoR (39:4) Wint 85, p. 769.
        "Great Blue." NewYorker (61:33) 7 O 85, p. 58.
        "Listening to September." ThRiPo (25/26) 85, p. 32.
        "Nests." ThRiPo (25/26) 85, p. 31.
        "October Flocks." QW (21) Fall-Wint 85, p. 20.
        "Robbing Clam Beds." MichQR (24:3) Sum 85, p. 420-421.
        "Sea Huns." PoetC (17:1) Fall 85, p. 26-33.
        "This Fog." MichQR (24:3) Sum 85, p. 418-419.
        "Willow, Wishbone, Warblers." NewYorker (61:29) 9 S 85,
            p. 42.
1653. GALVIN, James
        "About." Atlantic (256:4), O 85, p. 78.
        "Against the Rest of the Year." QW (20) Spr-Sum 85, p.
            102-103.
        "Avatar." Crazy (29) Fall 85, p. 36.
        "Genesis." Atlantic (256:4), O 85, p. 78.
        "Meteorology." Crazy (29) Fall 85, p. 37.
        "Riddle." Atlantic (256:4), O 85, p. 78.
        "To the Republic." AmerPoR (14:6) N-D 85, p. 48.
        "Whistle." Iowa (15:1) Wint 85, p. 34.
1654. GALVIN, John
        "Materialism." Atlantic (255:3), Mr 85, p. 93.
1655. GANDER, Forrest
        "But You Already Know That." Raccoon (17) Mr 85, p. 37-38.
        "Come Over Here and Say That." CharR (11:2) Fall 85, p.
            106.
        "Death's Self Portrait" (tr. of Veronica Volkow). Mund
            (16:1/2) 85, p. 33.
        "El Inicio" (Selections: X, I, tr. of Veronica Volkow).
            Mund (16:1/2) 85, p. 29, 31.
        "Kata: Bus Stop." Swallow (4) 85, p. 10.
        "Memory" (tr. of Veronica Volkow). Mund (16:1/2) 85, p.
            35.
        "The Moment When Your Name Is Pronounced." CharR (11:2)
            Fall 85, p. 107.
        "Realm of the Hungry Ghosts." CutB (23) Fall-Wint 85, p.
            68.
        "The Washerwoman" (tr. of Veronica Volkow). Mund (16:1/2)
            85, p. 27.
        "The Weariness of Eurylochus" (tr. of Veronica Volkow).
            Mund (16:1/2) 85, p. 25.

1656. GANZER, Carol
      "Bells." SpoonRQ (10:4) Fall 85, p. 45.
1657. GARCIA, Richard
      "The Contras." Imagine (1:2) Wint 84, p. 114.
      "Eternal Return." Imagine (1:2) Wint 84, p. 115.
1658. GARCIA R., Roberto
      "Oda a Cucamonga." BilingR (11:3) S-D 84, p. 47-48.
1659. GARCIA RAMOS, Reinaldo
      "Discurso al Odiador." LindLM (4:2) Ap-Je 85, p. 4.
      "Doinel en Sus Cuarenta" (A Truffaut, in memoriam).
      LindLM (4:1) Ja-Mr 85, p. 19.
1660. GARDNER, Geoffrey
      "Trout Fever." Paint (11:21/12:24) 84-85, p. 12.
1661. GARDNER, Stephen
      "Eva McCann's Diary: 1/2/80: Knoxville." CalQ (26) Sum
      85, p. 38.
      "Good Woman." TexasR (6:1/2) Spr-Sum 85, p. 106.
1662. GARELLI, Anna
      "Velamen" (tr. of Gianni Toti). LitR (28:2) Wint 85, p.
      309.
1663. GARFINKEL, Patricia
      "Hannah Counts." Vis (17) 85, p. 22-23.
1664. GARIN, Marita
      "The Encounter." MidAR (5:1) 85, p. 26.
      "Huskies." Verse (4) 85, p. 9.
1665. GARNEAU, Sylvain
      "Kings and Castles" (tr. by Julie Besonen). Mund (15:1/2)
      85, p. 139.
      "Rois et Châteaux." Mund (15:1/2) 85, p. 138.
1666. GARRETT-PETTS, Will
      "A Band of Hair beneath the Veil" (St. Peter's Square,
      1981). CanLit (106) Fall 85, p. 30-31.
1667. GARRIGUES, Lisa
      "Oasis." Cond (11/12) 85, p. 107-108.
      "Under Franco." Cond (11/12) 85, p. 106.
1668. GARSON, Karl
      "Search for a New Calf." SoDakR (23:1) Spr 85, p. 66.
1669. GARVER, Dan
      "Saying North and South." CarolQ (38:1) Fall 85, p. 37.
1670. GASH, Sandra
      "Ritual, 1957." USl (18/19) Wint 85, p. 13.
1671. GASKIN, Bob
      "A Need for Ceremony." TexasR (6:1/2) Spr-Sum 85, p. 99.
1672. GASPARINI, Len
      "Dream." CanLit (106) Fall 85, p. 40.
      "Homage to Walter Anderson 1903-1965." AntigR (60) Wint
      85, p. 31.
1673. GASS, Brian E.
      "Holston River." Wind (15:55) 85, p. 23.
1674. GASS, W. H.
      "Erection." RiverS (17) 85, p. 19.
1675. GASTIGER, Joseph
      "Why I Need Glasses." Poetry (146:3) Je 85, p. 156-157.
1676. GATES, Beatrix
      "The Balloonist" (David Edgerley Gates, 11/13/11-8/5/79).
      NegC (5:3) Sum 85, p. 130.
      "Falling." CutB (23) Fall-Wint 85, p. 36-38.
      "This Picture." GreenfR (13:1/2) Fall-Wint 85, p. 148.
1677. GATES, Edward
      "Death and Division." PottPort (7) 85-86, p. 30.
      "In the Beginning." PottPort (7) 85-86, p. 15.
      "Overnight." AntigR (61) Spr 85, p. 103.
GATTUTA, Margo la
      See LaGATTUTA, Margo
1678. GAVER, Chasen
      "Bar Americani" (for James Toms). JamesWR (2:2) Wint 85,

                    p. 2.
             "Mirror Images." JamesWR (2:3) Spr-Sum 85, p. 10.
1679. GAVIÑO de FRANCHY, Carlos
             "El orfebre ha concluido." LindLM (4:4) O-D 85, p. 6.
             "El párpado levanta." LindLM (4:4) O-D 85, p. 6.
1680. GAWRON, James
             "Still Life." Vis (17) 85, p. 27.
1681. GEAREN, Ann
             "Elegy for an Ex-Husband." Prima (9) 85, p. 72.
1682. GEDDES, Gary
             "For Bi Shouwang." Waves (13:2/3) Wint 85, p. 7.
             "Poem for the Fifth of May." Waves (13:2/3) Wint 85, p. 8-
                9.
             "To the Women of the Fo Shan Silk Commune." Waves
                (13:2/3) Wint 85, p. 10-11.
             "Wild Goose Pagoda." Waves (13:2/3) Wint 85, p. 11.
1683. GEEST, Berber van der
             "Birth" (tr. by Rod Jellema). PoetL (79:4) Wint 85, p.
                239.
1684. GELETA, Greg
             "For Kellianne, a Clarinetist at Nine." PaintedB (26/27)
                Sum-Fall 85, p. 26.
             "Jamaica Farewell." SecC (12:1) 84, p. 8.
             "The Price is Right." PaintedB (26/27) Sum-Fall 85, p. 27-
                28.
1685. GELFOND, Rhoda
             "The Most Calculated Error in the Universe." PoetL (80:3)
                Fall 85, p. 141.
1686. GELMAN, Juan
             "Anclao en París." Inti (18/19) Otoño 83-Prim. 84, p.
                180-181.
             "Arte Poética." Inti (18/19) Otoño 83-Prim. 84, p.
                184-185.
             "CCLXI." Inti (18/19) Otoño 83-Prim. 84, p. 182-183.
             "Comentario IV (Santa Teresa)." Inti (18/19) Otoño 83-
                Prim. 84, p. 189.
             "Comentario XXV (San Juan de la Cruz)." Inti (18/19)
                Otoño 83-Prim. 84, p. 189-190.
             "Confianzas." Inti (18/19) Otoño 83-Prim. 84, p. 184.
             "En la Carpeta." Inti (18/19) Otoño 83-Prim. 84, p. 181.
             "En la Fecha." Inti (18/19) Otoño 83-Prim. 84, p. 185-
                186.
             "Gotán." Inti (18/19) Otoño 83-Prim. 84, p. 181-182.
             "Madres." Inti (18/19) Otoño 83-Prim. 84, p. 186-188.
             "Nota XXII." Inti (18/19) Otoño 83-Prim. 84, p. 188.
             "Relaciones." Inti (18/19) Otoño 83-Prim. 84, p. 183-
                184.
             "Sobre las Despedidas." Inti (18/19) Otoño 83-Prim. 84,
                p. 185.
             "XVII." Inti (18/19) Otoño 83-Prim. 84, p. 182.
1687. GENEGA, Paul
             "Dragon." WebR (10:2) Fall 85, p. 73.
             "The Rainmaker." Nat (240:11) 23 Mr 85, p. 340.
             "Walking the Plank." WebR (10:2) Fall 85, p. 71-72.
GENNARO, Lorraine S. de
             See DeGENNARO, Lorraine S.
1688. GENOVESE, Alicia
             "Anónima." Imagine (2:1) Sum 85, p. 48.
             "Elementos." Imagine (2:1) Sum 85, p. 47.
             "Formas." Imagine (2:1) Sum 85, p. 47.
             "La Silenciosa Agonía." Imagine (2:1) Sum 85, p. 49.
1689. GENOVESE, Andrea
             "Like the Migrant" (In Italian and English, tr. by Ruth
                Feldman). CrossCur (4:2) 84, p. 54-55.
1690. GEORGE, Ann
             "Vernal Equinox (1984)." SouthernPR (25:1) Spr 85, p. 35.

1691. GEORGE, Anne
      "Aunt Nettie at the Well." NegC (5:3) Sum 85, p. 38-39.
      "The Bridge Foursome." NegC (5:1) Wint 85, p. 51-52.
      "Josie-in-the-Morning." NegC (5:1) Wint 85, p. 29-30.
1692. GEORGE, Christopher T.
      "Top Banana." Bogg (53) 85, p. 19.
1693. GEORGE, Stefan
      "Guardianship" (tr. by Peter Viereck). NewL (51:4) Sum
         85, p. 74.
      "Love Lyric" (tr. by Peter Viereck). NewL (51:3) Spr 85,
         p. 54.
      "The Year of the Soul" (Selection: "October Tints, tr. by
         Peter Viereck). NewL (51:4) Sum 85, p. 74.
1694. GEORGES, Victor
      "You Who Return" (tr. by Yann Lovelock). Verse (4) 85, p.
         23.
1695. GERBER, Dan
      "Adumbratio." PassN (6:1) Fall-Wint 85, p. 15.
      "Evening in Bangkok." Pequod (19/20/21) 85, p. 135.
      "February." PassN (6:1) Fall-Wint 85, p. 15.
      "January." NewL (51:3) Spr 85, p. 62.
      "Snow on the Backs of Animals." NewL (51:3) Spr 85, p. 62.
1696. GERLACH, Eva
      "De doden zijn in mijn kind opgestaan." Mund (16:1/2) 85,
         p. 8.
      "The dead are resurrected in my child" (tr. by Myra
         Heerspink Scholz). Mund (16:1/2) 85, p. 9.
      "Wereld die ik haar aanpraat, zekerheden." Mund (16:1/2)
         85, p. 8.
      "World I talk her into, certainties" (tr. by Myra Heerspink
         Scholz). Mund (16:1/2) 85, p. 9.
1697. GERMAN, Norman
      "Explanation 5." WindO (46) Fall 85, p. 9.
      "Impressions." WindO (46) Fall 85, p. 9-11.
      "Leaving, the Last Time." Wind (15:54) 85, p. 21.
      "Losers." WindO (46) Fall 85, p. 8.
1698. GERNER, Ken
      "The Moon Year" (after Li Ho, 791-817, for Kenneth Rexroth,
         1905-1982). CutB (24) Spr-Sum 85, p. 75-91.
1699. GERNES, Sonia
      "Birds That Do Not Fly." PoetryNW (26:4) Wint 85-86, p.
         32-33.
      "The Chinese Writers Visit Notre Dame." LaurelR (19:2)
         Sum 85, p. 10-11.
      "Family History." GeoR (39:1) Spr 85, p. 24.
      "First Notice." PoetryNW (26:4) Wint 85-86, p. 34-35.
      "Freight." LaurelR (19:2) Sum 85, p. 12.
      "Letter to an Insomniac." PoetryNW (26:4) Wint 85-86, p.
         33-34.
      "Playing the Bells." LaurelR (19:2) Sum 85, p. 11.
      "Women at Forty." GeoR (39:1) Spr 85, p. 23.
1700. GERRY, David
      "The Gift." KanQ (17:4) Fall 85, p. 110.
      "Marilyn, 244/300." KanQ (17:3) Sum 85, p. 25.
1701. GERRY, Thomas
      "Before the Word." AntigR (60) Wint 85, p. 104.
      "The Clouds Incline to Yearning Love." AntigR (60) Wint
         85, p. 103.
1702. GERSHON, David Ben
      "When Winter Comes" (tr. of David Jaffin, w. Menahem Ben).
         CrossCur (4:2) 84, p. 35-36.
1703. GERSTLER, Amy
      "Alice and Lewis." Gargoyle (27) 85, p. 80-81.
      "Decorum." Temblor (1) 85, p. 91.
      "Loomings." Temblor (1) 85, p. 91.
      "Soft Talk." Temblor (1) 85, p. 91.

1704. GERTH, Vel
    "Fall." <u>Wind</u> (15:54) 85, p. 22.
1705. GERVAIS, André
    "On Rideath" (a loose gloss). <u>Rampike</u> (4:2/3) 85-86, p.
      65.
1706. GERVAIS, C. H.
    "Letter to Goethe." <u>CrossC</u> (7:3/4) 85, p. 54.
    "Letter to Jean Cocteau." <u>CrossC</u> (7:3/4) 85, p. 54.
    "Letter to John Keats in Rome." <u>CrossC</u> (7:3/4) 85, p. 54.
1707. GERY, John
    "Dark Horse." <u>NoDaQ</u> (53:4) Fall 85, p. 188-189.
1708. GESSNER, Richard
    "The Ball" (a series of object-based texts). <u>Rampike</u>
      (4:2/3) 85-86, p. 126-127.
    "The Embezzler." <u>Oink</u> (19) 85, p. 111.
    "The Ink Device." <u>Oink</u> (19) 85, p. 110.
1709. GETZEL, Teddy
    "Debt of Thera." <u>Open24</u> (4) 85, p. 45.
1710. GHALIB
    "Freely in hidden fire" (Ghazal, tr. by Frances Pritchett).
      <u>NewL</u> (51:4) Sum 85, p. 126-127.
    "I'll go live somewhere" (Ghazal, tr. by Frances
      Pritchett). <u>NewL</u> (51:4) Sum 85, p. 127.
    "Stanzas from Ghalib" (tr. by Frances Pritchett). <u>NewL</u>
      (51:4) Sum 85, p. 127-130.
1711. GHELMEZ, Petre
    "Star Roar" (tr. by Tom Carlson and Vasile Poenaru). <u>Mund</u>
      (16:1/2) 85, p. 59.
    "Vuiet Stelar." <u>Mund</u> (16:1/2) 85, p. 58.
1712. GHIGNA, Charles
    "Painted Windows." <u>Verse</u> (2) 85, p. 19.
1713. GHIRADELLA, Robert
    "Existential." <u>KanQ</u> (17:4) Fall 85, p. 58.
    "Line Storm." <u>KanQ</u> (17:3) Sum 85, p. 75.
1714. GHISELIN, Brewster
    "Alexandrian." <u>QW</u> (21) Fall-Wint 85, p. 99.
1715. GHOSSEIN, Mirene
    "Your Eyes Are Autumn Grey" (from <u>Ashes on a Cold Earth</u>,
      tr. Abdel Kader Arnaut). <u>NewRena</u> (19) Fall 85, p. 79.
1716. GIANOLI, Paul
    "Shoes." <u>WebR</u> (10:2) Fall 85, p. 50.
    "Ted Hughes?" <u>WebR</u> (10:2) Fall 85, p. 51.
1717. GIBB, Robert
    "Elegy for Sam Peckinpah." <u>StoneC</u> (13:1/2) Fall-Wint 85-
      86, p. 14-15.
    "Field Mouse." <u>BlueBldgs</u> (9) [85?], p. 44.
    "Home Movies." <u>PoetryNW</u> (26:1) Spr 85, p. 35.
    "The Return to Standard Time." <u>BlueBldgs</u> (9) [85?], p. 44.
1718. GIBBON, Timothy
    "The Cold in May." <u>AntigR</u> (60) Wint 85, p. 7-9.
1719. GIBBONS, Reginald
    "Along with the Dust" (tr. of Stanislaw Baranczak, w. the
      author). <u>TriQ</u> (63) Spr-Sum 85, p. 566.
    "The Blue Dress." <u>DenQ</u> (20:2) Fall 85, p. 37-46.
    "If China" (tr. of Stanislaw Baranczak, w. the author).
      <u>TriQ</u> (63) Spr-Sum 85, p. 567.
    "A Large Heavy-Faced Woman, Pocked, Unkempt, in a Loose
      Dress." <u>Iowa</u> (15:1) Wint 85, p. 88-89.
1720. GIBBONS, Robert
    "The Oranges of Crete." <u>ConnPR</u> (3:1) 84, p. 15.
1721. GIBBS, Barbara
    "Accusatory Poem." <u>NewYorker</u> (61:19) 1 Jl 85, p. 32.
1722. GIBBS, Robert
    "Climbing Tr'er Ceiri and Other Welsh Adventures" (with Joe
      and Ann Sherman). <u>PoetryCR</u> (7:2) Wint 85-86, p. 33.
    "Does It Keep in Your Ear?" <u>CrossCur</u> (4:3) 84, p. 137.

"Going without Breakfast" (on Bach's 300th birthday).
    Germ (9:1) Spr-Sum 85, p. 31-32.
"Making Believe We're Real." PoetryCR (7:2) Wint 85-86,
    p. 33.
"Something to Be Divined" (for Bob Hawkes). PoetryCR
    (7:2) Wint 85-86, p. 33.
1723. GIBSON, Keiko Matsui
"Hill" (tr. of Itsuko Ishikawa). NewL (51:4) Sum 85, p.
    146.
"I Am How I breathe" (In Japanese, tr. of Morgan Gibson).
    CrossCur (4:4/5:1) 85, p. 54.
"One and All" (In Japanese, tr. of Elizabeth Bartlett).
    CrossCur (4:2) 84, p. 58.
"Where" (tr. of Itsuko Ishikawa). NewL (51:4) Sum 85, p.
    145.
1724. GIBSON, Margaret
"Carmen's Story." MichQR (24:3) Sum 85, p. 415-417.
"Fast Light" (5 May 1941). Crazy (28) Spr 85, p. 52-54.
"Madrid" (23 November 1941). MinnR (N.S. 25) Fall 85, p.
    50-52.
"Maria" (18 November 1941). MinnR (N.S. 25) Fall 85, p.
    49-50.
"Mother / Daughter." GeoR (39:1) Spr 85, p. 133-135.
"Still Lives" (7 July 1941). GrahamHR (8) Wint 85, p. 25-
    26.
"Tina's Story: Glass." MichQR (24:3) Sum 85, p. 413-414.
"Vocation" (16 August 1941). GrahamHR (8) Wint 85, p. 27-
    28.
1725. GIBSON, Morgan
"I Am How I breathe" (In English and Japanese, tr. by Keiko
    Matsui Gibson). CrossCur (4:4/5:1) 85, p. 54-55.
"Searching for Dawn." CrossCur (4:4/5:1) 85, p. 81.
1726. GIBSON, Stephen M.
"A Short History of Bread." SouthernHR (19:1) Wint 85, p.
    40-41.
"Wisconsin Death Trip" (after the 19th century photos by
    Charles Van Schaick). TexasR (6:1/2) Spr-Sum 85, p. 22-
    23.
1727. GILBERT, Celia
"Crossing." Poetry (147:3) D 85, p. 153.
"Persephone Ascending." Poetry (147:3) D 85, p. 150-153.
1728. GILBERT, Christina
"The Loft." PoeticJ (11) 85, p. 6.
1729. GILBERT, Gerry
"Last Word in February." Rampike (4:2/3) 85-86, p. 22-24.
1730. GILBERT, Jack
"A Close Call." Iowa (15:2) Spr-Sum 85, p. 76.
"Ghosts." Iowa (15:2) Spr-Sum 85, p. 77.
"In Umbria." Iowa (15:2) Spr-Sum 85, p. 74.
"Late Friday Night in Summer Iowa." Iowa (15:2) Spr-Sum
    85, p. 75.
"Not Getting Closer." Iowa (15:2) Spr-Sum 85, p. 76.
"Secrets of Poetry." Iowa (15:2) Spr-Sum 85, p. 76.
"Twenty Favorite Times." Iowa (15:2) Spr-Sum 85, p. 75.
"Why Get So Exited." Iowa (15:2) Spr-Sum 85, p. 74.
1731. GILBERT, Sandra M.
"For Miss Lewis and Miss Newton." Poetry (147:3) D 85, p.
    133-134.
"In the Golden Sala." Poetry (147:3) D 85, p. 132-133.
"Kleptomaniac." PoetryNW (26:3) Aut 85, p. 39-40.
"Spring/Songs." PoetryNW (26:3) Aut 85, p. 40-41.
1732. GILBERT, Virginia
"Hunters of the Lost Spirit." PoetryR (2:2) Ap 85, p. 41-
    42.
1733. GILDNER, Gary
"I Remember the Failing Light." SenR (15:2) 85, p. 121-

122.
"Pies." SenR (15:2) 85, p. 119-120.
"Sometimes We Throw Things in the Car, Fast." Geor (39:2)
    Sum 85, p. 370-371.
"When an Angry Stranger Saw Me Crawling." PoetryNW (26:1)
    Spr 85, p. 44.
1734. GILGUN, John
"Adolescent, 1952." Vis (17) 85, p. 38.
"Los Angeles." Raccoon (17) Mr 85, p. 16.
"Conversation with a New York Literary Agent." JamesWR
    (2:3) Spr-Sum 85, p. 7.
1735. GILKES, M. A.
"A Portrait of the Artist As an Older Woman." GreenfR
    (12:3/4) Wint-Spr 85, p. 152.
"The Syzygy." GreenfR (12:3/4) Wint-Spr 85, p. 153.
1736. GILLESPIE, Mary
"Father and Daughter." LitR (29:1) Fall 85, p. 25.
1737. GILLESPIE, Robert
"Second Person." NewL (52:1) Fall 85, p. 126.
1738. GILLETT, Michelle
"Childhood Illness." PassN (6:1) Fall-Wint 85, p. 20.
1739. GILLUM, Richard F.
"Death among the Ndebele." KanQ (17:4) Fall 85, p. 226-
    227.
"Trumpeter." KanQ (17:1/2) Wint-Spr 85, p. 145.
1740. GINSBERG, Allen
"Arguments." AmerPoR (14:6) N-D 85, p. 17.
"The Black Man." AmerPoR (14:6) N-D 85, p. 16.
"Empire Air" (Flying to Rochester Institute of Technology).
    AmerPoR (14:6) N-D 85, p. 18.
"Far Away." AmerPoR (14:6) N-D 85, p. 16.
"Homage Vajracarya." AmerPoR (14:6) N-D 85, p. 16.
"I Am Not." AmerPoR (14:6) N-D 85, p. 17.
"I'm a Prisoner of Allen Ginsberg." AmerPoR (14:6) N-D
    85, p. 17.
"In My Kitchen in New York" (for Bataan Faigao). PortLES
    (2:1) Sum 85, p. 29-30.
"Maturity." AmerPoR (14:6) N-D 85, p. 16.
"They Are All Phantoms of My Imagining." AmerPoR (14:6) N-
    D 85, p. 18.
"Those Two." AmerPoR (14:6) N-D 85, p. 16.
"Throw Out the Yellow Journalists of Bad Grammar & Terrible
    Manner" (for Anne Waldman). AmerPoR (14:6) N-D 85, p.
    16.
"What the Sea Throws Up at Vlissengen" (for Simon
    Vinkenoog). AmerPoR (14:6) N-D 85, p. 17.
1741. GIOIA, Dana
"Cruising with the Beachboys." Poetry (146:5) Ag 85, p.
    263-264.
"The End." Poetry (146:5) Ag 85, p. 264-265.
"Flying over Clouds." ParisR (27:97) Fall 85, p. 172.
"In Chandler Country." NewYorker (61:11) 6 My 85, p. 50.
"Instructions for the Afternoon." Pequod (19/20/21) 85,
    p. 137-138.
"The Next Poem." Poetry (146:5) Ag 85, p. 262-263.
"The Room Upstairs." PoetryR (5) S 85, p. 19-22.
"Waiting in the Airport." Pequod (19/20/21) 85, p. 136.
"The Worn Steps." Pequod (19/20/21) 85, p. 138.
1742. GIRARD, Linda Walvoord
"At the Loom." MidwQ (26:4) Sum 85, p. 449.
"August: Cooling Trend." Ascent (10:3) 85, p. 12.
"The Damned." MidwQ (26:4) Sum 85, p. 447.
"Nebuchadnezzar." MidwQ (26:4) Sum 85, p. 448.
"The Pied Piper." MidwQ (26:4) Sum 85, p. 450-451.
1743. GIRCZYC, Catherine
"Cells." AntigR (62/63) Sum-Aut 85, p. 68.

"Walker in the Wood." <u>AntigR</u> (62/63) Sum-Aut 85, p. 68.
1744. GIROUX, Robert
    "Cendres." <u>Os</u> (21) 85, p. 7.
1745. GIULIANI, Alfredo
    "And Then We Learn" (tr. by Giuliano Dego and Margaret
        Straus). <u>LitR</u> (28:2) Wint 85, p. 244.
    "Casuals" (Excerpt, tr. by P. F. Paolini). <u>LitR</u> (28:2)
        Wint 85, p. 241.
    "Chomsky Poem" (tr. by P. F. Paolini). <u>LitR</u> (28:2) Wint
        85, p. 240-241.
    "Friday Even Azure" (tr. by P. F. Paolini). <u>LitR</u> (28:2)
        Wint 85, p. 239.
    "Resurrection after the Rain" (tr. by P. F. Paolini).
        <u>LitR</u> (28:2) Wint 85, p. 241.
    "Songlet" (tr. by P. F. Paolini). <u>LitR</u> (28:2) Wint 85, p.
        242.
    "When I Was Young" (tr. by Giuliano Dego and Margaret
        Straus). <u>LitR</u> (28:2) Wint 85, p. 243.
1746. GIZZI, Art
    "August 2, 1983." <u>HiramPoR</u> (38) Spr-Sum 85, p. 13.
1747. GJUZEL, Bogomil
    "The Desert Woman" (Excerpt from a sequence of poems, tr.
        by Zoran Ancevski and James McKinley). <u>NewL</u> (51:4) Sum
        85, p. 27.
    "A Stranger at Home, at Home Elsewhere" (tr. by Zoran
        Ancevski and James McKinley). <u>NewL</u> (51:4) Sum 85, p.
        28.
1748. GLADDING, Jody
    "The Right Occasion." <u>WestB</u> (17) 85, p. 63.
    "Taughannock Falls." <u>WestB</u> (17) 85, p. 62.
1749. GLANCY, Diane
    "Against Dark Clouds." <u>Waves</u> (14:1/2) Fall 85, p. 68.
    "The Buzz." <u>Nimrod</u> (28:2) Spr-Sum 85, p. 48.
    "Curator of the Zoo" (for Bill Fiore, General Curator of
        the Tulsa Zoological Park). <u>Nimrod</u> (28:2) Spr-Sum 85,
        p. 49.
    "Daughter Who Lives with Her Father." <u>Nimrod</u> (28:2) Spr-
        Sum 85, p. 48.
    "The Eight O Five." <u>CrossCur</u> (4:4/5:1) 85, p. 82-83.
    "Escarpment." <u>Waves</u> (14:1/2) Fall 85, p. 69.
    "Fort Lancaster, Southwest Texas." <u>NoDaQ</u> (53:2) Spr 85,
        p. 107-108.
    "A Game of Scrabble." <u>NewL</u> (52:1) Fall 85, p. 37.
    "The Kansas-Oklahoma Border." <u>NoDaQ</u> (53:2) Spr 85, p. 108.
    "Moon Face." <u>PraS</u> (59:3) Fall 85, p. 73.
    "Muchow's Cry." <u>PraS</u> (59:3) Fall 85, p. 74-75.
    "Neighbor." <u>Nimrod</u> (28:2) Spr-Sum 85, p. 50.
    "Northern Texas Plains." <u>NoDaQ</u> (53:2) Spr 85, p. 108.
    "Roundup." <u>PraS</u> (59:3) Fall 85, p. 74.
    "Some Thoughts on Our Uncommon Language." <u>Sulfur</u> (14) 85,
        p. 39-41.
    "Stone Figure from an Ancient Dynasty" (Freer Gallery,
        Smithsonian). <u>Amelia</u> (2:1) Ap 85, p. 18.
    "Thanksgiving." <u>Amelia</u> (2:2) O 85, p. 66-68.
    "Three Ducks in the Marias des Cygnes Wildlife Reserve"
        (Highway 69, Kansas 12/25/84). <u>Nimrod</u> (28:2) Spr-Sum
        85, p. 47.
    "Trucker." <u>NoDaQ</u> (53:2) Spr 85, p. 109.
1750. GLASER, Elton
    "At the James Wright Poetry Festival." <u>PoetryNW</u> (26:2)
        Sum 85, p. 42-44.
    "Convention of Travelers." <u>LittleM</u> (14:4) 85, p. 35.
    "Ghost Excursion." <u>MemphisSR</u> (5:2) Spr 85, p. 11.
    "Homage to Gertrude Stein" (tr. of Raymond Queneau).
        <u>GrahamHR</u> (9) Fall 85, p. 64.
    "Homage to Jacques Prévert" (tr. of Raymond Queneau).

GrahamHR (9) Fall 85, p. 65.
"Homebound." MemphisSR (5:2) Spr 85, p. 12.
"Mathematics for Poets." WoosterR (3) Spr 85, p. 20.
"Memory" (tr. of Raymond Queneau). GrahamHR (9) Fall 85,
    p. 67.
"New Year's Fear." CapeR (20:2) Fall 85, p. 17.
"Prayer to Saint Uncumber." LittleM (14:4) 85, p. 36.
"Primitives." Field (32) Spr 85, p. 37.
"Pro and Con" (tr. of Raymond Queneau). GrahamHR (9) Fall
    85, p. 66.
"School of the Soldier" (tr. of Raymond Queneau).
    GrahamHR (9) Fall 85, p. 68.
1751. GLASER, Michael S.
    "Prizes." ChrC (102:17) 15 My 85, p. 485.
1752. GLASS, Jesse (See also GLASS, Jesse, Jr.)
    "Museum." CreamCR (10:2) [85?], p. 64-68.
1753. GLASS, Jesse, Jr. (See also GLASS, Jesse)
    "Carl Sandburg." SpoonRQ (10:2) Spr 85, p. 60.
    "On the Photograph of a Great-Aunt Who Died at Eighteen"
        (Flat Woods, Va. 1920). SpoonRQ (10:4) Fall 85, p. 48.
1754. GLASS, Malcolm
    "Another Story." StoneC (12:2/3) Spr-Sum 85, p. 49.
    "The Coat" (For Louis Gruenberg and King Baker). NegC
        (5:3) Sum 85, p. 90-91.
    "Drifting." Amelia (2:2) O 85, p. 65.
    "In the Shadow of the Gourd." ArizQ (41:2) Sum 85, p. 116-
        118.
    "Names of Death." CreamCR (10:1) 85, p. 31.
    "Star Trails." MichQR (24:2) Spr 85, p. 275-276.
    "Toes." NegC (5:1) Wint 85, p. 57-58.
    "Tongues." YellowS (14) Spr 85, p. 39.
1755. GLASSER, Jane Ellen
    "For the Good Children." VirQ (61:3) Sum 85, p. 424-425.
1756. GLATSTEIN, Jacob
    "Small Door of a Dream" (tr. by Doris Vidaver). Poetry
        (146:5) Ag 85, p. 256.
1757. GLAZE, Andrew
    "An Age Once Horrid." NegC (5:3) Sum 85, p. 17.
    "American." NegC (5:3) Sum 85, p. 14.
    "Bliss." NegC (5:3) Sum 85, p. 21.
    "Elected Reason." NegC (5:3) Sum 85, p. 15.
    "Firefly Evening." NegC (5:3) Sum 85, p. 19.
    "Honeymoon." NegC (5:3) Sum 85, p. 20.
    "Iron Mask." NegC (5:3) Sum 85, p. 10-13.
    "Palos." NegC (5:3) Sum 85, p. 18.
    "Pirate King." NegC (5:3) Sum 85, p. 16.
    "What's That You Say, Cesar?" (to Cesar Ortiz-Tinoco).
        TriQ (63) Spr-Sum 85, p. 168-170.
1758. GLAZER, Jane
    "Mother's Mother." MidAR (5:1) 85, p. 3.
    "Point of No Return." Calyx (9:1) Spr-Sum 85, p. 34-35.
1759. GLAZIER, Loss Pequeño
    "Vrouvelijkheid." Os (21) 85, p. 6.
1760. GLEN, Emilie
    "Sky Slate." SmPd (22:3) Fall 85, p. 9.
    "Take It from Poseidon." PoetryR (5) S 85, p. 42.
    "To Eagle." SmPd (22:3) Fall 85, p. 9.
1761. GLENN, Emilie
    "Every Inch of the Way." ConnPR (3:1) 84, p. 41.
1762. GLENN, Laura
    "Outside the Voting Booth." Chelsea (44) 85, p. 71.
    "Under the Leafless Tree." PoetL (80:3) Fall 85, p. 169.
1763. GLICKMAN, Susan
    "Arabia Deserta." CanLit (104) Spr 85, p. 6.
    "Birdwatching along the Humber." PoetryCR (7:1) Aut 85,
        p. 22.

"Chocolate: A Love Poem." PoetryCR (7:1) Aut 85, p. 22.
"Ignorance and Bliss." Quarry (34:3) Sum 85, p. 64.
"Like Billie Holiday." PoetryCR (7:1) Aut 85, p. 22.
"Two Callas" (after a photograph by Imogen Cunningham).
    PoetryCR (7:1) Aut 85, p. 22.
"Wind, 10:00." Quarry (34:3) Sum 85, p. 64.
1764. GLOVER, Jon
"The Deserted Lake." Stand (26:1) Wint 84-85, p. 40.
"Treasures." Stand (26:1) Wint 84-85, p. 41.
1765. GLOWNEY, John E.
"To a Woman in an Elevator." MichQR (24:4) Fall 85, p.
    621.
"A Wedding Dance at the Z.C.B.J. Hall." Northeast (Series
    4:1) Sum 85, p. 3-4.
1766. GLUCK, Louise
"Adult Grief." Pequod (18) 85, p. 22.
"The Reproach." Pequod (18) 85, p. 24-25.
"The Triumph of Achilles." Pequod (18) 85, p. 23.
1767. GLYNN, Daniel
"First Geese." KanQ (17:4) Fall 85, p. 205.
1768. GNIATCZYNSKI, Wojciech
"After Reading about Unusual Changes Taking Place in the
    Sun" (tr. by the author). AmerPoR (14:5) S-O 85, p. 48.
1769. GODFREY, John
"Encore." Oink (19) 85, p. 66.
"The Harp's Outside the Door." Oink (19) 85, p. 64.
"In the Chamber." Oink (19) 85, p. 62-63.
"Johnny Cash, Meet Johnny 'G'." Oink (19) 85, p. 65.
1770. GODWIN, Greg
"Speaking." PaintedB (26/27) Sum-Fall 85, p. 54.
1771. GOEBEL, Ulf
"Civility." WebR (10:1) Spr 85, p. 73.
"Debt." WebR (10:1) Spr 85, p. 73.
"Marriage." WebR (10:1) Spr 85, p. 72.
"Nautical Term." CumbPR (5:1) Fall 85, p. 44.
1772. GOEDICKE, Patricia
"Americans Shot at in Canyon." Tendril (19/20) 85, p. 148-
    150.
"Our 34th Anniversary" (by Patricia Grean, as told to
    Patricia Goedicke). Raccoon (17) Mr 85, p. 7-8.
"The Rain between Us." CutB (23) Fall-Wint 85, p. 30-31.
1773. GOFF, Charles Rice, III
"Henry K Performs Orwell in SF Commonwealth Club." SanFPJ
    (7:3) 84 [i.e. 85], p. 38.
"Mutiny." SanFPJ (7:3) 84 [i.e. 85], p. 39.
"Progress." SanFPJ (7:3) 84 [i.e. 85], p. 37.
1774. GOFREED, Howard
"Guns and Putter." SanFPJ (7:4) 85, p. 82-84.
1775. GOJMERAC-LEINER, Georgia
"Garden." Vis (19) 85, p. 19.
1776. GOLDBARTH, Albert
"Attempt at the Ultimate Postcard." Ascent (10:3) 85, p.
    13.
"Brotherly." Poetry (146:2) My 85, p. 78.
"By One" (for David Clewell). GeoR (39:1) Spr 85, p. 91-
    92.
"Comic Collecting." OhioR (35) 85, p. 74-75.
"Dancing." DenQ (19:4) Spr 85, p. 6-8.
"A Deep and Craving Hunger for the Past." NewEngR (7:3)
    Spr 85, p. 293-295.
"Different Reviewers: Different Poems." CarolQ (37:2)
    Wint 85, p. 96-98.
"Flute/The Ten Lost Tribes of Israel." SenR (15:1) 85, p.
    40-41.
"Glass." DenQ (19:4) Spr 85, p. 9-10.
"The Gulf." BelPoJ (35:3) Spr 85, p. 24-31.

"Ishango." <u>CarolQ</u> (37:2) Wint 85, p. 91-95.
"Jake." <u>CarolQ</u> (37:2) Wint 85, p. 85-90.
"Just Enough Moon." <u>Iowa</u> (15:1) Wint 85, p. 93.
"Mishipasinghan, Lumchipamudana, etc." <u>GeoR</u> (39:1) Spr
      85, p. 90-91.
"A Moment." <u>NewOR</u> (12:3) Fall 85, p. 53.
"The Nile in America." <u>DenQ</u> (19:4) Spr 85, p. 13-14.
"A Pantheon." <u>SouthwR</u> (70:4) Aut 85, p. 513-515.
"Personal." <u>OhioR</u> (35) 85, p. 72-73.
"Pheletos of Cos." <u>NewEngR</u> (7:3) Spr 85, p. 291-292.
"The Poem of the Praises." <u>BlackWR</u> (11:2) Spr 85, p. 7-10.
"Poem Whose Last Sentence Is 17 Syllables after a
      Suggestion." <u>Poetry</u> (146:2) My 85, p. 76-78.
"Problem Solving." <u>Poetry</u> (145:4) Ja 85, p. 212-214.
"Pulp." <u>PoetryNW</u> (26:1) Spr 85, p. 6.
"The Relationship." <u>SouthernPR</u> (25:1) Spr 85, p. 69.
"Some of the Reasons." <u>PoetryNW</u> (26:1) Spr 85, p. 3-4.
"Steerage." <u>Poetry</u> (146:2) My 85, p. 74-76.
"Waking." <u>NewOR</u> (12:3) Fall 85, p. 42.
"We're Just About to Observe the Edge of the Universe."
      <u>Poetry</u> (145:4) Ja 85, p. 210-212.
"Whole Heart." <u>DenQ</u> (19:4) Spr 85, p. 11-12.
"The Window." <u>PoetryNW</u> (26:1) Spr 85, p. 4-6.
"You Hum." <u>Poetry</u> (145:4) Ja 85, p. 214-215.
1777. GOLDBERG, Beckian Fritz
"Birdscaping." <u>PoetryNW</u> (26:4) Wint 85-86, p. 46-47.
"The Cloud by Desire." <u>PoetryNW</u> (26:4) Wint 85-86, p. 44-
      45.
"The Consolation of Celibacy." <u>Tendril</u> (19/20) 85, p. 151-
      152.
"Horses at Estero Beach." <u>Crazy</u> (28) Spr 85, p. 62-63.
"Nightgowns." <u>Crazy</u> (28) Spr 85, p. 60-61.
"The Perception of Motion." <u>Tendril</u> (19/20) 85, p. 154-
      156.
"State Street Motel." <u>Tendril</u> (19/20) 85, p. 153.
"Visiting the Stockyards." <u>Crazy</u> (28) Spr 85, p. 59.
1778. GOLDBERG, Bonni
"What Remains." <u>AntR</u> (43:4) Fall 85, p. 460-461.
1779. GOLDEN, Renny
"The Feast of the Saints, the Feast of the Dead, Guatemala
      1985." <u>ChrC</u> (102:38) 4 D 85, p. 1117.
1780. GOLDENSOHN, Barry
"Contra Botticelli." <u>MassR</u> (26:1) Spr 85, p. 118.
"Kerensky's Glasses." <u>NewRep</u> (192:18) 6 My 85, p. 40.
"Visionary Gifts." <u>Salm</u> (67) Sum 85, p. 34-35.
1781. GOLDERMAN, Cynthia R.
"After Shock - Just Thinking of the Neutron Bomb." <u>SanFPJ</u>
      (7:2) 85, p. 54-55.
"Neutronic Winter." <u>SanFPJ</u> (7:4) 85, p. 78-79.
"San Diego Off-White & Sacrifice." <u>ConnPR</u> (3:1) 84, p. 29-
      30.
1782. GOLDSBY, Marcie
"The Hot Ear of the Earth Is Tired of Hearing Your Bull
      Shit, Come Back to the Valley." <u>AmerPoR</u> (14:4) Jl-Ag
      85, p. 17.
1783. GOLDSMITH, Frederica
"Capes." <u>Kaleid</u> (11) Sum 85, p. 27.
1784. GOLDSTEIN, Henry
"Last Night." <u>Confr</u> (30/31) N 85, p. 177.
1785. GOLDSTEIN, Jonas L.
"Second Season." <u>SanFPJ</u> (7:3) 84 [i.e. 85], p. 72.
"Walls." <u>SanFPJ</u> (7:3) 84 [i.e. 85], p. 45.
1786. GOLDSTEIN, Laurence
"Homesick in Los Angeles." <u>Poetry</u> (146:2) My 85, p. 73.
"A Letter to Andrew and Jonathan and Other Poems." <u>OntR</u>
      (23) Fall-Wint 85-86, p. 59-70.

1787. GOM, Leona
"Silver Wedding Anniversary" (for Gina). Quarry (34:3)
Sum 85, p. 10.
"Surviving." Waves (13:4) Spr 85, p. 85.
"What Women Want." Waves (13:4) Spr 85, p. 85.
1788. GOMEZ, Alma
"To Open Up a Trunk" (a quien sabe). Imagine (2:1) Sum
85, p. 72-73.
1789. GOMEZ, Jewelle
"My Chakabuku Mama." OP (38/39) Spr 85, p. 58-59.
1790. GONNELLA, Joe
"The Lesson." LittleM (14:4) 85, p. 37.
"Poems for My Son." LittleM (14:4) 85, p. 38.
"Railbird." LittleM (14:4) 85, p. 39.
1791. GONZALES, Rebecca
"After the Sermon." Imagine (1:2) Wint 84, p. 58.
"The Difference." Imagine (1:2) Wint 84, p. 57.
"In Spite of a Fire and a Coat." Imagine (1:2) Wint 84,
p. 57-58.
1792. GONZALEZ, José Emilio
"A Francisco Matos Paoli" (al leer su libro Vestido para
la denudez). Mairena (7:19) 85, p. 102.
1793. GOODENOUGH, J. B.
"Hill Water." DeKalbLAJ (18:1/2) 85, p. 69.
"Imprecation." Wind (15:53) 85, p. 13.
"Inheritors." SpoonRQ (10:2) Spr 85, p. 48.
"Lines from the Interior." SouthernHR (19:1) Wint 85, p.
42.
"Moving into the Neighborhood." PaintedB (26/27) Sum-Fall
85, p. 32.
"Night Door." Wind (15:53) 85, p. 13.
"The Old Way." CrossCur (4:4/5:1) 85, p. 99.
"The Red Sow." DeKalbLAJ (18:1/2) 85, p. 69-70.
"Routines." DeKalbLAJ (18:1/2) 85, p. 70.
"Shrike." SouthernHR (19:1) Wint 85, p. 64.
"Strictures." Blueline (6:2) Wint-Spr 85, p. 40.
"This Is the Map." SpoonRQ (10:2) Spr 85, p. 49.
1794. GOODISON, Lorna
"Garden of the Women Once Fallen." GreenfR (12:3/4) Wint-
Spr 85, p. 157-158.
"Guinea Woman." GreenfR (12:3/4) Wint-Spr 85, p. 155-156.
"Jah Music" (For Michael Cooper). GreenfR (12:3/4) Wint-
Spr 85, p. 156.
1795. GOODMAN, Diane
"The Last New Town." NegC (5:4) Fall 85, p. 111.
1796. GOODMAN, Dottie
"Lady's Labor of Love." PoeticJ (10) 85, p. 2.
1797. GOODMAN, Frances
"At the Mill." SanFPJ (7:2) 85, p. 10-11.
1798. GOODMAN, Jeffrey
"New Epigrams." ChiR (35:1) Aut 85, p. 57.
1799. GOODMAN, Melinda
"Wedding Reception." Cond (11/12) 85, p. 17-20.
1800. GOODMAN, Michael
"Pisgah" (for Rob). PartR (52:2) 85, p. 70-71.
1801. GOODMAN, Ryah Tumakin
"Poetry Meeting." CumbPR (5:1) Fall 85, p. 45.
1802. GOODRUM, David
"Whimper." WindO (46) Fall 85, p. 24-25.
1803. GOODWIN, Douglas
"Caught Not Looking." Bogg (54) 85, p. 30.
"The Mad Women of Unemployment." WormR (25:1, issue 97)
85, p. 31-32.
"Morning Sickness." WormR (25:1, issue 97) 85, p. 32-33.
"Poetic Noise." WormR (25:1, issue 97) 85, p. 29-31.

1804. GOOSE, Mary
        "Sounds of Birds Passing." NoDaQ (53:2) Spr 85, p. 180.
        "Wood Carver" (For Luke Kapayou). NoDaQ (53:2) Spr 85, p.
            181.
1805. GORCZYNSKI, Renata
        "Franz Schubert: A Press Conference" (tr. of Adam
            Zagajewski). Thrpny (6:2, issue 22) Sum 85, p. 25.
        "In the Encyclopedias, No Room for Osip Mandelstam" (tr. of
            Adam Zagajewski). NewYRB (32:16) 24 O 85, p. 34.
        "Kierkegaard on Hegel" (tr. of Adam Zagajewski). NewYRB
            (32:16) 24 O 85, p. 34.
        "My Masters" (tr. of Adam Zagajewski). NewYRB (32:16) 24
            O 85, p. 34.
1806. GORDETT, Marea
        "Vanished." GeoR (39:4) Wint 85, p. 755-756.
1807. GORDON, Andra
        "August, 1983." HangL (48) Fall 85, p. 61.
        "Two on a Balance Beam." HangL (48) Fall 85, p. 60.
1808. GORDON, Carol
        "Message Home" (Centrum Writers' Conference, 1984).
            CrabCR (2:2) Wint 85, p. 21.
        "Midwives." Calyx (9:1) Spr-Sum 85, p. 41.
        "October." SnapD (8:2) Spr 85, p. 17.
        "Taking Our Anger to Bed." Calyx (9:1) Spr-Sum 85, p. 39.
        "Unwed Fathers' Home." Calyx (9:1) Spr-Sum 85, p. 40.
1809. GORDON, Coco
        "Your Smile" (for Ray). Confr (30/31) N 85, p. 272.
1810. GORDON, Kirpal
        "How, after Masturbating, the World Is Just a Dream." Sam
            (42:3, 167th release) 85, p. 13.
1811. GORDON, L. Suzanne
        "Listening." PoetL (79:4) Wint 85, p. 215.
1812. GORDON, Mark
        "The Cremation of Malloney's." PoetryCR (6:3) Spr 85, p.
            32.
        "Opening of the Shoe Museum." PoetryCR (7:2) Wint 85-86,
            p. 53.
1813. GORDON, Rebecca
        "Jalapa -- Soldier's Funeral." Calyx (9:1) Spr-Sum 85, p.
            25.
        "Nights in Siuna." Calyx (9:1) Spr-Sum 85, p. 26-27.
        "La Revolución Es una Chavala de Cinco Años" (The
            Revolution is like a five year old girl -- Nicaraguan
            saying). Calyx (9:1) Spr-Sum 85, p. 24-25.
1814. GORHAM, Sarah
        "Ghazal in Blue." SouthernPR (25:1) Spr 85, p. 56.
1815. GORLIN, Debra
        "Of a Feather." MassR (26:1) Spr 85, p. 27-28.
        "Slow Burial." MassR (26:1) Spr 85, p. 29.
1816. GORMAN, Leroy
        "Haiku" (5 selections). PoetryCR (7:2) Wint 85-86, p. 50.
1817. GORSKI, Andrew
        "Blind Intimacy" (tr. of Jerzy Ficowski). Os (21) 85, p.
            13.
        "A Sin Avoided" (tr. of Jerzy Ficowski). Os (21) 85, p.
            15.
1818. GOTT, George
        "Ho-Had-Hun." RagMag (4:2) Fall 85, p. 42.
        "Osiris." DeKalbLAJ (18:3/4) 85, p. 34.
        "A Poem with a Line of French." MidwQ (26:4) Sum 85, p.
            454-455.
        "Stasis." DeKalbLAJ (18:3/4) 85, p. 35.
1819. GOTTLIEB, Darcy
        "Letting Go." Outbr (14/15) Fall 84-Spr 85, p. 69.
1820. GOTTLIEB, Teresa
        "Cuando está un poco oscuro" ("Sin Título"). Imagine

(2:1) Sum 85, p. 45.
"Sólo puedo intentar." <u>Imagine</u> (2:1) Sum 85, p. 46.
1821. GOUMAS, Yannis
"Fitting Room" (tr. of Naná Issaìa). <u>NewRena</u> (19)
Fall 85, p. 57-65.
"Gazi Berkay Sokak, Sisli." <u>NewRena</u> (19) Fall 85, p. 41.
"To the Painter Leftéris Rórros" (tr. by Stavros
Tsimicalis). <u>Waves</u> (13:4) Spr 85, p. 98.
"Ucler Balik Restaurant." <u>NewRena</u> (19) Fall 85, p. 42.
1822. GOWAN, Lee
"Measures." <u>Grain</u> (13:4) N 85, p. 58.
1823. GRAHAM, David
"American Gothic." <u>Poetry</u> (146:1) Ap 85, p. 24.
"The Bad Season Makes the Poet Sad" (--Herrick).
<u>SouthernPR</u> (25:1) Spr 85, p. 49.
"Crickets in August." <u>PassN</u> (6:2) Spr-Sum 85, p. 19.
"In Praise of the Coelacanth." <u>PoetryNW</u> (26:1) Spr 85, p.
24-25.
"A Lot of Boys Bar." <u>Poetry</u> (146:1) Ap 85, p. 23.
"The Mohawk River: A Real Allegory of Twenty Years of My
Life As an Artist." <u>Blueline</u> (6:2) Wint-Spr 85, p. 14.
"The Outskirts of Everything." <u>Poetry</u> (146:1) Ap 85, p.
22.
"The Scholar Gypsy: A Progress Report." <u>SouthernPR</u> (25:1)
Spr 85, p. 48.
"This Temporary Map" (for Dennis Finnell). <u>Blueline</u> (7:1)
Sum-Fall 85, p. 16.
"When Clowns Go Bad" (variations on a theme by Gary
Larson). <u>PoetryNW</u> (26:1) Spr 85, p. 25.
1824. GRAHAM, Jorie
"The Artist's Model." <u>AmerPoR</u> (14:3) My-Je 85, p. 38-39.
"Noli Me Tangere." <u>AmerPoR</u> (14:3) My-Je 85, p. 40-41.
"Ravel and Unravel." <u>AmerPoR</u> (14:3) My-Je 85, p. 39-40.
"Self Portrait as Both Parties." <u>AmerPoR</u> (14:3) My-Je 85,
p. 38.
"Self Portrait as Demeter and Persephone." <u>AmerPoR</u> (14:3)
My-Je 85, p. 37.
"Self-portrait As the Gesture between Them" (Adam and Eve).
<u>Antaeus</u> (55) Aut 85, p. 101-105.
1825. GRAHAM, Matthew
"Romance." <u>Crazy</u> (29) Fall 85, p. 61.
1826. GRAHAM, Neile
"The Master of Winter." <u>Wind</u> (15:53) 85, p. 18.
1827. GRAHAM, Vicki
"A Woman Combing." <u>Thrpny</u> (6:2, issue 22) Sum 85, p. 16.
1828. GRAHN, Judy
"Descent to the Butch of the Realm." <u>Zyzzyva</u> (1:4) Wint
85, p. 40-46.
"Talkers in a Dream Door." <u>Zyzzyva</u> (1:1) Spr 85, p. 66-69.
1829. GRAMIGNA, Giuliano
"The (Portable) Rite of Sleep" (Selections: 1-4, 12, 17,
tr. by Giuliano Dego and Margaret Straus). <u>LitR</u> (29:1)
Fall 85, p. 101-103.
1830. GRANET, Roger B.
"Observations at a Family Dinner." <u>NegC</u> (5:3) Sum 85, p.
127.
1831. GRASS, Günther
"Clearance Sale" (tr. by Bruce Berlind). <u>Ploughs</u> (11:4)
85, p. 140-141.
GRAVELLES, Charles de
<u>See</u> DeGRAVELLES, Charles
1832. GRAVES, Michael
"Meditation, 10." <u>Wind</u> (15:53) 85, p. 14.
"Meditation, 25." <u>HolCrit</u> (22:2) Ap 85, p. 17.
1833. GRAY, Alasdair
"Old Negatives" (Selections: A Sequence of Four Poems).

Verse (1) 84, p. 36-37.
1834. GRAY, Alice Wirth
"He Was When He Died." AmerS (54:2) Spr 85, p. 179-180.
"What We Did on Your Vacation." Atlantic (255:6), Je 85,
p. 86.
1835. GRAY, Cecil
"Canals of England." GreenfR (12:3/4) Wint-Spr 85, p. 160.
"Moorings." GreenfR (12:3/4) Wint-Spr 85, p. 162-163.
"Surveyor" (For Cecil Herbert). GreenfR (12:3/4) Wint-Spr
85, p. 161.
1836. GRAY, Cecile G.
"The Lovers at Exeter." NegC (5:1) Wint 85, p. 19.
1837. GRAY, Elizabeth
"Ghazals" (10, 24, 26, 42, tr. of Hafiz). Ploughs (11:4)
85, p. 252-255.
1838. GRAY, Janet
"The calla lilies appear to have grown back into the
ground." RagMag (4:1) Spr 85, p. 7.
"To Resume." RagMag (4:1) Spr 85, p. 6.
"Year after Year the Same Things Come Down from My Sky"
(after Dr. Seuss). Open24 (4) 85, p. 31.
1839. GRAY, Martin
"Elegy for the Death of My Father." PoetryCR (6:3) Spr
85, p. 35.
1840. GRAY, Patrick Worth
"After a Painting by Paul Kircher." PoetryCR (6:3) Spr
85, p. 33.
"January in Omaha." CapeR (20:2) Fall 85, p. 43.
1841. GRAY, R. W.
"Good Muggage: The Bean Curd Yodel of Three Pirates."
Open24 (4) 85, p. 55.
1842. GREALY, Lucinda
"Ferrying Horses." Ploughs (11:1) 85, p. 104-105.
"My Brother." Ploughs (11:1) 85, p. 110.
"Poem" ("For years I've been trying to remember my
father"). Ploughs (11:1) 85, p. 108-109.
"Something Else." Ploughs (11:1) 85, p. 111-112.
"Stories from the Train." Ploughs (11:1) 85, p. 106-107.
1843. GREAN, Patricia
"Our 34th Anniversary" (as told to Patricia Goedicke).
Raccoon (17) Mr 85, p. 7-8.
1844. GREEN, Bob
"We Took the Kids in the Afternoon to See Him." LittleBR
(5:1) Fall-Wint 84-85, p. 13.
1845. GREEN, Connie J.
"Ars Poetica: Lessons in Bread Baking." Confr (29) Wint
85, p. 110.
1846. GREEN, David H.
"This sagging shed propped." Amelia (2:1) Ap 85, p. 37.
1847. GREEN, George
"The Ivory-Billed Woodpecker." GrahamHR (8) Wint 85, p.
35.
"Leopold Grumjian's Beast & Bird Almanac" (Selections:
"January," "April," "May," "August"). OntR (22) Spr-
Sum 85, p. 65-73.
1848. GREEN, Jim
"Wan-Li's First Year in Yellowknife." PraF (6:2) Spr 85,
p. 46.
1849. GREEN, Lori Susan
"Debbie." Poem (53) Mr 85, p. 60.
"A Taste." Poem (53) Mr 85, p. 59.
1850. GREEN, Tony
"Two Poems." Verse (1) 84, p. 11.
1851. GREEN, William H.
"Can She Help If Her Pale Glance." Poem (53) Mr 85, p. 50.
"Dionysus." LitR (29:1) Fall 85, p. 65.

"Hermes." <u>LitR</u> (29:1) Fall 85, p. 65.
"Icarus." <u>ChiR</u> (34:4) 85, p. 64.
"Narcissus." <u>LaurelR</u> (19:2) Sum 85, p. 72.
1852. GREENBAUM, Jessica
    "The Fault." <u>Geor</u> (39:2) Sum 85, p. 272.
1853. GREENBERG, Alvin
    "The Art of the Possible." <u>CrossCur</u> (4:2) 84, p. 17-18.
    "The Night of the Moving Men" (Second Pablo Neruda Prize
       for Poetry). <u>Nimrod</u> (29:1) Fall-Wint 85, p. 76-85.
    "Physics Can Be Fun." <u>MichQR</u> (24:2) Spr 85, p. 271-272.
1854. GREENBERG, Max
    "If you do it your way." <u>LittleM</u> (14:4) 85, p. 40.
1855. GREENE, Jeffrey
    "The Birdwatcher." <u>Iowa</u> (15:1) Wint 85, p. 32.
    "The Coat." <u>MissouriR</u> (8:3) 85, p. 20-21.
    "Fishing over Birds." <u>BlackWR</u> (11:2) Spr 85, p. 64-65.
    "Louisiana." <u>NewYorker</u> (60:53) 18 F 85, p. 120.
    "Mornings in Texas." <u>Telescope</u> (4:1) Wint 85, p. 16-17.
1856. GREENLEY, Emily
    "Morning, You." <u>HarvardA</u> (119:1) N 85, p. 22.
    "October/November." <u>HarvardA</u> (119:2) D 85, p. 15.
    "Poems." <u>HarvardA</u> (119:2) D 85, p. 12-13.
1857. GREENWALD, Roger
    "Interlocutor." <u>PoetryE</u> (18) Fall 85, p. 30.
    "Joel in His Son's Room." <u>PoetryE</u> (18) Fall 85, p. 29.
    "A Thing You're Saying." <u>PoetryE</u> (18) Fall 85, p. 31.
1858. GREENWAY, William
    "Nails." <u>LaurelR</u> (19:2) Sum 85, p. 18-19.
    "New Testament." <u>CapeR</u> (20:2) Fall 85, p. 11.
    "Stress Test." <u>GreenfR</u> (12:3/4) Wint-Spr 85, p. 46.
    "The Unities on North Avenue." <u>LaurelR</u> (19:2) Sum 85, p.
      20.
1859. GREENWOOD, C. P.
    "This Poem." <u>PoetryCR</u> (7:2) Wint 85-86, p. 20.
1860. GREGER, Debora
    "And." <u>SouthwR</u> (70:1) Wint 85, p. 109-110.
    "In the Elephant Folio." <u>NewYorker</u> (61:37) 4 N 85, p. 48.
    "Long Island Real Estate: Great Neck." <u>NewRep</u> (192:6) 11
      F 85, p. 36.
    "Newton Wonders." <u>NewRep</u> (193:20) 11 N 85, p. 38.
    "The Temperate House." <u>SouthwR</u> (70:1) Wint 85, p. 107-108.
    "There, There." <u>SouthwR</u> (70:1) Wint 85, p. 108-109.
1861. GREGERSON, Linda
    "Malbecco." <u>Agni</u> (22) 85, p. 95.
1862. GREGG, Linda
    "Alma in the Dark." <u>Iowa</u> (15:2) Spr-Sum 85, p. 79.
    "Balancing Everything." <u>AmerPoR</u> (14:5) S-O 85, p. 31.
    "Forget All That." <u>VirQ</u> (61:3) Sum 85, p. 431-432.
    "Innocents." <u>AmerPoR</u> (14:5) S-O 85, p. 31.
    "Late Afternoon in California." <u>Iowa</u> (15:2) Spr-Sum 85,
      p. 80.
    "Love for a Month." <u>AmerPoR</u> (14:5) S-O 85, p. 31.
    "Me and Aphrodite and the Other." <u>VirQ</u> (61:3) Sum 85, p.
      430-431.
    "New York Address." <u>Iowa</u> (15:2) Spr-Sum 85, p. 79.
    "Not the Moon nor Pretend." <u>AmerPoR</u> (14:5) S-O 85, p. 31.
    "Pictures of Marriage." <u>Iowa</u> (15:2) Spr-Sum 85, p. 78.
    "Safe and Beautiful." <u>AmerPoR</u> (14:5) S-O 85, p. 31.
1863. GREGOR, Arthur
    "The Fleeting." <u>NewL</u> (51:3) Spr 85, p. 117.
    "In Dark's Cover." <u>Hudson</u> (38:3) Aut 85, p. 442-444.
    "Old Offense." <u>Nat</u> (240:11) 23 Mr 85, p. 340.
1864. GREGORY, Michael
    "Examination." <u>Crazy</u> (29) Fall 85, p. 54-55.
    "June: The Smell of Death." <u>NoDaQ</u> (53:4) Fall 85, p. 190.
    "The Valley Floor." <u>NoDaQ</u> (53:4) Fall 85, p. 191-201.

1865. GREGORY, Robert
        "The Tiny Hooks." Oink (19) 85, p. 108-109.
1866. GREIF, Shirley
        "For Jamie." StoneC (13:1/2) Fall-Wint 85-86, p. 60.
1867. GREIG, David
        "Absolution." Waves (14:1/2) Fall 85, p. 110.
1868. GRENNAN, Eamon
        "All Souls' Morning." NewYorker (61:38) 11 N 85, p. 48.
        "Incident." NewYorker (61:34) 14 O 85, p. 40.
        "Lesson." Verse (3) 85, p. 7-8.
        "Soul Music: The Derry Air." NewYorker (60:48) 14 Ja 85,
            p. 32.
GRESTY, David Price
        See PRICE-GRESTY, David
1869. GREY, Robert
        "Fort Bragg." Poem (53) Mr 85, p. 16-18.
1870. GRIFFIN, Sheila
        "Visits." NegC (5:4) Fall 85, p. 76-77.
1871. GRIFFIN, Walter
        "Fish Leaves." Poem (53) Mr 85, p. 61.
        "Fish Leaves." PoetryR (2:2) Ap 85, p. 46.
        "Heritage." SouthwR (70:4) Aut 85, p. 485.
        "In Italy, Sons Kiss Their Fathers." Poem (53) Mr 85, p.
            62.
        "In Italy, Sons Kiss Their Fathers." PoetryR (2:2) Ap 85,
            p. 47.
1872. GRIFFITHS, Steve
        "Continuity." Stand (26:4) Aut 85, p. 66.
1873. GRIGSBY, Gordon
        "Wand Goldenrod." WestB (16) 85, p. 46.
1874. GRILL, Neil
        "Let Us Not Mince Worlds." CrossCur (5:3) 85, p. 153-154.
        "May" (for Genese). Amelia (2:1) Ap 85, p. 74.
        "The Sign." CrossCur (5:3) 85, p. 156-157.
        "When the Poems Came Home." CrossCur (5:3) 85, p. 155.
1875. GRILLO, Janet
        "Ruins: Pescara, Italy." NewRena (19) Fall 85, p. 80-81.
1876. GRIMM, Reinhold
        "About Some Who Got Away" (tr. of Günter Kunert, w. Felix
            Pollak). NewL (51:4) Sum 85, p. 51.
        "Bathroom" (tr. of Hans Magnus Enzensberger, w. Felix
            Pollak). NewL (51:4) Sum 85, p. 67.
        "The Dark Room" (tr. of Hans Magnus Enzensberger, w. Felix
            Pollak). NewL (51:4) Sum 85, p. 65.
        "Dirge for the Apple" (tr. of Hans Magnus Enzensberger, w.
            Felix Pollak). NewL (51:4) Sum 85, p. 68.
        "The Divorce" (tr. of Hans Magnus Enzensberger, w. Felix
            Pollak). NewL (51:4) Sum 85, p. 66.
        "In Memory of William Carlos Williams" (tr. of Hans Magnus
            Enzensberger, w. Felix Pollak). LitR (28:4) Sum 85, p.
            585.
        "Misogyny" (tr. of Hans Magnus Enzensberger, w. Felix
            Pollak). LitR (28:4) Sum 85, p. 584.
        "Report about Him" (tr. of Günter Kunert, w. Felix
            Pollak). NewL (51:4) Sum 85, p. 52-53.
1877. GRISWOLD, Jay
        "Landscape with Train." BlackWR (11:2) Spr 85, p. 87.
1878. GROFF, David
        "Addison Groff Chooses the Ministry" (Boonesboro, Maryland,
            August 1937). PraS (59:3) Fall 85, p. 49-50.
        "Daisy Buchanan, 1983." Iowa (15:1) Wint 85, p. 71.
        "Envoi." Confr (30/31) N 85, p. 137.
        "Leaving the Farm." ChiR (34:4) 85, p. 91-92.
        "Steamed Crabs." PraS (59:3) Fall 85, p. 51.
GRONDIN, Dana Keller
        See KELLER-GRONDIN, Dana

1879. GROSHOLZ, Emily
        "Exile." Hudson (38:3) Aut 85, p. 391-397.
        "Nietzsche in the Box of Straws." Pequod (18) 85, p. 43-
            46.
        "Theories of Vision." Hudson (38:3) Aut 85, p. 398-400.
1880. GROSSMAN, Allen
        "The Branch." GrahamHR (8) Wint 85, p. 22-23.
        "The Gate." YaleR (74:3) Spr 85, p. 447.
        "The House of Water." GrahamHR (8) Wint 85, p. 20-21.
        "In Ruin's House." YaleR (74:3) Spr 85, p. 448-449.
        "The Stream and the Canoe." GrahamHR (8) Wint 85, p. 24.
1881. GROSSMAN, Andrew J.
        "Trap." Abraxas (33) 85, p. 24-25.
        "The White Marches." DeKalbLAJ (18:1/2) 85, p. 72.
1882. GROSSMAN, Edith
        "The Anti-Lazarus" (tr. of Nicanor Parra). RiverS (18)
            85, p. 40-41.
        "At the Rate We're Going" (tr. of Nicanor Parra). RiverS
            (18) 85, p. 37.
        "Homework" (tr. of Nicanor Parra). RiverS (18) 85, p. 38.
        "The Man He Imagined" (tr. of Nicanor Parra). RiverS (18)
            85, p. 43.
        "The Mistake We Made Was Thinking" (tr. of Nicanor Parra).
            RiverS (18) 85, p. 37.
        "The Poems of the Pope" (tr. of Nicanor Parra). RiverS
            (18) 85, p. 42.
        "Rest in Peace" (tr. of Nicanor Parra). RiverS (18) 85,
            p. 39.
1883. GROSSMAN, Florence
        "Frostbite." ChiR (35:2) Wint 85, p. 22.
        "Gale Meadows." Nat (240:11) 23 Mr 85, p. 342.
        "High Meadow." ChiR (35:2) Wint 85, p. 21.
        "Signals" (East Dorset, Vermont). Nat (241:9) 28 S 85, p.
            284.
1884. GROTH, Brian J.
        "Sergeant York." SanFPJ (7:4) 85, p. 54.
        "Steinbeck's Beans." SanFPJ (7:4) 85, p. 29.
        "You Lied." SanFPJ (7:4) 85, p. 53.
1885. GROVE, Bob
        "In the War." SecC (12:1) 84, p. 3.
        "Lost Head / El Salvador / Our Sister." SecC (12:1) 84,
            p. 4.
1886. GROVER-ROGOFF, Jay
        "Dun Aengus." Hudson (38:1) Spr 85, p. 83.
        "A European Boyhood." Nimrod (29:1) Fall-Wint 85, p. 41-
            45.
        "The Invention of English." Hudson (38:1) Spr 85, p. 82-
            83.
        "Redon Discovers Color." PartR (52:4) 85, p. 432-433.
        "Vanishing Point." Hudson (38:1) Spr 85, p. 84.
1887. GRUBE, John
        "1622." Rampike (4:2/3) 85-86, p. 79.
1888. GRUENER, Jordan
        "Two Old." Open24 (4) 85, p. 60.
1889. GUDZEVIC, Sinan
        "Miraculous Tree" (tr. by Nina Zivancević). AmerPoR
            (14:3) My-Je 85, p. 28.
        "When God Understands" (tr. by Nina Zivancević).
            AmerPoR (14:3) My-Je 85, p. 28.
        "Whorehouse" (tr. by Nina Zivancević). AmerPoR (14:3)
            My-Je 85, p. 28.
1890. GUEDRON, Pierre
        "Cesses Mortels de Soupirer." NegC (5:1) Wint 85, p. 77.
        "You Mortals, Breathe Your Sighs No More" (tr. by W. D.
            Snodgrass and Leigh Banks). NegC (5:1) Wint 85, p. 78.

1891. GUENTHER, Charles
        "Course of Clay" (tr. of René Char). NewL (51:4) Sum
          85, p. 149.
        "Let's Dance at the Barronies" (tr. of René Char). NewL
          (51:4) Sum 85, p. 149.
        "On the Death of Marie" (From the Second Book of Loves,
          tr. of Pierre de Ronsard). WebR (10:1) Spr 85, p. 34.
        "Signs" (tr. of Pedro Salinas). CharR (11:1) Spr 85, p.
          93-94.
        "Sonnet XCVI" (From the First Book of Loves, tr. of
          Pierre de Ronsard). WebR (10:1) Spr 85, p. 33.
        "To Bloom in Winter" (From La Nuit Talismanique 1972, tr.
          of René Char). WebR (10:2) Fall 85, p. 39.
1892. GUEREÑA, Jacinto-Luis
        "Taller de Ritmos." Os (20) 85, p. 24-25.
      GUERNELLI, Adelaida Lugo
        See LUGO GUERNELLI, Adelaida
1893. GUESS, Jeff
        "Lighting the Incinerator." PoetryCR (7:2) Wint 85-86, p.
          42.
1894. GUEST, Barbara
        "The Wild Gardens Overlooked by Night Lights." Conjunc
          (8) 85, p. 146-147.
1895. GUEVARA, Ivan
        "U.S. Logging Company" (tr. by Kent Johnson). MinnR (N.S.
          25) Fall 85, p. 41.
1896. GUIDACCI, Margherita
        "Anniversary with Agaves" (tr. by Ruth Feldman). Ploughs
          (11:4) 85, p. 55.
        "Appointment to Look at the Moon" (from Hymn to Joy 1983,
          tr. by Ruth Feldman). WebR (10:1) Spr 85, p. 11.
        "A Different Latitude" (from Hymn to Joy 1983, tr. by
          Ruth Feldman). WebR (10:1) Spr 85, p. 10.
        "Libyan Sibyl" (br. by Ruth Feldman). Mund (15:1/2) 85,
          p. 167.
        "Sibilla Libica." Mund (15:1/2) 85, p. 166.
        "Sunflower" (from Hymn to Joy 1983, tr. by Ruth Feldman).
          WebR (10:1) Spr 85, p. 11.
1897. GUILFORD, Linda
        "Birds." StoneC (12:2/3) Spr-Sum 85, p. 11.
1898. GUILLEN, Jorge
        "Advenimiento." SinN (14:4) Jl-S 84, p. 14.
        "Afirmacion." SinN (14:4) Jl-S 84, p. 16.
        "Autor y Lector." SinN (14:4) Jl-S 84, p. 23.
        "Clamante." SinN (14:4) Jl-S 84, p. 21.
        "Clamor Estrellado." SinN (14:4) Jl-S 84, p. 22.
        "Desnudo." SinN (14:4) Jl-S 84, p. 15.
        "Equilibrio." Imagine (1:2) Wint 84, p. 223.
        "Estatua Ecuestre." SinN (14:4) Jl-S 84, p. 15-16.
        "Horas Marinas." SinN (14:4) Jl-S 84, p. 27-29.
        "Hormiga Sola." SinN (14:4) Jl-S 84, p. 19.
        "In Balance" (Adaption by David Ferry). Imagine (1:2)
          Wint 84, p. 224-225.
        "Inditos" (Oaxaca). SinN (14:4) Jl-S 84, p. 18.
        "Los Intranquilos." SinN (14:4) Jl-S 84, p. 17-18.
        "Los Jardines." SinN (14:4) Jl-S 84, p. 16.
        "Juan Ruiz." SinN (14:4) Jl-S 84, p. 23-25.
        "Una Margarita." SinN (14:4) Jl-S 84, p. 29-30.
        "Margen Vario: La Inmensidad, el Mar." SinN (14:4) Jl-S
          84, p. 22-23.
        "Meseta." SinN (14:4) Jl-S 84, p. 17.
        "Muerte de unos Zapatos." SinN (14:4) Jl-S 84, p. 18-19.
        "Los Nombres." SinN (14:4) Jl-S 84, p. 13.
        "Oido y Visto" (A Ignacio Prat, 1972). SinN (14:4) Jl-S
          84, p. 27.
        "Perfeccion." SinN (14:4) Jl-S 84, p. 16.

"Privilegiada Situacion." SinN (14:4) Jl-S 84, p. 26.
"La puerta da, bien cerrada." SinN (14:4) Jl-S 84, p. 25-26.
"Raices." SinN (14:4) Jl-S 84, p. 30.
"Sabor a Vida." SinN (14:4) Jl-S 84, p. 14-15.
"Supere a nuestro mundo en caos." SinN (14:4) Jl-S 84, p. 26-27.
"Treboles." SinN (14:4) Jl-S 84, p. 20-21.
"Vuelo." SinN (14:4) Jl-S 84, p. 19-20.
1899. GUILLEN, Nicolás
"Ana Maria" (tr. by John DuVal and Gastón Fernández-Torriente). NewEngR (7:4) Sum 85, p. 541.
"The Grand Zoo" (Selections: "Winds," "The Great Bear," "Aconcagua," "KKK," "Rivers", tr. by John DuVal and Gastón Fernández-Torriente). NewEngR (7:4) Sum 85, p. 542-544.
"Sensemayah" (Snake-killing song, tr. by John DuVal and Gastón Fernández-Torriente). NewEngR (7:4) Sum 85, p. 540-541.
"Un Son para Niños Antillanos." NewEngR (7:4) Sum 85, p. ix.
1900. GUILLEN, Rafael
"The Final Tenderness" (tr. by Sandy McKinney). Tendril (19/20) 85, p. 159-160.
"A Friend Comes Back" (tr. by Sandy McKinney). SenR (15:2) 85, p. 168-170.
"The Last Gesture" (tr. by Sandy McKinney). Pequod (18) 85, p. 109.
"Not Fear" (tr. by Sandy McKinney). Pequod (18) 85, p. 110-111.
"One Day with the Dawn" (tr. by Sandy McKinney). Tendril (19/20) 85, p. 157-158.
"Opening a Path for the Flash" (tr. by Sandy McKinney). SenR (15:2) 85, p. 164-165.
"Poem of No" (tr. by Sandy McKinney). Tendril (19/20) 85, p. 161.
"Road Show" (tr. by Sandy McKinney). SenR (15:2) 85, p. 166-167.
"To Be an Instant" (tr. by Sandy McKinney). SenR (15:2) 85, p. 162-163.
"Today Paris Doesn't Exist" (tr. by Sandy McKinney). SenR (15:2) 85, p. 171-173.
1901. GUILLEN LANDRIAN, Nicolas
"Cuanto Nos Cuesta." LindLM (4:4) O-D 85, p. 32.
"Del Loco y la Lagartija." LindLM (4:4) O-D 85, p. 32.
"Divago." LindLM (4:4) O-D 85, p. 32.
1902. GUILLEVIC (See also GUILLEVIC, Eugene)
"We Do Not Know" (tr. by David Kinloch). Verse (2) 85, p. 37.
1903. GUILLEVIC, Eugene (See also GUILLEVIC)
"Eight Fabliettes" (tr. by Norman Shapiro). Ploughs (11:4) 85, p. 109-111.
1904. GULLANS, Charles
"The Most Famous Waterfall in North America." Hudson (38:3) Aut 85, p. 448.
"Winter in Minnesota." Hudson (38:3) Aut 85, p. 447.
1905. GULLING, Dennis
"This Is What the Nights Become." Bogg (53) 85, p. 11.
1906. GUNDY, Jeff
"On Woody Crumbo's Deer and the Elements." NoDaQ (53:4) Fall 85, p. 202.
"Riding Bike at Night." WoosterR (3) Spr 85, p. 19.
1907. GUNERSEL, Tarik
"Concerto" (tr. by Talat Sait Halman). GreenfR (13:1/2) Fall-Wint 85, p. 91.

1908. GUNN, Genni
      "Developing." <u>PoetryCR</u> (7:2) Wint 85-86, p. 40.
      "In the End." <u>AntigR</u> (61) Spr 85, p. 10.
      "Often I Cup My Hands." <u>PoetryCR</u> (7:2) Wint 85-86, p. 40.
      "The Second Decision." <u>AntigR</u> (61) Spr 85, p. 9.
      "Sibling Collage." <u>PoetryCR</u> (7:2) Wint 85-86, p. 40.
1909. GUNN, Thom
      "From the Wave." <u>TriQ</u> (63) Spr-Sum 85, p. 98-99.
      "The Honesty." <u>Sulfur</u> (13) 85, p. 46.
      "The Hug." <u>YaleR</u> (74:4) Sum 85, p. 568-569.
      "In Time of Plague." <u>Sulfur</u> (13) 85, p. 47.
      "An Invitation" (from San Francisco to my brother).
          <u>Thrpny</u> (5:4, issue 20) Wint 85, p. 4.
      "J.V.C." <u>ChiR</u> (35:1) Aut 85, p. 21.
      "The Seabed" (for children). <u>Thrpny</u> (6:1, issue 21) Spr
          85, p. 4.
      "Tenderloin." <u>Sulfur</u> (13) 85, p. 44-45.
      "To a Friend in Time of Trouble." <u>YaleR</u> (74:4) Sum 85, p.
          567-568.
1910. GUNNARS, Kristjana
      "Because this is the workshop of the Universe." <u>PoetryCR</u>
          (6:3) Spr 85, p. 13.
      "Dead Splendor." <u>PoetryCR</u> (6:3) Spr 85, p. 13.
      "From a Distance." <u>PoetryCR</u> (6:3) Spr 85, p. 13.
      "I know how hard it is for you after 1300 years."
          <u>PoetryCR</u> (6:3) Spr 85, p. 13.
      "A Long Production." <u>PoetryCR</u> (6:3) Spr 85, p. 13.
      "Revealing Horse." <u>PoetryCR</u> (6:3) Spr 85, p. 13.
      "William Blake Receding." <u>PoetryCR</u> (6:3) Spr 85, p. 13.
1911. GUNSTROM, Nickie
      "Amulet against Oncoming Traffic." <u>CapeR</u> (20:1) Spr 85,
          p. 25.
1912. GURLEY, James
      "Stories for the Fire." <u>Paint</u> (11:21/12:24) 84-85, p. 22.
1913. GUSTAFSON, Ralph
      "At Urbino." <u>WestCR</u> (19:4) Ap 85, p. 12.
      "On the Island of Torcello." <u>WestCR</u> (19:4) Ap 85, p. 11.
      "One Cannot Overcome the Nature of Happiness." <u>WestCR</u>
          (19:4) Ap 85, p. 10.
      "A Visible Collection of Particles of Water." <u>PoetryCR</u>
          (6:3) Spr 85, p. 12.
1914. GUSTAVSON, Jeffrey
      "Easter Sunday" (Letter to Clyde Rykken). <u>Ploughs</u> (11:1)
          85, p. 114.
      "Minnesota." <u>Ploughs</u> (11:1) 85, p. 115. Errata in
          <u>Ploughs</u> (11:4) 85, p. 268.
      "Palm Sunday" (Letter to Gary in St. Paul). <u>Ploughs</u>
          (11:1) 85, p. 113.
      "Requiem Notes." <u>Ploughs</u> (11:1) 85, p. 116-117. Errata in
          <u>Ploughs</u> (11:4) 85, p. 268.
1915. GUTHRIE, Arlo
      "Prologue." <u>ClockR</u> (2:2) 85, p. 40.
1916. GUYOTAT, Pierre
      "Eden, Eden, Eden" (Excerpt, tr. by Graham Fox). <u>Temblor</u>
          (1) 85, p. 122-123.
1917. GUZMAN VEA, Judith
      "El Amor y el Deseo." <u>Imagine</u> (2:1) Sum 85, p. 45.
1918. GWILYM, Dafydd ap
      "A Recantation" (tr. by Leslie Norris). <u>QW</u> (21) Fall-Wint
          85, p. 103.
      "Trouble at a Tavern" (tr. by Leslie Norris). <u>QW</u> (21)
          Fall-Wint 85, p. 100-102.
1919. GWYNN, R. S.
      "Also to the Tower." <u>TexasR</u> (6:3/4) Fall-Wint 85, p. 90-
          92.

1920. HABOVA, Dana
        "In the Yard of the Policlinic" (tr. of Vladimir Holan, w.
          C. G. Hanzlicek). AmerPoR (14:4) Jl-Ag 85, p. 36.
        "Snow" (tr. of Vladimir Holan, w. C. G. Hanzlicek).
          AmerPoR (14:4) Jl-Ag 85, p. 36.
1921. HACKER, Marilyn
        "The Borgo Pinti Sonnets." Pequod (19/20/21) 85, p. 171-
          173.
        "Double Dactylics." OP (38/39) Spr 85, p. 190.
        "Joint Custody." Pequod (18) 85, p. 69.
        "June Sonnets." CreamCR (10:2) [85?], p. 46.
        "Lines for a Composer Who Will Play It for Me If I Hum a
          Few Bars, or in a Few" (for Elinor Armer). OP (38/39)
          Spr 85, p. 180-181.
        "L'Invitation au Voyage." OP (40) Fall-Wint 85, p. 24-25.
        "The Little Robber Girl Considers Some Options." Calyx
          (9:1) Spr-Sum 85, p. 53.
        "The Little Robber Girl Considers the Wide World."
          Chelsea (44) 85, p. 40-41.
        "The Little Robber Girl Gets on in the Wide World" (for
          Julie Fay). ParisR (27:95) Spr 85, p. 69-72.
        "Nights of 1964-66: The Old Reliable." GrandS (4:2) Wint
          85, p. 147-149.
        "Open Windows XVI." MassR (26:1) Spr 85, p. 57.
        "Open Windows XVII." MassR (26:1) Spr 85, p. 57.
        "The Robber Woman." Chelsea (44) 85, p. 38-39.
        "Rune of the Finland Woman" (for Sára Karig). Pequod
          (18) 85, p. 67-68.
1922. HADAS, Pamela White
        "Dear Lydia E. Pinkham" (for Robert Pack). TriQ (63) Spr-
          Sum 85, p. 458-466.
        "Walking Sophie in Your Absence" (for Naomi in Copenhagen).
          OP (38/39) Spr 85, p. 132-133.
1923. HADAS, Rachel
        "After the Stroke." PartR (52:3) 85, p. 242-244.
        "Alien Corn, II." DevQ (19:3) Wint 85, p. 11-12.
        "All That Blab." CrossCur (5:3) 85, p. 115-116.
        "Arranged in Summer Thus." DevQ (19:3) Wint 85, p. 13-14.
        "Between Worlds." Pequod (19/20/21) 85, p. 174-176.
        "Cupfuls of Summer." DenQ (20:2) Fall 85, p. 79-83.
        "Pass It On." CrossCur (5:3) 85, p. 112.
        "Teacher, Taught, Eater, Eaten." CrossCur (5:3) 85, p.
          113-114.
        "The Third Sex." DevQ (19:3) Wint 85, p. 15-16.
1924. HADEN, Jessica
        "Early Fall." Quarry (34:1) Wint 85, p. 64.
1925. HAECK, Philippe
        "L'Etudiante Rouge." Rampike (4:2/3) 85-86, p. 65.
1926. HAERLIN, A.
        "See, I Am Perfectly Disguised As Myself." CapeR (20:1)
          Spr 85, p. 24.
1927. HAFIZ
        "Ghazals" (10, 24, 26, 42, tr. by Elizabeth Gray).
          Ploughs (11:4) 85, p. 252-255.
1928. HAGEN, Cecelia
        "Snake Oil." PraS (59:4) Wint 85, p. 80.
        "Swimming." PraS (59:4) Wint 85, p. 78.
        "What I Don't Say to Darcy." PraS (59:4) Wint 85, p. 79.
1929. HAGINS, Jerry
        "Lubbock, 1961." YellowS (14) Spr 85, p. 30.
        "Reverie." YellowS (14) Spr 85, p. 30.
1930. HAHN, Kimiko
        "Coalfields (Text 2), 30 Seconds on Fred Carter." Cond
          (11/12) 85, p. 83.
        "Her First Language." Cond (11/12) 85, p. 84.

1931. HAHN, Oscar
    "Adolfo Hitler Medita en el Problema Judío." *Inti*
        (18/19) Otoño 83-Prim. 84, p. 206.
    "Agua Geométrica." *Inti* (18/19) Otoño 83-Prim. 84, p.
        205.
    "And Now What?" (tr. by Ina Cumpriano). *Mund* (15:1/2) 85,
        p. 105.
    "Birth of the Ghost" (tr. by Ina Cumpriano). *Mund*
        (15:1/2) 85, p. 111.
    "Cafiche de la Muerte." *Inti* (18/19) Otoño 83-Prim. 84,
        p. 202-203.
    "Comet" (tr. by James Hoggard). *NewL* (51:4) Sum 85, p.
        109.
    "De Tal Manera Mi Razón Enflaquece." *Inti* (18/19)
        Otoño 83-Prim. 84, p. 206.
    "Death Sits at the Foot of My Bed" (tr. by Ina Cumpriano).
        Mund (15:1/2) 85, p. 109.
    "Ecología del Espíritu." *Inti* (18/19) Otoño 83-
        Prim. 84, p. 208.
    "En la Vía Pública." *Inti* (18/19) Otoño 83-Prim.
        84, p. 208-209.
    "The Flaming Corpse" (tr. by James Hoggard). *NewL* (51:4)
        Sum 85, p. 109-110.
    "Fotografía." *Mund* (15:1/2) 85, p. 104.
    "Fragmentos de Heráclito al Estrellarse contra el Cielo."
        Inti (18/19) Otoño 83-Prim. 84, p. 203-205.
    "Gladiolos Junto al Mar." *Inti* (18/19) Otoño 83-Prim.
        84, p. 201.
    "Invocación al Lenguaje." *Inti* (18/19) Otoño 83-Prim.
        84, p. 203.
    "La Muerte Esta Sentada a los Pies de Mi Cama." *Mund*
        (15:1/2) 85, p. 108.
    "La Muerte Está Sentada a los Pies de Mi Cama." *Inti*
        (18/19) Otoño 83-Prim. 84, p. 200.
    "Nacimiento del Fantasma." *Mund* (15:1/2) 85, p. 110.
    "Ningu'n Lugar Está Aquí o Está Ahí." *Inti*
        (18/19) Otoño 83-Prim. 84, p. 207-208.
    "Photograph" (tr. by Ina Cumpriano). *Mund* (15:1/2) 85, p.
        105.
    "Reencarnación de los Carniceros." *Inti* (18/19) Otoño
        83-Prim. 84, p. 199--200.
    "Restriccion de los Desplazamientos Nocturnos." *Mund*
        (15:1/2) 85, p. 106, 107.
    "Restrictions against Night Travel" (tr. by Ina Cumpriano).
        Mund (15:1/2) 85, p. 107, 109.
    "Sabana de Arriba." *Mund* (15:1/2) 85, p. 106.
    "Top Sheet" (tr. by Ina Cumpriano). *Mund* (15:1/2) 85, p.
        107.
    "Tractatus de Sortilegiis." *Inti* (18/19) Otoño 83-Prim.
        84, p. 206-207.
    "Visión de Hiroshima." *Inti* (18/19) Otoño 83-Prim.
        84, p. 201-202.
    "Y Ahora Que?" *Mund* (15:1/2) 85, p. 104.
1932. HAHN, Steve
    "North of My Blood's Hometown" (Edenkoben, Germany). *PraS*
        (59:1) Spr 85, p. 15.
    "Oak Flowers: Nemaha County, Nebraska." *PraS* (59:1) Spr
        85, p. 16.
    "Wasps." *SouthernHR* (19:1) Wint 85, p. 23.
1933. HAHN, Susan
    "The Death of a Small Animal." *PraS* (59:1) Spr 85, p. 37.
1934. HAIDER, Daud
    "A Red Blossom" (tr. by Lila Ray). *NewL* (51:4) Sum 85, p.
        132-133.
    "You Threw a Stone" (tr. by Lila Ray). *NewL* (51:4) Sum
        85, p. 132.

1935. HAIL, Raven
        "The Hawk and the Raven." <u>LittleBR</u> (5:1) Fall-Wint 84-85,
            p. 25-26.
1936. HAINING, James
        "Back." <u>SpoonRQ</u> (10:4) Fall 85, p. 28.
        "Blue." <u>SpoonRQ</u> (10:4) Fall 85, p. 27.
        "Brothers." <u>SpoonRQ</u> (10:4) Fall 85, p. 31.
        "Cases" ("Dadoed with Don"). <u>SpoonRQ</u> (10:4) Fall 85, p.
            30.
        "His love." <u>SpoonRQ</u> (10:4) Fall 85, p. 27.
        "His pockets." <u>SpoonRQ</u> (10:4) Fall 85, p. 32.
        "Letter from Whitney." <u>SpoonRQ</u> (10:4) Fall 85, p. 32.
        "Martin Avenue." <u>SpoonRQ</u> (10:4) Fall 85, p. 29.
        "My son dances." <u>SpoonRQ</u> (10:4) Fall 85, p. 29.
        "No Sugar Tramps." <u>SpoonRQ</u> (10:4) Fall 85, p. 31.
        "A screen not stopping." <u>SpoonRQ</u> (10:4) Fall 85, p. 28.
        "Turning Dirt." <u>SpoonRQ</u> (10:4) Fall 85, p. 30.
1937. HAIR, Jennie
        "At Last." <u>CrabCR</u> (2:2) Wint 85, p. 6.
1938. HAISLIP, John
        "Interlude." <u>NowestR</u> (23:3) 85, p. 12.
        "Late Afternoon, Seal Rock: 1/25/84." <u>NowestR</u> (23:3) 85,
            p. 14.
        "The Wind Dolls." <u>NowestR</u> (23:3) 85, p. 13.
1939. HALDERMAN, M. Corder
        "Never Sold Real Estate." <u>JamesWR</u> (2:1) Fall 84, p. 11.
1940. HALL, Chris
        "Canadian Ice." <u>HiramPoR</u> (38) Spr-Sum 85, p. 14.
        "Canon in D" (for Ron Huza). <u>HiramPoR</u> (38) Spr-Sum 85, p.
            17-18.
        "Tribuni Plebis." <u>HiramPoR</u> (38) Spr-Sum 85, p. 15-16.
1941. HALL, Daniel
        "Love-Letter-Burning." <u>YaleR</u> (74:4) Sum 85, p. 520.
        "Tidal." <u>YaleR</u> (74:4) Sum 85, p. 520.
1942. HALL, David
        "For a Son Dead in the War." <u>NegC</u> (5:3) Sum 85, p. 92.
1943. HALL, Donald
        "The Baseball Players." <u>Verse</u> (1) 84, p. 8.
        "Couplet" (Old Timer's Day, Fenway Park, 1 May 1982).
            <u>NewL</u> (51:3) Spr 85, p. 60.
        "The Granite State: Contradiction and Resolution." <u>Verse</u>
            (1) 84, p. 7.
        "New Animals." <u>VirQ</u> (61:4) Aut 85, p. 636-637.
        "A Novel in Two Volumes." <u>Verse</u> (2) 85, p. 5.
1944. HALL, James B. (<u>See also</u> HALL, James Baker & HALL, Jim)
        "Rod McKuen Answers His Critics." <u>PoetL</u> (80:2) Sum 85, p.
            103.
1945. HALL, James Baker (<u>See also</u> HALL, James B. & HALL, Jim)
        "Downtown Local." <u>CharR</u> (11:1) Spr 85, p. 86-87.
        "Establishing Longitude." <u>Poetry</u> (146:1) Ap 85, p. 35.
        "Final." <u>Poetry</u> (146:2) My 85, p. 100.
        "Identifying the Body." <u>Poetry</u> (146:2) My 85, p. 99.
        "On the Day of Balanchine's Death." <u>Poetry</u> (146:2) My 85,
            p. 98.
        "Organdy Curtain, Window, South Bank of the Ohio." <u>Poetry</u>
            (146:1) Ap 85, p. 35-36.
        "The Realization." <u>CharR</u> (11:1) Spr 85, p. 85-86.
        "The Scavengers." <u>NewOR</u> (12:3) Fall 85, p. 20.
        "Welcoming the Season's First Insects." <u>Poetry</u> (146:1) Ap
            85, p. 37.
1946. HALL, Jim (<u>See also</u> HALL, James B. & HALL, James Baker)
        "The Boy." <u>CharR</u> (11:2) Fall 85, p. 82.
        "Here's One." <u>CharR</u> (11:2) Fall 85, p. 80-81.
        "Preposterous." <u>Geor</u> (39:2) Sum 85, p. 377.
        "The Purpose of Hair." <u>CutB</u> (24) Spr-Sum 85, back cover.
        "The Reel World." <u>Geor</u> (39:2) Sum 85, p. 378.

1947. HALL, Judith
"Movements, Giselle and Isadora." CalQ (26) Sum 85, p. 44-45.
1948. HALL, Kathryn
"The Accident." PoetC (16:3) Spr 85, p. 47.
"Accusations." PoetC (16:3) Spr 85, p. 53-55.
"Andante." PoetC (16:3) Spr 85, p. 48.
"Candlemas Day." PoetC (16:3) Spr 85, p. 45.
"The Carnival Unpacks." PoetC (16:3) Spr 85, p. 51-52.
"Double Cropping." PoetC (16:3) Spr 85, p. 44.
"Eclipse." PoetC (16:3) Spr 85, p. 50.
"Here and Then." PoetC (16:3) Spr 85, p. 41-43.
"Note in a Bottle." PoetC (16:3) Spr 85, p. 49.
"On Lighthouse Road." PoetC (16:3) Spr 85, p. 46.
1949. HALLERMAN, Victoria
"Walking through Rodin." IndR (8:1) Wint 85, p. 82.
1950. HALLEY, Anne
"Leda as Lena." NewRep (192:25) 24 Je 85, p. 36.
1951. HALMAN, Talat Sait
"Ban" (tr. of Ince Ozdemir). GreenfR (13:1/2) Fall-Wint
85, p. 94.
"Bit by Bit" (tr. of Ince Ozdemir). GreenfR (13:1/2) Fall-
Wint 85, p. 95.
"Body Language" (tr. of Ince Ozdemir). GreenfR (13:1/2)
Fall-Wint 85, p. 94.
"Classroom Notes" (Selections, tr. of Ferit Edgü).
GreenfR (13:1/2) Fall-Wint 85, p. 86-90.
"Concerto" (tr. of Tarik Günersel). GreenfR (13:1/2)
Fall-Wint 85, p. 91.
"The Dagger" (tr. of Ulkü Tamer). GreenfR (13:1/2) Fall-
Wint 85, p. 97.
"A Different Silence" (tr. of Ince Ozdemir). GreenfR
(13:1/2) Fall-Wint 85, p. 93.
"High Noon" (tr. of Cemal Süreya). GreenfR (13:1/2)
Fall-Wint 85, p. 96.
"History of the Vanquished" (tr. of Ulkü Tamer).
GreenfR (13:1/2) Fall-Wint 85, p. 98.
"In Praise of My Father" (tr. of Ince Ozdemir). GreenfR
(13:1/2) Fall-Wint 85, p. 92.
"Lot's Woman" (tr. of Enis Batur). GreenfR (13:1/2) Fall-
Wint 85, p. 84-85.
"Poet's Nonalignment" (tr. of Ince Ozdemir). GreenfR
(13:1/2) Fall-Wint 85, p. 93.
"The Sparrow" (tr. of Ulkü Tamer). GreenfR (13:1/2)
Fall-Wint 85, p. 99-102.
1952. HALPERIN, Joan
"Emergency." LaurelR (19:2) Sum 85, p. 40.
1953. HALPERN, Daniel
"After Wright at Ohrid." MissouriR (8:2) 85, p. 158-159.
"Dead Fish." RiverS (17) 85, p. 55.
"Ezra Pound." SouthernR (21:1) Wint 85, p. 122-123.
"Incident in Winter." Iowa (15:1) Wint 85, p. 77.
"Nightwork." SouthernR (21:1) Wint 85, p. 123-129.
"North Africa: Preparations for an Evening." NewYorker
(61:3) 11 Mr 85, p. 46.
"Señor Excellent." CrossCur (4:3) 84, p. 16-17.
"Summer Nights." NewRep (193:2) 8 Jl 85, p. 36.
"Walking in the Fifteenth Century." Thrpny (6:2, issue
22) Sum 85, p. 13.
1954. HALPERN, Sal
"Appraisal." WoosterR (3) Spr 85, p. 47.
1955. HALSEY, Alan
"An Epitaph." Conjunc (8) 85, p. 200.
1956. HAMBURGER, Michael
"Elder." SouthernHR (19:4) Fall 85, p. 309.
"Elder." Stand (26:1) Wint 84-85, p. 25.

171   HAMMER

"Everything's Different" (tr. of Paul Celan). <u>Stand</u>
    (26:3) Sum 85, p. 48.
"Matière de Bretagne" (tr. of Paul Celan). <u>Verse</u> (2)
    85, p. 40.
"Oak." <u>Stand</u> (26:1) Wint 84-85, p. 24.
"Uprising of Smoke Banners" (tr. of Paul Celan). <u>Stand</u>
    (26:3) Sum 85, p. 47.
"Windmills" (tr. of Paul Celan). <u>Stand</u> (26:3) Sum 85, p.
    49.
1957. HAMILL, Sam
"Every Understanding" (tr. of Jaan Kaplinski). <u>ParisR</u>
    (27:96) Sum 85, p. 101.
"Going to the Palace with a Friend at Dawn" (tr. of Tu Fu).
    <u>PoetryE</u> (18) Fall 85, p. 68.
"Historical Romance." <u>Pequod</u> (19/20/21) 85, p. 177-183.
"Looking at Mount T'ai" (tr. of Tu Fu). <u>PoetryE</u> (18) Fall
    85, p. 67.
"A Lover's Quarrel" (after Roethke). <u>PoetryE</u> (18) Fall
    85, p. 5-8.
"Non-being Pervades Everything" (tr. of Jaan Kaplinski).
    <u>ParisR</u> (27:96) Sum 85, p. 100.
"Our Shadows" (tr. of Jaan Kaplinski). <u>ParisR</u> (27:96) Sum
    85, p. 99.
"Passing Mr. Sung's Old House" (tr. of Tu Fu). <u>PoetryE</u>
    (18) Fall 85, p. 70.
"Random Pleasures, III" (tr. of Tu Fu). <u>PoetryE</u> (18) Fall
    85, p. 66.
"Random Pleasures, IV" (tr. of Tu Fu). <u>PoetryE</u> (18) Fall
    85, p. 69.
"Visiting the Monastery at Lung-men" (tr. of Tu Fu).
    <u>PoetryE</u> (18) Fall 85, p. 65.
1958. HAMILTON, Alfred Starr
"Allegiance." <u>WormR</u> (25:3, issue 99) 85, p. 105.
"Crooked Legs." <u>NewL</u> (51:3) Spr 85, p. 116.
"Ghosts." <u>WormR</u> (25:3, issue 99) 85, p. 105.
"Sky and Purposes." <u>WormR</u> (25:3, issue 99) 85, p. 106.
1959. HAMILTON, Bruce
"On an Ongoing Strangeness." <u>NegC</u> (5:3) Sum 85, p. 118.
1960. HAMILTON, Carol (<u>See also</u> HAMILTON, Carol S.)
"A Day of Lonely Dreamers." <u>Poem</u> (53) Mr 85, p. 21.
"End of the Season." <u>CapeR</u> (20:1) Spr 85, p. 50.
"Mapped." <u>StoneC</u> (13:1/2) Fall-Wint 85-86, p. 11.
1961. HAMILTON, Carol S. (<u>See also</u> HAMILTON, Carol)
"The Traveller" (in memory of my grandmother). <u>CumbPR</u>
    (5:1) Fall 85, p. 62-63.
"Verfall Einer Familie." <u>CumbPR</u> (5:1) Fall 85, p. 60-61.
1962. HAMILTON, Fritz
"Begetting a Birdman!" <u>GreenfR</u> (13:1/2) Fall-Wint 85, p.
    162-163.
"A Conciliatory Poem!" <u>SmPd</u> (22:3) Fall 85, p. 18.
"Happy No Housing." <u>SmPd</u> (22:2) Spr 85, p. 32.
"Mirror-Polisher!" <u>YellowS</u> (17) Wint 85, p. 34.
"Nature's Peculiar Mercy!" <u>KanQ</u> (17:4) Fall 85, p. 130.
"The Nigger of the Narcissus in San Francisco." <u>SmPd</u>
    (22:3) Fall 85, p. 19.
"A-Okay Guard" (for Phoebe). <u>SmPd</u> (22:3) Fall 85, p. 22.
"Who Started the Flood." <u>SmPd</u> (22:1) Wint 85, p. 27.
1963. HAMILTON, Judith
"Cathedral." <u>GreenfR</u> (12:3/4) Wint-Spr 85, p. 165.
"A Different Drummer." <u>GreenfR</u> (12:3/4) Wint-Spr 85, p.
    165-166.
1964. HAMILTON, Robin
"Family Influences." <u>Verse</u> (4) 85, p. 19.
1965. HAMMER, Patrick, Jr.
"Dead Air." <u>StoneC</u> (13:1/2) Fall-Wint 85-86, p. 30.

1966. HAMMOND, Mary Stewart
        "Hubris at White, Ga." (Winner, NER/BLQ Narrative Poetry
           Competition). NewEngR (8:1) Aut 85, p. 32-38.
1967. HAMMOND, Ralph
        "Homage to William Stafford." NegC (5:4) Fall 85, p. 47-
           48.
        "To Those Never Born Out of War." Amelia (2:2) O 85, p.
           62.
        "Whatever Happened to the Choicest of Virgins?" NegC
           (5:3) Sum 85, p. 145.
1968. HAMPL, Patricia
        "The Moment." NewYorker (61:43) 16 D 85, p. 133.
        "Summer Sublet." NewYorker (61:26) 19 Ag 85, p. 28.
1969. HANCOCK, Craig
        "The Owl." Blueline (6:2) Wint-Spr 85, p. 23.
1970. HAND, Jack
        "Driving Down a Missouri Two-Lane Blacktop, I Contemplate
           War, Sheep, and Death." RiverS (18) 85, p. 85.
        "Love of Our Times." RiverS (18) 85, p. 84.
        "This Poem Got a Gun in It." OP (38/39) Spr 85, p. 115.
1971. HANDY, Nixeon Civille
        "The Dowser." TexasR (6:1/2) Spr-Sum 85, p. 25.
        "River As Metaphor." StoneC (13:1/2) Fall-Wint 85-86, p.
           12.
        "Round and Round." Wind (15:54) 85, p. 23.
1972. HANFORD, Mary
        "John." BlueBldgs (9) [85?], p. 37.
1973. HANKLA, Susan
        "The Gourmet Laundress." OP (40) Fall-Wint 85, p. 40.
        "House with No Overhead." OP (40) Fall-Wint 85, p. 42-43.
        "Pedestrian." OP (40) Fall-Wint 85, p. 41.
        "Vacation." OP (40) Fall-Wint 85, p. 39.
        "Yellow Storybook." LaurelR (19:1) Wint 85, p. 74-75.
1974. HANNA, Deirdre
        "Resid(u)e." CapilR (37) Fall 85, p. 69.
        "Voices." CapilR (37) Fall 85, p. 68.
1975. HANSELL, Susan
        "Bareback" (Award of Excellence, first prize -- Non-
           Professional Poet). Kaleid (10) Spr 85, p. 58.
        "The Wolf" (Award of Excellence, first prize -- Non-
           Professional Poet). Kaleid (10) Spr 85, p. 57.
1976. HANSEN, Jorgen Christian
        "In the Night Which Is Black" (tr. Pia Tafdrup). Verse
           (3) 85, p. 43.
        "Ind" (Excerpt, tr. Juliane Preisler). Verse (3) 85, p.
           43.
        "Women in Black Dresses" (tr. of Anette Tranaes). Verse
           (3) 85, p. 42.
1977. HANSEN, Joseph
        "The Blue Planet." SoDakR (23:1) Spr 85, p. 17.
        "Listen -- The Rain." SoDakR (23:1) Spr 85, p. 19.
        "Years Falling Away." SoDakR (23:1) Spr 85, p. 18.
1978. HANSEN, Tom
        "At the End of His Winter Journey through the Pennsylvania
           Mountains, a Barefoot Man Wakes Up in Bed and Talks to
           His Feet One Last Time." WebR (10:1) Spr 85, p. 39.
        "The Ghost at Ragdale." KanQ (17:1/2) Wint-Spr 85, p. 43.
        "The Human Cannonball." StoneC (12:2/3) Spr-Sum 85, p. 70.
        "October." Confr (29) Wint 85, p. 138.
        "October Nocturne." KanQ (17:1/2) Wint-Spr 85, p. 42.
        "Three States of Water." WebR (10:1) Spr 85, p. 38.
        "Wooden Angel Nailed to a Tree." KanQ (17:1/2) Wint-Spr
           85, p. 42.
        "Words Disappearing from Descartes' Dictionary." KanQ
           (17:1/2) Wint-Spr 85, p. 41.

1979. HANSON, Charles
        "Death of Trees." <u>WoosterR</u> (3) Spr 85, p. 58.
        "The Glass Blower." <u>PoeticJ</u> (10) 85, p. 4.
        "Pomegranates." <u>CrabCR</u> (2:2) Wint 85, p. 16.
        "Solemn Creatures." <u>BelPoJ</u> (35:3) Spr 85, p. 1.
        "Young Man in a Flower Garden." <u>WoosterR</u> (3) Spr 85, p.
            59.
1980. HANSON, Howard G.
        "By Big Bald Creek." <u>ArizQ</u> (41:4) Wint 85, p. 292.
1981. HANSON, Julie Jordan
        "Science Hour." <u>MichQR</u> (24:2) Spr 85, p. 157-158.
1982. HANSON, Kenneth O.
        "Anniversary Photo." <u>NowestR</u> (23:2) 85, p. 72.
        "Graves at Mukilteo." <u>NowestR</u> (23:2) 85, p. 66.
        "Man Carrying an Object." <u>NowestR</u> (23:2) 85, p. 73.
        "On Buying an Ikon." <u>NowestR</u> (23:2) 85, p. 68-69.
        "Routine." <u>NowestR</u> (23:2) 85, p. 67.
        "Sian (Old Style)." <u>NowestR</u> (23:2) 85, p. 70-71.
1983. HANSON, Portia
        "Momentarily Sapphire." <u>CreamCR</u> (10:1) 85, p. 28.
        "Of Water." <u>CreamCR</u> (10:2) [85?], p. 63.
        "Thrift Fair." <u>CreamCR</u> (10:1) 85, p. 27.
1984. HANZLICEK, C. G.
        "In the Yard of the Policlinic" (tr. of Vladimir Holan, w.
            Dana Habova). <u>AmerPoR</u> (14:4) Jl-Ag 85, p. 36.
        "Snow" (tr. of Vladimir Holan, w. Dana Habova). <u>AmerPoR</u>
            (14:4) Jl-Ag 85, p. 36.
1985. HARA, Tamiki
        "Water Please" (tr. by Steven Forth). <u>AmerPoR</u> (14:4) Jl-
            Ag 85, p. 9.
1986. HARALSON, Carol
        "Anna John Counts Out the Biscuit Flour." <u>Nimrod</u> (28:2)
            Spr-Sum 85, p. 57.
        "Everything East of Us Has Already Happened." <u>Nimrod</u>
            (28:2) Spr-Sum 85, p. 58-59.
        "Mary." <u>Nimrod</u> (28:2) Spr-Sum 85, p. 61.
        "My Mother Watches a Total Eclipse of the Moon." <u>Nimrod</u>
            (28:2) Spr-Sum 85, p. 62.
        "Rapunzel." <u>Nimrod</u> (28:2) Spr-Sum 85, p. 59-60.
1987. HARARY, Helen B.
        "Survivors." <u>SouthernPR</u> (26, i.e. 25:2) Fall 85, p. 29.
1988. HARDENBROOK, Yvonne
        "Delirium." <u>Pig</u> (13) 85, p. 46.
1989. HARDER, Richard
        "Defense of the Night." <u>PraF</u> (6:1) Wint 85, p. 27.
        "I obscure pain." <u>PraF</u> (6:1) Wint 85, p. 27.
        "I've been up murdering flies." <u>PraF</u> (6:1) Wint 85, p. 26.
        "Winter: Its Regional Influence." <u>PraF</u> (6:1) Wint 85, p.
            26.
1990. HARDING, May
        "Nene." <u>PoeticJ</u> (11) 85, p. 42.
1991. HARDING, Robert
        "The Way We Do It." <u>PoetryCR</u> (7:2) Wint 85-86, p. 17.
1992. HARDY, Jonathan
        "Leaves shattered on black soil." <u>CrossCur</u> (4:1) 84, p.
            34.
        "A Skeleton in the Phone Booth." <u>CrossCur</u> (4:1) 84, p. 33.
HARE, Jannis Allan
        <u>See</u> ALLAN-HARE, Jannis
1993. HARGROVE, Steve
        "Racquette." <u>Open24</u> (4) 85, p. 13.
1994. HARJO, Joy
        "Anchorage." <u>NoDaQ</u> (53:2) Spr 85, p. 220-221.
        "Dancer." <u>Cond</u> (11/12) 85, p. 15-16.
        "Remember." <u>NoDaQ</u> (53:2) Spr 85, p. 233.
        "War Dog." <u>Cond</u> (11/12) 85, p. 13-14.

1995. HARKIANAKIS, Stylianos
      "The Fourth Dimension" (tr. by Peter Bien). Verse (1) 84,
         p. 42.
      "Keep Left" (tr. by Peter Bien). Verse (1) 84, p. 41.
1996. HARKLERODE, Katrinia A.
      "Night Crawler." SouthernPR (26, i.e. 25:2) Fall 85, p.
         36.
1997. HARKNESS, Edward
      "Grandma Shooting Moles." PoetryNW (26:4) Wint 85-86, p.
         14-15.
1998. HARLEY, Peter
      "Still Schooner." PoetryCR (6:4) Sum 85, p. 47.
1999. HARMON, Joan
      "Ring Ferryman after Dark: Cable Ferry Gagetown."
         PottPort (7) 85-86, p. 47.
      "To Manageable Size." PottPort (7) 85-86, p. 51.
2000. HARMON, William
      "20, 000 Fantods under the Sea." CarolQ (37:3) Spr 85, p.
         54.
      "Prose Poems" (Selections: 1-5). NewL (52:1) Fall 85, p.
         62-64.
      "To a Friend: A Translation." CarolQ (37:3) Spr 85, p. 53.
2001. HARN, John
      "I want to say the other word" ("Untitled"). PraS (59:1)
         Spr 85, p. 50.
      "The Problem Explained." PraS (59:1) Spr 85, p. 51.
2002. HARNACK, Curtis
      "The Nearness." Nat (241:21) 21 D 85, p. 690.
2003. HARPER, Michael S.
      "Bandstand." SouthernR (21:3) Sum 85, p. 816.
      "Engagements." SouthernR (21:3) Sum 85, p. 814.
      "Josh Gibson's Bat" (Cooperstown, N.Y., Doubleday Field).
         Antaeus (55) Aut 85, p. 106-107.
      "Lecturing on the Theme of Motherhood." Antaeus (55) Aut
         85, p. 109.
      "My Book on Trane" (for McCoy Tyner). SouthernR (21:3)
         Sum 85, p. 817-818.
      "My Students Who Stand in Snow" (In Memory of MLK, Jr.
         4/4/85). Antaeus (55) Aut 85, p. 108.
      "Obscurity." SouthernR (21:3) Sum 85, p. 813.
      "Polls." SouthernR (21:3) Sum 85, p. 812.
      "Sugarloaf." SouthernR (21:3) Sum 85, p. 815-816.
      "Village Blues." PoetryR (2:2) Ap 85, p. 18.
2004. HARRINGTON, Ann
      "The Coming of Darkness." YellowS (15) Sum 85, p. 29.
2005. HARRIS, Claire
      "Koan." Quarry (34:4) Aut 85, p. 11.
      "V(O)FR: to Limit or Bound in Respect of Space." Quarry
         (34:4) Aut 85, p. 12.
2006. HARRIS, Gail
      "Angel." MalR (71) Je 85, p. 10.
      "An Angel Looks Like This." MalR (71) Je 85, p. 15.
      "Archangel." MalR (71) Je 85, p. 10.
      "The Cherub Is a Bolder Creature." MalR (71) Je 85, p. 12.
      "The Heads of the Seraphim." MalR (71) Je 85, p. 13.
      "If You Try to Photograph an Angel." MalR (71) Je 85, p.
         14.
      "A Strange Bird, the Angel." MalR (71) Je 85, p. 11.
      "Sugar Boy BOY." MalR (71) Je 85, p. 16.
2007. HARRIS, Jana
      "The Scientist's Wife Has an Opinion on Her Rival." OntR
         (23) Fall-Wint 85-86, p. 90-92.
2008. HARRIS, Jay D.
      "Bittersweet." PoeticJ (9) 85, p. 36.
      "Pride to Prayer." PoeticJ (12) 85, p. 31.

2009. HARRIS, Joseph
       "Chinese Nightingale." Amelia (2:1) Ap 85, p. 84.
       "Mood." Poem (54) N 85, p. 22.
       "On Straightening Utrillo." CrossCur (4:4/5:1) 85, p. 74.
2010. HARRIS, Lyle G.
       "Evensong." PoetryCR (7:2) Wint 85-86, p. 55.
2011. HARRIS, Maureen
       "Snake in the Grass." PoetryCR (7:2) Wint 85-86, p. 42.
2012. HARRIS, Michael
       "Flowers for My Brother's Ashes." Grain (13:4) N 85, p.
         39.
       "The Last Stone Down." PoetryCR (6:3) Spr 85, p. 6.
       "The Light-house Keeper." AntigR (61) Spr 85, p. 25.
       "Out on the Road." AntigR (61) Spr 85, p. 24.
       "Punting on the Thames." AntigR (61) Spr 85, p. 23.
       "Spring" (For Jeffrey Harris, August 3, 1946 - New Year's
         Day, 1977). Grain (13:4) N 85, p. 38.
       "Spring" (For Jeffrey Harris, August 3, 1946 - New Year's
         Day, 1977). NewEngR (8:2) Wint 85, p. 236.
       "Turning Out the Light" (Excerpts). NewEngR (8:2) Wint
         85, p. 233-235.
2013. HARRIS, Peter
       "The Cross" (from Unfinished Crusade, The Voice of an
         Unknown Woman Poet, tr. Rafal Wojaczek, w. Danuta
         Lopozyko). Chelsea (44) 85, p. 116.
HARRIS, Robert von Dassanowsky
       See DASSANOWSKY-HARRIS, Robert von
2014. HARRIS, Robert
       "Nocturne." CrossCur (4:1) 84, p. 96.
       "Tango." Wind (15:54) 85, p. 24.
2015. HARRISON, Jeanne
       "The Closing Movement." Waves (13:2/3) Wint 85, p. 78-80.
       "In a window on a dark horizon." Quarry (34:1) Wint 85,
         p. 49.
2016. HARRISON, Jeffrey
       "Canoeing with My Brother." NewRep (193:22) 25 N 85, p.
         36.
2017. HARRY, Margaret
       "Rats." Waves (13:2/3) Wint 85, p. 98.
2018. HARSHMAN, Marc
       "Animation." Northeast (Series 4:2) Fall 85, p. 6.
       "Before and After." LaurelR (19:2) Sum 85, p. 16.
       "Having Watched the Road and Fields." Northeast (Series
         4:2) Fall 85, p. 7.
       "Knitting." Northeast (Series 4:2) Fall 85, p. 8.
       "Little Wars." SouthernPR (25:1) Spr 85, p. 26.
       "Oxford." Geor (39:2) Sum 85, p. 412-413.
       "Playgrounds." WoosterR (4) Fall 85, p. 58-59.
       "Still Life." SouthernPR (25:1) Spr 85, p. 24-25.
2019. HART, Henry
       "A Gift of Warblers." Verse (4) 85, p. 24.
       "The Sea Trout." Stand (26:4) Aut 85, p. 67.
       "The Spring Competitions." Poetry (146:5) Ag 85, p. 283-
         284.
       "Two Screams." Verse (1) 84, p. 10-11.
       "The Winter House." Verse (1) 84, p. 9.
2020. HART, Kathleen
       "Coming Down the Stairs." Calyx (9:1) Spr-Sum 85, p. 36.
       "The Fire in My Father's Chest." Calyx (9:1) Spr-Sum 85,
         p. 37.
2021. HART, William
       "Sheriff." Bogg (53) 85, p. 8.
       "Spring Thoughts." Amelia (2:1) Ap 85, p. 73.
2022. HARTMAN, Charles O.
       "Colloquy." QW (21) Fall-Wint 85, p. 42-43.
       "The Fire That Feeds." PraS (59:4) Wint 85, p. 70-71.

"Harm's Way." PraS (59:4) Wint 85, p. 69-70.
2023. HARTNETT, D. W.
    "Chestnuts." PoetryCR (7:1) Aut 85, p. 30.
    "Erntezeit" (A Painting by Valkenborch). PoetryCR (7:1)
        Aut 85, p. 30.
    "Floating World." PoetryCR (7:1) Aut 85, p. 30.
2024. HARTSFIELD, Carla
    "What We Want." PoetryCR (6:4) Sum 85, p. 39.
2025. HARTY, Callen
    "For Earl" (murdered in Superior, WI, July 1984). JamesWR
        (2:1) Fall 84, p. 15.
2026. HARVEY, Andrew
    "Any words I give you are my words." SenR (15:1) 85, p.
        61.
    "The Dormition of Aunt Menka" (tr. of Blazhe Koneski, w.
        Anne Pennington). SenR (15:1) 85, p. 59.
    "No Diamonds, No Hat, No Honey." PartR (52:2) 85, p. 56-
        60.
    "Sharks." SenR (15:1) 85, p. 62-64.
    "The true audience." SenR (15:1) 85, p. 60.
2027. HARVEY, Gayle Elen
    "All" (after Van Gogh's "Red Vineyard"). PoeticJ (10) 85,
        p. 35.
2028. HARVEY, Ken J.
    "Laughing at the Wrong Times." Bogg (54) 85, p. 8.
2029. HARWAY, Judith
    "Condolence" (for Suzanne). CapeR (20:2) Fall 85, p. 5.
    "The Fire." CreamCR (10:2) [85?], p. 54-55.
    "The Man Who Rings the Bell." MalR (71) Je 85, p. 29.
    "Navigator's Log." MalR (71) Je 85, p. 28.
    "Reflection." QW (21) Fall-Wint 85, p. 94.
    "Urban Deer." QW (21) Fall-Wint 85, p. 93.
    "Wash." CumbPR (5:1) Fall 85, p. 8.
2030. HASKINS, David
    "The Death of Marriages." Waves (13:4) Spr 85, p. 71.
2031. HASKINS, Lola
    "The Daily of Alma Lind." BelPoJ (35:4) Sum 85, p. 25-34.
    "Exteriors." BelPoJ (35:4) Sum 85, p. 17-24.
    "Loving a Son." Agni (22) 85, p. 68.
    "On Passing Forty." BelPoJ (35:4) Sum 85, p. 35.
2032. HASS, Robert
    "1913" (tr. of Czeslaw Milosz, w. the author). Thrpny
        (6:2, issue 22) Sum 85, p. 13.
    "After Paradise" (tr. of Czeslaw Milosz, w. the author).
        NewYorker (61:21) 15 Jl 85, p. 25.
    "Anka" (tr. of Czeslaw Milosz, w. the author). NewYorker
        (61:35) 21 O 85, p. 38.
    "At Noon" (tr. of Czeslaw Milosz, w. the author).
        NewYorker (61:21) 15 Jl 85, p. 24.25.
    "Consciousness" (tr. of Czeslaw Milosz, w. the author).
        Antaeus (55) Aut 85, p. 138-140.
    "Elegy for Y.Z." (tr. of Czeslaw Milosz, w. the author).
        NewYorker (61:21) 15 Jl 85, p. 25.
    "Into the Tree" (tr. of Czeslaw Milosz, w. the author).
        Antaeus (55) Aut 85, p. 135-136.
    "My-ness" (tr. of Czeslaw Milosz, w. the author).
        NewYorker (61:45) 30 D 85, p. 24.
    "On Prayer" (tr. of Czeslaw Milosz, w. the author).
        Antaeus (55) Aut 85, p. 137.
    "Preparation" (tr. of Czeslaw Milosz, w. the author).
        NewYRB (32:14) 26 S 85, p. 4.
    "Return to Cracow in 1880" (tr. of Czeslaw Milosz, w. the
        author). NewYorker (61:21) 15 Jl 85, p. 25.
    "Rustling Taffetas" (tr. of Czeslaw Milosz, w. the author).
        NewYorker (61:21) 15 Jl 85, p. 24.
    "Spring Drawing I." Thrpny (6:2, issue 22) Sum 85, p. 11.

"Table I" (tr. of Czeslaw Milosz, w. the author).
    NewYorker (61:21) 15 Jl 85, p. 24.
"Table II" (tr. of Czeslaw Milosz, w. the author).
    NewYorker (61:21) 15 Jl 85, p. 24.
"Winter" (tr. of Czeslaw Milosz, w. the author).
    NewYorker (61:21) 15 Jl 85, p. 24-25.
2033. HASTY, Palmer
    "Summer." Confr (29) Wint 85, p. 148.
2034. HATHAWAY, James
    "Americana." CapeR (20:2) Fall 85, p. 21.
    "Heat." CapeR (20:2) Fall 85, p. 20.
2035. HATHAWAY, William
    "American Gogol" (for Ronald Reagan). AmerPoR (14:6) N-D
        85, p. 6.
    "East Polk Street Park" (for Pat Screen). MemphisSR (5:2)
        Spr 85, p. 31-33.
    "Sleeping Bell." NewL (52:1) Fall 85, p. 67.
    "Timor Mortis: Sermo." NewEngR (7:3) Spr 85, p. 315-322.
2036. HAUCK, Chris
    "Digging Out Blackberry." CalQ (26) Sum 85, p. 51.
2037. HAUG, James
    "Afternoons." HangL (47) Spr 85, p. 20.
    "Dimes" (for Jean). PassN (6:2) Spr-Sum 85, p. 18.
    "Ticket Taker." HangL (47) Spr 85, p. 19.
2038. HAUGE, Olav
    "The Aspen" (tr. by Robin Fulton). Verse (3) 85, p. 41.
    "The Birch" (tr. by Robin Fulton). Verse (3) 85, p. 40.
    "A Grain" (tr. by Robin Fulton). Verse (3) 85, p. 40.
    "Stare Miasto" (the old part of Warsaw, tr. by Robin
        Fulton). Verse (3) 85, p. 40.
2039. HAUSER, Reine
    "Dill." Ploughs (11:1) 85, p. 121.
    "Liquor." Ploughs (11:1) 85, p. 118.
    "Still Farther Away" (L.K.). Ploughs (11:1) 85, p. 119-
        120.
2040. HAVEN, Stephen
    "Maria Francesca." RiverS (18) 85, p. 88-89.
2041. HAWK, Victor
    "Fourier." Wind (15:54) 85, p. 17.
2042. HAWKES, Robert
    "Correspondence" (Inspired by a talk on Faith and
        Conflict). Germ (9:1) Spr-Sum 85, p. 30.
2043. HAWKINS, Dwight
    "Third World Children." SanFPJ (7:2) 85, p. 40.
2044. HAWKINS, Hunt
    "Lawn Fertilizer." TriQ (64) Fall 85, p. 115.
    "Male Grief." TriQ (64) Fall 85, p. 116.
    "My Mother Writes in the Snow." TriQ (64) Fall 85, p. 117-
        118.
2045. HAWKINS, Thomas
    "The Tractor Driver." KanQ (17:4) Fall 85, p. 207.
2046. HAXTON, Brooks
    "Hand and Foot." Poetry (147:2) N 85, p. 92.
    "Happy Hour." ChiR (34:4) 85, p. 28.
    "Pond." BelPoJ (36:2) Wint 85-86, p. 20-22.
    "The Ring." ChiR (34:4) 85, p. 29.
    "Walking Home in the Dark." BelPoJ (36:2) Wint 85-86, p.
        23.
2047. HAYASHI, R. T.
    "Dusty." Vis (18) 85, p. 25.
    "Oh, the Concentration." CapeR (20:2) Fall 85, p. 23.
2048. HAYDEN, Dolores
    "Sprezzatura." StoneC (12:2/3) Spr-Sum 85, p. 57.
2049. HAYDEN, Nancy
    "Fringe Benefit." EngJ (74:1) Ja 85, p. 84.

2050. HAYDEN, Robert
"He had no time for pulling at his pipe" (Untitled). TriQ
(62) Wint 85, p. 183-184.
"I am the secret, midnight voice you do not hear"
(Untitled). TriQ (62) Wint 85, p. 180.
"Schizophrenia" (Ed Dalton, his poem). TriQ (62) Wint 85,
p. 185-186.
"They are sitting by the Cumberland" (Untitled). TriQ
(62) Wint 85, p. 181-182.
2051. HAYES, Alice Ryerson
"Japanese Plate." SpoonRQ (10:4) Fall 85, p. 42.
2052. HAYN, Annette
"Kinderfraulein." Wind (15:53) 85, p. 15.
2053. HAYNES, Pamela
"When." MemphisSR (5:2) Spr 85, p. 48.
2054. HAYS, Janice
"Academic Life on America's Branch Campuses: Again This
Year, Estelle and Harry Go to the Opera in Santa Fe."
BelPoJ (35:4) Sum 85, p. 12-13.
2055. HAYTON, Alan
"Milk Grass Idyll." Verse (4) 85, p. 43-44.
2056. HAZARD, James
"The Crow Call, February." ClockR (2:2) 85, p. 30.
"New Year's Eve in Whiting, Indiana." ClockR (2:2) 85, p.
28.
"Sidney Bechet at Six Years Old." ClockR (2:2) 85, p. 29.
2057. HAZARD, John
"For John, on the Mountain." WebR (10:1) Spr 85, p. 61.
"Getting a Bead." CrabCR (3:1) Fall-Wint 85, p. 22.
"Iphigenia." WebR (10:1) Spr 85, p. 60.
"On Existentialism." WebR (10:2) Fall 85, p. 67.
"The Problem of Still Life." CrabCR (3:1) Fall-Wint 85,
p. 22.
"The Waves." CrabCR (2:2) Wint 85, p. 6.
2058. HAZZARD, Shirley
"Lines written in the knowledge." OP (38/39) Spr 85, p.
178.
2059. HEAD, Gwen
"The Swans of Saigon." GrandS (4:4) Sum 85, p. 167-169.
"Wallenda, Falling." GrandS (4:2) Wint 85, p. 216.
2060. HEALY, Jack
"Holiday at Myall Lake." PoetryCR (7:1) Aut 85, p. 6.
2061. HEALY, Susan
"Red and Green If You Can't See Them." CreamCR (10:1) 85,
p. 8-9.
2062. HEANEY, Seamus
"The Ballad of the Bullets." Ploughs (11:4) 85, p. 38-40.
"Grotus and Coventina." Verse (1) 84, p. 3.
"The Master." GrahamHR (8) Wint 85, p. 9.
"The Mud Vision." Thrpny (6:3, issue 23) Fall 85, p. 8.
"Sweeney and the Cleric." GrahamHR (8) Wint 85, p. 7.
"Sweeney Remembers the Hermit." GrahamHR (8) Wint 85, p.
8.
2063. HEARD, Karen
"The Crossing." BlackALF (19:3) Fall 85, p. 128.
"Saltwater." BlackALF (19:3) Fall 85, p. 127.
2064. HEATH, Terrence
"Another Garden." PraF (6:2) Spr 85, p. 14.
2065. HEBALD, Carol
"Fantasy in a Floating Cafe Aboard a Cruise Ship Somewhere
near Southampton." KanQ (17:4) Fall 85, p. 44.
"Letter to a Gay Artist Aboard a Cruise Ship Somewhere near
Stockholm." KanQ (17:4) Fall 85, p. 43.
"Two Quatrains." NewL (51:3) Spr 85, p. 60-61.
2066. HEBBEL, Friedrich
"Aphorisms and Observations" (tr. by Jay Boggis). Ploughs

(11:4) 85, p. 148-150.
2067. HEBERT, Anne
"And There Was Light" (tr. by A. Poulin). GrahamHR (9)
Fall 85, p. 43-44.
"Cities Setting Out" (tr. by A. Poulin). GrahamHR (9)
Fall 85, p. 39.
"Crown of Joy" (tr. by A. Poulin). GrahamHR (9) Fall 85,
p. 40.
"End of the World" (tr. by A. Poulin, Jr.). AmerPoR
(14:2) Mr-Ap 85, p. 19.
"Noel" (tr. by A. Poulin, Jr.). AmerPoR (14:2) Mr-Ap 85,
p. 20.
"The Offended" (tr. by A. Poulin). GrahamHR (9) Fall 85,
p. 42.
"Original Earth" (tr. by A. Poulin). GrahamHR (9) Fall
85, p. 41.
"Rain" (tr. by A. Poulin, Jr.). AmerPoR (14:2) Mr-Ap 85,
p. 19.
2068. HECHT, Anthony
"Terms." NewYorker (61:9) 22 Ap 85, p. 44.
2069. HECHT, Jennifer
"Two Minutes to Midnight." Sam (42:4, 168th release) 85,
p. 14.
2070. HEDGES, Warren
"Nails." WoosterR (3) Spr 85, p. 84.
2071. HEDIN, Mary
"Moonstones." PoetryR (5) S 85, p. 43.
2072. HEDLIN, Robert
"Missing Children." SouthernPR (25:1) Spr 85, p. 70.
HEE, Yoo Ok
See YOO, Ok Hee
2073. HEFFERNAN, Michael
"Central States" (20 poems). MidwQ (26:3) Spr 85, p. 315-
342.
"Jim's Cafe." ColEng (47:7) N 85, p. 717.
"What I Did on My Vacation." PoetryNW (26:1) Spr 85, p.
32-34.
2074. HEFLIN, Jack
"The Sawmill." CutB (23) Fall-Wint 85, p. 24-25.
"The Sleepwalker." CutB (23) Fall-Wint 85, p. 26.
2075. HEIGHTON, Steven
"Cobalt Peak." AntigR (60) Wint 85, p. 91.
"The Gap." PoetryCR (7:1) Aut 85, p. 51.
"Restless." AntigR (60) Wint 85, p. 92.
2076. HEIM, S. W.
"Going Home." PaintedB (25) Spr 85, p. 13-14.
2077. HEINEMAN, W. F.
"In the Field." CrabCR (2:3) Sum 85, p. 3.
2078. HEINLEIN, David
"Kyoto-Otsu Visit, New Year's, 1985." USl (18/19) Wint
85, p. 10.
2079. HEINRICH, Colleen
"Found Conversations" ("Overheard in the Cafeteria,"
"Cafeteria II"). CapilR (36) 85, p. 70-73.
HEITER, Marcia Martin
See MARTIN-HEITER, Marcia
2080. HEJINIAN, Lyn
"Accidia" (tr. of Arkadii Dragomoshchenko, w. Michael
Molnar). Sulfur (14) 85, p. 116-122.
"I dread my dreams" (tr. of Arkadii Dragomoshchenko, w.
Michael Molnar). Sulfur (14) 85, p. 131.
"Obscure Bases of Narration" (example readings, tr. of
Arkadii Dragomoshchenko, w. Michael Molnar). Sulfur
(14) 85, p. 123-127.
"The Person." Zyzzyva (1:2) Sum 85, p. 45-48.
"The Person" (Selections: 2-4). Temblor (1) 85, p. 81-84.

"A Sentimental Elegy" (a gift for Anna, tr. of Arkadii
   Dragomoshchenko, w. Michael Molnar). Sulfur (14) 85,
   p. 128-130.
"Study of Dimension" (tr. of Arkadii Dragomoshchenko, w.
   Michael Molnar). Sulfur (14) 85, p. 131.
2081. HELLER, Peter
   "Winter Nights." PassN (6:1) Fall-Wint 85, p. 6.
2082. HELLERSTEIN, Kathryn
   "Writing." Imagine (2:1) Sum 85, p. 100-101.
2083. HELLEW, J. V.
   "Poem" (How come I feel like apologizing). LittleM (14:4)
   85, p. 57.
2084. HELLMAN, Kate
   "Warning: to you it may." PoetryCR (7:2) Wint 85-86, p.
   51.
   "We because we speak in speed." PoetryCR (7:2) Wint 85-
   86, p. 51.
2085. HELLMAN, Sheila
   "Ballet Positions." BelPoJ (35:3) Spr 85, p. 32-33.
   "Toe Shoes." BelPoJ (35:3) Spr 85, p. 34.
2086. HELMSTETLER, Yvonne
   "There Was a Time." PoeticJ (11) 85, p. 28.
2087. HELWIG, Maggie
   "Antics." Descant 48 (16:1) Spr 85, p. 23.
   "The Chemist in the Rockies -- for Kate." Grain (13:1) F
   85, p. 14.
   "Corpus Christi Sunday, Florence." Descant 48 (16:1) Spr
   85, p. 22.
   "Green Islands." Descant 48 (16:1) Spr 85, p. 21.
   "Painting Jacob -- for Maurice Denis." Grain (13:1) F 85,
   p. 15.
2088. HEMMINGSON, Michael (See also HEMMINGSON, Michael A.)
   "The Boss." SecC (12:1) 84, p. 5.
   "Nowhere Is Safe." Sam (42:2, 166th release) 85, 12 p.
2089. HEMMINGSON, Michael A. (See also HEMMINGSON, Michael)
   "#36." Bogg (53) 85, p. 31.
   "Composing to Gretchen." PoeticJ (9) 85, p. 24.
   "Crossing the Border." PoeticJ (10) 85, p. 34.
   "Gretchen, behind the Piano." PoeticJ (10) 85, p. 39.
   "Maybe Tonight." PoeticJ (11) 85, p. 12.
   "Most Poets." Bogg (54) 85, p. 32.
   "Prophecy." PoeticJ (9) 85, p. 25.
2090. HEMP, Christine
   "November Stone Walls." EngJ (74:1) Ja 85, p. 63.
2091. HEMPHILL, Essex
   "The Note." BlackALF (19:3) Fall 85, p. 111.
2092. HEMSCHEMEYER, Judith
   "Alexander at Thebes" (Zh. 471, tr. of Anna Akhmatova).
   NowestR (23:3) 85, p. 67.
   "And all day, terrified by its own moans" (Zh. 234, tr. of
   Anna Akhmatova). Ploughs (11:4) 85, p. 178.
   "Apparition" (Zh. 290, tr. of Anna Akhmatova). Ploughs
   (11:4) 85, p. 180.
   "Around the neck is a string of find beads" (Zh. 232, tr.
   of Anna Akhmatova). NowestR (23:3) 85, p. 55.
   "Because sin is what I glorified" (Zh. 516, tr. of Anna
   Akhmatova). NowestR (23:3) 85, p. 57.
   "Cast-iron fence" (Zh. 278, tr. of Anna Akhmatova).
   NowestR (23:3) 85, p. 59.
   "Chinese Baby." Hudson (38:1) Spr 85, p. 81.
   "Confusion" (tr. of Anna Akhmatova). NewL (51:4) Sum 85,
   p. 47.
   "Don't torment your heart with the joys of earth" (Zh. 244,
   tr. of Anna Akhmatova). Ploughs (11:4) 85, p. 178.
   "Farewell Song" (Zh. 461, tr. of Anna Akhmatova). NowestR
   (23:3) 85, p. 65.

"He whispers: I won't even apologize" (Zh. 255, tr. of Anna
    Akhmatova). Ploughs (11:4) 85, p. 179.
"How terribly the body has changed" (tr. of Anna
    Akhmatova). NewL (51:4) Sum 85, p. 47.
"I will leave your white house and peaceful garden" (Zh.
    113, tr. of Anna Akhmatova). Ploughs (11:4) 85, p. 177.
"It's Dead." Hudson (38:1) Spr 85, p. 80.
"Latest Return" (Zh. 408, tr. of Anna Akhmatova). NowestR
    (23:3) 85, p. 64.
"Like the angel moving upon the water" (tr. of Anna
    Akhmatova). NewL (51:4) Sum 85, p. 47-48.
"Listening to Singing" (Zh. 582, tr. of Anna Akhmatova).
    NowestR (23:3) 85, p. 68.
"Mayakovsky in 1913" (Zh. 330, tr. of Anna Akhmatova).
    NowestR (23:3) 85, p. 63.
"The Method." Hudson (38:1) Spr 85, p. 79.
"Native Land" (Zh. 478, tr. of Anna Akhmatova). NowestR
    (23:3) 85, p. 66.
"Over the snowdrift's hard crust" (tr of. Anna Akhmatova,
    "Tsarskoye Selo"). Mund (15:1/2) 85, p. 199.
"Parting (2)" (Zh. 328, tr. of Anna Akhmatova). NowestR
    (23:3) 85, p. 61.
"Parting (3)" (Zh. 329, tr. of Anna Akhmatova). NowestR
    (23:3) 85, p. 62.
"Suddenly it's become still in the house" (tr. of Anna
    Akhmatova). NewL (51:4) Sum 85, p. 48.
"Three times it came to torment me" (tr of. Anna Akhmatova,
    "Tsarskoye Selo"). Mund (15:1/2) 85, p. 199.
"To the Victor." Hudson (38:1) Spr 85, p. 80.
"Versailles." Hudson (38:1) Spr 85, p. 81.
"The Voice of Another" (tr of. Anna Akhmatova, "Tsarskoye
    Selo"). Mund (15:1/2) 85, p. 200.
"Wedding Night." Hudson (38:1) Spr 85, p. 79.
"Why then did I used to" (Zh. 196, tr. of Anna Akhmatova).
    NowestR (23:3) 85, p. 58.
"Willow" (Zh. 322, tr. of Anna Akhmatova). NowestR (23:3)
    85, p. 60.
"You know, I languish in captivity" (Zh. 83, tr. of Anna
    Akhmatova). NowestR (23:3) 85, p. 56.
2093. HENDERSHOT, Peggy
    "Dear." NegC (5:3) Sum 85, p. 42.
2094. HENDERSON, Brian
    "Smoking Mirror" (Selections: Five pieces). CanLit (107)
        Wint 85, p. 86-89.
2095. HENDRICKS, Brent
    "Night." PoetryE (18) Fall 85, p. 28.
    "The Night Garden." PoetryE (18) Fall 85, p. 26-27.
2096. HENDRIKS, A. L.
    "Sauteurs." GreenfR (12:3/4) Wint-Spr 85, p. 170.
    "Views from Ailys House" (for Barbara Hendriks). GreenfR
        (12:3/4) Wint-Spr 85, p. 168.
    "Villanelle of the Year's End" (To an English lady, from a
        Jamaican, December 1983). GreenfR (12:3/4) Wint-Spr
        85, p. 169.
2097. HENN, Mary Ann (Sister)
    "Fingers." SanFPJ (7:4) 85, p. 10.
    "Haiku" (3 poems). WindO (45) Spr 85, p. 42.
    "Jogging the Path of Life." WindO (46) Fall 85, p. 41.
    "Nothing But." WindO (46) Fall 85, p. 41.
    "Who's Really to Blame?" SanFPJ (7:4) 85, p. 11.
2098. HENNING, Barbara
    "For the Ghost Girl." MemphisSR (5:2) Spr 85, p. 14.
2099. HENRIE, Carol
    "A Coyote Runs Across My Path at Midnight in the Pine Loop
        Campground at Grand Canyon." NewRep (192:23) 10 Je 85,
        p. 38.

2100. HENRIKSON, Carol
      "Wanting Winter." <u>Geor</u> (39:2) Sum 85, p. 391.
2101. HENRIQUE-ORTIZ, Juana
      "Avocados, Lemons, Limes." <u>Imagine</u> (2:1) Sum 85, p. 81.
HENRIQUEZ, Eduardo Zepeda
      <u>See</u> ZEPEDA-HENRIQUEZ, Eduardo
2102. HENRY, Gordon
      "How Soon." <u>NoDaQ</u> (53:2) Spr 85, p. 36.
      "Pine Point: After Rain." <u>BlackWR</u> (11:2) Spr 85, p. 108-
         109.
      "Pine Point: Her Breath." <u>BlackWR</u> (11:2) Spr 85, p. 106-
         107.
2103. HENRY, Laurie
      "Fairyland." <u>AntR</u> (43:2) Spr 85, p. 204.
      "Restoring the Chateau of the Marquis de Sade." <u>SilverFR</u>
         (10) 85, 23 p.
2104. HENRY, Michael
      "Hanukah Bush." <u>AntigR</u> (61) Spr 85, p. 131-132.
2105. HENRY, Sarah
      "Valentine's Day." <u>HolCrit</u> (22:1) F 85, p. 17.
2106. HENTZ, Robert R.
      "The Stakes Are High." <u>SanFPJ</u> (7:3) 84 [i.e. 85], p. 87.
      "To Light a Candle Is Not Enough." <u>SanFPJ</u> (7:3) 84 [i.e.
         85], p. 21.
2107. HEPBURN, Margaret
      "Philadelphia 1937" (for Samuel). <u>NewL</u> (52:1) Fall 85, p.
         125-126.
HERBERT, Mary Sewall
      <u>See</u> SEWALL-HERBERT, Mary
2108. HERBERT, W. N.
      "As It Must" (After the Italian of Mario Luzi). <u>Verse</u> (3)
         85, p. 31.
      "The Boating Party." <u>Verse</u> (4) 85, p. 37.
      "Coco-de-Mer." <u>Verse</u> (3) 85, p. 31.
      "Grout and Pamisample." <u>Verse</u> (3) 85, p. 30.
      "The Hermitage." <u>Verse</u> (4) 85, p. 36-37.
      "Landscape." <u>Verse</u> (4) 85, p. 35.
      "What Graham Does." <u>Verse</u> (1) 84, p. 23.
2109. HERBERT, Zbigniew
      "Beethoven" (tr. by John and Bogdana Carpenter). <u>Antaeus</u>
         (55) Aut 85, p. 115.
      "Mr. Cogito -- the Return" (tr. by John and Bogdana
         Carpenter). <u>Antaeus</u> (55) Aut 85, p. 121-123.
      "Mr. Cogito's Soul" (tr. by John and Bogdana Carpenter).
         <u>Antaeus</u> (55) Aut 85, p. 119-120.
      "The Murderers of Kings" (tr. by John and Bogdana
         Carpenter). <u>Antaeus</u> (55) Aut 85, p. 118.
      "Pan Cogito and the Imagination" (In Polish and English,
         tr. by Leonard Kress). <u>CrossCur</u> (4:2) 84, p. 120-121.
      "The Power of Taste" (For Professor Izydora Dambska, tr. by
         John and Bogdana Carpenter). <u>Antaeus</u> (55) Aut 85, p.
         116-117.
      "Report from the Besieged City" (tr. by John and Bogdana
         Carpenter). <u>Antaeus</u> (55) Aut 85, p. 110-112.
      "To Ryszard Krynicki -- a Letter" (tr. by John and Bogdana
         Carpenter). <u>Antaeus</u> (55) Aut 85, p. 113-114.
2110. HERMAN, Grace
      "Cool." <u>PoetryR</u> (5) S 85, p. 58.
      "Dolly, Dolly." <u>PoetryR</u> (5) S 85, p. 59.
      "I Cannot Tell." <u>PoetryR</u> (5) S 85, p. 58.
2111. HERMSEN, Terry
      "Handing the Tool to Ignorance." <u>KanQ</u> (17:1/2) Wint-Spr
         85, p. 223.
      "Into Dry Land." <u>Vis</u> (17) 85, p. 5.
2112. HERNANDEZ, Antonio
      "Beside What Doesn't Die" (tr. by Frederick H. Fornoff).

<u>NewOR</u> (12:4) Wint 85, p. 44-46.
2113. HERNANDEZ, Samuel
      "A Pound of Clay." <u>CrossCur</u> (4:4/5:1) 85, p. 95-96.
2114. HERNDON, John
      "Broad sun at dead noon." <u>WormR</u> (25:4, issue 100) 85, p.
        124.
      "Okra and Coathangers." <u>WormR</u> (25:4, issue 100) 85, p.
        124.
      "Plumbing." <u>WormR</u> (25:4, issue 100) 85, p. 124.
      "Three Guitars." <u>WormR</u> (25:4, issue 100) 85, p. 125.
2115. HERNTON, Calvin
      "A Cat by Any Name" (for amiri). <u>RiverS</u> (17) 85, p. 56-57.
      "D Blues." <u>PoetryR</u> (2:2) Ap 85, p. 17.
2116. HERPORT, Susan Hall
      "Brush Fire." <u>PoetryNW</u> (26:4) Wint 85-86, p. 10-11.
      "Gift of a Dead Bird." <u>PoetryNW</u> (26:4) Wint 85-86, p. 11.
2117. HERRERA, Juan Felipe
      "Literary Asylums" (for Francisco X. Alarcón). <u>AmerPoR</u>
        (14:4) Jl-Ag 85, p. 32-33.
      "Photo-Poem of the Chicano Moratorium 1980/L.A." <u>AmerPoR</u>
        (14:4) Jl-Ag 85, p. 32.
2118. HERRERA-SOBEK, María
      "A la Muerte de un Hermano." <u>BilingR</u> (11:2) My-Ag 84
        [c1986], p. 15.
      "Chamomile Nights." <u>Imagine</u> (2:1) Sum 85, p. 69.
      "Memories." <u>Imagine</u> (2:1) Sum 85, p. 70.
2119. HERRICK, Robert
      "Fiat Justitia." <u>Atlantic</u> (256:5), N 85, p. 56.
2120. HERRINGTON, Neva
      "I Asked a Nearby Cuckoo" (tr. of Anna Akhmatova, w. Gale
        Vathing). <u>NewL</u> (51:4) Sum 85, p. 49.
      "I Didn't Ask for the Praise" (tr. of Anna Akhmatova, w.
        Gale Vathing). <u>NewL</u> (51:4) Sum 85, p. 48.
2121. HERSHON, Robert
      "The Department Head." <u>Confr</u> (30/31) N 85, p. 166.
      "Grover Cleveland High School." <u>PoetryNW</u> (26:3) Aut 85,
        p. 25.
      "I Tell My Mother's Daydream" (for Maureen Owen). <u>PoetryE</u>
        (18) Fall 85, p. 34.
      "New Driver." <u>PoetryNW</u> (26:3) Aut 85, p. 24.
      "Sailing around the Horn." <u>PoetryNW</u> (26:1) Spr 85, p. 43.
      "Walking from the Station." <u>Confr</u> (30/31) N 85, p. 166.
      "Water, for My Father." <u>PoetryE</u> (18) Fall 85, p. 35.
      "What Is Available, What Is Permitted, What Is Mandatory."
        <u>PoetryE</u> (18) Fall 85, p. 36.
2122. HERZ, Stephen E.
      "Light Exercise." <u>SmPd</u> (22:3) Fall 85, p. 25.
2123. HERZBERG, Judith
      "A Child's Mirror." <u>Vis</u> (18) 85, p. 4.
      "Dagrest" (Selections: "Vrouw, Eiseres," "Liedje,"
        "Rooster," "Je Hoopt,"Blijf Bij"). <u>PoetryCR</u> (7:1) Aut
        85, p. 23.
      "Old Age." <u>Vis</u> (18) 85, p. 4.
      "Quartz, Mica, Feldspar" (tr. by Scott Rollins). <u>Vis</u> (19)
        85, p. 35.
      "What's Left of the Day" (Selections, tr. by Maria Jacobs:
        "Wife, Claimant," "Time Table," "You Hope," "Song,"
        "Stay"). <u>PoetryCR</u> (7:1) Aut 85, p. 23.
2124. HESFORD, W. S.
      "Garden of Remembrance." <u>NegC</u> (5:2) Spr 85, p. 44.
2125. HESS, Mary
      "Exchanges." <u>SanFPJ</u> (7:3) 84 [i.e. 85], p. 44.
2126. HESSELBACH, Bruce
      "Dazzling." <u>PoeticJ</u> (12) 85, p. 14.
2127. HESTER, M. L.
      "All the Men Are Waiting." <u>Northeast</u> (Series 4:2) Fall

85, p. 11.
"Poem" (for Charles Eaton). StoneC (13:1/2) Fall-Wint 85-
86, p. 16.
2128. HESTER, William
"Old Man with a Horn." Amelia (2:1) Ap 85, p. 44-46.
2129. HETTICH, Michael
"Landscape." Wind (15:55) 85, p. 31.
2130. HETTINGA, Tsjebbe
"In the Enchantment of the Depth between Light and Light"
(Excerpt, tr. by Rod Jellema). PoetL (79:4) Wint 85,
p. 237.
2131. HEWETT, Gregory G.
"Day's End, Minden, Nebraska." CalQ (26) Sum 85, p. 47.
2132. HEWITT, Geof
"Miaking Light." NewL (52:1) Fall 85, p. 92.
2133. HEYEN, William
"Blackberries." Iowa (15:1) Wint 85, p. 42.
"Bobby Wine and the Championship Game." Confr (30/31) N
85, p. 123-125.
"Brockport Sunflowers." AmerPoR (14:2) Mr-Ap 85, p. 23.
"The Cabin." AmerPoR (14:2) Mr-Ap 85, p. 27.
"Cherry." VirQ (61:2) Spr 85, p. 257-258.
"The Coffin" (for Irene Drachowski, 1914-1982). VirQ
(61:2) Spr 85, p. 258-261.
"The Colony." AmerPoR (14:2) Mr-Ap 85, p. 27.
"The Confessions of Doc Williams." AmerPoR (14:2) Mr-Ap
85, p. 24-26.
"December Snow." Iowa (15:1) Wint 85, p. 43.
"Dresden Gals Won't You Come Out Tonight." Verse (3) 85,
p. 18.
"Lily." AmerPoR (14:2) Mr-Ap 85, p. 27.
"Memorial Day, Brockport, 1981." TriQ (63) Spr-Sum 85, p.
624.
"The New American Poetry." TriQ (63) Spr-Sum 85, p. 622-
623.
"The Shore." VirQ (61:2) Spr 85, p. 256-257.
"Sunflowers." AmerPoR (14:2) Mr-Ap 85, p. 28.
"That Summer." AmerPoR (14:2) Mr-Ap 85, p. 23.
"This Acre." Raccoon (17) Mr 85, p. 26.
2134. HEYM, Georg
"Final Vigil" (tr. by Peter Viereck). NewL (51:3) Spr 85,
p. 54.
"White Butterflies of Night, So Often near Me" (tr. by
Peter Viereck). NewL (51:4) Sum 85, p. 73.
2135. HEYMAN, Ann
"Damage" (Scholarship winner). DeKalbLAJ (18:3/4) 85, p.
25.
"Holy Wars" (Scholarship winner). DeKalbLAJ (18:3/4) 85,
p. 25.
"James" (2nd place scholarship winner). DeKalbLAJ
(18:1/2) 85, p. 59.
"Johnny's Falling Stars" (2nd place scholarship winner).
DeKalbLAJ (18:1/2) 85, p. 59.
"Michael's Dance" (2nd place scholarship winner).
DeKalbLAJ (18:1/2) 85, p. 60.
"Pride" (Scholarship winner). DeKalbLAJ (18:3/4) 85, p.
26.
2136. HICKEY, Dona J.
"Some Catastrophes." CreamCR (10:1) 85, p. 7.
2137. HICKMAN, Leland
"Tiresias" (Selections: 2 poems -- "Annotation for That
Which Follows," "He Who Delights in Signs"). Sulfur
(12) 85, p. 12-16.
2138. HICKMAN, Martha Whitmore
"Meditation of Mary, Mother of God." ChrC (102:34) 6 N
85, p. 988.

185 HILL

2139. HICKS, John V.
"Equines." Waves (13:2/3) Wint 85, p. 90-91.
"My Song" (during Mahler). CanLit (104) Spr 85, p. 94.
"A Night of Endless Rummaging." AntigR (60) Wint 85, p. 29.
"Night Tide (During Scriabin)." AntigR (60) Wint 85, p. 28.
"The Woman in the Web of My Thumb." KanQ (17:1/2) Wint-Spr 85, p. 40.
2140. HIERHOLZER, Bente
"Behind the Masks" (Excerpt, tr. of Marianne Larsen). Mund (15:1/2) 85, p. 91.
"Days Late in March" (tr. of Henrik Nordbrandt). Mund (15:1/2) 85, p. 67.
"Dear Living" (Excerpt, tr. of Marianne Larsen). Mund (15:1/2) 85, p. 93.
"Since Yesterday" (tr. of Henrik Nordbrandt). Mund (15:1/2) 85, p. 67.
2141. HIGGINS, Y.
"My Parents and the Summer Visit." SnapD (8:2) Spr 85, p. 40-41.
2142. HIGH, Maura
"Amboseli National Park: The Evening Game Run." Paint (11:21/12:24) 84-85, p. 29.
2143. HILBERRY, Jane
"Photography in the Nuclear Age." CrossCur (4:3) 84, p. 58-59.
"Relativity." MichQR (24:2) Spr 85, p. 288.
2144. HILDEBIDLE, John
"Dry Winter." CrossCur (5:2) 85, p. 115.
"For Nicholas, at Two." Poetry (145:5) F 85, p. 264-265.
"Leah's Morning Song." Poetry (145:5) F 85, p. 265-266.
"Thoreau: Some Times" (1984 AWP Award-Winning Poem). Tendril (19/20) 85, p. 29-34.
"To Begin With" (for my son). PraS (59:1) Spr 85, p. 68-69.
"Versions of August." PraS (59:1) Spr 85, p. 69-70.
2145. HILDEN, Julie
"John Harvard." HarvardA (119:1) N 85, p. 27.
2146. HILL, Beth Munroe
"A Line from Margaret Atwood." AntigR (62/63) Sum-Aut 85, p. 156.
2147. HILL, Brian Merrikin
"Chansons du Dé à Coudre" (Selections: "Autumn," "Somewhere in the empty house," tr. of Pierre Emmanuel). Verse (1) 84, p. 39.
"Magdalen in the Garden" (tr. of Pierre Emmanuel). Verse (1) 84, p. 38.
2148. HILL, Gerald
"In the City." PraF (6:2) Spr 85, p. 43.
"In the Jazz Lounge." PraF (6:2) Spr 85, p. 41-42.
"In the Lowered Night of Nuns." PraF (6:2) Spr 85, p. 42.
"In the Translucent Past." PraF (6:2) Spr 85, p. 43.
"Labour Day, Unemployed." MalR (72) S 85, p. 114-115.
"The Masseuse." Dandel (12:2) 85, p. 29.
"Metonymy." Dandel (12:2) 85, p. 30.
"The Ornamental Fig" (for Dave McFadden). MalR (72) S 85, p. 116.
"Upper Arrow Lake." MalR (72) S 85, p. 113.
2149. HILL, Jeanne Foster
"The Pearl River." Hudson (38:2) Sum 85, p. 271-275.
2150. HILL, John Meredith
"In Transit." LitR (28:4) Sum 85, p. 568-569.
2151. HILL, Kris
"Last Week in Your Room." Cond (11/12) 85, p. 160.

2152. HILL, Robert
      "Black Wings." <u>Piq</u> (13) 85, p. 13.
2153. HILLARD, Jeffrey
      "The Cartoonist." <u>SmPd</u> (22:1) Wint 85, p. 22.
2154. HILLES, Robert
      "Animal Mind." <u>PoetryCR</u> (7:2) Wint 85-86, p. 25.
      "Fourth Room." <u>PoetryCR</u> (7:2) Wint 85-86, p. 25.
      "God Has Not Sung in Wineries." <u>Waves</u> (13:4) Spr 85, p.
         69.
      "Your Hands Warm the Sun." <u>Waves</u> (13:4) Spr 85, p. 68-69.
2155. HILLMAN, A. J.
      "Chaconne." <u>SouthernR</u> (21:1) Wint 85, p. 135-137.
      "The Nostalgic Ones." <u>SouthernR</u> (21:1) Wint 85, p. 133-
         134.
2156. HILLMAN, Brenda
      "Arroyo." <u>MissouriR</u> (8:3) 85, p. 36-37.
      "Saguaro." <u>Thrpny</u> (5:4, issue 20) Wint 85, p. 8.
2157. HILLMAN, William S.
      "Round Trip." <u>Confr</u> (30/31) N 85, p. 196-197.
2158. HILLRINGHOUSE, Mark
      "In the Pine Barrens." <u>LittleM</u> (14:4) 85, p. 44.
      "June 9, 1982" (for Howard Moss). <u>LittleM</u> (14:4) 85, p.
         45.
2159. HILTON, David
      "Faery Mushrooms 1." <u>PoetL</u> (79:4) Wint 85, p. 222.
      "Faery Mushrooms 2." <u>PoetL</u> (79:4) Wint 85, p. 223.
      "The Neck." <u>PoetL</u> (79:4) Wint 85, p. 220-221.
2160. HIND, Steven
      "A Kind of Divorce." <u>KanQ</u> (17:4) Fall 85, p. 170.
2161. HINDLEY, Norman
      "Fan" (to Tai Babilonia). <u>HawaiiR</u> (17) Spr 85, p. 4-5.
      "Martha." <u>HawaiiR</u> (17) Spr 85, p. 3.
      "The Mature Male." <u>HawaiiR</u> (17) Spr 85, p. 6.
2162. HINES, Debra
      "Adam and Eve on a Raft." <u>QW</u> (20) Spr-Sum 85, p. 97.
      "Courtesty." <u>CutB</u> (23) Fall-Wint 85, p. 62.
      "Instructions from the Beibei, Congqing Sichuan Teachers
         College." <u>MassR</u> (26:4) Wint 85, p. 527-528.
2163. HINKHOUSE, David A.
      "Toilets." <u>KanQ</u> (17:1/2) Wint-Spr 85, p. 92.
2164. HINKLE, Charlie
      "Shadows." <u>Thrpny</u> (5:4, issue 20) Wint 85, p. 23.
2165. HINRICHSEN, Dennis
      "China Sea." <u>Telescope</u> (4:1) Wint 85, p. 20-21.
2166. HINSHELWOOD, Nigel
      "No Bark, Very Little Bite." <u>Gargoyle</u> (27) 85, p. 69.
2167. HIPPOLYTE, Kendel
      "Abstract #1." <u>GreenfR</u> (12:3/4) Wint-Spr 85, p. 174-175.
      "Mèl." <u>GreenfR</u> (12:3/4) Wint-Spr 85, p. 175-176.
      "Poem in a Manger." <u>GreenfR</u> (12:3/4) Wint-Spr 85, p. 172-
         173.
HIRO, Sato
      <u>See</u> SATO, Hiro
2168. HIRSCH, Edward
      "Birds-of-Paradise." <u>NewRep</u> (193:9) 26 Ag 85, p. 36.
      "Curriculum Vitae (1937)." <u>OntR</u> (22) Spr-Sum 85, p. 17-21.
      "The Emaciated Horse" (Chinese painting of the Yüan
         Dynasty). <u>Crazy</u> (29) Fall 85, p. 84-86.
      "Execution." <u>Atlantic</u> (256:6), D 85, p. 70.
      "Fast Break" (In Memory of Dennis Turner, 1946-1984).
         <u>Atlantic</u> (255:6), Je 85, p. 60.
      "In a Polish Home for the Aged" (Chicago, 1983). <u>GrandS</u>
         (5:1) Aut 85, p. 78-79.
      "My Grandfather's Poems." <u>Nat</u> (241:9) 28 S 85, p. 285.
      "My Grandmother's Bed." <u>NewYorker</u> (61:39) 18 N 85, p. 159.
      "The Skokie Theatre." <u>MissouriR</u> (8:3) 85, p. 127.

187 HOFFMAN

2169. HIRSCHFIELD, Robert
"Confession of a Christian Militia Commander -- October
1982." <u>Comm</u> (112:16) 20 S 85, p. 495.
2170. HIRSHFIELD, Jane
"Against Loss." <u>CrossCur</u> (5:2) 85, p. 107.
"How, on a Summer Night." <u>YellowS</u> (14) Spr 85, p. 11.
"In a Net of Blue and Gold." <u>AntR</u> (43:3) Sum 85, p. 337.
"In That World, the Angels Wear Fins." <u>AntR</u> (43:3) Sum
85, p. 336.
"My Maiden Aunt Goes to the Beach Alone." <u>YellowS</u> (17)
Wint 85, p. 10.
2171. HIRSHKOWITZ, Lois
"After Noon." <u>LaurelR</u> (19:2) Sum 85, p. 56-57.
"Angel." <u>EngJ</u> (74:2) F 85, p. 103.
2172. HIRZEL, David
"Awakening." <u>CapeR</u> (20:1) Spr 85, p. 33.
"I Said Yes." <u>StoneC</u> (13:1/2) Fall-Wint 85-86, p. 61.
"Peeping Tom." <u>CapeR</u> (20:1) Spr 85, p. 34.
"A Torso." <u>CapeR</u> (20:1) Spr 85, p. 35.
2173. HIX, Harvey
"Her: A Short Life of Kierkegaard." <u>Amelia</u> (2:2) O 85, p.
32.
"Sunset Sonnet." <u>Wind</u> (15:54) 85, p. 25.
2174. HJARTARSON, Snorri
"Cairn on the Moor" (tr. by Martin Regal). <u>LitR</u> (28:4)
Sum 85, p. 588-589.
"Staves" (tr. by Alan Boucher). <u>Vis</u> (18) 85, p. 20.
2175. HOAGLAND, Tony
"Between a Barn and a River." <u>Telescope</u> (4:1) Wint 85, p.
8.
2176. HOCHMAN, William S.
"Anywhere." <u>PortLES</u> (2:1) Sum 85, p. 53.
2177. HOCQUARD, Emmanuel
"Elegy 3" (tr. by Rosmarie Waldrop). <u>Verse</u> (2) 85, p. 29-
33.
2178. HODGE, Jan D.
"He Responds to His Analyst's Count" (a cardinal ideogram,
after May Swenson). <u>NegC</u> (5:3) Sum 85, p. 40-41.
2179. HODGE, Marion
"Good Afternoon." <u>BelPoJ</u> (36:2) Wint 85-86, p. 19.
2180. HODGINS, Philip
"Hotel Minerva." <u>Shen</u> (36:1) 85-86, p. 98.
2181. HOEFER, David
"Driving." <u>Wind</u> (15:53) 85, p. 16.
"Happy Survival." <u>IndR</u> (8:1) Wint 85, p. 74-75.
2182. HOEFT, Robert D.
"Creatures in a Different Light." <u>CrossCur</u> (5:3) 85, p.
75.
2183. HOEY, Allen
"Children of Paradise." <u>MidAR</u> (5:2) 85, p. 81.
"Fire in the Trees." <u>Hudson</u> (38:3) Aut 85, p. 424-425.
"Fishing the Hudson, Kingston Point, New York." <u>TexasR</u>
(6:1/2) Spr-Sum 85, p. 52-55.
"Icon." <u>TexasR</u> (6:3/4) Fall-Wint 85, p. 43.
"Parts of a Whole." <u>SouthernHR</u> (19:4) Fall 85, p. 312.
"The Simple Truth about Snow." <u>Hudson</u> (38:3) Aut 85, p.
425-426.
"Sunday Rock." <u>Blueline</u> (6:2) Wint-Spr 85, p. 34-35.
"To Open the Eternal Worlds." <u>Hudson</u> (38:3) Aut 85, p.
423-424.
"Toil" (for my father). <u>GeoR</u> (39:1) Spr 85, p. 129-132.
2184. HOFER, Mariann
"Alterable States." <u>HiramPoR</u> (38) Spr-Sum 85, p. 19.
2185. HOFFMAN, D. S.
"Chicken Pox." <u>OP</u> (38/39) Spr 85, p. 207.
"Marmalade." <u>OP</u> (38/39) Spr 85, p. 207.

2186. HOFFMAN, Daniel
    "The City of Satisfactions." <u>Pequod</u> (19/20/21) 85, p. 207-209.
    "A Trip." <u>Pequod</u> (19/20/21) 85, p. 206.
2187. HOFFMAN, N. M.
    "Figure of a Dead King, Sketch #3." <u>WindO</u> (45) Spr 85, p. 5.
2188. HOFFMAN, Ruth Cassel
    "The Closet." <u>PoetryNW</u> (26:3) Aut 85, p. 29.
2189. HOFFMANN, Roald
    "Cosmetic Company Buys Eisenhower College." <u>MichQR</u> (24:2) Spr 85, p. 217-221.
2190. HOFMANN, Michael
    "Don John of Austria." <u>ParisR</u> (27:98) Wint 85, p. 150-151.
    "Giro Account." <u>ParisR</u> (27:98) Wint 85, p. 152.
    "Not Talking." <u>Poetry</u> (146:4) Jl 85, p. 221-223.
    "Old Firm." <u>ParisR</u> (27:98) Wint 85, p. 146.
    "Vortex." <u>ParisR</u> (27:98) Wint 85, p. 147-148.
    "Withdrawn from Circulation." <u>ParisR</u> (27:98) Wint 85, p. 149.
2191. HOFMANN, P.
    "Exploring." <u>AntigR</u> (60) Wint 85, p. 89.
    "Fran." <u>AntigR</u> (60) Wint 85, p. 89.
2192. HOGAN, Linda
    "All Winter." <u>NoDaQ</u> (53:2) Spr 85, p. 121.
    "Evolution in Light and Water." <u>DevQ</u> (19:3) Wint 85, p. 17-18.
    "Gamble." <u>NoDaQ</u> (53:2) Spr 85, p. 119.
    "What Has Happened to These Working Hands?" <u>NoDaQ</u> (53:2) Spr 85, p. 120.
2193. HOGAN, Wayne
    "Into Haiku." <u>Amelia</u> (2:2) O 85, p. 70.
2194. HOGGARD, James
    "Comet" (tr. of Oscar Hahn). <u>NewL</u> (51:4) Sum 85, p. 109.
    "The Flaming Corpse" (tr. of Oscar Hahn). <u>NewL</u> (51:4) Sum 85, p. 109-110.
    "Night in Vienna." <u>NegC</u> (5:4) Fall 85, p. 126.
    "R. Lowell Had." <u>KanQ</u> (17:4) Fall 85, p. 172-173.
    "Split Papayas" (San Miguel de Allende, Mexico). <u>KanQ</u> (17:4) Fall 85, p. 172.
2195. HOGUE, Cynthia
    "The Nameless" (after "The Seal Woman"). <u>Raccoon</u> (17) Mr 85, p. 42.
    "Traces." <u>GreenfR</u> (13:1/2) Fall-Wint 85, p. 161-162.
2196. HOHEISEL, Peter
    "Another Easter for the Poet." <u>CentR</u> (29:2) Spr 85, p. 219-220.
    "Sheltered Currents." <u>KanQ</u> (17:4) Fall 85, p. 187.
2197. HOLAN, Vladimir
    "In the Yard of the Policlinic" (tr. by C. G. Hanzlicek and Dana Habova). <u>AmerPoR</u> (14:4) Jl-Ag 85, p. 36.
    "A Night with Hamlet" (Excerpts, tr. by Clayton Eshleman and Frantisek Galan). <u>Sulfur</u> (12) 85, p. 4-11.
    "A Night with Hamlet" (Excerpts, tr. by Clayton Eshleman and Frantisek Galan). <u>Sulfur</u> (13) 85, p. 129-134.
    "A Night with Hamlet" (Excerpts, tr. by Clayton Eshleman and Frantisek Galan). <u>Sulfur</u> (14) 85, p. 74-80.
    "Snow" (tr. by C. G. Hanzlicek and Dana Habova). <u>AmerPoR</u> (14:4) Jl-Ag 85, p. 36.
2198. HOLCOMBE, Emily G.
    "Not Ghosts." <u>LitR</u> (29:1) Fall 85, p. 66.
    "Tacking." <u>LitR</u> (29:1) Fall 85, p. 67.
2199. HOLDEN, Jonathan
    "Facing West." <u>MissouriR</u> (8:2) 85, p. 43.
    "Farm, Seen from Highway 24." <u>KanQ</u> (17:4) Fall 85, p. 40.
    "Landscapes" (near Moab, Utah). <u>MissouriR</u> (8:2) 85, p. 42.

"The Mercator Projection." <u>CrossCur</u> (5:2) 85, p. 93.
"Rereading Old Love Letters." <u>Poetry</u> (146:3) Je 85, p. 145-146.
"River Time." <u>Iowa</u> (15:3) Fall 85, p. 116-121.
"The Scientist." <u>CrossCur</u> (5:3) 85, p. 9.
"Sex without Love" (For X.). <u>Poetry</u> (146:3) Je 85, p. 146-147.
"Shoptalk." <u>Poetry</u> (146:3) Je 85, p. 144-145.
"Summer Horses." <u>CrossCur</u> (5:3) 85, p. 10.
"Tinkering." <u>Iowa</u> (15:3) Fall 85, p. 122.
"Wading." <u>Poetry</u> (146:3) Je 85, p. 147-148.
"Water Poem." <u>KanQ</u> (17:4) Fall 85, p. 39.
2200. HOLDSTOCK, P. J.
"Transpositions." <u>Rampike</u> (4:2/3) 85-86, p. 81.
2201. HOLINGER, Richard
"Communion." <u>WindO</u> (46) Fall 85, p. 38.
"June 21st." <u>NoDaQ</u> (53:4) Fall 85, p. 203-204.
"Notebook Entry on the Propagation of Sound." <u>PoetryR</u> (2:2) Ap 85, p. 83.
2202. HOLLAHAN, Eugene
"The Crossroads of the Thirteen Widows." <u>Verse</u> (3) 85, p. 10.
2203. HOLLANDER, John
"After a Sad Talk." <u>NewRep</u> (193:12/13) 16-23 S 85, p. 44.
"After Blossoming." <u>Verse</u> (3) 85, p. 16.
"Effet de Neige" (Claude Monet, <u>La Route de la Ferme St-Siméon</u>, Honfleur, about 1867). <u>GrandS</u> (4:3) Spr 85, p. 34-36.
"Hush!" <u>PartR</u> (52:4) 85, p. 421-422.
"Marks and Noises." <u>PartR</u> (52:4) 85, p. 421.
2204. HOLLINGS, Ken
"Lenin's Tomb." <u>Rampike</u> (4:2/3) 85-86, p. 73.
2205. HOLLIS, Jocelyn
"Hercules Builds Its New Corporate Headquarters on King Street, Wilmington, Delaware, 1981-82." <u>Sam</u> (42:3, 167th release) 85, p. 23.
"Like Fallen Angels." <u>Sam</u> (42:3, 167th release) 85, p. 24.
2206. HOLLO, Anselm
"Late Night Dream Movies" (for Chris Toll). <u>Open24</u> (4) 85, p. 61-62.
2207. HOLLOWAY, Geoffrey
"Mainline." <u>Bogg</u> (54) 85, p. 15.
"Railbar." <u>Bogg</u> (54) 85, p. 15.
2208. HOLLOWAY, Marcella M., CSJ
"The Risk." <u>ChrC</u> (102:5) 6-13 F 85, p. 118.
2209. HOLLOWAY, Mike
"Dr. Suess Grows Up in NY." <u>PortLES</u> (2:1) Sum 85, p. 35.
2210. HOLMAN, Amy
"Tea with Nora." <u>WoosterR</u> (3) Spr 85, p. 85-86.
2211. HOLMES, Elizabeth
"Something Out of a Fairy Tale." <u>CarolQ</u> (37:3) Spr 85, p. 80.
2212. HOLMES, John Clelton
"Old Pilate in His Rose Garden." <u>TexasR</u> (6:1/2) Spr-Sum 85, p. 36.
2213. HOLMES, Nancy
"Into the Halo." <u>Germ</u> (9:1) Spr-Sum 85, p. 36.
2214. HOLSTEIN, Michael
"Brass Rubbing." <u>Vis</u> (19) 85, p. 34.
"Daily Exercises." <u>RiverS</u> (17) 85, p. 21.
"Farm Wife's Almanac." <u>NoDaQ</u> (53:4) Fall 85, p. 205-206.
"Giant Kauri." <u>CrossCur</u> (4:4/5:1) 85, p. 141.
"Haka" (after the Mauri war chant). <u>BelPoJ</u> (35:4) Sum 85, p. 6-7.
"Revising Poems." <u>NegC</u> (5:3) Sum 85, p. 141.
"Sailing at the Corner of Elizabeth and John." <u>RiverS</u>

(17) 85, p. 20.
2215. HOLT, Rochelle Lynn
"Another Island." <u>Vis</u> (18) 85, p. 23.
2216. HOLT-FORTIN, Cher
"Morning in January." <u>Blueline</u> (6:2) Wint-Spr 85, p. 21.
2217. HOLTZMAN, Clark
"The Wreck of the Ice Cream Truck" (For A.W.). <u>NegC</u> (5:3)
Sum 85, p. 140.
2218. HOLUB, Miroslav
"The End of the World" (tr. by Ewald Osers). <u>Verse</u> (2)
85, p. 16.
"The Fly" (tr. by George Theiner). <u>TriQ</u> (63) Spr-Sum 85,
p. 94-95.
"Skeletons" (tr. by David Young and the author). <u>Ploughs</u>
(11:4) 85, p. 85-86.
"Spacetime" (tr. by David Young and the author). <u>Ploughs</u>
(11:4) 85, p. 87.
"Spice" (tr. by Ewald Osers). <u>Verse</u> (2) 85, p. 16.
"Voices in the Landscape" (tr. by Ewald Osers). <u>Verse</u> (2)
85, p. 15.
2219. HOMER, Art
"Hung-Over with Snow Clouds." <u>MidwQ</u> (26:4) Sum 85, p. 456.
"Incentives for Night Work." <u>Tendril</u> (19/20) 85, p. 170.
"Roads for High Places." <u>MidwQ</u> (26:4) Sum 85, p. 457.
2220. HOMER, Janet
"Driving toward Laramie Peak." <u>Amelia</u> (2:2) O 85, p. 74.
"I see it before I see it." <u>Amelia</u> (2:2) O 85, p. 74.
2221. HONGO, Garrett Kaoru
"96 Tears." <u>MinnR</u> (N.S. 24) Spr 85, p. 5-8.
"Morro Rock" (for M.J.). <u>Field</u> (32) Spr 85, p. 20-23.
2222. HOOD, Michael
"Bleeding Heart Flowers" (Chilmark). <u>LitR</u> (28:4) Sum 85,
p. 581.
"Chockalog Graveyard (Uxbridge)." <u>RagMag</u> (4:1) Spr 85, p.
42-43.
"Riverside Park (Agawaw)." <u>RagMag</u> (4:1) Spr 85, p. 41.
"Song Painting (Southwick)." <u>RagMag</u> (4:1) Spr 85, p. 40.
"Swans and Hounds" (Stoneham). <u>CapeR</u> (20:1) Spr 85, p. 15.
"Under Thin Arms (Yarmouth)." <u>RagMag</u> (4:1) Spr 85, p. 40.
2223. HOOGESTRAAT, Jane
"Bridges." <u>Tendril</u> (19/20) 85, p. 172-173.
"Crocuses." <u>KanQ</u> (17:4) Fall 85, p. 254.
"The Death of the Khan." <u>Tendril</u> (19/20) 85, p. 171.
"The Flowers from Someone Else's Funeral." <u>Poem</u> (53) Mr
85, p. 56.
"One Degree above Zero." <u>KanQ</u> (17:4) Fall 85, p. 261.
"Toward the Calm." <u>Poem</u> (53) Mr 85, p. 55.
2224. HOOPER, Patricia
"Glass." <u>AmerPoR</u> (14:6) N-D 85, p. 27.
"Reunion." <u>AmerS</u> (54:4) Aut 85, p. 484.
"Waking in an Upstairs Room near Elm Trees." <u>SouthernPR</u>
(25:1) Spr 85, p. 46.
2225. HOOVER, Paul
"Apology for the Senses." <u>MissR</u> (40/41) Wint 85, p. 126-
127.
"Being Mayakovsky." <u>OP</u> (40) Fall-Wint 85, p. 16-17.
"Long History of the Short Poem." <u>MissR</u> (40/41) Wint 85,
p. 124-125.
"Maudlin Confession." <u>OP</u> (40) Fall-Wint 85, p. 18-19.
"Written on Songs by Lawes." <u>OP</u> (40) Fall-Wint 85, p. 15.
2226. HOPES, David (<u>See also</u> HOPES, David Brendan)
"Who Runs the Winter Nights." <u>WindO</u> (46) Fall 85, p. 42.
2227. HOPES, David Brendan (<u>See also</u> HOPES, David)
"The Round of Cool Lovers." <u>SouthernPR</u> (25:1) Spr 85, p.
55-56.

2228. HOPKINS, Michael F.
       "Thelonious Monk" (for Jass, for this century, a high
       priest & an ultimate sphere of influence). MoodySI
       (15) Spr 85, p. 9.
2229. HOPKINSON, Thomas
       "Boxcie." JamesWR (3:1) Fall 85, p. 8-9.
       "Only the Need of a Want of a Cry." JamesWR (2:3) Spr-Sum
       85, p. 19.
2230. HOPPENTHALER, John
       "Poem" ("In this uncertain exile"). NewL (51:3) Spr 85,
       p. 112.
2231. HORNE, J. Phillip
       "Pastoral Poem." CarolQ (37:3) Spr 85, p. 26-27.
2232. HORNE, Lewis
       "The Churchhouse." TexasR (6:1/2) Spr-Sum 85, p. 58-59.
       "Conundrums of Color." Poetry (146:2) My 85, p. 93.
       "The Cry." CumbPR (5:1) Fall 85, p. 69.
       "Homage to G. G." Poetry (146:2) My 85, p. 95-96.
       "Perceiving a Season." CumbPR (5:1) Fall 85, p. 68.
       "Silent Things." Poetry (146:2) My 85, p. 94.
       "While Reading a Victorian Novel, or, Somebody Moved my
       Mango." Waves (14:1/2) Fall 85, p. 88-90.
2233. HORNIG, Doug
       "Like a Rolling Boulder." Bogg (53) 85, p. 45.
2234. HORNING, Ron
       "Around Town" (tr. of Jacques Rigaut). Ploughs (11:4) 85,
       p. 122.
2235. HORNOSTY, Cornelia C.
       "Notes from an Original Sinner" (in honour of Rilke).
       PoetryCR (7:1) Aut 85, p. 51.
2236. HORNSEY, Richard
       "What to Say to a Dying Man." CanLit (104) Spr 85, p. 64.
2237. HOROVITZ, Frances
       "Cancer Ward." Stand (26:1) Wint 84-85, p. 23.
       "Evening." Stand (26:1) Wint 84-85, p. 23.
       "Evening" (final form). Stand (26:2) Spr 85, p. 27.
2238. HOROWITZ, Mikhail
       "Love Song." YellowS (14) Spr 85, p. 18.
2239. HORTON, Barbara
       "I Dreamt of Flowers." Mund (15:1/2) 85, p. 203.
       "I Want to Describe Sunlight." SpoonRQ (10:4) Fall 85, p.
       46.
       "Naming Things." KanQ (17:4) Fall 85, p. 95.
       "Too Steady for Fear." SpoonRQ (10:4) Fall 85, p. 47.
2240. HORTON, Lisa
       "Avalon, 1962." CrossCur (4:1) 84, p. 107.
       "Covenant." WebR (10:1) Spr 85, p. 71.
       "Here in the Dark." IndR (8:3) Fall 85, p. 14-15.
2241. HORVATH, Elemér
       "A Chest with Painted Tulips" (tr. by Nicholas Kolumban).
       NewL (51:4) Sum 85, p. 34.
       "Execution" (tr. by Nicholas Kolumban). NewL (51:4) Sum
       85, p. 35.
       "The First Time" (tr. by Nicholas Kolumban). HawaiiR (17)
       Spr 85, p. 94.
       "It's Tangled But Accurate" (tr. by Nicholas Kolumban).
       NewL (51:4) Sum 85, p. 34-35.
2242. HORVATH, J.
       "For the Gerund Man" (1895-1962). DeKalbLAJ (18:1/2) 85,
       p. 73.
       "Gossip Fence." Poem (54) N 85, p. 40.
       "Lazarus Novotny Returns a Favor." Poem (54) N 85, p. 39.
2243. HOSKIN, William D.
       "I Could Not Find Him in That Lonely Place." HiramPoR
       (38) Spr-Sum 85, p. 21.
       "You Are Gone and I." HiramPoR (38) Spr-Sum 85, p. 20.

2244. HOUCHIN, Ron
      "Song of My Cells." Wind (15:54) 85, p. 26.
2245. HOUGHTON, Tim
      "Ghost Story." StoneC (13:1/2) Fall-Wint 85-86, p. 32.
      "Hide-and-Go-Seek." Amelia (2:1) Ap 85, p. 63.
2246. HOUSE, Tom
      "How It All Just Gets So Similar." Open24 (4) 85, p. 41.
      "Marlboro Mama." Bogg (54) 85, p. 38.
      "Mr. Chilled Perception Shivers." Open24 (4) 85, p. 19.
      "Story of the Full Moon." Vis (17) 85, p. 26.
      "Tequila's Gambit." Open24 (4) 85, p. 9.
2247. HOUSTON, Peyton
      "Impossibility of the Bee." OP (38/39) Spr 85, p. 209.
      "Looking at Tulips." ParisR (27:95) Spr 85, p. 77.
      "Question and Answer Session between Old Parties."
          Conjunc (8) 85, p. 203.
      "The Rower." ParisR (27:95) Spr 85, p. 78.
      "Sometimes in a House There Is No One." ParisR (27:95)
          Spr 85, p. 79-80.
HOUTEN, Lois van
      See Van HOUTEN, Lois
2248. HOUTS, Eric
      "Great Horned Owl." NewL (52:1) Fall 85, p. 38.
HOVANESSIAN, Diana der
      See Der HOVANESSIAN, Diana
2249. HOWARD, Ben
      "Ante." Geor (39:2) Sum 85, p. 352.
      "Fair Exchange." Poetry (146:5) Ag 85, p. 257-258.
      "Last Things." MidwQ (26:4) Sum 85, p. 458.
      "Views." Poetry (146:5) Ag 85, p. 257.
2250. HOWARD, Eugene
      "Looking through a Blind Spot." AmerPoR (14:3) My-Je 85,
          p. 43.
2251. HOWARD, Frances Minturn
      "Contrasts." CrossCur (4:2) 84, p. 53.
2252. HOWARD, Jim
      "Bread." NewL (51:3) Spr 85, p. 48.
2253. HOWARD, Lynne Cawood
      "I Write on My Lap." PassN (6:1) Fall-Wint 85, p. 16.
2254. HOWE, Fanny
      "The Bluff." Temblor (1) 85, p. 57-59.
      "Santa Monica." Temblor (1) 85, p. 55-56.
2255. HOWE, Marie
      "After the Flood" (For F.W.). Ploughs (11:1) 85, p. 123.
      "From Nowhere." Ploughs (11:1) 85, p. 126-127.
      "The Meadow." Ploughs (11:1) 85, p. 124-125.
      "Part of Eve's Discussion." Ploughs (11:1) 85, p. 122.
      "Retribution." Agni (22) 85, p. 103-104.
      "A Thin Smattering of Applause." AmerPoR (14:5) S-O 85,
          p. 32.
2256. HOWELL, Abigail
      "Again." WoosterR (4) Fall 85, p. 74-75.
2257. HOWELL, Christopher
      "Machado." MinnR (N.S. 24) Spr 85, p. 40.
      "Master Ronald Westman: Excluded from the Tea." HolCrit
          (22:3) Je 85, p. 16.
2258. HOWELL, John
      "Denizens." PraS (59:3) Fall 85, p. 80-81.
      "Last Break." PraS (59:3) Fall 85, p. 81.
      "Sugar Snap." PraS (59:3) Fall 85, p. 82.
2259. HOWELL, Kath
      "Eden in Apple Country." Comm (112:8) 19 Ap 85, p. 246.
2260. HOWELL, Sue
      "To a Gay Student." EngJ (74:3) Mr 85, p. 59.
2261. HOWES, Barbara
      "Being Me." Hudson (38:1) Spr 85, p. 101.

2262. HOWSARE, Katrine
    "This House." <u>AmerPoR</u> (14:2) Mr-Ap 85, p. 21.
2263. HOYT, Victoria
    "The Animal." <u>RiverS</u> (18) 85, p. 100-101.
    "Shade." <u>RiverS</u> (18) 85, p. 103.
    "Thievery." <u>RiverS</u> (18) 85, p. 102.
2264. HRYCIUK, Marshall
    "Mes Musiciennes" (un tableau pour Pablo). <u>Rampike</u>
       (4:2/3) 85-86, p. 76.
2265. HSIEH, Ling-Yün
    "From the Southern to the Northern Peak by Way of the Lake:
       Stopping to View the Scenery" (tr. by Bruce M. Wilson
       and Zhang Ting-chen). <u>NewL</u> (51:4) Sum 85, p. 143.
    "Scaling the Height of Stone Gate Mountain" (tr. by Bruce
       M. Wilson and Zhang Ting-chen). <u>NewL</u> (51:4) Sum 85, p.
       141.
    "A Solitary Islet, Alone in the Stream" (tr. by Bruce M.
       Wilson and Zhang·Ting-chen). <u>NewL</u> (51:4) Sum 85, p.
       142.
    "Spending the Night on the Cliff at Stone Gate Mountain"
       (tr. by Bruce M. Wilson and Zhang Ting-chen). <u>NewL</u>
       (51:4) Sum 85, p. 142.
2266. HSIN, Ch'i-chi
    "Late Spring" (tr. by Julie Landau). <u>MSS</u> (4:3) Spr 85, p.
       26.
2267. HSU, Wei
    "Painting Bamboo" (tr. by Jim Cryer). <u>CarolQ</u> (37:3) Spr
       85, p. 77.
    "Peach Leaf Ferry" (tr. by Jim Cryer). <u>CarolQ</u> (37:3) Spr
       85, p. 76.
    "Wind among Bamboos" (tr. by Graeme Wilson). <u>WestHR</u>
       (39:1) Spr 85, p. 63.
HU, Li Jia
    <u>See</u> LI, Jia Hu
HUA, Li Min
    <u>See</u> LI, Min Hua
2268. HUBBARD, Ann E.
    "Procrastinations." <u>AntigR</u> (62/63) Sum-Aut 85, p. 222.
2269. HUCKSTEP, Kecia
    "Guest Speaker." <u>EngJ</u> (74:3) Mr 85, p. 98.
2270. HUDDLE, David
    "Stopping by Home." <u>VirQ</u> (61:1) Wint 85, p. 63-68.
2271. HUDGINS, Andrew
    "Around the Campfire." <u>SouthernR</u> (21:2) Spr 85, p. 441-
       442.
    "Communion in the Asylum." <u>NewEngR</u> (8:2) Wint 85, p. 255.
    "Compost: An Ode." <u>Poetry</u> (147:1) O 85, p. 2-3.
    "Glyphs." <u>Crazy</u> (26) Spr 84, p. 34-35.
    "In the Night Garden." <u>Crazy</u> (29) Fall 85, p. 58-60.
    "The Last Time I Saw General Lee: An Idyll." <u>SouthernR</u>
       (21:2) Spr 85, p. 445-446.
    "Listen! The Flies." <u>SouthernR</u> (21:2) Spr 85, p. 443-445.
    "Memories of Lookout Prison: Sidney Lanier, 1864." <u>ChiR</u>
       (35:1) Aut 85, p. 73.
    "On the Killing Floor." <u>SouthernR</u> (21:2) Spr 85, p. 442-
       443.
    "Praying, Drunk." <u>NewEngR</u> (8:2) Wint 85, p. 253-254.
    "Rebuilding a Bird." <u>Crazy</u> (29) Fall 85, p. 56-57.
    "Saints and Strangers" (5 selections). <u>MissouriR</u> (8:3)
       85, p. 145-151.
    "Sentimental Dangers." <u>Poetry</u> (147:1) O 85, p. 1-2.
    "The Summer of the Drought: Macon, Georgia, 1874."
       <u>SouthernR</u> (21:2) Spr 85, p. 447.
    "A Waltz" (for Kevin McIlvoy). <u>ChiR</u> (35:1) Aut 85, p. 74-
       75.
    "What Moves Us." <u>ChiR</u> (35:2) Wint 85, p. 52-53.

2272. HUDSPITH, Vicki
      "From Lower Broadway." <u>RiverS</u> (17) 85, p. 54.
2273. HUFF, Robert
      "Auld Lang Syne." <u>Poetry</u> (147:3) D 85, p. 140-141.
2274. HUFF, Steven
      "Moving." <u>MSS</u> (4:3) Spr 85, p. 152.
      "Some Lifelong Doubts." <u>MSS</u> (4:3) Spr 85, p. 154.
      "Winter Voices, Music in Spring." <u>MSS</u> (4:3) Spr 85, p.
      156.
2275. HUFFSTICKLER, Albert
      "Kinfolk." <u>Sam</u> (42:4, 168th release) 85, p. 44.
      "The Passion." <u>Open24</u> (4) 85, p. 6.
      "Starlight." <u>Pig</u> (13) 85, p. 28.
2276. HUGHES, Anthony
      "Green and Pleasant." <u>Stand</u> (26:2) Spr 85, p. 23.
2277. HUGHES, Carolyn J. Fairweather
      "Communication." <u>Wind</u> (15:55) 85, p. 46.
2278. HUGHES, Glenn
      "The Disappointed Woman." <u>PoetryE</u> (18) Fall 85, p. 42.
      "Lament." <u>PoetryE</u> (18) Fall 85, p. 43.
2279. HUGHES, Henry John
      "Walking Henry Home." <u>Wind</u> (15:53) 85, p. 47.
2280. HUGHES, Mary Gray
      "Some Days in San Francisco." <u>CrossCur</u> (4:1) 84, p. 35.
      "Two Strings." <u>TriQ</u> (64) Fall 85, p. 94-97.
2281. HUGHES, Ora Wayne
      "Don't Feed Flynn Has Been" (for Harold). <u>AntigR</u> (62/63)
      Sum-Aut 85, p. 237.
      "Not a Watermelon Day." <u>AntigR</u> (62/63) Sum-Aut 85, p. 236.
      "Swamp Sojourn." <u>AntigR</u> (62/63) Sum-Aut 85, p. 238.
2282. HUGHES, Sophie
      "Credo." <u>Poem</u> (54) N 85, p. 44-45.
      "X." <u>Poem</u> (54) N 85, p. 46.
2283. HUGO, Richard
      "Montesano Unvisited." <u>TriQ</u> (63) Spr-Sum 85, p. 135.
2284. HUIDOBRO, Vicente
      "Express" (tr. by David Guss). <u>Pequod</u> (19/20/21) 85, p.
      210-211.
2285. HULL, Lynda (<u>See also</u> HULL, Lynda K.)
      "Jackson Hotel." <u>NewYorker</u> (61:6) 1 Ap 85, p. 44.
2286. HULL, Lynda K. (<u>See also</u> HULL, Lynda)
      "Tide of Voices." <u>Tendril</u> (19/20) 85, p. 174-175.
2287. HULSE, Michael
      "Correspondence Course." <u>AntigR</u> (61) Spr 85, p. 52.
      "Fear of Flying." <u>AntigR</u> (61) Spr 85, p. 53.
      "Kiki Zanzibar" (for the girls of the Crazy Horse Saloon,
      Paris). <u>AntigR</u> (61) Spr 85, p. 50-51.
      "The Kiss." <u>AntigR</u> (61) Spr 85, p. 52.
      "Nine Points of the Nation." <u>Waves</u> (14:1/2) Fall 85, p.
      76-77.
      "Table Talk." <u>PoetryCR</u> (7:1) Aut 85, p. 13.
2288. HUMES, Harry
      "At the Shad Festival." <u>Raccoon</u> (17) Mr 85, p. 9.
      "Blindsight." <u>PoetryNW</u> (26:3) Aut 85, p. 44.
      "Dead Bat." <u>WestB</u> (17) 85, p. 60.
      "Evening in the Small Park." <u>Salm</u> (66) Wint-Spr 85, p.
      137.
      "Hitting the Vulture." <u>CumbPR</u> (5:1) Fall 85, p. 71-74.
      "Hunting Pheasants in Lehigh County." <u>CutB</u> (24) Spr-Sum
      85, p. 44.
      "The Long Habit of Fire." <u>Salm</u> (66) Wint-Spr 85, p. 138.
      "Sorrow near the Old House." <u>WestB</u> (17) 85, p. 61.
      "Winter Solstice." <u>CumbPR</u> (5:1) Fall 85, p. 70.
2289. HUMMER, T. R.
      "An Abandoned Farm in the West." <u>WestHR</u> (39:1) Spr 85, p.
      47-48.

"Genealogy." <u>Harp</u> (271:1622) Jl 85, p. 26.
"The Immoralities: Drunk All Afternoon." <u>GeoR</u> (39:1) Spr
    85, p. 35-36.
"Legal Limit" (an adulterers' story). <u>Hudson</u> (38:2) Sum
    85, p. 268-270.
"Northeast: A Bend in the River." <u>Crazy</u> (26) Spr 84, p.
    33.
"Sister of Mercy Charity Ward, Lights Out." <u>Crazy</u> (26)
    Spr 84, p. 32.
"The Underworld" (Jefferson Island, Louisiana). <u>Hudson</u>
    (38:2) Sum 85, p. 265-267.
2290. HUMPHRIES, Jefferson
"Desire" (In memoriam: Tennessee Williams). <u>NegC</u> (5:4)
    Fall 85, p. 116-118.
2291. HUNT, Tim
"Stories." <u>SouthernPR</u> (26, i.e. 25:2) Fall 85, p. 30.
2292. HUNTER, Bruce
"An Honest Declaration of Love in the Latter Part of the
    20th Century." <u>Waves</u> (13:4) Spr 85, p. 70.
"January, 1966 Snowshoeing into Paradise Valley."
    <u>PoetryCR</u> (6:3) Spr 85, p. 25.
2293. HUNTER, Donnell
"Crosspollination." <u>CutB</u> (24) Spr-Sum 85, p. 31.
"Turkeys." <u>CutB</u> (23) Fall-Wint 85, p. 44-45.
2294. HURD, Michael R.
"On Visiting Jane Austen's Tomb." <u>KanQ</u> (17:4) Fall 85, p.
    101.
"Watering Hole." <u>KanQ</u> (17:4) Fall 85, p. 102.
2295. HURLEY, Tom
"The Subway Collector." <u>CreamCR</u> (10:1) 85, p. 58-59.
2296. HUSE, Russell
"Admonition." <u>CrossCur</u> (4:1) 84, p. 94-95.
2297. HUSS, David
"Express" (tr. of Vicente Huidobro). <u>Pequod</u> (19/20/21)
    85, p. 210-211.
2298. HUSS, Steven W.
"Frozen Spider." <u>WindO</u> (45) Spr 85, p. 7.
"Gladiators." <u>WindO</u> (45) Spr 85, p. 7.
"The Harvest." <u>GreenfR</u> (13:1/2) Fall-Wint 85, p. 160.
"The Political Influence of Mullet." <u>WebR</u> (10:2) Fall 85,
    p. 77.
"Timberton." <u>LaurelR</u> (19:2) Sum 85, p. 65.
2299. HUSTED, Bette
"Harry." <u>EngJ</u> (74:6) O 85, p. 46.
2300. HUTCHESON, M. R.
"Three Months After." <u>MissR</u> (13:3, issue 39) Spr 85, p.
    65.
2301. HUTCHINGS, Pat (<u>See also</u> HUTCHINS, Pat)
"Boxes: For a Cat Once Trapped in One." <u>SouthernHR</u> (19:2)
    Spr 85, p. 116.
"A Christmas Elsewhere." <u>SouthernHR</u> (19:4) Fall 85, p.
    334-335.
"Meditation on Adulthood." <u>CrabCR</u> (3:1) Fall-Wint 85, p.
    17.
"Sailing after Einstein." <u>Prima</u> (9) 85, p. 90.
"Sunday Dinner at the Mosley's." <u>BlueBldgs</u> (9) [85?], p.
    49.
"Tadpoles." <u>ClockR</u> (2:2) 85, p. 15.
2302. HUTCHINS, Pat (<u>See also</u> HUTCHINGS, Pat)
"April in Iowa City." <u>Wind</u> (15:53) 85, p. 17.
"A Short Exchange." <u>Wind</u> (15:53) 85, p. 17-18.
2303. HUTCHISON, Joseph
"Elemental Prayer in a Black Hour." <u>MissR</u> (40/41) Wint
    85, p. 131.
"The One-Armed Boy." <u>CrossCur</u> (4:3) 84, p. 133.
"Saint Vander Meer and the Dragon." <u>DenQ</u> (20:2) Fall 85,

p. 30-31.
"Vander Meer Crying Fowl." <u>DenQ</u> (20:2) Fall 85, p. 29.
"Vander Meer Holding On." <u>Tendril</u> (19/20) 85, p. 176.
2304. HUTERA, Donald
"Something's Burning." <u>JamesWR</u> (2:2) Wint 85, p. 10.
2305. HUWE, Dorothy
"Kailua Morning." <u>Amelia</u> (2:1) Ap 85, p. 32.
2306. HYDE, Lewis
"The Goldfish in the Charles River." <u>Thrpny</u> (6:1, issue
    21) Spr 85, p. 4.
"Three Black Kids Break & Wave, New York, 1984." <u>Thrpny</u>
    (5:4, issue 20) Wint 85, p. 27.
2307. HYETT, Barbara Helfgott
"Love Poem for My Husband." <u>Nat</u> (241:9) 28 S 85, p. 285.
2308. HYLAND, Gary
"Cell 43" (WQ Editors' Second Prize Winner -- Poetry).
    <u>CrossC</u> (7:1) 85, p. 19.
2309. HYMAN, Gabby
"Coming to Grips with Capitalism on a 4-H Afternoon."
    <u>PoetryNW</u> (26:3) Aut 85, p. 31.
2310. IACOBELLI, Luciano
"Dancing with the Young." <u>PoetryCR</u> (7:1) Aut 85, p. 51.
2311. IBAÑEZ, Soveig
"Sonetos a Sor Juana Inés de la Cruz." <u>LetFem</u> (11:1/2)
    Prim-Otoño 85, p. 99-100.
IBARRA, Beatriz Santiago
    <u>See</u> SANTIAGO-IBARRA, Beatriz
2312. IDLEMAN, Paul
"The Relationships Between." <u>BlueBldgs</u> (9) [85?], p. 63.
2313. IGNATOW, David
"Graves" (tr. of Bohdan Boychuk, w. the author). <u>GrandS</u>
    (4:3) Spr 85, p. 130.
"In Memoriam: For Sam." <u>NewL</u> (51:3) Spr 85, p. 44.
"In the Dawn." <u>Confr</u> (30/31) N 85, p. 77.
"Look into the Faces of Dead Poets" (tr. of Bohdan Boychuk,
    w. the author). <u>GrandS</u> (4:3) Spr 85, p. 131.
"Once upon a Time." <u>Confr</u> (30/31) N 85, p. 77.
"Scenario for a Movie." <u>Confr</u> (30/31) N 85, p. 78.
"Stone Women" (tr. of Bohdan Boychuk, w. the author).
    <u>GrandS</u> (4:3) Spr 85, p. 130.
2314. IGNATOW, Yaedi
"The Ashram." <u>Confr</u> (30/31) N 85, p. 144.
"Instead of Suicide." <u>PoetryR</u> (5) S 85, p. 48.
"Matching You to the Garden." <u>PoetryR</u> (5) S 85, p. 47-48.
2315. ILLAS, Juan Jorge
"Mi Nombre al Fin, Mi Nombre!" <u>LindLM</u> (4:2) Ap-Je 85, p.
    13.
2316. ILLYES, Gyula
"Grip" (tr. by Bruce Berlind). <u>NewL</u> (51:4) Sum 85, p. 38.
"The Salvation of the Damned" (tr. by Bruce Berlind).
    <u>NewL</u> (51:4) Sum 85, p. 37.
"World Collapse" (tr. by Bruce Berlind). <u>NewL</u> (51:4) Sum
    85, p. 38.
2317. INADA, Lawson Fusao
"It Takes an Aardvark." <u>OP</u> (38/39) Spr 85, p. 213-214.
2318. INCE, Ozdemir
"Ban" (tr. by Talat Sait Halman). <u>GreenfR</u> (13:1/2) Fall-
    Wint 85, p. 94.
"Bit by Bit" (tr. by Talat Sait Halman). <u>GreenfR</u> (13:1/2)
    Fall-Wint 85, p. 95.
"Body Language" (tr. by Talat Sait Halman). <u>GreenfR</u>
    (13:1/2) Fall-Wint 85, p. 94.
"A Different Silence" (tr. by Talat Sait Halman). <u>GreenfR</u>
    (13:1/2) Fall-Wint 85, p. 93.
"In Praise of My Father" (tr. by Talat Sait Halman).
    <u>GreenfR</u> (13:1/2) Fall-Wint 85, p. 92.

"Poet's Nonalignment" (tr. by Talat Sait Halman). GreenfR
   (13:1/2) Fall-Wint 85, p. 93.
INES DE LA CRUZ, Juana, Sor
   See CRUZ, Juana Inés de la, Sor
2319. INEZ, Colette
   "Cecilia at Odds in the North." CrossCur (5:2) 85, p. 117-
      118.
   "Hearing New Year's Eve." MassR (26:4) Wint 85, p. 501.
   "Men and Women in the Xingu Forest." PoetryNW (26:2) Sum
      85, p. 19.
   "Old Woman out of Iowa." Raccoon (17) Mr 85, p. 10.
   "The Orphans of Tangshan." CrossCur (5:2) 85, p. 119-120.
   "What Are the Days." PoetryNW (26:2) Sum 85, p. 20.
   "Word Circuits, Solitary." PoetryR (2:2) Ap 85, p. 93-94.
2320. INMAN, Sue Lile
   "Fall without Pattern." SoCaR (17:2) Spr 85, p. 64-65.
   "Something to Look For." SoCaR (17:2) Spr 85, p. 64.
2321. INMAN, Will
   "Being Sanitary." SecC (12:1) 84, p. 9-10.
   "The Jogger." WindO (46) Fall 85, p. 12-14.
2322. IOANNOU, Susan
   "A Woman Warped by Love." WestCR (20:2) O 85, p. 39.
2323. IODICE, Ruth G.
   "Aquarian" (For H.W.). NegC (5:3) Sum 85, p. 119.
2324. IRBY, Kenneth
   "Exercitatio / Praecipere." Conjunc (7) 85, p. 61.
   "A Set." Temblor (1) 85, p. 4-12.
   "Sophrosyne Spring Muse Overhang, Memorial Day" (Basil
      Bunting in memoriam). Conjunc (8) 85, p. 158.
2325. IRIE, Kevin
   "Crayfish." PoetryCR (6:3) Spr 85, p. 14.
   "In Praise of Damselflies." PoetryCR (6:3) Spr 85, p. 14.
   "The River." Waves (13:2/3) Wint 85, p. 94-95.
   "Tubifex Worms." CanLit (104) Spr 85, p. 51.
2326. IRION, Mary Jean
   "Pacem in Terris, Warick, New York." ChrC (102:34) 6 N
      85, p. 996.
2327. IRWIN, Kit
   "The Pinboys." Tendril (19/20) 85, p. 177.
2328. ISHII, Roger
   "A bunch of flowers." Amelia (2:1) Ap 85, p. 73.
   "How quick the chill night." Amelia (2:1) Ap 85, p. 73.
   "I take your hand." Amelia (2:1) Ap 85, p. 73.
   "She goes off." Amelia (2:1) Ap 85, p. 73.
   "Sipping from my cup." Amelia (2:1) Ap 85, p. 73.
2329. ISHIKAWA, Itsuko
   "Hill" (tr. by Keiko Matsui Gibson). NewL (51:4) Sum 85,
      p. 146.
   "Where" (tr. by Keiko Matsui Gibson). NewL (51:4) Sum 85,
      p. 145.
2330. ISOM, Joan Shaddox
   "The Hunt." NegC (5:2) Spr 85, p. 92-93.
2331. ISSA
   "Haiku" (19 poems). Germ (9:2) Fall-Wint 85, p. 47-49.
2332. ISSAIA, Nanà
   "Fitting Room" (in Greek). NewRena (19) Fall 85, p. 56-64.
   "Fitting Room" (tr. by Yannis Goumas). NewRena (19) Fall
      85, p. 57-65.
2333. ISSENHUTH, Jean-Pierre
   "L'Aster." Os (20) 85, p. 23.
   "Le Soir dans la Clairière." Os (20) 85, p. 23.
ITSUKO, Ishikawa
   See ISHIKAWA, Itsuko
2334. ITZIN, Charles F.
   "Bombs." Vis (17) 85, p. 30-31.

2335. IVANOV, Vyacheslav
        "To the Translator" (tr. by Richard Lourie). Ploughs
        (11:4) 85, p. 176.
2336. IVASK, Astrid
        "Jorge Guillén" (tr. of Ivar Ivask, w. the author).
        Imagine (1:2) Wint 84, p. 207.
2337. IVASK, Ivar
        "Jorge Guillén" (in Estonian). Imagine (1:2) Wint 84,
        p. 206.
        "Jorge Guillén" (tr. by Astrid Ivask and the author).
        Imagine (1:2) Wint 84, p. 207.
2338. IVEREM, Esther
        "The Time." AmerPoR (14:3) My-Je 85, p. 47.
2339. IVES, Rich
        "A Light in the Window." CrossCur (4:3) 84, p. 57.
2340. JACCCOTTET, Philippe
        "The Collared Dove" (tr. by Mark Treharne). Verse (2) 85,
        p. 24-25.
2341. JACKSON, Angela
        "Fannie" (of Fannie Lou Hamer). BlackALF (19:3) Fall 85,
        p. 101.
        "The Village Women and the Swinging Guests" (Of Tarzan and
        Jane). OP (38/39) Spr 85, p. 72-73.
        "The War Chant of the Architect" (Toni Cade Bambara).
        BlackALF (19:3) Fall 85, p. 100.
2342. JACKSON, Fleda Brown
        "The Catch." PoetryNW (26:4) Wint 85-86, p. 4-5.
        "Do Not Peel the Birches." IndR (8:2) Spr 85, p. 74-75.
        "Family Chronicles." PoetryNW (26:4) Wint 85-86, p. 3-4.
        "A Jogging Injury." WindO (46) Fall 85, p. 6.
        "Keeping Fit." PoetryR (2:2) Ap 85, p. 45.
2343. JACKSON, Haywood (See also JACKSON, William Haywood)
        "Falling Out." StoneC (12:2/3) Spr-Sum 85, p. 47.
2344. JACKSON, Richard
        "For the Nameless Man at the Nursing Home near the
        Shawsheen River." Ploughs (11:1) 85, p. 130-131.
        "Not the Right Place." ThRiPo (25/26) 85, p. 34-35.
        "What Doesn't Happen." ThRiPo (25/26) 85, p. 33-34.
        "Worlds Apart." Ploughs (11:1) 85, p. 128-129.
2345. JACKSON, Rodica S.
        "Post-Card." Mund (16:1/2) 85, p. 23.
2346. JACKSON, Travis E.
        "Linguistics Class at a City University." EngJ (74:6) O
        85, p. 60.
2347. JACKSON, William (Haywood) (See also JACKSON, Haywood)
        "Matthew Brady Visits an Admiring Charles Dodgson." Bogg
        (53) 85, p. 24.
2348. JACOB, Teresa
        "Bailando by Myself." Imagine (2:1) Sum 85, p. 51.
        "I'll never be an intellectual" ("Untitled"). Imagine
        (2:1) Sum 85, p. 50.
        "My Love Poem." Imagine (2:1) Sum 85, p. 51-52.
2349. JACOBOWITZ, Judah (See also JACOBOWITZ, Judah L.)
        "The Interpretation of Dreams." Poem (54) N 85, p. 10.
        "Near Catastrophe." Poem (54) N 85, p. 8-9.
        "Once I Was Old." CapeR (20:1) Spr 85, p. 42.
        "Too Early Winter." Poem (54) N 85, p. 7.
2350. JACOBOWITZ, Judah L. (See also JACOBOWITZ, Judah)
        "Artist Models at the Fair." JlNJPo (8:1) 85, p. 32-33.
2351. JACOBS, Maria
        "What's Left of the Day" (Selections, tr. of Judith
        Herzberg: "Wife, Claimant," "Time Table," "You Hope,"
        "Song," "Stay"). PoetryCR (7:1) Aut 85, p. 23.
        "Winter Roads" (Selections, tr. of J. Bernlef: "Hotel
        Guest," "Before It Starts," "Winter Roads," "With and
        Without Snow"). PoetryCR (7:1) Aut 85, p. 50.

2352. JACOBSEN, Josephine
    "Now." NewL (51:3) Spr 85, p. 47.
    "The Strangeness." CrossCur (4:4/5:1) 85, p. 57.
2353. JACOBSON, Bonnie
    "Romantic Pig." NegC (5:2) Spr 85, p. 22.
    "Wu Emigrates." NegC (5:2) Spr 85, p. 23.
2354. JACOBSON, Jeremy
    "Sunday Morning" (tr. of Raúl Zurita). Mund (15:1/2)
      85, p. 147, 149, 151.
2355. JACOBSON, Susan S.
    "Echo and Narcissus." NegC (5:2) Spr 85, p. 156.
2356. JACQUE, Valentina
    "I Knew at Once" (tr. of Liana Sturua). Nimrod (28:2) Spr-
      Sum 85, p. 40.
2357. JACQUOT, Martine
    "Boredom Cake" (tr. of Herménégilde Chiasson). Germ
      (9:2) Fall-Wint 85, p. 13.
    "Geography" (tr. of Gérald LeBlanc). Germ (9:2) Fall-
      Wint 85, p. 11.
    "Inventory Number Two" (tr. of Herménégilde Chiasson).
      Germ (9:2) Fall-Wint 85, p. 15.
    "November Song" (tr. of Gérald LeBlanc). Germ (9:2)
      Fall-Wint 85, p. 10.
    "October Song" (tr. of Gérald LeBlanc). Germ (9:2) Fall-
      Wint 85, p. 9.
    "Rimbaud from the Bottom of the Night" (tr. of
      Herménégilde Chiasson). Germ (9:2) Fall-Wint 85,
      p. 14.
    "September Song" (for my birthday, tr. of Gérald
      LeBlanc). Germ (9:2) Fall-Wint 85, p. 8.
2358. JAEGER, Ann
    "Dog Metal." CapilR (34) 85, p. 8.
    "Tracks." CapilR (34) 85, p. 9.
2359. JAEGER, Lowell L.
    "I Bump into Reality." Pig (13) 85, p. 30.
    "Let's Hope This Thing Blows over Soon." Pig (13) 85, p.
      37.
    "Peace Vigil in Love Park." Pig (13) 85, p. 31.
    "The War at Home." Pig (13) 85, p. 29.
2360. JAEGER, Sharon Ann
    "Body in Brightness" (tr. of Antônio Ramos Rosa).
      GrahamHR (9) Fall 85, p. 96.
    "In the Sphere of Repose" (tr. of Antônio Ramos Rosa).
      GrahamHR (9) Fall 85, p. 97.
    "Pulsations of the Earth" (tr. of Antônio Ramos Rosa).
      GrahamHR (9) Fall 85, p. 94-95.
    "To Write" (tr. of Antônio Ramos Rosa). GrahamHR (9)
      Fall 85, p. 93.
2361. JAFFE, Maggie
    "Eurydice in Hell." NegC (5:2) Spr 85, p. 150-153.
    "Everything Happens at Night" (In Memory, Stephen Biko, d.
      September 12, 1977). MinnR (N.S. 25) Fall 85, p. 100-
      101.
    "Still Life with Golem" (In Memoriam, Kathryn Griffin, 1944-
      1982). Blueline (7:1) Sum-Fall 85, p. 50-51.
2362. JAFFIN, David
    "When Winter Comes" (In Hebrew and English, tr. by Menahem
      Ben and David Ben Gershon). CrossCur (4:2) 84, p. 34-
      36.
2363. JAGODZINSKE, Marcia
    "Portrait of a Father." NegC (5:3) Sum 85, p. 121.
2364. JAMES, David
    "In Every Small Town." PassN (6:1) Fall-Wint 85, p. 20.
2365. JAMES, Joyce
    "Their Anniversary." Crazy (27) Fall 84, p. 33-34.

2366. JAMES, Norberto
       "Internal Conflict" (tr. by Beth Wellington). NewEngR
       (7:4) Sum 85, p. 578.
2367. JAMES, Pat
       "Letter to the General Who Wants to Write Loose and Lovely
       Prose." Outbr (14/15) Fall 84-Spr 85, p. 13.
2368. JAMES, Sapphina
       "Rozzelle Court" (For my brother Sam). NewL (52:1) Fall
       85, p. 127.
2369. JAMES, Sibyl
       "January 6, 1957" (Elvis makes his appearance on the Ed
       Sullivan Show). OP (38/39) Spr 85, p. 11.
       "Landscape with Cows and Dog." CrabCR (2:3) Sum 85, p. 5.
       "This is not Vienna, not the old country" (Ol, translitic
       based on the Love Sonnets of Louise Labè). Tendril
       (19/20) 85, p. 178.
2370. JAMES, T. Mathias
       "After the Laughter" (Hail to the Auto-chief!). SanFPJ
       (7:4) 85, p. 42-43.
       "Love Is Based on Trust / In God We Trust." SanFPJ (7:4)
       85, p. 70-71.
2371. JAMIESON, Leland
       "Gifts" (In memory of Medwin). PoeticJ (10) 85, p. 3.
2372. JAMIESON, Patrick
       "Yellow Bath." AntigR (62/63) Sum-Aut 85, p. 20.
2373. JAMIS, Fayad
       "Auschwitz Was Not My Playground" (tr. by Arnold Odio).
       NewEngR (7:4) Sum 85, p. 494.
2374. JAMISON, Martin
       "Picture of a Deer Browsing in Duckweed." HiramPoR (38)
       Spr-Sum 85, p. 22.
2375. JAMPOLE, Marc
       "Moses in the Suburbs." NegC (5:1) Wint 85, p. 15-16.
2376. JANEVSKI, Slavko
       "The Black Dream of the Elm" (tr. by Zoran Ancevski and
       James McKinley). NewL (51:4) Sum 85, p. 23-24.
       "Droughts" (tr. by Zoran Ancevski and James McKinley).
       NewL (51:4) Sum 85, p. 23.
2377. JANEWAY, Elizabeth
       "Chiasmus." OP (38/39) Spr 85, p. 188.
2378. JANKOLA, Beth
       "Shadow Casting." PoetryCR (6:4) Sum 85, p. 45.
       "Your/Self." PoetryCR (6:4) Sum 85, p. 45.
2379. JANKULAK, Mary
       "Early Thursday Morning." PoetryCR (7:2) Wint 85-86, p. 6.
       "For a Friend Who Doesn't Call." PoetryCR (7:2) Wint 85-
       86, p. 6.
2380. JANOWITZ, Phyllis
       "Aging in April" (1984 AWP Award-Winning Poem). Tendril
       (19/20) 85, p. 38-41.
       "Catch." NewYorker (61:30) 16 S 85, p. 101.
2381. JANZEN, Jean
       "Chrysanthemums." ChrC (102:28) 25 S 85, p. 822.
       "Leaf." ChrC (102:16) 8 My 85, p. 467.
2382. JARMAN, Mark (See also JARMAN, Mark Anthony)
       "Good Friday." Crazy (28) Spr 85, p. 23-26.
       "Gossamer" (for Dennis Sampson). QW (21) Fall-Wint 85, p.
       98.
       "Human Geography." MissouriR (8:3) 85, p. 40-42.
       "Liechtenstein" (to Audrey Rugg). MissouriR (8:2) 85, p.
       62-67.
       "Miss Urquhart's Tiara." Crazy (28) Spr 85, p. 18-22.
       "Sand." Crazy (28) Spr 85, p. 27-28.
       "The Unicycle." Crazy (28) Spr 85, p. 16-17.
2383. JARMAN, Mark Anthony (See also JARMAN, Mark)
       "Scissorbills with Jaegers." Grain (13:4) N 85, p. 25.

2384. JARRETT, Emmett
    "Christmas 1979." <u>HangL</u> (47) Spr 85, p. 21.
    "God" (1983). <u>HangL</u> (47) Spr 85, p. 27.
    "Letting Go" (1981). <u>HangL</u> (47) Spr 85, p. 25.
    "Six Poems for Carol." <u>HangL</u> (47) Spr 85, p. 21-27.
    "A Sort of a Psalm" (1980). <u>HangL</u> (47) Spr 85, p. 22-23.
    "Sunrise, Vineyard Haven" (1982). <u>HangL</u> (47) Spr 85, p. 26.
    "Tuesday Morning" (1981). <u>HangL</u> (47) Spr 85, p. 24.
2385. JASON, Philip K.
    "Flashpoint." <u>CrossCur</u> (4:3) 84, p. 14.
    "Post-Modern Windows." <u>CrossCur</u> (5:3) 85, p. 138-139.
    "Technique." <u>CrossCur</u> (4:3) 84, p. 13.
2386. JASTRUN, Tomasz
    "City" (tr. by Daniel Bourne). <u>CharR</u> (11:2) Fall 85, p. 107-108.
    "The Detention Camp" (a poem for a book published under censorship, tr. by Daniel Bourne). <u>CutB</u> (24) Spr-Sum 85, p. 52.
    "Freedom" (tr. by Daniel Bourne). <u>CharR</u> (11:2) Fall 85, p. 108.
2387. JAY, Peter
    "Poems" (Selections: 1, 2, 5, 15, 16, 31, 94, 104a, 105a, 105c, tr. of Sappho). <u>Iowa</u> (15:2) Spr-Sum 85, p. 90-95.
JEANNE, Ave
    See AVE JEANNE
2388. JEAYS, Linda
    "Double Exposure." <u>Quarry</u> (34:1) Wint 85, p. 20.
2389. JELLEMA, Rod
    "Birth" (tr. of Berber van der Geest). <u>PoetL</u> (79:4) Wint 85, p. 239.
    "Dictators" (tr. of Sikke Doele). <u>PoetL</u> (79:4) Wint 85, p. 238.
    "Experiments" (tr. Sjoerd Spanninga). <u>PoetL</u> (79:4) Wint 85, p. 236.
    "First and Last" (Selections: 6, 9, tr. of Theun de Vries). <u>PoetL</u> (79:4) Wint 85, p. 233.
    "Frisia Cantat" (tr. of Jelle Kaspersma). <u>PoetL</u> (79:4) Wint 85, p. 229.
    "In the Enchantment of the Depth between Light and Light" (Excerpt, tr. of Tsjebbe Hettinga). <u>PoetL</u> (79:4) Wint 85, p. 237.
    "Old Skipper" (tr. of Meindert Bylsma). <u>PoetL</u> (79:4) Wint 85, p. 234.
    "Stanzas for My Son" (tr. of Douwe A. Tamminga). <u>PoetL</u> (79:4) Wint 85, p. 230.
    "Stream" (tr. of Beart Oosterhaven). <u>PoetL</u> (79:4) Wint 85, p. 232.
    "Two Miniatures" (tr. of Douwe A. Tamminga). <u>PoetL</u> (79:4) Wint 85, p. 231.
    "When You're Fifteen" (tr. of Jan Bylsma). <u>PoetL</u> (79:4) Wint 85, p. 235.
2390. JELLINGS, Dale
    "Reflections." <u>WindO</u> (45) Spr 85, p. 31.
    "Sunset" (haiku). <u>Northeast</u> (Series 4:2) Fall 85, p. 48.
2391. JENDRZEJCZYK, L. M.
    "Prodigy." <u>ChrC</u> (102:25) 14-21 Ag 85, p. 726.
2392. JENKINS, Lee Clinton
    "Persistence of Memory." <u>PraS</u> (59:1) Spr 85, p. 71-72.
2393. JENKINS, Louis
    "Appointed Rounds." <u>CharR</u> (11:2) Fall 85, p. 102.
    "Automobile Repair." <u>PoetryE</u> (18) Fall 85, p. 32.
    "The Northern River." <u>VirQ</u> (61:3) Sum 85, p. 422-424.
    "Oklahoma." <u>CharR</u> (11:2) Fall 85, p. 101.
    "Stratus." <u>VirQ</u> (61:4) Aut 85, p. 633-634.

2394. JENKINS, Paul
        "If Space Is Curved." <u>CrossCur</u> (4:3) 84, p. 101.
2395. JENNINGS, Kate
        "Donor." <u>SouthernHR</u> (19:4) Fall 85, p. 336.
        "Equinox." <u>PraS</u> (59:3) Fall 85, p. 36.
        "Milwaukee" (for Maureen). <u>PraS</u> (59:3) Fall 85, p. 37.
        "Phone Call at Midnight." <u>PraS</u> (59:3) Fall 85, p. 38.
        "Surveyor." <u>PraS</u> (59:3) Fall 85, p. 39.
2396. JENNINGS, Lane
        "Inheritance (AD 2184)." <u>Bogg</u> (53) 85, p. 10.
2397. JENOFF, Marvyne
        "The Orphan and the Stranger." <u>Germ</u> (9:1) Spr-Sum 85, p.
            35.
2398. JENSEN, Laura
        "Child." <u>Field</u> (32) Spr 85, p. 12.
        "Eating Words." <u>Field</u> (32) Spr 85, p. 13-14.
        "Pinks." <u>Field</u> (32) Spr 85, p. 15-19.
2399. JERVIS, Austen
        "House of Cards." <u>Waves</u> (14:1/2) Fall 85, p. 102.
2400. JESUS, Luis F. de
        "La Vida." <u>Mairena</u> (7:19) 85, p. 104.
2401. JEWELL, Terri L.
        "Ha'nt." <u>CentR</u> (29:2) Spr 85, p. 207-208.
        "Ha'nt." <u>Cond</u> (11/12) 85, p. 135.
        "No News among Us." <u>BlackALF</u> (19:3) Fall 85, p. 110.
        "Returning Anymore." <u>Cond</u> (11/12) 85, p. 137.
        "Teda." <u>CentR</u> (29:2) Spr 85, p. 208-209.
        "Teda." <u>NegC</u> (5:2) Spr 85, p. 29.
        "Uxoricide." <u>Cond</u> (11/12) 85, p. 136.
2402. JIA, Dao
        "Early Start" (tr. by Miles W. Murphy). <u>BelPoJ</u> (36:2)
            Wint 85-86, p. 18.
        "On the Passion to 'Improve' a Garden Pavilion" (tr. by
            Miles W. Murphy). <u>BelPoJ</u> (36:2) Wint 85-86, p. 19.
        "Touched by Autumn" (tr. by Miles W. Murphy). <u>BelPoJ</u>
            (36:2) Wint 85-86, p. 18.
JIANG, Haicheng
        <u>See</u> AI, Qing
2403. JILES, Paulette
        "Aubade." <u>PoetryCR</u> (7:2) Wint 85-86, p. 28.
        "Charming: Or, the Witch." <u>PoetryCR</u> (7:2) Wint 85-86, p.
            29.
        "Cosmic Sentences." <u>PoetryCR</u> (7:2) Wint 85-86, p. 28.
        "Desperados: Missouri 1861-1882" (or The James Gang and
            Their Relations). <u>MalR</u> (72) S 85, p. 5-25.
        "Dirty Kittens." <u>PoetryCR</u> (7:2) Wint 85-86, p. 29.
        "The Elks Club." <u>PoetryCR</u> (7:2) Wint 85-86, p. 28.
        "Ocean Songs." <u>PoetryCR</u> (7:2) Wint 85-86, p. 29.
        "Snow White." <u>PoetryCR</u> (7:2) Wint 85-86, p. 28.
JINGRONG, Chen
        <u>See</u> CHEN, Jingrong
2404. JOEL, Janet
        "Alien Mac has not seen E.T." <u>LittleBR</u> (5:1) Fall-Wint 84-
            85, p. 64-65.
        "Tremors." <u>LittleBR</u> (5:1) Fall-Wint 84-85, p. 65.
2405. JOENS, Harley
        "I have a great and lonely spirit." <u>Northeast</u> (Series
            4:2) Fall 85, p. 9.
        "It's past midnight." <u>Northeast</u> (Series 4:2) Fall 85, p.
            10.
2406. JOHNSEN, Gretchen
        "Ice." <u>Bogg</u> (53) 85, p. 27.
2407. JOHNSON, Dan
        "The Road I See" (for Henry Taylor). <u>Gargoyle</u> (27) 85, p.
            47.

2408. JOHNSON, Denis
"The Throne of the Third Heaven of the Nations Millennium
General Assembly" (James Hampton, 1909, Elloree, S.C.--
1964, Washington, D.C.). ParisR (27:95) Spr 85, p. 73-
76.
2409. JOHNSON, Fred
"Escaping Dreams." NoDaQ (53:2) Spr 85, p. 212.
2410. JOHNSON, Greg
"A Death Suite: Three Poems" (in memory of E.R.W.). Poem
(54) N 85, p. 32-33.
"Ignorance." Poem (54) N 85, p. 35.
"Victims." Poem (54) N 85, p. 36.
2411. JOHNSON, Honor
"April. Year Seesawed to Year." Oink (19) 85, p. 104.
"You Place." Sulfur (14) 85, p. 110-111.
2412. JOHNSON, Jean Youell
"Credentials: 50 Years of Being." Bogg (53) 85, p. 30.
"Seasons Four Prelude." PoeticJ (9) 85, p. 6.
2413. JOHNSON, Jenny
"Tippex." Bogg (54) 85, p. 21.
2414. JOHNSON, Kent
"Caferino the Peasant" (tr. of Grethel Cruz). MinnR (N.S.
25) Fall 85, p. 42-43.
"Darling" (tr. of Abbey Melec Alvarado). MinnR (N.S. 25)
Fall 85, p. 47.
"During Somocismo" (tr. of Juan Ramon Falcon). MinnR
(N.S. 25) Fall 85, p. 40.
"Egrets" (tr. of Juan Bautista Paiz). MinnR (N.S. 25)
Fall 85, p. 47.
"I Had Heard about You" (tr. of Oscar Alonso). MinnR
(N.S. 25) Fall 85, p. 45.
"In Siuna" (tr. of Carlos Pineda). MinnR (N.S. 25) Fall
85, p. 44.
"The Last Day of Somoza's Liberal Party" (tr. of Juan
Antonio Lira). MinnR (N.S. 25) Fall 85, p. 41.
"Mad House" (I imagine New York, tr. of Anthony Campbell).
MinnR (N.S. 25) Fall 85, p. 46.
"Orlando" (tr. of Maria Pineda). MinnR (N.S. 25) Fall 85,
p. 43.
"The Pauses" (tr. of Eliseo Diego). BlueBldgs (9) [85?],
p. 8.
"Sandino" (tr. of Javier Ortiz). MinnR (N.S. 25) Fall 85,
p. 42.
"Tiscapa Hill" (tr. of Gerardo Torrente). MinnR (N.S. 25)
Fall 85, p. 48.
"U.S. Logging Company" (tr. of Ivan Guevara). MinnR (N.S.
25) Fall 85, p. 41.
"The Vase" (tr. of Eliseo Diego). BlueBldgs (9) [85?], p.
8.
"Versions" (tr. of Eliseo Diego). BlueBldgs (9) [85?], p.
9.
2415. JOHNSON, Larry
"Camera Obscura." StoneC (13:1/2) Fall-Wint 85-86, p. 57.
2416. JOHNSON, Linnea
"And Not to Keep." PraS (59:3) Fall 85, p. 61-62.
"Beside Me." PraS (59:3) Fall 85, p. 58-59.
"She Might Have Run Off into the Night Hedges." AmerPoR
(14:3) My-Je 85, p. 25.
"Slight Lecture to the Young Man on My Left." AmerPoR
(14:3) My-Je 85, p. 24.
"Yellow Pine Tree Poem for My Daughter, Morgan." PraS
(59:3) Fall 85, p. 59-60.
2417. JOHNSON, Manly
"A Beautiful Death" (tr. of Jansug Tcharkviani, w. Shota
Nishnianidze). Nimrod (28:2) Spr-Sum 85, p. 161.
"Betania" (tr. of Jansug Tcharkviani, w. Shota

Nishnianidze). <u>Nimrod</u> (28:2) Spr-Sum 85, p. 159.
"The Canary" (tr. of Jansug Tcharkviani, w. Shota
     Nishnianidze). <u>Nimrod</u> (28:2) Spr-Sum 85, p. 158.
"A Dream." <u>Nimrod</u> (28:2) Spr-Sum 85, p. 52.
"The Dream." <u>Nimrod</u> (28:2) Spr-Sum 85, p. 53.
"The Jug" (tr. of Jansug Tcharkviani, w. Shota
     Nishnianidze). <u>Nimrod</u> (28:2) Spr-Sum 85, p. 160.
"On the Avenue." <u>Nimrod</u> (28:2) Spr-Sum 85, p. 51.
"Spring" (tr. of Murman Lebanidze, w. Shota Nishnianidze).
     <u>Nimrod</u> (28:2) Spr-Sum 85, p. 162.
2418. JOHNSON, Markham
"Chain Letter Pantoum." <u>KanQ</u> (17:4) Fall 85, p. 252.
"The Dog" (tr. of Shota Nishnianidze, w. the author).
     <u>Nimrod</u> (28:2) Spr-Sum 85, p. 80.
"Euclidean Geometry & the First Born." <u>KanQ</u> (17:4) Fall
     85, p. 251.
"Fortune's Stones." <u>Nimrod</u> (28:2) Spr-Sum 85, p. 139.
"Fungoes." <u>Nimrod</u> (28:2) Spr-Sum 85, p. 137.
"Mimosa" (for Laurel, my daughter, at three). <u>Nimrod</u>
     (28:2) Spr-Sum 85, p. 138.
"On the Road." <u>Nimrod</u> (28:2) Spr-Sum 85, p. 135-136.
2419. JOHNSON, Michael (<u>See also</u> JOHNSON, Michael L.)
"Champion Swimmer" (tr. of Umberto Saba). <u>WebR</u> (10:1) Spr
     85, p. 35.
"Fetish." <u>WebR</u> (10:1) Spr 85, p. 37.
"Pomegranates" (tr. of Paul Valery). <u>WebR</u> (10:1) Spr 85,
     p. 36.
"Vacant House." <u>WebR</u> (10:1) Spr 85, p. 37.
"The Writer on Vacation." <u>WebR</u> (10:1) Spr 85, p. 37.
2420. JOHNSON, Michael L. (<u>See also</u> JOHNSON, Michael)
"Delirium Tremens." <u>KanQ</u> (17:4) Fall 85, p. 57.
"Homage to Max Ernst." <u>LaurelR</u> (19:2) Sum 85, p. 67.
"Moments at the Beach." <u>Wind</u> (15:55) 85, p. 24-25.
"Three Yarns from Ewell Yeager." <u>Wind</u> (15:55) 85, p. 24.
"Van Gogh, Self-Portrait." <u>TexasR</u> (6:1/2) Spr-Sum 85, p.
     95.
2421. JOHNSON, Robert (<u>See also</u> JOHNSON, Robert K.)
"Absences" (in memoriam, D.H. 1963-1985). <u>SnapD</u> (9:1)
     Fall 85, p. 12.
"Looking Glass Lake." <u>SnapD</u> (9:1) Fall 85, p. 13.
2422. JOHNSON, Robert K. (<u>See also</u> JOHNSON, Robert)
"My Daughter's Bedtime." <u>PoeticJ</u> (10) 85, p. 20.
"Otto: Old Age." <u>PoeticJ</u> (12) 85, p. 25.
"You, Remembered." <u>PoeticJ</u> (11) 85, p. 21.
JOHNSON, Robin Smith
     <u>See</u> SMITH-JOHNSON, Robin
2423. JOHNSON, Ronald
"Ark 53, the Balanchine Spire." <u>Conjunc</u> (8) 85, p. 43-45.
"A Flag for Bunting." <u>Conjunc</u> (8) 85, p. 197.
2424. JOHNSON, Sheila Golburgh
"Egnops." <u>PoeticJ</u> (12) 85, p. 37.
"Our Daily Bread." <u>PoeticJ</u> (9) 85, p. 37.
"The Princess of Ice Cream." <u>PoeticJ</u> (9) 85, p. 37.
2425. JOHNSON, Thomas (<u>See also</u> JOHNSON, Tom)
"The Physics of Dying." <u>Chelsea</u> (44) 85, p. 66.
2426. JOHNSON, Tom (<u>See also</u> JOHNSON, Thomas)
"John Colter (1773?-1813)." <u>SewanR</u> (93:3) Sum 85, p. 401.
"Motives." <u>SouthernR</u> (21:1) Wint 85, p. 115-118.
"Robert H. Haslam (1840-1912)." <u>SewanR</u> (93:3) Sum 85, p.
     402.
2427. JOHNSON, W. R. (<u>See also</u> JOHNSON, William R.)
"The Youth of Achilles." <u>Hudson</u> (38:2) Sum 85, p. 279-280.
2428. JOHNSON, William R. (<u>See also</u> JOHNSON, W. R.)
"Prayer." <u>AntR</u> (43:4) Fall 85, p. 459.
2429. JOHNSTON, George
"Maggie's Acrostic." <u>Quarry</u> (34:1) Wint 85, p. 26.

2430. JOHNSTON, Hilda
       "The Girl at the Museum." Calyx (9:1) Spr-Sum 85, p. 52.
2431. JOHNSTON, Mark
       "Nest." BallSUF (26:2) Spr 85, p. 79.
       "The Perennials." ConnPR (3:1) 84, p. 16.
2432. JOHNSTON, Wayne
       "That Summer." AntigR (62/63) Sum-Aut 85, p. 234-235.
2433. JOHNTZ, Katie
       "And This Is Andrea" (for Claudia). WebR (10:2) Fall 85,
           p. 65-66.
       "The Backs of Their Knees." WebR (10:2) Fall 85, p. 64-65.
       "Caesarian." WebR (10:2) Fall 85, p. 66.
2434. JONAS, Ann
       "The Moment." PoetryR (2:2) Ap 85, p. 28-29.
2435. JONES
       "Justina." Waves (14:1/2) Fall 85, p. 96.
2436. JONES, Andrew McCord
       "Birth Color." KanQ (17:4) Fall 85, p. 174.
       "Frustration." Wind (15:53) 85, p. 36.
2437. JONES, Arlene S.
       "Letter to My Aunt in Iowa from Berne." SmPd (22:3) Fall
           85, p. 24.
       "Modjur Rug, in Oslo." SmPd (22:3) Fall 85, p. 23.
2438. JONES, D. G.
       "Embers and Earth" (Selections: 6 Poems, tr. of Gaston
           Miron, w. Marc Plourde). PoetryCR (6:3) Spr 85, p. 23.
2439. JONES, Daryl E.
       "Maidenhair." NewOR (12:4) Wint 85, p. 82.
       "Thanksgiving." NewOR (12:4) Wint 85, p. 70.
2440. JONES, David
       "Terpsichore's Child" (For Gomer Jones). CentR (29:4)
           Fall 85, p. 444.
2441. JONES, Ethelene Dyer
       "Lincoln Speakes" (An Eulogy: Lincoln Speaks to a Grieving
           Mother). DeKalbLAJ (18:1/2) 85, p. 74.
2442. JONES, F. Whitney
       "The Voice of the Winter Poet." Conjunc (8) 85, p. 209.
2443. JONES, Glyn
       "Unentitled 4." Bogg (54) 85, p. 9.
2444. JONES, James
       "The Shrine" (Facsimile). Confr (30/31) N 85, p. 73-75.
2445. JONES, Janis Montgomery
       "Children of Silence and Slow Time." NegC (5:2) Spr 85,
           p. 155.
2446. JONES, Jordan
       "Cigar." CrossCur (4:1) 84, p. 51.
2447. JONES, Paula
       "Swan Myth." PoetryCR (6:4) Sum 85, p. 42.
2448. JONES, R. (See also JONES, Richard & Robert & Robert L. &
           Rodney & Roger)
       "Rhythms." CrossCur (4:1) 84, p. 53.
2449. JONES, Richard (See also JONES, R.)
       "A Beginning." NewL (52:1) Fall 85, p. 98.
       "The Decoy." CrossCur (5:3) 85, p. 53.
       "The Horses." NewL (52:1) Fall 85, p. 99.
       "Moving Day." CimR (73) O 85, p. 4.
2450. JONES, Robert (See also JONES, R. & JONES, Robert L.)
       "An Argument for Brass Ducks." Swallow (4) 85, p. 50.
       "Changing Names" (for my brother, David). PoetryNW (26:2)
           Sum 85, p. 18.
       "Delayed at Sea-Tac." PoetryNW (26:2) Sum 85, p. 17.
       "Drowning As a Spectator Sport." PoetryNW (26:2) Sum 85,
           p. 15-17.
2451. JONES, Robert L. (See also JONES, R. & JONES, Robert)
       "A Border Rose" (Tijuana/San Ysidro, returning). KanQ
           (17:1/2) Wint-Spr 85, p. 124.

2452. JONES, Rodney (See also JONES, R.)
        "After the Maquilisuat Tree." RiverS (18) 85, p. 56-58.
        "Curiosity." Swallow (4) 85, p. 33.
        "Dirt." RiverS (18) 85, p. 63.
        "Dry Socket." VirQ (61:1) Wint 85, p. 68-70.
        "Edisonesque." RiverS (18) 85, p. 62.
        "Friends of the Poor." Swallow (4) 85, p. 32.
        "Imagination." RiverS (18) 85, p. 60-61.
        "The Laundromat at the Bay Station." Swallow (4) 85, p.
            30-31.
        "The Man Who Thinks of Stallions." RiverS (18) 85, p. 59.
        "The Mosquito." Atlantic (255:2), F 85, p. 85.
        "Thoreau." VirQ (61:1) Wint 85, p. 70-71.
2453. JONES, Roger (See also JONES, R.)
        "Best Friend, Killed on a Rig" (to Jerry Long). HawaiiR
            (18) Fall 85, p. 99.
        "Seed." CimR (71) Ap 85, p. 62.
JONES, Tim Wynne
        See WYNNE-JONES, Tim
2454. JONESS, Wayne
        "The Mexican Baseball Player." PoetryE (18) Fall 85, p. 40.
2455. JORDAN, June
        "Deliza Questioning Perplexities." OP (38/39) Spr 85, p.
            77.
        "March Song." RiverS (18) 85, p. 69.
        "Poem on the Road" (for Alice Walker). RiverS (18) 85, p.
            66-68.
        "Politics of Identity." OP (38/39) Spr 85, p. 212.
        "A Song for Soweto." RiverS (18) 85, p. 70-71.
2456. JOSELOW, Beth
        "Black Room." Prima (9) 85, p. 19.
        "Playing the Magician." Gargoyle (27) 85, p. 79.
2457. JOSEPH, Lawrence
        "Any and All." Poetry (147:2) N 85, p. 87-88.
        "Curriculum Vitae." Poetry (147:2) N 85, p. 85-86.
        "I Pay the Price." Poetry (147:2) N 85, p. 89-91.
        "In the Beginning Was Lebanon." MichQR (24:4) Fall 85, p.
            568-569.
        "This Much Was Mine." PoetryE (18) Fall 85, p. 38-39.
2458. JOSEPHS, Laurence
        "Eccentric." Salm (66) Wint-Spr 85, p. 141-142.
        "Piero Della Francesca's Queen of Sheba at Arezzo." Salm
            (66) Wint-Spr 85, p. 142.
JOURNOUD, Claude Royet
        See ROYET-JOURNOUD, Claude
2459. JOYCE, Jane Wilson
        "Baskets." WoosterR (3) Spr 85, p. 32-33.
2460. JOYCE, William
        "Love Poem" (for Janet Sunderland). KanQ (17:4) Fall 85,
            p. 190.
        "We Laughed Because We Knew Pittsburgh, 1959" (For the
            storytellers of '59 -- F. Coletta, Sleepy, Fry, Woozy,
            and the late Bruiser). SouthernPR (25:1) Spr 85, p. 37-
            39.
JUANA INES de la CRUZ, Sor
        See CRUZ, Juana Inès de la, Sor
2461. JUANITA, Judy
        "Momma Love You Yepper Do." PaintedB (26/27) Sum-Fall 85,
            p. 24-25.
2462. JUARROZ, Roberto
        "Derivaciones de la luz." Mund (15:1/2) 85, p. 186, 188.
        "Derivations of light" (tr. by Mary Crow). Mund (15:1/2)
            85, p. 187, 189.
        "A fly walks head down on the roof" (To Paul Eluard, tr. by
            Mary Crow). Mund (15:1/2) 85, p. 189, 191.
        "Life sketches a tree" (tr. by Mary Crow). Mund (15:1/2)

85, p. 185, 187.
"Una mosca anda cabeza abajo por el techo" (A Paul Eluard).
    Mund (15:1/2) 85, p. 188, 190.
"La vida dibuja un árbol." Mund (15:1/2) 85, p. 184,
    186.
2463. JUERGENSEN, Hans
"The Other One." NegC (5:2) Spr 85, p. 12-14.
2464. JUNGIC, Zoran
"Roots of broker fingers." Quarry (34:4) Aut 85, p. 7-8.
2465. JUNKINS, Donald
"The German Word for Clown." Salm (68/69) Fall-Wint 85-
    86, p. 8-9.
"I Know a Child Called Forth." SewanR (93:1) Wint 85, p.
    60.
"A Note to Theodore, Leaving for America Next Week." Salm
    (68/69) Fall-Wint 85-86, p. 11-12.
"Running with My Son in Germany: Remembering My Father."
    Salm (68/69) Fall-Wint 85-86, p. 9-10.
"Spring in Freiburg, 1982: Forty Years and Many Boats
    Later." GrahamHR (8) Wint 85, p. 12-13.
"There Is a Kind of Grace." GreenfR (12:3/4) Wint-Spr 85,
    p. 13.
"There's a Mulberry Bush." SewanR (93:1) Wint 85, p. 59.
JUNKO, Yoshida
See YOSHIDA, Junko
2466. JUSTICE, Donald
"A Nineteenth-Century Portrait" (after Baudelaire and
    Winslow Homer). MemphisSR (5:2) Spr 85, p. 22.
2467. JUSTICE, Jack R.
"Wintering on Tanner's Creek." Wind (15:53) 85, p. 10.
2468. JUZYN, Olga Susana
"Costumbre de Traición." Inti (20) Otoño 84, p. 103.
"Un día encontré tirada una palabra." Inti (20)
    Otoño 84, p. 103.
"In Vitro." Inti (20) Otoño 84, p. 104.
"Lo veo, ahí, sentado como en un sueño." Inti (20)
    Otoño 84, p. 104.
"Madre." Inti (20) Otoño 84, p. 104-105.
2469. KABAKOW, Sara
"1407 Sunnyside Lane." HangL (47) Spr 85, p. 56-57.
"Again in Your White Chair." HangL (47) Spr 85, p. 59-60.
"When You Were Nowhere and Everywhere." HangL (47) Spr
    85, p. 58-59.
2470. KAFKA, Paul
"After." LittleM (14:4) 85, p. 26.
"Done Express." LittleM (14:4) 85, p. 24-25.
2471. KAHLO, Frida
"Recuerdo." Imagine (2:1) Sum 85, p. 1.
2472. KAHN, Alice
"Art Deco." YellowS (14) Spr 85, p. 23.
2473. KAISER-MARTIN, Billie
"The middle." SanFPJ (7:3) 84 [i.e. 85], p. 80.
"The MNC." SanFPJ (7:3) 84 [i.e. 85], p. 10-11.
"Nuclear deterrence." SanFPJ (7:3) 84 [i.e. 85], p. 81.
"R Sickness." SanFPJ (7:4) 85, p. 90-91.
2474. KALIKOFF, Beth
"On the Run." SpoonRQ (10:4) Fall 85, p. 40.
2475. KALINA, Gail
"Dance." CarolQ (38:1) Fall 85, p. 48.
2476. KALLET, Marilyn
"The Ladies" (August, Montgomery, Alabama). Tendril
    (19/20) 85, p. 179.
"Once upon a Time." NewL (52:1) Fall 85, p. 117-118.
2477. KALLSEN, T. J.
"Rousseau's 'The Sleeping Gypsy'." KanQ (17:3) Sum 85, p.
    40.

2478. KALMUS, Morris A.
      "Diary Entry June 10-11, 1984." SanFPJ (7:2) 85, p. 86-87.
2479. KALNOKY, László
      "Roving on a Celestial Body" (tr. by Ivan Halasz de Beky).
         Rampike (4:2/3) 85-86, p. 15.
      "Solitude" (tr. by Ivan Halasz de Beky). Rampike (4:2/3)
         85-86, p. 15.
      "What Man Could Do on Earth" (tr. by Ivan Halasz de Beky).
         Rampike (4:2/3) 85-86, p. 15.
2480. KAMAL, Daud
      "Do What You Have To" (tr. of Faiz Ahmad Faiz). PoetryE
         (18) Fall 85, p. 63.
      "The Frozen Country" (tr. of Faiz Ahmad Faiz). PoetryE
         (18) Fall 85, p. 62.
      "Where Will You Go" (tr. of Faiz Ahmad Faiz). PoetryE
         (18) Fall 85, back cover.
      "Why Pray for Eternal Life?" (tr. of Faiz Ahmad Faiz).
         PoetryE (18) Fall 85, p. 61.
2481. KAMENETZ, Rodger
      "After a Dry Spell." GrandS (4:4) Sum 85, p. 75.
      "On the Road to New Orleans." RiverS (18) 85, p. 65.
      "Sanitary Chicken Coop" (for Sharon Feinberg). RiverS
         (18) 85, p. 64.
2482. KANE, Paul
      "A Painting, Perhaps." Shen (36:1) 85-86, p. 13.
2483. KANFER, Allen
      "Climbing the Palm Tree." Wind (15:53) 85, p. 53.
2484. KANGAS, J. R.
      "Celestial Parties." WebR (10:1) Spr 85, p. 42.
      "A History." StoneC (12:2/3) Spr-Sum 85, p. 22.
      "View from a January Interior." WebR (10:1) Spr 85, p. 43.
2485. KANTCHEV, Nicolai (See also KUNCHEV, Nicolai)
      "All of them have gone away" (tr. by Jascha Kessler and
         Alexander Shurbanov). NewL (51:4) Sum 85, p. 40-41.
      "The Bees' Calendar" (tr. by Jascha Kessler and Alexander
         Shurbanov). Nimrod (29:1) Fall-Wint 85, p. 100.
      "Believe It or Not" (tr. by Jascha Kessler and Alexander
         Shurbanov). NewL (51:4) Sum 85, p. 40.
      "Birthplace" (tr. by Jascha Kessler and Alexander
         Shurbanov). Ploughs (11:4) 85, p. 223.
      "Declaration" (tr. by Jascha Kessler and Alexander
         Shurbanov). Nimrod (29:1) Fall-Wint 85, p. 98-99.
      "Field, Hand with Seeds" (tr. by Jascha Kessler and
         Alexander Shurbanov). Nimrod (29:1) Fall-Wint 85, p.
         98.
      "The Future" (tr. by Jascha Kessler and Alexander
         Shurbanov). Ploughs (11:4) 85, p. 223.
      "Nocturne" (tr. by Jascha Kessler and Alexander Shurbanov).
         NewL (51:4) Sum 85, p. 41.
      "Proof" (tr. by Jascha Kessler and Alexander Shurbanov).
         Ploughs (11:4) 85, p. 222.
      "Puzzle" (tr. by Jascha Kessler and Alexander Shurbanov).
         Ploughs (11:4) 85, p. 222.
      "Smile" (tr. by Jascha Kessler and Alexander Shurbanov).
         NewL (51:4) Sum 85, p. 40.
      "Time As Seen from Above" (tr. by Jascha Kessler and
         Alexander Shurbanov). Ploughs (11:4) 85, p. 221.
      "When a Woman" (tr. by Jascha Kessler and Alexander
         Shurbanov). Nimrod (29:1) Fall-Wint 85, p. 99.
      "Words" (tr. by Jascha Kessler and Alexander Shurbanov).
         Nimrod (29:1) Fall-Wint 85, p. 100.
      "Your Life" (tr. by Jascha Kessler and Alexander
         Shurbanov). Nimrod (29:1) Fall-Wint 85, p. 99.
2486. KAPLINSKI, Jaan
      "Every Understanding" (tr. by Sam Hamill). ParisR (27:96)
         Sum 85, p. 101.

"Non-being Pervades Everything" (tr. by Sam Hamill).
    ParisR (27:96) Sum 85, p. 100.
"Our Shadows" (tr. by Sam Hamill). ParisR (27:96) Sum 85,
    p. 99.
2487. KAPPEL, Andrew J.
    "The Idea of You." KanQ (17:4) Fall 85, p. 261-262.
    "One Kiss, Five Pups, and No Conclusion." Poetry (145:5)
    F 85, p. 285-286.
2488. KARLINS, Mark
    "At Matlock cave." Sulfur (12) 85, p. 17.
    "In the center of the labyrinth." Sulfur (12) 85, p. 21.
    "Pianist in Search of a Blue Note." Sulfur (12) 85, p. 20-
    21.
    "Thread." Sulfur (12) 85, p. 19.
    "The Village." Sulfur (12) 85, p. 17-19.
2489. KARNER, River
    "1975." Cond (11/12) 85, p. 85-86.
2490. KAROUZOS, Nikos
    "Anti-Nebula" (tr. by Kimon Friar). Mund (15:1/2) 85, p.
    133.
    "Behavior" (tr. by Kimon Friar). Mund (15:1/2) 85, p. 131.
    "Daredevil Motorcycling" (tr. by Kimon Friar). Mund
    (15:1/2) 85, p. 131-132.
    "Endless Winter" (tr. by Kimon Friar). Mund (15:1/2) 85,
    p. 132-133.
    "The Lesser Angel" (tr. by Kimon Friar). Mund (15:1/2)
    85, p. 130.
    "The Sum of Ambition" (tr. by Kimon Friar). Mund (15:1/2)
    85, p. 130-131.
2491. KARP, Vickie
    "On Your Birthday, Looking through a Telescope at Jupiter."
    NewYorker (61:4) 18 Mr 85, p. 48.
2492. KARR, Mary
    "Bazaar: Ethiopian Water Buffalo" (for Stratis Haviaras).
    SenR (15:2) 85, p. 88.
    "Courage" (for Lecia). SenR (15:2) 85, p. 90.
    "Home during a Tropical Snowstorm I Feed My Father Lunch."
    Ploughs (11:1) 85, p. 133-134.
    "Moving Days." Ploughs (11:1) 85, p. 132.
    "Night Answering Service." SenR (15:2) 85, p. 91.
    "Perspective: Anniversary, D-Day." SenR (15:2) 85, p. 92-
    93.
    "Sleepwalk, Infidelity." SenR (15:2) 85, p. 89.
2493. KASISCHKE, L. (See also KASISCHKE, Laura)
    "Their Hands into the Heat." PraS (59:2) Sum 85, p. 107-
    109.
    "Triona." PraS (59:2) Sum 85, p. 110.
2494. KASISCHKE, Laura (See also KASISCHKE, L.)
    "A Mother Says Good-Bye to Her Deaf Son" (St. Theresa Home
    for Children). PassN (6:1) Fall-Wint 85, p. 20.
2495. KASPERSMA, Jelle
    "Frisia Cantat" (tr. by Rod Jellema). PoetL (79:4) Wint
    85, p. 229.
2496. KASSELMANN, Barbara C.
    "The Blessed." Pig (13) 85, p. 9.
2497. KASTELAN, Jure
    "Stones' Lament" (tr. by Peter Kastmiler). WebR (10:2)
    Fall 85, p. 37.
2498. KASTMILER, Peter
    "Coral Returned to the Sea" (tr. of Vesna Parun, w. Vesna
    Dye). WebR (10:2) Fall 85, p. 38.
    "Stones' Lament" (tr. of Jure Kastelan). WebR (10:2) Fall
    85, p. 37.
2499. KASZUBA, Sophia
    "Abstract and Concrete." Dandel (12:2) 85, p. 41.
    "Letter from Father." Dandel (12:2) 85, p. 40.

"Preliminaries." <u>Waves</u> (13:4) Spr 85, p. 94.
"The Roped-Off Night." <u>Quarry</u> (34:3) Sum 85, p. 22.
2500. KATCHER, Antje
"To My Husband." <u>Calyx</u> (9:1) Spr-Sum 85, p. 38.
2501. KATES, J.
"Apologia for Separate Vacations." <u>Outbr</u> (14/15) Fall 84-
Spr 85, p. 45.
"Out." <u>MidAR</u> (5:1) 85, p. 22.
2502. KATHUSIAS
"On the Tomb of Aerobics of Rhodes, Weightlifter" (tr. by
Elliot Richman). <u>WindO</u> (46) Fall 85, p. 3.
2503. KATOPES, Peter
"The Child-Killer." <u>Confr</u> (30/31) N 85, p. 213.
2504. KATROVAS, Richard
"The Drag Show at Travis'." <u>Telescope</u> (4:2) Spr 85, p. 51-
52.
"Julia." <u>Crazy</u> (29) Fall 85, p. 40-41.
"One." <u>NoAmR</u> (270:4) D 85, p. 53.
"Shine." <u>MinnR</u> (N.S. 25) Fall 85, p. 86-87.
"The Waiter." <u>QW</u> (20) Spr-Sum 85, p. 100-101.
2505. KATZ, S. B.
"To a Computer at 3:00 A.M.: A Lovesong." <u>GreenfR</u>
(13:1/2) Fall-Wint 85, p. 149-150.
2506. KATZ, Susan A.
"The Remedy." <u>NegC</u> (5:4) Fall 85, p. 109.
2507. KATZ-LEVINE, Judy
"As She Speaks." <u>Imagine</u> (1:2) Wint 84, p. 67.
"Old Women" (II). <u>Imagine</u> (1:2) Wint 84, p. 68.
"Photo with Ed." <u>Imagine</u> (1:2) Wint 84, p. 67.
2508. KAUFFMAN, Janet
"The Child Comes In." <u>AmerPoR</u> (14:2) Mr-Ap 85, p. 13.
"God and His Sirens." <u>NewL</u> (52:1) Fall 85, p. 93-97.
"Harvest at Night." <u>AmerPoR</u> (14:2) Mr-Ap 85, p. 13.
"The Trees Move Apart." <u>AmerPoR</u> (14:2) Mr-Ap 85, p. 13.
2509. KAUFMAN, Shirley
"The Art of Reduction" (tr. of Dan Pagis). <u>NewL</u> (51:4)
Sum 85, p. 19-20.
"At the Station." <u>Field</u> (32) Spr 85, p. 30.
"Diary of a Woodcutter" (Excerpts, tr. of Fuad Rifka, w.
the author). <u>NewL</u> (51:4) Sum 85, p. 16-17.
"A Japanese Fan." <u>Field</u> (32) Spr 85, p. 31-32.
"Meatballs." <u>Field</u> (32) Spr 85, p. 29.
"Poem from Jerusalem." <u>CrossCur</u> (4:2) 84, p. 39.
"Seconal" (tr. of Dan Pagis). <u>NewL</u> (51:4) Sum 85, p. 19-
20.
"Three Songs of Love and Plenitude." <u>SouthernPR</u> (26, i.e.
25:2) Fall 85, p. 50-51.
2510. KAUNE, Gayle Rogers
"Blue Bridge" (4 A.M., February 5th). <u>CrabCR</u> (3:1) Fall-
Wint 85, p. 26.
2511. KAVANAGH, Paul
"Trees in Brittany." <u>Stand</u> (26:2) Spr 85, p. 51.
2512. KAZEMEK, Francis E.
"Holden." <u>EngJ</u> (74:3) Mr 85, p. 36.
2513. KAZUK, A. R.
"The Cowardice." <u>YellowS</u> (16) Aut 85, p. 12.
2514. KEARNEY, Lawrence
"Uncle God" (1984 AWP Award-Winning Poem). <u>Tendril</u>
(19/20) 85, p. 16-17.
2515. KEARNS, J. M. (<u>See also</u> KEARNS, Josie)
"Green Song." <u>CrossCur</u> (4:1) 84, p. 47.
2516. KEARNS, Josie (<u>See also</u> KEARNS, J. M.)
"Toast." <u>KanQ</u> (17:4) Fall 85, p. 162.
2517. KEARSEY, Greg
"Winter Footsteps." <u>PottPort</u> (7) 85-86, p. 21.

2518. KEEFAUVER, John
"Revolt." _CrossCur_ (4:4/5:1) 85, p. 58.
2519. KEEFER, Janice Kulyk
"Angels." _PoetryCR_ (7:1) Aut 85, p. 51.
"Cedar." _PottPort_ (7) 85-86, p. 51.
"City Spring." _PottPort_ (7) 85-86, p. 46.
"Cold Pastoral." _PottPort_ (7) 85-86, p. 16.
"Harvest." _Grain_ (13:3) Ag 85, p. 20.
"Requiem." _PoetryCR_ (7:1) Aut 85, p. 51.
"San Gimignano." _Germ_ (9:1) Spr-Sum 85, p. 37.
2520. KEELER, Julia
"Philosopher's Walk." _PraF_ (6:2) Spr 85, p. 30.
2521. KEELEY, Edmund
"After the Defeat" (tr. of Yannis Ritsos). _GrandS_ (5:1)
Aut 85, p. 196.
"After the Fact" (tr. of Yannis Ritsos). _OntR_ (23) Fall-
Wint 85-86, p. 93.
"Afternoon in the Old Neighborhood" (tr. of Yannis Ritsos).
NewL (51:4) Sum 85, p. 12.
"Aids" (tr. of Yannis Ritsos). _Iowa_ (15:2) Spr-Sum 85, p.
97.
"Alcmene" (tr. of Yannis Ritsos). _NewL_ (51:4) Sum 85, p.
9.
"Blockade" (tr. of Yannis Ritsos). _NewEngR_ (8:1) Aut 85,
p. 23.
"The Closed Circus" (tr. of Yannis Ritsos). _GrandS_ (5:1)
Aut 85, p. 193.
"Common Fate" (tr. of Yannis Ritsos). _NewL_ (51:4) Sum 85,
p. 11.
"Corners of Night" (tr. of Yannis Ritsos). _GrahamHR_ (9)
Fall 85, p. 49.
"The Craftsman" (tr. of Yannis Ritsos). _NewL_ (51:4) Sum
85, p. 13.
"The Day's End" (tr. of Yannis Ritsos). _GrahamHR_ (9) Fall
85, p. 46.
"The Discovery" (tr. of Yannis Ritsos). _NewL_ (51:4) Sum
85, p. 11.
"Disfigurement" (tr. of Yannis Ritsos). _Antaeus_ (55) Aut
85, p. 318.
"Double Sentencing" (tr. of Yannis Ritsos). _GrahamHR_ (9)
Fall 85, p. 50.
"Expanse" (tr. of Yannis Ritsos). _NewL_ (51:4) Sum 85, p.
12.
"Forbidden Territory" (tr. of Yannis Ritsos). _NewL_ (51:4)
Sum 85, p. 12.
"In Front of the Door" (tr. of Yannis Ritsos). _GrahamHR_
(9) Fall 85, p. 48.
"The Jester's Secret" (tr. of Yannis Ritsos). _NewL_ (51:4)
Sum 85, p. 10.
"Known Consequences" (tr. of Yannis Ritsos). _GrandS_ (5:1)
Aut 85, p. 194.
"Like Changes" (tr. of Yannis Ritsos). _Iowa_ (15:2) Spr-
Sum 85, p. 96.
"Marpessa's Choice" (tr. of Yannis Ritsos). _Antaeus_ (55)
Aut 85, p. 316.
"The Miracle" (tr. of Yannis Ritsos). _Iowa_ (15:2) Spr-Sum
85, p. 96.
"The Most Precious Things" (tr. of Yannis Ritsos).
NewEngR (8:1) Aut 85, p. 23.
"Moving" (tr. of Yannis Ritsos). _MissouriR_ (8:3) 85, p.
62.
"Nakedness" (tr. of Yannis Ritsos). _CrossCur_ (4:4/5:1)
85, p. 29.
"Night Episode" (tr. of Yannis Ritsos). _Iowa_ (15:2) Spr-
Sum 85, p. 97.
"One Sunday" (tr. of Yannis Ritsos). _GrandS_ (5:1) Aut 85,

p. 195.
"Paper Poems" (Athens-Kalamos, June, 1973-May, 1974, tr. of
    Yannis Ritsos). Ploughs (11:4) 85, p. 27-30.
"Penelope's Despair" (tr. of Yannis Ritsos). Antaeus
    (55) Aut 85, p. 315.
"Philomela" (tr. of Yannis Ritsos). Antaeus (55) Aut 85,
    p. 314.
"Precisely Now" (tr. of Yannis Ritsos). OntR (23) Fall-
    Wint 85-86, p. 94.
"Readiness" (tr. of Yannis Ritsos). GrandS (5:1) Aut 85,
    p. 194.
"The Real Reason" (tr. of Yannis Ritsos). GrandS (5:1)
    Aut 85, p. 195.
"A Road" (tr. of Yannis Ritsos). Iowa (15:2) Spr-Sum 85,
    p. 98.
"Short Review" (tr. of Yannis Ritsos). Iowa (15:2) Spr-
    Sum 85, p. 98.
"Signals" (tr. of Yannis Ritsos). Antaeus (55) Aut 85,
    p. 314.
"Spring 1971" (tr. of Yannis Ritsos). GrandS (5:1) Aut
    85, p. 192.
"Strange Times" (tr. of Yannis Ritsos). NewL (51:4) Sum
    85, p. 9-10.
"The Time Dimension" (tr. of Yannis Ritsos). GrahamHR (9)
    Fall 85, p. 51.
"The Tomb of Our Ancestors" (tr. of Yannis Ritsos).
    GrandS (5:1) Aut 85, p. 191.
"Transactions" (tr. of Yannis Ritsos). GrahamHR (9) Fall
    85, p. 47.
"Ultimate Contribution" (tr. of Yannis Ritsos). GrahamHR
    (9) Fall 85, p. 53.
"The Unhinged Shutter" (tr. of Yannis Ritsos, w. Mary
    Keeley). CrossCur (4:2) 84, p. 41.
"Unknown Obligation" (tr. of Yannis Ritsos). GrahamHR (9)
    Fall 85, p. 52.
"Vacant Lot" (tr. of Yannis Ritsos). Antaeus (55) Aut
    85, p. 317.
"A Walk in the Courtyard" (tr. of Yannis Ritsos).
    CrossCur (4:4/5:1) 85, p. 27.
2522. KEELEY, Mary
    "Mortgage" (tr. of Yannis Ritsos). CrossCur (4:4/5:1) 85,
        p. 28.
    "The Unhinged Shutter" (tr. of Yannis Ritsos, w. Edmund
        Keeley). CrossCur (4:2) 84, p. 41.
2523. KEEN, Suzanne
    "History, Pawtucket." GrahamHR (9) Fall 85, p. 18.
2524. KEENAN, Terrance
    "Common Mullein." GeoR (39:1) Spr 85, p. 110.
    "Wood Violet." GeoR (39:1) Spr 85, p. 109.
2525. KEENE-SANEL, Wendy
    "One Block In, Three Flights Up." AmerPoR (14:3) My-Je
        85, p. 48.
2526. KEENER, LuAnn
    "Drowning the Caller." SouthernPR (26, i.e. 25:2) Fall
        85, p. 38.
    "Security." NewOR (12:4) Wint 85, p. 90.
2527. KEEP, W. C.
    "Curse of the Old King Salmon, Returning for the Third Time
        to the River." CrabCR (2:3) Sum 85, p. 16.
2528. KEITH, W. J.
    "Archibald Lampman." CanLit (105) Sum 85, p. 17.
2529. KEITHLEY, George
    "A World Apart." DenQ (20:2) Fall 85, p. 63-64.
2530. KEIZER, Arlene R.
    "Arrivals" (for Elizabeth Bishop). LitR (29:1) Fall 85,
        p. 54.

2531. KELLER, Dana
        "Address Book." <u>DeKalbLAJ</u> (18:3/4) 85, p. 36.
2532. KELLER, David
        "After the First Snow." <u>PoetryNW</u> (26:3) Aut 85, p. 21-22.
        "At the Heart." <u>USl</u> (18/19) Wint 85, p. 9.
        "The Chinese Written Character As a Medium for Poetry."
            <u>USl</u> (18/19) Wint 85, p. 9.
        "Drawing a House." <u>SouthernPR</u> (25:1) Spr 85, p. 66-67.
        "Finding the Tennis Racquet." <u>PoetryE</u> (18) Fall 85, p. 22-
            23.
        "Going Back to the City." <u>BlackWR</u> (12:1) Fall 85, p. 59-
            60.
        "Lost in the Dictionary." <u>SouthernPR</u> (25:1) Spr 85, p. 67-
            68.
        "On the Beach." <u>PoetryE</u> (18) Fall 85, p. 20-21.
        "Pennsylvania Station." <u>USl</u> (18/19) Wint 85, p. 9.
        "Playing the Serpent." <u>BlueBldgs</u> (9) [85?], p. 61.
        "Thinking What to Say, for C. M." <u>IndR</u> (8:1) Wint 85, p.
            80-81.
        "True." <u>PoetryE</u> (18) Fall 85, p. 18-19.
        "Two Houses Down." <u>PoetryNW</u> (26:3) Aut 85, p. 22-23.
2533. KELLER-GRONDIN, Dana
        "Sanibel." <u>DeKalbLAJ</u> (18:1/2) 85, p. 75.
2534. KELLEY, Janine
        "Whispers" (For Vanessa). <u>MinnR</u> (N.S. 25) Fall 85, p. 17.
2535. KELLEY, Karen
        "In the Garden." <u>CutB</u> (23) Fall-Wint 85, p. 66-67.
2536. KELLEY, Shannon Keith
        "Sleepless Wishes." <u>CapeR</u> (20:1) Spr 85, p. 23.
2537. KELLY, Brigit Pegeen
        "Abbot Adelme of Malmesbury: His Conception and Three
            Miracles." <u>NowestR</u> (23:3) 85, p. 75-76.
        "Doing Laundry on Sunday." <u>Poetry</u> (146:3) Je 85, p. 159-
            160.
        "Ebenezer Hill." <u>NowestR</u> (23:3) 85, p. 73-74.
        "The Embarrassment of Faith." <u>WestB</u> (17) 85, p. 38-39.
        "Given the River." <u>NowestR</u> (23:3) 85, p. 72.
        "The Leader Swan of Music." <u>NowestR</u> (23:3) 85, p. 81-82.
        "Napa Valley." <u>Poetry</u> (146:1) Ap 85, p. 9-10.
        "Spring Musical, Harmony School" (song for Brother John).
            <u>NowestR</u> (23:3) 85, p. 70-71.
        "Sundays." <u>NowestR</u> (23:3) 85, p. 77-80.
2538. KELLY, Dave
        "Cycle for Pablo Neruda" (1984 AWP Award-Winning Poem).
            <u>Tendril</u> (19/20) 85, p. 18-24.
        "Dying." <u>OP</u> (38/39) Spr 85, p. 39.
        "Following the Accusation." <u>Swallow</u> (4) 85, p. 67.
        "Sport Sonnet." <u>Swallow</u> (4) 85, p. 66.
2539. KELLY, Joan Auer
        "The Dancer on the Down." <u>NegC</u> (5:2) Spr 85, p. 45-46.
2540. KELLY, Mary Lee
        "Word." <u>PoeticJ</u> (9) 85, p. 35.
2541. KELLY, Robert (<u>See also</u> KELLY, Robert A.)
        "Comes" (Selections: 88, 95). <u>Pequod</u> (19/20/21) 85, p.
            212-214.
        "Elegy." <u>Conjunc</u> (8) 85, p. 24-28.
        "A Woman with Flaxen Hair in Norfolk Heard" (A Sequence
            Set to Honor Basil Bunting, No More Mourning Than the
            Sea). <u>Conjunc</u> (8) 85, p. 214-216.
2542. KELLY, Robert A. (<u>See also</u> KELLY, Robert)
        "Lake Seminole." <u>AntigR</u> (61) Spr 85, p. 12.
2543. KELSEY, Laura
        "Bicycling to Linguistics." <u>HiramPoR</u> (39) Fall-Wint 85,
            p. 13.
        "Landsat Sees the Earth." <u>HiramPoR</u> (39) Fall-Wint 85, p.
            12.

2544. KEMP, Penny
    "The Charge." <u>Waves</u> (13:4) Spr 85, p. 80.
    "Coming Home." <u>Waves</u> (13:4) Spr 85, p. 81.
    "When We Could Be in Flight." <u>Waves</u> (13:4) Spr 85, p. 81.
2545. KEMPA, Rick
    "Sweeping the Gas Station Parking Lot, 4 A.M." <u>NewL</u>
        (52:1) Fall 85, p. 100.
2546. KEMPHER, Ruth Moon
    "Ending April." <u>Outbr</u> (14/15) Fall 84-Spr 85, p. 88.
2547. KENDALL, Robert
    "Claws." <u>IndR</u> (8:3) Fall 85, p. 70.
    "The Council." <u>PoetryR</u> (5) S 85, p. 65.
    "Eastbound on the Jersey Turnpike." <u>LitR</u> (29:1) Fall 85,
        p. 11.
    "Inside the Dream." <u>BlueBldgs</u> (9) [85?], p. 47.
    "Parade." <u>KanQ</u> (17:3) Sum 85, p. 26.
    "Understanding the Sound of Confetti." <u>BlueBldgs</u> (9)
        [85?], p. 45.
2548. KENDIG, Diane
    "Concordance." <u>Pig</u> (13) 85, p. 11.
    "Packing Your Bag for the Old College Town." <u>Pig</u> (13) 85,
        p. 22.
2549. KENDRICK, Debbie
    "Death on the Sidewalk outside Grand Central." <u>Kaleid</u>
        (10) Spr 85, p. 24.
    "A Question of Art." <u>Kaleid</u> (10) Spr 85, p. 24.
2550. KENNEDY, Alexandra
    "What I Meant to Say." <u>GrahamHR</u> (9) Fall 85, p. 23.
2551. KENNEDY, Martha
    "Coming Back from Bada Pass" (tr. of Chen Jingrong, w. Chiu
        Yee Ming). <u>DenQ</u> (19:3) Wint 85, p. 47-48.
    "Sowing" (tr. of Chen Jingrong, w. Chiu Yee Ming). <u>DenQ</u>
        (19:3) Wint 85, p. 47-48.
2552. KENNEDY, Terry
    "The Nun." <u>SecC</u> (12:1) 84, p. 27.
2553. KENNEDY, X. J.
    "A Beardsley Moment." <u>OP</u> (38/39) Spr 85, p. 182.
    "Normalcy." <u>OP</u> (38/39) Spr 85, p. 183.
2554. KENNEY, Richard
    "Crosshairs." <u>QW</u> (21) Fall-Wint 85, p. 14-15.
    "Easter." <u>Crazy</u> (27) Fall 84, p. 14.
    "The Encantadas" (Selection: 9. "Disappearing"). <u>Verse</u>
        (2) 85, p. 6.
    "The Encantadas" (Selections: 10. "Tic-Toc," 11. "Orders,"
        12. "Analog"). <u>Verse</u> (1) 84, p. 24-27.
    "Equinox." <u>NewYorker</u> (61:6) 1 Ap 85, p. 99.
    "Harvest." <u>Atlantic</u> (256:2), Ag 85, p. 40.
    "Hours" (Excerpt). <u>Verse</u> (3) 85, p. 17.
    "Late Light." <u>QW</u> (21) Fall-Wint 85, p. 18-19.
    "Open Hearth." <u>SewanR</u> (93:3) Sum 85, p. 403-404.
    "Shadow." <u>SouthernPR</u> (26, i.e. 25:2) Fall 85, p. 49-50.
    "Starling." <u>NewYorker</u> (61:17) 17 Je 85, p. 40.
    "Sweep." <u>SewanR</u> (93:3) Sum 85, p. 404-405.
    "Up Chimney." <u>Hudson</u> (38:1) Spr 85, p. 100.
    "Waterlogger." <u>QW</u> (21) Fall-Wint 85, p. 16-17.
2555. KENNY, Maurice
    "Eagle" (After a Drawing by Kahionhes). <u>Blueline</u> (6:2)
        Wint-Spr 85, p. 22.
    "Listening for the Elders." <u>NoDaQ</u> (53:2) Spr 85, p. 237.
    "Molly's Flight" (Degonwadonti). <u>NoDaQ</u> (53:2) Spr 85, p.
        238-239.
    "Passions" (From <u>Tekonwatonti: Molly Brant</u>). <u>RiverS</u>
        (18) 85, p. 92-93.
    "Sitting in the Waters of Grasse River." <u>RiverS</u> (18) 85,
        p. 94-95.
    "Sitting in the Waters of Grasse River, Canton, N.Y.--

7/1983." <u>NoDaQ</u> (53:2) Spr 85, p. 235-236.
"There Is a Need to Touch." <u>RiverS</u> (18) 85, p. 91.
2556. KENT, Rolly
"Part of the Night in Florida." <u>Thrpny</u> (6:1, issue 21)
Spr 85, p. 23.
2557. KENYON, Jane
"Apple Dropping into Deep Early Snow." <u>AmerPoR</u> (14:2) Mr-
Ap 85, p. 20.
"Campers Leaving: Summer 1981" (In memory of my father).
<u>GrandS</u> (4:4) Sum 85, p. 197.
"Depression." <u>AmerPoR</u> (14:2) Mr-Ap 85, p. 20.
"Drink, Eat, Sleep." <u>Verse</u> (3) 85, p. 15.
"Inertia." <u>Poetry</u> (146:3) Je 85, p. 133.
"No Steps." <u>NewRep</u> (192:22) 3 Je 85, p. 38.
"Things." <u>NewL</u> (51:3) Spr 85, p. 45-46.
"Trouble with Math in a One-Room Country School." <u>Poetry</u>
(146:3) Je 85, p. 134.
2558. KERCHEVAL, Jesse Lee
"New Caledonia." <u>SoDakR</u> (23:1) Spr 85, p. 21-22.
2559. KEROUAC, Jack
"To Edward Dahlberg." <u>TriQ</u> (63) Spr-Sum 85, p. 176.
2560. KERR, Don
"Body Replies to Many Insults." <u>PraF</u> (6:1) Wint 85, p. 25.
"Keynesianism Departs and We Drink All Night." <u>Quarry</u>
(34:4) Aut 85, p. 86-87.
"Landscape with Madonna." <u>Waves</u> (14:1/2) Fall 85, p. 100-
101.
"The Undeveloped Country." <u>AntigR</u> (62/63) Sum-Aut 85, p.
100-101.
2561. KERR, N. (<u>See also</u> KERR, Nora)
"Claiming Another History." <u>RagMag</u> (4:1) Spr 85, p. 11.
"A Day in Sanctuary." <u>RagMag</u> (4:1) Spr 85, p. 13.
"Harmonics." <u>RagMag</u> (4:1) Spr 85, p. 12.
2562. KERR, Nora (<u>See also</u> KERR, N.)
"Climbing Everest and Annapurna." <u>RagMag</u> (4:2) Fall 85,
p. 36.
"Nos et Mutamur in Illis" (And We Are Changed in Those
Things--Men, Women). <u>RagMag</u> (4:2) Fall 85, p. 35.
"Some Years after the Magic." <u>RagMag</u> (4:2) Fall 85, p. 37.
2563. KERRIGAN, T. S.
"Ancestors." <u>LaurelR</u> (19:2) Sum 85, p. 69.
2564. KESSLER, Jascha
"Albert Camus" (tr. of Kirsti Simonsuuri, w. the author).
<u>Ploughs</u> (11:4) 85, p. 249-251.
"All of them have gone away" (tr. of Nicolai Kantchev, w.
Alexander Shurbanov). <u>NewL</u> (51:4) Sum 85, p. 40-41.
"Arctic Journey" (tr. of Kirsti Simonsuuri, w. the author).
<u>NewL</u> (51:4) Sum 85, p. 79.
"Beast of Prey" (tr. of Ottó Orbán, w. Mária
Körösy). <u>GrahamHR</u> (9) Fall 85, p. 59.
"The Bee's Calendar" (tr. of Nicolai Kunchev, w. Alexander
Shurbanov). <u>CrossCur</u> (4:2) 84, p. 33.
"The Bees' Calendar" (tr. of Nicolai Kantchev, w. Alexander
Shurbanov). <u>Nimrod</u> (29:1) Fall-Wint 85, p. 100.
"Believe It or Not" (tr. of Nicolai Kantchev, w. Alexander
Shurbanov). <u>NewL</u> (51:4) Sum 85, p. 40.
"Birthplace" (tr. of Nicolai Kantchev, w. Alexander
Shurbanov). <u>Ploughs</u> (11:4) 85, p. 223.
"A Blade of Grass" (tr. of Ottó Orbán, w. Maria
Körösy). <u>Ploughs</u> (11:4) 85, p. 219.
"Builders" (tr. of Ottó Orbán, w. Mária Körösy).
<u>GrahamHR</u> (9) Fall 85, p. 57.
"Declaration" (tr. of Nicolai Kantchev, w. Alexander
Shurbanov). <u>Nimrod</u> (29:1) Fall-Wint 85, p. 98-99.
"Excerpts from the Modern Tragedy" (tr. of Sándor
Weöres, w. Maria Körösy). <u>GrahamHR</u> (8) Wint 85,

p. 41-42.
"An Excursion" (tr. of Ottó Orbán, w. Mária
    Körösy). GrahamHR (9) Fall 85, p. 60.
"Farewell" (tr. of Ottó Orbán, w. Mária Körösy).
    GrahamHR (9) Fall 85, p. 62.
"Field, Hand with Seeds" (tr. of Nicolai Kantchev, w.
    Alexander Shurbanov). Nimrod (29:1) Fall-Wint 85, p.
    98.
"The Finder" (tr. of Kirsti Simonsuuri, w. the author).
    Nimrod (29:1) Fall-Wint 85, p. 101.
"For Example" (tr. of Mihaly Ládanyi, w. Maria Korosy).
    NewL (51:4) Sum 85, p. 39.
"The Future" (tr. of Nicolai Kantchev, w. Alexander
    Shurbanov). Ploughs (11:4) 85, p. 223.
"Introduction to the Beyond" (tr. of Blaga Dimitrova, w.
    Alexander Shurbanov). Ploughs (11:4) 85, p. 220.
"The Lion" (tr. of Istbán Vas, w. Maria Körösy).
    Ploughs (11:4) 85, p. 215.
"Love Match" (tr. of Ottó Orbán, w. Mária
    Körösy). GrahamHR (9) Fall 85, p. 58.
"A Monk" (tr. of Kirsti Simonsuuri, w. the author). NewL
    (51:4) Sum 85, p. 80.
"Mythos" (tr. of Kirsti Simonsuuri, w. the author).
    Ploughs (11:4) 85, p. 248.
"Nocturne" (tr. of Nicolai Kantchev, w. Alexander
    Shurbanov). NewL (51:4) Sum 85, p. 41.
"Once More" (tr. of Istbán Vas, w. Maria Körösy).
    Ploughs (11:4) 85, p. 214.
"Painting" (tr. of Ottó Orbán, w. Mária Körösy).
    GrahamHR (9) Fall 85, p. 61.
"Proof" (tr. of Nicolai Kantchev, w. Alexander Shurbanov).
    Ploughs (11:4) 85, p. 222.
"Puzzle" (tr. of Nicolai Kantchev, w. Alexander Shurbanov).
    Ploughs (11:4) 85, p. 222.
"A Small Country" (tr. of Ottó Orbán, w. Mária
    Körösy). GrahamHR (9) Fall 85, p. 55.
"Smile" (tr. of Nicolai Kantchev, w. Alexander Shurbanov).
    NewL (51:4) Sum 85, p. 40.
"The Technique" (tr. of Ottó Orbán, w. Mária
    Körösy). GrahamHR (9) Fall 85, p. 56.
"The Technique" (tr. of Ottó Orbán, w. Maria
    Körösy). Ploughs (11:4) 85, p. 218.
"Three Nocturnes" (Selection: II, tr. of Kirsti Simonsuuri,
    w. the author). NewL (51:4) Sum 85, p. 79.
"Time As Seen from Above" (tr. of Nicolai Kantchev, w.
    Alexander Shurbanov). Ploughs (11:4) 85, p. 221.
"When a Woman" (tr. of Nicolai Kantchev, w. Alexander
    Shurbanov). Nimrod (29:1) Fall-Wint 85, p. 99.
"Words" (tr. of Nicolai Kantchev, w. Alexander Shurbanov).
    Nimrod (29:1) Fall-Wint 85, p. 100.
"Your Life" (tr. of Nicolai Kantchev, w. Alexander
    Shurbanov). Nimrod (29:1) Fall-Wint 85, p. 99.
2565. KESSLER, Stephen
    "The U.S. Congress Approves Aid to the Contras" (tr. of
    Ernesto Cardenal). Zyzzyva (1:4) Wint 85, p. 130-134.
2566. KESTENBAUM, Stuart
    "Angels on the Interstate." BelPoJ (35:3) Spr 85, p. 15.
    "Saint Francis." BelPoJ (35:3) Spr 85, p. 16-17.
2567. KESTER, Marcia
    "Missouri Rain." KanQ (17:1/2) Wint-Spr 85, p. 205.
    "Sunday." KanQ (17:1/2) Wint-Spr 85, p. 206.
2568. KETTNER, M.
    "Your bare legs." Amelia (2:1) Ap 85, p. 52.
2569. KEVORKIAN, Karen
    "Cleaning the Doves." CimR (70) Ja 85, p. 32.
    "How I Imagined It." VirQ (61:1) Wint 85, p. 75.

"The Wound." <u>VirQ</u> (61:1) Wint 85, p. 73-74.
2570. KEYES, Claire
"Vincent Selects the Sunflowers." <u>PassN</u> (6:2) Spr-Sum 85,
p. 8.
2571. KEYSER, Judy
"Through the Window" (for L.S.). <u>ConnPR</u> (3:1) 84, p. 50.
2572. KHALSA, Gurudain Singh
"The Tire Tracks behind the House." <u>BelPoJ</u> (36:2) Wint 85-
86, p. 30-31.
2573. KHARE, Vishnu
"Towards Delhi" (tr. of Kunwar Narayan). <u>NewL</u> (51:4) Sum
85, p. 135.
2574. KHIDR ("The Green One")
"For You, Marvin." <u>MoodySI</u> (15) Spr 85, p. 25.
2575. KHLEBNIKOV, Velimir
"Genghis Khan me, you midnight plantation!" ("Untitled,"
tr. by Paul Schmidt). <u>ParisR</u> (27:95) Spr 85, p. 127.
"I see them -- Crab, Ram, Bull" ("Untitled," tr. by Paul
Schmidt). <u>ParisR</u> (27:95) Spr 85, p. 128.
"The lice had blind faith, and they prayed to me" (from
<u>The King of Time</u>, tr. by Paul Schmidt). <u>PartR</u> (52:4)
85, p. 426.
"O Garden of Animals!" (tr. by Paul Schmidt). <u>ParisR</u>
(27:95) Spr 85, p. 129-130.
"Poem" (tr. by Paul Schmidt). <u>NewYRB</u> (32:15) 10 O 85, p.
4.
"Russia, I give you my divine white brain" (from <u>The King
of Time</u>, tr. by Paul Schmidt). <u>PartR</u> (52:4) 85, p.
426-427.
2576. KIENHOLZ, Philip
"Exit Weather." <u>Quarry</u> (34:4) Aut 85, p. 29.
"Home Poem." <u>PraF</u> (6:3) Sum 85, p. 23.
"Lands." <u>PraF</u> (6:3) Sum 85, p. 22.
"Spring Rain." <u>PraF</u> (6:3) Sum 85, p. 21.
2577. KIEVES, Tama J.
"Across the Way." <u>LindLM</u> (4:1) Ja-Mr 85, p. 30.
"Death Is Like the Morning." <u>LindLM</u> (4:1) Ja-Mr 85, p. 30.
"First Visit." <u>LindLM</u> (4:1) Ja-Mr 85, p. 30.
2578. KILMER, Anne
"For a Girl in the Library." <u>CentR</u> (29:4) Fall 85, p. 444-
445.
"Leaves for Jenny." <u>SouthernHR</u> (19:2) Spr 85, p. 115.
2579. KILMER, Nicholas
"Di Leo's Garages" (Excerpt). <u>Pequod</u> (18) 85, p. 61-66.
2580. KIM, Su-Jang
"Ravens" (Korean Sijo Poem, tr. by Graeme Wilson). <u>DenQ</u>
(20:1) Sum 85, p. 17.
2581. KIMBALL, Karen
"286" (tr. of Osip Mandelstam, w. Michael Cole). <u>MinnR</u>
(N.S. 24) Spr 85, p. 102.
"341" (tr. of Osip Mandelstam, w. Michael Cole). <u>MinnR</u>
(N.S. 24) Spr 85, p. 102.
"349" (tr. of Osip Mandelstam, w. Michael Cole). <u>MinnR</u>
(N.S. 24) Spr 85, p. 103.
"For me, winter feels like a belated gift" (tr. of Osip
Mandelstam, w. Michael Cole). <u>NewL</u> (51:4) Sum 85, p.
42.
"I don't know when this song began" (131, tr. of Osip
Mandelstam, w. Michael Cole). <u>StoneC</u> (12:2/3) Spr-Sum
85, p. 14-15.
"Poem" (tr. of Osip Mandelstam, w. Michael Cole). <u>Stand</u>
(26:2) Spr 85, p. 41.
"Today is yellow-beaked, inexperienced" (329, tr. of Osip
Mandelstam, w. Michael Cole). <u>StoneC</u> (12:2/3) Spr-Sum
85, p. 12-13.

2582. KIME, Peter
       "The Cherry Blossom Tree in My Neighbor's Yard." <u>WebR</u>
          (10:1) Spr 85, p. 82.
       "Lunar Eclipse" (for Beth). <u>WebR</u> (10:1) Spr 85, p. 83.
       "My Father's Visit." <u>PoetryNW</u> (26:3) Aut 85, p. 27.
2583. KIMMET, Gene
       "To the Health Farm." <u>SpoonRQ</u> (10:4) Fall 85, p. 58-59.
2584. KINCAID, Joan Payne
       "Archaeology." <u>PoeticJ</u> (12) 85, p. 33.
       "Eagle." <u>PoeticJ</u> (12) 85, p. 10.
       "Watching the Boats Sail Up and Down." <u>Confr</u> (30/31) N
          85, p. 162.
2585. KINDRED, Wendy
       "Letter from Addis Ababa, 1967." <u>BelPoJ</u> (36:2) Wint 85-
          86, p. 1.
2586. KING, Kenneth
       "The Furniture." <u>PoetryNW</u> (26:3) Aut 85, p. 7-8.
2587. KING, Linda
       "Stone Age." <u>PraF</u> (6:1) Wint 85, p. 42.
       "Unmasked." <u>PraF</u> (6:1) Wint 85, p. 41.
2588. KING, Lyn
       "Another Time." <u>AntigR</u> (62/63) Sum-Aut 85, p. 210.
       "Leap Year." <u>PoetryCR</u> (6:3) Spr 85, p. 27.
       "The Stone." <u>PoetryCR</u> (6:3) Spr 85, p. 34.
2589. KING, Robert
       "The Bus Cafe in Iowa." <u>PaintedB</u> (26/27) Sum-Fall 85, p.
          33.
2590. KINGSOLVER, Barbara
       "The Middle Daughter." <u>Calyx</u> (9:1) Spr-Sum 85, p. 20-21.
       "Remember the Moon Survives" (for Pamela). <u>Calyx</u> (9:1)
          Spr-Sum 85, p. 17-19.
       "Your Mother's Eyes" (for Maura and Lesbia Lopez). <u>Calyx</u>
          (9:1) Spr-Sum 85, p. 22-23.
2591. KINLOCH, David
       "Barents." <u>Verse</u> (4) 85, p. 39.
       "The Lych Gate." <u>Verse</u> (4) 85, p. 38-39.
       "Penembak Misterius." <u>Verse</u> (1) 84, p. 29.
       "Reformation." <u>Verse</u> (4) 85, p. 38.
       "We Do Not Know" (tr. of Guillevic). <u>Verse</u> (2) 85, p. 37.
2592. KINNELL, Galway
       "The Angel." <u>Verse</u> (4) 85, p. 4.
       "Break of Day." <u>Nat</u> (241:9) 28 S 85, p. 285.
       "Chamberlain's Porch." <u>ParisR</u> (27:96) Sum 85, p. 92.
       "Conception." <u>Antaeus</u> (55) Aut 85, p. 125.
       "December Day in Honolulu." <u>Antaeus</u> (55) Aut 85, p. 124.
       "Driftwood from a Ship." <u>Antaeus</u> (55) Aut 85, p. 127.
       "First Day of the Future." <u>NewYorker</u> (61:10) 29 Ap 85, p.
          40.
       "The Frog Pond." <u>ParisR</u> (27:96) Sum 85, p. 93-94.
       "The Geese." <u>ParisR</u> (27:96) Sum 85, p. 90.
       "The Man Splitting Wood in the Daybreak." <u>Antaeus</u> (55)
          Aut 85, p. 126.
       "Middle of the Night." <u>NewYorker</u> (61:32) 30 S 85, p. 34.
       "Milk." <u>SouthwR</u> (70:3) Sum 85, p. 360.
       "The Old Life." <u>ParisR</u> (27:96) Sum 85, p. 91.
       "The Olive Wood Fire." <u>NewL</u> (51:3) Spr 85, p. 45.
       "On the Oregon Coast" (In memorium Richard Hugo). <u>AmerPoR</u>
          (14:5) S-O 85, p. 7.
       "The Past." <u>Atlantic</u> (256:3), S 85, p. 84.
       "The Seekonk Woods." <u>NewYorker</u> (61:7) 8 Ap 85, p. 44-45.
       "The Shroud." <u>NewYorker</u> (61:29) 9 S 85, p. 70.
       "The Sow Piglet's Escapes." <u>Verse</u> (4) 85, p. 4.
       "The Waking." <u>AmerPoR</u> (14:5) S-O 85, p. 6.
2593. KINNETT, Elizabeth
       "Apocalypse." <u>Poem</u> (53) Mr 85, p. 38.
       "The Fields Are All Alight." <u>Poem</u> (53) Mr 85, p. 36.

"Irish Tune." Poem (53) Mr 85, p. 37.
"Triolet." Poem (53) Mr 85, p. 35.
2594. KINSLEY, Robert
"These Are the Sins." ThRiPo (25/26) 85, p. 36.
"Walking to the Sandstone Quarry behind Uncle Bo's." IndR
(8:3) Fall 85, p. 10-11.
2595. KINSOLVING, Susan
"The Forge" (Casco Bay, Maine. Fourth Prize, International
Poetry Contest). WestB (17) 85, p. 20.
2596. KINZIE, Mary
"1212 Wesley" (to a friend who is moving east). Salm (66)
Wint-Spr 85, p. 139-140.
"A Friend's Friend." ChiR (35:2) Wint 85, p. 31.
"Old Postcard" (She writes to him now dead 21 years).
Poetry (145:5) F 85, p. 257-258.
"Servile." Thrpny (6:3, issue 23) Fall 85, p. 20.
2597. KIRBY, David
"Dracula in Las Vegas." NegC (5:4) Fall 85, p. 142-144.
"Fallen Bodies." Amelia (2:1) Ap 85, p. 14.
"I Think I Am Going to Call My Wife Paraguay" (Guy Owen
Poetry Prize Winner, Peter Wild, Judge). SouthernPR
(26, i.e. 25:2) Fall 85, p. 5-6.
"Man Drowning in Restaurant." IndR (8:3) Fall 85, p. 67.
"Myopia." NegC (5:4) Fall 85, p. 139-140.
"Patience." Chelsea (44) 85, p. 111-112.
"Theology from the Viewpoint of a Younger Son." NegC
(5:4) Fall 85, p. 141.
2598. KIRCH, A. M.
"Faust at the Movies." YellowS (17) Wint 85, p. 14.
2599. KIRCHER, Pam
"Phototropic Life." Raccoon (17) Mr 85, p. 24.
2600. KIRKLAND, Will
"If I Had a Horse" (tr. of Carlos Edmundo de Ory). Mund
(15:1/2) 85, p. 15.
"The Kisses" (tr. of Carlos Edmundo de Ory). Mund
(15:1/2) 85, p. 11.
"Sob" (tr. of Carlos Edmundo de Ory). Mund (15:1/2) 85,
p. 13.
"A Song of Farewell" (tr. of Carlos Edmundo de Ory). Mund
(15:1/2) 85, p. 13.
"To a Woman" (tr. of Carlos Edmundo de Ory). Mund
(15:1/2) 85, p. 11.
2601. KIRKPATRICK, Robert
"A Guide to the Second Great World Exposition" (for William
Harmon). CarolQ (37:3) Spr 85, p. 55-57.
2602. KIRKUP, James
"Mornings in Whitby." NewYorker (60:50) 28 Ja 85, p. 32.
2603. KIRN, Walter
"Xenoi." SouthwR (70:4) Aut 85, p. 499.
2604. KIRSCH, Sarah
"The Birds Sing Best in the Rain" (in German and English,
tr. by Jean Pearson). StoneC (13:1/2) Fall-Wint 85-86,
p. 42-43.
"Blue Garden Ball" (tr. by Charles Fishman and Marina
Roscher). NewL (51:4) Sum 85, p. 70-71.
"Motionless" (tr. by Charles Fishman and Marina Roscher).
NewL (51:4) Sum 85, p. 72.
"Stoneheart" (tr. by Charles Fishman and Marina Roscher).
NewL (51:4) Sum 85, p. 70.
"Winter Promenade" (tr. by Charles Fishman and Marina
Roscher). NewL (51:4) Sum 85, p. 71.
2605. KIRSCHNER, Elizabeth
"She Outlives Us" (for Kelly Davis, February 1984).
BlueBldgs (9) [85?], p. 42-43.
2606. KISS, Marilyn
"Passion As." J1NJPo (8:1) 85, p. 34-35.

2607. KISTLER, William
"Ending near the Reservoir in Central Park." Nimrod
(28:2) Spr-Sum 85, p. 110.
"Form of Night." Nimrod (28:2) Spr-Sum 85, p. 105.
"Gate." Nimrod (28:2) Spr-Sum 85, p. 107.
"Seeing Her in the Street." Nimrod (28:2) Spr-Sum 85, p.
108.
"Song of Herself." Nimrod (28:2) Spr-Sum 85, p. 109.

2608. KITCHEN, Judith
"And So You Rise." PaintedB (26/27) Sum-Fall 85, p. 46.
"Largo." SenR (15:1) 85, p. 76.
"New Year." PaintedB (26/27) Sum-Fall 85, p. 47.
"Orange." ThRiPo (25/26) 85, p. 37.
"Winter Landscape." SenR (15:1) 85, p. 75.
"Working Definitions." PaintedB (26/27) Sum-Fall 85, p.
45.

2609. KITTELL, Linda
"Cleaning the Office, Twice." DeKalbLAJ (18:3/4) 85, p.
37.
"Walking on the Moon." SouthernPR (25:1) Spr 85, p. 64-65.

2610. KITTELL, Ronald (See also KITTELL, Ronald Edward)
"2." JamesWR (2:1) Fall 84, p. 15.

2611. KITTELL, Ronald Edward (See also KITTELL, Ronald)
"Mardi Gras." Open24 (4) 85, p. 7.

2612. KIZER, Carolyn
"Ingathering" (For Spain). Poetry (147:2) N 85, p. 66-68.
"The Singing Flower" (tr. of Shu Ting, w. Y. H. Zhao).
PoetryE (18) Fall 85, p. 72-78.
"The Valley of the Fallen." Poetry (147:2) N 85, p. 63-66.

2613. KLAMMER, Diane
"Captured Forest." SanFPJ (7:4) 85, p. 33.
"HUD." SanFPJ (7:4) 85, p. 41.
"Mushroom Cloud." SanFPJ (7:4) 85, p. 36.
"Sonnet Plea for Ecology." SanFPJ (7:4) 85, p. 59.
"Time." SanFPJ (7:4) 85, p. 41.

2614. KLAPPERT, Peter
"J'Accuse." StoneC (12:2/3) Spr-Sum 85, p. 50-51.
"A Sentimental Journey &c. &c." (Paris, 1939). StoneC
(12:2/3) Spr-Sum 85, p. 52-53.

2615. KLASS, David
"Sweet Helen." Poem (54) N 85, p. 26-27.
"Warp." Poem (54) N 85, p. 28.

2616. KLAVAN, Andre
"The Woman at the Window." CrossCur (4:4/5:1) 85, p. 72-
73.

2617. KLAWITTER, George
"Brian at the Y." JamesWR (2:2) Wint 85, p. 10.
"Scenes for a Movie Named 'Michael'." JamesWR (2:1) Fall
84, p. 3.

2618. KLEBECK, William J.
"Nine Years." PraF (6:3) Sum 85, p. 20.
"Sunflower." PraF (6:3) Sum 85, p. 20.
"Whistle." PraF (6:3) Sum 85, p. 20.

2619. KLECK, Judith
"Turning Stones" (for Joe). HawaiiR (18) Fall 85, p. 56.

2620. KLEINDL, Michael
"The Sum of Handles" (for my grandfather). Vis (18) 85,
p. 8.

2621. KLEINSCHMIDT, Edward
"Antagonisms." Poetry (146:6) S 85, p. 341-342.
"Arms and the Man." PoetryNW (26:2) Sum 85, p. 41-42.
"The Explanation." PoetC (17:1) Fall 85, p. 39.
"Grammatical Existence." ColEng (47:6) O 85, p. 610-611.
"A Poem You Might Have Written While Ploughing, 1925" (for
my father). PoetryNW (26:2) Sum 85, p. 39-40.
"Rebellion: Report of the Escaped Slaves" (after Czeslaw

Milosz). <u>Stand</u> (26:4) Aut 85, p. 57.
"She." <u>PoetryNW</u> (26:2) Sum 85, p. 38-39.
"Sickness unto Death." <u>MSS</u> (4:3) Spr 85, p. 120-121.
"Some Problems with the Mind/Body Problem." <u>PoetryNW</u>
    (26:4) Wint 85-86, p. 36-37.
"Tonight Insomnia." <u>Poetry</u> (145:4) Ja 85, p. 194-195.
"What Death Say." <u>PoetryNW</u> (26:4) Wint 85-86, p. 35-36.
"The World Without." <u>Poetry</u> (146:6) S 85, p. 343.
2622. KLEINZAHLER, August
"By the Tagus." <u>Sulfur</u> (13) 85, p. 82.
"Earthquake Weather." <u>Epoch</u> (34:3) 84-85, p. 216.
"Evenings, in A Minor." <u>Sulfur</u> (13) 85, p. 83.
"Nurses and Comedians." <u>Oink</u> (19) 85, p. 97.
"Poetics." <u>Epoch</u> (34:3) 84-85, p. 215.
"Poppies in the Wind." <u>Sulfur</u> (13) 85, p. 85.
"Workout, with Nib." <u>Sulfur</u> (13) 85, p. 84.
"Ye Olden Barge." <u>Sulfur</u> (13) 85, p. 85.
2623. KLEPETAR, Steve
"The Weary Man's Proposal for Sabbatical Leave." <u>PassN</u>
    (6:2) Spr-Sum 85, p. 16.
2624. KLINE, George L.
"Enigma for an Angel" (tr. of Joseph Brodsky). <u>TriQ</u> (63)
    Spr-Sum 85, p. 172-174.
2625. KLINGSOR, Tristan
"The Minuet" (tr. by Dorothy Aspinwall). <u>WebR</u> (10:2) Fall
    85, p. 35.
2626. KLOEFKORN, William
"Christmas 1940." <u>SpoonRQ</u> (10:2) Spr 85, p. 12-13.
"Mumps." <u>SpoonRQ</u> (10:2) Spr 85, p. 10-11.
"Summer 1942." <u>SpoonRQ</u> (10:2) Spr 85, p. 14.
"Threnody." <u>SpoonRQ</u> (10:2) Spr 85, p. 9.
2627. KNAUTH, Stephen
"Late Autumn Evening, Little Pigeon River." <u>SouthernPR</u>
    (26, i.e. 25:2) Fall 85, p. 33.
"Sermonette." <u>NegC</u> (5:4) Fall 85, p. 80.
2628. KNICKERBOCKER, H. E. (<u>See</u> <u>also</u> KNICKERBOCKER, Harry E.)
"Vendetta." <u>KanQ</u> (17:4) Fall 85, p. 254.
2629. KNICKERBOCKER, Harry E. (<u>See</u> <u>also</u> KNICKERBOCKER, H. E.)
"The Projectionist." <u>Amelia</u> (2:2) O 85, p. 86.
2630. KNIGHT, Arthur Winfield
"Born Again." <u>SpoonRQ</u> (10:2) Spr 85, p. 41-42.
"Brass Unicorns." <u>Blueline</u> (6:2) Wint-Spr 85, p. 6.
"Ennui." <u>Bogg</u> (53) 85, p. 28.
"First Thoughts." <u>NegC</u> (5:4) Fall 85, p. 112-113.
"Letter to Haslam in Petaluma." <u>Amelia</u> (2:1) Ap 85, p. 69-
    70.
"Letter to Joy in Bay City." <u>WebR</u> (10:1) Spr 85, p. 74-75.
"Letter to Shulman in Sherman Oaks." <u>SpoonRQ</u> (10:4) Fall
    85, p. 21-23.
"Loss." <u>DeKalbLAJ</u> (18:3/4) 85, p. 38.
"Lost." <u>WebR</u> (10:1) Spr 85, p. 75-76.
"Richmond." <u>Open24</u> (4) 85, p. 9.
"The Same Old Story." <u>Sam</u> (42:4, 168th release) 85, p. 52.
"Too Old." <u>Sam</u> (42:3, 167th release) 85, p. 48.
2631. KNIGHT, Elizabeth
"The Drowning Man." <u>Telescope</u> (4:2) Spr 85, p. 54.
"Landscape from a Boat at Night." <u>Telescope</u> (4:2) Spr 85,
    p. 53.
2632. KNIGHT, Etheridge
"Last Words by 'Slick'" (or a self/sung eulogy). <u>HangL</u>
    (47) Spr 85, p. 28.
2633. KNIGHT, Kit
"The Meeting." <u>SpoonRQ</u> (10:2) Spr 85, p. 43-44.
"Most Christians Have Shit for Brains." <u>SecC</u> (12:1) 84,
    p. 25-26.
"White-Out." <u>SpoonRQ</u> (10:4) Fall 85, p. 24-26.

2634. KNOBLOCH, Marta
    "Future Shock." <u>SanFPJ</u> (7:2) 85, p. 8.
    "Mediums of Exchange." <u>SanFPJ</u> (7:2) 85, p. 7.
2635. KNOELLER, Christian
    "Entering the Desert" (for Jamake Highwater). <u>CutB</u> (23)
        Fall-Wint 85, p. 47.
    "In the Country of Wind." <u>Ascent</u> (11:1) 85, p. 63.
    "Weighing Coal in Oaxaca." <u>CutB</u> (24) Spr-Sum 85, p. 59.
2636. KNOEPFLE, John
    "At the Sangamon Headwaters." <u>RiverS</u> (18) 85, p. 109.
    "Bath." <u>SpoonRQ</u> (10:2) Spr 85, p. 25.
    "Confluence." <u>SpoonRQ</u> (10:2) Spr 85, p. 26.
    "Decatur." <u>SpoonRQ</u> (10:2) Spr 85, p. 21-22.
    "Late Winter in Menard County." <u>SpoonRQ</u> (10:2) Spr 85, p.
        33-34.
    "Lincoln Tomb, a Report." <u>SpoonRQ</u> (10:2) Spr 85, p. 30-32.
    "Lines for the Tribe of Ben Ishmael." <u>RiverS</u> (18) 85, p.
        107-108.
    "Lunch Room New Berlin." <u>SpoonRQ</u> (10:2) Spr 85, p. 23-24.
    "Poem for Scott Lucas." <u>SpoonRQ</u> (10:2) Spr 85, p. 35-36.
    "Soundings in Glacial Drift." <u>SpoonRQ</u> (10:2) Spr 85, p.
        27-29.
2637. KNOLL, Michael
    "To those Still Waiting." <u>GreenfR</u> (12:3/4) Wint-Spr 85,
        p. 25.
    "Wonders." <u>GreenfR</u> (12:3/4) Wint-Spr 85, p. 24.
2638. KNOTT, Bill
    "Barren Precinct." <u>Iowa</u> (15:1) Wint 85, p. 19.
    "Brighton Rock by Graham Greene" (for Mary Karr). <u>SenR</u>
        (15:2) 85, p. 66-67.
    "Eros and Espionage in the Bent Center" (to Helen C., after
        reading D. G. Rossetti's "Troy Town"). <u>SenR</u> (15:2) 85,
        p. 65.
    "February/Freezeframe" (to X, with thanks for translating
        teardrops into handcuffs). <u>SenR</u> (15:2) 85, p. 62.
    "Up to the Minute." <u>SenR</u> (15:2) 85, p. 64.
    "Weltende Version" (for Jacob van Hoddis). <u>SenR</u> (15:2)
        85, p. 63.
2639. KNOWLTON, Lindsay
    "Central Park." <u>Ploughs</u> (11:1) 85, p. 135.
    "Closet." <u>SenR</u> (15:2) 85, p. 71-72.
    "Crib Bait." <u>SenR</u> (15:2) 85, p. 70.
    "Gardenia." <u>Ploughs</u> (11:1) 85, p. 136.
    "Marriage." <u>SenR</u> (15:2) 85, p. 68-69.
    "Passenger." <u>IndR</u> (8:3) Fall 85, p. 16-17.
    "Stuffed Rabbit." <u>Ploughs</u> (11:1) 85, p. 137.
2640. KNOX, Caroline
    "Angels." <u>MassR</u> (26:4) Wint 85, p. 579.
    "Lizzie Borden through Art and Literature." <u>MassR</u>
        (26:2/3) Sum-Aut 85, p. 446.
2641. KOCH, Kenneth
    "Impressions of Africa: The Congo." <u>Raritan</u> (4:3) Wint
        85, p. 26-41.
2642. KOCHHAR-LINDGREN, Gray
    "Women at the Crossroads." <u>CarolQ</u> (38:1) Fall 85, p. 54.
2643. KOERNER, Edgar
    "The Last Time I Played the Clarinet." <u>LittleM</u> (14:4) 85,
        p. 41.
2644. KOERTGE, Ron (<u>See</u> also KOERTGE, Ronald)
    "Dearly Beloved." <u>Oink</u> (19) 85, p. 99.
    "Desire" (for bianca). <u>WoosterR</u> (3) Spr 85, p. 24.
    "The Mummy." <u>Oink</u> (19) 85, p. 98.
    "Musée." <u>WoosterR</u> (3) Spr 85, p. 23.
    "On the Origin of Animal Demographics and Communication."
        <u>WoosterR</u> (3) Spr 85, p. 25.
    "To the Tune, 'The Cold, Instellar Spaces between Them'."

WoosterR (3) Spr 85, p. 26.
"Us & Them." WoosterR (3) Spr 85, p. 22.
2645. KOERTGE, Ronald (See also KOERTGE, Ron)
      "The Audio Portion." WormR (25:1, issue 97) 85, p. 2.
      "Ralph Nader." WormR (25:1, issue 97) 85, p. 2-3.
      "Roving Boy." WormR (25:1, issue 97) 85, p. 3.
      "Scot Free." WormR (25:1, issue 97) 85, p. 4.
      "Small Elegy." WormR (25:1, issue 97) 85, p. 4.
      "The Woman Who Married a Whale." WormR (25:1, issue 97)
          85, p. 1.
      "Written on Spotless Gauze." WormR (25:1, issue 97) 85,
          p. 3.
2646. KOESTENBAUM, Phyllis
      "Criminal Sonnets" (III). Tendril (19/20) 85, p. 197.
2647. KOESTENBAUM, Wayne
      "'Carmen' in Digital for a Deaf Woman." IndR (8:3) Fall
          85, p. 66.
2648. KOHLER, Sandra
      "First Day." AmerPoR (14:5) S-O 85, p. 32.
      "Love Poem #11." AmerPoR (14:5) S-O 85, p. 32.
2649. KOLUMBAN, Nicholas
      "A Chest with Painted Tulips" (tr. of Elemér Horváth).
          NewL (51:4) Sum 85, p. 34.
      "Execution" (tr. of Elemér Horváth). NewL (51:4) Sum
          85, p. 35.
      "The First Time" (tr. of Elemer Horvath). HawaiiR (17)
          Spr 85, p. 94.
      "Immigrants Wrestling with Sounds." PoetryR (2:2) Ap 85,
          p. 38.
      "In the Root Cellar" (tr. of Sándor Csoóri). NewL
          (51:4) Sum 85, p. 36.
      "It's Tangled But Accurate" (tr. of Elemér Horváth).
          NewL (51:4) Sum 85, p. 34-35.
      "Poppies." MichQR (24:1) Wint 85, p. 69.
2650. KOMUNYAKAA, Yusef
      "2527th Birthday of the Buddha." NoAmR (270:3) S 85, p.
          47.
      "After the Summer Fell Apart." MSS (4:3) Spr 85, p. 107-
          108.
      "Asking." RiverS (18) 85, p. 86.
      "Boat People." MSS (4:3) Spr 85, p. 109.
      "Born Pretty in a Poor Country." Ploughs (11:1) 85, p.
          138.
      "A Break from the Bush." Ploughs (11:1) 85, p. 140.
      "The Esoteric." RiverS (18) 85, p. 87.
      "Flashback." Ploughs (11:1) 85, p. 139.
2651. KONECKY, Edith
      "Poems for One-Handed Typists." OP (38/39) Spr 85, p. 102-
          103.
2652. KONESKI, Blazhe
      "The Dormition of Aunt Menka" (tr. by Anne Pennington and
          Andrew Harvey). SenR (15:1) 85, p. 59.
2653. KONG, Ann
      "Christ Going through the Wheatfield." Amelia (2:2) O 85,
          p. 24-25.
      "A Parable." Amelia (2:2) O 85, p. 25-26.
      "The Second Womb: The Story of Another City." Amelia
          (2:2) O 85, p. 27-28.
      "Sestina for My Wife." Amelia (2:2) O 85, p. 26-27.
2654. KONO, Juliet S.
      "Sulfur." HawaiiR (18) Fall 85, p. 73-74.
2655. KOOSER, Ted
      "A Perfect Heart." CreamCR (10:1) 85, p. 47.
2656. KOPEC, Carol
      "April." CrossCur (4:4/5:1) 85, p. 36-37.
      "Chinook Winds." WebR (10:1) Spr 85, p. 40.

"Illumination." <u>WebR</u> (10:1) Spr 85, p. 41.
"Winter Sky." <u>WebR</u> (10:1) Spr 85, p. 41.
2657. KOPELKE, Kendra
"Girl Asleep at a Table." <u>PartR</u> (52:4) 85, p. 427-428.
"Jonnie Richardson." <u>Tendril</u> (19/20) 85, p. 198-203.
"Sunday." <u>IndR</u> (8:3) Fall 85, p. 12.
2658. KOPP, Doug
"Moundville, Alabama: After the Battle." <u>NegC</u> (5:2) Spr
85, p. 63-64.
2659. KOPP, Karl
"Easter 1985 Sunrise." <u>CharR</u> (11:2) Fall 85, p. 102-103.
"News." <u>CharR</u> (11:2) Fall 85, p. 103-105.
2660. KOPPERL, Helga
"Go Out and Burn the Sun." <u>YellowS</u> (17) Wint 85, p. 4.
2661. KOROSY, Mária
"Beast of Prey" (tr. of Ottó Orbán, w. Jascha Kessler).
<u>GrahamHR</u> (9) Fall 85, p. 59.
"A Blade of Grass" (tr. of Ottó Orbán, w. Jascha
Kessler). <u>Ploughs</u> (11:4) 85, p. 219.
"Builders" (tr. of Ottó Orbán, w. Jascha Kessler).
<u>GrahamHR</u> (9) Fall 85, p. 57.
"Excerpts from the Modern Tragedy" (tr. of Sándor
Weöres, w. Jascha Kessler). <u>GrahamHR</u> (8) Wint 85, p.
41-42.
"An Excursion" (tr. of Ottó Orbán, w. Jascha Kessler).
<u>GrahamHR</u> (9) Fall 85, p. 60.
"Farewell" (tr. of Ottó Orbán, w. Jascha Kessler).
<u>GrahamHR</u> (9) Fall 85, p. 62.
"For Example" (tr. of Mihaly Ládanyi, w. Jascha Kessler).
<u>NewL</u> (51:4) Sum 85, p. 39.
"The Lion" (tr. of Istvån Vas, w. Jascha Kessler).
<u>Ploughs</u> (11:4) 85, p. 215.
"Love Match" (tr. of Ottó Orbán, w. Jascha Kessler).
<u>GrahamHR</u> (9) Fall 85, p. 58.
"Once More" (tr. of Istvån Vas, w. Jascha Kessler).
<u>Ploughs</u> (11:4) 85, p. 214.
"Painting" (tr. of Ottó Orbán, w. Jascha Kessler).
<u>GrahamHR</u> (9) Fall 85, p. 61.
"A Small Country" (tr. of Ottó Orbán, w. Jascha
Kessler). <u>GrahamHR</u> (9) Fall 85, p. 55.
"The Technique" (tr. of Ottó Orbán, w. Jascha Kessler).
<u>Ploughs</u> (11:4) 85, p. 218.
"The Technique" (tr. of Ottó Orbán, w. Jascha Kessler).
<u>GrahamHR</u> (9) Fall 85, p. 56.
2662. KORP, Maureen
"Good Friends." <u>CrossC</u> (7:1) 85, p. 12.
"The Publisher's Daughter." <u>CrossC</u> (7:1) 85, p. 12.
2663. KORZHAVIN, Naum
"Childhood Has Ended" (tr. by Richard Lourie). <u>Ploughs</u>
(11:4) 85, p. 174.
2664. KOSMICKI, Greg
"A Short History of Civilization." <u>GreenfR</u> (13:1/2) Fall-
Wint 85, p. 179.
2665. KOSS, A. Goldman
"The Appeal of Horror." <u>Pig</u> (13) 85, p. 43.
2666. KOSTELANETZ, Richard
"Dialogue, Dialect, Diaphragm, Dial." <u>MemphisSR</u> (5:2) Spr
85, p. 21.
"Duets, Duets, Trios, Trios, Trios, Choruses, . . ." <u>SmPd</u>
(22:2) Spr 85, p. 16-25.
"Epiphanies." <u>OP</u> (38/39) Spr 85, p. 110-112.
"Lovings" (Excerpts). <u>Open24</u> (4) 85, p. 59.
2667. KOVACIK, Karen
"Dorothy Wordsworth." <u>ColEng</u> (47:4) Ap 85, p. 374-375.
"Trains at Night." <u>PassN</u> (6:2) Spr-Sum 85, p. 16.

2668. KOZAK, Roberta
       "Dead Man." Crazy (29) Fall 85, p. 42-43.
       "On Brevity" (for Jim). BlackWR (12:1) Fall 85, p. 6-7.
       "On Listening." NoAmR (270:2) Je 85, p. 23.
       "Strait of Senyavin." Crazy (29) Fall 85, p. 44-45.
       "Ways of Walking." Crazy (26) Spr 84, p. 45-46.
2669. KRALC, Christina B.
       "The El Cajon Ranger." Open24 (4) 85, p. 36.
2670. KRAMER, Aaron
       "At Three in the Morning." Confr (30/31) N 85, p. 110.
       "Flood." CumbPR (5:1) Fall 85, p. 26-27.
       "Indigo." NewEngR (8:2) Wint 85, p. 178-179.
       "Metropolitan Forecast." Vis (17) 85, p. 25.
       "Southshore Line." Confr (30/31) N 85, p. 109.
2671. KRAMER, Matthew
       "Waking." HiramPoR (38) Spr-Sum 85, p. 23.
2672. KRAPF, Norbert
       "Breathing in Bogotá." AmerS (54:1) Wint 84-85, p. 98.
       "A Dream of Plum Blossoms." Sparrow (49) 85, 25 p.
       "Indigo Bunting." Raccoon (17) Mr 85, p. 28.
       "Meeting on Main Street." Confr (30/31) N 85, p. 130.
       "The Politics of Weeds." Confr (30/31) N 85, p. 128-129.
       "St. Meinrad Archabbey." Blueline (7:1) Sum-Fall 85, p. 6.
       "A Swabian Scene." NoDaQ (53:1) Wint 85, p. 112-113.
2673. KRATT, Mary
       "In the Time of John L. Lewis" (Selection: II. "I'd Have
          Waited a Lifetime for You, Greer Garson"). Nimrod
          (29:1) Fall-Wint 85, p. 57-58.
2674. KRAUSE, Judith
       "I Dream You Are Riding a Dolphin." PoetryCR (7:2) Wint
          85-86, p. 23.
2675. KRAUSS, Janet
       "Thoughts after Having a Bad Fall." BlueBldgs (9) [85?],
          p. 9.
2676. KRAWIEC, Richard
       "Love Runs Out." NegC (5:1) Wint 85, p. 119.
       "Shifting Layers." Wind (15:55) 85, p. 9.
2677. KREEGER, Walter
       "The Longest Day" (tr. of Hugo Dittberner). Mund (15:1/2)
          85, p. 159, 161.
       "On the Utility of Love" (tr. of Hugo Dittberner). Mund
          (15:1/2) 85, p. 159.
2678. KREITER-KURYLO, Carolyn
       "Take This on Authority." NegC (5:2) Spr 85, p. 24.
       "Touch." Wind (15:54) 85, p. 19.
2679. KRESH, David
       "Equinox." WebR (10:1) Spr 85, p. 44-48.
       "Goodnight. Goodnight." ChiR (35:2) Wint 85, p. 24.
       "Gray." ChiR (35:2) Wint 85, p. 23.
2680. KRESS, Leonard
       "N.N. Records Something on the Back of a Cigarette Pack"
          (tr. of Stanislaw Baranczak). CrossCur (4:2) 84, p. 13.
       "Pan Cogito and the Imagination" (tr. of Zbygniew Herbert).
          CrossCur (4:2) 84, p. 121.
       "The Piano of Chopin" (tr. of Cyprian Norwid). WebR
          (10:1) Spr 85, p. 18-21.
       "Psalm Ajar" (tr. of Tadeusz Nowak). BlueBldgs (9) [85?],
          p. 18.
       "Resumé" (tr. of Wislawa Szymborska). CrossCur (4:2)
          84, p. 163, 165.
       "Sennik." QW (21) Fall-Wint 85, p. 23-24.
2681. KRETZ, T. (See also KRETZ, Thomas)
       "Gretchen Grit." Bogg (53) 85, p. 7.
2682. KRETZ, Thomas (See also KRETZ, T.)
       "After Three Months in the Same Pew." WestCR (20:2) O 85,
          p. 24.

"Driving South from Madrid." SpoonRQ (10:4) Fall 85, p. 54.
"Fisherman's Prayer." NegC (5:4) Fall 85, p. 126.
"On Being a Foreigner." KanQ (17:1/2) Wint-Spr 85, p. 206.
"Same Prayer by Andre Breton." NegC (5:4) Fall 85, p. 126.
"Schwarzwald." Amelia (2:1) Ap 85, p. 81.
2683. KRICH, A. M.
"Memorial Day." MassR (26:4) Wint 85, p. 503-504.
2684. KRIESEL, Michael Allen
"Living with the Beast." PassN (6:1) Fall-Wint 85, p. 22.
2685. KRINSLEY, Jeanne
"In an Office with No Windows." Prima (9) 85, p. 74.
2686. KRISTOFCO, John
"Coal Miner." Wind (15:55) 85, p. 26.
2687. KROETSCH, Robert
"Excerpts from the Real World" (Selections). Dandel (12:1) 85, p. 33.
2688. KROK, Peter
"Toll." NegC (5:2) Spr 85, p. 79.
2689. KROLL, Ernest
"Ciphers" (In memoriam: Ralph Cory, Guadalcanal, 1942). TexasR (6:1/2) Spr-Sum 85, p. 38-39.
"Loren Eiseley" (1907-1977). WebR (10:2) Fall 85, p. 79.
"The Monument." LaurelR (19:1) Wint 85, p. 29.
"Rendezvous" (Or, The Reformation Revisited). LaurelR (19:2) Sum 85, p. 58.
"Silverado Revisited" (Mount Saint Helena, California). WebR (10:2) Fall 85, p. 78-79.
"Spanish Main." MidwQ (26:4) Sum 85, p. 459.
2690. KROLL, Judith
"After the Snowfall." Tendril (19/20) 85, p. 204.
"The Dream of Elizabeth Hartley." SouthernR (21:1) Wint 85, p. 104-110.
"Figures of Silence." NoAmR (270:4) D 85, p. 43.
"Lost Cause." WestHR (19:2) Sum 85, p. 132.
"Same Time, Next Life." Tendril (19/20) 85, p. 206.
"Summer Fractures." SenR (15:1) 85, p. 31-33.
"Winter Birth." Tendril (19/20) 85, p. 205.
2691. KROLOW, Karl
"Air" (tr. by Stuart Friebert). Ploughs (11:4) 85, p. 144.
"Haven't You Noticed?" (tr. by Stuart Friebert). Field (32) Spr 85, p. 38.
"In Flight" (tr. by Stuart Friebert). Ploughs (11:4) 85, p. 147.
"People on the Move" (tr. by Stuart Friebert). Ploughs (11:4) 85, p. 146.
"Some Exceptions" (tr. by Stuart Friebert). Field (32) Spr 85, p. 39.
"Stranger's Hand in Your Pocket" (tr. by Stuart Friebert). Ploughs (11:4) 85, p. 145.
"Think I Heard Something" (tr. by Stuart Friebert). Field (32) Spr 85, p. 40.
2692. KROMBEL, Raymond M.
"Circus Fool." RagMag (4:1) Spr 85, p. 46.
2693. KRONEN, Steve
"How the Birds Fly" (for Ellie). SouthernPR (25:1) Spr 85, p. 10.
"Life As It Really Is." SouthernPR (25:1) Spr 85, p. 11.
2694. KRONENBERG, Mindy
"Coming Clean." Bogg (53) 85, p. 30.
2695. KRONENBERG, Susan
"Lift Off." CrabCR (3:1) Fall-Wint 85, p. 4.
2696. KRONENFELD, Judy
"Again." NegC (5:1) Wint 85, p. 50.
"Her Hair." Wind (15:54) 85, p. 27.
"Reach Out and Touch Someone." CrossCur (4:4/5:1) 85, p.

136.
2697. KRUSOE, James
      "Bow Ties." <u>CrossCur</u> (5:2) 85, p. 121.
      "A Cloud." <u>Zyzzyva</u> (1:3) Fall 85, p. 57.
2698. KRYNICKI, Ryszard
      "The Answer" (tr. by Stanislaw Baranczak and Clare
          Cavanagh). <u>Ploughs</u> (11:4) 85, p. 134.
      "By Saying" (tr. by Stanislaw Baranczak and Clare
          Cavanagh). <u>Ploughs</u> (11:4) 85, p. 133.
      "The Heart" (tr. by Stanislaw Baranczak and Clare
          Cavanagh). <u>Ploughs</u> (11:4) 85, p. 135.
      "How Far" (tr. by Stanislaw Baranczak and Clare Cavanagh).
          <u>Ploughs</u> (11:4) 85, p. 135.
      "If It Comes to Pass" (tr. by Stanislaw Baranczak and Clare
          Cavanagh). <u>Ploughs</u> (11:4) 85, p. 136.
      "I'll Remember That" (tr. by Stanislaw Baranczak and Clare
          Cavanagh). <u>Ploughs</u> (11:4) 85, p. 136.
      "Inscription on a China Dish" (tr. by Stanislaw Baranczak
          and Clare Cavanagh). <u>Ploughs</u> (11:4) 85, p. 137.
      "Rumor Has It" (tr. by Stanislaw Baranczak and Clare
          Cavanagh). <u>Ploughs</u> (11:4) 85, p. 133.
      "This Moment" (tr. by Stanislaw Baranczak and Clare
          Cavanagh). <u>Ploughs</u> (11:4) 85, p. 134.
      "The Time of Trial" (tr. by Stanislaw Baranczak and Clare
          Cavanagh). <u>Ploughs</u> (11:4) 85, p. 137.
2699. KRYSL, Marilyn
      "The Foreign Woman Laments the Persistence of Ideal
          Systems." <u>OP</u> (38/39) Spr 85, p. 87-88.
      "People's Republic of China: Leaving -- The Open Ended
          Sestina." <u>DenQ</u> (20:1) Sum 85, p. 11-12.
      "Sestina: People's Republic of China, The No. 1 Machine
          Tool Factory Foreman's Wife." <u>DenQ</u> (20:1) Sum 85, p. 7-
          8.
      "West Lake, Hangzhou." <u>DenQ</u> (20:1) Sum 85, p. 9-10.
2700. KUBY, Lolette
      "To the Social Worker (Crazy Cousin Celia)." <u>PoetL</u> (80:2)
          Sum 85, p. 87-88.
      "The Wrong Side of the Bed." <u>MidwQ</u> (26:4) Sum 85, p. 460-
          461.
2701. KUDERKO, Lynne
      "Love Scene from an Unfinished Novel." <u>PoetryNW</u> (26:3)
          Aut 85, p. 43.
2702. KUMIN, Maxine
      "After the Harvest." <u>OntR</u> (22) Spr-Sum 85, p. 96-97.
      "In the Absence of Bliss" (Museum of the Diaspora, Tel
          Aviv). <u>Tendril</u> (19/20) 85, p. 207-209.
      "The Long Approach." <u>OntR</u> (22) Spr-Sum 85, p. 94-95.
      "My Elusive Guest." <u>MassR</u> (26:2/3) Sum-Aut 85, p. 175.
      "A New England Gardener Gets Personal." <u>MassR</u> (26:2/3)
          Sum-Aut 85, p. 176-177.
      "Pain." <u>TriQ</u> (63) Spr-Sum 85, p. 166-167.
      "Sundays in March" (For Celeste and Robert Klein). <u>Poetry</u>
          (145:6) Mr 85, p. 342-344.
      "Video Cuisine." <u>Nat</u> (240:2) 19 Ja 85, p. 54.
      "Visiting Professor." <u>Tendril</u> (19/20) 85, p. 210-211.
2703. KUNCHEV, Nicolai (<u>See also</u> KANTCHEV, Nicolai)
      "The Bee's Calendar" (In Bulgarian and English, tr. by
          Jascha Kessler and Alexander Shurbanov). <u>CrossCur</u>
          (4:2) 84, p. 33.
2704. KUNERT, Günter
      "About Some Who Got Away" (tr. by Felix Pollak and Reinhold
          Grimm). <u>NewL</u> (51:4) Sum 85, p. 51.
      "Answer to Questionnaire" (tr. by Agnes Stein). <u>DenQ</u>
          (19:4) Spr 85, p. 57-58.
      "Fellow Citizen" (tr. by Agnes Stein). <u>DenQ</u> (19:4) Spr
          85, p. 59.

KUNERT   228

"On the Archaeology of Our Interment" (tr. by Agnes Stein).
     DenQ (19:4) Spr 85, p. 55-56.
"Report about Him" (tr. by Felix Pollak and Reinhold
     Grimm). NewL (51:4) Sum 85, p. 52-53.
2705. KUNITZ, Stanley
"Passing Through" (on my 79th birthday). AmerPoR (14:5) S-
     O 85, p. 23.
"Raccoon Journal." NewYorker (61:22) 22 Jl 85, p. 32.
"The Round." AmerPoR (14:5) S-O 85, p. 23.
"The Scene" (After Alexander Blok). Antaeus (55) Aut 85,
     p. 128.
"Three Small Parables for My Poet Friends." Antaeus (55)
     Aut 85, p. 129.
"The Tumbling of Worms." AmerPoR (14:5) S-O 85, p. 24.
2706. KUNTZ, Bob
"After the Funeral." ChrC (102:1) 2-9 Ja 85, p. 5.
2707. KUNZE, Reiner
"Along the Danube in Fog" (tr. by Lori Fisher). NewL
     (51:4) Sum 85, p. 50.
"Erasmus of Rotterdam" (tr. by Lori Fisher). NewL (51:4)
     Sum 85, p. 50.
"Kleine Rechenschaft nach Mahren" (für Jan Skácel).
     Mund (16:1/2) 85, p. 14.
"Love Poem after Takeoff, or In the Same Plane with You"
     (tr. by Lori Fisher). NewL (51:4) Sum 85, p. 51.
"A Small Account of Moravia" (for Jan Skacel, tr. by Lori
     Fisher). Mund (16:1/2) 85, p. 15.
"Solace at Ten Thousand Meters" (tr. by Lori Fisher).
     NewL (51:4) Sum 85, p. 50.
2708. KUPFERBERG, Tuli
"Slum Landlord of the Lower East Side" (A a new Fug Song,
     to the tune of "Slum Goddess of the Lower East Side," an
     old Fug Song). PortLES (2:1) Sum 85, p. 9-10.
KURYLO, Carolyn Kreiter
     See KREITER-KURYLO, Carolyn
2709. KUSCH, Robert
"The Field." SewanR (93:4) Fall 85, p. 533-534.
2710. KUZMA, Greg
"Consciousness." ConnPR (3:1) 84, p. 12.
"The Dead." ConnPR (3:1) 84, p. 3.
"Deep Woods." GrahamHR (8) Wint 85, p. 32.
"Geronimo." CrabCR (2:2) Wint 85, p. 25.
"Goodbye." CharR (11:2) Fall 85, p. 93.
"A Monday in March." PraS (59:1) Spr 85, p. 55.
"The Mountains." CharR (11:2) Fall 85, p. 94.
"The Ownership of the River" (for Wendell Berry). NowestR
     (23:1) 85, p. 11.
"Physical Labor." OhioR (35) 85, p. 78.
"Pond." GrahamHR (8) Wint 85, p. 33.
"Roses." PraS (59:1) Spr 85, p. 56.
"The Snow." PraS (59:1) Spr 85, p. 57.
"So Far." PraS (59:1) Spr 85, p. 54.
"That Region." GrahamHR (8) Wint 85, p. 30-31.
"They." ConnPR (3:1) 84, p. 2.
2711. KVAM, Wayne
"Cafeteria Linemen." WindO (46) Fall 85, p. 26.
2712. KWAIN, Constance
"The Arrow in August." Oink (19) 85, p. 113.
"Xerox Sharks." CreamCR (10:2) [85?], p. 48.
2713. KWIATEK, JoEllen
"A Painting by Vermeer" (For R. Zannoni). AntR (43:4)
     Fall 85, p. 465.
2714. KWOCK, C. H.
"Lakeshore" (tr. of Ren Yu, w. G. G. Gach). Zyzzyva (1:1)
     Spr 85, p. 40.
"To the Tune of Half & Half" (tr. of Sung Fang-Hu, w. G. G.

Gach). <u>Zyzzyva</u> (1:1) Spr 85, p. 41.

KYOKO, Mori
   <u>See</u> MORI, Kyoko
KYU-BO, Yi
   <u>See</u> YI, Kyu-bo

LA . . .
   <u>See also</u> names beginning with "La" without the following
      space, filed below in their alphabetic positions, e.g.,
      LaSALLE.
La CRUZ, Juana Inès de, Sor
   <u>See</u> CRUZ, Juana Inès de la, Sor
La PUEBLA, Manuel de
   <u>See</u> PUEBLA, Manuel de la
2715. La ROQUE, Catherine
      "White Man." <u>SanFPJ</u> (7:2) 85, p. 85.
2716. LACERDA, Alberto de
      "Rhythm" (To Jorge Guillén, tr. by David Wevill).
         <u>Imagine</u> (1:2) Wint 84, p. 209.
      "Ritmo" (A Jorge Guillén). <u>Imagine</u> (1:2) Wint 84, p.
         208.
2717. LADANY, Mihàly (<u>See also</u> LADANYI, Mihaly)
      "Come Back" (tr. by Ivan Halasz de Beky). <u>Rampike</u> (4:2/3)
         85-86, p. 14.
      "Inventory" (tr. by Ivan Halasz de Beky). <u>Rampike</u> (4:2/3)
         85-86, p. 14.
      "The Pack" (tr. by Ivan Halasz de Beky). <u>Rampike</u> (4:2/3)
         85-86, p. 14.
2718. LADANYI, Mihaly (<u>See also</u> LADANY, Mihàly)
      "For Example" (tr. by Jascha Kessler and Maria Korosy).
         <u>NewL</u> (51:4) Sum 85, p. 39.
2719. LADHA, Yasmin
      "Your Inheritance Teacher." <u>Dandel</u> (12:1) 85, p. 19-21.
2720. LaGATTUTA, Margo
      "Swallowing Flowers." <u>PassN</u> (6:2) Spr-Sum 85, p. 19.
2721. LAIRD, R. Steven
      "Moses before Canaan." <u>Grain</u> (13:3) Ag 85, p. 13.
      "Slow River." <u>Grain</u> (13:3) Ag 85, p. 60.
LAJOIE, Rhea Mouledoux
   <u>See</u> MOULEDOUX-LAJOIE, Rhea
2722. LAKE, Paul
      "An Artist at Mid-Life." <u>KanQ</u> (17:3) Sum 85, p. 38-39.
      "Concerning Angels: A Poetry Reading" (for Robert Pinsky
         and Bob Hass). <u>PoetryNW</u> (26:1) Spr 85, p. 45-46.
      "Introduction to Poetry." <u>TexasR</u> (6:1/2) Spr-Sum 85, p.
         37.
      "While Watching the Ballet Folclorico Nacional de Mexico."
         <u>Pequod</u> (19/20/21) 85, p. 215-216.
2723. LALLY, Margaret
      "Tom's Hand." <u>LitR</u> (28:4) Sum 85, p. 580.
2724. LAMADRID, Lucas
      "Transmigracion." <u>LindLM</u> (4:2) Ap-Je 85, p. 29.
2725. LaMANNA, Richard
      "At Paul Metcalf's Poetry Reading." <u>CapeR</u> (20:2) Fall 85,
         p. 10.
2726. LAMANTIA, Philip
      "Death Jets." <u>Zyzzyva</u> (1:4) Wint 85, p. 136-138.
2727. LAMAR, Paul
      "Holiday in New Haven" (1965). <u>MidAR</u> (5:2) 85, p. 19.
      "Ultimata" (for Wayne). <u>MidAR</u> (5:2) 85, p. 18.
2728. LAMB, Margaret
      "Nature, How Supremely Orderly." <u>Blueline</u> (6:2) Wint-Spr
         85, p. 24.
2729. LAMBERT, Deborah
      "The Extravagance of the Real" (For Mary Wilkins Freeman,
         1852-1930). <u>SouthwR</u> (70:4) Aut 85, p. 496-497.

2730. LAMMON, Martin
    "Witness: A Mother's Labor." CharR (11:2) Fall 85, p. 109.
2731. LAMPELL, Jacqueline
    "Scene." Open24 (4) 85, p. 48.
2732. LANCE, Jeanne
    "Passionate Attention" (for Kathleen Fraser). LaurelR
        (19:2) Sum 85, p. 64.
2733. LANDALE, Zoë
    "100 Mile House: Duration." AntigR (61) Spr 85, p. 130.
    "Green Tomato Chutney Poem." Quarry (34:4) Aut 85, p. 33-
        34.
    "Leaning into Next Year." WestCR (20:2) O 85, p. 19.
2734. LANDAU, Julie
    "Late Spring" (tr. of Hsin Ch'i-chi). MSS (4:3) Spr 85,
        p. 26.
    "Ting Feng P'o: Ignore it!" (tr. of Su Shih). DenQ (20:1)
        Sum 85, p. 13.
    "Ting Feng P'o: Sing of the red flowering plum" (tr. of Su
        Shih). DenQ (20:1) Sum 85, p. 14.
2735. LANDER, Tim
    "I Am Tongue-Tied." WestCR (20:2) O 85, p. 20.
LANDRIAN, Nicolas Guillen
    See GUILLEN LANDRIAN, Nicolas
2736. LANDRY, John
    "From Sconticut." GreenfR (13:1/2) Fall-Wint 85, p. 34.
    "Letter from Paradise." GreenfR (13:1/2) Fall-Wint 85, p.
        33.
    "Proletarian Sonnet." GreenfR (13:1/2) Fall-Wint 85, p.
        35.
    "Stars Full of Trees" (after the Portuguese of Eugenio de
        Andrade). GreenfR (13:1/2) Fall-Wint 85, p. 35.
2737. LANDSMAN, Julie
    "Place Setting." PassN (6:2) Spr-Sum 85, p. 14.
2738. LANE, M. Travis
    "Looking at a Sculpture by Ulker Ozerdam" (Five Poems).
        Waves (13:4) Spr 85, p. 56-58.
2739. LANE, Pinkie Gordon
    "Old Photo from a Family Album, 1915." SouthernR (21:3)
        Sum 85, p. 862-863.
    "Two Poems for Gordon." SouthernR (21:3) Sum 85, p. 860-
        861.
2740. LANE, W.
    "The Goats at Dusk." JlNJPo (8:1) 85, p. 12.
    "Poster of Borges" (for S. Rabinowitz). JlNJPo (8:1) 85,
        p. 14.
    "Walking at Night" (for Lisa Portmess). JlNJPo (8:1) 85,
        p. 13.
2741. LANG, Stephen
    "Allegro con Brio." Poem (54) N 85, p. 24.
    "Grenadier." Poem (54) N 85, p. 25.
    "Hemophiliacs." Poem (53) Mr 85, p. 6.
    "On the Sabbath Morning." Poem (53) Mr 85, p. 5.
    "This Goodly Remembered Night." NegC (5:4) Fall 85, p.
        123.
    "The Virgins Were Gathered." Poem (53) Mr 85, p. 4.
    "The World's End." Poem (54) N 85, p. 23.
2742. LANG, Warren
    "In the Night." RagMag (4:2) Fall 85, p. 32.
    "The Palace of Joy and Longevity." RagMag (4:2) Fall 85,
        p. 31.
    "Turtle Eggs" (for Dan and Jane). RagMag (4:2) Fall 85,
        p. 33.
2743. LANGDON, Keith
    "A Nurse (Who Works with Dying Patients)." EngJ (74:2) F
        85, p. 39.

2744. LANGE, Art
      "As Seen at the Art Institute of Chicago, 5/3/84: Joan
         Mitchell's City Landscape Swept by Sorrow and
         Disillusionment." Oink (19) 85, p. 87-88.
      "To the Muse." Oink (19) 85, p. 86.
2745. LANGENDORF, Adele
      "The Sister Doll." NegC (5:2) Spr 85, p. 96.
2746. LANGTON, Daniel (See also LANGTON, Daniel J.)
      "The Perfect Country and Western Song." OP (38/39) Spr
         85, p. 168.
2747. LANGTON, Daniel J. (See also LANGTON, Daniel)
      "Near By." CapeR (20:2) Fall 85, p. 45.
2748. LANSING, Gerrit
      "Bracketing in City Thickets." Temblor (1) 85, p. 133.
      "The Orchards of Sleep" (Selections: Five Poems in Memory
         of Anna Kavan). Conjunc (7) 85, p. 59-60.
2749. LANZA, Carmela
      "The Vision." Cond (11/12) 85, p. 152-153.
2750. LAPIDUS, Jacqueline
      "Imported Gifts." HangL (48) Fall 85, p. 45.
2751. LAPINGTON, S. C.
      "Intensive Care." Stand (26:4) Aut 85, p. 40.
      "Traction." Stand (26:4) Aut 85, p. 41.
      "The Wanderer." Stand (26:4) Aut 85, p. 39.
2752. LARDAS, Konstantinos
      "Havoc." Wind (15:53) 85, p. 32.
      "Lilies." Wind (15:53) 85, p. 32.
2753. LARKIN, Joan
      "Notes on Sex without Love." HangL (48) Fall 85, p. 48.
      "A Qualification: Pat H." HangL (48) Fall 85, p. 49-50.
      "Rape Memory." HangL (48) Fall 85, p. 46-47.
      "Translation." HangL (48) Fall 85, p. 48.
2754. LARRAIN, Virginia
      "Friendship." Imagine (2:1) Sum 85, p. 105.
      "Potter's Song." Imagine (2:1) Sum 85, p. 105.
      "This May Not Seem Important, But." Imagine (2:1) Sum 85,
         p. 104.
      "Two Friends." Imagine (2:1) Sum 85, p. 104.
2755. LARSEN, Deborah
      "August Heat: Near Center City, Minnesota, 1958." HolCrit
         (22:5) D 85, p. 14-15.
2756. LARSEN, James
      "Icarus." CanLit (105) Sum 85, p. 16-17.
2757. LARSEN, Marianne
      "Ask" (In Danish and English, tr. by Alexander Taylor).
         CrossCur (4:2) 84, p. 108.
      "Bag Om Maskerne" (Excerpt). Mund (15:1/2) 85, p. 90.
      "Behind the Masks" (Excerpt, tr. by Bente Hierholzer).
         Mund (15:1/2) 85, p. 91.
      "Dear Living" (Excerpt, tr. by Bente Hierholzer). Mund
         (15:1/2) 85, p. 93.
      "Kaere Levende" (Excerpt). Mund (15:1/2) 85, p. 92.
2758. LARSON, Rustin
      "The Woman in the White Peugeot." IndR (8:3) Fall 85, p.
         68-69.
Las CASAS, Walter de
      See CASAS, Walter de las
2759. LaSALLE, Peter
      "A girl in a Bar after a Wedding." Wind (15:53) 85, p. 19-
         20.
2760. LASH, Kenneth
      "Topic of Cancer." NoAmR (270:4) D 85, p. 5.
2761. LASKEY, Michael
      "In Aldringham Churchyard, Suffolk." Stand (26:3) Sum 85,
         p. 27.

2762. LASKIN, Pamela I. (See also LASKIN, Pamela L.)
      "Unbraided." WindO (45) Spr 85, p. 6.
2763. LASKIN, Pamela L. (See also LASKIN, Pamela I.)
      "Beauty & the Beast." PoeticJ (11) 85, p. 14.
      "On Reading William Carlos Williams." Wind (15:55) 85, p.
         44.
2764. LASOEN, Patricia
      "Before the Revolution." Vis (18) 85, p. 21.
2765. LASSELL, Michael (See also LASSELL, Michael J.)
      "Aqua." Amelia (2:1) Ap 85, p. 65.
      "Armageddon Avenue." CrabCR (3:1) Fall-Wint 85, p. 18.
      "California Memories." Amelia (2:2) O 85, p. 37-38.
      "Death in Late Summer." Amelia (2:2) O 85, p. 38-39.
      "The Donald Years" (For Rudy Kikel). MidAR (5:1) 85, p.
         39-41.
      "How to Go to the Theater." Zyzzyva (1:4) Wint 85, p. 125-
         129.
      "Old Men at the Spa" (For Laud Humphreys). MidAR (5:2)
         85, p. 33-46.
      "Street Meat" (Excerpt). JamesWR (2:3) Spr-Sum 85, p. 10-
         11.
      "Unremembered Dreams." Amelia (2:2) O 85, p. 40.
2766. LASSELL, Michael J. (See also LASSELL, Michael)
      "The Indian Hunter" (bronze, 1860 by John Quincy Adams
         Ward, American, 1830-1910). CrabCR (2:2) Wint 85, p. 6.
2767. LATCHAW, Joan S.
      "The Dream." Pig (13) 85, p. 81.
2768. LATCHMAN, Paula
      "Day Care." Waves (13:2/3) Wint 85, p. 99.
      "Trouble." Waves (13:2/3) Wint 85, p. 99.
2769. LATTAK, Marjeanne
      "All Night Diner." Wind (15:54) 85, p. 28.
2770. LATTIMORE, Elaine
      "Fat Lady." PoetL (80:2) Sum 85, p. 80-81.
2771. LATTIMORE, Richmond
      "The Idea of a Town." Hudson (38:1) Spr 85, p. 56.
2772. LAU, Carolyn
      "#1 Plus #17." AmerPoR (14:5) S-O 85, p. 8.
      "Daphne Returning." AmerPoR (14:5) S-O 85, p. 8.
      "Guanyin." AmerPoR (14:5) S-O 85, p. 8.
      "How the Middle Kingdom Works." AmerPoR (14:5) S-O 85, p.
         8.
      "The Meaning 'Woman' translated from Chinese into English."
         AmerPoR (14:5) S-O 85, p. 8.
      LAUCANNO, Christopher Sawyer
         See SAWYER-LAUCANNO, Christopher
2773. LAUGHLIN, James
      "A la Testa Que Dansa Ela" (in Provençal, tr. by Guy
         Mathieu). Oink (19) 85, p. 40.
      "Les Amants." ParisR (27:98) Wint 85, p. 123.
      "The Beautiful Muttering." Iowa (15:2) Spr-Sum 85, p. 6.
      "The Believer." Chelsea (44) 85, p. 122.
      "The Bible Says." Chelsea (44) 85, p. 121.
      "The Care and Feeding of a Poet." AntigR (60) Wint 85, p.
         118.
      "The Casual Kiss." OP (38/39) Spr 85, p. 174.
      "C'est à Mourir de Rire." Antaeus (55) Aut 85, p. 130.
      "Domestic Nomenclature." AntigR (60) Wint 85, p. 119.
      "The Doppelgängers." ParisR (27:98) Wint 85, p. 124.
      "Elle A la Tete Qui Danse." Oink (19) 85, p. 39.
      "The End of It All." AntigR (60) Wint 85, p. 119.
      "The French." ParisR (27:98) Wint 85, p. 125.
      "I Have Heard." OP (38/39) Spr 85, p. 117.
      "If in the Night I Wake." Chelsea (44) 85, p. 121.
      "J'Ayme Donc Je Suis, Je Souffre Mais Je Vis." AntigR
         (60) Wint 85, p. 120.

"J'Ayme Donc Je Suis, Je Souffre Mais Je Vis." <u>Oink</u> (19)
    85, p. 43.
"J'Ayme Donc Je Suis, Je Souffre Mais Je Vis" (tr. into
    English by Reno Odlin). <u>AntigR</u> (60) Wint 85, p. 121.
"Je Suis le Comedien." <u>Oink</u> (19) 85, p. 41.
"Pour Bien Aimer." <u>Oink</u> (19) 85, p. 42.
"She's Not Exactly Like You." <u>Iowa</u> (15:2) Spr-Sum 85, p. 7.
"Some Memories of E.P." (Drafts & Fragments). <u>Iowa</u> (15:2)
    Spr-Sum 85, p. 3-5.
"Les Vieillards." <u>Os</u> (21) 85, p. 2.
2774. LAUTERBACH, Ann
"After the Storm." <u>Conjunc</u> (8) 85, p. 94.
"Betty Observed." <u>ParisR</u> (27:98) Wint 85, p. 103.
"Graffiti." <u>ParisR</u> (27:98) Wint 85, p. 100.
"Mountain Roads." <u>Conjunc</u> (8) 85, p. 92-93.
"Naming the House." <u>ParisR</u> (27:98) Wint 85, p. 101.
"Still." <u>ParisR</u> (27:98) Wint 85, p. 102.
"Uneasy Requital for Coleman Dowell." <u>ParisR</u> (27:98) Wint
    85, p. 104-106.
2775. LAUTERMILCH, Steven
"2.26" (tr. of Rainer Maria Rilke). <u>MalR</u> (71) Je 85, p.
    52.
"This Prayer I Pray in the Spring" (tr. of Rainer Maria
    Rilke). <u>MalR</u> (71) Je 85, p. 53.
2776. LAUX, Dorianne
"China." <u>YellowS</u> (15) Sum 85, p. 34.
"Quarter to Six." <u>PoetL</u> (80:2) Sum 85, p. 94-96.
"Skipping Stones." <u>Tendril</u> (19/20) 85, p. 228-229.
"Two Pictures of My Sister." <u>BelPoJ</u> (35:3) Spr 85, p. 22-
    23.
2777. LAVALLE, Tomás Guido
"As If Nothing But His Own Calamity" (tr. by Jason Weiss).
    <u>Temblor</u> (1) 85, p. 113.
"Tracing of the Dawn" (tr. by Jason Weiss). <u>Temblor</u> (1)
    85, p. 111-113.
2778. LAVANT, Christine
"Again I climb down into the crater of fear" (tr. by David
    Chorlton). <u>NegC</u> (5:2) Spr 85, p. 144.
"Buy us a grain of reality!" (tr. by David Chorlton).
    <u>NegC</u> (5:2) Spr 85, p. 140.
"Durch diese gläsernen Nachmittage" (from <u>Kunst Wie
    Meine Ist Nur Verstummeltes Leben</u>). <u>NegC</u> (5:2) Spr
    85, p. 143.
"Erhöre die Stelle, die dein gedenkt" (from <u>Kunst Wie
    Meine Ist Nur Verstummeltes Leben</u>). <u>NegC</u> (5:2) Spr
    85, p. 147.
"Fremdblütig im Herzen der Hacht" (from <u>Der
    Pfauenschrei</u>). <u>NegC</u> (5:2) Spr 85, p. 139.
"Das Ich Dem Mond Mein Gemüt Uberliess" ("Because I Leave
    My Spirit to the Moon," tr. by David Chorlton). <u>PoetL</u>
    (80:3) Fall 85, p. 173.
"Im Finsteren Hohlweg" ("Along the Dark Pass," tr. by David
    Chorlton). <u>PoetL</u> (80:3) Fall 85, p. 177.
"Kauf uns ein Körnchen Wirklichkeit!" (from <u>Der
    Pfauenschrei</u>). <u>NegC</u> (5:2) Spr 85, p. 141.
"Listen closely at the place that remembers you" (tr. by
    David Chorlton). <u>NegC</u> (5:2) Spr 85, p. 146.
"Nun steige ich wieder hinab in den Krater der Angst" (from
    <u>Kunst Wie Meine Ist Nur Verstummeltes Leben</u>). <u>NegC</u>
    (5:2) Spr 85, p. 145.
"So Eine Kopflose Nacht!" ("What a Headless Night," tr. by
    David Chorlton). <u>PoetL</u> (80:3) Fall 85, p. 172.
"Strange blood in the heart of the night" (tr. by David
    Chorlton). <u>NegC</u> (5:2) Spr 85, p. 138.
"Strenge Nächtigung über dem Ort" ("A Harsh Night's
    Rest over the Village," tr. by David Chorlton). <u>PoetL</u>

        (80:3) Fall 85, p. 175.
    "Through these glazed afternoons" (tr. by David Chorlton).
        NegC (5:2) Spr 85, p. 142.
    "Trotzdem der Himmel ein Bleisarg Wird" ("Although Heaven
        Turns," tr. by David Chorlton). PoetL (80:3) Fall 85,
        p. 174.
    "Zerschlage die Glocke in Meinem Gehör" ("Shatter the
        Bell in My Ear," tr. by David Chorlton). PoetL (80:3)
        Fall 85, p. 176.
2779. LAWDER, Douglas
    "Swimming before Sleep." PoetryR (2:2) Ap 85, p. 31-32.
2780. LAWLER, Patrick
    "Border Crossing." WestB (17) 85, p. 111.
    "Commerce." NoDaQ (53:4) Fall 85, p. 207.
    "Fat Lady." MalR (71) Je 85, p. 78-79.
    "Peeling Potatoes." NoDaQ (53:4) Fall 85, p. 207.
    "Plow." ConnPR (3:1) 84, p. 22.
    "Sleep." Nimrod (29:1) Fall-Wint 85, p. 87-95.
    "Tritanopia." CrossCur (4:4/5:1) 85, p. 38.
    "Veterans Hospital." PassN (6:2) Spr-Sum 85, p. 20.
    "The Woodworker's Daughter" (for Barbara). CimR (73) O
        85, p. 16.
2781. LAWRY, Mercedes
    "The Heart Grows Fonder." BlueBldgs (9) [85?], p. 23.
2782. LAWS, Kyle
    "Into the Soul of the Night." PoeticJ (12) 85, p. 21.
    "Metal on the Pinon Wood." PoeticJ (12) 85, p. 20.
    "Plum Sage." PoeticJ (9) 85, p. 20.
    "These Winter Bones." PoeticJ (9) 85, p. 21.
2783. LAWSON, Catherine
    "Flamenco" (tr. of Francisca Aguirre). Mund (15:1/2) 85,
        p. 163.
    "The Other Music" (tr. of Francisca Aguirre). Mund
        (15:1/2) 85, p. 165.
2784. LAYTON, Elizabeth
    "Run That Cycle of Birth Around Again." LittleBR (5:1)
        Fall-Wint 84-85, p. 84-85.
2785. LAYTON, Irving
    "Dionysians in a Bad Time." CanLit (105) Sum 85, p. 43.
    "Etruscan Tombs" (for Dante Gardini). Descant 48 (16:1)
        Spr 85, p. 25.
    "Fellini." CanLit (106) Fall 85, p. 15.
    "Judgement at Murrays." Descant 48 (16:1) Spr 85, p. 28.
    "Leopardi in Montreal." CanLit (106) Fall 85, p. 55.
    "The Massacre." Descant 48 (16:1) Spr 85, p. 27.
    "Una Scopata." Descant 48 (16:1) Spr 85, p. 26.
2786. LAZARD, Naomi
    "The Day Death Comes" (tr. of Faiz Ahmed Faiz, w. the
        author). NewL (51:4) Sum 85, p. 125.
    "If You Look at the City from Here" (tr. of Faiz Ahmed
        Faiz, w. the author). GrandS (4:4) Sum 85, p. 51.
    "Once Again the Mind" (tr. of Faiz Ahmed Faiz, w. the
        author). GrandS (4:4) Sum 85, p. 50.
    "The Ward for Children." Confr (30/31) N 85, p. 79-80.
    "You Tell Us What to Do" (tr. of Faiz Ahmed Faiz, w. the
        author). GrandS (4:4) Sum 85, p. 52.
2787. LAZEBNIK, Jack
    "All-Purpose Advising Letter." OP (38/39) Spr 85, p. 155.
2788. LAZER, Hank
    "1616 Hester Avenue." WoosterR (3) Spr 85, p. 17-18.
2789. LAZIC, Radmila
    "From Letter #57 Addressed to Lj.N." (tr. by Nina
        Zivancević). AmerPoR (14:3) My-Je 85, p. 29.
    "Joy" (tr. by Nina Zivancević). AmerPoR (14:3) My-Je
        85, p. 29.
    "Piano" (tr. by Nina Zivancević). AmerPoR (14:3) My-Je

85, p. 29.
"When You Need to Clean and Cut Your Finger Nails" (tr. by
Nina Živančević). AmerPoR (14:3) My-Je 85, p. 29.
2790. LAZIN, Sharlene
"One of Those Cold Afternoons in the Park." WestCR (19:4)
Ap 85, p. 40.
"Words from within a Cloud." WestCR (19:4) Ap 85, p. 39.
LE . . .
See also names beginning with "Le" without the following
space, filed below in their alphabetic positions, e.g.,
LeFEVRE.
2791. LEA, Sydney
"Conspiracy." Crazy (27) Fall 84, p. 56-59.
"Fall." NewRep (192:1/2) 7-14 Ja 85, p. 38.
"Insufficiencies." Crazy (26) Spr 84, p. 29-31.
"Midway." Atlantic (255:4), Ap 85, p. 89.
"Reckoning." Tendril (19/20) 85, p. 230-232.
"Telescope." SewanR (93:3) Sum 85, p. 406-407.
"Tough End." GeoR (39:1) Spr 85, p. 164-167.
"Waiting for Armistice" (after the Beirut massacres).
Iowa (15:1) Wint 85, p. 38-41.
2792. LEARDI, Jeanette
"Close to Dawn." CentR (29:3) Sum 85, p. 322-323.
"Single Love." Poem (54) N 85, p. 55.
"Still Life with Apples." Poem (54) N 85, p. 54.
"The Wall." Poem (54) N 85, p. 56.
2793. LEAVITT, Penelope
"Up and Away." PoetryCR (6:4) Sum 85, p. 42.
2794. LEBANIDZE, Murman
"Spring" (tr. by Shota Nishnianidze and Manly Johnson).
Nimrod (28:2) Spr-Sum 85, p. 162.
2795. LEBHERT, Margitt
"Exaggerated Consequence" (tr. of Michael Augustin).
Ploughs (11:1) 85, p. 36.
"An Excellent Sentence" (tr. of Michael Augustin).
Ploughs (11:1) 85, p. 38.
"Immaculatus" (tr. of Michael Augustin). Ploughs (11:1)
85, p. 37.
"Self-Portrait" (tr. of Michael Augustin). Ploughs (11:1)
85, p. 37.
"Sleepwalking" (tr. of Michael Augustin). Ploughs (11:1)
85, p. 36.
"A Terrible Disappointment" (tr. of Michael Augustin).
Ploughs (11:1) 85, p. 35.
2796. LeBLANC, Gérald
"Geography" (tr. by Martine Jacquot). Germ (9:2) Fall-
Wint 85, p. 11.
"November Song" (tr. by Martine Jacquot). Germ (9:2) Fall-
Wint 85, p. 10.
"October Song" (tr. by Martine Jacquot). Germ (9:2) Fall-
Wint 85, p. 9.
"September Song" (for my birthday, tr. by Martine Jacquot).
Germ (9:2) Fall-Wint 85, p. 8.
2797. LEDBETTER, J. T.
"Carlenda's Song" (Selections: 3, 5). CrossCur (4:1) 84,
p. 81-83.
2798. LEE, Dean
"200-Yard Inner Stampede." Sam (42:3, 167th release) 85,
p. 16.
2799. LEE, Dennis
"Jenny the Juvenile Juggler." Quarry (34:1) Wint 85, p. 7.
2800. LEE, John B.
"Tough Love." PraF (6:2) Spr 85, p. 56-57.
"When Sheep Sleep." Waves (14:1/2) Fall 85, p. 80.
2801. LEE, L. Barker
"Intended Flowers." Dandel (12:2) 85, p. 48-49.

"Pastoral 2." <u>Dandel</u> (12:2) 85, p. 46-47.
2802. LEE, Lance
"Garden Chant." <u>Poem</u> (54) N 85, p. 14-15.
"Matisse's Scissors in Napa Valley." <u>NegC</u> (5:3) Sum 85,
p. 24.
"Natural Movement." <u>HiramPoR</u> (38) Spr-Sum 85, p. 24.
"Reconcilement" (after Tyutchev). <u>Poem</u> (54) N 85, p. 16.
"Vocabulary Lesson." <u>Poem</u> (54) N 85, p. 17.
2803. LEE, Li-Young
"Eating Together." <u>Iowa</u> (15:1) Wint 85, p. 94.
2804. LEE, Susannah
"A Certain Reformatory." <u>Ploughs</u> (11:1) 85, p. 141-142.
"Living through the Heat Wave." <u>SenR</u> (15:2) 85, p. 61.
"On Walk." <u>Ploughs</u> (11:1) 85, p. 143.
"Wall Painting/Heirakonpolis." <u>SenR</u> (15:2) 85, p. 59-60.
2805. LEFCOWITZ, Barbara F.
"Aegean Balcony" (Myconos, 1984). <u>PaintedB</u> (25) Spr 85,
p. 21.
"The Amtrak Bathtub." <u>Outbr</u> (14/15) Fall 84-Spr 85, p. 25.
"Jodie's Heart." <u>Outbr</u> (14/15) Fall 84-Spr 85, p. 26-28.
"Sunday Night at the Gyldenlove Hotel, Oslo." <u>PaintedB</u>
(25) Spr 85, p. 23.
"Turning 50." <u>PaintedB</u> (25) Spr 85, p. 22.
2806. LEFEBURE, Stephen
"The Dying." <u>KanQ</u> (17:1/2) Wint-Spr 85, p. 70.
2807. LEHMAN, David
"Arbeit Macht Frei." <u>ParisR</u> (27:97) Fall 85, p. 162.
"The Evil Genius." <u>Epoch</u> (34:3) 84-85, p. 214.
"Nightmares with Happy Endings." <u>Stand</u> (26:1) Wint 84-85,
p. 57-59.
"Small Wonder." <u>Epoch</u> (34:3) 84-85, p. 213.
LEINER, Georgia Gojmerac
<u>See</u> GOJMERAC-LEINER, Georgia
2808. LEIPER, Esther M.
"Green Afterworld." <u>Amelia</u> (2:1) Ap 85, p. 35-37.
"Portrait of Cat." <u>Amelia</u> (2:1) Ap 85, p. 47.
2809. LEISER, Dorothy
"Rachel." <u>ChrC</u> (102:36) 20 N 85, p. 1066.
2810. LEITHAUSER, Brad
"An Actor Plays a Trumpet." <u>NewYRB</u> (32:3) 28 F 85, p. 23.
"In a Bonsai Nursery." <u>NewYorker</u> (61:36) 28 O 85, p. 34.
"In a Japanese Moss Garden." <u>Atlantic</u> (255:5), My 85, p.
86-87.
"Rabbits." <u>Atlantic</u> (256:6), D 85, p. 90.
"Recollections of an Irish Daybreak." <u>NewYorker</u> (61:13)
20 My 85, p. 46.
"Seahorses." <u>NewYRB</u> (32:10) 13 Je 85, p. 23.
"A Stuffed Tortoise." <u>NewYorker</u> (61:39) 18 N 85, p. 50.
2811. LEKIC-TRBOJEVIC, Anita
"A Critique of Metaphores" (tr. of Branko Miljković).
<u>Mund</u> (16:1/2) 85, p. 47.
"Drop of Ink" (tr. of Branko Miljković). <u>Mund</u> (16:1/2)
85, p. 49.
"To a Friend and Poet" (Tanasiju Mladenovicu, tr. of Branko
Miljković).Lekic-Trbojeciv). <u>Mund</u> (16:1/2) 85, p. 53.
"The Wretchedness of Poetry" (tr. of Branko Miljković).
<u>Mund</u> (16:1/2) 85, p. 51.
2812. LeMASTER, J. R.
"Chorale in December" (tr. of Claude Vigée, w. Kenneth
Lawrence Beaudoin). <u>Mund</u> (15:1/2) 85, p. 179, 181.
"Heart Lost in the World" (tr. of Claude Vigée, w.
Kenneth Lawrence Beaudoin). <u>Mund</u> (15:1/2) 85, p. 177,
179.
"Living Tomb" (tr. of Claude Vigée, w. Kenneth Lawrence
Beaudoin). <u>WebR</u> (10:1) Spr 85, p. 31-32.
"Patience" (tr. of Claude Vigée, w. Kenneth Lawrence

Beaudoin). <u>Mund</u> (15:1/2) 85, p. 183.
2813. LEMM, Pat
    "Metamorphosis." <u>Amelia</u> (2:2) O 85, p. 68.
2814. LENHART, Michael
    "100 Goddamned Poems from the Rexroth." <u>Bogg</u> (53) 85, p.
        20.
2815. LENSE, Edward
    "E." <u>HiramPoR</u> (39) Fall-Wint 85, p. 14.
LEON, Armando Rojo
    <u>See</u> ROJO LEON, Armando
2816. LEON, Grace de
    "Tire Shop Corner of San Joaquin and Highway 90."
        <u>Imagine</u> (2:1) Sum 85, p. 66.
LEON, Kathie de
    <u>See</u> De LEON, Kathie
2817. LEON, Nephtalí de
    "Gray." <u>Imagine</u> (1:2) Wint 84, p. 109.
    "Night Wind." <u>Imagine</u> (1:2) Wint 84, p. 110-112.
    "Pathfinder of the Soul" (Carol Cisneros). <u>Imagine</u> (1:2)
        Wint 84, p. 108-109.
    "Yo Caminé las Calles con Titanes" (Nueva york:
        Manhattan, the Bronx). <u>Imagine</u> (1:2) Wint 84, p. 112-
        113.
2818. LEPKOWSKI, Frank J.
    "Going Places." <u>KanQ</u> (17:1/2) Wint-Spr 85, p. 288.
    "Mid-February Love Song." <u>KanQ</u> (17:1/2) Wint-Spr 85, p.
        287.
2819. LEPORE, Dominick J.
    "Leonardo Da Vinci: Uomo Universale." <u>ArizQ</u> (41:4) Wint
        85, p. 369.
2820. LEPOVETSKY, Lisa
    "To Bill Stafford One Kind of Goodbye." <u>NegC</u> (5:4) Fall
        85, p. 53.
2821. LERNER, Laurence
    "Proteus." <u>CumbPR</u> (5:1) Fall 85, p. 1-2.
2822. LERNER, Linda
    "The Friendship." <u>KanQ</u> (17:4) Fall 85, p. 241-242.
    "Garden Justice." <u>CrossCur</u> (4:4/5:1) 85, p. 137-138.
    "A Writer's Legacy." <u>Confr</u> (30/31) N 85, p. 189.
2823. LERZUNDI, Patricio
    "Cancion de Ronda." <u>LindLM</u> (4:2) Ap-Je 85, p. 7.
    "Por la Razon o la Fuerza." <u>LindLM</u> (4:2) Ap-Je 85, p. 7.
    "Proclama General." <u>LindLM</u> (4:2) Ap-Je 85, p. 7.
    "XII." <u>LindLM</u> (4:2) Ap-Je 85, p. 7.
    "XIX." <u>LindLM</u> (4:2) Ap-Je 85, p. 7.
    "XVI." <u>LindLM</u> (4:2) Ap-Je 85, p. 7.
    "XX." <u>LindLM</u> (4:2) Ap-Je 85, p. 7.
    "XXII." <u>LindLM</u> (4:1) Ja-Mr 85, p. 5.
2824. LesCARBEAU, Mitchell
    "Hallows' Eve at the Narragansett Café." <u>NewEngR</u> (8:2)
        Wint 85, p. 206-207.
    "Inversions" (for Louise Glück). <u>LittleM</u> (14:4) 85, p.
        27.
    "Kafka Contemplates Suicide." <u>LittleM</u> (14:4) 85, p. 28.
    "Lycanthropy." <u>NegC</u> (5:2) Spr 85, p. 119.
    "Piano." <u>PoetL</u> (80:2) Sum 85, p. 93.
    "Winter Birds." <u>GrahamHR</u> (9) Fall 85, p. 13-14.
2825. LESLIE, Naton
    "The Choice in Sight." <u>StoneC</u> (12:2/3) Spr-Sum 85, p. 8.
    "The Furnace." <u>TexasR</u> (6:1/2) Spr-Sum 85, p. 84-85.
    "Hannibal." <u>IndR</u> (8:1) Wint 85, p. 46-47.
    "Masury, Ohio." <u>IndR</u> (8:1) Wint 85, p. 48-49.
    "Vatic." <u>WestB</u> (17) 85, p. 110-111.
2826. LESSER, Rika
    "Someone's stacking the leaves of an artichoke in heaps"
        (#11 from "Närmare underrättelser" in <u>En avlägsen</u>

likhet, tr. of Per Wästberg). PartR (52:4) 85, p.
    428-429.
"Summer has turned now" (tr. of Göran Sonnevi). SenR
    (15:1) 85, p. 57-58.
2827. LESSING, Karin
"In the Aviary of Voices." Sulfur (13) 85, p. 63-65.
"A Picture of Perfect Rest." Conjunc (8) 85, p. 58-61.
"A Winter's Dream Journal" (January 1984). Temblor (2)
    85, p. 56-59.
2828. LESSINGHAM, Ann (York)
"Real Silk." MalR (71) Je 85, p. 57.
2829. LESTER-MASSMAN, Gordon
"Daffodils." GreenfR (12:3/4) Wint-Spr 85, p. 109.
"Headgear." Abraxas (33) 85, p. 50.
"Night Calls." Abraxas (33) 85, p. 51.
"Nose Jobs." HolCrit (22:2) Ap 85, p. 15.
"Peacetime Benediction." SouthwR (70:3) Sum 85, p. 413-
    414.
2830. LETKO, Ken
"When Dawn Has Put Her White Cloak On" (7 poems, tr. of Ai
    Qing, w. Li Jia Hu and Michael Karl (Ritchie)). MidAR
    (5:2) 85, p. 47-63.
2831. LETONA SILVESTRE, Renè
"Cuando Pases." LindLM (4:1) Ja-Mr 85, p. 26.
2832. LEVENSON, Christopher
"Babushka." CrossC (7:1) 85, p. 12.
"Brink's Truck." PoetryCR (7:2) Wint 85-86, p. 54.
"Magnolias" (for Stan Rogers). CrossC (7:1) 85, p. 12.
"Physical." PoetryCR (7:2) Wint 85-86, p. 54.
2833. LEVERTOV, Denise
"Caedmon." SouthernHR (19:3) Sum 85, p. 203.
"During a Son's Dangerous Illness." MichQR (24:4) Fall
    85, p. 605-606.
"Every Day." MichQR (24:4) Fall 85, p. 607.
"The Well." MichQR (24:4) Fall 85, p. 608.
2834. LEVETT, John
"Exile" (Three pieces by béla egyedi). AntigR (62/63)
    Sum-Aut 85, p. 30-31.
2835. LEVI, Jan Heller
"Baltimore." BelPoJ (35:3) Spr 85, p. 6-14.
"Some Other Where." Pequod (19/20/21) 85, p. 217.
"This Is Not What You Think." Ploughs (11:1) 85, p. 145.
"Women." Ploughs (11:1) 85, p. 144.
2836. LEVI, Primo
"Chess I" (May 9, 1984, tr. by Ruth Feldman). Ploughs
    (11:4) 85, p. 50.
"Chess II" (June 23, 1984, tr. by Ruth Feldman). Ploughs
    (11:4) 85, p. 51.
"Flight" (tr. by Ruth Feldman). Stand (26:4) Aut 85, p. 7.
"Partisan" (tr. by Ruth Feldman). Stand (26:4) Aut 85, p.
    6.
"Passover" (tr. by Ruth Feldman). Stand (26:4) Aut 85, p.
    7.
"Unfinished Business" (April 19, 1981, tr. by Ruth
    Feldman). Ploughs (11:4) 85, p. 48-49.
2837. LEVI, Toni Mergentime
"The Deer-Blind." Blueline (7:1) Sum-Fall 85, p. 15.
"The Persistence of Ghosts." TexasR (6:1/2) Spr-Sum 85,
    p. 96-98.
2838. LEVIN, Amy
"The Flirt in American Literature." Confr (29) Wint 85,
    p. 122.
2839. LEVIN, Phillis (See also LEVIN, Phyllis)
"Animals." PoetryR (2:2) Ap 85, p. 52.
"The Lost Bee." ParisR (27:97) Fall 85, p. 166-167.
"The Shadow Returns." PoetryR (2:2) Ap 85, p. 51.

239   LEVITIN

2840. LEVIN, Phyllis (See also LEVIN, Phillis)
       "Lunch after Ruins." Pequod (19/20/21) 85, p. 218.
2841. LEVINE, Anne-Marie
       "Snakes Do It." BelPoJ (35:4) Sum 85, p. 1.
LEVINE, Judy Katz
       See KATZ-LEVINE, Judy
2842. LEVINE, Norm
       "Some Words for My Deaf Daughter." LaurelR (19:2) Sum 85,
       p. 66.
2843. LEVINE, Philip
       "Blue." Ploughs (11:1) 85, p. 148. Errata in Ploughs
       (11:4) 85, p. 268.
       "The Boys." AntR (43:3) Sum 85, p. 328.
       "Jewish Graveyards, Italy." Poetry (145:6) Mr 85, p. 320-
       323.
       "Look." Poetry (145:6) Mr 85, p. 315-316.
       "The Present." Poetry (145:6) Mr 85, p. 316-320.
       "Salt Peanuts." AntR (43:3) Sum 85, p. 325.
       "Salts and Oils." Iowa (15:1) Wint 85, p. 36-37.
       "Sweet Will." Poetry (145:6) Mr 85, p. 313-315.
       "Texel." AntR (43:3) Sum 85, p. 326-327.
       "Winter Words." Ploughs (11:1) 85, p. 146-147.
2844. LEVIS, Larry
       "The Assimilation of the Gypsies." MissouriR (8:2) 85, p.
       160-163.
       "In the City of Light." QW (20) Spr-Sum 85, p. 46-47.
       "The Poet at Seventeen." QW (20) Spr-Sum 85, p. 44-45.
       "Two Variations on a Theme by Kobayashi." AmerPoR (14:2)
       Mr-Ap 85, p. 29-30.
2845. LEVITIN, Alexis
       "Almost Mother-of-Pearl" (tr. of Eugenio de Andrade).
       PoetryR (2:2) Ap 85, p. 64.
       "Arson" (tr. of Alexandre O'Neill). HangL (47) Spr 85,
       p. 39-40.
       "At Fifty" (tr. of Jorge de Sena). AmerPoR (14:2) Mr-Ap
       85, p. 48.
       "Children" (tr. of Eugenio de Andrade). BlueBldgs (9)
       [85?], p. 25.
       "Christmas Letter to Murilo Mendes" (tr. of Sophia de Mello
       Breyner). SenR (15:1) 85, p. 29.
       "The House" (tr. of Eugenio de Andrade). BlueBldgs (9)
       [85?], p. 25.
       "I'm Satisfied" (tr. of Eugenio de Andrade). NowestR
       (23:1) 85, p. 50.
       "On Awakening" (tr. of Eugenio de Andrade). CumbPR (5:1)
       Fall 85, p. 57.
       "On the Greenness of Clover" (tr. of Eugenio de Andrade).
       SenR (15:1) 85, p. 28.
       "Other Afternoons" (tr. of Eugenio de Andrade). PoetryR
       (2:2) Ap 85, p. 64.
       "Paestum, with New Moon" (tr. of Eugenio de Andrade).
       NewL (51:4) Sum 85, p. 87.
       "Rain" (tr. of Eugenio de Andrade). SenR (15:1) 85, p. 24.
       "Sheltered from Harm" (tr. of Eugenio de Andrade). SenR
       (15:1) 85, p. 27.
       "Sometimes One Enters" (tr. of Eugenio de Andrade).
       NowestR (23:1) 85, p. 49.
       "South" (tr. of Eugenio de Andrade). BlueBldgs (9) [85?],
       p. 24.
       "Still-Life with Fruit" (tr. of Eugenio de Andrade). NewL
       (51:4) Sum 85, p. 87.
       "A Tale of Summer" (tr. of Eugenio de Andrade).
       SouthernHR (19:1) Wint 85, p. 39.
       "There Is No One at the Entrance of November" (tr. of
       Eugenio de Andrade). CumbPR (5:1) Fall 85, p. 59.
       "To the Memory of Ruy Belo" (tr. of Eugenio de Andrade).

<u>NewL</u> (51:4) Sum 85, p. 88.
"Torso" (tr. of Sophia de Mello Breyner). <u>SenR</u> (15:1) 85,
    p. 30.
"Vast Fields" (tr. of Eugenio de Andrade). <u>QW</u> (20) Spr-
    Sum 85, p. 115.
"The Visit of the Prince" (tr. of Eugenio de Andrade).
    <u>SenR</u> (15:1) 85, p. 26.
"Voyage" (tr. of Eugenio de Andrade). <u>SenR</u> (15:1) 85, p.
    25.
2846. LEVREAULT, Donna
    "The Old Ones." <u>ArizQ</u> (41:4) Wint 85, p. 305.
2847. LEVY, Bonnie
    "Rite of Passage." <u>Waves</u> (14:1/2) Fall 85, p. 92-93.
2848. LEVY, R. (<u>See</u> <u>also</u> LEVY, Robert J.)
    "Fitness." <u>HolCrit</u> (22:5) D 85, p. 18.
2849. LEVY, Robert J. (<u>See</u> <u>also</u> LEVY, R.)
    "American Country." <u>GeoR</u> (39:4) Wint 85, p. 735.
    "The Country of Enumerability" (for R. W. F.). <u>QW</u> (21)
        Fall-Wint 85, p. 44-45.
    "Hiatus Interruptus." <u>RiverS</u> (17) 85, p. 38.
    "Sestina: Perrier." <u>MichQR</u> (24:3) Sum 85, p. 477-478.
2850. LEVY, Thurber, Jr.
    "Night Watchman." <u>SnapD</u> (8:2) Spr 85, p. 42-43.
2851. LEWERENZ, Mark
    "Lines on a Christmas Card Depicting Hiroshige's Night Snow
        at Kambara." <u>Amelia</u> (2:1) Ap 85, p. 39.
2852. LEWIN, Roger A.
    "How I Became Worn." <u>AntigR</u> (62/63) Sum-Aut 85, p. 66.
    "The Openness That Freezes Us Taut, Frees Us." <u>Quarry</u>
        (34:3) Sum 85, p. 7-8.
    "Serengeti Plain." <u>AntigR</u> (62/63) Sum-Aut 85, p. 67.
    "The Snow Is Clairvoyance, 1976." <u>AntigR</u> (60) Wint 85, p.
        100-101.
    "The World Is Beautiful with Breezes." <u>AntigR</u> (60) Wint
        85, p. 100.
2853. LEWIS, J. Patrick
    "On Saltlick Pond." <u>MSS</u> (4:3) Spr 85, p. 113.
2854. LEWIS, James
    "Index." <u>ChiR</u> (35:1) Aut 85, p. 33-35.
2855. LEWIS, Janet
    "Comment in Passing." <u>NewRep</u> (192:7) 18 F 85, p. 36.
2856. LEWIS, Lisa
    "History of a Partial Cure." <u>Tendril</u> (19/20) 85, p. 238-
        239.
    "The Stories We Know." <u>CutB</u> (24) Spr-Sum 85, p. 28-30.
2857. LEWIS, Mary Gabriel
    "Age of Aquarius." <u>SanFPJ</u> (7:2) 85, p. 19.
    "Human Race." <u>SanFPJ</u> (7:2) 85, p. 18.
    "Judgement Day." <u>SanFPJ</u> (7:2) 85, p. 19.
    "Nineteen Eighty-Five." <u>SanFPJ</u> (7:2) 85, p. 19.
2858. LEWIS, Melvyn J.
    "In My Sleep." <u>PoeticJ</u> (10) 85, p. 5.
    "Seasons." <u>PoeticJ</u> (10) 85, p. 5.
2859. LEWIS, Stephen
    "Night." <u>Confr</u> (30/31) N 85, p. 136.
LEZAMA, Manuel Alvarez
    <u>See</u> ALVAREZ LEZAMA, Manuel

2860. LI, Jia Hu
    "When Dawn Has Put Her White Cloak On" (7 poems, tr. of Ai
        Qing, w. Ken Letko, and Michael Karl (Ritchie)). <u>MidAR</u>
        (5:2) 85, p. 47-63.
2861. LI, Min Hua
    "For 35 Cents." <u>Vis</u> (18) 85, p. 14.
2862. LIANNE, Lenny
    "Abide in Me, Billy James." <u>Bogg</u> (53) 85, p. 22-23.

"Killer-Pissed Work Ethic" (for David). Open24 (4) 85, p.
    8.
2863. LIATSOS, Sandra
    "Grandmother." CapeR (20:2) Fall 85, p. 18.
    "Maternal Garden." CapeR (20:2) Fall 85, p. 19.
2864. LIBRO, Antoinette
    "Meeting the Darkness" (for my mother). PaintedB (26/27)
        Sum-Fall 85, p. 21-22.
    "The Naked Dreamer." PaintedB (26/27) Sum-Fall 85, p. 20.
2865. LIDDELL, Eleanor P.
    "Recapturing." PoeticJ (11) 85, p. 10.
2866. LIDDELL, Norrie
    "Comet." PoeticJ (9) 85, p. 22.
    "Piano Recital." PoeticJ (10) 85, p. 38.
2867. LIEBENTHAL, Jean Z.
    "Migrant Worker, 1954." SnapD (8:2) Spr 85, p. 6-7.
    "Where Have You Gone." SnapD (8:2) Spr 85, p. 5.
2868. LIEBER, Ron
    "Crete: August." Nat (241:3) 3-10 Ag 85, p. 88.
2869. LIEBERMAN, Laurence
    "The Architect Monk." AmerPoR (14:1) Ja-F 85, p. 28-29.
    "The Banana Madonna." AmerPoR (14:1) Ja-F 85, p. 30-31.
    "Heartshot: One Page from the Cannoneer's Journal."
        MemphisSR (5:2) Spr 85, p. 6-10.
    "The Mural of Wakeful Sleep" (for Dunstan and Derek).
        AmerPoR (14:1) Ja-F 85, p. 23-27.
    "The Organist's Black Carnation." AmerPoR (14:1) Ja-F 85,
        p. 27-28.
    "The Queen's Last Fittings." AmerPoR (14:1) Ja-F 85, p.
        29-30.
    "Slave Platoons Gouging the Capitol." PartR (52:2) 85, p.
        71-73.
2870. LIEBERT, Dan
    "A Circle of Beads." Vis (18) 85, p. 29.
    "An Evening Service" (for Isaac Singer). Vis (19) 85, p.
        39.
2871. LIETZ, Robert
    "After the Company Moves Out, History Seeks Its Level."
        Geor (39:2) Sum 85, p. 392-393.
    "An Apology for Baseball in Upstate New York." MidAR
        (5:1) 85, p. 6-7.
    "For Gerald Coury." MidAR (5:2) 85, p. 14-15.
    "Palm Sunday Eve through Easter Monday." CharR (11:1) Spr
        85, p. 70-76.
    "Three Airmen Regroup at Casey's Topless." Poetry (146:5)
        Ag 85, p. 251-252.
2872. LIFSHIN, Lyn
    "Afterward, I." CentR (29:4) Fall 85, p. 438.
    "Afterward, II." CentR (29:4) Fall 85, p. 439.
    "Afterward, III." CentR (29:4) Fall 85, p. 439-440.
    "Annie's List of Last Things." HawaiiR (18) Fall 85, p.
        75.
    "Back Ache Madonna." WormR (25:3, issue 99) 85, p. 111.
    "Bad Stump Madonna." US1 (18/19) Wint 85, p. 19.
    "Ballet Class." CentR (29:2) Spr 85, p. 220-221.
    "Basket Madonna." WormR (25:3, issue 99) 85, p. 111.
    "Birch Madonna." WormR (25:3, issue 99) 85, p. 110.
    "Dead Battery Madonna." WormR (25:3, issue 99) 85, p. 110.
    "Depression." RagMag (4:2) Fall 85, p. 18.
    "Dream of the Lost Mother." LittleM (14:4) 85, p. 30-31.
    "Fed Up Madonna." WormR (25:3, issue 99) 85, p. 111.
    "Frost Madonna." WormR (25:3, issue 99) 85, p. 110.
    "The Glass Man Comes on to Me in a Restaurant." Bogg (53)
        85, p. 7.
    "He Said I Don't Enunciate Clearly." CentR (29:2) Spr 85,
        p. 221-222.

"Head Ache Madonna." <u>WormR</u> (25:3, issue 99) 85, p. 110.
"Her Last Night in the House." <u>KanQ</u> (17:1/2) Wint-Spr 85,
    p. 56-57.
"In the Dream." <u>LittleM</u> (14:4) 85, p. 32.
"Iron Pumping Madonna." <u>WormR</u> (25:3, issue 99) 85, p. 111.
"Kind of Like Pumping Iron Blues." <u>WindO</u> (46) Fall 85, p.
    37.
"Liquids." <u>LittleM</u> (14:4) 85, p. 33.
"Love Like Kitty Litter." <u>WindO</u> (45) Spr 85, p. 8-9.
"The Mad Girl Is Drawn to Inaccessible Men." <u>CapeR</u> (20:2)
    Fall 85, p. 15.
"The Mad Girl Is Drawn to What Has No Edges." <u>Amelia</u>
    (2:2) O 85, p. 76.
"The Mad Girl Is Flip, Uses Words." <u>RagMag</u> (4:2) Fall 85,
    p. 17.
"The Mad Girl Wakes Terrified at 3 AM." <u>CapeR</u> (20:2) Fall
    85, p. 14.
"The Mad Girl's Lover." <u>Vis</u> (18) 85, p. 37.
"Madonna of the Bully." <u>USl</u> (18/19) Wint 85, p. 19.
"Madonna of the Doodles." <u>WormR</u> (25:3, issue 99) 85, p.
    111.
"Madonna of the Married Man." <u>USl</u> (18/19) Wint 85, p. 19.
"Madonna Who Can't Stand to See Anything Age." <u>WormR</u>
    (25:3, issue 99) 85, p. 112.
"Magic Cube Madonna." <u>WormR</u> (25:3, issue 99) 85, p. 111.
"Mangled Madonna." <u>Bogg</u> (53) 85, p. 19.
"Manipulative Madonna" (1 & 2). <u>WormR</u> (25:3, issue 99)
    85, p. 110.
"Marilyn Monroe Would Be 56 Now." <u>CapeR</u> (20:2) Fall 85,
    p. 16.
"McDonald's Madonna." <u>WormR</u> (25:3, issue 99) 85, p. 109.
"Mountain Madonna." <u>WormR</u> (25:3, issue 99) 85, p. 110.
"My Mother Straightening Pots and Pans." <u>PoetryE</u> (18)
    Fall 85, p. 33.
"Necklace Madonna." <u>WormR</u> (25:3, issue 99) 85, p. 111.
"New Postage Rate Madonna." <u>WormR</u> (25:3, issue 99) 85, p.
    111.
"On a Day They Say They'll cut the Lights the Phone and the
    Doctor Threatens to Repossess Your Back Bone." <u>WindO</u>
    (45) Spr 85, p. 8.
"On the Second Cool August Wednesday." <u>KanQ</u> (17:1/2) Wint-
    Spr 85, p. 58.
"Pachelbel's Madonna." <u>WormR</u> (25:3, issue 99) 85, p. 110.
"Postage Due Madonna." <u>WormR</u> (25:3, issue 99) 85, p. 110.
"Postcards Falling Out of Books." <u>Amelia</u> (2:2) O 85, p.
    76.
"Rereading the Notes in a Green Book from Italy." <u>Amelia</u>
    (2:1) Ap 85, p. 6.
"Somewhere Blue Horses Nuzzle Leaves." <u>Open24</u> (4) 85, p.
    20.
"There Were Always Stars." <u>HawaiiR</u> (17) Spr 85, p. 95-96.
"Thinking of Kent State 13 Years Later." <u>PraF</u> (6:2) Spr
    85, p. 44.
"Thursday." <u>LittleM</u> (14:4) 85, p. 34.
"Time Deposit Madonna." <u>WormR</u> (25:3, issue 99) 85, p. 110.
"Unease." <u>KanQ</u> (17:1/2) Wint-Spr 85, p. 57.
"Using Words As a Cape." <u>RagMag</u> (4:2) Fall 85, p. 16.
"Valley Girl Madonna." <u>WormR</u> (25:3, issue 99) 85, p. 111.
"With So Many Voices." <u>CrabCR</u> (2:2) Wint 85, p. 6.
"Yellow Roses." <u>CreamCR</u> (10:1) 85, p. 19.
"Yellow Terry Cloth Bathrobes." <u>WindO</u> (45) Spr 85, p. 9.
"You, Baby." <u>HiramPoR</u> (39) Fall-Wint 85, p. 15.

2873. LIFSON, Martha
    "It Might As Well Be Spring: An Elegy." <u>Temblor</u> (1) 85,
        p. 119.
    "Reading Sappho." <u>GeoR</u> (39:4) Wint 85, p. 835.

"Still Life for My Mother" (after reading <u>Chardin</u> <u>and</u> <u>the</u>
   <u>Still-life</u> <u>Tradition</u> <u>in</u> <u>France</u>). <u>Temblor</u> (1) 85, p.
   119.
2874. LIGI
   "Countdown." <u>PaintedB</u> (26/27) Sum-Fall 85, p. 17.
   "Death." <u>Bogg</u> (53) 85, p. 6.
   "Five Notices." <u>Open24</u> (4) 85, p. 27.
   "Love." <u>Open24</u> (4) 85, p. 27.
   "Monday Night Football." <u>CrabCR</u> (2:2) Wint 85, p. 10.
2875. LIGNELL, Kathleen
   "Casals in Exile." <u>PraS</u> (59:2) Sum 85, p. 50-51.
2876. LIHN, Enrique
   "A Catulo." <u>LindLM</u> (4:3) Jl-S 85, p. 18.
   "Así Es la Vida." <u>Inti</u> (18/19) Otoño 83-Prim. 84, p.
     153.
   "El Bello Pánico." <u>Inti</u> (18/19) Otoño 83-Prim. 84, p.
     165.
   "Canto General." <u>Inti</u> (18/19) Otoño 83-Prim. 84, p. 166-
     168.
   "Carne del Insomnio." <u>Inti</u> (18/19) Otoño 83-Prim. 84,
     p. 164-165.
   "Cementerio de Punta Arenas." <u>Inti</u> (18/19) Otoño 83-
     Prim. 84, p. 158-159.
   "La Despedida." <u>Inti</u> (18/19) Otoño 83-Prim. 84, p. 161-
     164.
   "Disparan en la Noche." <u>LindLM</u> (4:3) Jl-S 85, p. 18.
   "Edward Hopper." <u>Inti</u> (18/19) Otoño 83-Prim. 84, p. 164.
   "Gallo." <u>Inti</u> (18/19) Otoño 83-Prim. 84, p. 158.
   "Monólogo del Viejo con la Muerte." <u>Inti</u> (18/19)
     Otoño 83-Prim. 84, p. 156-158.
   "No Hay Narciso Que Valga." <u>Inti</u> (18/19) Otoño 83-Prim.
     84, p. 165-166.
   "Obelisco." <u>LindLM</u> (4:3) Jl-S 85, p. 17.
   "La Pieza Oscura." <u>Inti</u> (18/19) Otoño 83-Prim. 84, p.
     153-156.
   "Porque Escribí." <u>Inti</u> (18/19) Otoño 83-Prim. 84, p.
     160-161.
   "Recuerdos de Matrimonio." <u>Inti</u> (18/19) Otoño 83-Prim.
     84, p. 159-160.
   "La Vejez de Narciso." <u>Inti</u> (18/19) Otoño 83-Prim. 84,
     p. 153.
LILLYWHITE, Eileen Silver
   <u>See</u> SILVER-LILLYWHITE, Eileen
2877. LILLYWHITE, Harvey
   "Believing." <u>NoDaQ</u> (53:1) Wint 85, p. 47.
   "The Gypsy King." <u>NoDaQ</u> (53:1) Wint 85, p. 46-47.
   "Song." <u>NoDaQ</u> (53:1) Wint 85, p. 48.
   "Three Kinds of Love." <u>NoDaQ</u> (53:1) Wint 85, p. 45-46.
   "Waking." <u>NoDaQ</u> (53:1) Wint 85, p. 47-48.
2878. LIMA, Robert
   "The Light." <u>LindLM</u> (4:3) Jl-S 85, p. 27.
   "Snow Geese." <u>LindLM</u> (4:3) Jl-S 85, p. 27.
   "Soft Focus." <u>LindLM</u> (4:3) Jl-S 85, p. 27.
2879. LINDAHL, David
   "Not Knowing Anything." <u>JamesWR</u> (2:1) Fall 84, p. 4.
2880. LINDEMAN, Jack
   "Letter to Bruce." <u>CrabCR</u> (3:1) Fall-Wint 85, p. 9.
   "Twenty Years" (for Vic and Barbara). <u>KanQ</u> (17:1/2) Wint-
     Spr 85, p. 273.
LINDGREN, Gray Kochhar
   <u>See</u> KOCHHAR-LINDGREN, Gray
2881. LINDNER, Carl
   "In the Forest the World." <u>NegC</u> (5:2) Spr 85, p. 158-159.
2882. LINDSAY, Frannie
   "Coming Awake Together." <u>BlackWR</u> (11:2) Spr 85, p. 68-69.

2883. LINDSEY, Robert
"Calypso and Penelope." Quarry (34:4) Aut 85, p. 61.
2884. LINEHAN, Don
"Channels." AntigR (62/63) Sum-Aut 85, p. 102.
LING-YÜN, Hsieh
See HSIEH, Ling-Yün
2885. LIOTTA, P. H.
"The Earth from This Distance." NoDaQ (53:1) Wint 85, p. 129.
"The Last Room of the Dream." NoDaQ (53:1) Wint 85, p. 128.
2886. LIPMAN, Ed "Foots"
"Nights Primarily Ill." SecC (12:1) 84, p. 30.
2887. LIPSITZ, Lou
"Abandoned House in the Country." PoetryE (18) Fall 85, p. 9-11.
"Afternoon Search." NewL (52:1) Fall 85, p. 36-37.
"Christmas Alone" (for Barbara). NewL (52:1) Fall 85, p. 35-36.
"Robert Frost House, Sugar Hill, NH" (for Peter Dubow). PoetryE (18) Fall 85, p. 12.
"Root." PoetryE (18) Fall 85, p. 13.
"Separation." NewL (52:1) Fall 85, p. 34-35.
"There Is a Lizard in Me." SouthernPR (26, i.e. 25:2) Fall 85, p. 37.
"They Are Dreaming a Lot in Warsaw These Days, March, 1982." MassR (26:1) Spr 85, p. 9.
2888. LIRA, Juan Antonio
"The Last Day of Somoza's Liberal Party" (tr. by Kent Johnson). MinnR (N.S. 25) Fall 85, p. 41.
2889. LISH, Gordon
"Mother Lish's Bologna Sandwich." OP (38/39) Spr 85, p. 13.
2890. LISHAN, Stuart
"The Coral" (From: The Body Bestiary). MidAR (5:1) 85, p. 56-59.
"The Cries of Birds" (From: The Body Bestiary). MidAR (5:2) 85, p. 97-100.
"Elegy." MissouriR (8:2) 85, p. 59.
"Five Tales of H's, Cherry George, and Kathy: A Love Poem." MidAR (5:1) 85, p. 54-55.
"From the Stories of God." QW (21) Fall-Wint 85, p. 95-96.
"My Father in the Merchant Marine." WestHR (39:4) Wint 85, p. 329-331.
2891. LISOWSKI, Joseph
"Black Rock Mountain." NegC (5:4) Fall 85, p. 114-115.
"The Coming of the Snake" (After Paul Klee). NegC (5:2) Spr 85, p. 30.
"In the Garden." Amelia (2:2) O 85, p. 64.
"The New Year." NegC (5:1) Wint 85, p. 100.
"On the Holy Mountain" (tr. of Wang Wei). Amelia (2:1) Ap 85, p. 29.
"Spring Street Blues" (3, 16). Vis (17) 85, p. 32.
2892. LISTON, Paul F.
"Sunflower Field" (Italy, 1984). Bogg (53) 85, p. 27.
2893. LITSEY, Sarah
"Retirement Home." Wind (15:54) 85, p. 29.
2894. LITTLE, Geraldine C.
"Learning." CrossCur (5:2) 85, p. 45-46.
"Sequence on Lady Ise (875? - 939)." Confr (30/31) N 85, p. 270-272.
"Vignettes: Suzanne Valadon." Nimrod (29:1) Fall-Wint 85, p. 70-73.
"Wild Ponies in Ireland." LitR (29:1) Fall 85, p. 51.
2895. LITTLEFOOT, Cassandra
"Clones." SanFPJ (7:2) 85, p. 52.

2896. LITTLETON, Mark R.
    "Corn." <u>CrossCur</u> (4:1) 84, p. 45.
LLOSA, Ricardo Pau
    <u>See</u> PAU-LLOSA, Ricardo
2897. LOCHHEAD, Douglas
    "At Jolicure." <u>PoetryCR</u> (6:4) Sum 85, p. 19.
    "Beausejour." <u>PoetryCR</u> (6:3) Spr 85, p. 26.
    "From Fort Lawrence Road." <u>PoetryCR</u> (6:3) Spr 85, p. 26.
    "Lost Stations." <u>PoetryCR</u> (6:4) Sum 85, p. 19.
    "Markings." <u>PoetryCR</u> (6:4) Sum 85, p. 19.
    "This Place." <u>PoetryCR</u> (6:4) Sum 85, p. 19.
    "The Three Components." <u>PoetryCR</u> (6:4) Sum 85, p. 19.
    "The Tree, the Pylon." <u>PoetryCR</u> (6:3) Spr 85, p. 26.
    "Vigils & Mercies." <u>AntigR</u> (62/63) Sum-Aut 85, p. 53-65.
    "What Harbours?" <u>PoetryCR</u> (6:4) Sum 85, p. 19.
2898. LOCKE, Duane
    "All Winter." <u>NegC</u> (5:4) Fall 85, p. 91.
    "The Sea Is Near." <u>Os</u> (20) 85, p. 12-14.
2899. LOCKLIN, Gerald
    "America Misses the Point, Again." <u>WormR</u> (25:3, issue 99)
      85, p. 82.
    "Androgen Misanthropy." <u>WormR</u> (25:1, issue 97) 85, p. 38.
    "Boola-Boola." <u>Bogg</u> (54) 85, p. 29.
    "Character Witness." <u>WormR</u> (25:3, issue 99) 85, p. 81.
    "Disneyland Revisited." <u>Open24</u> (4) 85, p. 49.
    "Don't Do Me Any Favors." <u>WormR</u> (25:3, issue 99) 85, p.
      83.
    "The Dynamics of Literary Response." <u>WormR</u> (25:3, issue
      99) 85, p. 81.
    "Family Drama." <u>WormR</u> (25:3, issue 99) 85, p. 82-83.
    "If Dirk Bogarde Had Never Been Born." <u>WormR</u> (25:3, issue
      99) 85, p. 81.
    "Its Time Has Come." <u>SecC</u> (12:1) 84, p. 6.
    "Izaak, Are You Grieving?" <u>WormR</u> (25:3, issue 99) 85, p.
      80.
    "The Kind of Year It's Been." <u>WormR</u> (25:1, issue 97) 85,
      p. 38.
    "Literary Capsule." <u>WormR</u> (25:3, issue 99) 85, p. 82.
    "Not Even Acne, Which Goes Deeper." <u>WormR</u> (25:1, issue
      97) 85, p. 38.
    "An Old Fashioned Barber Shop." <u>WormR</u> (25:1, issue 97)
      85, p. 37.
    "Old World / New World" (for Edmund Wilson and my aunts).
      <u>Wind</u> (15:55) 85, p. 28.
    "Pass the Hemlock, Please." <u>WormR</u> (25:3, issue 99) 85, p.
      83.
    "Persona Non Grata." <u>WormR</u> (25:3, issue 99) 85, p. 80.
    "Poetry Broker." <u>WormR</u> (25:3, issue 99) 85, p. 79.
    "Thank God for the Ones That Get Away." <u>Wind</u> (15:55) 85,
      p. 28-29.
    "The Thin Pink Line." <u>WormR</u> (25:1, issue 97) 85, p. 38.
    "The Uglier Side of a Hill." <u>Wind</u> (15:55) 85, p. 27.
    "The Ultimate Obscenity." <u>WormR</u> (25:1, issue 97) 85, p.
      38.
    "The Unkindest Haircut of All." <u>Wind</u> (15:55) 85, p. 27-28.
    "The Word Mnemonic." <u>Bogg</u> (53) 85, p. 44.
2900. LOCKWOOD, Sandra
    "The Missionary." <u>Waves</u> (13:2/3) Wint 85, p. 87.
2901. LOCKWOOD, Virginia
    "Nadir" (after a death). <u>US1</u> (18/19) Wint 85, p. 3.
2902. LOGAN, John
    "The Paperboys." <u>AmerPoR</u> (14:4) Jl-Ag 85, p. 37.
2903. LOGAN, William
    "Banana Republics." <u>DenQ</u> (19:3) Wint 85, p. 33-34.
    "California from England." <u>DenQ</u> (19:3) Wint 85, p. 38.
    "Elms and Antiques." <u>SewanR</u> (93:1) Wint 85, p. 61.

"From a Far Cry, a Return to the City." <u>Nat</u> (240:5) 9 F
    85, p. 154.
"The Inns and Outs of Irony." <u>DenQ</u> (19:3) Wint 85, p. 35.
"The New World." <u>SewanR</u> (93:1) Wint 85, p. 62.
"Propriety." <u>DenQ</u> (19:3) Wint 85, p. 36-37.
"Sutcliffe and Whilby." <u>Nat</u> (240:5) 9 F 85, p. 154.
"Travel." <u>Nat</u> (240:4) 2 F 85, p. 117.
"The Virus in Rude Weather." <u>NewYorker</u> (61:1) 25 F 85, p.
    32.
2904. LOGUE, Mary
    "Field Notes." <u>YellowS</u> (16) Aut 85, p. 18.
2905. LOHMANN, Jeanne
    "Home Stretch." <u>WestHR</u> (39:1) Spr 85, p. 75-76.
2906. LOMBARDO, Gian S.
    "I recall your smile, and it is a clear pool" (tr. of
        Eugenio Montale). <u>Germ</u> (9:2) Fall-Wint 85, p. 31.
    "My life, I do not ask of you fixed features" (tr. of
        Eugenio Montale). <u>Germ</u> (9:2) Fall-Wint 85, p. 32.
    "Perhaps one morning walking about in a crisp, glassy air"
        (tr. of Eugenio Montale). <u>Germ</u> (9:2) Fall-Wint 85, p.
        30.
2907. LONANO, Mari
    "More Than This." <u>GreenfR</u> (13:1/2) Fall-Wint 85, p. 16.
    "Sebastopol, 1980." <u>GreenfR</u> (13:1/2) Fall-Wint 85, p. 17.
2908. LONDON, Jonathan
    "First Pregnancy." <u>Wind</u> (15:53) 85, p. 21-22.
    "Suspecting the Mirror." <u>Wind</u> (15:53) 85, p. 21.
2909. LONDON, Sara
    "Cows' Eyes." <u>MichQR</u> (24:3) Sum 85, p. 479-481.
    "Rare Rhythms." <u>CarolQ</u> (37:2) Wint 85, p. 28-29.
2910. LONG, Rebecca
    "Are You Lonely?" <u>LindLM</u> (4:1) Ja-Mr 85, p. 13.
    "Returning from Washington" (For Stephen). <u>LindLM</u> (4:1)
        Ja-Mr 85, p. 13.
2911. LONG, Richard
    "Something about a Pine cone" (for cwhiii). <u>NegC</u> (5:4)
        Fall 85, p. 85.
    "The Way to the Magical Order." <u>TexasR</u> (6:1/2) Spr-Sum
        85, p. 108.
2912. LONG, Robert (<u>See also</u> LONG, Robert Hill)
    "East Ninth Street." <u>Crazy</u> (29) Fall 85, p. 82-83.
    "Have a Nice Day." <u>Crazy</u> (29) Fall 85, p. 80-81.
2913. LONG, Robert Hill (<u>See also</u> LONG, Robert)
    "Simple Holdings." <u>PassN</u> (6:1) Fall-Wint 85, p. 5.
2914. LONG, Virginia
    "The Indisputable Truth as Spoken by the Guru in Two
        Words." <u>Amelia</u> (2:1) Ap 85, p. 61.
2915. LONGINOVIC, Tomislav
    "Pain Sales I-X" (To Ksenija, tr. by the author and the U.
        of Iowa Translation Workshop). <u>Mund</u> (15:1/2) 85, p.
        201-202.
2916. LONGLEY, Judy
    "House in Maine at Dusk" (after a painting by Edward
        Hopper). <u>PoetL</u> (80:3) Fall 85, p. 168.
LOO, Jeff
    <u>See</u> CAYLE
2917. LOOMIS, Sabra
    "The Rain." <u>NegC</u> (5:4) Fall 85, p. 59.
2918. LOONEY, George
    "Sleepwalking into a Pool" (for Douglas Smith). <u>IndR</u>
        (8:2) Spr 85, p. 31.
2919. LOOTS, Barbara
    "Handling the Evidence." <u>NewL</u> (51:3) Spr 85, p. 113.
2920. LOPES, Michael
    "An Offering." <u>HangL</u> (48) Fall 85, p. 53.
    "She Said / I Said / We Said / I thought She Thought I

Thought." HangL (48) Fall 85, p. 52.
"T.W.A.M." HangL (48) Fall 85, p. 51.
LOPEZ, Antonio Dávila
     See DAVILA LOPEZ, Antonio
2921. LOPEZ, N.
     "In the Land of the Chained." SanFPJ (7:3) 84 [i.e. 85],
          p. 40.
     "Invisible." SanFPJ (7:3) 84 [i.e. 85], p. 43.
     "To Not Have." SanFPJ (7:3) 84 [i.e. 85], p. 42.
LOPEZ, Yolanda Porras
     See PORRAS LOPEZ, Yolanda
2922. LOPEZ ADORNO, Pedro
     "Atentado a las Neutralidades de los Nuestros." Mairena
          (7:19) 85, p. 39.
     "De la Oscilacion de un Caliban en Jarialito." Mairena
          (7:19) 85, p. 38.
     "De un 'Quijote' en un Lugar de Cuyo Nombre no Quiere
          Acordarse." Mairena (7:19) 85, p. 37.
     "De un Vigilante Nocturno en Quebrada." Mairena (7:19)
          85, p. 36.
     "Del Padre al Hijo en Alta Fiebre." Mairena (7:19) 85, p.
          36.
     "Del Sepulturero frente al Sol del Mediodia." Mairena
          (7:19) 85, p. 40.
     "Ejemplo de Los Que Se Despreocuparon en el Sueño."
          Mairena (7:19) 85, p. 39-40.
2923. LOPEZ-ALONSO, Emilio V.
     "El Ausente." LindLM (4:4) O-D 85, p. 29.
     "Douanier Rousseau." LindLM (4:4) O-D 85, p. 29.
     "Oración por un Enamorado de Espuma, Espejo y Ojo de Luna
          Recién Estrenados." LindLM (4:2) Ap-Je 85, p. 12.
2924. LOPEZ SURIA, Violeta
     "Vigilia a Corretjer." Mairena (7:19) 85, p. 88.
2925. LOPOZYKO, Danuta
     "The Cross" (from Unfinished Crusade, The Voice of an
          Unknown Woman Poet, tr. Rafal Wojaczek, w. Peter
          Harris). Chelsea (44) 85, p. 116.
2926. LORDAHL, Jo Ann
     "A Letter Home." NegC (5:1) Wint 85, p. 23.
2927. LORTS, Jack E.
     "A Space of Ignorance." EngJ (74:1) Ja 85, p. 44.
2928. LOSH, Elizabeth
     "Road Trip." HarvardA (118:4) My 85, p. 30.
     "Table for Two: Further Spelling Errors in Blank Verse."
          HarvardA (118:4) My 85, p. 26.
     "The Tanhakkaya of Old Marriages." HarvardA (118:4) My
          85, p. 8.
2929. LOTT, Rick
     "Coal Company Agent." CentR (29:4) Fall 85, p. 447-448.
     "Ruby and the Hummingbird." TexasR (6:1/2) Spr-Sum 85, p.
          56.
     "The Watchers." TexasR (6:1/2) Spr-Sum 85, p. 82-83.
2930. LOURIE, Richard
     "Adam" (tr. of Evgeny Vinokurov). Ploughs (11:4) 85, p.
          175.
     "Atlantis" (tr. of Stanislaw Baranczak). Ploughs (11:4)
          85, p. 138.
     "Childhood Has Ended" (tr. of Naum Korzhavin). Ploughs
          (11:4) 85, p. 174.
     "History" (The first protest leaflet, June, 1956, tr. of
          Stanislaw Baranczak). Ploughs (11:4) 85, p. 139.
     "To the Translator" (tr. of Vyacheslav Ivanov). Ploughs
          (11:4) 85, p. 176.
2931. LOUTHAN, Robert
     "The Dirt." AmerPoR (14:6) N-D 85, p. 27.
     "Here." AmerPoR (14:6) N-D 85, p. 27.

"So What." <u>AmerPoR</u> (14:6) N-D 85, p. 27.
"We're Good." <u>AmerPoR</u> (14:6) N-D 85, p. 27.
2932. LOVE, B. D.
"Nude, Cubist." <u>PoetryNW</u> (26:3) Aut 85, p. 28-29.
2933. LOVELOCK, Yann
"You Who Return" (tr. of Victor Georges). <u>Verse</u> (4) 85,
p. 23.
2934. LOWE, Frederick
"The Green Bird of 1982." <u>BelPoJ</u> (36:2) Wint 85-86, p. 29.
"More Atmosphere" (from <u>La Guitare Endormie</u>, 1929, tr. of
Pierre Reverdy). <u>RiverS</u> (17) 85, p. 44.
"No Farther" (From <u>Coeur de Chêne</u>, 1921, tr. of Pierre
Reverdy). <u>RiverS</u> (17) 85, p. 43.
"Nocturnal Panorama" (from <u>La Guitare Endormie</u>, 1929, tr.
of Pierre Reverdy). <u>RiverS</u> (17) 85, p. 45.
2935. LOWENSTEIN, Robert
"The Front Lawn Exacts Tithes." <u>Wind</u> (15:55) 85, p. 30.
"Last Night of a Cruise." <u>Wind</u> (15:55) 85, p. 30-31.
"Sound Effects." <u>SouthernPR</u> (25:1) Spr 85, p. 42-43.
2936. LOWEY, Mark
"Gone Astray, Souvenirs for Those" (St. Joseph's Oratory,
Montreal). <u>PoetryCR</u> (6:3) Spr 85, p. 35.
2937. LOWLAND, Jacob
"Insurrection." <u>JamesWR</u> (2:3) Spr-Sum 85, p. 14.
"A Tombstone for Tab." <u>JamesWR</u> (2:3) Spr-Sum 85, p. 14.
2938. LOWRY, Betty
"At les Baux de Provence." <u>DeKalbLAJ</u> (18:1/2) 85, p. 76.
2939. LOWRY, John
"Don't Ask." <u>HangL</u> (47) Spr 85, p. 29.
"The Easy Way." <u>HangL</u> (47) Spr 85, p. 30.
"The Joy of Serving." <u>HangL</u> (47) Spr 85, p. 31.
2940. LOYD, Marianne
"Intimation." <u>StoneC</u> (13:1/2) Fall-Wint 85-86, p. 64.
"Paradiso." <u>Wind</u> (15:54) 85, p. 30-31.
2941. LUBETSKY, Elsen
"Accident!" <u>SanFPJ</u> (7:4) 85, p. 9.
"Afterthought." <u>PoeticJ</u> (9) 85, p. 40.
"Another Giant Step." <u>PoeticJ</u> (10) 85, p. 21.
"Celebration." <u>PoeticJ</u> (12) 85, p. 26.
"Coverup." <u>SanFPJ</u> (7:4) 85, p. 7.
"Deliverer of Light." <u>PoeticJ</u> (10) 85, p. 20.
"The Disappeared." <u>SanFPJ</u> (7:2) 85, p. 13.
"A Found Elegy." <u>SanFPJ</u> (7:4) 85, p. 12.
"A Hard Act to Follow." <u>SanFPJ</u> (7:4) 85, p. 8.
"On Target." <u>SanFPJ</u> (7:4) 85, p. 25.
"A Petition to Congress." <u>SanFPJ</u> (7:2) 85, p. 15.
"Portrait of the Artist As a Very Young Dilettante."
<u>PoeticJ</u> (11) 85, p. 19.
"Power Outage." <u>SanFPJ</u> (7:2) 85, p. 16.
"Progress Report." <u>PoeticJ</u> (11) 85, p. 20.
"Rachel's Takin' Swimmin' Lessons." <u>PoeticJ</u> (9) 85, p. 31.
"Rebuttal to Restriding a Lyre." <u>SanFPJ</u> (7:2) 85, p. 35.
"The Way to Dusty." <u>SanFPJ</u> (7:2) 85, p. 14.
2942. LUCAS, Barbara
"Driving Home." <u>DeKalbLAJ</u> (18:1/2) 85, p. 77-78.
"Hempstead Harbor." <u>DeKalbLAJ</u> (18:1/2) 85, p. 78-79.
2943. LUCCHESI, M.
"Urban Nouns / Hollywood Duplex." <u>Rampike</u> (4:2/3) 85-86,
p. 75.
2944. LUCIA, Joseph
"Sunday Morning above Monocacy Creek." <u>StoneC</u> (12:2/3)
Spr-Sum 85, p. 65.
2945. LUCINA, Mary, Sister
"In Phases." <u>CrossCur</u> (4:4/5:1) 85, p. 111.
"Yearbook." <u>Vis</u> (19) 85, p. 4.

2946. LUDVIGSON, Susan
        "Miracles" (for Moni). GeoR (39:4) Wint 85, p. 824-825.
        "When Love Becomes." Poetry (145:5) F 85, p. 269.
        "The Will to Believe." SouthernPR (26, i.e. 25:2) Fall
            85, p. 62-70.
2947. LUECKE, Janemarie
        "Receiving the Message." NegC (5:2) Spr 85, p. 49-51.
        "Water Holes." Outbr (14/15) Fall 84-Spr 85, p. 23-24.
2948. LUEPTOW, Diana
        "Jeanne Moreau, 1963" (from Photographs by Beaton).
            Prima (9) 85, p. 10.
2949. LUGO GUERNELLI, Adelaida
        "Vuelo." Mairena (7:19) 85, p. 107.
2950. LUISI, Luciano
        "Am Being Called" (tr. by P. F. Paolini). LitR (29:1)
            Fall 85, p. 104.
        "To My Father" (tr. by P. F. Paolini). LitR (29:1) Fall
            85, p. 104.
2951. LUKENS, Randy
        "Refuge." PoeticJ (11) 85, p. 28.
        "Vanity." PoeticJ (11) 85, p. 5.
2952. LUM, Wing Tek
        "Urban Love Songs" (after Tzu Yeh). MissouriR (8:3) 85,
            p. 22-23.
2953. LUNA, Nita
        "Chispas." Imagine (2:1) Sum 85, p. 60.
        "Ponle ritmo" ("Sin Título"). Imagine (2:1) Sum 85, p.
            60.
2954. LUND, Orval
        "You've Heard This All Before." RagMag (4:1) Spr 85, p.
            34-35.
2955. LUNDE, David
        "Falling." Wind (15:53) 85, p. 31.
        "To a Friend 'in Love Again'." NegC (5:1) Wint 85, p. 103-
            104.
        "Weighing the Future." GreenfR (13:1/2) Fall-Wint 85, p.
            184.
2956. LUNETTA, Mario
        "Camel" (tr. by Giuliano Dego and Margaret Straus). LitR
            (28:2) Wint 85, p. 249-250.
2957. LUPACK, Alan
        "Bedivere Contemplates Camelot." NegC (5:2) Spr 85, p.
            162.
        "Guinevere's Farewell to Arthur." NegC (5:2) Spr 85, p.
            163.
2958. LUSK, Daniel
        "The Sheep Observe the Sabbath." KanQ (17:1/2) Wint-Spr
            85, p. 43.
2959. LUX, Thomas
        "The Ballet" (for Cathy Appel, who took me). Iowa (15:1)
            Wint 85, p. 49.
        "The Crows of Boston and New York." SenR (15:2) 85, p. 13.
        "Farmer Brown." SenR (15:2) 85, p. 11.
        "The Fourth Grade." SenR (15:2) 85, p. 10.
        "Names." OP (38/39) Spr 85, p. 187.
        "The Swimming Pool." SenR (15:2) 85, p. 8.
        "Via Posthumia." SenR (15:2) 85, p. 12.
        "Wife Hits Moose." SenR (15:2) 85, p. 9.
LUZ VILLANUEVA, Alma
        See VILLANUEVA, Alma Luz
2960. LUZI, Mario
        "Blows" (tr. by Nigel Thompson). Verse (2) 85, p. 39.
        "Ménage" (tr. by P. F. Paolini). LitR (28:2) Wint 85,
            p. 251-252.
LYNN, Elizabeth Cook
        See COOK-LYNN, Elizabeth

2961. LYNSKEY, Edward C.
       "Mechanized Dreams." _Amelia_ (2:1) Ap 85, p. 77.
       "The Risk of Green." _AntigR_ (61) Spr 85, p. 91.
2962. LYON, Adriane R.
       "Literary Lunch." _DeKalbLAJ_ (18:3/4) 85, p. 39.
2963. LYON, George Ella
       "Home Remedies." _Wind_ (15:53) 85, p. 23.
       "Stone." _Wind_ (15:53) 85, p. 24.
2964. LYON, Hillary
       "The Composer." _LitR_ (29:1) Fall 85, p. 27.
2965. LYONS, Richard
       "Hands." _Crazy_ (29) Fall 85, p. 75-77.
       "Land's End." _NewEngR_ (7:3) Spr 85, p. 340-341.
       "So Swiftly Past." _Crazy_ (26) Spr 84, p. 24-25.
       "The Whore & the Night." _NewEngR_ (7:3) Spr 85, p. 339-340.

Mac . . .
       See _also_ names beginning with Mc . . .
2966. MacCORMACK, Karen
       "Later, the Function of the Holy Place Was Assumed by
          Dragons" (--Julia Kristeva, About Chinese Women).
          PoetryCR (7:2) Wint 85-86, p. 43.
       "Love Is Not a Location." _PoetryCR_ (7:2) Wint 85-86, p.
          43.
       "A Singular Plurality." _Rampike_ (4:2/3) 85-86, p. 74.
2967. MacCREADY, Jean
       "Interpretation." _CrossCur_ (4:4/5:1) 85, p. 175.
2968. MacDONALD, Bernell
       "Upon Hearing of Your Death" (for Alden). _PottPort_ (7) 85-
          86, p. 48.
2969. MacDONALD, Errol
       "The Raccoon." _AntigR_ (62/63) Sum-Aut 85, p. 79.
       "Villa Imaginaire." _AntigR_ (62/63) Sum-Aut 85, p. 80.
2970. MacDOUGALL, Alan
       "The Bodhisattva Awakes." _NegC_ (5:2) Spr 85, p. 87-88.
2971. MacEWEN, Gwendolyn
       "Black Ice." _Descant_ 50 (16:3) Fall 85, p. 16.
       "Languages 2." _Descant_ 50 (16:3) Fall 85, p. 15.
       "Me and the Runner." _Descant_ 50 (16:3) Fall 85, p. 17.
2972. MacINNES, Mairi
       "Crossing the Channel" (for P.L.D., 1921-1984). _PraS_
          (59:4) Wint 85, p. 40-42.
2973. MACK, Joe
       "Condemned to Death." _SanFPJ_ (7:3) 84 [i.e. 85], p. 33-34.
       "Conventional Conservative Hogwash." _SanFPJ_ (7:4) 85, p.
          50-51.
       "Declaration of Independence" (The Real Thing). _SanFPJ_
          (7:4) 85, p. 23.
       "Miami! No Way Justice." _SanFPJ_ (7:4) 85, p. 22.
2974. MacKAY, Brent
       "Angle Iron." _Sulfur_ (13) 85, p. 88-90.
       "Baby Jazz." _Sulfur_ (13) 85, p. 87-88.
       "Fare-The-Well." _Sulfur_ (13) 85, p. 88.
       "Politics." _Sulfur_ (13) 85, p. 90.
       "Six Days Overdue." _Sulfur_ (13) 85, p. 86.
2975. MacKENZIE, Robert
       "Coinage." _Verse_ (3) 85, p. 13.
2976. MACKIN, Randy
       "Grandfather." _Vis_ (18) 85, p. 9.
2977. MACKLIN, Elizabeth
       "Where Inside Is Dark or Light." _NewYorker_ (61:5) 25 Mr
          85, p. 48.
2978. MACKRIDGE, Peter
       "The First Anatomist" (tr. of Aris Alexandrou). _Verse_ (4)
          85, p. 45.

"Make Sure" (tr. of Aris Alexandrou). Verse (4) 85, p. 44.
"Promotion" (tr. of Aris Alexandrou). Verse (4) 85, p. 44.
2979. MacLEAN, Sorley
"Raasay Wood" (English version by Sally Evans). Verse (3)
85, p. 44-49.
2980. MacLEOD, Alistair
"The Road to Rhu and Cairn an' Dorin" (The Cairn of
Sorrow). AntigR (61) Spr 85, p. 7-8.
2981. MACLEOD, Norman
"After the Real Jazz Went to Chinatown." WormR (25:4,
issue 100) 85, p. 123-124.
"A Cezanne of Shane the Gunslinger Riding toward Sainte-
Victoire." NewL (51:3) Spr 85, p. 107.
"From Shelled Out Frankfurt to Posterity." WormR (25:4,
issue 100) 85, p. 122-123.
"The Girl from Saks Fifth Avenue" (for Robert P. Mills).
NewL (51:3) Spr 85, p. 109.
"I'm Going to Shake, Rattle and Roll, the Prexy Said."
Confr (30/31) N 85, p. 254.
"Kris Stands There with Arms Akimbo" (for Kris Hotvedt).
NewL (51:3) Spr 85, p. 111.
"A Mad Micturator Way of Looking at Things." Confr
(30/31) N 85, p. 255.
"Taking Sophocles to Jesus, Jack" (For Ruth Peck). NewL
(51:3) Spr 85, p. 110.
"A Wake for Jack Sherby." NewL (51:3) Spr 85, p. 108-109.
2982. MacMANUS, Mariquita
"Count Vladimir." WebR (10:2) Fall 85, p. 55-56.
"Mission." WebR (10:2) Fall 85, p. 56.
2983. MacSWEEN, R. J.
"Angel Wings." AntigR (61) Spr 85, p. 62-63.
"The Awakening." AntigR (62/63) Sum-Aut 85, p. 12.
"The Gamble." AntigR (62/63) Sum-Aut 85, p. 9-10.
"In the Back Lots." AntigR (60) Wint 85, p. 102.
"A Summer Day." AntigR (62/63) Sum-Aut 85, p. 11.
"Turning Away." AntigR (61) Spr 85, p. 60.
"The Waters of Stillness." AntigR (61) Spr 85, p. 61.
MADHUSUDHAN, S. K.
See ATMANAM
2984. MADONICK, Michael
"Lines toward a Roundelay." StoneC (12:2/3) Spr-Sum 85,
p. 58.
"What We Know." StoneC (12:2/3) Spr-Sum 85, p. 58.
2985. MADSON, Arthur
"St. Patrick's Day in Rock County." SouthernHR (19:1)
Wint 85, p. 24.
2986. MAGEE, Kevin
"By the Inlet of the Infinitive to Amaze" (for Margitt).
Ploughs (11:1) 85, p. 149-150.
"The Inner Circle." Ploughs (11:1) 85, p. 151.
"Sioux River." Ploughs (11:1) 85, p. 152.
MAGGIO, Jill di
See DiMAGGIO, Jill
2987. MAGLIOCCO, Peter
"After the Sex Crime." Sam (42:3, 167th release) 85, p.
43.
"Quick Revenge." Sam (42:4, 168th release) 85, p. 49.
2988. MAGORIAN, James
"Flagpole Sitter." OP (38/39) Spr 85, p. 169.
"Hernia." OP (38/39) Spr 85, p. 101.
2989. MAHAPATRA, Jayanta
"The Corpse" (tr. of Jagannath Prasad Das). NewL (51:4)
Sum 85, p. 134.
"An Evening by the River." SewanR (93:2) Spr 85, p. 191.

"The Season of the Old Rain." SewanR (93:2) Spr 85, p.
    190-191.
2990. MAHER, Barry
    "Corrections" (Three Lines, Scratches, and Blotches).
    NegC (5:4) Fall 85, p. 95.
2991. MAHLER, Carol
    "When the Baby's Cried Herself to Sleep." PassN (6:2) Spr-
    Sum 85, p. 8.
2992. MAHONEY, MaryJo
    "B Unit." HangL (48) Fall 85, p. 54.
2993. MAHONY, Phillip
    "Bushwick Names." HangL (47) Spr 85, p. 32.
    "Fabien." HangL (47) Spr 85, p. 33.
2994. MAI-LAN
    "On the Way Home" (tr. of Che-Lan-Vien, w. Robert
    Crawford). Verse (1) 84, p. 40.
2995. MAILANDER, L. B.
    "The Tunnel of Love." JamesWR (2:3) Spr-Sum 85, p. 8.
2996. MAILER, Norman
    "I Got Two Kids and Another in the Oven." LittleBR (5:1)
    Fall-Wint 84-85, p. 1-2.
2997. MAILLARD, Claude
    "Wrecks" (tr. by Eric Sarner). Verse (2) 85, p. 36.
2998. MAIRE, Mark
    "Hawks' Wings." ArizQ (41:3) Aut 85, p. 214.
2999. MAIRS, Nancy
    "The Departure of the Women." Kaleid (10) Spr 85, p. 31.
    "Felo-de-se." Kaleid (10) Spr 85, p. 30.
    "For a Child Who Has Lost Her Cat" (for Susan Abbey).
    Kaleid (10) Spr 85, p. 30.
    "The Ice Palace." Kaleid (10) Spr 85, p. 30.
    "Montage." Kaleid (10) Spr 85, p. 30.
    "Moving Out of the Attic." Kaleid (10) Spr 85, p. 31.
    "Primipara." Kaleid (10) Spr 85, p. 31.
3000. MAIZELL, Sylvia
    "Black Poplar" (tr. of David Samojlov, w. Robert L. Smith).
    WebR (10:1) Spr 85, p. 12.
    "Inspiration" (tr. of David Samojlov, w. Robert L. Smith).
    WebR (10:1) Spr 85, p. 13.
    "Trace" (tr. of Leonid Martynov, w. Robert L. Smith).
    WebR (10:1) Spr 85, p. 13.
3001. MAJOR, Alice
    "Thirst." Quarry (34:4) Aut 85, p. 13.
3002. MAJOR, Deborah
    "What We Gonna Do 'bout Dem Youth?" Zyzzyva (1:1) Spr 85,
    p. 20-22.
3003. MAKEPIECE, E. Maria
    "Borne by the easterlies" ("Untitled"). Conjunc (8) 85,
    p. 182.
3004. MAKOFSKE, Mary
    "Bracing." CumbPR (5:1) Fall 85, p. 38.
    "Letter from an English Winter." CumbPR (5:1) Fall 85, p.
    37.
    "On an Island among Newlyweds." CumbPR (5:1) Fall 85, p.
    39-40.
3005. MAKSIMOVIC, Miroslav
    "Banovo Brdo*" (*a section of Belgrade, tr. by Nina
    Zivancević). AmerPoR (14:3) My-Je 85, p. 30.
    "Flooded into the Handbooks against My Wish" (tr. by Nina
    Zivancević). AmerPoR (14:3) My-Je 85, p. 30.
    "Indian Education" (tr. by Nina Zivancević). AmerPoR
    (14:3) My-Je 85, p. 30.
    "Movies and Universities" (tr. by Nina Zivancević).
    AmerPoR (14:3) My-Je 85, p. 30.
3006. MAKUCK, Peter
    "Dark Preface." AmerS (54:4) Aut 85, p. 466.

"Leavings" (In memory of Jean-Claude Rouiller). PraS
(59:1) Spr 85, p. 73-76.
3007. MALANGA, Gerard
"Two Variations and 3 Additional Parts" (for Lindsay).
Open24 (4) 85, p. 17-18.
3008. MALAQUAIS, Dominique
"Afternoon, Where the Fields." Imagine (2:1) Sum 85, p.
109, 111, 113.
"Après-midi, d'Où les Champs." Imagine (2:1) Sum 85,
p. 108, 110, 112.
"Phoem" (En Echo à André Breton). Imagine (2:1) Sum
85, p. 106.
"Pmoem" (Echoing André Breton). Imagine (2:1) Sum 85,
p. 107.
3009. MALASCHAK, Dolores
"Smog Age." PoeticJ (12) 85, p. 36.
"Song for the Unemployed." PoeticJ (12) 85, p. 16-17.
MALE, Belkis Cuza
See CUZA MALE, Belkis
3010. MALFAIERA, Anna
"Towards the Imperfect" (tr. by P. F. Paolini). LitR
(28:2) Wint 85, p. 257-259.
3011. MALIK (Delano Abdul Malik de Coteau)
"More-Weight." GreenfR (12:3/4) Wint-Spr 85, p. 178-179.
3012. MALLIN, Rupert
"The Fat of My Pursuits." HangL (48) Fall 85, p. 17.
"The Fear of Functions." HangL (48) Fall 85, p. 16.
"Soil." HangL (48) Fall 85, p. 18.
3013. MALLINSON, Anna
"Black Hole Poem." AntigR (60) Wint 85, p. 49-51.
3014. MALLOY, Vivian
"Once." WoosterR (4) Fall 85, p. 76-77.
3015. MALONE, Joe
"Ahi Ali Baba" (Bektashi dervish origin, tr. of anonymous
poem). Paint (11:21/12:24) 84-85, p. 57.
"The Visitor" (tr. of Nuala Ni Dhomhnaill). Paint
(11:21/12:24) 84-85, p. 56.
3016. MALTMAN, Kim
"Installation #12." PoetryCR (6:4) Sum 85, p. 10.
"Installation #21." PoetryCR (6:4) Sum 85, p. 10.
"The Technology of the Metal at the Heart of Sorrow."
PoetryCR (6:4) Sum 85, p. 10.
3017. MANAHAN, Margaret
"Father's Day." Outbr (14/15) Fall 84-Spr 85, p. 12.
3018. MANDEL, Charlotte
"Account." BlueBldgs (9) [85?], p. 22.
"Child with Pen." BlueBldgs (9) [85?], p. 21.
"The Shroud of Turin." NegC (5:2) Spr 85, p. 125.
"Touring the Mill." WestB (16) 85, p. 87-88.
3019. MANDEL, Eli
"Moon Dog." Dandel (12:1) 85, p. 40-43.
3020. MANDEL, Siegfried
"Nightflight" (tr. of Ingeborg Bachmann). CumbPR (5:1)
Fall 85, p. 32-33.
"Stars in March" (tr. of Ingeborg Bachmann). CumbPR (5:1)
Fall 85, p. 29.
3021. MANDEL, Tom
"Sonnet IV" (tr. of Paul Celan). Zyzzyva (1:3) Fall 85,
p. 129-130.
3022. MANDELKER, Barry
"The Polish Police Have Just Murdered Grzegorz Przemyk."
Rampike (4:2/3) 85-86, p. 73.
3023. MANDELSTAM, Osip
"286" (tr. by Michael Cole and Karen Kimball). MinnR
(N.S. 24) Spr 85, p. 102.
"341" (tr. by Michael Cole and Karen Kimball). MinnR

(N.S. 24) Spr 85, p. 102.
"349" (tr. by Michael Cole and Karen Kimball). MinnR
    (N.S. 24) Spr 85, p. 103.
"For me, winter feels like a belated gift" (tr. by Michael
    Cole and Karen Kimball). NewL (51:4) Sum 85, p. 42.
"I don't know when this song began" (131, in Russian and
    English, tr. by Michael Cole and Karen Kimball).
    StoneC (12:2/3) Spr-Sum 85, p. 14-15.
"My age, my animal" (tr. by Clarence Brown). TriQ (63)
    Spr-Sum 85, p. 175.
"Night outside. An uppercrust lie" (tr. by Clarence Brown).
    TriQ (63) Spr-Sum 85, p. 175.
"Poem" (tr. by Michael Cole and Karen Kimball). Stand
    (26:2) Spr 85, p. 41.
"Today is yellow-beaked, inexperienced" (329, in Russian
    and English, tr. by Michael Cole and Karen Kimball).
    StoneC (12:2/3) Spr-Sum 85, p. 12-13.
3024. MANDERSON, Monica
    "In Memory of Issac." Germ (9:2) Fall-Wint 85, p. 25.
3025. MANICOM, David
    "Pearl." Grain (13:2) My 85, p. 35.
    "Slow Portrait." Grain (13:2) My 85, p. 36.
3026. MANILLA, Saul
    "It's Always Darkest before Don." WormR (25:4, issue 100)
        85, p. 130.
    "The More the Terrier." WormR (25:4, issue 100) 85, p.
        130.
3027. MANLEY, Rachel
    "Marquez' One Hundred Years of Solitude." GreenfR
        (12:3/4) Wint-Spr 85, p. 199.
    "Poem" (The brown lady wakes). GreenfR (12:3/4) Wint-Spr
        85, p. 198.
    "Regardless" (for Mardi). GreenfR (12:3/4) Wint-Spr 85,
        p. 200.
MANNA, Richard la
    See LaMANNA, Richard
3028. MANNING, Nichola
    "Benjamin." WormR (25:3, issue 99) 85, p. 109.
    "Breakage." WormR (25:1, issue 97) 85, p. 28-29.
    "Cross Country." WormR (25:1, issue 97) 85, p. 27.
    "Cupboard." WormR (25:3, issue 99) 85, p. 109.
    "Drink." WormR (25:1, issue 97) 85, p. 27-28.
    "Fishy." WormR (25:3, issue 99) 85, p. 109.
    "Library Books." WormR (25:1, issue 97) 85, p. 27.
    "My Gas Heater." WormR (25:3, issue 99) 85, p. 108.
    "Nonsense." WormR (25:3, issue 99) 85, p. 108.
    "Obscenity." WormR (25:1, issue 97) 85, p. 29.
    "River Bed." WormR (25:1, issue 97) 85, p. 28.
    "Suspicion." WormR (25:3, issue 99) 85, p. 108.
    "Telephone Need." WormR (25:3, issue 99) 85, p. 108.
3029. MANSILLA, Sergio
    "Life" (tr. by Steven White). Stand (26:3) Sum 85, p. 59.
3030. MANUPELLI, George
    "Augusto Cesar Sandino." Rampike (4:2/3) 85-86, p. 68.
3031. MAQUIEIRA, Diego
    "No One Knows What I'm Talking About" (tr. by Steven
        White). PoetryR (2:2) Ap 85, p. 78.
3032. MARCHANT, Fred
    "Grief." Agni (22) 85, p. 39.
    "Rescue." Agni (22) 85, p. 40.
3033. MARCUS, Mordecai
    "American Elegance." Amelia (2:2) O 85, p. 60-61.
    "Lessons from Shakespeare." KanQ (17:1/2) Wint-Spr 85, p.
        93.
    "Still Points." KanQ (17:1/2) Wint-Spr 85, p. 93.

3034. MARCUS, Morton
    "Aunt Bertha." TriQ (64) Fall 85, p. 56-59.
    "Dinner at Grandpa's." TriQ (64) Fall 85, p. 60-61.
    "Father and Son." TriQ (63) Spr-Sum 85, p. 603-604.
    "Give Me Back My Rags" (tr. of Vasko Popa, w. Charles
        Simic). Ploughs (11:4) 85, p. 181-190.
    "The Women in the Photograph." TriQ (64) Fall 85, p. 54-
        55.
3035. MARE, Mauro
    "Eternity" (tr. by P. F. Paolini). LitR (29:1) Fall 85,
        p. 105.
    "The Feast" (tr. by P. F. Paolini). LitR (29:1) Fall 85,
        p. 105.
    "Remembrances" (tr. by P. F. Paolini). LitR (29:1) Fall
        85, p. 106.
3036. MARGOLIS, Gary
    "Between Us" (for my father). PraS (59:1) Spr 85, p. 89-
        90.
    "Beyond Resembling." AmerS (54:1) Wint 84-85, p. 118.
    "Borne Away." ColEng (47:5) S 85, p. 499-500.
    "Dancing at Bread Loaf." PraS (59:1) Spr 85, p. 90-95.
    "Her Apprehension." Tendril (19/20) 85, p. 251.
    "Inside." PraS (59:1) Spr 85, p. 88.
    "It's Something." ColEng (47:5) S 85, p. 500-501.
    "Knock Back." DenQ (20:2) Fall 85, p. 69-70.
    "Moon of Another Childhood." Crazy (27) Fall 84, p. 29-30.
    "Pearl of the Moon." DenQ (20:2) Fall 85, p. 65-66.
    "There." DenQ (20:2) Fall 85, p. 67-68.
3037. MARGOSHES, Dave
    "Beneath the Skin" (for Jon & Bernadette). Waves (14:1/2)
        Fall 85, p. 104.
    "Marking Time." PoetryCR (6:4) Sum 85, p. 46.
    "The Tone Was There." CrossC (7:2) 85, p. 12.
3038. MARIANI, Paul
    "Minneapolis: At the Summer Solstice." Tendril (19/20)
        85, p. 252-253.
    "Pentecost Sunday: Howard Beach." Verse (3) 85, p. 11-12.
    "Sarcophagus." Agni (22) 85, p. 65-67.
3039. MARION, Jeff Daniel
    "Gifts." SouthernPR (26, i.e. 25:2) Fall 85, p. 34.
    "A Lamp in the Window." LaurelR (19:2) Sum 85, p. 21.
3040. MARION, Paul
    "Meeting." WestB (17) 85, p. 109.
MARIS, Ron de
    See De MARIS, Ron
3041. MARISCAL, Jose Luis
    "Fielmente." LindLM (4:1) Ja-Mr 85, p. 15.
    "Hora Primera." LindLM (4:1) Ja-Mr 85, p. 15.
    "Sinceramente." LindLM (4:1) Ja-Mr 85, p. 15.
3042. MARKOS, Don
    "The Protestant Wedding." SouthernR (21:1) Wint 85, p.
        119.
3043. MARLIN, Daniel
    "In Brunem" (In Yiddish). Imagine (1:2) Wint 84, p. 98-99.
    "Mother" (In Yiddish, with tr. by the author). Imagine
        (1:2) Wint 84, p. 96-97.
    "This Is How We Are" (In Yiddish, with tr. by the author).
        Imagine (1:2) Wint 84, p. 94-95.
    "The Well" (In Yiddish, with tr. by the author). Imagine
        (1:2) Wint 84, p. 98-99.
3044. MARLING, William
    "Night Unending" (Dedicated to the memory of Francisco
        Morales Menendez, tr. of Armando Valladares). NewOR
        (12:2) Sum 85, p. 102.
    "Question" (for Fernando Arrabal, my friend, tr. of Armando
        Valladares). NewOR (12:2) Sum 85, p. 55.

"To the Preachers of Hate" (tr. of Armando Valladares).
    NewOR (12:2) Sum 85, p. 36-37.
3045. MARQUARDT, B. (See also MARQUARDT, Barbara)
    "November Remnants." NoDaQ (53:4) Fall 85, p. 208.
3046. MARQUARDT, Barbara (See also MARQUARDT, B.)
    "What a Mayfly May Not Do." KanQ (17:1/2) Wint-Spr 85, p.
    135.
MARQUEZ, Luis Diaz
    See DIAZ MARQUEZ, Luis
3047. MARRA, Sue
    "Remember." PoeticJ (9) 85, p. 15.
    "Sorcery." PoeticJ (10) 85, p. 40.
3048. MARRIOTT, Anne
    "In a Dark Green Rain." Waves (13:4) Spr 85, p. 60.
    "Story from Utah." Waves (13:4) Spr 85, p. 62.
    "Suddenly behind Svaneke." Waves (13:4) Spr 85, p. 61.
3049. MARSH, Tony
    "I Sing the Rented Rooms." StoneC (13:1/2) Fall-Wint 85-
    86, p. 27.
3050. MARSH, William
    "Cambodia." WormR (25:1, issue 97) 85, p. 12.
    "The Cool Guys." WormR (25:1, issue 97) 85, p. 12.
    "King for a Day." WormR (25:1, issue 97) 85, p. 14.
    "Little Buggers." WormR (25:1, issue 97) 85, p. 14.
    "Nowhere." WormR (25:1, issue 97) 85, p. 13.
    "Only in America." WormR (25:1, issue 97) 85, p. 11.
    "Vietnam." WormR (25:1, issue 97) 85, p. 12-13.
    "West Meets East" (Special Section). WormR (25:3, issue
    99) 85, p. 93-104.
3051. MARSHALL, Christina
    "He left you shattered visions." Open24 (4) 85, p. 23.
3052. MARSHALL, Jack
    "Arabian Nights." Confr (30/31) N 85, p. 252-253.
    "Harbor Music." Pequod (19/20/21) 85, p. 219-221.
3053. MARSHALL, John
    "Lagoon." CanLit (104) Spr 85, p. 108.
3054. MARSHALL, Nancy
    "Theodicy." Sam (42:3, 167th release) 85, p. 37.
3055. MARSHBURN, Sandra
    "Beetles and Bears." ThRiPo (25/26) 85, p. 41.
    "For All of Us." HiramPoR (38) Spr-Sum 85, p. 26.
    "Lula's Antique Shop." ThRiPo (25/26) 85, p. 40-41.
3056. MARTEAU, Robert
    "Sur la Seine lente." Os (20) 85, p. 2.
3057. MARTENS, Caroline Rowe
    "Penciled Thought." Amelia (2:2) O 85, p. 85-86.
    "Sea Sonnet." Amelia (2:2) O 85, p. 85.
MARTIN, Billie Kaiser
    See KAISER-MARTIN, Billie
3058. MARTIN, Charles Casey
    "Julia." Telescope (4:2) Spr 85, p. 38-39.
    "The Penalty for Guessing." Telescope (4:2) Spr 85, p. 40-
    41.
3059. MARTIN, Don Roger
    "What Do You Want to Be When You Grow Up?" Sam (42:4,
    168th release) 85, p. 42.
3060. MARTIN, Herbert Woodward
    "Atlanta." BlackALF (19:3) Fall 85, p. 110.
3061. MARTIN, Lynn
    "Air." PoetryNW (26:1) Spr 85, p. 40.
    "Fasting." IndR (8:3) Fall 85, p. 7.
    "A Guest of Fishes" (for J. C. 1956-1984). PoetryNW
    (26:1) Spr 85, p. 39.
    "It Is Sunny" (after Carlos Drummond de Andrade). Tendril
    (19/20) 85, p. 254.
    "Prayer." AntR (43:3) Sum 85, p. 329.

"Shaving." Tendril (19/20) 85, p. 255.
3062. MARTIN, Paul
"The Artist." Wind (15:54) 85, p. 32.
3063. MARTIN-HEITER, Marcia
"The Exterminator." NegC (5:4) Fall 85, p. 88-89.
3064. MARTIN URIOL, Miguel Angel
"Alguien Puso la Luz a los Colores." Mairena (7:19) 85,
p. 97.
3065. MARTINEZ, Daniel C.
"Field Gossip." BilingR (11:3) S-D 84, p. 65.
"La Gran Puta." BilingR (11:3) S-D 84, p. 65-66.
"The Lost Dance." BilingR (11:3) S-D 84, p. 61.
"El Menudero." BilingR (11:3) S-D 84, p. 66.
"Mi Perro Agringado." BilingR (11:3) S-D 84, p. 67-68.
"Polvos de Laredo." BilingR (11:3) S-D 84, p. 61-64.
"Sentado Pensando en la Filosofia." BilingR (11:3) S-D
84, p. 67.
"El Viejo Original." BilingR (11:3) S-D 84, p. 64.
3066. MARTINEZ, Dionisio D.
"The Arc of a Curve." Iowa (15:3) Fall 85, p. 67-68.
"Dream-of-the-Month Club." Iowa (15:3) Fall 85, p. 70-71.
"Fable." Iowa (15:3) Fall 85, p. 68-69.
"The Mouth Will Taste Its Own Fears." Iowa (15:3) Fall
85, p. 70.
"Pain" (for Armando Valladares). Iowa (15:3) Fall 85, p.
66.
"Rivers, Horses and Firewood." Iowa (15:3) Fall 85, p. 68.
MARTINEZ, Maria Isabel Arbona de
See ARBONA DE MARTINEZ, Maria Isabel
3067. MARTINEZ, Ramón E.
"The Light." CapeR (20:1) Spr 85, p. 45.
MARTINI, Brenda de
See DeMARTINI, Brenda
3068. MARTINI, Jim
"Death of a God." Amelia (2:2) O 85, p. 63.
3069. MARTINSON, Harry
"The Birch Heart" (tr. by William Jay Smith and Leif
Sjöberg). NewL (51:4) Sum 85, p. 78.
"Butterflies" (tr. by William Jay Smith and Leif
Sjöberg). NewL (51:4) Sum 85, p. 77.
"Cabbages" (tr. by William Jay Smith and Leif Sjöberg).
NewL (51:4) Sum 85, p. 77.
"The Final Year" (tr. by William Jay Smith and Leif
Sjöberg). NewL (51:4) Sum 85, p. 78.
"The Rooster" (tr. by William Jay Smith and Leif
Sjöberg). NewL (51:4) Sum 85, p. 77.
Wild Bouquet: Nature Poems (Selections, tr. by William
Jay Smith and Leif Sjöberg). AmerPoR (14:4) Jl-Ag
85, p. 23-25.
3070. MARTOS, Marco
"Rite" (tr. by Mary Crow). Mund (15:1/2) 85, p. 141.
"Rito." Mund (15:1/2) 85, p. 140.
3071. MARTYNOV, Leonid
"Trace" (tr. by Robert L. Smith and Sylvia Maizell). WebR
(10:1) Spr 85, p. 13.
MARY LUCINA, Sister
See LUCINA, Mary (Sister)
3072. MARZAN, Dinorah
"Un disparo y la locura." Mairena (7:19) 85, p. 108.
3073. MASARIK, Al
"California Coast October." CreamCR (10:2) [85?], p. 44.
"Runoff." PaintedB (26/27) Sum-Fall 85, p. 31.
"The Willow Tree." SecC (12:2) 84?, p. 10.
3074. MASEL, Carolyn
"Nocturne." Quarry (34:3) Sum 85, p. 21.

3075. MASON, David
    "Greek Primitive" (after a painting by Themis Tsironis).
        NegC (5:1) Wint 85, p. 32-33.
3076. MASON, Julian
    "Morning Lights" (for Marge Piercy 2-17-84). SouthernPR
        (26, i.e. 25:2) Fall 85, p. 55.
3077. MASON-BROWNE, Nicholas
    "The Gulf." MalR (71) Je 85, p. 64.
MASSAO, Nonagase
    See NONAGASE, Massao
MASSMAN, Gordon Lester
    See LESTER-MASSMAN, Gordon
MASTER, J. R. le
    See LeMASTER, J. R.
3078. MASTERSON, Dan
    "Breaking the Seal." DenQ (19:4) Spr 85, p. 71-72.
    "Rolling the Awning." DenQ (19:4) Spr 85, p. 70.
3079. MATHESON, William
    "Heron Variations" (Selections: II, III, VIII, for J.
        Thomas Rimer). RiverS (17) 85, p. 46.
3080. MATHIEU, Guy
    "A la Testa Que Dansa Ela" (in Provenç al, tr. of James
        Laughlin). Oink (19) 85, p. 40.
3081. MATHIS, Cleopatra
    "Dancer among the Constellations." USl (18/19) Wint 85,
        p. 20.
    "May Run" (for Tom). Iowa (15:1) Wint 85, p. 90.
    "Running Snow." NewRep (193:24) 9 D 85, p. 40.
    "Wings." USl (18/19) Wint 85, p. 20.
3082. MATHIS-EDDY, Darlene
    "Autumn Earth." BallSUF (24:4) Fall 83 [c1985], p. 54.
    "Lambing." BallSUF (24:4) Fall 83 [c1985], p. 14.
    "Starry Nights." BallSUF (24:4) Fall 83 [c1985], p. 41.
    "Thistle and Finch." BallSUF (24:4) Fall 83 [c1985], p.
        26.
MATRE, C. van
    See Van MATRE, C. (Connie)
3083. MATSON, Clive
    "Babes in a Cradle." YellowS (14) Spr 85, p. 19.
    "A Marriage." YellowS (14) Spr 85, p. 19.
3084. MATSUEDA, Pat
    "Six Poems about Artists" (for Hal Lum). HawaiiR (17) Spr
        85, p. 25-30.
3085. MATTAX, E. R.
    "Apple Trees in Arkansas." ChrC (102:29) 2 O 85, p. 861.
    "Between." ChrC (102:27) 11-18 S 85, p. 799.
3086. MATTERN, Evelyn
    "Barclay's Pond." Comm (112:6) 22 Mr 85, p. 186.
    "Sound and Sight." ChrC (102:38) 4 D 85, p. 1110.
3087. MATTHEWS, William
    "Scenic View." NewYorker (61:27) 26 Ag 85, p. 26.
    "The Theme of the Three Caskets." Iowa (15:1) Wint 85, p.
        28-30.
3088. MATTISON, Alice
    "Edges." Shen (36:1) 85-86, p. 24-25.
    "The Man at the Other Picnic." Shen (36:1) 85-86, p. 25-
        26.
    "The Phone Call." LittleM (14:4) 85, p. 59.
MATVEIEV, Ivan Venediktovich
    See ELAGIN, Ivan
3089. MATVEYEFF, Helen
    "Birch Tree" (tr. of Ivan Elagin). WoosterR (4) Fall 85,
        p. 33.
    "I Stand Here, Filled with Sawdust" (tr. of Ivan Elagin).
        WoosterR (4) Fall 85, p. 35, 37.

3090. MATZUREFF, Donna
        "Considerate Tim." PoetL (80:2) Sum 85, p. 85-86.
3091. MAURA, Gabriel Vicente
        "Nunca he visto cosa alguna." Mairena (7:19) 85, p. 108.
3092. MAURA, Sister
        "For My Students." AntigR (62/63) Sum-Aut 85, p. 35.
3093. MAUREN, Steven
        "Death." Wind (15:55) 85, p. 32.
3094. MAVIGLIA, Joseph
        "Accenti / Accents." CanLit (106) Fall 85, p. 4.
3095. MAXFIELD, Brad
        "Confession." PoetC (17:1) Fall 85, p. 40-41.
3096. MAXSON, Gloria
        "The Flamenco Guitarist." ChrC (102:10) 20-27 Mr 85, p.
        288.
3097. MAY, Kathy
        "Summer." PassN (6:2) Spr-Sum 85, p. 14.
3098. MAY, Michael
        "High Top Terrorists." Bogg (54) 85, p. 37.
        "Manhole." Sam (42:3, 167th release) 85, p. 45.
MAYANS, Fernando Sanchez
        See SANCHEZ MAYANS, Fernando
3099. MAYER, Bernadette
        "Approaching a City." Oink (19) 85, p. 75.
        "To Mr. Robt. Herrick & Another." Oink (19) 85, p. 76.
3100. MAYHALL, Jane
        "Sunlight on Fire Escapes." PartR (52:3) 85, p. 250-251.
3101. MAYHEW, Lenore
        "Haiku" (8 poems). WindO (45) Spr 85, p. 26.
        "The Leningrad Elegy" (tr. of Anna Akhmatova, w. William
        McNaughton). DevQ (19:3) Wint 85, p. 19-20.
        "Secrets of the Trade" (Excerpts, tr. of Anna Akhmatova).
        DevQ (19:3) Wint 85, p. 21-26.
3102. MAYNE, Seymour
        "Another Son." CanLit (105) Sum 85, p. 31.
        "Going Up." CanLit (105) Sum 85, p. 30.
3103. MAYO, Michael
        "America Revisited." JamesWR (2:1) Fall 84, p. 8-9.
3104. MAYS, John Bentley
        "A Chapter of Coming Forth by Day" (tr. of The Egyptian
        Book of the Dead, Spell XVII). Descant 50 (16:3) Fall
        85, p. 53-81.
3105. MAZUR, Gail
        "Early Winter." PraS (59:4) Wint 85, p. 37-38.
        "The Horizontal Man." Shen (36:1) 85-86, p. 30-31.
        "Summer Rain" (for Jane). PraS (59:4) Wint 85, p. 38-39.
3106. MAZZARI, Louis
        "Blues for Robert Johnson" (d. 1938). NewRena (19) Fall
        85, p. 93-94.
3107. MAZZARO, Jerome
        "Awakening to Fog." Hudson (38:2) Sum 85, p. 277.
        "Dream's End." Confr (30/31) N 85, p. 238.
        "Hard Listening." Confr (29) Wint 85, p. 23.
        "Morning Reflection." Hudson (38:2) Sum 85, p. 278.
        "Steps toward Unemployment." Confr (29) Wint 85, p. 24.
        "Summer Ties." CrossCur (5:3) 85, p. 168-169.
Mc . . .
        See also names beginning with Mac . . .
3108. McALEAVEY, David
        "1970." Vis (19) 85, p. 11.
        "Aegean Festival." LaurelR (19:2) Sum 85, p. 14.
        "Conches." RiverS (17) 85, p. 27.
        "Horse Feathers." LaurelR (19:2) Sum 85, p. 15.
        "Utter Pastoral." RiverS (17) 85, p. 26.
3109. McANALLY, Mary
        "The Luxury of Guilt" (for Carolyn Forché). Nimrod

        (28:2) Spr-Sum 85, p. 44.
        "Our Work." <u>Nimrod</u> (28:2) Spr-Sum 85, p. 43.
3110. McARTHUR, Mary
        "Jane Addams' Dream of a Wheel." <u>Nat</u> (240:18) 11 My 85,
            p. 566.
3111. McBRIDE, Elizabeth
        "Everyday Places." <u>GeoR</u> (39:3) Fall 85, p. 508.
3112. McBRIDE, Mekeel
        "The Kiss." <u>Tendril</u> (19/20) 85, p. 256-257.
        "The Plainest Signs." <u>Tendril</u> (19/20) 85, p. 258-259.
        "The Thief of Light." <u>Tendril</u> (19/20) 85, p. 260.
3113. McBRIDE, Regina
        "The Fair." <u>NegC</u> (5:2) Spr 85, p. 47-48.
3114. McCABE, Michael
        "Thought Maze." <u>NoDaQ</u> (53:2) Spr 85, p. 213.
        "A View from the Studio." <u>NoDaQ</u> (53:2) Spr 85, p. 213.
3115. McCABE, Victoria
        "Birthday." <u>AntigR</u> (60) Wint 85, p. 14.
        "Body: Irish-American." <u>AntigR</u> (60) Wint 85, p. 13.
        "The Failed Suicide." <u>AmerPoR</u> (14:3) My-Je 85, p. 48.
        "The Feet." <u>MemphisSR</u> (5:2) Spr 85, p. 52.
        "Hangover." <u>NewL</u> (52:1) Fall 85, p. 121.
        "The Marriage of Ear and Finger." <u>GreenfR</u> (13:1/2) Fall-
            Wint 85, p. 76.
        "The Marriage of Ear and Finger, Part II." <u>GreenfR</u>
            (13:1/2) Fall-Wint 85, p. 77-78.
        "Marriage Parable." <u>PraS</u> (59:1) Spr 85, p. 99.
        "Needy Relatives." <u>CutB</u> (23) Fall-Wint 85, p. 50-51.
        "On the Suicide of a Painter." <u>KanQ</u> (17:3) Sum 85, p. 55.
        "The Past." <u>HolCrit</u> (22:1) F 85, p. 18.
        "Radio Found Poem." <u>NewL</u> (52:1) Fall 85, p. 120-121.
        "The Woman Who Wished to Forget Her Throat." <u>KanQ</u> (17:3)
            Sum 85, p. 56.
3116. McCAFFREY, Phillip
        "The Dream of the Burning Child." <u>AntR</u> (43:3) Sum 85, p.
            334-335.
3117. McCANN, David
        "The Hippy Market in Sao Paulo" (tr. of So Chongju).
            <u>GrahamHR</u> (9) Fall 85, p. 71.
        "Kilimanjaro Sunrise" (tr. of So Chongju). <u>GrahamHR</u> (9)
            Fall 85, p. 72.
        "Nevada" (tr. of So Chongju). <u>GrahamHR</u> (9) Fall 85, p. 70.
        "New Year's Prayer, 1976" (tr. of So Chongju). <u>NewL</u>
            (51:4) Sum 85, p. 138-139.
        "The Pedlar Women of Wu-Lai" (tr. of So Chongju).
            <u>GrahamHR</u> (9) Fall 85, p. 74.
        "Song of the Indian Wanderers" (tr. of So Chongju).
            <u>GrahamHR</u> (9) Fall 85, p. 73.
3118. McCANN, Janet
        "Four Tickets to the Asylum." <u>RagMag</u> (4:1) Spr 85, p. 19.
        "Three Mile Island." <u>Sam</u> (42:4, 168th release) 85, p. 4.
        "We Wanted to Greet You." <u>WoosterR</u> (3) Spr 85, p. 69.
        "You Can't." <u>NewRena</u> (19) Fall 85, p. 108-109.
3119. McCARTHY, Gerald
        "The Hooded Legion." <u>TriQ</u> (63) Spr-Sum 85, p. 626.
3120. McCARTNEY, Sharon
        "October 1967." <u>Waves</u> (13:4) Spr 85, p. 93.
        "Rancho Santa Fe." <u>Waves</u> (13:4) Spr 85, p. 92.
3121. McCAUGHEY, Claire
        "Echoes." <u>Quarry</u> (34:4) Aut 85, p. 30.
3122. McCLANE, Kenneth A.
        "Birth Song." <u>NowestR</u> (23:2) 85, p. 47.
        "The Glowworm." <u>StoneC</u> (13:1/2) Fall-Wint 85-86, p. 38-39.
        "Paul." <u>BlackALF</u> (19:3) Fall 85, p. 128.
        "The Radio" (For Robert Morgan). <u>GreenfR</u> (13:1/2) Fall-
            Wint 85, p. 49.

"Rich beyond Cost." NowestR (23:2) 85, p. 48.
"Tree Fire." StoneC (13:1/2) Fall-Wint 85-86, p. 39.
3123. McCLATCHY, J. D.
"Above Beirut." AntR (43:3) Sum 85, p. 331.
"After a Visit." Nat (241:16) 16 N 85, p. 520.
"At a Reading" (Anthony Hecht's). ParisR (27:97) Fall 85,
p. 134-136.
"A Cold in Venice." NewYorker (61:34) 14 O 85, p. 46.
"The Cup." AntR (43:3) Sum 85, p. 332-333.
"The Family Circle." SouthwR (70:1) Wint 85, p. 69-70.
"Fiddlehead." NewRep (192:21) 27 My 85, p. 38.
"First Steps." Poetry (146:6) S 85, p. 311-323.
"The Palace Dwarf" (The Ducal Palace, Mantua). Pequod
(19/20/21) 85, p. 222-223.
3124. McCLEERY, Nancy
"By the Kits-Ka-Toos (The Platte)." KanQ (17:4) Fall 85,
p. 170.
"View of Pawnee Origins." KanQ (17:4) Fall 85, p. 171.
3125. McCLELLAND, James J.
"Across a Street." HiramPoR (38) Spr-Sum 85, p. 25.
3126. McCLOSKEY, Mark
"The Binding Glitter." PoetryNW (26:3) Aut 85, p. 3-4.
"Next Time." PoetryNW (26:3) Aut 85, p. 4-5.
3127. McCLURE, Keith
"Fireflies." BelPoJ (36:2) Wint 85-86, p. 26.
3128. McCOMBS, Judith
"Changeling Dream." Poetry (146:6) S 85, p. 340.
"Harvest." CentR (29:2) Spr 85, p. 207.
"Mirror." RiverS (17) 85, p. 50.
3129. McCORKLE, James
"The Flaying of Marsyas." MissouriR (8:2) 85, p. 122-123.
"Room in New York." MidAR (5:1) 85, p. 8-9.
"Rooms by the Sea." MidAR (5:1) 85, p. 10-11.
3130. McCORMACK, Catherine Savoy
"Matters of the Soul." SanFPJ (7:3) 84 [i.e. 85], p. 84.
"No Cast." SanFPJ (7:3) 84 [i.e. 85], p. 69.
"Shall We Tell Them?" SanFPJ (7:3) 84 [i.e. 85], p. 69.
"Voting." SanFPJ (7:3) 84 [i.e. 85], p. 83.
3131. McCOWN, Clint
"Bears." ConnPR (3:1) 84, p. 13-14.
"Wind over Water" (Section six). KanQ (17:4) Fall 85, p.
68-69.
3132. McCOY, Barbara
"Long Live the Tiger." Wind (15:55) 85, p. 10.
3133. McCULLOUGH, Ken
"Afternoon on the Broad River near Columbia, South
Carolina" (for L.S.A.). NewL (52:1) Fall 85, p. 59.
"Harbinger." NoDaQ (53:1) Wint 85, p. 61.
"Responses to Rilke." NoDaQ (53:1) Wint 85, p. 60-61.
"Where We Are" (for George Oppen). NewL (52:1) Fall 85,
p. 58.
3134. McCURDY, Harold
"Remembering Her." ChrC (102:25) 14-21 Ag 85, p. 728.
3135. McDANIEL, Judith (See also McDANIEL, Judith A.)
"Crossing the Border" (from Leaving Home). GreenfR
(13:1/2) Fall-Wint 85, p. 13-15.
"Deathdance." Cond (11/12) 85, p. 29-30.
"The Doe." Cond (11/12) 85, p. 27-28.
"The Fog." Cond (11/12) 85, p. 31-32.
"Lebenstanz." Cond (11/12) 85, p. 33-34.
3136. McDANIEL, Judith A. (See also McDANIEL, Judith)
"The Earthquake." NegC (5:1) Wint 85, p. 17.
3137. McDANIEL, Tom
"The Mud and Smoke." Wind (15:55) 85, p. 33.
"The Other Side of Okra." Wind (15:55) 85, p. 33.

3138. McDANIEL, Wilma Elizabeth
      "Bass at Migrant Creek." HangL (47) Spr 85, p. 34.
      "Fronie Has Lost the War." HangL (47) Spr 85, p. 35.
      "A Green Grape Pie." HangL (47) Spr 85, p. 37.
      "Writing Poetry on New Paper." HangL (47) Spr 85, p. 36.
3139. McDERMOTT, John
      "Boy." USl (18/19) Wint 85, p. 9.
      "Fast Song." USl (18/19) Wint 85, p. 17.
3140. McDERMOTT, Mary E.
      "Abundance." NegC (5:4) Fall 85, p. 87.
3141. McDONALD, Agnes
      "Beach Place." CarolQ (37:3) Spr 85, p. 40-41.
3142. McDONALD, Bray
      "First Song of Grago the Gypsy." NegC (5:2) Spr 85, p. 78.
3143. McDONALD, Ian
      "Axed Man." GreenfR (12:3/4) Wint-Spr 85, p. 182.
      "Granny Isaacs Versus Death." GreenfR (12:3/4) Wint-Spr
         85, p. 183.
      "A White Man Considers the Situation." GreenfR (12:3/4)
         Wint-Spr 85, p. 181-182.
3144. McDONALD, Peter
      "Short Story." Verse (2) 85, p. 20.
3145. McDONALD, Walt (See also McDONALD, Walter)
      "Danse Macabre." TexasR (6:3/4) Fall-Wint 85, p. 94.
3146. McDONALD, Walter (See also McDONALD, Walt)
      "After a Week in the Rockies." Poem (54) N 85, p. 52.
      "Black Wings Wheeling." ThRiPo (25/26) 85, p. 39.
      "Buzzing in a Biplane." Poetry (146:5) Ag 85, p. 275-276.
      "Children of All Ages." Vis (19) 85, p. 29.
      "The Circle." KanQ (17:1/2) Wint-Spr 85, p. 69.
      "Crosswind Landings." AntigR (62/63) Sum-Aut 85, p. 218.
      "Driving the Night Shift." WindO (45) Spr 85, p. 10.
      "Estacado." SoDakR (23:2) Sum 85, p. 71.
      "Falling Objects." Raccoon (17) Mr 85, p. 27.
      "Fishing the San Juan Wilderness." Ascent (11:1) 85, p.
         32.
      "The Flying Dutchman." TriQ (64) Fall 85, p. 113-114.
      "For Richard Hugo" (from his words). TriQ (64) Fall 85,
         p. 112.
      "Goat Ranching on Hardscrabble." CapeR (20:1) Spr 85, p.
         40.
      "In Winter." WebR (10:1) Spr 85, p. 68.
      "Leaving a Boat in the Water." Ascent (11:1) 85, p. 33.
      "Living on Scorched Earth." Poem (54) N 85, p. 51.
      "Looking Out on the Morning." CimR (73) O 85, p. 62.
      "The Middle Years." Poetry (146:5) Ag 85, p. 276.
      "Moon and Trees." ConnPR (3:1) 84, p. 47-48.
      "Morning in Glacier Park." SpoonRQ (10:2) Spr 85, p. 54.
      "Off Port Aransas." AntigR (62/63) Sum-Aut 85, p. 217.
      "Overnight." LaurelR (19:1) Wint 85, p. 45.
      "Rafting the Brazos." CutB (23) Fall-Wint 85, p. 22-23.
      "Report from the City." MidAR (5:2) 85, p. 16.
      "Retired Pilot." Vis (18) 85, p. 19.
      "Rigging the Windmill." MissouriR (8:3) 85, p. 24.
      "Rowing in Eden." MalR (71) Je 85, p. 82.
      "Scheduled Flights." WebR (10:1) Spr 85, p. 68.
      "Settling on Open Plains." CrossCur (5:3) 85, p. 33.
      "Shells." PassN (6:1) Fall-Wint 85, p. 15.
      "The Snowplow Driver." KanQ (17:1/2) Wint-Spr 85, p. 68.
      "Starting a Pasture." AmerPoR (14:5) S-O 85, p. 22.
      "Tracking on Hardscrabble." SpoonRQ (10:2) Spr 85, p. 53.
      "The Weatherman Reports the Weather." CharR (11:2) Fall
         85, p. 83.
      "Whatever It Takes." AmerPoR (14:5) S-O 85, p. 22.
      "Whatever It Takes." Poetry (146:5) Ag 85, p. 277.
      "Whatever the Stream Delivers." CrossCur (5:3) 85, p. 34-

35.
"Where the Aspens Go." ConnPR (3:1) 84, p. 46.
"Wildcatting on Hardscrabble." ThRiPo (25/26) 85, p. 38.
"Wind and Hardscrabble." Atlantic (256:1), Jl 85, p. 46.
"Witching on Hardscrabble" (Special Issue). SpoonRQ
    (11:1) Wint 85, 71 p.
3147. McDOWELL, John Nevin
"Advice on Making It Through a Nightmare." Dandel (12:2)
    85, p. 5.
3148. McDOWELL, Robert
"Quiet Money" (for Randy & Carole McDowell). Hudson
    (38:2) Sum 85, p. 235-246.
3149. McELROY, Colleen J.
"And That Which Is Sold unto Dow" (placenta, L. cake, PLAC,
    NA). SouthernPR (25:1) Spr 85, p. 31-34.
"Green River Prelude for a Serial Murder." MissouriR
    (8:3) 85, p. 56-57.
"Moon, Razor, Eye." GeoR (39:3) Fall 85, p. 523.
3150. McENEANEY, Kevin T.
"Symmetrical Portrait with Blue and Yellow Line" (for Paul
    Muldoon). ChiR (35:2) Wint 85, p. 43.
3151. McFALL, Gardner
"After a Fairy Tale by Oscar Wilde." Tendril (19/20) 85,
    p. 261.
"The Air Pilot's Wife." Crazy (29) Fall 85, p. 64-65.
"Along the St. John's." NewYorker (61:32) 30 S 85, p. 36.
"Everything You Need." Crazy (29) Fall 85, p. 66.
3152. McFARLAND, Ron
"The Poet Learns to Hear." WoosterR (4) Fall 85, p. 9-10.
"Spring Comes to the Clearwater." CutB (23) Fall-Wint 85,
    p. 46.
3153. McFARLANE, Basil
"Geography Lesson." GreenfR (12:3/4) Wint-Spr 85, p. 185.
"Season of the African Queen." GreenfR (12:3/4) Wint-Spr
    85, p. 186.
3154. McFERREN, Martha
"The Fall." OP (38/39) Spr 85, p. 74.
"Mabel Takes a Dive." PoetryR (2:2) Ap 85, p. 23-24.
3155. McGANN, Jerome
"How I Spent My Summer Vacation." AmerPoR (14:4) Jl-Ag
    85, p. 40.
3156. McGARRY, Bill
"Bobbing on Wheat Fields." SnapD (8:2) Spr 85, p. 8.
3157. McGOVERN, Martin
"All Hollows Eve / Anniversary." Poetry (147:1) O 85, p.
    16-18.
"Late Spring, Elegy, Early June." NoAmR (270:2) Je 85, p.
    53.
"Near San Gregorio." Tendril (19/20) 85, p. 262-263.
"Toward an Epithalamion." Poetry (147:1) O 85, p. 15-16.
3158. McGOVERN, Robert
"Sir Real Met a Physical." KanQ (17:1/2) Wint-Spr 85, p.
    78-79.
"Towards Eating." KanQ (17:1/2) Wint-Spr 85, p. 79.
3159. McGRATH, Thomas
"Columbus." NoDaQ (53:1) Wint 85, p. 26.
"The Edge of the River." NoDaQ (53:1) Wint 85, p. 28.
"Lament for Pablo Neruda." NoDaQ (53:1) Wint 85, p. 44.
"The Need for Stoicism in the Stoa of Attalus." NoDaQ
    (53:1) Wint 85, p. 28.
"Once We Meant It." NoDaQ (53:1) Wint 85, p. 28.
"Portents." NoDaQ (53:1) Wint 85, p. 26.
"Recall." NoDaQ (53:1) Wint 85, p. 27.
"Route Song and Epitaph." NewL (51:3) Spr 85, p. 46.
"The Sense of Being Incomplete" (for Sam Ray, and for those
    left behind). NewL (51:3) Spr 85, p. 46.

"That Week in the Desert." NoDaQ (53:1) Wint 85, p. 27.
3160. McGUCKIAN, Medbh
    "Children of the Mist." PoetryCR (7:1) Aut 85, p. 6.
    "The Fire Tower." PoetryCR (7:1) Aut 85, p. 6.
    "The Frame." PoetryCR (6:4) Sum 85, p. 42.
    "Sea or Sky." NewYorker (61:18) 24 Je 85, p. 38.
    "Ylang-Ylang." Poetry (146:4) Jl 85, p. 203.
3161. McHUGH, Heather
    "After You Left." AmerPoR (14:5) S-O 85, p. 13.
    "A Cup of Sky, a Foot of Fire." NewRep (193:27) 30 D 85,
        p. 48.
    "Gray Day." ParisR (27:97) Fall 85, p. 100.
    "Have or Love." NewRep (192:4) 28 Ja 85, p. 38.
    "Memento Vitae." AmerPoR (14:5) S-O 85, p. 13.
    "Pro Vita." Atlantic (256:2), Ag 85, p. 67.
    "Take Care." NewRep (193:3/4) 15-22 Jl 85, p. 41.
    "This Is the Life." ParisR (27:97) Fall 85, p. 101.
    "To the Quick." ParisR (27:97) Fall 85, p. 102.
    "Vacation." NewRep (192:14) 8 Ap 85, p. 40.
3162. McINTOSH, Joan
    "The Summer House." Wind (15:54) 85, p. 33-34.
    "There's a Place Called Wheatland." Wind (15:54) 85, p.
        33.
3163. McKAGUE, Thomas R.
    "Cabin Fever." Blueline (6:2) Wint-Spr 85, p. 15.
    "Midwinter and the Color Orange." Blueline (6:2) Wint-Spr
        85, p. 15.
3164. McKAIG, Kelly
    "About the Ballerina in the Jewelry Box." WoosterR (4)
        Fall 85, p. 13.
3165. McKAY, Don
    "Gulp." MalR (72) S 85, p. 92.
    "Homelite LX130." MalR (72) S 85, p. 93.
    "Styles of Fall." MalR (72) S 85, p. 87-91.
3166. McKEAN, James
    "An Apology to a Friend for Shooting a Hole in His
        Ceiling." Atlantic (255:3), Mr 85, p. 74.
    "Lost in Amsterdam." Poetry (145:5) F 85, p. 261.
3167. McKEE, Louis
    "The Bath." Amelia (2:2) O 85, p. 77.
    "Clandestine Exchange." PoeticJ (12) 85, p. 15.
    "Consideration." Bogg (53) 85, p. 31.
    "Emmaus." Wind (15:54) 85, p. 35.
    "Genesis." NegC (5:2) Spr 85, p. 135.
    "Girls from Scranton" (for M.M.). PoeticJ (12) 85, p. 34-
        35.
    "In the Morning." NegC (5:1) Wint 85, p. 107-108.
    "Luck." NegC (5:1) Wint 85, p. 106.
    "Name Poem." AmerPoR (14:3) My-Je 85, p. 46.
    "Sailing Back to Penelope." NegC (5:2) Spr 85, p. 149.
    "Summer Neighbor." Pig (13) 85, p. 24.
    "Three Stories." LitR (29:1) Fall 85, p. 30.
3168. McKENZIE, Earl
    "Flint." GreenfR (12:3/4) Wint-Spr 85, p. 189.
    "My Wise Old Lamp." GreenfR (12:3/4) Wint-Spr 85, p. 190.
    "Sabbath." GreenfR (12:3/4) Wint-Spr 85, p. 188.
3169. McKENZIE-PORTER, Patricia
    "Guns and Petals" (Selections: Six Poems). Germ (9:1) Spr-
        Sum 85, p. 40-47.
    "The Saint." AntigR (62/63) Sum-Aut 85, p. 221.
    "A Shadow." AntigR (62/63) Sum-Aut 85, p. 220.
    "Without Landmarks." AntigR (62/63) Sum-Aut 85, p. 219.
3170. McKIM, Elizabeth
    "News from the Globe." Imagine (2:1) Sum 85, p. 92-93.
3171. McKINLEY, James
    "The Black Dream of the Elm" (tr. of Slavko Janevski, w.

Zoran Ancevski). <u>NewL</u> (51:4) Sum 85, p. 23-24.
"The Carvers" (tr. of Zoran Ancevski, w. the author).
   <u>NewL</u> (51:4) Sum 85, p. 32.
"A Child Talking in Its Sleep" (tr. of Vlada Urosevic, w.
   Zoran Ancevski). <u>NewL</u> (51:4) Sum 85, p. 25.
"The Desert Woman" (Excerpt from a sequence of poems, tr.
   of Bogomil Gjuzel, w. Zoran Ancevski). <u>NewL</u> (51:4) Sum
   85, p. 27.
"Droughts" (tr. of Slavko Janevski, w. Zoran Ancevski).
   <u>NewL</u> (51:4) Sum 85, p. 23.
"For Aunt A.K." (tr. of Zoran Ancevski, w. the author).
   <u>NewL</u> (51:4) Sum 85, p. 30.
"Night Song" (tr. of Zoran Ancevski, w. the author). <u>NewL</u>
   (51:4) Sum 85, p. 31-32.
"Poem of the Inscriptions" (tr. of Vlada Urosevic, w. Zoran
   Ancevski). <u>NewL</u> (51:4) Sum 85, p. 25.
"Reader of Dreams" (tr. of Vlada Urosevic, w. Zoran
   Ancevski). <u>NewL</u> (51:4) Sum 85, p. 24.
"The Rebellion of the Seeds" (tr. of Radovan Pavlovski, w.
   Zoran Ancevski). <u>NewL</u> (51:4) Sum 85, p. 26.
"A Stranger at Home, at Home Elsewhere" (tr. of Bogomil
   Gjuzel, w. Zoran Ancevski). <u>NewL</u> (51:4) Sum 85, p. 28.
"Travelling to Ithaca" (tr. of Zoran Ancevski, w. the
   author). <u>NewL</u> (51:4) Sum 85, p. 29-30.
"The Turtle" (tr. of Radovan Pavlovski, w. Zoran Ancevski).
   <u>NewL</u> (51:4) Sum 85, p. 26-27.
3172. McKINNEY, Irene
   "Starlings in the Walls at Night." <u>NowestR</u> (23:1) 85, p.
   12.
3173. McKINNEY, Sandy
   "A Birthday" (J. McK. 1967-1976). <u>SenR</u> (15:2) 85, p. 52.
   "The Body of Desire." <u>Tendril</u> (19/20) 85, p. 277.
   "The Final Tenderness" (tr. of Rafael Guillen). <u>Tendril</u>
   (19/20) 85, p. 159-160.
   "A Friend Comes Back" (tr. of Rafael Guillen). <u>SenR</u>
   (15:2) 85, p. 168-170.
   "The Last Gesture" (tr. of Rafael Guillen). <u>Pequod</u> (18)
   85, p. 109.
   "The Neighbor." <u>SenR</u> (15:2) 85, p. 53.
   "Not Fear" (tr. of Rafael Guillen). <u>Pequod</u> (18) 85, p.
   110-111.
   "One Day with the Dawn" (tr. of Rafael Guillen). <u>Tendril</u>
   (19/20) 85, p. 157-158.
   "Opening a Path for the Flash" (tr. of Rafael Guillen).
   <u>SenR</u> (15:2) 85, p. 164-165.
   "Poem of No" (tr. of Rafael Guillen). <u>Tendril</u> (19/20) 85,
   p. 161.
   "Road Show" (tr. of Rafael Guillen). <u>SenR</u> (15:2) 85, p.
   166-167.
   "To Be an Instant" (tr. of Rafael Guillen). <u>SenR</u> (15:2)
   85, p. 162-163.
   "Today Paris Doesn't Exist" (tr. of Rafael Guillen). <u>SenR</u>
   (15:2) 85, p. 171-173.
3174. McKINNON, Patrick (<u>See</u> <u>also</u> McKINNON, Patrick J.)
   "The Bathtub Poem." <u>Open24</u> (4) 85, p. 50.
   "Casey Livingston Is an Epileptic." <u>Abraxas</u> (33) 85, p.
   44-45.
   "In My Head." <u>RagMag</u> (4:1) Spr 85, p. 14.
   "Its Fall." <u>RagMag</u> (4:2) Fall 85, p. 38.
   "The Lake." <u>RagMag</u> (4:1) Spr 85, p. 16.
   "Martha." <u>Open24</u> (4) 85, p. 51.
   "Mountains." <u>RagMag</u> (4:1) Spr 85, p. 17.
   "Owl Trash." <u>Open24</u> (4) 85, p. 50.
   "So." <u>RagMag</u> (4:1) Spr 85, p. 15.
   "Staggering toward Zimbabwe." <u>RagMag</u> (4:2) Fall 85, p. 39.

3175. McKINNON, Patrick J. (See also McKINNON, Patrick)
      "The Bathtub Poem." CrabCR (3:1) Fall-Wint 85, p. 25.
      "The Diaphragm Poem." Bogg (53) 85, p. 34.
      "Searching for Spiders." CrabCR (3:1) Fall-Wint 85, p. 26.
3176. McKINSEY, Martin
      "The Choice" (tr. of Yannis Ritsos). YaleR (74:3) Spr 85,
         p. 452-453.
      "Deep Blue" (tr. of Odysseus Elytis). Ploughs (11:4) 85,
         p. 16.
      "The Garden Was Entering the Sea" (tr. of Odysseus Elytis).
         Ploughs (11:4) 85, p. 18-19.
      "Our Life in Phares" (tr. of Yannis Ritsos). YaleR (74:3)
         Spr 85, p. 453.
      "Violet" (tr. of Odysseus Elytis). Ploughs (11:4) 85, p.
         17.
3177. McLANE, Robert
      "Upon the Recent Listing by a Group of College Professors
         of Ten Books Since 1940 Which Should be Required
         Reading: All of Them Prose." Wind (15:54) 85, p. 50.
3178. McLAREN, Lowell R.
      "Caution: Cunning Linguist" (for Robert Kroetsch). Dandel
         (12:1) 85, p. 10.
3179. McLATCHEY, Marilyn Bennett
      "The Peculiar Truth." Grain (13:2) My 85, p. 50.
3180. McLAUGHLIN, William
      "Chinese Children Read Porcelain to Me." PoetryNW (26:3)
         Aut 85, p. 20-21.
      "Old Man of the Backyard to His Dear Wife." SouthernHR
         (19:1) Wint 85, p. 20-21.
      "The Pigeons of Dubrovnik" (Anonymous, out of the Serbo-
         Croatian). KanQ (17:1/2) Wint-Spr 85, p. 147.
      "Secret Service" (Anonymous from the underground, out of
         the Serbo-Croatian). KanQ (17:1/2) Wint-Spr 85, p. 146.
      "The Subject in a Virtuoso Dark" (Anonymous, from the
         Croato-Serbian). WoosterR (3) Spr 85, p. 60-61.
      "Surfaces." CapeR (20:1) Spr 85, p. 44.
      "Two Writers at Sledmere House" (England). SouthernHR
         (19:1) Wint 85, p. 61.
3181. McLEOD, Joan
      "Alberta, Alberta." Quarry (34:4) Aut 85, p. 77-79.
      "Grace." Dandel (12:1) 85, p. 38-39.
3182. McLEOD, Stephen
      "Ars Poetica" (for Greg). Shen (36:1) 85-86, p. 15.
      "The Reason You Feel This Way." PoetryE (18) Fall 85, p.
         52.
3183. McMAHAN, Florence Myers
      "The Dispossessed." Wind (15:55) 85, p. 34-35.
      "Her Excuse for Complacency" (published, Summer 1953
         Westminster Magazine). Wind (15:55) 85, p. 34.
      "Or Sometimes Perverse." Nimrod (28:2) Spr-Sum 85, p. 111.
      "Red Warriors Return" (published, June 1938 in
         Kaleidograph). Wind (15:55) 85, p. 34.
      "Spring Storm Remembered." Wind (15:55) 85, p. 35-36.
3184. McMAHILL, Cheiron
      "Drunk" (tr. of Yoshihara Sachiko). Mund (16:1/2) 85, p.
         71.
      "Woman" (tr. of Yoshihara Sachiko). Mund (16:1/2) 85, p.
         69-70.
3185. McMAHON, Lynne
      "Pastoral." PraS (59:1) Spr 85, p. 40.
      "The Red Shoes" (for Anna Akhmatova). Tendril (19/20) 85,
         p. 278--279.
      "River." PraS (59:1) Spr 85, p. 41-42.
3186. McMANIS, Jack
      "Letter to a Friend before the February Thaw." ChrC
         (102:6) 20 F 85, p. 181.

3187. McMANUS, Fran, RSM
    "Masquerade." EngJ (74:5) S 85, p. 27.
3188. McMASTER, Arthur
    "Stones in a Still Pond." Blueline (7:1) Sum-Fall 85, p.
    33.
3189. McMILLAN, Ian
    "The Harsh Stink of Mythical European Gypsy Violins."
    HangL (48) Fall 85, p. 23.
    "The Politics of the Glimpse." HangL (48) Fall 85, p. 22.
    "Two Miners Pass in Opposite Directions at Daybreak."
    HangL (48) Fall 85, p. 20-21.
3190. McMILLAN, James A.
    "All the Poets My Brothers." StoneC (13:1/2) Fall-Wint 85-
    86, p. 13.
    "The Fanatic." JlNJPo (8:1) 85, p. 27.
3191. McMULLEN, Richard E.
    "Old Fanta." Wind (15:54) 85, p. 14.
    "Old Man in March." Wind (15:54) 85, p. 14.
3192. McNALL, Sally
    "Ice Storm." SpoonRQ (10:2) Spr 85, p. 44.
    "Sentinels." CapeR (20:1) Spr 85, p. 13.
3193. McNAUGHTON, William
    "The Leningrad Elegy" (tr. of Anna Akhmatova, w. Lenore
    Mayhew). DevQ (19:3) Wint 85, p. 19-20.
3194. McNEELY, Thomas
    "Juliet the Dominatrix." Rampike (4:2/3) 85-86, p. 83.
3195. McNEIL, Murray, 3
    "The Blimp Explodes." WormR (25:1, issue 97) 85, p. 8-9.
    "Safe Insane." WormR (25:1, issue 97) 85, p. 9-10.
3196. McNEILL, Anthony
    "After Seeing Zorba the Greek." GreenfR (12:3/4) Wint-
    Spr 85, p. 192.
    "From 'The First Mass' of the MS The Chapel of Death."
    GreenfR (12:3/4) Wint-Spr 85, p. 193.
    "From the MS The Cathedral of Names." GreenfR (12:3/4)
    Wint-Spr 85, p. 192.
3197. McPHERSON, Michael
    "The Alien Lounge." HawaiiR (18) Fall 85, p. 29.
    "February." HawaiiR (17) Spr 85, p. 58.
    "Lipstick in Your Volvo" (for D.L.S.). HawaiiR (18) Fall
    85, p. 27-28.
3198. McPHERSON, Sandra
    "American Footnote: Hiroshima." GrandS (4:4) Sum 85, p.
    154.
    "The Feather." NewYorker (61:16) 10 Je 85, p. 44.
    "Fringecups." GrandS (4:3) Spr 85, p. 56-57.
    "Hallucination." Field (32) Spr 85, p. 9-10.
    "In the Surgeon's Museum of Hands." Iowa (15:1) Wint 85,
    p. 33.
    "The Microscope in Winter." Field (32) Spr 85, p. 7-8.
    "Picketing Our Anti-Choice Senator at Reed College,
    September 1982." Crazy (29) Fall 85, p. 28.
    "Security Clearance" (Seattle 1966). Crazy (29) Fall 85,
    p. 26-27.
3199. McQUADE, Molly
    "For Mary." Prima (9) 85, p. 32.
3200. McQUAID, Theresa
    "Hitching a Dream Ride." PoetL (80:2) Sum 85, p. 79.
3201. McQUILKIN, Rennie
    "And When I've Had It Up to Here." MalR (72) S 85, p. 102.
    "Carrie Wolf." Wind (15:53) 85, p. 25-26.
    "Christmas in Cienfuegos" (for Jim Meyers). MalR (72) S
    85, p. 100-101.
    "The Dance of Charles Little Bear." KanQ (17:4) Fall 85,
    p. 160-161.
    "The Darkening." BelPoJ (36:2) Wint 85-86, p. 4-5.

"The Dealer." PoetL (79:4) Wint 85, p. 213.
"From Pan Am." Wind (15:53) 85, p. 26-27.
"Lizard." Wind (15:53) 85, p. 26.
"On Seeing My Son Dance in the West River Graveyard."
    Wind (15:53) 85, p. 25.
"A Poem to Condemn All Poems That Come In on Little Cat
    Feet." Wind (15:53) 85, p. 27.
"Regatta." Atlantic (256:4), O 85, p. 85.
"Sister Marie Angelica Plays Badminton." Atlantic
    (256:5), N 85, p. 93.
"Wood Man, Ice Man" (for Oscar and Gladys Egdahl). LitR
    (28:4) Sum 85, p. 573.
3202. McRAY, Paul
"Ashes." BlueBldgs (9) [85?], p. 51.
"Blue Period." CumbPR (5:1) Fall 85, p. 41-42.
"Tricks That Work." Abraxas (33) 85, p. 46.
3203. McREYNOLDS, Ronald
"Bartolommeo Murillo's 'The Immaculate Conception'."
    CharR (11:1) Spr 85, p. 89.
"Francisco Goya y Lucientes' 'Portrait of Don Ignacio
    Omulryan y Rourera'." CharR (11:1) Spr 85, p. 91.
"El Greco's 'Crucifix'." CharR (11:1) Spr 85, p. 90.
"El Greco's 'The Penitent Magdalene'." CharR (11:1) Spr
    85, p. 90.
"El Greco's 'Trinitarian Monk'." CharR (11:1) Spr 85, p.
    90-91.
3204. McWATT, Mark
"Hunting Light." GreenfR (12:3/4) Wint-Spr 85, p. 195.
"On Hallowed Ground." GreenfR (12:3/4) Wint-Spr 85, p.
    195-196.
3205. McWHIRTER, George
"Contaminations" (tr. of Jose Emillio Pacheco). PoetryCR
    (7:1) Aut 85, p. 18.
"Daybreak in Buenos Aires" (tr. of Jose Emillio Pacheco).
    PoetryCR (7:1) Aut 85, p. 18.
"The Georgia Strait" (tr. of Jose Emillio Pacheco).
    PoetryCR (7:1) Aut 85, p. 18.
"Hills." PoetryCR (7:2) Wint 85-86, p. 6.
3206. MEAD, Stephen X.
"Peacetime." IndR (8:2) Spr 85, p. 76.
3207. MEADE, Richard
"Degrees of Darkness." CrabCR (2:3) Sum 85, p. 27.
3208. MECKLENBORG, R. T.
"Ivry." LaurelR (19:1) Wint 85, p. 32-33.
3209. MEDEIROS, Jim
"My Wife at Thirty." CapeR (20:1) Spr 85, p. 10.
3210. MEDINA, Pablo
"4." LindLM (4:3) Jl-S 85, p. 15.
"Cosmology for the Beloved's Leg." USl (18/19) Wint 85,
    p. 3.
"Happiness." LindLM (4:3) Jl-S 85, p. 15.
"Mala Suerte." LindLM (4:3) Jl-S 85, p. 15.
3211. MEDINA, Rubén
"El Agua de Doña Nicolasa." RevChic (13:1) Spr 85, p.
    33-34.
"Después de Todo, Lonely" (para Efraín Huerta & Tom
    McGrath). RevChic (13:1) Spr 85, p. 40.
"Identidad." RevChic (13:1) Spr 85, p. 38-39.
"The Russians Are Coming! The Russians!" RevChic (13:1)
    Spr 85, p. 35-37.
3212. MEDINA SANCHEZ, Bethoven
"Lejana." Mairena (7:19) 85, p. 98.
3213. MEEK, Jay
"The Librettist." NoDaQ (53:1) Wint 85, p. 1-4.
"Voyager Music." Poetry (147:3) D 85, p. 154-155.

3214. MEEKS, Gretchen
   "Arachnid." PoeticJ (9) 85, p. 5.
   "Those with Wings." PoeticJ (10) 85, p. 30.
3215. MEHREN, Stein
   "The Cry" (tr. by Nadia Christensen). Ploughs (11:4) 85,
      p. 246.
   "Little Girls Riding Bikes on the Sidewalk" (tr. by Nadia
      Christensen). Ploughs (11:4) 85, p. 247.
3216. MEI, Francesco
   "Death in Viareggio" (tr. by Annalisa Saccà). LitR
      (29:1) Fall 85, p. 109.
   "Evening Ambush" (tr. by Annalisa Saccà). LitR (29:1)
      Fall 85, p. 107.
   "The Wind Will Tell" (tr. by Annalisa Saccà). LitR
      (29:1) Fall 85, p. 108.
3217. MEIER, Kay
   "Sequences in a Photo Album." EngJ (74:3) Mr 85, p. 93.
3218. MEINKE, Peter
   "Marathon Key." CrossCur (5:2) 85, p. 20-21.
   "Night Watch on the Chesapeake" (for Paul Van Dongen).
      VirQ (61:1) Wint 85, p. 62-63.
   "The Pin" (for Schwartz, Lowell, Berryman). VirQ (61:1)
      Wint 85, p. 61-62.
   "Les Temps Modernes." ChrC (102:21) 19-25 Je 85, p. 613.
   "Underneath the Lantern." CrossCur (5:2) 85, p. 13-19.
   "Weeds." SouthernPR (26, i.e. 25:2) Fall 85, p. 35.
3219. MEISTER, Peter
   "Our houses, our hills." Amelia (2:2) O 85, p. 54.
3220. MELANÇON, Charlotte
   "1981." Os (20) 85, p. 10.
   "La Fin des Lilas." Os (20) 85, p. 10.
   "Promenade Merveilleuse." Os (20) 85, p. 11.
3221. MELARTIN, Riikka
   "Everything Possible." SouthernPR (26, i.e. 25:2) Fall
      85, p. 27.
3222. MELEC ALVARADO, Abbey
   "Darling" (tr. by Kent Johnson). MinnR (N.S. 25) Fall 85,
      p. 47.
3223. MELENDEZ de ESPINOZA, Juana
   "You" (tr. by Bettina Escudero). NewL (51:4) Sum 85, p.
      114.
3224. MELFI, Mary
   "Canada Vs. Italy." CanLit (106) Fall 85, p. 56.
   "The Fashion Designer." PoetryCR (6:3) Spr 85, p. 15.
   "Free Lessons." PoetryCR (6:3) Spr 85, p. 15.
   "The Janitor." PoetryCR (6:3) Spr 85, p. 15.
   "School for the Dead." CanLit (106) Fall 85, p. 53.
3225. MELHEM, D. H.
   "Hudson Continuum." Confr (30/31) N 85, p. 286.
   "Visit." Confr (30/31) N 85, p. 262.
3226. MELNYCZUK, Askold
   "Chorale: In April." Poetry (146:1) Ap 85, p. 29-30.
3227. MELTON, Bill
   "2 Hours -- The Movie." JamesWR (2:2) Wint 85, p. 14.
   "So It Goes." JamesWR (2:1) Fall 84, p. 11.
3228. MENASHE, Samuel
   "In Focus." Confr (30/31) N 85, p. 141.
   "Spur of the Moment" (for John Thornton). Confr (30/31) N
      85, p. 141.
3229. MENDEZ SANTIAGO, Sabino
   "Hijo del Silencio." Mairena (7:19) 85, p. 101.
3230. MENDOZA, Nick
   "-Cide/(Side)." NoDaQ (53:2) Spr 85, p. 215.
3231. MENEBROKER, Ann
   "The Blue Fish." Bogg (54) 85, p. 55.
   "Love." Bogg (54) 85, p. 55.

"Quietly." <u>Bogg</u> (53) 85, p. 44.
"Torch Song." <u>Bogg</u> (54) 85, p. 55.
"White Elephants." <u>Open24</u> (4) 85, p. 12.
3232. MENESES, Vidaluz
"A Mis Hijos, Carlos y Karla, en Su Autoexilio." <u>Imagine</u>
     (2:1) Sum 85, p. 40.
"A Vidaluz, Ximena y Dorel Que Unidas a Muchos Hermanos
     Hacen Posible el Futuro." <u>Imagine</u> (2:1) Sum 85, p. 41.
"Ciclo Fatal." <u>Imagine</u> (2:1) Sum 85, p. 42.
"Postal para Alba Azucena." <u>Imagine</u> (2:1) Sum 85, p. 42.
3233. MENFI, John
"Green Apples." <u>NoDaQ</u> (53:4) Fall 85, p. 209-210.
"Mountain Fear." <u>NoDaQ</u> (53:4) Fall 85, p. 210-211.
"New Vineyard Graveyard, Maine." <u>NoDaQ</u> (53:4) Fall 85, p.
     211.
"Norton Hill, Strong, Maine." <u>NoDaQ</u> (53:4) Fall 85, p.
     212-213.
MENOZZI, Wallis Wilde
     <u>See</u> WILDE-MENOZZI, Wallis
3234. MERASTY, Billy
"Decisions." <u>PraF</u> (6:4) Aut-Wint 85, p. 99.
"Mother of Metis." <u>PraF</u> (6:4) Aut-Wint 85, p. 98.
"Pelagie & Joe Highway." <u>PraF</u> (6:4) Aut-Wint 85, p. 99.
"Subtle Pleading of Bird." <u>PraF</u> (6:4) Aut-Wint 85, p. 98.
3235. MERCHANT, Keith
"In Mr. Eliot's Library." <u>AntigR</u> (61) Spr 85, p. 96.
3236. MEREDITH, Joseph
"How It's Done." <u>PaintedB</u> (25) Spr 85, p. 18.
"The Old Man in the Garden." <u>SouthwR</u> (70:2) Spr 85, p.
     244.
3237. MERKIN, Daphne
"A Grandfather, Late Afternoon." <u>PartR</u> (52:4) 85, p. 429-
     430.
MERLO, Antonio Santiago
     <u>See</u> SANTIAGO MERLO, Antonio
3238. MERRIAM, Eve
"Cupid and Psyche." <u>OP</u> (38/39) Spr 85, p. 108.
3239. MERRICLE, William
"Chemistry Set." <u>Open24</u> (4) 85, p. 26.
"Crumbs." <u>Wind</u> (15:55) 85, p. 37.
"I Did It My Way." <u>Open24</u> (4) 85, p. 26.
3240. MERRILL, James
"The Fifteenth Summer." <u>SouthwR</u> (70:1) Wint 85, p. 68.
"Icecap." <u>NewYorker</u> (61:43) 16 D 85, p. 40.
"Midsummer Evening on the Prinsengracht" (for Hans).
     <u>Verse</u> (2) 85, p. 4.
"Nike" (Erratum: last 13 lines omitted from v. 35, no. 2-3,
     p. 214). <u>Shen</u> (36:1) 85-86, p. 100.
"Six Bits." <u>Ploughs</u> (11:4) 85, p. 131-132.
3241. MERRIN, Jeredith
"Lunar Eclipse" (July 5, 1982). <u>Thrpny</u> (6:2, issue 22)
     Sum 85, p. 16.
3242. MERWIN, W. S.
"After School." <u>NewYorker</u> (61:41) 2 D 85, p. 48.
"Anniversary on the Island." <u>MemphisSR</u> (5:2) Spr 85, p. 4.
"Before Us." <u>GrandS</u> (4:3) Spr 85, p. 83-84.
"Footprints on the Glacier." <u>TriQ</u> (63) Spr-Sum 85, p. 138.
"Glasses." <u>NewYorker</u> (61:13) 20 My 85, p. 40.
"Koa." <u>Antaeus</u> (55) Aut 85, p. 131-134.
"Life" (tr. of Jean Follain). <u>TriQ</u> (63) Spr-Sum 85, p.
     137.
"Now Renting." <u>NewYorker</u> (60:50) 28 Ja 85, p. 26.
"The Salt Pond." <u>NewYorker</u> (61:31) 23 S 85, p. 34.
"Shadow Passing." <u>GrandS</u> (5:1) Aut 85, p. 40.
"Touching the Tree." <u>GrandS</u> (4:4) Sum 85, p. 82.

3243. MESA, Lauren
"All the Embraces." <u>Amelia</u> (2:1) Ap 85, p. 39.
"Remo." <u>Amelia</u> (2:1) Ap 85, p. 38.
3244. MESLER, Corey
"Jane." <u>Wind</u> (15:55) 85, p. 52.
3245. MESSERLI, Douglas
"Maxims from My Mother's Milk" (5 Selections: "Pandora's
Box," "From Here to Air," "On the Line," "Ear Endow,"
"Aller et Retour"). <u>Conjunc</u> (7) 85, p. 107-109.
3246. METCALF, Paul
"Firebird" (Excerpts). <u>Conjunc</u> (8) 85, p. 81-91.
3247. METCALFE, Robin
"Dream Poem: Gertrude Stein Gives an Interview to a Woman
from the BBC." <u>JamesWR</u> (2:2) Wint 85, p. 1.
3248. METRAS, Gary
"Destiny's Calendar." <u>Sam</u> (42:1, 165th release) 85, 66 p.
"The Ruins of Dreams" (Selection: 2). <u>GreenfR</u> (13:1/2)
Fall-Wint 85, p. 72.
3249. METZ, Jarred
"The Four Tongues of Castor Bernard." <u>PoetL</u> (80:2) Sum
85, p. 106-109.
3250. MEYER, Bruce
"Monet's Rouen Cathedral." <u>Quarry</u> (34:3) Sum 85, p. 76.
3251. MEYER, Thomas
"Ode." <u>Conjunc</u> (8) 85, p. 180.
3252. MEYER, William
"Cold Morning Run." <u>WindO</u> (46) Fall 85, p. 39.
"Exercizing My Sissical Muscles." <u>WindO</u> (46) Fall 85, p.
39.
"Pineapple Clear Evening." <u>WindO</u> (45) Spr 85, p. 30.
"The Power of Blackness." <u>WindO</u> (46) Fall 85, p. 40.
"Train Wreck at Nome, Texas." <u>BallSUF</u> (26:2) Spr 85, p.
33.
"Turquoise Shrouds Are Floating in the Hay Fresco Oles."
<u>Gargoyle</u> (27) 85, p. 33.
3253. MEZEY, Robert
"Charge on Transience" (tr. of Hamdija Demirovič, w. the
author). <u>AmerPoR</u> (14:2) Mr-Ap 85, p. 21.
"From the water, life" (tr. of Hamdija Demirovič, w. the
author). <u>AmerPoR</u> (14:2) Mr-Ap 85, p. 21.
"Shit Creek Days." <u>OP</u> (38/39) Spr 85, p. 90-92.
"Your nights are all too clear" (tr. of Hamdija
Demirovič, w. the author). <u>AmerPoR</u> (14:2) Mr-Ap 85,
p. 21.
3254. MICHAEL KARL (RITCHIE)
"When Dawn Has Put Her White Cloak On" (7 poems, tr. of Ai
Qing, w. Li Jia Hu and Ken Letko). <u>MidAR</u> (5:2) 85, p.
47-63.
3255. MICHAELS, Anne
"Lake of Two Rivers" (from <u>The Weight of Oranges</u>).
<u>PoetryCR</u> (7:2) Wint 85-86, p. 5.
"Words for the Body." <u>Waves</u> (13:2/3) Wint 85, p. 58-61.
3256. MICHAELS, Larry R.
"At the Window." <u>Wind</u> (15:54) 85, p. 10.
MICHELE, Mary di
<u>See</u> Di MICHELE, Mary
3257. MICHELSON, Richard
"Interrogation." <u>Nimrod</u> (29:1) Fall-Wint 85, p. 49.
"The March of the Orphans" (August 5, 1942). <u>Nimrod</u>
(29:1) Fall-Wint 85, p. 46-47.
"Young Men Painting, Warsaw Ghetto - 1943." <u>Nimrod</u> (29:1)
Fall-Wint 85, p. 48.
3258. MICHELUTTI, Dorina
"New Year's Resolution -- 85." <u>CanLit</u> (106) Fall 85, p.
75.

3259. MIDDLETON, Christopher
"Another Village." <u>Verse</u> (4) 85, p. 6.
"Coral Snake." <u>Verse</u> (4) 85, p. 6-7.
"Minim." <u>Verse</u> (2) 85, p. 9.
"The Mol." <u>Verse</u> (2) 85, p. 8.
3260. MIDDLETON, David
"Shrewsbury Abbey." <u>Poem</u> (54) N 85, p. 12-13.
"To the Demiurge." <u>Poem</u> (54) N 85, p. 11.
3261. MIERAU, Maurice
"The Martyrdom Method" (Selections: 2 poems -- "Leonhard
    Keyser, Who Would Not Burn," "When the Russians Came
    into the Village"). <u>PraF</u> (6:1) Wint 85, p. 75-76.
3262. MIFFLIN, Margot
"The Dolphin Race." <u>YellowS</u> (15) Sum 85, p. 43.
"My Feet Have All Gone for a Walk in the Light." <u>Cond</u>
    (11/12) 85, p. 150-151.
"September 12." <u>YellowS</u> (16) Aut 85, p. 16.
"The Sun Humping the Moon." <u>YellowS</u> (15) Sum 85, p. 42.
3263. MIGONE, Christof
"Reward famous dead police . . ." (Image/Text). <u>Rampike</u>
    (4:2/3) 85-86, p. 106.
3264. MILBERG, Jeannie
"For an Abused Child." <u>Wind</u> (15:53) 85, p. 28.
3265. MILBURN, Michael
"Acts of Love." <u>Crazy</u> (26) Spr 84, p. 47.
"All Autumn." <u>Crazy</u> (27) Fall 84, p. 44-45.
"Depot." <u>Agni</u> (22) 85, p. 32.
"Details (Wanting a Child)." <u>Ploughs</u> (11:1) 85, p. 153-
    154.
"The Electric Fly-Trap." <u>SenR</u> (15:2) 85, p. 54.
"False Night." <u>PraS</u> (59:3) Fall 85, p. 63.
"First Steps." <u>Crazy</u> (27) Fall 84, p. 43.
"In Weather." <u>Ploughs</u> (11:1) 85, p. 155.
"Milton and Paradise Lost." <u>SenR</u> (15:2) 85, p. 55-56.
"A Photograph of Yeats's Lapis Lazuli." <u>Agni</u> (22) 85, p.
    33.
"Rachmaninoff Plays Chopin." <u>Agni</u> (22) 85, p. 34.
"Reunion." <u>PraS</u> (59:3) Fall 85, p. 64.
"Separation." <u>SenR</u> (15:2) 85, p. 57-58.
3266. MILICI, Jim
"Explosion in the Corporate Research Facility, June, 1981."
    <u>JlNJPo</u> (8:1) 85, p. 20-21.
3267. MILJKOVIC, Branko
"Beda Poezije." <u>Mund</u> (16:1/2) 85, p. 50.
"A Critique of Metaphores" (tr. by Anita Lekic-Trbojeciv).
    <u>Mund</u> (16:1/2) 85, p. 47.
"Drop of Ink" (tr. by Anita Lekic-Trbojeciv). <u>Mund</u>
    (16:1/2) 85, p. 49.
"Kap Mastila." <u>Mund</u> (16:1/2) 85, p. 48.
"Kritika Metafore." <u>Mund</u> (16:1/2) 85, p. 46.
"Prijatelju Pesniku" (Tanasiju Mladenovicu). <u>Mund</u>
    (16:1/2) 85, p. 52.
"To a Friend and Poet" (Tanasiju Mladenovicu, tr. by Anita
    Lekic-Trbojeciv). <u>Mund</u> (16:1/2) 85, p. 53.
"The Wretchedness of Poetry" (tr. by Anita Lekic-
    Trbojeciv). <u>Mund</u> (16:1/2) 85, p. 51.
3268. MILLER, Carolyn Reynolds
"At Night, Spirits Come Out of the Trees." <u>PoetryNW</u>
    (26:1) Spr 85, p. 7-8.
"Could the Wolf Be Presented As a Sympathic Character?"
    <u>PoetryNW</u> (26:1) Spr 85, p. 8-9.
"A Turn to the Right, a Little White Light." <u>PoetryNW</u>
    (26:1) Spr 85, p. 10-11.
3269. MILLER, Ceci
"First One Thing and Then Another." <u>Telescope</u> (4:1) Wint
    85, p. 5-6.

"The Moths." <u>CarolQ</u> (38:1) Fall 85, p. 23-24.
3270. MILLER, E. Ethelbert
    "Juanita." <u>Vis</u> (17) 85, p. 40.
3271. MILLER, E. S.
    "Age." <u>OP</u> (38/39) Spr 85, p. 104.
    "Bore." <u>OP</u> (38/39) Spr 85, p. 175.
    "The Periad" (Editor's Note). <u>OP</u> (38/39) Spr 85, p. 154.
3272. MILLER, Edmund
    "The High Tide of the East." <u>Confr</u> (30/31) N 85, p. 161.
3273. MILLER, Elizabeth Gamble
    "Nocturnes of Trafalgar Place" (Selections: III, V, tr. of
        David Escobar Galindo). <u>Mund</u> (16:1/2) 85, p. 11, 13.
    "Picture Postcard" (tr. of David Escobar Galindo). <u>Mund</u>
        (16:1/2) 85, p. 13.
3274. MILLER, Gary
    "Jean-Louis." <u>MoodySI</u> (15) Spr 85, p. 15.
3275. MILLER, Hugh
    "Aubade for Nadine." <u>AntigR</u> (60) Wint 85, p. 45.
    "Mowing Nellie's Lawn." <u>AntigR</u> (60) Wint 85, p. 46.
    "Rag-Tag in Cazadero: Sue's New/Old House/Summer Cabin"
        (for Sue). <u>AntigR</u> (61) Spr 85, p. 42.
3276. MILLER, James A.
    "Downriver." <u>NoDaQ</u> (53:4) Fall 85, p. 216.
    "Easter, D.C." <u>LaurelR</u> (19:1) Wint 85, p. 37.
    "Epistolary Epistemology." <u>NoDaQ</u> (53:4) Fall 85, p. 216.
    "Odyssey" (for Lynne). <u>NoDaQ</u> (53:4) Fall 85, p. 214-216.
    "On Honored Streets." <u>BlackALF</u> (19:3) Fall 85, p. 112.
3277. MILLER, Jane
    "Are You Home?" <u>AmerPoR</u> (14:3) My-Je 85, p. 6.
    "The Cover of Mars." <u>Iowa</u> (15:3) Fall 85, p. 72-73.
    "High Holy Days." <u>AmerPoR</u> (14:3) My-Je 85, p. 6.
    "Imitation at Twilight." <u>MissouriR</u> (8:2) 85, p. 32-33.
    "Lunar Flock." <u>AmerPoR</u> (14:3) My-Je 85, p. 5.
    "Meadow with Standing Crows." <u>MissouriR</u> (8:2) 85, p. 31.
    "Memory at These Speeds." <u>AmerPoR</u> (14:3) My-Je 85, p. 3.
    "Near You Are Heavenly Bodies." <u>AmerPoR</u> (14:3) My-Je 85,
        p. 3.
    "O'Keeffian." <u>AmerPoR</u> (14:3) My-Je 85, p. 7.
    "Ozone Avenue." <u>Tendril</u> (19/20) 85, p. 280-281.
    "Race Point Polaroids." <u>Iowa</u> (15:3) Fall 85, p. 73-77.
    "Romeo Void." <u>AmerPoR</u> (14:3) My-Je 85, p. 8.
    "Sunset over Hand-Made Church." <u>Iowa</u> (15:1) Wint 85, p.
        26-27.
    "Sycamore Mall." <u>AmerPoR</u> (14:3) My-Je 85, p. 4.
    "Sympathètique." <u>AmerPoR</u> (14:3) My-Je 85, p. 7.
    "Tilt." <u>AmerPoR</u> (14:3) My-Je 85, p. 5.
    "Timing for What." <u>AmerPoR</u> (14:3) My-Je 85, p. 4.
    "Whitecaps, Black Beach." <u>AmerPoR</u> (14:3) My-Je 85, p. 5.
3278. MILLER, Jauren
    "Wind Run." <u>Wind</u> (15:53) 85, p. 29.
3279. MILLER, John N.
    "Drought." <u>NoDaQ</u> (53:4) Fall 85, p. 217.
    "Poland." <u>CharR</u> (11:1) Spr 85, p. 92-93.
    "Sentences." <u>CharR</u> (11:1) Spr 85, p. 91-92.
3280. MILLER, Leslie F.
    "Friedhof Verkehr" (cemetery traffic). <u>Open24</u> (4) 85, p.
        22.
3281. MILLER, Michael
    "Leafing Out." <u>CrossCur</u> (4:4/5:1) 85, p. 161.
    "The Maker" (James Wright, 1927-1980). <u>Confr</u> (30/31) N
        85, p. 264.
3282. MILLER, Philip
    "Dusting." <u>CapeR</u> (20:1) Spr 85, p. 2.
    "The Follies." <u>CapeR</u> (20:1) Spr 85, p. 3.
    "Mornings." <u>CapeR</u> (20:1) Spr 85, p. 1.

3283. MILLER, Stephen M.
        "July Is Green and Thick with Lust." <u>Abraxas</u> (33) 85, p.
            42.
        "Mallards Departing from the Great Splash." <u>Abraxas</u> (33)
            85, p. 42.
        "Stopover." <u>Abraxas</u> (33) 85, p. 43.
3284. MILLER, Stuart
        "Full Circle" (tr. by Stuart Miller). <u>NewL</u> (51:4) Sum 85,
            p. 68.
        "Pet Peeves" (tr. by Stuart Miller). <u>NewL</u> (51:4) Sum 85,
            p. 69.
3285. MILLER, Vassar
        "Every Night." <u>SewanR</u> (93:1) Wint 85, p. 63.
        "No Hiding Place." <u>SewanR</u> (93:1) Wint 85, p. 63.
3286. MILLER, Warren C.
        "Billy." <u>Amelia</u> (2:1) Ap 85, p. 85.
        "Mother." <u>Amelia</u> (2:2) O 85, p. 61.
        "Protestant Ethic 82." <u>Wind</u> (15:55) 85, p. 38-39.
        "Sunday Afternoon under the Oaks." <u>Wind</u> (15:55) 85, p. 38.
        "Thankless Job." <u>Bogg</u> (53) 85, p. 9.
        "Ultimately." <u>Open24</u> (4) 85, p. 54.
3287. MILLER, William
        "Sex Education." <u>NegC</u> (5:4) Fall 85, p. 121.
3288. MILLIS, Christopher
        "Cassandra at the Car Lot." <u>GreenfR</u> (13:1/2) Fall-Wint
            85, p. 180.
        "Driving at Midnight." <u>HangL</u> (47) Spr 85, p. 38.
        "The Fisherman and the Genie." <u>PoetL</u> (80:2) Sum 85, p.
            112.
        "The House of My Babysitter" (tr. of Umberta Saba). <u>NewL</u>
            (51:4) Sum 85, p. 170.
        "Ulysses." <u>GreenfR</u> (13:1/2) Fall-Wint 85, p. 181.
        "Warning" (tr. of Umberta Saba). <u>NewL</u> (51:4) Sum 85, p.
            170-171.
3289. MILLMAN, Lawrence
        "Hoy Windsong" (For George Mackay Brown). <u>NowestR</u> (23:1)
            85, p. 9.
        "Parliament of Ravens." <u>CutB</u> (23) Fall-Wint 85, p. 43.
        "St. Kilda: Leavetaking." <u>NowestR</u> (23:1) 85, p. 10.
3290. MILLS, Paul
        "Children of Auschwitz and Elsewhere" (tr. of André
            Verdet). <u>Stand</u> (26:2) Spr 85, p. 50.
3291. MILLS, Ralph J., Jr.
        "9/81." <u>SpoonRQ</u> (10:2) Spr 85, p. 38.
        "Early Sun's." <u>Northeast</u> (Series 4:2) Fall 85, p. 13.
        "End of December." <u>SpoonRQ</u> (10:2) Spr 85, p. 37.
        "June Rains." <u>SpoonRQ</u> (10:2) Spr 85, p. 40.
        "Sun's Along." <u>Northeast</u> (Series 4:2) Fall 85, p. 14.
        "This Sky's." <u>Northeast</u> (Series 4:2) Fall 85, p. 12.
        "Yard Song." <u>SpoonRQ</u> (10:2) Spr 85, p. 39.
3292. MILLS, Robert
        "Ball Game." <u>SpoonRQ</u> (10:4) Fall 85, p. 38.
        "The Day They Closed Down the Lottery." <u>SpoonRQ</u> (10:4)
            Fall 85, p. 37.
        "Sleep Therapy." <u>SpoonRQ</u> (10:4) Fall 85, p. 39.
        "Spring Song." <u>SpoonRQ</u> (10:2) Spr 85, p. 50.
3293. MILLS, Sparling
        "After George Sand." <u>PoetryCR</u> (6:4) Sum 85, p. 16.
        "Waking with You in My Head." <u>PoetryCR</u> (7:2) Wint 85-86,
            p. 36.
        "Water Music" (remembering George Whalley). <u>Quarry</u> (34:3)
            Sum 85, p. 26.
        "Women in South Africa." <u>Rampike</u> (4:2/3) 85-86, p. 70-71.
3294. MILLS, William
        "Oklahoma, As You Break to Beauty." <u>CimR</u> (71) Ap 85, p. 9-
            10.

"Oklahoma Yoga." <u>CimR</u> (71) Ap 85, p. 21-22.
3295. MILOSZ, Czeslaw
"1913" (tr. by the author and Robert Hass). <u>Thrpny</u> (6:2,
issue 22) Sum 85, p. 13.
"After Paradise" (tr. by the author and Robert Hass).
<u>NewYorker</u> (61:21) 15 Jl 85, p. 25.
"Anka" (tr. by the author and Robert Hass). <u>NewYorker</u>
(61:35) 21 O 85, p. 38.
"At Noon" (tr. by the author and Robert Hass). <u>NewYorker</u>
(61:21) 15 Jl 85, p. 24.25.
"Consciousness" (tr. by the author and Robert Hass).
<u>Antaeus</u> (55) Aut 85, p. 138-140.
"A Damned Man" (tr. of Aleksander Wat). <u>TriQ</u> (63) Spr-Sum
85, p. 97.
"Elegy for Y.Z." (tr. by the author and Robert Hass).
<u>NewYorker</u> (61:21) 15 Jl 85, p. 25.
"Into the Tree" (tr. by the author and Robert Hass).
<u>Antaeus</u> (55) Aut 85, p. 135-136.
"My-ness" (tr. by the author and Robert Hass). <u>NewYorker</u>
(61:45) 30 D 85, p. 24.
"On Prayer" (tr. by the author and Robert Hass). <u>Antaeus</u>
(55) Aut 85, p. 137.
"Poet at Seventy" (tr. by the author). <u>Antaeus</u> (55) Aut
85, p. 141-142.
"Preparation" (tr. by the author and Robert Hass). <u>NewYRB</u>
(32:14) 26 S 85, p. 4.
"Return to Cracow in 1880" (tr. by the author and Robert
Hass). <u>NewYorker</u> (61:21) 15 Jl 85, p. 25.
"Rustling Taffetas" (tr. by the author and Robert Hass).
<u>NewYorker</u> (61:21) 15 Jl 85, p. 24.
"Table I" (tr. by the author and Robert Hass). <u>NewYorker</u>
(61:21) 15 Jl 85, p. 24.
"Table II" (tr. by the author and Robert Hass). <u>NewYorker</u>
(61:21) 15 Jl 85, p. 24.
"Winter" (tr. by the author and Robert Hass). <u>NewYorker</u>
(61:21) 15 Jl 85, p. 24-25.
3296. MINARD, Murielle
"Bedtime Story." <u>Kaleid</u> (10) Spr 85, p. 39.
"The Children." <u>Kaleid</u> (10) Spr 85, p. 38.
"Fairy Tales." <u>Kaleid</u> (10) Spr 85, p. 39.
"Let's Pretend." <u>Kaleid</u> (10) Spr 85, p. 38.
"The Magic Shoes." <u>Kaleid</u> (10) Spr 85, p. 39.
"The Visit." <u>Kaleid</u> (10) Spr 85, p. 38.
3297. MINARELLI, Enzo
"Polypoetry" (tr. by the author). <u>Rampike</u> (4:2/3) 85-86,
p. 112-114.
MING, Chiu Yee
<u>See</u> CHIU, Yee Ming
3298. MINIC, Snezana
"Action" (tr. by Nina Zivancević). <u>AmerPoR</u> (14:3) My-Je
85, p. 29.
"After Coming Home" (tr. by Nina Zivancević). <u>AmerPoR</u>
(14:3) My-Je 85, p. 28.
"Water Flower" (tr. by Nina Zivancević). <u>AmerPoR</u> (14:3)
My-Je 85, p. 28.
3299. MINOR, James
"Light of moon" (haiku). <u>Northeast</u> (Series 4:1) Sum 85,
p. 49.
"Seaside" (haiku). <u>Northeast</u> (Series 4:1) Sum 85, p. 49.
"Sugar maple" (haiku). <u>Northeast</u> (Series 4:1) Sum 85, p.
49.
"Windward" (haiku). <u>Northeast</u> (Series 4:1) Sum 85, p. 49.
3300. MINORE, Renato
"The Franciscan Convent" (Excerpts, tr. by P. F. Paolini).
<u>LitR</u> (29:1) Fall 85, p. 110-111.

MINORU, Yoshioka
    See YOSHIOKA, Minoru
3301. MINTON, Helena
    "The Field by the Tew-Mac Airport." ConnPR (3:1) 84, p.
      37.
3302. MINTY, Judith
    "The Gray Whale." Poetry (146:1) Ap 85, p. 3-5.
    "Meeting My Father at the River." PassN (6:1) Fall-Wint
      85, p. 8.
    "The Mount Pleasant Journal." PassN (6:1) Fall-Wint 85,
      p. 8.
    "Small Deaths." IndR (8:3) Fall 85, p. 92.
3303. MIRAKENTZ, Claire
    "The Mute Who Lives in the Airport." PoeticJ (11) 85, p.
      25.
3304. MIRANDA, Gary
    "This Temporary Appearance" (for Gregory Pikouras).
      CrossCur (4:2) 84, p. 37.
3305. MIRELES, Oscar
    "The Marriage Proposal." RevChic (13:2) Sum 85, p. 44-45.
    "Smells Just Like Yesterday." RevChic (13:2) Sum 85, p.
      46-47.
3306. MIRON, Gaston
    "Embers and Earth" (Selections: 6 Poems, tr. by Marc
      Plourde and D. G. Jones). PoetryCR (6:3) Spr 85, p. 23.
3307. MIRSKIN, Jerry
    "Cold." Paint (11:21/12:24) 84-85, p. 10.
    "My Friends at the Lake" (Gary, Jeff). CimR (71) Ap 85,
      p. 31.
3308. MISHKIN, Julia
    "The Passion of Uncertainty." Crazy (26) Spr 84, p. 54-56.
    "Tabula Rasa." Crazy (26) Spr 84, p. 53.
3309. MITCHAM, Judson
    "Birthday at 35" (for Fred Chappell). NegC (5:1) Wint 85,
      p. 118.
    "Couples in the New Year." SouthernPR (25:1) Spr 85, p.
      53.
    "Home." Tendril (19/20) 85, p. 282.
    "How They Stood." SouthernPR (25:1) Spr 85, p. 52.
    "Notes for a Prayer in June" (for Glenn Hawkins, Jr.).
      Geor (39:2) Sum 85, p. 239-241.
    "The Smell of Rain." Tendril (19/20) 85, p. 283.
    "Surviving in Tolstoy's Dream" (for John Gardner). GeoR
      (39:4) Wint 85, p. 736-737.
3310. MITCHELL, Beverly
    "Hiccups" (tr. of Léon Damas). NewEngR (7:4) Sum 85, p.
      495-497.
3311. MITCHELL, Margaret L.
    "Knowing Your Niggers" (for Louis). BlackALF (19:3) Fall
      85, p. 126.
    "When Midday Is." BlackALF (19:3) Fall 85, p. 126.
3312. MITCHELL, Nora
    "Driving to Florida with a Parrot in the Back." Calyx
      (9:1) Spr-Sum 85, p. 13.
    "The Ghost on Chocorua." Calyx (9:1) Spr-Sum 85, p. 14-15.
    "Ursa Major." Calyx (9:1) Spr-Sum 85, p. 10-12.
3313. MITCHELL, Pat
    "Ash Wednesday" (Hiroshima). SanFPJ (7:3) 84 [i.e. 85],
      p. 66.
    "July 5, 1983." SanFPJ (7:3) 84 [i.e. 85], p. 68.
    "Status Quo." SanFPJ (7:3) 84 [i.e. 85], p. 67.
3314. MITCHELL, Roger
    "Know Ye That We." TriQ (64) Fall 85, p. 168-171.
3315. MITCHELL, Stephen
    "And That Is Your Glory" (Phrase from the liturgy of the
      Days of Awe, tr. of Yehuda Amichai). ParisR (27:98)

Wint 85, p. 20.
"The Bull Returns" (tr. of Yehuda Amichai). <u>ParisR</u>
    (27:98) Wint 85, p. 22.
"Farewell" (tr. of Yehuda Amichai). <u>ParisR</u> (27:98) Wint
    85, p. 19.
"My Mother Told Me Once" (tr. of Yehuda Amichai). <u>MissR</u>
    (40/41) Wint 85, p. 114.
"National Thoughts" (tr. of Yehuda Amichai). <u>ParisR</u>
    (27:98) Wint 85, p. 23.
"Now in the Storm" (tr. of Yehuda Amichai). <u>MissR</u> (40/41)
    Wint 85, p. 115.
"A Pity. We Were Such a Good Invention" (tr. of Yehuda
    Amichai). <u>MissR</u> (40/41) Wint 85, p. 116.
"Poems for a Woman" (tr. of Yehuda Amichai). <u>Zyzzyva</u>
    (1:4) Wint 85, p. 74-77.
"Resurrection" (tr. of Yehuda Amichai). <u>ParisR</u> (27:98)
    Wint 85, p. 21.
"Six Poems for Tamar" (tr. of Yehuda Amichai). <u>ParisR</u>
    (27:98) Wint 85, p. 17-18.
"The U.N. Headquarters in the High Commissioner's House in
    Jerusalem" (tr. of Yehuda Amichai). <u>Thrpny</u> (6:3, issue
    23) Fall 85, p. 8.
3316. MITCHELL, Susan
"A Story." <u>Crazy</u> (26) Spr 84, p. 7-8.
3317. MITCHNER, Gary
"Morgan Becomes a Horse." <u>Shen</u> (36:1) 85-86, p. 33.
"Shakespeare in San Francisco" (a traveling exhibition).
    <u>Shen</u> (36:1) 85-86, p. 32-33.
3318. MLADINIC, Peter
"GI." <u>MSS</u> (4:3) Spr 85, p. 55.
"Music and Silence." <u>MSS</u> (4:3) Spr 85, p. 54.
3319. MOBLEY, Carla
"Sisters." <u>Quarry</u> (34:3) Sum 85, p. 42.
"Summer Visit." <u>AntigR</u> (62/63) Sum-Aut 85, p. 250.
3320. MOFFEIT, Tony
"Billy the Kid." <u>Open24</u> (4) 85, p. 19.
"Billy the Kid." <u>Vis</u> (17) 85, p. 28.
"Coyote Moans and Quarter Moons." <u>PoeticJ</u> (10) 85, p. 29.
"Crazy Horse." <u>PoeticJ</u> (9) 85, p. 18.
"Death Cutting the Air Like Grease." <u>Open24</u> (4) 85, p. 19.
"For the Liquid Dark." <u>Vis</u> (18) 85, p. 22.
"Highway 3." <u>PoeticJ</u> (11) 85, p. 22.
"The Moon a Molten Orange." <u>Amelia</u> (2:2) O 85, p. 80.
"My Breath Is Lightning, My Laughter Is Thunder." <u>PoeticJ</u>
    (11) 85, p. 23.
"On the Edge of Smoke." <u>Amelia</u> (2:2) O 85, p. 80.
"Shooting Chant." <u>PoeticJ</u> (9) 85, p. 19.
"The Spider Who Walked Underground." <u>PoeticJ</u> (10) 85, p.
    28.
"Stalking the Midnight Sun." <u>PoeticJ</u> (10) 85, p. 28.
"To Be Born Again." <u>PoeticJ</u> (12) 85, p. 18.
"We Walked in the Rain of Juarez." <u>Amelia</u> (2:1) Ap 85, p.
    76.
"While the Lightning Beats." <u>Bogg</u> (54) 85, p. 45.
"The Wind My Will, My Will the Wind." <u>PoeticJ</u> (12) 85, p.
    19.
"Yellow Lamps of Questa." <u>CrabCR</u> (2:3) Sum 85, p. 4.
3321. MOFFET, Penelope
"The Body Makes Love Possible" (--Galway Kinnell).
    <u>YellowS</u> (15) Sum 85, p. 41.
3322. MOFFETT, Martha
"Who's Who of American Children." <u>OP</u> (38/39) Spr 85, p.
    12.
3323. MOFFI, Larry
"Naming a Star." <u>PoetL</u> (80:2) Sum 85, p. 113-114.

3324. MOFFIT, John (<u>See also</u> MOFFITT, John)
"In Flower Bed or Sky." <u>CrossCur</u> (4:3) 84, p. 41.
3325. MOFFITT, John (<u>See also</u> MOFFIT, John)
"My Drongo." <u>NegC</u> (5:3) Sum 85, p. 85.
3326. MOHRING, Ron
"Working beside My Father." <u>HangL</u> (48) Fall 85, p. 55-56.
3327. MOIR, James M.
"Getting Out Wood." <u>PraF</u> (6:4) Aut-Wint 85, p. 90.
"Necessity." <u>PraF</u> (6:4) Aut-Wint 85, p. 91.
3328. MOLLOHAN, Terrie
"Vomiting Princes on the Bathroom Floor." <u>Bogg</u> (54) 85,
p. 31.
3329. MOLNAR, Gwen
"The Tale of the Worms." <u>Quarry</u> (34:1) Wint 85, p. 12-13.
3330. MOLNAR, Michael
"Accidia" (tr. of Arkadii Dragomoshchenko, w. Lyn
Hejinian). <u>Sulfur</u> (14) 85, p. 116-122.
"Elegies on the Cardinal Points" (for M. Sh., I. Burikhim,
E. Feoktistov, tr. of Elena Shvarts). <u>Mund</u> (15:1/2)
85, p. 195-198.
"I dread my dreams" (tr. of Arkadii Dragomoshchenko, w. Lyn
Hejinian). <u>Sulfur</u> (14) 85, p. 131.
"Obscure Bases of Narration" (example readings, tr. of
Arkadii Dragomoshchenko, w. Lyn Hejinian). <u>Sulfur</u> (14)
85, p. 123-127.
"A Sentimental Elegy" (a gift for Anna, tr. of Arkadii
Dragomoshchenko, w. Lyn Hejinian). <u>Sulfur</u> (14) 85, p.
128-130.
"Study of Dimension" (tr. of Arkadii Dragomoshchenko, w.
Lyn Hejinian). <u>Sulfur</u> (14) 85, p. 131.
3331. MOLTON, Warren Lane
"Attic Window at Advent." <u>ChrC</u> (102:39) 11 D 85, p. 1140.
3332. MONACO, Cory
"Army Memory." <u>StoneC</u> (13:1/2) Fall-Wint 85-86, p. 68-69.
"Crime Statistic." <u>WormR</u> (25:4, issue 100) 85, p. 129.
"M-79 Rocket." <u>WormR</u> (25:4, issue 100) 85, p. 129.
3333. MONAGHAN, Patricia
"The Fates among Us." <u>PoetL</u> (80:2) Sum 85, p. 76-78.
"The Maps of Magic." <u>NegC</u> (5:2) Spr 85, p. 17.
3334. MONFREDO, Louise
"First Star." <u>CapeR</u> (20:2) Fall 85, p. 7.
3335. MONROE, Kent, Jr.
"Dogwoods and Lilacs." <u>StoneC</u> (12:2/3) Spr-Sum 85, p. 59.
"Easter" (Prison, 1984). <u>VirQ</u> (61:4) Aut 85, p. 632.
"Six Times I Have Circled the Yard." <u>VirQ</u> (61:4) Aut 85,
p. 631-632.
3336. MONTALE, Eugenio
"Boats on the Marne" (tr. by William Arrowsmith). <u>Pequod</u>
(18) 85, p. 131-132.
"Correspondences" (tr. by William Arrowsmith). <u>SenR</u>
(15:1) 85, p. 89.
"Cuttlefish Bones" (tr. by Jonathan Galassi). <u>Ploughs</u>
(11:4) 85, p. 43-47.
"Eastbourne" (tr. by William Arrowsmith). <u>GrandS</u> (4:4)
Sum 85, p. 138-139.
"Gerti's Carnival" (tr. by William Arrowsmith). <u>SenR</u>
(15:1) 85, p. 84-86.
"I recall your smile, and it is a clear pool" (tr. by Gian
S. Lombardo). <u>Germ</u> (9:2) Fall-Wint 85, p. 31.
"In the Rain" (tr. by William Arrowsmith). <u>SenR</u> (15:1)
85, p. 87.
"Motet" (tr. by Michael O'Brien). <u>NewL</u> (51:4) Sum 85, p.
169.
"My life, I do not ask of you fixed features" (tr. by Gian
S. Lombardo). <u>Germ</u> (9:2) Fall-Wint 85, p. 32.
"New Stanzas" (tr. by William Arrowsmith). <u>Pequod</u> (18)

85, p. 135-136.
"News from Amiata" (tr. by William Arrowsmith). PartR
    (52:2) 85, p. 60-62.
"Old Verses" (tr. by William Arrowsmith). SenR (15:1) 85,
    p. 82-83.
"Perhaps one morning walking about in a crisp, glassy air"
    (tr. by Gian S. Lombardo). Germ (9:2) Fall-Wint 85, p.
    30.
"A Poem" (tr. by Jonathan Galassi). NewYRB (32:13) 15 Ag
    85, p. 14.
"Stanzas" (tr. by William Arrowsmith). Pequod (18) 85, p.
    133-134.
"Summer" (tr. by William Arrowsmith). SenR (15:1) 85, p.
    88.
3337. MONTE, Bryan (See also MONTE, Bryan R.)
    "The Crocuses." JamesWR (2:2) Wint 85, p. 5.
3338. MONTE, Bryan R. (See also MONTE, Bryan)
    "In Envy of Naturalism." JamesWR (3:1) Fall 85, p. 4.
    "The Visit." JamesWR (3:1) Fall 85, p. 4.
3339. MONTEJO, Eugenio
    "Acacias." Inti (18/19) Otoño 83-Prim. 84, p. 216.
    "Un Año." Inti (18/19) Otoño 83-Prim. 84, p. 220-221.
    "Cancion." Inti (18/19) Otoño 83-Prim. 84, p. 226-227.
    "Cementerio de Vaugirard" (a Teófilo Tortolero). Inti
        (18/19) Otoño 83-Prim. 84, p. 217-218.
    "Dos Ciudades." Inti (18/19) Otoño 83-Prim. 84, p. 225.
    "Dos Rembrandt." Inti (18/19) Otoño 83-Prim. 84, p. 219.
    "Duracion." Inti (18/19) Otoño 83-Prim. 84, p. 224-225.
    "En el Norte." Inti (18/19) Otoño 83-Prim. 84, p. 220.
    "El Esclavo." Inti (18/19) Otoño 83-Prim. 84, p. 222-223.
    "Hotel Antiguo." Inti (18/19) Otoño 83-Prim. 84, p. 221.
    "Manoa." Inti (18/19) Otoño 83-Prim. 84, p. 227-228.
    "Orfeo." Inti (18/19) Otoño 83-Prim. 84, p. 215-216.
    "Pajaros." Inti (18/19) Otoño 83-Prim. 84, p. 228.
    "Regreso." Inti (18/19) Otoño 83-Prim. 84, p. 216-217.
    "Setiembre" (a Alejandro Oliveros). Inti (18/19) Otoño
        83-Prim. 84, p. 223.
    "Solo la Tierra" (a Reynaldo Pérez-So). Inti (18/19)
        Otoño 83-Prim. 84, p. 226.
    "Soy Esta Vida." Inti (18/19) Otoño 83-Prim. 84, p. 224.
    "La Terredad de un Pajaro." Inti (18/19) Otoño 83-Prim.
        84, p. 222.
    "Uccello, Hoy 6 de Agosto." Inti (18/19) Otoño 83-Prim.
        84, p. 218-219.
3340. MONTERROSO, Augusto
    "The Fox Is Wiser" (tr. by Linda Scheer). Chelsea (44)
        85, p. 52.
    "The Frog Who Wanted to Be an Authentic Frog" (tr. by Linda
        Scheer). Chelsea (44) 85, p. 53.
    "The Mirror Who Couldn't Sleep" (tr. by Linda Scheer).
        Chelsea (44) 85, p. 53.
    "On Attributions" (tr. by Linda Scheer). Chelsea (44) 85,
        p. 51-52.
    "The Thunderbolt Who Struck Twice in the Same Spot" (tr. by
        Linda Scheer). Chelsea (44) 85, p. 53.
3341. MONTEZ, Susan
    "Hardware." LittleM (14:4) 85, p. 15.
3342. MONTGOMERY, Carol
    "Susan." BlueBldgs (9) [85?], p. 53.
3343. MONTGOMERY, George
    "Poe Pats My Soul." Open24 (4) 85, p. 39.
3344. MONTGOMERY, Roy F.
    "Fantasie Impromptu" (Composed on My Son Jim's 23rd
        Birthday). NegC (5:2) Spr 85, p. 168-169.
3345. MONTGOMERY, Shirley
    "Death Leave for a Teacher." EngJ (74:3) Mr 85, p. 93.

3346. MONTOYA, José
    "How Great Was My Valley." <u>Imagine</u> (1:2) Wint 84, p. 92-
    93.
    "The Telling Signs of Downtown." <u>Imagine</u> (1:2) Wint 84,
    p. 89-91.
3347. MOODY, Shirley
    "I Want to Say to You." <u>SouthernPR</u> (26, i.e. 25:2) Fall
    85, p. 44-45.
3348. MOOLTEN, David
    "Visiting Silence." <u>CreamCR</u> (10:1) 85, p. 43.
3349. MOORE, Barbara
    "In Gratitude to Pissaro for His <u>Woman</u> <u>and</u> <u>Child</u> <u>at</u> <u>the</u>
    <u>Well</u>." <u>LitR</u> (28:4) Sum 85, p. 590.
    "These Days." <u>SouthwR</u> (70:3) Sum 85, p. 361.
3350. MOORE, Frank D.
    "Burning the Tobacco Bed." <u>PassN</u> (6:2) Spr-Sum 85, p. 11.
3351. MOORE, George
    "Anarchy." <u>JlNJPo</u> (8:1) 85, p. 39.
    "Late April." <u>LitR</u> (29:1) Fall 85, p. 68.
    "Mexico Firsthand." <u>Tendril</u> (19/20) 85, p. 284-285.
    "Sitting in the Garden Courtyard." <u>JlNJPo</u> (8:1) 85, p. 40-
    41.
3352. MOORE, Janice Townley
    "Under the Earth." <u>SouthernHR</u> (19:2) Spr 85, p. 158.
3353. MOORE, Lenard D.
    "Haiku" (2 selections: "Sleety rain," "All the cherry
    blossoms"). <u>PoetryCR</u> (6:3) Spr 85, p. 33.
    "Haiku" (3 poems). <u>WindO</u> (46) Fall 85, p. 17.
    "Her Breath Smokes." <u>Amelia</u> (2:2) O 85, p. 65.
    "Poem on Viewing a Mountain Stream." <u>KanQ</u> (17:4) Fall 85,
    p. 128.
    "The Way of Feet in the Heat." <u>BlackALF</u> (19:3) Fall 85,
    p. 111.
    "Where the Road Ends." <u>CrossCur</u> (4:4/5:1) 85, p. 131.
3354. MOORE, Opal
    "Landscapes: Shakin'." <u>BlackALF</u> (19:3) Fall 85, p. 113.
3355. MOORE, Richard
    "For Gertrude." <u>Poetry</u> (146:3) Je 85, p. 149.
    "Signals." <u>Poetry</u> (146:3) Je 85, p. 149-150.
3356. MOORE, Roger
    "Columbus Square." <u>Waves</u> (14:1/2) Fall 85, p. 107.
    "Eggs." <u>Waves</u> (14:1/2) Fall 85, p. 106.
    "The Naples Manuscript." <u>PoetryCR</u> (6:3) Spr 85, p. 27.
    "So Impossible." <u>AntigR</u> (62/63) Sum-Aut 85, p. 96.
3357. MOORE, Todd
    "Drinker's Golf." <u>Open24</u> (4) 85, p. 35.
    "I Was sitting." <u>Open24</u> (4) 85, p. 35.
    "She Came." <u>Open24</u> (4) 85, p. 36.
    "She Knew." <u>Bogg</u> (53) 85, p. 18.
    "Watching" (A Wormwood Chapbook). <u>WormR</u> (25:2, issue 98)
    85, p. 41-76.
    "Whenever Jack Edwards." <u>Open24</u> (4) 85, p. 36.
3358. MOORHEAD, Andrea
    "Ionisation." <u>Os</u> (21) 85, p. 16-21.
    "Paris I." <u>Os</u> (20) 85, p. 3-4.
    "Paris II." <u>Os</u> (20) 85, p. 5.
    "Paris III." <u>Os</u> (20) 85, p. 6.
3359. MOOSE, Ruth
    "The Mountain." <u>SouthernPR</u> (25:1) Spr 85, p. 60.
3360. MORA, Pat
    "Mothering Me." <u>BilingR</u> (11:2) My-Ag 84 [c1986], p. 16.
3361. MORAES, Vinicius de
    "Recipe for a Woman" (tr. by Celso de Oliveira). <u>Verse</u>
    (3) 85, p. 50-51.
3362. MORAFF, Barbara
    "Bees. Honey." <u>Sulfur</u> (14) 85, p. 114-115.

"Domestic Culinary Text." <u>GreenfR</u> (13:1/2) Fall-Wint 85,
    p. 25.
"Imagine." <u>Sulfur</u> (14) 85, p. 112-113.
"Island." <u>Sulfur</u> (14) 85, p. 113-114.
"Sukhavati" (for Nancy Harrison, who had Lupus and could
    not go into the sun until she died). <u>Sulfur</u> (14) 85,
    p. 114.
"The World." <u>Sulfur</u> (14) 85, p. 112.
3363. MORALES, Gladys
    "Flowers Wither." <u>Imagine</u> (2:1) Sum 85, p. 73.
3364. MORAN, Ronald
    "An Act of God." <u>Northeast</u> (Series 4:1) Sum 85, p. 7.
    "The Mall Culture." <u>Northeast</u> (Series 4:1) Sum 85, p. 6.
    "The Paperman." <u>Wind</u> (15:54) 85, p. 55.
3365. MORDECAI, Pamela
    "Road to Saratoga" (Excerpt). <u>GreenfR</u> (12:3/4) Wint-Spr
        85, p. 204.
    "Southern Cross" (Selections: I. "Wareika," IV. "Sans
        Souci"). <u>GreenfR</u> (12:3/4) Wint-Spr 85, p. 202-203.
3366. MOREAU, June
    "I opened the door this morning." <u>StoneC</u> (12:2/3) Spr-Sum
        85, p. 65.
3367. MOREJON, Nancy
    "Black Woman" (tr. by Elena B. Odio). <u>NewEngR</u> (7:4) Sum
        85, p. 576-577.
3368. MORGAN, Clifford
    "Outside." <u>AntigR</u> (61) Spr 85, p. 64.
    "Wild Blueberries." <u>AntigR</u> (61) Spr 85, p. 64.
3369. MORGAN, David R.
    "Lonely As a Warewolf." <u>Bogg</u> (54) 85, p. 16.
    "Road Works." <u>Bogg</u> (54) 85, p. 20.
3370. MORGAN, Edwin
    "Nineteen Kinds of Barley." <u>Verse</u> (1) 84, p. 4-5.
    "Sonnets from Scotland" (Selections: "The Mirror," "Matthew
        Paris"). <u>Verse</u> (1) 84, p. 6.
    "A Trace of Wings." <u>Conjunc</u> (8) 85, p. 152.
3371. MORGAN, Frederick
    "Greenwich 1930s." <u>Nat</u> (240:4) 2 F 85, p. 123.
    "Meditations for Autumn." <u>PoetryR</u> (5) S 85, p. 12-13.
3372. MORGAN, Jean
    "Floodsong." <u>SouthernPR</u> (26, i.e. 25:2) Fall 85, p. 41-42.
3373. MORGAN, John (<u>See also</u> MORGAN, John H.)
    "Ambush." <u>TriQ</u> (63) Spr-Sum 85, p. 543-544.
    "Letter from the Camp: the Pearl Fishers." <u>Antaeus</u> (55)
        Aut 85, p. 143.
3374. MORGAN, John H. (<u>See also</u> MORGAN, John)
    "Abandoned Mine." <u>SanFPJ</u> (7:3) 84 [i.e. 85], p. 75.
    "Emigre Succeeder." <u>SanFPJ</u> (7:3) 84 [i.e. 85], p. 48.
    "Imperial Smiler." <u>SanFPJ</u> (7:3) 84 [i.e. 85], p. 75.
    "Junta Drama." <u>SanFPJ</u> (7:3) 84 [i.e. 85], p. 74.
3375. MORGAN, Robert
    "Books in the Attic." <u>OntR</u> (22) Spr-Sum 85, p. 28-29.
    "Chicken Scratches." <u>CarolQ</u> (37:3) Spr 85, p. 9.
    "Floating Water." <u>CarolQ</u> (37:3) Spr 85, p. 12.
    "The Gift of Tongues." <u>Verse</u> (3) 85, p. 13.
    "Indigo Culture." <u>CarolQ</u> (37:3) Spr 85, p. 7.
    "Jet Trails." <u>CarolQ</u> (37:3) Spr 85, p. 11.
    "Nail Bag." <u>Poetry</u> (146:5) Ag 85, p. 290-291.
    "The Road Up Pinnacle." <u>CarolQ</u> (37:3) Spr 85, p. 8.
    "Rockpile." <u>Poetry</u> (146:5) Ag 85, p. 290.
    "School Ground." <u>Poetry</u> (146:5) Ag 85, p. 289.
    "Standing Chimneys." <u>CarolQ</u> (37:3) Spr 85, p. 10.
    "The Swing." <u>OntR</u> (22) Spr-Sum 85, p. 30.
    "Vietnam War Memorial." <u>Poetry</u> (146:5) Ag 85, p. 291-292.
3376. MORGAN, S. K.
    "Annie Hasn't Called Recently." <u>Bogg</u> (53) 85, p. 38.

"Drizzle." <u>Pig</u> (13) 85, p. 11.
"The Druid Wind." <u>PoeticJ</u> (10) 85, p. 18.
"The Mickey Mouse Club Ramble." <u>Bogg</u> (53) 85, p. 29.
"No Poem." <u>PassN</u> (6:1) Fall-Wint 85, p. 7.
3377. MORGENTHALER, Sharon
"One Man's Smell." <u>Bogg</u> (54) 85, p. 39.
3378. MORI, Kyoko
"The Bee Sting." <u>BelPoJ</u> (36:2) Wint 85-86, p. 16-17.
"The Japanese Earthquake." <u>GrahamHR</u> (9) Fall 85, p. 19-20.
"The Nightgown." <u>GrahamHR</u> (9) Fall 85, p. 21-22.
3379. MORICONI, Alberto M.
"Huddle with a Hyena" (tr. by Giuliano Dego and Margaret
Straus). <u>LitR</u> (29:1) Fall 85, p. 112.
3380. MORIN, Edward
"The Monogram" (Selection: VII, tr. of Odysseus Elytis, w.
Lefteris Pavlides). <u>NewL</u> (51:4) Sum 85, p. 13.
3381. MORISON, Ted
"Jewel." <u>SouthernHR</u> (19:3) Sum 85, p. 220.
"Volunteer." <u>SouthernHR</u> (19:1) Wint 85, p. 63.
3382. MORITZ, A. F.
"The Explorer." <u>WebR</u> (10:1) Spr 85, p. 50.
"The Moth." <u>MalR</u> (71) Je 85, p. 27.
"Snow in May." <u>WebR</u> (10:1) Spr 85, p. 51.
"Tithonus." <u>WebR</u> (10:1) Spr 85, p. 49.
"The Tradition" (Selections: "Mahler Symphony No. 4 ...,"
"Days along the Banks," "The Secret Maker"). <u>PoetryCR</u>
(7:1) Aut 85, p. 48.
3383. MORLEY, Hilda
"Egrets, Antigua." <u>Poetry</u> (146:1) Ap 85, p. 2.
"For Cèsar Vallejo" (Zivogosce, Yugoslavia, 1983).
<u>Pequod</u> (19/20/21) 85, p. 224-225.
"The Leaf." <u>Conjunc</u> (8) 85, p. 141-145.
"The Whiteness." <u>Poetry</u> (146:1) Ap 85, p. 1.
3384. MORRILL, Donald
"Betrothal Park: Iowa." <u>CimR</u> (70) Ja 85, p. 54.
"Grief." <u>Ascent</u> (10:3) 85, p. 10-11.
3385. MORRIS, Beth
"Conversations with Prather." <u>JlNJPo</u> (8:1) 85, p. 24-26.
3386. MORRIS, Herbert
"Latin." <u>Poetry</u> (147:3) D 85, p. 135-139.
"The Mystery of Your Appearance in My Life." <u>Crazy</u> (28)
Spr 85, p. 39-49.
3387. MORRIS, John N.
"The Country beyond the Hill." <u>NewYorker</u> (61:28) 2 S 85,
p. 32.
"Hamlet at Sea." <u>GrandS</u> (4:2) Wint 85, p. 118-119.
"His Will." <u>GrandS</u> (4:2) Wint 85, p. 120.
"The Parson's Tale." <u>SewanR</u> (93:4) Fall 85, p. 535.
"The Unburied." <u>SewanR</u> (93:4) Fall 85, p. 536.
3388. MORRIS, Mervyn
"Jamaica." <u>GreenfR</u> (12:3/4) Wint-Spr 85, p. 206.
"Peace-Time." <u>GreenfR</u> (12:3/4) Wint-Spr 85, p. 207.
"Sister." <u>GreenfR</u> (12:3/4) Wint-Spr 85, p. 206.
3389. MORRIS, Tony
"Children of Light." <u>Bogg</u> (54) 85, p. 21.
3390. MORRIS, Yaakov
"The Belfast Boat." <u>Poem</u> (54) N 85, p. 41.
"Dawn and Dusk." <u>Poem</u> (54) N 85, p. 42.
"Metamorphosis." <u>Poem</u> (54) N 85, p. 43.
3391. MORRISON, Lillian
"Mother." <u>PoetryR</u> (2:2) Ap 85, p. 65.
3392. MORSE, Cheryl
"Riding the Creek Road, Heartland." <u>KanQ</u> (17:4) Fall 85,
p. 228.
"Waiting for Annie." <u>KanQ</u> (17:4) Fall 85, p. 227.

3393. MORSE, Ruth
"In the Granary Burying Ground." <u>Shen</u> (36:1) 85-86, p. 26.
3394. MORSTEIN, Petra von
"For C. S. Lewis" (Who imagines hell is like the vast slums
of Oldham, England, I've been told. Tr. by Rosemarie
Waldrop). <u>NewL</u> (51:4) Sum 85, p. 76.
"Justice" (tr. by Rosemarie Waldrop). <u>NewL</u> (51:4) Sum 85,
p. 75.
3395. MORTON, Grace
"What Howard Moss Has Just Mailed You." <u>OP</u> (38/39) Spr
85, p. 100.
3396. MOSBY, Katherine
"Finding My Mother's Copy of Hart Crane." <u>OntR</u> (23) Fall-
Wint 85-86, p. 98.
"The Letter" (for my father). <u>OntR</u> (23) Fall-Wint 85-86,
p. 97-98.
3397. MOSER, Stephanie
"Villanelle." <u>WebR</u> (10:2) Fall 85, p. 76.
3398. MOSES, David
"I Heard a Poet Once Say." <u>PottPort</u> (7) 85-86, p. 41.
"Tug." <u>PottPort</u> (7) 85-86, p. 42.
"Winter Is One Less Assumption." <u>PottPort</u> (7) 85-86, p.
46.
3399. MOSS, Greg
"Logodrama." <u>AmerS</u> (54:1) Wint 84-85, p. 62.
"To a Little Girl Dying of Cancer." <u>NegC</u> (5:4) Fall 85,
p. 75.
3400. MOSS, Howard
"Going Under." <u>NewYorker</u> (60:52) 11 F 85, p. 36.
"It." <u>AntR</u> (43:1) Wint 85, p. 65.
"Two Moons at the Same Beach." <u>Confr</u> (30/31) N 85, p. 76.
3401. MOSS, Stanley
"Homing." <u>Pequod</u> (19/20/21) 85, p. 230.
"Lenin, Gorky and I." <u>Pequod</u> (19/20/21) 85, p. 226-227.
"Travels." <u>Pequod</u> (19/20/21) 85, p. 228-229.
3402. MOSS, Thylias
"Back to the Hyena." <u>IndR</u> (8:2) Spr 85, p. 28-29.
"Doubts during Catastrophe." <u>IndR</u> (8:2) Spr 85, p. 26-27.
"The Dromedary of My Dreams." <u>IndR</u> (8:2) Spr 85, p. 30.
3403. MOTT, Elaine
"The Clothes of Hiroshima." <u>CumbPR</u> (5:1) Fall 85, p. 4.
"Dracula and the Photographer." <u>PoetL</u> (80:3) Fall 85, p.
144.
"The Imagination in Winter." <u>CumbPR</u> (5:1) Fall 85, p. 3.
"Somewhere near the Swamp." <u>CutB</u> (24) Spr-Sum 85, p. 57.
3404. MOTT, Michael
"Mozambique." <u>PartR</u> (52:3) 85, p. 247-248.
3405. MOUL, Keith
"They had agreed that her crime" ("Untitled", from a
Sequence, "The Taking Poems"). <u>CapeR</u> (20:2) Fall 85,
p. 29.
3406. MOULEDOUX-LAJOIE, Rhea
"The Muse." <u>Quarry</u> (34:3) Sum 85, p. 43.
"The Poetic Eye." <u>PoetryCR</u> (7:2) Wint 85-86, p. 25.
"Why Is It Always Winter." <u>CrossC</u> (7:1) 85, p. 13.
3407. MOULES, Sue
"Moving." <u>PoetryCR</u> (7:1) Aut 85, p. 46.
"Roseships." <u>PoetryCR</u> (7:1) Aut 85, p. 46.
3408. MOURE, Erin
"Eleftherias Street." <u>MalR</u> (71) Je 85, p. 22.
"Famous." <u>CapilR</u> (34) 85, p. 44.
"Four Propositions for Climate." <u>CapilR</u> (34) 85, p. 43.
"Goodbye to Beef." <u>CapilR</u> (34) 85, p. 46.
"Paleohora Wind." <u>MalR</u> (71) Je 85, p. 23.
"Remembering Sheep." <u>MalR</u> (71) Je 85, p. 24-25.
"Resilience." <u>Dandel</u> (12:1) 85, p. 12.

"Snow Door." <u>CapilR</u> (34) 85, p. 44-45.
"The Water." <u>Dandel</u> (12:1) 85, p. 13.
3409. MOUSTAKAS, John
       "Dream on Ice." <u>PoeticJ</u> (12) 85, p. 38.
3410. MOUW, Gudrun
       "A Kind of Marriage." <u>KanQ</u> (17:1/2) Wint-Spr 85, p. 253.
3411. MOVIUS, Geoffrey
       "5 x 8 Card." <u>LittleM</u> (14:4) 85, p. 7.
       "Bloodlines." <u>LittleM</u> (14:4) 85, p. 8.
       "He Asks Her Out." <u>LittleM</u> (14:4) 85, p. 9.
       "He Is Part of a Moebius Strip." <u>LittleM</u> (14:4) 85, p. 7.
3412. MOYER, Jennifer
       "When Girls Were Girls" (Excerpts from the booklength
          manuscript). <u>OP</u> (40) Fall-Wint 85, p. 26-32.
3413. MUELLER, Lisel
       "For a Thirteenth Birthday." <u>IndR</u> (8:2) Spr 85, p. 56-58.
       "Fulfilling the Promise." <u>TriQ</u> (63) Spr-Sum 85, p. 652-
          653.
       "Imaginary Still Lives." <u>OP</u> (38/39) Spr 85, p. 97.
3414. MUELLER, Teresa
       "Winter Procession." <u>PassN</u> (6:2) Spr-Sum 85, p. 16.
3415. MULLANY, Stephen W.
       "Fish Hawk." <u>Vis</u> (19) 85, p. 15.
3416. MULLEN, Laura
       "Denial." <u>Ploughs</u> (11:1) 85, p. 157.
       "Letter." <u>Ploughs</u> (11:1) 85, p. 156.
3417. MULLINS, Cecil J.
       "Teacher." <u>CapeR</u> (20:1) Spr 85, p. 4.
3418. MULRANE, Scott H.
       "Rejoining the Pack." <u>StoneC</u> (13:1/2) Fall-Wint 85-86, p.
          58.
3419. MUMFORD, Erika
       "Ashram in Pandukeshwar" (1984 Narrative Poetry Prize).
          <u>PoetL</u> (80:1) Spr 85, p. 5-25.
       "The Embodiment: Six Ghazals." <u>NewL</u> (52:1) Fall 85, p. 86-
          90.
3420. MURA, David
       "The Emergency Room." <u>Crazy</u> (28) Spr 85, p. 7-8.
       "Nantucket Honeymoon." <u>Crazy</u> (28) Spr 85, p. 9.
3421. MURABITO, Stephen
       "Twice the Magic of Grape Juice to Wine." <u>LaurelR</u> (19:2)
          Sum 85, p. 78-79.
3422. MURATORI, Fred
       "The Casket Maker's Proposal." <u>Tendril</u> (19/20) 85, p. 286.
       "The Relatives Will Not Be Stopped." <u>PoetryNW</u> (26:3) Aut
          85, p. 5-7.
3423. MURAWSKI, Elisabeth (<u>See also</u> MURAWSKI, Elizabeth)
       "Amvet." <u>Vis</u> (17) 85, p. 37.
       "Artist at Landmark Mall." <u>MSS</u> (4:3) Spr 85, p. 56.
       "Carousel." <u>Vis</u> (18) 85, p. 7.
       "Cow: With Landscape." <u>CarolQ</u> (37:2) Wint 85, p. 47.
       "The Octogenarians." <u>Comm</u> (112:1) 11 Ja 85, p. 15.
       "Perspective." <u>CarolQ</u> (37:2) Wint 85, p. 48.
3424. MURAWSKI, Elizabeth (<u>See also</u> MURAWSKI, Elisabeth)
       "Depression." <u>HolCrit</u> (22:3) Je 85, p. 19.
3425. MURPHY, Dorothy
       "Let's Hear It for the Poor White Trash!" <u>SanFPJ</u> (7:3) 84
          [i.e. 85], p. 14-15.
       "Things Been Jus' Fine aroun' Here up to Now" (Small Town,
          Texas, 1960). <u>SanFPJ</u> (7:4) 85, p. 34-35.
3426. MURPHY, James
       "Emptying." <u>HiramPoR</u> (38) Spr-Sum 85, p. 27.
       "Reading Dreiser at the Laundromat." <u>HiramPoR</u> (38) Spr-
          Sum 85, p. 28.
3427. MURPHY, Kay
       "The Autopsy" (for Martha. Special issue). <u>SpoonRQ</u> (10:3)

Sun 85, 58 p.

"Friday Nights 1964 / Pat O'Brien 1984." <u>SpoonRQ</u> (10:2)
Spr 85, p. 57.

"Jazz Quartet." <u>SenR</u> (15:1) 85, p. 65.

3428. MURPHY, Miles W.

"Early Start" (tr. of Jia Dao). <u>BelPoJ</u> (36:2) Wint 85-86,
p. 18.

"On the Passion to 'Improve' a Garden Pavilion" (tr. of Jia
Dao). <u>BelPoJ</u> (36:2) Wint 85-86, p. 19.

"Touched by Autumn" (tr. of Jia Dao). <u>BelPoJ</u> (36:2) Wint
85-86, p. 18.

3429. MURPHY, P. D.

"Central America Could Never Be Another Vietnam." <u>SanFPJ</u>
(7:4) 85, p. 68.

"Days and Days." <u>SanFPJ</u> (7:4) 85, p. 63.

"News Item." <u>SanFPJ</u> (7:2) 85, p. 12.

"You Never Say Never." <u>SanFPJ</u> (7:2) 85, p. 72.

3430. MURPHY, Rich

"City Welfare." <u>NewL</u> (51:3) Spr 85, p. 91.

3431. MURPHY, Sheila E.

"Detox." <u>DeKalbLAJ</u> (18:3/4) 85, p. 40.

"I Watch You Get Thin." <u>CentR</u> (29:3) Sum 85, p. 321.

"Indiana." <u>PassN</u> (6:2) Spr-Sum 85, p. 16.

"Instructions for an Etch-a-sketch." <u>CentR</u> (29:3) Sum 85,
p. 321-322.

"Language." <u>Chelsea</u> (44) 85, p. 45.

"Letter to Sleep." <u>Open24</u> (4) 85, p. 7.

"Meeting." <u>LaurelR</u> (19:1) Wint 85, p. 17.

"Raison D'Etre." <u>PoeticJ</u> (10) 85, p. 37.

"Resumé." <u>Chelsea</u> (44) 85, p. 43-44.

"Runner's High." <u>WindO</u> (46) Fall 85, p. 5.

"Saying Goodbye." <u>DeKalbLAJ</u> (18:1/2) 85, p. 79.

"Taking Out the Trash." <u>CrabCR</u> (3:1) Fall-Wint 85, p. 15.

"Unwanted Facial Hair Phantoum." <u>DeKalbLAJ</u> (18:1/2) 85,
p. 80-81.

3432. MURRAY, Gloria G.

"Funeral." <u>Amelia</u> (2:1) Ap 85, p. 80.

3433. MURRAY, Joan

"The Grotte des Enfants" (November 1983). <u>OntR</u> (22) Spr-
Sum 85, p. 47-52.

"Under Everything, Something Else" (Itineraries, Paris
1983). <u>OntR</u> (22) Spr-Sum 85, p. 40-46.

3434. MURRAY, Les (<u>See</u> <u>also</u> MURRAY, Les A.)

"Machine Portraits with Pendant Spaceman" (For Valerie).
<u>PartR</u> (52:3) 85, p. 237-241.

3435. MURRAY, Les A. (<u>See</u> <u>also</u> MURRAY, Les)

"1980 in a Street of Federation Houses." <u>PoetryCR</u> (7:2)
Wint 85-86, p. 49.

"The Butter Factory." <u>PoetryCR</u> (7:2) Wint 85-86, p. 48.

"Louvres." <u>Thrpny</u> (6:3, issue 23) Fall 85, p. 11.

"The Milk Lorry." <u>PoetryCR</u> (7:2) Wint 85-86, p. 48.

"The Vol Sprung from Heraldry." <u>PoetryCR</u> (7:2) Wint 85-
86, p. 49.

3436. MURRAY, Marilyn

"Mourning with the Wallflowers." <u>PoetryE</u> (18) Fall 85, p.
48.

3437. MURRAY, Virginia R.

"Urgent." <u>NegC</u> (5:2) Spr 85, p. 154.

3438. MUSGRAVE, Susan

"Rolling Boil." <u>PoetryCR</u> (6:3) Spr 85, p. 19.

"Three Witches Go for Lunch in Elora." <u>PoetryCR</u> (6:4) Sum
85, p. 22.

3439. MUSICK, Martin

"The Greatest Salesman in the World." <u>PoeticJ</u> (11) 85, p.
40.

"Wave of Words." <u>PoeticJ</u> (11) 85, p. 40.

3440. MUSINSKY, Gerald
        "Sometimes Men." Wind (15:54) 85, p. 36.
3441. MUSKAT, Timothy
        "Encomium for Cows." CutB (24) Spr-Sum 85, p. 63.
3442. MUSKE, Carol
        "A Former Love, a Lover of Form." AmerPoR (14:4) Jl-Ag
        85, p. 10.
3443. MUTIS, Alvaro
        "204." Inti (18/19) Otoño 83-Prim. 84, p. 91-92.
        "Amen." Inti (18/19) Otoño 83-Prim. 84, p. 94.
        "Cada Poema." Inti (18/19) Otoño 83-Prim. 84, p. 96-97.
        "Cinco Imagenes." Inti (18/19) Otoño 83-Prim. 84, p.
        101-102.
        "Cita." Inti (18/19) Otoño 83-Prim. 84, p. 96.
        "Ciudad." Inti (18/19) Otoño 83-Prim. 84, p. 95-96.
        "Estela Para Arthur Rimbaud." Inti (18/19) Otoño 83-
        Prim. 84, p. 104-105.
        "Hija Eres de los Lágidas." Inti (18/19) Otoño 83-
        Prim. 84, p. 103-104.
        "Invocacion." Inti (18/19) Otoño 83-Prim. 84, p. 100-
        101.
        "Letania." Inti (18/19) Otoño 83-Prim. 84, p. 99-100.
        "El Miedo." Inti (18/19) Otoño 83-Prim. 84, p. 92-93.
        "La Muerte de Alexandr Sergueievitch." Inti (18/19)
        Otoño 83-Prim. 84, p. 102-103.
        "La Muerte de Matias Aldecoa." Inti (18/19) Otoño 83-
        Prim. 84, p. 94-95.
        "Las Plagas de Maqroll." Inti (18/19) Otoño 83-Prim.
        84, p. 99.
        "Pregon de los Hospitales." Inti (18/19) Otoño 83-Prim.
        84, p. 97-98.
3444. MYCUE, Edward
        "The Dead Will Sleep." Open24 (4) 85, p. 11.
        "Harvest." Wind (15:53) 85, p. 9.
        "Not This Freight." YellowS (14) Spr 85, p. 35.
3445. MYERS, Douglas
        "Halves of One Abstraction." CutB (23) Fall-Wint 85, p.
        39.
3446. MYERS, Gary
        "For Now and Always" (Dachau, West Germany, 1979).
        NewYorker (61:36) 28 O 85, p. 40.
        "Lily of Intense Dreaming." IndR (8:2) Spr 85, p. 104-105.
3447. MYERS, George, Jr.
        "Ode to Working the Night Shift with a Dead Surrealist."
        PoetC (17:1) Fall 85, p. 6.
        "Odette." PoetC (17:1) Fall 85, p. 7.
        "Tonal Odes." PoetC (17:1) Fall 85, p. 8-9.
3448. MYERS, Jack
        "Hardware." Crazy (29) Fall 85, p. 34-35.
        "Inducement." Crazy (26) Spr 84, p. 20.
        "Poem against Good Health." Crazy (26) Spr 84, p. 19.
        "The Poet as Househusband." Telescope (4:2) Spr 85, p. 48.
        "The Watchdog." CrossCur (5:3) 85, p. 73.
3449. MYERS, Joan Rohr
        "After Honey Bees." Comm (112:6) 22 Mr 85, p. 170.
        "Fertility." Comm (112:13) 12 Jl 85, p. 399.
        "Foggy Morning Run." Comm (112:14) 9 Ag 85, p. 428.
        "Green Apples." Comm (112:13) 12 Jl 85, p. 399.
        "In His Image." ChrC (102:13) 17 Ap 85, p. 375.
        "Sometimes." PoeticJ (11) 85, p. 3.
3450. MYRSIADES, Kostas
        "Opposite the Rock" (tr. of Yannis Ritsos, w. Kimon Friar).
        ArizQ (41:4) Wint 85, p. 318.
3451. MYSZKOWSKI, Marian A.
        "Let's Talk." SanFPJ (7:4) 85, p. 13.
        "Remembrances" (Widows). SanFPJ (7:4) 85, p. 14.

3452. NADELMAN, Cynthia
      "Cold Water and a Boy." <u>ParisR</u> (27:98) Wint 85, p. 86.
3453. NAGAYAMA, Mokuo
      "Lake" (in the Canadian Rockies). <u>Waves</u> (14:1/2) Fall 85,
      p. 17.
3454. NAGEL, Gwen Lindberg
      "The Framer." <u>CentR</u> (29:4) Fall 85, p. 441-442.
      "Vita." <u>CentR</u> (29:4) Fall 85, p. 442-443.
3455. NAHHAT, Edward
      "Heart of the Home." <u>Vis</u> (17) 85, p. 10-12.
3456. NAKELL, Martin
      "How It Will Be for You." <u>Blueline</u> (6:2) Wint-Spr 85, p.
      16.
3457. NAMEROFF, Rochelle
      "Matinee in Winter." <u>MidAR</u> (5:2) 85, p. 82-83.
3458. NAMJOSHI, Suniti
      "I Have the Power?" <u>Descant</u> 48 (16:1) Spr 85, p. 13.
      "Lapis Ludens." <u>Descant</u> 48 (16:1) Spr 85, p. 11.
      "Meru." <u>Descant</u> 48 (16:1) Spr 85, p. 10.
      "Narrative Distance." <u>Descant</u> 48 (16:1) Spr 85, p. 14.
      "Postscript to Meru." <u>Descant</u> 48 (16:1) Spr 85, p. 12.
3459. NANCE, Thomas
      "To My Son." <u>Amelia</u> (2:2) O 85, p. 49.
3460. NANFITO, Bryanne
      "Declaration of War." <u>KanQ</u> (17:4) Fall 85, p. 206-207.
      "Phases of the Moon." <u>GreenfR</u> (13:1/2) Fall-Wint 85, p.
      152-153.
3461. NARANJO, Teresa Mae
      "All Souls' Day." <u>NoDaQ</u> (53:2) Spr 85, p. 216.
      "Duck Down" (Summer Cacique or Chief). <u>NoDaQ</u> (53:2) Spr
      85, p. 217.
3462. NARAYAN, Kunwar
      "Towards Delhi" (tr. by Vishnu Khare). <u>NewL</u> (51:4) Sum
      85, p. 135.
3463. NASH, David
      "Hearth." <u>RiverS</u> (18) 85, p. 44.
3464. NASH, Roger
      "C.N. Tower: Revolving Restaurant." <u>AntigR</u> (60) Wint 85,
      p. 112.
      "Evening on a Half-Mile Lake." <u>MalR</u> (71) Je 85, p. 58-59.
      "The Instinct of Hydrangeas." <u>WestCR</u> (20:2) O 85, p. 40.
      "The Sea Cliff of Summer." <u>WestCR</u> (20:2) O 85, p. 41.
      "Women at Windows." <u>Waves</u> (13:4) Spr 85, p. 84.
      "The World's Last Poem." <u>AntigR</u> (60) Wint 85, p. 111.
3465. NASIO, Brenda
      "At the Corner of Grant and Clay" (following the massacre
      at the golden dragon restaurant). <u>CutB</u> (24) Spr-Sum
      85, p. 34-35.
      "At the Phillips Collection." <u>Amelia</u> (2:1) Ap 85, p. 24.
      "From the Non-Smoking Compartment." <u>Amelia</u> (2:1) Ap 85,
      p. 23.
      "Money Matters." <u>SmPd</u> (22:3) Fall 85, p. 25.
      "The Time I Pointed Out Diane Keaton to My Mother in Soho."
      <u>OP</u> (38/39) Spr 85, p. 30.
      "The Wintering of Summer People." <u>Amelia</u> (2:1) Ap 85, p.
      25.
3466. NASSO, Enzo
      "Bridge" (tr. by P. F. Paolini). <u>LitR</u> (29:1) Fall 85, p.
      115.
      "Fragment" (tr. by P. F. Paolini). <u>LitR</u> (29:1) Fall 85,
      p. 115.
      "Manhattan's Balcony" (to Franco Desideri, tr. by Annalisa
      Saccà). <u>LitR</u> (29:1) Fall 85, p. 113.
      "Nostalgia" (tr. by P. F. Paolini). <u>LitR</u> (29:1) Fall 85,
      p. 114.
      "Perhaps the Whistling of the Trains" (tr. by Annalisa

Saccà). <u>LitR</u> (29:1) Fall 85, p. 114.
3467. NATHAN, Leonard
"Mocking Bird Song." <u>Salm</u> (68/69) Fall-Wint 85-86, p. 7.
"The One." <u>CrossCur</u> (4:2) 84, p. 151.
"Romance." <u>Salm</u> (68/69) Fall-Wint 85-86, p. 6.
3468. NATHAN, Norman
"Enclosed." <u>Poem</u> (54) N 85, p. 3.
"The Enemy at Midnight." <u>Poem</u> (54) N 85, p. 1.
"In the Presence." <u>KanQ</u> (17:1/2) Wint-Spr 85, p. 222.
"Jigsaw." <u>Poem</u> (54) N 85, p. 4.
"Lava Thoughts." <u>KanQ</u> (17:1/2) Wint-Spr 85, p. 222-223.
"Mine and I." <u>Poem</u> (54) N 85, p. 2.
3469. NATIONS, Opal Louis
"Proverbial Tale" (a text composed entirely of proverbs).
<u>OP</u> (38/39) Spr 85, p. 122-123.
3470. NAUGLE, Mike
"Frontiers." <u>StoneC</u> (12:2/3) Spr-Sum 85, p. 57.
"Lovemaking in Early Morning." <u>Vis</u> (18) 85, p. 22.
"To My Son, on Visiting My Campus." <u>Vis</u> (17) 85, p. 39.
3471. NEAL, Larry
"Don't Say Goodbye to the Porkpie Hat" (Mingus, Bird, Prez,
Langston, and them). <u>Callaloo</u> (8:1, issue 23) Wint 85,
p. 243-247.
3472. NEELD, Judith
"1938 -- Washington, DC: Dreams of the Chinese Torture
Party." <u>PoetryR</u> (5) S 85, p. 63-64.
"The Chosen." <u>Outbr</u> (14/15) Fall 84-Spr 85, p. 53.
"Falling into the Dream." <u>CrossCur</u> (4:3) 84, p. 103.
"Hawk." <u>PoetryR</u> (5) S 85, p. 62.
"Her Topography." <u>CrossCur</u> (5:2) 85, p. 143.
"Of Six Young Tomato Plants." <u>CrossCur</u> (4:3) 84, p. 104.
"When They Pull You from My River Caroling." <u>Calyx</u> (9:1)
Spr-Sum 85, p. 42.
3473. NEELON, Ann
"Principia Bubonica." <u>MichQR</u> (24:2) Spr 85, p. 269-270.
"Tree of an Emigre." <u>Pequod</u> (19/20/21) 85, p. 231.
"Whatever Crept Away." <u>MassR</u> (26:2/3) Sum-Aut 85, p. 445.
NEJAT, Murat Nemet
<u>See</u> NEMET-NEJAT, Murat
3474. NELMS, Sheryl L.
"Come On into Apple." <u>LaurelR</u> (19:1) Wint 85, p. 21.
"How About." <u>Confr</u> (29) Wint 85, p. 159.
"One Oklahoma Farmer." <u>Wind</u> (15:55) 85, p. 40.
"Pushed." <u>Wind</u> (15:55) 85, p. 40.
3475. NELSON, Howard
"From an Old Appalachian Song." <u>WestB</u> (16) 85, p. 61.
"An Outpost in the Snow." <u>WestB</u> (16) 85, p. 60-61.
3476. NELSON, John S.
"The Feeder." <u>KanQ</u> (17:4) Fall 85, p. 80.
3477. NELSON, Liza
"Wild Salad." <u>BlackWR</u> (11:2) Spr 85, p. 90.
3478. NELSON, Lonnie
"Farm Woman." <u>SanFPJ</u> (7:4) 85, p. 85-86.
3479. NELSON, Michael
"A Call for Celebration." <u>JamesWR</u> (3:1) Fall 85, p. 3.
"In Unlimited Cadence." <u>JamesWR</u> (3:1) Fall 85, p. 3.
"The Lesson." <u>JamesWR</u> (3:1) Fall 85, p. 3.
"Phantom Reality." <u>JamesWR</u> (3:1) Fall 85, p. 3.
3480. NELSON, Paul
"Rhodos." <u>Poetry</u> (145:6) Mr 85, p. 329-330.
3481. NELSON, Riki Kölbl
"Bodies Laugh." <u>RagMag</u> (4:2) Fall 85, p. 23.
"Silly Song." <u>RagMag</u> (4:2) Fall 85, p. 22.
"Smooth." <u>RagMag</u> (4:2) Fall 85, p. 24-25.
3482. NELSON, Robert E.
"The Making of a Body Flute." <u>CapeR</u> (20:2) Fall 85, p. 39.

3483. NELSON, Shannon
    "Handed Down: The Snowball Bush" (Laura Hall Peters, Port
        Angeles, Washington, 1890's). CrabCR (3:1) Fall-Wint
        85, p. 16.
    "Handed Down: The Teaspoons" (Susanna Slover McFarland,
        Connor Creek, Washington Territory, circa 1878).
        CrabCR (3:1) Fall-Wint 85, p. 16.
    "Late Summer, Fort Worden" (for Penney McNeff). Calyx
        (9:1) Spr-Sum 85, p. 47.
    "Nisqually Journal" (Derived from the journal of Joseph
        Heath, circa 1849). CrabCR (2:3) Sum 85, p. 10.
3484. NELSON, W. Dale
    "Handling the Serpents." Quarry (34:4) Aut 85, p. 56.
    "Rehearsal for a Nativity." SouthernHR (19:1) Wint 85, p.
        42.
    "Reporting about the Volcano." Vis (19) 85, p. 37-38.
3485. NEMEROV, Howard
    "TV." TriQ (63) Spr-Sum 85, p. 80-81.
3486. NEMET-NEJAT, Murat
    "Orthodoxies I" (Excerpts, tr. of Ece Ayhan). Chelsea
        (44) 85, p. 148.
3487. NEPO, Mark
    "Mountain Berries." GreenfR (12:3/4) Wint-Spr 85, p. 47-
        48.
3488. NEREM, Marc
    "Continued Cases." SanFPJ (7:2) 85, p. 84.
    "Telescopy." SanFPJ (7:2) 85, p. 82-83.
    "The Will of the People." SanFPJ (7:2) 85, p. 81.
3489. NERUDA, Pablo
    "House" (adapted from "Casa" by Kevin Orth). PoetryR
        (2:2) Ap 85, p. 68.
    "Letter to Miguel Otero Silva, in Caracas (1948)" (From
        Canto General, Section 12, tr. by Robert Bly). NewL
        (51:4) Sum 85, p. 103-106.
    "La Rosa Separada" (Selecciones: I. "Los Hombres," VIII.
        "La Isla," IX. "Los Hombres," XVI. "Los Hombres," XX.
        "La Isla"). NowestR (23:2) 85, p. 6-14.
    "La Rosa Separada" (Selections: I. "Men," VIII. "The
        Island," IX. "Men," XVI. "Men," XX. "The Island," tr. by
        William O'Daly). NowestR (23:2) 85, p. 7-15.
    "Youth" (adapted from "Juventud" by Kevin Orth). PoetryR
        (2:2) Ap 85, p. 68.
3490. NEUER, Kathleen
    "Winter of the Swimming Pool." BlueBldgs (9) [85?], p. 54.
3491. NEURON, Vesta
    "Candle Heart." PoeticJ (12) 85, p. 23.
    "Chrysalis." PoeticJ (9) 85, p. 2.
    "Colors and Seasons." PoeticJ (12) 85, p. 23.
    "Outlander." PoeticJ (9) 85, p. 23.
    "A Tree, a Stone." PoeticJ (10) 85, p. 23.
3492. NEVILLE, Tam Lin
    "Reading Po-Chui." AmerPoR (14:4) Jl-Ag 85, p. 48.
3493. NEVO, Ruth
    "Travels" (Excerpt, tr. of Yehuda Amichai). Pequod
        (19/20/21) 85, p. 19-24.
3494. NEW, Elisa
    "Cul-de-sac." Raritan (5:2) Fall 85, p. 103-104.
    "Pathetic Fallacy." Raritan (5:2) Fall 85, p. 106.
    "Through the Keyhole" (after Edgar Degas' "The Morning
        Bath"). Raritan (5:2) Fall 85, p. 104-105.
3495. NEWALL, Liz
    "Simile." EngJ (74:1) Ja 85, p. 84.
3496. NEWELL, Mike
    "Children at Recess Are Like Ships in Choppy Seas."
        Sulfur (13) 85, p. 73-74.
    "First Frost." Sulfur (13) 85, p. 72.

"Lawn Lions in Early August." <u>Sulfur</u> (13) 85, p. 73.
"The Quiet Monopoly All Poets Share." <u>Sulfur</u> (13) 85, p. 75.
"The Soil around the Root." <u>Sulfur</u> (13) 85, p. 74-75.
"Twaddle in a Public Shrine." <u>EngJ</u> (74:7) N 85, p. 30.
"Twaddle in a Public Shrine." <u>Sulfur</u> (13) 85, p. 72.
3497. NEWLOVE, John
"Cold Heat." <u>Quarry</u> (34:3) Sum 85, p. 62.
"The Light of History: This Rhetoric against That Jargon." <u>Quarry</u> (34:3) Sum 85, p. 62-63.
"Like Water." <u>Quarry</u> (34:3) Sum 85, p. 63.
"Report on Absence." <u>Quarry</u> (34:3) Sum 85, p. 62.
"Speech about a Blackfoot Woman with Travois" (Photo by R. H. Trueman, ca. 1890). <u>CanLit</u> (104) Spr 85, p. 23.
"Syllables via Sanskrit." <u>CapilR</u> (36) 85, p. 4-8.
3498. NEWMAN, Christopher
"So to Speak" (tr. of Eugene Dubnov). <u>Rampike</u> (4:2/3) 85-86, p. 74.
3499. NEWMAN, P. B.
"Great-Grandfather Gibson: Artist." <u>SouthernPR</u> (25:1) Spr 85, p. 23.
3500. NEWMAN, Wade
"The Summons." <u>NegC</u> (5:1) Wint 85, p. 24.
"A Young Priest Writes to Gerard Manley Hopkins." <u>MidAR</u> (5:2) 85, p. 96.
3501. NIATUM, Duane
"Snowy Owl near Ocean Shores." <u>CharR</u> (11:2) Fall 85, p. 28.
"To the Lark at New Place." <u>NewL</u> (52:1) Fall 85, p. 102.
"Words for Awkward Departures" (for Patricia). <u>CrabCR</u> (2:2) Wint 85, p. 17.
3502. NICCOLAI, Giulia
"The Duchess." <u>LitR</u> (28:2) Wint 85, p. 274.
"E. V. Ballad" (To Emilio Villa). <u>LitR</u> (28:2) Wint 85, p. 273-274.
"S. L. Ballad" (To Steve Lacy). <u>LitR</u> (28:2) Wint 85, p. 275-276.
"Utah." <u>LitR</u> (28:2) Wint 85, p. 274.
3503. NICHOLS, Grace
"Walking with My Brother in Georgetown after Being Away for Nearly Seven Years, August 1984." <u>NewEngR</u> (7:4) Sum 85, p. 615-616.
3504. NICHOLSON, D. H.
"Landgrant Orgy at Illinois." <u>EngJ</u> (74:6) O 85, p. 62.
3505. NICHOLSON, Joseph
"El Salvador Dolly." <u>WestB</u> (17) 85, p. 78.
"The Humming Dead." <u>WestB</u> (17) 85, p. 79.
3506. NICHOLSON, Ruth
"Expedition." <u>PassN</u> (6:2) Spr-Sum 85, p. 14.
3507. NICKERSON, Sheila
"On Trying to Explain Reality, Zoos, and Sadness." <u>CrabCR</u> (3:1) Fall-Wint 85, p. 3.
"Why Poets Need to Eat Meat." <u>CrabCR</u> (2:2) Wint 85, p. 14.
3508. NICOLLS, Alix
"Bone's Edge." <u>NegC</u> (5:1) Wint 85, p. 45.
"The Watcher." <u>NegC</u> (5:4) Fall 85, p. 78.
3509. NIDITCH, B. Z.
"1944, for Czeslaw Milosz." <u>NewL</u> (52:1) Fall 85, p. 19-20.
"Climbing the Mt. of Olives." <u>Os</u> (20) 85, p. 22.
"Communication." <u>AntigR</u> (62/63) Sum-Aut 85, p. 119.
"An Ex Communication." <u>AntigR</u> (62/63) Sum-Aut 85, p. 120.
"Haydn String Quartet." <u>PoeticJ</u> (11) 85, p. 7.
"It's 1984." <u>AntigR</u> (62/63) Sum-Aut 85, p. 120.
"The Last Bergmann." <u>AntigR</u> (61) Spr 85, p. 27.
"Listening to Vivaldi's 'Seasons'." <u>AntigR</u> (61) Spr 85, p. 26.

"Miklos Radnoti" (In Memoriam). AntigR (61) Spr 85, p. 27.
"Open City." Open24 (4) 85, p. 10.
"Prague, 1984." Vis (19) 85, p. 33.
"Return to Dachau." NewL (52:1) Fall 85, p. 19.
"Traverse Laps." WindO (46) Fall 85, p. 37.
"Tribute to McLuhan." AntigR (62/63) Sum-Aut 85, p. 119.
"Visiting a Russian Exile." PoetryR (5) S 85, p. 41.
3510. NIELSEN, Christine
"A Baby Is a Poem." PottPort (7) 85-86, p. 15.
"Homecoming." PottPort (7) 85-86, p. 24.
3511. NIELSEN, Nancy L.
"Neighbors Strangers to One Another." Blueline (6:2) Wint-
Spr 85, p. 32.
3512. NIETO, Benigno
"A Su Imagen y Semejanza." LindLM (4:2) Ap-Je 85, p. 8.
"Al Despertar." LindLM (4:2) Ap-Je 85, p. 8.
"Ella, La Dulzura Misma." LindLM (4:2) Ap-Je 85, p. 8.
"Manos de Curandera." LindLM (4:2) Ap-Je 85, p. 9.
"La Protesta de Quevedo." LindLM (4:2) Ap-Je 85, p. 8.
"Retrato de Miranda en la Carraca" (Oleo de A. Michelena,
1863-1898). LindLM (4:2) Ap-Je 85, p. 8.
"Retrato de una Desconocida." LindLM (4:2) Ap-Je 85, p. 9.
"El Viento." LindLM (4:2) Ap-Je 85, p. 8.
NIETO, Catherine Rodriguez
See RODRIGUEZ-NIETO, Catherine
NIETZCHE, Vicente Rodriguez
See RODRIGUEZ NIETZCHE, Vicente
3513. NIGHTINGALE, Barbara
"Insomnia." CrossCur (4:1) 84, p. 36-37.
3514. NIJMEIJER, Peter
"Two Thirds Air" (tr. of Eddy van Vliet). Vis (19) 85, p.
17.
3515. NIMNICHT, Nona
"Anna Alone." CalQ (26) Sum 85, p. 50.
"Hysteropotmoi." CalQ (26) Sum 85, p. 49.
3516. NIMS, John Frederick
"Few Things to Say." TriQ (63) Spr-Sum 85, p. 101.
"Gravity." SewanR (93:3) Sum 85, p. 408-409.
"Keeping Change." Geor (39:2) Sum 85, p. 394-396.
"Optimist." OP (38/39) Spr 85, p. 185.
"Spacial Metrics." OP (38/39) Spr 85, p. 185.
NIORD, Chard de
See DeNIORD, Chard
3517. NISETICH, Frank J.
"In the Mausoleum" (for my Grandmother). KanQ (17:1/2)
Wint-Spr 85, p. 81.
"January." PartR (52:3) 85, p. 249-250.
"New Haven Cemetery." KanQ (17:1/2) Wint-Spr 85, p. 80.
"The Recidivist." PartR (52:2) 85, p. 63-68.
"Recognition." NegC (5:1) Wint 85, p. 25.
3518. NISHNIANIDZE, Shota
"A Beautiful Death" (tr. of Jansug Tcharkviani, w. Manly
Johnson). Nimrod (28:2) Spr-Sum 85, p. 161.
"Betania" (tr. of Jansug Tcharkviani, w. Manly Johnson).
Nimrod (28:2) Spr-Sum 85, p. 159.
"The Canary" (tr. of Jansug Tcharkviani, w. Manly Johnson).
Nimrod (28:2) Spr-Sum 85, p. 158.
"The Dog" (tr. by the author and Markham Johnson). Nimrod
(28:2) Spr-Sum 85, p. 80.
"The Jug" (tr. of Jansug Tcharkviani, w. Manly Johnson).
Nimrod (28:2) Spr-Sum 85, p. 160.
"Spring" (tr. of Murman Lebanidze, w. Manly Johnson).
Nimrod (28:2) Spr-Sum 85, p. 162.
3519. NIXON, John, Jr.
"Three Golds." KanQ (17:4) Fall 85, p. 108.

3520. NOBLE, Charles
"III Interview" (from a five part poem). <u>Grain</u> (13:3) Ag
85, p. 27-31.
3521. NOEL, Bernard
"Vertical Letter" (tr. by Paul Buck). <u>Temblor</u> (1) 85, p.
130-132.
3522. NOIPROX, Max
"Marseille before the War." <u>Bogg</u> (54) 85, p. 14.
3523. NOLAN, Pat
"From Exile in Paradise." <u>Oink</u> (19) 85, p. 103.
3524. NOLAN, Timothy
"Elephants at the Airport." <u>Nat</u> (241:9) 28 S 85, p. 285.
3525. NOLAND, John
"Dog Days." <u>DeKalbLAJ</u> (18:3/4) 85, p. 41.
3526. NOLD, John
"Black Heaven." <u>Quarry</u> (34:3) Sum 85, p. 23-24.
"Long Distance." <u>Quarry</u> (34:3) Sum 85, p. 23.
"Migrations." <u>PoetryCR</u> (6:4) Sum 85, p. 40.
"Owls." <u>Waves</u> (13:2/3) Wint 85, p. 92-93.
"Smell Spring." <u>PoetryCR</u> (6:3) Spr 85, p. 30.
"To Hold a Hawk." <u>PoetryCR</u> (6:3) Spr 85, p. 30.
3527. NOMEZ, Nain
"Cuando Acabe Esta Guerra." <u>Waves</u> (13:2/3) Wint 85, p. 71-
73.
"When This War Should End" (tr. by Augusta Dwyer). <u>Waves</u>
(13:2/3) Wint 85, p. 70, 72.
3528. NONAGASE, Massao
"A Day Dream" (tr. by Junko Yoshida). <u>HiramPoR</u> (39) Fall-
Wint 85, p. 17.
"Old Age Blues in the Sunset" (Selections: 3 poems, tr. by
Junko Yoshida). <u>HiramPoR</u> (39) Fall-Wint 85, p. 16-18.
"An Old Man's Amorous Monologue" (tr. by Junko Yoshida).
<u>HiramPoR</u> (39) Fall-Wint 85, p. 16.
"To You, My Gentle One" (tr. by Junko Yoshida). <u>HiramPoR</u>
(39) Fall-Wint 85, p. 18.
3529. NORD, Gennie
"Remembering Clara." <u>CreamCR</u> (10:1) 85, p. 29-30.
3530. NORDBRANDT, Henrik
"Dage Sent I Marts." <u>Mund</u> (15:1/2) 85, p. 66.
"Days Late in March" (tr. by Bente Hierholzer). <u>Mund</u>
(15:1/2) 85, p. 67.
"Ode to an Old Wine" (tr. by Alexander Taylor and the
author). <u>Ploughs</u> (11:4) 85, p. 242-244.
"The Post Office" (tr. by Alexander Taylor and the author).
<u>Ploughs</u> (11:4) 85, p. 245.
"Siden I Gaar." <u>Mund</u> (15:1/2) 85, p. 66.
"Since Yesterday" (tr. by Bente Hierholzer). <u>Mund</u>
(15:1/2) 85, p. 67.
3531. NORDHAUS, Jean
"Adirondack Return." <u>PraS</u> (59:3) Fall 85, p. 79.
"Caballos." <u>WestB</u> (17) 85, p. 108-109.
"Electrician." <u>PraS</u> (59:3) Fall 85, p. 78.
3532. NORDSTROM, Lars
"Apples of Knowledge" (tr. of Rolf Aggestam, w. Erland
Anderson). <u>GreenfR</u> (12:3/4) Wint-Spr 85, p. 120.
"I took strands of hair from your heads" (tr. of Rolf
Aggestam, w. Erland Anderson). <u>GreenfR</u> (12:3/4) Wint-
Spr 85, p. 119.
"It Has Taken Me Many Years to Build This House" (tr. of
Rolf Aggestam, w. Erland Anderson). <u>LitR</u> (29:1) Fall
85, p. 26-27.
"Proof of God" (tr. of Rolf Aggestam, w. Erland Anderson).
<u>NowestR</u> (23:2) 85, p. 36.
"The recalcitrant" ("Untitled, tr. of Rolf Aggestam, w.
Erland Anderson). <u>NowestR</u> (23:2) 85, p. 36.

3533. NORGREN, Constance
"Muriel, County Galway." GreenfR (12:3/4) Wint-Spr 85, p. 110.
"Visit." PoetryR (2:2) Ap 85, p. 60.
"What Changes and What Doesn't." GreenfR (12:3/4) Wint-Spr 85, p. 110-111.

3534. NORMOLLE, Su
"Cat Talk." WebR (10:2) Fall 85, p. 70.
"The Quickening." WebR (10:2) Fall 85, p. 70.

3535. NORRIS, Helen
"Portrait of Mother and Sorrowing Child." NegC (5:3) Sum 85, p. 36.
"Visit." NegC (5:3) Sum 85, p. 37.

3536. NORRIS, Kathleen
"The Bride." VirQ (61:4) Aut 85, p. 628.
"Saturday Afternoon at the Library." VirQ (61:4) Aut 85, p. 629-630.
"Thinking about Louise Bogan." Agni (22) 85, p. 101-102.
"Three Dreams." SoDakR (23:1) Spr 85, p. 15-16.
"What I Want to Be." VirQ (61:4) Aut 85, p. 630-631.

3537. NORRIS, Ken
"The Defects of Sexual Anatomy." Waves (13:4) Spr 85, p. 72.
"Guy Lafleur and Me." PoetryCR (6:3) Spr 85, p. 30.
"Heartbreak Hotel." Waves (13:4) Spr 85, p. 72.
"If I had a vocabulary for this sorrow." PoetryCR (7:2) Wint 85-86, p. 22.
"Propaganda." Rampike (4:2/3) 85-86, p. 75.
"This Island, My Home" (Montreal Island). PoetryCR (7:2) Wint 85-86, p. 22.
"You never lose the ability." PoetryCR (6:3) Spr 85, p. 30.

3538. NORRIS, Leslie
"A Recantation" (tr. of Dafydd ap Gwilym). QW (21) Fall-Wint 85, p. 103.
"Trouble at a Tavern" (tr. of Dafydd ap Gwilym). QW (21) Fall-Wint 85, p. 100-102.

3539. NORTH, Mick
"Pictures in the Fire." Stand (26:3) Sum 85, p. 26.

3540. NORTHNAGEL, E. W.
"End of Summer Play." Wind (15:54) 85, p. 52.

3541. NORTHUP, Harry E.
"Enough the Great Running Chapel" (Poem 6-13-1976, excerpts). Temblor (2) 85, p. 124-131.

3542. NORTON, Glenn
"Tracks." OhioR (34) 85, p. 103.

3543. NORTON, Scott
"The Tao of Levittown." USl (18/19) Wint 85, p. 8.

3544. NORTON, W. D. Herter
"Lovesong" (tr. of Rainer Maria Rilke). YellowS (14) Spr 85, p. 49.

3545. NORWID, Cyprian
"The Piano of Chopin" (tr. by Leonard Kress). WebR (10:1) Spr 85, p. 18-21.

3546. NORWOOD, Kyle
"July Third." SenR (15:2) 85, p. 123-125.
"Prayer for the Flood." SenR (15:2) 85, p. 126-127.

3547. NOSTRAND, Jennifer
"In the shadow of the Cathedral." Amelia (2:1) Ap 85, p. 42.
"October fills the park" ("Untitled"). Amelia (2:2) O 85, p. 33.
"The tree in the orchard." Amelia (2:1) Ap 85, p. 42.
"Under a string of Japanese lanterns." Amelia (2:1) Ap 85, p. 42.

3548. NOVAK, Carolyn
        "Friendly Foe." AntigR (61) Spr 85, p. 40.
        "Weaknesses." AntigR (61) Spr 85, p. 41.
3549. NOVAK, Michael Paul
        "Building a Fire." StoneC (13:1/2) Fall-Wint 85-86, p. 17.
        "Long Enough." KanQ (17:4) Fall 85, p. 57.
        "Nightingales, Cave Drawings." KanQ (17:4) Fall 85, p. 56.
3550. NOVAK, Robert
        "Olympic Poem." WindO (46) Fall 85, p. 56.
        "Running Past the Houses of the Orchard's Patrons." WindO
            (46) Fall 85, p. 1.
3551. NOWAK, Nancy
        "The Faithful." SmPd (22:3) Fall 85, p. 33.
3552. NOWAK, Tadeusz
        "Psalm Ajar" (tr. by Leonard Kress). BlueBldgs (9) [85?],
            p. 18.
3553. NOWLAN, Michael O.
        "Lines for a Forty-Seventh Birthday." CanLit (104) Spr
            85, p. 23.
3554. NOYES, H. F.
        "Just now the sound." Amelia (2:1) Ap 85, p. 19.
3555. NOYES, Steve
        "John & Light." AntigR (62/63) Sum-Aut 85, p. 268.
        "Moving across Election." AntigR (62/63) Sum-Aut 85, p.
            267.
        "Photograph." AntigR (62/63) Sum-Aut 85, p. 265-266.
        "She Does the Love Poem." PoetryCR (7:2) Wint 85-86, p.
            55.
3556. NUGENT, Macushla
        "The End of the Day." NegC (5:2) Spr 85, p. 90-91.
        "Loch Raven Reservoir." CapeR (20:1) Spr 85, p. 12.
3557. NURKSE, D.
        "The Clearing in the Forest." SouthernHR (19:1) Wint 85,
            p. 62.
        "The Demolition Contract." GWR (6:1) 85?, p. 29.
        "The Demotion." MassR (26:1) Spr 85, p. 83-84.
        "Home from the Fair." YellowS (15) Sum 85, p. 36.
        "The Old Resort." YellowS (16) Aut 85, p. 17.
        "Privates." MassR (26:1) Spr 85, p. 83.
3558. NWOKO, Egbuniwe John
        "Old February." CalQ (26) Sum 85, p. 41-42.
3559. NYE, Naomi Shihab
        "At Mother Teresa's." ChrC (102:31) 16 O 85, p. 920.
3560. NYHART, Nina
        "Jack Looks Back." Shen (36:1) 85-86, p. 14-15.
3561. NYMAN, Mary M.
        "Concerning the Eaglets' Release at Quabbin Reservoir."
            PoeticJ (9) 85, p. 3.
3562. NYSTROM, Debra
        "Bonin Drowned." Ploughs (11:1) 85, p. 161.
        "Driving Home." Ploughs (11:1) 85, p. 160.
        "Eurydice." SenR (15:2) 85, p. 157.
        "Flooded Breaks." AmerPoR (14:6) N-D 85, p. 6.
        "From Her Diary." SenR (15:2) 85, p. 156.
        "A Game." Ploughs (11:1) 85, p. 159.
        "Pheasant Weather." Ploughs (11:1) 85, p. 158.
        "A Terror." SenR (15:2) 85, p. 155.
        "With You Gone." AmerPoR (14:6) N-D 85, p. 6.
3563. OAKEY, Shawn
        "Elegy." Quarry (34:3) Sum 85, p. 25.
3564. OAKS, Jeff
        "First Frost." Blueline (6:2) Wint-Spr 85, p. 7.
3565. OANDASAN, William
        "The Arrowhead." NoDaQ (53:2) Spr 85, p. 219.
3566. OATES, David
        "East Alexander." YellowS (15) Sum 85, p. 40.

"Kouros." YellowS (17) Wint 85, p. 16.
3567. OATES, Joyce Carol
"Ancient Aphorisms." PoetryR (5) S 85, p. 10-11.
"Dead Friends." PoetryR (5) S 85, p. 6.
"The Heir." MassR (26:4) Wint 85, p. 605.
"Midsummer, Night." PoetryR (5) S 85, p. 5-6.
"My Grandfather's Stone Well." PoetryR (5) S 85, p. 7.
"North Sea." PoetryR (5) S 85, p. 8-9.
"Winter Aphorisms, Uncoded." GeoR (39:4) Wint 85, p. 823.
3568. O'BRIEN, Geoffrey
"Tibet." Sulfur (13) 85, p. 80-81.
3569. O'BRIEN, John
"Summer Dusk in Oswego, New York." Wind (15:53) 85, p. 33.
"Upon Looking at Three Polaroid Pictures of Myself . . ."
Wind (15:53) 85, p. 33-34.
3570. O'BRIEN, Margaret
"A Homing." PoetL (80:3) Fall 85, p. 148.
3571. O'BRIEN, Michael
"Cur Secessisti?" (tr. of René Char). NewL (51:4) Sum
85, p. 150.
"The Legitimate Order Is Sometimes Inhuman" (tr. of René
Char). NewL (51:4) Sum 85, p. 150.
"Motet" (tr. of Eugenio Montale). NewL (51:4) Sum 85, p.
169.
"Penumbra" (tr. of René Char). NewL (51:4) Sum 85, p.
150.
"Say" (tr. of René Char). NewL (51:4) Sum 85, p. 151.
3572. O'BRIEN, Sherry
"Barefoot and Pregnant." Waves (14:1/2) Fall 85, p. 94.
3573. O'BRIEN, Sylvia
"Museum of Modern Art Sculpture Garden in the Rain."
Amelia (2:2) O 85, p. 69.
3574. O'BRIEN, William P.
"Hopper's Early Sunday Morning" (For Joe DiTucci). KanQ
(17:3) Sum 85, p. 68.
"The Ice Palace." KanQ (17:1/2) Wint-Spr 85, p. 255.
3575. O'CALLAGHAN, Julie
"Getting through the Night." PoetryCR (6:4) Sum 85, p. 42.
3576. OCHESTER, Ed
"The Canaries in Uncle Arthur's Basement." VirQ (61:2)
Spr 85, p. 249.
"Conversation on Lady Day." VirQ (61:2) Spr 85, p. 248.
"Entirely Because of the Growing Confusion" (tr. of Bertolt
Brecht). NewL (51:4) Sum 85, p. 62.
"A Famous Literary Couple." OP (38/39) Spr 85, p. 99.
"On Swimming in Lakes and Rivers" (tr. of Bertolt Brecht).
CharR (11:2) Fall 85, p. 85-86.
"On the Infanticide: Marie Farrar" (tr. of Bertolt Brecht).
Telescope (4:2) Spr 85, p. 55-58.
"Poem for Basho." NoAmR (270:2) Je 85, p. 45.
"Poem for Dr. Spock." WestHR (19:2) Sum 85, p. 154.
"The Relatives." Poetry (147:3) D 85, p. 130-131.
"Rock Hill." CharR (11:2) Fall 85, p. 84-85.
"The Ship" (tr. of Bertolt Brecht). NewL (51:4) Sum 85,
p. 63-64.
"The Shopper" (tr. of Bertolt Brecht). NewL (51:4) Sum
85, p. 62-63.
"Traveling in a Comfortable Car" (tr. of Bertolt Brecht).
NewL (51:4) Sum 85, p. 61.
3577. O'CONNELL, Bill
"South on Eel River" (for J.B.). CutB (24) Spr-Sum 85, p.
58.
3578. O'CONNELL, George
"First Cutting." AntR (43:2) Spr 85, p. 199.
"Western Nebraska, 1870." AntR (43:2) Spr 85, p. 198.

3579. O'CONNOR, Conleth
"Night Is an Age." Waves (13:2/3) Wint 85, p. 101.
"To Us, a Son." Waves (13:2/3) Wint 85, p. 100-101.
3580. O'CONNOR, Mark
"The Watchers" (Vulcano Island, Aeolian Straits). Quarry
(34:4) Aut 85, p. 60.
3581. O'CONNOR, Michael (See also O'CONNOR, Michael Edward)
"Shining." Pig (13) 85, p. 78.
"To My Friend." Pig (13) 85, p. 35.
3582. O'CONNOR, Michael Edward (See also O'CONNOR, Michael)
"Sean Scanlon." JamesWR (2:2) Wint 85, p. 11.
3583. O'DALY, William
"La Rosa Separada" (Selections: I. "Men," VIII. "The
Island," IX. "Men," XVI. "Men," XX. "The Island," tr. of
Pablo Neruda). NowestR (23:2) 85, p. 7-15.
3584. ODENBAUGH, Jen
"Who the Hell Cares?" Kaleid (10) Spr 85, p. 39.
3585. ODERMAN, Kevin
"Does Too." PoetC (17:1) Fall 85, p. 11.
"The Foggiest." PoetC (17:1) Fall 85, p. 12.
"Gummed." PoetC (17:1) Fall 85, p. 13.
"Small Life and." PoetC (17:1) Fall 85, p. 14.
"This Alone." PoetC (17:1) Fall 85, p. 15.
3586. ODIO, Arnold
"Auschwitz Was Not My Playground" (tr. of Fayad Jamís).
NewEngR (7:4) Sum 85, p. 494.
"Cuban Poets Have Stopped Dreaming" (tr. of Heberto
Padilla). NewEngR (7:4) Sum 85, p. 603.
"The Man Who Consumes Today's Newspapers" (tr. of Heberto
Padilla). NewEngR (7:4) Sum 85, p. 604.
"The Other" (tr. of Roberto Fernández Retamar). NewEngR
(7:4) Sum 85, p. 521.
"Out of the Game" (To Yannis Ritsos, in a Greek jail, tr.
of Heberto Padilla). NewEngR (7:4) Sum 85, p. 602-603.
3587. ODIO, Elena B.
"Black Woman" (tr. of Nancy Morejón). NewEngR (7:4) Sum
85, p. 576-577.
3588. ODLIN, Reno
"J'Ayme Donc Je Suis, Je Souffre Mais Je Vis" (English tr.
of J. Laughlin). AntigR (60) Wint 85, p. 121.
3589. O'DONOGHUE, Bernard
"The Migrant Workers." Verse (1) 84, p. 14.
3590. O'DRISCOLL, Dennis
"Normally Speaking." Poetry (146:4) Jl 85, p. 213.
"Time Sharing." Poetry (146:4) Jl 85, p. 212.
3591. OERKE, Andrew
"Diary of Death, Beirut, New Year's 1984." NegC (5:4)
Fall 85, p. 69-72.
3592. OESAU, Patricia
"Conversation over Dinner." Chelsea (44) 85, p. 141.
"Near a Decision." Chelsea (44) 85, p. 141.
"Oasis." Chelsea (44) 85, p. 142.
3593. O'FLAHERTIE, Fingall
"The Clones of Academe" (to the tune of "The Vicar of
Bray"). OP (38/39) Spr 85, p. 162-163.
3594. OGDEN, Hugh
"I Remember Thinking They Would Save Him." NoDaQ (53:1)
Wint 85, p. 120.
3595. O'HERN, Phillip
"In the Post Office" (Title in Greek). NegC (5:1) Wint
85, p. 128.
3596. OLDER, Julia
"Daughters." PoetryR (5) S 85, p. 79.
"Spare Parts." OP (38/39) Spr 85, p. 172.
"There Are Some Who Have Trumpets" (tr. of Boris Vian).
NewL (51:4) Sum 85, p. 152.

"There Was a Copper Lamp" (tr. of Boris Vian). NewL
     (51:4) Sum 85, p. 151.
3597. OLDKNOW, Antony
     "Talking with Her." CreamCR (10:1) 85, p. 24.
3598. OLDS, Peter
     "The People of Spring Street." SecC (12:1) 84, p. 29.
3599. OLDS, Sharon
     "12 Years Old." ParisR (27:96) Sum 85, p. 98.
     "The Blue Dress." OP (40) Fall-Wint 85, p. 10-11.
     "The Cast." Poetry (146:5) Ag 85, p. 278.
     "Death." OP (40) Fall-Wint 85, p. 12-13.
     "Death and Morality." Iowa (15:1) Wint 85, p. 75-76.
     "Feelings." AmerPoR (14:6) N-D 85, p. 5.
     "The First Night My Son Is at Camp." OP (40) Fall-Wint
          85, p. 14.
     "The Glass." AmerPoR (14:6) N-D 85, p. 3.
     "I Cannot Forget the Woman in the Mirror." ParisR (27:96)
          Sum 85, p. 97.
     "I Go Back to May 1937." AmerPoR (14:6) N-D 85, p. 3.
     "In the Hospital, near the End." AmerPoR (14:6) N-D 85,
          p. 4.
     "Little Things." AmerPoR (14:6) N-D 85, p. 3.
     "Making Love." Atlantic (256:1), Jl 85, p. 72.
     "The Moment of My Father's Death." AmerPoR (14:6) N-D 85,
          p. 4.
     "The Moment the Two Worlds Meet." AmerPoR (14:6) N-D 85,
          p. 5.
     "My Parents' Wedding Night, 1937." Iowa (15:1) Wint 85,
          p. 72-73.
     "On the Subway." Nat (241:9) 28 S 85, p. 284.
     "The Planned Child." Poetry (146:5) Ag 85, p. 279.
     "Poem for My Son, Aged 10, After a High Fever." NewYorker
          (60:53) 18 F 85, p. 44.
     "The Present Moment." Iowa (15:1) Wint 85, p. 73-75.
     "The Race." NewYorker (61:40) 25 N 85, p. 44.
     "The Solution." ParisR (27:96) Sum 85, p. 95-96.
     "Still Life." Iowa (15:1) Wint 85, p. 76.
     "That Moment." OP (40) Fall-Wint 85, p. 9.
     "Topography." OP (38/39) Spr 85, p. 193.
     "True Love." AmerPoR (14:6) N-D 85, p. 5.
3600. O'LEARY, Patrick
     "Pornography." LittleM (14:4) 85, p. 11.
     "Theology." LittleM (14:4) 85, p. 10.
3601. OLES, Carole
     "2 A.M., Summer Storm, Alarm." DenQ (19:4) Spr 85, p. 34.
     "At Nightfall in Vermont." DenQ (19:4) Spr 85, p. 35.
     "For a Friend at Dusk, 22 Useless Lines." IndR (8:1) Wint
          85, p. 22.
     "High Heels." Poetry (146:5) Ag 85, p. 281-282.
     "Maria Observes Halley's Comet, 1835." AmerPoR (14:4) Jl-
          Ag 85, p. 38.
     "Maria's Ghost Considers Interpretation by Freud."
          AmerPoR (14:4) Jl-Ag 85, p. 38.
     "Maria's Ghost Considers the Reappearance of Halley's Comet
          in 1985." ClockR (2:2) 85, p. 34.
     "Maria's Ghost Haunts Phyllis Schlafly." AmerPoR (14:4)
          Jl-Ag 85, p. 38-39.
     "Maria's Mother Falls Ill." ClockR (2:2) 85, p. 32.
     "Night Watches: Inventions on the Life of Maria Mitchell"
          (A Group of Poems: 11 selections). PraS (59:2) Sum 85,
          p. 19-35.
     "On the Cliff Walk at Newport, Rhode Island, Thinking of
          Percy Bysshe Shelley." IndR (8:1) Wint 85, p. 23.
     "Quintet in C Major for Two Listeners." DenQ (19:4) Spr
          85, p. 36.
     "Rough Passage." ClockR (2:2) 85, p. 33.

"Stitches" (For my son). <u>Poetry</u> (146:5) Ag 85, p. 280.
3602. OLGA
        "Undone." <u>Imagine</u> (2:1) Sum 85, p. 63.
        "Wisemen." <u>Imagine</u> (2:1) Sum 85, p. 63.
3603. OLIVEIRA, Celso de
        "Recipe for a Woman" (tr. of Vinicius de Moraes). <u>Verse</u>
            (3) 85, p. 50-51.
3604. OLIVER, Mary
        "Banyan." <u>Poetry</u> (146:1) Ap 85, p. 7-8.
        "Cleaning the Fish." <u>WestHR</u> (39:4) Wint 85, p. 324.
        "Ich Bin der Welt Abhanden Gekommen." <u>WestHR</u> (39:4) Wint
            85, p. 355-356.
        "Milkweed." <u>Atlantic</u> (255:5), My 85, p. 52.
        "The Shark." <u>Poetry</u> (146:1) Ap 85, p. 6-7.
        "Sunrise." <u>PartR</u> (52:2) 85, p. 62-63.
3605. OLIVER, Merrill
        "Beauty." <u>WestB</u> (16) 85, p. 23.
3606. OLIVER, Raymond
        "Epigrams on Mortality" (in homage to J. V. Cunningham).
            <u>ChiR</u> (35:1) Aut 85, p. 22.
3607. OLIVEROS, Chuck
        "Engine Noises." <u>RagMag</u> (4:1) Spr 85, p. 45.
3608. OLSEN, David
        "Rusty redwood leaf." <u>Amelia</u> (2:1) Ap 85, p. 62.
        "Tanka." <u>Amelia</u> (2:2) O 85, p. 20.
3609. OLSEN, Don
        "The Dinosaur" (by Gagaway Kennel). <u>SpoonRQ</u> (10:2) Spr
            85, p. 15-16.
3610. OLSEN, William
        "Saint Paul the Hermit, Saint Anthony, and the
            Pipistrelles." <u>Crazy</u> (29) Fall 85, p. 78-79.
3611. OLSON, Charles
        "Abstract #1, Yucatan." <u>Sulfur</u> (12) 85, p. 77.
        "The Advantage." <u>Sulfur</u> (12) 85, p. 75-76.
        "The Alba." <u>Sulfur</u> (12) 85, p. 94.
        "As Though There Were No Flowering." <u>Sulfur</u> (13) 85, p. 4-
            5.
        "The Civil War." <u>Sulfur</u> (12) 85, p. 79-80.
        "Dramatis Personae." <u>Sulfur</u> (12) 85, p. 85-87.
        "The Drum II" (for John Clarke). <u>Sulfur</u> (13) 85, p. 19-20.
        "The Drum World." <u>Sulfur</u> (13) 85, p. 16-19.
        "Evil" (1-4). <u>Sulfur</u> (12) 85, p. 92-93.
        "Ferrini." <u>Sulfur</u> (13) 85, p. 7-14.
        "Friday, Good Friday." <u>Sulfur</u> (12) 85, p. 77.
        "From the Inca." <u>Sulfur</u> (12) 85, p. 84.
        "I met my Angel last night or it was the corner of
            Reservoir Road." <u>Sulfur</u> (13) 85, p. 15-16.
        "I saw, from under Him, the beginning of the web of God."
            <u>Sulfur</u> (13) 85, p. 7.
        "In an Automotive Store." <u>Sulfur</u> (13) 85, p. 5-7.
        "Issues from the Hand of God." <u>Sulfur</u> (12) 85, p. 78-79.
        "Jas Jargon." <u>Sulfur</u> (12) 85, p. 87-88.
        "New Poem." <u>Sulfur</u> (12) 85, p. 91.
        "The Real." <u>Sulfur</u> (12) 85, p. 90.
        "A Story." <u>Sulfur</u> (12) 85, p. 89.
        "The Thing Was Moving." <u>Sulfur</u> (12) 85, p. 82-84.
        "War on the Mind in a Time of Love." <u>Sulfur</u> (12) 85, p.
            81-82.
        "The Writ." <u>Sulfur</u> (12) 85, p. 94-95.
3612. OLSON, Elder
        "Mad Girl." <u>TriQ</u> (63) Spr-Sum 85, p. 629.
        "Returning a Knife to a 'Friend'." <u>TriQ</u> (63) Spr-Sum 85,
            p. 629.
        "Revenant." <u>TriQ</u> (63) Spr-Sum 85, p. 629.
3613. OLSON, Kristina
        "The Girls in the Schoolyard." <u>AntigR</u> (61) Spr 85, p. 113.

3614. OLSON, Ruth
       "Diphtheria." IndR (8:2) Spr 85, p. 70.
       "John Rides a Horse." NoDaQ (53:4) Fall 85, p. 218-219.
       "Their Time." NoDaQ (53:4) Fall 85, p. 220.
3615. O'NEILL, Alexandre
       "Arson" (tr. by Alexis Levitin). HangL (47) Spr 85, p. 39-
       40.
3616. O'NEILL, Brian
       "Blackbird." ColEng (47:1) Ja 85, p. 56-57.
       "The Coffee Pot." ColEng (47:1) Ja 85, p. 55-56.
       "For Old Classmates Finding No Easy Deliverance."
       WoosterR (3) Spr 85, p. 29.
       "Photograph: Father and Grandfather Fishing the Pier at
       Michigan City." AmerS (54:1) Wint 84-85, p. 42-43.
       "A Poem for Fly Tiers." Chelsea (44) 85, p. 72.
       "Revise, Revise." PartR (52:3) 85, p. 251.
       "Sodbusters." WoosterR (3) Spr 85, p. 30-31.
       "Visitation at Fox River." Chelsea (44) 85, p. 73.
3617. O'NEILL, John
       "Birds." Grain (13:2) My 85, p. 25.
       "River and Mountain." Grain (13:2) My 85, p. 24.
3618. O'NEILL, Patrick
       "God's Boot Camp." SanFPJ (7:2) 85, p. 37.
       "On the 5th Chapter of St. Matthew" (Especially for
       parents, teachers, clergymen, administrators, and other
       god-like creatures). SanFPJ (7:2) 85, p. 44.
3619. O'NEILL, Paul
       "Harvest-Time." PottPort (7) 85-86, p. 24.
3620. ONUORA, Oku
       "Mada." GreenfR (12:3/4) Wint-Spr 85, p. 210.
       "Watch di Moon." GreenfR (12:3/4) Wint-Spr 85, p. 209.
3621. OOSTERHAVEN, Beart
       "Stream" (tr. by Rod Jellema). PoetL (79:4) Wint 85, p.
       232.
3622. OPENGART, Bea Carol
       "Erotica." Tendril (19/20) 85, p. 287.
3623. OPPENHEIMER, Joel
       "For Bunting" (1 march 1900 -- 17 april 1985). Conjunc
       (8) 85, p. 183-184.
3624. ORBAN, Ottó
       "Beast of Prey" (tr. by Jascha Kessler and Mária
       Körösy). GrahamHR (9) Fall 85, p. 59.
       "A Blade of Grass" (tr. by Jascha Kessler and Maria
       Körösy). Ploughs (11:4) 85, p. 219.
       "Builders" (tr. by Jascha Kessler and Mária Körösy).
       GrahamHR (9) Fall 85, p. 57.
       "An Excursion" (tr. by Jascha Kessler and Mária
       Körösy). GrahamHR (9) Fall 85, p. 60.
       "Farewell" (tr. by Jascha Kessler and Mária Körösy).
       GrahamHR (9) Fall 85, p. 62.
       "Love Match" (tr. by Jascha Kessler and Mária
       Körösy). GrahamHR (9) Fall 85, p. 58.
       "Painting" (tr. by Jascha Kessler and Mária Körösy).
       GrahamHR (9) Fall 85, p. 61.
       "A Small Country" (tr. by Jascha Kessler and Mária
       Körösy). GrahamHR (9) Fall 85, p. 55.
       "The Technique" (tr. by Jascha Kessler and Mária
       Körösy). GrahamHR (9) Fall 85, p. 56.
       "The Technique" (tr. by Jascha Kessler and Maria
       Körösy). Ploughs (11:4) 85, p. 218.
3625. OREN, Miriam
       "Meeting" (tr. by Ruth Whitman). Ploughs (11:4) 85, p.
       173.
3626. ORESICK, Peter
       "American Landscape with Unemployed." MinnR (N.S. 25)
       Fall 85, p. 67-68.

"In a Time of Peace" (Excerpt). <u>MinnR</u> (N.S. 24) Spr 85,
p. 38.
"Thirst." <u>MinnR</u> (N.S. 25) Fall 85, p. 66.
3627. ORFALEA, Greg
"Winter Orange" (for Pablo Medina). <u>LindLM</u> (4:1) Ja-Mr
85, p. 29.
3628. ORLEN, Steve
"Acts of Will" (For Jon Anderson). <u>Crazy</u> (29) Fall 85, p.
24-25.
"Alternative Lives." <u>Crazy</u> (29) Fall 85, p. 23.
"At the Indoor Shopping Mall." <u>SenR</u> (15:2) 85, p. 98-99.
"Down at the Harvest Bar." <u>SenR</u> (15:2) 85, p. 101.
"Even the Smallest Death." <u>Iowa</u> (15:1) Wint 85, p. 95.
"In the Park." <u>SenR</u> (15:2) 85, p. 102.
"Like All the World." <u>SenR</u> (15:2) 85, p. 103.
"Snapshot from an Album." <u>SenR</u> (15:2) 85, p. 100.
3629. ORLOWSKY, Dzvinia
"Anesthesia." <u>Ploughs</u> (11:1) 85, p. 164.
"Praying." <u>Ploughs</u> (11:1) 85, p. 162-163.
3630. OROZCO, Olga
"En el Final Era el Verbo." <u>LindLM</u> (4:3) Jl-S 85, p. 10.
"Esa Es Tu Pena." <u>LindLM</u> (4:3) Jl-S 85, p. 10.
"El Obstáculo." <u>LindLM</u> (4:3) Jl-S 85, p. 10.
3631. ORR, Ed
"Clouds" (after Anais Nin). <u>YellowS</u> (14) Spr 85, p. 6.
"Eroticism." <u>Sam</u> (42:3, 167th release) 85, p. 11.
"Leaves, Moon, Mustache" (after Miró). <u>Open24</u> (4) 85,
p. 4.
"Metamorphoses Part I" (variation on line by William
Carpenter). <u>YellowS</u> (14) Spr 85, p. 6.
"The Song of Vowels" (after Miró). <u>Open24</u> (4) 85, p. 4.
"Ulysses S. Grant." <u>CrabCR</u> (2:2) Wint 85, p. 24.
3632. ORR, Gregory
"Amor As a God of Death on Roman Stone Coffins." <u>Pequod</u>
(19/20/21) 85, p. 250.
"Variation on 'The Discovery and Conquest of Mexico'."
<u>Pequod</u> (19/20/21) 85, p. 251-252.
3633. ORR, Linda
"Journal from the Rue" (Selections). <u>Pequod</u> (19/20/21)
85, p. 253-259.
3634. ORR, Verlena
"The Auctioneer." <u>CutB</u> (24) Spr-Sum 85, p. 70.
3635. ORTELLI, Rosana María
"Caminando Mis Huellas." <u>Mairena</u> (7:19) 85, p. 99.
3636. ORTENBERG, Neil
"Meditation in Upstate N.Y." <u>GreenfR</u> (13:1/2) Fall-Wint
85, p. 176.
3637. ORTH, Kevin
"House" (from the Spanish of Pablo Neruda's "Casa").
<u>PoetryR</u> (2:2) Ap 85, p. 68.
"The Labyrinth" (from the Spanish of Jorge Luis Borges).
<u>PoetryR</u> (2:2) Ap 85, p. 67.
"A Treatise on Comedy." <u>PoetryE</u> (18) Fall 85, p. 37.
"Youth" (from the Spanish of Pablo Neruda's "Juventud").
<u>PoetryR</u> (2:2) Ap 85, p. 68.
3638. ORTIZ, Javier
"Sandino" (tr. by Kent Johnson). <u>MinnR</u> (N.S. 25) Fall 85,
p. 42.
ORTIZ, Juana Henrique
See HENRIQUE-ORTIZ, Juana
3639. ORTIZ, Simon J.
"Uncle Bunk's Beans." <u>RiverS</u> (17) 85, p. 15-18.
ORTIZ COFER, Judith
See COFER, Judith Ortiz
3640. ORTOLANI, Al
"Old Timer on the Girard Square with Pickers." <u>SpoonRQ</u>

(10:4) Fall 85, p. 55.
"Willows." WindO (45) Spr 85, p. 16.
3641. ORY, Carlos Edmundo de
"A una Mujer." Mund (15:1/2) 85, p. 10.
"Los Besos." Mund (15:1/2) 85, p. 10.
"Canto de Despedida." Mund (15:1/2) 85, p. 12.
"If I Had a Horse" (tr. by Will Kirkland). Mund (15:1/2)
85, p. 15.
"The Kisses" (tr. by Will Kirkland). Mund (15:1/2) 85, p.
11.
"Llanto." Mund (15:1/2) 85, p. 12.
"Si Tuviera un Caballo." Mund (15:1/2) 85, p. 14.
"Sob" (tr. by Will Kirkland). Mund (15:1/2) 85, p. 13.
"A Song of Farewell" (tr. by Will Kirkland). Mund
(15:1/2) 85, p. 13.
"To a Woman" (tr. by Will Kirkland). Mund (15:1/2) 85, p.
11.
3642. OSBEY, Brenda Marie
"The Bone Step-Women." SouthernR (21:3) Sum 85, p. 831.
"Devices of Icons" (to Charles H. Rowell, after hearing
Audre Lorde read on 10 April 1980, a preliminary).
SouthernR (21:3) Sum 85, p. 834-836.
"In These Houses of Swift Easy Women." SouthernR (21:3)
Sum 85, p. 830.
"Portrait" (1984 AWP Award-Winning Poem). Tendril (19/20)
85, p. 25-28.
"The Wastrel-Woman Poem." SouthernR (21:3) Sum 85, p. 832-
833.
3643. OSBORN, Karen
"Women, Listening." PassN (6:2) Spr-Sum 85, p. 19.
3644. OSBORN, Marijane
"The Avenger's Wife" (tr. of the Old English poem called
"The Wife's Lament"). LitR (28:4) Sum 85, p. 586-587.
3645. OSERS, Ewald
"The End of the World" (tr. of Miroslav Holub). Verse (2)
85, p. 16.
"Even the raven belongs to the song bird family" (tr. of
Jaroslav Seifert). CrossCur (5:2) 85, p. 72.
"Everything on earth has happened before" (tr. of Jaroslav
Seifert). CrossCur (5:2) 85, p. 71.
"For you I would like to bring a little white dove" (tr. of
Jaroslav Seifert). CrossCur (5:2) 85, p. 73.
"I remember the days when it was much darker in the cinemas
than today" (tr. of Jaroslav Seifert). CrossCur (5:2)
85, p. 75.
"I used to yearn for distant cities" (tr. of Jaroslav
Seifert). CrossCur (5:2) 85, p. 78.
"Nocturnal Divertimento" (tr. of Jaroslav Seifert).
Ploughs (11:4) 85, p. 90-95.
"Not till old age did I learn" (tr. of Jaroslav Seifert).
CrossCur (5:2) 85, p. 69.
"On a forgotten stone block in the garden" (tr. of Jaroslav
Seifert). CrossCur (5:2) 85, p. 70.
"Our lives run like fingers over sandpaper" (tr. of
Jaroslav Seifert). CrossCur (5:2) 85, p. 76.
"Reminiscence 1939 (Boats in the Desert)" (tr. of Josef
Simon). Verse (2) 85, p. 18.
"Return from Aloft" (tr. of Josef Simon). Verse (2) 85,
p. 18.
"Spice" (tr. of Miroslav Holub). Verse (2) 85, p. 16.
"To all those million verses in the world" (tr. of Jaroslav
Seifert). CrossCur (5:2) 85, p. 79.
"To Be a Poet" (tr. of Jaroslav Seifert). Ploughs (11:4)
85, p. 88-89.
"To the Eternal Inhabitants of Category 4" (tr. of Josef
Simon). Verse (2) 85, p. 17.

"To the Twenty-Year-Old Angels of Hopelessness" (tr. of
    Josef Simon). <u>Verse</u> (2) 85, p. 17.
"View from Charles Bridge" (tr. of Jaroslav Seifert).
    <u>Ploughs</u> (11:4) 85, p. 96-98.
"Voices in the Landscape" (tr. of Miroslav Holub). <u>Verse</u>
    (2) 85, p. 15.
"The worst is over now" (tr. of Jaroslav Seifert).
    <u>CrossCur</u> (5:2) 85, p. 77.
"You can stay silent if you don't feel like talking" (tr.
    of Jaroslav Seifert). <u>CrossCur</u> (5:2) 85, p. 74.
3646. OSHEROW, Jacqueline
    "Looking for Angels in New York." <u>NewYorker</u> (61:25) 12 Ag
        85, p. 32.
3647. OSING, Gordon
    "Burlesco" (Garibaldi Square). <u>KanQ</u> (17:1/2) Wint-Spr 85,
        p. 217.
    "Que Hora Es?" <u>KanQ</u> (17:1/2) Wint-Spr 85, p. 217.
    "Seeing the End of the World" (poems on themes in Borges).
        <u>Raccoon</u> (18) Jn 85 (Monograph 5), p. 11-15.
    "'Snow at Giverny' -- Monet" (with a little help from
        Rilke). <u>CharR</u> (11:1) Spr 85, p. 67.
3648. OSOINACH, John Campbell
    "Aging." <u>YellowS</u> (17) Wint 85, p. 20.
3649. OSTASZEWSKI, Krzysztof
    "Opus 80, a Tragedy." <u>Waves</u> (13:4) Spr 85, p. 101.
3650. OSTRIKER, Alicia
    "The Anniversary Dinner." <u>OP</u> (38/39) Spr 85, p. 51.
    "April One." <u>OP</u> (38/39) Spr 85, p. 210-211.
    "April One." <u>USl</u> (18/19) Wint 85, p. 10-11.
    "Encountering the Dead." <u>Poetry</u> (147:1) O 85, p. 21.
    "Evening Rush Hour: Three Images." <u>LittleM</u> (14:4) 85, p.
        61.
    "The Game." <u>Tendril</u> (19/20) 85, p. 288-289.
    "He Gets Depressed Whenever We Argue." <u>USl</u> (18/19) Wint
        85, p. 10.
    "The Imaginary Lover" (Selections: "Cows," "Poem Beginning
        with a Line by Fitzgerald/Hemingway"). <u>OntR</u> (22) Spr-
        Sum 85, p. 22-27.
    "Listen." <u>AmerPoR</u> (14:5) S-O 85, p. 7.
    "Sex." <u>Poetry</u> (147:1) O 85, p. 20.
    "Telling the Daughters." <u>LittleM</u> (14:4) 85, p. 60.
    "Where Trees Come From." <u>LittleM</u> (14:4) 85, p. 62.
    "Widow in a Stone House." <u>Nat</u> (240:2) 19 Ja 85, p. 59.
    "The Woman Who Ran Away." <u>Poetry</u> (147:1) O 85, p. 19-20.
3651. OSTROM, Hans
    "High School Football." <u>SoCaR</u> (18:1) Fall 85, p. 9.
    "In January." <u>Wind</u> (15:55) 85, p. 41.
    "In the Sierra." <u>LaurelR</u> (19:1) Wint 85, p. 38.
3652. OTIS, Emily (<u>See also</u> OTIS, Emily T.)
    "Aunt Anne." <u>WestB</u> (17) 85, p. 37.
    "Transition." <u>WestB</u> (17) 85, p. 36.
3653. OTIS, Emily T. (<u>See also</u> OTIS, Emily)
    "Long Distance to the Old House." <u>Wind</u> (15:54) 85, p. 37.
    "Trace." <u>Wind</u> (15:54) 85, p. 37-38.
3654. OTTEN, Charlotte F.
    "A friend dreamed I had given birth" ("Untitled"). <u>Comm</u>
        (112:13) 12 Jl 85, p. 399.
3655. OUELLETTE, Fernand
    "Depuis la Musique" (Extraits). <u>Os</u> (20) 85, p. 8-9.
3656. OUGHTON, John
    "Living in Edville." <u>Rampike</u> (4:2/3) 85-86, p. 107.
3657. OUGHTON, Libby
    "Cape Traverse." <u>PottPort</u> (7) 85-86, p. 41.
3658. OUTRAM, Richard
    "Herrings" (for Alberto). <u>Descant</u> 51 (16:4/17:1) Wint 85-
        86, p. 156-167.

"Sherlock Holmes" (tr. of Jorge Luis Borges). <u>Descant</u> 51
(16:4/17:1) Wint 85-86, p. 10-11.

3659. OVERALL, Suzanne
"Destination." <u>PoeticJ</u> (10) 85, p. 19.

3660. OVERTON, Ron
"The Infant" (for Ned). <u>HangL</u> (48) Fall 85, p. 58.
"Turning 39 Thinking of Jackie Jensen." <u>HangL</u> (48) Fall
85, p. 57.
"Why Tom Continually Runs after Jerry." <u>OP</u> (38/39) Spr
85, p. 203-204.

3661. OWEN, Maureen
"Gossip Notes of Court Life, or the Irises of Loyang"
(Excerpt, for Mary Kelly). <u>Oink</u> (19) 85, p. 71.
"The Hens/Twyla Story." <u>OP</u> (38/39) Spr 85, p. 38.
"Internal Damage." <u>Oink</u> (19) 85, p. 72.
"The Jam Wars." <u>OP</u> (38/39) Spr 85, p. 37.

3662. OWEN, Sue
"Bone Soup." <u>Iowa</u> (15:3) Fall 85, p. 112-113.
"Cat in the Corner." <u>Iowa</u> (15:3) Fall 85, p. 113-114.
"My Graveyard Poem." <u>Iowa</u> (15:3) Fall 85, p. 111-112.
"Recipe for Night." <u>Iowa</u> (15:3) Fall 85, p. 110-111.
"Tattletale." <u>Iowa</u> (15:3) Fall 85, p. 114-115.

3663. OWENS, Rochelle
"Ode to a Tea-Serving Set" (Norman, Oklahoma). <u>OP</u> (38/39)
Spr 85, p. 138-139.

3664. OWER, John
"Cactuses." <u>AntigR</u> (61) Spr 85, p. 28.
"Eichmann's Final Prayer." <u>Wind</u> (15:53) 85, p. 14.
"For A.M." <u>KanQ</u> (17:1/2) Wint-Spr 85, p. 254-255.
"Halloween." <u>AntigR</u> (61) Spr 85, p. 28.

3665. OXENDINE, Pam
"Grandma's Flowers." <u>PoetryCR</u> (7:2) Wint 85-86, p. 17.

3666. OXENHANDLER, Noelle
"Only a Child Can Make You Feel So Thin." <u>OhioR</u> (34) 85,
p. 102.

3667. OXENHORN, Harvey
"On Y Danse." <u>NewEngR</u> (8:2) Wint 85, p. 262-264.

3668. OXHOLM, José M.
"Este Llanto." <u>Mairena</u> (7:19) 85, p. 98.

3669. OZAROW, Kent Jorgensen
"Blues Running -- S'Conset Beach." <u>PoetC</u> (17:1) Fall 85,
p. 37.
"Second Hand." <u>PoetC</u> (17:1) Fall 85, p. 36.

3670. OZER, Kemal
"At the Beach" (tr. by O. Yalim, W. Fielder and Dionis
Riggs). <u>NewL</u> (51:4) Sum 85, p. 14.

3671. OZICK, Cynthia
"An Urgent Exhortation to His Admirers and Dignifiers" (. .
. Transcript of an Address before the Mark Twain
Association, by Samuel Clemens, Shade). <u>OP</u> (38/39) Spr
85, p. 134-135.

3672. PACE, Rosalind
"This Is English and I Am Speaking It No Matter What."
<u>ThRiPo</u> (25/26) 85, p. 42.

3673. PACERNICK, Gary
"Omen." <u>CrossCur</u> (5:3) 85, p. 99.
"Turning Inward." <u>CrossCur</u> (4:3) 84, p. 109.

3674. PACEY, Michael
"At My Feet an Orient." <u>Germ</u> (9:1) Spr-Sum 85, p. 29.
"Border Papers." <u>Germ</u> (9:1) Spr-Sum 85, p. 28.

3675. PACHECO, José Emilio
"Aceleración de la Historia." <u>Inti</u> (18/19) Otoño 83-
Prim. 84, p. 258.
"Alta Traición." <u>Inti</u> (18/19) Otoño 83-Prim. 84, p.
258.
"The '&'" (tr. by Linda Scheer). <u>Chelsea</u> (44) 85, p. 161.

"Bitch on Earth" (tr. by Linda Scheer). Chelsea (44) 85,
    p. 159-160.
"Contaminations" (tr. by George McWhirter). PoetryCR
    (7:1) Aut 85, p. 18.
"Crónica de Indias." Inti (18/19) Otoño 83-Prim. 84,
    p. 258-259.
"Daybreak in Buenos Aires" (tr. by George McWhirter).
    PoetryCR (7:1) Aut 85, p. 18.
"Descripción de un Naufragio en Ultramar" (agosto 1966).
    Inti (18/19) Otoño 83-Prim. 84, p. 255-256.
"The Georgia Strait" (tr. by George McWhirter). PoetryCR
    (7:1) Aut 85, p. 18.
"Homenaje a Nezahualcóyotl" (A partir de las traducciones
    de Angel María Garibay y Miguel León-Portilla).
    Inti (18/19) Otoño 83-Prim. 84, p. 262-263.
"Idilio." Inti (18/19) Otoño 83-Prim. 84, p. 259-260.
"In Defense of Anonymity" (a refusal to grant George B.
    Moore an interview, tr. by Linda Scheer). Chelsea (44)
    85, p. 46-48.
"José Luis Cuevas Hace un Autorretrato." Inti (18/19)
    Otoño 83-Prim. 84, p. 261-262.
"Malpaís." Inti (18/19) Otoño 83-Prim. 84, p. 263-264.
"Malpaís" (tr. by Linda Scheer). Chelsea (44) 85, p. 49-
    50.
"Qué Tierra Es Esta" (Homenaje a Juan Rulfo con sus
    palabras). Inti (18/19) Otoño 83-Prim. 84, p. 265-
    268.
"Silence" (tr. by Linda Scheer). Chelsea (44) 85, p. 50.
"Torre de Naipes." Inti (18/19) Otoño 83-Prim. 84, p.
    264-265.
3676. PACK, Robert
"Clayfeld among the Quarks." PraS (59:2) Sum 85, p. 15-17.
"Clayfeld Holds On." Tendril (19/20) 85, p. 290-292.
"Clayfeld Is Summoned." DenQ (20:1) Sum 85, p. 30-32.
"Clayfeld's Campaign." DenQ (20:1) Sum 85, p. 27-29.
"Clayfeld's Duck" (for Mark Strand). QW (21) Fall-Wint
    85, p. 25-27.
"Clayfeld's Madonna." NewEngR (7:3) Spr 85, p. 380-381.
"Clayfeld's Recipe." PraS (59:2) Sum 85, p. 12-14.
"Narrator's Prologue." PraS (59:2) Sum 85, p. 10-12.
3677. PACKIE, Susan
"Canal Cover." SanFPJ (7:2) 85, p. 77.
"Human Rights Testimony." SanFPJ (7:2) 85, p. 80.
"Opportunity?" SanFPJ (7:2) 85, p. 78-79.
"Southern Anachronism." Sam (42:4, 168th release) 85, p.
    36.
3678. PADGETT, Ron
"Dog." Oink (19) 85, p. 67.
"Goethe." Sulfur (13) 85, p. 91.
"The Little Past Midnight Snack." Sulfur (13) 85, p. 92.
"The Rue de Rennes." Oink (19) 85, p. 68.
"The Way of All Handwriting." Sulfur (13) 85, p. 92.
"Who and Each." Sulfur (13) 85, p. 93.
3679. PADHI, Bibhu
"Grandmother's Soliloquy." AntigR (62/63) Sum-Aut 85, p.
    13.
3680. PADILLA, Heberto
"Cuban Poets Have Stopped Dreaming" (tr. by Arnold Odio).
    NewEngR (7:4) Sum 85, p. 603.
"The Man Who Consumes Today's Newspapers" (tr. by Arnold
    Odio). NewEngR (7:4) Sum 85, p. 604.
"Out of the Game" (To Yannis Ritsos, in a Greek jail, tr.
    by Arnold Odio). NewEngR (7:4) Sum 85, p. 602-603.
3681. PAGE, Judith
"The Poem about the Rape." StoneC (13:1/2) Fall-Wint 85-
    86, p. 59.

3682. PAGE, P. K.
        "In Class We Create Ourselves -- Having Been Told to Shut
            Our Eyes and Given a Piece of Plasticene with Which to
            Model a Person" (For Judith). CanLit (105) Sum 85, p.
            6.
        "Suffering." CanLit (105) Sum 85, p. 58.
3683. PAGE, Tom
        "Black Magnolias." MinnR (N.S. 24) Spr 85, p. 61.
3684. PAGE, William
        "Champions." MissR (40/41) Wint 85, p. 128-129.
        "Chrome, Feathers, and Glory." WindO (46) Fall 85, p. 16.
        "How Can I Explain." WebR (10:1) Spr 85, p. 88.
        "Static." WindO (46) Fall 85, p. 16-17.
        "Work." CharR (11:1) Spr 85, p. 81.
3685. PAGIS, Dan
        "The Art of Reduction" (tr. by Shirley Kaufman). NewL
            (51:4) Sum 85, p. 19-20.
        "Seconal" (tr. by Shirley Kaufman). NewL (51:4) Sum 85,
            p. 19-20.
3686. PAGLIARANI, Elio
        "Physic's Lesson" (to Helen, tr. by Giuseppe Perricone).
            LitR (28:2) Wint 85, p. 277-279.
3687. PAINTER, Charlotte
        "The Visiting Poet of Great Charm." OP (38/39) Spr 85, p.
            107.
PAIZ, Juan Bautista
        See BAUTISTA PAIZ, Juan
3688. PALADINO, Thomas
        "Metaphysician at the River." Telescope (4:1) Wint 85, p.
            7.
3689. PALANDER, John
        "Dandy-Long-Legs." AntigR (62/63) Sum-Aut 85, p. 29.
3690. PALAZZESCHI, Aldo
        "Annoying Doubt" (tr. by Annalisa Saccà). LitR (28:2)
            Wint 85, p. 280.
PALCHI, Alfredo de
        See De PALCHI, Alfredo
3691. PALIJ, Lydia
        "Autumn Letters." PoetryCR (6:3) Spr 85, p. 16.
        "First Snow on the Humber." PoetryCR (6:3) Spr 85, p. 16.
        "It Hurts No More." PoetryCR (6:3) Spr 85, p. 16.
        "We Walked." PoetryCR (6:3) Spr 85, p. 16.
        "Winter in Black and White." PoetryCR (6:3) Spr 85, p. 16.
3692. PALLANT, Marilee Lehman
        "An Omnipotent & Nervy Thing to Do" (for June Langford
            Berkley). EngJ (74:4) Ap 85, p. 76.
3693. PALMER, Michael
        "The Baudelaire Series" (5 selections). Temblor (2) 85,
            p. 51-55.
3694. PALMER, William
        "Desire." CentR (29:4) Fall 85, p. 445-446.
3695. PALMER, Winthrop
        "July 4." Confr (30/31) N 85, p. 32.
        "Mill Pond Spring." Confr (30/31) N 85, p. 32.
        "When the Word Was God." Confr (30/31) N 85, p. 21.
3696. PANKEY, Eric
        "The Guard, 1934." Tendril (19/20) 85, p. 296-300.
        "Late August." Tendril (19/20) 85, p. 294-295.
        "Rhododendron." Tendril (19/20) 85, p. 293.
3697. PAOLA, Suzanne
        "Death by Water." StoneC (13:1/2) Fall-Wint 85-86, p. 52-
            53.
        "Fatima." WestB (17) 85, p. 95.
        "Soon." Paint (11:21/12:24) 84-85, p. 11.
        "The Way Down" (St. Patrick's Cathedral, New York 1982).
            CutB (23) Fall-Wint 85, p. 61.

3698. PAOLINI, P. F.
"Am Being Called" (tr. of Luciano Luisi). LitR (29:1)
Fall 85, p. 104.
"Ambiguous Solitude" (tr. of Gabriella Sobrino). LitR
(29:1) Fall 85, p. 120.
"Bridge" (tr. of Enzo Nasso). LitR (29:1) Fall 85, p. 115.
"Casuals" (Excerpt, tr. of Alfredo Giuliani). LitR (28:2)
Wint 85, p. 241.
"Chomsky Poem" (tr. of Alfredo Giuliani). LitR (28:2)
Wint 85, p. 240-241.
"Descriptions Underway" (Excerpt, tr. of Roberto Roversi).
LitR (28:2) Wint 85, p. 304-305.
"Easter at Pieve di Soligo" (tr. of Andrea Zanzotto).
LitR (28:2) Wint 85, p. 320-322.
"Eternity" (tr. of Mauro Mare). LitR (29:1) Fall 85, p.
105.
"The Feast" (tr. of Mauro Mare). LitR (29:1) Fall 85, p.
105.
"Fragment" (tr. of Enzo Nasso). LitR (29:1) Fall 85, p.
115.
"The Franciscan Convent" (Excerpts, tr. of Renato Minore).
LitR (29:1) Fall 85, p. 110-111.
"Friday Even Azure" (tr. of Alfredo Giuliani). LitR
(28:2) Wint 85, p. 239.
"Geometry Is in the Air" (tr. of Elio Filippo Accrocca).
LitR (29:1) Fall 85, p. 92.
"If I Could Know" (tr. of Gabriella Sobrino). LitR (29:1)
Fall 85, p. 119.
"Market -- Damned" (tr. of Daniela Ripetti). LitR (29:1)
Fall 85, p. 116.
"Ménage" (tr. of Mario Luzi). LitR (28:2) Wint 85, p.
251-252.
"My Fair Ladies" (tr. of Daniela Ripetti). LitR (29:1)
Fall 85, p. 116.
"Nostalgia" (tr. of Enzo Nasso). LitR (29:1) Fall 85, p.
114.
"Notifying One's Presence on the Euganean Hills" (tr. of
Andrea Zanzotto). LitR (28:2) Wint 85, p. 318.
"Remembrances" (tr. of Mauro Mare). LitR (29:1) Fall 85,
p. 106.
"Resurrection after the Rain" (tr. of Alfredo Giuliani).
LitR (28:2) Wint 85, p. 241.
"September 13, 1959" (a variant, tr. of Andrea Zanzotto).
LitR (28:2) Wint 85, p. 319.
"Skyey Navigation" (tr. of Andrea Zanzotto). LitR (28:2)
Wint 85, p. 318.
"Songlet" (tr. of Alfredo Giuliani). LitR (28:2) Wint 85,
p. 242.
"To My Father" (tr. of Luciano Luisi). LitR (29:1) Fall
85, p. 104.
"Towards the Imperfect" (tr. of Anna Malfaiera). LitR
(28:2) Wint 85, p. 257-259.
3699. PAPE, Greg
"The Horses of Santo Domingo." MissouriR (8:3) 85, p. 58-
59.
"No Visible Stars." Iowa (15:1) Wint 85, p. 100.
3700. PAPELL, Helen
"At the Street Fair on the South St. Dock." Vis (17) 85,
p. 14.
"The Beggar in the Subway." Vis (18) 85, p. 16.
3701. PAPINCHAK, Robert Allen
"Recovering on the Lawn." KanQ (17:1/2) Wint-Spr 85, p.
259.
3702. PAPPAS, Theresa
"First Night in Athens." PoetC (16:3) Spr 85, p. 10-11.
"Hellas-Souvenir." Abraxas (33) 85, p. 18.

"In America, Grandmother." <u>Abraxas</u> (33) 85, p. 19.
"Main Street." <u>PoetC</u> (16:3) Spr 85, p. 12-13.
"River Styx." <u>Abraxas</u> (33) 85, p. 21.
"Wedding Song." <u>Abraxas</u> (33) 85, p. 20-21.
"Wet." <u>LaurelR</u> (19:2) Sum 85, p. 30.
3703. PARA, Nicanor
"España." <u>LindLM</u> (4:1) Ja-Mr 85, p. 16-17.
3704. PARADIS, Philip
"First Trout." <u>ColEng</u> (47:2) F 85, p. 139.
3705. PARE, Terence P.
"The Shape of Things." <u>Poetry</u> (146:6) S 85, p. 348.
3706. PARFAIR, Daniel
"Loin de Pietraperzia" (tr. of Vincenzo Rindone). <u>Os</u> (21)
    85, p. 11.
"Violence" (tr. of Vincenzo Rindone). <u>Os</u> (21) 85, p. 9.
3707. PARHAM, Robert
"Cops and Detectives." <u>HawaiiR</u> (17) Spr 85, p. 59.
"A Sonnet for Henry." <u>HawaiiR</u> (17) Spr 85, p. 60.
"Told by Candles in Decline." <u>SouthwR</u> (70:1) Wint 85, p.
    70.
"Warm Water Dreams." <u>SoCaR</u> (18:1) Fall 85, p. 90.
"Waxed Paper and Nickel Cokes." <u>SoCaR</u> (18:1) Fall 85, p.
    89.
3708. PARINI, Jay
"The House Not Home." <u>OntR</u> (23) Fall-Wint 85-86, p. 86-88.
"Skiing Home at Dusk." <u>OntR</u> (23) Fall-Wint 85-86, p. 85.
"Solstice, Entering Capricorn." <u>OntR</u> (23) Fall-Wint 85-
    86, p. 89.
3709. PARIS, Cindy
"Slow Dancing with a Burglar." <u>CarolQ</u> (37:3) Spr 85, p.
    68.
3710. PARK, Clara Claiborne
"Refusing to Testify." <u>Comm</u> (112:16) 20 S 85, p. 495.
3711. PARK, In-whan
"As Time Goes By." <u>AntigR</u> (62/63) Sum-Aut 85, p. 76.
"As Time Goes By" (In Korean). <u>AntigR</u> (62/63) Sum-Aut 85,
    p. 77.
3712. PARKER, David G.
"Freeway through the Mountains." <u>Amelia</u> (2:1) Ap 85, p.
    46.
3713. PARKER, Doris
"Professor Bock Recalls His Best Dig." <u>PoetL</u> (79:4) Wint
    85, p. 203-204.
"Trout Don't Walk on the C&O Canal." <u>PoetL</u> (79:4) Wint
    85, p. 204-205.
3714. PARKER, Lizbeth
"Gloria in Excelsis Deo." <u>Bogg</u> (53) 85, p. 24.
3715. PARKER, Martha
"Away from Home." <u>Outbr</u> (14/15) Fall 84-Spr 85, p. 91.
"Borders." <u>DeKalbLAJ</u> (18:1/2) 85, p. 81.
3716. PARKS, Richard
"Dear James." <u>YellowS</u> (16) Aut 85, p. 12.
3717. PARLATO, Stephen
"Do Small Things with Great Love." <u>Open24</u> (4) 85, p. 3.
3718. PARLATORE, Anselm
"Helix at Mecox at Night." <u>Confr</u> (30/31) N 85, p. 188.
3719. PARMETER, Sarah-Hope
"Summer near Point Lobos." <u>CalQ</u> (26) Sum 85, p. 37.
3720. PARRA, Nicanor
"The Anti-Lazarus" (tr. by Edith Grossman). <u>RiverS</u> (18)
    85, p. 40-41.
"At the Rate We're Going" (tr. by Edith Grossman). <u>RiverS</u>
    (18) 85, p. 37.
"Homework" (tr. by Edith Grossman). <u>RiverS</u> (18) 85, p. 38.
"The Man He Imagined" (tr. by Edith Grossman). <u>RiverS</u>
    (18) 85, p. 43.

"The Mistake We Made Was Thinking" (tr. by Edith Grossman).
RiverS (18) 85, p. 37.
"The Poems of the Pope" (tr. by Edith Grossman). RiverS
(18) 85, p. 42.
"Rest in Peace" (tr. by Edith Grossman). RiverS (18) 85,
p. 39.
3721. PARRY, Norm
"Dancing at the Yates." HiramPoR (38) Spr-Sum 85, p. 29.
3722. PARSON, Julie
"Response to Pornography in Literature." Imagine (2:1)
Sum 85, p. 101-103.
3723. PARSONS, Bruce
"My Grandfather Had a Wooden Leg." PottPort (7) 85-86, p.
22-23.
"That Summer Philosophy." PottPort (7) 85-86, p. 14.
3724. PARSONS, J. H.
"Innocence on the Rebound." WormR (25:4, issue 100) 85,
p. 150.
"More Innocence on the Rebound." WormR (25:4, issue 100)
85, p. 151.
"The Neighbors." WormR (25:4, issue 100) 85, p. 150.
"Simple Static." WormR (25:4, issue 100) 85, p. 150.
3725. PARTRIDGE, Dixie
"What We Took from Red Mountain." SouthernHR (19:2) Spr
85, p. 169.
"Why We Climbed." SouthernHR (19:2) Spr 85, p. 144.
3726. PARUN, Vesna
"Coral Returned to the Sea" (tr. by Vesna Dye and Peter
Kastmiler). WebR (10:2) Fall 85, p. 38.
3727. PARVIN, Betty
"Don't Waken Us!" (Etching by Goya of victims of the
Inquisition). Stand (26:2) Spr 85, p. 39.
3728. PASOLINI, Pier Paolo
"To an Unborn Son" (tr. by N. S. Thompson). Verse (1) 84,
p. 43.
3729. PASOS, Joaquín
"Canción de Cama." Inti (18/19) Otoño 83-Prim. 84, p.
18.
"Canto de Guerra de las Cosas." Inti (18/19) Otoño 83-
Prim. 84, p. 11-17.
"Cementerio." Inti (18/19) Otoño 83-Prim. 84, p. 24-25.
"Dulces Seres Monstruosos." Inti (18/19) Otoño 83-Prim.
84, p. 17.
"Los Indios Viejos." Inti (18/19) Otoño 83-Prim. 84, p.
18-19.
"Liebpostal." Inti (18/19) Otoño 83-Prim. 84, p. 24.
"Pasión y Muerte." Inti (18/19) Otoño 83-Prim. 84, p.
20-22.
"Patíbulo." Inti (18/19) Otoño 83-Prim. 84, p. 24.
"Perrito." Inti (18/19) Otoño 83-Prim. 84, p. 19.
"Pintura de la Guerra sobre un Muro." Inti (18/19)
Otoño 83-Prim. 84, p. 22.
"Poema a Pie." Inti (18/19) Otoño 83-Prim. 84, p. 17-18.
"Revolución por el Descubrimiento del Mar." Inti
(18/19) Otoño 83-Prim. 84, p. 22-23.
"Solsticio." Inti (18/19) Otoño 83-Prim. 84, p. 20.
PASQUALE, E. di
See DiPASQUALE, E.
3730. PASTAN, Linda
"Clinic." Agni (22) 85, p. 98.
"Departures." TriQ (63) Spr-Sum 85, p. 665.
"Family Scene: Mid Twentieth Century" (Corrected line).
Ploughs (11:1) 85, p. 238.
"The Flowering of New England." OP (38/39) Spr 85, p. 171.
"Green Thumb." Atlantic (256:3), S 85, p. 58.
"Japanese Lantern." Agni (22) 85, p. 96-97.

"Last Will." <u>VirQ</u> (61:3) Sum 85, p. 425-426.
"Market Day." <u>Poetry</u> (146:1) Ap 85, p. 18.
"Mother Eve." <u>GeoR</u> (39:3) Fall 85, p. 574.
"Orpheus." <u>CrossCur</u> (4:2) 84, p. 11.
"Realms of Gold." <u>MSS</u> (4:3) Spr 85, p. 57-58.
"The Seven Deadly Sins." <u>Poetry</u> (146:1) Ap 85, p. 19-21.
"Snowing: A Triptych." <u>SouthernPR</u> (26, i.e. 25:2) Fall
        85, p. 25-26.
3731. PASTERNAK, Boris
"How life lulls us" (tr. by Mark Rudman and Bohdan
        Boychuk). <u>Pequod</u> (19/20/21) 85, p. 260-263.
3732. PATERSON, Andrea
"April in Colorado." <u>PoetL</u> (80:3) Fall 85, p. 147.
3733. PATT, John
"American Capillary." <u>StoneC</u> (13:1/2) Fall-Wint 85-86, p.
        73.
"The Beggar." <u>SanFPJ</u> (7:2) 85, p. 28.
"No Escape." <u>SanFPJ</u> (7:2) 85, p. 27.
"Smiley." <u>SanFPJ</u> (7:2) 85, p. 26.
3734. PATTEN, Karl
"Winter Possibilities." <u>LaurelR</u> (19:1) Wint 85, p. 36.
3735. PATTERSON, Raymond R.
"Computer Blues." <u>PoetryR</u> (2:2) Ap 85, p. 16.
3736. PATTERSON, Tom
"Bye Basil Bunting" (April 17, 1985). <u>Conjunc</u> (8) 85, p.
        202.
3737. PATTON, David
"Voodoo Won't Work." <u>JamesWR</u> (3:1) Fall 85, p. 11.
3738. PAU-LLOSA, Ricardo
"Battlefields." <u>CarolQ</u> (38:1) Fall 85, p. 13.
"Brooms" (After the photograph by Mario Algaze). <u>Agni</u>
        (22) 85, p. 25.
"Homage to Vesalius" (After the paintings of Armando
        Morales). <u>Ascent</u> (11:1) 85, p. 18.
"The Room." <u>BlackWR</u> (12:1) Fall 85, p. 41.
"The View from Altos de Chavón" (for Dominique). <u>Ascent</u>
        (11:1) 85, p. 19.
"What Is a Face?" <u>BlackWR</u> (12:1) Fall 85, p. 42-43.
3739. PAULENICH, Craig
"Working hte Long Shift." <u>Raccoon</u> (17) Mr 85, p. 41.
3740. PAULSEN, Kathryn
"Dreamers." <u>NewL</u> (51:3) Spr 85, p. 114-115.
3741. PAVESE, Cesare
"The Night You Slept" (tr. by Alan Williamson). <u>Ploughs</u>
        (11:4) 85, p. 54.
"You, Wind of March" (tr. by Alan Williamson). <u>Ploughs</u>
        (11:4) 85, p. 52-53.
3742. PAVLICH, Walter
"Damage Report" (For the Bohunks). <u>Vis</u> (17) 85, p. 16.
"Remembering St. Regis" (for Wayne Challeen, on the West
        Zone Helitack fire crew, St. Regis, Montana). <u>Swallow</u>
        (4) 85, p. 28-29.
"Ruth, Mt. Tabor Nursing Home, 1972." <u>CutB</u> (24) Spr-Sum
        85, p. 50.
3743. PAVLIDES, Lefteris
"The Monogram" (Selection: VII, tr. of Odysseus Elytis, w.
        Edward Morin). <u>NewL</u> (51:4) Sum 85, p. 13.
3744. PAVLOVSKI, Radovan
"The Rebellion of the Seeds" (tr. by Zoran Ancevski and
        James McKinley). <u>NewL</u> (51:4) Sum 85, p. 26.
"The Turtle" (tr. by Zoran Ancevski and James McKinley).
        <u>NewL</u> (51:4) Sum 85, p. 26-27.
3745. PAWLOWSKI, Robert
"Flying Time." <u>LaurelR</u> (19:2) Sum 85, p. 13.
3746. PEABODY, Richard
"Attachments." <u>Bogg</u> (53) 85, p. 17.

"Penelope: The Movie." <u>Bogg</u> (53) 85, p. 11.
3747. PEACOCK, Molly
"Don't Fix It Again." <u>Nat</u> (241:9) 28 S 85, p. 284.
"One Being, One Place." <u>MichQR</u> (24:4) Fall 85, p. 567.
"The Surge." <u>Shen</u> (36:1) 85-86, p. 22.
"There Must Be." <u>MichQR</u> (24:4) Fall 85, p. 565.
"What's Blue and Huge?" <u>MichQR</u> (24:4) Fall 85, p. 566-567.
"Why Are We All Clothed?" <u>NewL</u> (51:3) Spr 85, p. 48-49.
3748. PEARLSON, Fredda S.
"Returning to Ice (Mountain Sounds)." <u>StoneC</u> (12:2/3) Spr-
Sum 85, p. 10.
3749. PEARSON, Jean
"The Birds Sing Best in the Rain" (tr. of Sarah Kirsch).
<u>StoneC</u> (13:1/2) Fall-Wint 85-86, p. 42-43.
"Finding Her Roots, She Starts to Sing." <u>AmerPoR</u> (14:3)
My-Je 85, p. 43.
3750. PEATTIE, Noel
"The Flight Home." <u>SecC</u> (12:2) 84?, p. 4.
3751. PECK, Claude
"Stun." <u>JamesWR</u> (3:1) Fall 85, p. 5.
3752. PECK, Gail J.
"Legacy." <u>MissR</u> (13:3, issue 39) Spr 85, p. 64.
3753. PECK, J. (<u>See also</u> PECK, John)
"Ashes." <u>AntigR</u> (61) Spr 85, p. 126.
3754. PECK, John (<u>See also</u> PECK, J.)
"Campagna." <u>YaleR</u> (74:4) Sum 85, p. 571.
"He, She, All of them, Ay." <u>TriQ</u> (63) Spr-Sum 85, p. 666-
667.
"Interleaved Lines on Jephthah and His Daughter." <u>YaleR</u>
(74:4) Sum 85, p. 570.
"Street of Tents." <u>NewRep</u> (192:3) 21 Ja 85, p. 41.
3755. PECK, Mary
"Unwanted Birth." <u>NegC</u> (5:1) Wint 85, p. 117.
3756. PEDEN, Margaret Sayers
"Man Like a Pomegranate" (tr. of Luisa Valenzuela).
<u>Chelsea</u> (44) 85, p. 94.
"Origin of the Species" (tr. of Luisa Valenzuela).
<u>Chelsea</u> (44) 85, p. 95.
"The Salt of Life" (tr. of Luisa Valenzuela). <u>Chelsea</u>
(44) 85, p. 94.
3757. PEELER, Tim
"An Elegy." <u>Amelia</u> (2:1) Ap 85, p. 59-60.
3758. PELENSKY, Olga
"Home Town." <u>Imagine</u> (2:1) Sum 85, p. 75.
3759. PENDARVIS, Jack
"Muscling in on Valentine's." <u>NegC</u> (5:1) Wint 85, p. 129.
3760. PENFOLD, Nita
"Declaration." <u>Imagine</u> (2:1) Sum 85, p. 90.
"In Grandmother's Garden." <u>Imagine</u> (2:1) Sum 85, p. 91.
3761. PENNANT, Edmund
"Rocky Mountain Triptych." <u>NegC</u> (5:1) Wint 85, p. 63-65.
"Voices." <u>CrossCur</u> (4:2) 84, p. 119.
3762. PENNINGTON, Anne
"The Burning Hands" (tr. of Vasko Popa). <u>TriQ</u> (63) Spr-
Sum 85, p. 96.
"The Dormition of Aunt Menka" (tr. of Blazhe Koneski, w.
Andrew Harvey). <u>SenR</u> (15:1) 85, p. 59.
"The Homeless Head" (tr. of Vasko Popa). <u>TriQ</u> (63) Spr-
Sum 85, p. 96.
3763. PEON, Roberta
"Glass Dialogue." <u>MalR</u> (71) Je 85, p. 26.
3764. PEOPLE'S REPUBLIC OF POETRY
"Antisocial Surrealism." <u>Rampike</u> (4:2/3) 85-86, p. 25.
3765. PEPIN, Mylene
"Land of Morning Calm." <u>PoetryCR</u> (7:2) Wint 85-86, p. 18.
"Red Leaves and Winter." <u>PoetryCR</u> (7:2) Wint 85-86, p. 18.

3766. PEPPER, Pat
      "Slang Dictionary." <u>Bogg</u> (54) 85, p. 40.
3767. PERCHES, Ana
      "Amor." <u>Imagine</u> (2:1) Sum 85, p. 56.
      "Contrato." <u>Imagine</u> (2:1) Sum 85, p. 56.
3768. PERCHIK, Simon
      "Again the sun leading the world by the neck." <u>BelPoJ</u>
         (35:3) Spr 85, p. 20-21.
      "As a narrow breeze." <u>Os</u> (21) 85, p. 27-28.
      "Egg." <u>Confr</u> (30/31) N 85, p. 131.
      "Eight months your heart that blinking flag." <u>Abraxas</u>
         (33) 85, p. 22.
      "Even the sun is terrified." <u>Os</u> (21) 85, p. 28-29.
      "Face up this darkness." <u>Os</u> (21) 85, p. 30-31.
      "Footsteps." <u>Confr</u> (30/31) N 85, p. 132.
      "From this lacquered dish." <u>CapeR</u> (20:2) Fall 85, p. 24.
      "I never saw Death so neat." <u>Bogg</u> (54) 85, p. 41-42.
      "I should ware gloves, these white pages." <u>Mund</u> (16:1/2)
         85, p. 78-80.
      "Listen to Your Tears." <u>Nimrod</u> (29:1) Fall-Wint 85, p. 74.
3769. "PERCHIK, Simon
      "My far garbled, some musician gunned down." <u>Wind</u> (15:53)
         85, p. 37.
3770. PERCHIK, Simon
      "The plumage in this narwhal's side." <u>CapeR</u> (20:2) Fall
         85, p. 25.
      "So Many Bones." <u>SoDakR</u> (23:1) Spr 85, p. 20.
      "This Barbarous Water." <u>Nimrod</u> (29:1) Fall-Wint 85, p. 75.
      "This room needs a door, a knob." <u>RagMag</u> (4:2) Fall 85,
         p. 12.
      "With every omelet some placenta." <u>JlNJPo</u> (8:1) 85, p. 36.
      "You are called Beads." <u>JlNJPo</u> (8:1) 85, p. 37.
      "You are called Beads." <u>RagMag</u> (4:2) Fall 85, p. 13.
      "Your lips overtake." <u>Mund</u> (16:1/2) 85, p. 81.
      "Your name mangled in this gate." <u>JlNJPo</u> (8:1) 85, p. 38.
3771. PERDEW, Kermit
      "No Tell Motel." <u>WoosterR</u> (4) Fall 85, p. 47.
      PEREGRINO, José Flores
         <u>See</u> FLORES PEREGRINO, José
3772. PERELMAN, Bob
      "Anti-Oedipus." <u>Temblor</u> (2) 85, p. 87.
      "Cliff Notes." <u>Temblor</u> (2) 85, p. 88.
      "Fable." <u>Oink</u> (19) 85, p. 74.
      "Streets." <u>Temblor</u> (2) 85, p. 89.
      "Word World." <u>Oink</u> (19) 85, p. 73.
3773. PERET, Benjamin
      "Je Sublime" (Selections: 4 poems -- "The Square of the
         Hypotenuse," "I," "A H," "Nebula," tr. by Rachel Stella
         and John Yau). <u>Sulfur</u> (13) 85, p. 76-79.
3774. PEREZ, Estela
      "Abortion." <u>Imagine</u> (2:1) Sum 85, p. 44.
      "Childbirth" (To Tanya, on her christening day). <u>Imagine</u>
         (2:1) Sum 85, p. 44.
3775. PEREZ, Hidelbrado
      "Mutatis Mutandis" (tr. by John Olver Simon). <u>Chelsea</u>
         (44) 85, p. 89.
3776. PEREZ FIRMAT, Gustavo
      "A Mi Hermano el Impostor." <u>LindLM</u> (4:2) Ap-Je 85, p. 3.
      "Before I Was a Writer." <u>BilingR</u> (11:3) S-D 84, p. 59.
      "Seeing Snow." <u>BilingR</u> (11:3) S-D 84, p. 60.
3777. PERISH, Melanie
      "Fall Thoughts." <u>Swallow</u> (4) 85, p. 95.
3778. PERKINS, James A. (<u>See also</u> PERKINS, James Ashbrook)
      "Antonio Salieri." <u>PoetL</u> (80:2) Sum 85, p. 70-71.
      "December Morning." <u>AntigR</u> (61) Spr 85, p. 83.
      "Spring Encounters the Physics of Light." <u>AntigR</u> (61) Spr

                          85, p. 83.
3779. PERKINS, James Ashbrook (See also PERKINS, James A.)
          "Lambertville Lace." USl (18/19) Wint 85, p. 17.
3780. PERLBERG, Mark
          "The Heron." Hudson (38:2) Sum 85, p. 276.
3781. PERLIS, Alan (See also PERLIS, Alan D.)
          "For Charles." Poem (53) Mr 85, p. 63.
          "Telling Stories." Poem (53) Mr 85, p. 65.
          "Your Passage." Poem (53) Mr 85, p. 64.
3782. PERLIS, Alan D. (See also PERLIS, Alan)
          "A Detailed Autobiography of 500wds or Less." LitR (29:1)
          Fall 85, p. 44-45.
3783. PERLMAN, John
          "For the earliest spikes of lilac." Northeast (Series
          4:2) Fall 85, p. 16.
          "In sun arraying." Northeast (Series 4:2) Fall 85, p. 15.
          "See ! the wind so constant." Northeast (Series 4:2) Fall
          85, p. 17.
3784. PERLMAN, Orren
          "Walking in Galilee." PaintedB (26/27) Sum-Fall 85, p. 34.
3785. PERRICONE, Giuseppe
          "Document" (tr. of Amelia Rosselli). LitR (28:2) Wint 85,
          p. 301-303.
          "Maladie D'Amour" (tr. of Antonio Porta). LitR (28:2)
          Wint 85, p. 295.
          "Physic's Lesson" (to Helen, tr. of Elio Pagliarani).
          LitR (28:2) Wint 85, p. 277-279.
          "The Sources of Deceit" (tr. of Antonio Porta). LitR
          (28:2) Wint 85, p. 296.
3786. PERRIN, Judith N.
          "After the Weekend." KanQ (17:3) Sum 85, p. 96.
          "Diptych, circa 1485, Oil and Tempera on Panel, by
          Memling." KanQ (17:3) Sum 85, p. 96.
3787. PERRY, Elaine
          "The Invention of Eve." Vis (18) 85, p. 36-37.
3788. PERRY, Madilane
          "Carbon Date, Columbia River." SnapD (9:1) Fall 85, p. 61.
3789. PERSAUD, Steve
          "The Versions of John Crow." GreenfR (13:1/2) Fall-Wint
          85, p. 103-104.
3790. PESATA, Susan
          "Song in the Desert." NoDaQ (53:2) Spr 85, p. 218.
3791. PESSOLANO, Linda
          "Late Afternoon City Scene." StoneC (13:1/2) Fall-Wint 85-
          86, p. 65.
3792. PETERS, Mary Ann
          "Chaco Canyon Love Song." KanQ (17:1/2) Wint-Spr 85, p.
          185.
3793. PETERS, Robert
          "Cape Misery." PoetL (80:3) Fall 85, p. 162.
          "Christian Ohlson, Ship's Carpenter." PoetL (80:3) Fall
          85, p. 161.
          "Every Man As His Own Tailor: Preparations for the Escape
          South." PoetL (80:3) Fall 85, p. 159.
          "Kane" (Excerpt). PoetryR (2:2) Ap 85, p. 25-27.
          "Kane Is Dumped into Icy Water." PoetL (80:3) Fall 85, p.
          160.
          "Nippings." TexasR (6:1/2) Spr-Sum 85, p. 40.
          "Playing Seal." MidAR (5:1) 85, p. 125.
3794. PETERSEN, Karen
          "Death to the Fascist Insect Who Preys on the Blood of the
          People." Rampike (4:2/3) 85-86, p. 85.
          "Maybe." AntigR (62/63) Sum-Aut 85, p. 178.
3795. PETERSEN, Paulann
          "I Listen to Alice Walker on a Pocket Radio." Calyx (9:1)
          Spr-Sum 85, p. 9.

3796. PETERSON, Bruce B.
    "Keeping Secrets." ColEng (47:6) O 85, p. 608-609.
3797. PETERSON, Eugene H.
    "Nests in Its Shade." ChrC (102:13) 17 Ap 85, p. 381.
3798. PETERSON, Jim
    "Names That Are Not Names." GreenfR (13:1/2) Fall-Wint
        85, p. 24.
3799. PETERSON, Karen
    "She Cleans His Fish." Prima (9) 85, p. 57.
3800. PETERSON, Mare
    "Muscatel Flats" (To Char). CrabCR (2:2) Wint 85, p. 13.
3801. PETERSON, Marsha
    "August 18, 1980" (for my mother and for my sister, Lue).
        Prima (9) 85, p. 22.
3802. PETESCH, Donald A.
    "For Mr. Federman, a Kosher Butcher." KanQ (17:1/2) Wint-
        Spr 85, p. 187-188.
    "The Girl in the University of Idaho Bookstore." KanQ
        (17:1/2) Wint-Spr 85, p. 186-187.
3803. PETOSKEY, Barbara J.
    "Repertory." CrossCur (4:1) 84, p. 121.
3804. PETRAKOS, Chris
    "Here and Now." PoetryE (18) Fall 85, p. 53.
    "Our World." PoetryE (18) Fall 85, p. 54.
    "Response." PoetryE (18) Fall 85, p. 55-56.
PETRICK, Mary Philipp
    See PHILIPP-PETRICK, Mary
3805. PETRIE, Paul
    "Backyard, West Kingston." ColEng (47:5) S 85, p. 502.
    "Checkmate." KanQ (17:1/2) Wint-Spr 85, p. 260.
    "The Conversation." KanQ (17:1/2) Wint-Spr 85, p. 260-261.
    "The Death of Couperin." Atlantic (256:5), N 85, p. 103.
    "Family at Sundown." PoetryR (5) S 85, p. 73.
    "In the Tower" (For the Earl of Warwick, imprisoned as a
        child, executed in early manhood). SouthernHR (19:2)
        Spr 85, p. 132.
    "Last Words of Don Quixote" ("I am no longer Don Quixote de
        la Mancha"). AmerS (54:2) Spr 85, p. 248-249.
    "Lazarus." PoetryR (5) S 85, p. 72.
    "On a Child's Slate." LitR (29:1) Fall 85, p. 86.
    "Platonic Poem to a Young Girl Just Married." Comm
        (112:13) 12 Jl 85, p. 399.
3806. PETROSKY, Anthony
    "Beginning with a Journal Entry and a History Book."
        Stand (26:2) Spr 85, p. 25.
    "Poem." Stand (26:2) Spr 85, p. 24.
3807. PETROUSKE, Rosalie
    "The Show Must Go On" (The Circus Boss Said). PassN (6:2)
        Spr-Sum 85, p. 14.
3808. PETTEYS, D. F.
    "Gedankenexperiment." LitR (29:1) Fall 85, p. 52.
    "Gulls." LitR (29:1) Fall 85, p. 52.
    "Payment in Kind." Confr (30/31) N 85, p. 165.
3809. PETTINGELL, Phoebe
    "Speech Problems." BelPoJ (35:4) Sum 85, p. 2-4.
3810. PETTIT, Michael
    "Home again." MissouriR (8:3) 85, p. 133-134.
    "So Long, Tuscaloosa." MissouriR (8:2) 85, p. 156-157.
    "Sparrow of Española." MissouriR (8:2) 85, p. 152-153.
    "The Uncompahgre Range." MassR (26:4) Wint 85, p. 577-578.
    "Virginia Evening." MissouriR (8:2) 85, p. 154-155.
    "Watson at the Railroad Crossing." MissouriR (8:3) 85, p.
        130-131.
    "Watson Quits the Track." MissouriR (8:3) 85, p. 132.
PETTS, Will Garrett
    See GARRETT-PETTS, Will

3811. PETTUS, Ruth
       "The Afterlife at Breakfast." <u>Open24</u> (4) 85, p. 5.
       "Lemons." <u>Open24</u> (4) 85, p. 5.
3812. PETURSSON, Hannes
       "A Habitat by the Sea" (Excerpt, tr. by Alan Boucher).
          <u>Vis</u> (19) 85, p. 7.
3813. PEVEAR, Richard
       "The Almond Tree" (tr. of Yves Bonnefoy). <u>NewYorker</u>
          (60:49) 21 Ja 85, p. 36.
       "The Lure of the Threshold" (tr. of Yves Bonnefoy).
          <u>ParisR</u> (27:95) Spr 85, p. 117-126.
       "The River" (tr. of Yves Bonnefoy). <u>Pequod</u> (18) 85, p. 26-
          28.
3814. PFINGSTON, Roger
       "The Buckeye Bush." <u>PaintedB</u> (26/27) Sum-Fall 85, p. 23.
3815. PFLUG, Ursula
       "Alligator Wars." <u>Rampike</u> (4:2/3) 85-86, p. 85.
3816. PHELPS, Dean
       "Endurance." <u>CrossCur</u> (4:4/5:1) 85, p. 31.
3817. PHIFER, Marjorie Maddox
       "Dividing a Dying Woman's Land." <u>Wind</u> (15:54) 85, p. 39.
       "God Goes Fishing." <u>Wind</u> (15:54) 85, p. 39.
       "Moments Before." <u>CreamCR</u> (10:1) 85, p. 60.
3818. PHILIPP-PETRICK, Mary
       "Her Work in the Greenhouse." <u>PassN</u> (6:2) Spr-Sum 85, p.
          21.
3819. PHILLIPPY, Patricia A.
       "Astrophel" (what should have been an elegy). <u>MissouriR</u>
          (8:3) 85, p. 102-105.
       "Bermuda High." <u>MissouriR</u> (8:3) 85, p. 97.
       "The Garden." <u>MissouriR</u> (8:3) 85, p. 99-100.
       "Jewels" (In Three Acts). <u>MissouriR</u> (8:3) 85, p. 101.
       "Monuments." <u>MissouriR</u> (8:3) 85, p. 98.
3820. PHILLIPS, Ben
       "Three Gulls Break Apart." <u>PoetryCR</u> (6:4) Sum 85, p. 17.
3821. PHILLIPS, Dennis
       "The Hero Is Nothing" (Selections: 1-2). <u>Temblor</u> (1) 85,
          p. 117.
       "A World" (Selections: 1-13). <u>Temblor</u> (2) 85, p. 104-109.
3822. PHILLIPS, James
       "The Winds meet at the heart of roads." <u>WebR</u> (10:2) Fall
          85, p. 85.
3823. PHILLIPS, Jayne Anne
       "Counting" (Selections: 11. "Possessions," 12. "Camera,"
          20. "Letters," 22. "Counting"). <u>RiverS</u> (17) 85, p. 24-
          25.
3824. PHILLIPS, Louis
       "Bear in Mind." <u>HawaiiR</u> (18) Fall 85, p. 30.
       "Cristobel Colon, Instead of Setting Sail to India, Runs
          His Morning Errands." <u>HawaiiR</u> (17) Spr 85, p. 54.
       "Freud, in His Garden, Contemplates Suicide." <u>CentR</u>
          (29:3) Sum 85, p. 320-321.
       "I Have No Choice in the Matter." <u>HawaiiR</u> (18) Fall 85,
          p. 31.
       "Lament for the Destruction of Ur." <u>WebR</u> (10:1) Spr 85,
          p. 70.
       "Lord, I Am the Running Man." <u>WindO</u> (46) Fall 85, p. 48-
          49.
       "New Year's Eve, Somewhere in New Jersey." <u>Wind</u> (15:53)
          85, p. 35-36.
       "Noah's Flude." <u>HawaiiR</u> (17) Spr 85, p. 52-53.
3825. PHILLIPS, Robert
       "The Announcing Man." <u>GrahamHR</u> (8) Wint 85, p. 15-16.
       "Old People." <u>ThRiPo</u> (25/26) 85, p. 47.
       "Portrait of a Lady" (Color Snapshot, circa 1960). <u>ThRiPo</u>
          (25/26) 85, p. 46.

"The Wounded Angel." GrahamHR (8) Wint 85, p. 17-19.
3826. PHILLIPS, Walt
"Anima." WindO (45) Spr 85, p. 32.
"Calendar." Amelia (2:1) Ap 85, p. 66.
"Canyon." WindO (45) Spr 85, p. 32.
"Cashier." Amelia (2:1) Ap 85, p. 66.
"The Cup." Sam (42:3, 167th release) 85, p. 32.
"Genius Is Only Resignation in Disguise." Sam (42:3,
    167th release) 85, p. 22.
"Most of a Day." PoeticJ (11) 85, p. 17.
"Places and Times." Amelia (2:2) O 85, p. 32.
"The Relative Silence at 14 Cotter Lane." Sam (42:4,
    168th release) 85, p. 30.
"Rhapsody." Sam (42:4, 168th release) 85, p. 9.
3827. PHILLIS, Randy
"The End of the Line." CutB (23) Fall-Wint 85, p. 54-55.
3828. PHILLIS, Yannis
"Almost Hysteria" (tr. of Nikos Spanias). StoneC (12:2/3)
    Spr-Sum 85, p. 54-55.
3829. PICANO, Felice
"Birth Marks." ConnPR (3:1) 84, p. 31-32.
"Cain and Abel: An Update." ConnPR (3:1) 84, p. 32-33.
3830. PICARD, Maureen
"Long Train Rides." TexasR (6:1/2) Spr-Sum 85, p. 109.
3831. PICCIONE, Anthony
"With Whitman at the Friendship Hotel." Iowa (15:1) Wint
    85, p. 31.
3832. PICHASKE, David (See also PICHASKE, David R.)
"Kawinogans Lake, Ontario 6/7/85" (for Bob Aufenthie, with
    thanks). SpoonRQ (10:4) Fall 85, p. 56.
3833. PICHASKE, David R. (See also PICHASKE, David)
"The Father, Lonely in His Exile, Blesses the Children for
    Whom He Waits." KanQ (17:1/2) Wint-Spr 85, p. 82.
3834. PICKARD, Deanna Louise
"A Gift from Another Country." PassN (6:2) Spr-Sum 85, p.
    7.
3835. PICKARD, Tom
"Spring Tide" (For Basil Bunting, Spring 1900 to Spring
    1985). Conjunc (8) 85, p. 199-200.
3836. PIDGEON, Beverly Brown
"Gardener." Vis (19) 85, p. 18.
3837. PIERCE, Neal
"Trilobites." Wind (15:55) 85, p. 36.
3838. PIERCY, Marge
"Dartmoor." MassR (26:4) Wint 85, p. 544-545.
"The Faithless." Atlantic (255:4), Ap 85, p. 117.
"How Divine Is Forgiving." MassR (26:4) Wint 85, p. 545-
    546.
"Moves on the Ceiling." AmerV (1) 85, p. 16-17.
3839. PIERMAN, Carol J.
"Beginning Perspective." PaintedB (25) Spr 85, p. 5.
"Cinema Vérité." ThRiPo (25/26) 85, p. 44-45.
"Rocket Athletic Boosters." ThRiPo (25/26) 85, p. 43.
PIERO, W. S. di
    See Di PIERO, W. S.
3840. PIKE, Earl C.
"The Intellectual Confronts the Apocalypse." SanFPJ (7:3)
    84 [i.e. 85], p. 46-47.
3841. PILIBOSIAN, Helene
"Acculturation." KanQ (17:1/2) Wint-Spr 85, p. 256.
3842. PILINSZKY, János
"Adominition" (by Ivan Halasz de Beky). Rampike (4:2/3)
    85-86, p. 17.
"Scaffold in Winter" (by Ivan Halasz de Beky). Rampike
    (4:2/3) 85-86, p. 17.
"Through a Whole Life" (by Ivan Halasz de Beky). Rampike

     (4:2/3) 85-86, p. 17.
3843. PILKINGTON, Kevin
     "Falling Asleep in a Town near Beach." Ploughs (11:1) 85,
        p. 170-171.
     "I sit alone in the kitchen" ("Untitled"). Ploughs (11:1)
        85, p. 168-169.
     "More Than Blue and Cloud." Ploughs (11:1) 85, p. 172-173.
     "Walking Home" (Amagansette, L.I.). Ploughs (11:1) 85, p.
        165-167.
3844. PINDAR
     "Olympians 3" (For Theron of Akragas, winner in the chariot
        race, tr. by Elroy L. Bundy, edited and revised by Helen
        Pinkerton). ChiR (35:1) Aut 85, p. 88-90.
PINEDA, Barbara Brinson
     See BRINSON-PINEDA, Barbara
3845. PINEDA, Carlos
     "In Siuna" (tr. by Kent Johnson). MinnR (N.S. 25) Fall
        85, p. 44.
3846. PINEDA, Maria
     "Orlando" (tr. by Kent Johnson). MinnR (N.S. 25) Fall 85,
        p. 43.
3847. PINEGAR, Pat
     "South of Kuwait." Paint (11:21/12:24) 84-85, p. 16-17.
3848. PINKERTON, Helen
     "Olympians 3" (For Theron of Akragas, winner in the chariot
        race, tr. of Pindar by Elroy L. Bundy, edited and
        revised by Helen Pinkerton). ChiR (35:1) Aut 85, p. 88-
        90.
PINO, Salvador Rodriguez del
     See RODRIGUEZ DEL PINO, Salvador
PIÑON, Evangelina Vigil
     See VIGIL-PIÑON, Evangelina
3849. PINSKER, Sanford
     "If Precision Always Had a Point." KanQ (17:1/2) Wint-Spr
        85, p. 173.
     "On Hot Summer Days." CentR (29:3) Sum 85, p. 320.
     "On Hot Summer Days." KanQ (17:1/2) Wint-Spr 85, p. 173.
3850. PINSKY, Robert
     "The Cold." StoneC (12:2/3) Spr-Sum 85, p. 36-37.
     "Flowers." StoneC (12:2/3) Spr-Sum 85, p. 38-39.
     "A Long Branch Song." StoneC (12:2/3) Spr-Sum 85, p. 35.
     "Ralegh's Prizes." StoneC (12:2/3) Spr-Sum 85, p. 43-44.
     "The Saving." StoneC (12:2/3) Spr-Sum 85, p. 45-46.
     "Sonnet." Verse (4) 85, p. 5.
     "The Street." StoneC (12:2/3) Spr-Sum 85, p. 40-42.
     "The Superb Lily." Antaeus (55) Aut 85, p. 144.
     "The Want Bone." Thrpny (6:2, issue 22) Sum 85, p. 7.
     "The Want Bone." Verse (4) 85, p. 5.
3851. PITKIN, Anne
     "Ian, Aged 10, Dying of Cancer." BlueBldgs (9) [85?], p.
        36.
     "Rainbow." BlueBldgs (9) [85?], p. 37.
3852. PITTS, R. Evan
     "Ear Evolution." Open24 (4) 85, p. 46.
3853. PIZARNIK, Alejandra
     "Caminos del Espejo." Inti (18/19) Otoño 83-Prim. 84,
        p. 234-236.
     "El Corazón de lo Que Existe." Inti (18/19) Otoño 83-
        Prim. 84, p. 240.
     "En Esta Noche, en Este Mundo" (a Martha Isabel Moia).
        Inti (18/19) Otoño 83-Prim. 84, p. 241-242.
     "Fragmentos para Dominar el Silencio." Inti (18/19)
        Otoño 83-Prim. 84, p. 233-234.
     "Inminencia." Inti (18/19) Otoño 83-Prim. 84, p. 236.
     "Lazo Mortal." Inti (18/19) Otoño 83-Prim. 84, p. 240.
     "Linterna Sorda." Inti (18/19) Otoño 83-Prim. 84, p.

240.
"Niña en Jardín." <u>Inti</u> (18/19) Otoño 83-Prim. 84,
p. 239.
"Presencia de Sombra." <u>Inti</u> (18/19) Otoño 83-Prim. 84,
p. 243.
"Reloj." <u>Inti</u> (18/19) Otoño 83-Prim. 84, p. 240.
"Rescate." <u>Inti</u> (18/19) Otoño 83-Prim. 84, p. 239.
"Sortilegios." <u>Inti</u> (18/19) Otoño 83-Prim. 84, p. 234.
"El Sueño de la Muerte o el Lugar de los Cuerpos
Poéticos." <u>Inti</u> (18/19) Otoño 83-Prim. 84, p. 237-
239.
"Texto de Sombra." <u>Inti</u> (18/19) Otoño 83-Prim. 84, p.
243.
3854. PIZZINI, Tony
"The Angles of the Eclipse." <u>Amelia</u> (2:1) Ap 85, p. 83.
3855. PLACOTARI, Alexandra
"Platytera" (Byzantize Madonna, tr. by Rae Dalven).
<u>Poetry</u> (145:6) Mr 85, p. 335.
3856. PLANCHAT, Henry-Luc
"A Blaise Cendrars" (tr. of James Sallis). <u>Rampike</u>
(4:2/3) 85-86, p. 45.
3857. PLANCON, Jehan
"Pretty Rosy May Dew" (tr. by W. D. Snodgrass and Michael
Valentin). <u>NegC</u> (5:1) Wint 85, p. 70, 72, 74.
"La Rousée du Joly Mois de May." <u>NegC</u> (5:1) Wint 85, p.
69, 71, 73.
3858. PLANTIER, Thérèse
"If it rains, what will we do?" (tr. by Frances Driscoll).
<u>WebR</u> (10:1) Spr 85, p. 29.
"Night on earth and love" (tr. by Frances Driscoll). <u>WebR</u>
(10:1) Spr 85, p. 30.
"There is no one season to sow the body" (tr. by Frances
Driscoll). <u>WebR</u> (10:1) Spr 85, p. 29.
3859. PLANTOS, Ted
"Names." <u>Waves</u> (13:4) Spr 85, p. 90-91.
3860. PLATH, James
"The Hawk." <u>CreamCR</u> (10:1) 85, p. 44.
3861. PLOURDE, Marc
"Embers and Earth" (Selections: 6 Poems, tr. of Gaston
Miron, w. D. G. Jones). <u>PoetryCR</u> (6:3) Spr 85, p. 23.
3862. PLUMLY, Stanley
"Above Barnesville." <u>Antaeus</u> (55) Aut 85, p. 145-147.
"Against Starlings." <u>ParisR</u> (27:98) Wint 85, p. 126-128.
"The Foundry Garden." <u>OhioR</u> (35) 85, p. 70-71.
3863. PLUMPP, Sterling D.
"First Annual Chicago Blues Festival, 1984." <u>BlackALF</u>
(19:3) Fall 85, p. 121.
"Streets" (for Gregory Powell). <u>BlackALF</u> (19:3) Fall 85,
p. 121-123.
3864. PLYMELL, Charles
"Vernal Equinox" (Excerpt). <u>Bogg</u> (54) 85, p. 43.
3865. POBO, Kenneth
"Building a Shelter." <u>SanFPJ</u> (7:3) 84 [i.e. 85], p. 76.
"Nicaragua." <u>SanFPJ</u> (7:3) 84 [i.e. 85], p. 73.
"Raspberries." <u>IndR</u> (8:1) Wint 85, p. 50.
3866. POENARU, Vasile
"Bas-Relief with Heroes" (tr. of Nichita Stanescu, w. Tom
Carlson). <u>Mund</u> (16:1/2) 85, p. 75.
"Burned Forest" (tr. of Nichita Stanescu, w. Thomas C.
Carlson). <u>StoneC</u> (13:1/2) Fall-Wint 85-86, p. 46-47.
"My Mother and Her Soldier" (tr. of Nichita Stanescu, w.
Tom Carlson). <u>Mund</u> (16:1/2) 85, p. 73.
"Of Course" (tr. of Nichita Stanescu, w. Tom Carlson).
<u>Mund</u> (16:1/2) 85, p. 77.
"Star Roar" (tr. of Petre Ghelmez, w. Tom Carlson). <u>Mund</u>
(16:1/2) 85, p. 59.

3867. POETKER, Audrey
    "For the Poetkers." PraF (6:2) Spr 85, p. 58.
    "The Healer." Quarry (34:3) Sum 85, p. 39-40.
    "The Notorious Other Woman." Quarry (34:3) Sum 85, p. 39.
3868. POIRIER, Thelma
    "Coyote Man." PraF (6:4) Aut-Wint 85, p. 85.
    "Tasunka Topa Naunkewin" (From 1885--A True Story).
        PraF (6:4) Aut-Wint 85, p. 128.
    "Wilderness Begins with a W." PraF (6:4) Aut-Wint 85, p.
        84.
3869. POLENTZ, Kirsten
    "Hard Winter" (DeKalb County High Schools, Literary award
        winners: third place, poetry). DeKalbLAJ (18:3/4) 85,
        p. 47.
3870. POLIZZOTTI, Mark
    "Legend" (tr. of Jean Senac). ParisR (27:96) Sum 85, p.
        136-137.
    "Ode to Black America" (for Marc Baudon, tr. of Jean
        Senac). ParisR (27:96) Sum 85, p. 141-143.
    "Ode to Cernuda" (tr. of Jean Senac). ParisR (27:96) Sum
        85, p. 137-139.
    "Talisman for Patrick" (tr. of Jean Senac). ParisR
        (27:96) Sum 85, p. 139-141.
    "Young Deluge" (K.T. from Oran, tr. of Jean Senac).
        ParisR (27:96) Sum 85, p. 135-136.
3871. POLLAK, Felix
    "Abgesang." Kaleid (10) Spr 85, p. 14.
    "About Some Who Got Away" (tr. of Günter Kunert, w.
        Reinhold Grimm). NewL (51:4) Sum 85, p. 51.
    "Astigmatism." Kaleid (10) Spr 85, p. 14.
    "Bathroom" (tr. of Hans Magnus Enzensberger, w. Reinhold
        Grimm). NewL (51:4) Sum 85, p. 67.
    "The Dark Room" (tr. of Hans Magnus Enzensberger, w.
        Reinhold Grimm). NewL (51:4) Sum 85, p. 65.
    "Dirge for the Apple" (tr. of Hans Magnus Enzensberger, w.
        Reinhold Grimm). NewL (51:4) Sum 85, p. 68.
    "The Divorce" (tr. of Hans Magnus Enzensberger, w. Reinhold
        Grimm). NewL (51:4) Sum 85, p. 66.
    "The Finger." Kaleid (10) Spr 85, p. 17.
    "Galileo." Kaleid (10) Spr 85, p. 16.
    "In Memory of William Carlos Williams" (tr. of Hans Magnus
        Enzensberger, w. Reinhold Grimm). LitR (28:4) Sum 85,
        p. 585.
    "Incident." Kaleid (10) Spr 85, p. 16.
    "Misogyny" (tr. of Hans Magnus Enzensberger, w. Reinhold
        Grimm). LitR (28:4) Sum 85, p. 584.
    "Reality." Kaleid (10) Spr 85, p. 15.
    "Report about Him" (tr. of Günter Kunert, w. Reinhold
        Grimm). NewL (51:4) Sum 85, p. 52-53.
    "Talking Books." Kaleid (10) Spr 85, p. 15.
    "Tunnel Visions." Kaleid (10) Spr 85, p. 15.
    "Waiting Room with Horses." Kaleid (10) Spr 85, p. 17.
3872. POLLITT, Katha
    "Abandoned Poems." NewYorker (61:8) 15 Ap 85, p. 44.
    "Lives of the Nineteenth-Century Poetesses." NewYorker
        (61:38) 11 N 85, p. 44.
    "Maya." GrandS (5:1) Aut 85, p. 149.
    "Milkweed." NewYorker (61:28) 2 S 85, p. 36.
    "Old Sonnets." GrandS (5:1) Aut 85, p. 150.
3873. POLSON, Don
    "Falling Back." PoetryCR (6:3) Spr 85, p. 34.
    "River Home." AntigR (62/63) Sum-Aut 85, p. 162.
    "A Small Ache Healed." PoetryCR (6:3) Spr 85, p. 34.
    "Symbiosis." AntigR (62/63) Sum-Aut 85, p. 163.
3874. POND, Lily
    "I am heavy with desire." YellowS (16) Aut 85, p. 29.

"On the Chapter Titles of Alexander Lowen." YellowS (14)
      Spr 85, p. 32-33.
3875. PONGE, Francis
      "The Jug" (tr. by Larry Weirather). Amelia (2:1) Ap 85,
      p. 40.
3876. PONIEWAZ, Jeff
      "The Tomb of the Unknown Poet." Abraxas (33) 85, p. 45.
3877. PONSOT, Marie
      "The Avignon Train, Afternoon, September." Pequod
      (19/20/21) 85, p. 272-273.
      "I Ask Myself a Few Real Historical Questions." OP (40)
      Fall-Wint 85, p. 3-8.
3878. POOLE, Thomas
      "Easter." Agni (22) 85, p. 38.
3879. POPA, Vasko
      "The Burning Hands" (tr. by Anne Pennington). TriQ (63)
      Spr-Sum 85, p. 96.
      "Give Me Back My Rags" (tr. by Charles Simic and Morton
      Marcus). Ploughs (11:4) 85, p. 181-190.
      "The Homeless Head" (tr. by Anne Pennington). TriQ (63)
      Spr-Sum 85, p. 96.
3880. PORRAS LOPEZ, Yolanda
      "My Cottage by the Sea." Imagine (2:1) Sum 85, p. 57.
      "Nightfall." Imagine (2:1) Sum 85, p. 57.
3881. PORTA, Antonio
      "Maladie D'Amour" (tr. by Giuseppe Perricone). LitR
      (28:2) Wint 85, p. 295.
      "The Sources of Deceit" (tr. by Giuseppe Perricone). LitR
      (28:2) Wint 85, p. 296.
3882. PORTER, Anne
      "A Biography of Flowers." Comm (112:9) 3 My 85, p. 266.
      "Four Seasons Carol." Comm (112:9) 3 My 85, p. 266.
      "My Anastasia." Comm (112:21) 29 N 85, p. 674-675.
      "November Sunrise." Comm (112:9) 3 My 85, p. 267.
      "Oaks and Squirrels, Genesis 18:27." Comm (112:9) 3 My
      85, p. 267.
      "Refugee Servant." Comm (112:9) 3 My 85, p. 267.
3883. PORTER, Caryl
      "Homage to Johann Sebastian" (Three Centuries Later)."
      ChrC (102:10) 20-27 Mr 85, p. 299.
      "She Answers the Philosopher's Letter." NegC (5:3) Sum
      85, p. 49.
      "Shoes." ChrC (102:1) 2-9 Ja 85, p. 13.
3884. PORTER, Josie
      "3.00 A.M." HangL (47) Spr 85, p. 61.
      "Portrait of the Artist." HangL (47) Spr 85, p. 61.
PORTER, Patricia McKenzie
      See McKENZIE-PORTER, Patricia
3885. PORTER, Peter
      "Susannah and the Elders." Poetry (146:4) Jl 85, p. 209-
      210.
      "To Be on the Safe Side." Poetry (146:4) Jl 85, p. 210-
      211.
3886. PORTLEY, Fran
      "Decision Time." StoneC (12:2/3) Spr-Sum 85, p. 31.
3887. PORTMAN, Clem
      "Crossing the Border." Wind (15:55) 85, p. 7.
3888. POSNER, David
      "Deep-Sea Study" (for Robert Wishoff). Chelsea (44) 85,
      p. 74-76.
3889. POST, Ron
      "Channel Course." CrabCR (2:2) Wint 85, p. 7.
3890. POSTER, Carol
      "Interlude." BallSUF (26:2) Spr 85, p. 66.
3891. POTASH, L.
      "The Sunshine Warriors." SanFPJ (7:2) 85, p. 88.

3892. POTTER, Carol
"The Children Who Haven't Stopped Moving." <u>MissouriR</u>
(8:2) 85, p. 99.
"Diving the Shoals" (for Msika). <u>MissouriR</u> (8:2) 85, p.
105.
"News from the North" (for my brother). <u>MissouriR</u> (8:2)
85, p. 103-104.
"Releasing the Herd." <u>MissouriR</u> (8:2) 85, p. 100-101.
"Tales of a Four-Legged Land." <u>MissouriR</u> (8:2) 85, p. 106-
107.
"That Not So Certain Feeling." <u>MissouriR</u> (8:2) 85, p. 102.
"Un-Buckling the Lines." <u>MassR</u> (26:1) Spr 85, p. 157.
3893. POTTIER, Anna
"To the Broad-Hipped Italian Woman." <u>CanLit</u> (106) Fall
85, p. 54.
3894. POULIN, A., Jr.
"And There Was Light" (tr. of Anne Hébert). <u>GrahamHR</u>
(9) Fall 85, p. 43-44.
"Cities Setting Out" (tr. of Anne Hébert). <u>GrahamHR</u> (9)
Fall 85, p. 39.
"Crown of Joy" (tr. of Anne Hébert). <u>GrahamHR</u> (9) Fall
85, p. 40.
"End of the World" (tr. of Anne Hébert). <u>AmerPoR</u> (14:2)
Mr-Ap 85, p. 19.
"Noel" (tr. of Anne Hébert). <u>AmerPoR</u> (14:2) Mr-Ap 85,
p. 20.
"The Offended" (tr. of Anne Hébert). <u>GrahamHR</u> (9) Fall
85, p. 42.
"Original Earth" (tr. of Anne Hébert). <u>GrahamHR</u> (9)
Fall 85, p. 41.
"Rain" (tr. of Anne Hébert). <u>AmerPoR</u> (14:2) Mr-Ap 85,
p. 19.
3895. POUND, Ezra
"Credo." <u>Iowa</u> (15:2) Spr-Sum 85, p. 2.
3896. POUND, Omar
"Battle with Demons." <u>AntigR</u> (62/63) Sum-Aut 85, p. 33.
"Do not write too clearly." <u>Conjunc</u> (8) 85, p. 201.
"Hopi Spring Song." <u>AntigR</u> (62/63) Sum-Aut 85, p. 34.
"On a Poet Who Watches Paintings Go By" (for R.E.S.).
<u>AntigR</u> (62/63) Sum-Aut 85, p. 33.
"Standing outside my hut I gaze." <u>Conjunc</u> (8) 85, p. 201.
"Tit for Tat" (940 A.D.). <u>Conjunc</u> (8) 85, p. 201.
3897. POWELL, Amanda
"Consuelo" (for Chelo de Muñoz). <u>Imagine</u> (2:1) Sum 85,
p. 94.
"Philosophical Satire" (tr. of Sor Juana Inés de la
Cruz). <u>Imagine</u> (2:1) Sum 85, p. 95-96.
3898. POWELL, Gregory
"Fragments of a Dream" (for Martin Luther King, Jr.).
<u>BlackALF</u> (19:3) Fall 85, p. 124-125.
3899. POWELL, Janice L.
"Don't Tell Me." <u>SanFPJ</u> (7:3) 84 [i.e. 85], p. 26-27.
"The Miracle of Me." <u>SanFPJ</u> (7:3) 84 [i.e. 85], p. 25.
3900. POWELL, Jim
"Inscriptions" (a letter, for my sister, Kath). <u>Thrpny</u>
(5:4, issue 20) Wint 85, p. 10.
"It Was Fever That Made the World." <u>ParisR</u> (27:97) Fall
85, p. 109-110.
"Memory, Recognition." <u>ParisR</u> (27:97) Fall 85, p. 113-114.
"Revisiting the Haight." <u>ParisR</u> (27:97) Fall 85, p. 111-
112.
3901. POWELL, Joseph
"Ode to Simplicity." <u>HawaiiR</u> (18) Fall 85, p. 85.
"Something Visible." <u>Poetry</u> (146:6) S 85, p. 335.
"Stevens in a Stark Wood." <u>HawaiiR</u> (18) Fall 85, p. 86-87.

3902. POWELL, Lynn
    "Descant." <u>CarolQ</u> (38:1) Fall 85, p. 38-39.
3903. POWER, Marjorie
    "Her Clues." <u>CutB</u> (23) Fall-Wint 85, p. 42.
    "P.T.A. Matron Greets Poet." <u>CapeR</u> (20:1) Spr 85, p. 5.
3904. POWERS, Jack
    "My God Don't Hate Gooks." <u>Sam</u> (42:3, 167th release) 85,
       p. 40.
3905. POWERS, John Margaret
    "Carving a Crooked Line of Apartheid with Their Flight."
       <u>Sam</u> (41:4, 164rd release) 85, p. 2-4.
3906. POYNER, Ken
    "The Carnival." <u>PoetL</u> (80:3) Fall 85, p. 167.
    "The Gift." <u>Wind</u> (15:53) 85, p. 30-31.
    "The Primitive." <u>WestB</u> (16) 85, p. 24.
3907. POZARZYCKI, Julia Rhodes
    "Watching the Storm." <u>CrossCur</u> (4:4/5:1) 85, p. 165.
3908. PRATT, C. W.
    "Balloon Flight." <u>Comm</u> (112:6) 22 Mr 85, p. 186.
    "Evening Meditation in a Cathedral Town." <u>Comm</u> (112:6) 22
       Mr 85, p. 186.
    "The Quiet of the Country." <u>LitR</u> (29:1) Fall 85, p. 42.
    "Two Poets in Vermont." <u>LitR</u> (29:1) Fall 85, p. 43.
    "Winter Squash." <u>PoetryNW</u> (26:1) Spr 85, p. 40.
3909. PREISLER, Juliane
    "Ind" (Excerpt, tr. by Jorgen Christian Hansen). <u>Verse</u>
       (3) 85, p. 43.
3910. PRELER, Horacio
    "Baratijas." <u>Mairena</u> (7:19) 85, p. 51.
    "Casa Vacia." <u>Mairena</u> (7:19) 85, p. 55.
    "La Hoja del Otoño." <u>Mairena</u> (7:19) 85, p. 54.
    "Laderas." <u>Mairena</u> (7:19) 85, p. 51.
    "Oficio." <u>Mairena</u> (7:19) 85, p. 54.
    "Paises." <u>Mairena</u> (7:19) 85, p. 53.
    "Penurias Personales." <u>Mairena</u> (7:19) 85, p. 52.
    "Proyeccion." <u>Mairena</u> (7:19) 85, p. 53.
    "Residuos de la Muerte." <u>Mairena</u> (7:19) 85, p. 55.
    "Las Urnas." <u>Mairena</u> (7:19) 85, p. 52.
3911. PREUSS, R. S.
    "Atmosphere." <u>GreenfR</u> (13:1/2) Fall-Wint 85, p. 170.
    "Yes, It Persists." <u>GreenfR</u> (13:1/2) Fall-Wint 85, p. 169-
       170.
3912. PREVERT, Jacques
    "Free Pass" (tr. by Harriet Zinnes). <u>Oink</u> (19) 85, p. 44.
    "Signs" (tr. by Harriet Zinnes). <u>Oink</u> (19) 85, p. 44.
3913. PRICE, Alice L.
    "January's Two Faces." <u>Nimrod</u> (28:2) Spr-Sum 85, p. 128.
    "Twice-Born" (for Ruth Nelson and Philip Kaiser). <u>Nimrod</u>
       (28:2) Spr-Sum 85, p. 126-127.
3914. PRICE, Gale
    "7 Questions." <u>SanFPJ</u> (7:2) 85, p. 94-96.
    "Firecracker." <u>SanFPJ</u> (7:3) 84 [i.e. 85], p. 50.
    "Old Friends." <u>Wind</u> (15:55) 85, p. 18.
    "Upstream." <u>SanFPJ</u> (7:3) 84 [i.e. 85], p. 51.
3915. PRICE, Reynolds
    "Hawk Hill." <u>Poetry</u> (147:2) N 85, p. 99.
    "Lighthouse, Mosquito Inlet." <u>Poetry</u> (147:2) N 85, p. 98.
    "Rincón." <u>Poetry</u> (147:2) N 85, p. 97.
3916. PRICE, Ron
    "After a Storm." <u>PaintedB</u> (26/27) Sum-Fall 85, p. 65.
    "All Things Come." <u>PaintedB</u> (26/27) Sum-Fall 85, p. 70.
    "Brother Song." <u>PaintedB</u> (26/27) Sum-Fall 85, p. 64.
    "Brother Songs." <u>PaintedB</u> (26/27) Sum-Fall 85, p. 67-69.
    "Elegy for My Father." <u>AmerPoR</u> (14:3) My-Je 85, p. 44-45.
    "Rita Warns Her Daughter-in-Law." <u>PaintedB</u> (26/27) Sum-
       Fall 85, p. 63.

"Singing the Blues" (For Ma Rainey III). <u>PaintedB</u> (26/27)
    Sum-Fall 85, p. 60.
"Singing to Everything around Us." <u>PaintedB</u> (26/27) Sum-
    Fall 85, p. 61.
"Sitting on an Eastern Bluff along the Mississippi River."
    <u>PaintedB</u> (26/27) Sum-Fall 85, p. 66.
"Three Kinds of Inheritance." <u>PaintedB</u> (26/27) Sum-Fall
    85, p. 62.
3917. PRICE, Trevor
"Portrait of the Artist As a False Prophet." <u>PoetryCR</u>
    (7:1) Aut 85, p. 51.
3918. PRICE-GRESTY, David
"The Hum." <u>Amelia</u> (2:1) Ap 85, p. 11-12.
"Rehearsal." <u>Amelia</u> (2:1) Ap 85, p. 12-13.
3919. PRIEST, Robert
"If You Just Want to Drop Something." <u>Waves</u> (13:2/3) Wint
    85, p. 75.
"My Huge Voice." <u>Waves</u> (13:2/3) Wint 85, p. 76.
"Wedding Poem." <u>Waves</u> (13:2/3) Wint 85, p. 74.
3920. PRIMM, Sandy
"Sunset over Beaver Creek." <u>NoDaQ</u> (53:4) Fall 85, p. 221-
    222.
3921. PRITCHETT, Frances
"Freely in hidden fire" (Ghazal, tr. of Ghalib). <u>NewL</u>
    (51:4) Sum 85, p. 126-127.
"I'll go live somewhere" (Ghazal, tr. of Ghalib). <u>NewL</u>
    (51:4) Sum 85, p. 127.
"Stanzas from Ghalib" (tr. of Ghalib). <u>NewL</u> (51:4) Sum
    85, p. 127-130.
3922. PRIVETT, Katharine
"A Matter of Education" (for Austin). <u>CreamCR</u> (10:2)
    [85?], p. 58-59.
3923. PROCSAL, Gloria H.
"Three Runners" (Senryu and haiku). <u>WindO</u> (46) Fall 85,
    p. 26.
"Wild Animal Park." <u>PoeticJ</u> (9) 85, p. 10.
3924. PROPER, Stan
"At What Time Hence?" <u>SanFPJ</u> (7:2) 85, p. 22-23.
"Cambridge Plan." <u>SanFPJ</u> (7:3) 84 [i.e. 85], p. 71.
"Give Me Your Hungry." <u>SanFPJ</u> (7:4) 85, p. 45.
"Green Grenada." <u>SanFPJ</u> (7:4) 85, p. 16.
"Isolation." <u>PoeticJ</u> (12) 85, p. 39.
"Labor Day Surge." <u>SanFPJ</u> (7:3) 84 [i.e. 85], p. 70.
"Rat Race." <u>SanFPJ</u> (7:2) 85, p. 24.
"The Ultimate Bomb." <u>SanFPJ</u> (7:2) 85, p. 21.
"Until the Bomb." <u>SanFPJ</u> (7:2) 85, p. 25.
3925. PROPHET, Barry
"Hypothesis, Hypothalamus." <u>Rampike</u> (4:2/3) 85-86, p. 27.
3926. PROSPERE, Susan
"Passion." <u>Antaeus</u> (55) Aut 85, p. 150.
"Sophronia and the Wild Turkey." <u>Nat</u> (240:11) 23 Mr 85,
    p. 342.
"Star of Wonder." <u>Antaeus</u> (55) Aut 85, p. 148-149.
3927. PROVOST, Sarah
"Obie." <u>MassR</u> (26:1) Spr 85, p. 117.
"PFC." <u>HolCrit</u> (22:2) Ap 85, p. 18.
3928. PRUITT, Gladys
"My Grandmother's Hand." <u>PoeticJ</u> (11) 85, p. 2-3.
3929. PRUITT, Paul
"The Medium." <u>NegC</u> (5:2) Spr 85, p. 121.
3930. PRUNTY, Wyatt
"Rooms without Walls." <u>Tendril</u> (19/20) 85, p. 301-303.
"Sleep." <u>NewRep</u> (192:12) 25 Mr 85, p. 36.
"What Doesn't Go Away." <u>Verse</u> (2) 85, p. 7.
"The Whore Mother." <u>PraS</u> (59:2) Sum 85, p. 61-62.

3931. PUCKETT, John R.
    "Clear." KanQ (17:1/2) Wint-Spr 85, p. 259.
    "Shine." KanQ (17:1/2) Wint-Spr 85, p. 258.
3932. PUEBLA, Manuel de la
    "Viene de Adentro." Mairena (7:19) 85, p. 86.
3933. PULTZ, Constance
    "Marcher." SanFPJ (7:4) 85, p. 96.
    "Rift." StoneC (13:1/2) Fall-Wint 85-86, p. 54.
    "Riot." Sam (42:4, 168th release) 85, p. 18.
    "Urban Renewal." Sam (42:4, 168th release) 85, p. 26.
    "The Year of St. Swithin." StoneC (13:1/2) Fall-Wint 85-
        86, p. 55.
3934. PUMPHREY, Patricia
    "Eve Knows." Amelia (2:2) O 85, p. 79.
3935. PURDY, Al
    "Death Approaches." CrossC (7:1) 85, p. 7.
    "For Steve McIntyre, 1912-1984." PoetryCR (6:4) Sum 85,
        p. 27.
    "Home Thoughts." PoetryCR (6:4) Sum 85, p. 27.
    "Letter to Morley Callaghan." PoetryCR (6:4) Sum 85, p.
        27.
    "The Mother." PoetryCR (6:4) Sum 85, p. 27.
    "Orchestra." CrossC (7:1) 85, p. 6.
    "Yes and No." CrossC (7:1) 85, p. 6-7.
3936. PURSIFULL, Carmen M.
    "Compose Me." RevChic (13:1) Spr 85, p. 48.
    "P. Is for Pedophile." RevChic (13:1) Spr 85, p. 47.
3937. PYLE, Dan
    "Summery Paragraph." EngJ (74:8) D 85, p. 60.
3938. PYRCZ, Heather
    "Windsurfer Lost on Fundy." PottPort (7) 85-86, p. 9.
QING, Ai
    See AI, Qing
3939. QUAGLIANO, Tony
    "The Condo Marxist." HawaiiR (18) Fall 85, p. 77.
    "Post Op." HawaiiR (18) Fall 85, p. 76.
    "To Kerouac" (August 1982). MoodySI (15) Spr 85, p. 4.
3940. QUALLS, Becky
    "But with No Moon." DeKalbLAJ (18:1/2) 85, p. 82.
3941. QUASIMODO, Salvatore
    "Milan, August 1943" (tr. by Rina Ferrarelli). NewL
        (51:4) Sum 85, p. 165.
3942. QUENEAU, Raymond
    "Hand on Pen" (In French and English, tr. by Teo Savory).
        CrossCur (4:4/5:1) 85, p. 128-129.
    "Homage to Gertrude Stein" (tr. by Elton Glaser).
        GrahamHR (9) Fall 85, p. 64.
    "Homage to Jacques Prèvert" (tr. by Elton Glaser).
        GrahamHR (9) Fall 85, p. 65.
    "Memory" (tr. by Elton Glaser). GrahamHR (9) Fall 85, p.
        67.
    "Pro and Con" (tr. by Elton Glaser). GrahamHR (9) Fall
        85, p. 66.
    "School of the Soldier" (tr. by Elton Glaser). GrahamHR
        (9) Fall 85, p. 68.
3943. QUIGG, Peter
    "Winter Roofs." PoetryR (5) S 85, p. 66.
3944. QUILTER, Sarah M.
    "Church at Abo." Poem (54) N 85, p. 48.
    "New Romance." Poem (54) N 85, p. 49.
    "Saving Grace." Poem (54) N 85, p. 47.
3945. QUINN, Bernetta (Sister)
    "For Primus St. John." NewL (51:3) Spr 85, p. 95.
    "Gerard Manley Hopkins." GreenfR (13:1/2) Fall-Wint 85,
        p. 153.
    "Here in Your Wheelchair." KanQ (17:4) Fall 85, p. 20.

QUINN 324

"To Ezra Pound, before the Sun Rose." <u>NewL</u> (51:3) Spr 85, p. 95.
3946. QUINN, Doris Kerns
"Summer at the Core." <u>Wind</u> (15:54) 85, p. 40.
"The Unexpected Tribute." <u>Wind</u> (15:54) 85, p. 40-42.
3947. QUINN, Fran
"Delano's Bar and Restaurant, Amherst, Mass, Good Friday, 1984" (1:25 P.M.). <u>PaintedB</u> (26/27) Sum-Fall 85, p. 19.
"Why They Told Us What They Have." <u>PaintedB</u> (26/27) Sum-Fall 85, p. 18.
3948. QUINN, James P.
"Runner's Axis." <u>WindO</u> (46) Fall 85, p. 45-46.
"When Love Is" (For Pat). <u>PoeticJ</u> (11) 85, p. 21.
3949. QUINN, John (<u>See also</u> QUINN, John R. & John Robert)
"All Free Will and No St. Francis." <u>ThRiPo</u> (25/26) 85, p. 48.
"Mendeltna Creek: Down from Old Man Lake." <u>CutB</u> (24) Spr-Sum 85, p. 46.
"Odd-Man-Out." <u>CutB</u> (24) Spr-Sum 85, p. 47.
"The Printer's Hands" (for Harry Duncan). <u>PoetryR</u> (5) S 85, p. 51.
3950. QUINN, John R. (<u>See also</u> QUINN, John & John Robert)
"Summer Kitchen." <u>KanQ</u> (17:4) Fall 85, p. 127.
3951. QUINN, John Robert (<u>See also</u> QUINN, John & John R.)
"Good Morning." <u>KanQ</u> (17:1/2) Wint-Spr 85, p. 261.
"Monuments." <u>KanQ</u> (17:1/2) Wint-Spr 85, p. 261.
"Together." <u>ChrC</u> (102:17) 15 My 85, p. 493.
3952. QUINN, Shelley
"Les Irreals Omegues" (Selection: XVI, tr. of Foix, J. V.). <u>AntigR</u> (61) Spr 85, p. 55.
3953. QUIÑONES, Magaly
"Lluvia." <u>BilingR</u> (11:2) My-Ag 84 [c1986], p. 14.
3954. QUIROGA, J. (<u>See also</u> QUIROGA, Jose)
"Seran." <u>LindLM</u> (4:2) Ap-Je 85, p. 26.
3955. QUIROGA, Jose (<u>See also</u> QUIROGA, J.)
"Octubre." <u>LindLM</u> (4:4) O-D 85, p. 13.
3956. R. C. (<u>See also</u> CLOKE, Richard)
22 poems. <u>SanFPJ</u> (7:2-4) 85.
3957. RA, Carol
"My Brother's Keeper." <u>PassN</u> (6:2) Spr-Sum 85, p. 18.
3958. RAAB, Lawrence
"Desire and Revenge." <u>Crazy</u> (26) Spr 84, p. 12.
"Romanticism." <u>Crazy</u> (26) Spr 84, p. 13.
"What We Should Have Known." <u>OhioR</u> (34) 85, p. 87.
3959. RABINOWITZ, Paula
"All Summer Long." <u>PassN</u> (6:1) Fall-Wint 85, p. 10.
3960. RABORG, Frederick A., Jr.
"Big Trees." <u>PoeticJ</u> (11) 85, p. 43.
"Conyland." <u>CrabCR</u> (3:1) Fall-Wint 85, p. 21.
"The Dark, and the Man upon the Bridge." <u>Open24</u> (4) 85, p. 48.
"A Long Story." <u>Bogg</u> (54) 85, p. 29-30.
"Modeling Clay." <u>DeKalbLAJ</u> (18:1/2) 85, p. 82.
"The Morning Moon." <u>PoeticJ</u> (12) 85, p. 17.
"The Patron." <u>Wind</u> (15:55) 85, p. 42.
"Queenie on Her Haunted Corner." <u>ClockR</u> (2:2) 85, p. 14.
"That Last Letter from a Friend." <u>PoeticJ</u> (10) 85, p. 26.
3961. RACHEL, Naomi
"Early Spring: Cultural Practices in Our Community." <u>Wind</u> (15:53) 85, p. 38-39.
"To the Dark." <u>PoetryR</u> (2:2) Ap 85, p. 75-76.
RACHEWILTZ, Mary de
<u>See</u> De RACHEWILTZ, Mary
3962. RACINE, Jean Baptiste
"Phaedra" (Selections: Scene 2 & 5, tr. by Richard Wilbur).

Ploughs (11:4) 85, p. 99-108.
3963. RADAIKIN, Norine
"Good Man." KanQ (17:4) Fall 85, p. 104.
3964. RADISON, Garry
"As a Lover." Grain (13:2) My 85, p. 47.
"Dream of Survival." Grain (13:2) My 85, p. 46.
"Reflections on Oedipus, Gloucester, et al." Grain (13:2)
My 85, p. 46-47.
3965. RADKE, Don Van
"Still Life." SouthwR (70:4) Aut 85, p. 545.
3966. RADNER, Rebecca
"Apartment Building." MinnR (N.S. 24) Spr 85, p. 89.
"Signs, Blessings." NegC (5:2) Spr 85, p. 43.
3967. RADTKE, Rosetta
"Invitation." PassN (6:2) Spr-Sum 85, p. 15.
3968. RADU, Kenneth
"Bad Weather." AntigR (61) Spr 85, p. 86.
"Bird in the Hall." AntigR (61) Spr 85, p. 84.
"The Frog Prince." AntigR (62/63) Sum-Aut 85, p. 143-144.
"Letters." MalR (72) S 85, p. 110-112.
"Priorities." AntigR (61) Spr 85, p. 85.
3969. RAFFA, Joseph
"Remembering Childhood." DeKalbLAJ (18:3/4) 85, p. 42.
3970. RAFFANIELLO, Robert
"Thornbush." Confr (30/31) N 85, p. 267.
3971. RAGAN, James
"Let's Say You Like Horses." CrossCur (5:3) 85, p. 117.
3972. RAHMANN, Pat
"The Big Bad Wolf." KanQ (17:4) Fall 85, p. 19.
"The Great Ape House" (Chicago's Lincoln Park, "Second to
None"). KanQ (17:4) Fall 85, p. 20.
3973. RAINE, Craig
"The Explorers." Poetry (146:4) Jl 85, p. 193-196.
3974. RAISOR, Philip
"Hoosier Schoolmaster." MidwQ (26:4) Sum 85, p. 466.
3975. RAIZISS, S.
"& as in the bible I betroth" (tr. of Alfredo de Palchi).
NewL (51:4) Sum 85, p. 162.
"In the fluster of buds & birds" (tr. of Alfredo de
Palchi). NewL (51:4) Sum 85, p. 162.
"Smokestacks fertilizer" (tr. of Alfredo de Palchi). NewL
(51:4) Sum 85, p. 162.
3976. RAKOSI, Carl
"A Man of Unwavering Integrity." Oink (19) 85, p. 60.
"A Minor Poet Not Conspicuoulsy Dishonest." Conjunc (8)
85, p. 153.
"Modules." Sulfur (13) 85, p. 42-43.
"The Natives Are Restless Tonight." Oink (19) 85, p. 60.
"Parallel Lines Crossing in a Mystique" (from Homages).
Oink (19) 85, p. 61.
3977. RALEIGH, Richard
"All of God's Children." CumbPR (5:1) Fall 85, p. 50.
"Las Casas Colgadas." CumbPR (5:1) Fall 85, p. 48-49.
"The Philosopher." WindO (45) Spr 85, p. 29.
"Royal Couple." Vis (17) 85, p. 41.
3978. RAMANUJAN, A. K.
"Extended Family." AmerS (54:2) Spr 85, p. 181-182.
3979. RAMASWAMI, M. S.
"Reconsideration" (tr. of Atmanam). Stand (26:3) Sum 85,
p. 6.
RAMIREZ BERG, Charles
See BERG, Charles Ramirez
3980. RAMKE, Bin
"According to Ovid." Poetry (147:1) O 85, p. 11.
"The Cats of Balthus." DenQ (19:3) Wint 85, p. 30-31.
"Home for the Funeral." OhioR (35) 85, p. 97-99.

"Hospital Food." <u>Shen</u> (36:1) 85-86, p. 87-89.
"Il Pleure dans la Ville." <u>DenQ</u> (19:3) Wint 85, p. 32.
"The Language Student." <u>DenQ</u> (20:1) Sum 85, p. 41.
"The Last of the Lullabies." <u>OhioR</u> (35) 85, p. 93-94.
"A Man Tells a Story." <u>MissR</u> (40/41) Wint 85, p. 120-121.
"The Man Whose Wife Had Hobbies." <u>MissR</u> (40/41) Wint 85,
     p. 122.
"Optical Illusion." <u>CrossCur</u> (5:3) 85, p. 135.
"A Polite Young Man in Therapy." <u>DenQ</u> (19:3) Wint 85, p.
     29.
"Sine and Cosine." <u>GeoR</u> (39:4) Wint 85, p. 784.
"The Triumph of the Narrow-Minded Novelist." <u>DenQ</u> (20:1)
     Sum 85, p. 42-43.
"Why We Must Forgive One Another." <u>OhioR</u> (35) 85, p. 95-
     96.
RAMOS, Reinaldo Garcia
     <u>See</u> GARCIA RAMOS, Reinaldo
RAMOS ROSA, Antônio
     <u>See</u> ROSA, Antônio Ramos
3981. RAMSEY, Paul
     "Death in the Museum." <u>ArizQ</u> (41:3) Aut 85, p. 270.
3982. RANDALL, Dudley
     "Love Song of a Hippo." <u>OP</u> (38/39) Spr 85, p. 184.
3983. RANDALL, Julia
     "Moving in Memory." <u>AmerPoR</u> (14:2) Mr-Ap 85, p. 14-15.
     "The Wilderness of This World." <u>AmerPoR</u> (14:2) Mr-Ap 85,
          p. 14.
3984. RANDALL, Neil
     "A Courtroom Fancy" (Excerpt from a long poem entitled <u>The
          Divorce of Heaven and Hell</u>). <u>Rampike</u> (4:2/3) 85-86,
          p. 124-125.
3985. RANKIN, Paula
     "How Much." <u>PoetryNW</u> (26:2) Sum 85, p. 9-10.
     "The Loneliness Bird." <u>PoetryNW</u> (26:2) Sum 85, p. 11-12.
     "Sad Music." <u>PoetryNW</u> (26:2) Sum 85, p. 10-11.
3986. RANKIN, Ricky
     "About Gay Christians." <u>JamesWR</u> (2:1) Fall 84, p. 9.
     "Just My Type." <u>JamesWR</u> (2:3) Spr-Sum 85, p. 11.
     "Noah's Ark." <u>JamesWR</u> (2:2) Wint 85, p. 3.
     "Why I Left You: the Short Version." <u>JamesWR</u> (2:3) Spr-
          Sum 85, p. 10-11.
3987. RANKIN, Rush
     "For Men Only." <u>ThRiPo</u> (25/26) 85, p. 49.
     "Three Flights." <u>Stand</u> (26:3) Sum 85, p. 7.
3988. RAO, K. Raghavendra
     "The Image" (tr. of V. G. Bhat). <u>NewL</u> (51:4) Sum 85, p.
          133.
3989. RAPHAEL, Dan
     "Starting the Year with the Flu." <u>Bogg</u> (54) 85, p. 38.
3990. RASULA, Jed
     "Arched Like the Back of a Hissing Cat." <u>Temblor</u> (1) 85,
          p. 92.
     "The Tent of Times." <u>Sulfur</u> (12) 85, p. 58-61.
3991. RATCH, Jerry
     "Sonnet 95." <u>CarolQ</u> (38:1) Fall 85, p. 55.
     "Sonnet 98." <u>CarolQ</u> (38:1) Fall 85, p. 56.
     "Sonnet 110." <u>CarolQ</u> (37:2) Wint 85, p. 72.
     "Sonnet 111." <u>CarolQ</u> (37:2) Wint 85, p. 73.
     "Sonnet 112." <u>CarolQ</u> (37:2) Wint 85, p. 74.
3992. RATNER, Rochelle
     "Finding the Words" (for my parents). <u>ConnPR</u> (3:1) 84, p.
          20-21.
3993. RATTEE, Michael
     "Grade School / A Daydream of Birds." <u>PoetL</u> (79:4) Wint
          85, p. 219.
     "His Silence." <u>PoetL</u> (79:4) Wint 85, p. 218.

3994. RATZLAFF, Keith
  "Closing the Illinois River." <u>PoetryNW</u> (26:4) Wint 85-86,
   p. 39.
  "For Treva, to Be Read to Her on Our Tenth Anniversary."
   <u>PoetryNW</u> (26:4) Wint 85-86, p. 40.
  "The Husband." <u>Telescope</u> (4:2) Spr 85, p. 46-47.
  "Necessity." <u>IndR</u> (8:1) Wint 85, p. 76.
3995. RAWLINS, Susan
  "At Home." <u>ColEng</u> (47:7) N 85, p. 715.
  "Bad Press." <u>Zyzzyva</u> (1:4) Wint 85, p. 49.
  "My Aunt, Whose '64 Mustang Suits Her." <u>PoetryNW</u> (26:2)
   Sum 85, p. 34-35.
3996. RAWSON, Eric
  "The Arbor." <u>WebR</u> (10:2) Fall 85, p. 60.
  "Not Old Russia." <u>CutB</u> (24) Spr-Sum 85, p. 53.
3997. RAY, David
  "The Absences." <u>PoetryE</u> (18) Fall 85, p. 47.
  "Autumn, 1984." <u>NewL</u> (51:3) Spr 85, p. 42.
  "Billiards." <u>PoetryE</u> (18) Fall 85, p. 46.
  "Brief Song." <u>NewL</u> (51:3) Spr 85, p. 41.
  "For an Old Dog." <u>Amelia</u> (2:2) O 85, p. 30-31.
  "Haiku." <u>NewL</u> (51:3) Spr 85, p. 43.
  "How to Be Loved." <u>NewL</u> (51:3) Spr 85, p. 41.
  "Mom." <u>NewL</u> (51:3) Spr 85, p. 42.
  "Past Mid-Century." <u>Amelia</u> (2:2) O 85, p. 31.
  "Sam's Song." <u>PoetryR</u> (2:2) Ap 85, p. 35.
  "Stupid Animal Tricks." <u>CharR</u> (11:2) Fall 85, p. 99.
  "Thanksgiving 1984." <u>NewL</u> (51:3) Spr 85, p. 43.
  "Three Prayers" (Adaption of Rabindranath Tagore's
   Bengali/English). <u>NewL</u> (51:4) Sum 85, p. 130-131.
  "Treasuring the Snapshot" (In Memoriam, Samuel Cyrus David
   Ray, 1965-1984). <u>Geor</u> (39:2) Sum 85, p. 411.
  "The Wedding Party." <u>PoetryR</u> (2:2) Ap 85, p. 33-34.
3998. RAY, Judy
  "Downtown Art." <u>ClockR</u> (2:2) 85, p. 59.
  "For Sam: Looking Back." <u>PoetryR</u> (2:2) Ap 85, p. 36-37.
3999. RAY, Lila
  "A Red Blossom" (tr. of Daud Haider). <u>NewL</u> (51:4) Sum 85,
   p. 132-133.
  "You Threw a Stone" (tr. of Daud Haider). <u>NewL</u> (51:4) Sum
   85, p. 132.
4000. RAY, Robbie (<u>See</u> also RAY, Robert Beverly)
  "Betrayed." <u>AntigR</u> (62/63) Sum-Aut 85, p. 36.
  "Betrayed II." <u>AntigR</u> (62/63) Sum-Aut 85, p. 36.
4001. RAY, Robert Beverly (<u>See</u> <u>also</u> RAY, Robbie)
  "19 June 1984." <u>AntR</u> (43:1) Wint 85, p. 73.
  "The Canonization of the Imaginary." <u>AntR</u> (43:1) Wint 85,
   p. 76-77.
  "The Theory of Interruptions." <u>AntR</u> (43:1) Wint 85, p. 74-
   75.
4002. RAY, Sam
  "A Child and a Man." <u>NewL</u> (51:3) Spr 85, p. 36.
  "Dreammaker" (For Kristi). <u>NewL</u> (51:3) Spr 85, p. 33-34.
  "Every Night." <u>NewL</u> (51:3) Spr 85, p. 36.
  "Is There Time to Compose." <u>NewL</u> (51:3) Spr 85, p. 34.
  "Late Words." <u>NewL</u> (51:3) Spr 85, p. 35.
  "Looking Ahead." <u>NewL</u> (51:3) Spr 85, p. 33.
  "Magic" (For Cindy). <u>NewL</u> (51:3) Spr 85, p. 35.
  "Not Leaving This City." <u>NewL</u> (51:3) Spr 85, p. 37.
4003. RAYFORD, Julian Lee
  "Eternal in Me." <u>NewL</u> (51:3) Spr 85, p. 55.
4004. RAZ, Hilda
  "A Meeting." <u>DenQ</u> (20:1) Sum 85, p. 68-69.
  "My Dream, Your Dream." <u>DenQ</u> (20:1) Sum 85, p. 70.
  "What Happened This Summer." <u>DenQ</u> (20:1) Sum 85, p. 71.

4005. REA, Susan
"Gathering Grape Hyacinths." _Amelia_ (2:1) Ap 85, p. 70.
"Listening to Mozart." _PassN_ (6:2) Spr-Sum 85, p. 18.
"Miscarriage." _Prima_ (9) 85, p. 87.
"Weather Report" (for Archie Ammons). _AmerS_ (54:2) Spr
   85, p. 220.
4006. REA, Tom
"Calvin on the Lake Shore." _NowestR_ (23:3) 85, p. 16-17.
"Leaving Cheyenne." _GreenfR_ (13:1/2) Fall-Wint 85, p. 168.
4007. REANEY, James
"Clown Clown." _PoetryCR_ (7:1) Aut 85, p. 24.
"The Granary." _PoetryCR_ (7:1) Aut 85, p. 24.
"The Roof." _PoetryCR_ (7:1) Aut 85, p. 24.
"The Skaters, the Skippers." _PoetryCR_ (7:1) Aut 85, p. 24.
4008. REARDON, Henry
"Clouded Perspective." _PoeticJ_ (12) 85, p. 7.
"Found in This Vicinity." _PoeticJ_ (12) 85, p. 6.
4009. REAVEY, Jean
"Mapping for Tempo." _SanFPJ_ (7:4) 85, p. 60.
"The Un Facto." _SanFPJ_ (7:4) 85, p. 57-58.
4010. RECTENWALD, Michael
"All the Beds in the County Are Full." _Pig_ (13) 85, p. 60.
"Duffy." _Pig_ (13) 85, p. 67.
4011. RECTOR, Liam
"Office: Devoid of Ornament or Rhetoric of Any Kind" (for
   Robert Venturi). _PoetryE_ (18) Fall 85, p. 14-16.
4012. REDA, Jacques
"Les Bretelles Etoilees." _Verse_ (2) 85, p. 27.
"The Spangled Braces" (tr. by Thomas Dauzat). _Verse_ (2)
   85, p. 28.
4013. REDEL, Victoria
"Sightseeing." _PoetryE_ (18) Fall 85, p. 57.
"That Summer, New York." _NewEngR_ (7:3) Spr 85, p. 296.
4014. REDGROVE, Peter
"Eden's Medicine" (For Alan and Su Bleakley). _Poetry_
   (146:4) Jl 85, p. 198-199.
"More Than Meets the Eye." _Poetry_ (146:4) Jl 85, p. 197-
   198.
4015. REDICAN, Dan
"Emerald Lake." _PoetryCR_ (6:3) Spr 85, p. 35.
4016. REED, Alison (_See also_ REED, Alison T.)
"The Escalator." _CarolQ_ (38:1) Fall 85, p. 46.
"The Parental Factor: A Woman in White Goes Wild Fearing
   the Baby Lost." _LaurelR_ (19:2) Sum 85, p. 54-55.
"The Sensitive Husband." _HolCrit_ (22:1) F 85, p. 11.
4017. REED, Alison T. (_See also_ REED, Alison)
"A Garden in Usufruct." _Outbr_ (14/15) Fall 84-Spr 85, p. 67.
"A Nabokovian Chaperones a Trip Out West." _Outbr_ (14/15)
   Fall 84-Spr 85, p. 65-66.
"Small Chapels and Sunday Afternoons" (dedicated to Erich
   Groos). _Outbr_ (14/15) Fall 84-Spr 85, p. 63-64.
4018. REED, Cecilia
"Smelt Fevah." _SmPd_ (22:1) Wint 85, p. 29--30.
4019. REED, Jeremy
"Apprehension." _Verse_ (3) 85, p. 34.
"Blackberrying." _PoetryCR_ (6:3) Spr 85, p. 29.
"Cornering." _Verse_ (3) 85, p. 33.
"Crossed Wires." _PoetryCR_ (7:1) Aut 85, p. 6.
"Horse Chestnuts." _PoetryCR_ (7:1) Aut 85, p. 6.
"Lamorna Cove." _PoetryCR_ (6:3) Spr 85, p. 29.
"Momentum." _PoetryCR_ (6:3) Spr 85, p. 29.
"Rabbits." _PoetryCR_ (6:3) Spr 85, p. 29.
4020. REED, John (_See also_ REED, John R.)
"Forgetting." _Tendril_ (19/20) 85, p. 304-305.
4021. REED, John R. (_See also_ REED, John)
"A Drink of Water." _AmerS_ (54:1) Wint 84-85, p. 44.

"Dry Earth" (Ethiopia, 1985). PoetryR (5) S 85, p. 35.
4022. REES, Elizabeth
     "Ode to Empty Israeli Bus Stations." GreenfR (12:3/4)
        Wint-Spr 85, p. 23.
4023. REES, Ennis
     "Daniel Boone in New York City, March 1979." SoCaR (17:2)
        Spr 85, p. 33.
4024. REEVE, F. D.
     "Georgian Bay." SewanR (93:1) Wint 85, p. 65-66.
     "Sailboats in Hazy Sun." SewanR (93:1) Wint 85, p. 66.
     "Skirting the House." SewanR (93:1) Wint 85, p. 64-65.
     "The Tall Tree." NewYorker (61:37) 4 N 85, p. 44.
4025. REEVES, Trish
     "After Nature." SenR (15:2) 85, p. 116-117.
     "And Then." Ploughs (11:1) 85, p. 177.
     "Driving Through." SenR (15:2) 85, p. 115.
     "Gathering." SenR (15:2) 85, p. 114.
     "Goodbye." Ploughs (11:1) 85, p. 174-175.
     "I Say, Not Here, Not There, So Where?" Pequod (18) 85,
        p. 53-54.
     "My Parents." SenR (15:2) 85, p. 118.
     "Passion." Ploughs (11:1) 85, p. 179-180.
     "Pure and Rapid." SenR (15:2) 85, p. 113.
     "Rural Childhood." Ploughs (11:1) 85, p. 176.
     "Secret Communication." SenR (15:2) 85, p. 112.
     "The Silver Coin." Ploughs (11:1) 85, p. 178.
     "Watching." Pequod (18) 85, p. 56.
     "When I Awakened Out of My Head." Pequod (18) 85, p. 55.
     "Window." Pequod (18) 85, p. 52.
4026. REGAL, Martin
     "Cairn on the Moor" (tr. of Snorri Hjartarson). LitR
        (28:4) Sum 85, p. 588-589.
4027. REGAN, Jennifer
     "Poor Baby." OhioR (35) 85, p. 90-91.
     "Who Feeds and Shelters Us." OhioR (35) 85, p. 88-89.
4028. REIBSTEIN, Regina
     "Bargain." Confr (30/31) N 85, p. 118.
4029. REICH, Karen
     "Anna's Prologue." PoetL (80:2) Sum 85, p. 115-117.
4030. REID, Christopher
     "Eyebrows Almost Spoke." GrandS (5:1) Aut 85, p. 15.
     "History and Parody." GrandS (5:1) Aut 85, p. 18.
     "Katerina Brac" (Selections: 8 poems). GrandS (5:1) Aut
        85, p. 13-21.
     "On the Subject of Fingers and Thumbs." GrandS (5:1) Aut
        85, p. 16.
     "Screens." GrandS (5:1) Aut 85, p. 20-21.
     "The South." GrandS (5:1) Aut 85, p. 19.
     "A Tune." GrandS (5:1) Aut 85, p. 13.
     "What the Uneducated Old Woman Told Me." GrandS (5:1) Aut
        85, p. 17.
     "When the Bullfrogs Are in Love." GrandS (5:1) Aut 85, p.
        14.
4031. REID, Dennis
     "Epiphanies and the Larger Scheme of Things." PraF (6:2)
        Spr 85, p. 59.
4032. REID, Monty
     "Echo." CapilR (36) 85, p. 84.
     "The Fern." CapilR (36) 85, p. 85-86.
     "Squatters' Rights." Dandel (12:1) 85, p. 14-18.
4033. REIDEL, James
     "Cincinnati." PaintedB (26/27) Sum-Fall 85, p. 57.
     "A Couple Playing in the Shower with a Gooseneck Shower
        Head, A Couple Waiting for Water Pressure So They May
        Cleanse Themselves." Ploughs (11:1) 85, p. 185.

"Czechs." <u>Ploughs</u> (11:1) 85, p. 183.
"Kitsch." <u>Ploughs</u> (11:1) 85, p. 181.
"Norman Rockwell." <u>Ploughs</u> (11:1) 85, p. 184.
"Pronounced Bell Fountain." <u>PaintedB</u> (26/27) Sum-Fall 85,
    p. 56.
"Reforestation." <u>PaintedB</u> (26/27) Sum-Fall 85, p. 55.
"Week of January." <u>Ploughs</u> (11:1) 85, p. 182.
4034. REINFELD, Linda
    "Dogturds emerging" (After Basho). <u>Amelia</u> (2:2) O 85, p.
        14.
    "Notes from the Faculty of Arts and Science." <u>Amelia</u>
        (2:1) Ap 85, p. 28-29.
4035. REINHARD, John
    "Burning the Prairie" (Easter 1985). <u>Abraxas</u> (33) 85, p.
        38.
    "Epiphany." <u>Abraxas</u> (33) 85, p. 35-37.
    "The Fundamentalist Argues against Darwin." <u>PassN</u> (6:2)
        Spr-Sum 85, p. 3.
4036. REISNER, Barbara
    "Sabbath on Martha's Vineyard." <u>StoneC</u> (12:2/3) Spr-Sum
        85, p. 56.
4037. REISS, James
    "Demolition." <u>Nat</u> (240:11) 23 Mr 85, p. 341.
    "Tie." <u>Iowa</u> (15:1) Wint 85, p. 85.
    "Whitman at a Grain Depot." <u>Antaeus</u> (55) Aut 85, p. 151.
4038. REITER, David
    "At Mormon Square, Salt Lake." <u>Quarry</u> (34:4) Aut 85, p.
        80-82.
    "His Children." <u>CanLit</u> (107) Wint 85, p. 19.
4039. REITER, Thomas
    "Bathsheba, Barbados." <u>TexasR</u> (6:1/2) Spr-Sum 85, p. 94.
    "Coal." <u>Raccoon</u> (17) Mr 85, p. 20.
    "Daybook Entry." <u>PoetryR</u> (2:2) Ap 85, p. 30.
    "Dragonfly." <u>PoetL</u> (79:4) Wint 85, p. 206.
4040. RELIN, Louis
    "Arrogance." <u>SanFPJ</u> (7:2) 85, p. 92.
    "Mea Culpa." <u>SanFPJ</u> (7:3) 84 [i.e. 85], p. 28.
    "Memo for Election Day" (File and Forget). <u>SanFPJ</u> (7:3)
        84 [i.e. 85], p. 30-31.
    "To a PhD. Candidate in Physiological Psychology." <u>SanFPJ</u>
        (7:2) 85, p. 89.
4041. REMBOLD, Kristen Staby
    "Home: Crisis That Brings Me Back." <u>CimR</u> (72) Jl 85, p.
        39.
4042. REMPE, Lee
    "The Awful Sorrow of Research." <u>EngJ</u> (74:7) N 85, p. 48.
4043. REN, Yu
    "Lakeshore" (in Chinese and English, tr. by G. G. Gach and
        C. H. Kwock). <u>Zyzzyva</u> (1:1) Spr 85, p. 40.
4044. RENAUD, Jorge Antonio
    "Leaning over the new stove." <u>RevChic</u> (12:2) Sum 84, p.
        27.
4045. RENDALL, Barbara
    "Camucima." <u>PoetryCR</u> (6:4) Sum 85, p. 23.
4046. RENDLEMAN, Danny
    "Scripture." <u>PassN</u> (6:2) Spr-Sum 85, p. 3.
4047. RENFRO, Elizabeth
    "The Plaza in San Martin." <u>CutB</u> (23) Fall-Wint 85, p. 57.
4048. RENKER, Skip
    "The Horses of Snowy River." <u>PassN</u> (6:2) Spr-Sum 85, p.
        16.
4049. RENNIE, Michael
    "Masks." <u>PraF</u> (6:2) Spr 85, p. 18.
4050. REPLOGLE, Justin
    "It's 29 Below." <u>CreamCR</u> (10:1) 85, p. 20-21.
    "Who Do You Think Is Coming to Town." <u>CreamCR</u> (10:1) 85,

p. 22-23.
REPOSA, Carol Coffee
    See COFFEE REPOSA, Carol
4051. REPP, John
    "Loaves." PassN (6:2) Spr-Sum 85, p. 10.
4052. RESCH, Jennifer
    "So what is this" ("Untitled"). Amelia (2:1) Ap 85, p. 26.
4053. RESS, Lisa
    "Depending on You." Outbr (14/15) Fall 84-Spr 85, p. 89.
    "Splitting Maul." Outbr (14/15) Fall 84-Spr 85, p. 90.
RETAMAR, Roberto Fernández
    See FERNANDEZ RETAMAR, Roberto
4054. RETTEW, David
    "Asteroids." HangL (48) Fall 85, p. 66.
    "Gibbig." HangL (48) Fall 85, p. 65.
    "Lava." HangL (48) Fall 85, p. 65.
    "The Long Walk Home." HangL (48) Fall 85, p. 62-64.
4055. REVARD, Carter
    "That Lightning's Hard to Climb." GreenfR (12:3/4) Wint-
        Spr 85, p. 78-79.
4056. REVEAL, David
    "Is Constipation Part of Growing Older?" Swallow (4) 85,
        p. 48-49.
    "Time Flees in Our Disarray." Swallow (4) 85, p. 49.
4057. REVELL, Donald
    "Birthplace." DenQ (19:3) Wint 85, p. 41-42.
    "Extracts: For Celine." Crazy (27) Fall 84, p. 52.
    "From an Interview." Crazy (27) Fall 84, p. 53.
    "The Gaza of Winter." ParisR (27:98) Wint 85, p. 84-85.
    "The Mean Time." Crazy (27) Fall 84, p. 51.
    "The Melville Scholar." DenQ (19:3) Wint 85, p. 43-44.
    "The More Lustrous." DenQ (19:3) Wint 85, p. 39-40.
4058. REVERDY, Pierre
    "More Atmosphere" (from La Guitare Endormie, 1929, tr. by
        Frederick Lowe). RiverS (17) 85, p. 44.
    "No Farther" (From Coeur de Chêne, 1921, tr. by
        Frederick Lowe). RiverS (17) 85, p. 43.
    "Nocturnal Panorama" (from La Guitare Endormie, 1929, tr.
        by Frederick Lowe). RiverS (17) 85, p. 45.
4059. REVERE, Elizabeth
    "Astarte." CapeR (20:1) Spr 85, p. 17.
    "Lilacs." CapeR (20:1) Spr 85, p. 16.
4060. REYES DAVILA, Marcos
    "A Juan Antonio Corretjer." Mairena (7:19) 85, p. 85.
4061. REYNOLDS, Diane
    "Consummation." CutB (24) Spr-Sum 85, p. 37.
    "That Which Isn't Flint Is Tinder" (--Annie Dillard).
        LitR (28:4) Sum 85, p. 576-577.
4062. RHENISCH, Harold
    "Rose." CanLit (105) Sum 85, p. 45-46.
    "The Year." CanLit (105) Sum 85, p. 131134.
4063. RHODENBAUGH, Suzanne
    "Baggin." LaurelR (19:1) Wint 85, p. 19-20.
    "Scrub Palmetto." Gargoyle (27) 85, p. 32.
4064. RICE, Nicky
    "Strawberries." CumbPR (5:1) Fall 85, p. 76.
    "Transplant." CumbPR (5:1) Fall 85, p. 75.
4065. RICHARDS, G. D.
    "Evening on Eighth Avenue." NegC (5:2) Spr 85, p. 76-77.
4066. RICHARDSON, Michael
    "At This Kind of Time / 41.46N., 50.14W." (from A Night to
        Remember (1956), written by Walter Lord). Descant 49
        (16:2) Sum 85, p. 29.
    "In Days When" (for Jeannie). Descant 49 (16:2) Sum 85,
        p. 26.
    "Last Year" (from Last Year at Marienbad (1961), directed

by Alain Resnais, written by Alain Robbe-Grillet).
Descant 49 (16:2) Sum 85, p. 30.
"Snapshot: Brighton, 1948." _Descant_ 49 (16:2) Sum 85, p.
28.
"These Stories." _Descant_ 49 (16:2) Sum 85, p. 27.
4067. RICHARDSON, Miles
"And Then What?" _PoeticJ_ (12) 85, p. 8.
"Get Rid of That Thing." _PoeticJ_ (12) 85, p. 9.
4068. RICHER, Luc
"Onze Heures." _Rampike_ (4:2/3) 85-86, p. 13.
4069. RICHMAN, Elliot
"After the Poetry Disappears." _WindO_ (45) Spr 85, p. 37.
"Camp Airy, August 17, 1953." _WindO_ (45) Spr 85, p. 33-35.
"On the Tomb of Aerobics of Rhodes, Weightlifter" (tr. of
Kathusias). _WindO_ (46) Fall 85, p. 3.
"On the Tomb of Another Cuckold, Antilochosos of Athens"
(tr. of Sappho). _WindO_ (46) Fall 85, p. 4.
"On the Tomb of Gladiator Butchweldedes" (tr. of
Edgarleechiades of Spoonia). _WindO_ (46) Fall 85, p. 4.
"On the Tomb of Kalamachius, the Jogger" (tr. of Timeon of
Corinth). _WindO_ (46) Fall 85, p. 3.
"On the Tomb of the Cuckold Menoitios" (tr. of anonymous).
WindO (46) Fall 85, p. 3.
"Poem." _PoetryR_ (5) S 85, p. 39-40.
"Spring." _WindO_ (45) Spr 85, p. 27.
"Summer." _PoetryR_ (5) S 85, p. 40.
"To My Head Expander, Not My Shrink." _WindO_ (45) Spr 85,
p. 35-36.
4070. RICHMOND, Kevin
"Winter Images 2." _Bogg_ (54) 85, p. 20.
4071. RICHMOND, Steve
"For Jim Callahan" (Special Section). _WormR_ (25:1, issue
97) 85, p. 15-26.
4072. RICKEL, Boyer
"Elegy" (Clayton Rickel, April 19-August 11, 1984).
Poetry (147:2) N 85, p. 74-75.
"From Where It's Dark" (For Gail). _Poetry_ (145:4) Ja 85,
p. 199-201.
"Two Mothers in the Cloisters." _NoAmR_ (270:1) Mr 85, p.
27.
4073. RICKERTSEN, Anne
"Opal." _Cond_ (11/12) 85, p. 159.
4074. RIDGE, Melissa
"Fou, Fou Beauty." _Gargoyle_ (27) 85, p. 81.
4075. RIDGE, Pat
"Mathematics Made Simple." _Open24_ (4) 85, p. 41.
4076. RIDL, Jack
"A Father." _LaurelR_ (19:1) Wint 85, p. 69.
4077. RIDLAND, John
"It Said in the L.A. Times." _Thrpny_ (6:1, issue 21) Spr
85, p. 11.
4078. RIEDEMANN, Clemente
"The Man from Leipzig" (tr. by Steven White). _GreenfR_
(12:3/4) Wint-Spr 85, p. 118.
"The Tree of the World" (tr. by Steven White). _GreenfR_
(12:3/4) Wint-Spr 85, p. 114-115.
"Wekufe's Dream" (tr. by Steven White). _GreenfR_ (12:3/4)
Wint-Spr 85, p. 116-117.
4079. RIEL, Steven
"Notes on Paranoia" (Excerpt, for Neil). _JamesWR_ (2:1)
Fall 84, p. 12.
4080. RIFAT, Oktay
"In Clouded Water" (in Turkish and English, tr. by Ozcan
Yalim, William Fielder and Dionis Coffin Riggs).
StoneC (13:1/2) Fall-Wint 85-86, p. 44-45.

333   RIOS

4081. RIFKA, Fuad
"Diary of a Woodcutter" (Excerpts, tr. by the author and
Shirley Kaufman). NewL (51:4) Sum 85, p. 16-17.
4082. RIGAUT, Jacques
"Around Town" (tr. by Ron Horning). Ploughs (11:4) 85, p.
122.
4083. RIGGS, Dionis (See also RIGGS, Dionis Coffin)
"At the Beach" (tr. of Kemal Ozer, w. O. Yalim and W.
Fielder). NewL (51:4) Sum 85, p. 14.
"Night and Night" (tr. of Ismail Uyaroglu, w. O. Yalim and
W. Fielder). NewL (51:4) Sum 85, p. 14.
"To My Wife" (tr. of Ozcan Yalim, w. O. Yalim and W.
Fielder). NewL (51:4) Sum 85, p. 15.
4084. RIGGS, Dionis Coffin (See also RIGGS, Dionis)
"In Clouded Water" (tr. of Oktay Rifat, w. Ozcan Yalim and
William Fielder). StoneC (13:1/2) Fall-Wint 85-86, p.
44-45.
"No One Knows." StoneC (13:1/2) Fall-Wint 85-86, p. 22.
4085. RIGSBEE, David
"Anymore." DenQ (20:2) Fall 85, p. 27-28.
"Autobiography." NewYorker (61:27) 26 Ag 85, p. 34.
"The Hopper Light." DenQ (20:2) Fall 85, p. 23-24.
"Sunbathing." GeoR (39:3) Fall 85, p. 536.
"Trawlers at Montauk." Crazy (27) Fall 84, p. 42.
"The Word 'World' in Jarrell" (for Sister Bernetta Quinn).
DenQ (20:2) Fall 85, p. 25-26.
4086. RILEY, Joanne (See also RILEY, Joanne M.)
"Running at Night." WebR (10:2) Fall 85, p. 84.
4087. RILEY, Joanne M. (See also RILEY, Joanne)
"Immigrant Silver." CapeR (20:2) Fall 85, p. 48.
"Suds and Stones." CapeR (20:2) Fall 85, p. 49.
4088. RILKE, Rainer Maria
"2.26" (tr. by Steven Lautermilch). MalR (71) Je 85, p.
52.
"Liebeslied." YellowS (14) Spr 85, p. 49.
"Lovesong" (tr. by W. D. Herter Norton). YellowS (14) Spr
85, p. 49.
"This Prayer I Pray in the Spring" (tr. by Steven
Lautermilch). MalR (71) Je 85, p. 53.
4089. RIND, Sherry
"Taking Home a Rhinoceros from London Zoo." PoetryNW
(26:1) Spr 85, p. 26-27.
4090. RINDONE, Vincenzo
"Loin de Pietraperzia" (tr. by Daniel Parfait). Os (21)
85, p. 11.
"Lontano da Pietraperzia." Os (21) 85, p. 10.
"Violence" (tr. by Daniel Parfait). Os (21) 85, p. 9.
"Violenza." Os (21) 85, p. 8.
4091. RINGOLD, Francine
"Georgia, the Caucasus." Nimrod (28:2) Spr-Sum 85, p. 21.
"Now in Maine." Nimrod (28:2) Spr-Sum 85, p. 23.
"The Ruins of Narikala" (for Shota Rustaveli, 12th Century
Georgian poet. Set to music after a Georgian theme by
Manly Johnson). Nimrod (28:2) Spr-Sum 85, p. 19-20.
"Seat in Vermont." Nimrod (28:2) Spr-Sum 85, p. 22.
4092. RINGOLD, Leslie
"Carving with Bone." Nimrod (28:2) Spr-Sum 85, p. 140.
4093. RINGQUIST, Kurt
"Gray Light." KanQ (17:4) Fall 85, p. 208.
4094. RIORDAN, P.
"The Girl over the Road." Bogg (54) 85, p. 19.
4095. RIOS, Alberto
"Five Indiscretions, or." RevChic (13:1) Spr 85, p. 24-28.
"The Night Would Grow Like a Telescope Pulled Out." OhioR
(34) 85, p. 81-82.
"On January 5, 1984, El Santo the Wrestler Died, Possibly."

RevChic (13:1) Spr 85, p. 29-31.
"One Woman Turns Her Lips Away." BlueBldgs (9) [85?], p. 14.
"Playing." BlueBldgs (9) [85?], p. 15.
"Taking Away the Name of a Nephew." RevChic (13:1) Spr 85, p. 21-23.

4096. RIPETTI, Daniela
"Market -- Damned" (tr. by P. F. Paolini). LitR (29:1) Fall 85, p. 116.
"My Fair Ladies" (tr. by P. F. Paolini). LitR (29:1) Fall 85, p. 116.

4097. RISSET, Jacqueline
"The Translation Begins" (tr. by Paul Buck). Temblor (1) 85, p. 124-129.

4098. RITCHIE, Elisavietta
"Tying It On." Prima (9) 85, p. 59.

4099. RITCHIE, Michael Karl (See also MICHAEL KARL (RITCHIE))
"Getting to Know You" (w. F. Keith Wahle). YellowS (16) Aut 85, p. 19-20.
"Presidential Statues" (w. F. Keith Wahle & Michael Shay). YellowS (15) Sum 85, p. 8-9.

4100. RITSOS, Yánnis
"After the Defeat" (tr. by Edmund Keeley). GrandS (5:1) Aut 85, p. 196.
"After the Fact" (tr. by Edmund Keeley). OntR (23) Fall-Wint 85-86, p. 93.
"Afternoon in the Old Neighborhood" (tr. by Edmund Keeley). NewL (51:4) Sum 85, p. 12.
"Aids" (tr. by Edmund Keeley). Iowa (15:2) Spr-Sum 85, p. 97.
"Alcmene" (tr. by Edmund Keeley). NewL (51:4) Sum 85, p. 9.
"Blockade" (tr. by Edmund Keely). NewEngR (8:1) Aut 85, p. 23.
"The Choice" (tr. by Martin McKinsey). YaleR (74:3) Spr 85, p. 452-453.
"The Closed Circus" (tr. by Edmund Keeley). GrandS (5:1) Aut 85, p. 193.
"Common Fate" (tr. by Edmund Keeley). NewL (51:4) Sum 85, p. 11.
"Corners of Night" (tr. by Edmund Keeley). GrahamHR (9) Fall 85, p. 49.
"The Craftsman" (tr. by Edmund Keeley). NewL (51:4) Sum 85, p. 13.
"The Day's End" (tr. by Edmund Keeley). GrahamHR (9) Fall 85, p. 46.
"Degrees of Sensation" (tr. by Kimon Friar). Mund (15:1/2) 85, p. 52.
"The Discovery" (tr. by Edmund Keeley). NewL (51:4) Sum 85, p. 11.
"Disfigurement" (tr. by Edmund Keeley). Antaeus (55) Aut 85, p. 318.
"Double Sentencing" (tr. by Edmund Keeley). GrahamHR (9) Fall 85, p. 50.
"Expanse" (tr. by Edmund Keeley). NewL (51:4) Sum 85, p. 12.
"Forbidden Territory" (tr. by Edmund Keeley). NewL (51:4) Sum 85, p. 12.
"Greek Horse-Drawn Cart" (In Greek and English, tr. by Minas Savvas). CrossCur (4:2) 84, p. 42-45.
"The Idiot" (tr. by Kimon Friar). Mund (15:1/2) 85, p. 51.
"In Front of the Door" (tr. by Edmund Keeley). GrahamHR (9) Fall 85, p. 48.
"An Invalid's Day" (tr. by Kimon Friar). Mund (15:1/2)

85, p. 52.
"The Jester's Secret" (tr. by Edmund Keeley). <u>NewL</u> (51:4)
    Sum 85, p. 10.
"Known Consequences" (tr. by Edmund Keeley). <u>GrandS</u> (5:1)
    Aut 85, p. 194.
"Like Changes" (tr. by Edmund Keeley). <u>Iowa</u> (15:2) Spr-
    Sum 85, p. 96.
"Marpessa's Choice" (tr. by Edmund Keeley). <u>Antaeus</u> (55)
    Aut 85, p. 316.
"The Miracle" (tr. by Edmund Keeley). <u>Iowa</u> (15:2) Spr-Sum
    85, p. 96.
"Mortgage" (tr. by Mary Keeley). <u>CrossCur</u> (4:4/5:1) 85,
    p. 28.
"The Most Precious Things" (tr. by Edmund Keely). <u>NewEngR</u>
    (8:1) Aut 85, p. 23.
"Moving" (tr. by Edmund Keeley). <u>MissouriR</u> (8:3) 85, p.
    62.
"Nakedness" (tr. by Edmund Keeley). <u>CrossCur</u> (4:4/5:1)
    85, p. 29.
"Need of Proof" (tr. by Kimon Friar). <u>Mund</u> (15:1/2) 85,
    p. 50.
"Night Episode" (tr. by Edmund Keeley). <u>Iowa</u> (15:2) Spr-
    Sum 85, p. 97.
"One Sunday" (tr. by Edmund Keeley). <u>GrandS</u> (5:1) Aut 85,
    p. 195.
"Opposite the Rock" (tr. by Kimon Friar and Kostas
    Myrsiades). <u>ArizQ</u> (41:4) Wint 85, p. 318.
"Our Life in Phares" (tr. by Martin McKinsey). <u>YaleR</u>
    (74:3) Spr 85, p. 453.
"Paper Poems" (Athens-Kalamos, June, 1973-May, 1974, tr. by
    Edmund Keeley). <u>Ploughs</u> (11:4) 85, p. 27-30.
"Penelope's Despair" (tr. by Edmund Keeley). <u>Antaeus</u>
    (55) Aut 85, p. 315.
"Philomela" (tr. by Edmund Keeley). <u>Antaeus</u> (55) Aut 85,
    p. 314.
"Precisely Now" (tr. by Edmund Keeley). <u>OntR</u> (23) Fall-
    Wint 85-86, p. 94.
"Process" (tr. by Kimon Friar). <u>Mund</u> (15:1/2) 85, p. 50.
"Readiness" (tr. by Edmund Keeley). <u>GrandS</u> (5:1) Aut 85,
    p. 194.
"The Real Reason" (tr. by Edmund Keeley). <u>GrandS</u> (5:1)
    Aut 85, p. 195.
"A Road" (tr. by Edmund Keeley). <u>Iowa</u> (15:2) Spr-Sum 85,
    p. 98.
"Short Review" (tr. by Edmund Keeley). <u>Iowa</u> (15:2) Spr-
    Sum 85, p. 98.
"Signals" (tr. by Edmund Keeley). <u>Antaeus</u> (55) Aut 85,
    p. 314.
"Spring 1971" (tr. by Edmund Keeley). <u>GrandS</u> (5:1) Aut
    85, p. 192.
"Strange Times" (tr. by Edmund Keeley). <u>NewL</u> (51:4) Sum
    85, p. 9-10.
"The Suspect" (tr. by Kimon Friar). <u>Mund</u> (15:1/2) 85, p.
    51.
"The Time Dimension" (tr. by Edmund Keeley). <u>GrahamHR</u> (9)
    Fall 85, p. 51.
"The Tomb of Our Ancestors" (tr. by Edmund Keeley).
    <u>GrandS</u> (5:1) Aut 85, p. 191.
"Transactions" (tr. by Edmund Keeley). <u>GrahamHR</u> (9) Fall
    85, p. 47.
"Ultimate Contribution" (tr. by Edmund Keeley). <u>GrahamHR</u>
    (9) Fall 85, p. 53.
"The Unhinged Shutter" (In Greek and English, tr. by Edmund
    and Mary Keeley). <u>CrossCur</u> (4:2) 84, p. 40-41.
"Unknown Obligation" (tr. by Edmund Keeley). <u>GrahamHR</u> (9)
    Fall 85, p. 52.

"Vacant Lot" (tr. by Edmund Keeley). <u>Antaeus</u> (55) Aut
   85, p. 317.
"A Walk in the Courtyard" (tr. by Edmund Keeley).
   <u>CrossCur</u> (4:4/5:1) 85, p. 27.
4101. RITTY, Joan
"In March." <u>PoeticJ</u> (11) 85, p. 35.
"In Words of One Syllable." <u>PoeticJ</u> (12) 85, p. 2.
"Masks." <u>PoeticJ</u> (10) 85, p. 31.
"Mother's First Communion." <u>PoeticJ</u> (9) 85, p. 27.
"Mountain Climber." <u>PoeticJ</u> (10) 85, p. 16.
"Sheila and I." <u>PoeticJ</u> (11) 85, p. 32.
"Villanelle: Denial." <u>PoeticJ</u> (9) 85, p. 26.
4102. RIVARD, David
"The Fast Long Time." <u>Crazy</u> (29) Fall 85, p. 73-74.
"Lies." <u>Crazy</u> (29) Fall 85, p. 71-72.
4103. RIVARD, Ken
"The Ostrich Is a Blonde Wearing Glasses." <u>PraF</u> (6:2) Spr
   85, p. 45.
"Semblance." <u>PoetryCR</u> (6:3) Spr 85, p. 25.
4104. RIVERA, Diana
"The Peacock." <u>HawaiiR</u> (18) Fall 85, p. 57-58.
"The Rose." <u>BilingR</u> (11:2) My-Ag 84 [c1986], p. 50.
"Six Windows and One Moon." <u>CrabCR</u> (2:2) Wint 85, p. 8-9.
4105. RIVERA, Etnairis
"Andar en el cuerpo." <u>Mairena</u> (7:19) 85, p. 13-17.
4106. RIVERA, George, Jr.
"All of Her Dreams" (for grandmother). <u>RevChic</u> (12:1) Spr
   84, p. 40.
"Mexican Dreams / Mexican Shadows." <u>RevChic</u> (12:1) Spr
   84, p. 39-40.
"La Rosita." <u>RevChic</u> (12:1) Spr 84, p. 41.
"Vaquero del Hacha" (for my father). <u>RevChic</u> (12:1) Spr
   84, p. 41.
4107. RIVERO, Eliana
"Anticipo." <u>BilingR</u> (11:2) My-Ag 84 [c1986], p. 11.
"Para Alguien Que No Sabe Cantar." <u>BilingR</u> (11:2) My-Ag
   84 [c1986], p. 77.
"Presagio." <u>BilingR</u> (11:2) My-Ag 84 [c1986], p. 39-40.
4108. RIVERS, J. W.
"Modesty Silsbee Finds Her Father's Bible in a Chest."
   <u>SpoonRQ</u> (10:4) Fall 85, p. 57.
4109. RIVERS, Pamela Canyon
"Regaining the Womb." <u>SanFPJ</u> (7:2) 85, p. 61.
"Stolen Ground." <u>SanFPJ</u> (7:2) 85, p. 64.
ROBATTO, Matilde Albert
<u>See</u> ALBERT ROBATTO, Matilde
4110. ROBBINS, Anthony
"Mindfulness." <u>AmerPoR</u> (14:6) N-D 85, p. 19.
4111. ROBBINS, Martin
"In a Heat Wave." <u>CapeR</u> (20:1) Spr 85, p. 28.
"On Grid Mornings." <u>WebR</u> (10:1) Spr 85, p. 84.
4112. ROBBINS, Richard
"Neighborhoods, 1965." <u>CharR</u> (11:2) Fall 85, p. 73-74.
"On First Being Startled on Armed Forces Day." <u>PoetryNW</u>
   (26:3) Aut 85, p. 26.
"Roethke on Film." <u>CharR</u> (11:2) Fall 85, p. 73.
"Salvations." <u>ChrC</u> (102:30) 9 O 85, p. 886.
"Spotted Bear Ranger Station, Montana." <u>PoetryNW</u> (26:3)
   Aut 85, p. 26-27.
4113. ROBBINS, Tim
"Afternoon." <u>HangL</u> (48) Fall 85, p. 59.
"Confession." <u>HangL</u> (47) Spr 85, p. 47.
"Decorations." <u>HangL</u> (47) Spr 85, p. 42.
"Intimacy." <u>HangL</u> (47) Spr 85, p. 41.
"My Grandmother's Songs." <u>HangL</u> (47) Spr 85, p. 44-45.
"Two Friends." <u>HangL</u> (47) Spr 85, p. 46.

"Why Do I Worry?" HangL (47) Spr 85, p. 43.
4114. ROBERTS, Betty
"Walk Softly." Bogg (54) 85, p. 19.
4115. ROBERTS, Bonnie
"Grandfather Was a Farmer." Amelia (2:1) Ap 85, p. 82.
"How Aliens Survive on This Planet" (why mother and I
garden). YellowS (15) Sum 85, p. 12.
"The Long Black Jagged Crack in the Counselor's Wall."
Bogg (53) 85, p. 35.
"Looking for Our Old Woman" (On Christmas Eve in the
Nursing Home). SanFPJ (7:3) 84 [i.e. 85], p. 82-83.
"The Seduction Isn't Over until the Door is Barred." Bogg
(53) 85, p. 37.
4116. ROBERTS, Katrina
"Line." HarvardA (119:2) D 85, p. 39.
4117. ROBERTS, Kim
"Birthday: Elyria Ohio, 1957." CarolQ (37:3) Spr 85, p.
78.
"The Smell of What's Gone On." Amelia (2:2) O 85, p. 23.
4118. ROBERTS, Len
"Cutting Down the Old Shed." SouthernPR (26, i.e. 25:2)
Fall 85, p. 12.
"The Driving." MissouriR (8:3) 85, p. 117.
"Killing the Mole." WestB (16) 85, p. 21.
"Pretending in Paestum." GeoR (39:4) Wint 85, p. 838.
"White Flower." WestB (16) 85, p. 20.
"The White Towel." SouthernPR (25:1) Spr 85, p. 61.
4119. ROBERTS, Sheila
"For a Granddaughter." DenQ (20:2) Fall 85, p. 47.
"My Egg-plant Poem" (for Robert Kroetsch). DenQ (20:2)
Fall 85, p. 48-49.
4120. ROBERTSON, William B.
"Men." Waves (14:1/2) Fall 85, p. 97.
"My Business." Grain (13:1) F 85, p. 4.
"Shovelling Out." PoetryCR (6:3) Spr 85, p. 14.
4121. ROBINER, Mel
"Extremely Louie's Bar / Adding It Up." SouthernPR (25:1)
Spr 85, p. 36.
4122. ROBINS, Corinne
"Letter Not to Be Sent Abroad" (for Joyce). NewL (52:1)
Fall 85, p. 116.
4123. ROBINSON, Bruce
"Lodging." GreenfR (13:1/2) Fall-Wint 85, p. 23.
4124. ROBINSON, James Miller
"Flood." KanQ (17:4) Fall 85, p. 228.
"Fortune Cookies." GreenfR (12:3/4) Wint-Spr 85, p. 42.
"Knocking." GreenfR (12:3/4) Wint-Spr 85, p. 43.
"Mr. Cornet." Wind (15:54) 85, p. 44.
"What the Preacher Says." Wind (15:54) 85, p. 43.
4125. ROBINSON, Leonard Wallace
"The Arch Bishop." OP (38/39) Spr 85, p. 179.
"A Sensitive Chap." OP (38/39) Spr 85, p. 179.
4126. ROBINSON, Michael N.
"I Heard It" (On the Death of Marvin Gaye). SanFPJ (7:2)
85, p. 60.
"The Politics of Riot Commissions" (a twentieth anniversary
poem). SanFPJ (7:2) 85, p. 69-71.
"Riot Commissions." SanFPJ (7:2) 85, p. 57.
4127. ROBINSON, Olivia H.
"Ars Poetica." DeKalbLAJ (18:1/2) 85, p. 83.
4128. ROBINSON, Sondra Till
"Not Yet Dark." WebR (10:1) Spr 85, p. 56.
"Onion." WebR (10:1) Spr 85, p. 55.
4129. ROBINSON, Steven Richard
"The Griot." BlackALF (19:3) Fall 85, p. 112.

4130. ROBLES, Doreen Breheney
       "Contentment is." Amelia (2:2) O 85, p. 84.
       "Memory." Amelia (2:1) Ap 85, p. 86.
       "Moonlight and the white cat watches." Amelia (2:2) O 85,
          p. 12.
4131. ROBSON, Ruthann
       "Because of Blanche." NegC (5:2) Spr 85, p. 15-16.
4132. ROCHE, Judith
       "Desire." YellowS (16) Aut 85, p. 28.
4133. RODEFER, Stephen
       "Fidelity." Conjunc (8) 85, p. 117-118.
       "Flowering." Sulfur (12) 85, p. 48-49.
       "Hart Crane." Zyzzyva (1:1) Spr 85, p. 102-103.
       "Passing Duration" (4 selections). Temblor (2) 85, p. 92-
          95.
4134. RODIER, Katharine
       "Reply." AntR (43:3) Sum 85, p. 330.
4135. RODRIGUEZ, Eugenio
       "Win Wenders, Los Reyes de la Carretera." LindLM (4:2) Ap-
          Je 85, p. 27.
4136. RODRIGUEZ, Norman
       "Ramona." Mairena (7:19) 85, p. 105.
4137. RODRIGUEZ DEL PINO, Salvador
       "On Problems." Imagine (1:2) Wint 84, p. 135.
       "The View from El Capricho." Imagine (1:2) Wint 84, p.
          136.
4138. RODRIGUEZ-NIETO, Catherine
       "Marina" (tr. of Lucha Corpi). AmerPoR (14:4) Jl-Ag 85,
          p. 31.
       "The Protocol of Vegetables" (tr. of Lucha Corpi).
          AmerPoR (14:4) Jl-Ag 85, p. 31.
4139. RODRÍGUEZ NIETZSCHE, Vicente
       "A Juan Antonio Corretjer." Mairena (7:19) 85, p. 84.
4140. ROESKE, Paulette
       "The Bus Driver Dreams of Blue Island." Ascent (11:1) 85,
          p. 51-52.
       "How the Twentieth Century Betrayed the Last Christian
          Martyr." Ascent (11:1) 85, p. 52-53.
       "Lost." IndR (8:2) Spr 85, p. 100-101.
       "Mother, Retelling the News." Ascent (11:1) 85, p. 54.
       "A Plan to Circumvent the Death of Beauty." Tendril
          (19/20) 85, p. 306.
       "Venus de Milo: Her Final Complaint." ChiR (35:2) Wint
          85, p. 50-51.
       "Waiting for This." IndR (8:2) Spr 85, p. 98-99.
4141. ROGAL, Stanley
       "Juno." WestCR (20:2) O 85, p. 26.
       "Measuring." WestCR (20:2) O 85, p. 26.
       "Transition." WestCR (20:2) O 85, p. 26.
4142. ROGERS, Anne
       "Subterranean Blueprint." GrahamHR (8) Wint 85, p. 10-11.
       "Three Poems." KanQ (17:1/2) Wint-Spr 85, p. 216.
4143. ROGERS, C. D.
       "The Mark." SanFPJ (7:2) 85, p. 31.
       "Pestilence." SanFPJ (7:2) 85, p. 30.
4144. ROGERS, Jalane
       "Dream Image." DeKalbLAJ (18:1/2) 85, p. 83.
4145. ROGERS, Linda
       "The Bridge." PoetryCR (7:2) Wint 85-86, p. 15.
       "Cadenza for Wallace Stevens." PoetryCR (7:2) Wint 85-86,
          p. 15.
       "Eat the Apple." PoetryCR (7:2) Wint 85-86, p. 15.
       "Embouchure." PoetryCR (7:2) Wint 85-86, p. 15.
       "Idiot Savant." PoetryCR (7:2) Wint 85-86, p. 15.
       "Invention of the World." CanLit (107) Wint 85, p. 111.
       "Muskrat." PoetryCR (7:2) Wint 85-86, p. 15.

"Rhinestone Madonna." <u>PoetryCR</u> (7:2) Wint 85-86, p. 15.
4146. ROGERS, Pattiann
"Coming Back." <u>PoetryNW</u> (26:2) Sum 85, p. 29-30.
"The Creation of Protest" (Stan Engelke, September 1965-May
1983). <u>VirQ</u> (61:1) Wint 85, p. 60-61.
"Finding the Tattooed Lady in the Garden." <u>PoetryNW</u>
(26:2) Sum 85, p. 30-31.
"How the Whale Forgets the Love of Felicia." <u>MissouriR</u>
(8:3) 85, p. 18-19.
"Inside God's Eye." <u>VirQ</u> (61:1) Wint 85, p. 59-60.
"The Nature of Winter." <u>PoetryNW</u> (26:2) Sum 85, p. 31-32.
"The Revolution of the Somersault." <u>Crazy</u> (26) Spr 84, p.
48.
"Stripes of the Sea: Multiple Images and the Spaces
Between." <u>Crazy</u> (26) Spr 84, p. 49.
ROGOFF, Jay Grover
<u>See</u> GROVER-ROGOFF, Jay
4147. ROGOW, Zack
"Earthlight" (Selections: 15 poems, tr. of André Breton,
w. Bill Zavatsky). <u>AmerPoR</u> (14:1) Ja-F 85, p. 3-10.
"Maps on the Dunes" (To Giuseppe Ungaretti, tr. of André
Breton, w. Bill Zavatsky). <u>Antaeus</u> (55) Aut 85, p. 90.
"The Reptile Houseburglars" (To Janine, tr. of André
Breton, w. Bill Zavatsky). <u>Antaeus</u> (55) Aut 85, p. 88-
89.
"Shrivelled Love" (tr. of André Breton, w. Bill
Zavatsky). <u>Antaeus</u> (55) Aut 85, p. 90.
"The Verb to Be" (tr. of André Breton, w. Bill Zavatsky).
<u>ParisR</u> (27:95) Spr 85, p. 131-132.
4148. ROHLFS, Bruce
"Chicago Alley." <u>MidAR</u> (5:2) 85, p. 93.
4149. ROHRER, Jane
"Bad Truth." <u>AmerPoR</u> (14:1) Ja-F 85, p. 40.
"Orchard in the Spring." <u>AmerPoR</u> (14:1) Ja-F 85, p. 40.
4150. ROJAS, Gonzalo
"A Veces Pienso Quién." <u>Inti</u> (18/19) Otoño 83-Prim.
84, p. 41.
"Al Silencio." <u>Inti</u> (18/19) Otoño 83-Prim. 84, p. 34.
"Carbón." <u>Inti</u> (18/19) Otoño 83-Prim. 84, p. 37-38.
"Celia." <u>Inti</u> (18/19) Otoño 83-Prim. 84, p. 39-40.
"Contra la Muerte." <u>Inti</u> (18/19) Otoño 83-Prim. 84, p.
36-37.
"Los Días Van Tan Rápidos" (A Vicente Gerbasi en
Venezuela, en Chile, antes, despuées). <u>Inti</u> (18/19)
Otoño 83-Prim. 84, p. 38-39.
"Escrito con L." <u>Inti</u> (18/19) Otoño 83-Prim. 84, p. 34-
35.
"Fosa con Paul Celan." <u>Inti</u> (18/19) Otoño 83-Prim. 84,
p. 41-42.
"Oscuridad Hermosa." <u>Inti</u> (18/19) Otoño 83-Prim. 84, p.
33.
"Qué Se Ama Cuando Se Ama?" <u>Inti</u> (18/19) Otoño 83-
Prim. 84, p. 35-36.
"Requiem de la Mariposa." <u>Inti</u> (18/19) Otoño 83-Prim.
84, p. 40-41.
"Una Vez el Azar Se Llamo Jorge Cáceres." <u>Inti</u> (18/19)
Otoño 83-Prim. 84, p. 33-34.
4151. ROJO LEON, Armando
"A Jorge Guillén, Enamorado da la Vida" (A Málaga).
<u>SinN</u> (14:4) Jl-S 84, p. 106.
4152. ROLLINGS, Alane
"In the Days inside the Night." <u>AntR</u> (43:2) Spr 85, p.
202-203.
"Where Single Rooms Can Spring to Life So Easily." <u>AntR</u>
(43:2) Spr 85, p. 200-201.

4153. ROLLINS, Scott
"Before the Revolution" (tr. of Patricia Lasoen). <u>Vis</u>
(18) 85, p. 21.
"Quartz, Mica, Feldspar" (tr. of Judith Herzberg). <u>Vis</u>
(19) 85, p. 35.

4154. ROMAINE, E.
"Zeno Proves That the Stone He Just Dropped and Which Hit
the Ground Did Not Fall." <u>TexasR</u> (6:1/2) Spr-Sum 85,
p. 24.

4155. ROMERO, Julia
"Amor Muerto." <u>Mairena</u> (7:19) 85, p. 106.

4156. ROMTVEDT, David
"Black Beauty, a Praise." <u>Raccoon</u> (17) Mr 85, p. 45-48.
"To Make It Now." <u>CrabCR</u> (3:1) Fall-Wint 85, p. 24-25.

4157. ROMUALDO, Alejandro
"Almost a Fable" (tr. by John Olver Simon). <u>Chelsea</u> (44)
85, p. 88.

4158. RONCI, Ray
"For Mary." <u>Ploughs</u> (11:1) 85, p. 187.
"Providence." <u>Ploughs</u> (11:1) 85, p. 186.
"Rilke's Waif." <u>Ploughs</u> (11:1) 85, p. 188-189.

4159. RONER, C. J.
"Child of the Cong." <u>SanFPJ</u> (7:3) 84 [i.e. 85], p. 85-86.
"No Surrender at the Summit" (8-26-84). <u>SanFPJ</u> (7:3) 84
[i.e. 85], p. 88.

4160. RONSARD, Pierre de
"On the Death of Marie" (From the <u>Second</u> <u>Book</u> <u>of</u> <u>Loves</u>,
tr. by Charles Guenther). <u>WebR</u> (10:1) Spr 85, p. 34.
"Sonnet XCVI" (From the <u>First</u> <u>Book</u> <u>of</u> <u>Loves</u>, tr. by
Charles Guenther). <u>WebR</u> (10:1) Spr 85, p. 33.

4161. ROOP, Laura
"The Locked Room." <u>MichQR</u> (24:4) Fall 85, p. 624.

4162. ROOT, Judith
"Barnstormer's Loop." <u>AmerPoR</u> (14:4) Jl-Ag 85, p. 15.
"Naming the Shells." <u>Nat</u> (241:2) 20-27 Jl 85, p. 61.

4163. ROOT, William Pitt
"An Artist at the Death of His First Wife" (Claude Monet to
Georges Clemenceau). <u>CrabCR</u> (2:3) Sum 85, p. 26.
"Monet in Cleveland." <u>AmerPoR</u> (14:1) Ja-F 85, p. 47.
"Newswalkers of Swidnik." <u>Tendril</u> (19/20) 85, p. 307-310.
"Terriblita." <u>NewL</u> (52:1) Fall 85, p. 13-14.

ROQUE, Catherine la
<u>See</u> La ROQUE, Catherine

4164. RORICK, Robert
"For the Vice Officer I Kissed in the Wood near Lake
Harriet." <u>JamesWR</u> (2:2) Wint 85, p. 5.

4165. ROSA, Antônio Ramos
"Body in Brightness" (tr. by Sharon Ann Jaeger). <u>GrahamHR</u>
(9) Fall 85, p. 96.
"In the Sphere of Repose" (tr. by Sharon Ann Jaeger).
<u>GrahamHR</u> (9) Fall 85, p. 97.
"Pulsations of the Earth" (tr. by Sharon Ann Jaeger).
<u>GrahamHR</u> (9) Fall 85, p. 94-95.
"To Write" (tr. by Sharon Ann Jaeger). <u>GrahamHR</u> (9) Fall
85, p. 93.

4166. ROSADO, Gabriel
"Epitafio 2." <u>Inti</u> (20) Otoño 84, p. 109-110.
"Homenaje a Góngora." <u>Inti</u> (20) Otoño 84, p. 109.
"El Sueño de Endimión." <u>Inti</u> (20) Otoño 84, p. 109.

4167. ROSALES, Héctor
"Sobre Los Angeles." <u>Imagine</u> (1:2) Wint 84, p. 137-138.

4168. ROSALES, Mauricio
"You Have what I Want" (tr. of Jaime Sabines). <u>Mund</u>
(15:1/2) 85, p. 157.

4169. ROSBERG, Rose
"Closed Accounts." <u>Quarry</u> (34:4) Aut 85, p. 14.

"Imaging Waters." <u>Wind</u> (15:55) 85, p. 32.
4170. ROSBOROUGH, Jeff
     "Thomas Hardy Speaks One Night Not Long before His Death."
        <u>BlueBldgs</u> (9) [85?], p. 18.
     "Where Do We Come From? What Are We? Where Are We Going?"
        <u>BlueBldgs</u> (9) [85?], p. 19.
4171. ROSCHER, Marina
     "Blue Garden Ball" (tr. of Sarah Kirsch, w. Charles
        Fishman). <u>NewL</u> (51:4) Sum 85, p. 70-71.
     "Motionless" (tr. of Sarah Kirsch, w. Charles Fishman).
        <u>NewL</u> (51:4) Sum 85, p. 72.
     "Stoneheart" (tr. of Sarah Kirsch, w. Charles Fishman).
        <u>NewL</u> (51:4) Sum 85, p. 70.
     "Winter Promenade" (tr. of Sarah Kirsch, w. Charles
        Fishman). <u>NewL</u> (51:4) Sum 85, p. 71.
4172. ROSE, Jennifer
     "Eastham Sonnets." <u>Nat</u> (240:18) 11 My 85, p. 567.
4173. ROSE, Jonathan
     "Indecisive." <u>PoeticJ</u> (9) 85, p. 40.
4174. ROSE, Mike
     "Elise." <u>Bogg</u> (53) 85, p. 8.
     "He Used Sweet Wine in Place of Life Because He Didn't Have
        Any More Life to Use" (Richard Brautigan, in memoriam).
        <u>ColEng</u> (47:6) O 85, p. 610.
4175. ROSE, Wilga
     "Sea Song." <u>Bogg</u> (54) 85, p. 13.
4176. ROSEN, Aaron
     "Self-Portrait: Alberto Giacometti." <u>Epoch</u> (34:2) 84-85,
        p. 101.
     "Self-Portrait: Milton Avery." <u>Epoch</u> (34:2) 84-85, p. 100.
4177. ROSEN, Kenneth
     "Bluejay." <u>SenR</u> (15:2) 85, p. 133-134.
     "Earthworm and Slug." <u>Pequod</u> (18) 85, p. 119-120.
     "Forgetting Ogunquit" (for Jane Hardy, d. summer 1983).
        <u>SenR</u> (15:2) 85, p. 128-132.
     "The Foxes." <u>Pequod</u> (18) 85, p. 117-118.
     "Performances." <u>Telescope</u> (4:2) Spr 85, p. 42-45.
     "Polar Bear." <u>SenR</u> (15:2) 85, p. 135-136.
     "Red Pilot." <u>AmerPoR</u> (14:6) N-D 85, p. 19.
     "White Dove." <u>Pequod</u> (18) 85, p. 121-122.
4178. ROSEN, Michael (<u>See also</u> ROSEN, Michael J.)
     "Child's Play." <u>Tendril</u> (19/20) 85, p. 311-312.
     "Walden Pond." <u>ChiR</u> (34:4) 85, p. 66.
4179. ROSEN, Michael J. (<u>See also</u> ROSEN, Michael)
     "En Route." <u>Epoch</u> (34:2) 84-85, p. 120.
     "Holding Pattern." <u>GreenfR</u> (13:1/2) Fall-Wint 85, p. 30.
     "A Tough Act to Follow." <u>Epoch</u> (34:2) 84-85, p. 118-119.
     "The Year Penn's Elevator Is Converted." <u>Epoch</u> (34:2) 84-
        85, p. 121.
4180. ROSENBERG, David
     "Pentecostal." <u>Nat</u> (240:12) 30 Mr 85, p. 376.
     "TV of Sun." <u>VirQ</u> (61:4) Aut 85, p. 624-625.
4181. ROSENBERG, L. M.
     "The Accident." <u>PraS</u> (59:2) Sum 85, p. 88-90.
     "Another Sleepless Night among the Ruins." <u>Crazy</u> (27)
        Fall 84, p. 16.
     "Dread." <u>NewYorker</u> (61:16) 10 Je 85, p. 115.
     "First Heat." <u>Crazy</u> (27) Fall 84, p. 17.
     "The Grief Machine." <u>NewL</u> (51:3) Spr 85, p. 55.
     "Thanksgiving Company." <u>Crazy</u> (27) Fall 84, p. 15.
     "Wearing His Old Boots." <u>MissouriR</u> (8:2) 85, p. 58.
4182. ROSENBERG, Liz
     "Into the Territories." <u>Nat</u> (241:18) 30 N 85, p. 592.
     "What's in the Air." <u>ThRiPo</u> (25/26) 85, p. 51.
     "Why Plato Hated the Poets." <u>ThRiPo</u> (25/26) 85, p. 50.

4183. ROSENBERGER, Francis Coleman
"Poetry Reading." SouthernPR (25:1) Spr 85, p. 58.
4184. ROSENBLATT, Judith
"Child." CrossCur (4:1) 84, p. 101-102.
4185. ROSENFELD, Natania
"Annele's Girl." SenR (15:1) 85, p. 74.
4186. ROSENSTOCK, Carl
"Legend in My Lifetime." PoetL (80:3) Fall 85, p. 157-158.
4187. ROSENTHAL, Abby
"Instructions to My Husband, Snipping Mint in Our Tiny City
Backyard." HolCrit (22:2) Ap 85, p. 16.
4188. ROSENTHAL, M. L.
"The Blonde on the Beach." PoetryR (5) S 85, p. 23-25.
"Six Titles for Songs of the Balkan Peoples." OP (38/39)
Spr 85, p. 158.
4189. ROSENZWEIG, Gerry
"Atlantic Tides." PoeticJ (10) 85, p. 8.
"First Summer Visit." PoetL (80:3) Fall 85, p. 149.
"He Put the Burned Matches Back into the Box" (Title from
Yehuda Amichai. For Gary, 1932-1956). PoeticJ (10) 85,
p. 9.
4190. ROSS, Michael Lance
"Jo-burg II: Spring." HarvardA (118:3) Mr 85, p. 11.
"A Little Transaction." HarvardA (118:3) Mr 85, p. 9.
4191. ROSSELLI, Amelia
"Document" (tr. by Giuseppe Perricone). LitR (28:2) Wint
85, p. 301-303.
4192. ROSSER, J. Allyn
"The Ex." NegC (5:4) Fall 85, p. 122.
4193. ROSTWOROWSKI, Boguslaw
"The Belly of Barbara N." (tr. of Wiktor Woroszylski).
TriQ (63) Spr-Sum 85, p. 565.
4194. ROTELLA, Alexis
"Mother's Milk." Wind (15:54) 85, p. 45.
"Separated." SmPd (22:1) Wint 85, p. 15.
"Soup." LaurelR (19:1) Wint 85, p. 18.
4195. ROTH, Daniel
"Ringside Seats." WindO (45) Spr 85, p. 38.
4196. ROTHENBERG, Jerome
"A Danube Vision." RiverS (18) 85, p. 51.
"Dreamwork One" (for Barbara Einzig). Sulfur (12) 85, p.
106-108.
"Dreamwork Three." Sulfur (12) 85, p. 109-111.
"Dreamwork Two." Sulfur (12) 85, p. 109.
"Shaman Dreamwork Four." RiverS (18) 85, p. 50.
"Shaman Dreamwork One." RiverS (18) 85, p. 48.
"Shaman Dreamwork Three." RiverS (18) 85, p. 49.
"Shaman Dreamwork Two." RiverS (18) 85, p. 48.
"Visions of Jesus." Sulfur (14) 85, p. 22-24.
4197. ROTHHOLZ, Amy
"Hieroglyphics." PoetL (80:3) Fall 85, p. 134.
"John Ashbery in the East End." Confr (30/31) N 85, p. 17.
4198. ROTHMAN, David
"Honor." QW (20) Spr-Sum 85, p. 98.
4199. ROUGHTON, Becke
"In the Wilderness." SouthernPR (25:1) Spr 85, p. 54.
4200. ROUNTREE, Thomas
"Over Fifty." NegC (5:4) Fall 85, p. 144.
4201. ROVERSI, Roberto
"Descriptions Underway" (Excerpt, tr. by P. F. Paolini).
LitR (28:2) Wint 85, p. 304-305.
4202. ROWAN, Phyllis
"But Still." Germ (9:1) Spr-Sum 85, p. 27.
4203. ROWE, Kelly
"Eurydice in the Garden." SenR (15:2) 85, p. 31-32.
"The Faithful." SenR (15:2) 85, p. 33.

"Fear." <u>SenR</u> (15:2) 85, p. 30.
"Hangover." <u>SenR</u> (15:2) 85, p. 35-36.
"Instructions on How to Fall Asleep." <u>SenR</u> (15:2) 85, p.
   37.
"The Traveling Salesman's Wife." <u>SenR</u> (15:2) 85, p. 34.
4204. ROWELL, Charles H.
"Grandpa Paul." <u>SouthernR</u> (21:3) Sum 85, p. 837-838.
"Window" (for Brenda Marie Osbey). <u>SouthernR</u> (21:3) Sum
   85, p. 839-841.
4205. ROYET-JOURNOUD, Claude
"Love in the Ruins" (tr. by Keith Waldrop). <u>Conjunc</u> (8)
   85, p. 108-115.
4206. ROYSTER, Philip M.
"Love Song from a Plain Brown Rapper." <u>BlackALF</u> (19:3)
   Fall 85, p. 110.
4207. RUBENSTEIN, Elaine
"Aubade." <u>Poetry</u> (145:5) F 85, p. 267-268.
"Deborah's Lament." <u>Poetry</u> (145:5) F 85, p. 267.
4208. RUBIA, Geraldine
"Autumn Song." <u>CanLit</u> (107) Wint 85, p. 4.
"Skating among the Graves." <u>CanLit</u> (107) Wint 85, p. 32-
   33.
4209. RUBIN, Larry
"Alternatives." <u>CrossCur</u> (4:2) 84, p. 140.
"The Cold Front Passes." <u>Wind</u> (15:53) 85, p. 40.
"Dirge for Autumn." <u>MassR</u> (26:4) Wint 85, p. 502.
"The Drowning (II)." <u>Wind</u> (15:53) 85, p. 40-41.
"Final Maps." <u>SewanR</u> (93:4) Fall 85, p. 537.
"Imperfect Dissolution." <u>Wind</u> (15:53) 85, p. 40.
"Lines to a Middle-Aged Cousin Who Has Just Had Her Face
   Lifted." <u>PoetryR</u> (2:2) Ap 85, p. 59.
"The Mantra." <u>Amelia</u> (2:1) Ap 85, p. 57.
"Sunday at Sea." <u>SewanR</u> (93:4) Fall 85, p. 537.
"Words to a Disciple." <u>PoetryR</u> (2:2) Ap 85, p. 59.
4210. RUBIN, Mark
"1973 Cabernet." <u>NoAmR</u> (270:1) Mr 85, p. 72.
4211. RUDD, Gail
"She Is Wearing Her Sad Coat." <u>USl</u> (18/19) Wint 85, p. 18.
4212. RUDMAN, Mark
"First Glances." <u>Pequod</u> (19/20/21) 85, p. 285-286.
"How life lulls us" (tr. of Boris Pasternak, w. Bohdan
   Boychuk). <u>Pequod</u> (19/20/21) 85, p. 260-263.
"Landscapes" (tr. of Bohdan Boychuk, w. the author).
   <u>GrandS</u> (4:3) Spr 85, p. 132.
"Last Morning." <u>Pequod</u> (19/20/21) 85, p. 289.
"The Morning After." <u>PoetryE</u> (18) Fall 85, p. 17.
"Perspective." <u>Pequod</u> (19/20/21) 85, p. 284.
"Rome 1." <u>Pequod</u> (19/20/21) 85, p. 287.
"Rome 2: Recovering from Michelangelo." <u>Pequod</u> (19/20/21)
   85, p. 288.
4213. RUDNIK, Raphael
"On the Train." <u>Pequod</u> (19/20/21) 85, p. 290-292.
4214. RUDOLF, Anthony
"Hier Règnant Désert" (tr. of Yves Bonnefoy). <u>Stand</u>
   (26:3) Sum 85, p. 46.
4215. RUESCHER, Scott
"Blue Anniversary." <u>SenR</u> (15:2) 85, p. 38-39.
"The Cold Garage." <u>SenR</u> (15:2) 85, p. 40-41.
"From a Log Fallen in the Shade of a Lilac Bush." <u>SenR</u>
   (15:2) 85, p. 42-43.
"Get Well Card with Wild Bouquet." <u>PoetryNW</u> (26:3) Aut
   85, p. 32-33.
4216. RUFF, John
"How I Left the Fish Tank." <u>SenR</u> (15:1) 85, p. 69-70.
4217. RUFFIN, Paul
"Drought." <u>SouthernPR</u> (25:1) Spr 85, p. 44.

"The Fox." <u>NoDaQ</u> (53:4) Fall 85, p. 225-226.
"Gigging Frogs." <u>SoCaR</u> (17:2) Spr 85, p. 73.
"His Grandfather Talks about Naming." <u>KanQ</u> (17:4) Fall
    85, p. 149.
"His Grandmother Kills a Snake." <u>NoDaQ</u> (53:4) Fall 85, p.
    224.
"His Grandmother Talks about God." <u>NoDaQ</u> (53:4) Fall 85,
    p. 223.
"The Land." <u>GreenfR</u> (13:1/2) Fall-Wint 85, p. 165.
"On the Green of Your Grave." <u>CentR</u> (29:4) Fall 85, p.
    443.
"River Swing." <u>GreenfR</u> (13:1/2) Fall-Wint 85, p. 164.
"The Warmth of Stone." <u>KanQ</u> (17:4) Fall 85, p. 148-149.
RUGERIS, C. K. de
    <u>See</u> DeRUGERIS, C. K.
RUIZ, José O. Colón
    <u>See</u> COLON RUIZ, José O.
4218. RUKEYSER, Muriel
    "Effort at Speech between Two People." <u>PoetryE</u> (16/17)
        Spr-Sum 85, p. 17-18.
    "A Little Stone in the Middle of the Road, in Florida."
        <u>PoetryE</u> (16/17) Spr-Sum 85, p. 23.
    "Myth." <u>PoetryE</u> (16/17) Spr-Sum 85, p. 24.
    "Nine Poems for the Unborn Child." <u>PoetryE</u> (16/17) Spr-
        Sum 85, p. 18-22.
    "Place Poems -- New York." <u>PoetryE</u> (16/17) Spr-Sum 85, p.
        27-43.
    "St. Roach." <u>PoetryE</u> (16/17) Spr-Sum 85, p. 25.
    "Then." <u>PoetryE</u> (16/17) Spr-Sum 85, p. 26.
    "An Unborn Poet" (for Alice Walker). <u>PoetryE</u> (16/17) Spr-
        Sum 85, p. 13-16.
    "The War Comes into My Room." <u>PoetryE</u> (16/17) Spr-Sum 85,
        back cover.
4219. RUKSTELIS, Michael
    "At the Monastery of the Holy Spirit, Conyers, GA." <u>Wind</u>
        (15:54) 85, p. 46.
4220. RUMENS, Carol
    "Camouflage." <u>Poetry</u> (146:4) Jl 85, p. 208.
4221. RUMMEL, Mary Kay
    "How Trees Grow." <u>Northeast</u> (Series 4:1) Sum 85, p. 28.
    "This Is Our Inheritance." <u>Vis</u> (18) 85, p. 35-36.
4222. RUNCIMAN, Lex
    "Postcard." <u>QW</u> (20) Spr-Sum 85, p. 119.
    "Repetitions." <u>MissouriR</u> (8:2) 85, p. 22-23.
    "Waiting for Nothing" (Tom Kromer, American Century
        Series). <u>MinnR</u> (N.S. 25) Fall 85, p. 18.
    "Walkers." <u>NewEngR</u> (7:3) Spr 85, p. 337-338.
4223. RUSH, Jerry (<u>See also</u> RUSH, Jerry M.)
    "Hedgerows Steel Themselves." <u>PoetryCR</u> (6:4) Sum 85, p.
        21.
4224. RUSH, Jerry M. (<u>See also</u> RUSH, Jerry)
    "Heia Safari!" <u>WestCR</u> (20:2) O 85, p. 25.
    "Pastel IV." <u>WestCR</u> (20:2) O 85, p. 25.
4225. RUSS, Biff
    "A Physics of Postwar Music" (for M.T.). <u>Outbr</u> (14/15)
        Fall 84-Spr 85, p. 8.
    "Something Harder." <u>Outbr</u> (14/15) Fall 84-Spr 85, p. 6-7.
    "The Spring before Your Father Leaves." <u>Outbr</u> (14/15)
        Fall 84-Spr 85, p. 5.
4226. RUSS, Lawrence
    "Down the Road." <u>NegC</u> (5:1) Wint 85, p. 55-56.
    "The Food of Fairyland." <u>BelPoJ</u> (36:2) Wint 85-86, p. 32-
        34.
4227. RUSS, Lisa
    "Blind Boy on Skates." <u>Crazy</u> (27) Fall 84, p. 36-37.
    "It All Comes Back to You." <u>PoetryE</u> (18) Fall 85, p. 58-

59.
4228. RUSSAKOFF, Molly
        "September 3, Philadelphia." ParisR (27:97) Fall 85, p.
        170-171.
4229. RUSSELL, Bill
        "The Trapeze." Open24 (4) 85, p. 37.
4230. RUSSELL, Carol Ann
        "Burning the Sweatlodge" (for Jeremiah McSparron). CharR
        (11:1) Spr 85, p. 88.
        "Ibeji." CharR (11:1) Spr 85, p. 87.
4231. RUSSELL, Frank
        "Another Rib." Chelsea (44) 85, p. 145.
        "Of Goners at Key West." KanQ (17:1/2) Wint-Spr 85, p.
        275.
        "Past the Everybodies." Chelsea (44) 85, p. 69.
        "Sand Key." Chelsea (44) 85, p. 68.
        "Sunday Occasionally." KanQ (17:1/2) Wint-Spr 85, p. 274-
        275.
4232. RUSSELL, Hilary
        "The Boy, Back Home." GWR (6:1) 85?, p. 9.
        "Singing School." GWR (6:1) 85?, p. 11.
        "The Widow Gets Her Boy to Plow." GWR (6:1) 85?, p. 10.
4233. RUSSELL, Norman H.
        "Botanist." DeKalbLAJ (18:1/2) 85, p. 84.
        "God Writes Accidents." WestB (16) 85, p. 64.
        "In the Forest." WestB (16) 85, p. 65.
4234. RUSSELL, R. F. Gillian (Harding)
        "Delta." Quarry (34:3) Sum 85, p. 41.
4235. RUSSELL, Timothy
        "Biding Time." PoetryNW (26:1) Spr 85, p. 42.
        "In Haec Verba." WestB (17) 85, p. 58.
        "In Vino Veritas." WestB (17) 85, p. 59.
4236. RUST, Laurel
        "This Room of the House." Calyx (9:1) Spr-Sum 85, p. 48-
        49.
4237. RUTER, Anthony H.
        "Carpe Diem" (Winner of the poetry prize in the Ohio High
        School Creative Writing Contest). WoosterR (3) Spr 85,
        p. 70-71.
4238. RUTH, Steve
        "Graduation Marriage, Anniversary Five." Wind (15:55) 85,
        p. 43.
4239. RUTSALA, Vern
        "An American Morning." Poetry (145:4) Ja 85, p. 196-197.
        "Cards from My Aunt." Crazy (27) Fall 84, p. 31-32.
        "Coming Home." Poetry (145:4) Ja 85, p. 197-198.
        "The Goodbye Series: A Memoir." MassR (26:1) Spr 85, p.
        81-82.
        "Hard Cases." NewYorker (61:27) 26 Ag 85, p. 65.
        "Once Again." PoetryR (2:2) Ap 85, p. 49-50.
        "Relatives." MissouriR (8:3) 85, p. 129.
        "Slinging Hash." MissouriR (8:3) 85, p. 128.
4240. RYAN, Dennis
        "Clouds caught in mist" ("Untitled"). Blueline (6:2) Wint-
        Spr 85, p. 48.
4241. RYAN, Gina
        "White Trains." NoDaQ (53:2) Spr 85, p. 218.
4242. RYAN, Kay
        "Asylum." NegC (5:3) Sum 85, p. 43.
        "For Virginia Woolf." SoDakR (23:2) Sum 85, p. 61.
        "It Has Been Said That the Greeks Were Great Because They
        Never Drew from the Antique" (Book of Tea). SoDakR
        (23:2) Sum 85, p. 62.
        "On the Primacy of Green." Zyzzyva (1:2) Sum 85, p. 20-21.
        "The Proof of God" (from Meditations I: The Sun That
        Burns). Pig (13) 85, p. 82.

"Road and Houses, Cape Cod" (Edward Hopper). AntigR (60)
Wint 85, p. 94.
"Six Persimmons" (Mu ch'i, 13th century). WebR (10:2)
Fall 85, p. 53.
"Something." Pig (13) 85, p. 82.
"What Nets But Words." WebR (10:2) Fall 85, p. 52.
"Winter Technique" ("Bamboo Trees," watercolor, Wang Tseng-
tsu). WebR (10:2) Fall 85, p. 53.
"The Zouave" (oil, Van Gogh). AntigR (60) Wint 85, p. 93.
4243. RYAN, Michael
"The Gladiator" (a tintinnabulae from Pompeii). AmerPoR
(14:1) Ja-F 85, p. 40.
"Switchblade." NewYorker (61:24) 5 Ag 85, p. 34.
4244. RYERSON, Alice
"Butterfly Man." Confr (30/31) N 85, p. 265.
"Is It True That Only Children Marry." Swallow (4) 85, p.
21.
"A Line from Tennyson Eludes Two Old English Professors in
July." Prima (9) 85, p. 71.
"May Floods." Prima (9) 85, p. 25.
4245. RYOKAN, Priest
"Retrospect" (tr. by Graeme Wilson). WestHR (39:1) Spr
85, p. 64.
4246. SABA, Umberto
"Champion Swimmer" (tr. by Michael L. Johnson). WebR
(10:1) Spr 85, p. 35.
"The House of My Babysitter" (tr. by Christopher Millis).
NewL (51:4) Sum 85, p. 170.
"Warning" (tr. by Christopher Millis). NewL (51:4) Sum
85, p. 170-171.
4247. SABINES, Jaime
"Tú Tienes Lo Que Busco." Mund (15:1/2) 85, p. 156.
"You Have what I Want" (tr. by Mauricio Rosales). Mund
(15:1/2) 85, p. 157.
4248. SACCA, Annalisa
"Annoying Doubt" (tr. of Aldo Palazzeschi). LitR (28:2)
Wint 85, p. 280.
"Birthday" (tr. of Giorgio Caproni). LitR (28:2) Wint 85,
p. 222.
"The Cock on the Barrel" (tr. of Franco Desideri). LitR
(28:2) Wint 85, p. 232.
"Death in Viareggio" (tr. of Francesco Mei). LitR (29:1)
Fall 85, p. 109.
"Details" (tr. of Cesare Vivaldi). LitR (28:2) Wint 85,
p. 310.
"Evening Ambush" (tr. of Francesco Mei). LitR (29:1) Fall
85, p. 107.
"Excessus" (tr. of Edoardo Cacciatore). LitR (28:2) Wint
85, p. 214.
"Experience" (tr. of Giorgio Caproni). LitR (28:2) Wint
85, p. 222.
"Five Poems" (tr. by the author). LitR (29:1) Fall 85, p.
117-118.
"Homecoming" (tr. of Giorgio Caproni). LitR (28:2) Wint
85, p. 221.
"I Have Nothing to Give You" (tr. of Franco Desideri).
LitR (28:2) Wint 85, p. 231.
"In This Scent" (tr. of Franco Desideri). LitR (28:2)
Wint 85, p. 231.
"Instinct of Self-preservation" (tr. of Nanni Balestrini).
LitR (28:2) Wint 85, p. 207.
"The Last Hamlet" (tr. of Giorgio Caproni). LitR (28:2)
Wint 85, p. 220-221.
"Manhattan's Balcony" (to Franco Desideri, tr. of Enzo
Nasso). LitR (29:1) Fall 85, p. 113.
"Not Even the Greeting" (tr. of Franco Desideri). LitR

(28:2) Wint 85, p. 231.
"Nothingness, Part II" (tr. of Edoardo Cacciatore). LitR
   (28:2) Wint 85, p. 213.
"Perhaps the Whistling of the Trains" (tr. of Enzo Nasso).
   LitR (29:1) Fall 85, p. 114.
"Portrait of a Sick Man" (tr. of Attilio Bertolucci).
   LitR (28:2) Wint 85, p. 208.
"Postcard 22" (tr. of Edoardo Sanguineti). LitR (28:2)
   Wint 85, p. 306.
"Postcard 46" (tr. of Edoardo Sanguineti). LitR (28:2)
   Wint 85, p. 306.
"The Squalor" (tr. of Franco Desideri). LitR (28:2) Wint
   85, p. 232.
"'Stracciafoglio': 34" (tr. of Edoardo Sanguineti). LitR
   (28:2) Wint 85, p. 307.
"'Stracciafoglio': 41" (tr. of Edoardo Sanguineti). LitR
   (28:2) Wint 85, p. 307.
"Sure Direction" (To the foreigner who had asked for the
   hotel, tr. of Giorgio Caproni). LitR (28:2) Wint 85,
   p. 221.
"The Wind Will Tell" (tr. of Francesco Mei). LitR (29:1)
   Fall 85, p. 108.
"You Rest Also" (tr. of Cesare Vivaldi). LitR (28:2) Wint
   85, p. 311.
4249. SACHA, Amy Harder
   "Marie Meyer at 83." Vis (17) 85, p. 21.
SACHIKO, Yoshihara
   See YOSHIHARA, Sachiko
4250. SACKS, Peter
   "Arles: The Bulls." NewRep (192:10) 11 Mr 85, p. 36.
   "In These Mountains." SenR (15:1) 85, p. 42-54.
   "Machadodorp." Crazy (29) Fall 85, p. 10-11.
   "Valerie." Crazy (29) Fall 85, p. 7-9.
4251. SADLER, Janet
   "A Case against Old Habits: A Vision." GeoR (39:4) Wint
      85, p. 714-715.
   "High Noon." GeoR (39:4) Wint 85, p. 715.
   "When We Are Denied." GeoR (39:4) Wint 85, p. 716.
4252. SADOFF, Ira
   "The Romance of the Radish" (From Palm Reading in
      Winter). Telescope (4:2) Spr 85, p. 34.
   "The Way of All Flesh." Antaeus (55) Aut 85, p. 152.
4253. SAENZ, Jaime
   "Este cuerpo, esta alma, están aquí." Inti (18/19)
      Otoño 83-Prim. 84, p. 81-82.
   "El Frío." Inti (18/19) Otoño 83-Prim. 84, p. 72-74.
   "Muerte por el Tacto" (Selection: II). Inti (18/19)
      Otoño 83-Prim. 84, p. 69-71.
   "Recorrer Esta Distancia" (A la imagen de Puraduralubia.
      Selections: I-II, VI-X). Inti (18/19) Otoño 83-Prim.
      84, p. 74-81.
4254. SAFARIK, Allan
   "Above the Bones." Dandel (12:2) 85, p. 54.
   "Being Human Is More Dangerous Than Being Mineral."
      Dandel (12:2) 85, p. 56-57.
   "The Bloodletting." Waves (13:4) Spr 85, p. 73.
   "Folk Song." Dandel (12:2) 85, p. 55.
   "Naked in the Fields by Lantern Light" (for Ian and Linda).
      Dandel (12:2) 85, p. 58-59.
4255. SAGAN, Miriam
   "Calistoga, July 21, 1983." Sam (42:4, 168th release) 85,
      back cover.
   "Chamber Music Concert, Dublin, New Hampshire." StoneC
      (13:1/2) Fall-Wint 85-86, p. 56.
   "Elsewhere." Amelia (2:1) Ap 85, p. 79.
   "Leaving the Temple." Sam (42:3, 167th release) 85, p. 34-

35.
"Ruins" (For Daniel). <u>Sam</u> (42:4, 168th release) 85, p. 28-29.
"Women in the Country of the Rain." <u>Imagine</u> (2:1) Sum 85, p. 83.
4256. SAGARIS, Lake
"Carmen Gloria" (a young woman murdered in Valparaiso while participating in the third national protest against Chile's military regime). <u>PoetryCR</u> (6:4) Sum 85, p. 41.
"Night." <u>PoetryCR</u> (6:4) Sum 85, p. 41.
4257. SAHAKIAN, Yuri
"Portrait" (tr. by Diana Der Hovanessian). <u>GrahamHR</u> (8) Wint 85, p. 45-46.
"Your Shadow Falls on My Life" (tr. by Diana Der Hovanessian). <u>Mund</u> (15:1/2) 85, p. 69.
SAINT
See also ST. (filed as spelled)
4258. SALEH, Dennis
"Chin." <u>LittleM</u> (14:4) 85, p. 16-17.
"Number Seven Dust." <u>LittleM</u> (14:4) 85, p. 18.
4259. SALINAS, Luis Omar
"Back in Town Again." <u>Crazy</u> (26) Spr 84, p. 16-17.
"Come Pick Up My Body." <u>Crazy</u> (26) Spr 84, p. 18.
4260. SALINAS, Pedro
"Signs" (tr. by Charles Guenther). <u>CharR</u> (11:1) Spr 85, p. 93-94.
4261. SALINERO, Amelia
"Poemas Sensibles." <u>Imagine</u> (2:1) Sum 85, p. 50.
4262. SALING, Joseph
"Encounter." <u>PoetL</u> (79:4) Wint 85, p. 212.
4263. SALISBURY, Ralph
"Death of ____ _____, Chief without a Tribe." <u>NoDaQ</u> (53:2) Spr 85, p. 45-46.
"A Descendant of 'Savage' Nature Worshipping Cherokees Visits Christian Venice." <u>CharR</u> (11:1) Spr 85, p. 82.
"For Prairie Chicken, Now Extinct." <u>GreenfR</u> (12:3/4) Wint-Spr 85, p. 82.
"Green Dragon Mine." <u>CrossCur</u> (5:3) 85, p. 52.
"One-Past." <u>PoetC</u> (17:1) Fall 85, p. 38.
"Ranch Sleep-Out." <u>CrossCur</u> (4:2) 84, p. 19.
"The Soldier Who Would Ask." <u>GreenfR</u> (12:3/4) Wint-Spr 85, p. 80-82.
"Some Answers." <u>NoDaQ</u> (53:2) Spr 85, p. 46.
"The Ultimate Mountain." <u>CrossCur</u> (5:3) 85, p. 51.
4264. SALKEY, Andrew
"Cement Mixer." <u>GrandS</u> (5:1) Aut 85, p. 132.
"The President-Reject and the Last Lady." <u>MassR</u> (26:1) Spr 85, p. 85-92.
"Winnie Mandela." <u>GrandS</u> (5:1) Aut 85, p. 132.
SALLE, Peter la
See LaSALLE, Peter
4265. SALLEE, Hyun-jae Yee
"Reed Flowers" (tr. of Ahn-Jinn Yoo). <u>AntigR</u> (62/63) Sum-Aut 85, p. 78.
4266. SALLEE, Marjorie L.
"Committee Meeting." <u>EngJ</u> (74:8) D 85, p. 21.
4267. SALLEE, Wayne Allen
"Midday at the Twilight of the Words." <u>Open24</u> (4) 85, p. 10.
4268. SALLI, Doreen
"Echoes" (for Mummu, my grandmother). <u>NegC</u> (5:1) Wint 85, p. 114.
4269. SALLIS, James
"A Blaise Cendrars" (In French, tr. by Henry-Luc Planchat). <u>Rampike</u> (4:2/3) 85-86, p. 45.
"At Night." <u>CharR</u> (11:2) Fall 85, p. 75-76.

"Country Music." <u>NoDaQ</u> (53:4) Fall 85, p. 227.
"Leda." <u>NegC</u> (5:2) Spr 85, p. 167.
"Love, Again, at Forty." <u>CharR</u> (11:2) Fall 85, p. 76.
"Neighbor." <u>Confr</u> (29) Wint 85, p. 155.
"Shorecrest" (for Cathy L.). <u>NegC</u> (5:1) Wint 85, p. 101-102.
"The Surrealist Announces His Despair." <u>CharR</u> (11:2) Fall 85, p. 74.
"To a Russian Friend." <u>KanQ</u> (17:4) Fall 85, p. 124-125.
"What It Was Like in Boston." <u>ConnPR</u> (3:1) 84, p. 23.
4270. SALTER, Mary Jo
"The Cherry Blossoms at Mitsubishi." <u>Nat</u> (240:11) 23 Mr 85, p. 342.
"Dead Letters." <u>NewRep</u> (193:18) 28 O 85, p. 52.
4271. SAM, David A.
"Drifts." <u>StoneC</u> (13:1/2) Fall-Wint 85-86, p. 71.
4272. SAMARAS, Nicholas
"The Alcoholic's Wife." <u>Confr</u> (30/31) N 85, p. 164.
4273. SAMMONS, Toni
"If Winter, If Summer." <u>AntigR</u> (62/63) Sum-Aut 85, p. 89-90.
"The Otter." <u>AntigR</u> (62/63) Sum-Aut 85, p. 90.
4274. SAMOJLOV, David
"Black Poplar" (tr. by Robert L. Smith and Sylvia Maizell). <u>WebR</u> (10:1) Spr 85, p. 12.
"Inspiration" (tr. by Robert L. Smith and Sylvia Maizell). <u>WebR</u> (10:1) Spr 85, p. 13.
4275. SAMS, Jeffrey
"Leaving an After." <u>Open24</u> (4) 85, p. 7.
4276. SAMUELSON, Janet
"Letter to Mrs. Ramsay." <u>CentR</u> (29:3) Sum 85, p. 323.
"Sleeper." <u>CentR</u> (29:3) Sum 85, p. 323-324.
4277. SANAZARO, Leonard
"Nietzsche" (after Peter Zweig). <u>SouthwR</u> (70:1) Wint 85, p. 54.
"Remembrance" (Margaret Bunnell Young, 1906-1980). <u>KanQ</u> (17:1/2) Wint-Spr 85, p. 177.
SANCHEZ, Bethoven Medina
    <u>See</u> MEDINA SANCHEZ, Bethoven
4278. SANCHEZ, Enrique
"Origins of Cave Art" (tr. by John Olver Simon). <u>Chelsea</u> (44) 85, p. 90.
4279. SANCHEZ, Sonia
"Blues." <u>PoetryR</u> (2:2) Ap 85, p. 14.
4280. SANCHEZ MAYANS, Fernando
"Monologo del Soneto." <u>LindLM</u> (4:4) O-D 85, p. 13.
4281. SANDERS, David
"Mayflies." <u>NewOR</u> (12:4) Wint 85, p. 33.
4282. SANDERS, Mark
"The Creighton Pool Hall." <u>PraS</u> (59:1) Spr 85, p. 39.
"Digging for Fossils." <u>PraS</u> (59:1) Spr 85, p. 38.
4283. SANDERS, Patricia
"Seven." <u>CrossCur</u> (4:1) 84, p. 84-85.
4284. SANDERS, Shelly
"Poem in Two Parts." <u>CutB</u> (24) Spr-Sum 85, p. 38-41.
4285. SANDERSON, Gertrude
"Within the Mystery" (Excerpt, tr. of Jacques Brault). <u>AntigR</u> (61) Spr 85, p. 92-95.
4286. SANDLER, Warren
"Cosmic Debate." <u>SanFPJ</u> (7:4) 85, p. 66.
"Feast of Flies and Cats." <u>SanFPJ</u> (7:4) 85, p. 65.
"War Flashes." <u>SanFPJ</u> (7:4) 85, p. 67.
4287. SANDRY, Ellen S.
"The Loon." <u>SanFPJ</u> (7:2) 85, p. 39.
"Wildlife Only Please." <u>SanFPJ</u> (7:2) 85, p. 38.

4288. SANDS, Leslie
        "Fragments." PoeticJ (10) 85, p. 12.
4289. SANDY, Stephen
        "Egyptian Onions." Atlantic (256:6), D 85, p. 78.
        "From Away." Salm (66) Wint-Spr 85, p. 143-144.
        "Grenadine." CarolQ (37:2) Wint 85, p. 57.
        "The News and the Weather." QW (20) Spr-Sum 85, p. 76.
        "Ray's Garden Shop." GrandS (4:4) Sum 85, p. 31-33.
        "To Ammons." GrandS (4:4) Sum 85, p. 29-30.
SANEL, Wendy Keene
        See KEENE-SANEL, Wendy
4290. SANELLI, Mary Lou
        "Bloodmeat Each July" (For the Tsimshian Women of
          Metlakatla, Alaska). CrabCR (2:3) Sum 85, p. 11-12.
4291. SANER, Reg
        "Dear Reg." OP (38/39) Spr 85, p. 3.
        "Dragonfly Aspect." CrossCur (5:2) 85, p. 36-37.
        "If Space Were Curved." NoAmR (270:4) D 85, p. 55.
        "North Inlet, Jacob's Ladder." WoosterR (4) Fall 85, p. 7.
        "Of the Gods." SouthernPR (25:1) Spr 85, p. 6.
        "Sailor." CutB (24) Spr-Sum 85, p. 45.
        "Spangled." WoosterR (4) Fall 85, p. 8.
        "Visiting Petrarch at Arquà." IndR (8:1) Wint 85, p. 69-
          71.
        "What the Stream Said." LittleM (14:4) 85, p. 42.
        "You Have To." SouthernPR (25:1) Spr 85, p. 5.
4292. SANFORD, Christy Sheffield
        "8 mm Wedding, Spliced." Vis (18) 85, p. 5-6.
4293. SANGER, Peter
        "Crabapple Blossoms." AntigR (62/63) Sum-Aut 85, p. 166.
        "Fisherman." AntigR (62/63) Sum-Aut 85, p. 165.
        "Kestrel." AntigR (62/63) Sum-Aut 85, p. 164.
4294. SANGUINETI, Edoardo
        "Laborintus" (Selections: 8, 11, 23, tr. by Lawrence R.
          Smith). Iowa (15:2) Spr-Sum 85, p. 85-87.
        "Postcard 22" (tr. by Annalisa Saccà). LitR (28:2) Wint
          85, p. 306.
        "Postcard 46" (tr. by Annalisa Saccà). LitR (28:2) Wint
          85, p. 306.
        "'Stracciafoglio': 34" (tr. by Annalisa Saccà). LitR
          (28:2) Wint 85, p. 307.
        "'Stracciafoglio': 41" (tr. by Annalisa Saccà). LitR
          (28:2) Wint 85, p. 307.
SANKICHI, Toge
        See TOGE, Sankichi
4295. SANSIRENE, Teresa
        "Por un Brindis a la Nostalgia" (a mi madre). LindLM
          (4:3) Jl-S 85, p. 5.
4296. SANSOM, Peter
        "Relax." Bogg (54) 85, p. 10.
4297. SantaVICCA, Ed
        "Asymmetrical Ambivalence." JamesWR (2:1) Fall 84, p. 4.
        "There Is Disagreement." JamesWR (2:2) Wint 85, p. 1.
4298. SANTEK, Jerry
        "Desert Walk." Wind (15:53) 85, p. 42.
SANTIAGO, Sabino Méndez
        See MENDEZ SANTIAGO, Sabino
4299. SANTIAGO-IBARRA, Beatriz
        "Escuechen a la Poeta." Mairena (7:19) 85, p. 110.
4300. SANTIAGO MERLO, Antonio
        "A la Mujer Sensible." Mairena (7:19) 85, p. 105.
SANTO, Alex di
        See DiSANTO, Alex
4301. SANTOS, Sherod
        "After the Island Fighting." NewYorker (61:26) 19 Ag 85,
          p. 32.

"Apollinaire's Epitaph." PoetryCR (7:1) Aut 85, p. 37.
"At the All-Clear." NewYorker (61:31) 23 S 85, p. 40.
"Farmland on the North Coast." PoetryCR (7:1) Aut 85, p.
    36.
"Ghosts." PoetryCR (7:1) Aut 85, p. 37.
"Married Love." Atlantic (255:1), Ja 85, p. 66.
"Saying Goodbye to a Friend" (for Catherine Parke).
    PoetryCR (7:1) Aut 85, p. 36.
"The Sea Change." Antaeus (55) Aut 85, p. 153-154.
"The Unsleeping Genius of Misfortune." Poetry (147:1) O
    85, p. 22-24.
4302. SANTOS SILVA, Loreina
"A Victoria Urbano." LetFem (11:1/2) Prim-Otoño 85, p.
    100-101.
"Porque aquí, donde estoy." Mairena (7:19) 85, p. 107.
4303. SANTOS TIRADO, Adrián
"Esta Dura Tristeza." Mairena (7:19) 85, p. 106.
4304. SAPIA, Yvonne
"La Desconocida." RevChic (13:1) Spr 85, p. 43.
"The Distant Figure, Approaching." RevChic (13:1) Spr 85,
    p. 46.
"La Mujer, Her Back to the Spectator." RevChic (13:1) Spr
    85, p. 45.
"Perdida" (for Miriam). PraS (59:2) Sum 85, p. 91.
"La Persona." RevChic (13:1) Spr 85, p. 44.
"Prepositional Phases." NegC (5:3) Sum 85, p. 86-87.
"Return to the Sanctuary." PartR (52:4) 85, p. 423-424.
"Rosario's Fault." RevChic (13:1) Spr 85, p. 41-42.
4305. SAPINKOPF, Lisa
"The Beautiful Summer" (tr. of Yves Bonnefoy). Ploughs
    (11:4) 85, p. 112.
"Delphi the Second Day" (tr. of Yves Bonnefoy). Ploughs
    (11:4) 85, p. 113.
"Dialogue of Anguish and Desire" (Excerpts, from Words in
    Stone, tr. of Yves Bonnefoy). PartR (52:3) 85, p. 241-
    242.
"The Foliage Lit Up" (from Yesterday's Barren Kingdom,
    tr. of Yves Bonnefoy). Abraxas (33) 85, p. 30-31.
"I believe in the trees whose roots sink" (tr. of Sophia de
    Mello Breyner Andresen). StoneC (13:1/2) Fall-Wint 85-
    86, p. 50-51.
"Inert margins spread their arms" (tr. of Sophia de Mello
    Breyner Andresen). StoneC (13:1/2) Fall-Wint 85-86, p.
    48-49.
"The Iron Bridge" (tr. of Yves Bonnefoy). Ploughs (11:4)
    85, p. 115.
"Nine Poems" (tr. of Sophia de Mello Breyner Andresen).
    Ploughs (11:4) 85, p. 230-232.
"Our fingers opened closed hands" (tr. of Sophia de Mello
    Breyner Andresen). StoneC (13:1/2) Fall-Wint 85-86, p.
    48-49.
"The pinetrees moan at the passing wind" (tr. of Sophia de
    Mello Breyner Andresen). StoneC (13:1/2) Fall-Wint 85-
    86, p. 50-51.
"The Ravine" (tr. of Yves Bonnefoy). Ploughs (11:4) 85,
    p. 114.
"Shake off the clouds that settle on your hair" (from
    Coral, tr. of Sophia de Mello Breyner Andresen).
    Abraxas (33) 85, p. 27.
"Threats of the Witness" (from Yesterday's Barren
    Kingdom, tr. of Yves Bonnefoy). Abraxas (33) 85, p.
    28-29.
"Veneranda" (tr. of Yves Bonnefoy). Ploughs (11:4) 85, p.
    113.
"A Voice" (tr. of Yves Bonnefoy). Ploughs (11:4) 85, p.
    115.

"Yes, To your rooms lined with moonlight" (from Coral,
    tr. of Sophia de Mello Breyner Andresen). Abraxas (33)
    85, p. 27.
4306. SAPPHO
"On the Tomb of Another Cuckold, Antilochosos of Athens"
    (tr. by Elliot Richman). WindO (46) Fall 85, p. 4.
"Poems" (Selections: 1, 2, 5, 15, 16, 31, 94, 104a, 105a,
    105c, tr. by Peter Jay). Iowa (15:2) Spr-Sum 85, p. 90-
    95.
4307. SARGENT, Colin
"Virga." PoetL (79:4) Wint 85, p. 224-225.
4308. SARGENT, Robert
"Stage Direction." PoetryR (2:2) Ap 85, p. 90.
4309. SARNER, Eric
"Wrecks" (tr. of Claude Maillard). Verse (2) 85, p. 36.
4310. SARTON, May
"The Cosset Lamb." CreamCR (10:2) [85?], p. 50.
"The Skilled Man" (for Bill Vaughan). CreamCR (10:2)
    [85?], p. 49.
4311. SASANOV, Catherine
"Becoming America." BelPoJ (36:2) Wint 85-86, p. 28.
4312. SATCHER, Mike
"No Charge." NegC (5:1) Wint 85, p. 130.
4313. SATO, Hiro
"Darkness falls to darkness, valley to valley" (tr. of
    Takahashi). NewL (51:4) Sum 85, p. 147.
"Forest, trees" (tr. of Takahashi). NewL (51:4) Sum 85,
    p. 147.
"Loves become torn apart" (tr. of Takahashi). NewL (51:4)
    Sum 85, p. 148.
4314. SAUL, Brandon
"Skepticism." ArizQ (41:3) Aut 85, p. 230.
4315. SAULS, Roger
"Charleston." Raccoon (17) Mr 85, p. 13.
"The Concept of Sorrow." PoetryE (18) Fall 85, p. 50.
4316. SAUNDERS, Clifford
"Blood of Sorrow, Blood of Light." Poem (54) N 85, p. 18-
    19.
4317. SAUNDERS, David
"Dressing the Pheasant." PoetryE (18) Fall 85, p. 51.
4318. SAUNDERS, Geraldine
"I Think of a Wild Horse Dancing." USl (18/19) Wint 85,
    p. 3.
"If Luck Comes Around." GreenfR (12:3/4) Wint-Spr 85, p.
    44-45.
4319. SAVAGE, Gail
"Tradeoffs." CrabCR (2:2) Wint 85, p. 11.
4320. SAVAGE, Tom
"Birthday Poem." LittleM (14:4) 85, p. 23.
"For Alice, a Miracle on Astor Place." PortLES (2:1) Sum
    85, p. 25.
4321. SAVARD, Jeannine
"The Blue Donkey." PoetryNW (26:4) Wint 85-86, p. 24.
"Burial." AmerPoR (14:5) S-O 85, p. 4.
"Feud." AmerPoR (14:5) S-O 85, p. 3.
"Figment." AmerPoR (14:5) S-O 85, p. 5.
"The Florist's Widow." AmerPoR (14:5) S-O 85, p. 5.
"For the Uncles." QW (21) Fall-Wint 85, p. 22.
"The Inheritance." AmerPoR (14:5) S-O 85, p. 5.
"Listening to Mozart's 'Jupiter' near the Desert Airport."
    AmerPoR (14:5) S-O 85, p. 5.
"A Mill Town in Late Autumn." QW (21) Fall-Wint 85, p. 21.
"October Nights." AmerPoR (14:5) S-O 85, p. 4.
"Postpartum." AmerPoR (14:5) S-O 85, p. 4.
"Shadow of the Ox." AmerPoR (14:5) S-O 85, p. 3.
"Six O'Clock in Nova Scotia." AmerPoR (14:5) S-O 85, p. 4.

4322. SAVOIE, Terry
    "Arsenal Island." ConnPR (3:1) 84, p. 42.
4323. SAVORY, Teo
    "Hand on Pen" (tr. of Raymond Queneau). CrossCur
        (4:4/5:1) 85, p. 129.
    "Pigeons" (tr. of Eich Günter). CrossCur (4:4/5:1) 85,
        p. 101.
4324. SAVVAS, Minas
    "Greek Horse-Drawn Cart" (tr. of Yannis Ritsos). CrossCur
        (4:2) 84, p. 43, 45.
4325. SAWYER-LAUCANNO, Christopher
    "Art." NegC (5:4) Fall 85, p. 108.
    "Bird." NegC (5:4) Fall 85, p. 108.
4326. SBROCCHI, F. A.
    "Oasis, N.S.W. 1981." AntigR (60) Wint 85, p. 71-72.
    "Too Many of Us." AntigR (60) Wint 85, p. 72.
4327. SCALAPINO, Leslie
    "That They Were at the Beach -- Aeolotropic Series."
        AmerPoR (14:6) N-D 85, p. 23-26.
    "That They Were at the Beach -- Aeolotropic Series"
        (Excerpts). Conjunc (7) 85, p. 54-58.
4328. SCALF, Sue
    "The Cheerleader." Poem (53) Mr 85, p. 11.
    "Early Autumn, 1944." Vis (17) 85, p. 9.
    "Less That Greek." Poem (53) Mr 85, p. 12.
    "Ovum." Poem (53) Mr 85, p. 10.
    "Prodigals." NegC (5:1) Wint 85, p. 120.
4329. SCAMMELL, Michael
    "Don't Tell Me You Have No Soul" (tr. of Veno Taufer).
        Vis (18) 85, p. 21.
4330. SCARFE, Francis
    "In Memoriam." Stand (26:3) Sum 85, p. 58.
4331. SCARPA, Viven C.
    "Mountains." Wind (15:55) 85, p. 44.
4332. SCATES, Maxine
    "Dreams." PoetryE (18) Fall 85, p. 24-25.
    "A Ferry Crossing." QW (21) Fall-Wint 85, p. 76-77.
4333. SCHAEFFER, Susan Fromberg
    "Damp." LitR (29:1) Fall 85, p. 28.
    "Geraniums." CentR (29:2) Spr 85, p. 218-219.
    "In the Water." MemphisSR (5:2) Spr 85, p. 43-44.
    "The Magnolia, Nine Years Later." CentR (29:2) Spr 85, p.
        209-211.
    "On Learning of Your Death." CentR (29:2) Spr 85, p. 217-
        218.
    "The Smallest Angel." MemphisSR (5:2) Spr 85, p. 44-45.
    "Trying to Think." CentR (29:2) Spr 85, p. 211-215.
    "Two Elders in the Country." CentR (29:2) Spr 85, p. 215-
        217.
    "Visitors." LitR (29:1) Fall 85, p. 29.
4334. SCHAPER, Dorothy Jo
    "Riding the Twister." Sam (43:2, 170th release) 85, 36 p.
4335. SCHAST, David
    "Some Soldiers I Saw." AmerPoR (14:3) My-Je 85, p. 21.
4336. SCHEELE, Roy
    "At a Country Wedding" (for Julie and David Bathgate).
        PraS (59:2) Sum 85, p. 18.
    "Drawing Water." PraS (59:2) Sum 85, p. 17-18.
4337. SCHEER, Linda
    "The '&'" (tr. of José Emilio Pacheco). Chelsea (44)
        85, p. 161.
    "Bitch on Earth" (tr. of José Emilio Pacheco). Chelsea
        (44) 85, p. 159-160.
    "The Fox Is Wiser" (tr. of Augusto Monterroso). Chelsea
        (44) 85, p. 52.
    "The Frog Who Wanted to Be an Authentic Frog" (tr. of

Augusto Monterroso). <u>Chelsea</u> (44) 85, p. 53.
"In Defense of Anonymity" (a refusal to grant George B.
   Moore an interview, tr. of José Emilio Pacheco).
   <u>Chelsea</u> (44) 85, p. 46-48.
"Malpaís" (tr. of José Emilio Pacheco). <u>Chelsea</u> (44)
   85, p. 49-50.
"The Mirror Who Couldn't Sleep" (tr. of Augusto
   Monterroso). <u>Chelsea</u> (44) 85, p. 53.
"On Attributions" (tr. of Augusto Monterroso). <u>Chelsea</u>
   (44) 85, p. 51-52.
"Silence" (tr. of José Emilio Pacheco). <u>Chelsea</u> (44)
   85, p. 50.
"The Thunderbolt Who Struck Twice in the Same Spot" (tr. of
   Augusto Monterroso). <u>Chelsea</u> (44) 85, p. 53.
4338. SCHEINOHA, Gary A.
"Brain Storm." <u>PoeticJ</u> (10) 85, p. 36.
"Pathway." <u>PoetryCR</u> (7:1) Aut 85, p. 42.
"Typewriter Guerrilla." <u>PoeticJ</u> (11) 85, p. 17.
4339. SCHELLER, Linda
"For Wallace Stevens." <u>Waves</u> (14:1/2) Fall 85, p. 19.
4340. SCHELSTRAETE, Joyce
"Captive Audience." <u>EngJ</u> (74:1) Ja 85, p. 91.
4341. SCHERZER, Joel
"Sundance." <u>CrabCR</u> (2:3) Sum 85, p. 6.
4342. SCHEVILL, James
"Oklahoma Farming Song." <u>OP</u> (38/39) Spr 85, p. 206.
"Windowshade Vision." <u>CentR</u> (29:2) Spr 85, p. 206.
4343. SCHEXNAYDER, Kenneth
"The Last Bitten." <u>Raccoon</u> (17) Mr 85, inside back cover.
4344. SCHIFF, Jeff
"Articulating the Familiar." <u>Tendril</u> (19/20) 85, p. 313.
"The Dead Skunk Poem." <u>GreenfR</u> (13:1/2) Fall-Wint 85, p.
   156.
4345. SCHIFF, Laura
"By the Gypsies' Graves" (tr. of Károly Bari). <u>Zyzzyva</u>
   (1:4) Wint 85, p. 79.
4346. SCHIFF, Morty
"Time Turned" (thoughts on the film "2001"). <u>Outbr</u>
   (14/15) Fall 84-Spr 85, p. 11.
4347. SCHILDHOUSE, Amy
"Party at Vassar College." <u>PoetryR</u> (2:2) Ap 85, p. 84.
4348. SCHLEY, Jim
"Nicki's View." <u>GrahamHR</u> (8) Wint 85, p. 39-40.
"Perennials." <u>Crazy</u> (29) Fall 85, p. 38-39.
4349. SCHLOSS, David
"The Crying Room." <u>Crazy</u> (29) Fall 85, p. 20.
"My Parents, 1939." <u>Crazy</u> (29) Fall 85, p. 18-19.
4350. SCHLOSSER, Robert
"This Spring." <u>PoeticJ</u> (11) 85, p. 34.
4351. SCHMIDT, Paul
"Genghis Khan me, you midnight plantation!" ("Untitled,"
   tr. of Velimir Khlebnikov). <u>ParisR</u> (27:95) Spr 85, p.
   127.
"I see them -- Crab, Ram, Bull" ("Untitled," tr. of Velimir
   Khlebnikov). <u>ParisR</u> (27:95) Spr 85, p. 128.
"The lice had blind faith, and they prayed to me" (from
   <u>The King of Time</u>, tr. of Velimir Khlebnikov). <u>PartR</u>
   (52:4) 85, p. 426.
"O Garden of Animals!" (tr. of Velimir Khlebnikov).
   <u>ParisR</u> (27:95) Spr 85, p. 129-130.
"Poem" (tr. of Velimir Khlebnikov). <u>NewYRB</u> (32:15) 10 O
   85, p. 4.
"Russia, I give you my divine white brain" (from <u>The King
   of Time</u>, tr. of Velimir Khlebnikov). <u>PartR</u> (52:4) 85,
   p. 426-427.

4352. SCHMIDT, Steven
       "Porch of Light." <u>StoneC</u> (13:1/2) Fall-Wint 85-86, p. 33.
4353. SCHMITZ, Barbara
       "She." <u>Wind</u> (15:54) 85, p. 47.
4354. SCHMITZ, Dennis
       "Gill Boy" (for John, my son). <u>TriQ</u> (63) Spr-Sum 85, p.
           547-548.
       "Instructions for Fishing the Eel." <u>Antaeus</u> (55) Aut 85,
           p. 155-156.
4355. SCHNACKENBERG, Gjertrud
       "Kremlin of Smoke" (Chopin in the Faubourg Saint-Germain,
           Winter, 1831). <u>YaleR</u> (74:2) Wint 85, p. 253-258.
4356. SCHNEIDER, Aaron
       "Helmet." <u>AntigR</u> (62/63) Sum-Aut 85, p. 88.
       "Prairie." <u>Vis</u> (19) 85, p. 40.
       "Tornado and the Truck Stop." <u>AntigR</u> (62/63) Sum-Aut 85,
           p. 87.
4357. SCHNEIDER, Lauren
       "On Stuttering" (for my brother). <u>CimR</u> (70) Ja 85, p. 27.
4358. SCHOEBERLEIN, Marion
       "Needles." <u>Amelia</u> (2:1) Ap 85, p. 68.
4359. SCHOENBERGER, Nancy
       "Cypresses." <u>CutB</u> (24) Spr-Sum 85, p. 26.
       "Flambeaux." <u>CutB</u> (23) Fall-Wint 85, p. 70-71.
       "Girl on a White Porch." <u>CutB</u> (23) Fall-Wint 85, p. 69.
4360. SCHOFIELD, Fred
       "The Art of the Naked Woman" (dedicated to "readers" of
           certain magazines). <u>Bogg</u> (54) 85, p. 7.
4361. SCHOLZ, Myra Heerspink
       "The dead are resurrected in my child" (tr. of Eva
           Gerlach). <u>Mund</u> (16:1/2) 85, p. 9.
       "World I talk her into, certainties" (tr. of Eva Gerlach).
           <u>Mund</u> (16:1/2) 85, p. 9.
4362. SCHOONOVER, Amy Jo
       "That Other Kind" (for William Stafford). <u>NegC</u> (5:4) Fall
           85, p. 49.
4363. SCHOR, Sandra
       "The Doctrine of the Last Hour." <u>Comm</u> (112:15) 6 S 85, p.
           458.
4364. SCHORR, Laurie
       "Choked." <u>HiramPoR</u> (39) Fall-Wint 85, p. 19.
       "Conversation." <u>HiramPoR</u> (39) Fall-Wint 85, p. 20.
4365. SCHOTT, John
       "Living the Present Life." <u>GeoR</u> (39:4) Wint 85, p. 713.
4366. SCHOTT, Penelope Scambly
       "Album in Several Voices." <u>StoneC</u> (12:2/3) Spr-Sum 85, p.
           18-21.
       "Album in Several Voices" (Excerpts. The Phillips Poetry
           Award, Spring/Summer 1985). <u>StoneC</u> (13:1/2) Fall-Wint
           85-86, p. 2.
4367. SCHOUWENAARS, Clem
       "The Dying" (in Flemish and English, tr. by C. J. Stevens).
           <u>StoneC</u> (13:1/2) Fall-Wint 85-86, p. 40-41.
4368. SCHRADER, Alfred
       "Two Poets / Realtor / Sailor / Me." <u>Bogg</u> (53) 85, p. 37.
4369. SCHRADER, Peggy
       "Overcoming the Ordinary" (w. Carol Barrett). <u>WoosterR</u>
           (4) Fall 85, p. 73.
4370. SCHREIBER, Ron
       "Tie" (var, Ty, Tighe, Thai). <u>Tendril</u> (19/20) 85, p. 314.
       "Travel." <u>JamesWR</u> (2:3) Spr-Sum 85, p. 19.
4371. SCHROEDER, Gary
       "My Town." <u>NoDaQ</u> (53:4) Fall 85, p. 228.
4372. SCHULER, Robert
       "Gacela for a Late May." <u>Northeast</u> (Series 4:2) Fall 85,
           p. 29.

"Mappemonde." <u>Abraxas</u> (33) 85, p. 39.
"Matisse Time." <u>SpoonRQ</u> (10:4) Fall 85, p. 10.
"Matisse Time." <u>SpoonRQ</u> (10:4) Fall 85, p. 12.
"Matisse Time: California, December, Coast." <u>SpoonRQ</u>
    (10:4) Fall 85, p. 13.
"Matisse Time: Jazz No. 2." <u>SpoonRQ</u> (10:4) Fall 85, p. 12.
"Matisse Time: Living Quietly" (for Want Wei). <u>SpoonRQ</u>
    (10:4) Fall 85, p. 13.
"Matisse Time: Miles Davis' 'Star People', Jazz No. 1."
    <u>SpoonRQ</u> (10:4) Fall 85, p. 11.
"Matisse time: Report on the Old Garden, July." <u>SpoonRQ</u>
    (10:4) Fall 85, p. 10.
"Matisse Time: The Studio Window." <u>SpoonRQ</u> (10:4) Fall
    85, p. 11.
"Planting." <u>Abraxas</u> (33) 85, p. 39.
4373. SCHULER, Ruth Wildes
"Caro Il Mio Pappa." <u>PoeticJ</u> (12) 85, p. 28.
"Historical Data." <u>PoeticJ</u> (12) 85, p. 24.
"Journey of a Modest Inquirer." <u>PoeticJ</u> (11) 85, p. 39.
"Russian River." <u>PoeticJ</u> (9) 85, p. 11.
"William Butler." <u>PoeticJ</u> (9) 85, p. 39.
4374. SCHULMAN, Grace
"Application." <u>OP</u> (38/39) Spr 85, p. 29.
"Waking to Song." <u>CrossCur</u> (4:2) 84, p. 109.
4375. SCHULMAN, Norma
"Aging." <u>MidAR</u> (5:1) 85, p. 123-124.
"Nathan." <u>CrossCur</u> (4:4/5:1) 85, p. 163-164.
"Raskolnikov's Dream." <u>MSS</u> (4:3) Spr 85, p. 110-111.
4376. SCHULTZ, Robert
"The Moths." <u>VirQ</u> (61:3) Sum 85, p. 420-421.
4377. SCHUMACHER, Rose
"Nuptial." <u>ConcPo</u> (18:1/2) 85, p. 19-20.
4378. SCHUYLER, James
"Fauré Second Piano Quartet." <u>NewYRB</u> (32:17) 7 N 85, p.
    22.
"A Few Days." <u>ParisR</u> (27:96) Sum 85, p. 52-80.
4379. SCHWARTZ, Hillel
"Backing into the Water." <u>PoetryNW</u> (26:2) Sum 85, p. 26-
    27.
"Changelings." <u>Thrpny</u> (6:1, issue 21) Spr 85, p. 22.
"Continence." <u>StoneC</u> (12:2/3) Spr-Sum 85, p. 60-64.
"Fair." <u>NoDaQ</u> (53:1) Wint 85, p. 87-88.
"Fire Sermon." <u>KanQ</u> (17:4) Fall 85, p. 23.
"For Linda, Who Will Not Know Why." <u>CentR</u> (29:4) Fall 85,
    p. 446-447.
"Headings." <u>PoetryNW</u> (26:2) Sum 85, p. 27-28.
"Housemates." <u>PraS</u> (59:1) Spr 85, p. 52-53.
"Khan's Custom Painting." <u>CutB</u> (23) Fall-Wint 85, back
    cover.
"Loft." <u>PoetryR</u> (2:2) Ap 85, p. 66.
"Looking Glass" (the name given by the Strategic Air
    Command to its perpetually airborne control center."
    <u>PassN</u> (6:1) Fall-Wint 85, p. 7.
"Max the Tire King." <u>CutB</u> (23) Fall-Wint 85, p. 34.
"News of the World." <u>IndR</u> (8:2) Spr 85, p. 71-73.
"Specific for Insomnia." <u>LitR</u> (28:4) Sum 85, p. 570-571.
"Talking the Deer Down from the Mountain." <u>PoetryNW</u>
    (26:4) Wint 85-86, p. 26-27.
"Trapper Nelson." <u>TexasR</u> (6:1/2) Spr-Sum 85, p. 60-61.
"Visiting My Daughter at Summer Camp." <u>HolCrit</u> (22:1) F
    85, p. 19.
"Wailing Women at Greenham Common As the Cruise Missiles
    Come in Their Separate Pieces." <u>ChiR</u> (34:4) 85, p. 68-
    69.
4380. SCHWARTZ, Lloyd
"Simple Questions." <u>Shen</u> (36:1) 85-86, p. 91-96.

4381. SCHWARTZ, Naomi
"Scattering" (for George Oppen). CalQ (26) Sum 85, p. 42-
43.
4382. SCHWARTZ, Stephen
"L'Envoi" (After Blake). LindLM (4:1) Ja-Mr 85, p. 7.
"Floral Games V: California 3." LindLM (4:1) Ja-Mr 85, p.
7.
"For the Cuban Exiles." LindLM (4:3) Jl-S 85, p. 4.
"Poland." LindLM (4:1) Ja-Mr 85, p. 7.
4383. SCHWARTZBERG, Cindie
"The Hallowed Magician, 1977" (for Joseph Chassler).
AmerPoR (14:3) My-Je 85, p. 25.
"Measles (At the Last Minute)." Chelsea (44) 85, p. 143.
4384. SCHWEITZER, Lea
"Rebekah's Dream." CrossCur (4:4/5:1) 85, p. 10-11.
4385. SCHWERNER, Armand
"Tablet XXV." Conjunc (8) 85, p. 116.
4386. SCOFIELD, Sandra
"Incarceration." MinnR (N.S. 24) Spr 85, p. 63.
4387. SCOTELLARO, Rocco
"The Catherine-Wheels" (tr. by Ruth Feldman and Brian
Swann). Ploughs (11:4) 85, p. 58.
"Greeting" (tr. by Ruth Feldman and Brian Swann). Ploughs
(11:4) 85, p. 56-57.
4388. SCOTT, Dawn Catherine
"Highway One." CumbPR (5:1) Fall 85, p. 34.
"The Lump in My Throat." CumbPR (5:1) Fall 85, p. 35.
4389. SCOTT, Dennis
"Fallsong." GreenfR (12:3/4) Wint-Spr 85, p. 218.
"Givingsong." GreenfR (12:3/4) Wint-Spr 85, p. 217.
"Lovestorey." GreenfR (12:3/4) Wint-Spr 85, p. 219.
"Pulse." GreenfR (12:3/4) Wint-Spr 85, p. 218.
4390. SCOTT, Hugh
"Embryo in a School Laboratory." Verse (3) 85, p. 34.
4391. SCOTT, Mark Murphy
"Doings in the Garden." USl (18/19) Wint 85, p. 20.
"With Fitzers in Mind." USl (18/19) Wint 85, p. 20.
4392. SCOTT, Paul
"Lovers." CreamCR (10:1) 85, p. 61.
"To Scribble a Journey." Blueline (6:2) Wint-Spr 85, p.
25.
4393. SCOTT, Shelley
"Dreams of a Childless Woman." PoetryR (5) S 85, p. 61.
"La Femme" (To Jane Clark). PoetryR (5) S 85, p. 60.
4394. SCOTT, Virginia
"Caressed by Light." AntigR (62/63) Sum-Aut 85, p. 208-
209.
4395. SCUPHAM, Peter
"A Box of Ghosts." Poetry (146:4) Jl 85, p. 216-217.
"Observer Corps, 1940." Poetry (146:4) Jl 85, p. 217-218.
4396. SCUTELLARO, Guy
"The Dreamers." CrossCur (4:4/5:1) 85, p. 166.
4397. SEAMAN, Michael
"The Lord of Chou." KanQ (17:1/2) Wint-Spr 85, p. 274.
4398. SEARLE, John
"Belt." Ploughs (11:1) 85, p. 191.
"Heart." Ploughs (11:1) 85, p. 191.
"I Found Some Pennies and Brought Them Home" (for M.).
Ploughs (11:1) 85, p. 192.
"Poem" ("In the lit room, an inkblot runs," for Hilary).
Ploughs (11:1) 85, p. 190.
4399. SEATON, Maureen
"Room 22." Amelia (2:2) O 85, p. 70.
"Summer Solstice." MissR (40/41) Wint 85, p. 123.
4400. SEATOR, Lynette
"Transvestite II." OP (38/39) Spr 85, p. 76.

4401. SEELIG, Helen
        "Reflections on a Nursing Home." Northeast (Series 4:1)
          Sum 85, p. 20.
4402. SEEMAN, Julianne
        "The Day the Words Came Back." KanQ (17:3) Sum 85, p. 67.
        "Henry Moore Sculptures." KanQ (17:3) Sum 85, p. 66-67.
        "The Way We Carry On." CrabCR (2:3) Sum 85, p. 17.
4403. SEETCH, Beth
        "When We Meet in the Middle of the Night." PoetryNW
          (26:1) Spr 85, p. 37.
4404. SEGALL, Pearl B. (See also SEGALL, Pearl Bloch)
        "I Screamed." SanFPJ (7:3) 84 [i.e. 85], p. 7.
        "Rubber." SanFPJ (7:3) 84 [i.e. 85], p. 6.
4405. SEGALL, Pearl Bloch (See also SEGALL, Pearl B.)
        "Beirut, Free-Fire Zone." PoeticJ (11) 85, p. 37.
        "Newteen: Arrival at Disenchantment's Door." PoeticJ (12)
          85, p. 11.
        "A Slight Misinterpretation." PoeticJ (10) 85, p. 27.
        "Without Siblings." PoeticJ (9) 85, p. 4.
4406. SEGARRA, Samuel
        "Poema a una Mujer Actriz." Mairena (7:19) 85, p. 109.
4407. SEGOVIA, Tomas
        "Versos de Verdad." LindLM (4:2) Ap-Je 85, p. 15.
4408. SEIBLES, Tim
        "Hope." Mund (15:1/2) 85, p. 79.
        "The Snail." Mund (15:1/2) 85, p. 79-80.
        "Stranger" (for everyone who listens). Mund (15:1/2) 85,
          p. 78.
4409. SEIDMAN, Hugh
        "8.1.83." ParisR (27:95) Spr 85, p. 68.
        "I Dream of You As the Mother and of the Poet of She Who Is
          the Death of Orpheus in Your Dream." ParisR (27:95)
          Spr 85, p. 65-67.
4410. SEIFERLE, Rebecca
        "Building Rabbit Cages." Poem (53) Mr 85, p. 33.
        "Let's Pretend." CutB (24) Spr-Sum 85, p. 66-67.
        "The Poinsettia." Poem (53) Mr 85, p. 34.
        "Rumors of Suicide." IndR (8:2) Spr 85, p. 32-33.
4411. SEIFERT, Jaroslav
        "Autobiography." Harp (270:1617) F 85, p. 32-33.
        "Burning Ship" (tr. by Jeffrey Fiskin and Erik Vestville).
          Antaeus (55) Aut 85, p. 158.
        "Even the raven belongs to the song bird family" (tr. by
          Ewald Osers). CrossCur (5:2) 85, p. 72.
        "Everything on earth has happened before" (tr. by Ewald
          Osers). CrossCur (5:2) 85, p. 71.
        "For you I would like to bring a little white dove" (tr. by
          Ewald Osers). CrossCur (5:2) 85, p. 73.
        "I remember the days when it was much darker in the cinemas
          than today" (tr. by Ewald Osers). CrossCur (5:2) 85,
          p. 75.
        "I used to yearn for distant cities" (tr. by Ewald Osers).
          CrossCur (5:2) 85, p. 78.
        "Mortar Salvos" (tr. by Jeffrey Fiskin and Erik Vestville).
          Antaeus (55) Aut 85, p. 159-160.
        "Nocturnal Divertimento" (tr. by Ewald Osers). Ploughs
          (11:4) 85, p. 90-95.
        "Not till old age did I learn" (tr. by Ewald Osers).
          CrossCur (5:2) 85, p. 69.
        "On a forgotten stone block in the garden" (tr. by Ewald
          Osers). CrossCur (5:2) 85, p. 70.
        "Our lives run like fingers over sandpaper" (tr. by Ewald
          Osers). CrossCur (5:2) 85, p. 76.
        "To all those million verses in the world" (tr. by Ewald
          Osers). CrossCur (5:2) 85, p. 79.
        "To Be a Poet" (tr. by Ewald Osers). Ploughs (11:4) 85,

p. 88-89.
"View from Charles Bridge" (tr. by Ewald Osers). <u>Ploughs</u>
(11:4) 85, p. 96-98.
"When the Ashes" (tr. by Jeffrey Fiskin and Erik
Vestville). <u>Antaeus</u> (55) Aut 85, p. 157.
"The worst is over now" (tr. by Ewald Osers). <u>CrossCur</u>
(5:2) 85, p. 77.
"You can stay silent if you don't feel like talking" (tr.
by Ewald Osers). <u>CrossCur</u> (5:2) 85, p. 74.
4412. SEILER, Sheila (<u>See</u> also CLARK, Sheila Seiler)
"After Your Suicide" (for Ray, 9-8-59/9-12-82). <u>Amelia</u>
(2:1) Ap 85, p. 86.
"Desert Home." <u>PoeticJ</u> (11) 85, p. 24.
"Luna in Traction." <u>PoeticJ</u> (11) 85, p. 24.
"Rootless." <u>PoeticJ</u> (9) 85, p. 29.
"There Was No Note." <u>PoeticJ</u> (10) 85, p. 36.
"Three Candles for Elaine." <u>PoeticJ</u> (11) 85, p. 18.
"Through the Trap Door." <u>PoeticJ</u> (9) 85, p. 28.
4413. SELAWSKY, John T.
"Autumnal." <u>LittleBR</u> (5:1) Fall-Wint 84-85, p. 76.
"The Bloom." <u>Poem</u> (53) Mr 85, p. 48.
"Coming upon Many Tracks by a Stream." <u>CumbPR</u> (5:1) Fall
85, p. 43.
"Indian Summer." <u>WestB</u> (16) 85, p. 68.
"March." <u>Poem</u> (53) Mr 85, p. 49.
"The Orchard." <u>LaurelR</u> (19:1) Wint 85, p. 62.
"Pastoral." <u>LittleBR</u> (5:1) Fall-Wint 84-85, p. 63.
"The Prize." <u>Poem</u> (53) Mr 85, p. 47.
"The Tadpoles." <u>WestB</u> (17) 85, p. 96.
"Under Gemini." <u>WestB</u> (17) 85, p. 97.
"Upon Waking and Seeing My Breath One cold Morning."
<u>SoDakR</u> (23:1) Spr 85, p. 65.
4414. SELERIE, Gavin
"Azimuth" (Selections). <u>NoDaQ</u> (53:3) Sum 85, p. 119-157.
4415. SELF, Lynda
"Variant Textures." <u>Confr</u> (29) Wint 85, p. 136.
4416. SELINGER, Eric
"Letters from Avignon." <u>HarvardA</u> (118:3) Mr 85, p. 24-25.
"Poem on a Line by Jorge Guillen." <u>HarvardA</u> (119:2) D 85,
p. 35.
4417. SELLAND, Eric
"Kusudama" (5 selections, tr. of Minoru Yoshioka).
<u>Temblor</u> (2) 85, p. 60-67.
4418. SELMAN, Robyn
"Conversation with My Father." <u>Ploughs</u> (11:1) 85, p. 194.
"The First Snow." <u>Ploughs</u> (11:1) 85, p. 195.
"Used Books." <u>Ploughs</u> (11:1) 85, p. 193.
"Yours and Something Different." <u>OP</u> (40) Fall-Wint 85, p.
20-23.
SELO, Tsarskoye
<u>See</u> AKHMATOVA, Anna
4419. SEMENOVICH, Joseph
"Mother." <u>Abraxas</u> (33) 85, p. 26.
"Sentimentale." <u>WebR</u> (10:1) Spr 85, p. 65-66.
"Why Jimmy doesn't have a telephone." <u>Wind</u> (15:53) 85, p.
20.
4420. SEMONES, Charles
"Henry Thoreau Writes to Us from Deep Creek." <u>Wind</u>
(15:54) 85, p. 48-49.
"Poem before an Equinox" (for J.L.R.). <u>Wind</u> (15:54) 85,
p. 49.
4421. SENA, Jorge de
"At Fifty" (tr. by Alexis Levitin). <u>AmerPoR</u> (14:2) Mr-Ap
85, p. 48.
4422. SENAC, Jean
"Legend" (tr. by Mark Polizzotti). <u>ParisR</u> (27:96) Sum 85,

p. 136-137.
"Ode to Black America" (for Marc Baudon, tr. by Mark
    Polizzotti). ParisR (27:96) Sum 85, p. 141-143.
"Ode to Cernuda" (tr. by Mark Polizzotti). ParisR (27:96)
    Sum 85, p. 137-139.
"Talisman for Patrick" (tr. by Mark Polizzotti). ParisR
    (27:96) Sum 85, p. 139-141.
"Young Deluge" (K.T. from Oran, tr. by Mark Polizzotti).
    ParisR (27:96) Sum 85, p. 135-136.
4423. SENIOR, Olive
"The Mother" (from Island Crosses). GreenfR (12:3/4)
    Wint-Spr 85, p. 222-223.
"Nansi 'Tory." GreenfR (12:3/4) Wint-Spr 85, p. 221.
"One Night, the Father." GreenfR (12:3/4) Wint-Spr 85, p.
    224-225.
4424. SEPULVEDA, Arnaldo
"Capital" (tr. of José Lis Vega). RiverS (17) 85, p.
    42.
4425. SERCHUK, Peter
"The Children Must Come." KanQ (17:1/2) Wint-Spr 85, p.
    149.
"A Note Found after the Storm." MissouriR (8:2) 85, p.
    124.
4426. SERENI, Vittorio
"The Elm's Disease" (tr. by Ann Snodgrass). ParisR
    (27:98) Wint 85, p. 89-90.
"The Seashore" (tr. by Ann Snodgrass). NewL (51:4) Sum
    85, p. 160.
"Those Children" (tr. by Ann Snodgrass). NewL (51:4) Sum
    85, p. 161.
"Via Scarlatti" (tr. by Ann Snodgrass). NewL (51:4) Sum
    85, p. 160-161.
4427. SERGEANT, Howard
"Double Knife-Throwing Act." GreenfR (13:1/2) Fall-Wint
    85, p. 151-152.
4428. SESHADRI, Viji
"An Oral History of Migration" (Excerpt). Thrpny (5:4,
    issue 20) Wint 85, p. 16.
4429. SESSIONS, W. A.
"Some News for Mark." GeoR (39:4) Wint 85, p. 848.
4430. SETH, Vikram
"The Gentle Waves Pavilion." NewRep (193:17) 21 O 85, p.
    36.
"The Golden Gate: A Novel in Verse" (Selections: 1-41).
    Raritan (5:1) Sum 85, p. 107-127.
"The North Temple Tower." NewRep (193:17) 21 O 85, p. 36.
"The Tarrying Garden." NewRep (193:17) 21 O 85, p. 36.
4431. SEVOV, Kolyo
"Song between the Sea and Sky" (tr. by John Balaban).
    Mund (15:1/2) 85, p. 143.
4432. SEWALL-HERBERT, Mary
"I Am a Third and Younger Soul." Poem (54) N 85, p. 53.
4433. SEXTON, Anne
"Live." TriQ (63) Spr-Sum 85, p. 51-52.
"Man and Wife." TriQ (63) Spr-Sum 85, p. 49-50.
4434. SEXTON, Tom
"December Walk." CutB (24) Spr-Sum 85, p. 62.
"Low Tide." CutB (24) Spr-Sum 85, p. 62.
"Waitress." CharR (11:1) Spr 85, p. 84.
4435. SEYFRIED, Robin
"Elegy for Two Young Robins." PraS (59:2) Sum 85, p. 85-
    87.
"The Wives of the Poets." Poetry (147:1) O 85, p. 9-10.
4436. SEYLER, Deborah
"A.P. Photo." Vis (19) 85, p. 33.
"Because I know." Bogg (54) 85, p. 40.

"Spring Harvest." Quarry (34:4) Aut 85, p. 32.
"Too." RagMag (4:1) Spr 85, p. 47.
4437. SEYMOUR, A. J.
    "For My Father." GreenfR (12:3/4) Wint-Spr 85, p. 228-229.
    "New Year's Day." GreenfR (12:3/4) Wint-Spr 85, p. 227.
SHADDOX, Brenda Davidson
    See DAVIDSON-SHADDOX, Brenda
SHADEED
    See WHITAKER, Romous
4438. SHAFTON, Anthony
    "On Weather." StoneC (13:1/2) Fall-Wint 85-86, p. 37.
SHAHID ALI, Agha
    See ALI, Agha Shahid
4439. SHAKELY, Lauren
    "First Light." Sulfur (13) 85, p. 114-115.
    "From the Train." Sulfur (13) 85, p. 116.
    "May 3, 1984." Sulfur (13) 85, p. 114.
    "Mother's Method." Sulfur (13) 85, p. 115.
    "With a View." Sulfur (13) 85, p. 115.
4440. SHANER, Richard Clark
    "Grandfather." PassN (6:2) Spr-Sum 85, p. 7.
4441. SHANKEN, Zev
    "Piaf on Stereo." Confr (29) Wint 85, p. 147.
4442. SHANNON, Beth Tashery
    "Legands." ChiR (35:1) Aut 85, p. 86-87.
4443. SHANTZ, Christine
    "Fragment IX" (tr. of Jorge Etcheverry). Waves (13:4) Spr
        85, p. 102.
    "Rue de Grand Pre" (tr. of Jorge Etcheverry). Waves
        (13:4) Spr 85, p. 103.
4444. SHAPIRO, Alan
    "Astronomy Lesson." NewRep (193:11) 9 S 85, p. 38.
    "A Christmas Story." Crazy (29) Fall 85, p. 14-15.
    "Extra." TriQ (64) Fall 85, p. 7-11.
    "His Happy Hour." TriQ (63) Spr-Sum 85, p. 605-606.
    "Lace Fern." SouthwR (70:3) Sum 85, p. 385-386.
    "Other Hands." Crazy (29) Fall 85, p. 12-13.
    "Otter Island" (Cape Breton, Nova Scotia). SouthwR (70:3)
        Sum 85, p. 384.
4445. SHAPIRO, David
    "House (Blown Apart)" (for John Hejduk). AmerPoR (14:4)
        Jl-Ag 85, p. 3-6.
4446. SHAPIRO, Gregg
    "Standing Still in Motion." LittleM (14:4) 85, p. 53.
    "Wash." WoosterR (3) Spr 85, p. 40.
4447. SHAPIRO, Norman
    "Eight Fabliettes" (tr. of Eugene Guillevic). Ploughs
        (11:4) 85, p. 109-111.
SHARAT CHANDRA, G. S.
    See CHANDRA, G. S. Sharat
4448. SHARE, Don
    "Lunch at my desk." Amelia (2:2) O 85, p. 9.
4449. SHARP, Loretta
    "First Spring on Roosevelt Drive." CutB (24) Spr-Sum 85,
        p. 54-55.
4450. SHARP, Paula
    "The Grand Jury." MinnR (N.S. 24) Spr 85, p. 85-88.
4451. SHARPE, Neil F.
    "Canon." PoetryCR (7:2) Wint 85-86, p. 25.
    "Dialogue with Dali." PoetryCR (6:3) Spr 85, p. 35.
4452. SHAVER, Shelley
    "Dusters." SouthwR (70:3) Sum 85, p. 350-351.
    "Mid-day." SouthwR (70:3) Sum 85, p. 351-353.
    "Mrs. Mack." SouthwR (70:3) Sum 85, p. 356-358.
    "To Bed." SouthwR (70:3) Sum 85, p. 353-356.

4453. SHAW, Janet Beeler
      "A Major American Bacon Love Poem." OP (38/39) Spr 85, p.
         194.
4454. SHAW, Robert B.
      "Echo." Poetry (145:5) F 85, p. 281-282.
      "Family Album." Poetry (145:5) F 85, p. 279-280.
      "Narcissus." Poetry (145:5) F 85, p. 280-281.
      "Things We Will Never Know." Poetry (145:5) F 85, p. 278-
         279.
      "Toll Call." ParisR (27:98) Wint 85, p. 87.
4455. SHAWGO, Lucy
      "A Distant Cry." AmerS (54:4) Aut 85, p. 536.
      "The Olive Tree." DeKalbLAJ (18:3/4) 85, p. 42-43.
      "Shadings." NegC (5:3) Sum 85, p. 123.
4456. SHAY, Michael
      "Presidential Statues" (w. F. Keith Wahle & Michael Karl
         Ritchie). YellowS (15) Sum 85, p. 8-9.
4457. SHAY, Timothy
      "Wounding the Robin." Quarry (34:4) Aut 85, p. 31.
4458. SHEARD, Norma (See also SHEARD, Norma V. & Norma Voorhees)
      "Five Haiku." USl (18/19) Wint 85, p. 17.
4459. SHEARD, Norma V. (See also SHEARD, Norma & Norma Voorhees)
      "The Man / The Woman." SmPd (22:1) Wint 85, p. 28.
4460. SHEARD, Norma Voorhees (See also SHEARD, Norma & Norma V.)
      "Sacred Rituals." CapeR (20:1) Spr 85, p. 14.
4461. SHEARER, Ellen
      "Mr Brown." AntigR (62/63) Sum-Aut 85, p. 15.
4462. SHECK, Laurie
      "Main Street." OntR (22) Spr-Sum 85, p. 103-105.
      "New England Graveyard." MidwQ (26:4) Sum 85, p. 464-465.
      "Noble, Also, of the Beautiful Hair, Thought of Eating."
         AntR (43:4) Fall 85, p. 457.
      "Persephone to Demeter." MidwQ (26:4) Sum 85, p. 462-463.
      "Poem Beginning with a Line from Sappho." OntR (22) Spr-
         Sum 85, p. 102-103.
      "Watching Television." Iowa (15:1) Wint 85, p. 78-79.
      "Wounded Whale." NewYorker (61:14) 27 My 85, p. 34.
4463. SHEDD, Ken
      "The Inheritance." KanQ (17:4) Fall 85, p. 253.
      "We Were Drinking Margaritas." KanQ (17:4) Fall 85, p.
         252-253.
4464. SHEEHAN, Marc J.
      "Paris Boulevard, 1839." MichQR (24:4) Fall 85, p. 623.
4465. SHEEHAN, Thomas (See also SHEEHAN, Tom)
      "Faces Old Ponds Have." IndR (8:2) Spr 85, p. 34-35.
      "Old Saugus Town." SoDakR (23:2) Sum 85, p. 68-70.
4466. SHEEHAN, Tom (See also SHEEHAN, Thomas)
      "Discovery of an Asterisk." Poem (54) N 85, p. 62-63.
      "Octobering." BlueBldgs (9) [85?], p. 52.
      "Solo Shot." Poem (54) N 85, p. 61.
4467. SHEFFER, Roger
      "Bathroom Mirror." CapeR (20:1) Spr 85, p. 9.
      "The Straw Bed." CapeR (20:1) Spr 85, p. 8.
4468. SHEFTEL, Harry B.
      "Diorama." NegC (5:2) Spr 85, p. 52.
4469. SHEIRER, John Mark
      "Confronted with Modernism" (Four Previously Indifferent
         Cows Become Religious, and Start a Church -- for James
         Wright). LaurelR (19:1) Wint 85, p. 67.
      "Revelation While Walking in Winter." Wind (15:54) 85, p.
         31.
4470. SHELDON, Glenn
      "Impulse." StoneC (13:1/2) Fall-Wint 85-86, p. 37.
4471. SHEPARD, Neil
      "North Platte to Chicago, November Nights, Rte #80." KanQ
         (17:1/2) Wint-Spr 85, p. 136.

4472. SHEPARD, Roy
"Easter Monday." ChrC (102:12) 10 Ap 85, p. 348.
"Park in Passing." JlNJPo (8:1) 85, p. 22-23.
4473. SHEPHERD, Delilah
"Drunk at 3 A.M." (Obscene Acrostic, w. Keith Blue).
Open24 (4) 85, p. 44.
4474. SHEPHERD, Gail
"For a Lost Child." Poetry (145:6) Mr 85, p. 336.
4475. SHEPHERD, J. Barrie
"All Hallows' Eve." ChrC (102:33) 30 O 85, p. 972.
"Father, into Thy Hands." ChrC (102:7) 27 F 85, p. 205.
"Hanging the Greens." ChrC (102:39) 11 D 85, p. 1143.
"Lent Four." ChrC (102:9) 13 Mr 85, p. 267.
"Overslip." ChrC (102:37) 27 N 85, p. 1085.
"Penitential." ChrC (102:10) 20-27 Mr 85, p. 286.
"Vote of Thanks." ChrC (102:36) 20 N 85, p. 1055.
4476. SHEPHERD, Jamie
"At Birkenau." SnapD (8:2) Spr 85, p. 34-35.
4477. SHEPPARD, Susan
"Crossing Water." BlueBldgs (9) [85?], p. 57.
"Crossing Water." GreenfR (13:1/2) Fall-Wint 85, p. 1-2.
"Howler's Moon." PaintedB (26/27) Sum-Fall 85, p. 38.
"Odalisque." PaintedB (26/27) Sum-Fall 85, p. 36-37.
"Unspeakable Sabbat." PaintedB (26/27) Sum-Fall 85, p. 39-
40.
4478. SHER, Steven
"Empty Rooms." Blueline (6:2) Wint-Spr 85, p. 41.
"How No One Gets Away." GreenfR (13:1/2) Fall-Wint 85, p.
167.
"Smoke in the Distance." CrabCR (3:1) Fall-Wint 85, p. 28.
"Winter Morning in Kentucky, Puckett's Market." GreenfR
(13:1/2) Fall-Wint 85, p. 166.
4479. SHERMAN, Kenneth
"Anderson the Ice Man." Descant 49 (16:2) Sum 85, p. 9-10.
"Bluzhov." PoetryCR (7:2) Wint 85-86, p. 46.
"Bob Ulmer's Household." PoetryCR (7:2) Wint 85-86, p. 46.
"Cleaning Fish." PoetryCR (7:2) Wint 85-86, p. 46.
"The Comedy of the Wyrd Ladies." Waves (13:2/3) Wint 85,
p. 63.
"Demons." Waves (13:2/3) Wint 85, p. 64.
"The New Country." PoetryCR (7:2) Wint 85-86, p. 46.
"The Nouvelle Cuisine." Descant 49 (16:2) Sum 85, p. 11-
13.
"Nymphs." Waves (13:2/3) Wint 85, p. 62.
4480. SHERMAN, Nan
"Don't Open This Invitation!" PoeticJ (10) 85, p. 33.
4481. SHERMAN, Susan
"Testament." HangL (47) Spr 85, p. 48.
4482. SHIFFRIN, Nancy
"Spirare." Prima (9) 85, p. 73.
SHIH, Su
See SU, Shih
4483. SHIPLEY, Vivian
"Seeing with Sound: Ultrasound." MichQR (24:2) Spr 85, p.
326.
4484. SHIRAZ, Hovhaness
"Orphan" (tr. by Diana Der Hovanessian). Mund (15:1/2)
85, p. 70.
4485. SHIRLEY, Aleda
"The Blown Glass Souvenir among the Maps and Old Deeds" (w.
Alex Stevens). Chelsea (44) 85, p. 144.
"Chinese Architecture." GeoR (39:3) Fall 85, p. 601-602.
"Magical Thinking." VirQ (61:1) Wint 85, p. 72-73.
"My Parents, When They Were Young." IndR (8:1) Wint 85,
p. 72-73.
"Open Ending." VirQ (61:1) Wint 85, p. 71-72.

"The Subject Is 'You Understood'." <u>GeoR</u> (39:3) Fall 85,
    p. 602-603.
"Talking in Bed." <u>Chelsea</u> (44) 85, p. 104-105.
"Tertium Quid." <u>Poetry</u> (145:5) F 85, p. 283-284.
4486. SHOAF, Diann Blakely
"Gauguin in Alaska." <u>Verse</u> (4) 85, p. 25.
"Go in Good Health." <u>SouthernHR</u> (19:3) Sum 85, p. 242.
"Mirror." <u>SouthernHR</u> (19:4) Fall 85, p. 324.
4487. SHOEMAKER, Lynn
"Dance of the Fox Fur / My Daughter and the No-Child."
    <u>KanQ</u> (17:1/2) Wint-Spr 85, p. 221.
4488. SHOENIGHT, Aloise Tracy
"Companion." <u>NegC</u> (5:4) Fall 85, p. 74.
4489. SHOLL, Betsy
"6 A.M." <u>Agni</u> (22) 85, p. 107-108.
"Edges." <u>Agni</u> (22) 85, p. 105-106.
"Forsythia." <u>WestB</u> (16) 85, p. 17-18.
"Hanging Out the Wash" (for my grandmother). <u>Agni</u> (22)
    85, p. 109-110.
"Releasing Grandfather." <u>WestB</u> (16) 85, p. 18-19.
4490. SHOMER, Enid
"At the End." <u>NegC</u> (5:1) Wint 85, p. 18.
"Customs." <u>PoetL</u> (79:4) Wint 85, p. 198.
"Early Morning." <u>PoetL</u> (79:4) Wint 85, p. 199.
"Finding the Ocean." <u>NegC</u> (5:3) Sum 85, p. 23.
"Grandmother's Story." <u>CalQ</u> (26) Sum 85, p. 35.
"Luncheonette, Live Oak, Florida." <u>PoetL</u> (79:4) Wint 85,
    p. 200.
"The Promise." <u>CalQ</u> (26) Sum 85, p. 36-37.
"Women of Herculaneum." <u>PoetL</u> (80:2) Sum 85, p. 118-123.
SHOPTAW, John Willett
    <u>See</u> WILLETT-SHOPTAW, John
4491. SHORB, Michael
"Entering the Water." <u>KanQ</u> (17:4) Fall 85, p. 126-127.
"Furnaces in the Pines." <u>KanQ</u> (17:4) Fall 85, p. 125.
"Wild Rice Country." <u>Vis</u> (17) 85, p. 4.
4492. SHORE, Jane
"The Game of Jack Straws." <u>YaleR</u> (74:4) Sum 85, p. 572-
    573.
"The Island." <u>Pequod</u> (19/20/21) 85, p. 314-315.
4493. SHORR, Kathy
"Falling." <u>NegC</u> (5:4) Fall 85, p. 125.
4494. SHREVE, Sandy
"Baskets." <u>PoetryCR</u> (7:2) Wint 85-86, p. 40.
"Hunting Season." <u>PottPort</u> (7) 85-86, p. 34.
"Missaquash Memories." <u>PoetryCR</u> (7:2) Wint 85-86, p. 40.
"Petroglyphs." <u>PoetryCR</u> (7:2) Wint 85-86, p. 40.
"The Potter's Wheel." <u>PottPort</u> (7) 85-86, p. 30.
"The Tantramar." <u>PottPort</u> (7) 85-86, p. 51.
"Vacation, I." <u>PottPort</u> (7) 85-86, p. 30.
4495. SHU, Ting
"The Singing Flower" (tr. by Carolyn Kizer and Y. H. Zhao).
    <u>PoetryE</u> (18) Fall 85, p. 72-78.
4496. SHUGRUE, Jim
"11-22-63." <u>PaintedB</u> (26/27) Sum-Fall 85, p. 52.
4497. SHULL, Ellen M.
"Naming of Nouns" (With Apologies to Henry Reed). <u>EngJ</u>
    (74:4) Ap 85, p. 93.
4498. SHULMAN, Susie
"Constant, at 50 Yards" (Judy Youngblud, 1946-1983).
    <u>Imagine</u> (1:2) Wint 84, p. 70-71.
"I Am the Skeptic." <u>Imagine</u> (1:2) Wint 84, p. 72-73.
"A Little More Than Kin" (for my father). <u>Imagine</u> (1:2)
    Wint 84, p. 74.
"Muses and Unknown Sailors." <u>Imagine</u> (1:2) Wint 84, p. 69-
    70.

4499. SHURBANOV, Alexander
    "All of them have gone away" (tr. of Nicolai Kantchev, w.
        Jascha Kessler). NewL (51:4) Sum 85, p. 40-41.
    "The Bee's Calendar" (tr. of Nicolai Kunchev, w. Jascha
        Kessler). CrossCur (4:2) 84, p. 33.
    "The Bees' Calendar" (tr. of Nicolai Kantchev, w. Jascha
        Kessler). Nimrod (29:1) Fall-Wint 85, p. 100.
    "Believe It or Not" (tr. of Nicolai Kantchev, w. Jascha
        Kessler). NewL (51:4) Sum 85, p. 40.
    "Birthplace" (tr. of Nicolai Kantchev, w. Jascha Kessler).
        Ploughs (11:4) 85, p. 223.
    "Declaration" (tr. of Nicolai Kantchev, w. Jascha Kessler).
        Nimrod (29:1) Fall-Wint 85, p. 98-99.
    "Field, Hand with Seeds" (tr. of Nicolai Kantchev, w.
        Jascha Kessler). Nimrod (29:1) Fall-Wint 85, p. 98.
    "The Future" (tr. of Nicolai Kantchev, w. Jascha Kessler).
        Ploughs (11:4) 85, p. 223.
    "Introduction to the Beyond" (tr. of Blaga Dimitrova, w.
        Jascha Kessler). Ploughs (11:4) 85, p. 220.
    "Nocturne" (tr. of Nicolai Kantchev, w. Jascha Kessler).
        NewL (51:4) Sum 85, p. 41.
    "Proof" (tr. of Nicolai Kantchev, w. Jascha Kessler).
        Ploughs (11:4) 85, p. 222.
    "Puzzle" (tr. of Nicolai Kantchev, w. Jascha Kessler).
        Ploughs (11:4) 85, p. 222.
    "Smile" (tr. of Nicolai Kantchev, w. Jascha Kessler).
        NewL (51:4) Sum 85, p. 40.
    "Time As Seen from Above" (tr. of Nicolai Kantchev, w.
        Jascha Kessler). Ploughs (11:4) 85, p. 221.
    "When a Woman" (tr. of Nicolai Kantchev, w. Jascha
        Kessler). Nimrod (29:1) Fall-Wint 85, p. 99.
    "Words" (tr. of Nicolai Kantchev, w. Jascha Kessler).
        Nimrod (29:1) Fall-Wint 85, p. 100.
    "Your Life" (tr. of Nicolai Kantchev, w. Jascha Kessler).
        Nimrod (29:1) Fall-Wint 85, p. 99.
4500. SHURIN, Aaron
    "Codex" (8 selections). Temblor (1) 85, p. 73-80.
4501. SHUTTLE, Penelope
    "The Hell-Bender." Poetry (146:4) Jl 85, p. 202.
    "The Knife Knows How." Poetry (146:4) Jl 85, p. 201.
4502. SHUTTLEWORTH, Paul
    "Born of Nothingness" (after Sartre's Saint Genet).
        WestB (16) 85, p. 66.
    "Bullpen Catcher & Friends" (For Luke). Sam (43:1, 169th
        release) 85, 24 p.
    "The Bullpen Catcher Considers His Condition." TexasR
        (6:1/2) Spr-Sum 85, p. 72.
    "The Darkest Day of the Year." WestB (16) 85, p. 66.
    "Life in Primitive Times." CapeR (20:1) Spr 85, p. 6.
    "One Seems Frightened." Sam (42:4, 168th release) 85, p.
        51.
4503. SHVARTS, Elena
    "Elegies on the Cardinal Points" (for M. Sh., I. Burikhim,
        E. Feoktistov, tr. by Michael Molnar). Mund (15:1/2)
        85, p. 195-198.
4504. SIAMANTO (Adom Yarjanian)
    "The Bath" (tr. by Diana Der Hovanessian). GrahamHR (9)
        Fall 85, p. 77-78.
    "A Handful of Ash" (To the Memory of Akn, tr. by Diana Der
        Hovanessian). GrahamHR (9) Fall 85, p. 84-85.
    "The Mulberry Tree" (tr. by Diana Der Hovanessian).
        GrahamHR (9) Fall 85, p. 81-83.
    "The Strangling" (tr. by Diana Der Hovanessian). GrahamHR
        (9) Fall 85, p. 79-80.
    "Thirst" (tr. by Diana Der Hovanessian). GrahamHR (9)
        Fall 85, p. 76.

4505. SIBLEY, Frederic
    "Open-Heart." NegC (5:1) Wint 85, p. 21-22.
4506. SIBUM, Norm
    "Breakfast at Guenther's." CapilR (37) Fall 85, p. 70-73.
    "An Evening in the Park." CapilR (37) Fall 85, p. 74-78.
4507. SICOLI, Dan
    "The Girl Who Loves Me." Amelia (2:1) Ap 85, p. 77.
    "Spy." Open24 (4) 85, p. 23.
    "Sunday Morning Fails Again." Bogg (53) 85, p. 34.
4508. SIEBERT, Charles
    "The Lament of the Air Traffic Controller." Tendril
        (19/20) 85, p. 339-340.
4509. SIEGEL, Joan I.
    "Snow." HiramPoR (38) Spr-Sum 85, p. 30.
4510. SIEGEL, Melanie
    "Municipal Rites." Vis (17) 85, p. 24.
4511. SIEGEL, Robert
    "Red Wings." CreamCR (10:1) 85, p. 26.
    "Something Else." Verse (3) 85, p. 12.
4512. SIEMS, Larry
    "Three Poems from a Period of Limited War." GrahamHR (8)
        Wint 85, p. 36-38.
4513. SILEN, Ivan
    "La Mascara." Mairena (7:19) 85, p. 103.
    "Mascara -II." Mairena (7:19) 85, p. 103.
4514. SILESKY, Barry
    "Fumbling with the Fire." GreenfR (13:1/2) Fall-Wint 85,
        p. 159.
    "The Other." Abraxas (33) 85, p. 41.
    "Sailing in December." Ascent (11:1) 85, p. 31.
4515. SILKIN, Jon
    "Herodias." WoosterR (4) Fall 85, p. 30.
    "Herod's Life." WoosterR (4) Fall 85, p. 28.
    "A Man from the Shipyards." Stand (26:2) Spr 85, p. 38.
    "Salome's Herod." WoosterR (4) Fall 85, p. 26.
    "Salome's John the Baptist." WoosterR (4) Fall 85, p. 29.
    "Salome's Self." WoosterR (4) Fall 85, p. 27.
4516. SILVA, Beverly
    "A Chicano in a Monte Carlo." RevChic (12:1) Spr 84, p.
        37.
    "I Always Loved the Wild Ones." RevChic (12:1) Spr 84, p.
        38.
    "It's an Unlikely Match, Those Two." Imagine (2:1) Sum
        85, p. 65.
    "La Magnolia Blanca." RevChic (12:1) Spr 84, p. 38.
    "Palabras." Imagine (2:1) Sum 85, p. 65.
    "Tentación." RevChic (12:1) Spr 84, p. 37.
4517. SILVA, Eddie
    "On My Father's Gun Rack Is a Japanese Sword." CutB (23)
        Fall-Wint 85, p. 27.
4518. SILVA, Humberto da
    "The Love Club." Rampike (4:2/3) 85-86, p. 84.
SILVA, Loreina Santos
    See SANTOS SILVA, Loreina
4519. SILVER, William
    "My Father's Cure." LittleM (14:4) 85, p. 58.
4520. SILVER-LILLYWHITE, Eileen
    "Vanish." OhioR (35) 85, p. 87.
SILVESTRE, René Letona
    See LETONA SILVESTRE, René
4521. SIMEONI, Piera
    "The Life That Has Made You" (from Contrappunto, in
        Italian and English, tr. by Ruth Feldman). StoneC
        (12:2/3) Spr-Sum 85, p. 32-33.
    "To Don Quixote" (In Italian and English, tr. by Ruth
        Feldman). CrossCur (4:2) 84, p. 90-91.

4522. SIMIC, Charles
    "Ancient Engines and Beasts." <u>SenR</u> (15:1) 85, p. 11.
    "The Ant and the Bird." <u>SenR</u> (15:1) 85, p. 13.
    "At the Night Court." <u>TriQ</u> (64) Fall 85, p. 84.
    "Avenue of the Americas." <u>TriQ</u> (64) Fall 85, p. 87.
    "Bedtime Story." <u>OP</u> (38/39) Spr 85, p. 173.
    "Caravan." <u>Iowa</u> (15:1) Wint 85, p. 83.
    "Dear Friedrich." <u>TriQ</u> (64) Fall 85, p. 85.
    "Down the Alleymouth." <u>YaleR</u> (74:4) Sum 85, p. 521-522.
    "First Frost." <u>YaleR</u> (74:4) Sum 85, p. 522.
    "Give Me Back My Rags" (tr. of Vasko Popa, w. Morton
      Marcus). <u>Ploughs</u> (11:4) 85, p. 181-190.
    "In the Blue of the Evening." <u>SenR</u> (15:1) 85, p. 12.
    "In Times of Irremediable Evil." <u>TriQ</u> (64) Fall 85, p. 86.
    "The Little Pins of Memory." <u>Field</u> (32) Spr 85, p. 11.
    "To Helen." <u>YaleR</u> (74:4) Sum 85, p. 521.
    "Winter Flies." <u>Iowa</u> (15:1) Wint 85, p. 84.
4523. SIMMERMAN, Jim
    "Against Derrida." <u>CimR</u> (72) Jl 85, p. 21.
    "Almost Dancing." <u>Poetry</u> (145:5) F 85, p. 287-289.
    "Bad Weather." <u>MemphisSR</u> (5:2) Spr 85, p. 49.
    "Daedalus Aground." <u>Tendril</u> (19/20) 85, p. 344-345.
    "Fetch." <u>Poetry</u> (146:3) Je 85, p. 136-137.
    "Finally." <u>Poetry</u> (145:5) F 85, p. 290.
    "The Gulls." <u>Poetry</u> (146:3) Je 85, p. 139.
    "Lighthouse." <u>Poetry</u> (146:3) Je 85, p. 138.
    "The Reluctant Angels." <u>Tendril</u> (19/20) 85, p. 343.
    "Rock 'n' Roll." <u>Tendril</u> (19/20) 85, p. 341-342.
    "Roden Crater." <u>QW</u> (21) Fall-Wint 85, p. 79-82.
    "Sure the Oak." <u>Crazy</u> (26) Spr 84, p. 38-39.
    "Then Again." <u>Crazy</u> (26) Spr 84, p. 40-41.
4524. SIMMONS, Cherie
    "White." <u>HangL</u> (48) Fall 85, p. 66.
4525. SIMMONS, James
    "Elegy for Two Students I Did Not Know." <u>NewEngR</u> (7:3)
      Spr 85, p. 297.
4526. SIMMS, Colin
    "18.4.85 Northumberland, for B.B." <u>Conjunc</u> (8) 85, p. 184.
4527. SIMON, John Oliver
    "Almost a Fable" (tr. of Alejandro Romualdo). <u>Chelsea</u>
      (44) 85, p. 88.
    "The Last Crusader" (tr. of Eduardo Chirirnos). <u>Chelsea</u>
      (44) 85, p. 89.
    "Mutatis Mutandis" (tr. of Hidelbrado Perez). <u>Chelsea</u>
      (44) 85, p. 89.
    "Origins of Cave Art" (tr. of Enrique Sanchez). <u>Chelsea</u>
      (44) 85, p. 90.
4528. SIMON, Josef
    "Reminiscence 1939 (Boats in the Desert)" (tr. by Ewald
      Osers). <u>Verse</u> (2) 85, p. 18.
    "Return from Aloft" (tr. by Ewald Osers). <u>Verse</u> (2) 85,
      p. 18.
    "To the Eternal Inhabitants of Category 4" (tr. by Ewald
      Osers). <u>Verse</u> (2) 85, p. 17.
    "To the Twenty-Year-Old Angels of Hopelessness" (tr. by
      Ewald Osers). <u>Verse</u> (2) 85, p. 17.
4529. SIMON, Maurya
    "A Door in the Wind." <u>Poetry</u> (147:1) O 85, p. 27-28.
    "Madras Insomnia." <u>CutB</u> (24) Spr-Sum 85, p. 27.
    "The Way We Are." <u>Poetry</u> (147:1) O 85, p. 27.
    "Winter Song." <u>KanQ</u> (17:1/2) Wint-Spr 85, p. 111.
4530. SIMONS, Michelle Blake
    "Acts of Imagination." <u>PoetryNW</u> (26:1) Spr 85, p. 41.
    "For My Brother" (1949-1967). <u>SenR</u> (15:2) 85, p. 104-105.
    "Letters from a Journey." <u>MidAR</u> (5:1) 85, p. 42-44.

4531. SIMONSUURI, Kirsti
"Albert Camus" (tr. by Jascha Kessler and the author).
Ploughs (11:4) 85, p. 249-251.
"Arctic Journey" (tr. by the author and Jascha Kessler).
NewL (51:4) Sum 85, p. 79.
"The Finder" (tr. by Jascha Kessler and the author).
Nimrod (29:1) Fall-Wint 85, p. 101.
"A Monk" (tr. by the author and Jascha Kessler). NewL
(51:4) Sum 85, p. 80.
"Mythos" (tr. by Jascha Kessler and the author). Ploughs
(11:4) 85, p. 248.
"Three Nocturnes" (Selection: II, tr. by the author and
Jascha Kessler). NewL (51:4) Sum 85, p. 79.
4532. SIMPSON, Astor
"Homeplace." Wind (15:55) 85, p. 45.
4533. SIMPSON, Grace
"Sleeping Too Late." NegC (5:4) Fall 85, p. 54-55.
4534. SIMPSON, Louis
"A Bramble Bush." SouthernHR (19:4) Fall 85, p. 310-311.
"Clippings." Verse (3) 85, p. 9.
"The Flaubert Pavilion." Hudson (38:1) Spr 85, p. 57-61.
"A Fuse Link." Pequod (19/20/21) 85, p. 334-335.
"The Naturalist and the Volcano." Hudson (38:1) Spr 85,
p. 61-62.
"Numbers and Dust." VirQ (61:4) Aut 85, p. 634-636.
"The Victor Book of the Opera." Iowa (15:1) Wint 85, p.
47-48.
4535. SIMPSON, Nancy
"Approaching Home." NegC (5:2) Spr 85, p. 20.
"Grass." SouthernPR (25:1) Spr 85, p. 39.
"Leaving in the Dead of Winter." IndR (8:1) Wint 85, p.
78.
"On the River." NegC (5:2) Spr 85, p. 21.
4536. SINISGALLI, Leonardo
"San Babila" (tr. by Rina Ferrarelli). NewL (51:4) Sum
85, p. 172.
"September's New Moon" (tr. by Rina Ferrarelli). NewL
(51:4) Sum 85, p. 172.
"The Sun Will Not Stop" (tr. by Rina Ferrarelli). NewL
(51:4) Sum 85, p. 173.
4537. SIRETT, Neff
"Burning Shoes." Grain (13:4) N 85, p. 59.
4538. SIROWITZ, Hal
"Army of Ants." Open24 (4) 85, p. 28.
"The Morning After." PaintedB (26/27) Sum-Fall 85, p. 29.
"Submerging." Bogg (53) 85, p. 56.
"Too Much Space." PaintedB (26/27) Sum-Fall 85, p. 30.
SISTER MARY LUCINA
See LUCINA, Mary, Sister
SISTER MAURA
See MAURA, Sister
4539. SJOBERG, Leif
"The Birch Heart" (tr. of Harry Martinson, w. William Jay
Smith). NewL (51:4) Sum 85, p. 78.
"Butterflies" (tr. of Harry Martinson, w. William Jay
Smith). NewL (51:4) Sum 85, p. 77.
"Cabbages" (tr. of Harry Martinson, w. William Jay Smith).
NewL (51:4) Sum 85, p. 77.
"The Final Year" (tr. of Harry Martinson, w. William Jay
Smith). NewL (51:4) Sum 85, p. 78.
"The Rooster" (tr. of Harry Martinson, w. William Jay
Smith). NewL (51:4) Sum 85, p. 77.
"Wild Bouquet: Nature Poems" (Selections, tr. of Harry
Martinson, w. William Jay Smith). AmerPoR (14:4) Jl-Ag
85, p. 23-25.

4540. SJOGREN, Lennart
"The Barn" (tr. by Robin Fulton). <u>Verse</u> (3) 85, p. 42.
4541. SKAU, Michael
"De Chirico Exhibit." <u>KanQ</u> (17:3) Sum 85, p. 76.
"Winter Scenes." <u>KanQ</u> (17:3) Sum 85, p. 76.
4542. SKEEN, Anita
"Driving through Kansas, Eating a Pear." <u>KanQ</u> (17:1/2)
Wint-Spr 85, p. 94.
4543. SKELLEY, Jack
"To Marie Osmond." <u>Harp</u> (271:1626) N 85, p. 27.
4544. SKELTON, Robin
"Birch Tree in Winter" (tr. of George Faludy). <u>PoetryCR</u>
(7:1) Aut 85, p. 17.
"Closed Freight Car" (tr. of George Faludy). <u>PoetryCR</u>
(7:1) Aut 85, p. 17.
"Reading Chinese Poems" (tr. of George Faludy). <u>PoetryCR</u>
(7:1) Aut 85, p. 17.
"Refugee in Morocco 1940" (tr. of George Faludy).
<u>PoetryCR</u> (7:1) Aut 85, p. 17.
"Sonnet Twenty Seven" (tr. of George Faludy). <u>PoetryCR</u>
(7:1) Aut 85, p. 17.
4545. SKILLMAN, Judith
"Floods and Madness." <u>PoetryNW</u> (26:4) Wint 85-86, p. 41.
"Still Life with Death." <u>CrabCR</u> (3:1) Fall-Wint 85, p. 26.
4546. SKINNER, Jeffrey
"Hey, Nineteen." <u>Poetry</u> (146:6) S 85, p. 330-331.
"Prayer to Owl Hiding in Daylight." <u>NewYorker</u> (61:45) 30
D 85, p. 66.
4547. SKINNER, Knute
"Bailey." <u>PoetryR</u> (5) S 85, p. 76.
"February in Bellingham." <u>Amelia</u> (2:2) O 85, p. 29.
"How It Seems Today Anyway." <u>Amelia</u> (2:2) O 85, p. 29.
"The Sound of His Voice from Childhood." <u>NewL</u> (52:1) Fall
85, p. 119.
"Water and Rock: Three Voices" (from a Photograph by Becky
Bolen-Rubey). <u>PoetryR</u> (5) S 85, p. 74-75.
4548. SKLAR, Morty
"Making Beans to Bruckner's 9th." <u>OP</u> (38/39) Spr 85, p.
114.
4549. SKLAREW, Myra
"After Stalin." <u>SenR</u> (15:1) 85, p. 14-15.
"At Yehuda's Wedding." <u>CrossCur</u> (4:4/5:1) 85, p. 71.
4550. SKLOOT, Floyd
"Old Stories." <u>Chelsea</u> (44) 85, p. 140.
"A Working Marriage." <u>Chelsea</u> (44) 85, p. 138-139.
"The Yeon Building." <u>Raccoon</u> (17) Mr 85, p. 14.
4551. SKOYLES, John
"Against Autumn." <u>Ploughs</u> (11:1) 85, p. 197.
"Front Street." <u>Ploughs</u> (11:1) 85, p. 198.
"In the Hospital." <u>YaleR</u> (74:2) Wint 85, p. 259-260.
"Self-Portrait in Spring." <u>YaleR</u> (74:2) Wint 85, p. 259.
"Snowfall." <u>Ploughs</u> (11:1) 85, p. 196.
4552. SLACK, Ellen
"Deep South, Long Fall." <u>AmerPoR</u> (14:3) My-Je 85, p. 43.
4553. SLACK, Nathan
"The Famous Catch" (for Ryne Sandburg). <u>NegC</u> (5:1) Wint
85, p. 125-126.
4554. SLATE, Ron
"The Partygoers." <u>VirQ</u> (61:2) Spr 85, p. 252-253.
4555. SLAUGHTER, Adele
"Poem to Save a Marriage." <u>Confr</u> (30/31) N 85, p. 43.
"The Waves." <u>Waves</u> (13:4) Spr 85, p. 95.
4556. SLAUGHTER, Lynne
"Nespelum, Colville Reservation." <u>CrabCR</u> (2:3) Sum 85, p.
3.

SLAUGHTER 370

4557. SLAUGHTER, William
"The Cripple-Maker" (after Naguib Mahfouz). GreenfR
(13:1/2) Fall-Wint 85, p. 26-27.
"In My Dream / 20 Years Ago." HolCrit (22:4) O 85, p. 14.
"The Man Who Buried His Books." CrossCur (5:3) 85, p. 76-
77.
4558. SLAVITT, David R.
"Excursion to Pergamon." PoetryNW (26:1) Spr 85, p. 31-32.
"Parodos." PraS (59:3) Fall 85, p. 106-107.
"The Shadow." SouthernPR (25:1) Spr 85, p. 41-42.
"The Whippets." Chelsea (44) 85, p. 155-158.
4559. SLAVOV, Atanas
"The Dough of America Is Rising in Me." Vis (17) 85, p. 43.
4560. SLEADD, Marcie
"High Bridge" (after a painting by Paul Sawyier). KanQ
(17:3) Sum 85, p. 24.
4561. SLEIGH, Tom
"Don't Go to the Barn" (For Rose Sleigh). Antaeus (55)
Aut 85, p. 161-162.
"Hope" (For Aunt Hope, corrected version). Ploughs (11:1)
85, p. 239-240.
4562. SLESINGER, Warren
"Our Garden of Words." WoosterR (3) Spr 85, p. 7-8.
4563. SLOMKOWKSI, Lusia
"For Jurek." GreenfR (12:3/4) Wint-Spr 85, p. 22.
4564. SLUMSTRUP, Finn
"Aalborg." MoodySI (15) Spr 85, p. 26.
4565. SMALL, Mary Wren
"For Delmore Schwartz." Wind (15:54) 85, p. 50.
4566. SMALLWOOD, Randy
"On the Savannah." Wind (15:53) 85, p. 44-45.
"To a Soldier Undressing in the Window." Wind (15:53) 85,
p. 43-44.
"The Wilderness of Transition" (after Prokosch). JamesWR
(3:1) Fall 85, p. 13.
4567. SMALLWOOD, Vivian
"Advice to a Moon-Child." NegC (5:2) Spr 85, p. 9.
4568. SMART, Carolyn
"Dancing in the Light of the Moon." (for Angus Smart).
Waves (13:4) Spr 85, p. 76-77.
4569. SMART, Marjory
"October Cocktail." AntigR (60) Wint 85, p. 90.
4570. SMITH, Allen
"Graveyard Shift." PoetryCR (6:3) Spr 85, p. 34.
4571. SMITH, Arthur
"Hurricane Warning." NewYorker (61:24) 5 Ag 85, p. 28.
"Western Roll." Poetry (145:6) Mr 85, p. 338-339.
4572. SMITH, Barbara
"Replay at the Holiday Inn." WoosterR (4) Fall 85, p. 48.
"Request for Remission." LaurelR (19:1) Wint 85, p. 44.
4573. SMITH, Bill (See also SMITH, William Jay)
"Windy Bank." Poetry (146:4) Jl 85, p. 214-215.
4574. SMITH, Bob (See also SMITH, Robert L.)
"Sultan School for Handicapped Children." ClockR (2:2)
85, p. 58.
4575. SMITH, Bruce
"Geometry and Sea Air." NewRep (192:8) 25 F 85, p. 34.
"'It Was Foul and I Loved It.' -- Augustine." Crazy (27)
Fall 84, p. 24.
"The Ocean." Crazy (27) Fall 84, p. 22-23.
"One Note Rage Can Understand" (Louise Bogan). AmerPoR
(14:4) Jl-Ag 85, p. 47.
"The Woman in Me, a Drink, a Dream, the Sea, a Heart
Beating." AmerPoR (14:4) Jl-Ag 85, p. 47.
4576. SMITH, Charles C. (See also SMITH, Charlie)
"Sight in the Distance." Dandel (12:2) 85, p. 36-37.

"Starting Points" (for Nicholas Guillen). <u>Dandel</u> (12:2)
    85, p. 38-39.
4577. SMITH, Charlie (<u>See also</u> SMITH, Charles C.)
    "Doctor Auchincloss Bids Good-bye to His Wife." <u>BlackWR</u>
        (11:2) Spr 85, p. 50-51.
    "Homerun." <u>Crazy</u> (27) Fall 84, p. 40-41.
    "Jehovah's Witness." <u>BlackWR</u> (11:2) Spr 85, p. 53.
    "Kings." <u>BlackWR</u> (11:2) Spr 85, p. 54-55.
    "The Major" (after Hawthorne). <u>Crazy</u> (27) Fall 84, p. 38-
        39.
    "Monkey Bridge." <u>BlackWR</u> (11:2) Spr 85, p. 52.
    "The New World." <u>BlackWR</u> (11:2) Spr 85, p. 57.
    "Red Roads." <u>BlackWR</u> (11:2) Spr 85, p. 56.
    "White and Scarlet." <u>Tendril</u> (19/20) 85, p. 346-347.
4578. SMITH, Dale
    "Haiku." <u>WindO</u> (45) Spr 85, p. 28.
4579. SMITH, Dave (<u>See also</u> SMITH, David)
    "Camellias." <u>NewYorker</u> (61:45) 30 D 85, p. 28.
    "Cooking Eggs." <u>Antaeus</u> (55) Aut 85, p. 163-164.
    "Cuba Night." <u>Antaeus</u> (55) Aut 85, p. 167-168.
    "DeSoto." <u>Nat</u> (240:7) 23 F 85, p. 216.
    "Drag Race" (For Norman Dubie). <u>Antaeus</u> (55) Aut 85, p.
        165-166.
    "Ear Ache." <u>NewRep</u> (192:15) 15 Ap 85, p. 36.
    "Guinea Hens." <u>NewYorker</u> (60:47) 7 Ja 85, p. 26.
    "James River Storm." <u>NewRep</u> (192:5) 4 F 85, p. 38.
    "Just Married." <u>AmerPoR</u> (14:4) Jl-Ag 85, p. 28.
    "Little Birthday Ode" (For William Heyen). <u>Nat</u> (240:3) 26
        Ja 85, p. 90.
    "Little League Opening Day." <u>ThRiPo</u> (25/26) 85, p. 52-53.
    "Loneliness." <u>ThRiPo</u> (25/26) 85, p. 53-56.
    "New England Mill." <u>Antaeus</u> (55) Aut 85, p. 169-170.
    "Night Traffic near Winchester." <u>TriQ</u> (63) Spr-Sum 85, p.
        600-601.
    "On Looking into Neruda's <u>Memoirs</u>." <u>AmerPoR</u> (14:4) Jl-
        Ag 85, p. 27.
    "Sawmill." <u>Iowa</u> (15:1) Wint 85, p. 99.
    "Skunked." <u>AmerPoR</u> (14:4) Jl-Ag 85, p. 27.
    "Treading Clams at Egg Island." <u>AmerPoR</u> (14:4) Jl-Ag 85,
        p. 28.
4580. SMITH, David (<u>See also</u> SMITH, Dave)
    "The Overdose." <u>DeKalbLAJ</u> (18:3/4) 85, p. 43.
4581. SMITH, Douglas
    "At Sand Cut Beach" (For Marjory Fee and Mark Baker).
        <u>Germ</u> (9:1) Spr-Sum 85, p. 11.
    "Dream: After Seeing 'The Chant of Jimmy Blacksmith."
        <u>Germ</u> (9:1) Spr-Sum 85, p. 12.
    "Gathering Stones for the Sauna." <u>Germ</u> (9:1) Spr-Sum 85,
        p. 18.
    "Inside the Whirlpool." <u>Germ</u> (9:1) Spr-Sum 85, p. 16.
    "Living in Poems." <u>Germ</u> (9:1) Spr-Sum 85, p. 13.
    "Meeting Alex Colville." <u>Germ</u> (9:1) Spr-Sum 85, p. 8.
    "Old Recipe." <u>Germ</u> (9:1) Spr-Sum 85, p. 10.
    "The Psychiatrist Tree." <u>Germ</u> (9:1) Spr-Sum 85, p. 19.
    "Reaching for Apples." <u>Germ</u> (9:1) Spr-Sum 85, p. 15.
    "Reading Late at Night, a Ladybug Lands on My Chest."
        <u>Germ</u> (9:1) Spr-Sum 85, p. 9.
    "Running in Flames." <u>Germ</u> (9:1) Spr-Sum 85, p. 17.
    "We Are Drawn Down." <u>Germ</u> (9:1) Spr-Sum 85, p. 14.
    "Weather Pigs" (Earl's Gulf Station, Rose Valley, P.E.I,
        April, 1984). <u>PottPort</u> (7) 85-86, p. 52.
    "A Woman Named Experience" (Port Lorne Cemetery, Nova
        Scotia, December 22, 1983). <u>PottPort</u> (7) 85-86, p. 4.
4582. SMITH, Elvet
    "Tuning-up." <u>AntigR</u> (62/63) Sum-Aut 85, p. 177.

4583. SMITH, Iain Crichton
        "Doing Well." <u>Verse</u> (3) 85, p. 4.
        "Drunk." <u>Verse</u> (1) 84, p. 13.
        "Incident." <u>Stand</u> (26:2) Spr 85, p. 7.
        "Old Woman." <u>Stand</u> (26:2) Spr 85, p. 6-7.
        "Poems from an Asylum." <u>Verse</u> (1) 84, p. 12.
4584. SMITH, J. D.
        "Margins." <u>CutB</u> (23) Fall-Wint 85, p. 33.
        "Scrub Pines." <u>CutB</u> (23) Fall-Wint 85, p. 32.
4585. SMITH, James Steel
        "Bus Depot." <u>Amelia</u> (2:2) O 85, p. 55.
      SMITH, James Sutherland
        <u>See</u> SUTHERLAND-SMITH, James
4586. SMITH, Jan
        "The Joining of Ways." <u>NegC</u> (5:3) Sum 85, p. 124-125.
4587. SMITH, Jared
        "A Day in August." <u>Wind</u> (15:53) 85, p. 46.
        "Finding Love." <u>Wind</u> (15:53) 85, p. 46-47.
4588. SMITH, Jennifer E.
        "Preceding Our Arrival." <u>BlackALF</u> (19:3) Fall 85, p. 112.
4589. SMITH, Jordan
        "At Arnold's Monument." <u>NewEngR</u> (7:3) Spr 85, p. 384-385.
        "Burnt Hills." <u>SenR</u> (15:1) 85, p. 38-39.
        "Country Blues." <u>QW</u> (20) Spr-Sum 85, p. 78-80.
        "Fell Street." <u>GrandS</u> (4:3) Spr 85, p. 66-67.
        "Free Verse" (for Liam Rector). <u>NewEngR</u> (7:3) Spr 85, p.
            382-383.
        "Silverlake: A Theater Song for Kurt Weill." <u>GrandS</u> (4:3)
            Spr 85, p. 68-70.
4590. SMITH, Katherine
        "Found." <u>StoneC</u> (13:1/2) Fall-Wint 85-86, p. 15.
4591. SMITH, Larry (<u>See also</u> SMITH, Lawrence R.)
        "Burning Sand Creek Bridge." <u>Wind</u> (15:55) 85, p. 5.
4592. SMITH, Lawrence R. (<u>See also</u> SMITH, Larry)
        "Contributors." <u>CharR</u> (11:2) Fall 85, p. 109.
        "Footnotes" (Excerpts: 12, 14, 23). <u>WormR</u> (25:4, issue
            100) 85, p. 156-157.
        "Laborintus" (Selections: 8, 11, 23, tr. of Edoardo
            Sanguineti). <u>Iowa</u> (15:2) Spr-Sum 85, p. 85-87.
4593. SMITH, LeRoy, Jr.
        "The Shriving of the Serpent." <u>Comm</u> (112:16) 20 S 85, p.
            495.
4594. SMITH, Melinda B.
        "Reading Old Letters." <u>Wind</u> (15:55) 85, p. 3.
4595. SMITH, Patrick
        "A Neighbors Tale." <u>NewL</u> (52:1) Fall 85, p. 55-57.
4596. SMITH, R. T. (<u>See also</u> SMITH, Rod & Ron)
        "An Antidote for Fear and Trembling." <u>NoDaQ</u> (53:3) Sum
            85, p. 43-44.
        "Appeal to Shrew." <u>Poem</u> (53) Mr 85, p. 26-27.
        "Aspera." <u>Poem</u> (53) Mr 85, p. 32.
        "Birch-light, Abandoning Wittgenstein." <u>NoDaQ</u> (53:3) Sum
            85, p. 41-43.
        "Can a Flower?" <u>HolCrit</u> (22:2) Ap 85, p. 11.
        "Carnival." <u>Poem</u> (53) Mr 85, p. 28.
        "A Custon in Umbria." <u>CrabCR</u> (2:2) Wint 85, p. 23.
        "From Spring to Stream." <u>NoDaQ</u> (53:3) Sum 85, p. 47-48.
        "The Hollow Log Lounge" (For Steve Harrelson. 1985 Texas
            Review Poetry Award Chapbook). <u>TexasR</u> (6:3/4) Fall-
            Wint 85, p. 65-80.
        "Hostage." <u>Poem</u> (53) Mr 85, p. 25.
        "January 7." <u>Poem</u> (53) Mr 85, p. 30-31.
        "Matins." <u>PoetL</u> (80:3) Fall 85, p. 138.
        "Moonset." <u>NoDaQ</u> (53:3) Sum 85, p. 45-46.
        "New Stove." <u>KanQ</u> (17:4) Fall 85, p. 92-93.
        "When the Sun Sets, Your Shadow Embraces the World" (for

Vic). <u>Poem</u> (53) Mr 85, p. 29.
"Winter Visit." <u>KanQ</u> (17:4) Fall 85, p. 91.
4597. SMITH, Robert L. (<u>See also</u> SMITH, Bob)
"Black Poplar" (tr. of David Samojlov, w. Sylvia Maizell).
<u>WebR</u> (10:1) Spr 85, p. 12.
"Inspiration" (tr. of David Samojlov, w. Sylvia Maizell).
<u>WebR</u> (10:1) Spr 85, p. 13.
"Song about a Dog" (tr. of Sergey Esenin). <u>BlueBldgs</u> (9)
[85?], p. 24.
"Trace" (tr. of Leonid Martynov, w. Sylvia Maizell). <u>WebR</u>
(10:1) Spr 85, p. 13.
4598. SMITH, Rod (<u>See also</u> SMITH, R. T.)
"The Honeymoon." <u>Bogg</u> (53) 85, p. 18.
4599. SMITH, Ron (<u>See also</u> SMITH, R. T.)
"Railroad Track." <u>PoetryNW</u> (26:4) Wint 85-86, p. 9-10.
"When My Father." <u>GeoR</u> (39:1) Spr 85, p. 78-79.
SMITH, Sybil Woods
<u>See</u> WOODS-SMITH, Sybil
4600. SMITH, Thomas R.
"Hungry Ghost." <u>Germ</u> (9:1) Spr-Sum 85, p. 39.
"In the Lambing Season." <u>YellowS</u> (16) Aut 85, p. 15.
"Laughing with You." <u>YellowS</u> (15) Sum 85, p. 13.
"The South Shore." <u>Germ</u> (9:1) Spr-Sum 85, p. 38.
"The Sun." <u>Abraxas</u> (33) 85, p. 25.
4601. SMITH, Timothy M.
"Apple Bees." <u>Poem</u> (53) Mr 85, p. 52.
"The Cellar." <u>Poem</u> (53) Mr 85, p. 51.
"Rainy April Night." <u>Poem</u> (53) Mr 85, p. 53.
4602. SMITH, Troy S.
"Life among the Clouds." <u>KanQ</u> (17:4) Fall 85, p. 239.
4603. SMITH, William Jay (<u>See also</u> SMITH, Bill)
"The Birch Heart" (tr. of Harry Martinson, w. Leif
Sjöberg). <u>NewL</u> (51:4) Sum 85, p. 78.
"Butterflies" (tr. of Harry Martinson, w. Leif Sjöberg).
<u>NewL</u> (51:4) Sum 85, p. 77.
"Cabbages" (tr. of Harry Martinson, w. Leif Sjöberg).
<u>NewL</u> (51:4) Sum 85, p. 77.
"The Final Year" (tr. of Harry Martinson, w. Leif
Sjöberg). <u>NewL</u> (51:4) Sum 85, p. 78.
"The Rooster" (tr. of Harry Martinson, w. Leif Sjöberg).
<u>NewL</u> (51:4) Sum 85, p. 77.
"A Sculptor, Welding." <u>SouthernR</u> (21:2) Spr 85, p. 430-
431.
"Wild Bouquet: Nature Poems" (Selections, tr. of Harry
Martinson, w. Leif Sjöberg). <u>AmerPoR</u> (14:4) Jl-Ag
85, p. 23-25.
4604. SMITH-JOHNSON, Robin
"The Season When." <u>PoetryR</u> (2:2) Ap 85, p. 43.
4605. SMITHERS, Glenda Stroup
"Things to See While Running the 10 K" (in the rain).
<u>WindO</u> (46) Fall 85, p. 14.
4606. SMITS, Lia
"Greetings, death, you great sparkler!" (tr. of Imants
Ziedonis). <u>Os</u> (21) 85, p. 23.
"Heavens, I've dropped my sun!" (tr. of Imants Ziedonis).
<u>Os</u> (21) 85, p. 25.
4607. SMUKLER, Linda
"He touched me and the shivery circle came around my head."
<u>NewEngR</u> (8:1) Aut 85, p. 45.
"The Shower." <u>NewEngR</u> (8:1) Aut 85, p. 45-47.
4608. SNIDER, Clifton
"Taos, New Mexico." <u>Vis</u> (19) 85, p. 9.
4609. SNIVELY, Susan
"Four Poems for Brontë and Dickinson." <u>MassR</u> (26:1) Spr
85, p. 141-145.
"Haply I Think on Thee." <u>MassR</u> (26:4) Wint 85, p. 603-604.

"Mary Queen of Scots." <u>MassR</u> (26:4) Wint 85, p. 604.
4610. SNODGRASS, Ann
"The Elm's Disease" (tr. of Vittorio Sereni). <u>ParisR</u>
(27:98) Wint 85, p. 89-90.
"First Pieta." <u>BlackWR</u> (12:1) Fall 85, p. 8-9.
"The Seashore" (tr. of Vittorio Sereni). <u>NewL</u> (51:4) Sum
85, p. 160.
"Those Children" (tr. of Vittorio Sereni). <u>NewL</u> (51:4)
Sum 85, p. 161.
"Via Scarlatti" (tr. of Vittorio Sereni). <u>NewL</u> (51:4) Sum
85, p. 160-161.
4611. SNODGRASS, W. D.
"Credo." <u>NegC</u> (5:4) Fall 85, p. 102-104.
"Disguised As Cock Robin, W. D. Escapes." <u>Salm</u> (67) Sum
85, p. 11.
"Eva Braun" (10 April 1945). <u>MichQR</u> (24:1) Wint 85, p. 48-
50.
"Helga Goebbels" (29 April, 1945). <u>MichQR</u> (24:1) Wint 85,
p. 50-51.
"Interrogation" (from The Death of Cock Robin). <u>Salm</u> (67)
Sum 85, p. 5-6.
"Old Jewelry." <u>Stand</u> (26:4) Aut 85, p. 5.
"Pretty Rosy May Dew" (tr. of Jehan Planç on, w. Michael
Valentin). <u>NegC</u> (5:1) Wint 85, p. 70, 72, 74.
"Reichsmarschal Hermann Göring" (16 April, 1945).
<u>MichQR</u> (24:1) Wint 85, p. 46-47.
"W. D. Attempts to Save Cock Robin." <u>NegC</u> (5:4) Fall 85,
p. 105.
"W. D. Creates a Device for Escaping." <u>Salm</u> (67) Sum 85,
p. 9.
"W. D. Creates a Device for Inverting Mr. Evil." <u>NegC</u>
(5:4) Fall 85, p. 96.
"W. D. Disguised As Cock Robin and Hidden Deep in Crimson."
<u>Salm</u> (67) Sum 85, p. 12.
"W. D. Don't Fear That Animal" (after the painting by
DeLoss McGras). <u>NegC</u> (5:4) Fall 85, p. 97.
"W. D. Finds Cock Robin." <u>Salm</u> (67) Sum 85, p. 7.
"W. D. Is Concerned about the Character Assassination of
Cock Robin." <u>NegC</u> (5:4) Fall 85, p. 100-101.
"W. D. Meets Mr. Evil While Removing the Record of Bartok .
. ." <u>NegC</u> (5:4) Fall 85, p. 98-99.
"Who Wants to Cure a Migraine?" (tr. of Gabriel Bataille).
<u>NegC</u> (5:1) Wint 85, p. 82.
"You Mortals, Breathe Your Sighs No More" (tr. of Pierre
Guedron, w. Leigh Banks). <u>NegC</u> (5:1) Wint 85, p. 78.
4612. SNOW, Carol
"Aria." <u>Pequod</u> (18) 85, p. 124-126.
"Prospect" (The Graces)." <u>Pequod</u> (18) 85, p. 123.
4613. SNOW, Karen
"Fifty-Two." <u>BelPoJ</u> (36:2) Wint 85-86, p. 10-11.
4614. SNOW, Phoebe
"Stand-up on the Rock." <u>Kaleid</u> (10) Spr 85, p. 46.
4615. SNYDER, J. K.
"In the Public Gardens." <u>AntigR</u> (60) Wint 85, p. 10.
"Ketch Harbour: 'Owt of thise blake wawes for to sayle':
Troilus and Criseyde." <u>AntigR</u> (60) Wint 85, p. 12.
"Maritime." <u>AntigR</u> (60) Wint 85, p. 11.
"Muse: for Robert." <u>AntigR</u> (60) Wint 85, p. 11.
"Nova Scotia." <u>AntigR</u> (60) Wint 85, p. 10-12.
"Smith's Beach." <u>AntigR</u> (60) Wint 85, p. 10.
4616. SO, Chongju
"The Hippy Market in Sao Paulo" (tr. by David McCann).
<u>GrahamHR</u> (9) Fall 85, p. 71.
"Kilimanjaro Sunrise" (tr. by David McCann). <u>GrahamHR</u> (9)
Fall 85, p. 72.
"Nevada" (tr. by David McCann). <u>GrahamHR</u> (9) Fall 85, p.

70.
"New Year's Prayer, 1976" (tr. by David McCann). <u>NewL</u>
    (51:4) Sum 85, p. 138-139.
"The Pedlar Women of Wu-Lai" (tr. by David McCann).
    <u>GrahamHR</u> (9) Fall 85, p. 74.
"Song of the Indian Wanderers" (tr. by David McCann).
    <u>GrahamHR</u> (9) Fall 85, p. 73.
SOBEK, Maria Herrera
    <u>See</u> HERRERA-SOBEK, Maria
4617. SOBIN, Gustaf
    "Fragment: from a Blossoming Almond." <u>Temblor</u> (1) 85, p.
        17.
    "On Imagerie: Esther Williams, 1944." <u>Temblor</u> (1) 85, p.
        19.
    "A Portrait of the Self As Instrument of Its Syllables"
        (for Robert Duncan). <u>Sulfur</u> (14) 85, p. 45-64.
    "Where the Pine-Needles Bristle." <u>Temblor</u> (1) 85, p. 18.
4618. SOBRINO, Gabriella
    "Ambiguous Solitude" (tr. by P. F. Paolini). <u>LitR</u> (29:1)
        Fall 85, p. 120.
    "If I Could Know" (tr. by P. F. Paolini). <u>LitR</u> (29:1)
        Fall 85, p. 119.
4619. SOCOLOW, Elizabeth
    "To Newton: Reading His <u>Opticks</u> Again." <u>USl</u> (18/19)
        Wint 85, p. 11.
4620. SOKAD, Jerry
    "Heritage Letter." <u>SanFPJ</u> (7:2) 85, p. 20.
    "The Palace Guard." <u>SanFPJ</u> (7:2) 85, p. 29.
    "Penal Colony." <u>SanFPJ</u> (7:2) 85, p. 32.
    "Seventh Body Washed Ashore." <u>SanFPJ</u> (7:2) 85, p. 17.
4621. SOLARI, Rose
    "I'm Not Afraid for You, Though I Wish." <u>MissR</u> (13:3,
        issue 39) Spr 85, p. 79-80.
    "Three Poems for Grace." <u>MissR</u> (13:3, issue 39) Spr 85,
        p. 75-78.
4622. SOLDO, John J.
    "Repose" (in memory of Jeanne Bonnette). <u>DeKalbLAJ</u>
        (18:1/2) 85, p. 85.
4623. SOLHEIM, James
    "Existence One Thursday." <u>Poetry</u> (147:1) O 85, p. 25-26.
    "Variations: Couple Seen through a Window." <u>Poetry</u>
        (146:6) S 85, p. 336-337.
    "The World to a Fake Stuffed Zebra on Display outside a
        Missouri Gas Station." <u>MissR</u> (40/41) Wint 85, p. 132-
        133.
4624. SOLLERS, John F.
    "Rubber Road." <u>SnapD</u> (8:2) Spr 85, p. 4.
    "Talking Money." <u>SnapD</u> (8:2) Spr 85, p. 3.
4625. SOLLFREY, Stacey
    "Artificial Insemination." <u>Open24</u> (4) 85, p. 45.
    "Bubbled Over." <u>Open24</u> (4) 85, p. 12.
4626. SOLOMON, Carl
    "Nary a Louse." <u>Oink</u> (19) 85, p. 107.
4627. SOLONCHE, J. R.
    "My Shorts, My Undershirts, Drying on the Line." <u>PoetryNW</u>
        (26:4) Wint 85-86, p. 21-22.
    "Suggested Entries for a Diary." <u>NegC</u> (5:4) Fall 85, p.
        110.
4628. SOLORIO, Luis
    "Perdon." <u>BilingR</u> (11:3) S-D 84, p. 46-47.
4629. SOLWAY, David
    "Islands." <u>SewanR</u> (93:2) Spr 85, p. 193.
    "Kithnos." <u>SewanR</u> (93:2) Spr 85, p. 195.
    "Reflections." <u>SewanR</u> (93:2) Spr 85, p. 194.
    "What I Was Looking For." <u>SewanR</u> (93:2) Spr 85, p. 192.

4630. SOMERVILLE, Jane
        "Shapes of Stars" (for Beulah Powell). <u>PoetryR</u> (2:2) Ap
          85, p. 40.
4631. SONDE, Susan
        "Letters from the Poet Zhang Jie." <u>NewL</u> (52:1) Fall 85,
          p. 14-15.
4632. SONG, Cathy
        "Frameless Windows, Squares of Light." <u>SenR</u> (15:2) 85, p.
          139-141.
        "Waterwings." <u>SenR</u> (15:2) 85, p. 137-138.
4633. SONIAT, Katherine
        "Cantata for Christmas Children." <u>SouthwR</u> (70:4) Aut 85,
          p. 516.
        "Death Watch." <u>SouthwR</u> (70:4) Aut 85, p. 517.
        "Necktie, and So Forth." <u>Poetry</u> (146:5) Ag 85, p. 249-250.
        "Something You Could Almost See." <u>ColEng</u> (47:7) N 85, p.
          714.
        "The Woodworker" (for C.B.C., 1909-1984). <u>NewOR</u> (12:4)
          Wint 85, p. 27.
4634. SONNEVI, Göran
        "Summer has turned now" (tr. by Rika Lesser). <u>SenR</u> (15:1)
          85, p. 57-58.
4635. SORENSEN, Sally Jo
        "Northern Liberties." <u>AmerPoR</u> (14:3) My-Je 85, p. 43.
        "Seining Minnow." <u>WestB</u> (17) 85, p. 99.
4636. SORESTAD, Glen
        "First Ice." <u>Descant</u> 48 (16:1) Spr 85, p. 7.
        "Moments from the Past." <u>Descant</u> 48 (16:1) Spr 85, p. 8.
        "Saskatchewan Town at Night." <u>Descant</u> 48 (16:1) Spr 85,
          p. 9.
4637. SORNBERGER, Judith
        "Amelia Earhart Rag Doll." <u>PraS</u> (59:3) Fall 85, p. 45.
        "Bisque Doll Family." <u>PraS</u> (59:3) Fall 85, p. 42-43.
        "The First, Second, and Last Scene of Mortality" (A needle
          picture by Prudence Punderson). <u>PraS</u> (59:3) Fall 85,
          p. 41.
        "French Young Lady Doll ca. 1845." <u>PraS</u> (59:3) Fall 85,
          p. 42.
        "Judith Beheading Holofernes." <u>PraS</u> (59:3) Fall 85, p. 40-
          41.
        "Pioneer Child's Doll." <u>PraS</u> (59:3) Fall 85, p. 44.
        "Women on Thanksgiving." <u>Calyx</u> (9:1) Spr-Sum 85, p. 43-45.
4638. SORRELL, John Edward
        "Sidewalk Cafe, Thinking of the Fuehrer." <u>Stand</u> (26:1)
          Wint 84-85, p. 32.
4639. SOTO, Aida Guisela
        "Un Pueblecito Magico." <u>LindLM</u> (4:2) Ap-Je 85, p. 27.
4640. SOTO, Gary
        "Another Time." <u>Stand</u> (26:4) Aut 85, p. 23.
        "As It Is." <u>Stand</u> (26:4) Aut 85, p. 22.
        "At the Door." <u>SenR</u> (15:1) 85, p. 7.
        "Behind Grandma's House." <u>OP</u> (38/39) Spr 85, p. 14.
        "Blue." <u>OP</u> (40) Fall-Wint 85, p. 54-55.
        "The Concert." <u>OP</u> (40) Fall-Wint 85, p. 49-50.
        "Good Morning, Fresno." <u>MSS</u> (4:3) Spr 85, p. 27.
        "Small Town with One Road." <u>Poetry</u> (147:2) N 85, p. 94-95.
        "Sorrow in French." <u>Poetry</u> (147:2) N 85, p. 93-94.
        "Taking Notice." <u>OP</u> (40) Fall-Wint 85, p. 51-53.
        "That Girl." <u>Poetry</u> (147:2) N 85, p. 95-96.
        "Thinking Like a Child." <u>Thrpny</u> (6:3, issue 23) Fall 85,
          p. 13.
4641. SOUSTER, Raymond
        "High Divers." <u>Waves</u> (13:2/3) Wint 85, p. 89.
        "More Impressions from Mr. Colville's Picture Gallery" (2.
          "Nude and Dummy," 3. "Horse and Train," 4. "Skater," 12.
          Ocean Limited"). <u>PoetryCR</u> (6:3) Spr 85, p. 25.

"New Moon." <u>Waves</u> (13:2/3) Wint 85, p. 89.
4642. SOUTH, Karen
        "The Abattoir." <u>Ploughs</u> (11:1) 85, p. 200.
        "Sleep Song." <u>Ploughs</u> (11:1) 85, p. 199.
4643. SPACKS, Barry
        "At Bedtime." <u>Confr</u> (29) Wint 85, p. 34.
        "Flying Horses" (For Seth, Horsemaster). <u>CalQ</u> (26) Sum
            85, p. 46.
        "He to Her." <u>CalQ</u> (26) Sum 85, p. 46.
        "Images." <u>SewanR</u> (93:1) Wint 85, p. 67.
        "Silk Stockings." <u>SewanR</u> (93:1) Wint 85, p. 68.
        "Slowness and Apricots." <u>SewanR</u> (93:1) Wint 85, p. 67.
        "The Snow Camper" (For Michael Sollazzo). <u>CalQ</u> (26) Sum
            85, p. 45.
        "What Eugenia Said." <u>Confr</u> (29) Wint 85, p. 34.
SPANCKEREN, Kathryn van
        See Van SPANCKEREN, Kathryn
4644. SPANGLE, Douglas
        "This Is the Way." <u>CrabCR</u> (3:1) Fall-Wint 85, p. 8-9.
4645. SPANIAS, Nikos
        "Almost Hysteria" (in Greek and English, tr. by Yannis
            Phillis). <u>StoneC</u> (12:2/3) Spr-Sum 85, p. 54-55.
4646. SPANNINGA, Sjoerd
        "Experiments" (tr. by Rod Jellema). <u>PoetL</u> (79:4) Wint 85,
            p. 236.
4647. SPARKS, Amy
        "Counting." <u>AmerPoR</u> (14:4) Jl-Ag 85, p. 7.
        "Feast Day." <u>AmerPoR</u> (14:4) Jl-Ag 85, p. 7.
        "The Horticulturist." <u>AmerPoR</u> (14:4) Jl-Ag 85, p. 7.
4648. SPARSHOTT, Francis
        "Possum Non Potes" (Footnote on a Sunday Morning Service).
            <u>PoetryCR</u> (7:2) Wint 85-86, p. 10.
        "Windy City." <u>PoetryCR</u> (6:4) Sum 85, p. 46.
4649. SPEAKES, Richard
        "Pelicans." <u>MemphisSR</u> (5:2) Spr 85, p. 33.
4650. SPEAR, Roberta
        "Chartres." <u>AmerPoR</u> (14:2) Mr-Ap 85, p. 16.
        "Just South." <u>Poetry</u> (147:1) O 85, p. 29-30.
        "Men Back Then." <u>AmerPoR</u> (14:2) Mr-Ap 85, p. 16.
4651. SPEARS, Heather
        "2nd Letter for Steen." <u>CanLit</u> (105) Sum 85, p. 99.
        "The Eye of the Lion." <u>PoetryCR</u> (6:3) Spr 85, p. 27.
        "Fox Cubs at Play." <u>CanLit</u> (105) Sum 85, p. 98.
        "Letter for Steen." <u>CanLit</u> (105) Sum 85, p. 99.
        "Procedure." <u>CanLit</u> (105) Sum 85, p. 97-98.
4652. SPEARS, Monroe K.
        "Acoustic Isolation." <u>SewanR</u> (93:4) Fall 85, p. 538.
        "Against Commitment." <u>Hudson</u> (38:3) Aut 85, p. 418.
        "The Banquet" (Allen Tate's 75th birthday, Sewanee, 1974).
            <u>SewanR</u> (93:4) Fall 85, p. 539.
        "A Horror Story." <u>Hudson</u> (38:3) Aut 85, p. 417-418.
        "A Painful Subject." <u>Hudson</u> (38:3) Aut 85, p. 415-417.
4653. SPEER, Laurel
        "The Boy with Scars on His Arms." <u>NewL</u> (51:3) Spr 85, p.
            118-119.
        "The Owner of a Green Hudson" (an anachronism). <u>KanQ</u>
            (17:4) Fall 85, p. 24.
        "Rolling in from California." <u>ConnPR</u> (3:1) 84, p. 39-40.
        "Three Ways to Tell a Story." <u>IndR</u> (8:3) Fall 85, p. 64-
            65.
        "To My Daughter Blooming Red beside Me in the Street."
            <u>WindO</u> (46) Fall 85, p. 43-45.
4654. SPEIDEL, Joanne
        "On Hearing the 5th." <u>PassN</u> (6:2) Spr-Sum 85, p. 21.
4655. SPENCE, Betty
        "Negative Capability." <u>NegC</u> (5:3) Sum 85, p. 148.

4656. SPENCE, Michael
    "The Discarded." <u>MinnR</u> (N.S. 24) Spr 85, p. 37.
    "First Love in Two Dimensions." <u>Poetry</u> (146:6) S 85, p.
        329.
    "Montana Snowstorm with Esther" (for Emily Warn). <u>SnapD</u>
        (9:1) Fall 85, p. 6-7.
4657. SPENCER, Tony
    "Back to Sleep." <u>Descant</u> 48 (16:1) Spr 85, p. 18.
    "Dialogue." <u>Descant</u> 48 (16:1) Spr 85, p. 15.
    "Sticks in My Mind." <u>Descant</u> 48 (16:1) Spr 85, p. 19-20.
    "What I Wear." <u>Descant</u> 48 (16:1) Spr 85, p. 16-17.
4658. SPENDER, Stephen
    "Perhaps" (original and revised versions). <u>ParisR</u> (27:96)
        Sum 85, p. 190-191.
    "The Sign Faehre nach Wilm" (original and revised
        versions). <u>ParisR</u> (27:96) Sum 85, p. 188-189.
    "To a Spanish Poet" (to Manuel Altolaguirre). <u>ParisR</u>
        (27:96) Sum 85, p. 200, 202.
    "To Manuel Altolaguirre." <u>ParisR</u> (27:96) Sum 85, p. 201,
        203.
    "The Town" (tr. of C. P. Cavafy, w. Nikos Stangos). <u>TriQ</u>
        (63) Spr-Sum 85, p. 102.
    "The Uncreating Chaos." <u>ParisR</u> (27:96) Sum 85, p. 192,
        194, 196, 198.
    "The Uncreating Chaos" (Double Portrait in a Mirror).
        <u>ParisR</u> (27:96) Sum 85, p. 193, 195, 197, 199.
4659. SPICER, David
    "Bert." <u>GreenfR</u> (13:1/2) Fall-Wint 85, p. 108.
    "The Desperado's Last Escape." <u>GreenfR</u> (13:1/2) Fall-Wint
        85, p. 109.
4660. SPICER, Russell
    "What Brought Him." <u>Vis</u> (19) 85, p. 16.
4661. SPICHER, Julia
    "Dying with Amish Uncles." <u>WestB</u> (17) 85, p. 53.
    "Onion, Fruit of Grace." <u>WestB</u> (17) 85, p. 52.
4662. SPINGARN, Lawrence P.
    "No Backward Step." <u>Amelia</u> (2:1) Ap 85, p. 16.
4663. SPIRES, Elizabeth
    "Apology." <u>Crazy</u> (26) Spr 84, p. 37.
    "The Bearers of Bad Tidings." <u>Crazy</u> (26) Spr 84, p. 36.
    "A Book of Hours." <u>Pequod</u> (18) 85, p. 80-81.
    "Espresso." <u>SenR</u> (15:1) 85, p. 66.
    "Ever-Changing Landscape" (Ladew topiary gardens: Monkton,
        Maryland). <u>Verse</u> (4) 85, p. 21-23.
    "Ocean City: Early March." <u>Pequod</u> (18) 85, p. 77-78.
    "Storyville Portrait" (New Orleans red light district,
        1912, a photo by E. J. Bellocq). <u>Pequod</u> (18) 85, p. 79.
    "Storyville Portrait" (New Orleans Red Light District,
        1912, a photograph by E. J. Bellocq). <u>VirQ</u> (61:3) Sum
        85, p. 427-428.
    "Storyville Portrait" (New Orleans red-light district,
        1912, a photograph by E. J. Bellocq). <u>AmerPoR</u> (14:3)
        My-Je 85, p. 19.
    "Swan's Island" (Selections: "Bread & Water," "Love's
        Body"). <u>OntR</u> (23) Fall-Wint 85-86, p. 95-96.
    "Whodunit." <u>MissouriR</u> (8:2) 85, p. 151.
    "Woman Weighing Pearls." <u>Pequod</u> (18) 85, p. 76.
4664. SPIVACK, Karla
    "Joan." <u>CentR</u> (29:3) Sum 85, p. 324-325.
4665. SPIVACK, Kathleen
    "Because of Her." <u>StoneC</u> (12:2/3) Spr-Sum 85, p. 71.
    "Car Crash in Greece" (for Mania Seferi). <u>CapeR</u> (20:2)
        Fall 85, p. 46-47.
    "The Drive: Crossing the Sierras." <u>GWR</u> (6:1) 85?, p. 3-6.
    "Escape Artist." <u>SenR</u> (15:1) 85, p. 16.
    "Getting the Message." <u>GreenfR</u> (13:1/2) Fall-Wint 85, p.

62-63.
"The Unmentionable Subject." OP (38/39) Spr 85, p. 217-
218.
"The Yellow House, My Friends." Prima (9) 85, p. 70.
4666. SPIVACK, Susan Fantl
"November Is Not Grateful." GreenfR (13:1/2) Fall-Wint
85, p. 51-52.
4667. SPOONER, Michael
"The Woodcutter's Widow." CapeR (20:2) Fall 85, p. 6.
4668. SPRACKLIN, Sahara
"Marry Me!" Rampike (4:2/3) 85-86, p. 109.
4669. SPRAGER, Venceslav
"Fall" (tr. by Gisela Argyle). Waves (14:1/2) Fall 85, p.
74.
"Frühling." Waves (14:1/2) Fall 85, p. 72.
"Herbst." Waves (14:1/2) Fall 85, p. 74.
"Sommer." Waves (14:1/2) Fall 85, p. 73.
"Spring" (tr. by Gisela Argyle). Waves (14:1/2) Fall 85,
p. 72.
"Summer" (tr. by Gisela Argyle). Waves (14:1/2) Fall 85,
p. 73.
"Winter" (In German and English, tr. by Gisela Argyle).
Waves (14:1/2) Fall 85, p. 75.
4670. SPRECHER, Lorrie
"Last Judgment -- A Cow." Chelsea (44) 85, p. 54-56.
4671. SPROXTON, Birk
"Phantom Lake." PraF (6:1) Wint 85, p. 65.
"Return Visit." PraF (6:1) Wint 85, p. 66.
"Return Visit." PraF (6:4) Aut-Wint 85, p. 71-74.
"Wandering men" ("Untitled"). CapilR (34) 85, p. 34.
4672. SQUIER, Donna
"Dark Ages." Open24 (4) 85, p. 38.
4673. ST. CLAIR, Philip
"Coyote Fatalism." PoetryNW (26:2) Sum 85, p. 47.
"Coyote in Law School." PoetryNW (26:2) Sum 85, p. 46.
"Coyote Insomnia." PraF (6:2) Spr 85, p. 17.
"Coyote on Retreat." PoetryNW (26:2) Sum 85, p. 45.
"Coyote Repose." PraF (6:2) Spr 85, p. 16.
4674. ST. JOHN, Bruce
"5 A.M. -- Barbados." GreenfR (12:3/4) Wint-Spr 85, p.
212-213.
"Crosses." GreenfR (12:3/4) Wint-Spr 85, p. 213-215.
"Jealousy." GreenfR (12:3/4) Wint-Spr 85, p. 212.
4675. ST. JOHN, David
"Black Poppy (At the Temple)." AmerPoR (14:2) Mr-Ap 85,
p. 4.
"An Essay on Liberation." PartR (52:2) 85, p. 69-70.
"A Hard & Noble Patience." AmerPoR (14:2) Mr-Ap 85, p. 4.
"The Lemons." Crazy (26) Spr 84, p. 50.
"Meridian." Crazy (26) Spr 84, p. 51-52.
"A Temporary Situation." AmerPoR (14:2) Mr-Ap 85, p. 3.
"Two Sorrows." AmerPoR (14:2) Mr-Ap 85, p. 3.
"Wavelength." AmerPoR (14:2) Mr-Ap 85, p. 4.
"Winter Fires." Iowa (15:1) Wint 85, p. 18.
4676. STAFFORD, June Billings
"Waiting for a Grade" (for Pam Stratton). EngJ (74:5) S
85, p. 92.
4677. STAFFORD, Kim R.
"There Are No Names But Stories." PoetryNW (26:1) Spr 85,
p. 47.
4678. STAFFORD, William
"Any Time." SouthwR (70:2) Spr 85, p. 212-213.
"At Memorial Park." CrossCur (4:2) 84, p. 77.
"Browser." SouthwR (70:2) Spr 85, p. 213.
"Chicory." SouthwR (70:2) Spr 85, p. 212.
"Deserters." NeqC (5:4) Fall 85, p. 12.

"Facing Dawn at OSU." <u>CimR</u> (70) Ja 85, p. 62.
"How It Can Be." <u>QW</u> (20) Spr-Sum 85, p. 77.
"A Life, a Ritual." <u>SouthernR</u> (21:1) Wint 85, p. 138.
"On Their Blindness." <u>OP</u> (38/39) Spr 85, p. 131.
"Saying 'Light, ' Saying 'Corazon'." <u>MemphisSR</u> (5:2) Spr 85, p. 50.
"Some Day." <u>NewL</u> (51:3) Spr 85, p. 50.
"The Summer We Didn't Die." <u>NegC</u> (5:4) Fall 85, p. 11.
"A Thought That Is Real." <u>NewL</u> (51:3) Spr 85, p. 50.
"Two People." <u>PaintedB</u> (26/27) Sum-Fall 85, p. 7.
"The Way Trees Began." <u>SouthernR</u> (21:1) Wint 85, p. 139.
"Wrong Number." <u>NegC</u> (5:4) Fall 85, p. 10.

4679. STALLWORTHY, Jon
"Windfalls." <u>Hudson</u> (38:2) Sum 85, p. 270.

4680. STAMBLER, Peter
"Head of a Girl" (Vermeer). <u>ChiR</u> (35:1) Aut 85, p. 70.
"Practicing." <u>ChiR</u> (35:1) Aut 85, p. 71.
"A Year Afterwards, in the Gallery." <u>ChiR</u> (35:1) Aut 85, p. 69.

4681. STANCICH, C. P.
"A Sage, and Bitter." <u>Wind</u> (15:54) 85, p. 51.

4682. STANDING, Sue
"The Bones of the Plagiarist." <u>QW</u> (20) Spr-Sum 85, p. 48.
"How to Use a Coma Kit." <u>PoetryNW</u> (26:3) Aut 85, p. 30.
"Palinode." <u>QW</u> (20) Spr-Sum 85, p. 49.
"Quarry." <u>PoetryNW</u> (26:3) Aut 85, p. 30.
"Waterlilies in the Muddy River." <u>PartR</u> (52:3) 85, p. 246-247.

4683. STANESCU, Nichita
"Bas-Relief with Heroes" (tr. by Tom Carlson and Vasile Poenaru). <u>Mund</u> (16:1/2) 85, p. 75.
"Basorelief cu Eroi." <u>Mund</u> (16:1/2) 85, p. 74.
"Burned Forest" (in Romanian and English, tr. by Thomas C. Carlson and Vasile Poenaru). <u>StoneC</u> (13:1/2) Fall-Wint 85-86, p. 46-47.
"Desigur." <u>Mund</u> (16:1/2) 85, p. 76.
"Mama Mea Si Soldatul Ei." <u>Mund</u> (16:1/2) 85, p. 72.
"My Mother and Her Soldier" (tr. by Tom Carlson and Vasile Poenaru). <u>Mund</u> (16:1/2) 85, p. 73.
"Of Course" (tr. by Tom Carlson and Vasile Poenaru). <u>Mund</u> (16:1/2) 85, p. 77.

4684. STANFORD, Frank
"Bullshit." <u>Raccoon</u> (17) Mr 85, p. 36.
"Friend of the Enemy." <u>Raccoon</u> (17) Mr 85, p. 40.
"Pits." <u>Raccoon</u> (17) Mr 85, p. 33.
"Porch Chair." <u>Raccoon</u> (17) Mr 85, p. 34-35.

4685. STANFORD, Janet Holmes
"Editorial." <u>LittleM</u> (14:4) 85, p. 49.

4686. STANGOS, Nikos
"The Town" (tr. of C. P. Cavafy, w. Stephen Spender). <u>TriQ</u> (63) Spr-Sum 85, p. 102.

4687. STANHOPE, Patrick
"The Arrangement." <u>KanQ</u> (17:4) Fall 85, p. 24.

4688. STANIZZI, John L.
"Stream Fear." <u>PoetL</u> (80:1) Spr 85, p. 41-42.

4689. STANNARD, Martin
"An Empty Summer." <u>HangL</u> (48) Fall 85, p. 26.
"Heart Deep in Bargain Bags." <u>HangL</u> (48) Fall 85, p. 27-28.
"The Ingredient." <u>HangL</u> (48) Fall 85, p. 25-26.

4690. STANSBERGER, Richard
"How to Approach a Poem" (for the Seniors of Bell 2). <u>EngJ</u> (74:3) Mr 85, p. 90.

4691. STANTON, Joseph
"Dojoji." <u>HawaiiR</u> (18) Fall 85, p. 92.

4692. STANTON, Maura
        "Good People." <u>Crazy</u> (26) Spr 84, p. 9.
        "March." <u>Ploughs</u> (11:1) 85, p. 201.
        "Modern Lives." <u>Poetry</u> (146:1) Ap 85, p. 25-26.
        "Overnight in St. Louis." <u>Crazy</u> (26) Spr 84, p. 10-11.
        "Space." <u>Ploughs</u> (11:1) 85, p. 202-203.
        "Spring." <u>Poetry</u> (146:1) Ap 85, p. 27.
        "Trees, Trees." <u>SenR</u> (15:1) 85, p. 55-56.
        "Twelve Below." <u>Poetry</u> (146:1) Ap 85, p. 27.
4693. STAP, Don
        "The Big People." <u>PassN</u> (6:1) Fall-Wint 85, p. 3.
        "Jacob Stap" (1893-1976). <u>PassN</u> (6:2) Spr-Sum 85, p. 7.
        "Letter to a Friend." <u>PassN</u> (6:1) Fall-Wint 85, p. 3.
        "Remember?" <u>PassN</u> (6:1) Fall-Wint 85, p. 3.
        "A Terrible Life." <u>QW</u> (20) Spr-Sum 85, p. 99.
        "Tonight, Sitting Down to Write." <u>PassN</u> (6:1) Fall-Wint
            85, p. 3.
4694. STARBUCK, George
        "Hardearned Overturned Caribbean Basin Stomp." <u>Harp</u>
            (271:1625) O 85, p. 30.
        "Washington International." <u>NewYorker</u> (61:32) 30 S 85, p.
            111.
        "The Word" (fugue on a theme by Dugan, a theme by Stevens).
            <u>PartR</u> (52:4) 85, p. 425-426.
4695. STARK, Sharon Sheehe
        "The Movers." <u>WestB</u> (17) 85, p. 56-57.
        "Small Game Season." <u>WestB</u> (17) 85, p. 54-55.
        "Uncut Fields." <u>PraS</u> (59:1) Spr 85, p. 58-60.
4696. STARZEC, Larry
        "Another Gin and Tonic at the Last Chance Saloon." <u>Vis</u>
            (18) 85, p. 31.
        "Bridging the Birth Canal." <u>CapeR</u> (20:2) Fall 85, p. 34.
        "Waiting for the 10:29." <u>CapeR</u> (20:2) Fall 85, p. 32.
        "The Welder." <u>CapeR</u> (20:2) Fall 85, p. 33.
4697. STEELE, Peggy
        "Grandma Clicks Her Needles." <u>AmerV</u> (1) 85, p. 5.
4698. STEELE, Timothy
        "Eros." <u>Poetry</u> (145:5) F 85, p. 262.
        "Ethics." <u>Poetry</u> (145:5) F 85, p. 263.
4699. STEFANILE, Felix
        "Andrew." <u>NewL</u> (51:3) Spr 85, p. 90-91.
4700. STEFFENS, Bradley
        "Centaur's Visit." <u>CrossCur</u> (4:4/5:1) 85, p. 35.
4701. STEFFLER, John
        "The Grey Islands" (Selections: 9 Poems). <u>PoetryCR</u> (6:3)
            Spr 85, p. 21.
4702. STEIN, Agnes
        "Answer to Questionnaire" (tr. of Gunter Kunert). <u>DenQ</u>
            (19:4) Spr 85, p. 57-58.
        "The Brave Blondes." <u>KanQ</u> (17:4) Fall 85, p. 129.
        "Fellow Citizen" (tr. of Gunter Kunert). <u>DenQ</u> (19:4) Spr
            85, p. 59.
        "On the Archaeology of Our Interment" (tr. of Gunter
            Kunert). <u>DenQ</u> (19:4) Spr 85, p. 55-56.
4703. STEIN, Charles
        "The Sad Machines" (From <u>theforestforthetrees</u>). <u>Conjunc</u>
            (7) 85, p. 197-208.
        "Theforestforthetrees" (3 selections). <u>Temblor</u> (1) 85, p.
            23-32.
STEIN, Hadassah
        <u>See</u> STEIN, Hannah (Hadassah)
4704. STEIN, Hannah (Hadassah Stein)
        "Deathbed" (For Mary and Arthur Child). <u>CalQ</u> (26) Sum 85,
            p. 33.
        "The Game of 'Statues'." <u>CutB</u> (23) Fall-Wint 85, p. 53.
        "Invisible." <u>PoetryNW</u> (26:2) Sum 85, p. 33.

4705. STEIN, Harvey
        "Executions" (Guilin, Guangxi Province). CrabCR (2:2)
        Wint 85, p. 26.
4706. STEIN, Jill
        "The Doll Dream." USl (18/19) Wint 85, p. 8.
        "My Grandfather and the Bee Sting Coma." WestB (16) 85,
        p. 36-37.
        "My Great-Aunt Speaks through the Clairvoyant." WestB
        (16) 85, p. 38-39.
        "One Man Shares His Grief at the Seminar on Death." WestB
        (16) 85, p. 35.
        "Santo Domingo, Sunday." USl (18/19) Wint 85, p. 8.
4707. STEIN, Kevin
        "Past Thirty." PoetryNW (26:2) Sum 85, p. 37.
        "The WPA in Anderson, Indiana." PoetryNW (26:2) Sum 85,
        p. 36.
4708. STEIN, Rachel
        "I hate strolling" ("Untitled"). AmerPoR (14:3) My-Je 85,
        p. 21.
4709. STEINBERGH, Judith
        "Past Time." Tendril (19/20) 85, p. 348.
4710. STEINKE, Russell
        "The Flowers." Confr (30/31) N 85, p. 134.
        "It Was Murder." Confr (30/31) N 85, p. 135.
4711. STEINLE, Rita Juul
        "Cora's Baby." Confr (30/31) N 85, p. 176.
4712. STEINMAN
        "Inheriting the Earth." Vis (17) 85, p. 27.
4713. STEINMAN, Lisa
        "Driving to Buffalo." Thrpny (5:4, issue 20) Wint 85, p.
        26.
4714. STELLA, Rachel
        "Je Sublime" (Selections: 4 poems -- "The Square of the
        Hypotenuse," "I," "A H," "Nebula," tr. of Benjamin
        Peret, w. John Yau). Sulfur (13) 85, p. 76-79.
4715. STELMACH, Marjorie
        "Grace Notes." CapeR (20:2) Fall 85, p. 36.
        "Halley's Coming." CapeR (20:2) Fall 85, p. 37.
        "The Shapes We Make to Protect Us" (First Prize,
        International Poetry Contest). WestB (17) 85, p. 6-12.
4716. STEPANCHEV, Stephen
        "John Bowne of Flushing." Confr (30/31) N 85, p. 119-121.
        "A Nun in Mesic, Yugoslavia." NewL (52:1) Fall 85, p. 20.
4717. STEPHENS, M. G.
        "Moo Goong Hwa (Rose of Sharon)" (tr. of Yoo Ok Hee).
        NewL (51:4) Sum 85, p. 139.
4718. STEPHENSON, Shelby
        "Recognition." SouthernPR (26, i.e. 25:2) Fall 85, p. 42-
        43.
        "Round and Out." PoetC (17:1) Fall 85, p. 42.
        "Who Would Tell His Story." TexasR (6:1/2) Spr-Sum 85, p.
        57.
4719. STEPTOE, Lamont B.
        "Cooperation" (Abidjan, Ivory Coast). PaintedB (26/27)
        Sum-Fall 85, p. 13.
        "A Long Ride Back" (Philadelphia, Pa.). PaintedB (26/27)
        Sum-Fall 85, p. 12.
4720. STERN, Gerald
        "At Jane's" (For Gil Orlovitz, 1919-1974). Iowa (15:1)
        Wint 85, p. 22-23.
4721. STERN, Joan
        "Rooms." NewL (52:1) Fall 85, p. 66.
4722. STERNLIEB, Barry
        "First Lesson" (16th-Century Japan). Poetry (146:2) My
        85, p. 86-87.
        "Fission." MidAR (5:2) 85, p. 20-21.

"A Prayer for Many Worlds." <u>Outbr</u> (14/15) Fall 84-Spr 85, p. 9.
"Still Life: Dissecting the Shark." <u>Outbr</u> (14/15) Fall 84-Spr 85, p. 10.

4723. STERRETT, Jane
"Five Blue Japanese Iris." <u>PoetryNW</u> (26:2) Sum 85, p. 12-13.
"Instructions for a Walking Tour." <u>PoetryNW</u> (26:2) Sum 85, p. 14-15.

4724. STETLER, Charles
"A Classic." <u>WormR</u> (25:3, issue 99) 85, p. 114.
"Commission." <u>WormR</u> (25:3, issue 99) 85, p. 113.
"Dead to Rights." <u>WormR</u> (25:3, issue 99) 85, p. 114.
"Paddle Your Own Camus." <u>WormR</u> (25:3, issue 99) 85, p. 113.
"A World Out of Joint." <u>WormR</u> (25:3, issue 99) 85, p. 112.

4725. STEVEN, I. M.
"Wileminia." <u>AntigR</u> (61) Spr 85, p. 114.

4726. STEVENS, Alex
"The Blown Glass Souvenir among the Maps and Old Deeds" (w. Aleda Shirley). <u>Chelsea</u> (44) 85, p. 144.

4727. STEVENS, C. J.
"The Dying" (tr. of Clem Schouwenaars). <u>StoneC</u> (13:1/2) Fall-Wint 85-86, p. 40-41.

4728. STEVENSON, Anne
"The Ballad of the Made Maid" (To my Feminist Friends). <u>Poetry</u> (146:4) Jl 85, p. 206-207.
"Calendar." <u>Poetry</u> (146:4) Jl 85, p. 205.
"In the Tunnel of Summers." <u>Poetry</u> (146:4) Jl 85, p. 204-205.
"A Love Sequence." <u>Stand</u> (26:4) Aut 85, p. 21.

4729. STEVENSON, Diane
"Ascension." <u>PraS</u> (59:3) Fall 85, p. 46.
"Crossing Over." <u>PraS</u> (59:3) Fall 85, p. 47-48.

4730. STEVENSON, Richard
"Baby Tears" (Pilea depressa, from <u>Houseplant Series</u>, 29). <u>Germ</u> (9:2) Fall-Wint 85, p. 43.
"Chocolate Soldier" (Episcia cupreata, from <u>Houseplant Series</u>, 25). <u>Germ</u> (9:2) Fall-Wint 85, p. 42.
"The Coats." <u>Germ</u> (9:2) Fall-Wint 85, p. 46.
"Dracaena" (from <u>Houseplant Series</u>, 32). <u>Germ</u> (9:2) Fall-Wint 85, p. 44.
"Even before the Fated Phone Call Comes." <u>Germ</u> (9:2) Fall-Wint 85, p. 45.
"Houseplant Series" (Selections: 20. "Ghost Plant," 22. "Drunkard's Dream"). <u>PoetryCR</u> (6:4) Sum 85, p. 17.
"Meniscus." <u>Waves</u> (13:2/3) Wint 85, p. 81.
"Oxtongue Gasteria" (from <u>Houseplant Series</u>, 15). <u>Germ</u> (9:2) Fall-Wint 85, p. 41.
"Staghorn Fern." <u>BelPoJ</u> (35:4) Sum 85, p. 5.
"Waka II." <u>CrossCur</u> (4:3) 84, p. 94-95.

4731. STEWARD, D. E.
"Control." <u>Bogg</u> (53) 85, p. 56.
"Small Press." <u>Bogg</u> (54) 85, p. 43.

4732. STEWART, Dolores
"Dusting, de Beauvoir to Dickens." <u>DenQ</u> (20:1) Sum 85, p. 65-66.

4733. STEWART, Frank
"Above June Lake." <u>HawaiiR</u> (18) Fall 85, p. 103-104.
"The Backwater Poets." <u>MissR</u> (40/41) Wint 85, p. 117.
"The Backwater Poets" (for us all). <u>HawaiiR</u> (18) Fall 85, p. 102.
"Don Giovanni." <u>MissR</u> (40/41) Wint 85, p. 119.
"Flight." <u>MissR</u> (40/41) Wint 85, p. 118.
"Flying the Red Eye." <u>HawaiiR</u> (17) Spr 85, p. 1.
"Hard Yellow." <u>HawaiiR</u> (18) Fall 85, p. 100-101.

"On the Pali Coast, Hawaii" (for Michael Sykes). GrahamHR
    (8) Wint 85, p. 34.
"Stroke." HawaiiR (17) Spr 85, p. 2.
4734. STEWART, Robert
"The Job Left to Do." NewL (52:1) Fall 85, p. 85.
"Understanding." NewL (52:1) Fall 85, p. 85.
"What I Do Sundays Since the Divorce." NewL (52:1) Fall
    85, p. 84.
4735. STEWART, Susan
"André Derain, Woman in Chemise." SenR (15:1) 85, p. 35-
    36.
"The Last Prince of Urbino." Crazy (26) Spr 84, p. 57-62.
"The Summer before the Moon." SenR (15:1) 85, p. 34.
4736. STICKNEY, John
"101 Things to Do with Plastic Plants." WormR (25:4,
    issue 100) 85, p. 126.
"House of Worship." WormR (25:4, issue 100) 85, p. 125.
"Lonely Dental Behavior." Bogg (53) 85, p. 45.
"Open Range." Bogg (53) 85, p. 36.
"Our Passage Is the Passage of Liberation." Pig (13) 85,
    p. 76.
"Thelonious Vowels." Bogg (54) 85, p. 45.
"Wedding Night." Bogg (53) 85, p. 29.
"With Ché in Slumberland." PaintedB (26/27) Sum-Fall
    85, p. 35.
"Your Freudian African Dream." Pig (13) 85, p. 84.
4737. STILLMAN, Peter
"A Winter Death." Blueline (6:2) Wint-Spr 85, p. 46.
4738. STILLWELL, Mary Kathryn
"Waiting, 1976: Color Lithograph" (from The Barnet Poems).
    Nimrod (29:1) Fall-Wint 85, p. 20.
"You of the soft body rock into me like the sea." PraS
    (59:3) Fall 85, p. 62.
4739. STIPE, Shirley
"Methodist Retirement Home." SouthernPR (26, i.e. 25:2)
    Fall 85, p. 14-15.
4740. STIRLING, Mary
"Memoirs." ArizQ (41:3) Aut 85, p. 246.
4741. STIX, Judith Saul
"Two Creatures" (in gratitude to Paul Tillich). WebR
    (10:1) Spr 85, p. 67.
4742. STOCK, Bud
"Crimson Current." Poem (53) Mr 85, p. 9.
"Farmhouse Walls." Poem (53) Mr 85, p. 7.
"Retrieval." Poem (53) Mr 85, p. 8.
4743. STOCKLAND, Will
"In a Blue Steel World." SanFPJ (7:4) 85, p. 44.
"The Plastic Patriotic Church of the Air Inc." SanFPJ
    (7:3) 84 [i.e. 85], p. 8.
"Polemic." SanFPJ (7:4) 85, p. 37-38.
"A Psalm for Threadbare Images." SanFPJ (7:3) 84 [i.e.
    85], p. 63-64.
"The Suicide Seed." SanFPJ (7:3) 84 [i.e. 85], p. 18-19.
4744. STOICHEFF, Jim, Jr.
"Last Words." SnapD (8:2) Spr 85, p. 24-25.
4745. STOKES, Terry
"The Permanent Fixtures." Shen (36:1) 85-86, p. 16.
"Soupbone Sandwiches." Shen (36:1) 85-86, p. 17.
4746. STOKESBURY, Leon
"Lauds." Crazy (27) Fall 84, p. 54-55.
4747. STONE, Arlene
"His Grace." YellowS (14) Spr 85, p. 20-21.
"Nefertittie: Erotic Anti-Goddess" (A Collaboration, w.
    Harry Weisburd). YellowS (15) Sum 85, p. 14-21.
4748. STONE, Ellen
"Under Water." KanQ (17:4) Fall 85, p. 152.

4749. STONE, Joan
"Morning Song." SpoonRQ (10:4) Fall 85, p. 41.
4750. STONE, John
"Argument and After." MidwQ (26:2) Wint 85, p. 206.
"The Circuit." MidwQ (26:2) Wint 85, p. 207.
"Comparative Anatomy" (The possum has an os penis). MidwQ
(26:2) Wint 85, p. 208.
"The Dead Pigeon." AmerS (54:3) Sum 85, p. 402.
"Early Sunday Morning" (title of painting by Edward Hopper,
1930). AmerS (54:1) Wint 84-85, p. 119-120.
"The Hands." MidwQ (26:2) Wint 85, p. 210-211.
"November." MidwQ (26:2) Wint 85, p. 204.
"Seeing Double after Eye Surgery" (for Sister Bernetta
Quinn). MidwQ (26:2) Wint 85, p. 205.
"Trying to Remember Even a Small Dream Much Less the Big
Gaudy Ones in Color with Popcorn and High Ticket
Prices." MidwQ (26:2) Wint 85, p. 209.
4751. STONE, Ken
"Again an Iago Plays." Wind (15:55) 85, p. 20.
"Broken Hero." PoeticJ (9) 85, p. 17.
"Flying." PoeticJ (12) 85, p. 27.
"Meditation." PoeticJ (9) 85, p. 16.
"Natural Design." NegC (5:1) Wint 85, p. 105.
4752. STORACE, Patricia
"Pamina's Marriage Speech." Harp (271:1621) Je 85, p. 30-
31.
"Translations from the American." Pequod (19/20/21) 85,
p. 339-341.
4753. STORNI, Alfonsina
"Saturday" (tr. by Maria Bennett). CrabCR (3:1) Fall-Wint
85, p. 7.
4754. STOUT, Robert Joe
"Transformation." KanQ (17:4) Fall 85, p. 129.
"Two Nights with the Gypsy Guitarist." KanQ (17:1/2) Wint-
Spr 85, p. 80.
4755. STRAHAN, Bradley R.
"Child." NegC (5:2) Spr 85, p. 10.
"Horizon." CrabCR (2:3) Sum 85, p. 6.
4756. STRAND, Mark
"A Brief Introduction to Winter." NewYorker (61:42) 9 D
85, p. 44.
"The Empire of Chance." NewYorker (61:29) 9 S 85, p. 36.
"Itself Now." NewYorker (61:20) 8 Jl 85, p. 24.
"Travel." MemphisSR (5:2) Spr 85, p. 51.
4757. STRAUS, Austin
"The Critic." Open24 (4) 85, p. 44.
"The Dictator." PoeticJ (11) 85, p. 38.
"History." PoeticJ (11) 85, p. 38.
4758. STRAUS, Margaret
"And Then We Learn" (tr. of Alfredo Giuliani, w. Giuliano
Dego). LitR (28:2) Wint 85, p. 244.
"Camel" (tr. of Mario Lunetta, w. Giuliano Dego). LitR
(28:2) Wint 85, p. 249-250.
"Delft" (tr. of Elio Filippo Accrocca w. Giuliano Dego).
LitR (29:1) Fall 85, p. 91.
"Even in Dickens" (tr. of Carlo Villa). LitR (29:1) Fall
85, p. 122.
"Faces by Rembrandt" (tr. of Elio Filippo Accrocca, w.
Giuliano Dego). LitR (29:1) Fall 85, p. 90.
"George Washington" (tr. of Carlo Villa). LitR (29:1)
Fall 85, p. 121.
"God Calling the Holy Ghost" (tr. of Carlo Villa). LitR
(29:1) Fall 85, p. 121-122.
"Huddle with a Hyena" (tr. of Alberto M. Moriconi, w.
Giuliano Dego). LitR (29:1) Fall 85, p. 112.
"North Sea" (tr. of Elio Filippo Accrocca w. Giuliano

Dego). <u>LitR</u> (29:1) Fall 85, p. 91.
"The (Portable) Rite of Sleep" (Selections: 1-4, 12, 17,
    tr. of Giuliano Gramigna, w. Giuliano Dego). <u>LitR</u>
    (29:1) Fall 85, p. 101-103.
"A Private Story" (Excerpt, tr. of Dario Bellezza w.
    Giuliano Dego). <u>LitR</u> (29:1) Fall 85, p. 93-94.
"Provos" (tr. of Elio Filippo Accrocca w. Giuliano Dego).
    <u>LitR</u> (29:1) Fall 85, p. 90.
"Psychograph" (tr. of Mariella Bettarini, w. Giuliano
    Dego). <u>LitR</u> (29:1) Fall 85, p. 94.
"La Storia in Rima" (an epic poem, in progress: Excerpt,
    tr. of Giuliano Dego, w. the author). <u>LitR</u> (29:1) Fall
    85, p. 97-100.
"When I Was Young" (tr. of Alfredo Giuliani, w. Giuliano
    Dego). <u>LitR</u> (28:2) Wint 85, p. 243.
4759. STRAYER, Jean
    "The Procedure." <u>TexasR</u> (6:3/4) Fall-Wint 85, p. 103.
4760. STRECKER, James
    "Billie Holiday on the Sound of Jazz." <u>PoetryCR</u> (7:2)
        Wint 85-86, p. 26.
    "Buying Lester's Records on Queen Street." <u>PoetryCR</u> (7:2)
        Wint 85-86, p. 26.
    "Jimmie Lunceford's Band." <u>PoetryCR</u> (7:2) Wint 85-86, p.
        26.
    "Miles Davis: Saeta." <u>PoetryCR</u> (6:4) Sum 85, p. 11.
4761. STRESSMAN, S. P.
    "Fire at Night." <u>CrossCur</u> (4:1) 84, p. 48-49.
    "Orlando: October, 1927." <u>CrossCur</u> (4:1) 84, p. 50.
4762. STREZNEWSKI, Marylou Kelly
    "Final Exam: English 10." <u>EngJ</u> (74:7) N 85, p. 97.
4763. STRICKLAND, Stephanie
    "In April." <u>Tendril</u> (19/20) 85, p. 349.
    "Love Affair: Fourth Century." <u>PraS</u> (59:4) Wint 85, p. 65-
        68.
    "Shadow." <u>PraS</u> (59:2) Sum 85, p. 93-94.
    "She Doesn't Care." <u>PraS</u> (59:2) Sum 85, p. 92-93.
4764. STRINGER, A. E.
    "The Work." <u>Nat</u> (241:7) 14 S 85, p. 220.
4765. STROBLAS, Laurie
    "How To Read a Woman Like a Book." <u>Outbr</u> (14/15) Fall 84-
        Spr 85, p. 41.
4766. STRUTHERS, Ann
    "Ambition." <u>GreenfR</u> (13:1/2) Fall-Wint 85, p. 157.
    "Bread Rising" (for Mary's Baby). <u>GreenfR</u> (13:1/2) Fall-
        Wint 85, p. 157.
4767. STRUTHERS, Betsy
    "The Baker's Daughter." <u>Descant</u> 49 (16:2) Sum 85, p. 32-
        33.
    "The Butcher's Boy." <u>Descant</u> 49 (16:2) Sum 85, p. 34.
    "Late Night Mirror" (for Ally). <u>Descant</u> 49 (16:2) Sum 85,
        p. 31.
4768. STRYK, Dan
    "Cat in the Rain." <u>AntigR</u> (61) Spr 85, p. 20.
4769. STRYK, Lucien
    "Rooms." <u>Poetry</u> (146:1) Ap 85, p. 14-17.
4770. STUART, Dabney
    "Getting What She Wants." <u>SouthernR</u> (21:2) Spr 85, p. 435.
    "The Hospital of Lies." <u>PoetryNW</u> (26:4) Wint 85-86, p. 5-
        8.
    "Listening." <u>Poetry</u> (146:2) My 85, p. 97.
    "One Woman, Seen Twice." <u>SouthernR</u> (21:2) Spr 85, p. 436.
    "Taking the Wheel." <u>SouthernR</u> (21:2) Spr 85, p. 432-435.
    "This Is No Dream, This Is My Life." <u>MemphisSR</u> (5:2) Spr
        85, p. 46-47.
    "Turning Forty in a New Town." <u>VirQ</u> (61:2) Spr 85, p. 255-
        256.

"What He Did with the New Egg." VirQ (61:2) Spr 85, p.
        254-255.
4771. STUART, Katherine
        "Naglfar." NegC (5:4) Fall 85, p. 56.
4772. STUART, Lavina Claire
        "Green Card" (To Dariusz). Vis (17) 85, p. 15.
4773. STUCKERT, Steven Lawson
        "Strolling for the Truth." Abraxas (33) 85, p. 31.
4774. STUDEBAKER, William
        "Hunting the Dead: A Shoshone Tradition." OhioR (34) 85,
        p. 44.
4775. STURUA, Lia
        "Women 1941" (tr. by Peter Tempest). Nimrod (28:2) Spr-
        Sum 85, p. 41.
4776. STURUA, Liana
        "I Knew at Once" (tr. by Valentina Jacque). Nimrod (28:2)
        Spr-Sum 85, p. 40.
4777. STYERS, Steven W.
        "Returning." WestB (17) 85, p. 107.
4778. SU, Adrienne
        "Of the Elements" (DeKalb County High Schools, Literary
        award winners: third place, poetry). DeKalbLAJ
        (18:3/4) 85, p. 46.
4779. SU, Shih
        "Ting Feng P'o: Ignore it!" (tr. by Julie Landau). DenQ
        (20:1) Sum 85, p. 13.
        "Ting Feng P'o: Sing of the red flowering plum" (tr. by
        Julie Landau). DenQ (20:1) Sum 85, p. 14.
SU-JANG, Kim
        See KIM, Su-Jang
4780. SUBLETT, Dyan
        "The Women Who Teach Languages." Poetry (145:6) Mr 85, p.
        328.
4781. SUBRAMAN, Belinda
        "Frustrared People [sic]." Bogg (53) 85, p. 39.
        "Quiz Time." Bogg (54) 85, p. 39.
        "We Say." Open24 (4) 85, p. 14.
4782. SUDERMAN, Elmer
        "Job and the Donkey." ChrC (102:4) 30 Ja 85, p. 99.
        "Saturday Night in the Depression." KanQ (17:4) Fall 85,
        p. 40.
4783. SUEN, Sam
        "After Rain, I Stay at a Pond-Pagoda of Liu, Minister of
        War" (tr. of Chia Tao). NewL (51:4) Sum 85, p. 144.
        "Lamenting the Monk, P'o-yen" (tr. of Chia Tao). NewL
        (51:4) Sum 85, p. 144.
        "Thoughts on Hearing the Cicada" (tr. of Chia Tao). NewL
        (51:4) Sum 85, p. 144.
4784. SUK, Julie
        "Growing into Hard Times." MissR (40/41) Wint 85, p. 134.
4785. SUKNASKI, Andrew
        "Divining for West" (Excerpt). PoetryCR (6:4) Sum 85, p.
        37.
        "Life Fragment in Progress" (From Part II of Celestial
        Madness). Waves (14:1/2) Fall 85, p. 64-65.
4786. SULLIVAN
        "The Eagles." KanQ (17:1/2) Wint-Spr 85, p. 148-149.
4787. SULLIVAN, Chuck
        "A Dream Come True Song: For Sr. Martin Anthony SSJ."
        SouthernPR (26, i.e. 25:2) Fall 85, p. 60-61.
4788. SULLIVAN, Francis
        "Enigma #6." LittleM (14:4) 85, p. 54-55.
        "Enigma #8." LittleM (14:4) 85, p. 56.
4789. SULLIVAN, Gerald
        "The Far End of the Track." Comm (112:4) 22 F 85, p. 115.

4790. SULLIVAN, Janet
        "Second Birth." NegC (5:3) Sum 85, p. 35.
4791. SULLIVAN, Olive L.
        "Avebury." LittleBR (5:1) Fall-Wint 84-85, p. 21.
        "Grandmother's Ghosts." LittleBR (5:1) Fall-Wint 84-85,
            p. 21.
4792. SULLIVAN, Patricia
        "April." CimR (72) Jl 85, p. 60-61.
4793. SULLIVAN, Rosemary
        "Aristophanes' Hermaphrodite." MalR (72) S 85, p. 62-63.
        "Double Exposure." MalR (72) S 85, p. 56.
        "Euclid Street." MalR (72) S 85, p. 60-61.
        "The Fugitive Heart." MalR (72) S 85, p. 53.
        "The Green Hat." MalR (72) S 85, p. 57.
        "Sisters." MalR (72) S 85, p. 58-59.
        "Story of a House." MalR (72) S 85, p. 54.
        "Tree Man" (for Juan). MalR (72) S 85, p. 55.
4794. SUMMERHAYES, Don
        "Green Butterflies Ascending." MalR (71) Je 85, p. 56.
        "The Onion Pickers." MalR (71) Je 85, p. 54-55.
4795. SUMMERS, Hollis
        "Epithalamion." SewanR (93:1) Wint 85, p. 69.
        "A Special Hunger." CrossCur (4:2) 84, p. 89.
        "Wraith." SewanR (93:1) Wint 85, p. 70-71.
4796. SUMNER, Melody
        "A Dog at Evening" (Excerpts from Mein Kampf and the
            Bible). Rampike (4:2/3) 85-86, p. 69.
4797. SUMRALL, Amber Coverdale
        "Keams Canyon, Black Mesa." GreenfR (13:1/2) Fall-Wint
            85, p. 2-3.
SUNDERLAND-SMITH, James
        See SUTHERLAND-SMITH, James
4798. SUNG, Fang-Hu
        "To the Tune of Half & Half" (in Chinese and English, tr.
            by G. G. Gach and C. H. Kwock). Zyzzyva (1:1) Spr 85,
            p. 41.
SUNITI, Namjoshi
        See NAMJOSHI, Suniti
4799. SUPERVIELLE, Jules
        "The Sleeping Lake" (tr. by Philip Cranston). GrahamHR
            (9) Fall 85, p. 88.
        "Sleepless" (tr. by Philip Cranston). GrahamHR (9) Fall
            85, p. 90-91.
        "This Pure Child" (tr. by Philip Cranston). GrahamHR (9)
            Fall 85, p. 87.
        "Whisper in Agony" (tr. by Philip Cranston). GrahamHR (9)
            Fall 85, p. 89.
4800. SUPRANER, Robyn
        "The Nannies." Tendril (19/20) 85, p. 350-351.
        "Someone Else's Window" (for Kathleen). Confr (30/31) N
            85, p. 139.
4801. SUREYA, Cemal
        "High Noon" (tr. by Talat Sait Halman). GreenfR (13:1/2)
            Fall-Wint 85, p. 96.
SURIA, Violeta López
        See LOPEZ SURIA, Violeta
4802. SUSSMAN, Marjorie
        "During a Brief Visit Home" (for my sister). SenR (15:1)
            85, p. 73.
4803. SUTHERLAND, E. L.
        "In Time." CrabCR (3:1) Fall-Wint 85, p. 5.
4804. SUTHERLAND, Judith
        "Easter." ChrC (102:11) 3 Ap 85, p. 324.
        "A Recovery." ChrC (102:5) 6-13 F 85, p. 127.
4805. SUTHERLAND, Kenneth
        "Great Shot." Bogg (53) 85, p. 38.

"A Poet's Vacation in Postcards." <u>Bogg</u> (54) 85, p. 33-36.
4806. SUTHERLAND, W. Mark
        "I Talk Like a Spray Gun." <u>Rampike</u> (4:2/3) 85-86, p. 75.
4807. SUTHERLAND-SMITH, James
        "Emergency Section." <u>Chelsea</u> (44) 85, p. 67.
        "Ferns." <u>KanQ</u> (17:1/2) Wint-Spr 85, p. 146.
        "His and Hers." <u>Chelsea</u> (44) 85, p. 109-110.
        "In Libya." <u>KanQ</u> (17:4) Fall 85, p. 41.
        "In the Harbor at Lepcis Magna." <u>KanQ</u> (17:4) Fall 85, p.
            42.
        "Incident in Guatemala." <u>PoetL</u> (79:4) Wint 85, p. 210.
        "Ladies of the Bundesrepublik." <u>PoetL</u> (79:4) Wint 85, p.
            208-209.
        "Preparations for a Mural." <u>WestB</u> (16) 85, p. 41.
        "A Violin Playing in Cairo." <u>Outbr</u> (14/15) Fall 84-Spr
            85, p. 61-62.
4808. SUTSKEVER, Abraham
        "Poems from a 1984 Diary" (Selections: 3-6, tr. by Ruth
            Whitman). <u>Ploughs</u> (11:4) 85, p. 167-170.
4809. SUVIN, D. R.
        "If." <u>Amelia</u> (2:2) O 85, p. 18.
4810. SVOBODA, Terese
        "As Told to Me." <u>PraS</u> (59:1) Spr 85, p. 62.
        "Carwash Kiss." <u>Ploughs</u> (11:1) 85, p. 204.
        "Drive-In." <u>PoetryR</u> (2:2) Ap 85, p. 77.
        "Putenga, Polynesian for 'the Sound of Thighs Slapping
            Together in Sex.'" <u>PraS</u> (59:1) Spr 85, p. 60-61.
        "Transformer." <u>Ploughs</u> (11:1) 85, p. 205-206.
4811. SWAIM, Alice Mackenzie
        "Peace or Peanut Butter" (A Sestina for the Sullen
            Housewife). <u>Amelia</u> (2:1) Ap 85, p. 56-57.
4812. SWANBERG, Christine
        "A False Front in the Midwest." <u>SpoonRQ</u> (10:4) Fall 85,
            p. 34.
        "Hospital Visit." <u>SpoonRQ</u> (10:4) Fall 85, p. 33.
4813. SWANDER, Mary
        "Driving the Body Back" (for Cousin Eileen. Selection: 1.
            "Jim"). <u>Crazy</u> (29) Fall 85, p. 29-33.
        "Driving the Body Back" (Selections: "Ed," "Nell,"
            "Grandma"). <u>PoetC</u> (16:3) Spr 85, p. 16-40.
        "Nailing Down the Vegetable Cave Door." <u>OhioR</u> (34) 85, p.
            88-89.
        "Phil." <u>OP</u> (38/39) Spr 85, p. 31-36.
        "Two Skulls." <u>Nat</u> (241:3) 3-10 Ag 85, p. 90.
4814. SWANGER, David
        "Dispensable." <u>PoetryNW</u> (26:2) Sum 85, p. 4.
        "Ending It." <u>PoetryNW</u> (26:2) Sum 85, p. 5.
        "Grandma." <u>NegC</u> (5:4) Fall 85, p. 79.
        "The Limitations of Light." <u>PoetryNW</u> (26:2) Sum 85, p. 3.
        "Practice, Father and Son." <u>NegC</u> (5:1) Wint 85, p. 127.
        "Scar." <u>GeoR</u> (39:1) Spr 85, p. 111-112.
4815. SWANN, Brian
        "The Catherine-Wheels" (tr. of Rocco Scotellaro, w. Ruth
            Feldman). <u>Ploughs</u> (11:4) 85, p. 58.
        "Coyote." <u>PraS</u> (59:2) Sum 85, p. 83.
        "The Devil's Skin." <u>SewanR</u> (93:3) Sum 85, p. 411.
        "An Existential Song." <u>AmerPoR</u> (14:1) Ja-F 85, p. 17.
        "God's Helmet." <u>SewanR</u> (93:3) Sum 85, p. 410.
        "Greeting" (tr. of Rocco Scotellaro, w. Ruth Feldman).
            <u>Ploughs</u> (11:4) 85, p. 56-57.
        "Late Fruit." <u>PraS</u> (59:2) Sum 85, p. 84.
        "Rain of the Waldensians" (for my grandmother, née
            Elizabeth Tilney, and for my wife). <u>AmerS</u> (54:2) Spr
            85, p. 204-205.
        "Songs of the Bones." <u>SewanR</u> (93:3) Sum 85, p. 410-411.
        "The Truth." <u>AmerPoR</u> (14:1) Ja-F 85, p. 17.

"Underwood Five." <u>SouthernPR</u> (26, i.e. 25:2) Fall 85, p. 7.

4816. SWANN, Roberta M.
"Create a Good Impression above All." <u>Oink</u> (19) 85, p. 106.
"Gifts." <u>Oink</u> (19) 85, p. 106.

4817. SWANNELL, Anne
"War." <u>PoetryCR</u> (6:4) Sum 85, p. 8.
"Wings." <u>PoetryCR</u> (6:4) Sum 85, p. 8.

4818. SWARTS, William
"Boston Common" (for Robert Lowell). <u>SmPd</u> (22:1) Wint 85, p. 9.
"Go-Go." <u>SmPd</u> (22:1) Wint 85, p. 10.
"Jumbo Deus ex Machina." <u>SmPd</u> (22:1) Wint 85, p. 12.
"Stapling Machine." <u>SmPd</u> (22:1) Wint 85, p. 11.

4819. SWEDE, George
"Early morning." <u>Quarry</u> (34:1) Wint 85, p. 21.
"Saw Loon Con Verse Ay Shun." <u>Rampike</u> (4:2/3) 85-86, p. 106.

4820. SWEENEY, Anne
"Family Secrets." <u>MissouriR</u> (8:2) 85, p. 21.

4821. SWEENEY, Kevin
"Cunt Is Just Another Foreign Country." <u>WormR</u> (25:4, issue 100) 85, p. 153-154.
"Mexico." <u>WormR</u> (25:4, issue 100) 85, p. 152-153.
"Proposition 2-1/2" (or 13, depending upon your state). <u>SanFPJ</u> (7:2) 85, p. 49.
"Relationships." <u>WormR</u> (25:4, issue 100) 85, p. 151-152.

4822. SWEET, Nanora
"The Northern Provinces." <u>WebR</u> (10:2) Fall 85, p. 82-83.
"The Rungs." <u>RiverS</u> (17) 85, p. 52-53.

4823. SWENSEN, Cole
"Fade to Light." <u>Zyzzyva</u> (1:2) Sum 85, p. 31.
"The Immigrant Carries Her Painting." <u>AmerPoR</u> (14:1) Ja-F 85, p. 46.
"Stop." <u>AmerPoR</u> (14:1) Ja-F 85, p. 46.

4824. SWENSON, Karen
"Gardens." <u>DenQ</u> (19:4) Spr 85, p. 73-74.
"Henry Moore's Statue at Lincoln Center." <u>SouthernPR</u> (26, i.e. 25:2) Fall 85, p. 24.
"The Highway Death Toll." <u>DenQ</u> (19:4) Spr 85, p. 75.

4825. SWENSON, Nancy E.
"Material at Hand." <u>NegC</u> (5:1) Wint 85, p. 121-122.

4826. SWICK, David
"Winter." <u>AntigR</u> (62/63) Sum-Aut 85, p. 176.

4827. SWICKARD, David
"Johannes Brahms Reads the Brothers Grimm." <u>CutB</u> (24) Spr-Sum 85, p. 68-69.
"Opus Posthumous: Sonatensatz." <u>Confr</u> (30/31) N 85, p. 140.
"Raining Frogs." <u>Confr</u> (30/31) N 85, p. 288.

4828. SWIFT, Joan
"His Sister." <u>AmerPoR</u> (14:2) Mr-Ap 85, p. 15.

4829. SWIR, Anna
"Myself and My Person." <u>Thrpny</u> (6:3, issue 23) Fall 85, p. 5.
"What Is a Pineal Gland." <u>Thrpny</u> (6:3, issue 23) Fall 85, p. 5.

4830. SWISS, Thomas
"Fragments from a Childhood" (1954-57, 1983). <u>Crazy</u> (28) Spr 85, p. 12-13.
"In the Late Spring, Cutting Tulips" (for Mark). <u>Crazy</u> (28) Spr 85, p. 14-15.
"Measure: For Jacob." <u>Crazy</u> (28) Spr 85, p. 10-11.
"Prologue." <u>NewEngR</u> (8:2) Wint 85, p. 141.

4831. SWIST, Wally
        "Among the litter" (haiku). <u>Northeast</u> (Series 4:2) Fall
            85, p. 18.
        "Father's day off" (haiku). <u>Northeast</u> (Series 4:2) Fall
            85, p. 18.
        "That patch of snow" (haiku). <u>Northeast</u> (Series 4:2) Fall
            85, p. 18.
        "Young lovers" (haiku). <u>Northeast</u> (Series 4:2) Fall 85,
            p. 18.
4832. SYLVESTER, Janet
        "Avocados." <u>SenR</u> (15:2) 85, p. 109-111.
        "Mrs. Gardner's Picture." <u>PraS</u> (59:1) Spr 85, p. 34.
        "What Happened to Janet." <u>SenR</u> (15:2) 85, p. 106-108.
4833. SZE, Arthur
        "Crush an Apple." <u>Tendril</u> (19/20) 85, p. 352.
4834. SZUMIGALSKI, Anne
        "Cicatrice." <u>Waves</u> (14:1/2) Fall 85, p. 60.
        "The Varying Hare." <u>Waves</u> (14:1/2) Fall 85, p. 59-60.
4835. SZUMOWSKI, Margaret (<u>See also</u> SZUMOWSKI, Margaret C.)
        "We Have No Ambassador Here" (1984 AWP Award-Winning Poem).
            <u>Tendril</u> (19/20) 85, p. 35-36.
4836. SZUMOWSKI, Margaret C. (<u>See also</u> SZUMOWSKI, Margaret)
        "The Head and Hoof Barber Shop: 'We Sell Shoes, Too'."
            <u>MassR</u> (26:1) Spr 85, p. 26.
4837. SZYMBORSKA, Wislawa
        "Resumé" (In Polish and English, tr. by Leonard Kress).
            <u>CrossCur</u> (4:2) 84, p. 162-165.
4838. TADIC, Novica
        "The Cabin" (tr. by Nina Zivancevič). <u>AmerPoR</u> (14:3) My-
            Je 85, p. 30.
        "Campaign" (tr. by Nina Zivancevič). <u>AmerPoR</u> (14:3) My-
            Je 85, p. 30.
        "Clock" (tr. by Nina Zivancevič). <u>AmerPoR</u> (14:3) My-Je
            85, p. 30.
        "Raven Snow" (tr. by Nina Zivancevič). <u>AmerPoR</u> (14:3)
            My-Je 85, p. 30.
4839. TAFDRUP, Pia
        "In the Night Which Is Black" (tr. by Jorgen Christian
            Hansen). <u>Verse</u> (3) 85, p. 43.
4840. TAGGART, John
        "For Jerry Lee Lewis." <u>Sulfur</u> (13) 85, p. 135.
        "The Rothko Chapel Poem." <u>Temblor</u> (2) 85, p. 16-50.
        "Strip or Ribbon." <u>Temblor</u> (1) 85, p. 60-61.
4841. TAGLIABUE, Grace
        "So How Can You, Reader, Be Forgotten?" <u>NewL</u> (51:4) Sum
            85, p. 140.
4842. TAGLIABUE, John
        "China Travel Journal" (Selections). <u>GreenfR</u> (13:1/2)
            Fall-Wint 85, p. 27-28.
        "China Travel Journal" (Selections: 1-8). <u>NewL</u> (51:3) Spr
            85, p. 92-95.
4843. TAGORE, Rabindranath
        "Three Prayers" (Adapted from the author's Bengali/English
            by David Ray). <u>NewL</u> (51:4) Sum 85, p. 130-131.
4844. TAKACS, Nancy
        "March 6" (for my father). <u>MissouriR</u> (8:2) 85, p. 121.
4845. TAKAHASHI
        "Darkness falls to darkness, valley to valley" (tr. by Hiro
            Sato). <u>NewL</u> (51:4) Sum 85, p. 147.
        "Forest, trees" (tr. by Hiro Sato). <u>NewL</u> (51:4) Sum 85,
            p. 147.
        "Loves become torn apart" (tr. by Hiro Sato). <u>NewL</u> (51:4)
            Sum 85, p. 148.
4846. TAKSA, Mark
        "Jogging for Success." <u>WindO</u> (46) Fall 85, p. 18.
        "Knight Dreaming." <u>Wind</u> (15:53) 85, p. 45.

"Love among the Joggers." <u>WindO</u> (46) Fall 85, p. 19.
4847. TALL, Deborah
    "Prayer." <u>GeoR</u> (39:3) Fall 85, p. 571.
4848. TAM, Reuben
    "Inter-Island Flight." <u>HawaiiR</u> (18) Fall 85, p. 105.
4849. TAMBUZI
    "Sestina: A Stupid Poem." <u>NewRena</u> (19) Fall 85, p. 97-98.
4850. TAMER, Ulkü
    "The Dagger" (tr. by Talat Sait Halman). <u>GreenfR</u> (13:1/2)
        Fall-Wint 85, p. 97.
    "History of the Vanquished" (tr. by Talat Sait Halman).
        <u>GreenfR</u> (13:1/2) Fall-Wint 85, p. 98.
    "The Sparrow" (tr. by Talat Sait Halman). <u>GreenfR</u>
        (13:1/2) Fall-Wint 85, p. 99-102.
TAMIKI, Hara
    <u>See</u> HARA, Tamiki
4851. TAMMARO, Thom
    "Faces at an Intersection." <u>SoDakR</u> (23:2) Sum 85, p. 59.
    "Leaving Friends Behind." <u>CrossCur</u> (4:3) 84, p. 105.
    "Unfinished Business" ("Four dead in Ohio" --Crosby,
        Stills, Nash, Young). <u>SpoonRQ</u> (10:4) Fall 85, p. 8.
    "Violets on Lon Halverson's Grave." <u>SoDakR</u> (23:2) Sum 85,
        p. 57-58.
    "Walking the Trestle." <u>SpoonRQ</u> (10:4) Fall 85, p. 9.
    "Watching Snow Fall and Thinking of Friends." <u>SoDakR</u>
        (23:2) Sum 85, p. 60-61.
4852. TAMMINGA, Douwe A.
    "Stanzas for My Son" (tr. by Rod Jellema). <u>PoetL</u> (79:4)
        Wint 85, p. 230.
    "Two Miniatures" (tr. by Rod Jellema). <u>PoetL</u> (79:4) Wint
        85, p. 231.
4853. TAMMINGA, Frederick W.
    "A Sonnet a la Honka" (For my daughter Theresa Lois).
        <u>CrabCR</u> (2:2) Wint 85, p. 22.
4854. TANA, Patti
    "Sewing the Bullet Holes." <u>SanFPJ</u> (7:3) 84 [i.e. 85], p.
        89-90.
4855. TANDORI, Deszö
    "The Christmas of Long Walks" (tr. by Bruce Berlind).
        <u>Ploughs</u> (11:4) 85, p. 216-217.
4856. TANIGUCHI, Chris K.
    "Eating Alone." <u>HawaiiR</u> (17) Spr 85, p. 31.
    "A Winter Nocturne." <u>HawaiiR</u> (17) Spr 85, p. 32.
TAO, Chia
    <u>See</u> CHIA, Tao
4857. TAPSCOTT, Stephen
    "Elegance." <u>GeoR</u> (39:3) Fall 85, p. 524.
    "Letter to an Immigrant" (Excerpts). <u>Pequod</u> (19/20/21)
        85, p. 342-346.
    "Transitive." <u>GeoR</u> (39:3) Fall 85, p. 525.
4858. TARACIDO, Susan L.
    "Antonia's Questions" (tr. of Marjorie Agosin). <u>NewL</u>
        (51:4) Sum 85, p. 111.
    "Barren Land" (tr. of Jaime Torres Bodet). <u>PraS</u> (59:2)
        Sum 85, p. 56-57.
    "Gina's Lover" (tr. of Marjorie Agosin). <u>NewL</u> (51:4) Sum
        85, p. 113.
    "Letters" (tr. of Marjorie Agosin). <u>NewL</u> (51:4) Sum 85,
        p. 111.
    "The Married Woman" (tr. of Marjorie Agosin). <u>NewL</u> (51:4)
        Sum 85, p. 112.
    "Medieval House" (tr. of Marjorie Agosin). <u>NewL</u> (51:4)
        Sum 85, p. 113-114.
4859. TARN, Nathaniel
    "The Book of Songs" (Provisionally Entitled . . . "All
        These Shitty Little Places in New Jersey." Selections:

13 poems. For Cleo McNelly). <u>Conjunc</u> (7) 85, p. 210-223.

4860. TARRANT, John
"Flute." <u>ParisR</u> (27:97) Fall 85, p. 168-169.

TASSEL, Katrina van
See Van TASSEL, Katrina

4861. TATE, James
"The Chaste Stranger." <u>Tendril</u> (19/20) 85, p. 353-354.
"Dear Customer." <u>Ploughs</u> (11:1) 85, p. 15-16.
"The Eagle Exterminating Company." <u>TriQ</u> (63) Spr-Sum 85, p. 139.
"Islands of Lunch." <u>Ploughs</u> (11:1) 85, p. 13.
"Jo Jo's Fireworks -- Next Exit." <u>Ploughs</u> (11:1) 85, p. 14.
"The Little Sighs Bite a Sheet." <u>Tendril</u> (19/20) 85, p. 355.
"Made in Holland." <u>Ploughs</u> (11:1) 85, p. 19.
"No Rest for the Gambler." <u>Tendril</u> (19/20) 85, p. 356.
"The Sadness of My Neighbors." <u>Tendril</u> (19/20) 85, p. 357.
"Short March, Teeny Wall." <u>Tendril</u> (19/20) 85, p. 359-360.
"Stella Maris." <u>Ploughs</u> (11:1) 85, p. 17-18.
"Tuesday's Child Is: Full of Grace." <u>Ploughs</u> (11:1) 85, p. 12.
"We'll Burn That Bridge When We Come to It." <u>Tendril</u> (19/20) 85, p. 358.

4862. TAUFER, Veno
"Don't Tell Me You Have No Soul." <u>Vis</u> (18) 85, p. 21.

4863. TAYLOR, Alexander
"Ask" (tr. of Marianne Larsen). <u>CrossCur</u> (4:2) 84, p. 108.
"Ode to an Old Wine" (tr. of Henrik Nordbrandt, w. the author). <u>Ploughs</u> (11:4) 85, p. 242-244.
"The Post Office" (tr. of Henrik Nordbrandt, w. the author). <u>Ploughs</u> (11:4) 85, p. 245.

4864. TAYLOR, Brian
"La Gare Saint-Lazare as Europe Falls." <u>SewanR</u> (93:1) Wint 85, p. 72-73.

4865. TAYLOR, Bruce
"Dire Portent." <u>MalR</u> (72) S 85, p. 106-107.
"Four Perspectives on Elf." <u>MalR</u> (72) S 85, p. 103-105.
"Reminiscence of My Childhood: Viking Winter." <u>MalR</u> (72) S 85, p. 108-109.

4866. TAYLOR, Eleanor Ross
"Enter Daughter." <u>VirQ</u> (61:2) Spr 85, p. 247.
"Sibyl." <u>VirQ</u> (61:2) Spr 85, p. 246.

4867. TAYLOR, Henry
"Wineberries." <u>WestHR</u> (39:1) Spr 85, p. 20-21.

4868. TAYLOR, Kent
"Proofreader." <u>CreamCR</u> (10:1) 85, p. 6.

4869. TAYLOR, Laurie
"Happiness." <u>CapeR</u> (20:2) Fall 85, p. 26.
"Menopause Poem." <u>CapeR</u> (20:2) Fall 85, p. 27.

4870. TAYLOR, Maurice
"Everlasting Peace" (tr. of Wolf Biermann). <u>MalR</u> (71) Je 85, p. 80.

4871. TAYLOR, Peter
"A Difficult Birth." <u>Waves</u> (14:1/2) Fall 85, p. 105.

4872. TAYLOR, Susan
"Snowman." <u>Stand</u> (26:4) Aut 85, p. 56.

4873. TCHARKVIANI, Jansug
"A Beautiful Death" (tr. by Shota Nishnianidze and Manly Johnson). <u>Nimrod</u> (28:2) Spr-Sum 85, p. 161.
"Betania" (tr. by Shota Nishnianidze and Manly Johnson). <u>Nimrod</u> (28:2) Spr-Sum 85, p. 159.
"The Canary" (tr. by Shota Nishnianidze and Manly Johnson). <u>Nimrod</u> (28:2) Spr-Sum 85, p. 158.
"The Jug" (tr. by Shota Nishnianidze and Manly Johnson).

Nimrod (28:2) Spr-Sum 85, p. 160.
4874. TEILLIER, Jorge
"Despedida." BlackWR (12:1) Fall 85, p. 84, 86.
"End of the World" (tr. by Carolyne Wright). GrahamHR (9)
Fall 85, p. 37.
"End of the World" (tr. by Mary Crow). NewL (51:4) Sum
85, p. 108.
"In Order to Talk to the Dead" (tr. by Carolyn Wright).
BlackWR (12:1) Fall 85, p. 79.
"The Last Island" (tr. by Carolyn Wright). BlackWR (12:1)
Fall 85, p. 81.
"The Last Island" (tr. by Carolyne Wright). GrahamHR (9)
Fall 85, p. 36.
"The Last Island" (tr. by Carolyne Wright). Mund (15:1/2)
85, p. 99, 101.
"Narratives" (tr. by Carolyne Wright). GrahamHR (9) Fall
85, p. 33-34.
"Narratives" (tr. by Carolyne Wright). Mund (15:1/2) 85,
p. 97, 99.
"Otoño Secreto." BlackWR (12:1) Fall 85, p. 74, 76.
"Otoño Secreto." Mund (15:1/2) 85, p. 100, 102.
"Para Hablar con los Muertos." BlackWR (12:1) Fall 85, p.
78.
"Platforms" (tr. by Mary Crow). NewL (51:4) Sum 85, p.
107.
"Poema de Invierno." Mund (15:1/2) 85, p. 94.
"Relatos." Mund (15:1/2) 85, p. 96, 98.
"Secret Autumn" (tr. by Carolyn Wright). BlackWR (12:1)
Fall 85, p. 75, 77.
"Secret Autumn" (tr. by Carolyne Wright). GrahamHR (9)
Fall 85, p. 31.
"Secret Autumn" (tr. by Carolyne Wright). Mund (15:1/2)
85, p. 101, 103.
"Señales." BlackWR (12:1) Fall 85, p. 82.
"Signals" (tr. by Carolyn Wright). BlackWR (12:1) Fall
85, p. 83.
"So Long" (tr. by Carolyn Wright). BlackWR (12:1) Fall
85, p. 85, 87.
"Tango Lyric" (tr. by Carolyne Wright). GrahamHR (9) Fall
85, p. 32.
"To a Child in a Tree" (tr. by Carolyne Wright). GrahamHR
(9) Fall 85, p. 35.
"La Ultima Isla." BlackWR (12:1) Fall 85, p. 80.
"La Ultima Isla." Mund (15:1/2) 85, p. 98, 100.
"Winter Poem" (tr. by Carolyne Wright). Mund (15:1/2) 85,
p. 95.
"Wooden Mill" (tr. by Carolyne Wright). GrahamHR (9) Fall
85, p. 30.
4875. TEM, Steve Rasnic
"In the Bean Line." SanFPJ (7:2) 85, p. 90-91.
4876. TEMPEST, Peter
"Women 1941" (tr. of Lia Sturua). Nimrod (28:2) Spr-Sum
85, p. 41.
4877. TERPSTRA, John
"James Joyce and the Equator." Waves (13:4) Spr 85, p.
100.
4878. TERRANOVA, Elaine
"The Cult of the Right Hand." AmerPoR (14:3) My-Je 85, p.
42.
4879. TERRILL, Kathryn
"X." PoetryNW (26:2) Sum 85, p. 21-23.
4880. TERRIS, Virginia R.
"Lunch in the Lower Grades." Confr (30/31) N 85, p. 142.
"To a Son." NewL (51:3) Spr 85, p. 49.
4881. TERRY, Chris
"The Fall in That City." AntigR (62/63) Sum-Aut 85, p. 16-

17.
4882. TETI, Zona
"In Summer in the House." <u>Quarry</u> (34:3) Sum 85, p. 19.
"Milly Hayes, Free from the Shacks." <u>MissR</u> (40/41) Wint
    85, p. 130.
"Needles." <u>Quarry</u> (34:3) Sum 85, p. 19-20.
4883. THALMAN, Mark
"Cabin Fever." <u>CharR</u> (11:2) Fall 85, p. 78-79.
"Mirror in the Forest." <u>CharR</u> (11:2) Fall 85, p. 77.
"Opening Day of Fishing Season: Diamond Lake." <u>Blueline</u>
    (6:2) Wint-Spr 85, p. 33.
4884. THEINER, George
"The Fly" (tr. of Miroslav Holub). <u>TriQ</u> (63) Spr-Sum 85,
    p. 94-95.
4885. THENON, Susana
"Distances" (3 selections: 2 in Spanish & English, 1 in
    English, tr. by Renata Treitel). <u>Nimrod</u> (28:2) Spr-Sum
    85, p. 133-134.
4886. THESEN, Sharon
"Adults." <u>MalR</u> (72) S 85, p. 40.
"Charm." <u>PoetryCR</u> (7:1) Aut 85, p. 47.
"The Drift." <u>MalR</u> (72) S 85, p. 39.
"Every Atom Belonging to Me." <u>PoetryCR</u> (7:1) Aut 85, p.
    47.
"Giving It All You've Got." <u>PoetryCR</u> (7:1) Aut 85, p. 47.
"Ladies Advice." <u>MalR</u> (72) S 85, p. 41.
"The Landlord's Flower Beds." <u>PoetryCR</u> (7:1) Aut 85, p.
    47.
"Making a Break." <u>MalR</u> (72) S 85, p. 37.
"May Day." <u>PoetryCR</u> (7:1) Aut 85, p. 47.
"New Year's." <u>MalR</u> (72) S 85, p. 42.
"Saved." <u>MalR</u> (72) S 85, p. 38.
4887. THIBAUDEAU, Colleen
"Throgmogle Fordful: A Day in the Country." <u>Quarry</u> (34:1)
    Wint 85, p. 19.
4888. THIEL, Marek
"The End of the Earth" (for Rob d'Italian). <u>GWR</u> (6:1)
    85?, p. 30.
4889. THOMAS, Calvin
"Day after Easter." <u>Swallow</u> (4) 85, p. 9.
4890. THOMAS, Charles Philip
"Drought" (tr. of Aguinaldo Fonseca). <u>WebR</u> (10:2) Fall
    85, p. 36.
4891. THOMAS, Debra
"Michael's Direction." <u>HawaiiR</u> (17) Spr 85, p. 45.
"The Turning of the Year." <u>MissouriR</u> (8:2) 85, p. 125-132.
4892. THOMAS, Evelyn
"The Jailer" (Merit Award, 2nd Prize, Non-Professional).
    <u>Kaleid</u> (11) Sum 85, p. 48.
4893. THOMAS, Fran
"The Rout of San Romano." <u>ConcPo</u> (18:1/2) 85, p. 84.
4894. THOMAS, Jim
"Father's Confession." <u>CimR</u> (72) Jl 85, p. 48.
"Hay Crop." <u>EngJ</u> (74:3) Mr 85, p. 93.
"In Exile Triumphant." <u>KanQ</u> (17:1/2) Wint-Spr 85, p. 224.
"More Jays." <u>KanQ</u> (17:1/2) Wint-Spr 85, p. 224.
"Scraping through Dry Grass." <u>CharR</u> (11:1) Spr 85, p. 84.
"Square Yard." <u>CimR</u> (72) Jl 85, p. 62.
"Sun's Mercy." <u>CapeR</u> (20:1) Spr 85, p. 47.
4895. THOMAS, John
"Camp Starvation Aug 5." <u>Temblor</u> (1) 85, p. 121.
"They're Wrong to Call It the Little Death and To Hell with
    the Here and Now." <u>Temblor</u> (1) 85, p. 120.
"Underwater Interlude." <u>Temblor</u> (1) 85, p. 120.
4896. THOMAS, Linda
"Cherry Patricia." <u>GWR</u> (6:1) 85?, p. 8.

"Mister Man" (for K.D.). <u>GWR</u> (6:1) 85?, p. 7.
4897. THOMAS, M. J.
"Recollections." <u>PoetryR</u> (2:2) Ap 85, p. 88-89.
4898. THOMAS, R. S.
"Apostrophe." <u>Stand</u> (26:4) Aut 85, p. 4.
"The Banquet." <u>Stand</u> (26:4) Aut 85, p. 4.
4899. THOMASON, Wanda
"Winter Sundays." <u>Wind</u> (15:54) 85, p. 23.
4900. THOMPSON, Earle
"Ceremony." <u>GreenfR</u> (12:3/4) Wint-Spr 85, p. 53.
"Origin." <u>GreenfR</u> (12:3/4) Wint-Spr 85, p. 52.
4901. THOMPSON, Henrietta Moser
"The Collector." <u>CrossCur</u> (4:4/5:1) 85, p. 15.
4902. THOMPSON, John
"Most Bones Are Bowed a Bit." <u>CrossCur</u> (4:4/5:1) 85, p. 9.
4903. THOMPSON, Jon
"The State of the Art." <u>SoCaR</u> (17:2) Spr 85, p. 92.
4904. THOMPSON, Kathleen
"The Baptism." <u>Bogg</u> (53) 85, p. 21.
4905. THOMPSON, N. S. (<u>See also</u> THOMPSON, Nigel)
"To an Unborn Son" (tr. of Pier Paolo Pasolini). <u>Verse</u>
(1) 84, p. 43.
4906. THOMPSON, Nance E.
"In Family Court Corridor." <u>Sam</u> (42:3, 167th release) 85,
p. 26.
4907. THOMPSON, Nigel (<u>See also</u> THOMPSON, N. S.)
"Blows" (tr. of Mario Luzi). <u>Verse</u> (2) 85, p. 39.
4908. THOMPSON, Perry
"All That He Has Chosen" (1st place scholarship winner).
<u>DeKalbLAJ</u> (18:1/2) 85, p. 61.
"Fishermen Are Coming Home" (1st place scholarship winner).
<u>DeKalbLAJ</u> (18:1/2) 85, p. 62.
"I Go in Rooms" (1st place scholarship winner). <u>DeKalbLAJ</u>
(18:1/2) 85, p. 62.
"Insensitive Poet" (Scholarship winner). <u>DeKalbLAJ</u>
(18:3/4) 85, p. 26.
"Let the Strangers" (1st place scholarship winner).
<u>DeKalbLAJ</u> (18:1/2) 85, p. 63.
"Midwinter Surgery" (Scholarship winner). <u>DeKalbLAJ</u>
(18:3/4) 85, p. 27.
"The Punjah Is Lazy" (Scholarship winner). <u>DeKalbLAJ</u>
(18:3/4) 85, p. 27-28.
4909. THOMPSON, Phil
"The Fence." <u>AntigR</u> (62/63) Sum-Aut 85, p. 190.
"Sea of Slaughter" (for Farley Mowat). <u>PottPort</u> (7) 85-
86, p. 46.
"Thirty/Twenty Vision." <u>AntigR</u> (62/63) Sum-Aut 85, p. 191.
"Thirty/Twenty Vision." <u>PottPort</u> (7) 85-86, p. 42.
"The Trucks." <u>AntigR</u> (62/63) Sum-Aut 85, p. 192.
4910. THOMPSON, Ralph Bonner
"Behind My Back, They Whisper." <u>NegC</u> (5:2) Spr 85, p. 27.
"Now I Dare Look." <u>NegC</u> (5:3) Sum 85, p. 126.
4911. THOMPSON, Robert
"Flower Dust." <u>Oink</u> (19) 85, p. 112.
4912. THOMSON, B. R.
"Poetry: Sometimes it writes itself." <u>Confr</u> (30/31) N 85,
p. 147.
4913. THORNBERRY, Suzanne
"Reflections." <u>NegC</u> (5:3) Sum 85, p. 129.
4914. THORNTON, Russell
"The Dogwood." <u>AntigR</u> (62/63) Sum-Aut 85, p. 189.
"A Hidden Full Moon." <u>CrossC</u> (7:1) 85, p. 13.
"I Never Answered Her nntil Now." <u>Quarry</u> (34:3) Sum 85,
p. 38.
4915. THORPE, Michael
"Here." <u>PottPort</u> (7) 85-86, p. 47.

"How We Wanted to Punch His Eyes Out." <u>PottPort</u> (7) 85-
     86, p. 48.
4916. THRONE, Marilyn
     "Bobwhite Lives." <u>Outbr</u> (14/15) Fall 84-Spr 85, p. 92.
     "The Star That Is Not There." <u>Outbr</u> (14/15) Fall 84-Spr
        85, p. 92.
4917. THURSTON, Harry
     "Kindling." <u>Germ</u> (9:1) Spr-Sum 85, p. 33-34.
4918. TICHY, Susan
     "Event on Grape Creek." <u>SouthernPR</u> (26, i.e. 25:2) Fall
        85, p. 30-32.
     "Liquidation Is a Metaphor." <u>NowestR</u> (23:3) 85, p. 18-21.
4919. TIERNEY, Terry
     "The Museum of Personal History." <u>CentR</u> (29:4) Fall 85,
        p. 441.
     "Never Trust the Weather Reports." <u>BlueBldgs</u> (9) [85?],
        p. 55.
     "The Poisoned Blood." <u>Abraxas</u> (33) 85, p. 49.
     "Two Women Leaving the Church." <u>BlueBldgs</u> (9) [85?], p.
        55.
4920. TIFFANY, Georgia
     "The Greenhouse Bar." <u>NoDaQ</u> (53:3) Sum 85, p. 4-5.
     "Spirit Lake" (for M.B. and Molly). <u>NoDaQ</u> (53:3) Sum 85,
        p. 1-2.
     "Three Poems for an Autumn Birthday" (I. "The Gum Tree,"
        II. "Long Distance," III. "Fall's a Beginning"). <u>NoDaQ</u>
        (53:3) Sum 85, p. 6-9.
     "Wrong Time." <u>NoDaQ</u> (53:3) Sum 85, p. 3-4.
4921. TIHANYI, EVA
     "Analogue." <u>Waves</u> (13:4) Spr 85, p. 79.
     "Faith." <u>Waves</u> (13:4) Spr 85, p. 78.
4922. TILLINGHAST, David
     "Degrees of Freedom." <u>SoCaR</u> (18:1) Fall 85, p. 114.
     "The Science of Hitting (Ted Williams)" (For my youngest
        son). <u>TexasR</u> (6:1/2) Spr-Sum 85, p. 70-71.
4923. TILLINGHAST, Richard
     "On the Road to San Romano" (tr. of André Breton).
        <u>Ploughs</u> (11:4) 85, p. 123-124.
     "Savannah, Sleepless." <u>Crazy</u> (27) Fall 84, p. 12-13.
4924. TIMEON OF CORINTH
     "On the Tomb of Kalamachius, the Jogger" (tr. by Elliot
        Richman). <u>WindO</u> (46) Fall 85, p. 3.
4925. TIMMINS, Michael
     "Spiral Fractures." <u>AntigR</u> (62/63) Sum-Aut 85, p. 18.
     "The Surveyor." <u>AntigR</u> (62/63) Sum-Aut 85, p. 19.
     "Wednesday at the Reference Library." <u>AntigR</u> (62/63) Sum-
        Aut 85, p. 18.
TING, Shu
     <u>See</u> SHU, Ting
TING-CHEN, Zhang
     <u>See</u> ZHANG, Ting-chen
TIRADO, Adrián Santos
     <u>See</u> SANTOS TIRADO, Adrián
4926. TISDALE, Charles
     "Because they are not dead, trees." <u>Swallow</u> (4) 85, p. 2.
     "Gregor Mendel: A Meditation on the Variety of Peas."
        <u>MichQR</u> (24:2) Spr 85, p. 267-268.
     "In This Backyard." <u>KanQ</u> (17:1/2) Wint-Spr 85, p. 144.
4927. TISERA, Mary
     "Earth Bound." <u>BlueBldgs</u> (9) [85?], p. 50.
     "The Out of Commission Navigator." <u>Hudson</u> (38:3) Aut 85,
        p. 419-420.
     "A Precarious Peace." <u>WestB</u> (17) 85, p. 76.
     "A Question of Faith." <u>WestB</u> (17) 85, p. 74-75.
     "School in the Bird's Eye" (Second Award Poem, 1984/1985).
        <u>KanQ</u> (17:1/2) Wint-Spr 85, p. 9-10.

"The Star." <u>LaurelR</u> (19:1) Wint 85, p. 35.
"Three Voices in a Diner." <u>Hudson</u> (38:3) Aut 85, p. 420-
    422.
"Waiting for the Bread to Rise." <u>WestB</u> (17) 85, p. 72-73.
4928. TOBIN, Juanita
"The Banjo Player." <u>StoneC</u> (12:2/3) Spr-Sum 85, p. 69.
4929. TODD, A. L.
"Granville Mall." <u>WestCR</u> (19:4) Ap 85, p. 41.
4930. TOGE, Sankichi
"Give the People Back" (tr. by Steven Forth). <u>AmerPoR</u>
    (14:4) Jl-Ag 85, p. 9.
4931. TOHEE, Mahtoh-Ge
"O." <u>NoDaQ</u> (53:2) Spr 85, p. 214.
4932. TOLEDO, Tommy
"Pepsi or Coke" (for Clara Melman). <u>Outbr</u> (14/15) Fall 84-
    Spr 85, p. 68.
4933. TOME, Jesús
"Las Voces del Deseo." <u>Mairena</u> (7:19) 85, p. 95.
4934. TOMLINSON, Charles
"Interpretations." <u>Pequod</u> (19/20/21) 85, p. 351.
"Macchu Picchu." <u>PartR</u> (52:2) 85, p. 56.
"This." <u>Pequod</u> (19/20/21) 85, p. 352.
"Traveller." <u>Pequod</u> (19/20/21) 85, p. 347.
4935. TOMPKINS, R. D. Wayne
"Walking Down Country Roads." <u>PoetryCR</u> (6:3) Spr 85, p.
    35.
4936. TOMPKINS, Wayne
"Man and Boy at Howland Ridge." <u>PottPort</u> (7) 85-86, p. 34.
4937. TONEY, Mitchell
"Explanation." <u>SenR</u> (15:1) 85, p. 81.
"Legerdemain." <u>SenR</u> (15:1) 85, p. 78.
"The Matter with Stairs." <u>SenR</u> (15:1) 85, p. 77.
"Subtraction." <u>SenR</u> (15:1) 85, p. 79.
"Tailor's Song." <u>SenR</u> (15:1) 85, p. 80.
4938. TONGUE, Margaret
"Black Cats, etc." (for Lori). <u>HiramPoR</u> (38) Spr-Sum 85,
    p. 31.
"Help Wanted." <u>HiramPoR</u> (38) Spr-Sum 85, p. 32.
4939. TORNES, Beth
"Goya." <u>MissouriR</u> (8:2) 85, p. 60-61.
"In <u>The</u> <u>Testament</u> <u>of</u> <u>Orpheus</u>." <u>AntR</u> (43:4) Fall 85, p.
    466-467.
4940. TORNLUND, Niklas
"The Break of Light" (tr. by John Tritica). <u>RiverS</u> (17)
    85, p. 48-49.
"Portrait of a Portrait" (Rembrandt 1655, tr. by John
    Tritica). <u>RiverS</u> (17) 85, p. 47.
"The Riddle That Never" (In Swedish and English, tr. by
    John Tritica). <u>CrossCur</u> (4:2) 84, p. 148-149.
4941. TORRENTE, Gerardo
"Tiscapa Hill" (tr. by Kent Johnson). <u>MinnR</u> (N.S. 25)
    Fall 85, p. 48.
4942. TORRES, Margaret D.
"Dido." <u>KanQ</u> (17:1/2) Wint-Spr 85, p. 289-290.
"Eurydice." <u>KanQ</u> (17:1/2) Wint-Spr 85, p. 290.
4943. TORRES BODET, Jaime
"Barren Land" (tr. by Susan L. Taracido). <u>PraS</u> (59:2) Sum
    85, p. 56-57.
4944. TORRESON, Rodney
"The Semidivine Beings." <u>PassN</u> (6:1) Fall-Wint 85, p. 22.
TORRIENTE, Gastón Fernández
    <u>See</u> FERNANDEZ-TORRIENTE, Gastón
4945. TOSTESON, Heather
"Attendants." <u>MidAR</u> (5:1) 85, p. 122.
"The Fountain." <u>SmPd</u> (22:1) Wint 85, p. 15.
"Gallery." <u>SmPd</u> (22:1) Wint 85, p. 13.

"Maple Seeds." SmPd (22:1) Wint 85, p. 14.
4946. TOTI, Gianni
"Velamen" (tr. by Anna Garelli). LitR (28:2) Wint 85, p. 309.
4947. TOURE, Askia M.
"Scarifications 1" (Afro/Abstract: Blue). BlackALF (19:3) Fall 85, p. 99.
4948. TOWELL, Larry
"A Death in the Family." Dandel (12:2) 85, p. 16-17.
"The First Year of Exile." Dandel (12:2) 85, p. 18-19.
"Highlands." Dandel (12:2) 85, p. 14-15.
"In Memory of Remijio Rivera." Dandel (12:2) 85, p. 10-12.
"Insomnia & Lovers." Dandel (12:2) 85, p. 9.
"Sonsonate." Dandel (12:2) 85, p. 6-8.
"Tree Planting in Nueva Segovia." Dandel (12:2) 85, p. 13.
4949. TOWERS, Peggy
"For Huck and Jim on the Raft." PoetryR (5) S 85, p. 49.
"Icarus." PoetryR (5) S 85, p. 50.
4950. TOWNER, Daniel
"Count Tolstoy's New Gymnasium." AmerPoR (14:4) Jl-Ag 85, p. 40.
"Three Whistles." NoAmR (270:1) Mr 85, p. 31-33.
4951. TOWNSEND, Ann
"The Singer." CharR (11:2) Fall 85, p. 80.
4952. TOWNSEND, Cheryl
"My First Marriage." Amelia (2:1) Ap 85, p. 85.
"Rut." Open24 (4) 85, p. 41.
"Still." PoeticJ (12) 85, p. 29.
4953. TRAINER, Yvonne
"At the Woodmen's Museum" (for Robert Gibbs). Germ (9:2) Fall-Wint 85, p. 28.
"Drought / Prairie / '85." Germ (9:2) Fall-Wint 85, p. 29.
4954. TRAKL, Georg
"Grodek" (Trakl's last poem, tr. by Thomas Frick). Ploughs (11:4) 85, p. 143.
"Melancholia" (tr. by Thomas Frick). Ploughs (11:4) 85, p. 142.
4955. TRAMMELL, Robert
"Cherokee" (Excerpts). Temblor (1) 85, p. 94-103.
4956. TRANAES, Anette
"Women in Black Dresses" (tr. by Jorgen Christian Hansen). Verse (3) 85, p. 42.
4957. TRANSTROMER, Tomas
"Black Postcards" (tr. by Joanna Bankier). Thrpny (6:2, issue 22) Sum 85, p. 6.
"The Boat -- The Village" (tr. by Samuel Charters). Antaeus (55) Aut 85, p. 172.
"For Mats and Laila" (tr. by Samuel Charters). Antaeus (55) Aut 85, p. 173.
"The Forgotten Captain" (tr. by Robin Fulton). Verse (3) 85, p. 37.
"The Forgotten Commander" (tr. by Robert Bly). Ploughs (11:4) 85, p. 240-241.
"The Gallery" (tr. by Samuel Charters). Antaeus (55) Aut 85, p. 176-179.
"Gogol" (tr. by Samuel Charters). Antaeus (55) Aut 85, p. 171.
"Memory Sees Me" (tr. by Samuel Charters). Antaeus (55) Aut 85, p. 174.
"Molokai" (tr. by Samuel Charters). Antaeus (55) Aut 85, p. 175.
"The Nightingale in Badelunda" (tr. by Robin Fulton). Verse (3) 85, p. 38.
"The Station" (tr. by Samuel Charters). Antaeus (55) Aut 85, p. 174.
"The Winter's Glance" (tr. by Samuel Charters). Antaeus

(55) Aut 85, p. 175.
4958. TRANTER, John
        "At the Criterion." <u>PoetryCR</u> (7:2) Wint 85-86, p. 53.
        "High School Confidential." <u>Verse</u> (4) 85, p. 20.
        "A Jackeroo in Kensington." <u>PoetryCR</u> (7:2) Wint 85-86, p.
        53.
        "Reversal Process." <u>PoetryCR</u> (7:1) Aut 85, p. 41.
        "The Un-American Women." <u>PoetryCR</u> (7:1) Aut 85, p. 41.
        "The Water." <u>PoetryCR</u> (7:1) Aut 85, p. 41.
4959. TRASK, JoDiane
        "Bear." <u>PassN</u> (6:1) Fall-Wint 85, p. 11.
4960. TRAVIS, Terry
        "How His Vigilance Became the Night." <u>Nat</u> (240:11) 23 Mr
        85, p. 342.
4961. TREBY, Ivor (<u>See</u> <u>also</u> TREBY, Ivor C.)
        "Small Differences." <u>JamesWR</u> (2:3) Spr-Sum 85, p. 8.
4962. TREBY, Ivor C. (<u>See</u> <u>also</u> TREBY, Ivor)
        "Tight-Rope Artist." <u>CrabCR</u> (2:3) Sum 85, p. 25.
4963. TREGEBOV, Rhea
        "Vienna, November 1983." <u>CarolQ</u> (38:1) Fall 85, p. 28.
4964. TREHARNE, Mark
        "The Collared Dove" (tr. of Philippe Jaccottet). <u>Verse</u>
        (2) 85, p. 24-25.
4965. TREITEL, Margot
        "The Best of Both Worlds" (Ibadan, Nigeria, 1965). <u>WebR</u>
        (10:1) Spr 85, p. 64.
        "Chance Encounters." <u>HolCrit</u> (22:3) Je 85, p. 14-15.
        "Dancing in the Dark." <u>LitR</u> (29:1) Fall 85, p. 43.
        "Engineers." <u>Pig</u> (13) 85, p. 45.
        "False Bravado." <u>ColEng</u> (47:4) Ap 85, p. 375.
        "The Lifeguard at Cacapon Lake." <u>LaurelR</u> (19:2) Sum 85,
        p. 62-63.
        "Self-Consciousness." <u>StoneC</u> (12:2/3) Spr-Sum 85, p. 48.
        "Sleep." <u>StoneC</u> (12:2/3) Spr-Sum 85, p. 48.
4966. TREITEL, Renata
        "Brides of Bohemia." <u>Nimrod</u> (28:2) Spr-Sum 85, p. 132-133.
        "Distances" (3 selections, tr. of Susana Thênon).
        <u>Nimrod</u> (28:2) Spr-Sum 85, p. 133-134.
        "The Valet" (Oil Painting, after Chaim Soutine, 1894-1943).
        <u>Nimrod</u> (28:2) Spr-Sum 85, p. 132.
4967. TREMMEL, Robert
        "From the Coaches' Box: Little Girls at the Ballgame."
        <u>CumbPR</u> (5:1) Fall 85, p. 53-54.
        "Your First Time Driving the Milford Blacktop." <u>CumbPR</u>
        (5:1) Fall 85, p. 51-52.
        "Your First Time Making Iced Mint Delight." <u>Poem</u> (54) N
        85, p. 20-21.
4968. TRETHEWEY, Eric
        "The Man Who Smiles." <u>CrossCur</u> (4:3) 84, p. 55.
        "What Remains." <u>CanLit</u> (105) Sum 85, p. 135.
4969. TRILUSSA
        "Abbitudine." <u>Mund</u> (15:1/2) 85, p. 152.
        "Felicità." <u>Mund</u> (15:1/2) 85, p. 152.
        "Force of Habit" (tr. by John DuVal). <u>Mund</u> (15:1/2) 85,
        p. 153.
        "Happiness" (tr. by John DuVal). <u>Mund</u> (15:1/2) 85, p. 153.
4970. TRIMPER, Jack
        "Sitting in the Mirage." <u>Open24</u> (4) 85, p. 24.
4971. TRINIDAD, David
        "Dreams." <u>Oink</u> (19) 85, p. 114-115.
4972. TRIPOULAS, John
        "At the Circus." <u>HiramPoR</u> (39) Fall-Wint 85, p. 21.
4973. TRITICA, John
        "The Break of Light" (tr. of Niklas Törnlund). <u>RiverS</u>
        (17) 85, p. 48-49.
        "Portrait of a Portrait" (Rembrandt 1655, tr. of Niklas

Törnlund). <u>RiverS</u> (17) 85, p. 47.
"The Riddle That Never" (tr. of Niklas Tornlund).
    <u>CrossCur</u> (4:2) 84, p. 149.
"Searching for the Language" (for Jerome Rothenberg).
    <u>CrossCur</u> (4:4/5:1) 85, p. 139.
4974. TRIVELPIECE, Laurel
    "At the Demonstration." <u>IndR</u> (8:2) Spr 85, p. 77.
    "At Weeping Rock." <u>ConnPR</u> (3:1) 84, p. 49.
    "Ink Blots." <u>Poetry</u> (145:4) Ja 85, p. 205.
    "Morning Mists." <u>Poetry</u> (145:4) Ja 85, p. 203-204.
    "Progress." <u>Poetry</u> (145:4) Ja 85, p. 202-203.
    "Unborn" (For Ann, The Believer). <u>Poetry</u> (145:4) Ja 85,
        p. 204-205.
4975. TROENDLE, Yves
    "Anxiety: A Song." <u>PoetryCR</u> (6:4) Sum 85, p. 6.
    "Noon" (from "Mazatlan"). <u>PoetryCR</u> (6:4) Sum 85, p. 6.
    "The Storm." <u>PoetryCR</u> (6:4) Sum 85, p. 6.
4976. TROUBETZKOY, Ulrich
    "The Time We Drove All Night." <u>CrossCur</u> (4:2) 84, p. 51.
4977. TROUPE, Quincy
    "Transformation." <u>PoetryR</u> (2:2) Ap 85, p. 13.
4978. TROWBRIDGE, William
    "G.I. Joe from Kokomo." <u>MissouriR</u> (8:3) 85, p. 118.
    "Saint's Life." <u>GeoR</u> (39:3) Fall 85, p. 617-618.
    "Sunday School Lesson from Capt. Daniel Mayhew, USAAF,
        Ret." <u>MissouriR</u> (8:3) 85, p. 119.
4979. TROWELL, Ian (<u>See also</u> TROWELL, Ian Douglas)
    "A Penchant for Beginnings." <u>AntigR</u> (61) Spr 85, p. 127-
        129.
4980. TROWELL, Ian Douglas (<u>See also</u> TROWELL, Ian)
    "Seeing Neil MacKenzie." <u>PoetryCR</u> (7:2) Wint 85-86, p. 55.
4981. TRUCK, Fred
    "Purge Revolution" (Textual Image). <u>Rampike</u> (4:2/3) 85-
        86, p. 99.
4982. TRUHLAR, Richard
    "Memo from Minoa" (with Mara Zibens). <u>Rampike</u> (4:2/3) 85-
        86, p. 48-49.
4983. TRUNCELLITO, Barbara
    "The Gift." <u>SnapD</u> (9:1) Fall 85, p. 16-17.
TSARSKOYE SELO
    <u>See</u> AKHMATOVA, Anna
4984. TSIMICALIS, Stavros
    "To the Painter Leftèris Rörros" (tr. by Yannis
        Goumas). <u>Waves</u> (13:4) Spr 85, p. 98.
    "Under the Heavybranched Tree of Old Age" (tr. of Christos
        Ziatas). <u>Waves</u> (13:4) Spr 85, p. 99.
TSUNEKO, Yoshikawa
    <u>See</u> YOSHIKAWA, Tsuneko
4985. TSVETAEVA, Marina (Tsvetayeva, Marina)
    "344" (tr. by Linda Barrett). <u>GrahamHR</u> (8) Wint 85, p. 43-
        44.
    "I met the new year alone" (tr. by Joan Aleshire). <u>NewL</u>
        (51:4) Sum 85, p. 42.
4986. TUCKER, Jim
    "Block Island." <u>AntigR</u> (62/63) Sum-Aut 85, p. 161.
    "Blue, All the Way to Canada." <u>LitR</u> (28:4) Sum 85, p. 582.
    "Dead Fathers." <u>Poem</u> (54) N 85, p. 37.
    "The Glass Piano." <u>Wind</u> (15:54) 85, p. 52.
    "Smoke from Cold Fires." <u>Poem</u> (54) N 85, p. 38.
4987. TUCKER, Martin
    "Saturday Morning in East Hampton." <u>Confr</u> (30/31) N 85,
        p. 155.
4988. TUCKER, Memye Curtis
    "Days with William Stafford." <u>NegC</u> (5:4) Fall 85, p. 50-
        51.
    "Ritual." <u>NegC</u> (5:2) Spr 85, p. 97.

4989. TUDOR, Stephen
        "Protest." OP (38/39) Spr 85, p. 208.
4990. TUFTY, Duke
        "Teeter-Totter." PoeticJ (11) 85, p. 13.
4991. TUINSTRA, Nancy
        "Home Improvements." PoetryCR (7:1) Aut 85, p. 49.
4992. TULLOSS, Rodham
        "I Love to Read Lives of the Self-Taught." USl (18/19)
          Wint 85, p. 17.
        "Princeton Junction Station." USl (18/19) Wint 85, p. 17.
        "There Should be More Poetry about the Breakfast Oranges of
          Thomas Jefferson." USl (18/19) Wint 85, p. 17.
4993. TUMBLESON, Ray
        "Donne's Death." Quarry (34:3) Sum 85, p. 29.
4994. TURCO, Lewis
        "On Lines from Emily Dickinson's Letters." OntR (22) Spr-
          Sum 85, p. 98-101.
4995. TURNBULL, Gael
        "A Last Poem." Conjunc (8) 85, p. 223.
4996. TURNBULL, Harry
        "Time to Get Up in Texas." Bogg (53) 85, p. 23.
4997. TURNER, Frederick
        "At the Front of the Jet." DenQ (20:1) Sum 85, p. 22.
        "The Blessing." Poetry (147:2) N 85, p. 71-72.
        "Bone China Broken." Poetry (147:2) N 85, p. 69-71.
        "The Curse." DenQ (20:1) Sum 85, p. 25-26.
        "The Distribution" (For Victor Turner). Poetry (147:2) N
          85, p. 73.
        "Glass." OntR (22) Spr-Sum 85, p. 33.
        "Maine Summer, with Friends." DenQ (20:1) Sum 85, p. 23-
          24.
        "Pheromones." OntR (22) Spr-Sum 85, p. 31-32.
        "Spirit-Marriage." DenQ (20:1) Sum 85, p. 2-021.
4998. TURNER, Lisa Ann
        "Cheek Biter." Nat (240:18) 11 My 85, p. 567.
4999. TWICHELL, Chase
        "400 ASA." BlackWR (12:1) Fall 85, p. 44-45.
        "A Fire in the Mind." Antaeus (55) Aut 85, p. 180-181.
        "Heart As Kamikaze." BlackWR (12:1) Fall 85, p. 46.
        "The Late Comers." Crazy (27) Fall 84, p. 26.
        "Meteor Showers, August, 1968." Tendril (19/20) 85, p.
          369-370.
        "The Moon in the Pines." Tendril (19/20) 85, p. 368.
        "The Odds." Tendril (19/20) 85, p. 361-366.
        "Translations from the Rational." Tendril (19/20) 85, p.
          367.
5000. TYLER, Margaret
        "Small Graces." PassN (6:1) Fall-Wint 85, p. 15.
5001. TYLER, Robert L.
        "Close-Up." Vis (19) 85, p. 38.
        "Overlooking Interstate 95 in New London, Connecticut."
          NegC (5:3) Sum 85, p. 25.
5002. UBA, George
        "The Riddle" (after a poem by Yannis Ritsos). CarolQ
          (37:2) Wint 85, p. 32.
5003. UBERMAN, Leonard
        "Aubade." KanQ (17:1/2) Wint-Spr 85, p. 242.
        "Goldberg." KanQ (17:1/2) Wint-Spr 85, p. 241.
        "Readiness." Thrpny (6:1, issue 21) Spr 85, p. 27.
        "Spleen." KanQ (17:1/2) Wint-Spr 85, p. 240.
5004. UCEDA, Julia
        "España, Eres un Largo Invierno" (tr. by Noel M. Valis).
          PraS (59:4) Wint 85, p. 44-45.
        "Eternal Waves" (tr. by Noel M. Valis). PraS (59:4) Wint
          85, p. 42-43.

5005. UDRY, Susan
    "Making." CarolQ (37:3) Spr 85, p. 52.
5006. UFOLLA, Florence
    "What Have I Become?" Imagine (2:1) Sum 85, p. 78.
5007. ULMER, James
    "Blackberries." BlackWR (11:2) Spr 85, p. 88-89.
    "Brass Bed." Crazy (29) Fall 85, p. 46-47.
    "Distance, Light" (First Prize, Pablo Neruda Prize for
       Poetry). Nimrod (29:1) Fall-Wint 85, p. 7-12.
5008. UNGER, Barbara
    "New Year's Eve." GreenfR (13:1/2) Fall-Wint 85, p. 4-5.
5009. UNGER, Randy
    "The Ghost of Dashiell Hammett." SnapD (8:2) Spr 85, p.
       33.
5010. UNIVERSITY OF IOWA TRANSLATION WORKSHOP
    "Pain Sales I-X" (To Ksenija, tr. of Tomislav Longinović,
       w. the author). Mund (15:1/2) 85, p. 201-202.
5011. UNTERECKER, John
    "Grafton Landscape" (in memory of Dorothy and Granville
       Hicks). Blueline (7:1) Sum-Fall 85, p. 18-21.
    "The Lava." CarolQ (37:2) Wint 85, p. 67-68.
    "The Sail." CarolQ (37:2) Wint 85, p. 69-70.
    "Spanish Landscape: Near LaEscala, But Nearer the
       Mountains." AntR (43:4) Fall 85, p. 458.
5012. UPDIKE, John
    "Another Dog's Death." Harp (270:1618) Mr 85, p. 34.
    "Ode to Crystallization." NewYorker (60:49) 21 Ja 85, p.
       30-31.
    "Ode to Entropy." MichQR (24:2) Spr 85, p. 327-328.
    "Ode to Rot." Atlantic (255:1), Ja 85, p. 83.
    "The Sea" (tr. of Jorge Luis Borges). TriQ (63) Spr-Sum
       85, p. 111.
5013. UPTON, Lee
    "A Bowl of Shells." NewEngR (7:3) Spr 85, p. 335-336.
    "A Daughter." ThRiPo (25/26) 85, p. 59-60.
    "The Debt." ThRiPo (25/26) 85, p. 57.
    "Destruction of Daughters." Ploughs (11:1) 85, p. 207-208.
    "Extract of Angels." MassR (26:1) Spr 85, p. 115-116.
    "Hog Roast." Ploughs (11:1) 85, p. 209-210.
    "The How and Why of Rocks and Minerals." Ploughs (11:1)
       85, p. 211-212.
    "Lost Child." ThRiPo (25/26) 85, p. 58.
    "Miniatures." Poetry (146:3) Je 85, p. 154-155.
    "The Mountain." CentR (29:3) Sum 85, p. 326-327.
    "The Net." VirQ (61:3) Sum 85, p. 429-430.
    "Paperweights." Poetry (146:3) Je 85, p. 153.
    "The Quality of Mercy." PoetryE (18) Fall 85, p. 44-45.
    "The Snowflake Motel." VirQ (61:3) Sum 85, p. 428-429.
    "The Wives." ConnPR (3:1) 84, p. 27.
5014. URDANG, Constance
    "Alternative Lives." OntR (23) Fall-Wint 85-86, p. 42.
    "Benjamin Robert Haydon (1786-1846) and the Two Blue
       Glasses." OntR (23) Fall-Wint 85-86, p. 43.
    "In the Prairie Cemetery." DenQ (19:4) Spr 85, p. 53.
    "Mornings in Mexico." NewL (52:1) Fall 85, p. 60.
    "The Old Ladies of Amsterdam." NewL (52:1) Fall 85, p. 60-
       61.
    "Red's Landlady." DenQ (19:4) Spr 85, p. 52.
    "Returning to the Port of Authority: A Picaresque."
       Tendril (19/20) 85, p. 371-372.
    "Waiting for the Earthquake." DenQ (19:4) Spr 85, p. 54.
5015. URIARTE, Miriam de
    "Chant Number One." BilingR (11:2) My-Ag 84 [c1986], p.
       55.
    "Chant Number Three." BilingR (11:2) My-Ag 84 [c1986], p.
       57.

"Chant Number Two." <u>BilingR</u> (11:2) My-Ag 84 [c1986], p.
    56.
URIOL, Miguel Angel Martin
    <u>See</u> MARTIN URIOL, Miguel Angel
5016. URISTA, Xelina R.
    "Beauty Tips." <u>Imagine</u> (2:1) Sum 85, p. 71.
5017. UROSEVIC, Vlada
    "A Child Talking in Its Sleep" (tr. by Zoran Ancevski and
        James McKinley). <u>NewL</u> (51:4) Sum 85, p. 25.
    "Poem of the Inscriptions" (tr. by Zoran Ancevski and James
        McKinley). <u>NewL</u> (51:4) Sum 85, p. 25.
    "Reader of Dreams" (tr. by Zoran Ancevski and James
        McKinley). <u>NewL</u> (51:4) Sum 85, p. 24.
5018. URQUHART, Jane
    "Charlotte Bronte Waits for a Letter." <u>PoetryCR</u> (6:3) Spr
        85, p. 8.
    "Emily's Dog Keeper." <u>PoetryCR</u> (6:3) Spr 85, p. 8.
    "The Hook." <u>PoetryCR</u> (6:3) Spr 85, p. 8.
    "Mad Wife in the Attic." <u>PoetryCR</u> (6:3) Spr 85, p. 8.
    "Perma Frost." <u>PoetryCR</u> (6:3) Spr 85, p. 8.
5019. UYAROGLU, Ismail
    "Night and Night" (tr. by O. Yalim, W. Fielder and Dionis
        Riggs). <u>NewL</u> (51:4) Sum 85, p. 14.
5020. VACLAVICEK, Susan
    "Pursuit" (for Richard and Kate and for their house).
        <u>BlueBldgs</u> (9) [85?], p. 29.
5021. VAIL, Constance A.
    "On Seeing Hills" (For L.D.). <u>Blueline</u> (7:1) Sum-Fall 85,
        p. 52.
5022. VAISIUS, Andrew
    "For Megan at five." <u>PoetryCR</u> (6:4) Sum 85, p. 6.
    "Poets." <u>PoetryCR</u> (6:4) Sum 85, p. 6.
    "So Radically Different." <u>PoetryCR</u> (6:4) Sum 85, p. 6.
    "We Are an Unusual Love." <u>Waves</u> (13:4) Spr 85, p. 66-67.
VAL, John du
    <u>See</u> DuVAL, John
5023. VALDES, Gina
    "Creative Oppression." <u>Imagine</u> (2:1) Sum 85, p. 62.
    "My Mother Sews Blouses." <u>Imagine</u> (2:1) Sum 85, p. 61.
5024. VALENTI, Dan
    "In My Room It Was Dark." <u>NegC</u> (5:2) Spr 85, p. 165-166.
5025. VALENTIN, Michael
    "La Rousèe du Joly Mois de May" (tr. of Jehan Planç on,
        w. W. D. Snodgrass). <u>NegC</u> (5:1) Wint 85, p. 70, 72, 74.
5026. VALENTINE, Maggie
    "River Poem." <u>PassN</u> (6:2) Spr-Sum 85, p. 10.
5027. VALENZUELA, Luisa
    "Man Like a Pomegranate" (tr. by Margaret Sayers Peden).
        <u>Chelsea</u> (44) 85, p. 94.
    "Origin of the Species" (tr. by Margaret Sayers Peden).
        <u>Chelsea</u> (44) 85, p. 95.
    "The Salt of Life" (tr. by Margaret Sayers Peden).
        <u>Chelsea</u> (44) 85, p. 94.
5028. VALERY, Paul
    "Pomegranates" (tr. by Michael L. Johnson). <u>WebR</u> (10:1)
        Spr 85, p. 36.
5029. VALIS, Noël M.
    "And in the Air." <u>WindO</u> (45) Spr 85, p. 41.
    "Boston." <u>SmPd</u> (22:1) Wint 85, p. 23.
    "España, Eres un Largo Invierno" (tr. of Julia Uceda).
        <u>PraS</u> (59:4) Wint 85, p. 44-45.
    "Eternal Waves" (tr. of Julia Uceda). <u>PraS</u> (59:4) Wint
        85, p. 42-43.
    "Light." <u>RagMag</u> (4:1) Spr 85, p. 20.
    "Something Fine." <u>RagMag</u> (4:1) Spr 85, p. 20.
    "Ticket to Victoria." <u>Wind</u> (15:55) 85, p. 46.

"Tiger Lillies." <u>WindO</u> (45) Spr 85, p. 40.
VALL, Sally de
     <u>See</u> DeVALL, Sally
5030. VALLADARES, Armando
     "Night Unending" (Dedicated to the memory of Francisco
        Morales Menendez, tr. by William Marling). <u>NewOR</u>
        (12:2) Sum 85, p. 102.
     "Question" (for Fernando Arrabal, my friend, tr. by William
        Marling). <u>NewOR</u> (12:2) Sum 85, p. 55.
     "To the Preachers of Hate" (tr. by William Marling).
        <u>NewOR</u> (12:2) Sum 85, p. 36-37.
5031. VALLEJOS BARTLETT, Catherine
     "We moon women bathe ourselves" ("Untitled"). <u>Imagine</u>
        (2:1) Sum 85, p. 53-54.
Van . . .
     <u>See</u> <u>also</u> names beginning with "Van" without the following
        space, filed below in their alphabetic positions, e.g.,
        VANDERBILT.
5032. Van BEEK, Edith
     "Fisherman." <u>CapilR</u> (34) 85, p. 7.
5033. Van BRUNT, H. L.
     "Hitchhikers, 1936, Walker Evans." <u>Wind</u> (15:53) 85, p. 48-
        49.
     "The Ten O'Clock Wrestling Show." <u>Wind</u> (15:53) 85, p. 48.
5034. Van BRUNT, Lloyd
     "Wyoming Suite" (Selection: 9. "Last Exit"). <u>SouthernPR</u>
        (25:1) Spr 85, p. 43.
5035. Van BUREN, David
     "Footprints." <u>Wind</u> (15:54) 85, p. 53.
     "The Sky." <u>Wind</u> (15:54) 85, p. 53.
Van der Geest, Berber
     <u>See</u> GEEST, Berber van der
5036. Van HOUTEN, Lois
     "Wanderers." <u>GreenfR</u> (13:1/2) Fall-Wint 85, p. 5-7.
5037. Van MATRE, C. (Connie)
     "Reality." <u>SanFPJ</u> (7:4) 85, p. 72.
     "War of Minds." <u>SanFPJ</u> (7:4) 85, p. 69.
Van RADKE, Don
     <u>See</u> RADKE, Don Van
5038. Van SPANCKEREN, Kathryn
     "Dutch Rubber Plantations" (N. Sumatra). <u>RiverS</u> (18) 85,
        p. 81.
     "Pasar Ikan Canal" (Jakarta). <u>RiverS</u> (18) 85, p. 82-83.
5039. Van TASSEL, Katrina
     "This Day I Walk Here." <u>StoneC</u> (13:1/2) Fall-Wint 85-86,
        p. 31.
Van VLIET, Eddy
     <u>See</u> VLIET, Eddy van
5040. Van WALLEGHEN, Michael
     "What's Wrong with UFO's?" <u>Ascent</u> (10:3) 85, p. 35-43.
5041. Van WERT, William
     "The Disarray on the Sheltered Side." <u>PoetryE</u> (18) Fall
        85, p. 49.
5042. Van WINCKEL, Nance
     "First Things, Last Things." <u>PoetryNW</u> (26:3) Aut 85, p.
        33-35.
     "From the Distant Tomb of the Weatherman." <u>Ascent</u> (11:1)
        85, p. 76.
     "Leftover Passion." <u>CreamCR</u> (10:2) [85?], p. 57.
     "Now, Boys and Girls." <u>PoetryNW</u> (26:3) Aut 85, p. 35-36.
     "The Parts to the Whole" (For Samuel Palmer, illustrator,
        1853). <u>CrabCR</u> (2:3) Sum 85, p. 26-27.
     "Somewhere: How Can We Leave It Now?" <u>SouthernPR</u> (26,
        i.e. 25:2) Fall 85, p. 46.

5043. VANDERBILT, Heidi
       "Note from a Lost Child." StoneC (12:2/3) Spr-Sum 85, p.
       17.
5044. VANDERLIP, Brian
       "After Eden." PoetryCR (6:4) Sum 85, p. 47.
       "Nightwalk." PoetryCR (6:4) Sum 85, p. 47.
       "Nightwalk." PoetryCR (7:2) Wint 85-86, p. 55.
5045. VANDO, Gloria
       "Los Alamos." NewL (52:1) Fall 85, p. 15-16.
       "Promesas." NewL (52:1) Fall 85, p. 16-18.
5046. VANGELISTI, Paul
       "For Giuliano." Temblor (2) 85, p. 135.
       "The Woman with the Green Face." Temblor (2) 85, p. 133-
       134.
5047. VARGA, Jon
       "Moments Musicaux." CapeR (20:2) Fall 85, p. 38.
5048. VARGO, Beth Copeland
       "Ghost Story." PassN (6:2) Spr-Sum 85, p. 7.
5049. VARN, Jim
       "Pulled Apart." Paint (11:21/12:24) 84-85, p. 13.
5050. VAS, István
       "The Lion" (tr. by Jascha Kessler and Maria Körösy).
       Ploughs (11:4) 85, p. 215.
       "Once More" (tr. by Jascha Kessler and Maria Körösy).
       Ploughs (11:4) 85, p. 214.
5051. VASQUEZ, Enriqueta L.
       "Worldly and Innocence Meet in a Poem." Imagine (2:1) Sum
       85, p. 76-78.
5052. VATHING, Gale
       "I Asked a Nearby Cuckoo" (tr. of Anna Akhmatova, w. Neva
       Herrington). NewL (51:4) Sum 85, p. 49.
       "I Didn't Ask for the Praise" (tr. of Anna Akhmatova, w.
       Neva Herrington). NewL (51:4) Sum 85, p. 48.
VEA, Judith Guzman
       See GUZMAN VEA, Judith
5053. VEASEY, Jack
       "Children at Play." PaintedB (25) Spr 85, p. 6-8.
       "Going to Fires." PaintedB (25) Spr 85, p. 9-10.
5054. VEENENDAAL, Cornelia
       "What Can I Surrender?" ConnPR (3:1) 84, p. 17.
5055. VEGA, José Luis
       "Capital" (tr. by Arnaldo Sepúlveda). RiverS (17) 85,
       p. 42.
VEGA, Mario Enrique Contreras
       See CONTRERAS VEGA, Mario Enrique
5056. VEIGA, Marisella L.
       "An Exercise." WindO (46) Fall 85, p. 35.
5057. VEINBERG, John
       "Children Asleep in a Treehouse." MissouriR (8:2) 85, p.
       34.
5058. VEINSTEIN, Alain
       "Archeology of the Mother" (tr. by Rosmarie Waldrop).
       Verse (2) 85, p. 34-35.
5059. VELEZ, Guillermo
       "Amigo." RevChic (13:2) Sum 85, p. 37.
       "Busqueda." RevChic (13:2) Sum 85, p. 38.
       "Encuentro." RevChic (13:2) Sum 85, p. 39.
5060. VELEZ, Lydia
       "A las Mujeres." Mairena (7:19) 85, p. 104.
5061. VENABLE, Peter
       "Charge of Quarters." Bogg (53) 85, p. 23.
5062. VENTADOUR, Fanny
       "Blast." NegC (5:4) Fall 85, p. 107.
       "Every House, Guardian Snake." CapeR (20:1) Spr 85, p. 36.
       "I Never Saw Your Face So Clearly As Last Night." Wind
       (15:53) 85, p. 22.

"Lower Level." NegC (5:4) Fall 85, p. 106.
VENTI, Tom di
     See DiVENTI, Tom
5063. VENUTI, Lawrence
     "The Dream of the Dancing Cat" (tr. of Milo De Angelis).
          AmerPoR (14:1) Ja-F 85, p. 48.
     "Foreweb" (tr. of Milo De Angelis). AmerPoR (14:1) Ja-F
          85, p. 48.
     "Neither Point nor Line" (tr. of Milo De Angelis).
          AmerPoR (14:1) Ja-F 85, p. 48.
     "The Train Corridor" (tr. of Milo De Angelis). AmerPoR
          (14:1) Ja-F 85, p. 48.
5064. VERBA, Karen
     "Commercial Break." SecC (12:1) 84, p. 24.
5065. VERDET, André
     "Children of Auschwitz and Elsewhere" (tr. by Paul Mills).
          Stand (26:2) Spr 85, p. 50.
5066. VERDICCHIO, Pasquale
     "Formentera." CanLit (106) Fall 85, p. 74.
     "Moving East." CanLit (106) Fall 85, p. 28.
5067. VERE, John
     "Nocturne." Bogg (54) 85, p. 26.
5068. VERHULST, Pat
     "Dogs Bark." CrabCR (2:2) Wint 85, p. 14.
5069. VERNON, William J.
     "Chalk Drawings Outside." PoeticJ (11) 85, p. 31.
     "Equipment Room Manager." WindO (46) Fall 85, p. 34.
     "Far from Home." WindO (46) Fall 85, p. 33.
     "Getting the Old House in Order." WestB (17) 85, p. 81-82.
     "Horace Talks about Leroy Duncan." WestB (17) 85, p. 80-
          81.
     "Housebuilding." Wind (15:55) 85, p. 47.
     "The Struggle." WindO (46) Fall 85, p. 33-34.
5070. VERTREACE, Martha
     "Elegy Written on Bastille Day." Vis (19) 85, p. 6-7.
5071. VESTVILLE, Erik
     "Burning Ship" (tr. of Jaroslav Seifert, w. Jeffrey
          Fiskin). Antaeus (55) Aut 85, p. 158.
     "Mortar Salvos" (tr. of Jaroslav Seifert, w. Jeffrey
          Fiskin). Antaeus (55) Aut 85, p. 159-160.
     "When the Ashes" (tr. of Jaroslav Seifert, w. Jeffrey
          Fiskin). Antaeus (55) Aut 85, p. 157.
5072. VIAN, Boris
     "There Are Some Who Have Trumpets" (tr. by Julia Older).
          NewL (51:4) Sum 85, p. 152.
     "There Was a Copper Lamp" (tr. by Julia Older). NewL
          (51:4) Sum 85, p. 151.
VICCA, Ed Santa
     See SantaVICCA, Ed
VICENTE, Arminda Arroyo
     See ARROYO VICENTE, Arminda
5073. VIDAVER, Doris
     "Small Door of a Dream" (tr. of Jacob Glatstein). Poetry
          (146:5) Ag 85, p. 256.
5074. VIEIRA, John
     "The Lake Swan, the Tom." Agni (22) 85, p. 73.
5075. VIENNA, Darrell
     "The Saturday Men." ChiR (35:2) Wint 85, p. 68-69.
5076. VIERECK, Peter
     "Final Vigil" (tr. of Georg Heym). NewL (51:3) Spr 85, p.
          54.
     "Guardianship" (tr. of Stefan George). NewL (51:4) Sum
          85, p. 74.
     "Love Lyric" (tr. of Stefan George). NewL (51:3) Spr 85,
          p. 54.

"New England Seventeeners." <u>Confr</u> (30/31) N 85, p. 236.
"Portrait of the Artist As an Old Dog" (Excerpted from
    <u>Archer in the Marrow</u>). <u>PoetryR</u> (2:2) Ap 85, p. 53-54.
"Rogue" (excerpted from <u>Archer in the Marrow: The
    Applewood Cycles</u>). <u>PoetryR</u> (5) S 85, p. 14-18.
"White Butterflies of Night, So Often near Me" (tr. of
    Georg Heym). <u>NewL</u> (51:4) Sum 85, p. 73.
"The Year of the Soul" (Selection: "October Tints, tr. of
    Stefan George). <u>NewL</u> (51:4) Sum 85, p. 74.
VIEW, Lucille S. de
    <u>See</u> DeVIEW, Lucille S.
5077. VIGEE, Claude
    "A Coeur Perdu." <u>Mund</u> (15:1/2) 85, p. 176, 178.
    "Choral en Décembre." <u>Mund</u> (15:1/2) 85, p. 178, 180.
    "Chorale in December" (tr. by J. R. LeMaster and Kenneth
        Lawrence Beaudoin). <u>Mund</u> (15:1/2) 85, p. 179, 181.
    "Heart Lost in the World" (tr. by J. R. LeMaster and
        Kenneth Lawrence Beaudoin). <u>Mund</u> (15:1/2) 85, p. 177,
        179.
    "Living Tomb" (tr. by J. R. LeMaster and Kenneth Lawrence
        Beaudoin). <u>WebR</u> (10:1) Spr 85, p. 31-32.
    "Patience." <u>Mund</u> (15:1/2) 85, p. 182.
    "Patience" (tr. by J. R. LeMaster and Kenneth Lawrence
        Beaudoin). <u>Mund</u> (15:1/2) 85, p. 183.
5078. VIGIL-PIÑON, Evangelina
    "Legacy" (for Tomás Rivera). <u>RevChic</u> (13:3/4) 85, p. 15.
    "Misterio: Creaking Bed, Moans from behind Closed Door."
        <u>Imagine</u> (2:1) Sum 85, p. 74-75.
    "Necesidad." <u>Imagine</u> (2:1) Sum 85, p. 74.
5079. VILLA, Carlo
    "Even in Dickens" (tr. by Margaret Straus). <u>LitR</u> (29:1)
        Fall 85, p. 122.
    "George Washington" (tr. by Margaret Straus). <u>LitR</u> (29:1)
        Fall 85, p. 121.
    "God Calling the Holy Ghost" (tr. by Margaret Straus).
        <u>LitR</u> (29:1) Fall 85, p. 121-122.
5080. VILLAMIL, Antonietta
    "Tiempo." <u>LindLM</u> (4:2) Ap-Je 85, p. 3.
VILLAMIL, Maria de los A. Diaz
    <u>See</u> DIAZ VILLAMIL, Maria de los A.
5081. VILLANI, Jim
    "Network." <u>SecC</u> (12:1) 84, p. 11-12.
5082. VILLANUEVA, Alma Luz
    "The Labor of <u>Buscando la Forma</u>." <u>AmerPoR</u> (14:4) Jl-Ag
        85, p. 34.
    "Sassy." <u>AmerPoR</u> (14:4) Jl-Ag 85, p. 35.
VILLEGAS, Nestor Diaz de
    <u>See</u> DIAZ de VILLEGAS, Nestor
5083. VILLIAS, Josette Lilliane
    "'Gross' National Product Breakfast." <u>SanFPJ</u> (7:3) 84
        [i.e. 85], p. 65.
    "Indian Mother" (in memory of my father, Red Horse).
        <u>SanFPJ</u> (7:3) 84 [i.e. 85], p. 53-57.
    "Legacy of Red Horse." <u>SanFPJ</u> (7:2) 85, p. 76.
    "The Mitre of Death's Head." <u>SanFPJ</u> (7:2) 85, p. 73.
    "Primed." <u>SanFPJ</u> (7:2) 85, p. 74-75.
5084. VINCEK, Martha M.
    "Sailing the Inlets." <u>PoeticJ</u> (11) 85, p. 15.
5085. VINOKUROV, Evgeny
    "Adam" (tr. by Richard Lourie). <u>Ploughs</u> (11:4) 85, p. 175.
5086. VINZ, Mark
    "Good Fridy. Just West of Here." <u>OhioR</u> (34) 85, p. 60.
    "Homesteaders." <u>NoDaQ</u> (53:4) Fall 85, p. 229.
5087. VIVALDI, Cesare
    "Details" (tr. by Annalisa Saccà). <u>LitR</u> (28:2) Wint 85,
        p. 310.

"You Rest Also" (tr. by Annalisa Saccà). LitR (28:2)
    Wint 85, p. 311.
5088. VLASAK, Keith
    "Lost Faces." Poem (53) Mr 85, p. 58.
    "Morning." StoneC (12:2/3) Spr-Sum 85, p. 68.
    "Saints." Poem (53) Mr 85, p. 57.
5089. VLIET, Eddy van
    "Two Thirds Air" (tr. by Peter Nijmeijer). Vis (19) 85,
    p. 17.
5090. VOGEL, Constance
    "Marginal Images." SpoonRQ (10:4) Fall 85, p. 60.
5091. VOIGT, Ellen Bryant
    "The Bee Tree." Nat (240:22) 8 Je 85, p. 710.
    "The Chosen." SenR (15:2) 85, p. 159-161.
    "The Cusp." SenR (15:2) 85, p. 158.
    "Dancing with Poets." NewYorker (61:30) 16 S 85, p. 38.
    "Equinox." Iowa (15:1) Wint 85, p. 25.
    "The Farmer." Ploughs (11:1) 85, p. 216-217.
    "The Last Class." TriQ (63) Spr-Sum 85, p. 607-608.
    "The Lesson." Poetry (146:3) Je 85, p. 135-136.
    "The Pendulum." Pequod (18) 85, p. 128.
    "The Photograph." Atlantic (255:3), Mr 85, p. 56.
    "The Riders." Nat (240:8) 2 Mr 85, p. 251.
    "Separate Houses." Nat (240:19) 18 My 85, p. 602.
    "Short Story." Ploughs (11:1) 85, p. 213-214.
    "Song." Nat (241:3) 3-10 Ag 85, p. 91.
    "Stone Pond." Nat (240:11) 23 Mr 85, p. 341.
    "The Trust." Pequod (18) 85, p. 127.
    "Visiting the Graves." Ploughs (11:1) 85, p. 215.
    "The Waterfall." Pequod (18) 85, p. 129-130.
    "The Wide and Varied World." Atlantic (256:1), Jl 85, p.
    84.
    "The Witness." YaleR (74:4) Sum 85, p. 569.
5092. VOLBORTH, J.
    "Vision from Cedar Moon" (For Lorraine). NoDaQ (53:2) Spr
    85, p. 247.
5093. VOLKOW, Veronica
    "Autorretrato Muerta." Mund (16:1/2) 85, p. 32.
    "Death's Self Portrait" (tr. by Forrest Gander). Mund
    (16:1/2) 85, p. 33.
    "El Inicio" (Selecciones: X, I). Mund (16:1/2) 85, p. 28,
    30.
    "El Inicio" (Selections: X, I, tr. by Forrest Gander).
    Mund (16:1/2) 85, p. 29, 31.
    "La Lavandera." Mund (16:1/2) 85, p. 26.
    "La Memoria." Mund (16:1/2) 85, p. 34.
    "Memory" (tr. by Forrest Gander). Mund (16:1/2) 85, p. 35.
    "El Tedio de Euriloco." Mund (16:1/2) 85, p. 24.
    "The Washerwoman" (tr. by Forrest Gander). Mund (16:1/2)
    85, p. 27.
    "The Weariness of Eurylochus" (tr. by Forrest Gander).
    Mund (16:1/2) 85, p. 25.
5094. Von BRIESEN, Alice
    "Peacock." Amelia (2:2) O 85, p. 84.
Von DASSANOWSKY-HARRIS, Robert
    See DASSANOWSKY-HARRIS, Robert von
Von MORSTEIN, Petra
    See MORSTEIN, Petra von
5095. VREELAND, Elizabeth
    "Noon." NewYRB (32:8) 9 My 85, p. 37.
    "Three Poems from Morocco" ("We fly above Kenitra,"
    "Ladders," "Stick to Your Own Kind"). ParisR (27:97)
    Fall 85, p. 163-165.
VRIES, Carrow de
    See De VRIES, Carrow

VRIES, N. de
   <u>See</u> De VRIES, N.
5096. VRIES, Theun de
   "First and Last" (Selections: 6, 9, tr. by Rod Jellema).
      <u>PoetL</u> (79:4) Wint 85, p. 233.
5097. WADDEN, Paul
   "Five Senses Are Not Enough." <u>StoneC</u> (12:2/3) Spr-Sum 85,
      p. 72.
   "Lake of the Woods." <u>StoneC</u> (12:2/3) Spr-Sum 85, p. 72.
   "Reflection: A Painting of a Young Man by Degas." <u>KanQ</u>
      (17:1/2) Wint-Spr 85, p. 178.
5098. WADE, Evelyn Amuedo
   "April Afternoon." <u>Vis</u> (19) 85, p. 25-27.
5099. WADE, Michael
   "Una Dormienda." <u>Conjunc</u> (8) 85, p. 203.
5100. WADE, Seth
   "Where Do Old Poems Go?" <u>Bogg</u> (53) 85, p. 39.
5101. WADE, Sidney
   "The Impress of Evening." <u>PraS</u> (59:3) Fall 85, p. 53.
   "In the Garden." <u>NewYorker</u> (61:23) 29 Jl 85, p. 28.
   "Kirkeskibe - The Ship in the Church" (Denmark, Kansas).
      <u>PraS</u> (59:3) Fall 85, p. 52.
   "What Can't Be Said." <u>PraS</u> (59:3) Fall 85, p. 53-54.
5102. WAGNER, Anneliese
   "Butterfly." <u>WestB</u> (17) 85, p. 71.
   "Greek Courtyard." <u>Confr</u> (29) Wint 85, p. 69.
   "Little Rain in Zimbabwe." <u>Confr</u> (30/31) N 85, p. 263.
   "The Song" (tr. of Elisabeth Borchers). <u>Paint</u>
      (11:21/12:24) 84-85, p. 58.
   "Summer Begins" (tr. of Elisabeth Borchers). <u>Paint</u>
      (11:21/12:24) 84-85, p. 59.
5103. WAGNER, Kathleen
   "Ferry Poem." <u>Amelia</u> (2:2) O 85, p. 82.
   "Night Baseball." <u>WoosterR</u> (4) Fall 85, p. 14-15.
5104. WAGNER, Linda
   "The Story of Stones." <u>PoetryR</u> (5) S 85, p. 44-45.
5105. WAGONER, David
   "At Peace." <u>LitR</u> (28:4) Sum 85, p. 567.
   "By a Waterfall." <u>YaleR</u> (74:3) Spr 85, p. 452.
   "Eulogy for Richard Hugo." <u>Atlantic</u> (255:5) My 85, p. 62.
   "In Enemy Territory." <u>LitR</u> (28:4) Sum 85, p. 564-565.
   "In the Dream House." <u>VirQ</u> (61:3) Sum 85, p. 419-420.
   "Kissing Cousins." <u>OhioR</u> (35) 85, p. 92.
   "Mockingbird." <u>Poetry</u> (146:2) My 85, p. 63-64.
   "Our Father." <u>Poetry</u> (146:2) My 85, p. 65-66.
   "Our Model." <u>Poetry</u> (146:2) My 85, p. 64-65.
   "The Play." <u>Poetry</u> (146:2) My 85, p. 67.
   "The Return of Icarus." <u>TriQ</u> (63) Spr-Sum 85, p. 287-288.
   "Securing a House." <u>LitR</u> (28:4) Sum 85, p. 566.
   "Sharp-Shin." <u>VirQ</u> (61:3) Sum 85, p. 418-419.
5106. WAHLE, F. Keith
   "Getting to Know You" (w. Michael Karl Ritchie). <u>YellowS</u>
      (16) Aut 85, p. 19-20.
   "The Pictures." <u>YellowS</u> (16) Aut 85, p. 21.
   "Presidential Statues" (w. Michael Karl Ritchie & Michael
      Shay). <u>YellowS</u> (15) Sum 85, p. 8-9.
   "The Shadow." <u>Confr</u> (29) Wint 85, p. 39.
5107. WAINRIGHT, Carol Scott
   "Haiku" (5 poems). <u>WindO</u> (46) Fall 85, p. 46.
5108. WAINWRIGHT, Jeffrey
   "Transitive" (in memory of Daniel Richardson). <u>Stand</u>
      (26:1) Wint 84-85, p. 4-5.
5109. WAKOSKI, Diane
   "Braised Leeks & Framboise" (for Annette Smith). <u>VirQ</u>
      (61:4) Aut 85, p. 626-628.
   "The Fear of Fat Children" (upon the return of a much

foodstained copy of Bukowski's *Dangling in the
Tournefortia*, by a fat student). <u>DenQ</u> (19:4) Spr 85,
p. 37-39.
"On the Boardwalk in Atlantic City." <u>VirQ</u> (61:4) Aut 85,
p. 625-626.
"Reading the Pharmacist's Daughter's Letters" (for Chase
Twichell). <u>Raccoon</u> (17) Mr 85, p. 11.
5110. WAKULICH, Bob
"Leona Camp wanted a husband badly" (Textual/Image).
<u>Rampike</u> (4:2/3) 85-86, p. 108.
5111. WALCOTT, Derek
"Days." <u>PartR</u> (52:4) 85, p. 423.
"A Letter from the Old Guard." <u>NewYRB</u> (32:15) 10 O 85, p.
31.
"The Lighthouse." <u>NewYorker</u> (61:6) 1 Ap 85, p. 38-39.
"Marina Tsvetayeva." <u>Antaeus</u> (55) Aut 85, p. 182-183.
"Night-Fishing." <u>PartR</u> (52:3) 85, p. 236-237.
"Roseau Valley." <u>NewRep</u> (193:7/8) 12-19 Ag 85, p. 36.
"Saint Lucia's First Communion." <u>PartR</u> (52:3) 85, p. 236.
"Storm Figure." <u>Antaeus</u> (55) Aut 85, p. 184-185.
"To Norline." <u>PartR</u> (52:4) 85, p. 422-423.
"The Villa Restaurant." <u>GrahamHR</u> (9) Fall 85, p. 10-12.
"Winter Lamps." <u>GrahamHR</u> (9) Fall 85, p. 7-9.
5112. WALDROP, Keith
"Love in the Ruins" (tr. of Claude Royet-Journoud).
<u>Conjunc</u> (8) 85, p. 108-115.
5113. WALDROP, Rosmarie
"Archeology of the Mother" (tr. of Alain Veinstein).
<u>Verse</u> (2) 85, p. 34-35.
"Before Margins" (tr. of Heiner Bastian). <u>NewL</u> (51:4) Sum
85, p. 59.
"Elegy 3" (tr. of Emmanuel Hocquard). <u>Verse</u> (2) 85, p. 29-
33.
"For C. S. Lewis" (Who imagines hell is like the vast slums
of Oldham, England, I've been told. Tr. of Petra von
Morstein). <u>NewL</u> (51:4) Sum 85, p. 76.
"Justice" (tr. of Petra von Morstein). <u>NewL</u> (51:4) Sum
85, p. 75.
"Observations in the Aerial Ocean" (tr. of Heiner Bastian).
<u>NewL</u> (51:4) Sum 85, p. 60-61.
"Opening an Absence." <u>ConcPo</u> (18:1/2) 85, p. 36-38.
"The Reproduction of Profiles" (4 selections). <u>Temblor</u>
(1) 85, p. 85-86.
5114. WALKENSTEIN, Eileen
"Black Is." <u>SanFPJ</u> (7:4) 85, p. 26-27.
"The Four-Letter Word." <u>SanFPJ</u> (7:3) 84 [i.e. 85], p. 91.
"Men Against the Sky." <u>SanFPJ</u> (7:3) 84 [i.e. 85], p. 92.
"One Day Vietnam -- Tomorrow the World" (The John Birch
Prayer). <u>SanFPJ</u> (7:3) 84 [i.e. 85], p. 13.
5115. WALKER, Alice
"S M." <u>Zyzzyva</u> (1:1) Spr 85, p. 93.
5116. WALKER, Jeanne (<u>See</u> <u>also</u> WALKER, Jeanne Murray)
"The Child Molester." <u>PaintedB</u> (26/27) Sum-Fall 85, p. 50.
5117. WALKER, Jeanne Murray (<u>See</u> <u>also</u> WALKER, Jeanne)
"Nursing." <u>NowestR</u> (23:3) 85, p. 15.
"Parkers Prairie, Minnesota." <u>GeoR</u> (39:4) Wint 85, p. 759.
"The Shawl." <u>Poetry</u> (147:2) N 85, p. 76-77.
5118. WALKER, Leigh Anne
"My Father's Chair." <u>NegC</u> (5:3) Sum 85, p. 128.
5119. WALKER, Lynne
"Coffins at Kaufman's" (A Found Poem). <u>MidAR</u> (5:2) 85, p.
24-25.
"That Woman." <u>MidAR</u> (5:2) 85, p. 23.
5120. WALKER, Margaret
"Birmingham 1963." <u>SouthernR</u> (21:3) Sum 85, p. 829.
"Black Paramour." <u>SouthernR</u> (21:3) Sum 85, p. 828-829.

"My Mississippi Spring." <u>SouthernR</u> (21:3) Sum 85, p. 827.
5121. WALKER, Sue (<u>See</u> <u>also</u> WALKER, Susan Russo)
      "Imagine How It Will Be." <u>Vis</u> (19) 85, p. 35.
5122. WALKER, Susan Russo (<u>See</u> <u>also</u> WALKER, Sue)
      "Bottom of the Deck." <u>PoetryNW</u> (26:1) Spr 85, p. 28-30.
5123. WALKONEN, Dale
      "Oars." <u>Prima</u> (9) 85, p. 89.
5124 WALLACE, Bronwen
      "Common Magic" (Selections: "Learning from the Hands,"
      "Thinking with the Heart," for Mary di Michele).
      <u>PoetryCR</u> (6:3) Spr 85, p. 24.
      "Melons at the Speed of Light" (for Carolyn Smart).
      <u>PoetryCR</u> (6:4) Sum 85, p. 13.
5125. WALLACE, Linda
      "Breathing the Mountain and Field Gatherings." <u>SnapD</u>
      (9:1) Fall 85, p. 8.
      "Places of Wild Greens." <u>SnapD</u> (9:1) Fall 85, p. 9.
5126. WALLACE, Naomi
      "Child and Mother." <u>NewL</u> (52:1) Fall 85, p. 91.
5127. WALLACE, Robert
      "Divorce." <u>OP</u> (38/39) Spr 85, p. 189.
      "In Brussels." <u>OP</u> (38/39) Spr 85, p. 189.
      "Song of the Open Road." <u>OP</u> (38/39) Spr 85, p. 189.
5128. WALLACE, Ronald
      "The Anatomy of the Hand." <u>PoetryNW</u> (26:3) Aut 85, p. 15-
      17.
      "Bat." <u>PoetryNW</u> (26:2) Sum 85, p. 44.
      "Fawn." <u>CrossCur</u> (5:3) 85, p. 111.
      "Grouse." <u>PraS</u> (59:4) Wint 85, p. 35.
      "Poppies." <u>PraS</u> (59:4) Wint 85, p. 36.
5129. WALLACE, T. S. (<u>See</u> <u>also</u> WALLACE, Terry S.)
      "Euphrates." <u>SouthernPR</u> (26, i.e. 25:2) Fall 85, p. 56-57.
      "Then You Understand the Saints We Fear." <u>PaintedB</u> (25)
      Spr 85, p. 15.
5130. WALLACE, Terry S. (<u>See</u> <u>also</u> WALLACE, T. S.)
      "The People We Were We Hardly Remember." <u>CrabCR</u> (2:2)
      Wint 85, p. 15.
5131. WALLACE-CRABBE, Chris
      "Spire." <u>Verse</u> (2) 85, p. 5.
WALLEGHEN, Michael van
      <u>See</u> Van WALLEGHEN, Michael
5132. WALLENSTEIN, Barry
      "Sugar." <u>ConnPR</u> (3:1) 84, p. 38.
5133. WALLER, Gary
      "Of the 497 Kinds of Love, This Is #43." <u>Poetry</u> (145:5) F
      85, p. 255-256.
      "Why I Like All-Night Coffee Shops." <u>LaurelR</u> (19:1) Wint
      85, p. 22.
5134. WALLERSTEIN, Barry
      "Liberty, N.Y." <u>SecC</u> (12:2) 84?, p. 5.
5135. WALSH, Des
      "The Kitchen" (127 Gower St., St. John's, February 21,
      1985). <u>CanLit</u> (107) Wint 85, p. 102.
5136. WALSH, Joy
      "Praised Be Imagination" (for Jazzpoet Ted Joans).
      <u>BlackALF</u> (19:3) Fall 85, p. 111.
5137. WALTER, Eugene
      "Memento Mori." <u>NegC</u> (5:2) Spr 85, p. 123.
5138. WALTON, Gary
      "Cock-tale Party." <u>WoosterR</u> (4) Fall 85, p. 49-50.
5139. WANDERER, Ralph
      "Counting." <u>PoetryCR</u> (6:4) Sum 85, p. 42.
5140. WANG, Onc
      "The Poor Calumet." <u>SpoonRQ</u> (10:4) Fall 85, p. 51-52.
5141. WANG, V. S. M.
      "Divination by Bamboo" (An Old Ritual). <u>HarvardA</u> (118:3)

Mr 85, p. 18-20.
5142. WANG, Wei
"On the Holy Mountain" (tr. by Joseph Lisowski). _Amelia_
(2:1) Ap 85, p. 29.
5143. WANGBERG, Mark
"Driving to the Bank." _USl_ (18/19) Wint 85, p. 2.
5144. WANIEK, Marilyn Nelson
"The Century Quilt" (for Sarah Mary Taylor, Quilter).
SouthernR (21:3) Sum 85, p. 825-826.
"I Send Mama Home." _SouthernR_ (21:3) Sum 85, p. 823-825.
"Mama's Promise." _SouthernR_ (21:3) Sum 85, p. 821-823.
5145. WANTLING, William
"On the streets, he'd lived" (For Ernie Marshall if he's
still around). _SecC_ (12:2) 84?, p. 3.
5146. WARD, Dave
"Smoky City Girl" (Selections). _Bogg_ (54) 85, p. 52.
5147. WARD, Robert
"The Last Audience of the Hapsburgs" (from an unfinished
painting by Arthur von Ferrais, Museum of Art,
University of Oregon). _BlueBldgs_ (9) [85?], p. 30.
5148. WARD, Tom
"July Night on Sandy Lake." _WoosterR_ (4) Fall 85, p. 78.
5149. WARD, William J., Jr.
"Butchers." _HangL_ (48) Fall 85, p. 68.
"Little Big Things." _HangL_ (48) Fall 85, p. 67.
5150. WARDEN, Marine Robert
"Alger Creek." _NegC_ (5:3) Sum 85, p. 94.
"At the Poetry Reading." _Abraxas_ (33) 85, p. 48.
"Disorder at Sea." _SpoonRQ_ (10:4) Fall 85, p. 35.
"For Shelley." _SpoonRQ_ (10:4) Fall 85, p. 36.
"In a Field of Lightning." _SpoonRQ_ (10:4) Fall 85, p. 36.
"In Glendale." _Abraxas_ (33) 85, p. 48.
"Rio Grande, 1933" (For Billy at age 6). _NegC_ (5:3) Sum
85, p. 93.
5151. WARN, Emily
"Labor Day." _CrabCR_ (2:3) Sum 85, p. 28.
5152. WARNER, Barrett
"Modeling Nude." _CalQ_ (26) Sum 85, p. 39.
5153. WARNER, Catherine A.
"Mother's Day." _Paint_ (11:21/12:24) 84-85, p. 8.
5154. WARNER, Gale
"Turner." _Agni_ (22) 85, p. 72.
5155. WARNER, James
"Riding West, Again." _WestCR_ (20:2) O 85, p. 42.
5156. WARNER, Val
"Corned-Beef Legs." _Verse_ (3) 85, p. 32.
5157. WARREN, Larkin
"Rituals of the Ordinary." _Tendril_ (19/20) 85, p. 373.
"Vermont, Triptych, 1978." _Tendril_ (19/20) 85, p. 374.
5158. WARREN, Robert Penn
"John's Birches." _NewYorker_ (61:25) 12 Ag 85, p. 26.
"The Loose Shutter." _NewYorker_ (61:4) 18 Mr 85, p. 42.
"Re-Interment: Recollection of a Grandfather." _Atlantic_
(255:2), F 85, p. 48.
"The Smile." _MemphisSR_ (5:2) Spr 85, p. 5.
"Tulip-Tree in Bloom." _Iowa_ (15:1) Wint 85, p. 20-21.
"Uncertain Season in High Country." _SouthernR_ (21:2) Spr
85, p. 428-429.
5159. WARREN, Rosanna
"Funere Mersit Acerbo." _ChiR_ (34:4) 85, p. 65.
5160. WARREN, Shirley
"For Carlos Who Used to Compare Me with Roses." _Prima_ (9)
85, p. 9.
5161. WARREN, Tony
"I am a wizard" (DeKalb County High Schools, Literary award
winners: first place, poetry). _DeKalbLAJ_ (18:3/4) 85,

p. 45.
5162. WARSH, Lewis
"White Oak." Oink (19) 85, p. 77.
5163. WARWICK, Joanna
"Handling the Python." BelPoJ (36:2) Wint 85-86, p. 24-25.
"Wheat." BlueBldgs (9) [85?], p. 20.
5164. WASICZKO, Donna
"Bananas." PassN (6:1) Fall-Wint 85, p. 22.
5165. WASSON, Kirsten
"Spell." CreamCR (10:2) [85?], p. 47.
5166. WASTBERG, Per
"Someone's stacking the leaves of an artichoke in heaps"
(#11 from "Närmare underrättelser" in En avlägsen
likhet, tr. by Rika Lesser). PartR (52:4) 85, p. 428-
429.
5167. WAT, Aleksander
"A Damned Man" (tr. by Czeslaw Milosz). TriQ (63) Spr-Sum
85, p. 97.
5168. WATERMAN, Cary
"At the Chicago Zoo" (for Ellen). WoosterR (3) Spr 85, p.
10-11.
"At the Vietnam Memorial" (for Caroline Marshall). LitR
(29:1) Fall 85, p. 46.
"Morning Rowers, Summer Palace, Peking, China" (from a
photograph by Bokman Dong). WoosterR (3) Spr 85, p. 9.
5169. WATERS, Mary Ann
"Casualties." PoetryNW (26:1) Spr 85, p. 18.
"Four Women Sitting in the Mineral Mud." PoetryNW (26:1)
Spr 85, p. 19.
"When I Was Ten, at Night." Raccoon (17) Mr 85, p. 21.
5170. WATERS, Michael
"Bonwit Teller." Crazy (27) Fall 84, p. 7-8.
"Burning the Dolls." SenR (15:2) 85, p. 86-87.
"The Fire Balloon" (in memoriam Elizabeth Bishop). SenR
(15:2) 85, p. 85.
"John Sloan." GreenfR (13:1/2) Fall-Wint 85, p. 172.
"Morpho." GeoR (39:3) Fall 85, p. 534-535.
"Night Windows" (after the etching by John Sloan).
GreenfR (13:1/2) Fall-Wint 85, p. 171-172.
"Reading Dickens." Poetry (146:2) My 85, p. 71-72.
"The Story of the Krit." MemphisSR (5:2) Spr 85, p. 39.
5171. WATHALL, Agnes
"The Lie." PoeticJ (11) 85, p. 9.
5172. WATSON, Ellen
"Once." MassR (26:1) Spr 85, p. 62.
"A Pinhole of Blue." MassR (26:1) Spr 85, p. 61.
5173. WATSON, Harold
"Norm & Richie at the Lite Beer Bar." AmerPoR (14:3) My-
Je 85, p. 46.
5174. WATSON, Lawrence
"Becoming a Writer." IndR (8:3) Fall 85, p. 9.
"Midwest." IndR (8:3) Fall 85, p. 8.
5175. WAUGAMAN, Charles A.
"A Bouquet by Degas" ("The Woman with Chrysanthemums"
1865). Wind (15:55) 85, p. 48.
"Garden Musing." CapeR (20:1) Spr 85, p. 48.
"In Samuel Johnson's Garret." Wind (15:55) 85, p. 49.
"Too Long the Silence." CapeR (20:1) Spr 85, p. 49.
"Walk with My Son." Wind (15:55) 85, p. 48.
5176. WAYMAN, Tom
"Along Highway 97." TriQ (64) Fall 85, p. 91.
"Clearing the Trash." OntR (22) Spr-Sum 85, p. 106-107.
"The Hands." TriQ (64) Fall 85, p. 88.
"Lecture." TriQ (64) Fall 85, p. 92-93.
"The Music in the Silos." Nat (240:5) 9 F 85, p. 152.
"One Lump or Two." PoetryNW (26:4) Wint 85-86, p. 30-31.

"Sea-Cat." <u>PoetryNW</u> (26:4) Wint 85-86, p. 31-32.
"The Three Brains." <u>LittleM</u> (14:4) 85, p. 5-6.
"Why You Only Got 'B Plus'." <u>TriQ</u> (64) Fall 85, p. 89-90.
5177. WAYNE, Jane O.
"Filling the Terrarium." <u>CrossCur</u> (5:2) 85, p. 89.
"Insomniac." <u>IndR</u> (8:2) Spr 85, p. 97.
"Kiyomizu." <u>IndR</u> (8:2) Spr 85, p. 96.
5178. WEATHERS, Winston
"Little Boy Lost." <u>Nimrod</u> (28:2) Spr-Sum 85, p. 99-100.
"Morbus ab Ovo." <u>Nimrod</u> (28:2) Spr-Sum 85, p. 102.
"Nativity, 1926." <u>Nimrod</u> (28:2) Spr-Sum 85, p. 103-104.
"Objets d'Art, d'Amour." <u>SewanR</u> (93:1) Wint 85, p. 74-75.
"Le Saltimbanque." <u>Nimrod</u> (28:2) Spr-Sum 85, p. 100-101.
5179. WEAVER, Michael S.
"Messages: For Ntozake Shange, Secrets in Prophecy."
   <u>BlackALF</u> (19:3) Fall 85, p. 103-104.
"A New Nephilim." <u>SouthernR</u> (21:3) Sum 85, p. 843.
"Paradise Revisited." <u>SouthernR</u> (21:3) Sum 85, p. 842-843.
"A Tin Roof Song." <u>SouthernR</u> (21:3) Sum 85, p. 844.
"The Underground Railroad." <u>BlackALF</u> (19:3) Fall 85, p.
   104.
5180. WEBB, Jane
"Love Poem with Persimmons." <u>NegC</u> (5:3) Sum 85, p. 136-
   137.
5181. WEBB, John
"Columbia River." <u>AntigR</u> (60) Wint 85, p. 60.
"Ghost Town." <u>AntigR</u> (60) Wint 85, p. 59.
"Place Names." <u>AntigR</u> (60) Wint 85, p. 58.
5182. WEBER, Elizabeth
"Kansas, 1920." <u>GrahamHR</u> (9) Fall 85, p. 25.
5183. WEBER, Mark
"3 Sisters." <u>WormR</u> (25:4, issue 100) 85, p. 155.
"The Photograph." <u>WormR</u> (25:4, issue 100) 85, p. 156.
5184. WEBER, R. B. (<u>See also</u> WEBER, Ron)
"The Revolt of Frankenstein. And the Monster." <u>Confr</u>
   (30/31) N 85, p. 148.
5185. WEBER, Ron (<u>See also</u> WEBER, R. B.)
"Slash and Burn." <u>Gargoyle</u> (27) 85, p. 48-49.
5186. WEBSTER, Diane
"Gingerbread Man." <u>Bogg</u> (53) 85, p. 28.
5187. WEBSTER, Ronald
"Writing Poems." <u>CrabCR</u> (3:1) Fall-Wint 85, p. 4-5.
5188. WEDGE, George F.
"Letter to a Lost Friend." <u>KanQ</u> (17:1/2) Wint-Spr 85, p.
   174-176.
5189. WEDGE, Philip
"Her Pregnancy." <u>KanQ</u> (17:1/2) Wint-Spr 85, p. 145.
5190. WEEDON, Syd
"A Child Not Yet Born" (Meditations on a new life coming
   into the World). <u>RagMag</u> (4:2) Fall 85, p. 14-15.
"Weedon's Proverbs #089376451-1/2." <u>Sam</u> (42:4, 168th
   release) 85, p. 21.
5191. WEEKS, Laurie
"Seahorse." <u>Sulfur</u> (14) 85, p. 25-26.
5192. WEEKS, Ramona (<u>See also</u> WEEKS, Ramona M. & Ramona Maher)
"Air for Music Boxes." <u>CapilR</u> (36) 85, p. 77-78.
"The Moviewatcher." <u>PassN</u> (6:1) Fall-Wint 85, p. 22.
"Swimming." <u>CapilR</u> (36) 85, p. 75-76.
"The Tie." <u>CapilR</u> (36) 85, p. 74.
5193. WEEKS, Ramona M. (<u>See also</u> WEEKS, Ramona & Ramona Maher)
"Butter-and-Egg Men." <u>SnapD</u> (8:2) Spr 85, p. 10-11.
"Gem and Rock Show." <u>SnapD</u> (8:2) Spr 85, p. 9.
5194. WEEKS, Ramona Maher (<u>See also</u> WEEKS, Ramona & Ramona M.)
"Florencio Molina Campos." <u>BallSUF</u> (26:2) Spr 85, p. 78-
   79.

5195. WEI, Chuang
        "Composed by the Ferry at Night over the Chien-ch'ang
            River" (tr. by Robin D.S. Yates). Ploughs (11:4) 85,
            p. 200.
        "Mourning at the Strings of My Concubine, Miss Yang's
            Zither" (tr. by Robin D.S. Yates). Ploughs (11:4) 85,
            p. 202.
        "Night Thoughts at Chang Terrace" (tr. by Robin D.S.
            Yates). Ploughs (11:4) 85, p. 198.
        "Plucking Out White Hairs" (tr. by Robin D.S. Yates).
            Ploughs (11:4) 85, p. 200.
        "Recording Events" (tr. by Robin D.S. Yates). Ploughs
            (11:4) 85, p. 203.
        "Recording Events in the Village Where I Live" (tr. by
            Robin D.S. Yates). Ploughs (11:4) 85, p. 199.
        "Refusing Wine, I Leave My Mat" (tr. by Robin D.S. Yates).
            Ploughs (11:4) 85, p. 199.
        "Remembering My Daughter Silver Maid (Ah Yin)" (tr. by
            Robin D.S. Yates). Ploughs (11:4) 85, p. 201.
        "Tune: Echoing Heaven's Everlastingness. No. 1" (tr. by
            Robin D.S. Yates). Ploughs (11:4) 85, p. 202.
        "Tune: Raise the Cup. No. 1" (tr. by Robin D.S. Yates).
            Ploughs (11:4) 85, p. 203.
        "Tune: Raise the Cup. No. 2" (tr. by Robin D.S. Yates).
            Ploughs (11:4) 85, p. 204.
        "Tune: Song of an Immortal. No. 2" (tr. by Robin D.S.
            Yates). Ploughs (11:4) 85, p. 204.
        "Tune: Song of Waterclock at Night" (tr. by Robin D.S.
            Yates). Ploughs (11:4) 85, p. 205.
        "Withering" (tr. by Robin D.S. Yates). Ploughs (11:4) 85,
            p. 201.
WEI, Hsü
        See HSÜ, Wei
5196. WEIDMAN, Phil
        "April Snow." WormR (25:3, issue 99) 85, p. 85.
        "Call." WormR (25:3, issue 99) 85, p. 85.
        "Crisp's Eye." WormR (25:3, issue 99) 85, p. 85.
        "Hand Cream." WormR (25:3, issue 99) 85, p. 85.
        "Limited." WormR (25:3, issue 99) 85, p. 84.
        "Locked Out." WormR (25:3, issue 99) 85, p. 84.
        "Safe Keeping." WormR (25:3, issue 99) 85, p. 84.
        "Second Reading." WormR (25:3, issue 99) 85, p. 84.
        "Speakers." WormR (25:3, issue 99) 85, p. 84.
        "Valentine." WormR (25:3, issue 99) 85, p. 84.
5197. WEIGEL, James
        "Astronaut Song." Kaleid (11) Sum 85, p. 39.
        "Diana." Kaleid (11) Sum 85, p. 39.
        "Haiku." Kaleid (11) Sum 85, p. 39.
        "Testaments" (Selections). Kaleid (11) Sum 85, p. 36-37.
        "Werewolf's Lament" (from: Five Variations on a Theme).
            Kaleid (11) Sum 85, p. 39.
5198. WEIGEL, Tom
        "After Mayakovsky & Frank O'Hara" (for Nina Zivancevic).
            LittleM (14:4) 85, p. 20.
        "Lorelei." LittleM (14:4) 85, p. 21.
5199. WEIGL, Bruce
        "The Act." Tendril (19/20) 85, p. 375-376.
        "Snowy Egret." TriQ (63) Spr-Sum 85, p. 627-628.
        "Song of Napalm" (for my wife). TriQ (63) Spr-Sum 85, p.
            467-468.
        "To the Dog Dying." Tendril (19/20) 85, p. 377.
5200. WEINBERG, Viola
        "Krupa with the Lights On." YellowS (14) Spr 85, p. 25.
5201. WEINBERGER, Eliot
        "The Dream of India" (c. 1492). Sulfur (12) 85, p. 118-
            126.

5202. WEINGARTEN, Roger
       "Apples." Poetry (145:4) Ja 85, p. 191-193.
       "New Year's, Montpelier, 1885." Poetry (145:4) Ja 85, p.
          189-190.
       "Not Quite a Love Poem." Poetry (145:4) Ja 85, p. 190.
       "Personal Holiday." NoAmR (270:3) S 85, p. 48-49.
       "Premature Elegy by Firelight." Poetry (145:4) Ja 85, p.
          193.
       "Water Music." Tendril (19/20) 85, p. 378-379.
5203. WEINMAN, Paul
       "Band-Aids Will Do." SanFPJ (7:4) 85, p. 15.
       "Clean Up Your Frontage." SanFPJ (7:4) 85, p. 24.
       "Curled Up Tight." Sam (42:4, 168th release) 85, p. 39.
       "He Swings a Straight Stick." Sam (43:3, 171st release)
          85, 19 p.
       "No Idea of Mine." Wind (15:55) 85, p. 51-52.
       "Obscenity of Silence." Wind (15:55) 85, p. 50.
       "Sweet Berries Sour." Open24 (4) 85, p. 24.
       "Tree Frogs Clung." Wind (15:55) 85, p. 50.
       "Turn Off." Paint (11:21/12:24) 84-85, p. 19.
       "When He Stared." Wind (15:55) 85, p. 50-51.
       "When Him Came." DeKalbLAJ (18:1/2) 85, p. 86-87.
       "Where It Had Been Oiled." Sam (42:3, 167th release) 85,
          p. 18.
5204. WEIRATHER, Larry
       "The Jug" (tr. of Francis Ponge). Amelia (2:1) Ap 85, p.
          40.
5205. WEISBURD, Harry
       "Nefertittie: Erotic Anti-Goddess" (A Collaboration, w.
          Arlene Stone). YellowS (15) Sum 85, p. 14-21.
5206. WEISMAN, Ann
       "As the Sun Moves into Leo." Nimrod (28:2) Spr-Sum 85, p.
          112.
       "Love Will Happen." Nimrod (28:2) Spr-Sum 85, p. 114.
       "When the Owl Calls You." Nimrod (28:2) Spr-Sum 85, p.
          113.
5207. WEISS, David
       "Medicine Chest." Crazy (27) Fall 84, p. 27-28.
       "Val-de-Grâce." PartR (52:2) 85, p. 68-69.
5208. WEISS, Irving
       "Graffiti Poem." Rampike (4:2/3) 85-86, p. 36.
5209. WEISS, Jason
       "As If Nothing But His Own Calamity" (tr. of Tomás Guido
          Lavalle). Temblor (1) 85, p. 113.
       "Kafka." DenQ (20:2) Fall 85, p. 61-62.
       "Tracing of the Dawn" (tr. of Tomás Guido Lavalle).
          Temblor (1) 85, p. 111-113.
5210. WEISS, Sigmund
       "Mara's Realm." Open24 (4) 85, p. 45.
       "Strangers at the Job." SanFPJ (7:2) 85, p. 65-66.
5211. WEISS, Theodore
       "Coming Attractions." Iowa (15:1) Wint 85, p. 91-92.
5212. WEISSBORT, Daniel
       "Play." Stand (26:4) Aut 85, p. 64.
       "Resolution." NewOR (12:1) Spr 85, p. 48.
5213. WEITZMAN, Sarah Brown
       "After Reading John Updike's Poem Entitled 'Cunts'."
          YellowS (15) Sum 85, p. 37.
5214. WELBURN, Ron
       "Dear Old Stockholm" (in memory of Paul Laurence Dunbar
          Chambers, died 4 January 1969). AmerPoR (14:3) My-Je
          85, p. 46.
       "Insignia." GreenfR (13:1/2) Fall-Wint 85, p. 75.
       "Lens of Memory." GreenfR (13:1/2) Fall-Wint 85, p. 73-75.
5215. WELCH, Don
       "Apartheid." CutB (24) Spr-Sum 85, p. 33.

"The Ferret." <u>PraS</u> (59:1) Spr 85, p. 67.
"First Book Apocrypha." <u>Tendril</u> (19/20) 85, p. 380.
"Portent." <u>CutB</u> (24) Spr-Sum 85, p. 32.
"The Woman in the Beige Ranchstyle Down the Street."
    <u>CapeR</u> (20:2) Fall 85, p. 9.
5216. WELCH, Jennifer
    "When Editors Go Dancing." <u>NegC</u> (5:4) Fall 85, p. 92-93.
5217. WELCH, Liliane
    "The Bridge." <u>AntigR</u> (60) Wint 85, p. 56-57.
    "The Fall" (For Ghigno Timillero). <u>PottPort</u> (7) 85-86, p.
    48.
    "First Winter Ascension of the Sass Maor" (for Ghigno
    Timillero, December 1972). <u>PoetryCR</u> (6:3) Spr 85, p.
    30.
    "Fundy Bay in December." <u>PottPort</u> (7) 85-86, p. 19.
    "Raspberry Picking." <u>AntigR</u> (60) Wint 85, p. 57.
    "Return to Canada 1984." <u>PottPort</u> (7) 85-86, p. 4.
    "Wife of a Climber." <u>PoetryCR</u> (6:3) Spr 85, p. 30.
    "Zoccolo Pala Canali, South Chimney Wall" (October 1975).
    <u>PoetryCR</u> (6:3) Spr 85, p. 30.
5218. WELISH, Marjorie
    "The Movies among the Days." <u>Oink</u> (19) 85, p. 70.
    "Skin." <u>Oink</u> (19) 85, p. 69.
    "Talking about Here." <u>Conjunc</u> (7) 85, p. 62-67.
5219. WELLINGTON, Beth
    "Internal Conflict" (tr. of Norberto James). <u>NewEngR</u>
    (7:4) Sum 85, p. 578.
5220. WELLS, Paula A.
    "Apple." <u>MidAR</u> (5:1) 85, p. 118-119.
    "The Linear Dark." <u>MidAR</u> (5:1) 85, p. 120-121.
5221. WELLS, Will
    "Beatings." <u>SouthernPR</u> (25:1) Spr 85, p. 27.
    "Insomnia." <u>WebR</u> (10:2) Fall 85, p. 69.
    "The Lesson." <u>CapeR</u> (20:1) Spr 85, p. 27.
    "The Lesson." <u>WebR</u> (10:2) Fall 85, p. 68.
    "Night Baptism / Sandusky Shoals." <u>CapeR</u> (20:1) Spr 85,
    p. 26.
    "Night Train to Naples" (For Varda). <u>Swallow</u> (4) 85, p.
    57-58.
5222. WELSH, Harlen
    "Caladium." <u>YellowS</u> (16) Aut 85, p. 10-11.
5223. WEN, I-To
    "Confession" (tr. by Robert Dorsett). <u>LitR</u> (28:4) Sum 85,
    p. 589.
5224. WENDELL, Julia
    "Fireside." <u>MissouriR</u> (8:2) 85, p. 24.
    "The Rope" (In Memory of Frances Cole). <u>Crazy</u> (29) Fall
    85, p. 48-53.
5225. WENDT, Ingrid
    "Learning the Silence." <u>CrossCur</u> (4:2) 84, p. 14-15.
5226. WENTHE, William
    "Shadblow." <u>GeoR</u> (39:4) Wint 85, p. 757-758.
5227. WENTWORTH, Don
    "Demythology." <u>JlNJPo</u> (8:1) 85, p. 29.
    "Foreign Correspondences" (for b). <u>JlNJPo</u> (8:1) 85, p. 29.
    "Lot & the Burning Bush" (for mk). <u>JlNJPo</u> (8:1) 85, p. 30.
    "Upon Last Evening's Staff, Stars" (for WS). <u>JlNJPo</u> (8:1)
    85, p. 28.
5228. WEORES, Sándor
    "Excerpts from the Modern Tragedy" (tr. by Jascha Kessler
    and Maria Körösy). <u>GrahamHR</u> (8) Wint 85, p. 41-42.
WERT, William van
    <u>See</u> Van WERT, William
5229. WESCOTT, Mary
    "San Cristobal de las Casas." <u>GWR</u> (6:1) 85?, p. 31.

5230. WESLOWSKI, Dieter
       "After a Motet by Eugenio Montale." <u>Gargoyle</u> (27) 85, p.
          13.
       "After a Night Raid on a Border Village." <u>WestB</u> (16) 85,
          p. 63.
       "All I Need Now." <u>MSS</u> (4:3) Spr 85, p. 150.
       "The Arriver." <u>IndR</u> (8:1) Wint 85, p. 54.
       "Because Nothing." <u>DeKalbLAJ</u> (18:1/2) 85, p. 87.
       "The Bird Who Steals Everything Shining." <u>WebR</u> (10:1) Spr
          85, p. 54.
       "The Boy to the Spider, the Spider to the Boy." <u>WebR</u>
          (10:1) Spr 85, p. 54.
       "Crazy the Sun." <u>BallSUF</u> (26:2) Spr 85, p. 80.
       "Feeding the Angel." <u>AmerPoR</u> (14:5) S-O 85, p. 35.
       "How Bears Came to Calabria" (for Daniel Sargo). <u>HangL</u>
          (47) Spr 85, p. 49.
       "If the Bahamas." <u>Gargoyle</u> (27) 85, p. 13.
       "Manolo." <u>Abraxas</u> (33) 85, p. 23.
       "The Oracle." <u>WormR</u> (25:4, issue 100) 85, p. 121.
       "The Split." <u>Abraxas</u> (33) 85, p. 23.
       "When Silence Turns the Last Hour of Night" (for Carlos
          Fuentes). <u>WormR</u> (25:4, issue 100) 85, p. 122.
       "When the Angel Returned to Sue D." <u>LaurelR</u> (19:1) Wint
          85, p. 71.
5231. WESSEL, Peter
       "American Dairy Farm" (For John Bennett). <u>NegC</u> (5:1) Wint
          85, p. 58.
       "The Train-Whistle." <u>NegC</u> (5:3) Sum 85, p. 147.
       "Winter in the Vineyards." <u>WebR</u> (10:1) Spr 85, p. 76.
5232. WEST, Charles
       "Teacher, This Is Just to Say" (A Variation on a Theme by
          William Carlos Williams). <u>EngJ</u> (74:2) F 85, p. 39.
5233. WEST, Kathleene
       "Nebraska Hide-Out." <u>PoetryNW</u> (26:4) Wint 85-86, p. 27.
5234. WEST, Michael
       "Renaming the Animals That Threaten Our Dreams."
          <u>DeKalbLAJ</u> (18:1/2) 85, p. 88-89.
5235. WESTERFIELD, Nancy (<u>See also</u> WESTERFIELD, Nancy G.)
       "Cleaning Ladies" (Eve of Saint Agnes Contest Winner).
          <u>NegC</u> (5:1) Wint 85, p. 14.
5236. WESTERFIELD, Nancy G. (<u>See also</u> WESTERFIELD, Nancy)
       "The Breakfast Table." <u>TexasR</u> (6:1/2) Spr-Sum 85, p. 107.
       "Changelings." <u>NegC</u> (5:2) Spr 85, p. 11.
       "Comic Strip." <u>PoetryR</u> (2:2) Ap 85, p. 48.
       "Fetishes." <u>RiverS</u> (18) 85, p. 97.
       "Symptoms." <u>RiverS</u> (18) 85, p. 98.
       "Three Colors of Snow." <u>KanQ</u> (17:1/2) Wint-Spr 85, p. 178.
       "Toys in the Attic." <u>Confr</u> (29) Wint 85, p. 61.
5237. WESTERGAARD, Diane
       "Gudrun Himmler Visits Dachau." <u>PraS</u> (59:1) Spr 85, p. 14.
       "September 1942." <u>PraS</u> (59:1) Spr 85, p. 13.
5238. WESTON, Ruth D.
       "The Mark of the Plow" (for Darcy O'Brien). <u>Nimrod</u> (28:2)
          Spr-Sum 85, p. 42.
5239. WEVILL, David
       "Other Names for the Heart." <u>Shen</u> (36:1) 85-86, p. 90-91.
       "Rhythm" (To Jorge Guillén, tr. of Alberto de Lacerda).
          <u>Imagine</u> (1:2) Wint 84, p. 209.
5240. WHEALDON, Everett
       "Tideland Cattle Drive." <u>Sam</u> (42:3, 167th release) 85, p.
          27-29.
5241. WHEAT, Maxwell Corydon
       "Hoboes." <u>Confr</u> (30/31) N 85, p. 179.
5242. WHEELER, Alice H.
       "A Shakespeare Sampler." <u>WestB</u> (16) 85, p. 69.

5243. WHIPPLE, George
   "Birdolatry." _PoetryCR_ (6:4) Sum 85, p. 43.
   "Offertory." _PoetryCR_ (6:4) Sum 85, p. 43.
5244. WHITAKER, Romous (a.k.a. Shadeed)
   "A Farewell Salute to Marvin." _MoodySI_ (15) Spr 85, p. 24.
5245. WHITE, Claire Nicolas
   "Saving the Baby." _Prima_ (9) 85, p. 76-77.
5246. WHITE, Gail
   "Coverlets." _Poem_ (54) N 85, p. 60.
   "Midwinter." _Poem_ (54) N 85, p. 59.
   "Perhaps My Daughter Is Anorexic." _Wind_ (15:53) 85, p. 50-
      51.
   "The Way We Come Home." _Sparrow_ (48) 85, 23 p.
5247. WHITE, J. P. (_See also_ WHITE, Joan)
   "1984." _MinnR_ (N.S. 24) Spr 85, p. 120.
   "Apple Blossom, Oriole, Lilac" (for David Mura). _NoAmR_
      (270:3) S 85, p. 55.
   "Christmas Eve without Starlight." _CumbPR_ (5:1) Fall 85,
      p. 46.
   "In a Rowboat on a Lake in Minnesota." _Poetry_ (146:3) Je
      85, p. 142-143.
   "The Nightingale Lights at My Window and Tells Me How the
      Soldiers Had Their Fun." _CreamCR_ (10:1) 85, p. 39-42.
   "Su Tung P'o Awakens in Moonlight to Write a Letter to His
      Wife." _Poetry_ (146:3) Je 85, p. 140.
   "We Who Set Out for the New World." _Poetry_ (146:3) Je 85,
      p. 141-142.
5248. WHITE, Joan (_See also_ WHITE, J. P.)
   "Lucy." _PoetL_ (80:2) Sum 85, p. 99-100.
5249. WHITE, Roger
   "Can. Lit. Committee Meeting." _CrossC_ (7:2) 85, p. 8.
5250. WHITE, S. Lauderdale
   "House of Persuasion." _HolCrit_ (22:3) Je 85, p. 15.
5251. WHITE, Steven
   "Beach" (tr. of Juan Cameron). _Mund_ (15:1/2) 85, p. 37.
   "Canto 7" (from the long poem _Cámera Oscura_, tr. of
      Juan Cameron). _Mund_ (15:1/2) 85, p. 41.
   "Event" (tr. of Juan Cameron). _Mund_ (15:1/2) 85, p. 39.
   "Hard Work" (tr. of Juan Cameron). _Mund_ (15:1/2) 85, p.
      39.
   "Heraclitus" (tr. of Juan Cameron). _Mund_ (15:1/2) 85, p.
      37.
   "Life" (tr. of Sergio Mansilla). _Stand_ (26:3) Sum 85, p.
      59.
   "The Man from Leipzig" (tr. of Clemente Riedemann).
      GreenfR (12:3/4) Wint-Spr 85, p. 118.
   "Mosquito" (tr. of Juan Cameron). _Mund_ (15:1/2) 85, p. 39.
   "No One Knows What I'm Talking About" (tr. of Diego
      Maquieira). _PoetryR_ (2:2) Ap 85, p. 78.
   "Of the Nameless Birds" (tr. of Teresa Calderón). _Mund_
      (15:1/2) 85, p. 205.
   "September: The Shark" (tr. of Pablo Antonio Cuadra).
      NowestR (23:1) 85, p. 95-113.
   "The Tree of the World" (tr. of Clemente Riedemann).
      GreenfR (12:3/4) Wint-Spr 85, p. 114-115.
   "Wekufe's Dream" (tr. of Clemente Riedemann). _GreenfR_
      (12:3/4) Wint-Spr 85, p. 116-117.
   "When It's Over" (tr. of Juan Cameron). _Mund_ (15:1/2) 85,
      p. 35.
5252. WHITE, Todd
   "On the Last Day of the 1983 Deer Season, I Have a
      Successful Hunt." _PassN_ (6:2) Spr-Sum 85, p. 15.
5253. WHITE, William M.
   "After Letting Go." _Swallow_ (4) 85, p. 59.
   "After the Killing." _SouthernR_ (21:2) Spr 85, p. 448.

5254. WHITEHOUSE, Anne Cherner
    "Anti-Dirge." <u>Confr</u> (30/31) N 85, p. 266.
5255. WHITEMAN, Roberta Hill
    "Home before Dark" (for Ramona Compton). <u>Abraxas</u> (33) 85,
        p. 9-10.
    "Van Gogh in the Olive Grove." <u>Abraxas</u> (33) 85, p. 8-9.
    "A Visit." <u>Abraxas</u> (33) 85, p. 11.
5256. WHITEN, Clifton
    "Cabbages & PeeWee Baseball." <u>CrossC</u> (7:2) 85, p. 15.
    "Conversations with Poets." <u>CrossC</u> (7:2) 85, p. 15.
    "The Day Stories." <u>CrossC</u> (7:2) 85, p. 15.
    "Hands." <u>CrossC</u> (7:2) 85, p. 15.
    "Pear on Doorstep." <u>CrossC</u> (7:2) 85, p. 15.
5257. WHITING, Nathan
    "4 Steel Plates." <u>Wind</u> (15:53) 85, p. 52-53.
    "The Brooklyn Bridge Is My Favorite Playground Apparatus."
        <u>Wind</u> (15:53) 85, p. 52.
    "The Echo's Age." <u>WindO</u> (46) Fall 85, p. 20-21.
    "Half a Humingbird's Retina." <u>GreenfR</u> (13:1/2) Fall-Wint
        85, p. 32.
    "A Late Threat to Maybe." <u>GreenfR</u> (13:1/2) Fall-Wint 85,
        p. 31.
5258. WHITLOW, Carolyn Beard
    "Mercedes." <u>MassR</u> (26:1) Spr 85, p. 153-156.
5259. WHITMAN, Ruth
    "Basic Training, 1942." <u>Tendril</u> (19/20) 85, p. 381.
    "Cracow." <u>OntR</u> (23) Fall-Wint 85-86, p. 36.
    "Les Enfants du R. P. G." (Rocket-Propelled Grenade, tr. of
        Rami Ditzani). <u>Ploughs</u> (11:4) 85, p. 171-172.
    "From West Beirut" (September 1982, in connection with non-
        standard and negligent building in Lebanon, tr. of Rami
        Ditzani). <u>Ploughs</u> (11:4) 85, p. 172.
    "Meeting" (tr. of Miriam Oren). <u>Ploughs</u> (11:4) 85, p. 173.
    "Poems from a 1984 Diary" (Selections: 3-6, tr. of Abraham
        Sutskever). <u>Ploughs</u> (11:4) 85, p. 167-170.
    "The Red Roof on Tuckerman Avenue." <u>MassR</u> (26:2/3) Sum-
        Aut 85, p. 359.
    "Skiathos." <u>CrossCur</u> (4:2) 84, p. 87-88.
    "Uncle Harry at the Tar Pits." <u>Confr</u> (29) Wint 85, p. 40-
        41.
    "The Wedding." <u>OntR</u> (23) Fall-Wint 85-86, p. 35.
5260. WHITNEY, J. D.
    "For Ed on-the-Hour Dorn." <u>Northeast</u> (Series 4:2) Fall
        85, p. 30-31.
5261. WHITTINGHAM, Nechia
    "Discretion." <u>EngJ</u> (74:3) Mr 85, p. 64.
5262. WICKERS, Brian
    "Fathoming." <u>AntigR</u> (61) Spr 85, p. 22.
    "Giacometti's Sculpture." <u>AntigR</u> (61) Spr 85, p. 21.
    "Pastorals." <u>Quarry</u> (34:4) Aut 85, p. 27.
5263. WIEDER, Laurance
    "Ink." <u>NewYorker</u> (60:51) 4 F 85, p. 50.
5264. WIELAND, Liza
    "Oil Painting for Beginners." <u>BlackWR</u> (12:1) Fall 85, p.
        10-11.
    "The Polygamist's Daughter." <u>CutB</u> (24) Spr-Sum 85, p. 64-
        65.
    "The Woman and Her Tale." <u>CarolQ</u> (38:1) Fall 85, p. 40.
5265. WIER, Dara
    "Late Afternoon on a Good Lake." <u>AmerPoR</u> (14:1) Ja-F 85,
        p. 47.
    "Lot's Wife." <u>ThRiPo</u> (25/26) 85, p. 60-61.
5266. WIGGINS, Jean
    "Sunflower." <u>Wind</u> (15:54) 85, p. 26.
5267. WILBORN, William
    "French Doors for Allen Varney's Mother" (Eve of Saint

Agnes Contest Winner). <u>NegC</u> (5:1) Wint 85, p. 13.
"Glaziery" (Boston 1679, Joseph Hood on his death-bed
　　receives a shipment from Leyden). <u>NegC</u> (5:1) Wint 85,
　　p. 39.
"Is It Art to Make Art Out of Celery." <u>Shen</u> (36:1) 85-86,
　　p. 97-98.
"Love's Mansion." <u>NegC</u> (5:1) Wint 85, p. 37-38.
"On Welfare." <u>TriQ</u> (63) Spr-Sum 85, p. 621.
"A View of the Panama-Pacific Exposition, San Francisco."
　　<u>MidAR</u> (5:2) 85, p. 94-95.
5268. WILBUR, Richard
"All That Is." <u>NewYorker</u> (61:12) 13 My 85, p. 44.
"A Finished Man." <u>NewYorker</u> (61:2) 4 Mr 85, p. 42.
"Phaedra" (Selections: Scene 2 & 5, tr. of Jean Baptiste
　　Racine). <u>Ploughs</u> (11:4) 85, p. 99-108.
5269. WILD, Peter
"Acolytes." <u>SouthernPR</u> (25:1) Spr 85, p. 7.
"A Bouquet." <u>CharR</u> (11:2) Fall 85, p. 100-101.
"Chicken Chimichangas." <u>SouthernPR</u> (25:1) Spr 85, p. 8.
"The Concert." <u>MidAR</u> (5:1) 85, p. 23.
"Home Gardening." <u>MidAR</u> (5:2) 85, p. 92.
"Majorettes." <u>LittleM</u> (14:4) 85, p. 29.
"Optometrists." <u>LitR</u> (29:1) Fall 85, p. 53.
"Pete the Last Tastykake Horse." <u>AmerPoR</u> (14:5) S-O 85,
　　p. 35.
"Postmen." <u>Raccoon</u> (17) Mr 85, p. 31.
"Real Stars." <u>PoetryR</u> (2:2) Ap 85, p. 71-72.
"Restaurants." <u>HawaiiR</u> (17) Spr 85, p. 56-57.
"Robbers." <u>HawaiiR</u> (17) Spr 85, p. 55.
"Someone Your Own Age Named Violet." <u>MidAR</u> (5:1) 85, p.
　　24-25.
"Transplant." <u>AmerPoR</u> (14:5) S-O 85, p. 35.
5270. WILDE-MENOZZI, Wallis
"Matisse's Interiors." <u>KanQ</u> (17:3) Sum 85, p. 98.
"School for Pears." <u>KanQ</u> (17:3) Sum 85, p. 97-98.
"Then I Come Alive." <u>KanQ</u> (17:4) Fall 85, p. 56.
5271. WILDER, Rex
"Watching the Boy Watching the Funeral from the Riverbed."
　　<u>Geor</u> (39:2) Sum 85, p. 250.
5272. WILEY, Christopher
"Coming Out." <u>JamesWR</u> (3:1) Fall 85, p. 10.
5273. WILJER, Robert
"Death Angels." <u>KanQ</u> (17:1/2) Wint-Spr 85, p. 254.
"Leisurely Lunch." <u>AntigR</u> (62/63) Sum-Aut 85, p. 32.
5274. WILK, David
"President's Commission on Holiday Verse, Directive #81-A-
　　406." <u>OP</u> (38/39) Spr 85, p. 105-106.
5275. WILKERSON, James C.
"January." <u>NegC</u> (5:1) Wint 85, p. 99.
5276. WILKINSON, Claude
"Like da Blues-Man Do" (The Heritage). <u>BlackALF</u> (19:3)
　　Fall 85, p. 127.
5277. WILKINSON, Robin J.
"Climb." <u>Wind</u> (15:54) 85, p. 54-55.
"Lorraine." <u>Wind</u> (15:54) 85, p. 54.
5278. WILLARD, Nancy
"Psalm to the Newt." <u>NewYorker</u> (61:41) 2 D 85, p. 52.
5279. WILLERTON, Chris
"Camera in the Bush." <u>SouthernPR</u> (25:1) Spr 85, p. 40-41.
5280. WILLETT-SHOPTAW, John
"Sleeping through the Midwest." <u>HarvardA</u> (119:2) D 85, p.
　　30.
"While You Were Out." <u>HarvardA</u> (119:1) N 85, p. 20-21.
5281. WILLEY, Edward
"The Mystery of Life." <u>OP</u> (38/39) Spr 85, p. 167.
"The Ninth Life." <u>OP</u> (38/39) Spr 85, p. 167.

423   WILLIAMSON

5282. WILLIAMS, C. K. (See also WILLIAMS, Christie)
      "Artemis." NewEngR (8:2) Wint 85, p. 153.
      "Books." Antaeus (55) Aut 85, p. 188.
      "The Dirty Talker, Boston." NewEngR (8:2) Wint 85, p. 155.
      "Drought." Antaeus (55) Aut 85, p. 192.
      "Elms." SenR (15:2) 85, p. 145.
      "From the Next Book by." SenR (15:2) 85, p. 146.
      "Girl Meets Boy." Antaeus (55) Aut 85, p. 187.
      "Guatemala: 1964" (For Loren Crabtree). Antaeus (55) Aut
         85, p. 193.
      "Love: Intimacy." Antaeus (55) Aut 85, p. 194.
      "Medusa." SenR (15:2) 85, p. 142.
      "Neglect." TriQ (63) Spr-Sum 85, p. 609-611.
      "Normality." SenR (15:2) 85, p. 144.
      "Nostalgia." SenR (15:2) 85, p. 143.
      "Philadelphia: 1978." Antaeus (55) Aut 85, p. 189.
      "Rungs." Antaeus (55) Aut 85, p. 191.
      "Self-knowledge." Antaeus (55) Aut 85, p. 190.
      "Shame." NewEngR (8:2) Wint 85, p. 156.
      "Souls." NewEngR (8:2) Wint 85, p. 154.
      "Travelers." Antaeus (55) Aut 85, p. 186.
      "Waking Jed." TriQ (63) Spr-Sum 85, p. 612-613.
      "Winter." NewEngR (8:2) Wint 85, p. 157.
5283. WILLIAMS, Christie (See also WILLIAMS, C. K.)
      "Night Watch." KanQ (17:4) Fall 85, p. 84.
5284. WILLIAMS, Daniel
      "Deus ex Machina." NoDaQ (53:4) Fall 85, p. 230.
      "Father's Truck." NoDaQ (53:4) Fall 85, p. 231.
      "For a Silent Woman, Alone." NoDaQ (53:4) Fall 85, p. 233.
      "Trout/Man." NoDaQ (53:4) Fall 85, p. 234.
      "Woodcutters/Blue Flame." NoDaQ (53:4) Fall 85, p. 232.
5285. WILLIAMS, David
      "Privacy." Atlantic (255:2), F 85, p. 68.
5286. WILLIAMS, Ernie
      "Jogging Interruptus" (Two Limericks). WindO (46) Fall
         85, p. 25.
5287. WILLIAMS, Frances Howell
      "Haiku Symphony." NegC (5:4) Fall 85, p. 68.
      "The Wind Clan Princess." NegC (5:1) Wint 85, p. 61-62.
5288. WILLIAMS, Hugo
      "Unfinished Poem." Poetry (146:4) Jl 85, p. 219-220.
      "Waiting to Go On." Poetry (146:4) Jl 85, p. 219.
5289. WILLIAMS, John (See also WILLIAMS, John A.)
      "The Aged Lover Again." NewL (51:3) Spr 85, p. 119.
5290. WILLIAMS, John A. (See also WILLIAMS, John)
      "1:2.8 at f 30: Diana in Chelsea." NewL (51:3) Spr 85, p.
         116.
      "Alejo's Poem." NewL (51:3) Spr 85, p. 116.
5291. WILLIAMS, Juliet
      "Escape." AmerPoR (14:3) My-Je 85, p. 21.
5292. WILLIAMS, Miller
      "After the Revolution for Jesus, the Associate Professor
         Prepares His Final Remarks." AmerPoR (14:3) My-Je 85,
         p. 9.
      "A Poem for Emily." Poetry (145:4) Ja 85, p. 219.
      "Ruby Tells All." GeoR (39:3) Fall 85, p. 548-549.
5293. WILLIAMS, Randall
      "Out of Bounds." Wind (15:54) 85, p. 56.
5294. WILLIAMS, William Carlos
      "The Semblances" (Excerpt). Tendril (19/20) 85, p. 5.
5295. WILLIAMSON, Alan
      "The Chair." Poetry (145:5) F 85, p. 275-277.
      "East Arlington." Pequod (18) 85, p. 70-71.
      "Fallings from Us, Vanishings." NewRep (193:5) 29 Jl 85,
         p. 34.
      "The Night You Slept" (tr. of Cesare Pavese). Ploughs

(11:4) 85, p. 54.
"Paris: Late Fall." <u>Pequod</u> (18) 85, p. 75.
"The Prayer of the Cathars." <u>Pequod</u> (18) 85, p. 72-74.
"You, Wind of March" (tr. of Cesare Pavese). <u>Ploughs</u>
    (11:4) 85, p. 52-53.
5296. WILLISON, Andrea
    "The Kiss." <u>Amelia</u> (2:1) Ap 85, p. 75-76.
5297. WILLITTS, Martin, Jr.
    "Running Away from Home." <u>NewRena</u> (19) Fall 85, p. 95.
5298. WILMARTH, Richard Norman
    "Colleen." <u>RagMag</u> (4:1) Spr 85, p. 21.
5299. WILNER, Eleanor
    "Concerto." <u>ChiR</u> (34:4) 85, p. 30-31.
5300. WILOCH, Thomas
    "A Flower Custom." <u>BlueBldgs</u> (9) [85?], p. 25.
    "The Gift of a Mirror." <u>NegC</u> (5:2) Spr 85, p. 25.
5301. WILSON, Bill
    "With Anastasia at Rumplemeyer's." <u>BlueBldgs</u> (9) [85?],
        p. 48.
5302. WILSON, Bruce M.
    "From the Southern to the Northern Peak by Way of the Lake:
        Stopping to View the Scenery" (tr. of Hsieh Ling-Yün,
        w. Zhang Ting-chen). <u>NewL</u> (51:4) Sum 85, p. 143.
    "Scaling the Height of Stone Gate Mountain" (tr. of Hsieh
        Ling-Yün, w. Zhang Ting-chen). <u>NewL</u> (51:4) Sum 85,
        p. 141.
    "A Solitary Islet, Alone in the Stream" (tr. of Hsieh Ling-
        Yün, w. Zhang Ting-chen). <u>NewL</u> (51:4) Sum 85, p. 142.
    "Spending the Night on the Cliff at Stone Gate Mountain"
        (tr. of Hsieh Ling-Yün, w. Zhang Ting-chen). <u>NewL</u>
        (51:4) Sum 85, p. 142.
5303. WILSON, D. H.
    "Childhood Image" (tr. of Hans Georg Bulla, w. the author).
        <u>Stand</u> (26:2) Spr 85, p. 22.
5304. WILSON, Eric
    "Passing." <u>CrossCur</u> (5:3) 85, p. 136-137.
5305. WILSON, Graeme
    "Chalice" (Korean Sijo Poem, tr. of Chong Chol). <u>DenQ</u>
        (20:1) Sum 85, p. 18.
    "Choosing a Plum-Branch" (Ki no Tomonori,   -905). <u>MalR</u>
        (72) S 85, p. 99.
    "Cock" (Korean Sijo Poem, tr. of Anonymous). <u>DenQ</u> (20:1)
        Sum 85, p. 16.
    "Dawn" (Korean Sijo Poem, tr. of Anonymous). <u>DenQ</u> (20:1)
        Sum 85, p. 15.
    "Disinterest" (Ki no Tomonori,   -905). <u>MalR</u> (72) S 85,
        p. 99.
    "In the Mountains" (Priest Ryokan, 1757-1831). <u>MalR</u> (72)
        S 85, p. 99.
    "Ravens" (Korean Sijo Poem, tr. of Kim Su-Jang). <u>DenQ</u>
        (20:1) Sum 85, p. 17.
    "Retrospect" (tr. of Priest Ryokan). <u>WestHR</u> (39:1) Spr
        85, p. 64.
    "Tiger" (tr. of Yi Kyu-bo). <u>WestHR</u> (39:1) Spr 85, p. 63.
    "Virtue Rewarded" (Korean Sijo Poem, tr. of Anonymous).
        <u>DenQ</u> (20:1) Sum 85, p. 19.
    "Wind among Bamboos" (tr. of Hsu Wei). <u>WestHR</u> (39:1) Spr
        85, p. 63.
5306. WILSON, Jack Lowther
    "A Moment." <u>Quarry</u> (34:4) Aut 85, p. 28.
    "Owl Glass." <u>Quarry</u> (34:4) Aut 85, p. 28.
5307. WILSON, Jeffrey
    "Blackberries" (for t. batt). <u>YellowS</u> (15) Sum 85, p. 35.
5308. WILSON, John T.
    "Stanley Knife." <u>Bogg</u> (54) 85, p. 18-19.

5309. WILSON, Joseph
       "Cecilia's Song." PoetL (80:2) Sum 85, p. 104-105.
5310. WILSON, Keith
       "Chantey." GreenfR (13:1/2) Fall-Wint 85, p. 70.
       "The Charted Destinies" (for Ted Enslin). GreenfR
          (13:1/2) Fall-Wint 85, p. 68.
       "The Ending, and What Comes." GreenfR (13:1/2) Fall-Wint
          85, p. 69.
       "Tunnel Mountain Campground" (Banff, Alberta, August 12,
          1984 -- for Ted). GreenfR (13:1/2) Fall-Wint 85, p. 71.
5311. WILSON, Michael
       "Still Life." PoetryCR (6:4) Sum 85, p. 44.
5312. WILSON, Miles
       "Nights in Crosley." NoDaQ (53:4) Fall 85, p. 235.
5313. WILSON, Ralph
       "The Garden of Eden." Geor (39:2) Sum 85, p. 367-369.
       "The Nightmare." QW (20) Spr-Sum 85, p. 81.
5314. WILSON, Rob (See also WILSON, Robert N.)
       "As the Day." HawaiiR (17) Spr 85, p. 91.
5315. WILSON, Robert N. (See also WILSON, Rob)
       "Death Dancing." LaurelR (19:1) Wint 85, p. 70.
5316. WILSON, Steve
       "At the Well of Sacrifices" (Kukulcan, the Rain God).
          StoneC (13:1/2) Fall-Wint 85-86, p. 36.
       "Mandala." WebR (10:2) Fall 85, p. 63.
       "Sunday Night at the Turkey Hotel." WebR (10:2) Fall 85,
          p. 62.
       "What in This Life Is Hardest to Accept." WebR (10:2)
          Fall 85, p. 61.
5317. WILSON, Ted
       "Take It Again" (this time from the top). Callaloo (8:1,
          issue 23) Wint 85, p. 257-259.
5318. WIMP, Jet
       "The Ultimate Resolution of Pi." BelPoJ (35:4) Sum 85, p.
          8-9.
5319. WINANS, A. D.
       "Bad Luck Gambler." KanQ (17:4) Fall 85, p. 65.
       "Class Reunion." PaintedB (26/27) Sum-Fall 85, p. 9-10.
       "For James Evans." PaintedB (26/27) Sum-Fall 85, p. 11.
       "For Joanie Whitebird." SecC (12:2) 84?, p. 9.
       "Graveyard Shift." Bogg (53) 85, p. 46.
       "Politics." SecC (12:1) 84, p. 31.
       "The Reagan Psalms" (San Francisco: Integrity Times Press).
          Distributed as SecC (13:1?) 84, 89 p.
       "An ulcer" ("Untitled"). KanQ (17:4) Fall 85, p. 66.
WINCKEL, Nance van
       See Van WINCKEL, Nance
5320. WINFIELD, William
       "Days of Glass." IndR (8:3) Fall 85, p. 90-91.
       "Immortality." HolCrit (22:3) Je 85, p. 17.
       "The Lesson." Pig (13) 85, p. 36.
       "The Lover." KanQ (17:1/2) Wint-Spr 85, p. 54.
       "Tracks in January." Pig (13) 85, p. 47.
       "Yours." Abraxas (33) 85, p. 14.
WING, Tek Lum
       See LUM, Wing Tek
5321. WINKLER, Kristin
       "Ornament." LittleM (14:4) 85, p. 46.
       "Song of the Fishwife." LittleM (14:4) 85, p. 47-48.
5322. WINN, Howard
       "Kent State." Vis (19) 85, p. 34.
       "Mystery." KanQ (17:4) Fall 85, p. 96.
       "Prayer." KanQ (17:4) Fall 85, p. 96.
5323. WINNER, Robert
       "Home." Ploughs (11:1) 85, p. 219-220.
       "Home Early." Ploughs (11:1) 85, p. 218.

"Still Life." Ploughs (11:1) 85, p. 221.
"Thanksgiving Day, 1983" (On the decision to deploy
    Pershing II Missiles in Europe). Ploughs (11:1) 85, p.
    222.
5324. WINTERS, Anne
    "The Billboard Man." Thrpny (6:3, issue 23) Fall 85, p.
    13.
5325. WINTERS, Kirk
    "Another Poet-Runner." WindO (46) Fall 85, p. 32.
    "Dream." WindO (46) Fall 85, p. 31.
    "The Machine and the Rose." WindO (46) Fall 85, p. 31.
    "What Mother Said." Vis (19) 85, p. 28.
5326. WINWOOD, David
    "Girl." BlueBldgs (9) [85?], p. 10.
5327. WISEMAN, Christopher
    "Abundances" (for J.C.). Dandel (12:1) 85, p. 6-7.
    "The Other Face." Dandel (12:1) 85, p. 5.
    "Scarborough Again." Dandel (12:1) 85, p. 8.
    "Task Force." Dandel (12:1) 85, p. 9.
5328. WITKOSKI, Michael
    "The Map of Charleston: Memory." CapeR (20:2) Fall 85, p.
    28.
5329. WITT, Harold
    "American Lit.: O e. e." HiramPoR (38) Spr-Sum 85, p. 34.
    "American Lit.: 'Our Town' on the Barge." HiramPoR (38)
        Spr-Sum 85, p. 33.
    "Aunt Tisnelda Sees 'On Golden Pond'." WormR (25:3, issue
        99) 85, p. 86.
    "Ballade of the Bodybuilders." WindO (46) Fall 85, p. 28.
    "Effie." Thrpny (6:1, issue 21) Spr 85, p. 25.
    "Exercycling to Beethoven." NegC (5:1) Wint 85, p. 53-54.
    "The Happy Journey." Amelia (2:2) O 85, p. 73.
    "Len Sylvester, S. & L. Clerk." WebR (10:2) Fall 85, p.
        74.
    "Mighty Wheeler: Used Car Dealer." WormR (25:3, issue 99)
        85, p. 86-87.
    "Miss Orange County." Bogg (54) 85, p. 42.
    "Mobile." WebR (10:2) Fall 85, p. 75.
    "Mrs. Asquith Takes Up Jogging." WindO (46) Fall 85, p.
        27.
    "Mrs. Asquith's Faith Is Restored by the Afterschool
        Special." LaurelR (19:2) Sum 85, p. 31.
    "Paul's Case." Amelia (2:2) O 85, p. 73.
    "The Runner." WindO (46) Fall 85, p. 27-28.
    "Some Rattlers." PoetryR (5) S 85, p. 69.
    "Watching Wasps." PoetryR (5) S 85, p. 70.
5330. WITTE, George
    "The Country of Perfect Weekends." Atlantic (256:5), N
        85, p. 112.
5331. WITTER, Alice
    "The Mad Woman." AntigR (61) Spr 85, p. 56.
    "Mowing." AntigR (61) Spr 85, p. 56.
5332. WITTLINGER, Ellen
    "Blue Murder." Tendril (19/20) 85, p. 391-392.
5333. WOESSNER, Warren
    "Grand Marais." PraS (59:4) Wint 85, p. 68.
    "Jungle Music." Pig (13) 85, p. 23.
    "Lessons." GreenfR (13:1/2) Fall-Wint 85, p. 28-29.
    "Storm Lines." GreenfR (13:1/2) Fall-Wint 85, p. 29.
5334. WOESTER, Janice
    "Millie's Auto Wreckers, Slab Fork, West Virginia."
        ThRiPo (25/26) 85, p. 62.
5335. WOHLFELD, Valerie
    "The Pharoah's Bones" (For Edwin Arthur Lowry, 1924-1944,
        drowned while serving in the Navy). Nimrod (29:1) Fall-
        Wint 85, p. 17-19.

5336. WOHMANN, Gabriele
        "Everything Went Quite Well Again" (tr. by Allen H.
        Chappel). NewOR (12:1) Spr 85, p. 90-91.
5337. WOJACZEK, Rafal
        "The Cross" (from Unfinished Crusade, The Voice of an
        Unknown Woman Poet, tr. by Danuta Lopozyko and Peter
        Harris). Chelsea (44) 85, p. 116.
5338. WOJAHN, David
        "250 Bradford." GeoR (39:3) Fall 85, p. 572-573.
        "A Game of Croquet" (After Eakins). GrandS (4:3) Spr 85,
        p. 169-170.
5339. WOLCOTT, Jamie
        "Under the Maple." Nimrod (29:1) Fall-Wint 85, p. 52-56.
5340. WOLFERT, Adrienne
        "Seasons." Confr (30/31) N 85, p. 251.
5341. WOLFF, Daniel
        "How Old Men Get Old." YellowS (17) Wint 85, p. 9.
5342. WOLFKILL, R. T. (See also WOLFKILL, Robert)
        "Blue: (Poem)." Bogg (53) 85, p. 6.
5343. WOLFKILL, Robert (See also WOLFKILL, R. T.)
        "Dreams of Wheels and Lights." Amelia (2:2) O 85, p. 41.
        "This Kimono." Amelia (2:2) O 85, p. 41.
5344. WONDOLOWSKI, Rupert
        "Testify." Open24 (4) 85, p. 55.
5345. WONDRA, Janet
        "Testing: By the Knife" (From a sequence, Darwin Said).
        MichQR (24:2) Spr 85, p. 265-266.
5346. WONG, Nellie
        "Pillow Talk." OP (38/39) Spr 85, p. 84-85.
5347. WOOD, Bill
        "Wet Grass." BlueBldgs (9) [85?], p. 8.
5348. WOOD, Clem
        "For James Jones." Confr (30/31) N 85, p. 30-31.
5349. WOOD, Peter
        "Clutching at a Lollipop Stick." USl (18/19) Wint 85, p.
        2.
5350. WOOD, Silviana
        "El Chubasco." Imagine (1:2) Wint 84, p. 144.
        "Like a Thief." Imagine (1:2) Wint 84, p. 145.
        "Sweet Revenge." Imagine (1:2) Wint 84, p. 146-147.
5351. WOODRUFF, William
        "North Carolina, 1955." PoeticJ (9) 85, p. 12-13.
5352. WOODS, Phil
        "The Little Tramp Goes to Spain." NewL (52:1) Fall 85, p.
        102-103.
5353. WOODS-SMITH, Sybil
        "Mississippi and the Three Banes." PoetryR (5) S 85, p.
        71.
        "The Nightmare Deer." SouthernPR (25:1) Spr 85, p. 28-29.
5354. WORLEY, James
        "Masochist." ChrC (102:21) 19-25 Je 85, p. 605.
5355. WORLEY, Jeff
        "The Death of Chang Eng." PoetryCR (6:3) Spr 85, p. 33.
        "Worley Meeting Zimmer under the Neon of an MLA
        Convention." PoetL (80:3) Fall 85, p. 163-164.
5356. WORMSER, Baron
        "An Advent of Paganism." Poetry (146:5) Ag 85, p. 267.
        "Fans." NewEngR (7:3) Spr 85, p. 342-343.
        "Getting Ready." SewanR (93:1) Wint 85, p. 77.
        "In a Cab." Poetry (146:5) Ag 85, p. 269-270.
        "Lament upon the Closing of the Northern Conservatory in
        Bangor, Maine." Poetry (146:5) Ag 85, p. 268-269.
        "Married Sex." Poetry (146:5) Ag 85, p. 268.
        "Mencken." SewanR (93:1) Wint 85, p. 76-77.
        "The Single Urge." NewEngR (7:3) Spr 85, p. 342.
        "Well-Being." PartR (52:4) 85, p. 430-431.

5357. WOROSZYLSKI, Wiktor
"The Belly of Barbara N." (tr. by Boguslaw Rostworowski).
TriQ (63) Spr-Sum 85, p. 565.
5358. WOROZBYT, Theodore (See also WOROZBYT, Theodore, Jr.)
"Birthday." BlackWR (12:1) Fall 85, p. 57-58.
5359. WOROZBYT, Theodore, Jr. (See also WOROZBYT, Theodore)
"Another Chest." HiramPoR (39) Fall-Wint 85, p. 22-23.
"The Kiss." HiramPoR (39) Fall-Wint 85, p. 24.
5360. WORTH, Douglas
"April 25" (From the book, Once Around Bullough's Pond).
PoeticJ (10) 85, p. 24.
"Ascent." Vis (19) 85, p. 12-13.
5361. WRAY, Bettye K.
"Grandpa Lane." NegC (5:3) Sum 85, p. 131-133.
5362. WRIGHT, C. D. (See also WRIGHT, Carolyne & Charles)
"The Cinematographers Faro Island Log." ThRiPo (25/26)
85, p. 64.
"Glowworm." Raccoon (17) Mr 85, p. 32.
"Handfasting." ThRiPo (25/26) 85, p. 65.
"Hotels." ThRiPo (25/26) 85, p. 65.
"Kahlo." Imagine (2:1) Sum 85, p. 114.
"The Legend of Hell" (homage to Barbara McClintock).
Raccoon (17) Mr 85, p. 17-18.
"This Couple." NewYorker (61:42) 9 D 85, p. 48.
"Vestigal Love Poem." ThRiPo (25/26) 85, p. 63.
5363. WRIGHT, Carolyne (See also WRIGHT, C. D. & Charles)
"After We Received the News of the 100-Mile Wind" (Cheyenne
to Laramie, Wyoming). GreenfR (13:1/2) Fall-Wint 85,
p. 41.
"End of the World" (tr. of Jorge Teillier). GrahamHR (9)
Fall 85, p. 37.
"Eugenia." Tendril (19/20) 85, p. 393-395.
"Eulene Enters the Me Generation." PoetryNW (26:3) Aut
85, p. 41-42.
"In Order to Talk to the Dead" (tr. of Jorge Teillier).
BlackWR (12:1) Fall 85, p. 79.
"The Last Island" (tr. of Jorge Teillier). BlackWR (12:1)
Fall 85, p. 81.
"The Last Island" (tr. of Jorge Teillier). GrahamHR (9)
Fall 85, p. 36.
"Logos of the Sentimentalist." Poetry (145:4) Ja 85, p.
220-221.
"Narratives" (tr. of Jorge Teillier). GrahamHR (9) Fall
85, p. 33-34.
"Post-Revolutionary Letter." GreenfR (13:1/2) Fall-Wint
85, p. 42-43.
"Secret Autumn" (tr. of Jorge Teillier). BlackWR (12:1)
Fall 85, p. 75, 77.
"Secret Autumn" (tr. of Jorge Teillier). GrahamHR (9)
Fall 85, p. 31.
"The Ship in the Bottle." Poetry (145:4) Ja 85, p. 222-
223.
"Signals" (tr. of Jorge Teillier). BlackWR (12:1) Fall
85, p. 83.
"So Long" (tr. of Jorge Teillier). BlackWR (12:1) Fall
85, p. 85, 87.
"The Stroke Victim." GreenfR (13:1/2) Fall-Wint 85, p. 40.
"Talking Politics" (Ouro Preto, Brasil: February 1972."
Tendril (19/20) 85, p. 396-399.
"Tango Lyric" (tr. of Jorge Teillier). GrahamHR (9) Fall
85, p. 32.
"To a Child in a Tree" (tr. of Jorge Teillier). GrahamHR
(9) Fall 85, p. 35.
"Wooden Mill" (tr. of Jorge Teillier). GrahamHR (9) Fall
85, p. 30.

5364. WRIGHT, Charles (See also WRIGHT, C. D. & Carolyne)
      "A Journal of True Confessions." ParisR (27:97) Fall 85,
         p. 72-80.
      "A Journal of True Confessions" (Selections: 25 August
         1984, 9 September 1984). Verse (3) 85, p. 14-15.
      "Mantova." Pequod (19/20/21) 85, p. 355.
      "Streams." Pequod (19/20/21) 85, p. 353-354.
      "Yard Journal." NewYorker (61:35) 21 O 85, p. 44-45.
5365. WRIGHT, Franz
      "Audience." Ploughs (11:1) 85, p. 225.
      "Rooms I (I will not say worked in) once heard in"
         ("Untitled). Ploughs (11:1) 85, p. 226.
      "The Street." Ploughs (11:1) 85, p. 223.
      "There." Ploughs (11:1) 85, p. 224. Errata in Ploughs
         (11:4) 85, p. 268.
      "Waiting Up." Crazy (26) Spr 84, p. 28.
      "Winter: Twilight & Dawn." Crazy (26) Spr 84, p. 27.
5366. WRIGHT, Jeff (See also WRIGHT, Jeffrey C.)
      "Paint the Horses and Ride." Open24 (4) 85, p. 40.
      "Rush" (for John Godfrey). Open24 (4) 85, p. 14.
5367. WRIGHT, Jeffrey C. (See also WRIGHT, Jeff)
      "Homeward." Poem (53) Mr 85, p. 42-44.
5368. WRIGLEY, Robert
      "Pheasant Hunting" (for Hugh Nichols). NewEngR (8:2) Wint
         85, p. 180.
      "A Photo of Immigrants, 1903." CrabCR (2:3) Sum 85, p. 18.
      "The Skull of a Snowshoe Hare." CharR (11:2) Fall 85, p.
         71.
      "Stardust." NewEngR (8:2) Wint 85, p. 181.
      "Torch Songs." GeoR (39:1) Spr 85, p. 66.
5369. WRONSKY, Gail
      "Ceci N'Est Pas un Morç eau de Fromage." Calyx (9:1)
         Spr-Sum 85, p. 51.
      "Longings, Salt Lake City." Calyx (9:1) Spr-Sum 85, p. 50.
      "Weird Beach." QW (21) Fall-Wint 85, p. 46.
5370. WUEST, Barbara
      "Mass." ParisR (27:95) Spr 85, p. 160-167.
5371. WULF, Frida
      "Hypotheticals." Imagine (2:1) Sum 85, p. 68.
      "Losses." Imagine (2:1) Sum 85, p. 67-68.
5372. WYATT, Bill
      "In Winter." Sam (42:3, 167th release) 85, p. 17.
5373. WYATT, David
      "Omaha" (for P.W.G.). ColEng (47:4) Ap 85, p. 373-374.
5374. WYGAL, Jane
      "Fowl in Winter." SouthernPR (25:1) Spr 85, p. 50-51.
5375. WYNAND, Derk
      "Heat Wave." Grain (13:4) N 85, p. 49.
      "Heat Waves." Descant 49 (16:2) Sum 85, p. 7-8.
WYNNE, Diane Carmody
      See CARMODY-WYNNE, Diane
5376. WYNNE-JONES, Tim
      "Holes." Quarry (34:1) Wint 85, p. 11.
5377. WYTTENBERG, Victoria
      "The Abandoned Wife." PoetryNW (26:4) Wint 85-86, p. 18-19.
      "The Boy with Two Frogs." PoetryNW (26:4) Wint 85-86, p.
         17-18.
      "St. Joseph Hospital: Fourth Floor." PoetryNW (26:4) Wint
         85-86, p. 17.
      "To My Son on His Twentieth Birthday." PoetryNW (26:4)
         Wint 85-86, p. 16.
5378. YALIM, Ozcan
      "At the Beach" (tr. of Kemal Ozer, w. W. Fielder and Dionis
         Riggs). NewL (51:4) Sum 85, p. 14.
      "In Clouded Water" (tr. of Oktay Rifat, w. William Fielder
         and Dionis Coffin Riggs). StoneC (13:1/2) Fall-Wint 85-

86, p. 44-45.
"Night and Night" (tr. of Ismail Uyaroglu, w. W. Fielder
    and Dionis Riggs). NewL (51:4) Sum 85, p. 14.
"To My Wife" (tr. by O. Yalim, W. Fielder and Dionis
    Riggs). NewL (51:4) Sum 85, p. 15.
5379. YALKUT, Carolyn
    "The Literate Listener." WebR (10:1) Spr 85, p. 79.
    "The Literature of Baseball." WebR (10:1) Spr 85, p. 77-
        78.
YAMPERT, Rick de
    See De YAMPERT, Rick
5380. YAMRUS, John
    "I Did a Poem Tonight." Bogg (54) 85, p. 28-29.
    "My Shirts Don't Fit." Bogg (53) 85, p. 33.
YARJANIAN, Adom
    See Siamanto
5381. YARROW, Bill
    "Life with Fish." LitR (28:4) Sum 85, p. 583.
5382. YARROW, Susan
    "Conception." Grain (13:2) My 85, p. 11.
    "Early Spring." Grain (13:2) My 85, p. 10.
5383. YATES, J. Michael
    "Poem: It must speak of things." CrossCur (4:3) 84, p. 84.
    "Reversal." CrossCur (4:3) 84, p. 83.
5384. YATES, Robin D. S.
    "Composed by the Ferry at Night over the Chien-ch'ang
        River" (tr. of Wei Chuang). Ploughs (11:4) 85, p. 200.
    "Mourning at the Strings of My Concubine, Miss Yang's
        Zither" (tr. of Wei Chuang). Ploughs (11:4) 85, p. 202.
    "Night Thoughts at Chang Terrace" (tr. of Wei Chuang).
        Ploughs (11:4) 85, p. 198.
    "Plucking Out White Hairs" (tr. of Wei Chuang). Ploughs
        (11:4) 85, p. 200.
    "Recording Events" (tr. of Wei Chuang). Ploughs (11:4)
        85, p. 203.
    "Recording Events in the Village Where I Live" (tr. of Wei
        Chuang). Ploughs (11:4) 85, p. 199.
    "Refusing Wine, I Leave My Mat" (tr. of Wei Chuang).
        Ploughs (11:4) 85, p. 199.
    "Remembering My Daughter Silver Maid (Ah Yin)" (tr. of Wei
        Chuang). Ploughs (11:4) 85, p. 201.
    "Tune: Echoing Heaven's Everlastingness. No. 1" (tr. of Wei
        Chuang). Ploughs (11:4) 85, p. 202.
    "Tune: Raise the Cup. No. 1" (tr. of Wei Chuang). Ploughs
        (11:4) 85, p. 203.
    "Tune: Raise the Cup. No. 2" (tr. of Wei Chuang). Ploughs
        (11:4) 85, p. 204.
    "Tune: Song of an Immortal. No. 2" (tr. of Wei Chuang).
        Ploughs (11:4) 85, p. 204.
    "Tune: Song of Waterclock at Night" (tr. of Wei Chuang).
        Ploughs (11:4) 85, p. 205.
    "Withering" (tr. of Wei Chuang). Ploughs (11:4) 85, p.
        201.
5385. YAU, John
    "Je Sublime" (Selections: 4 poems -- "The Square of the
        Hypotenuse," "I," "A H," "Nebula," tr. of Benjamin
        Peret, w. Rachel Stella). Sulfur (13) 85, p. 76-79.
    "Words from & for Basil Bunting." Conjunc (8) 85, p. 221-
        222.
YEE SALLEE, Hyun-jae
    See Sallee, Hyun-jae Yee
5386. YENSER, Jon Kelly
    "Death Mars Wedding Party." MassR (26:1) Spr 85, p. 31.
    "Prayer." MassR (26:1) Spr 85, p. 31-32.
    "Short Story" (for Murray Moulding). MassR (26:1) Spr 85,
        p. 30-31.

5387. YEO, Wilma
      "Yugen." <u>Amelia</u> (2:2) O 85, p. 44.
5388. YI, Kyu-bo
      "Tiger" (tr. by Graeme Wilson). <u>WestHR</u> (39:1) Spr 85, p.
         63.
5389. YOO, Ahn-Jinn
      "Reed Flowers" (In Korean). <u>AntigR</u> (62/63) Sum-Aut 85, p.
         78.
      "Reed Flowers" (tr. by Hyun-jae Yee Sallee). <u>AntigR</u>
         (62/63) Sum-Aut 85, p. 78.
5390. YOO, Ok Hee
      "Moo Goong Hwa (Rose of Sharon)" (tr. by M. G. Stephens).
         <u>NewL</u> (51:4) Sum 85, p. 139.
5391. YOSHIDA, Junko
      "A Day Dream" (tr. of Massao Nonagase). <u>HiramPoR</u> (39)
         Fall-Wint 85, p. 17.
      "Old Age Blues in the Sunset" (Selections: 3 poems, tr. of
         Massao Nonagase). <u>HiramPoR</u> (39) Fall-Wint 85, p. 16-18.
      "An Old Man's Amorous Monologue" (tr. of Massao Nonagase).
         <u>HiramPoR</u> (39) Fall-Wint 85, p. 16.
      "To You, My Gentle One" (tr. of Massao Nonagase).
         <u>HiramPoR</u> (39) Fall-Wint 85, p. 18.
5392. YOSHIHARA, Sachiko
      "Drunk" (tr. by Cheiron McMahill). <u>Mund</u> (16:1/2) 85, p.
         71.
      "Woman" (tr. by Cheiron McMahill). <u>Mund</u> (16:1/2) 85, p.
         69-70.
5393. YOSHIKAWA, Tsuneko
      "Glass Country" (in Japanese and English, tr. by Steven
         Forth). <u>Waves</u> (13:2/3) Wint 85, p. 84-85.
      "If You" (tr. by Steven Forth). <u>AmerPoR</u> (14:4) Jl-Ag 85,
         p. 10.
      "Long Summer" (in Japanese and English, tr. by Steven
         Forth). <u>Waves</u> (13:2/3) Wint 85, p. 85-86.
5394. YOSHIOKA, Minoru
      "Kusudama" (5 selections, tr. by Eric Selland). <u>Temblor</u>
         (2) 85, p. 60-67.
5395. YOUMANS, Marlene
      "The Arabic Lesson" (For Amal). <u>CarolQ</u> (37:2) Wint 85, p.
         31.
      "Children of Summer." <u>Blueline</u> (7:1) Sum-Fall 85, p. 22-
         23.
      "The Gourd Tepee" (Fincastle, Virginia). <u>LaurelR</u> (19:2)
         Sum 85, p. 70-71.
      "Lepidopteran." <u>CarolQ</u> (37:2) Wint 85, p. 30.
      "Lethargy at Otter Lake." <u>LittleM</u> (14:4) 85, p. 52.
      "Letters from Elsewhere." <u>LittleM</u> (14:4) 85, p. 50-51.
      "Rite: Six for the Fears." <u>Blueline</u> (7:1) Sum-Fall 85, p.
         34.
      "Snow House Stories." <u>CarolQ</u> (38:1) Fall 85, p. 22.
5396. YOUNG, Al
      "Sweet Sixteen Lines." <u>TriQ</u> (63) Spr-Sum 85, p. 602.
      "What Is the Blues." <u>PoetryR</u> (2:2) Ap 85, p. 15.
5397. YOUNG, Anne
      "Drowning." <u>Calyx</u> (9:1) Spr-Sum 85, p. 16.
5398. YOUNG, David
      "Skeletons" (tr. of Miroslav Holub, w. the author).
         <u>Ploughs</u> (11:4) 85, p. 85-86.
      "Spacetime" (tr. of Miroslav Holub, w. the author).
         <u>Ploughs</u> (11:4) 85, p. 87.
      "Suite for Jean Follain." <u>Iowa</u> (15:1) Wint 85, p. 96-97.
5399. YOUNG, Dean
      "Painting the House." <u>OhioR</u> (35) 85, p. 69.
      "A Pure Room." <u>KanQ</u> (17:1/2) Wint-Spr 85, p. 70.
      "Thank You, Teachers." <u>Crazy</u> (29) Fall 85, p. 69-70.
      "That Way Things Come, and Go." <u>KanQ</u> (17:1/2) Wint-Spr

85, p. 69.
"Threshold." <u>Crazy</u> (29) Fall 85, p. 67-68.
"Twice First Light." <u>Telescope</u> (4:1) Wint 85, p. 14-15.
5400. YOUNG, Geoffrey
"Elegy." <u>Sulfur</u> (12) 85, p. 36-41.
"Rocks and Deals." <u>Oink</u> (19) 85, p. 89-92.
5401. YOUNG, Jim
"Dawn." <u>NegC</u> (5:1) Wint 85, p. 31.
"The Pond." <u>Wind</u> (15:55) 85, p. 53.
"Shadows." <u>StoneC</u> (13:1/2) Fall-Wint 85-86, p. 63.
"The Stray." <u>Wind</u> (15:55) 85, p. 53.
5402. YOUNG, Merlene
"Smoke Signals." <u>SecC</u> (12:1) 84, p. 28.
5403. YOUNG, Patricia
"Beginning of Me." <u>PoetryCR</u> (7:2) Wint 85-86, p. 40.
"He Left Me." <u>PoetryCR</u> (7:2) Wint 85-86, p. 40.
"Jenny and the Beast." <u>Descant</u> 48 (16:1) Spr 85, p. 24.
"Sin-Eater." <u>Waves</u> (14:1/2) Fall 85, p. 66-67.
"Tin Suitcase." <u>Waves</u> (14:1/2) Fall 85, p. 67.
5404. YOUNG, Ree
"Gaydelle Turns Fifteen." <u>LaurelR</u> (19:1) Wint 85, p. 72-
73.
5405. YOUNG, Reggie
"Love Veins." <u>SpoonRQ</u> (10:4) Fall 85, p. 49.
5406. YOUNG, Tom
"Marshall." <u>JamesWR</u> (2:1) Fall 84, p. 15.
"Visit Me." <u>JamesWR</u> (2:3) Spr-Sum 85, p. 7.
5407. YOUNG BEAR, Ray A.
"Emily Dickinson, Bismarck, and the Roadrunner's Inquiry."
<u>NoDaQ</u> (53:2) Spr 85, p. 24-27.
5408. YOURIL, John A.
"Hieroglyph 35." <u>StoneC</u> (13:1/2) Fall-Wint 85-86, p. 64.
5409. YOVU, Peter
"First Death." <u>Ploughs</u> (11:1) 85, p. 229.
"Negative." <u>Ploughs</u> (11:1) 85, p. 227.
"Site." <u>Ploughs</u> (11:1) 85, p. 230.
"South Beach." <u>Ploughs</u> (11:1) 85, p. 231-232.
"Wind and Rain." <u>Ploughs</u> (11:1) 85, p. 228.
YU, Ren
See Ren, Yu
5410. YUND, Ted
"The Boredom Line." <u>NegC</u> (5:1) Wint 85, p. 59-60.
"Peeking True" (A Warrior's Fan Again). <u>NegC</u> (5:2) Spr
85, p. 100-102.
"When I Wish Someone Back to Take Me Fishing." <u>NegC</u> (5:2)
Spr 85, p. 98-99.
5411. YUP, Paula
"The Music." <u>BlueBldgs</u> (9) [85?], p. 60.
"That Time Again." <u>PassN</u> (6:1) Fall-Wint 85, p. 16.
5412. YURKIEVICH, Saúl
"Edifice Dedicated to Silence" (tr. by Cola Franzen).
<u>Sulfur</u> (14) 85, p. 107-109.
"I Myself" (tr. by Cola Franzen). <u>Sulfur</u> (14) 85, p. 106.
"Ratifica." <u>Temblor</u> (1) 85, p. 114.
"Ratifies" (tr. by Cola Franzen). <u>Temblor</u> (1) 85, p. 115.
"Reverieriver" (tr. by Cola Franzen). <u>Temblor</u> (1) 85, p.
115.
"Rolling Stones" (tr. by Cola Franzen). <u>Temblor</u> (1) 85,
p. 116.
"Sentence" (tr. by Cola Franzen). <u>Sulfur</u> (14) 85, p. 106-
107.
"Story" (tr. by Cola Franzen). <u>Temblor</u> (1) 85, p. 116.
"Sueñocieno." <u>Temblor</u> (1) 85, p. 114.
"They force me to play" (tr. by Cola Franzen). <u>Sulfur</u>
(14) 85, p. 106.
"Tumbles and Rumbles" (tr. by Cola Franzen). <u>Temblor</u> (1)

85, p. 116.
5413. ZABELSKIS, Peter
"Inscription on an Old Wall." Sam (42:3, 167th release)
85, p. 47.
5414. ZABLE, Jeffrey
"Incident at the Supermarket." Open24 (4) 85, p. 46.
5415. ZACHARIN, Noah
"Canadoze" (By Noah Zacharin, alias Nelson Sacrebutt).
Rampike (4:2/3) 85-86, p. 106.
5416. ZAGAJEWSKI, Adam
"Franz Schubert: A Press Conference" (tr. by Renata
Gorczynski). Thrpny (6:2, issue 22) Sum 85, p. 25.
"In the Encyclopedias, No Room for Osip Mandelstam" (tr. by
Renata Gorczynski). NewYRB (32:16) 24 O 85, p. 34.
"Kierkegaard on Hegel" (tr. by Renata Gorczynski). NewYRB
(32:16) 24 O 85, p. 34.
"My Masters" (tr. by Renata Gorczynski). NewYRB (32:16)
24 O 85, p. 34.
5417. ZAHN, Curtis
"Gloucester / You / Malibu." YellowS (15) Sum 85, p. 31.
"Wanda" (#5). YellowS (15) Sum 85, p. 30-31.
5418. ZAKOSEK, Chris
"After First Grade." HangL (48) Fall 85, p. 69.
5419. ZALUSKI, John
"Postcard from San Francisco." JamesWR (3:1) Fall 85, p.
5.
5420. ZAMORA, Daisy
"Commander Two" (tr. by Sesshu Foster). NewL (51:4) Sum
85, p. 95.
"Commander Two" (tr. by Sesshu Foster). Open24 (4) 85, p.
31.
5421. ZAMORA, Silvia Rosa
"De Martí, para Martí." Mester (14:1/2) Prim-Otoño
85, p. 74.
5422. ZANCANELLA, Don
"The University Bowling Alley and Lounge." CapeR (20:2)
Fall 85, p. 1.
5423. ZANZOTTO, Andrea
"Easter at Pieve di Soligo" (tr. by P. F. Paolini). LitR
(28:2) Wint 85, p. 320-322.
"Notifying One's Presence on the Euganean Hills" (tr. by P.
F. Paolini). LitR (28:2) Wint 85, p. 318.
"September 13, 1959" (a variant, tr. by P. F. Paolini).
LitR (28:2) Wint 85, p. 319.
"Skyey Navigation" (tr. by P. F. Paolini). LitR (28:2)
Wint 85, p. 318.
5424. ZAPATA, Miguel Angel
"Aquí en las Sierras Yo Me Levanto." LindLM (4:2) Ap-Je
85, p. 18.
5425. ZARANKA, William
"Diorama." Poetry (146:3) Je 85, p. 152.
"Twenty-Two Motels." Poetry (146:3) Je 85, p. 151.
5426. ZAREMBA, Donald
"Coming into the World." Pig (13) 85, p. 57.
5427. ZARIN, Cynthia
"Colophon." ParisR (27:98) Wint 85, p. 82-83.
5428. ZARZYSKI, Paul
"Pete Briskie's Creel." MidAR (5:1) 85, p. 1-2.
"Riding Double: 16 & Beating the Heat" (For James Dickey).
CutB (24) Spr-Sum 85, p. 43.
5429. ZAVATSKY, Bill
"Maps on the Dunes" (To Giuseppe Ungaretti, tr. of André
Breton, w. Zack Rogow). Antaeus (55) Aut 85, p. 90.
"The Reptile Houseburglars" (To Janine, tr. of André
Breton, w. Zack Rogow). Antaeus (55) Aut 85, p. 88-89.
"Shrivelled Love" (tr. of André Breton, w. Zack Rogow).

Antaeus (55) Aut 85, p. 90.
"The Verb to Be" (tr. of André Breton, w. Zack Rogow).
    ParisR (27:95) Spr 85, p. 131-132.
"Earthlight" (Selections: 15 poems, tr. of André Breton,
    w. Zack Rogow). AmerPoR (14:1) Ja-F 85, p. 3-10.
5430. ZAVRIAN, Suzanne
"The Book of Daniel." OP (38/39) Spr 85, p. 49-50.
5431. ZAWADIWSKY, Christine
"All Smoke Will Rise." LittleM (14:4) 85, p. 43.
"Breaking Chains." BlueBldgs (9) [85?], p. 58.
5432. ZAZUYER, Leah
"Walking Rosey Hill Road." Blueline (6:2) Wint-Spr 85, p.
    5.
5433. ZEGERS, Kip
"Ceilings." HangL (47) Spr 85, p. 50-51.
5434. ZEIGER, David
"Early Morning." Confr (30/31) N 85, p. 143.
5435. ZEIGER, L. L.
"The Fish Cellar." Confr (30/31) N 85, p. 114.
"Northern State." Confr (30/31) N 85, p. 37.
"Refusal." GreenfR (13:1/2) Fall-Wint 85, p. 183.
5436. ZEIS, Gabriel, T.O.R.
"I Can See the Angel Dancing." ChrC (102:23) 17-24 Jl 85,
    p. 676.
5437. ZEKOWSKI, Arlene
"En Route to Auron Winter Ski Station" (Part of a Neo-
    Narrative trilogy, selections: "More of But Not the
    Same," "The Eternal City"). SoDakR (23:1) Spr 85, p.
    99-106.
5438. ZELCER, Brook
"The Women of 1997." SanFPJ (7:2) 85, p. 87.
5439. ZEND, Robert
"Two Letters." Rampike (4:2/3) 85-86, p. 5.
5440. ZENITH, Richard
"The Art of Starving." GeoR (39:3) Fall 85, p. 507.
"The Fashion Designer." GeoR (39:3) Fall 85, p. 506.
"Groundwork." GeoR (39:3) Fall 85, p. 505.
5441. ZEPEDA-HENRIQUEZ, Eduardo
"Mis Estaciones en la Naturaleza." LindLM (4:1) Ja-Mr 85,
    p. 9.
5442. ZERFAS, Jan
"Directions for Bathing a Man" (Eve of Saint Agnes Contest
    Winner). NegC (5:1) Wint 85, p. 12.
"Liquid Face." NegC (5:1) Wint 85, p. 36.
5443. ZETTLEMOYER, Ron
"A Day Late, and a Dollar Short." SanFPJ (7:3) 84 [i.e.
    85], p. 94.
"Good Morning." SanFPJ (7:4) 85, p. 92.
"Has There Really Been Enough Written of Vietnam? SanFPJ
    (7:3) 84 [i.e. 85], p. 95.
5444. ZHANG, Ting-chen
"From the Southern to the Northern Peak by Way of the Lake:
    Stopping to View the Scenery" (tr. of Hsieh Ling-Yün,
    w. Bruce M. Wilson). NewL (51:4) Sum 85, p. 143.
"Scaling the Height of Stone Gate Mountain" (tr. of Hsieh
    Ling-Yün, w. Bruce M. Wilson). NewL (51:4) Sum 85,
    p. 141.
"A Solitary Islet, Alone in the Stream" (tr. of Hsieh Ling-
    Yün, w. Bruce M. Wilson). NewL (51:4) Sum 85, p. 142.
"Spending the Night on the Cliff at Stone Gate Mountain"
    (tr. of Hsieh Ling-Yün, w. Bruce M. Wilson). NewL
    (51:4) Sum 85, p. 142.
5445. ZHAO, Y. H.
"The Singing Flower" (tr. of Shu Ting, w. Carolyn Kizer).
    PoetryE (18) Fall 85, p. 72-78.

5446. ZIATAS, Christos
        "Under the Heavybranched Tree of Old Age" (tr. by Stavros
          Tsimicalis). <u>Waves</u> (13:4) Spr 85, p. 99.
5447. ZIBENS, Mara
        "Memo from Minoa" (with Richard Truhlar). <u>Rampike</u> (4:2/3)
          85-86, p. 48-49.
5448. ZIEDONIS, Imants
        "Greetings, death, you great sparkler!" (tr. by Lia Smits).
          <u>Os</u> (21) 85, p. 23.
        "Heavens, I've dropped my sun!" (tr. by Lia Smits). <u>Os</u>
          (21) 85, p. 25.
        "Milo debestin, man izbira saule." <u>Os</u> (21) 85, p. 24.
        "Sveika, nave, tu liela brinumsvecite!" <u>Os</u> (21) 85, p. 23.
5449. ZIEROTH, Dale
        "House in the Night." <u>CapilR</u> (34) 85, p. 33.
        "Last Night's Owl." <u>CapilR</u> (34) 85, p. 30.
        "This Side." <u>CapilR</u> (34) 85, p. 32.
        "What Is Given." <u>CapilR</u> (34) 85, p. 31.
5450. ZIMELE-KEITA, Nzadi
        "Poem for Maurice Bishop." <u>AmerPoR</u> (14:3) My-Je 85, p. 46.
5451. ZIMMER, Paul
        "The Poet's Strike." <u>OP</u> (38/39) Spr 85, p. 124.
        "Skywriters" (for Jodie Slothower). <u>GeoR</u> (39:3) Fall 85,
          p. 561.
        "Zimmer Closes His Family Home." <u>GeoR</u> (39:3) Fall 85, p.
          562.
5452. ZIMMERMAN, Robert N.
        "Beehive in the Woods." <u>PoeticJ</u> (10) 85, p. 6.
        "Early Dawn." <u>PoeticJ</u> (9) 85, p. 7.
        "Falling Snow Flakes." <u>PoeticJ</u> (11) 85, p. 33.
        "Streaming Sea Gulls." <u>PoeticJ</u> (10) 85, p. 7.
5453. ZIMMERMAN, Ruth
        "Reflecting." <u>PassN</u> (6:2) Spr-Sum 85, p. 18.
5454. ZINNES, Harriet
        "Free Pass" (tr. by Harriet Zinnes). <u>Oink</u> (19) 85, p. 44.
        "Signs" (tr. by Harriet Zinnes). <u>Oink</u> (19) 85, p. 44.
5455. ZIOLKOWSKI, Thad
        "Like an Open Letter in a Foreign Tongue." <u>LaurelR</u> (19:2)
          Sum 85, p. 59.
5456. ZIOLKOWSKI, Thaddeus
        "The North American Wrass." <u>Gargoyle</u> (27) 85, p. 98.
5457. ZISQUIT, Linda
        "A Beginning." <u>Paint</u> (11:21/12:24) 84-85, p. 23.
        "Betrayal" (from Summer at War). <u>Nimrod</u> (29:1) Fall-Wint
          85, p. 50.
        "The New Dress." <u>PoetL</u> (80:3) Fall 85, p. 145-146.
5458. ZITTAU, Herbert
        "Why Peking?" <u>NegC</u> (5:2) Spr 85, p. 28.
5459. ZIVANCEVIC, Nina
        "Action" (tr. of Snezana Minić). <u>AmerPoR</u> (14:3) My-Je
          85, p. 29.
        "After Coming Home" (tr. of Snezana Minić). <u>AmerPoR</u>
          (14:3) My-Je 85, p. 28.
        "Banovo Brdo*" (*a section of Belgrade, tr. of Miroslav
          Maksimović). <u>AmerPoR</u> (14:3) My-Je 85, p. 30.
        "The Cabin" (tr. of Novica Tadić). <u>AmerPoR</u> (14:3) My-Je
          85, p. 30.
        "Campaign" (tr. of Novica Tadić). <u>AmerPoR</u> (14:3) My-Je
          85, p. 30.
        "Clock" (tr. of Novica Tadić). <u>AmerPoR</u> (14:3) My-Je 85,
          p. 30.
        "Flooded into the Handbooks against My Wish" (tr. of
          Miroslav Maksimović). <u>AmerPoR</u> (14:3) My-Je 85, p. 30.
        "From Letter #57 Addressed to Lj.N." (tr. of Radmila
          Lazić). <u>AmerPoR</u> (14:3) My-Je 85, p. 29.
        "Indian Education" (tr. of Miroslav Maksimović).

AmerPoR (14:3) My-Je 85, p. 30.
"Joy" (tr. of Radmila Lazić). AmerPoR (14:3) My-Je 85,
    p. 29.
"Miraculous Tree" (tr. of Sinan Gudzević). AmerPoR
    (14:3) My-Je 85, p. 28.
"La Morte d'Arthur (or As You Like It)." LittleM (14:4)
    85, p. 22.
"Movies and Universities" (tr. of Miroslav Maksimović).
    AmerPoR (14:3) My-Je 85, p. 30.
"Piano" (tr. of Radmila Lazić). AmerPoR (14:3) My-Je
    85, p. 29.
"Raven Snow" (tr. of Novica Tadić). AmerPoR (14:3) My-
    Je 85, p. 30.
"Water Flower" (tr. of Snezana Minić). AmerPoR (14:3)
    My-Je 85, p. 28.
"When God Understands" (tr. of Sinan Gudzević). AmerPoR
    (14:3) My-Je 85, p. 28.
"When You Need to Clean and Cut Your Finger Nails" (tr. of
    Radmila Lazić). AmerPoR (14:3) My-Je 85, p. 29.
"Whorehouse" (tr. of Sinan Gudzević). AmerPoR (14:3) My-
    Je 85, p. 28.
5460. ZOLLER, Ann
    "The Privacy of Corn." Nimrod (28:2) Spr-Sum 85, p. 45-46.
5461. ZOLLER, James A.
    "The Evil Rose." GreenfR (13:1/2) Fall-Wint 85, p. 154-
    155.
    "This, This." Blueline (6:2) Wint-Spr 85, p. 13.
5462. ZONAILO, Carolyn
    "The Geese." PoetryCR (6:4) Sum 85, p. 23.
    "The Red Alabaster Heart." Waves (14:1/2) Fall 85, p. 98.
    "White Cat, Sunday Morning." PoetryCR (6:4) Sum 85, p. 23.
5463. ZOOK, Amy Jo
    "Neither Delighteth He in Any Man's Legs." WindO (46)
    Fall 85, p. 15.
    "To a Jogger on I - 44." WindO (46) Fall 85, p. 15.
5464. ZUCKER, David
    "Encountering Henry Moore's Nudes in Public Places."
    GrahamHR (9) Fall 85, p. 26.
    "In Memory of Antoine de Saint-Exupery." GreenfR (13:1/2)
    Fall-Wint 85, p. 64.
    "Lines While Drunk." GreenfR (13:1/2) Fall-Wint 85, p. 65.
5465. ZUCKER, Jack
    "Adams Hardware, Watson, Ohio." WoosterR (4) Fall 85, p.
    18.
5466. ZULAGER, Ried R.
    "Dogmatic Poems." WoosterR (4) Fall 85, p. 45-46.
5467. ZULAUF, Sander
    "Daybreak in Succasunna." JlNJPo (8:1) 85, p. 18.
    "Morning in Succasunna." JlNJPo (8:1) 85, p. 28.
    "One for the Old Roosters." JlNJPo (8:1) 85, p. 19.
5468. ZURITA, Raúl
    "Domingo en la Mañana." Mund (15:1/2) 85, p. 146, 148,
    150.
    "Sunday Morning" (tr. by Jeremy Jacobson). Mund (15:1/2)
    85, p. 147, 149, 151.
5469. ZVIBLEMAN, Jana
    "When she is 18, of whichever moon." Calyx (9:1) Spr-Sum
    85, p. 33.
5470. ZYDEK, Frederick (See also ZYDEK, Fredrick)
    "Chilkat Mask." PoetryCR (7:1) Aut 85, p. 14.
    "The Thinnest Wounds." PoetryCR (7:1) Aut 85, p. 14.
5471. ZYDEK, Fredrick (See also ZYDEK, Frederick)
    "32nd Meditation: Advice to the Would-Be Poet." SpoonRQ
    (10:4) Fall 85, p. 14-17.
    "At the Altar of the Unknown God." Amelia (2:2) O 85, p.
    42-43.

"Gray Missoula Lady." <u>AntigR</u> (62/63) Sum-Aut 85, p. 158.
"Lines." <u>CapeR</u> (20:2) Fall 85, p. 22.
"Making a Joyful Noise." <u>AntigR</u> (62/63) Sum-Aut 85, p.
    159.
"Mummy." <u>Amelia</u> (2:2) O 85, p. 42.
"Specializing in Rumors" (for Gary Numan). <u>AntigR</u> (62/63)
    Sum-Aut 85, p. 157.
"Those Who Survive, Survive." <u>Amelia</u> (2:2) O 85, p. 43-44.

TITLE INDEX

Titles are arranged alphanumerically, with numerals filed in numerical order before letters. Each title is followed by one or more author entry numbers, which refer to the numbered entries in the first part of the volume.

At Birkenau: 4476.
At Bomosan Temple: 657.
At Clem's Cabin: 1086.
At day's end, when the sun
    paints the familiar
    roundness of the barrels
    red: 908, 1023.
At Dinas: 919.
At Fifty: 2845, 4421.
At Home: 3995.
At Jane's: 4720.
At Jolicure: 2897.
At Kasuga Shrine: 1494.
At Klondike Bluffs, Utah: 891.
At Last: 1937.
At les Baux de Provence: 2938.
At Matlock cave: 2488.
At Memorial Park: 4678.
At Mormon Square, Salt Lake:
    4038.
At Mother Teresa's: 3559.
At My Desk / Fri. Night: 1175.
At My Feet an Orient: 3674.
At Night: 4269.
At Night, Spirits Come Out of
    the Trees: 3268.
At Nightfall in Vermont: 3601.
At Noon: 2032, 3295.
At Paul Metcalf's Poetry
    Reading: 2725.
At Peace: 5105.
At Sand Cut Beach: 4581.
At the All-Clear: 4301.
At the Altar of the Unknown
    God: 5471.
At the Back of the North Wind:
    735.
At the Beach: 1483, 3670,
    4083, 5378.
At the Boulderado: 1286.
At the Chicago Zoo: 5168.
At the Circus: 4972.
At the Corner of Grant and
    Clay: 3465.
At the Criterion: 4958.
At the Demonstration: 4974.
At the Door: 4640.
At the Duncan Turn-Off: 757.
At the End: 4490.
At the End of His Winter
    Journey through the
    Pennsylvania Mountains, a
    Barefoot Man Wakes Up in
    Bed and Talks to His Feet
    One Last Time: 1978.
At the Faculty Christmas
    Party: 508.
At the Frederic Inn: 526.
At the Front of the Jet: 4997.
At the Heart: 2532.
At the Indoor Shopping Mall:
    3628.
At the James Wright Poetry
    Festival: 1750.
At the Knacker's: 174.
At the Loom: 1742.

At the Mill: 1797.
At the Monastery of the Holy
    Spirit, Conyers, GA: 4219.
At the Night Court: 4522.
At the Ninth Grade Prom: 1282.
At the Nursing Home: 296.
At the Park after Work,
    Listen: 182.
At the Phillips Collection:
    3465.
At the Poetry Reading: 5150.
At the Rate We're Going: 1882,
    3720.
At the Sangamon Headwaters:
    2636.
At the Shad Festival: 2288.
At the Smithville Methodist
    Church: 1284.
At the Station: 825, 2509.
At the Street Fair on the
    South St. Dock: 3700.
At the Summit: 1192.
At the Union Picnic: 879.
At the Vietnam Memorial: 5168.
At the Vietnam War Memorial:
    1050.
At the Well of Sacrifices:
    5316.
At the Window: 3256.
At the Woodmen's Museum: 4953.
At This Kind of Time /
    41.46N., 50.14W: 4066.
At Thoreau's Grave, 1974:
    1153.
At Three in the Morning: 2670.
At times a flight of doves
    arrives: 908, 1023.
At Urbino: 1913.
At Weeping Rock: 4974.
At What Time Hence?: 3924.
At Work: 468.
At Yehuda's Wedding: 4549.
At Your Hanging: 1288.
El Atarantado: 353.
Atentado a las Neutralidades
    de los Nuestros: 2922.
Athene: 837.
Athens: 705.
Atlanta: 3060.
Atlantic Tides: 4189.
Atlantic Window: 747.
Atlantis: 254, 2930.
Atmosphere: 3911.
Attachments: 3746.
Attack of the Polka-Dot Girls:
    474.
Attempt at the Ultimate
    Postcard: 1776.
Attendants: 4945.
Attending the Garage Sale:
    228.
Attending Toas: 250.
Attic Window at Advent: 3331.
Au Travers de L'Ecriture: 631.
Aubade: 273, 787, 1540, 1625,
    2403, 4207, 5003.

Birch Tree: 1343, 3089.
Birch Tree in Winter: 1438,
    4544.
Bird: 4325.
The Bird Cage Bunch: 541.
Bird I Was: 1194.
Bird in Paradise: 1038.
Bird in the Hall: 3968.
The Bird Who Steals Everything
    Shining: 5230.
Birdcall: 931.
Birdolatry: 5243.
Birds: 1897, 3617.
Birds-of-Paradise: 2168.
Birds on a Pond at Dust,
    Turnbull Wildlife Refuge,
    May 1984: 191.
The Birds Sing Best in the
    Rain: 2604, 3749.
Birds That Do Not Fly: 1699.
Birdscaping: 1777.
The Birdwatcher: 1855.
Birdwatching: 725.
Birdwatching along the Humber:
    1763.
Birmingham 1963: 5120.
Birth: 1683, 2389.
Birth Color: 2436.
Birth Marks: 3829.
Birth of the Ghost: 1931.
Birth Song: 3122.
Birthday: 701, 3115, 4248,
    5358.
A Birthday: 3173.
Birthday at 35: 3309.
Birthday: Elyria Ohio, 1957:
    4117.
Birthday Poem: 4320.
Birthplace: 2485, 2564, 4057,
    4499.
Bisque Doll Family: 4637.
Bit by Bit: 1951, 2318.
Bitch on Earth: 3675, 4337.
Bits of Perfection: 845.
Bittersweet: 2008.
Black and White: 825.
Black Beauty, a Praise: 4156.
Black Cats, etc: 4938.
The Black Dream of the Elm:
    96, 2376, 3171.
Black Heaven: 3526.
Black Hole Poem: 3013.
Black Ice: 1227, 2971.
Black Is: 5114.
Black Magnolias: 3683.
The Black Man: 1740.
Black Market, 1944: 1023.
The Black Nebula: 1531.
Black Paramour: 5120.
Black Poplar: 3000, 4274,
    4597.
Black Poppy (At the Temple):
    4675.
Black Postcards: 247, 4957.
Black River: 428.
Black Rock Mountain: 2891.

Black Room: 2456.
Black Roses: 520.
Black Sheep, Red Stars: 265.
Black Star: 1640.
Black Widow: 1141.
Black Wings: 636.
Black Wings: 2152.
Black Wings Wheeling: 3146.
Black Woman: 3367, 3587.
Blackberries: 2133, 5007,
    5307.
Blackberries in the China
    Cabinet: 270.
Blackberry Morning: 291.
Blackberrying: 4019.
Blackbird: 3616.
Blackbirds Flocked in
    Evergreens: 1185.
A Blade of Grass: 2564, 2661,
    3624.
Blast: 5062.
Bleeding Heart Flowers: 2222.
The Blessed: 2496.
Blessing: 891.
The Blessing: 4997.
The Blimp Explodes: 3195.
The Blind: 121.
Blind Boy on Skates: 4227.
The Blind Girl Speaks of the
    Marvelous Things: 292.
Blind Intimacy: 1480, 1817.
Blind-Spot: 1499.
Blindsight: 2288.
Bliskość Niewidoma: 1480.
Bliss: 1757.
Blisters: 397.
Block Island: 4986.
Blockade: 2521, 4100.
The Blond Nets: 51.
The Blonde on the Beach: 4188.
Blood: 742.
Blood House: 1287.
Blood of Sorrow, Blood of
    Light: 4316.
Blood or Time: 707.
Blood Test: 697.
The Bloodletting: 4254.
Bloodlines: 3411.
Bloodmeat Each July: 4290.
Bloodstorm: 610.
Bloody Horse: 9.
The Bloom: 4413.
The Blowgun: 1309.
The Blown Glass Souvenir among
    the Maps and Old Deeds:
    4485, 4726.
Blows: 2960, 4907.
Blue: 1936, 2843, 4640.
Blue, All the Way to Canada:
    4986.
Blue and White: 998.
Blue Anniversary: 4215.
The Blue Boat: 155.
Blue Brassieres: 1162.
Blue Bridge: 2510.
Blue City: 31.

Blue Collar: 1132.
The Blue Donkey: 4321.
The Blue Dress: 1719, 3599.
The Blue Fish: 3231.
Blue Garden Ball: 1516, 2604, 4171.
Blue Moon of Ixtab: 880.
Blue Murder: 5332.
Blue Mystery: 630.
Blue Period: 3202.
The Blue Planet: 1977.
Blue: (Poem): 5342.
Blue Room: 1021.
Bluebeard's Theatre: 1306.
Bluebell Canyon: 983.
Bluejay: 1615, 4177.
Blues: 4279.
Blues for Robert Johnson: 3106.
Blues on Elegy: 1412.
Blues Running -- S'Conset Beach: 3669.
The Bluff: 2254.
Blur in the Attic: 506.
Bluzhov: 4479.
The Boat -- The Village: 793, 4957.
Boat People: 2650.
Boat Race Speculation: 1310.
The Boating Party: 2108.
Boats near Luxor: 893.
Boats on the Marne: 157, 3336.
Bob Ulmer's Household: 4479.
Bobbing on Wheat Fields: 3156.
Bobby Wine and the Championship Game: 2133.
Bobwhite Lives: 4916.
Boda de la Pluma y la Letra: 353.
The Bodhisattva Awakes: 2970.
Bodies: 1433.
Bodies Laugh: 3481.
The Body As Concept: 1251.
Body in Brightness: 2360, 4165.
Body: Irish-American: 3115.
Body Language: 1951, 2318.
The Body Makes Love Possible: 3321.
The Body of Desire: 3173.
Body Replies to Many Insults: 2560.
The Bog: 637.
Bolero: 1166.
Bombs: 2334.
The Bone Bank: 984.
Bone China Broken: 4997.
Bone Soup: 3662.
The Bone Step-Women: 3642.
Bone Structures There in the Sky: 1569.
Bones: 336.
Bone's Edge: 3508.
The Bones of the Plagiarist: 4682.
Bonin Drowned: 3562.

Bonnard's Nudes: 742.
Bonwit Teller: 5170.
Book Circle: 1204.
The Book of Daniel: 5430.
A Book of Hours: 4663.
The Book of Songs: 4859.
A Book of Spells II: 640.
Books: 5282.
Books in the Attic: 3375.
Boola-Boola: 2899.
Border Crossing: 2780.
Border Papers: 3674.
A Border Rose: 2451.
Borders: 3715.
Bore: 3271.
Boredom Cake: 805, 2357.
The Boredom Line: 5410.
The Borgo Pinti Sonnets: 1921.
Born Again: 2630.
Born of Nothingness: 4502.
Born Pretty in a Poor Country: 2650.
Borne Away: 3036.
Borne by the easterlies: 3003.
The Borrowed Ones: 1646.
The Boss: 2088.
Boston: 5029.
Boston Common: 4818.
Botanist: 4233.
The Bottle Garden: 483.
Bottom of the Deck: 5122.
A Bouquet: 5269.
A Bouquet by Degas: 5175.
The Bouquet: 150.
Bow Ties: 2697.
Bowing to the Rigid Applause: 1617.
A Bowl of Shells: 5013.
A Box of Ghosts: 4395.
Boxcie: 2229.
Boxes: For a Cat Once Trapped in One: 2301.
Boy: 3139.
The Boy: 1946.
Boy at Seven: 861.
The Boy, Back Home: 4232.
The Boy to the Spider, the Spider to the Boy: 5230.
The Boy with Scars on His Arms: 4653.
The Boy with Two Frogs: 5377.
The Boys: 2843.
The Bracelet: 720.
Bracing: 3004.
Bracketing in City Thickets: 2748.
Brain Storm: 4338.
Braised Leeks & Framboise: 5109.
A Bramble Bush: 4534.
The Branch: 1880.
Brass Bed: 5007.
Brass Rubbing: 2214.
Brass Unicorns: 2630.
Brave: 1535.
The Brave Blondes: 4702.

Car Crash in Greece: 4665.
La Cara de Mis Hijas: 353.
Caravan: 4522.
Carbón: 4150.
Carbon Date, Columbia River:
    3788.
Cards from My Aunt: 4239.
Cards, Kielbasy: 1029.
The Care and Feeding of a
    Poet: 2773.
Caressed by Light: 4394.
Carl Sandburg: 1753.
Carlenda's Song: 2797.
Carlisle School: 215.
Carmen Gloria: 4256.
'Carmen' in Digital for a Deaf
    Woman: 2647.
Carmen's Story: 1724.
Carnations for C: 735.
Carne del Insomnio: 2876.
Carnival: 4596.
The Carnival: 3906.
The Carnival Unpacks: 1948.
Caro Il Mio Pappa: 4373.
Carolina, Coltrane, and Love:
    227.
Carousel: 3423.
Carpe Diem: 4237.
Carrie Wolf: 3201.
Cars: 1429.
The Cartoonist: 2153.
The Carvers: 96, 3171.
Carving a Crooked Line of
    Apartheid with Their
    Flight: 3905.
Carving with Bone: 4092.
Carvings: 100.
Carwash Kiss: 4810.
Casa Vacia: 3910.
Casals in Exile: 2875.
Las Casas Colgadas: 3977.
A Case against Old Habits: A
    Vision: 4251.
Cases: 1936.
Casey Livingston Is an
    Epileptic: 3174.
Cashier: 3826.
Casi un Sueño: 84.
The Casket Maker's Proposal:
    3422.
Caso: 688.
Cassandra at the Car Lot:
    3288.
The Cast: 3599.
Cast-iron fence: 42, 2092.
Castaway: 1141.
The Casual Kiss: 2773.
Casuals: 1745, 3698.
Casualties: 5169.
A Cat by Any Name: 2115.
Cat in the Corner: 3662.
Cat in the Rain: 4768.
Cat Talk: 3534.
Catalina: 1285.
A Catalogue for Cooks: 1235.
Catch: 2380.

The Catch: 2342.
Catching Fireflies: 728.
Catching the Sunrise: 132.
The Caterpillar: 1617.
Cathedral: 1963.
The Catherine-Wheels: 1463,
    4387, 4815.
Cathy: 88.
Cats: 1086.
The Cats of Balthus: 3980.
The Cat's Revenge: 1064.
A Catulo: 2876.
The Caught Fish Speaks: 481.
Caught Not Looking: 1803.
Caution: Cunning Linguist:
    3178.
Ceci N'Est Pas un Morç eau
    de Fromage: 5369.
Cecilia at Odds in the North:
    2319.
Cecilia's Song: 5309.
Cedar: 2519.
Cedar Crest Lodge: 1321.
Ceilings: 5433.
Celebration: 2941.
Celestial Parties: 2484.
Celia: 4150.
Céline Blues: 545.
Cell 43: 2308.
The Cellar: 4601.
Cellblock Blues: 1414.
Cells: 1743.
Cement-Man: 1545.
Cement Mixer: 4264.
Cementerio: 3729.
Cementerio de Punta Arenas:
    2876.
Cementerio de Vaugirard: 3339.
Cemetery Nights III: 1206.
Cemetery Nights IV: 1206.
Cendres: 1744.
Cenno (I): Genova: 354.
Cenno (II): Venezia: 354.
Cenno (III): Milano: 354.
Cenno (IV): Siena: 354.
The Centauress: 606.
Centaur's Visit: 4700.
Centipede on Chop Suey: 1503.
Central America Could Never Be
    Another Vietnam: 3429.
Central Park: 2639.
Central States: 2073.
The Century Quilt: 5144.
Cepo de Lima: 353.
Ceremony: 4900.
A Certain Reformatory: 2804.
Cesses Mortels de Soupirer:
    1890.
C'est à Mourir de Rire:
    2773.
A Cezanne of Shane the
    Gunslinger Riding toward
    Sainte-Victoire: 2981.
Chaco Canyon Love Song: 3792.
Chaconne: 2155.
Chain Letter Pantoum: 2418.

461   CURRIER

Crabapple Blossoms: 4293.
Cracow: 5259.
The Craftsman: 2521, 4100.
Cragsmen: 596.
The Cranes: 742.
Crayfish: 2325.
Crazy Horse: 3320.
Crazy July: 674.
Crazy the Sun: 5230.
Cream o' Wheat: 655.
Create a Good Impression above
    All: 4816.
Creation: 728, 1283.
The Creation: 85.
The Creation of Protest: 4146.
Creative Oppression: 5023.
Creativity: 42, 116.
Creatures in a Different
    Light: 2182.
Credentials: 50 Years of
    Being: 2412.
Credo: 2282, 3895, 4611.
The Creek Book: A Week on the
    Chunky and Chickasawhay:
    397.
Creeping Intelligence: 1206.
The Creighton Pool Hall: 4282.
The Cremation of Malloney's:
    1812.
Crete: August: 2868.
Crib Bait: 2639.
Crickets in August: 1823.
The Cries of Birds: 2890.
Crime and the Classics: 1389.
Crime Statistic: 3332.
Crimes: 1178.
Crimes or Genesis II: 1111,
    1601.
Criminal Sonnets: 2646.
Crimson Current: 4742.
The Cripple-Maker: 4557.
Crisp's Eye: 5196.
Cristobel Colon, Instead of
    Setting Sail to India, Runs
    His Morning Errands: 3824.
The Critic: 4757.
A Critique of Metaphores:
    2811, 3267.
Crocuses: 2223.
The Crocuses: 3337.
Crónica de Indias: 3675.
Crooked Legs: 1958.
The Cross: 2013, 2925, 5337.
Cross Country: 425, 3028.
Cross My Heart: 940.
Crossed Wires: 4019.
Crosses: 4674.
Crosshairs: 2554.
Crossing: 1727.
The Crossing: 282, 828, 2063.
Crossing Indian Land: 1558.
Crossing Over: 4729.
Crossing the Border: 2089,
    3135, 3887.
Crossing the Channel: 2972.
Crossing the Front Campus,

October 21: 1353.
Crossing the Ice: Acapulco:
    345.
Crossing the River: 76.
Crossing Water: 592, 4477,
    4477.
Crosspollination: 2293.
The Crossroads of the Thirteen
    Widows: 2202.
Crosswind Landings: 3146.
The Crow Call, February: 2056.
Crow Mother Songs: 273.
Crown of Joy: 2067, 3894.
Crown Prince Rudolph Stands
    over the Body of Mary
    Vetsera in the Hunting
    Lodge at Mayerling: 817.
The Crows of Boston and New
    York: 2959.
Cruising with the Beachboys:
    1741.
Crumbs: 3239.
Crush an Apple: 4833.
The Cry: 820, 1431, 2232,
    3215.
The Crying Room: 4349.
Cuando Acabe Esta Guerra:
    3527.
Cuando el Amor se Acaba: 952.
Cuando el Diablo Me Rondaba
    Anunciando Tus Rigores:
    834.
Cuando está un poco oscuro:
    1820.
Cuando la Luz Se Cuaja sobre
    la Geografia: 752.
Cuando Llegue la Hora: 158.
Cuando Pases: 2831.
Cuando Se Acabe: 688.
Cuanta Existencia Menos!: 353.
Cuanto Nos Cuesta: 1901.
Cuba Night: 4579.
Cuban Poets Have Stopped
    Dreaming: 3586, 3680.
Cul-de-sac: 3494.
The Cult of the Right Hand:
    4878.
Cumbrian Herd: 1518.
Cunt Is Just Another Foreign
    Country: 4821.
The Cup: 3123, 3826.
A Cup of Chai: 1618.
A Cup of Sky, a Foot of Fire:
    3161.
Cupboard: 3028.
Cupfuls of Summer: 1923.
Cupid and Psyche: 3238.
Cur Secessisti?: 788, 3571.
The Curable Romantic: 1625.
Curator of the Zoo: 1749.
Cure: 1268.
Curiosity: 2452.
Curled Up Tight: 5203.
Curriculum Vitae (1937): 2168.
Curriculum Vitae: 2457.
Currier & Ives: 1262.

462

Daybreak in Succasunna: 5467.
Days: 5111.
Days and Days: 3429.
The Day's End: 2521, 4100.
Day's End, Minden, Nebraska:
   2131.
Days Late in March: 2140,
   3530.
Days of Glass: 5320.
Days with William Stafford:
   4988.
Daystar: 1238.
Dazzling: 2126.
DC Berry, Sr: 397.
De Chirico Exhibit: 4541.
De doden zijn in mijn kind
   opgestaan: 1696.
De la Oscilacion de un Caliban
   en Jarialito: 2922.
De las Aves sin Nombre: 679.
De Martí, para Martí:
   5421.
De Tal Manera Mi Razón
   Enflaquece: 1931.
De un 'Quijote' en un Lugar de
   Cuyo Nombre no Quiere
   Acordarse: 2922.
De un Vigilante Nocturno en
   Quebrada: 2922.
The Dead: 2710.
Dead Air: 1965.
The dead are resurrected in my
   child: 1696, 4361.
Dead Bat: 2288.
Dead Battery Madonna: 2872.
Dead Dog: 1374.
Dead Elm: 993.
Dead Fathers: 4986.
Dead Fish: 1953.
Dead Friends: 3567.
Dead Letters: 4270.
Dead Man: 2668.
The Dead Pigeon: 4750.
The Dead Skunk Poem: 4344.
The Dead Speak: 1189.
Dead Splendor: 1910.
Dead to Rights: 4724.
The Dead Will Sleep: 3444.
Dead Wood: 770.
The Dealer: 3201.
Dear: 2093.
Dear Customer: 4861.
Dear Friedrich: 4522.
Dear Ginger: 1275.
Dear James: 3716.
Dear Living: 2140, 2757.
Dear Lydia E. Pinkham: 1922.
Dear Old Stockholm: 5214.
Dear Reg: 4291.
Dear Valentine: 926.
Dearly Beloved: 2644.
Death: 1424, 2874, 3093, 3599.
Death among the Ndebele: 1739.
Death and Division: 1677.
Death and Morality: 3599.
Death Angels: 5273.

Death Approaches: 3935.
Death by Water: 3697.
Death Cutting the Air Like
   Grease: 3320.
Death Dancing: 5315.
Death in Late Summer: 2765.
A Death in the Family: 4948.
Death in the Museum: 3981.
Death in Viareggio: 3216,
   4248.
A Death in Winter: 965.
Death Is Like the Morning:
   2577.
Death Jets: 2726.
Death Leave for a Teacher:
   3345.
Death Mars Wedding Party:
   5386.
Death of ____ _____, Chief
   without a Tribe: 4263.
The Death of a Cow: 1137.
Death of a God: 3068.
Death of a Scientist, Birth of
   a Believer: 1604.
The Death of a Small Animal:
   1933.
Death of a White-Haired
   Friend: 1532.
The Death of Chang Eng: 5355.
The Death of Couperin: 3805.
The Death of Marriages: 2030.
The Death of Orpheus: 1233.
The Death of Rachel: 1274.
Death of the Houses in Ouro
   Preto: 114, 881.
The Death of the Khan: 2223.
Death of Trees: 1979.
Death of Your Baby: 169.
Death on the Sidewalk outside
   Grand Central: 2549.
Death Sits at the Foot of My
   Bed: 1931.
A Death Suite: Three Poems:
   2410.
Death this great impediment:
   1338.
Death to the Fascist Insect
   Who Preys on the Blood of
   the People: 3794.
Death Watch: 4633.
Death Wish: 33.
Deathbed: 4704.
Deathdance: 3135.
Death's Garden: 625.
Death's Self Portrait: 1655,
   5093.
Debbie: 1849.
Deborah's Lament: 4207.
Debt: 1771.
The Debt: 5013.
Debt of Thera: 1709.
The Decade: 142.
Decades: 268.
Decatur: 2636.
December Day in Honolulu:
   2592.

Divago: 1901.
Dividing a Dying Woman's Land: 3817.
Divination by Bamboo: 5141.
Diving for the Cripples at the VFW Lake: 1117.
Diving the Shoals: 3892.
Divining for West: 4785.
Divorce: 5127.
The Divorce: 1385, 1876, 3871.
Do Not Peel the Birches: 2342.
Do not write too clearly: 3896.
Do Small Things with Great Love: 3717.
Do What You Have To: 1432, 2480.
Doctor Auchincloss Bids Good-bye to His Wife: 4577.
The Doctrine of the Last Hour: 4363.
Document: 3785, 4191.
The Doe: 3135.
Does It Keep in Your Ear?: 1722.
Does Too: 3585.
Dog: 3678.
The Dog: 2418, 3518.
A Dog at Evening: 4796.
Dog Days: 3525.
Dog Days, Jerusalem: 1238.
The Dog Man: 1088.
Dog Metal: 2358.
Dog, This Dog: 1153.
Dogmatic Poems: 5466.
Dogs Bark: 5068.
Dogturds emerging: 4034.
The Dogwood: 4914.
Dogwoods and Lilacs: 3335.
Doinel en Sus Cuarenta: 1659.
Doing Laundry on Sunday: 2537.
Doing Time: 430.
Doing Well: 4583.
Doings in the Garden: 4391.
Dojoji: 4691.
Dolce Maria: 678, 771.
Doldrums: 1239.
The Doll Dream: 4706.
Dolly, Dolly: 2110.
The Dolphin Race: 3262.
Domestic Comforts: 891.
A Domestic Crisis: 1128.
Domestic Culinary Text: 3362.
Domestic Nomenclature: 2773.
Domesticity: 968.
Dominance: A Museum Guide: 1118.
Domingo en la Mañana: 5468.
Domingo en Santa Cristina de Budapest y Frutería al Lado: 834.
Don Giovanni: 4733.
Don John of Austria: 2190.
The Donald Years: 2765.
The Donation: 1288.
Done Express: 2470.

Donne's Death: 4993.
Donor: 2395.
Donovan's Tarot: 1223.
Don't Ask: 2939.
Don't Do Me Any Favors: 2899.
Don't Feed Flynn Has Been: 2281.
Don't Fix It Again: 3747.
Don't Go to the Barn: 4561.
Don't Let It End Here: 349.
Don't Open This Invitation!: 4480.
Don't Say Goodbye to the Porkpie Hat: 3471.
Don't Tell Me: 3899.
Don't Tell Me You Have No Soul: 4329, 4862.
Don't torment your heart with the joys of earth: 42, 2092.
Don't Waken Us!: 3727.
Doomed: 1418.
A Door in the Wind: 4529.
Doorway: 188.
The Doppelgängers: 2773.
Una Dormienda: 5099.
The Dormition of Aunt Menka: 2026, 2652, 3762.
Dorothy Wordsworth: 2667.
Dos Ciudades: 3339.
Dos Rembrandt: 3339.
Douanier Rousseau: 2923.
Double Cropping: 1948.
Double Dactylics: 1921.
Double Distance: 1546.
The Double Dream of Spring: 172.
Double Exposure: 2388, 4793.
Double Knife-Throwing Act: 4427.
Double Sentencing: 2521, 4100.
Double South Spring: 227.
Doubts during Catastrophe: 3402.
The Dough of America Is Rising in Me: 4559.
Down at the Harvest Bar: 3628.
Down by the Riverside: 1309.
Down by the Station, Early in the Morning: 172.
Down the Alleymouth: 4522.
Down the block: 1338.
Down the Road: 4226.
Downriver: 3276.
Downtown: 55.
Downtown Art: 3998.
Downtown Local: 1945.
The Dowser: 1971.
The Doyennes: 381.
Dr. Suess Grows Up in NY: 2209.
Dracaena: 4730.
Dracula and the Photographer: 3403.
Dracula in Las Vegas: 2597.
Drag Race: 4579.

roof: 998, 2462.
Flying: 4751.
The Flying Dutchman: 3146.
Flying Horses: 4643.
Flying into Billings to Read
  My Poetry: 836.
Flying over Clouds: 1741.
Flying over Nebraska by Night:
  341.
Flying the Red Eye: 4733.
Flying Time: 3745.
Flying to the Moon: 1331.
Foam Post: 396.
The Fog: 3135.
The Foggiest: 3585.
Foggy Morning Run: 3449.
The Foliage Lit Up: 493, 4305.
Folk Song: 1309, 4254.
The Follies: 3282.
Following the Accusation:
  2538.
The Food of Fairyland: 4226.
Fool's Week: 1611.
Footnotes: 693, 4592.
Footprints: 5035.
Footprints on the Glacier:
  3242.
Footsteps: 3768.
For 35 Cents: 2861.
For a Certified Public
  Accountant: 856.
For a Child Who Has Lost Her
  Cat: 2999.
For a Friend at Dusk, 22
  Useless Lines: 3601.
For a Friend, Randomly
  Murdered in L.A: 1123.
For a Friend Who Doesn't Call:
  2379.
For a Girl in the Library:
  2578.
For a Granddaughter: 4119.
For a Lost Child: 4474.
For a Silent Woman, Alone:
  5284.
For a Son Dead in the War:
  1942.
For a Thirteenth Birthday:
  3413.
For Alice, a Miracle on Astor
  Place: 4320.
For All of Us: 3055.
For all that time he asked
  her: 1651.
For A.M: 3664.
For an Abused Child: 3264.
For an Old Dog: 3997.
For Aunt A.K: 96, 3171.
For Basil Bunting: 332.
For Bi Shouwang: 1682.
For Bunting: 1074, 3623.
For C. S. Lewis: 3394, 5113.
For Carlos Who Used to Compare
  Me with Roses: 5160.
For César Vallejo: 3383.
For Charles: 3781.

For Charlie Howard: 197.
For Daile: 221.
For Dan: 1255.
For Delmore Schwartz: 4565.
For E.K: 1605.
For Earl: 2025.
For Ed on-the-Hour Dorn: 5260.
For Example: 2564, 2661, 2718.
For Frank Robinson: 954.
For G. and A: 1437.
For Gerald Coury: 2871.
For Gertrude: 3355.
For Giuliano: 5046.
For Huck and Jim on the Raft:
  4949.
For James Evans: 5319.
For James Jones: 5348.
For Jamie: 1866.
For Jerry Lee Lewis: 4840.
For Jim Callahan: 4071.
For Joanie Whitebird: 5319.
For John, on the Mountain:
  2057.
For Joy: 1525.
For Jude's Lebanon: 200.
For Jurek: 4563.
For Katie: Some Notes on These
  Times: 1443.
For Kellianne, a Clarinetist
  at Nine: 1684.
For Linda, Who Will Not Know
  Why: 4379.
For Louis Dudek: 1041.
For Maggie: 205.
For Mary: 3199, 4158.
For Mats and Laila: 793, 4957.
For me, winter feels like a
  belated gift: 884, 2581,
  3023.
For Megan at five: 5022.
For Men Only: 3987.
For Miss Lewis and Miss
  Newton: 1731.
For Months: 437.
For Moses, Who Must Have
  Learned It on the Mountain:
  1519.
For Mr. Federman, a Kosher
  Butcher: 3802.
For My Brother: 4530.
For My Daughter's Birthday:
  1630.
For My Father: 4437.
For My Irish Grandfather: 200.
For My Son, Adolescent: 233.
For My Students: 3092.
For Nelly: 1287.
For Nicholas, at Two: 2144.
For Now and Always: 3446.
For Old Classmates Finding No
  Easy Deliverance: 3616.
For Papa: 735.
For Phyllis, Whose Name Means
  'Leafy': 1627.
For Prairie Chicken, Now
  Extinct: 4263.

Fragile Hardware: 124.
Fragment: 3466, 3698.
Fragment IX: 1402, 4443.
Fragment: from a Blossoming
    Almond: 4617.
Fragment from the Seventies:
    1009, 1096.
Fragmento: 1174.
Fragmentos: 754.
Fragmentos de Heráclito al
    Estrellarse contra el
    Cielo: 1931.
Fragmentos para Dominar el
    Silencio: 3853.
Fragments: 754, 1126, 1583,
    4288.
Fragments from a Childhood:
    4830.
Fragments of a Dream: 3898.
The Frame: 3160.
Frameless Windows, Squares of
    Light: 4632.
The Framer: 3454.
Fran: 2191.
Frances and Elizabeth: 1285.
Frances at Virginia Beach:
    369.
The Franciscan Convent: 3300,
    3698.
Francisco Goya y Lucientes'
    'Portrait of Don Ignacio
    Omulryan y Rourera': 3203.
Franz Schubert: A Press
    Conference: 1805, 5416.
Freak: 1206.
Free Lessons: 3224.
Free Pass: 3912, 5454.
Free Verse: 4589.
Freedom: 515, 866, 2386.
Freely in hidden fire: 1710,
    3921.
Freeway through the Mountains:
    3712.
Freight: 1699.
Freighter: 220.
Fremdblütig im Herzen der
    Hacht: 2778.
The French: 2773.
French Doors for Allen
    Varney's Mother: 5267.
French Impressionists: 643.
French Young Lady Doll ca.
    1845: 4637.
Frente al Espejo: 1174.
Freud: 1136.
Freud, in His Garden,
    Contemplates Suicide: 3824.
Friday Even Azure: 1745, 3698.
Friday, Good Friday: 3611.
Friday Nights 1964 / Pat
    O'Brien 1984: 3427.
Friedhof Verkehr: 3280.
A Friend Comes Back: 1900,
    3173.
A friend dreamed I had given
    birth: 3654.

Friend of the Enemy: 4684.
Friendly Foe: 3548.
A Friend's Friend: 2596.
Friends of the Poor: 2452.
Friendship: 36, 2754.
The Friendship: 2822.
Fringe Benefit: 2049.
Fringecups: 3198.
El Frío: 4253.
Frisia Cantat: 2389, 2495.
The Frog Pond: 2592.
The Frog Prince: 3968.
The Frog Who Wanted to Be an
    Authentic Frog: 3340, 4337.
From a Boat, Neosho River:
    189.
From a Distance: 1910.
From a Frar Cry, a Return to
    the City: 2903.
From a Log Fallen in the Shade
    of a Lilac Bush: 4215.
From a Shipyard in a Bottle:
    515.
From an Interview: 4057.
From an Old Appalachian Song:
    3475.
From Away: 4289.
From Berkshire Elegy: 552.
From Exile in Paradise: 3523.
From Fort Lawrence Road: 2897.
From Her Diary: 3562.
From Letter #57 Addressed to
    Lj.N: 2789, 5459.
From Lower Broadway: 2272.
From Nowhere: 2255.
From Pan Am: 3201.
From Sconticut: 2736.
From Scratch: 657.
From Shelled Out Frankfurt to
    Posterity: 2981.
From Spring to Stream: 4596.
From the Ancient Chinese:
    1409.
From the Biography of the
    Hummingbird: 351.
From the Bridge: 380.
From the Coaches' Box: Little
    Girls at the Ballgame:
    4967.
From the Distant Tomb of the
    Weatherman: 5042.
From 'The First Mass' of the
    MS The Chapel of Death:
    3196.
From the Inca: 3611.
From the Journal of an Unknown
    Lady-in-Waiting: 1114.
From the MS The Cathedral of
    Names: 3196.
From the Next Book by: 5282.
From the Non-Smoking
    Compartment: 3465.
From the Southern to the
    Northern Peak by Way of the
    Lake: Stopping to View the
    Scenery: 2265, 5302, 5444.

King Street, Wilmington,
Delaware, 1981-82: 2205.
Here: 2931, 4915.
Here and Here: 1342.
Here and Now: 3804.
Here and Then: 1948.
Here in every house there are
little family cemeteries:
908, 1023.
Here in Oklahoma: 141.
Here in the Dark: 2240.
Here in Your Wheelchair: 3945.
Heredity: 937.
Here's One: 1946.
Heritage: 1871.
Heritage Letter: 4620.
Hermes: 1851.
A Hermit Thrush: 837.
The Hermitage: 2108.
Hernia: 2988.
The Hero Is Nothing: 3821.
Herodias: 4515.
Herod's Life: 4515.
Heroes: 36.
The Heron: 3780.
Heron Variations: 3079.
Herrings: 3658.
Hey, Nineteen: 4546.
Hiatus Interruptus: 2849.
Hiccups: 1047, 3310.
A Hidden Full Moon: 4914.
Hide-and-Go-Seek: 2245.
Hide and Seek: 1286.
Hiding: 462.
Hier Régnant Désert: 493,
4214.
Hierarchy: 1400.
Hieroglyph 35: 5408.
Hieroglyphics: 15, 4197.
High Bridge: 4560.
High Divers: 4641.
High Heels: 3601.
High Holy Days: 3277.
High Meadow: 1883.
High Noon: 1951, 4251, 4801.
High Potato Land: 1419.
High School: 146.
High School Confidential:
4958.
High School Football: 3651.
The High Tide of the East:
3272.
High Top Terrorists: 3098.
Highlands: 4948.
Highway 3: 3320.
The Highway a Mile from Home:
1496.
The Highway Death Toll: 4824.
Highway One: 4388.
Hija Eres de los Lágidas:
3443.
Hijo del Silencio: 3229.
Hilary Our Kitten: 1266.
Hilde's Birth, Pappy's Diary,
March 4, 1914: 955.
Hill: 1723, 2329.

Hill Water: 1793.
Hills: 3205.
The Hindenberg: 574.
Hippocrene: 837.
The Hippy Market in Sao Paulo:
3117, 4616.
Hips: 527.
His Alamo of Crocketts: 1146.
His and Hers: 4807.
His Children: 4038.
His Grace: 4747.
His Grandfather Talks about
Naming: 4217.
His Grandmother Kills a Snake:
4217.
His Grandmother Talks about
God: 4217.
His Happy Hour: 4444.
His love: 1936.
His pockets: 1936.
His Sermon to the Graduates:
1279.
His Shining Helmet, Its
Horsehair Crest: 1646.
His Silence: 3993.
His Sister: 4828.
His Will: 3387.
História de Verão: 115.
Historical Data: 4373.
Historical Romance: 1957.
History: 254, 2930, 4757.
A History: 2484.
History and Parody: 4030.
History Lessons: 1192.
History of a Partial Cure:
2856.
The History of Electricity:
1598.
History of the Vanquished:
1951, 4850.
History, Pawtucket: 2523.
Hitchhikers, 1936, Walker
Evans: 5033.
Hitching a Dream Ride: 3200.
Hitting the Vulture: 2288.
Ho-Had-Hun: 1818.
Hoboes: 5241.
Hog Roast: 5013.
The Hohntor: 1548.
La Hoja del Otoño: 3910.
Holden: 2512.
Holden Caulfield at the Car
Wash: 1140.
Holding Hands at the Mall:
1603.
Holding Pattern: 4179.
Holes: 5376.
Holiday at Myall Lake: 2060.
Holiday in New Haven: 2727.
Holiday in Tokyo: 1328.
Holi/day Sho(pping): 173.
The Hollow Log Lounge: 4596.
Holly: 870.
Hollywood Extra: 283.
Holocene Memories: 1322.
Holston River: 1673.

The Long Habit of Fire: 2288.
Long History of the Short
    Poem: 2225.
Long Island: 349.
Long Island (N.Y.) Images:
    758.
Long Island Real Estate: Great
    Neck: 1860.
Long Live the Tiger: 3132.
A Long Production: 1910.
A Long Ride Back: 4719.
A Long Story: 3960.
Long Summer: 1562, 5393.
Long Train Rides: 3830.
The Long Walk Home: 4054.
Longboat Key: 588.
The Longest Day: 1198, 2677.
Longings, Salt Lake City:
    5369.
Lontano da Pietraperzia: 4090.
Look: 2843.
Look into the Faces of Dead
    Poets: 523, 2313.
The Look of Things: 1105,
    1641.
Looking Ahead: 4002.
Looking at a Sculpture by
    Ulker Ozerdam: 2738.
Looking at Mount T'ai: 1261,
    1957.
Looking at Schiller's Pen:
    1075, 1336.
Looking at Tulips: 2247.
Looking Eastward: 1360.
Looking for Angels in New
    York: 3646.
Looking for Our Old Woman:
    4115.
Looking Glass: 4379.
Looking Glass Lake: 2421.
Looking Out on the Morning:
    3146.
Looking through a Blind Spot:
    2250.
Loomings: 1703.
The Loon: 4287.
Loose: 1406.
The Loose Shutter: 5158.
Lord, I Am the Running Man:
    3824.
The Lord of Chou: 4397.
Lord Randal's Wife Tells Her
    Story: 937.
Lorelei: 5198.
Loren Eiseley: 2689.
Lorena Faber (Known as
    'Linda'): 1434, 1566.
Lorraine: 5277.
Los Angeles: 1734.
Losers: 1697.
Losing Altitude: 825.
Losing Her: 1557.
Losing the Sea at Last: 1175.
Loss: 2630.
Loss of a Child: 1375.
Losses: 519, 5371.

Lost: 2630, 4140.
The Lost Bee: 2839.
Lost Cause: 2690.
Lost Child: 5013.
The Lost Children of Abergan:
    219.
Lost Creek: 818.
The Lost Dance: 3065.
Lost Faces: 5088.
The Lost Glove Is Happy: 141.
Lost Head / El Salvador / Our
    Sister: 1885.
Lost Horizon: 1093.
Lost in Amsterdam: 3166.
Lost in the Dictionary: 2532.
A Lost Memory of Delhi: 62.
Lost Sisters: 111.
Lost Stations: 2897.
Lot & the Burning Bush: 5227.
A Lot of Boys Bar: 1823.
Lot's Wife: 5265.
Lot's Woman: 311, 1951.
Lou Reed: 1217.
Louisiana: 1855.
Louvres: 3435.
Love: 2874, 3231.
Love Affair: Fourth Century:
    4763.
Love, Again, at Forty: 4269.
Love among the Joggers: 4846.
The Love and Fear of Fire:
    1257.
The Love Club: 4518.
Love for a Month: 1862.
Love in the Ruins: 4205, 5112.
Love: Intimacy: 5282.
Love Is Based on Trust / In
    God We Trust: 2370.
Love Is Not a Location: 2966.
Love-Letter-Burning: 1941.
Love Like Kitty Litter: 2872.
Love Lyric: 1693, 5076.
Love Match: 2564, 2661, 3624.
Love of Our Times: 1970.
Love Poem: 953, 2460.
Love Poem #11: 2648.
Love Poem after Takeoff,:
    1514, 2707.
Love Poem for My Husband:
    2307.
Love Poem with Persimmons:
    5180.
Love Potion No 9: 926.
Love Runs Out: 2676.
Love Scene from an Unfinished
    Novel: 2701.
A Love Sequence: 4728.
Love Song: 2238.
Love Song for Oscillating
    Universe: 738.
Love Song from a Plain Brown
    Rapper: 4206.
Love Song of a Hippo: 3982.
Love Veins: 5405.
Love Will Happen: 5206.
Lovemaking in Early Morning:

Moving Quiety, Cautiously
    toward a Drink: 1561.
Mowing: 5331.
Mowing Italy: 463.
Mowing Nellie's Lawn: 3275.
Mozambique: 3404.
Mozart: 899.
Mr Brown: 4461.
Mr. Chilled Perception
    Shivers: 2246.
Mr. Cogito -- the Return: 724,
    726, 2109.
Mr. Cogito's Soul: 724, 726,
    2109.
Mr. Cornet: 4124.
Mr. Electric: 457.
Mrs. Asquith Takes Up Jogging:
    5329.
Mrs. Asquith's Faith Is
    Restored by the Afterschool
    Special: 5329.
Mrs. Gardner's Picture: 4832.
Mrs. Leach: 1053.
Mrs. Mack: 4452.
Muchow's Cry: 1749.
The Mud and Smoke: 3137.
The Mud Vision: 2062.
Muddy Waters: 146.
La Muerte de Alexandr
    Sergueievitch: 3443.
La Muerte de Ate: 941.
La Muerte de Matias Aldecoa:
    3443.
La Muerte de Piro: 941.
Muerte de unos Zapatos: 1898.
Una Muerte del Niño Jesús:
    834.
La Muerte Está Sentada a los
    Pies de Mi Cama: 1931.
La Muerte Esta Sentada a los
    Pies de Mi Cama: 1931.
Muerte por el Tacto: 4253.
Mujer: 695.
La Mujer, Her Back to the
    Spectator: 4304.
Mujer sin Tiempo ni Edad: 721.
The Mulberry Tree: 1144, 4504.
Multicultural Blues: 1161.
Mummy: 5471.
The Mummy: 2644.
Mumps: 2626.
Municipal Rites: 4510.
The Mural of Wakeful Sleep:
    2869.
A Murder of Crows: 1496.
The Murderer: 1079.
The Murderers of Kings: 724,
    726, 2109.
Muriel, County Galway: 3533.
Muscatel Flats: 3800.
Muscling in on Valentine's:
    3759.
The Muse: 3406.
Muse: for Robert: 4615.
Musèe: 2644.
Museo del Oro, Bogotá: 519.

Muses and Unknown Sailors:
    4498.
Museum: 1752.
Museum of Modern Art Sculpture
    Garden in the Rain: 3573.
The Museum of Personal
    History: 4919.
Museum Piece: 1614.
Mushroom Cloud: 2613.
The Music: 5411.
Music and Silence: 3318.
The Music in the Silos: 5176.
Music Lessons: 1482.
Music Lover: 196.
The Music Miser: 621.
The Music of Wolves: 520.
Musica para Dos: 84.
The Musician Plays for
    Richard: 447.
Musicians, Aware: 621.
Muskrat: 4145.
Mutation: 1355.
Mutatis Mutandis: 3775, 4527.
The Mute Who Lives in the
    Airport: 3303.
Mutiny: 1773.
My age, my animal: 594, 3023.
My Anastasia: 3882.
My Aunt, Whose '64 Mustang
    Suits Her: 3995.
My Baby: 1503.
My Big Fling: 622.
My Book on Trane: 2003.
My Breath Is Lightning, My
    Laughter Is Thunder: 3320.
My Brother: 1842.
My Brothers: 1039.
My Brother's Keeper: 1603,
    3957.
My Brother's Son: 870.
My Business: 4120.
My Chakabuku Mama: 1789.
My Cottage by the Sea: 3880.
My Cousin's Heart Attack: 937.
My Crow: 742.
My Dark Darling, My Dolphin:
    1300.
My Daughter's Bedtime: 2422.
My Death: 742.
My Dentist, Running: 1279.
My Dream, Your Dream: 4004.
My Drongo: 3325.
My Egg-plant Poem: 4119.
My Elusive Guest: 2702.
My Fair Ladies: 3698, 4096.
My Family: 923.
My far garbled, some musician
    gunned down: 3769.
My Father in the Merchant
    Marine: 2890.
My Father's Chair: 5118.
My Father's Cure: 4519.
My Father's Greenhouse: 560.
My Father's Violin: 836.
My Father's Visit: 2582.
My Father's Visits: 606.

The Sheep Observe the Sabbath: 2958.
Sheila and I: 4101.
Shelley and the Romantics: 758.
Shells: 3146.
Sheltered Currents: 2196.
Sheltered from Harm: 115, 2845.
Shepherd's Song: 357.
Sheriff: 2021.
Sherlock Holmes: 502, 3658.
She's Not Exactly Like You: 2773.
Shifting Layers: 2676.
Shiftless: 742.
Shine: 2504, 3931.
Shining: 3581.
The Ship: 544, 3576.
The Ship in the Bottle: 5363.
Shit Creek Days: 3253.
Shiva Winding a Wreath of Victory Round a Devotee-King's Head: 784.
Shivo: 33.
The Shoe: 940.
Shoe Boiling: 363.
Shoes: 1716, 3883.
Shooting Chant: 3320.
The Shopper: 544, 3576.
Shoptalk: 2199.
The Shore: 2133.
Shorecrest: 4269.
A Short Exchange: 2302.
A Short History: 1484.
A Short History of Bread: 1726.
A Short History of Civilization: 2664.
Short March, Teeny Wall: 4861.
Short Review: 2521, 4100.
Short Story: 3144, 5091, 5386.
Shortwave: 223.
Shovelling Out: 4120.
The Show Must Go On: 3807.
The Shower: 4607.
Shrewsbury Abbey: 3260.
Shrike: 1793.
Shrine: 1192.
The Shrine: 2444.
Shrine of the Blessed Virgin Mary Still Life, Montreal, Canada 1963: 758.
Shrivelled Love: 555, 4147, 5429.
The Shriving of the Serpent: 4593.
Shroud: 625.
The Shroud: 2592.
The Shroud of Turin: 3018.
Si Tuviera un Caballo: 3641.
Sian (Old Style): 1982.
Sibilla Libica: 1896.
Sibling Collage: 1908.
Sibyl: 4866.
Sic Transit Gloria Mundi: 790.

Sickness, or Quilt: 474.
Sickness unto Death: 2621.
Sicut Minerva Strix: 1186.
Side with Stars: 636.
Siden I Gaar: 3530.
Sidewalk Cafe, Thinking of the Fuehrer: 4638.
Sidney Bechet at Six Years Old: 2056.
The Siege of Atlanta: 1501.
Sight in the Distance: 4576.
Sightseeing: 4013.
The Sign: 1874.
The Sign Faehre nach Wilm: 4658.
Signaling: 649.
Signals: 1883, 2521, 3355, 4100, 4874, 5363.
The Signing: 122.
Signs: 4, 170, 1891, 3912, 4260, 5454.
Signs, Blessings: 3966.
Signs of Life: 1512.
Silence: 3675, 4337.
The Silence: 1485.
Silence Is Golden: 1144, 1368.
The Silence of the World: 1350.
The Silence of Things in Their Place: 1451.
La Silenciosa Agonía: 1688.
Silent Things: 2232.
Silk Stockings: 4643.
Silly Song: 3481.
A Silly Syndicate of Lies Comes Forth: 294.
Silo: 189.
The Silver Coin: 4025.
Silver Wedding Anniversary: 1787.
Silverado Revisited: 2689.
Silverlake: A Theater Song for Kurt Weill: 4589.
The Silversmith: 715.
Simile: 3495.
Simple: 33.
A Simple Death: 589.
Simple Holdings: 2913.
Simple Questions: 4380.
Simple Static: 3724.
The Simple Truth about Snow: 2183.
A Sin Avoided: 1480, 1817.
Sin-Eater: 5403.
Since Yesterday: 2140, 3530.
Sinceramente: 3041.
Sine and Cosine: 3980.
The Singer: 4951.
The Singer of Manoa Street: 1617.
Singing: 652.
The Singing Flower: 2612, 4495, 5445.
Singing School: 4232.
Singing the Blues: 3916.
Singing to Everything around

Us: 3916.
Singing You Simply: 1386.
Single Love: 2792.
The Single Urge: 5356.
A Singular Plurality: 2966.
Sinking in the Botannical
    Gardens: 880.
Sioux River: 2986.
Sipping from my cup: 2328.
Sir Real Met a Physical: 3158.
Sir Thomas Tucker: 1603.
Sir Walter Ralegh and the
    Milkweed: 397.
Sister: 3388.
The Sister Doll: 2745.
Sister Marie Angelica Plays
    Badminton: 3201.
Sister Mary Appassionata
    Addresses the Eighth Grade
    Boys and Girls during a
    Field Trip to the Museums
    of Natural History and Art:
    836.
Sister Mary Appassionata
    Addresses the Psychic
    Research Guild of Marion,
    Ohio: 836.
Sister Mary Appassionata
    Addresses the V. F. W: 836.
Sister Mary Appassionata
    Lectures the Biology Class:
    Natural Selection and the
    Evolution of Fear: 836.
Sister Mary Appassionata
    Lectures the Criminology
    Class: Homage to the
    Coroner: 836.
Sister Mary Appassionata
    Lectures the Eighth Grade
    Girls: Cooking with Sweet
    Basil: 836.
Sister Mary Appassionata
    Lectures the Eighth Grade
    Girls: Furrow, Cave, Cowry,
    Home: 836.
Sister Mary Appassionata
    Lectures the Ethics Class:
    836.
Sister Mary Appassionata
    Lectures the History of
    Film Class: Rebel without a
    Cause: 836.
Sister Mary Appassionata
    Lectures the Meteorology
    Class: 836.
Sister Mary Appassionata
    Lectures the Mortuary
    Science Class: Feeding the
    Dead: 836.
Sister Mary Appassionata
    Lectures the Studio Art
    Class: Doctrines of
    Nakedness: 836.
Sister Mary Appassionata on
    the Nature of Sound: 836.
Sister Mary Appassionata

Responds to Questions from
    the Floor: 836.
Sister Mary Appassionata
    Speaks During the Retreat
    of the Eighth Grade Boys
    and Girls: 836.
Sister Mary Appassionata to
    the Human Awareness Class:
    One Fate Worse: 836.
Sister Mary Appassionata to
    the Ornithology Class: 836.
Sister of Mercy Charity Ward,
    Lights Out: 2289.
Sisters: 482, 3319, 4793.
Sisyphus in Parsippany: 304.
Site: 5409.
Sitting in the Garden
    Courtyard: 3351.
Sitting in the Mirage: 4970.
Sitting in the Waters of
    Grasse River: 2555.
Sitting in the Waters of
    Grasse River, Canton, N.Y.--
    7/1983: 2555.
Sitting on an Eastern Bluff
    along the Mississippi
    River: 3916.
Six Bits: 3240.
Six Days Overdue: 2974.
Six O'Clock in Nova Scotia:
    4321.
Six Persimmons: 4242.
Six Poems about Artists: 3084.
Six Poems for Carol: 2384.
Six Poems for Tamar: 91, 3315.
Six Post-scripts: 1069.
Six Times I Have Circled the
    Yard: 3335.
Six Titles for Songs of the
    Balkan Peoples: 4188.
Six White Birds: 880.
Six Windows and One Moon:
    4104.
The Skaters, the Skippers:
    4007.
Skating after School: 994.
Skating among the Graves:
    4208.
A Skeleton in the Phone Booth:
    1992.
Skeleton Song: 1618.
Skeletons: 2218, 5398.
Skepticism: 4314.
Sketch of an Angel: 1494.
Skiathos: 5259.
Skiing Home at Dusk: 3708.
The Skilled Man: 4310.
Skin: 5218.
Skins: 520.
Skipping Stones: 2776.
Skirting the House: 4024.
The Skokie Theatre: 2168.
The Skull of a Snowshoe Hare:
    5368.
Skulls: 155.
Skunked: 4579.